Theotokos

A Theological Encyclopedia of the Blessed Virgin Mary

Fragment of papyrus of an early (third or fourth century) Greek version of the *Sub Tuum* preserved in the John Rylands Library in Manchester.

Theotokos

A Theological Encyclopedia of the Blessed Virgin Mary

by

Michael O'Carroll, C.S.Sp.

A Michael Glazier Book
THE LITURGICAL PRESS
Collegeville, Minnesota

Dedication

To the Most Sacred Heart of Jesus, Eternal Son of the Father, Son of the Virgin Mary, and to three Archangels, Michael, Gabriel, Raphael.

A Michael Glazier Book
published by
THE LITURGICAL PRESS

Frontispiece is a reproduction of the oldest known prayer to the Theotokos (see entry under Sub Tuum). Reproduced by the kind permission of John Rylands Library, University of Manchester, England.

Copyright © 1982 by Michael O'Carroll, C.S.Sp. All rights reserved.

Cover design by Lilian Brulc

6	7	8	9

Library of Congress Cataloging-in-Publication Data

O'Carroll, Michael.
    Theotokos : a theological encyclopedia of the Blessed Virgin Mary
/ by Michael O'Carroll.
        p.   cm.
    Reprint. Originally published: Wilmington, Del. : M. Glazier,
1990.
    "A Michael Glazier book."
    Includes bibliographical references.
    ISBN 0-8146-5268-9
    1. Mary, Blessed Virgin, Saint—Dictionaries, indexes, etc.
I. Title.
BT599.032   1990
232.91'03—dc20   90-38452
                                                    CIP

Foreword

The purpose of this note is to render thanks. My thanks to Canon René Laurentin who read a number of articles from the letter E in a first draft and made very helpful suggestions. I am also deeply grateful to those in charge of the libraries of the following institutions: the Franciscan House of Studies, Dun Mhuire, Killiney, Co. Dublin; Trinity College, Dublin; Manchester University (including the John Rylands collection); Heythrop College, London; the Medieval Institute, Toronto; the Jesuit Houses of Studies at Chantilly, France and Eegenhoven, Belgium. In particular I wish to thank Fr. Auguste Cerckel, S.J., librarian to the Bollandistes, Brussels and all the Bollandistes for the unfailing courtesy and generosity I have received at their hands over the years. I have the same tribute of gratitude to express to Fr. Dermot Fleury, S.J., librarian to the Jesuit Institute of Theology, Milltown, Co. Dublin. There, apart from my own books, most of the reading for the present work was done. Nowhere could one work in happier conditions.

Michael Glazier and the editor he chose, Joseph Hopkins, took a personal interest in the book for which I wish to thank them warmly. Finally I ask the librarian of the John Rylands University of Manchester Library to accept my gratitude for the permission, graciously accorded, to reproduce as frontispiece to my book the priceless manuscript, Papyrus 470, most carefully preserved, as I have been privileged to see, in that great institution.

Michael O'Carroll, C.S.Sp.
Blackrock College
1 January, 1982

v

Abbreviations

AAS	*Acta Apostolicae Sedis.*
AB	*Analecta Bollandiana.*
ACO	*Acta Conciliorum Oecumenicorum,* ed. E. Schwartz, Strasburg, 1914—.
Acta Synodalia	*Acts of the Second Vatican Council.*
AER	American Ecclesiastical Review, Washington.
AH	*Analecta Hymnica Medii Aevi,* ed. G. M. Dreves, Leipzig, 1886—.
Anton	Antonianum, Rome.
ArchIbAm	Archivo Ibero-Americano, Madrid.
ASC	*Alma Socia Christi,* Proceedings of Rome International Mariological Congress, 1950.
ASS	*Acta Sanctae Sedis.*
Auctarium	*Auctarium Bibliothecae Hagiographicae Graecae,* ed. F. Halkin, S.J., Brussels.
Barré, H. Prières Anciennes	H. Barré, C.S.Sp., *Prières Anciennes de l'Occident à la Mère du Sauveur,* Paris, 1962.
BB	Biblica, Rome.
Beck	H.-G. Beck, *Kirche und theologische Literatur im byzantinischen Reich,* Munich, 1959.
BHG	*Bibliotheca Hagiographica Graeca,* ed. F. Halkin, S.J., Brussels.
BSFEM	*Études Mariales,* Bulletin de la Société française d'Études Mariales, Paris.
ByzZeitschr	Byzantinische Zeitschrift, Leipzig.
BZ	Byzantion, Brussels.
CahJos	*Cahiers de Josephologie,* Montréal.
Caro, R. La Homilética	R. Caro, S.J., "La Homilética Mariana Griega en el Siglo V," *Marian Library Studies,* Dayton. I, 1971, II, 1972.
CBQ	The Catholic Biblical Quarterly, Washington.
CCCM	*Corpus Christianorum Continuatio Medievalis,* Turnhout.
CCSL	*Corpus Christianorum, Series Latina,* Turnhout, 1953—.
ClavisG	Maurice Geerard, *Clavis Patrum Graecorum,* Turnhout, 1974—.
CM	Cahiers Marials, Paris.
CMP	*Corpus Marianum Patristicum,* ed. S. A. Campos, O.F.M., Burgos, 1970—.
CR	*Corpus Reformatorum.*
CRev	Clergy Review, London.
CSCO	*Corpus Scriptorum Christianorum Orientalium,* Louvain, 1903—.
CSEL	*Corpus Scriptorum Ecclesiasticorum Latinorum,* Vienna, 1866—.
DACL	*Dictionnaire d'Archéologie Chrétienne et de Liturgie,* ed. F. Cabrol, O.S.B. and H. Leclercq, O.S.B., Paris, 1907—.
DBS	*Dictionnaire de la Bible,* Supplement.
DCath	La Documentation Catholique, Paris.
DHGE	*Dictionnaire d'Histoire et de Géographie Ecclésiastiques,* Paris, 1912—.

Dillenschneider, Cl., St. Alphonse	Cl. Dillenschneider, C.SS.R., *La Mariologie de S. Alphonse de Liguori*, Fribourg, Switzerland, 2 vols. 1931, 1934.
DM	Documentos Marianos, Madrid.
DS	*Enchiridion Symbolorum*, Denziger-Bannwart, ed. 33, A. Schönmetzer, S.J.
DSp	*Dictionnaire de Spiritualité*, Paris, 1937—.
DTC	*Dictionnaire de Théologie Catholique*, Paris, 1903—.
EclXaver	Eclesiastica Xaveriana, Bogota.
EMBP	*Enchiridion Marianum Biblicum Patristicum*, ed. D. Casagrande, Rome, 1974.
EphLit	Ephemerides Liturgicae, Rome.
EphMar	Ephemerides Mariologicae, Madrid.
EstBib	Estudios Bíblicos, Madrid.
Est Ecl	Estudios Eclesiasticos, Madrid.
EstJos	Estudios Josefinos, Valladolid.
EstM	Estudios Marianos, Madrid.
ETL	Ephermides Theologicae Lovanienses, Louvain.
FranzSt	Franziskanische Studien, Werl (Wesph.).
FS	Franciscan Studies, New York.
GCS	*Die griechischen christlichen Scriftsteller der ersten drei Jahrhunderte*, Leipzig-Berlin, 1897—.
GeistLeb	Geist und Leben, Wurzburg.
Graef, H. Mary	H. Graef, *Mary, A History of Doctrine and Devotion*, London, Vol. I, 1963, II, 1965.
Gregor	Gregorianum, Rome.
Hennecke	E. Hennecke and W. Schneemelcher, *New Testament Apocrypha*, Philadelphia, 1963, 1965.
IER	Irish Ecclesiastical Record, Maynooth.
ITQ	Irish Theological Quarterly, Maynooth.
James, Apocryphal	M. R. James, *The Apocryphal New Testament*, Oxford, 1960.
Jerome Commentary	Jerome Biblical Commentary.
Jugie, M., L'Assomption	M. Jugie, A.A., *La mort et l'Assomption de la Sainte Vierge, ST 114*, Rome, 1944.
Jugie, M., L'Immaculée Conception	M. Jugie, A.A., *L'Immaculée Conception dans L'Ecriture Sainte et dans la Tradition orientales*, Rome, 1952.
Laurentin, R., Traité I	R. Laurentin, *Court Traité de théologie mariale*, Paris, 1953.
Laurentin, R., Traité V	R. Laurentin, *Court Traité sur la Vierge Marie*, Paris, 1968.
LexMar	Lexikon der Marienkunde, Regensburg, 1957—.
LG	Lumen Gentium, Dogmatic Constitution on the Church (Vatican Council II).
Mansi	Sacrorum Conciliorum Nova et Amplissima Collectio.
Maria	*Maria, Études sur la Sainte Vierge*, ed. H. du Manoir, S.J., (8 vols.), 1949—.
Mariology	*Mariology*, ed. J. Carol, O.F.M., Milwaukee, 1955-1961.
MariolSt	*Mariologische Studien* (Proceedings of German Society for Marian Studies), Essen, 1952—.
Mary in NT	*Mary in the New Testament*, ed. R. E. Brown, K. P. Donfried, J. A. Fitzmyer, S.J., J. Reumann. London, 1978.

McHugh, J., the Mother	J. McHugh, *The Mother of Jesus in the New Testament*, London, 1975.
ME	*Maria et Ecclesia*, Proceedings of the Lourdes International Mariological Congress, 1958.
MGH	*Monumenta Germaniae Historica*
MM	Marianum, Rome.
MO	*De Mariologia et Oecumenismo*, ed. K. Balic, O.F.M., Rome, 1962.
MSS	*Maria in Sacra Scriptura*, Proceedings of the International Mariological Congress, San Domingo.
MSt	*Marian Studies*. Proceedings of the American Mariological Society, Tampa, Florida.
Mus	Le Muséon, Louvain.
NCE	*New Catholic Encyclopedia*, New York.
NewCathComm	*A New Catholic Commentary on Holy Scripture*, London, 1969.
NovT	Novum Testamentum, Leiden.
NRT	Nouvelle Révue Théologique, Louvain.
NT	New Testament.
NTS	New Testament Studies, London.
OCP	Orientalia Christiana Periodica, Rome.
OL	Papal Teachings, Our Lady, ed. at Solesmes. (Trans. publ., Boston)
OT	Old Testament.
PCM	*Primordia Cultus Mariani*, Proceedings of the Lisbon International Mariological Congress, 1967.
PG	*Patrologia Graeca* (Migne).
PL	*Patrologia Latina* (Migne).
PO	*Patrologia Orientalia*.
PS	*Patrologia Syriaca*.
RAM	Révue d'Ascétique et Mystique, Toulouse.
RB	Révue Biblique, Paris.
REA	Révue des Études Augustiniennes, Paris.
REB	Révue des Études Byzantines, Paris.
RevBen	Révue Bénédictine, Maredsous.
RevSR	Révue des Sciences Religieuses, Strasbourg.
RHE	Révue d'Histoire Ecclésiastique, Louvain.
Rome Congress, 1975	*Devotion to Mary from the 12th to 15th century*. Proceedings of the Rome International Mariological Congress.
Roschini, G.M., Maria Santissima	G. M. Roschini, O.S.M., *Maria Santissima nella Storia della Salvezza* (4 vols.), Rome, 1969.
RSPT	Révue des Sciences Philosophiques et Théologiques, Paris.
RSR	Recherches de Science Religieuse, Paris.
RTAM	Recherches de Théologie Ancienne et Mediévale, Louvain.
Saragossa Congress	*Devotion to Mary in 16th Century*. Proceedings of the Saragossa International Mariological Congress.
SC	Sources Chrétiennes, Lyons.
ScEccl	Sciences Ecclésiastiques, Montreal.
Scheffczyk, Das Mariengeheimnis	L. Scheffczyk, *Das Mariengeheimnis in Frömmigkeit und Lehre der Karolingerzeit*, Leipzig, 1959.

SK	Scholastik, Freiburg.
ST	Studi e Testi, Rome.
TheolGlaube	Theologie und Glaube, Paderborn.
TheolSt	Theological Studies, Woodstock, Maryland.
Theotocos	*Enciclopedia Mariana, Theotocos*, Genoa-Milan (2nd ed.), 1958.
TU	Texte und Untersuchungen, Leipzig, 1882—.
V.I.	*Virgo Immaculata*. Proceedings of Rome Congress, 1954.
VieSp	La Vie Spirituelle, Paris.
WA	Weimar edition of Martin Luther's Works.
Wenger, A., L'Assomption	A. Wenger, A.A., *L'Assomption de la Très Sainte Vierge dans la Tradition Byzantine du Vie au Xe siècle,* Paris, 1955.
Zagreb Congress	*Devotion to Mary from 6th to 11th century*. Proceedings of the International Mariological Congress at Zagreb, 1971.

A

ABBO OF ST. GERMAIN (d. after 922)

A Benedictine poet of the abbey of St. Germain-des-Prés. In his *De bello parisiano,* which deals with the Norman attack on Paris in 885-86, he reproduces a prayer to Our Lady for help uttered by the bishop, Goscelin: "O loving Mother of the Redeemer and of the salvation of the world, gleaming star of the sea, more outstanding than all stars . . ." In the same passage, the bishop, urging "incomparable thanks" from his fellow-citizens to Our Lady, speaks thus of Paris: "The city shines in honour of Mary so exalted, to whom it is sacred, through whose help we enjoy life, [and] are now safe." In his prayer to her, he stresses her titles (*qv*) of power: "Queen of the heavens." "Mistress of the world," "Mother to be celebrated whose offspring is the High King." All the heavenly court "rejoice in you, are mindful of you, praise, revere, and worship you." She, the shining moon, has poured on earth the sun brighter than herself. She is "holier than all others, more blessed than any of her sex." "All glory, praise, honour, and radiant distinction be to her forever." She restored our fallen race, A. tells us; but this, in the context, is related to the Saviour.[1]

A *Florilegium,* assembling some 150 items, allegedly from A., has points of interest to Marian doctrine. According to scholars, however, the contents are scarcely of uniform authorship, and the sermon *On the twelve privileges of Mary* which affirms not only the Immaculate Conception (*qv*) but also the Assumption (*qv*) and Mary's omniscience (see KNOWLEDGE, OUR LADY'S) is certainly spurious. A.'s importance is for the doctrine of Mary's intercession (*qv*).[2]

[1]MGM, *Poet. Lat.,* IV, 89-90; PL 132, 733. [2]Cf. J. Leclercq, O.S.B., "Le Florilège d'Abbon de S. Germain," in *Revue du Moyen Age Latin,* 3(1947), 119-40; and H. Barré, C.S.Sp., in BSFEM, 7(1949), 85.

ABELARD, PETER (1079-1142)

A challenging figure whose philosophical and theological work is not so well known as his love affair with Héloise, A. was well in the current of thinking on Mary in his own time, and ahead with respect to one important question. His thought is found in six chapters of his *Sic et Non,* in hymns and sequences, and especially in four sermons—one for Christmas day, and three others for feasts of Our Lady (the Annunciation, the Purification, and the Assumption).[1]

A. thought that the "conception by the Lord's Mother was the beginning of our redemption." Mary was "chosen from the whole mass of mankind that in her [God] should work the mystery of our restoration and achieve the most high secret of His plan."[2] God wished that grace should be manifest through each sex. "We read that Adam was created outside paradise, Eve in paradise . . . . Eve was created from the old Adam; the new Adam, the redeemer of the old, was born of Mary."[3] A. recalls Ez 44:2. Mary's singular conception and childbirth give him an opportunity to insist on God's grace, and he has intuitions of interest on the Holy Spirit (*qv*).

With such a profound view of Mary's destiny, A. expresses a doctrine of her total purification (*qv*) by Christ[4]—but not the Immaculate Conception (*qv*). It was in regard to the Assumption (*qv*) that he rejected the current view. Although he thought Pseudo-Jerome (*qv*) authentic, he disagreed with him on the bodily resurrection; he does not appear to have known Pseudo-Augustine (*qv*). God may reveal to the lesser what He has not revealed to the greater; what was hidden may become manifest later "through the revealing Spirit." A. thinks in terms of the apocryphal imagery of the Assumption, with the Apostles assembling, the Lord giving the soul to Michael, but without a three-day delay before it is united to the body.

Mary is "our Mediatress (qv) to the Son as he is to the Father." The Son, who especially commends honour to parents, cannot refuse her prayers: witness Cana (qv) and the Theophilus (qv) legend. All the gifts of the Church are concentrated in Mary.[6]

---

[1]PL 178, 388-398 (*Serm. 2 in Natali Dom.*); *op. cit.*, 379-388 (*Serm. 1 in Ann. B.V.M.*); *op. cit.*, 417-425 (*Serm. in Purific. S.M.*); *op. cit.*, 539-547 (*Serm. in Assumpt. B.M.*).   [2]PL 178, 396C.   [3]PL 178, 542CD; on Eve, cf. also 545B.   [4]PL 178, 390B, 394A.   [5]PL 178, 542-543.   [6]PL 178, 544B, 540B.

ABELLY, LOUIS (1603-1691)

A disciple of St. Vincent de Paul, whose biography he would write, A. was involved in the Jansenistic and Marian controversies of the 17th century. He was bishop of Rodez for three years from 1664. Among some forty titles, his principal work is *Medulla Theologica* (Paris, 1650; latest edn., 1839).[1] There were several editions of his *La Tradition de L'Eglise touchant la dévotion particulière des chrétiens envers la très Sainte Vierge Marie, Mère de Dieu . . . la pratique de cette dévotion, selon le véritable esprit du christianisme (Paris, 1652)*. When an apologist for Port Royal referred in 1665 to heated Spanish discussion of the Immaculate Conception (qv) in an *Apologie pour les religieuses de Port Royal du Saint Sacrement contre les injustices et les violences du procédé dont on a usé contre ce monastère*, A. replied with *Défense de l'honneur de la Sainte Mère de Dieu contre un attentat de l'Apologiste de Port Royal, avec un projet d'examen de son apologie* (Paris, 1666; 2nd edn., 1690, with the title *Défense de l'honneur de la Très Sainte Mere de Dieu contre les ennemis de son Immaculée Conception*).

When Adam Widenfeld published the *Avis Salutaires* (qv), A. was one of the first to reply with *Sentiments des Saints Pères et Docteurs de l'Eglise touchant les excellences et prérogatives de la Très Sainte Vierge Marie, pour servir de réponse à un libelle intitulé: "Advertissements salutaires de la Bienheureuse Vierge Marie à ses dévots indiscrets"* (Paris, 1674; enlarged from 70 pages to 218 in the 1675 edn.). Dom Gabriel Gerberon, who had translated Widenfeld's booklet into French, dealt with the bishop's critique in an 18-page *Lettre à Mgr. Abelly, évêque de Rodez, touchant son livre des excellences de la Sainte Vierge* (1674). Within a month, A. issued his rejoinder in 16 pages, entitled *Réponse de Mgr. de Rodez à la lettre qu'on lui a écrite sur le sujet du Livre des Advertissements salutaires*. In these writings, the polemical intent has occasionally a hardening and limiting effect.

---

[1]Cl. Dillenschneider, *St. Alphonse*, 118-122; P. Hoffer, S.M., *La dévotion à Marie au déclin du XVIIe siècle* (Paris, 1938), 225-227; A. Vogt in DHGE, I, 97-103; R. Daeschler in DSp, I, 65-67.

ABERCIUS, Epitaph of, (2nd Century)

This is an early Christian inscription which was discovered in Phrygia in 1883 by Sir W. Ramsay and is now in the Lateran Museum. It is the self-composed epitaph of Abercius, who was probably bishop of Hierapolis in Asia Minor in the 2nd century and had traveled widely in the east and to Rome.[1] Theologians of Our Lady are interested in this passage: "I followed Paul and faith led me everywhere, and she gave me for food fish from the spring, mighty and pure, whom a spotless virgin (*parthenos agne*) took in her hands and gave to her friends to eat forever, having sweet wine and giving the mixed cup with bread."

The mystical, symbolical language may have been dictated by the "discipline of the secret" since the inscription stood in a public place; or it may be simply contemporary style, evident in the writings of Tertullian (qv) and St. Clement and in the frescoes of the Catacombs. If *partheons agne* referred to Our Lady, we have a testimony to Mary's virginity and holiness and a suggestion of the link between her and the Eucharist (qv). But it has been argued by A. Greiff and A. Abel that the Church is intended by the phrase. J. B. Lightfoot wavered and admitted that 2 Cor 11:2 where the very phrase is applied to the Church, and a kindred description in Eph 5:27, "will suggest a doubt whether it is not rather a designation of the Church." Defenders of the Church sense also contend that, although *parthenos* is applied to Mary in 2nd century texts, *agne* is not. The most recent, exhaustive monograph on the subject[2] considers these and other arguments in detail, examines the opposing interpretations, and, from a collation of all relevant contemporary texts, notably the Sibylline Oracles (see APOCRYPHA), wherein *parthenos agne* is found, affirms the entire validity of the Marian interpretation.

---

[1]J. B. Lightfoot, *Apostolic Fathers*, II, Vol. 1, 481; H. P. V. Nunn, *Christian Inscriptions* (Texts for Students 11),

(London, SPCK, 1920), 23-25. A photograph faces page 24; A. Abel, "Etudes sur l'inscription d'Abercius," in BN, 3(1926), 321-405; A. Greiff, "Zum Verständnis der Aberkiosinschrift," in *TheolGlaube*, 18(1926), 78-88; J. Quasten, *Patrology* (Washington, 1949), I, 171-173; G. Bardy, *Catholicisme*, I, s.v.; S. Grill in LexMar, I, 21-23; H. Gregoire in BN, 25-27(1955-1957), 363-368. [2]B. Emmi, O.P., "La testimonianza mariana dell'epitaffio di Albercio," in *Angelicum*, 46(1969), 232-302. A separate issue under same title, Rome, 1970.

ABRAHAM OF EPHESUS (6th Century)

A monastic founder in Constantinople and Jerusalem, he became bishop of Ephesus about the mid-sixth century.[1] Author of two homilies on Our Lady—for the Annunciation, and for the *Hypapante* or Presentation of the Lord—which were published by Fr. Martin Jugie.[2] A. held that Mary is *Theotokos*, the Virgin, and that her virginity was preserved *in partu*. He speaks of Simeon's prophecy, departing from the eastern tradition deriving from Origen on the meaning of the sword (*qv*). As Mary recalled Christ's miracles while she beheld his sufferings and humiliation on Calvary "there was enough from each side, to cause the soul of the most pure one to be torn as by a sword."[3] There is here no explicit question of doubt.

[1]S. Vailhé, in DHGE, 1, 173; Beck, 398. [2]PO, XVI, 442-454. [3]PO, XVI, 452.

ABSALON OF SPRINCKIRSBACH (d. 1205)

A Canon Regular of St. Augustine, who may have spent some time at the abbey of St. Victor as well as at Sprinckirsbach, A. gave three sermons each on the feasts of the Purification, the Annunciation and the Assumption of Mary and one on the Nativity.[1] The treatment is at times leisurely and includes general moral or spiritual thoughts. He exalts Mary's greatness, elaborates her role, and affirms her intercession; the last thought tends to recur. Mary, star of the sea, is above all creatures, by her loftiness, her immutability and the sharing of her light. "O Mary," he cries out, "O Star of the sea who guides the travellers, brings back those who wander, returns those in danger to the port of salvation."[2] The thought is worthy of St. Bernard, though not the rhetoric. "For since Mary is queen of all, so she is their patron and, for as much as is in her, equally approachable to all, for over all she has received the fullness of dignity."[3] The rays of her mercy shine on those far and near; the just and sinners pray to her; angels and archangels turn to her.

A. goes deeper into the mystery of Mary's influence. By intervention (*interventus*, a frequent substitute at the time for mediation) she effects our reconciliation, she gives us an example to imitate, and by her help protects us. "Her first benefit," he says elsewhere, "was to remove the yoke of ancient slavery from us, the second that she took from us the wrath of divine outrage, the third that she effaced the mark of human iniquity."[4]

Mary is exalted above every creature. A. will say that she is so bodily, for if this be error, "the error is most pleasing to me, since it meets and is excusable by the source of my devotion to the Mother of Mercy (*qv*)."[5] He argues positively too for this thesis. Assuming that Elias was taken up to heaven in a fiery chariot, he asks will the Son deny to his Mother what he would not refuse to a servant. If she were not bodily assumed would the Son deny to her relics veneration which he allows to those of John the Baptist? The precept "Honour thy father and thy mother" is, he thinks, relevant. Should Mary's body be treated as if it were neither in heaven or on earth? Does not this imply disrespect? The arguments for the Assumption (*qv*) which finally prevailed were stronger than this, but a thread of thought is here which would remain.

[1]PL 211, 87-102, 118-137, 245-260, 265-270. On A., cf. E. Vacant, DTC I, s.v.; A. Sage, A. A., *Maria*, II, 686-693. [2]*Serm. 44*, PL 211, 251B. [3]*Serm. 44, op. cit.*, 253C. [4]*Serm. 45, op. cit.*, 259B. [5]*Serm. 44, op. cit.*, 255D, 256A.

ADAM THE ELDER (SENIOR) (d. before 1581)

A. had obtained his *Magister Artium* degree in Paris and in 1535 entered the Cistercian monastery of Kinloss in Scotland. He has been erroneously ascribed to the 13th century.[1] This is impossible to reconcile with a letter to Robert Reid, bishop of Orkney, which appeared as a preface to his work *Strenae seu Conciones capitulares* (Paris, 1558); therein he shows acquaintance with Luther, Calvin, Zwingli, and elsewhere refers to the Council of Basle (*qqv*). The book contains five Marian homilies: for the Purification, Annunciation, Assumption, Nativity of Mary, and her Immaculate Conception. A. thought the decree of Basle valid; he defends the Immaculate Conception and likewise the bodily Assumption.

[1]Cf. E. Toniolo, O.S.M., "I sermoni mariani di Adam Senior," in MM, 21(1959), 298-305.

ADAM OF PERSEIGNE (d. 1221)

Adam was a Canon Regular, then a Benedictine (librarian at Marmoutier), finally a Cistercian; he was Abbot of Perseigne for 33 years until his death. An ascetical leader, he embodied the Marian ideals of the Cistercians—"*vir totus Mariae.*" His Marian writings are: passages in the Letters;[1] a *Mariale* composed of 5 sermons (on the Annunciation, on the Nativity of Christ [2], on the Purification of the B.V., and on the Assumption);[2] some fragments concerning Our Lady. A sermon on the Nativity of Mary is unpublished.

For A., Mary is the Mother of grace and the Mother of mercy (*qv*). He combines an exalted idea of her privileges with warm insistence on her interest in us and her power to help us. Thus, she is "the gate of heaven, the beauty of paradise, the sovereign of angels, queen of the world, joy of saints, advocate of believers, strength of combatants, recall of the straying, medicine of the repentant."[3] He, who, through her, came as a Child to the humble, has constituted Mary as advocate on our behalf. "He chose you as the way by which he would come to us; he made you the path by which we should come home."[4] Thus, A. calls her Mediatress (*qv*) between heaven and earth, God and man. She is certain salvation, unique hope of clemency, fullness of all good things. We are her adopted children; her Only-begotten Son becomes through her our brother, for she is "mother of the exile and of the king, of the culprit and the judge, of God and man."[5] A. saw a link between Mary and the Eucharist, sacrifice implicit in the Presentation. Mary is the Mother and the spouse (*qv*) of God.

---

[1]SC, 66, J. Bouvet. [2]PL 211, 699-744. [3]Letters, 3, page 78. [4]PL 211, 744C. [5]*Serm. 1, In Annunt., op. cit.,* 703C. See also, K. Romaniuk, "La Sainte Vierge Marie, Médiatrice de toutes les graces d'après Adam de Pers.," in MM 25(1963), 139-146. Also, E. Lamirande, "Le rôle de Marie à l'égard des hommes d'après Adam de Pers.," in *Maternité Spirituelle de la B.V.M.* (Ottawa, 1958), 81-121.

ADAM OF ST. VICTOR (12th Century)

Little is known for certain of this important liturgical poet save that he entered the Abbey of St. Victor and that he died either in 1177 or 1192.[1] In regard to his works, the critical position is as yet imperfect. Compositions principally relevant to Marian doctrine or piety are: three on the Nativity of the Lord, one on the Purification of Our Lady, three on the Assumption, and two on Blessed Mary. A. evokes the Eve (*qv*) – Mary contrast: "Eve brought forth grief, joyfully the Virgin brought forth the fruit of life." Mary was the chosen one: "First chosen by the beloved, first loved by the chosen one." "He who powerfully all things rules foresaw you and he chose you." A. likes to use OT symbols of Mary, the throne of Solomon, Gideon's fleece, the burning bush. Especially he calls Mary star of the sea. Though she is "without spot or wrinkle," though he insists on her virginity, especially the virginity *in partu* (*qqv*), it is her intercession which appeals most to him, based as it is on her mediation (*qv*) and her power. "O Mary, Mother of God, you after God are the height of hope, sweet refuge, consoler of the afflicted, one who raises up the dead, breaks the nets of death." "Hail honour of virgins, Mediatress of men" (some Mss have "Restorer" of men). "O queen, Mother of the king, appease the judge for us; through you, may your only offspring be for us a restorer, a consoler." Through many images, with rhyme and assonance, A. pursues this theme optimisitically.

---

[1]Cf. L. Gautier, *Oeuvres Poétiques d'Adam de St. Victor, texte critique,* (3rd ed., Paris, 1894); text used here, AH 54. Cf. esp., A. Mirot, in *Dict. de Biographie française,* 1, 495-497; F. Wellner, *Adam a Sancto Victore, Sämtliche Sequenzen, Lateinisch und deutsch Einführung und formegetreue Übertragung,* (Munich, 1955).

ADAM OF SCOTLAND (d. *c.* 1214)

A. was a Premonstratensian in Dryburg from 1184 to 1188 when he entered the Cistercian abbey of Witham. His works are found in PL 198, 91-872, in *Sermones fratris Adae* (ed. Walter Gray, London, 1901), and 14 sermons published at Tongerloo in 1934, *Ad viros religiosos,* ed. P. Petit, O. Prem.[1]

---

[1]G. Marocco, S.D.B., "*Nuovi documenti sull'Assunzione nel Medio Evo Latino,*" in MM 12(1950), 437-439.

ADAMANTIUS (4th Century)

A. appears in the dialogue *De recta in Deum fide,* an anti-Gnostic document of the early fourth century. The relevant Marian passages insist on the virginal conception and the reality of Mary's motherhood.

---

[1]PG 11; GCS 4; CMPI, 127-129; cf. G. Söll, S.D.B., Lex-Mar., 39.

ADAMNAN, ST. (625-704)

He was the ninth Abbot of Iona monastery, founded by St. Columba whose life he wrote. In his book *De Locis Sanctis* he recounts the visit to the Holy Land of Arculf, a French bishop, of whom nothing but this is known. Brief passages are relevant to Marian doctrine and piety.[1] The book was written between 679 and 682. Arculf saw that Mary's memory was recalled at Bethlehem. He describes a "quadrangular church of the holy Mary, Mother of the Lord," on the right of the round church of the Resurrection.[2] Arculf used also to visit the two-storied church of holy Mary in the valley of Jehoshaphat. "In the eastern portion of [the lower church] is an altar and at the right-hand side of the altar is the empty stone sepulchre of holy Mary, where she was once laid to rest. But how and when or by what persons her holy remains were removed from this sepulchre and where she awaits the resurrection no one, it is said, can know for certain."[3]

This passage influenced Bede (*qv*) and may have halted development of the doctrine of the Assumption.[4]

Arculf brought back from Constantinople a story of a miraculous icon of Our Lady. It was an image in wood which had been torn from its place and shockingly defiled. It was rescued, cleaned and set in a place of honour. Then wonderfully "there was an issue of genuine oil from the tablet with the picture of the blessed Mary." Arculf used to say that he saw it with his own eyes.[5] The incident is to be seen against the background of the iconoclastic controversy.

---

[1]CSEL 39, ed. P. Geyer. Recent critical ed. of Adamnan's *De Locis Sanctis*, in *Scriptores Latini Hiberniae*, 3, D. Meehan (Dublin, 1958). [2]*Lib*. I, c.4, in Geyer p. 232, Meehan p.49. [3]*Lib*. I, c.12, in Geyer, p.240, Meehan, p.59. [4]Cf. C. Balic, O.F.M., *Testimonia de Assumptione BVM*, I (Rome, 1948), 175ff; G. Quadrio, *Il Trattato 'De Assumptione Beatae Mariae Virginis' dello Pseudo-Agostino e il suo influsso nella Teologia Assunzion. Latina* (Rome, 1951), 99. [5]*Lib*. 3, c.5, in Geyer, pp.294-295, Meehan, p.119.

AD CAELI REGINAM (11 October, 1954)

Pius XII's Encyclical for the queenship (*qv*) of Mary. It is in four parts: preliminaries, history, doctrine, practical conclusions. The Pope having recalled his address on 13 May, 1946, reviews patristic testimony, previous papal teaching, evidence from the Liturgy (*qv*), and Christian art (*qv*). With Scripture and Tradition interwoven, the truth is based on the divine motherhood, on Mary's part in the Redemption, and on her eminence in grace. The Pope touches on the question of Mary's influence on souls. As at the International Mariological Congress, 24 October, 1954, Pius XII warned theologians and preachers against two dangers (excess and defect) in words later borrowed by *Lumen Gentium* 67. Finally he referred to the new feast and urged appropriate devotion.[1]

---

[1]AAS 46(1954), 625-640; OL, 384-399; CTS London. Cf. also *Allocution for the institution of the feast*, 1 November, 1954, AAS, 662-666; OL, 409-415. Cf. *La Royauté de l'Immaculée*, Canadian Congress, 1955, ed. Ottawa, 1957; also H. du Manoir, S.J.,, *La royauté de Marie. Etat de la question après l'Encyclique "Ad caeli Reginam"*, with bibliography, in ME V, 1-37.

AD DIEM ILLUM (2 February, 1904)

St. Pius X's Encyclical for the Golden Jubilee of *Ineffabilis Deus* (*qv*).[1] It related the spiritual motherhood (*qv*) to the mystery of the Incarnation, dealt with Mary's role in the Redemption and in the distribution of graces, adopted the distinction *de condigno* and *de congruo* in regard to Christ's and Mary's merit (*qv*). Rev 12 (see WOMAN IN) is interpreted in a Marian sense. Only Latin Fathers and church writers are quoted.

---

[1]ASS, 36(1903-1904), 449-462; OL, 165-182.

ADJUTRICEM POPULI (5 September, 1895)

Leo XIII's Encyclical on Our Lady in the context of Christian unity, particularly directed to the eastern Christians.[1] Eastern Fathers and liturgies are quoted, and "the prodigious things" done by the churches of the Orient in honour of Mary. Mary is entitled Mother of the Church. Constants in Leo's thinking appear—mediation, spiritual motherhood, the value of the Rosary (*qqv*).

---

[1]ASS 28 (1895-1896), 129-136; OL, 133-145.

ADVOCATE

From medieval times the word *Advocata* signifies Mary's special power of intercession. It is first found in the Latin (largely the only) version of the *Adversus Haereses* by St. Irenaeus (*qv*) "that the Virgin Mary should become the advocate of the virgin Eve."[1] It has been assumed that the Greek word used was *Paracletos*.[2] When, at the beginning of the present century, the text of another work of the saint, the *Epideixis*, or *Demonstration of apostolic preaching*, was discovered in an Armenian rendering, it yielded the same idea, "that a virgin, advocate of a virgin should undo and destroy virginal disobedience by virginal obedience."[3] In view of the differences of interpretation proposed by expert patrologists, it is difficult to decide what exactly St. Irenaeus meant by the word. The greatest of them, Mgr. G. Jouassard, a lifelong specialist in St. Irenaeus, arguing from the fact that intercession by Christians was already an element of belief in the community of Lyons, interpreted the word *Advocata* in the sense of "an action, a kind of intercession (*qv*) perhaps, performed by Our Lady on behalf of the one, towards whom she had an opposing role, to gain her heavenly bliss."[4] Others think the reference is to the restoration effected by the new Eve, not to intercession.[5]

The word *Paraclesis* is found in St. John of Damascus' second sermon on the Dormition; the faithful are imagined as present at the scene of Mary's death and, as they beg her not to leave them, they give her this name;[6] it is generally translated as consolation. The word *presbis* and its cognate forms will be used in later ages. St. Romanos the Singer (*qv*), in the sixth century pictures Mary addressing our first parents thus: "Cease your lamentations, I shall be your advocate with my son."[7] Towards the end of the century, Theoteknos of Livias (*qv*) calls Mary assumed into heaven "advocate of the human race" (the editor, Fr. A. A. Wenger, translates *ambassadrice*).[8] The usage is found in the next century with John of Thessalonica (d. *c*.630), Modestus of Jerusalem (d. 634) and later with John V of Jerusalem, and John the Monk. It enters eastern hymnography.[10]

St. Ambrose (*qv*) does not apply the word to Mary; he has an explicit reference to Christ as our Advocate.[11] In a passing way he admits the possibility of one Christian (Gratian) who has died becoming the advocate of another (Valentinian).[12] St. Augustine (*qv*) speaks of the martyrs as our advocates (*advocati*) "not in themselves, but in the Head, to whom they cling as perfect members. He is the one Advocate, but one as he is one Pastor"; and he goes on to show how others, Peter for example, share in the role of Pastor.[13]

Advocata applied to Mary is certainly found in the twelfth century. It is in the *Salve Regina*, and was taken up by St. Bernard: "You wish to have an advocate (*advocatum*) with him [Christ]," he asks in the *De Aqueductu* and answers, "Have recourse to Mary."[14] In the second sermon for Advent he exclaims: "Our Lady, our Mediatress, our Advocate (*Advocata*), reconcile us to your Son, commend us to your Son, represent us before your Son."[15]

The title remained in the literature and devotions thereafter. It was used by Leo X in the Bull *Pastoris Aeterni* (October 6, 1520), "the cult and sentiment of piety towards the unsullied Mother of God, our Advocate with him."[16] Sixtus V included the title in the Bull *Gloriosae* (June 8, 1587), as did Clement IX in the Brief *Sincera Nostra* (October 21, 1667), and Clement XI in the Bull *Commissi Nobis* (December 8, 1708), which established the feast of the Immaculate Conception (*qv*) in the universal calendar of the Church.[17]

In the nineteenth century the title was used by Pius VII,[18] and in the present century by St. Pius X,[19] Pius XI[20], and by Pius XII[21] several times. It was chosen for inclusion with Mediatress in LG(62) as were Helper and Aid-giver to reconcile differences of opinion on that word and idea (see VATICAN II).

A theology of Mary's mediation and intercession and of her relationship with the Holy Spirit must give the full meaning of the word Advocate as applied to her.

---

[1]*Adv. Haer.*, V, 19, 1; SC 153 (A. Rousseau, L. Doutreleau, C. Mercier, 1969), 248.   [2]Cf. reconstructed text *ibid.*; J. H. Newman, *Letter to Pusey*, in *Difficulties of Anglicans* (London, 1866), 37.   [3]tr. J. P. Smith, S. J. for *Ancient Christian Writers*, (1952), 33, p.69; L. M. Froideveaux, SC 62 (1958), 84-86.   [4]BSFEM, 16(1959), 57.   [5]For debate, cf. M. Jourjon in BSFEM, 23(1966), 38ff; and PCM, II, 143-148.   [6]PG 96, 733D.   [7]*Hymn on the Nativity*, II, SC 110, 100.   [8]*L'Assomption*, page 280.   [9]Cf. Lampe, s.v. *Presbis*, page 1129.   [10]Cf. E. Eustriades, *The Theotokos in Hymnography* (in Greek, Paris, 1930), 64.   [11]*In Ps.* 118, 20, 34, in PL 15, 1494.   [12]*De Obitu Valent.* 71, PL 16, 1379.   [13]*Serm. 184* PL 38, 996.   [14]*De Aquaeduc. 7*, ed. J. Leclercq. V, 279.   [15]PL 183, 43C.   [16]DMar, 76.   [17]DMar, 93, 115, 124.   [18]OL, 42.   [19]OL, 165.   [20]OL, 209, 223, 224.   [21]OL 265, 278, 463.

AELFRIC OF EYNSHAM (d.1025)

He was made abbot of the Benedictine house of Eynsham in 1005. An important preacher in Anglo-Saxon, he left three sermons on the

Assumption (*qv*).¹ As he did not know of the Immaculate Conception (*qv*), so in these sermons he was strongly influenced by Pseudo-Jerome (*qv*) and did not accept the bodily Assumption. But he says much in praise of Mary. The Assumption (of Mary's soul) is the highest feast, since Mary surpassed all the saints. Her immense love for Christ brought her martyrdom. Heaven closed by Eve was opened by her. She is the greatest help of Christians. A., in his second sermon, reflects on the active and contemplative life; in the third he recounts the legend of Emperor Julian's overthrow through Mary's intervention.

¹R. Warner, *Early English Homilies (Early English Texts Society* 152, London 1917); G. Marocco, S.D.B. "Nuovi documenti sull' Assunzione nel Medio Aevo Latino" in MM, 12(1950), 407-408; O. Stegmuller, LexMar, 54-55.

AELRED OF RIEVAULX, ST. (1109-1167)

Abbot of the Cistercian monastery of Rievaulx in Yorkshire, A. came under the influence of St. Bernard (*qv*). Marian doctrine is found in sermons for the feasts of Our Lady, in his instructions for anchoresses and in his treatise on the boy Jesus at twelve years old,¹ a short work which was at one time attributed to St. Bernard. Nothing about Mary occurs in his best known work, the treatise on spiritual friendship; a Marian passage from his pen is in PL in the works of St. Augustine.

A. spoke of Mary in bridal terms (see SPOUSE). "The Virgin in this marriage did not lose her virginity, God, by this marriage did not lose his divinity, the angel [called earlier *paranymphus*] by this marriage did not lose his dignity. There is still greater miracle in this marriage. The Son is Spouse and the Mother is spouse because the Son united the soul of the most holy Virgin to his divinity, since God himself made man went forth from her womb as a Spouse from his bridal chamber."²

Due perhaps to Bernard's influence. A. says nothing about the Immaculate Conception directly. But his portrait of Mary seems to exclude all imperfection: "Full of God, greater than the world, higher than heaven more fruitful than paradise, the honour of virgins, the glory of women, the praise of men, the joy of angels"; ". . . thus her holiness was above that of all others. She was the only in the world, to whom it could truly be said 'Thou art all fair, my beloved, and there is no stain in thee'." (Song 4:7).³

Of Mary's bodily Assumption, A. in a sermon found in PL says: "I have no means whereby I could carry conviction were someone to oppose me." In a sermon first published in 1952, he shows another influence: "nor is it wonderful if the holy Mother of God, who remained with him in his infancy, in his trials, should even in the body be assumed to heaven and exalted above the choirs of angels."⁴ He uses the symbolism of the Ark of the Covenant. Commenting, in another context, on Is 7:14, he suggests that Mary may have been reading the words at the moment of the Annunciation.

Mary is the craft which helps us to reach Christ across the sea of the world; she is the way to him. A. was clear on the mediation: "Through this grace [Mary's fullness of grace] the elements are renewed, the lower regions despoiled and those above restored, men are set free and demons trodden upon."⁵ "Note that whoever is praised in the Lord merits solely through the mediating merits of Mary that he should be praised."⁶ ". . . as her Son is known to be a Mediator between the Father and men, so she is mediatress between us and her son."⁷

A. shows a marked advance over Bernard in thinking on the spiritual motherhood: "But through blessed Mary we have a much better birth than through Eve, from the fact that Christ was born of her . . . She is our Mother, the Mother of our light . . . She is, therefore, more our Mother than our natural Mother."⁸

We, for our part, must render service to Mary: "For the Spouse of our Lord is our Lady; the Spouse of our King is our Queen; let us, therefore, serve her." Any possible abuse is excluded: "Let no one say: although I may do this or that against God I am not worried; I shall serve holy Mary and be safe. Thus things are not. As soon as ever a man offends the Son, then and there he offends the Mother." Mary is to be imitated.⁹ Mary is found at every stage of the spiritual life. We should pray, that he who through her was born would, through her, have mercy on us. Through her excellence she can help us, through her mercy she wills to do so. "No one can ever fail who can rely on such assistance."¹⁰ She is a singular refuge, solace in every tribulation, help in adversity, advice in times of doubt, remedy in pain.

The saint desires through prayer to achieve communion of mind with Mary: "Tell me, O most sweet lady, Mother of my Lord, what were your feelings, what your wonder, your joy when you found your sweetest Son, the boy Jesus."[11] For the anchoress, A. shows how prayer may benefit by reflection on and close identification with the scenes of Mary's life from the Annunciation to Calvary.[12]

---

[1]Works in PL 195 and CCCM 1; *Sermones inediti B. Aelredi Abbatis Rievallensis*, ed. C. H. Talbot (*Series Script. S. Ord. Cist.*, Rome, 1952); SC 60, 76. For Marian passage *inter op.* S. Augustini, cf. R. Laurentin, *Traité*, I, 126. On Aelred's Marian teaching, cf. A. Agius, O.S.B., "St. Aelred and Our Blessed Lady," *Downside Review*, 64(1946), 32-38; Ch. Dumont, O.C.R., "St. Aelred and the Assumption," *Life of the Spirit*, 8(1953), 205-210; "Aspects de la dévotion du Bx. Aelred à Notre Dame," *Collect. Ord. Cist. Ref.*, 20(1958), 313-326; A. Haller, S.O.Cist., *Un Educateur Monastique: Aelred de Rievaulx* (Paris, Gabalda, 1959); H. Graef, *Mary*, I, 249-250; A. Squire, O.P., *St. Aelred of Rievaulx* (London, 1967); A. Bail in DSp, I, 1109-1166. [2]*Serm. in Purif.*, PL 195, 254A. [3]*Serm. in Assumpt.*, in *Ser. Ined.*, 162. [4]*ibid.* [5]*Serm. in Annunt.*, *op. cit.*, 82. [6]*Serm. in Assumpt.*, *op. cit.*, 162. [7]*Serm. in Annunt.*, *op. cit.*, 82. [8]*Serm. 2 in Nativ.*, PL 195. 323C. [9]*ibid.*, and 324A. [10]*Serm. 3 in Assumpt.*, PL 195, 336. [11]*De Jesu Puero deperd.*, CCCM 1, 256. [12]*De Inst. Incl.*, CCCM 1, 662.

AKATHISTOS HYMN, THE

Few will challenge the judgment that this is "the most beautiful, the most profound, the most ancient Marian hymn of all Christian literature."[1] The authorship is still unknown. It appears in PG under the name of George of Pisidas, but his claim, as that of St. Germanus (*qv*) of Constantinople, asserted in the Latin versions, is discounted. The opening dedication thanks the *Theotokos* (*qv*) for her protection and deliverance of Constantinople under siege. Sergius was patriarch during the siege of 626, but he could not have composed this elaborate work which was sung during the siege; the dedication is a later addition. Scholars for a while favoured St. Romanos the Singer (*qv*) as author. This is no longer so, and his recent editor for SG (Fr. Grosdidier de Matons) rightly rejects the *Akathistos* from his hymns. Fr. E. M. Toniolo, O.S.M., states the entire argument against authorship by Romanos exhaustively. No critical edition of the text exists; Fr. Meersseman has made a judicious choice from existing texts. Since the hymn is sung standing (*a-cathistos* means "not sitting"), wholly on the fifth Saturday of Lent, and often by monks as a Little Office of Our Lady, it constitutes a singular medium of Christian tradition. Its influence in the eastern churches, and through translation, in the west, has been immense. It unites liturgical form, doctrinal statement and popular piety in a way until now unequalled.

The structure hinges on the number twelve. The first twelve stanzas are narrative, drawn from the infancy gospels and, in one instance, from the Apocrypha (*qv*). When the Holy Family entered a pagan temple in the Egyptian town of Sotines (now unknown), three hundred-and-sixty-five idols fell to the ground. This incident, which is related in Pseudo-Matthew 23, echoes Is 19:1. The second twelve stanzas are doctrinal. After each alternate stanza, beginning with the first, there are litanies, composed of twelve items, each of which begins with the word *Chaire* (i.e. "Hail"); the group ending with the almost untranslatable phrase, *Chaire, nymphe anympheute* ("unespoused Spouse," according to Miss Graef: "Bride unbrided," Fr. V. McNabb). Each of the even-numbered stanzas ends with *Alleluia*, which, therefore, like the litanies, is said twelve times. Fr. Meersseman links the twelve motif with Rev 12 (see WOMAN IN REV.).

The hymn was composed for the feast of the Annunciation, extolling the Incarnation as an act of "divine condescension" (I). In that sure setting Mary is extolled with Byzantine enthusiasm; images newly chosen or biblical are interwoven with theological attributes that evoke an entire homiletic corpus. Mary is the "tree of delightful fruit" (XIII), the "wood of welcome shade" (XIII), the "bridal chamber of pure nuptials" (XIX), the "mixing-cup that mingleth gladness" (XIX); or again, with OT in mind she is the "incense of prayer" (V), the "land of promise" (XI), the "food superseding the manna" (XI), the "rock that waters those thirsting for life" (XI), the "sea that drowned the spiritual Pharaoh" (XI), the "pillar of fire" (XI) and, of course, the "living temple" and the "ark gilded by the Spirit" (XXIII).

Theologically, the emphasis on Mary's enlightening power is of special interest. One phrase, "summary of all the tenets about God" (III), seems to have an echo in Vatican II; "Mary . . . in a certain way unites in her person and diffuses the highest imperatives of the faith" (LG, 65). But Mary is also said to "outsoar the learning of the wise, to enlighten the mind of the faithful" (III). She "shows the ignorance of the philosophers" and "makes speechless the men of science" (XVII). She is "faith's firm foundation" (VIII).

The article of LG already quoted speaks of Mary as "entering profoundly salvation history." The *Akathistos* springing from the mental categories of Byzantium is more ample in its assertions. It would be unjustified to dissect it in a search for texts in support of the Latin systematic theology of mediation and co-redemption (*qqv*). The reality is indubitably there. Mary is the "reconciliation of many sinners" (XIII), the "stole of those stripped of the right to appeal," the one by whom "was paid the ransom for transgression" (XV), the "gate of salvation," and "who has begotten anew those who were born in sin" (XIX). More significantly she is the one "by whom all creation is renewed" (I), "the whole world's redeeming" (V), the "opening of the gates of heaven . . .", and "the one by whom hell is despoiled" (VII). She is the "heavenly ladder by which God came down; the bridge that carries the earthborn to heaven" (III).

[1]Text, PG 92, 1335-1348; W. Christ and M. Parakinas, *Anthologia graeca carminum Christianorum* (Leipzig, 1871); E. Wellesz, *The Akathistos Hymn, Monumenta Musicae Byzantinae transcripta*, IX (2nd ed., Copenhagen, 1960); esp. G. G. Meersseman; O.P., *Hymnos Akathistos* (Greek text with English tr., Fribourg, 1958), and the English tr. by V. McNabb, O.P. (ed. D. Attwater, St. Dominic's Press, Ditchling, Sussex, 1934). Cf. M. Huglo, O.S.B., *L'Ancienne version latine de l'Acathiste*, Mus 64(1951), 27-61; R. Laurentin, *Traité* 1, 169-170; G. G. Meersseman, O.P., "Der Hymnos Akathistos im Abendland" in *Spicilegium Friburgense* (2 vols., Fribourg, 1958), 60; D. Montagna in MM, 24(1962), 499-500; G. M. Ellero, *La Madonna nel Culto* (Rome, 1966), 46; E. M. Toniolo, O.S.M., *Akathistos. Inno alla Madre di Dio. Traduzione per uso corale con brevi note esplicative* (Ed. Paoline, Catania, 1968), and by the same author *L'inno acatisto, monumento di teologia e di culto mariano nella Chiesa bizantina*, Zagreb Congress, IV, 1-39; I. Ortiz de Urbina, S. J., "En los albores de la devoción mariana. El himno 'Akatistos'", EstM, 35(1970), 9-20; under same title as preceding in C. Balic, *Festschrift*, 589-595; H. Graef, *Mary*, I, 127-129.

ALAN OF LILLE (d.1203)
Born in Lille, A. studied in Paris where he also taught. Later he taught in Montpellier, was engaged in combating the Catharist heresy, and towards the end of his life entered the Cistercian monastery of Citeaux. In his commentary on the Song of Songs (*qv*)[1] he follows a Marian interpretation, allowing for an ecclesial sense too. Thus he sees remarkable similarity between Mary and the Church (*qv*): "The Virgin Mary is like the Church of God in many ways. As the Church is the mother of Christ in his members through grace, the Virgin is the Mother of Christ the head through his human nature. And as the Church is without spot and wrinkle, so is the Virgin in glory (see *Lumen Gentium*, 65). As the Church has in different persons universality of gifts, so the Virgin Mary has in herself the universality of charisms."[2] A. also relates Mary to the Synagogue: "The Synagogue is called the mother of the Virgin, from which Christ too descended."

A. repeats the Augustinian phrase, Mary conceived Christ in her mind and in her womb. He recalls that though "the disciples fell away from faith, the Virgin did not fall away from the fixity of faith."[3] Christ revealed greater and lesser things to his disciples, but especially "to the glorious Virgin. Consequently he endured his Passion for the human race, and in this Passion the Virgin Mother especially shared his suffering. Therefore after the Resurrection he consoled his Mother."[4] A. says that Mary used to visit the places of the Passion after the Ascension. She had frequent visits from angels.

A. knows Pseudo-Augustine (*qv*) whom he quotes on the bodily Assumption (*qv*). Yet he later says that it is uncertain "whether she rose and ascended to heaven in the flesh or when." He thinks that Christ did not wish "the churches" to decide this, as the prophets and doctors of old had not done so. Then changing his approach, he writes: "It is reserved to the will of the Virgin, which is in harmony with the divine will, to wish it to be known that she was raised up."[5] Mary's influence on Christians is manifold for, to sum up, A. says we are "enlightened by the pattern of her life."[6]

In two of his sermons, A. speaks of the predestination of Mary and gives a picturesque twist to the Eve (*qv*) - Mary parallel and contrast.[7]

[1]PL 210, 51-110. Cf. P. Glorieux, "Alain de Lille, docteur de l'Assomption," in *Mélanges de Sc. Rel.*, 8(1951), 5-18; A. Garzia, "'Integritas carnis' e 'virginitas mentis'", in MM, 16(1954), 125-149, and by the same author "La mediazione universale in Alano de l'Isle," in EphMar, 6(1956), 299-321. [2]PL 210, 60AB. [3]PL 210, 58B. [4]PL 210, 69BC. [5]PL 210, 74D. [6]PL 210, 55B. [7]*Serm. I*, PL 210, 198B; *Serm. II in Annunt. B.M.*, Pl 210, 202A.

ALAN DE LA ROCHE (1428-1475)
Apostle of the Rosary (*qv*), an indefatigable preacher, A. was born in Brittany in 1428. He entered the Dominican order in 1450, transferring to the Dutch branch in 1464. He founded

the first confraternity of the Rosary at Douai in 1470; the Dominican James Sprenger founded the influential one at Cologne on September 8, 1475, the day after Alan died. A.'s success in spreading the prayer was considerable.[1] His writings, adaptations of which were widely diffused, helped to spread many legends, most notable was the origin of the Rosary in St. Dominic's life. We must look for his ideas, as he preached them, in: 1. *Quodlibet de veritate fraternitatis Rosarii seu Psalterii beatae Mariae Virginis* by his disciple Michel Francois (Cologne, 1479). A Lyons edition of 1488 has in addition a *Compendium Psalterii Trinitatis; 2. Magister Alanus de Rupe . . . Sponsus novellus beatissimae Virginis, Doctor Sacrae Theologiae devotissimus ordiis fratrum praedicatorum, de immensa et ineffabili dignitate psalterii precelsae ac intemeratae virginis Mariae*, published by the Carthusians in Stockholm, 1498; 3. a five-part treatise brought out by the Dominican A. Coppenstein in Freiburg, 1610 (reissued in Cologne, 1624 and in Naples, 1630, 1642, 1660), entitled *Beatus Alanus, redivivus, de Psalterio seu Rosario Christi et Mariae, tractatus in quinque partes distributus.* There seems to have been some editing in the Stockholm collection. Coppenstein covers his handling of the works with the statement, "The material is from Alain; the form is mine."[2] The five parts deal with: a reply to Bishop Ferri of Tournai on questions raised by him about the Rosary; narratives, revelations and visions of the Rosary; St. Dominick's sermons revealed to A; A.'s sermons and treatises; examples or miracles of the Rosary. An exceedingly rare work, of which a copy exists in the British Museum, was drawn up for the Breton confraternities and printed several times during the 15th century, *Le livre et ordonnance de la dévote confrarie du psaultier de la glorieuse Vierge Marie.*[2] A satisfactory critical edition of the works of A. may well be impossible.

---

[1]Cf. A. Willmart, "Comment Alain de la Roche prêchait le Rosaire ou Psautier de la Vierge," *La Vie et les Arts Liturgiques,* 11(1924-25), 108-115; A. Duval, O.P., *Maria,* II, 768-775; R. Coulon, DHGE, I, 1306-1312; M. Viller, DSp, I, 269-270. [2]Ed. by P. Marchegay in *Revue des Provinces de l'Ouest (Bretagne, Poitou et Anjou),* VI(1858), 129-146, 270-286.

ALBERT THE GREAT, ST. (before 1200-1280) Doctor of the Church. A man of universal knowledge, remembered as teacher of St. Thomas Aquinas (*qv*), A. wrote abundantly on Our Lady. Until 1625 he was thought to be the author of the *De Laudibus Sanctae Mariae*, by Richard of St. Laurent (*qv*). In the fifties of the present century it was shown that he was not the author of the *Mariale super Missus Est.* (see PSEUDO-ALBERT). On the other hand, research has discovered important Mss which now appear in the critical edition of his works by the *Albertus Magnus* Institute of Cologne; this was begun in 1951. Works not yet published in this edition are in the Borgnet edition (Paris, 1890-1899)[1]

Marian doctrine is found in twenty-three of A.'s works, sometimes in brief passages, principally in: a) the commentary on the Sentences of Peter Lombard, b) the treatises on the Incarnation, the Resurrection, the Good, the Nature of the Good, c) the exegetical passages in the biblical commentaries, especially the *Postilla super Isaiam* and the lengthy exposition of the first chapters in Mt and Lk. The commentary on the infancy narrative in Mt occupies 89 double-column pages in the Borgnet edition; that on the Annunciation, 70 double column pages. A. was the first to deal with the Annunciation (*qv*) in the treatise on the Incarnation, thus incorporating Marian theology in Christology.[2] He returns often to the same ideas.

A. shows the influence of Origen (*qv*) and John of Damascus (*qv*) among the Greek Fathers, and of the principal Latin Fathers. Anselm of Canterbury (*qv*), Bernard of Clairvaux (*qv*) and Peter Lombard (*qv*) of the more recent writers influenced him. He was intensely biblical, referring to many OT texts, often allegorically, the two Arks, Ex 3:2; 25:10, 1 Kings 2:19, Song 6:9, Is 7:14; 11:1; 66:7-8, Jer 31:22, Ez 44:2, Dan 2:34. Besides the obvious NT passages A. applies to Mary Col 2:9, and Phil 2:10; but this use is strictly related to Christ.

A. comments on the fourfold meaning then given to the name of Mary, Illuminatress, Star of the sea, Bitter sea, Lady. He denied the Immaculate Conception, since it was condemned by "Blessed Bernard in the letter to the Lyonnese and by all the masters of Paris."[3] But Mary was sanctified in the womb in an exceptional way, her sanctification greater than that given by the Sacraments, than that of Jeremiah or St. John the Baptist. It removed from her the tendency not only to mortal but to venial sin, giving her purity closest of all to Christ's: A.

thought that it took place "quickly after animation."[4] Mary was further sanctified by the descent of the Spirit and the coming of her divine Son.

The marriage (*qv*) between Mary and Joseph (*qv*) was genuine "and all the holier in that it was free from desire for intercourse of the flesh, for marriages of those bound to continence by equal vow are holier, as Augustine says."[5] On the "doubt" of Joseph A. took the view that the saint felt unworthy in presence of one so honoured by God – but he mistranslated the word *traducere* as to lead or take to his home.[6]

The great Dominican wrote at length on Mary's virginity.[7] He thought that she was the first to take a vow of virginity, becoming the "leader, rule, exemplar and teacher"[8] of virginity. He held that she was a virgin before, in and after childbirth.[9]

Mary was prepared by God for the mystery of the Annunciation and this was a means of ensuring that her consent should be from free choice – otherwise it would not be praiseworthy. Through her virtues she merited that she should be the Mother of God "by way of suitability (*per modum congruitatis*) not of the necessity of justice."[10] The dignity of divine motherhood is exalted. A. finds a place also for the bridal theme (see SPOUSE). He speaks of the heavenly king about to espouse our nature and then: "From the bridal chamber of the womb he (Christ) went forth as a spouse, when born of her he did not violate her as a mother, but loved her, consecrating her as a spouse without spot or wrinkle."[11]

On Mary's part in our salvation A. distinguished so sharply – not unlike recent theologians on the objective and subjective redemption (*qv*) – between general and particular justification, and stated so clearly that "general justification bears on the debt of nature from Adam and this only Christ could pay" that he seems poles apart from his spurious name-sake. He admits that particular justification is related to the merits of the saints and, by inference to those of Mary.[12] He also insists on Mary's redemption by Christ: "The work of redemption belongs only to the Head. Hence being redeemed belongs to the members. Since, therefore, the Blessed Virgin was a member, it was fitting for her to be redeemed."[13]

Mary is the type of the Church: "The Mother is a type (*figura*) of the Church as she conceives in her chaste womb and brings forth; the Son is the type of the reborn."[14] "She is the model of the Church as Joseph is the model of prelates of the Church."[15] "She was espoused that she might symbolize the Church, which is a virgin and spouse."[16]

The spiritual motherhood of Mary (*qv*) is by Vatican II (*qv*) linked with the divine motherhood, beginning with "the consent she gave in faith at the Annunciation" (LG 62). "She conceived us in her heart" says A. "at the same time as she conceived the divine Word in her womb."[17] In a subtle study of Gal 4:19 and Rev 12 (see Woman in), which is interpreted in a singular Marian sense, he sees Mary "bringing forth continuously her only Son, whom she forms in all that he may be carried off to the throne of God."[18] Elsewhere A. speaks of Mary nourishing "with her sweetness Christ who is formed in the hearts of many" and he continues, "if she did not nourish them, He who was recently formed would perish."[19] Pope Paul's title, Mother of the Church (*qv*) is found in A.'s work *De Sacrificio Missae*, which Fr. Fries thought doubtfully authentic, but the Cologne editors intend to issue.[20]

A. as he believed that the risen Jesus first appeared to her[21] believed that Mary was assumed into heaven, body and soul.[22] In the *De Natura Boni* he elaborates her role as an essential link in the continuing work of our salvation: "The axis of mercy supporting the world turns on these hinges or poles, that through the Mother we have access to the Son and through the Son to the Father, so that being thus led we should have no fear that our reconciliation would be rejected."[23] On the range of Mary's intercession A. set no limit: "She is the hope for forgiveness of those in the world who regret and expiate their sins. As to those in hell, the miracle of Theophilus (*qv*) whom she restored by the grace of mercy will be taken as an example. The innocent who are high up in grace consider her as the channel of grace, by which they have been preserved from sin. Prelates venerate her as the Lady, to whom nothing is denied by the supreme Pastor her Son . . . The blessed attribute their glory to her as the cause of their bliss."[24] The particulars of such manifold help are recalled by the saint elsewhere in his works.

---

[1]Cf. B. Korosak, O.F.M., *Mariologia S. Alberti Magni ejusque coaequalium* (Rome, 1954); G. M. Roschini, O.S.M.,

ALCUIN

"De Mariologia S. Alberti M.," in MM, 19(1957), 241-244;
R. Buschmiller, *The maternity of Mary in the Mariology of St. Albert the Great*, (Carthagena, 1957). Also 5 references by A. Fries, C.SS.R., *Die Gedanken des Heiligen Albertus Magnus über die Gottesmutter*, (Freiburg, 1958); and "Des Albertus Magnus Gedanken über Maria-Kirche," in ME III, 319-374; and *Was Albertus Magnus von Maria sast*, (Cologne, 1962); and "Zur Verwertung und Erklärung der Schrift in der 'Mariologie' Alberts des Grossen," in *Mariolog. Stud.* II, 53-79; and "Albert der Grosse," in LexMar, 111-121;; R. Masson, O.P., "Les réflexions théologiques de S. Albert le Grand sur la Sainte Vierge," in MM, 23(1961), 106-113. ²*De Incar.,* Cologne ed., vol.26, Tr.2; *De Annunt.,* 172-192. ³*In III Sent.,* dist. IIIA, a.4, 47a. ⁴*In III Sent.,* dist. IIIA, a.5, 48b. ⁵*In Mt.,* B.ed. 20, 34b. ⁶*In Mt.,* B.ed., 44b. ⁷*De natura boni,* Cologne ed., 25,1; *De virginitate divina beatae Virginis,* 44-103; also *De Bono,* Cologne ed., vol.28, 168-170. ⁸*De Bono,* 168. ⁹*De Bono,* 170. ¹⁰*De Incar.,* Cologne ed., vol.26, q.1, a.5, 176-177, and a.6,13, 180. ¹¹*In Lk. 1:35,* 103-104, B.ed. 22. ¹²*In III Sent.,* dist. 19A, a.1, 337a, B.ed. 28. ¹³*In III Sent.,* dist. 3, a.3, ad 1, 45. ¹⁴*Post. sup. Is.,* 11:1, Cologne ed. 19, 163. ¹⁵*Super Lk. 2:5,* B.ed. 22, 197b. ¹⁶*Super Mt. 1:18,* B.ed. 20, 35a. ¹⁷*Super Lk. 10:42,* B.ed. 23, 90b. ¹⁸*Super Lk. 11:27,* B.ed. 23, 163b. ¹⁹*Super Lk.,* 173a. ²⁰B.ed. 38, 156a; also cf. A. Fries, *ME,* III, 344. ²¹*In IV Sent.,* dist. 13, a.14, q.2, B.ed. 28, 360a; also *De Ressurect.,* Cologne, ed. vol.26, tr.2, q.5, 263. ²²*De Resurrect.,* Cologne ed., vol.26, tr.2, q.8, 285. ²³*De Natura Boni,* 59. ²⁴*In Lk. 1:49,* 130a.

ALCUIN (d.804)

The leading spirit in the Carolingian renaissance, Charlemagne's "Minister for Education" (Guizot), A. came from York in England to the imperial court at Aix-la-Chapelle, and ended his life in Tours where his creative influence continued. In Marian theology and devotion, his contribution is relevant to a debate on the Carolingian Age: in doctrine, the practice of prayer and Liturgy. Spurious works listed with his writings are now identified as such; some genuine items are lost. An authentic passage on Jn 2 was wrongly attributed to Venerable Bede (*qv*).¹

Opposing the adoptionist heresy, A. expounded the divine maternity and affirmed the virginity (*qv*): "The Blessed Virgin Mary who, without loss of the integrity of her body brought forth God and man, was the purest wool, renowned in her virginity, incomparable before all other virgins on earth, and of such character and greatness was she that she alone became worthy to receive into herself the divinity of the Son of God." A. then uses the metaphor of dyed wool to illustrate Mary's divinisation and concludes, "And thus the Blessed Virgin became the *Theotokos* as well as *Christotokos* (Greek words in the original)."²

His succinct summary of the doctrine of Ephesus is admirable: "She who was a virgin before birth, in birth and after birth, brought forth God, the Son of God, coequal and consubstantial with the Father."³

On the Cana (*qv*) episode he reflects too on the two natures: "For he would not dishonour his Mother, he who orders us to honour father and mother; nor would he deny that she was his Mother, from whose virginal flesh he did not shrink from taking flesh .... But when, about to work a miracle, he says 'Woman, what is it to me and thee' he means that he had not taken the principle of his divinity, by which he was to work the miracle, from his Mother in the order of time, but had eternity from his Father .... 'What is there in common between the divinity which I have eternally from my Father and your flesh, from which I have taken [my] flesh? ... I must first display the power of the eternal deity by performing works ...' The hour will come when he will show that which he has in common with his Mother, when dying on the Cross he will entrust the Virgin to the virgin disciple."³

Though the request of the Mother seemed to have been denied, she "None the less new the devotion of the Son and that he would not deny it."⁴ A.'s trust in Mary's mediation (*qv*) and intercession (*qv*) is manifest especially in the *Tituli*, poetic inscriptions composed for chapels or altars of Our Lady: "May devotion and honour remember you here, Queen of heaven, greatest hope of our life. May you regard with accustomed pity the children of God who implore you, Virgin most meek. In your clemency ever heed our prayers and by your prayers rule our days everywhere and at all times."⁵ "You are my sweet love, my jewel, and the great hope of my salvation. Help your servant, Virgin most illustrious. My voice sounds with tears, my heart burns with love. Heed too the prayers of all my brothers who cry to you: 'Virgin, you who are full of grace, through you may the grace of Christ preserve us.'"⁶ Here are sobriety and tenderness; belief in Mary's constant presence to her children, in her queenship (elsewhere he calls her "Queen of our salvation") and the sense of mediation in the phrase "through you (per te)."

For private devotion A. composed a *Liber Sacramentorum*, which assigns two votive Masses of the Blessed Virgin to Saturday.⁷ The Wisdom text from Eccl 24 is found in it. Letters

12

to the monks of St. Vaast and Fulda referring to the Mass are extant.[8] On the Saturday Mass of Our Lady, we await the publication of Fr. H. Barré's (qv) work. The text of the Mass appears in Lectionaries and Missals towards the end of the tenth century.

---

[1]For authenticity, cf. R. Laurentin, *Traité*, I, 142-143; H. Barré, C.S.Sp., *Prières Anciennes*, 50-51, and 109; G. Ellard, *Master Alcuin, Liturgist*, (Chicago, 1956); H. Barré and J. Deshusses, "A la recherche du Missel d'Alcuin," *Eph. Lit.*, 81(1968), 3-44; H. Barré, "Homéliaires" in DSp. [2]*De Fide Trinit., 3, 14*, in PL 101, 46. [3]*In Jn. Lib I, 2, 3-4*, PL 100, 766-767. [4]*In Jn. Lib I.* [5]MGH, I *Poetae*, (99, 12) 325; PL 101, 749D(86). [6]MGH, I *Poetae*, 313-314; PL 101, 771E(174); cf. MGH, I *Poetae*, 220, 241 and PL 101, 724BC, 790A. [7]PL 101, 455-456. [8]MGH *Epist.* IV, Ep. 296, 454-455; Ep. 250 to the monks of Fulda, 404-406. Cf. for the Saturday Mass, G. Frénaud, O.S.B., in *Maria*, VI, 190; J. Leclercq, O.S.B., "Formes successives de l'Office votif de la Vierge," *Eph. Lit.*, 72(1958), 29-301.

ALDAMA, JOSEPH DE (1904-1980)

A notable representative of the recent Spanish school of Marian theology, Patrologist, expert in St. John Chrysostom (qv), and the age of St. Ambrose (qv); a Jesuit he has taught theology for over 35 years in Granada.[1] Contributor to the review of the Spanish Mariological Society, *Estudios Marianos*, to *Ephemerides Mariologicae* and *Marianum*, as well as other reviews. Works include over 80 articles on subjects currently debated—Patrology, Spanish theology, especially Suarez (qv), the Assumption (qv), coredemption (qv), the virginity (qv), Vatican II and Mary's motherhood (qv) of the Church; also *Mariologia seu de Matre Redemptoris* in *Sacrae Theologiae Summa*, by Spanish Jesuit Professors (1950 and later editions); *Virgo Mater* (1963), *Temas de Teologia Mariana* (1966); *Maria e la Teologia* (1967); *De Quaestione Mariali in Hodierna vita Ecclesiae* (1964); *Maria en la Patristica* I, (1970).

---

[1]A. Rivera, C.M.F., "Homenaje al R. P. José A. De Aldama, S. J., en su sexagésimo quinto ano," *Eph Mar*, 20(1970), 241-245.

ALEXANDER VII (1599-1667; Pope *post* 1655)

A. played an important part in the development of the doctrine of the Immaculate Conception (qv). He replied to the embassies of the kings of Spain, in particular that of Philip IV and his legate, Crespi Borgia, who sought clarification of the precise object of the feast. His essential words, which were subsequently written into *Ineffabilis Deus* (qv) were: "Concerning the Most Blessed Virgin Mary, Mother of God, ancient indeed is that devotion of the faithful who have the sentiment that her soul, in the first instant of its creation and of its infusion into the body was, by a special grace and privilege of God, in view of the merits of Jesus Christ her Son, the Redeemer of the human race, preserved free from all stain of original sin, and with this meaning they have solemnly honoured and celebrated the feast of her Conception."[1] This statement bears close resemblance to the dogmatic formula of Pius IX (qv). The points of difference are: A. approves a pious belief or sentiment (see SENTIMENT OF THE FAITHFUL), whereas Pius defines a revealed doctrine; A. speaks of the soul, Pius of the Most Blessed Virgin Mary, that is of the person; A. speaks of the stain (*macula*) of original sin, Pius of all stain of original guilt, (*ab omni originalis culpae labe*). At the time there was opposition even to the very words Immaculate Conception. A. intervened twice to ensure that the Master of the Sacred Palace would give the *Imprimatur* to books by Fr. Esparza, S. J., and Luke Wadding, O.F.M. (qv), which had the words in their titles.

---

[1]Bull *Sollicitudo omnium ecclesiarum*, 8 December, 1661; cf. *Bullarium Taurinense*, 16, 789; DS 1, 100; Bourassé VII, 251; cf. C. Gutierrez, "Espana por el dogma de la Inmaculada. La ambajada a Roma de 1659 y la Bula 'Sollicitudo' de Alejandro VII," *Miscellanea Comilas*, 24(1955); R. Laurentin, *Traité* V, 85-86, 114; R. Laurentin, "Le Magistère et le développement du dogme de l'Immaculée Conception," in *V.I.*, II, 50ff.

ALEXANDER OF ALEXANDRIA, ST.(d. 328)

Patriarch of the greatest see in the east in his time, A. was an opponent of Arianism; with his deacon Athanasius, his renowned successor in the patriarchate, he defended orthodoxy at the Council of Nicaea (325). Author of a capital text: "In these things we know the resurrection of the dead; of this the first fruits was our Lord Jesus Christ, who truly and not merely in appearance bore flesh, taken from Mary *Theotokos*."[1] This is the first known use of the most important title ever given to Mary (see THEOTOKOS). Athanasius implies some dependence on A. in his own *Letter to the Virgins*: "I heard it from the lips of our Father Alexander . . . 'He was born of the Virgin Mary, for in her he took flesh made man . . . You have the conduct of Mary, who is the example and image of the heavenly life' (virginity evidently)."[2] The portrait given by Athanasius (later reproduced with correction by St. Ambrose) also bears resemblance to the *gnomai* or proverbs of the Council of Nicaea, attended by A.[3]

---

[1]*Epist. ad Alexand. Byzant.*, 1, 12, PG 18, 568C; cf. S. Söll, S.D.B., LexMar., 125. [2]*Letter to the Virgins*, ed. Th. Lefort, *Le Museon*, 42(1929), 256-259; CSCO 151, 72-76. [3]F. Haase, "Die koptischen Quellen Zum Nonzil von Nicaea," in *Studien zur Geschichte und Kultur des Altertums*, 10, 4(Paderborn, 1920), 50-52.

ALONSO, J. M., C. M. F. (1913-1981)

A Claretian, professor of Mariology and of the Introduction to Theology in the *Studium Theologicum Claretianum*, Madrid; also attached to the Theological Faculty of the Catholic University of Lisbon. Has contributed very many papers marked by rigorous scientific accuracy to reviews of Marian theology and Marian theological congresses (see FATIMA; SWORD; VIRGINITY)[1]; submitted a draft Marian schema to Vatican II (*qv*); has specialised in the subject of Fatima, and in recent controversies on the virgin birth (*qv*), in which he has engaged in direct dialogue with Fr. Schoonenberg.[2] Editor since 1969 of *Ephemerides Mariologicae*, to which he frequently contributes, and which he has brought fully into the aggiornamento, on patristic and biblical lines recommended by the Council.

---

[1]For bibliography cf. *Claretianum*, 6(1966), 1-15. [2]Cf. Eph.Mar, 21(1971), 161-216.

ALPHONSUS LIGUORI, ST., DOCTOR OF THE CHURCH (1696-1787)

St. Alphonsus was the most important writer on Our Lady in the eighteenth century, an age of decline in Marian theology and devotion. His contribution was enhanced by his reputation in Moral and Pastoral Theology and as a great religious founder.[1] A.'s principal Marian work is *The Glories of Mary*, the most widely distributed book on Our Lady in modern times—over 800 editions, in many languages, since 1750. The saint was convinced that he had received extraordinary graces from Our Lady. Piety born of this conviction led him to deal frequently with Marian themes, especially in his spiritual works.[2] Through sixteen years, crowded with many tasks, he worked at the *Glories*. His intention was "that devout souls may, with little trouble and little expense, read of the glories of Mary and be inflamed with love for Mary" and "to provide priests with material for sermons, so that they may spread devotion to the Mother of God."[3] To this pastoral end he would leave other prerogatives of Mary to other authors and confine himself to her mercy and intercession. Hence the plan of the work: Part One deals with phrase after phrase of the Salve Regina; Part Two is made up of sermons of feasts of Mary (Immaculate Conception, Nativity, Presentation, Annunciation, Visitation, Purification, two on the Assumption) and meditations on the seven sorrows of Our Lady and on ten virtues characteristic of her (humility, love of God, love of our neighbour, faith, hope, chastity, poverty, obedience, patience, spirit of prayer) with, to conclude, advice on traditional devotional practices. Later editions (after 1775) carried the saint's replies to a work by Abbé Rolli and to a critic, *Lamindus Pritanius redivivus*. To each chapter section of the first part and each chapter of the second, the author added edifying stories and prayers.

The text of the *Glories of Mary* abounds in references to past authors, who are often quoted in brief excerpts. The Fathers are there but the medieval writers are much favoured, St. Bernard most of all. St. Bridget of Sweden (*qv*) appears surprisingly often. The author did not have critical texts of these. He has been criticised for his interpretation of Scripture and for his use of dubious material in the edifying stories. On a higher level, Marian "minimalists" have attacked his theory of Mary's mediation and the language in which it was expressed. His phenomenal success in communication indicates a favourable response from the Sentiment of the Faithful (*qv*) to the core of the book. It was a successful challenge to Jansenism.

The emphasis on Mary's powerful role as Mediatress (*qv*) and Advocate (*qv*) is dominant and manifold. Part One opens with the queenship —on which A. is quoted in *Ad Caeli Reginam* (*qv*)—and the spiritual motherhood (*qv*). A. adopts the medieval view of the kingdom of justice ruled by Jesus and that of mercy by Mary. Gerson and St. Bonaventure are his authorities here and he invokes the example of Esther and Ahasuerus. With amazing dexterity the saint moves around the idea of motherhood, affirming, explaining, exhorting, applying his ideas to human need, to one universal need, help in the hour of death.

Chapters V and VI are centered on St. Bernard's axiom that all graces come to us through Mary. A. clarifies that "Jesus Christ is the only Mediator of justice" and "Mary is the mediatress of grace" for "mediation of justice by way of merit is one thing and mediation of grace is another."[4] In dealing with the use of the word "omnipotent" A. has something similar to say. "Mary then is called omnipotent in the sense in which it can be understood of a creature who is incapable of a divine attribute: that she is omnipotent because by her prayers she obtains whatever she wishes."[5] Though stating that "Mary, now in heaven, can no longer command her Son," A. later quotes St. Antoninus: "Since the prayers of the Blessed Virgin are those of a mother, they necessarily have, to a certain extent, the nature of a command."[6]

The hopeful theme, help for sinners, continues: Mary's saving role is expressed in concrete terms without too systematic a theology and without use of the word Coredemptress, which occurs elsewhere in his works.[7]

In the sermons on the feasts (Part Two), A. goes into points of theology. He argues that the Immaculate Conception (qv) was fitting to the first-born daughter of the Father, the Mother of the Son and the spouse of the Holy Ghost; but his history is in places defective. Speaking of Mary's birth he raises the question of her pre-eminence in grace over all others, even in the moment of the Immaculate Conception, and defends the view that she possessed the use of reason in her mother's womb. The Presentation (qv) stimulates reflections on her self-offering to God and the vow of virginity she took; the Annunciation on the dignity of the divine motherhood; the Visitation on Mary as the dispenser of graces; the Purification on her part in the final sacrifice to which her present offering looked. Mary, then, "by the merit of her sorrows and by sacrificing her Son became the Mother of all the redeemed."Again Bernard's idea, so often on A.'s lips, recurs: all graces come through Mary.

The passage on the Assumption quoted in *Munificentissimus Deus* (qv) is from the sermon on the Immaculate Conception: "It would have redounded to his dishonour if the virginal flesh with which he had clothed himself had rotted away."[8] A. refers to Pseudo-Augustine, not doubting its authenticity. The sermons on the feast of the Assumption are imaginative and picturesque. The Apostles come to the death; Mary entering heaven is greeted by the saints – foremost among them her parents and St. Joseph – and by the angels.

Intensity of feeling and helpful insights mark the remaining chapters of the book, notably on the sorrow of Mary on Calvary, and on Mary's faith (qv). A. recommends traditional devotions and the soundness of his devotion is evident in the formulas of consecration in which the key phrase is "that I (we) may never offend Jesus."

[1]Cf. esp. Cl. Dillenschneider, C.SS.R., *S. Alphonse*, 2 vols., (Fribourg, 1931), 34; *Pietas Alphonsiana erga Matrem gloriosam Mariam*, a symposium, (Louvain, 1941); S. Starowieyski, *De conjunctione Mariae cum Filio Secundum "Le Glorie di Maria" S. Alphonsi*, (Vatican City Press, 1954); G. M. Roschini, O.S.M., "La Corredentrice negli scritti di S. Alfonso M. de Liguori," in MM 18(1956), 314-336; L.R.P. Angel, S.SS.R., "La corredención objetiva in San Alfonso Maria de Liguori," in EstM 19(1958), 337-348; O. Gregorio, C.SS.R., "Caráttere pastorale della Mariologia di S. Alfonso," in *Asprenas* 10(1963), 215-228; D. J. Lowery, C.SS.R., "The spiritual maternity of Mary and St. Alphonsus Liguori," AER, 151(1964), 248-255; A. Muccino, C.SS.R., *La Regalità di Maria nella dottrina di S. Alfonso de Liguori*, (Naples, ed. Redenzione, 1965); H. Graef, *Mary*, II, 74-77; P. Hitz, C.SS.R., *Maria*, III, 277-305; LexMar I, 128-131; "Dans l'espirit de S. Alphonse, une pastorale mariale pour notre temps," *Studia Moralia*, 9(1971), 179-232. [2]Cf. *History of Heresies*, (London, 1851), on Helvidius, Jovinian and Nestorius; *Sermons on Various Subjects*, (London, 1858); various Marian items in the 18-vol. centenary edition (ed. E. Grimm, C.SS.R.) e.g., chapters in *The Way of Salvation, The Preparation for Death, The Dignity and Duties of Priests, The True Spouse of Christ, Sermons for Sundays of the Year, The Incarnation of Jesus Christ and Miscellaneous Subjects*. [3]English tr. of critical ed. rendered by Redemptorists of New York, (Baltimore, Dublin, 1962), vol. 1, 7,8. [4]V, 1, 97,96, cf. also *Declaration of the Author*, 11. [5]VI, 1,113. [6]VI, 1, 116. [7]*Opera dommatica contra gli eretici*, (Naples, 1871), apud C. Dillenschneider, op. cit., 127.

ALVA Y ASTORGA, PETER DE (d. 1667)

A Spanish Franciscan who specialized in the historical documentation of his own order's history and embarked on immense publishing activity on the Immaculate Conception (qv), object at the time of acute controversy.[1] He unearthed masses of materials in libraries and archives at a cost of tremendous labour and then assembled them in forty large works, in some cases digested or grouped around his own theses, in others—the series entitled *Monumenta*—reproduced textually. Owing to clashes with the Dominicans he moved to Belgium (then the

Spanish Netherlands) and continued publication, working for a while with his own printing house.[2] He worked in a crusading spirit, as the title of some of his works forcibly manifested; he did not see the appearance of all his compositions in print. The Roman Inquisition which had taken action against his equally prolific contemporary, I. Marracci (*qv*) issued one ban on two of his works, 22 June, 1665.

Titles chosen from this voluminous output are: 1. *Bibliotheca Virginalis*, 3 vols., (Madrid, 1649); 2. *Opusculum pro conficiendo armamentario majori pro Immaculata Conceptione V.*, (Madrid, 1649); 3. *Armamentarium seraphicum, pro tuendo I.C. titulo*, (Madrid, 1648); 4. *Sol Veritatis cum ventilabro seraphico pro candida aurora Maria etc.*, (Madrid, 1660); 5. *Nodus indissolubilis de conceptu mentis et de conceptu ventris*, (Brussels, 1661), 6. *Exsufflationes pro defensione I.C. Deiparae etc.*, (Saragossa, 1662); 7. *Risus Aurorae*, (Louvain, 1663); 8. *Radii Solis veritatis caeli atque zeli etc.*, (Louvain, 1663); 9. *Militia universalis pro Immaculata Conceptione ex diversis auctoribus etc.*, (Louvain, 1663); 10. *Allegationes et avisamenta J. de Segovia ad patres Concilii Basileensis, a.1436, circa V.M.I.C.*, (Madrid, 1664); 11. *Monumenta antiqua I. C. ex variis auctoribus antiquis*, (Louvain, 1664); 12. *Monumenta seraphica*, (Louvain, 1664); 13. *Monumenta Dominicana; Monumenta Italo-Gallica*, 2 vols., (Louvain, 1666); 14. *Expositio nova litteralis cantici Magnificat*, (Madrid, 1661). Full details are given about these and other published and unpublished works of the indefatigable knight of the Immaculate One in the excellent monograph noted.[3] Some works were massive, running to over 700 or 800 pages. The *Militia* occupies 1534 folio columns; it reproduces 6,000 testimonies, draws on 615 breviaries, 200 missals, records of universities, churches, liturgical ceremonies, councils, institutes. Present-day facsimile reproduction of Fr. de Alva's works is under way for *Culture et Civilisation*, Brussels.

---

[1] Cf. A. de Eguiluz, O.F.M., "El P. Alva y Astorga y sus escritos inmaculistas," in *Arch. Iber-Americ.*, 15(1955), 497-594. [2] Cf. L. Ceyssens, O.F.M., "Pedro de Alva y Astorga y su imprenta de la Inmaculada Concepcion de Lovania," in *Arch. Iber-Americ.*, 11(1951), 5-35. [3] A. de Eguiluz, *Arch. Iber-Americ.*, 15(1955), 552-594.

AMADEUS OF LAUSANNE, ST. (1110-1159)

A novice trained by St. Bernard (*qv*) at Clairvaux, A. became Abbot of Hautecombe in 1139, and five years later bishop of Lausanne. His eight sermons on Our Lady have a certain doctrinal substance.[1] The first situates Mary between the two Testaments. The remaining seven are on the phases and mysteries of her life, each one related to a Gift of the Holy Spirit: her justification to Fear of the Lord; the virginal conception to Piety; Christ's birth to Knowledge; the "martyrdom" of Mary to Fortitude; her Easter joy to Counsel; the Ascension and Assumption to Understanding; and her heavenly intercession to Wisdom.

A., convinced of Mary's perfection, left aside the question of the Immaculate Conception (*qv*). He gives much human detail in his account of Mother and Child as in describing Mary's sufferings on Calvary. But he explains the compassion (*qv*) by love: "Abyss calling to abyss two loves met, in and from the two was made one love when the Virgin Mother gave to her Son her love for God and to God love as to her Son. She suffered then all the more because she loved more; the intensity of her love stirred the fire of her suffering."[2] He recalls Ambrose's dictum *Lego stantem et non flentem* to show the Mother's strength.

Mary's joy in the Resurrection was complete: "You have then, O Blessed Virgin, your joy; your desire is fulfilled and Christ, crown of your head, has brought you supremacy over heaven through grace, queenship of the world through mercy, domination over hell in revenge."[3] Jesus wished her to remain on after the Ascension so that the Apostles would enjoy material comfort and instruction—though taught by the Spirit they still had much to learn from her; the Church too would be consoled by her presence. As *Munificentissimus Deus* (*qv*) says, A. taught the bodily Assumption. In Heaven she takes the place of the fallen Satan, "in the realm of eternal light and on the highest throne, first after her divine Son, who had taken flesh from her as from a humble servant."[4]

A. is not explicit on Mary as the spouse of Christ, but very much so on this relationship with the Spirit. "Your Creator has become your Spouse, he has loved your beauty .... Go out for the nuptial chamber is already prepared, and your Spouse is coming, the Holy Spirit comes to you." [5] Interestingly A. speaks of Mary's beauty, a theme proposed by Paul VI (qv) to the 1975 Rome Mariological Congress (qv).

The saint expressed Mediation by the metaphor of the neck, through which the vital grace of the Head, Christ, comes to the other parts of the Body. Mary had crushed the head of the serpent "that she should kill death and restore life." "As in Eve all died, so in Mary all would arise."[6] Five times, A. invokes the Eve (qv)—Mary parallel.

Mary's care extends to all. She is the Queen of heaven, source of life and especially the source of mercy. She has pity on the afflicted, relieves the unfortunate, knows our needs and prays for us. She turns all evil from those whose prayers she welcomes, assuring not only salvation but—miraculously if need be—health as well.[7] She is the Star of the Sea.

---

[1]PL 188, 1303-1346; SC 72; G. Bavaud, J. Deschusses, O.S.B., A. Dumas, O.S.B., A. Dimier, M. Cocherill, T. Robert, O.C.R., "Textes Mariales" in *Coll. Ord. Cist. Ref.*, 19(1957), 34-43, 122-132; R. Thomas, O.S.C.O., tr. "Amadeus Lausanensis," *Mariale*, (Chambarand, 1960). Cf. A. Dimier, *Amédée de Lausanne*, (S. Wandrille, 1949); *Coll. Ord. Cist. Ref.*, 21, 1-65; the same author in LexMar. Cf. also A. Louf, "Marie dans la Parole de Dieu selon S. Amédée de Lausanne," in *Coll. Ord. Cist. Ref.*, 21(1959), 29-63; M. A. Gomez, "Las homilias marianas de S. Amadeo de Lausana," in *Cistercium*, 11(1959), 123-129. [2]SC, V, 152. [3]SC, VI, 162. [4]SC, VIII, 210. [5]SC, III, 102-104. [6]SC, II, 80. [7]SC, VIII, 212-216.

AMBROSE, ST., DOCTOR OF THE CHURCH (339-397)

A.'s corpus of Marian writing is substantial.[1] After the dramatic event which was to change him from being a Roman consular official in Milan to ruling the city as bishop, he studied the writings of the Greek Fathers, the better to equip himself for his task. He is thus an example of the debt the West owes to the East in Marian theology. One whole section of his work *De Virginibus* is taken from the *Letter to Virgins* of St. Athanasius (qv).[2] (see EASTERN INFLUENCE)

As with many of the Fathers, controversy was a stimulus to his thinking. On Our Lady's virginity he resisted the heretical views of Jovinian, an apostate monk, and Bonosus, bishop of Sardica. He finally achieved the first major contribution of the Latin genius to Marian theology, in association with St. Jerome (qv) who outlived him, and his disciple, St. Augustine (qv).[3] Renewed interest in the Fathers has brought his ideas to prominence and into the documents of Vatican II (qv).

Marian theology is found in A.'s biblical commentaries, in his essays on virginity, in letters and other works. He repeats himself, sometimes in the very words, in different passages. Virginity as an ascetical ideal engaged the attention of all great pastors in his age. Though interested in many aspects of the mystery of Mary, A. gave pride of place to her virginity: titles referring to Christ as the Son or offspring (*partus*) of the Virgin are found 40 times in his works.[4] As in another area of thought he would remove doubt about Mary's personal sinlessness, in this domain he would establish the *virginitas in partu* (qv).

A. preached this doctrine to his flock as did Zeno of Verona. But a passage in the commentary on St. Luke, based on the sermons, is ambiguous and has caused controversy. A. does use the words "he opened his mother's womb" to conclude some reflections on Ex 13:12, on the virgin church whose womb Christ made fruitful to have the peoples of God as children, and on the sanctification of Jeremiah in the womb. A. may have been influenced here by Origen (qv), whose commentary on the same passage runs contrary to the *virginitas in partu*.[5]

Before long the saint's views would be affirmed in a public manner and in terms entirely explicit. Around 390 Jovinian, already condemned in Rome, sought refuge and support in Milan. A. had him and his followers expelled from the imperial city. He then convened an episcopal council to consider Jovinian's ideas. The latter's denial of the virginity in *partu* was brought to light and the true doctrine set forth in the letter sent to Pope Siricius: "So a virgin could conceive and a virgin could not give birth, though the conception comes first and the birth follows? But if the teachings of the priests are not believed, let the sayings of Christ be believed, let the admonitions of angels be believed when they say 'For no word is impossible with God'. Let the Apostles' Creed be believed as the Roman Church has ever kept and preserved it untouched . . . This is the Virgin who conceived in the womb: the Virgin who brought forth a Son."[6]

The same epistle applies to Mary the image of Ez 44:2, "the outer gate of the sanctuary, which faces east and was shut," a typology found in the same age in Amphilochius (qv). "This gate is Blessed Mary, of whom it is written that 'the

Lord shall pass through it and it shall be closed'; after childbirth; for as a virgin she conceived and brought forth." Elsewhere A. sums up a passage on the same idea with the words, "Christ passed through it, but did not open it."[7]

Not long after the Jovinian affair, A. was faced with another eruption of error. Bonosus, from a diocese in Illyricum, asserted that Mary, after the birth of Christ, had other children. A., appealed to, composed for the Illyrican bishops a letter which was approved by his own bishops, suggesting how the matter should be dealt with: "The Lord Jesus would not have chosen to be born of a virgin if he judged that she would become promiscuous, that ordinary sexual intercourse would permeate the origin of the Lord's body, the palace of the eternal king."[8] An argument is also drawn from the Saviour's action on Calvary, entrusting his Mother to John. In the commentary on St. Luke, A. had dealt with the objection to Mary's perpetual virginity based on Mt 1, 25, "but [Joseph] knew her not until she had borne a Son," showing from similar examples of biblical usage that the words need not at all mean that Joseph did know her. In the *De Institutione Virginis*, he deals similarly with an adverse interpretation of "before they came together" (Mt 1:18), rejects any difficulty arising from the Saviour's use of the word "Woman" in Jn 2:4, and also considers the "Brothers of the Lord" (*qv*).

A. insisted on the just character of St. Joseph, but he did no further thinking on the saint's personality and role. He thought that there was a true marriage between Mary and Joseph, for the essence of marriage was for him mutual consent (*pactio conjugalis*), not physical union.[9] He accepted the possibility that Joseph did not think Mary still a virgin after he knew of her pregnancy—he even uses the word guilty (*ream*). The purpose of the marriage he considered the preservation of Mary's good name, "For the Lord preferred that some should doubt his own origin, rather than the chastity of his Mother."[10] —that is, should take him for Joseph's son. He also reproduces the view of Origen (*qv*) which ultimately goes back to St. Ignatius of Antioch (*qv*), that Satan was kept in ignorance of the virginal conception.[11]

In regard to the "Brothers of the Lord" he lacks the precision of St. Jerome (*qv*). He admits that brothers in Sacred Scripture can refer to those of the same race or kindred or people,

quoting PS 21:23 and St. Paul (Rom 9:3) and then goes on: "But the brothers could have been from Joseph, not from Mary. Whoever wishes to investigate this matter more carefully, will find the answer. We did not think we should investigate these things, since the name of brother may be common to several."[12] There is an echo here of the eastern opinion that Joseph had been previously married: a view which St. Jerome and St. Augustine would resolutely oppose.

Not only the gate that faces to the east, but many other Old Testament images appealed to A. as symbols of Mary; they helped him to develop his thought. He was particularly attracted by the image of the "light cloud" mentioned by Is 19:1, which he links, in a remarkable passage, with the pillar of cloud going before the Israelites in the desert: "That pillar of cloud, did, in its outward appearance, go before the children of Israel, but as mystery it signified the Lord Jesus, who was to come in a light cloud [*levis*, swift or light, taken by A. in the latter sense], as Isaiah said; that is in the Virgin Mary, who was a cloud on account of the inheritance of Eve, but light because of her virginal integrity. She was light because she did not seek to please man, but God. She was light because she did not conceive in iniquity, but begot [a child] under the overshadowing Spirit; nor did she bring forth in fault, but with grace."[13]

A. seems to have been the first to apply images from the Song of Songs (*qv*) to Mary: "O that you would kiss me with the kiss of your mouth" (1:1) symbolizes the grace of the Spirit at the Annunciation. "Your name is oil poured out" (1:3) is referred to the virginal conception and birth, "as a virgin she brought forth good odour, that is to say the Son of God."[14]

The Latin doctor corrected certain eastern interpretations of biblical texts relating to Mary. The sword (*qv*) of Simeon (Lk 2:35) did not mean any future doubt of failure on her part. The awkward text in Lk 8:21 ("My mother and my brothers are those who hear the word of God and keep it") is thus explained: "Here, therefore, the Mother, who is acknowledged from the cross is not denied, but the form of heavenly commandments is preferred to physical relationship. This may also be understood that he shows through the figure of parents that the Church which believed is to be preferred to the Jews, from whom Christ came in the flesh."[15] On

Calvary, Mary was to show in her wisdom she was "not ignorant of the heavenly mystery."[16] She was also to manifest fortitude of soul and, in A.'s view already, a quality like the compassion (qv) which would figure so much in medieval literature. "But holy Mary stood by the cross of her Son, and the Virgin beheld the passion of her only-begotten. I read that she stood, not that she wept."[17] "The Mother stood before the cross, and as the men fled, she stood fearless. Consider whether the Mother of Jesus could alter her chaste behaviour when she did not alter her spirit. With loving eyes she gazed at the wounds of her Son, through whom she knew that redemption would come to all. The Mother stood, no unworthy sight, and did not fear the slayer. The Son hung on the cross, the Mother offered herself to the persecutors."[18] "We have here a teaching on devotion; the reading teaches us what maternal love should imitate, what filial reverence should follow, that the former should come forward in a moment of danger to their sons, while for these anxiety for the mother should be a greater grief than the sadness of their own death."[19]

Mary's spiritual purity is expressed by another Old Testament image, which would pass into the Liturgy, as it is also related to Mary's choice of virginity: "She is the rod which brings forth a flower. For she is pure, and her virginity is directed to God with a free heart and is not deflected by the dissipation of worldly cares."[20] A. first used the Latin word *sancta*, holy, about Mary – it is found sixteen times in his writings; the corresponding Greek word *hagia* was already in use. He spoke of Mary as "not from this earth but from heaven," without denying her genuine humanity. But all this perfecton was rooted in Christ. "Mary was not less than became the Mother of Christ."[21] "Who was there on whom the Lord had bestowed greater merit, from whom he held a greater reward than his Mother?"[22] It was Christ who chose for himself the vessel which was not from this earth but from heaven.[23] She was first beneficiary of the redemption: "Nor is it to be wondered at that when the Lord was about to redeem the world, he began his work from Mary, so that she, through whom salvation was being prepared for all, should be the first to draw salvation from her Son."[24] This passage bears comparison with the oft-quoted phrase of St. Irenaeus (qv): "(Mary)

. . . became the cause of salvation both for herself and the whole human race."

A. uses one striking description of Mary as "an incorrupt virgin, a virgin free through grace from every stain of sin."[25] Did he think her then free from Original Sin? Fr. J. Huhn, in an excellent monograph, inclines towards the negative opinion.[26] The saint was not faced with the problem which his disciple St. Augustine would present to generations of theologians, because of his particular explanation of the doctrine. In the spiritual portrait which A. took over from St. Athanasius every vestige of fault is eliminated; the picture is one of flawless perfection, characteristically set in the frame of virginity. "What can be nobler than the Mother of God? What is more splendid than her whom splendour chose? And what shall I say of her other virtues . . . This is the image of virginity. For such was Mary that her life alone is an example to all."[27]

Faith shines forth especially in this all-perfect one. Contrasting Mary's response to the angelic message with that of Zechariah, the great Latin doctor continues: "For because she had believed that it would be done, she asked how it would be done. Hence she deserved to hear 'Blessed art thou for believing'. And she was truly blessed who excelled the priest for if the priest had expressed denial, the virgin remedied his fault."[28]

A wider vision opens, which would be taken up and clarified by Augustine. There is in Mary's faith an exemplary, quasi-creative quality, one that must be found in every human heart: "See that Mary did not doubt, but believed and gathered the fruit of faith. 'Blessed' says [Elizabeth] because thou hast believed'. But you are blessed, who have heard and believed; for every soul that has believed both conceives and engenders the word of God and recognises his works . . . if, according to the flesh, there is one Mother of Christ, according to faith, Christ is the fruit of all."[29]

How did Mary's destiny known by faith link her with the central fact of salvation history, the Incarnation? A. had a strong Trinitarian sense and was resolutely anti-Arian. Many of his references to the Holy Spirit's role may be summarized in the pithy phrase: "The offspring of the Virgin is therefore the work of the Spirit."[30] He was the first to use the title *Mater Dei*, Mother of God, in the West; *Theotokos* (qv) was in widespread use in the East, and it is a matter of conjecture why A. in fact employed the Latin rendering only twice, whether he was reserved because of the cult of the Latin mother-goddess, Kybele.

The explanation given in the treatise on the Incarnation is in language which anticipates Ephesus and Chalcedon: "... Christ is the Son of God, both eternal from the Father and born from the Virgin Mary... Spouse of the soul according to the Word; giant of the earth because he performed the duties of our condition; since as God he was ever eternal, he undertook the mysteries of the Incarnation, not as divided, but as one; because each was one and he was one in each, that is in divinity and in the body; for he was not one [person] from the Father and another from the Virgin; but the same in one way from the Father, in another from the Virgin."[31] Elsewhere he uses the following phrases. "That you should know that there are not two Christs, but one: who was born before the ages from the Father, and in these last times created from the Virgin"[32]; "he who was from the Father took flesh from the Virgin: he took the physical disposition from his Mother so that he might adopt our infirmities"[33]; "she who had given birth to God"[34]; "God has been born of a Virgin."[35]

A. spoke in realistic terms of the flesh given by Mary. One is reminded of Vatican II's (qv) words "the Son of God took human nature from her that he might in the mysteries of his flesh free us from sin." (LG,55). "Flesh was born of flesh. The Virgin had something of her own to give; the Mother did not give anything foreign to herself, but from within her own inner physique [visceribus suis] she bestowed, in a manner unexampled though by a normal function, what was her own. The Virgin, therefore, had flesh which she transferred to her offspring by the right of sacred nature. According to the flesh, therefore, the nature of Mary who gave birth and of her Son was the same, nor was he unlike his brethren; for the Scripture says, so that he might be in all things like his brethren."[36] Here he has added the patristic image of the virgin earth.

Even in his handling of the Eve (qv)—Mary antithesis, A. emphasised the virginal theme: "Folly through a woman, through the Virgin wisdom"[37]; "Through the woman came anxiety, through the Virgin salvation arrived"; "He came to give salvation to the world through a Virgin and by his birth of a Virgin remedied the fault

of the woman."[38] "By a man and a woman flesh was driven from paradise, by a Virgin it was joined with God."[39] "Human nature says: I am black, because I have sinned, beautiful because Christ loves me; what he exiled in Eve, he took back from the Virgin, he accepted from Mary."[40] Here the author had the Song of Songs in mind.

Few writers in Christian antiquity, or for a long time after, wrote of womankind with such sensitive respect and insight as A. — witness not only his treatises on virginity, but his lengthy essay on widows, with its fine analysis of the Old and New Testament biblical exemplars. Sarah, Abraham's wife, the mother of the Old Covenant, he looked on as an intermediate type between Eve and Mary, all the more to show the latter's preeminence: "If she [Sarah] by giving birth from a man deserves to be heard as a type of Christ, how much did the sex accomplish who gave birth to Christ while keeping her virginity intact. Come then Eve, now Mary, who not only gave us a motive for virginity but brought us God."[41] "Adopt me in the flesh which fell in Adam. Adopt me, however, not from Sarah but from Mary."[42]

From the doctrine of Mary, the new Eve, one is led to consider her role in salvation and redemption (qv): A. saw it in the context of the Incarnation: "She was alone when the Holy Spirit came upon her and the power of the Most High overshadowed her. She was alone and she wrought the salvation of the world and conceived the redemption of all."[43] "The Virgin gave birth to the salvation of the world, the Virgin brought forth the life of all."[44]

Echoing Genesis 3:15 (see WOMAN IN), the saint attributes to Mary a share in the overthrow of Satan's power: "Mary conquered you, who gave birth to the Victor, who, without her virginity being lessened, brought forth him who when crucified would defeat you and when dead would bring you into subjection. You will be conquered today so that the woman should defeat your attacks [insidias]."[45]

Mary influenced those she encountered; she conferred the grace of virginity on some. John the Evangelist because of her companionship, "spoke more than others of divine mysteries." Yet the uniqueness and sufficiency of Christ's redemptive act must be maintained. "But Jesus had no need of a helper for the redemption of all, he who said 'I am become like a man without help, free among the dead'. So he accepted indeed the love [*affectum*] of a Mother, but did not seek the help of a human being."[46] The idea recurs elsewhere. An official report of Vatican II recalled the texts as a help to the Fathers in the subject of Mary's mediation. But in three of these texts A. imagines Mary as wishing to die with her Son, expecting thus "to add something to the public gift." In this precise context he says that Jesus did not need a helper. This is a different problem from that discussed by modern theologians on Mary's part in the Redemption. Some of them have been embarrassed by A.'s words.

Vatican II quotes A. on Mary as type of the Church: "Rightly," he says, "is she betrothed, yet a virgin, because she is a type of the Church which is immaculate yet married. The virgin [Church] has conceived us by the Spirit, the virgin brings us forth without pain. And therefore perhaps is holy Mary married to one [Joseph] but filled by another [the Holy Spirit], because the individual churches too are filled by the Spirit and his grace, but are externally joined to a mortal priest." "How beautiful are the things spoken in prophecy of Mary as a figure of the Church; that is if you look to the mysteries of generation and not the members of the body."[47]

Conceiving Christ, Mary conceived Christians: "From that womb of Mary was brought in the world the heap of wheat surrounded by lilies when Christ was born of her." ". . . by the very fact that she conceived and brought him forth for the salvation of all, she placed on his head the crown of eternal mercy that by the faith of believers Christ should become the Head of every man."[48] The relationship between Mary and the Church merges almost into identity on Calvary: "You will be 'a son of thunder' if you are a son of the Church. May Christ also say of you from the wood of the cross, 'Behold your Mother', for you will be a son of the Church when you see Christ victorious on the cross."[49]

A. warned against a certain kind of excess: "Without doubt the Holy Spirit too must be adored when we adore him who is born of the Spirit according to the flesh. But let none apply this to Mary: for Mary was the temple of God, not the God of the temple. And therefore he alone is to be adored, who worked in the temple."[50]

Imitation of Mary, A. proposed fully. Vatican II quotes (in the Decree on Religious) his statement that Mary is an example to all. He urged imitation of her on virgins, saintly mothers; he linked the idea of her virginity with our faith. "Christ is created from the Virgin so that it should be believed that he was born of God." "Let the soul of Mary be in all that she may magnify the Lord, let the spirit of Mary be in all that she may exult in God, for if according to the flesh there is one Mother of Christ, according to faith, none the less, the fruit of all is Christ."[51]

[1]Works in PL, 14-17; CSEL, 32, 62, 64, 73, 78, 79, 82; CCL, 14; *Corp. Script. Lat. Parav.*; CMP, III, 74-146; EMBP, 330-376. Cf. R. H. Connolly, *The Explanatio Symboli ad initiandos, a Work of St. Ambrose: Texts and Studies*, (Cambridge, 1962). [2]Cp. PL, 16, 208C-211C; also CSCO, 151, 59ff. [3]Cf. A. Pagnamento, *La Mariologia di S. Ambrogio*, (Milan, 1932); P. Friedrich, "Ambrosius von Mailand: über die Jungfräulickeit Marias vor der Geburt," in *Der Katholik*, 19-20(1917), 145-169, 232-258, 319-333. Cf. also, L. M. Canziani, *Maria SS. nella vita religiosa: Commentario ascetico alle virtù della Madonna sulla guida di S. Ambrogio*, 2nd ed., (Venegono, 1952); G. Jouassard, "Un portrait de la Sainte Vierge, par S. Ambroise," in VieSp, 90(1954), 477-489; G. Jouassard, "Deux chefs de file en théologie mariale dans la seconde moitié du IVe siècle: S. Epiphane et S. Ambroise," in Gregor 42(1961), 5-361. Note especially the following by J. Huhn: *Das Geheimnis der Jungfrau-Mutter: Maria nach dem Kirchenvater Ambrosius*, (Wurzburg, 1954); ASC, Vol. 1, 101-128; *Münchener theol. Zeitschrift*, 2(1951), 130-146; *Liturgie und Monchtum*, 15(1954), 40-46; *Maria est typus Ecclesiae secundum Patres, imprimis secundum S. Ambrosium et S. Augustinum*, in ME, III, 163-200; LexMar, 178-185. Cf. also C. W. Neumann, S.M., *The Virgin Mary in the Works of St. Ambrose*, (Fribourg, 1962); Rhaudenses (pseud.), *Maria ideale di vita cristiana nella dottrina di S. Ambrogio*, (Milan, 1970); M. Bertagna, "Elementa cultus mariani apud S. Ambrosium," PCM, III, 1-15; M. S. Ducci, "Senso della tipologia mariana in S. Ambrogio e suo rapporto con lo sviluppo storico e dottrinale," in EclXaver, 21(1971), 137-192; D. Bertetto, S.D.B., "De cultu imitationis B. M. V. apud Patres Latinos," in PCM, III, 101-111. [4]C. W. Neumann, PCM, III, 62. [5]*In Lucam II, 57*, CCL 14, 56; CSEL 32, IV, 73; cf. G. Jouassard, in *Maria*, I, 109, n.32; C. W. Neumann, *op.cit.*, 113ff. [6]*Ep. 42, 4-5*, PL, 16, 1125; cp. *De Instit. Virg.*, VIII, 53, PL, 16, 320. [8]*Ep. De Bonoso*, PL, 16, 1173C; for authenticity cf. J. de Aldama, *La carta ambrosiana De Bonoso*, in MM, 25, (1963), 1-22. [9]*De Inst. Virg.*, VI, 41, 42, PL, 16, 316C. [10]*Exp. Luc. II, 1*, CSEL, 32(iv), 41. [11]*Exp. Luc. II, 3*, CSEL 32(iv), 42. [12]*De Inst. Virg.*, VI, 43, PL, 16, 317. [13]*In Ps., 118, V, 3*, PL, 15, 1251-1252. [14]*De Virg., II, 65*, PL, 16. 282C. [15]*Exp. in Luc. VI, 38*, CSEL, 32(iv), 247-248. [16]*In Luc. II, 61*, CSEL, 32(iv), 74. [17]*De Obit. Val., 39*, PL, 16, 1371B. [18]*De Inst. Virg., 49*, PL, 16, 318C. [19]*Exp. in Luc. X, 132*, CSEL, 32(iv), 506. [20]*Exhort. Virg. V, 31*, PL, 16, 345. [21]*Exp.*

in Luc. X, 132, CSEL, 32(iv), 505. [22]De Inst. Virg., VI, PL, 16, 317B. [23]De Inst. Virg., V, 33, PL, 16, 313. [24]Exp. in Luc. X, 42, CSEL, 32(iv), 470. [25]In Ps. 118, 22, 30, PL, 15, 1521. [26]Op.cit., 242-253. [27]De Virg., ed. E. Cazzaniga, Corp. Script. Lat. Parav., (1948), 2, 7-15, 36-40. [28]Exp. in Luc. II, 17, CSEL, 32, 51. [29]Exp. in Luc. II, 26, op.cit., 55. [30]De Spirit. Sanct. II, 38, CSEL, 79, 101. [31]De Incar. I, 35, PL, 16, 827. [32]De Fide, III, 9, 60, CSEL, 78, 130; cf. Ep. 63, 49. [33]Explan. in Ps. 61, 5. [34]In Lk., 10, 130, CSEL, 32, 504. [35]De Inst. Virg., 17, 104, PL, 16, 331. [36]De Incar. I, 9, 104, PL, 16, 843CD. [37]In Lk., 4, 7, CSEL, 32, 142. [38]Ep. 42, 3, PL, 16, 173; Exhort. Virg., 26, PL, 16, 343C. [39]Ep. 63, 33, PL, 16, 1198. [40]In Ps. 118, 2, 8, PL, 15, 1212A. [41]De Inst. Virg., V, PL, 16, 313B. [42]In Ps. 118, 22,30, PL, 15, 1521. [43]Ep. 49, 2, PL, 16, 1154. [44]Ep. 63, 33, PL, 16, 1198. [45]De Obitu Theod., 44, PL, 16, 1400. [46]In Luc. X, 132, CSEL, 505; cp. De Inst. Virg. VI, PL, 16, 319; Ep. 63, 110, PL, 16, 1218; Ep. 49, PL, 16, 1155. [47]In Luc. II, 7, CSEL, 32, 45; De Inst. Virg., 89, PL, 16, 326C. [48]De Inst. Virg., 94, PL, 16, 327; De Inst. Virg., 98, PL, 16, 329. [49]In Luc. VII, 5, CSEL, 284. [50]De Spirit. Sancto, III, 80, CSEL, 79, 183; PL, 16, 795A. [51]In Luc. II, 26, CSEL, 55.

AMBROSE AUTPERT (d.784)

Born in southern Gaul early in the eighth century, A. entered the Benedictine monastery of St. Vincent's on the Volturno in southern Italy in 754.[1] He became Abbot, resigned soon after and, in 784, journeying to Rome to help solve a disputed abbatial succession, he died. Critical research has restored one important sermon on the Assumption to him. It is divided about the attribution of others. With the sermon on the Purification[2] and the Marian passages in his great work on the Book of Revelation,[3] the Assumption text confirms his status as a theologian of Our Lady. The disputed sermon on the Nativity of Mary[4] is not here considered, as the opinion of H. Barré, C.S.Sp. is preferred to that of J. Winandy, O.S.B.; nor is that on the Annunciation, despite a recent plea for authenticity.[5]

A. lived in a monastery not very distant from the Greek communities of monks who had fled to Sicily from the iconoclastic emperors. Dom Winandy thought that he was not thereby doctrinally influenced by the Greek Fathers; Miss H. Graef took the opposite view.[6]

A. was an innovator in the direct Marian themes of his sermons. Previous Latin preachers had spoken of Mary on feasts of the Lord. On the Assumption, he thought that the Church disregarded the Apocrypha and he thought curiosity about the fate of Mary's body improper, noting that no Latin writer had dealt formally with the subject of her death. He does refer to St. Ambrose's oblique allusion thereto—St. John the Evangelist (qv) was better placed than any to narrate the event "if God wished it made known." "It remains then that man should not lyingly indulge in open fiction about what God wished kept secret. The truth about her Assumption is found to be that—to use the Apostle's words—'whether in the body or out of the body we know not' (2 Cor, XII, 2). We should believe that she has been assumed above the angels." His earlier reference to Mary as "Queen of the Heavens" (the queenship recurs elsewhere) and the sustained high-flown eulogy which follows, show that his discretion on the bodily assumption in no way affected his exalted concept of Mary. His language is unexampled among the Latins known to us before him, as Dom Winandy rightly asserted.

No tongue can possibly praise her as she is "higher than heaven . . . deeper than the abyss." "This is the one who alone deserved to be called mother and spouse (qv); she undid the wrong of our first mother, she brought redemption to man who was lost." The mystery of salvation is then set forth in the Eve-Mary context: "For the mother of our race brought punishment to the world; the Mother of our Lord gave forth salvation to the world. Eve was the author of sin; Mary was the author of merit. Eve injured by bringing death; Mary helped by giving life."[7]

Mary was the spouse. But A. has too another intuition which has relevance to recent theology. The word associate (socia) became a keyword in the literature on Our Lady's part in the Redemption. A. uses it in verbal form (sociata) of Mary's union with angels and archangels, and says that those she associates (consociat) by divine grace with Christ are her sons. He uses a derivative verb in regard to Mary's own union with Christ in glory: "For you the royal throne is set up by angels in the hall of the eternal King and the King of Kings himself, loving you before all others, associates (associat) you with himself, in the embrace of love, as a true Mother and fair spouse."[8]

A. thought that the "offering made on the eve of the Lord's day, that is the Passion, by which we were reconciled to God, was prefigured in the offering made by Mary in the moment of the Purification." He goes on to show how Mary, having made her offering, continues it on our behalf, uniting Jesus with us by her holy intercession. He is led to a statement of the spiritual motherhood: "How should she not be the mother of the elect who gave birth to their brother? I say that if Christ is the brother of believers, why is she who gave birth to him not the mother of believers? Therefore, I implore you, my most blessed Virgin, offer us to Christ by your merciful supplications, you who do not hate your sons nor even mind the insults of those sons who do not honour you as they ought."[9]

The quality of Mary's intercession springs from her part in the Incarnation: "Nor is there any doubt that she who merited to set forth the price for those to be freed has more power than all the saints in offering prayers for those who are freed."[10] There is a hint of association in the Redemption in A.'s words on Simeon's prophecy: "It was necessary that the tender heart of the Mother should be pierced by the sword through the Passion of the Redeemer."[11] The prayer he composed was widely adopted, as it was believed to be Augustine's: "Help the miserable, assist the faint-hearted, cherish the tearful; pray for the people, intervene on behalf of the clergy, intercede for the choir of monks, pray for the devout female sex; may all feel your help whosoever celebrate your name."[12]

Through Rev 12, A. saw the Mary-Church relationship. The woman represents each: "Whether, therefore, we sometimes say that the Virgin Mary, sometimes the virgin mother Church, has borne or is bringing forth Christ, we shall not stray from the truth. For the one gave birth to the Head, the other brings forth the members." He drew this conclusion from his principle: "In this place the blessed and pious Virgin stands for (*personam agit*) the Church which daily brings forth new peoples, from whom the whole body of the Mediator is formed."[13]

[1]Cf. J. Winandy, O.S.B., *Ambroise Autpert, Moine at Théologien*, (Paris, 1953); J. Winandy, O.S.B., "L'Oeuvre littéraire d'Ambroise Autpert," in RevBen, 69(1950), 93-119; U. Berliére, in DHGE, II, 1115-1116; L. Bergeron, in DSp., I, 429; F. Buck, S.J., "Ambrose Autpert, the first Mariologist in the western Church," in Zagreb Congress, III, 277-318. [2]*Purification*, PL 89, 1291-1304; *Assumption*, PL 39, 2129-2134. Cf. R. Laurentin, *Traité* I, 129, 137. [3]*Maxima Bibliotheca Patrum*, (Lyons, 1677), vol. 13, 403-657; critical edition, (R. Weber, O.S.B., ed.), CCCM, 27, 27A. [4]*Inter op.* Alcuin, PL 101, 1300D-1308C. Cf. R.

Laurentin, *Traité* I, 143; J. Winandy, in RevBen, 69(1950), 111-116; H. Barré, *Prières Anciennes*, 109, n.41; H. Barré, in MM, 27(1965), 27-28. [5]F. Buck, *op.cit.*, 297. [6]J. Winandy, *Ambroise Autpert*, (Paris, 1953), 47-48; H. Graef, *Mary*, I, 65, n.2. [7]PL 39, 2130, 2131. [8]PL 39, 2134. [9]PL 89, 1297B. [10]PL 39, 2134. [11]PL 89, 1301. [12]PL 39, 2134. [13]*In Apoc.*, in *Maxima Bibl. Patrum*, 532G, 530H; CCCM, 27, 450, 443.

AMBROSIASTER (4th Century)

Erasmus gave this name to an unknown exegete whose commentaries on the epistles of St. Paul were ascribed to St. Ambrose (*qv*), and whose *Quaestiones Veteris et Novi Testamenti* appears in PL ed. of St. Augustine (*qv*).[1] A. has an apologetic of the virginal conception, which he thinks "folly to the gentiles" as was the Son of God crucified. He follows the Marian interpretation of Is 7:14, dismisses the idea that Mary had other sons as "madness" (*insania*), and sums up the Eve (*qv*)-Mary contrast thus: "He was born of God before all things that he should create all that did not exist. Secondly taking flesh from a virgin he was born that he should wipe out the sin which had entered the world from a virgin, Eve."[2] God sent his Son that he should be born of the Virgin, made like man.[3]

[1]Texts, PL 17, 35; CSEL 81, 50; CMP, III, 146-151; EMBP, 380-385. Cf. R. Laurentin, *Traité* I, 126; C. Martini, O.F.M., *Ambrosiaster*, Rome, Antonianum, 1944; G. Bardy in *Dict. B. Suppl.*, 1, 225-241; Clavis PL 184; B. Fischer, *Verzeichnis der Sigel fur Kirchenschriftsteller*, 2nd ed., (Freiburg, 1963), 72. [2]*In Ep. ad Col. 1, 19*, CSEL 81, 3, 173; PL 17, 425BC. [3]*In Ep. ad Gal. 4, 4*, CSEL 81, 3, 43; PL 17, 359C.

AMPHILOCHIUS OF ICONIUM, ST. (after 394)

A., bishop of Iconium, was friendly with the great Cappadocians, St. Basil (*qv*), St. Gregory of Nyssa (*qv*), and St. Gregory of Nazianzus (*qv*) who was his cousin.[1] His warm exclamation, "O Mary, O Mary, you who possess the maker of all things as your firstborn," indicates personal devotion.

A. taught the virginal conception, invoking as did so many of the Fathers, Is 7:14 (see EMMANUAL). He used the word *aeiparthenos* (ever-virgin) to express the perpetual virginity. He was among the first, if not the first, to adapt Ez 44:2 on the closed door to the virginity *in partu*. It was used in the same century by St. Ambrose (*qv*). His opinion has been controversed despite this fairly clear passage: "In what concerns the virginal nature, the doors are in no way opened, by the will of him who was until then borne in the womb, according to what was said of him: 'This is the door of the Lord, which he will enter and come through and the door will be closed.' (Ez 44:2 freely). Therefore in what relates to the virginal nature the virginal doors were not at all opened; as regards the power of the Lord who was born, nothing is closed to the Lord, but all things are open to him."[2]

A. praises Mary whom he calls holy and undefiled (*achrantos*). Though he does not use the word *Theotokos* he knows the dignity of Mary's motherhood: "He who gave the heavenly powers above their existence was given milk at the breasts of the holy Virgin."[3] Her role he saw as the antithesis of Eve's (*qv*): "The world is freed through a Virgin as formerly through a virgin it fell under sin."[4]

A. is in the Origen (*qv*) tradition in his understanding of the "sword" (*qv*) of Simeon: "The Virgin Mary lapsed into these [questioning thoughts], because she had not yet known the power of the resurrection, because she did not know whether the resurrection was near. Hence after the resurrection there is no longer a sword of doubt but joy and exultation. Therefore Simeon called the sign of the Cross the sign of contradiction when the sword of [questioning] thoughts pierced the Virgin."[5] A. tried to imagine the thoughts that crossed Mary's mind. This opinion of the "sword" was not adopted by A.'s contemporary, St. Ambrose.

---

[1]Homilies, PG, 39, 36A-44C, 44C-60A; fragments etc. CMP, II, 293-299; EMBP, 325-330. Cf. R. Laurentin, *Traité* I, 160; Clavis, PG, II, 230; H. Graef, *Mary* I, 69; K. Holl, *Amphilochius von Ikonium in seinem Verhältnis zu der Grosser Kappadoziern*, (Tubingen, 1904); G. Ficker, *Amphilochiana*, (Leipzig, 1906); C. Moss, in Mus, 43(1930), 317-364; I. Ortiz de Urbina, S.J., "Mariologia Amphilochii Iconiensis," in OCP, 23(1957), 186-191; G. Söll, S.D.B., in LexMar, 186. [2]PG, 39, 49. [3]PG, 39,40. [4]PG, 39, 41A. [5]PG, 39, 57.

ANASTASIUS OF ANTIOCH (d. 599)

Two homilies on the Annunciation are attributed to him.[1] Research is needed on the question of authenticity, for patrologists differ.

---

[1]PG, 89, 1376D-1385C, 1385C-1389B. Cf. R. Laurentin, *Traité*, I, 169; O. Stegmüller, in LexMar, 192.

ANDREW OF CRETE, ST. (c. 660-740)

With St. Germanus of Constantinople (*qv*) and St. John of Damascus (*qv*), A. forms a notable group. A native of Damascus, he had been a monk in Jerusalem and Constantinople before becoming Archbishop of Gortyna of Crete. He was the most prolific of all the Fathers on Our Lady; a complete critical edition of his works is regrettably lacking.[1] Migne has published four homilies on the Nativity (BHG 1080, 1082, 1092, 1127), one on the Annunciation (BHG 1093g), three on the Dormition (BHG 1109, 1115, 1122), and a short homily on Images (BHG 1125). The following eleven, all but one unpublished, must be added: on the Conception (BHG 1148g), on the Annunciation (BHG Auctarium 66a, 1115a), on the Presentation (BHG 1089d, 1110k, 1111e, 1140p, Auctarium 44b, 1093b), on the Dormition (BHG 1109c, 1121), on the Presentation of the Lord (BHG 1956n), on the Akathistos (BHG 1140). A. invented the liturgical Canon and composed three on Our Lady: for the Conception of Anne, for the Nativity of Mary and for the Annunciation— the latter first published in 1962. *Theotokia* in the Great Canon are also relevant.

Restricted publication limits completeness and certainty on A.'s thought; he is at times prolix. The great themes are emphasized. Mary is *Theotokos* (*qv*): "You had in your womb him who cannot be held by nature; you bore him who bears all things; you gave milk, O chaste one, to Christ who nourishes all creatures, the author of life."[2] Mary was brought into special relationship with the Holy Trinity: "God alone excepted, she excels all things."[3] "Of you," says A. to Mary, "all interpreters of the Spirit sang." Nowhere in the divinely inspired Scripture can one look without seeing some allusion to her. "Hail, Mediatress (*qv*) of the law and of grace, seal of the Old and New Testament, clear fulfilment of the whole of prophecy, of the truth of Scriptures inspired by God, the living and most pure book of God and the Word in which, without voice or writing, the writer himself, God and Word, is everyday read."[4] Here Mary is represented as God's revelation (*qv*), subject to Christ.

A. praised Mary's holiness in such terms that he has been claimed as a supporter of the Immaculate Conception (*qv*): "Beauty outstanding, she was a statue carved by God, the image of the divine archetype superbly expressed."[5] Mary, whom A. thought miraculously born to a sterile mother, was "the first fruits" of the renewed race. "Today the pure nobility of men receives the grace of the first creation by God and thus returns to itself: and the [human] nature, which clings to the [newly] born Mother of the Beautiful One, receives back the glorious beauty, which had been dimmed by the degradation of evil, and the best and most marvelous new formation. And this new formation is truly a re-formation, and the re-formation a deification, and this restoration to the first state."[6] Though A. is here speaking of the birth of Mary, since he did not have the Latin idea of original sin then prevailing in the West, he appears to think Mary uniquely God's handiwork, stainless, immaculate; elsewhere he says that she was "deified in Christ, the image completely resembling the original beauty."[7]

He taught the threefold aspect of Mary's virginity. For the virginal conception he used the partristic image of the virgin earth from which Adam was formed, to show how, from Mary, in a new way "the new Adam, maker of Adam, came."[8]

More than once A. applies to Mary the typology of the ancient Ark, joining with it Ps 131:8, faithful in this to the Assumptionist tradition from early times. His opinion on the Assumption is controverted in the recent literature. Mary, he thought, must have had a death different from that of others. He was puzzled by the death of one sinless.

Puzzled too by the silence of Scripture, he noted that the feast of the Dormition was honoured and loved by all. He has passages which seem to favour bodily Assumption, others which suggest separate existence for the soul in heaven and the incorrupt body in an earthly paradise. Again he thought God could have kept the matter from us.

Great things are associated with Mary by A.: "Blessed in heaven, and glorified on earth. For every tongue with grateful sentiment and piously, preaches about thee, glorifying thee as Mother of life. Every creature is filled with thy glory. All things have been made holy by the odour of thy fragrance; through thee the occasion of sin has been abolished; the woes of the first parent have been transformed into joy. Through thee all the angels sing with us: 'Glory in heaven; peace on earth.'"[9]

A. is an early, probably first, witness to the feast of the Conception celebrated in the East on 9 December. He composed a Canon for it.

[1]Works in PG, 97; EMBP, 1433-1577; Ballerini, *Sylloge Monumentorum*, BHG, 1121; "Un Canone inedito di S. Andrea di Creta per l'Annunciazione," ed. E. Follieri, in *Collectanea Vaticana in honorem Cardinalis Albaredo*, (Vatican, 1962), 337-357. Cf. M. Jugie, *L'Immaculée Conception*, 105-114; L'Assomption, 234-245. Also G. Grecu, *Doctrina marialis juxta S. Andream Cretensem*, Doctorate thesis, Propaganda University, (Rome, 1938); C. Coni, *La Mariologia di S. Andrea di Creta*, Doctorate thesis, Gregorian University, (Rome, 1950). Cf. esp. R. Laurentin, *Marie, l'Eglise et le Sacerdoce*, I, (Paris, 1953), 24-25, n.24; R. Garcia, O.P., "Andres de Creta; doctor de la Inmaculada Concepción y teólogo clásico de la Asunción de Maria a los cielos," in *Studium*, 10(1970), 3-52 (also separate issue); Beck, 500-502; O. Stegmüller and J. Tyciak, in LexMar, 209-211; H. Graef, *Mary*, I, 150-153; ClavisG, III, 541-553. [2]*Great Canon*, PG, 97, 1373C. [3]*Hom. III in Dorm.*, 1100A. [4]*Hom. IV in Dorm.*, 865A. [5]*Hom. III in Dorm.*, 1092D. [6]*Hom. I in Nativ.*, 812A, tr. H. Graef. [7]*Hom. I in Dorm.*, 1068C. [8]*Hom. I in Nativ.*, 816A. [9]*Hom. III in Dorm.*, 1100.

ANGELS, THE.
Reference here is to the angels of the Old Testament and New Testament as personal beings. As a devout Jewess, Mary would have grown up in a religious world wherein angels had important functions. They had intervened, in the history of her people, to promulgate the law (Acts 7:38; Gal 3:19), to protect God's faithful, act as destroyers (Ex 23:20; 2 K 19:35; Ps 78:49; Dan 10:13), to interpret prophecy (Ez 40:3; Dan 8:16; Zc 1:8; 2:2 etc.).[1] The thought of angels came easily to St. Stephen and to St. Paul, and the community of Qumran considered themselves brought into "a common destiny with the angels of the Presence."[2] Qumran also had an intuition, given some prominence in recent times, and accepted by Vatican II, that divine worship is accompanied by the angels. We have no direct evidence that such an outlook and the practice it dictates characterised Mary, but there is room for reasonable conjecture.

Two Old Testament texts stimulate discussion —Gen 3:15 and Is 7:14. Let it be just mentioned that an important Daughter of Zion text occurs in Zechariah, a book notable for its emphasis on angels as helpers of men, mediators and interpreters of divine revelation: "Sing and rejoice O daughter of Zion; for lo, I come and I will dwell in the midst of you, says the Lord." (Zc 2:10)

Two New Testament passages are relevant, the Annunciation (*qv*) and Rev 12. Gabriel was fulfilling a role traditional among God's people. There is a difference between this appearance to Zechariah and to Mary. Zechariah was afraid of him; Mary apparently was not. He gave his name to Zechariah; the evangelist gives his name to us, which may mean that Mary identified him herself. He had of course a message for her of immeasurably greater import than the one he gave to Zechariah. The encounter is a high point in the coalition of human and angelic society around the Word Incarnate. Such close union, identity of interests, is manifest also in the warlike narrative of Rev 12: it is Michael who fights with and overcomes the dragon who "stood before the woman who was about to bear a child, that he might devour her child when she brought it forth." (Rev 12:4,7,8)

Angels figure otherwise in the infancy narratives (qv). In Matthew, it is St. Joseph who is visited by them. At the Visitation Mary meets her cousin Elizabeth, beneficiary of such an angelic mission, and after the birth of Christ, the shepherds summoned to Bethlehem by an angelic choir met Mary and Joseph and saw the Child, and "they made known the saying which had been told them concerning this Child" (Lk 2:18). It must be assumed that Mary was among those told, for "she kept all these things, pondering them in her heart." (Lk 2:19)

The Assumption was Mary's full and direct encounter with the angels. The Assumption Apocrypha (qv) give a most important place to angels, in particular to St. Michael. The Ethopian *Book of Rest*, for example, speaks of many angels, accompanying Jesus and Michael to the death scene as the Apostles surrounded Mary's bed. Psalms were sung. After Mary had "completed her ministry," the Lord "took her soul and placed it in the hand of Michael and they wrapped it in a shroud, of whose glory silence is impossible."[3] Mary was buried and after three days Jesus came "and Michael with him." First he pacified the disputing Apostles. "Then our Lord gave a sign to Michael and he, Michael, spoke with the voice of the faithful angels and they came down in three clouds and their number above the cloud appeared to be ten thousand before the Saviour. And Our Lord told them to bear Mary's body in the clouds . . . And when they had together reached paradise they placed Mary's body by the tree of life. And they brought her soul and placed it on her body. And the Lord sent the angels back to their own place."[4]

Thus reads the text which is nearest to the source of the Transitus story; thus, with variations, the story comes down through the different versions. The Syriac one shows Michael in conversation with Mary—after the episode of the visit to the damned and their pitiful prayers—telling her how the bones of the patriarch Joseph were hidden from Pharaoh in the bed of the Nile but found by Moses. We have but a fragment but may surmise that Mary may have asked Michael about the future destiny of her own body: "And when these things were said by Moses and by the whole people, I came and spoke, I, Michael the angel, and said to Moses: "Moses, Moses, God hath heard your groaning. Rise and go to the river, and smite the waters with your staff, and the hidden treasure shall be laid bare before you.' What thinkest thou, Mary? As soon as Moses smote the river, did not the box in which Joseph was placed, appear and come to dry land? And Moses opened it, and found the roll in which it was written, 'These are the bones of Joseph' and he took them and conveyed them to their land unto their fathers."[5]

Here is Michael, the angel of God's power in Old Testament times, binding to Mary's person, in the moment of her Assumption, the capital event in Jewish salvation history, the exodus from Egypt. For plainly the preservation of Joseph's bones is seen as a type of her bodily glorification. The popular piety mirrored in the Apocrypha sprang from deep reflection on Mary as the culmination of saintly Judaism, wherein angelic presence and bounty were assumed. Thanks to the early Jewish Christians, the legacy passed to the Church.

Intercession by Mary, Michael and the Apostles is already adumbrated, for, when the damned cry out for help, when Michael, "their governor," weeps for them, when they implore Mary and the Apostles, the Lord takes note and thus replies: "Because of the tears of Michael and because of my holy Apostles and because of Mary my Mother, since they have come and seen you I have given you for three days rest of the Sabbath day."[6] Thus, in the Ethiopian *Book of Rest*. In the Irish *Testament of Mary*, the text reads: "Nevertheless, because of the tears of Mary, the honour of the Apostles, and the prayers of Michael, I shall give you respite for three hours each Sunday."[7]

History: Two concepts about Mary served to clarify her relationship with the angels, the queenship (*qv*) and the primacy (*qv*). An eight century liturgical antiphon for the feast of the Assumption says: "The holy Virgin Mary is exalted above the choirs of angels to the heavenly kingdom."[8] The eleventh century will bring the hymns, *Regina Caeli*, *Ave Regina Caelorum*, and *Ave Domina angelorum*; similar titles occur in local or particular liturgies of that time. At the beginning of the eleventh century too, St. Fulbert of Chartres (*qv*) used the title Queen of Angels as did St. Anselm (*qv*) about the same time. It will frequently recur thereafter.

The Palamite theologians took Mary's primacy in creation, after that of Christ, as fundamental. For Gregory Palamas (*qv*), since Mary is Mother of the Creator, supreme therefore over all creatures, all graces are, without her, inaccessible to angels and men; through her, men are associates of angels. Nicholas Cabasilas (*qv*) thinks that Mary is Mediatress between God and angels. Theophanes of Nicae (*qv*) is more explicit: Mary is the Mediatress of divinization to angels and men. He follows Pseudo-Dionysius' view that inferior orders are illuminated by the higher and asserts that Mary surpasses all the orders of angels; she is angel, archangel, power, cherubim and seraphim.[9]

Bernardine of Siena (*qv*) saw Mary as the channel of grace from the soul of Christ to angels; he saw her as their spiritual mother, Christ's partner at the centre of the one, the unitary *Civitas Dei*. He would be followed by the whole Franciscan school of the seventeeth century.[10] St. Lawrence of Brindisi (*qv*) sees Mary as exalted above all the angels by Christ; he is the foundation of the whole created universe.

Teaching Authority: The modern Popes freely use phrases like "exalted above all the choirs of angels," "Queen and sovereign of angels." Pius XII referred to Mary six times as Queen of angels. Vatican II is discreet about the angels. They will accompany the Lord when he comes in his majesty (*Lumen Gentium*, 49). The Church has venerated the martyrs with "special devotion, together with the Blessed Virgin Mary and the holy angels." (*Lumen Genium*, 50). Mary's excellence over them is stated: "She far surpasses all other creatures, both in heaven and on earth"; "She was exalted by the Lord as Queen of the universe"; "As the most holy Mother of God she was exalted by divine grace above all angels and men." (*Lumen Gentium*, 53, 59, 66)

---

[1]On Angels, cf. E. Peterson, *Le livre des anges*, (Paris, 1953); J. Cardinal Daniélou, *Les anges et leur mission*, (Chevetogne, 1951); J. Duhr, in DSp, I, 580-625; J. Daniélou, *La Théologie du Judéo-Christianisme*, (Paris, 1958), Ch. IV, V; A. de Villamonte, "Maria y los Angeles," in ME, VI, 401-438. [2]G. Vermes, *Discovery in the Judean Desert*, (New York, 1956), 214; also his *Jesus the Jew*, (London, Fontana Books, 1976), 61ff. On Qumran angelology, cf. J. Fitzmyer, S.J. in *Paul and Qumran*, ed. J. Murphy-O'Connor, O.P., (London, 1968), 31-47. [3]"De Transitu Mariae Apocrypha Aethiopice," ed. V. Arras, I, CSCO 343, 67, p.26. [4]CSCO 343, 89, pp.34-35. [5]W. Wright, *Contributions to the apocryphal Literature of the NT*, (London, 1865), 49-50. [6]CSCO 343, 38. [7]*Testament of Mary*, ed. C. Donahue, (New York, 1942), 55. [8]*Apud* G. Frenaud, O.S.B., in ME, V, 74. [9]*Serm. in Sanctiss. Deiparam*, ed. M. Jugie, (Rome, 1955), 80ff. [10]W. Sebastian, O.F.M., *De B. V. Maria universali gratiarum mediatrice ab 1600 at 1700*, (Rome, 1952).

ANGELUS, THE — See Supplement, p. 379.

ANGLICANISM (16th Century)

The collapse of Marian devotion in England was due to many causes.[1] England did not escape the decline which was widespread in Europe at the time, a decline due to weak theology from which came reliance on unwarranted legends, the Apocrypha, and similar things. In places, piety degenerated into superstition. St. Thomas More gives examples of the strange deviations which could be found at the time: a religious, hiring assassins, used to get them to recite the Hail Mary first in his private chapel; a Franciscan preached that anyone who daily recited the Rosary could not lose his soul.

In the sixteenth century, however, official attitudes and policies in regard to Marian doctrine and piety did not change at once. The formularies of faith drawn up during Henry VIII's reign were, in the context, unobjectionable. The initial confession of faith, *The Ten Articles* (1536), enjoined respect for the authority of the Fathers and of the "four holy Councils," which, of course, included Ephesus. More important still was the approval of images as "kindlers and stirrers of mens' minds," helping them to lament their sins and offences. This, it was stated, applied especially to images of Christ and Our Lady. But there was a warning about "censing, kneeling or offering unto them."

ANGLICANISM

Intercession of the saints was thus encouraged: "Yet it is very laudable to pray to saints in heaven everlastingly living whose charity is ever permanent to be intercessors and to pray for us and with us unto the Father, that is for his dear Son Jesus Christ's sake we may have grace of him and remission of our sins with an earnest purpose (not wanting ghostly strength) to observe and keep his holy commandments and never to decline from the same again unto our life's end; and in this manner we may pray to our Blessed Lady, to St. John the Baptist, to all and ever of the apostles and any other saint particularly as our devotion doth serve us."[2]

The entire doctrine of Mary's virginity is found in the *Institution of a Christian Man, The Bishops' Book* (1537): "She both in the conception and also in the birth and nativity of this her blessed Child and ever after retained still her virginity pure and immaculate and as clear without blot as she was at the time she was first born . . . pure, holy, undefiled." Five pages are devoted to interpretation of the Hail Mary (*qv*) said in honour of the Lord and "partly of the Blessed Virgin for her humble consent given and expressed to the angel at this salutation." Mary was full of grace because "she conceived and bore him that is the author of all grace." Again we read that "this Blessed Virgin was elect to be the instrument of our reparation in that she was chosen to bear the Saviour and Redeemer of the world."[3]

English and Lutheran divines agreed first, in 1536, on Seventeen Articles; then, in 1538, on Thirteen. Despite Melanchthon's pleas "to have the Roman piety taken out of our churches," Henry rejected the statements, passed the Act of Six Articles opposed to the Confession of Augsburg, and ignored Melanchthon's protest. Redman, an able theologian, had a hand in the final Henrican formulary: *The Necessary Doctrine and Erudition for any Christian Man, The King's Book* (1543). His view on Our Lady is thus expressed: "Some imagine that all the faithful, irrespective of the faith with which they have been endowed, are, none the less, equal in virtue and justice, so that they do not fear to place all women on an equal footing with the Blessed Virgin. Far from Christian minds be any such blasphemy."[4] The formulary retained Marian ideas of the previous texts. Henry VIII began his will invoking Our Lady, after God.

Things changed after his death, with official orders against images, pilgrimages, and shrines "because health and grace are to be sought from God alone." Still, the first Book of Prayer brought out in the reign of Edward VI (1539), mentioned Mary in the Communion Service. Two feasts of Our Lady were retained, the Purification and the Annunciation. These remained, but with Cranmer's influence dominant, everything else was swept away. German divines and their ideas were introduced to England. After Mary's brief reign, successive formulations led to *The Thirty Nine Articles* (1571)[5] The relevant Articles are: *Art. VI:* "Holy Scripture containeth all things necessary to salvation; so that whatsoever is not read therein, nor may be proved thereby, is not to be required of any man that it should be believed as an article of faith, or be thought requisite to salvation." *Art. XV:* . . . "But all we the rest, although baptised and born again in Christ, yet offend in many things, and if we say we have no sin, we deceive ourselves and the truth is not in us." *Art. XXII*: "The Romish doctrine concerning Purgatory, Pardons, Worshipping and Adoration as well of Images as of Reliques, and also the invocation of Saints, is a fond thing, vainly invented, and grounded upon no warranty of Scripture, but rather repugnant to the Word of God." In different ways these articles would be used against Marian theology and devotion.

Why did the influence of Bede, St. Anselm of Canterbury, Eadmer, Aelred of Rievalux, Nicholas of St. Albans, Robert Grosseteste, William of Ware, and Duns Scotus count for so little in the sixteenth century? Adaptation to the vernacular had been lacking. The Dissolution of the Monasteries achieved by Henry deprived the Church of important Marian centres fostered hitherto by the monks and friars.

Later times: Things worsened during the Cromwellian interlude, yet the Caroline divines kept Marian ideas alive through the seventeenth century: Bishop Hooker (d. 1600); Bishop Lancelot Andrewes (d. 1627); John Donne the poet, at one time a Catholic then an Anglican minister (d. 1631); Bishop Forbes (d. 1635); Anthony Stafford, (d. 1640) whose life of Mary, *The Femall Glory*, appeared with Archbishop Laud's *Imprimatur*; Bishop Montague (d. 1641); Bishop Hall (d. 1656); Bishop Ussher (d. 1656); Bishop Bramhall (d. 1663); Mark Frank (d.

1664), Master of Pembroke College, Cambridge, possibly the most illuminating of all; Bishop Ken (d. 1711); and Bishop Hickes (d. 1715). The corpus of writing and preaching from these men coincided in time with a golden age in the Catholic theology of Mary through seventeenth century Europe.

The Oxford Movement of the nineteenth century was a watershed in English religious history. Its members found their strength in a return to the Fathers, and in this source the *Theotokos* is a dominant, inescapable theme. Mary was honoured in public—for example in John Keble's (d.1866) *Ave Maria*, for the Annunciation of the Blessed Virgin Mary—and in the sermons and writings of J. H. Newman before his reception into the Catholic Church.

Newman while an Anglican contended that the Thirty Nine Articles did not compel denial of the doctrine of the Immaculate Conception. Later, A. T. Wirgman pointed out to Cardinal Lepicier that some Anglicans did not see Art. XV as an obstacle to the belief. It has also been suggested that the words "all we the rest, although baptised" need not apply to Mary since she was not baptised. Though Bishop Gore, prominent among Anglicans of his day, considered the Thirty Nine Articles as "an interesting historical document" and not "in any sense as a theological standard," he refused to accept the Immaculate Conception as an object of faith.

A similar response was to meet the dogma of the Assumption; polemical essays at the time were unyielding.[6]

Anglo-Catholics have returned to certain Marian devotions including the Rosary. Walsingham has become a place of Anglican pilgrimage. Marian literature has appeared. Early in this century specialists, who were members of the Anglican body, were making a contribution to Marian studies which passed largely unnoticed. Such was E. A. Wallis Budge (*qv*). Such was E. Hoskyns, whose insights into Johannine theology have been welcomed by competent Catholic scholars. Reflection on the Daugher of Zion (*qv*) theme was furthered by A. G. Herbert.

A more significant and in some ways surprising event was the foundation by an interfaith group (Catholic, Orthodox and Protestant, including Anglican) in 1967 in England, of the Ecumenical Society of the Blessed Virgin Mary.

The success of the venture, shown in the annual assemblies and in the literature it sponsors, has been one of the notable events of the postconciliar period.[7]

---

[1]Sources: *Formularies of Faith put forth by authority during the reign of Henry VIII*, (Oxford, Clarendon Press, 1825); C. Hardwick's *History of the Ten Articles*, (ed. F. Procter, London, 1904); *The First Book of Common Prayer of Edward VI, The Second Book of Common Prayer of Edward VI*, Westminster Library. Cf. G. Constant, *The Reformation in England*, ch. VIII, (London, 1934); P. Hughes, *The Reformation in England*, (London, 1950, 1954), Vol. I, 348-369, Vol. II, 22-60. [2]*Formularies*, xxviii, xxix; *Hardwick*, 252-253. [3]*Formularies*, xxxvii, 203-208. [4]*Apud* G. Constant, *The Reformation in England*, 430-431. [5]On the Thirty Nine Articles cf. G. F. McLear, *An Introduction to the Articles of the Church of England*, (London, 1895, ed. W. W. Williams, 1909); E. J. Bicknell, *The Thirty Nine Articles of the Church*, ed. H. J. Carpenter, (London, 1961); E. G. Wilson and J. H. Templeton, *Anglican Teaching: An Exposition of the Thirty Nine Articles* (Dublin, 1962). On Henry VIII and the Lutherans, cf. N. S. Tjernagel, *Henry VIII and the Lutherans*, (St. Louis, 1965). On general history of Anglican attitudes to Our Lady, cf. E. L. Mascall and H. S. Box, *The Blessed Virgin Mary*, (London, 1963); H Nicholson, *The Caroline Divines*, (London, the Ecumenical Society of Our Lady). On recent and present-day attitudes, cf. Bishop Gore, *The Holy Spirit and the Church*, (London, 1924), 354ff; C. M. Corr, *Maria*, III, 713, 731; S. Cwiertniak, *La Vierge Marie dans la Tradition anglicane*, (Paris, 1957). [6]Cf. Bishop Gore, *The Holy Spirit and the Church*, (London, 1924), 192-193, 354. On the Assumption, cf. *Declaration of the Archbishops of Canterbury and York*, in Church Times, August 18, 1950, p. 601; V. Bennett and R. Winch, *The Assumption of Our Lady and Catholic Theology*, (London, 1950). [7]For Hoskyns, cf. F. M. Braun, O.P., *La Mère des Fidèles*, passim; E. Hoskyns, *Journal of Theol. St.*, 1920, 210-218. Marian literature, in J. N. Ward, *Five for Sorrow, Ten for Joy*, (on the Rosary, London, 1973); D. Edwards, *The Virgin Birth in History and Faith*, (London, 1940) with extensive bibliographies, including the Ecumenical Society publications, E. Carroll, *Understanding the Mother of Jesus*, (Dublin, 1979), 111-159.

ANNUNCIATION, THE (Lk 1:26-38)

(26) In the sixth month the angel Gabriel was sent from God to a city of Galilee named Nazareth, (27) to a virgin betrothed to a man whose name was Joseph, a descendant of David, and the virgin's name was Mary. (28) He went in to her and said: 'Rejoice, most favoured one, the Lord is with you.' (29) But she was deeply troubled at the saying, and considered in her mind what this greeting might mean. (30) And the angel said to her, 'Do not be afraid, Mary, for you have found favour with God. (31) And behold you will conceive in your womb and bear a son, and you shall call his name Jesus.

(32) He will be great, and will be called the Son of the Most High; and the Lord God will give to him the throne of his father David, (33) and he will reign over the house of Jacob forever; and of his kingdom there will be no end.' (34) And Mary said to the angel, 'How shall this be, since I am a virgin?' (35) And the angel said to her, 'The Holy Spirit will come upon you and the power of the Most High will overshadow you and for that reason the holy child to be born will be called the Son of God. (36) And behold, your kinswoman Elizabeth in her old age has also conceived a son; and this is the sixth month with her who was called barren. (37) For with God nothing is impossible.' (38) And May said, 'Behold, I am the handmaid of the Lord; let it be to me according to your word.' And the angel departed from her."

History: This narrative tells of the most important event in world history, the Incarnation of the eternal Son of God, and links inseparably with it a unique human moment and personal decision.[1] Consequently it is a fabric which can sustain indefinite commentary and theological reflection, as many articles in this work show (see e.g., CONSENT, COREDEMPTION, DAUGHTER OF ZION, FAITH, FULL OF GRACE, HANDMAID OF THE LORD, HOLINESS, HOLY SPIRIT, KNOWLEDGE, MEDIATION, MOTHER OF GOD, MOTHER OF THE CHURCH, QUEENSHIP, VIRGINITY, VOW). The focus of interest has changed from age to age, as different intellectual demands, thought patterns, and methods of inquiry have succeeded each other within the Church.

From the outset the Eve (*qv*) – Mary parallel and contrast was studied in the Annunciation text and compared with the story of the Fall in Genesis. This insight of St. Irenaeus (*qv*) remained basic. Direct commentary of the Lucan text was provided by influential teachers, Origen (*qv*) in the East and Ambrose (*qv*) in the West, and a constant stimulus was to come from the Liturgy. There are twenty patristic homilies on the Annunciation. The flow continued by Byzantine times and was very much increased in the West from the Middle Ages on, witness St. Bernard's (*qv*) series *Super missus est*. With the appearance of systematic theologies, in the great age of Scholasticism, emphasis was placed on the conceptual content of single words and phrases. As Mariology

emerged to almost separate status as a theological discipline, the way was open for a wealth of theory. The Annunciation was a prime moment in Mary's life where all her power, gifts and destiny converged. Devotional practice kept pace with this development, as the Ave Maria (see HAIL MARY), the Rosary and the Angelus (*qqv*) show.

Modern Scholarship: The "New Theology," which urged a return to the sources, brought the Annunciation passage into prominence, examining the patristic testimony and the text itself in the light of modern techniques. Catholic writers since the liberating Encyclical of Pius XII (*qv*) in 1943 and Vatican II (*qv*) have made a substantial contribution to this investigation. Some, like E. Burrows, S.J. and S. Lyonnet, S.J., were in the field already.[2] R. Laurentin's work, relevant to the Infancy Narratives, was another landmark. With the Santo Domingo Congress, held just after the promulgation of the conciliar Constitution on the Church, Catholic commitment to scientific study of Marian passages in the Bible, especially Lk 1:26-38, was established. Catholic writers even went as far as assimilating the results of valid research outside the Church; of this the best example is the title, Daughter of Zion.

Scholars debate questions of authorship, sources and historicity. If historicity is accepted, the ultimate source of the Annunciation narrative must have been the Blessed Virgin Mary.

The episode is compared, in the context of biblical theology, with Old Testament stories of miraculous births: of Isaac (Gen 17:16; 18:10), Joseph (Gen 30:1-2; 22), Samson (Jg 13:3-4), Samuel (1 Sam 1:17-20),[3] and with that recorded by Luke, of John the Baptist (1:1-13). The mother in each case was married and either aged or otherwise sterile.[2] Mary was not married, which suggests the parallel with Is 7:14 (see EMMANUEL); the resemblance with v.31 is striking. In only one Old Testament instance is an angel mentioned, the announcement of Samson's birth.

The angel is an Old Testament element. "Angel of Yahweh" may mean, in some Old Testament passages, a divine word or action. Despite recent suggestions that the angel of the Annunciation was a literary device used to describe Mary's sublime experience, we may accept the traditional opinion that Gabriel was a personal messenger from God. Luke declared his intention to write history. Why should he alter the whole character of a concrete narrative, in which historical figures are named and entirely identifiable as is the place, by a piece of fiction — fiction in regard to the personal agent, fiction about the name? There is evidence that in that age angels were considered as personal beings. Gabriel's name is found in Dan 8:16 and 9:21; in Lk 1:19 he says to Zechariah, "I am Gabriel who stand in God's presence." Luke, in the gospel and Acts, mentions angels fifteen times, often in the same fullness of circumstance.

Gabriel is found in both parts of the diptych of the Annunciaton. Commentators emphasize the common features: the heavenly visitor, the greeting, the human reaction, the question, the angel's reply, and the sign. The differences are very striking. To Zechariah the first words are, "Do not be afraid," to Mary, "Rejoice"; he is called first by his own name, she by a glorious title, "Highly favoured One." He is told that his prayer has been heard, she that the Lord is with her; he was troubled at the sight of the angel, she at what the angel said, which she immediately thought over. His question, "How shall I know this?" implied doubt, whereas her "How shall this be?" sought fuller information. The sign in his case is a punishment, in hers a revelation; his Son will be filled with the Holy Spirit from his mother's womb, on Mary the Holy Spirit will descend. His son will be conceived as a result of normal human relations which are assumed; in her case, that formal consent is awaited and given, "Fiat . . .". Many other differences must be added which are inherent in her unique destiny as outlined in the dialogue, and in the exalted character of the Son she will miraculously conceive. He will be great and will be called the Son of the Most High, the Son of God, whereas John will be "great before the Lord." John will turn many of the sons of Israel to the Lord their God, but Mary's Son will rule forever over the house of Jacob.

The Annunciation is a unique summit in salvation history (qv), marking a unique calling. It will bear comparison with all such moments, not only the birth stories, in the Old Testament, and the call of Abraham and of Moses, but also the initial episode in Genesis which so seized the attention of the Fathers. Light has been sought in the call of Gideon (Jg 6:11-24), which

also opens with a special title, "valiant warrior";[4] and again, this time by a specialist in Rabbinic literature, in the story of Ruth and Boaz. "In Rabbinic literature, Ruth is celebrated as representative of the true proselyte and as an ancestress of David and the Messiah. Her life is often interpreted as prefiguring Messianic events, and where this is done, Boaz sometimes stands for God himself, or at least speaks and acts as God himself would."[5]

The Davidic point is explicit, not merely a literary parallel. The words "the throne of his father David" and "he will rule over the house of David forever" recall the oracle of Nathan to David (2 Sam 7:8-16; cp. Ps 89:20ff, Dan 2:44) and show that Mary's Son will be the spiritual David fulfilling Messianic hope bound to the royal name. This note is strengthened by the reference to her betrothed, Joseph, a descendant of David. He is sometimes strangely overlooked as is Mary's obligation to him as her betrothed. This duty must have a bearing on her question to the angel and on her final consent.

Relevant articles previously cited deal with recent theories on *Chaire* (DAUGHTER OF ZION), *Kecharitomene* (FULL OF GRACE), on v.34 (VOW OF VIRGINITY), v.35a (HOLY SPIRIT), v.35b (MARY'S KNOWLEDGE). On each of these points Old Testament echoes are much emphasized by scholars, as is Is 7:14 in regard to v.31. Attention may be drawn to two other phrases rich in meaning. "The Lord is with you" is not a statement of God's presence of the kind that is common in the Psalms, but a guarantee of help in a task or mission assigned by God and momentous in salvation history (Gen 26:24; 28:15; 39:2-3, 21-23; Jg 6:12-16; Jer 1:8; 30:11; Is 41:10, 43:5). The promise accords with the name given to Mary's Son, Jesus, a name meaning "God is Salvation." It places her Annunciation on a much higher level that Zechariah's. Her uniqueness in this moment is further emphasized by the choice of words to signify her conception, *sullemphe en gastri*, "you will conceive in the womb" In the promise of a child to Elizabeth there is but one word, *gennesi*. Lk 2:21 repeats the same idea about Mary, "before he was conceived in the womb," *hen te koilia*. Is this an application of the Old Testament image of Yahweh abiding at the heart of his people? (Zeph 3:15; Joel 2:27; Zc 2:11).

Mary links her consent with the servant theme of the Old Testament, and her "fiat" likewise recalls Old Testament words (Josh 2:21; 1 Macc 3:60), as well as similar phrases in the Psalms. What is singular, and so suggestive theologically and spiritually, is the immense programme to which she did, in that submissive and creative word, pledge her entire being.

Teaching Authority: It is the words "Full of Grace" which assume importance in pronouncements of the Church. In major documents it has been mostly interpreted along with the testimony of the Fathers. Thus Pius IX writes in *Ineffabilis Deus* (*qv*), "they [the Fathers] thought that this singular and solemn salutation, never heard before, showed that the Mother of God is the seat of all divine graces and is adorned with all gifts of the Holy Spirit."[6] Pius XII in *Munificentissimus Deus* (*qqv*), speaks of the Scholastic Doctors: "Similarly they have given special attention to these words of the New Testament: 'Hail, full of grace, the Lord is with you, blessed are you among women' since they saw, in the mystery of the Assumption, the fulfilment of that most perfect grace granted to the Blessed Virgin and the special blessing that countered the curse of Eve."[7] The same Pope, in proclaiming the queenship (*qv*) appealed to the words of the angel, "he will reign over the house of Jacob forever" as they and other biblical phrases were interpreted by "ancient writers." Having quoted a sentence from St. John of Damascus (*qv*) he says: "And we can also say that the first to proclaim the royal office of Mary was the heavenly messenger, the Archangel Gabriel."[8]

Vatican II (*qv*) on the Annunciation is a topic of interest. When, after the vote in October, 1963, it was decided to prepare a new schema, the biblical approach, by now highly acceptable to the Council, was adopted. Consequently much thought was given to Lk 1:26-38. In the draft text distributed to the Fathers, a section was entitled, "Mary in the Annunciation." The notes supplied to the report contained a great deal of patristic quotation under the heading *The meaning of the Annunciation*. It was the responsible commission's wish that Mary's consent should be positively stated. The grace with which she was endowed was exemplified from the writings of the eastern Fathers. Her perfection, by which she was full of grace, says the report, was functional and ordered to the Redemption. But it was not mere ornament. "Mary, by personal and free faith and obedience, gave her consent and is not brought out as a passive instrument."[9] The notes then show, again with quotations and references, how the doctrine of the new Eve arose.

The text submitted to the Fathers contained the words: "Adorned from the first instant of her conception with the splendours of an entirely new holiness, the Virgin of Nazareth is, on God's command, greeted by an angel messenger as 'full of grace.' (Lumen Gentium, 56). The article had opened with the words "The Father of mercies willed that the consent of the predestined mother should precede the Incarnation," and the words earlier quoted were followed by the assertion that, "By thus consenting to the divine utterance, Mary, a daughter of Adam, became the Mother of Jesus."

At the *Modi* stage, suggestions were made that *gratia plena* (full of grace) should be replaced by some other translation of *Kecharitomene*: e.g., *gratia plenissima, gratia perfecte impleta, gratia perfecte informata, summe Deo grata seu gratia plena*. Twenty-two Fathers asked that the reference to Luke's gospel be deleted for full of grace.[10] The commission appealed to widespread use in the Church and refused to change the text.

[1]Besides bibliographies to related articles, e.g., INFANCY NARRATIVES and ST. LUKE, cf. general commentaries, esp. Jerome Commentary and New Catholic Commentary. Cf. M. J. Lagrange, O.P., "La conception surnaturelle du Christ d'après S. Luc," in RB, 1914, 60-71, 188-208. Cf. also the following by S. Lyonnet, S.J.: "Chaire Kecharitomene," in BB, 20(1939), 131-141; "Le récit de l'Annonciation et la maternité divine de la Sainte Vierge," in L'Ami du Clergé, 66(1956), 33-48; "L'Annonciation et la mariologie biblique," in MSS, IV, 59-72. Cf. J. P. Audet, "L'Annonce à Marie," in RB, 63(1956), 346-374; S. del Paramo, S.J., El Fiat de la Anunciación punto de enlace entre el Antiguo y Nuevo Testamento en la historia de la Salud, (Semana Biblica Internacional, Madrid, 1965), 189-213; S. Munoz Iglesias, "S. Lucas 1:35b," in Est. Bibl., 27(1968), 275-299; M. Jourjon and J. P. Bouhout, "Luc 1:35 dans la patristique grecque," in BSFEM, 25(1968), 65-76; P. Gaechter, S.J., "Der Verkündigungsbericht Lk 1:26-38," in Zeits. Chr. Kath. Theo., 91(1969), 322-363, 567-586; J. Vogt, "Ecce Ancilla Domini. Eine Untersuchung zum sozialen Motiv des antiken Marienbildes," in VigChrist., 23(1969), 241-263; P. Benoit, O.P., "L'Annonciation. Lc 1:26-38," in Assemblées du Seigneur, 8(1972), 39-50; N. Garcia Garces, "De annuntiatione in theologia," in MSS, IV, 137-162; C. Stuhlmueller, "Annunciation," in NewCathEncycl., 562-565; P. Grelot, in DSp, X, 415-416; R. Laurentin, Structure et Théologie de Luc I-II, (Paris, 1957); J. McHugh, The Mother, 37-67; R. E.

Brown, *The Birth*, 286-329. [2] E. Burrows, *The Gospel of the Infancy*, (London, 1940); S. Lyonnet, "Chaire Kecharitomene," in BB, 20(1939), 131-141. [3] Cf. S. Munoz Iglesias, "El Evangelio de la Infancia en San Lucas y las infancias de los heroes biblicos," in *Est. Bibl.*, 16(1958), 329-382. [4] J. P. Audet, "L'Annonce 'a Marie," in RB, 63(1956), 346-374. [5] D. Daube, "Ruth and Boaz," in *The New Testament and Rabbinic Judaism*, (London, 1956), 33. [6] OL, 74. [7] OL, 312. [8] OL, 392; cf. also 386, 391. [9] Schema *De Ecclesia*, 1964, 212. [10] *Modi*, 1964, 10-11.

ANSELM, ST., DOCTOR OF THE CHURCH (1033-1109)

A., a European figure, born in Aosta, was a Benedictine monk and abbot of Le Bec; from 1093, he was archbishop of Canterbury. He marked, in Marian thought and piety, a transition to the flowering of the twelfth century. The "Father of Scholasticism" was in prayer a contemplative. Marian ideas will appear not only in sermons, scriptures, commentaries and prayers, but in formal treatises. He composed one such treatise on "The virginal conception and original sin"; his theology of Mary is also found in the treatise on the Incarnation, *Cur Deus homo*, and in the three great prayers.[1] The questions of authenticity have now been solved by A. Wilmart, O.S.B. and the critical editor, F. S. Schmitt, O.S.B. Rejected from the canon are the *Hymni et Psalterium de Sancta Virgine Maria* (PL 158, 1035-1050) and the *Tractatus de conceptione sanctae Mariae*, which was the work of Eadmer (*qv*), secretary, disciple and biographer of A. A. did not teach the Immaculate Conception. "For though the conception of the Man himself was pure and without any sin of carnal pleasure, nevertheless the Virgin from whom he was assumed was conceived in iniquity and her mother conceived her in sin, and she was born with original sin, since she sinned in Adam 'in whom all have sinned.'" "The Virgin from whom that Man of whom we speak was assumed was one of those who were purified by him from sins before his birth and in that very purity of his giving he was assumed from her ... For since his mother's purity through which he was pure was solely from him, he was pure through and from himself."[2]

A. did not have the intuition of Duns Scotus (*qv*) that the purity he spoke of could be conferred by preventing or preserving grace before conception. Yet he stated a general principle relevant to the privilege which would substantially find its way into *Ineffabilis Deus* (*qv*): "It was fitting that this Virgin should shine with a purity than which under God no greater can be understood ..." *Ineffabilis Deus*, in reference to the entire sinlessness of Mary speaks of "that fullness of holy innocence and sanctity than which, under God, one cannot understand anything greater."[3]

The saint exhausts his rhetoric in writing of Mary's excellence. But the basis of his thinking is strictly theological. The passage just quoted goes on to show Mary's relationship to each person of the Most Holy Trinity. The Father disposed things so as to give her his only Son, whom as his equal he loved as himself "that there should be naturally one identical Son of God the Father and the Virgin"; [the] "Holy Spirit willed and operated that from her would be conceived and born he from whom he himself proceeded."[4]

Insisting on divine transcendence, A., nevertheless, showed the immense role of Mary in salvation: "Nothing is equal to Mary, nothing but God is greater than Mary ... Every nature is created by God and God is born of Mary. God created all things and Mary gave birth to God. God who made all things made himself from Mary and thus he remade everything he had made ... God is the Father of created things and Mary is the Mother of recreated things. God is therefore the Father of the constitution of all things and Mary is the Mother of the restoration (*restitutionis*) of all things. God begot him through whom all things were made and Mary brought forth him through whom all things were saved." A. then enters the mystery of Mary's mediation: "For there is no reconciliation save what you the chaste one conceived; there is no justification save what you intact in the womb fostered, there is no salvation save what you as a virgin brought forth. Therefore, O Lady, you are the Mother of justification and of the justified, Mother of reconciliation and the reconciled, parent of salvation and the saved." For A., the spiritual motherhood follows logically, and, in development of the idea, he marks an advance: "The Mother of God is our Mother. The Mother of the one in whom alone we hope and whom alone we fear, is our Mother. The Mother, I say, of him who alone saves, alone condemns, is our Mother." [5]

A. does not use the word Mediatress (*qv*), but "reconciler of the world."[6] The title Mediatress was in use in his milieu. His thought on the subject, implicit in the passage quoted, is explicit in such eulogies as these: "Through your fruitfulness the sinful world is justified, the damned are saved, those in exile brought home. Your offspring, O Lady, ransomed the captive world, healed the sick, raised the dead." "O woman, wonderfully singular and singularly wonderful, through whom the elements are renewed, the lower world is restored, demons are crushed, men are saved, angels are raised anew."[7]

A. expresses courtly devotion and love to the one he so frequently calls Lady. "Merciful Lord, spare the slave (*servo*) of your Mother. Merciful Lady spare the slave of your Son." "Let this slave of yours be kept under your protection until the end."[8] This is the idea of servitude already expressed by St. Ildefonsus of Toledo (*qv*), later developed in seventeenth century Spain and France—servitude unique to Mary, "beautiful to behold, lovable to contemplate, delightful to love," surpassing the capacity of his heart.

These prayers, widely diffused, had immense effect in the monasteries. Through the monks, they were communicated to the faithful and were most persuasive in teaching the power of Mary's intercession (*qv*).

[1]*Anselmi Opera Omnia*, ed. F. S. Schmitt, O.S.B., (Edinburgh, 1946; photolithograph ed., Stuttgart-Bad Canstatt, 1968). Cf. R. Laurentin, *Traité*, I, 146-149; A. Wilmart, O.S.B., "Les propres corrections de S. Anselme dans sa grande prière à la Vierge Marie," in RTAM, 2(1930), 189-204; H. Barré, C.S.Sp., *Prières Anciennes*, 287-307; R. T. Jones, *Sancti Anselmi Mariologia*, (Mundelein Seminary, Chicago, 1937); J. Bruder, S.M., *The Mariology of Saint Anselm of Canterbury*, (Dayton, Ohio, 1939); S. Alameda, O.S.B., "Escritos mariológicos de San Anselmo," in *Liturgia*, 1(1946), 153-157; E. Burke, "Beginnings of a scientific Mariology," in MariolSt, 1(1950), 119-137; C. Borntrager, O.S.M., "The Service of Our Lady according to S. A.," in *Studi Storici dell'Ordine dei S. d. Maria*, 12(1963), 17-56; *Why God became man and the Virgin Conception*, etc., ed. J. M. Colleran, (New York, Magi books, 1969). Cf. also These articles in Zagreb Congress: H. Chavannes, "Quelle lumière les 'Orationes' de S. A. projettent-elles sur la preuve du Prosologion," III, 651-664; H. du Manoir, S.J., "La piété mariale de S. A.," III, 597-611; A. Krupa, O.F.M., "De Maria Matre misericordiae Sancti Anselmi Cantuariensis doctrina," IV, 487-498; P. Meinhold, "Die Stellung der Gottesmutter in der Theologie des Anselm von Canterbury," III, 631-650; M. Schmaus, "Die dogmatischen Grundlagen des Marienkultes nach A. von C.," III, 613-629. [2]*Cur Deus Homo*, in *Opera Omnia*, ed. F. S. Schmitt, O.S.B., II, 16, vol. 2, 116, 119. [3]*De Concep. virg., ibid.*, XVIII, vol. II, 159; OL, 61(tr. corrected). [4]*De Concep. virg.*, XVIII, vol. II, 159. [5]*Opera Omnia*, ed., F. S. Schmitt, III, 21-23; H. Barré, C.S.Sp., *Prières Anciennes*, 304-305. [6]*Opera Omnia*, ed. F. S. Schmitt, III, 17; Barré, 301. Cf. "Memorials of St. Anselm," ed. R .W. Southern and F. S. Schmitt, O.S.B. in *Auctores Brittanici Medii Aevi*, (London, 1969), I, 25, 267. [7]Or. VII, *Schmitt*, as above, 21; H. Barré, *Prières Anciennes*, 303-304. [8]Or. VI, *Schmitt*, as above, 16; Barré, 301; Or. VII, *Schmitt*, as above, 20; Barré 303.

ANSELM OF LUCCA, ST. (d.1086)

A. was a contemporary, friend and supporter of St. Gregory VII, who entrusted to him the spiritual direction of Countess Mathilda of Tuscany, a powerful ally of the Papacy. For her A. composed five prayers, which were discovered and publishd by Dom A. Wilmart (*qv*).[1] Three of them are addressed to Our Lady and the doctrine in them has a certain historical significance. With St. Peter Damian (*qv*) and Gottschalk of Limburg (*qv*), A. is the prelude to his namesake of Canterbury, with whom the twelfth century renewal begins. A. may be the pioneer in the West of the spiritual interpretation of Jn 19:25-27 (see WOMAN IN), which would be later defended by Rupert of Deutz (*qv*) and thereafter become common teaching: "Mary, there is your son, apostle, here is your mother—so that the glorious mother should intercede with such great and merciful affection for all true believers and guard by her patronage the redeemed slaves adopted as her sons, removing all fear from the unfortunate ones, to whom he granted the great consolation and joy of glorying in the name of the Mother of the Lord and exulting in association with your Son, co-heirs with Jesus Christ."[2]

Stressing the intercessory power of Mary, whom he calls Advocate (*qv*) and Lady, A. has a hint of the later medieval contrast between Christ as the King of justice and Mary as the Queen of mercy—being set in contrast by her Son with his own severity. "By your mediation (*interventione*) forced as it were, he would repeal the sentence of most just condemnation so that through you the kingdom of heaven would suffer violence and by your intercession, the violent would bear it away."[3] A.'s "sole trust" is in Mary after Jesus Christ the Saviour, and he pleads for her "alleviating remedy for his wounds." She has never despised those who cry to her; and then, this memory of consecration (*qv*): "You know that I have entrusted myself to you with entire devotion, that I have taken the symbols of your service, am more ready to die than go against your will."[4]

[1]"Cinq textes de prière composés par Anselme de Lucques pour la comtesse Mathilde," in RAM, 19(1938), 23-72; texts, 49-72. Cf. H. Barré, Prières Anciennes, 225-235. [2]I, ed. Wilmart, in RAM as cited above, 53; H. Barré, op. cit., 226. For spurious works, see PL 149, 577-590; cf. R. Laurentin, Traité, I, 146. [3]I, ed. Wilmart, in RAM as cited above, 51. [4]IV, in RAM as cited above, 68.

ANTHONY OF PADUA, ST., DOCTOR OF THE CHURCH (1195-1231)

A charismatic preacher, A. remains widely popular. His Marian teaching is found in six sermons, In Laudem B. Mariae: one on the Nativity of Mary; two on the Annunciation; two on the Purification; and one on the Assumption. In addition, A.'s Marian teaching can be found in passages in the Sunday sermons or those for feasts of the Lord and in passing references elsewhere in his works.[1]

The Blessed Virgin, "the throne of the glory of the most high from the beginning, that is, from the foundation of the world, was predestined as Mother of God in the sanctifying power of the Spirit."[2] Did A. see the Immaculate Conception (qv) in this destiny? Commentators are divided. A. did not deny the privilege as did so many Latin doctors. He must have known of the debate and of the opinion of St. Bernard (qv) and Peter Lombard (qv); he had not the Scotist intuition.

The texts which cause difficulty for defenders of the positive opinion are: "But the glorious Virgin had no stain in her birth, for she was sanctified in her mother's womb."[3] "[The Holy Spirit] overshadowed her, that is provided coolness and entirely extinguished in her the fomes of sin."[4] "After the assent of the holy Virgin the Holy Spirit came upon her purifying [purgans] her through the power receptive to the Godhead and at the same time preparing her capacity for generation"[5]—an involved idea which derived from St. John of Damascus (qv). On the other hand, A. quotes St. Augustine's text on Mary's sinlessness "because of the honour due to the Lord" and adds these words: "The glorious Virgin was prepared [praeventa] and filled with a singular grace that she should have as the fruit of her womb the One whom she had from the outset as Lord of the Universe."[6] By praeventa, he scarcely meant preservation in the Scotist sense. He had an image of Mary as a new paradise.

A. has a fleeting reference to the Eve-Mary (qv) contrast and he deals with the bridal theme: "The Father agreed and sent his Son who in the bridal chamber of the Blessed Virgin united our nature to himself."[7] In this mystical marriage in which Mary's Son was her spouse (qv), there were unique privileges and shining benefits: "virginity and motherhood, chastity and fruitfulness." Mary received great graces and virtues, never yielding to the evil one or the world.

A. taught the threefold virginity; the reasons given for the marriage with St. Joseph (qv) are traditional. The Holy Spirit created the body of the Redeemer in the womb of the Virgin Mary; A. calls her the "sanctuary of the Holy Spirit."[8]

A. speaks of Mary as our hope, the gate of heaven and door of Paradise. Though he used the words "the Blessed Virgin Mary our mediatress remade peace between God and the sinner," and said that her "birth enlightened the world covered with darkness and the shadow of death," his interest was not to elaborate theory, but to stir devotion. His opinion on the Assumption is quoted in Munificentissimus Deus (qv): "Thus you have it clearly that the Blessed Virgin in her body . . . was assumed."[9] Mary, exalted above the angels, was queen of all. All, especially sinners, should turn to "the city of refuge." She is the Star of the sea, shining on those shaken by the storm, leading them to the port. We must praise her, contemplate and imitate her virtuous life.

[1]Sermons, ed. A. Locatelli, (Padua, 1895). Cf. G. Catini, O.F.M., "Il pensiero di S. A. di P. intorno al concepimento immacolato di Maria," in Studi Francescani, S. 3, III, Vol. 28(1931), 129-144; G. Stano, O.F.M.,Conv., "Il pensiero di S. A. Sul Dogma dell'Immacolata Concezione di Maria," in La Voce del Padre S. Francesco, 10(1933), 441-446; L. Guidaldi, Il pensiero mariano di S. A. di P., (Padua, 1938); P. Bayart, "La prédication mariale de S. A. de P.," in France francisc., 21(1938), 223ff; G. M. Roschini, O.S.M., "La Mariologia di S. A. da P.," in MM, 8(1946), 16-67; V. Schaaf, O.F.M., De S. A. P. Ecclesiae Doctore, (Rome, 1946); B. M. Hess, O.F.M.Conv., De S. A. P. Doctore Evangelico, (Rome, 1946); L. di Fonzo, O.F.M.Conv., "La Mariologia di S. A.," in S. A. Dottore della Chiesa, (Vatican City, 1947), 85-172; B. Costa, O.F.M., La Mariologia di S. A. di P., (Padua, 1950); E. Zolli, "'Ubique de ipsa'. Una pagina di Mariologia Antoniana," in MM, 13(1951), 474-477; R. M. Huber, O.F.M.Conv., "The Mariology of S. A. of P.," in Studia Mariana, VII, 188-268; F. M. Bauducco, S.J., "Mariologia cherigmatica di S. A. di P.," in Civiltà Cattolica, 1952, 547-551; S. Clasen, L. Aswerus, E. v. Witzleben, A. Borer, in LexMar, 288-296. [2]In Assumpt., Sermons ed. Locatelli, 729. [3]In Nativ., ibid., 696. [4]Dom V p. Pascha, ibid., 199a. [5]Dom XX p. Pent., ibid., 515ab. [6]Dom III Quadrag., ibid., 89b. Cf. Roschini, O.S.M., "La Mariologia di S. A. da P.," in MM, 8(1946), 51ff; Di Fonzo, "La Mariologia di S. A.," in S. A. Dottore della Chiesa, (Vatican City, 1947), 119ff. [7]Dom XX p. Pent., ibid., 515. [8]Hom III Quadrag., ibid., 90. [9]In Assumpt., ibid., 729. Cf. AAS, 42(1950), 763; OL, 313.

ANTIPATER OF BOSTRA (d. c. 458)

A. was Bishop of Bostra in Arabia sometime after the Council of Chalcedon (451), which was attended by his predecessor Constantine. An important figure, he was one of seventy counselors of Emperor Leo I. A personal friend of St. Euthymius (d. 473), he was involved in the Origen (qv) controversy. Nothing else is known of him. He was cited as an approved author at the second Council of Nicaea.[1]

PG has two Marian homilies by Antipater: *On St. John the Baptist, the silence of Zechariah, and the greeting of the Mother of God,*[2] and *On the Annunciation of the most holy Mother of God* (also in BHG 1137).[3] The critical position is not fully established. A section of the first is probably genuine.[4] Too many questions still await an answer in regard to the second.[5] A third homily, for the Assumption, recently published by R. Grégoire in the Latin version, which alone exists, is still more fragile in point of authenticity.[6] It could belong to the second half of the fifth century, and the Latin version may have been made from a Syrian rendering of the Greek. Composed first for the primitive feast of Our Lady (see LITURGY AND MARY), it may have been enlarged to deal with the Visitation (qv). Whether for the fifth Sunday of the Jacobite Advent or for the later feast of the Visitation, remains questionable.

A number of manuscripts from, or claiming to be from, Antipater remain to be published. They include five Marian homilies. The Marian content of the reliably genuine text deals amply with the virginity (qv), soberly with the holiness (qv). But it is explicit on Mary's saving mission, which is set in the context of the Eve-Mary parallel, and, interestingly, Antipater uses *mesiteuousa*,[7] which, before long, with other preachers, would lead to *Mesites* (see MEDIATRESS).

[1]R. Caro, *La Homiletica*, I, 226-265; R. Laurentin, *Traité*, I, 167; S. Vailhé in DTC, 1, 1330; B. Laurès, in DHGE, 3, 713ff; C. Vona, *Le due orazioni di Antipatro di Bostra sulla natività di Giovanni Battista e sull'Annunziazione,* (Rome, 1967); ClavisG, III, 283-286. [2]PG, 85, 1764-1776. [3]PG, 85, 1776-1792. [4]R. Caro, *La Homilética*, I, 236-240; PG, 85, 1772C-1776A. [5]R. Caro, *op. cit.*, 264ff. [6]"Sermo sancti Antipatris nostri ad matutinum in adsumptione sanctae Mariae," in *La Parole de l'Orient*, 1(1970), 102-117. [7]PG, 85, 1772C.

ANTONINUS, ST. (1389-1459)

Dominican archbishop of Florence, church reformer and apostle of social charity, A. preached forty-six sermons on Our Lady and commented at length on Lk I. His Marian theology is found in a short chapter in Part One and in Titulus XV, Part Four, of his *Summa Theologica*.[1] He did not aim at originality, followed the Dominican tradition, and was particularly influenced by Pseudo-Albert (qv), whom he thought was St. Albert (qv). In Part One, he rejects the Immaculate Conception (qv) holding that Mary was sanctified shortly after animation.

The theology of Mary set out in Part Four is linked with the Gift of Piety, taking forty-five chapters.[2] The order of topics is somewhat arbitrary. A. begins with the spiritual motherhood (qv), interpreting Jn 19:26 in this sense (see WOMAN IN). Prone to divisions and subdivisions, he analyzes the different ways in which this motherhood is expressed within the Church.[3] Curiously his use of Scripture prompts him to apply to Mary a text on Mother Zion from Ps 87. He tries to keep his plentiful metaphors and images within biblical limits—his comparison of Mary with an immense book limps. Dealing with Mary's nativity, he asserts firmly that she has "become the middle term (*media*) or Mediatress between God and men."[4]

A. was convinced that Mary had many graces of perfection, many gifts and privileges. In keeping with tradition, he defended the vow of virginity (qv). For the marriage (qv), he adduces the reasons given by St. Thomas. On St. Joseph's doubt (qv), he follows St. Bernard (qv).[5] Though he deals with theological aspects of the Annunciation (qv), the influence of Pseudo-Albert is felt in the questions he raises on precise details of time, place, and appearance. Later he takes over Pseudo-Albert's theory of Mary as helper of our redemption. He especially repeats Pseudo-Albert on the *associatio* (see ASSOCIATE) between Jesus and Mary: *associatio* in being, suffering and acting.[6] Mary is Mother of all, Ark (qv) of the treasures, Queen (qv) of the heavens and Queen of the Church, Sword against enemies, Advocate (qv) of sinners. A. speaks of her as having absolved us of our guilt and punishment "through her Son." He taught the Assumption and Mary's supremacy over the angels. He liked to see similarity between the Magnificat and the Our Father; he saw a threefold meaning in Simeon's prophecy on the sword: the sword of sorrow, the sword of the divine word, the sword of virtuous love.[7] The marriage at Cana for him typified the marriage between God and the Church.

---

[1]*Summa Theologica*, (Verona, 1740; photolithograph ed., Graz, 1959). [2]*op. cit.*, 916-1250. Cf. E. Brand, *Die Mitwirkung der seligsten Jungfrau zur Erlösung nach dem hl. Antonin von Florenz*, (Rome, 1945); G. Defrenza, "Maria, Madre della Chiesa, nel pensiero di S. Antonino, Arcivesco di Firenze," in *Rivista asc. mist.*, 11(1966), 172-180. [3]*Summa Theologica*, 919. [4]*op. cit.*, 937. [5]*op. cit.*, 957. [6]*op.cit.*, 1058-1059. [7]*op.cit.*, 1183.

APHRAATES (4th Century)

A. is of importance to Marian theology since he is the first of the Syrian Fathers. Known as the Persian sage, he was probably a monk, possibly a bishop. Brief passages on Mary occur in the course of his twenty-three treatises, "Demonstrations" on the faith.[1] He speaks of her as a "prophetess" and "Mother of the great Prophet." Though no single word existed in Syriac for the Mother of God, the truth is clear enough: "For when Gabriel evangelised blessed Mary, his [Jesus'] Mother, then the Word went forth from on high and came and the Word was made a body and dwelt among us."[2] "He is the first-begotten, born of Mary."[3]

A., as the other Syrians (see EPHRAEM, ST. and JACOB OF SARUG), even St. Romanos (*qv*) who wrote in Greek, has a lively sense of St. Joseph's (*qv*) role and in this context emphasizes the virginal motherhood: "Jacob begot Joseph and Joseph was called the father of Jesus Christ; but Jesus was born of the Virgin Mary, of the seed of the house of David, of the Holy Ghost as it is written: Joseph with his espoused, both of the house of David. And the Apostle bears witness that *Jesus Christ* was of Mary *of the seed of David in the Holy Spirit*. Joseph was called the father of Jesus, though not born of his seed. The real paternal name was passed down from Adam to Joseph through sixty-three generations. The paternal name was taken up by Joseph and applied to Jesus. From Joseph, therefore, he received a paternal name, from John a priestly name, and from Mary he took on a body and adopted a name of generation."[4]

Mary's humility was singled out by the Sage for special praise, with a strong hint that, in this, she is our model (See IMITATION): "The humble are sons of the Almighty and brothers of Christ, who after he had been announced to us for our peace, came and Mary, because of her humility, received him. For when Gabriel evangelised most blessed Mary he said to her: *Peace be with you, you are blessed among women*. Gabriel therefore took peace. He bore down the blessed fruit and the beloved Offspring was sown in Mary. But she praised the Lord and magnified him *because he hath regarded the humility of his handmaid*; the proud and the powerful did not please him; and the Most High *exalts the humble*. See then, dearest, that peace hastens to the humble."[5]

Mary's spirit of prayer is lauded. Gabriel offered her prayers to God and "evangelised the [future] nativity, saying: *You have found grace before God*. Nor would Mary have found grace otherwise than by her fasting and prayer."[6]

The contrast between Eve and Mary is suggested in that between the curse brought by woman—death, child-bearing in pain, the earth itself bearing thorns and thistles—with the change thus described: "But now through the coming of the Offspring of blessed Mary the thorns are uprooted, the sweat wiped away, the fig tree cursed; the dust has become salt, the curse tied to the cross and the sword tip removed from the tree of life, which is given as food to believers; to the blessed and virgins and chaste, paradise is promised."[7]

---

[1]Cf. Ortiz de Urbina, S.J., "La Mariologia nei Padri Siriaci," in OCP, 1(1935), 102-103. [2]PS, 1, *Demonst.*, VI, 10, 281-282. [3]PS, 1, *Demonst.*, XIV, 683-684. [4]PS, 2, *Demonst.*, XXIII, 20, 63-66. [5]PS, 1, *Demonst.*, IX, 5, 418. [6]PS, 1, *Demonst.*, III, 14, 130-131. [7]PS, 1, *Demonst.*, VI, 6, 265-266.

APOCRYPHA, THE NEW TESTAMENT

This article deals with the group of disparate writings on biblical subjects appearing in the age of the New Testament or within immediate memory of it, and sometimes claiming a similar warrant. The simple test is their exclusion from the *canonical* writings. Contemporary interest in history and improved method in this area, important recent documentary finds and evidence that the texts were more ancient than had been hitherto believed, now ensure a respect for them previously denied. Another factor counts in Marian theology. They are at the origin of three feasts of Our Lady: the Conception, the Nativity and the Presentation. Their influence on literature, on art especially, has often been more marked than that of the canonical gospels. They tend to affect the fabric of private revelations. While often demonstrably unreliable on fact, they have influenced the development of doctrine, notably in the Assumption (qv) of Our Lady; they are particularly valuable as evidence of popular piety, which too is a factor in doctrinal growth. They are dealt with here in broadly identifiable categories.[1] The Assumption Apocrypha are treated in a separate article.

1. *Jewish Christian Apocrypha* of the first and second centuries. Jewish Christian gospels of a Synoptic kind have been given different names: *Gospel according to the Hebrews; Gospel of the Ebionites; Gospel of the Nazaraeans [or Nazorites]; Hebrew Gospel according to Matthew; Gospel of the Twelve* [Apostles]. What works actually correspond to these titles is not certain.[2] Passages of Marian interest are the following: "When Christ wished to come upon the earth to men, the good Father summoned a mighty heavenly power called Michael, and entrusted Christ to its care. And the power came into the world, and it was called Mary, and Christ was in her womb seven months." Such exchangeable appelations of angels and sacred figures occur in Jewish Christian literature. Origen (qv) had noted that the Holy Spirit was called Christ's mother—an error due probably to the feminine gender of *Ruah*. "Even so did my mother, the Holy Spirit, take me by one of my hairs and carry me away on to the great mountain Tabor."[3]

Thus, the *Gospel according to the Hebrews*. The *Gospel of the Nazaraeans* has an interesting passage on the Mother of the Lord and his brothers: "Behold, the mother of the Lord and his brothers said to him: 'John the Baptist baptizes unto the remission of sins, let us go and be baptized by him'. But he said to them: 'Wherein have I sinned that I should go and be baptized by him? Unless what I have said is ignorance.'"[4]

The *Gospel of the Ebionites* has a fragment which resembles the Synoptic account of Jesus' true family. It also has heretical elements. Christ is said to be born of human seed and to be the adopted Son of God—after the baptism by John the voice from heaven said "This day have I begotten thee." A *Gospel of Peter* is mentioned by Origen who thought that from it or, the *Book of James* (i.e. the *Protevangelium*), came the idea that the "Brothers of the Lord" were sons of Joseph by a former marriage—the idea is in the *Book of James*. A fragment in the *Gospel*

of Peter on the Passion and Resurrection makes no mention of Mary at the foot of the Cross.[5]

The *Testaments of the Twelve Patriarchs*, unlike the previous apocrypha which exist only in fragments, is textually complete, though partially in different versions. Theories on authorship differ, whether it is the work of a Jew with later Christian interpolations, or of a Christian working on Jewish documents. It was complete certainly before 200 A.D. The relevant Marian passage is in ch. 19, v.8 of the *Testament of Joseph*, an unusual vision: "And I saw that a virgin was born from Judah (and I saw in the midst of the horns a virgin) wearing a robe of fine linen (a many-coloured robe); and from her was born a spotless lamb and he had at his right, as it were, a lion and all the beasts (and all the reptiles) rushed against him and the lamb overcame them, trampling on them."[6] Variants are indicated but the word *parthenos* (virgin) is common to both versions.

The fine linen is, according to Rev 19:8, the distinctive attire of the Church, spouse of the Lamb. Psalm 44:14, echoed in the phrase "a many-coloured robe," refers in general to the spouse of the royal Messiah and was understood by the Fathers of the Church in terms of the Church as the spouse of Christ. We have then hint of the Mary-Church (qv) typology.

The *Ascension of Isaiah* is a Jewish composition to which a Jewish Christian writer, probably in the second century, added a vision of the prophet.[7] A passage on the miraculous appearance of the Christ child is a further interpolation of uncertain date. The prophet saw Mary of the house of David who was betrothed to Joseph of the same lineage. He tells of Mary's pregnancy, which, he says, was found when she was betrothed, and of Joseph's wish to put her away. "But the angel of the Spirit appeared in this world; and after that, Joseph did not put Mary away. He kept her but did not reveal the matter to anyone. And he did not approach Mary but kept her as a holy virgin, although she was with child. And he did not [yet] live with her for two months. After two months Joseph was in his house, with his wife Mary, the two of them alone. It came to pass, while they were alone, that Mary suddenly beheld with her eyes and saw a little child; and she was amazed. When her amazement wore off, her womb was found as it was before she was with child. And when her husband Joseph said to her 'What amazed you?', his eyes were opened; and he saw the child and praised God that the Lord had come to his portion. And a voice came to them: 'Tell this vision to no one.' But the report concerning the child was noised abroad in Bethlehem. Some said, 'The Virgin Mary has given birth before she was married two months'; and many said: 'She has not given birth; the midwife has not gone up to her, and we heard no cries of pain.'"[8]

A later phrase "he was like any other child, lest anyone should know him" (11:17) recalls St. Ignatius of Antioch's opinion that Mary's virginity was unknown to the prince of this world. There is also an explicit mention of the *virginitas in partu* (*qv*): the birth was painless. "We did not hear any cries of pain," say the inhabitants; Mary's womb was unchanged.

The absence of a midwife is also affirmed in the *Odes of Solomon*, a Jewish Christian hymnbook of first or early second century origin.[9] They were discovered in a Syriac manuscript in 1909 and the original language has been the subject of much debate; it may have been Syriac. The Marian passage is in Ode 19: "The womb of the Virgin took [it] and she received conception and brought forth: and the Virgin became a mother with great mercy; and she travailed and brought forth a Son without incurring pain. And it did not happen without purpose, and she had not sought a midwife, for he brought her to bear. She brought forth, as a man, of her own will, and she brought him forth as a sign and acquired him in great power. And she loved him in salvation, and guarded him in kindness and showed him in majesty." [10]

The phrase, "acquired him in great power," may echo Gen 4:1 when Eve says, "I have gotten a man with the help of the Lord." The sign may be a reference to Is 7:14 (see EMMANUEL); "as a man" could indicate Mary's consent, her co-operation with God.

Book Eight of the *Sibylline Oracles* has material which may have been added in the late second century to a work of Jewish-Hellenistic origin: Mary is a "pure virgin," (*parthenos agne*). Some unusual elements are added to the Lucan Annunciation narrative: "And the maiden laughed, her cheeks flushed scarlet, gladly rejoicing and touched in her heart with shame; then she took courage. The Word flew into her body, was made flesh in time and brought forth to life in her womb, was moulded to mortal form and became a boy by virgin birth-pangs. This, a great wonder to mortals, is not greater wonder to God the Father and to God the Son. When the child was born, delight came upon the earth, the heavenly throne laughed, and the world rejoiced; a new-shining star, God-appointed, was revered by the Magi."[11] Some lines recovered from the so-called Sibylline Theosophy, probably to be read towards the end of Book One, refer to the "maid who will give birth to the Logos of God Most High but as wedded wife shall give to the Logos a name." A star will shine from the East. There is a touching addition to the story of the loaves and fishes: Christ had the twelve baskets of fragments gathered "for the holy Virgin." There is a hint too of Mary's intercession: "For he gave seven periods for penance to men astray, thanks to the Holy Virgin."

2. *Mary in the Nativity and Infancy Gospels.* The original title of *The Book of James* or *Protevangelium* was *The Nativity of Mary.* The name, *The Book of James*, was first used by Guillaume Postel in the 16th century; the author poses as "James," probably James the "brother of the Lord." Accepted scholarly opinion was completely upset by the discovery in 1958 of a third century papyrus of the work.[12] The critical edition was made by Fr. de Strycker on the basis of three papyri, several manuscripts (including a ninth century palimpsest), Syrian, Sahidic and Armenian versions, and a Georgian version of an Armenian text.

Until then, critical opinion, deriving from Harnack, saw the text as a composite product of three separate documents, of differing dates. According to Fr. de Strycker, "the theory of the three documents is devoid of any foundation either in the domain of external or internal evidence."[13] The whole work is from before 200 A. D. and may be decades earlier than this date.

The influence of the *Protevangelium* has been considerable through a large family of texts which borrowed from it.[14] The first seventeen chapters of the Latin gospel of Pseudo-Matthew draw on it as a principal source. The work is hagiography composed to match the piety of the age towards Mary. Obviously influenced by the gospels it has additional biographical elements.

Mary is a descendant of David. Her parents are named, Joachim and Anne—Old Testament names (Susanna, 4; and 1 Sam 1:19,20). They receive their child, Mary, in answer to prayers. Joseph, her husband, is an aged widower with children—he is chosen for her miraculously; the *virginitas in partu* is affirmed by a midwife. The *Protevangelium* differs from the gospel record in some points—the Annunciation is made in Jerusalem, but Jesus' birth takes place in a cave near Bethlehem—and adds considerably elsewhere to the narrative, especially in the sequel for Joseph and Mary to the virginal conception.

Three feasts of Mary—the Conception, the Nativity and the Presentation in the Temple—and the feasts of her parents derive from the apocrophon. The narrative of Anne's conception of Mary implies strongly that the conception must be virginal, from which special preservation from sin would follow. Doctrine was affected in another way. The Presentation of Mary in the Temple and the details added to it serve not only to emphasize Mary's holiness, but, by inspiring the feast, influenced continuous reflection and an immense homiletic literature in the eastern Church.[15]

No such profound and permanent effect can be traced to the apocryphal gospels of the infancy: the *Gospel of Thomas*, described as an Israelite and philosopher[16]; the *Arabic gospel of the Infancy*[17]; and the *Armenian gospel of the Infancy*.[18] The analysis of these compilations, of their origins and inter-relations, would be a long enterprise. They aim at filling in the gap left by the canonical gospels between the Flight into Egypt and the Public Life of the Saviour. Invention is at times unbridled and if the result here and there is touching, it is more often bizarre, distasteful and shocking. There is an occasional flash of light. Thus, in the Armenian gospel, Joseph, as he sought the midwife, met Eve (*qv*) who came to see the promise of redemption fulfilled (VIII); in the *Protevangelium*, Joseph himself recalls that "the serpent came and found Eve alone and deceived her" (XIII).

The Arabic gospel narrates two miracles wrought by the Infant Jesus after a petition addressed to his Mother: a woman, oppressed by a demon, asks Mary to give her the divine Child, and when her request is granted, the demon is put to flight; three women whose brother has been changed into a mule beg Mary's pity. When the Mother places the Child on the mule, he returns to his human condition. The *Gospel of Thomas* concludes its account of the Finding in the Temple (*qv*) with words from Lk 1:42: "Blessed art thou among women, because God hath blessed the fruit of thy womb. For such glory and such excellence and wisdom we have neither seen nor heard at any time." (XIX)

The *History of Joseph the Carpenter* is an Egyptian composition sprung from the cult of the saint in that area. The work, at least in its present form, is now dated in the seventh century, a radical revision of the opinion deriving from Tischendorf, who placed it about the fourth century. The work is complete in Arabic and Bohairic, and exists in fragments in Sahidic, including some discovered in the present century.[19] Variations in the versions point to a more ancient original text, possibly more detailed—Greek according to some authorities, Sahidic for others.

The book falls into two parts, of which the first (Ch 1-11) deals with the early life of St. Joseph, the Holy Family and the infancy of Jesus, and the second (Ch 12-32) with the sickness, death and burial of the saint. Each part contains unusual elements. Joseph, a native of Bethlehem, was married at the age of forty. His wife died after forty nine years of marriage and, after one year, the priests of the Temple, casting lots among twelve old men of the tribe of Juda, entrusted Mary, then twelve years old, as fiancée to him, on whom the lot had fallen. She cared for James, the youngest of his six children—four sons and two daughters. There is no mention of the Annunciation (*qv*) or Visitation (*qv*), nor later of the Magi. The mystery of the Incarnation took place two years after Mary's entry to Joseph's home and the saint's anxiety, poignantly described, was lifted by an angelic visitation. Mary's Child was due to the operation of the Holy Spirit. The sojourn in Egypt lasted one year.

The second part of the work tells, with much detail, the story of Joseph approaching death at the age of one hundred and eleven, disturbed by strange fears. Mary and Jesus are present, and Jesus, by his prayer, assures relief. Joseph's soul is borne aloft by angels, led by Michael and Gabriel, and his body will be preserved from corruption. Those who commemorate the saint, honour his sanctuary, give alms in his name or write his life, or of his death, will be blessed. They will be entrusted to him in life and at death have their sins wiped out—a remarkable sign of devotion to the saint in early times. The poor are to give Joseph's name to their sons, ensuring thus preservation from famine and disease.

Mary's threefold virginity is emphasized. Joseph refers to the "seal of her virginity" (XVII) which she preserved, and if the title, Mother of God, is not used, her Son is called by Joseph "my Lord and my God," "my Saviour and truly the Son of God."

The apocrophon most diffused in the West, the *Gospel of Pseudo-Matthew*, in its first seventeen chapters, draws heavily on the *Protevangelium* and, in chapters twenty-five to the end, on the *Gospel of Thomas*.[20] There are omissions and much additional material, the latter sometimes reflecting patristic thought. The accepted date was the eighth century, but the most recent critical editor, G. Gijsel, colleague of E. de Strycker, places it about 550, hoping to reach a more precise year when the history of this basic adaptation of the *Protevangelium* is disentangled from that of translations which in fact preceded it.[21] A short *Liber de Nativitate Mariae*, spuriously attributed to St. Jerome (qv), may have been composed by Paschasius Radbert (qv).[22]

3. *Apocrypha of the Passion and Resurrection.* Mary figures in the dialogues which make up the *Questions of Bartholomew*, which may represent the *Gospel of Bartholomew*, mentioned by St. Jerome (qv). Through a complicated textual ancestry, scholars point to a third or fourth century Egyptian origin.[23] Marian piety at the time is strikingly illustrated. Already, titles of Mary begin to appear. She is called *Kecharitomene* (highly favoured) almost as a proper name. "Tabernacle of the most High," "salvation of the world," "Mother, Queen, Servant," "Mother of the heavenly King." Mary is asked by Bartholomew on behalf of the apostles "how thou didst conceive the incomprehensible, or how thou didst bear him that cannot be carried, or how thou didst bring forth so much greatness." Here is an early expression of Mary's role in divine revelation, of her influence on the Apostles (qv). They ask her to pray, after which she recounts the Annunciation in a strangely amplified form, alleging that God himself had told her three years before

the event: "I will send my Word unto thee." Her intercession (qv) is assumed when Peter asks her to "entreat the Lord that he would reveal unto us the things that are in the heavens," and the Mary-Eve (qv) contrast is recalled when Peter says to Mary: "Thou art she who hast brought to nought the transgression of Eve, changing it from shame into joy." (IV)

In Coptic only, there is further material, attributed to Bartholomew—a book of the resurrection—notable for an account of the risen Christ's appearance to Mary[24] (see RESURRECTION). When Mary made her act of faith, Jesus addresses her in terms of praise and of such theological import that the precise dating of the Coptic version would be helpful: "Hail to thee who hast borne the life of the whole world. Hail, my Mother, my saintly Ark (qv) . . . The whole of paradise rejoices because of thee. I tell thee, my Mother, whoever loves thee, loves life."[25]

Another set of fourth century documents bears the title *Gospel of Nicodemus* or *Acts of Pilate*, originating in the belief that Pilate had sent to the Roman emperor an account of the trial and death of Christ. Again, the textual history is complicated.[26] Inset in the alleged story of the trial of Jesus by the Roman governor is an accusation by the Jews that the Saviour was illegitimate (II, 3). Chapter X of the long recension enlarges the story of the carrying of the Cross: Mary, informed by John, met Jesus on the way, cried out in anguish and fainted (whence the fourth Station of the Cross). A long poignant lament by Mary at the foot of the Cross is given.[27] With the cycle of Pilate stories is also grouped the *Gospel of Gamaliel*, which also recounts Mary's lament, compared to that of Jacob for Joseph, and, with much detail, an apparition of the risen Jesus to his Mother.[28]

4. *Acts and Apocalypses.* The *Acts of John*, in their extant condition, have no reference to Mary. The *Acts of Paul*, composed by a priest in Asia Minor in the second century (c. 160-170), mention Mary's virginity in the part dealing with St. Thecla, and in the apocryphal letter of the saint to the Corinthians. A Greek papyrus, published in 1959, clears up a problem raised by the previously known manuscripts—the "Holy Ghost being sent forth from heaven from the Father unto her by the angel Gabriel." The papyrus reads: "Our Lord Jesus Christ was born of Mary, of the race of David, the Holy

Spirit having been sent to her from heaven by the Father that he might appear in this world and free all flesh by his flesh."[29]

The *Acts of Peter*, possibly originating also in Asia Minor, between 150-200, have a lengthy passage on the virginal motherhood. The author adduces a number of texts which he calls prophetic: "Who shall declare his generation" (Is 53:8); "In the last times shall a child be born of the Holy Ghost: his mother knoweth not a man, neither doth any man say that he is his father" (a composite text from Mt 1:18-19 and Lk 1:34-35); "Behold a virgin shall conceive in the womb" (Is 7:14 according to the LXX); "Neither did we hear her voice, neither did a midwife come in" (the *Ascension of Isaiah*); "A stone was cut out without hands, and smote all the kingdoms" (Dan 2:34, commonly applied by the Fathers to the virginal conception). Before this last quotation, occurs an alleged prophecy, echo of Jn 3:13, which seems to favour Docetism: "Born not of the womb of a woman, but from a heavenly place he came down." The general context does not favour Docetism. The strange medley of "prophetic" quotations shows the author's deficiency; his belief in the virginal conception is rock solid.[30]

In writings kindred to these Acts, the *Passion of St. Andrew* and the *Passion of Bartholomew*, there is reference to the virginal motherhood with the patristic image of the virgin earth (qv). The author of the second work speaks of Mary as the first to take the vow of virginity (qv). Both writings may have been influenced by St. Irenaeus (qv).[31]

The *Apocalypse of Peter* contains nothing about Our Lady, but the *Apocalypse of Paul* does. This work, from the latter half of the fourth century, describing Paul's visions when he was taken up to the "third heaven" (2 Cor 12:2), was widely popular, known to St. Augustine (qv), and quoted by Dante (qv).[32] There is manuscript variation and the Latin version enlarges on the references to Mary: a) in XLI, stating that those who are cast into the sealed well of the abyss are they who have not confessed that the Virgin Mary gave birth to Jesus Christ (the Greek version adds the word *Theotokos*); b) in XLVI, describing the vision of the Virgin Mary, coming in glory accompanied by angels, greeting Paul as one "dearly beloved of God and angels and men," and informing him of his high repute among the blest. The saints besought Jesus, "her Son and Lord," that they might see Paul in the flesh, because he had led so many into the Kingdom. Then Latin manuscripts add: "But I say unto thee, Paul, that for this cause I come first to meet them that have performed the will of my Son and my Lord Jesus Christ, even I come first to meet him and leave them not as strangers until they meet with him in peace."[33] This is a remarkable statement of the power of Mary, of her status in the realm of the blest.

There are *Apocalypses of the Virgin*, kindred to the *Assumption Apocrypha*, but branching off to a special theme—Mary's visit to the lower regions and her prayers on behalf of the damned. As in the *Assumption Apocrypha*, St. Michael is prominent in these compositions. Dialogue between him and Mary is a device, as a dialogue between her and her divine Son. The Ethiopian version shows the influence of the *Apocalypse of Paul*. Abundant evidence is found in these texts of Mary's intercession which, in the loosely defined Byzantine picture of the hereafter, could embrace those in hell. One present-day specialist, A. A. Wenger, dates them earlier than the first editors; there is still much scope for research.[34]

5. *Nag Hammadi Apocrypha*. Two of the Coptic Gnostic texts found in the neighbourhood of Nag Hammadi in 1945 are "gospels": the *Gospel of Philip* and the *Gospel of Thomas*. The *Gospel of Philip*, clearly dependent on the infancy narratives of Matthew and Luke, interprets the gospel persons symbolically. Mary and Joseph are spoken of as the parents of Jesus, but the Virgin Mother is presented as a heavenly power, the Holy Spirit. Jesus' true Father is the Father in heaven. Examples are: "Adam came into being from two virgins, from the Spirit and from the virgin earth. Christ, therefore, was born from a virgin to rectify the fall which occurred at the beginning." "It was he [Joseph] who made the cross from the trees which he planted. His own offspring hung on that which he planted. His offspring was Jesus, and the planting was the cross . . ."[35]

The *Gospel of Philip* may in part go back to the second century. The *Gospel of Thomas* is a collection of 114 sayings or *logia* of Jesus which in its present Coptic version is dated, at latest, about the first half of the fifth century. The primitive text may go back to 140 A. D., and come from sources still more ancient. A number of the *logia* refer to Mary. *Logion* 79 adds

LK 23:29 to Lk 11:27-28. In *Logion* 99, Jesus, in answer to the word from his disciples that his brothers and mother were standing outside, said: "Those here who do the will of my Father, they are my brothers and my mother; these are they who shall enter the kingdom of my Father." *Logion* 101 reads: "Whoever does not hate his father and his mother as I do cannot become my disciple. And whoever does [not] love his father and his mother as I do cannot become my disciple, for my mother [gave me falsehood] but [my] true [mother] gave me life." *Logion* 105 reads: "Whoever knows father and mother shall be called the son of a harlot."[36] The concluding passage, *Logion* 114, reads thus "Simon Peter said to them: Let Mary go out from among us, because women are not worthy of the Life. Jesus said: See, I shall lead her, so that I shall make her male, that she too may become a living spirit, resembling you males. For every woman who makes herself male will enter the Kingdom of Heaven."[37]

6. A different document is the *Epistula Apostolorum*, of which an Ethiopic version was found in 1895. Fragmentary Coptic papyri and later Latin fragments also exist.[38] Scholars differ on the date, some placing it in the second century. It contains a story also found in the Infancy *Gospel of Thomas*, of the boy Jesus challenging his teacher—when asked to say Alpha he would have answered "First you tell me what Beta is." Much more important is the creedal statement in the beginning of the work: "We believe that the word that became flesh through the holy Virgin Mary, was carried [conceived] in her womb by the Holy Spirit, was born not of the lust of the flesh but by the will of God, was wrapped [in swaddling clothes], made known at Bethlehem; and that he was reared and grew up, as we saw."[39]

[1]Cf. esp. E. Cothenet, "Marie dans les Apocryphes," in *Maria*, VI, 73-156; R. Laurentin, "Mythe et Dogme dans les Apocryphes," in PCM, IV, 13-29; P. E. Langevin, S.J., "Les écrits apocryphes du Nouveau Testament et la Vierge Marie," in PCM, IV, 233-252. General works with texts: K. Tischendorf, *Evangelia apocrypha*, 2nd ed., (Leipzig, 1876, reprinted, Hildesheim, Olms, 1966); C. Michael and P. Peeters, *Evangiles apocryphes*, 2 vols., (Paris, 1920); M. R. James, *The Apocryphal New Testament*, (Oxford, 1960); A. de Santos Otero, *Los Evngelios apocrifos*, 2nd ed., (Madrid, 1963); A. Hamman, *Littératures chrétiennes*, 1, *Naissance des Lettres chrétiennes*, II, *L'Empire et la croix*, (Paris, 1957); E. Hennecke and W. Schneemelcher, *New Testament Apocrypha*, ed. R. McL. Wilson, 2 vols., (London, 1963, 1965); L. Moraldi, *Apocrifi del Nuovo Testamento*, 2 vols., (Turin, 1971); M. Craveri, *I Vangeli Apocrifi*, with study by G. Pampaloni, (Turin, 1970). Cf. also R. E. Brown, S.S., in *Jerome Comm.*, II, 543ff; R. J. Foster in *Cath. Comm.*, 88; P. Vielhauer, *Geschichte der urchristlichen Literatur: Einleitung in das Neue Testament, die Apokryphen und die apostolischen Vater*, (Berlin, de Gruyter, 1975). [2]M. R. James, *The Apocryphal New Testament*, (Oxford, 1960), 1-8; E. Hennecke et al, *New Testament Apocrypha*, 1, (London 1963, 1965), 117-165. Cf. G. Bardy, "S. Jérome et l'Evangile aux Hébreux," in *Melanges Sc. Rel.*, 3(1946), 5-36; M. E. Boismard, O.P., "Evangile des Ebionites et problème synoptique," in RB, 73(1966), 321-352. For background cf. J. Daniélou, *The Theology of Jewish Christianity*, (Chicago, 1964). [3]"Gos. Heb., 1, 3," in E. Hennecke et al, *New Testament Apocrypha*, I, 163-164; M. R. James, *The Apocryphal New Testament*, (Oxford, 1960), 8. [4]"Gos. Nazaraeans, 2," in E. Hennecke, *op. cit.*, I, 146-147; M. R. James, *op. cit.*, 2. [5]E. Hennecke, *op. cit.*, I, 179-187; M. R. James, *op. cit.*, 13-14, 90-94. Cf. L. Vaganay, "L'Evangile de Pierre," (*Etudes Bibliques*, Paris, 1930); O. Perler, "L'Evangile de Pierre et Meliton de Sardes," in RB, 71(1964), 584-590. [6]Cf. M. de Jonge, "Testament of Joseph," in *The Testaments of the Twelve Patriarchs*, (Assen, Holland and Manchester University Press, 1958); A. N. Denis, *Introduction aux pseudepigraphes grecs de l'Ancien Testament*, (Leiden, 1970), 49-59. [7]Cf. J. Daniélou, *The Theology of Jewish Christianity*, 22-23; A. Vaillant, "Un Apocryphe pseudo-bogomile, La Vision d'Isaie?" in *Rev. Et. Slaves*, 42(1963), 109-121; F. Buck, S.J., "Are the 'Ascension of Isaiah' and the 'Odes of Solomon' witnesses to an early cult of Mary?" in PCM, IV, 373-380. [8]E. Hennecke et al, *New Testament Apocrypha*, I, 661 (11:4-14). [9]R. Harris and A. Mingana, *The Odes and Psalms of Solomon*, I, II, (Manchester, 1916, 1920). Cf. J. Daniélou, S.J., in SDB, 6, 677-684; J. Quasten, *Patrology*, I, (Maryland, 1950), 160-168; J. H. Charlesworth, 'The Odes of Solomon—not Gnostic," in CBQ, 31(1969), 356-369; *ibid.*, "Les Odes de Salomon et les manuscrits de la ner morte," in RB, 77(1970), 522-549. [10]Tr., F. Buck, *op. cit.*, 390. Cf. J. M. Bover, S.J., "La Mariologia en las odas de Salomon," in EstEcl, 1931, 349-363. [11]E Hennecke et al, *New Testament Apocrypha*, II, 740 (8:467-476). Cf. J. B. Bauer, "Die Messiasmutter in den Oracula Sibyllina," in MM, 18(1956), 118-124. [12]*Papyrus Bodmer V. Nativité de Marie*, ed. M. Testuz, (Cologny, Geneva, 1958); E. de Strycker, S.J., *La forme la plus ancienne du Protévangile de Jacques*, (Brussels, 1961); Georgian versions, G. Garitte, in Mus, 70(1957), 233-265; J. N. A. Birdsall, in Mus, 83(1970), 49-72. Cf. J. de Aldama, S.J., "Il Protevangelio de Santiago y sus problemas," in EphMar, 12(1962), 107-130; E. de Strycker, "Le Protévangile de Jacques, Problèmes critiques et exégétiques," in TU, (Berlin: Akademie, 1964), 343-359; *ibid.*, *Le Grieske handschriften van het Protévangile van Jacobus, De Protevangelii Jacobi codicibus graecis*, (Brussels, Paleis der Academien, 1968), list, 31-46; L. M. Peretto, O.S.M., *La Mariologia del Protovangelo di Giacomo*, (Rome, 1955). P.A. van Stempvoort, *The Protevangelium Jacobi: The Sources of its Theme and Style and their Bearing on its date, SE III/2, in TU, 88; 410-426*; N. Radovich, *Un Frammento slavo del Protovangelo di Giacomo* (Naples, ed. Cymba, 1969); G. M. Roschini, O.S.M., "I fondamenti dogmatici del culto mariano nel 'protovangelo di Giacomo'," in PCM,

IV, 253-271; E. Cothenet, "Protévangile de Jacques," in SDB, 8(1972), 1374-1384; H. R. Smid, *Protevangelium Jacobi: A Commentary*, (Assen, 1975). [13]E. de Strycker, *La forme la plus ancienne* etc., (Brussels, 1961), 403-404. [14]Cf. E. Amann, *Le Protévangile de Jacques et ses remaniements latins,* (Paris, 1910); I. M. Peretto, O.S.M., "Influsso del Protovangelo di Giacomo nei secoli II-IV," in MM, 19(1957), 66-70; *id.,* "Recenti ricerche sul Protovangelo di Giacomo," in MM, 24(1962), 131-132; *id.,* "Criteri d'impegno di alcune citazioni bibliche nel 'Protovangelo di Giacomo,'" in PCM, IV, 273-293; *id.,* "Espressioni del 'Protovangelo di Giacomo' nella eortologia bizantina," in Zagreb Congress, IV, 65-80; J. de Aldama, "Fragmentos de una versión latina del Protovangelo de Santiago y una neuva adaptación de sus primeros capítulos," in BB, 43(1962), 57-74; J. M. Canal, C.M.F., "Antiguas versiones latinas del Protovangelo de Santiago," in EphMar, 18(1968), 431-473. [15]Cf. R. Laurentin, *Traité,* V, 168-169. [16]M. R. James, *Apocryphal New Testament*, (Oxford, 1960), 49-70; E. Hennecke et al, *New Testament Apocrypha*, I, 392-401; S. Gero, "The Infancy Gospel of Thomas: A Study of the Textual and Literary Problems," in NovT, 13(1971), 46-80. [17]M. R. James, *Apocryphal New Testament*, 80-82; E. Hennecke et al, *New Testament Apocrypha*, I, 408-409. [18]M. R. James, *Apocryphal New Testament*, 83-84. [19]C. Michel and P. Peeters, *Evangiles Apocryphes,* I, (Paris, 1920), 192-245; M. R. James, *op. cit.,* (summary) 84-86. Cf. esp. R. Gauthier, C.S.C., "La Vierge Marie d'après l'Histoire de Joseph le Charpentier," in PCM, IV, 353-369; G. Giamberardini, O.F.M., *San Giuseppe nella Tradizione copta,* (Cairo, 1966), 93-113; L. T. Lefort, "A propos de 'L'Histoire de Joseph le Charpentier'," in Mus, 66(1953), 201-223. [20]M. R. James, *The Apocryphal New Testament*, 73-79 (summary); C. Michel and P. Peeters, *Evangiles Apocryphes,*I, text and French tr., 60-159. [21]Cf. R. Laurentin, in RSPT, 52(1968), 489; *ibid.,* in Zagreb Congress, II, 21. [22]Cf. E. Cothenet, "Marie dans les Apocryphes," in *Maria*, VI, 90, n.70; C. Lambot, O.S.B., in RevBen (1934), 279-283. [23]M. R. James, *Apocryphal New Testament*, 166-186; E. Hennecke et al, *New Testament Apocrypha*, I, 484-508. Cf. A. Wilmart and E. Tisserant, "Fragments grecs et latins de l'Evangile de Barthélémy," in RB, 10(1913), 161-190, 321-368; U. Moricca, "Un nuovo testo dell' 'Evangelo di Bartolomeo'," in RB, 30(1921), 481-516, also in RB, 31(1922), 20-30. [24]M. R. James, *Apocryphal New Testament*, 181-186; E. Revillout, in PO, 2; E. W. Budge, *Coptic Apocrypha in the Dialect of Upper Egypt*, (London, 1913), 1-48, 179-230 (*The Coptic "Book of the Resurrection"*). [25]E. Revillout, *op. cit.,* 190. [26]Text in E. Hennecke et al, *New Testament Apocrypha*, I, 444-484; P. Vannutelli, *Actorum Pilati textus synoptici,* (Rome, 1938). Cf. J. Quasten, *Patrology*, I, 115-118. [27]P. Vannutelli, *op. cit.,* 94ff. [28]Cf. A. Mingana, "The Lament of the Virgin and the martyrdom of Pilate," in *Woodbroke Studies,* (Manchester, 1928). For Ethiopian version, cf. M. A. van den Oudenrijn, *Gamaliel, Äthiopische Texte zur Pilatusliteratur,* (Fribourg, Switzerland, 1959); French tr. in *Le Figaro littéraire,* (13 April, 1957). [29]Quotations in M. R. James, *Apocryphal New Testament*, 289; M. Testuz, "Papyrus Bodmer X-XII," in Bodmer Libary, (Cologny-Geneva, 1959), p. 34; text of *Acts,* in M. R. James, *op. cit.,* 270-299; E. Hennecke et al, *New Testament Apocrypha*, II, 322-390. [30]M. R. James, *Apocryphal New Testament*, 325. [31]Cf. E. Cothenet, in *Maria*, VI, 15-116. [32]M. R.

James, *op. cit.,* 525-555; E. Hennecke et al, *New Testament Apocrypha*, II, 755-798. Cf. J. Quasten, *Patrology*, I, 146-149. [33]M. R. James, *Apocryphal New Testament*, 550. [34]Cf. H. Pernot, "Descente de la Vierge aux enfers d'après les manuscrits grecs de Paris," in *Rev. des Études Grecques,* 13(1900), 233-257; M. R. James, *op. cit.,* 563-564. Cf. esp. A. Wenger, in *Maria*, V, 956-961. [35]R. McL. Wilson, *The Gospel of Philip,* (New York: Harper and Row, 1962), 47, 49. [36]*The Gospel according to Thomas,* ed. and tr. by A. Guillaumont et al., (Leiden and London, 1959), 51, 53. Cf. H. Quecke, "L'Evangile de Thomas. État de Recherche," in *La venue du Messie,* ed. by E. Massaux (RechBib, 6, Bruges), 217-241. [37]Guillaumont, *The Gospel according to Thomas,* 57. [38]Cf. M. Hornschuh, *Studien zur Epistula Apostolorum,* (Berlin de Gruyter, 1965). [39]E. Hennecke et al, *New Testament Apocrypha*, I, 192-193.

APOLLINARIS OF LAODICEA (*c.*310-*c.* 390)

An author from whom a heresy bearing his name emerged, A., in the works restored to him by H. Leitzmann, frequently mentions Mary.[1] Occasionally his view that the Word assumed a human body and soul but not spirit, slightly affects his thinking on Our Lady, just as his insistence on the divine nature of Christ against the Arians also led him astray. But he can write thus: "Nor do we say that the flesh of our Lord Jesus Christ came from heaven, but we confess that God the Word was incarnate of the holy Virgin Mary; and we do not separate him from her flesh, but there is one person, one substance, one complete man, one complete God. If, therefore, we believe that he came in the likeness of man from the virginal conception, by which the Virgin is proved to be *Theotokos* (*qv*), he is not separated or divided from his own flesh . . ."[2] The use of *Theotokos* is significant. A. offers occasional comments on the gospel scenes in which Mary appears.

[1]For works restored to A., cf. H. Lietzmann, *Apollinaris von Laodicäa und seine Schule,* (Tübingen, 1904); R. Devreesse, *Les anciens commentateurs de l'Octateuche et des Rois,* in ST, 201; J. Reuss, *Mattheus-Kommentare aus der griechischen Kirche,* in TU, 61; *ibid., Johannes-Kommentare aus der griechischen Kirche,* in TU, 89; CMP, II, 215-228; EMBP, 301-305. Cf. G. Söll, in LexMar, 322; ClavisG, II, 301-316. [2]*De Fide et incarnatione*, 3, CMP, II, 221. Cf. H. Lietzmann, *op. cit.,* 194.

APOSTLES, THE

Scripture: Mary's association with the Apostles may appear slight in the New Testament. Quantitatively they wrote little about her; but it is the quality that matters. St. Paul (*qv*) was first with the text: "But when the time had fully come, God sent forth his Son, born of woman, born under the law, to redeem those who were under the law, so that we might receive adoption as sons." (Gal 4:4-5). Mary is here seen as the one through whom transition is effected from Old Testament to New Testament. Matthew (*qv*) has an infancy narrative and he relates the same episode as Mk 3:31-35, the encounter between the Mother and the "brothers" and Jesus during the public ministry (Mt 12:46-50). There is a bare mention in Jn 6:42. But John has his distinctive contribution in the Cana (*qv*) and Calvary passages (Jn 2:1-11 and 19:25-27) as well as Rev 12 (see *Woman in*), which came at least from a Johannine milieu.

Luke, not an Apostle, has much to say about Mary in his infancy narrative. He gives us, in Acts, the text which most significantly relates her to the Apostles: "All these [the Apostles just named] with one accord devoted themselves to prayer, together with the women and Mary, the Mother of Jesus, and with his brothers." (1:14). This text is capital in the theology of Mary and the Spirit (*qv*). Noteworthy, too, is the fact that, as at Cana, the disciples believed in Jesus after the sign wrought at his Mother's request, so Matthias, who would take the place made vacant by Judas, was chosen in the atmosphere of prayer wherein Mary was central.

The Apocrypha: There is much in these works about Mary and the Apostles, apart from the fact that some of them are attributed to Apostles as authors, notably the one which speaks most of her life, the *Protevangelium*. In the Gospel of Bartholomew, they gather around her to question her about the Incarnation. In the Assumption narratives, the Apostles are present, summoned miraculously, at the final scene, before Mary enters into glory. In Pseudo-Melito they are given a quasi-judicial role. Mary is mentioned twice in the Apocalypse of Paul.

Doctrine: With such beliefs spread through the body of the faithful, a climate of opinion arose in which a title like "Queen of Apostles" would be thought of. Through the ages, theologians have sought to describe the influence which Mary had on the privileged group, especially by way of enlightenment, as a source of comfort and as a sustenance by her prayer. Vatican II associates Mary and Apostles of her Son in what it says about the Holy Spirit. (LG 59, Missionary Decree, 4).

Mary's superiority to the Apostles is not controverted: Mary was chosen by God, the Apostles by God incarnate; she received her mission directly from God, they from Christ the Mediator; she received the Spirit at her conception, at the Annunciation and at Pentecost, they only on the latter occasion; in mediating the Incarnation she alone was a "cause of salvation to herself and the whole human race," they were dependent on her mediation; she by physical presence took part in the redemptive death of the Saviour, they as a group did not; her role vis-a-vis mankind remains personal, theirs is strongest as a group; her faith was antecedent to the Incarnation, a condition of the event, theirs consequent to it; Mary's love for Jesus was totally natural and supernatural, theirs principally supernatural; they were ministers of the Sacraments and Sacrifice of the New Law, she brought forth the Word incarnate, God's supreme Sacrament to men.

APOSTOLATE, THE

The apostolate is inherent in the mission of the Church to mankind; exercise of the apostolate flows from fidelity to that mission. Vatican II (*qv*) puts it clearly: "For this was the Church founded: that by spreading the kingdom of Christ everywhere for the glory of God the Father she might bring all men to share in Christ's saving Redemption; and that through them the whole world might in fact be brought into relationship with him. All activity of the Mystical Body directed to the attainment of this goal is called the apostolate, and the Church carries it on in various ways through all her members." (Decree on the Apostolate of the Laity, 2.) Several other Council documents treat of the subject.[1] This teaching was the culmination and summary of many papal pronouncement in the present century, which, for many reasons, caused an urgent examination of the doctrine. Reflection on the lay apostolate led to fuller awareness of the apostolate as such.

The Marian content of the lay apostolate in certain associations, in a similar way, prompted examination of Mary's role in the whole apostolate of the Church.[2] It will help to distinguish different historical forms of the Marian apostolate: that wholly directed to her own praise and glory; that pursued towards Christian goals with a formal reference to her as inspiration, protectress, helper; and exercise of the apostolate without such formal, public or conscious direction to Mary, but with acceptance of Catholic teaching and traditional practice in her regard. Cultural levels and milieus vary in each area. In the first category come the preachers and doctors of Our Lady: the eighth century Byzantine trio, the vast medieval company, St. Louis Marie de Montfort (qv) and St. Alphonsus Liguori (qv); so do the advocates of Marian devotions, the Rosary crusaders from Alan de la Roche (qv) to Fr. Patrick Peyton, and the vast army of those who in every way promote shrines and pilgrimages of Our Lady. In the *Teaching Authority*, the Popes from Pius IX (qv) to the present time—Pius XII (qv) most conspicuous among them—have been apostles of Mary in this sense.

In the second category are the great orders, like the Servites, and the religious congregations, especially numerous in the nineteenth and twentieth centuries, all of which have combined commitment to the religious life with the apostolate under the sign of Mary openly proclaimed. Here too must be noted the lay associations, from the Marian Congregations founded by the Jesuits in the sixteenth century to the great contemporary associations, the Legion of Mary (qv) and the Militia of Mary Immaculate, founded by Blessed Maximilian Kolbe (qv). Pius XII said: "For centuries the Church has had associations placed under the patronage of Mary, which have played a providential role, often praised by our predecessors and ourselves, in the personal sanctification of many Christians and the exercise of apostolic zeal. We should like to speak among other things of the Marian Congregations, which we have called Catholic Action in the spirit of the Blessed Virgin. Their nature and spirit is defined by the Apostolic Constitution *Bis Saeculari* of 27 September, 1948."[3] *Bis Saeculari* justifies the title Marian "not only because they take their name from the Blessed Virgin, but most of all because each and every member professes special devotion to the Mother of God and consecrates himself or herself, not of course under pain of sin, to work most seriously for his or her own Christian perfection and eternal salvation and for that of others under the standard of the Blessed Virgin Mary; by virtue of that consecration the member is attached

forever to the service of the Blessed Virgin Mary, unless he or she is expelled for some unworthy action or through instability, he or she leaves the association."[4]

Three modern apostles of Mary framed their purpose in words which illustrate the papal thesis. Fr. Chaminade (qv), founder of the Marianists, wrote: "We have enrolled ourselves under her banner as her soldiers and her ministers and we have bound ourselves by a special vow, that of stability, to support (*seconder*) her with all our strength, until the end of our lives, in the noble struggle against hell."[5] Francis Libermann affirming his "very special consecration . . ." "of the whole Society, of each of its members, of all the works and undertakings to the most holy Heart of Mary, a heart eminently apostolic and wholly inflamed with desires for the glory of God and the salvation of souls . . ." added: "We consider her as a perfect model of the apostolic zeal with which we must be consumed and as an abundant source, one always open, where we must draw. We shall have recourse to it ceaselessly with the greatest confidence, so that it may deign to pour out on us the motherly tenderness it feels for us and obtain an abundance of graces for us and for all our works."[6] The author of the *Handbook* of the Legion of Mary, Mr. Frank Duff (qv), writes thus: "The Legion of Mary is an Association of Catholics who, with the sanction of the Church and under the powerful leadership of Mary Immaculate, Mediatress of all graces (who is fair as the moon, bright as the sun, and—to Satan and his legionaries—terrible as an army set in battle array) have formed themselves into a Legion for service in the warfare which is perpetually waged by the Church against the world and its evil powers."[7] Elsewhere he speaks of the great purpose ". . . to bring Mary to the world."

Vatican II: The Council provides a concise doctrine of Mary and the apostolate: "Hence the Church in her apostolic work also rightly looks to her who brought forth Christ, conceivd by the Holy Spirit and born of the Virgin so that, through the Church, Christ may be born and grow in the hearts of the faithful also. The Virgin Mary in her own life lived an example of that maternal love by which all should be fittingly animated who cooperate in the apostolic mission of the Church on behalf of the rebirth of man." (LG, 65). This passage was added after the debate in September 1964. A report circulated to the Council Fathers said that Cardinal Suenens had proposed the addition on the apostolate "with insistence." The Cardinal had developed his thought on the subject through contact with the Legion of Mary. His work on the theology of the apostolate was a commentary on the legionary promise, and he had written the life of Edel Quin, a legionary envoy, Servant of God.

None the less, at the Modi stage, "several Fathers ask that the phrase 'who brought forth . . . and grow' be either deleted or corrected, as it is not clear. It should not be said that the conception and birth of the Son of God took place because of his spiritual birth in the hearts of men." The reply was, "The idea is patristic." For clarity, slight redrafting was proposed, the word Church being repeated. Two Fathers objected to the phrase, "maternal love," as applied to all apostolic activity, "especially when men are in question;" they suggested the words "outstanding charity." The answer was: "Maternal love is, as it were, the high point of the view. There is no difficulty in regard to men as is clear from St. Paul's manner of speaking." The Pauline text (Gal 4:19) referred to is: "My little children, with whom I am again in travail until Christ be formed in you!"[8]

The general truth, stated in LG, is given concrete expression in the Decree on the Laity. All are urged to venerate Mary devoutly, and to commend their life and apostolate to her: "The perfect example of this type of spiritual and apostolic life is the most Blessed Virgin Mary, Queen of Apostles. While leading on earth a life common to all men, one filled with family concerns and labours, she was always intimately united with her Son and cooperated in the work of the Saviour in a manner altogether special." (Art. 4). Mary's heavenly intercession is recalled in the words of LG 62.

[1]For example: LG, 33; Decree on Bishops, 17; on Priests, 5; on Priestly Training, 20; on Religious, 8; on the Lay Apostolate, *passim*; and on Social Communications, 13. Cf. "The Lay Apostolate," in *Papal Teachings*, St. Paul ed., Boston; Chautard, *L'Ame de tout apostolat*, (Paris, 1915. English tr., London, 1948). Cf. also Y. M. Congar, O.P., *Jalons pour une théologie du laïcat*, (Paris, 1953, 488ff; published in English as *Laymen in the Church*, London, 1957, 333ff). [2]Cf. L. Cardinal Suenens, *La Théologie de l'Apostolat*, (Bruges, 1952); F. Duff, *The Spirit of the Legion of Mary*, (Dublin, 1948); *id., Mary shall reign*, (Dublin, 1961); *ibid., Walk with Mary*, (Dublin, 1967); E. Neubert, S.M., *La Mission apostolique de Marie et la nôtre*, (Paris, 1956); K. Rahner, S.J., "Mary and the Apostolate," in *Mission and Grace*, I, (London, 1963), 172-202; J. J. McQuade, S.J., "Mary and the Apostolate," in MSt, 22(1971), 54-74. [3]*Bis Saeculari*, in OL, 374. [4]*op. cit.*, in AAS, 40(1948), 393. [5]*Apud* B. M. Morineau, in *Maria*, III, 347. [6]*Régle Provisoire de la Société du Saint Coeur de Marie*, (Amiens, 1845). [7]*Handbook of the Legion of Mary*, (Dublin, 1969), 1. [8]*Modi* VIII, LG, (Vatican Press, 1964), 19.

APPARITIONS

History: Apparitions of Our Lady have been recorded from patristic times.[1] Apart from legends, there is an account given by St. Gregory of Nyssa (*qv*) of Our Lady's apparition to St. Gregory the Wonderworker (d. *c.* 270). Mary appeared with St. John the Apostle, and she tells him to make known to the young man (that is, Gregory) "the mystery of true piety," to which the Apostle replied that he was willing in this matter to give pleasure to the Mother of the Lord since she so desired.[2] Not all narratives of the kind are as credible as this one. Legend mingles with history too in the medieval phase—which does not mean that they can be lightly dismissed.

The great modern series of well-known apparitions, with a public effect on the life of the Church, begin with that of the Miraculous Medal in 1830. Three hundred years before that, occurred the event in Guadalupe which is at the origin of the best-known Marian centre in the Americas. The Rue du Bac was not to be isolated in its time. In 1846 Our Lady appeared at La Salette, in 1858 at Lourdes, in 1871 at Pontmain, in 1879 at Knock in Ireland, in 1917 at Fatima, in 1932 at Beauraing and next year at Banneux in Belgium. Meanwhile reported apparitions and similar prodigies increased in number and, between 1928 and 1971, totalled 210.[3] The vast majority of these alleged apparitions have been repudiated by ecclesiastical authority.

Such a negative response is more frequent than a positive approval, even where there are many signs of acceptance by the official and praying Church.

Theology: The Church's attitude follows from its consciousness of its essential duty, the custody, interpretation and defence of public revelation. Theologians are agreed that God can grant private revelations, that he can suspend the normal laws which veil from mortals the persons and realities of the supernatural world and manifest these to direct sensory or intellectual perception. Thus there may be a vision, corporeal, imaginative or intellectual of Jesus Christ, his Blessed Mother, an angel or saint. The Old and New Testament record such happenings; so do the lives of saints, and it would be rash surely to eliminate, on an *a priori* basis, from such sacred or holy history such a considerable wealth of experience.

Private revelation for private use involves no one but the individual so favoured. Private revelation made public for any reason—because, for example, of a message intended for others—claims the attention of the Church for different reasons, principally because it must be related to public revelation and must not upset right public order. Then the first task is to establish genuineness. The norms of critical history must be strictly applied; the resources, of normal and paranormal psychology, fully used. Error can enter at any stage of the alleged communication. If error is clearly discovered, through deceitful testimony, psychiatric disease, mistaken observation, or defect in a spoken or written narrative, an adverse judgment may be pronounced to avert further harm. If a message or meaning contrary to church teaching is attributed to the event, the decision will be stricter.

If there is no reason for an intervention of this negative kind, the Church authorities may still show nothing more than tolerance, permission for the common acts of worship on the spot where the apparition is said to have taken place, and approval of certain prayers linked with it. Competence lies with the bishop of the diocese. Commissions of inquiry have generally been established to help the local authorities to reach a decision. A favourable decision has been formally delivered in certain cases: La Salette, Pontmain, Lourdes (*qv*), Fatima (*qv*), Beauraing, Banneux. Cumulative acts of veneration and public worship by ecclesiastical authorities amount to similar approval in other cases, such as Knock.

Popes have visited shrines of Our Lady associated with apparitions. Paul VI went to Fatima in 1967 for the Golden Jubilee of the apparitions and appeared before the multitude with the surviving witness, Sister Lucy; he also published a special Apostolic Exhortation, *Signum Magnum* (*qv*), for the occasion. John Paul II (*qv*) has gone to Guadalupe and Knock and announced his intention of going to Lourdes

(*qv*). At Knock, he spoke of the moment of grace on the day of the apparition. Pius XII, in the centenary documents for Lourdes, the Encyclical and the Apostolic Constitution, used such language as: "Bernadette was the first to drink at the spring, in obedience to Our Lady's command," and "The Blessed Virgin Mary, when she appeared in the grotto of Lourdes to an innocent and unspoiled child . . ."[4]

Benedict XIV (*qv*), in his classic treatise on the Beatification and Canonization of the Servants of God, insisted on the fact that the assent to apparitions was of human faith following the rules of prudence. Two replies, in 1875 and 1877 respectively, by the Sacred Congregation of Rites on the subject of apparitions are, for practical purposes thus summarized in St. Pius X's Encyclical *Pascendi*: "Such apparitions or revelations have neither been approved or condemned by the Apostolic See, but it has been permitted piously to believe them merely with human faith, with due regard to the tradition they bear . . ."[5]

On the other hand, Canon 1399, number 5, of the Code of Canon Law, bans books and articles on "apparitions, revelations, visions, prophecies, miracles," or which introduce "new devotions," if they do not have the ecclesiastical *Imprimatur*. Two decrees of the Holy Office were issued to condemn alleged apparitions; on 13 June, 1934, concerning Ezquioga in Spain; on 18 July, 1951, concerning Heroldsbach. Mostly the Roman authorities leave the decision to the bishop of the diocese.

In summary the extremes of naive credulity and irreverent scepticism are to be avoided. Charity must be observed to all, even to authentic visionaries. The Teaching Authority and the Sentiment of the Faithful (*qqv*) must work together.

[1]On Apparitions, cf., for bibliography, G. M. Besutti, O.S.M., in MM, 34(1973), 42-141; K. Rahner, S.J., *Visions and Prophecies*, (London, 1963); L. Volken, M.S., *Visions, revelations and the Church*, (New York, 1963); B. Billet, O.S.B., "Le dossier des apparitions non reconnues par l'Eglise," in CM, 15(1971), 93-123; A. Rivera, C.M.F., "Las apariciones marianas no reconocidas por la Iglesia," in EphMar, 22(1972), 405-413. Cf. ME, 12; papers of French Society for Marian Studies, *Vraies et fausses apparitions dans l'Eglise*, (J. M. Alonso, B. Billet, B. Bobrinskoy, R. Laurentin, M. Oraison), (Paris, 1973). [2]PG, 46, 912. Cf. P. A. Martinez, M.S., "De apparitionibus marianis in antiquitate Christiana," in PCM, V, 195-211; K. Balic, O.F.M., "Apparizioni mariane dei secoli XIX-XX," in

Teotocos, 234-254; M. Castellano, "La Prassi canonica circa le apparizioni mariane," in Teotocos, 486-505. For literature on ancient or recent apparitions, cf. R. Laurentin, in RSPT, 62(1978), 286-298. [3]Cf. table with dates and characteristics apud B. Billet, O.S.B., in BSFEM record j. cit., 9-20. [4]OL, 442, 452. [5]Pascendi, in ASS, 40(1907), 649. Cf. M. Castellano, "La Prassi canonica circa le apparizioni mariane," in Teotocos, 498, for all the Roman texts with references.

ARCHAEOLOGY

Archaeological research throws light on the origins of devotion to Our Lady. A church was built in her honour by Theonas, who was consecrated Patriarch of Alexandria in about 285 A.D.[1] Investigation in Nazareth indicates that on the site of the present church of the Annunciation where the twelfth century Basilica had stood, there had been a Byzantine church dating from the fifth century. There are remains of an earlier place of worship, in the manner of a synagogue, which cannot be later than the third century in origin, and parts of crypts much earlier still. Such underground crypts, which were apparently used for worship, are dated between 90 A.D. and mid-third century. There is evidence of a holy place erected by Jewish Christians between the third and fifth century, sacred to a woman whose name began with the letter M. A pilgrim linked this with XE Maria, adapted from St. Luke's gospel.

In the light of recent research the traditional site of the birth of Christ in Bethlehem is acceptable; so is Gethsemani as the place Mary's burial. The tradition, which names Meryem Ana near Ephesus, still lingers.

Burial inscriptions in the Roman Catacombs, and graffiti in the underground recesses of St. Peter's suggest that, from the second or early third century, Mary was considered a protectress of the dead and their kindly mediatress with Christ; she was honoured with Christ and St. Peter. The frescoes in the Catacombs of St. Priscilla, particularly rich in representation of Our Lady, confirm this view. Claims are made for a church in early times as far from Rome as Glastonbury.

Of a different kind is the Jewish burial inscription found in Egypt, dating from the first century, which helps to answer the objection against Mary's perpetual virginity based on St. Luke's use of the word "first-born" (prototokos) (2:7). That the word did not imply other children is shown by its use in this case to describe a woman who died after the birth of her first child, who could not obviously have had others.

Another important inscription, the epitaph of Abercius, is dealt with separately.

[1]Cf. J. B. Frey, C.S.Sp., "La signification du terme prototokos d'après une inscription juive," in BB, 11(1930), 369-372; J. Euzet, Historique de la Maison de la Sainte Vierge près d'Ephèse, (Istanbul, 1961); M. Guarducci, "Maria nelle epigrafi paleocristiane di Roma," in MM, 25(1963), 248-261; E. Testa, O.F.M., "Cultus marianus in textibus nazarethanis primorum saeculorum," in PCM, V, 21-34; A. Prandi, "Ricerche archeologiche a 'Meryem Ana Evi' presso Efeso," in PCM, V, 35-42; J. M. Salgado, O.M.I., "Le culte de Marie et les fresques de la catacombe de Priscille," in PCM, V, 43-62; F. de P. Sola, S.J., "La Santísima Virgen en las inscripciones principalmente sepulcrales en los primeros siglos del Cristianismo," in PCM, V, 63-77; H. M. Gillet, "Primordia cultus mariani in Britannia," in PCM, V, 125-128. B. Bagatti, O.F.M., "De Beatae Mariae Virginis cultu in monumentis palaeochristianis palaestinensibus," in PCM, V, 1-20; id., "Le origini della tomba della Vergine al Getsemani," in Rivista Biblica, 11(1963), 38-52; id., "Nuove scoperte alla tomba della Vergine a Getsemani," in Studii biblici franciscani liber annuus, 22(1972), 236-290. B. Bagatti with M. Piccirillo and A. Podroma, English tr. of previous entry, New Discoveries at the Tomb of the Virgin Mary in Gethsemane, (Jerusalem, 1975).

ARK OF THE COVENANT

Sacred Scripture: The New Testament references to the Ark of the Covenant do not bear explicitly on Our Lady.[1] Heb 9:4 recalls Jewish cultic history. Rev 11:19 reads: "Then God's temple in heaven was opened, and the ark of his covenant was seen within his temple; and there were flashes of lightning, loud noises, peals of thunder, an earthquake and heavy hail." This verse is followed immediately by the opening words of Rev 12: "And a great portent appeared in heaven . . ." (see WOMAN IN).

The typological interpretation has been exercised on Luke's infancy narrative (qqv). The angel's words in the Annunciation (qv) scene, "you will conceive in your womb" (1:31), echoed in 2:21, "before he was conceived in the womb," are related to Old Testament phrases signifying God's presence among his people. "This theme, initiated in Ex 33:3 (cf. 33:5) and 34:9, is Yahweh's dwelling in the bosom of Israel: in the Ark of the Covenant. With Zeph 3 and Is 12:6 it takes on an eschatalogical import. In Zion, restored Yahweh will dwell again: 'great in the midst of Israel.' Luke identifies the fulfilment of this promise with Mary's conception. He sees in this wonderful conception the eschatalogical accomplishment of the oracle of Zeph: Yahweh will dwell in the womb of the

Daughter of Zion [qv]."[2] Here the typology of the Daughter of Zion meets that of the Ark. Similarly the Visitation (qv) narrative, Lk 1:39-44, is typologically related to 2 Sam 6:2-11. "And why" said Elizabeth "is this granted to me, that the Mother of my Lord should come to me?" (1:43). "How," said David, "can the Ark of the Lord come to me?" (2 Sam 6:9). "And Mary remained with her about three months, and returned to her home." (Lk 1:56). "And the Ark of the Lord remained in the house of Obededom the Gittite three months." (2 Sam 6:11).

The typology, so subtly presented, is not accepted unreservedly by all. Luke, one author suggests, may have taken over an early Christian midrash about the Ark and toned it down to show that he was writing history.[3]

In patristic times the biblical text, which was used liturgically and stimulated homiletic treatment, was Ps 131:8: "Arise, O Lord, and go to thy resting-place, thou and the Ark of thy might." The Fathers did not derive the typology of the Ark from the Lucan texts which appeal to modern exegetes, nor from Rev 11:19 which would be used by medieval writers.

History: In a fragment from St. Irenaeus (qv) we read: "That Ark is shown to be a type of the body of Christ pure and undefiled . . ."[4] It was Hippolytus of Rome (qv) who first related the Ark to Our Lady: "Now the Lord was without sin, being in his human nature from incorruptible wood, that is from the Virgin, and being sheathed, as it were, with the pure gold of the Word within and of the Spirit without."[5] In the Coptic sermon attributed to Athanasius (qv), which if not authentic is probably of the fourth century, Our Lady is addressed thus: "O Ark of the new covenant, clad on all sides with purity in place of gold; the one in whom is found the golden vase with its true manna, that is the flesh in which lies the God-head."[6] In a Pseudo Athanasian sermon for the Presentation of the Lord, which is certainly fifth century, David is said to call Mary the Ark of sanctification.

Palestine was important at this time in development of doctrine and liturgy. Noteworthy then are the homilies of Hesychius (qv) and Chrysippus (qv). Adverting to Ps 131:8, Hesychius says: "The Ark of thy sanctification, the Virgin theotokos surely. If thou art the pearl then she must be the Ark."[7] Chrysippus too has Ps 131:8 in mind. He says: "The truly royal Ark, the most precious Ark, was the ever-Virgin *Theotokos*; the Ark which received the treasure of all sanctification . . . You and the Ark of your sanctification; for when you shall have arisen and sealed the Ark of your sanctification, then that Ark will arise with all from the fallen state in which relationship with Eve has set her."[8] There is a hint here of what the incorruptible wood of the Ark would eventually signify, immunity from the corruption of the grave.

The Jerusalem Liturgy had a feast of the Ark on 2 July; no other Old Testament treasure was commemorated thus. The date is seen to coincide with that chosen for the later feast of the Visitation (qv).

In the same century Proclus of Constantinople (qv) speaks of Mary as the Ark.[9] From the sixth century on, the typology recurs in eastern patristic writings: in the hymns of Romanos[10] (qv) and in the *Akathistos*[11] (qv) and in the homilies of Theoteknos of Livias (qv)[12], Severus of Antioch (qv), St. Andrew of Crete (qv)[13], St. John of Damascus (qv)[14], in John the Geometer's (qv) Life of Mary.[15]

In the West with the Carolingians we get the application of Rev 11:19 to Mary: "She was seen in the temple, that is in the Church of God" says Ambrose Autpert (qv). Paschasius Radbert is more explicit: "The temple of God was open and the Ark of the Covenant was seen. This certainly was not the Ark made by Moses, but is the Blessed Virgin, which [title] has already been transferred to her."[16]

Thereafter the idea is part of Christian thought at every level. It is found in the great prayer of Ekbert of Schönau (qv) to the Heart of Mary (qv); it enters the Litany of Loreto. St. Albert the Great will mention it. *Munificentissimus Deus* (qv) reminds us of St. Anthony of Padua's reference to Ps 131:8. St. Lawrence of Brindisi used the title itself repeatedly. Pius XII (qv) brought it into the Apostolic Constitution just mentioned: ". . . some [Fathers] have employed the words of the Psalmist: 'Arise, O Lord, and go into thy resting place, thou and the ark of thy might' and have looked upon the Ark of the Covenant, built of incorruptible wood and placed in the Lord's temple, as a type of the most pure body of the Virgin Mary, preserved and exempted from all corruption of the tomb and raised up to such glory in heaven."[17]

---

[1]Cf. Arndt and Gingrich, *A Greek English Lexicon etc.*, s. v. *kibotos*. Cf. Lampe, s. v.; EMBP, 2003. J. H. Crehan,

S.J., "The Ark of the Covenant," in *Clergy Review*, 35(1951), 301-311; *id.*, "The Assumption and the Jerusalem Liturgy," in TheolSt, 30(1969), 312-325. R. Laurentin, *Marie l'Eglise et le Sacerdoce*, (Paris, 1953), II, 214; *ibid.*, *Structure et Théologie de Luc I-II*, (Paris, 1957), 159-161, 228. Y. M. Congar, O.P., *The Mystery of the Temple*, (London, 1963), Appendix, 256-261; J. McHugh, *The Mother*, 56-63; R. E. Brown, *The Birth*, 327-328, 344-345. [2]R. Laurentin, *Structure et Théologie de Luc I-II*, (Paris, 1957), 70-71. [3]J. McHugh, *The Mother*, 62-63. [4]Fragment 8, ed. W. W. Harvey, (1857). [5]*In Ps, 23(22), apud* Theodoret. "Dial I," in GCS 1, 2, 147 (tr. adjusted by J. H. Crehan). Cf. *In Daniel 4*, in GCS 1, 1, 246; SC 14, 188,. [6]Coptic sermon, ed. L. Lefort, in Mus, 71(1958), 216. [7]*De S. Maria Deip.*, in PG, 93, 1464. [8]*In S. Mariam Deip.*, in PO, 19, 338. [9]*Hom. VI*, in PG, 65, 720C (authenticity of this passage confirmed by R. Caro, in *La Homilética*, II, 339. [10]Hymns, in Sc, 110, 122-3. [11]PG, 92, 1345D. [12]A. Wenger, *L'Assomption*, 282. [13]Homilies, in PG, 97, 869C. [14]Homilies, in PG, 96, 724.[15]A. Wenger, *L'Assomption*, 32, 386; also 67, 412. [16]PL, 96, 250A. [17]Pius XII, in OL, 311.

ARNOLD OF BONNEVAL (d. after 1156)

A Benedictine abbot, of Bonneval in the diocese of Chartres. A. deals with Marian themes in two works: in the third part of his treatise on the seven words of the Lord on the Cross[1]; and in the short essay *On the praises of the Blessed Virgin Mary*.[2] Though St. Bernard, whose friend he was, had written of Mary offering her Son to the Father in the moment of the Presentation (*qv*), A. seems to have been the first in the West to enunciate a theory of her part in the redemption, of coredemption (*qv*), some would say. He was mindful of the view of St. Ambrose (*qv*) that "Jesus had no need of a helper for the redemption of all." Though he begins then with a reference to the two altars, "one in the heart of Mary, the other in the body of Christ," and says that Mary immolated her soul, but desired to add "the blood of her flesh to the blood of her spirit," and "with the Lord Jesus to achieve the mystery of our redemption by [her] bodily death," he has to point out that this was the privilege of the high priest alone, with whom none could share dignity or authority.[3]

Ambrose had said that the Lord "received the affection" of the mother, so Arnold uses this as the basis of his theory. "Nevertheless that mother's affection cooperated very much according to its manner in propitiating God since the charity of Christ bore his own and his mother's offerings to the Father in such wise that the mother begged, the Son approved, and the Father granted."[4]

In his other work Arnold says "there was one single will of Christ and Mary, both together offered one holocaust to God; she in the blood of her heart, he in the blood of his flesh."[5] Thus the important step was taken. Mary was shown to have a role in the very moment of Calvary. John the Geometer (*qv*) had in the East, a century-and-a-half previously, seen the truth. Within another hundred years it would, in the West, be amply developed.

[1]*De verbo illo Domini: Mulier, ecce filius tuus*, in PL, 189, 1693-1698; R. Struve Haker, "Arnoldo de Bonavalle. Primero teológo de la Coredención mariana," in *Regina Mundi* (Bogotà), 7(1963), 48-75. [2]*On the praises of the Blessed Virgin Mary*, in PL, 189, 1725-1734. [3]*op. cit.*, in PL, 189, 1694B. [4]*op. cit.*, in PL, 189, 1694C. [5]*op. cit.*, in PL, 189, 1727A.

ART

History: Artistic representation of Our Lady is very abundant and begins early in Christian history.[1] Besides symbolic use of lines and letters, the Roman Catacombs (see ARCHAEOLOGY) contain some very striking representations of the Mother and Child: several of the Magi scenes, one from the second century; and the very remarkable and much discussed group composed of a mother and child, a figure with a roll in his left hand while his right points to a star above the woman's head. The group, which is in the Catacombs of St. Priscilla, dates from the second century. Not all scholars identify the standing figure as Isaiah; it has been suggested that he could be St. John. But there can be no reasonable doubt on the identity of the woman. There is also little doubt either in regard to the *Orantes* depicted in frescoes in the Catacombs, notably that in the *Cemeterium majus* on the Via Nomentana.

Ephesus (*qv*) was a landmark in artistic creation as in other domains. Pope Xystus ordered, in the year following the Council, the splendid mosaics in St. Mary Major's—the inscription *Xystus episcopus plebi Dei* is taken to indicate a kind of catechetical purpose. But cult must also have been implied, for here, as in the earlier images, faith was confessed in persons linked with salvation. From the end of the sixth century, royalty was a strong theme in Marian iconography. From the seventh to the twelfth centuries the idea of Mary as Empress had followed from a first instance in Santa Maria Antiqua. The Popes liked this conception and were eager to figure in suppliant posture before the powerful sovereign. John VII (*qv*), a Greek, proclaimed himself "the servant [slave] of the Mother of God." The Byzantine influence on the whole development is clear.

For a long time before this, the Byzantines themselves had produced a wealth of Marian imagery. It had begun before Ephesus and Constantine must have commissioned such work, for it is reported that during his reign the Arians burned an effigy of Mary. Eventually the conception and style was fixed in the eastern Icon, which is religious art brought to a height of purity and spirituality unmatched elsewhere. In the East the controversy over such objects arose and was fought out: whether images have a rightful place in Christian worship. The heat, indeed the ferocity, engendered, is almost unimaginable. Among the defenders of the view that prevailed were two noted Marian preachers, St. Germanus of Constantinople (*qv*) and St. John of Damascus (*qv*). The Council which decided the debate, Nicaea II, was recalled by Vatican II, which ordered that "those decrees issued in earlier times regarding the veneration of images of Christ, the Blessed Virgin, and the saints, be religiously observed." (LG 67). "For the honour of the image passes to the original," said the earlier Council, quoting St. Basil, and it added, "he who shows reverence to the image, shows reverence to the substance of him depicted in it." As the Icon passed with the Christian faith from Byzantium to Russia, the various types already elaborated were influential. The meaning was more profound in Russia than in Byzantium. Icons were decisive in the conversion of some areas to Christianity. A theology of the Icon would emerge; this was a permanent expression of religious symbolism.

The West, in late medieval times, exhibits the contrast between the spiritualized Madonnas, supreme with Fra Angelico, and the invasion of naturalism in Renaissance times. Hence the debate between mystics and naturalists. In the high Middle Ages Mary was a presence in the whole of life. Her image was wrought in every material—wood, stone, marble, stained glass, pigment, fabric; her person inspired the communal achievement of the great cathedrals, was recalled in the Miracle plays and evoked in shrines where the central effigy was often a product of true craftsmanship. Witness the assembly of carved wooden statues in the Museum of Popular Art in Barcelona. The Renaissance made the Marian theme a subject of patrons and artists, of studio performance. But the highest genius was involved, and, again and again, the greatest artists sought to depict this subject.

As have those in succeeding ages. But other elements entered in to complicate the role of the religious artist and his clients, eventually mass-production tending to debase the exchange. Inspiration in such circumstances has been sporadic; but it never dies. Stained glass has recently proved a helpful medium, and genius comes to its ends from unsuspected sources. Witness Epstein's Madonna and Child in Cavendish Square, London. Missionary art has made its contribution and the humble handmaid of beauty, philately, has occasionally passed from imitation to creative design.

Theology: Religious art, in the Madonna theme as in others, must resolve manifold tension and satisfy many claims. It can reveal the way of beauty in religious worship; it can respond to the yearning of the faithful for symbolic expression of truths, which, because of their mysterious content, almost defy statement. It can be the outlet for self-expression at the level of genius, giving evidence of profound religious, perhaps mystic, experience; it can teach truths of importance. It can affirm faith and call for acceptance; it can also be directed by the artist or the owner of his work, to ends not religious, possibly harmful to religion—the profit motive, for example.

The historian of Marian theology and devotion can find light in the art of succeeding ages and different cultures. The popular preacher may note the achievement of perfection in the varied media: the Icon of Our Lady of Vladimir; the stained glass of Notre Dame de la Belle Verrière in Chartres; Michaelangelo's Pieta and Raphael's Sistine Madonna. The theologian has available in the work of Serge Bulgakov, an introduction to theology deriving from a famous Icon.

[1]Besides the revelant articles in the *Lexicon der christlichen Ikonographie*, (Rome-Freiburg, 1968), vols. I, II, III, IV, cf. A. Munoz, *Iconografia della Madonna*, (Florence, 1905); L. Birchler and O. Karrer, *Maria, Die Madonna in der Kunst*, (Zurich, 1941); E. Tea, *La Vergine nell'Arte*, (Brescia, 1953); E. Sabbe, "Le culte marial et la genèse de la sculpture mediévale," in *Rev. belge d'arch. et de l'histoire de l'art*, 20(1951), 101-125; M. Belvianes, *La Vergine nella pittura*, (Novara, 1951). Cf. also M. Vloberg, O.S.B., *La Vierge notre*

Médiatrice, (Grenoble, 1938); id., "Les types iconographiques de la Mère de Dieu dans l'art byzantin," in Maria, II, 403-443; id., "Les types iconographiques de la Vierge dans l'art occidental," in Maria, II, 483-540; ibid., La Vierge et l'Enfant dans l'art français, (Paris-Grenoble, 1954); J. Lafontaine-Dosogne, "Iconography of the Blessed Virgin Mary," in NCE, 9, 369-384; ibid., Iconographie de l'enfance de la Vierge dans l'Empire byzantin et en Occident, 2 vols., (Brussels, 1964, 1965). P. Becker, Das Bild der Madonna. Skulpturen von der Romanik bis zum Barock, (Salzburg, 1965); E. Guldan, Eva und Maria. Eine Antithese als Bildmotiv, (Graz-Cologne, 1966). Cf. also G. Fallani, "La Madonna: Profilo iconografico," in Orientamenti dell'Arte Sacra dopo il Vaticano II, (Bergamo, 1969), 393-405; ibid., "Maria Santissima, Regina di tutti i santi. Iconografia," in Bibliotheca Sanctorum, vol. 8, (1967), 932-946; J. Fournée, Les orientations doctrinales de l'iconographie mariale à la fin de l'époque romane, Centre international d'études romanes, (1971), 23-60. [2] J. M. Salgado, O.M.I., "Le culte rendu à la très sainte Vierge Marie durant les premiers siècles à la lumière des fresques de la Catacombe de Priscille," in PCM, V, 51ff.

ASSOCIATE (SOCIA)

Sacred Scripture: Associate is a key word in the modern theology of Our Lady.[1] It is not applied to her in the Bible. *Socius*, of which the feminine form is used, occurs ten times in the Vulgate. In 2 Cor 1:7, *socii passionis* which will eventually be related to Mary, refers to 1:5 which is Christological.

Since *socia* has occasionally in early Christian literature a marriage connotation, the Eve (qv)-Mary parallel has been invoked to justify the principle of association, especially with the medieval intuition, first suggested probably by Hermann of Tournai, drawing Gen 2:18 into the theory, a "helper fit for him." A woman close to the Messiah is a recurring theme in the Old Testament; it seems to link Gen 3:15 (see WOMAN IN) and Is 7:14 (see EMMANUEL). "For him [Isaiah] and the Yahwist the Saviour and the woman called to give birth are closely united: they form the predestined group on which the hope of salvation rests."[2] Study of the mother figure in the patriarchal and kingly traditions recorded in the Old Testament has led another exegete to this conclusion: "Mary is the associate of her Son born of God, in his earthly birth, in his royal government, in his glory."[3]

History: None of the Latin Fathers speaks of Mary as *socia* of Christ; it is not found, for example, in the list of titles in EMBP. In a sermon where the Mary-Church typology is explained by St. Augustine, Christ's association with the Church is mentioned: "For the Only-begotten Son of God deigned to join human nature to himself that he might associate [consociaret] the immaculate Church with himself the immaculate Head; which the Apostle Paul calls a virgin not thinking only of those in it who are virgins in the body, but yearning for incorrupt minds in all. For I betrothed you to Christ to present you as a pure virgin to her husband (2 Cor 11:2). The Church, therefore, imitating the Mother of her Lord, is a mother and virgin in mind since she cannot be so bodily."[4]

In an explicitly Marian context the idea first occurs in the writings of Ambrose Autpert (qv); but it is the verb not the noun which expresses the idea. He uses *sociata* to describe Mary's union with the angels and archangels; he says those she associates (consociat) by divine grace with Christ are her sons. On her union with Christ in glory he writes: "For you the royal throne is set up in the hall of the eternal King, and the King of Kings himself, loving you before all others, associates [associat] you with himself as a true Mother and fair spouse."[5] Hermann of Tournai, in the passage where he evokes Gen 2:18, uses the primary verb *sociavit*, but it is "our flesh as a spouse which he associated with his Only-begotten Son in the womb of the blessed Virgin as in a bridal chamber."[6]

As present knowledge goes, it is Ekbert of Schönau (qv) who first uses the noun *socia* of Mary. He does so, moreover, in the context of salvation: "The Lord is with you [Lk 1:18], as one loving you, glorifying you, helping you in all things, taking you to himself as an associate, completing with you and in you the work of saving Incarnation, which cannot be accomplished without him, nor becomingly so without you."[7]

Pseudo-Albert (qv) elaborates the theory considerably. In a passage wherein he excludes the Sacrament of Orders from Mary he continues: "But the Blessed Virgin was not a vicar but a helper and associate, sharing in the kingdom as she shared in the sufferings for the human race when, as all the ministers and disciples fled, she stood alone beneath the Cross and received in her heart the wounds which Christ received in his body; so that a sword pierced her soul."[8] In another lengthier passage, Pseudo-Albert treats of Mary's association with Jesus, developing his thought with many distinctions and sub-distinctions: association in being which may be absolute—*in substantiali, in quali* and *in quanto*—or relative—of two each to the other, or both to another, with further subdivisions of the latter, all covering many aspects of Christ's life; association *in patiendo* and association *in agendo*—of *contrahentes, generantes* and *adjuvantes*.[9] Though the thought seems at time contrived, it is clear that Pseudo Albert viewed Mary's association with Jesus in the most comprehensive way.

The words *socia* or *sociata* occur in late medieval hymns: *In passione socia/ Regni consors in gloria*[10]; *O socia fidelis/ Adjutrix indefessa*.[11] But other titles—*mediatrix, sponsa, domina*, even *salvatrix* and *imperatrix*—are more frequently found. The great scholastics, St. Thomas (*qv*), St. Bonaventure (*qv*), St. Albert the Great (*qv*) and Duns Scotus (*qv*) did not see a place for the idea in their systems. It persists in a different stream of Marian theology—that represented in the fourteenth century by Englebert of Admont (*qv*) and Ubertino da Casale (*qv*). Englebert summarizes the redemptive aspect: ". . . being with [the crucified One] the single associate of his passion to which she was predestined and the chosen minister and supporter of the whole work of our redemption, partner through Christ in the perfect consolation that was to come."[12] She was "the inseparable [*indivisa*] associate of the passion and sorrow and toil of Christ."[13] Ubertino speaks of Mary as "Mother, associate, of the Son of God" and "worthy associate of the dying One." There are fleeting mentions in St. Bernardine and Bernardine of Busti. St. Antoninus of Florence takes over and reproduces with slight alterations the lengthy treatment of association by Pseudo-Albert, whom he thought to be St. Albert. Denis the Carthusian, as many before him, quoted Ambrose Autpert as St. Augustine, and he varies the context in which *socia* occurs; Mary is the associate of Christ, of the Father, of the Trinity.

Thereafter the idea recurs—for example with the Counter-Reformation doctors and with the French school of spirituality—more as an idea borne along by tradition than as a positive element in systematic thinking. This was to come in the present century, though as early as 1892 Louis Billot, S.J., a dogmatic theologian, wrote of the Virgin "standing by the Cross, as the new Eve associated with the new Adam" making a contribution to our redemption.[14] In the early decades of this century, Mary's association with the redemptive work of Christ was being proposed as either a main or secondary principle of Marian theology. When the debate on Mary's part in the Redemption (*qv*) was active after the second World War, "Coredemptress" was the most widely used title. As will presently be seen, it was not officially encouraged, whereas *socia* was. Marian theologians, especially French, developed the idea, each in his own manner: M. J. Nicolas, O.P., saw it rooted in the divine motherhood; Cl. Dillenschneider, C.SS.R., incorporated it in his exposition of coredemption as he saw it, Church-type, in his final mature synthesis; R. Laurentin, in the post-conciliar edition of his work *Court Traité*, bases Mary's association with Christ on her consent at the Annunciation and considers three important aspects of it: it was in the name of the redeemed, in virtue of her holiness, in her role as Mother.

Teaching Authority: The inseparable union between Mary and Christ is a constant in modern ecclesiastical teaching, papal and conciliar. *Socia* does not appear, however, until St. Pius X's (*qv*) *Ad diem illum*; Pius XI (*qv*) used the verb *associare* in regard to Mary and the work of Christ. It was Pius XII (*qv*) who gave prominence to the word and concept. As Pope, he never took up the title Coredemptress, which he had used as Secretary of State; he would not sanction this title for the Rome Congress of 1950, so *Alma Socia Christi* was substituted. In the Apostolic Constitution on the Assumption (*qv*), Mary was spoken of as the "noble associate of the divine Redeemer" (*generosam divini Redemptoris sociam*).[15] Similar phrases are used in *Haurietis Aquas* and *Ad Coeli Reginam* (*qv*); the latter Encyclical has been called the charter of Mary's association with Christ. Note that Pius generally integrated the doctrine very closely with his theory of Mary's part in the Redemption; so much so that he appeared to believe her a participant in the objective redemption. John XXIII (*qv*) and Paul VI (*qv*) are broadly in the same line.

The first schema prepared for Vatican Council II emphasized Mary's association with Christ.[16] The second schema, as rewritten on orders from the Theological Commission in June, 1964, contained the words: "In the design of divine Providence she was, here on earth, for Christ the Redeemer the humble 'handmaid of the Lord' and, in a singular way before others, a noble associate." In the final text submitted to the Council, account was taken of a *Modus* which, with other changes, had suggested insertion of the words *exstitit alma ejusdem Redemptoris mater.* The Modus was supported by 120 Fathers; one Father had asked for deletion of *humilis ancilla Domini.* The amended version read "she was here on earth the loving Mother of the divine Redeemer, singularly before others the noble associate and humble handmaid of the Lord." (LG 61).

Associate is not a word to stir controversy. In the comments sent to the Preparatory Commission of the Council on the first schema, there were queries on many things: on mediation, for example, and on the title Mediatress; as even on Coredemptress, mentioned only in the notes; none on associate. Christ is never spoken of as *socius* so there was no danger of attributing to his Mother a title which may or may not be proper or restricted to him. But, if the debate was thus freed from sterile tension and immobility, it may have been because the word associate was vague or even neutral. We may not yet have reached a satisfactory doctrine.

---

[1]For philology, cf. Forcellini, *Totius Latinitatis Lexicon,* (1845), IV, 192-193; Du Cange, *Glossarium mediae et infimae Latinitatis,* (1938), VII, 505; A. Blaise, *Dictionnaire Latin Français des Auteurs Chrétiens,* (Turnhout, 1953), 763; *Dictionnaire Etymologique de la Langue Latine,* (ed. 1967), 631. See bibliography under *Titles of Mary, infra;* see also I Marracci (with caution), *Encomia Mariana,* and Bourassé, *Summa Aurea,* 10, 274-275. Cf. J. M. Bover, S.J., *Síntesis orgánica de la Mariologia en función de la association de Maria a la obra redentora de Jesu Cristo,* (Madrid, 1929); J. Bittremieux, "De principio supremo Mariologiae," in *Eph. Theol. Lov.,* 8(1931), 249-251; E. Druwé, S.J., "Position et structure du traité marial," in BSFEM, 2(1936), 26 G. M. Roschini, O.S.M., *Mariologia,* (Rome, 1947), I, 373-375; *id., Maria Santissima,* 178-184. Cl. Dillenschneider C.SS.R., *Marie au service de notre rédemption,* (Hagenau, 1947), 331-364; *id., Marie dans l'économie de la création rénovée,* (Paris, 1957), ch. V., esp. 140-149; *ibid.,* "Marie est-elle l'associée de son Fils dans l'humaine rédemption?" in *Marie Corédemptrice,* (French 1946 National Congress, Lyons, 1948), 68-104; M. J. Nicolas, O.P., "Essai de synthèse mariale," in *Maria,* I, 732-734; *id.,* in BSFEM, 12(1954), 4-5; *id.,* "Mater et Socia," in *Theotokos,* (Paris, 1964), 81-88; *id.,* "Associée à la Rédemption," in *Théotokos,* 150-169; *id.,* "Socia du Christ ressuscité," in *Théotokos,* 169-183. H. du Manoir, S.J., in ME, V, 22-24; R. Laurentin, *Traité,* I, 89-91; *id., Traité,* V, 141-145. M. O'Carroll, C.SS.p., "Socia: the word and idea in regard to Mary," in EphMar, 25(1975), 337-357; *id., Maria Socia, Consors, Adjutrix, Christi,* (Rome Congress, 1975), IV, 27-51. [2]F. M. Braun, O.P., in BSFEM, 15(1954), 19. [3]H. Cazelles, P.S.S., in ME, V, 56. [4]*Serm. 191, 3,* in PL, 38, 1010.

[5]Ambrose Autpert, in PL, 39, 2134. [6]*De Incar. 11,* in PL, 180, 36. [7]"Super missus est," in *Die Visionen der hl. Elizabeth und die Schriften der Aebte Ekbert und Emencho,* ed. F. W. E. Roth, (Brun, 1884), 252. [8]*Mariale,* (inter op. Alberti Magni, 37), q. 42, p. 81. [9]*op. cit.,* 248. [10]"Sequence from Augsburg Missal," (1489), in AH, 4, n.85, p.46. [11]AH, 20, n.181, p.139. [12]*De Gratiis et Virtutibus B.V.M.,* Pt. I, 33, 556. [13]"De officio ancillari B.V.M.," ed. G. B. Fowler, in *Mitteil. des Inst. fur Oesterreichische Geschichtsforschung,* 92(1954), 389. [14]*De Verbo incarnato,* 281; cf. *op. cit.,* 5th ed. (1912), 400. [15]AAS, 42(1950), 768. [16]Cf. EphMar, 25(1975), 351-352.

ASSUMPTION OF OUR LADY, THE

Dogma: By the Apostolic Constitution, *Munificentissimus Deus* (qv), Pius XII on 1 November, 1950, defined the Assumption of Our Lady as a dogma of faith.[1] The essential passage was: "We pronounce, declare and define it to be a divinely revealed dogma: that the Immaculate Mother of God, the ever Virgin Mary having completed the course of her earthly life, was assumed body and soul to heavenly glory."[2]

The dogma was part of a programme planned by Pius XII (qv), as he confided to Mgr. (later Cardinal) Tardini shortly after he had become Pope. It came as a climax to a movement of piety and theology centred on Our Lady, and prompted continuity and expansion of this movement. Literature on the subject had increased in the present century; in the decade prior to the definition, two works—by Fr. M. Jugie, A.A. (qv) and Fr. C. Balic, O.F.M. (qv)— were conspicuous for exhaustive, scientific scholarship. Theological congresses (qv), notably those organized by Fr. Balic in different countries and by the French Society for Marian Studies, stimulated research and reflection with a considerable corpus of writing as a result.

Due largely to Fr. Jugie's expertise and influence, the question of Mary's death (qv) was removed from the scope of the dogma. The idea of tracing a historical tradition from apostolic times was abandoned. It was thought better to concentrate on the whole of divine revelation so as to bring to an explicit stage what it contained implicitly. Again, though the Pope said that all the "proofs and considerations of the Holy Fathers and the theologians are based upon the Sacred Scriptures as their ultimate foundation,"[3] he appealed principally to the faith of the Church rather than any particular biblical text as the basis of the definition. A drafting committee, whose names are known, worked on *Munificentissimus Deus* (qv). The proceedings were kept secret but the members were known publicly to differ as to what the biblical argument should be.

The faith of the Church had been manifest in different ways. Between 1849 and 1950, numerous petitions for the dogma arrived in Rome. They came from 113 Cardinals, eighteen Patriarchs, 2,505 archbishops and bishops, 32,000 priests and men religious, 50,000 religious women, 8,000,000 lay people. On 1 May, 1946 the Pope had sent to the bishops of the world the Encyclical *Deiparae Virginis* (*qv*), putting this question to them: "More especially we wish to know if you, Venerable Brethren, with your learning and prudence consider that the bodily Assumpton of the Immaculate Blessed Virgin can be proposed and defined as a dogma of faith and whether in addition to your own wishes this is desired by your clergy and people." When the replies were collated, it was found that twenty-two residential bishops out of 1181 dissented, but only six doubted that the Assumption was revealed truth—the others questioned the opportuneness. Figures for dissent among other categories were: Abbots and Prelates *nullius*, two out of fifty-nine; Vicars Apostolic, three out of 206; titular bishops, five out of 381.

The Pope interpreted the universal agreement of the "ordinary teaching authority" as a "certain and firm proof" that the Assumption is a truth that has been revealed by God. He goes on to outline "various testimonies, indications and signs of this common belief of the Church." Sacred buildings are mentioned. The witness of the Liturgy is recalled with a reminder from the Pope that it does not "engender the Catholic faith, but rather springs from it." When he passes in review the opinions of the Fathers and Doctors, he states that "they spoke of this doctrine as something already known and accepted by Christ's faithful."

The Pope is significantly silent on the *Transitus* stories. His list of prominent writers from early times does not include all who had supported the doctrine; it was rather a representative group to reflect the thought of successive ages. Suarez is the last in order of time, and he is said to be "supported by the common faith of the entire Church."

Dealing with Scripture, the Apostolic Constitution for the reason given does not appeal directly to any one text as conclusive evidence of the truth. Fr. Jugie had in writing expressed the view that Rev 12 on the great sign in heaven was the chief scriptural witness to the doctrine. The Pope speaks of the union between the Son and the Mother, especially during the infancy of Jesus. This union must have continued beyond the grave: "It seems impossible" to think of her bodily separated from him. Recalling the filial duty which bound the Redeemer "to honour not only his eternal Father, but also his beloved Mother," Pius concludes, "And since it was within his power to grant her this great honour, to preserve her from the corruption of the tomb, *we must believe*, that he really acted in this way."

St. Paul's (*qv*) doctrine on the Saviour's victory over sin and death is, in the text, linked with the patristic teaching on the new Eve (*qv*) and with the "struggle with the infernal foe" foretold in the *Protoevangelium,* to lead to the conclusion that "the struggle which was common to the Blessed Virgin and her divine Son should be brought to a close by the glorification of her virginal body." The Pope then shows how the Assumption is a fitting culmination of Mary's other privileges, and returns to the central idea of the document that the Church "has expressed its belief many times over in the course of the centuries." He adds later that the idea is "thoroughly rooted in the minds of the faithful."

History: Research will continue on the origin and development of the belief in the Assumption. The *Transitus* family is being traced. We know something about the tomb of Mary and the part played by Jewish Christians in the traditions descending from the tomb, as well as the attitude of Gentile Christians towards them. (See ASSUMPTION, APOCRYPHA and ARCHAEOLOGY.)

St. Epiphanius who, first among the Fathers, raised the question of Mary's passing from this world, leaves us with an enigma (see DEATH OF MARY). Epiphanius was dealing with heretics and may have felt inhibited. He speaks of the silence of the Scriptures, "because of the exceeding great marvel, so that the minds of men should not be perplexed," and he keeps silence. Elsewhere he puts forward three possibilities: death and burial, death by martyrdom, "or she remained alive, since nothing is impossible with God"; and he concludes, "for her end no one knows." Was he aware of the stories already current?

The Liturgy *(qv)* was to play a part in the development of doctrine (*qv*). The origins of the feast are far from clear. The starting-point was

Jerusalem. There was hesitancy and variation even in the name used for the feast as time passed: Dormition, Passing, Assumption. Certain facts are fixed, but evidence from the lectionaries and from homiletics has still to be sifted. The feast of the Dormition was decreed for Constantinople on 15 August by the emperor Maurice in 600; about fifty years later it was introduced in Rome and is mentioned in a papal decree of Sergius (687-701) who fixed a procession for the feast modelled on that already existing for the feast of 2 February. He did likewise for the Annunciation and the Nativity of Mary.

The homily of Theodosius, Monophysite patriarch of Alexandria (d. 566), reflects the influence of the dual Coptic celebration, the feast or memory of Mary's death on 16 January, of her resurrection or Assumption on 9 August. He allows a delay of 206 days between the two events.[4] As to whether Our Lady's body during this time was incorrupt or incorruptible, Theodosius is noncommittal. To justify the bodily resurrection, he argues from the divine maternity and he sees Mary's constant intercession on behalf of all as a direct result of her final glory.

More explicit on the fact and more comprehensive in theology is the homily of Theoteknos of Livias (qv), first published by Fr. Wenger in 1955.[5] Livias was a bishopric on the left bank of the Jordan, and Theoteknos ruled it between 550 and 650. He speaks of the feast as the Assumption (Analepsis), not Dormition (Koimesis). "If the Godbearing body of the saint has known death," he says, "it has not, nevertheless, suffered corruption; it has been preserved from corruption and kept free from stain and it has been raised to heaven with her pure, spotless soul by the holy angels and powers." "It was fitting," he says later, "that the most-holy body of Mary, God-bearing body, receptacle of God, divinised, incorruptible, illuminated by divine grace and full of glory . . . should be entrusted to the earth for a little while and raised up to heaven in glory, with her soul pleasing to God."[6]

The homily of Modestus of Jerusalem (qv), even if genuine, can scarcely be prior to that of Theoteknos. Modestus is quoted by Pius XII as "a very ancient writer." John of Thessalonica (qv) reproduces a Transitus, but he truncated his source in the epilogue and forfeited its essential value. By the eighth century, the Assumption was fully accepted in the East, taught by St.

Germanus of Constantinople (qv), Cosmas Vestitor (qv) and St. John of Damascus (qv).

Doctrinal progress in the West was to be irregular. The feast, introduced from the East, commemorated the dies natalis, but tended towards belief in the bodily Assumption. The liturgical prayer, Veneranda, in the Sacramentary sent by Pope Adrian to Charlemagne, spoke of the Mother of God who "suffered temporal death, but nevertheless could not be held back by the bonds of death, she who brought forth your Son, Our Lord, incarnate from herself." Some time before that, St. Gregory of Tours (d. 593), using the imagery of the Apocrypha, had spoken of Mary's body "taken up and borne on a cloud into Paradise, where now, reunited with her soul and rejoicing with the elect, it enjoys the good things of eternity which shall never come to an end."[7]

For a long time there was little progress from this hopeful beginning. Doubt was expressed by Adamnan (qv), echoed by Bede (qv). It was a pseudo-Augustinian sermon, written by Ambrose Autpert, and especially the forged letter Cogitis me of Pseudo-Jerome (qv), which halted development. Autpert urged men not to fake a "lying disclosure of what God had willed to be secret." "But," he said, "the true opinion about her Assumption is this, that we believe her to be assumed above the heavens, not knowing, to use the apostle's phrase, whether in the body or out of it."[8]

PASCHASIUS RADBERT, author of Cogitis me, had more substance in his text. He rejected the apocryphal story, admitted the empty tomb, but declared that nothing was certain about the end of the Virgin's life, save that she left the body. The letter contains much in praise of Mary. It arrested development of thought on the Assumption for two-and-a-half centuries through the authority of St. Jerome, falsely claimed. Another delaying factor was Usuard's ninth century Martyrology. Usuard was a monk of St. Germain des Prés in Paris, and his martyrology was very popular. Part of the entry for the feast of the Assumption was: "But where that venerable temple of the Holy Spirit was, by divine prompting and plan, hidden, the Church in her restraint has preferred to remain in ignorance reverently rather than to teach something frivolous and apocryphal, which she would hold about it."

ASSUMPTION APOCRYPHA

There was a counter-current. It has been known that, towards the end of the tenth century, a number of Greek homilies on the Dormition—by St. Andrew of Crete, Cosmas Vestitor, St. Germanus of Constantinople— were already translated into Latin in the influential monastery of Reichenau, an island in Lake Constance, and at the same time a De Assumptione based largely on them was put into circulation. It was given wider influence by Gerhoh of Reichersberg, who copied it for nuns who were his spiritual disciples. Recent research has shown that this commendation was not the decisive factor; thus H. Barré against A. Wenger, who edited the manuscript.[9] Quite recently G. Phillippart has shown that the author of the text was John, bishop of Arezzo, who lived in the second half of the ninth century. The attribution pushes back the date of the whole Reichenau corpus.[10]

Towards the end of the eleventh or beginning of the twelfth century a still more important work appeared, a treatise on the Assumption, theologically profound and claiming the authorship of St. Augustine. Pseudo-Augustine gradually eclipsed Pseudo-Jerome. By the thirteenth century, the great doctors taught the truth of Mary's bodily Assumption; so did theologians of stature thereafter, until agreement was practically universal.

Vatican II repeated the essential words of the dogma "having completed the course of her earthly life [Mary] was assumed in body and soul to heavenly glory." (LG 59). It linked the doctrine discreetly with the Mary-Church typology: "In the most holy Virgin the Church has already reached that perfection whereby she exists without spot or wrinkle." (LG 65). It is more strongly suggestive in eschatology: "In the bodily and spiritual glory which she possesses in heaven, the Mother of Jesus continues in this present world as the image and first flowering of the Church as it is to be perfected in the world to come. Likewise Mary shines forth until the day the Lord shall come [2 Pet 3:10] as a sign of sure hope and comfort for the pilgrim People of God." (LG 68).

In an age which has sought to demythologize so much, theologians and preachers must be ready to expound the Assumption in a way that respects truth and meets the valid requests of the modern mind. It is a question of pedagogy, not of altering the content of dogma.

ASSUMPTION APOCRYPHA

Textual History: Scholarly interest has been deeply stirred in the Transitus stories, as the apocryphal narratives of Mary's death are called.[1] The papal text promulgating the dogma of the Assumption made no reference to the

Transitus stories, but the event stimulated research into early testimony to belief in the truth. Progress in regard to the *Transitus* was furthered by the discovery of unpublished texts which, in turn, pointed to much earlier dates of origin than had been hitherto accepted. The relevant section in M. R. James' *Apocryphal New Testament*, brought out in 1923, is a useful starting-point from which to measure research.[2] He reproduced or summarized Coptic, Greek, Latin and Syriac texts from the early editions cited in the footnote herewith. He thought that the "legend was first elaborated, if it did not originate, in Egypt." He mentioned the Arabic, Ethiopian and Armenian versions; he knew of the Irish text and its intriguing similarity to the Syriac.

M. Jugie (*qv*) considered the Transitus stories in his major work, and, in 1925, he edited critically John of Thessalonica's homily, which was thought to be a development from Pseudo-John, then still considered the first Greek text. In 1933, Dom A. Wilmart (*qv*) published a Latin *Transitus*, earlier in composition than any hitherto known. C. Donahue critically edited the Irish version in 1942, but it attracted little attention until recently; he dated it before 715.

However, the landmark in manuscript publication was Fr. A. A. Wenger's *L'Assomption* in 1955. He had found, in the Vatican library, a Greek manuscript which seemed to fulfill a remarkable scholarly conjecture made by Dom B. Capelle, and, by a singular stroke of good fortune, in Karlsruhe, a Latin translation of the same text. Dom Capelle had surveyed the whole manuscript position and concluded that a basic text prior to all must be postulated; it was desirable that it be found.

The manuscript, discovered and published by Wenger, did seem to correspond to Capelle's description; it was John of Thessalonica's source. Some years later, M. Haibach-Reinisch added to the dossier an early version of Pseudo-Melito, the most influential text in use in the Latin Church. This could now, it was clear, be dated earlier than the sixth century. Meanwhile, the search went on for the primordial composition from which the Wenger manuscript derived. V. Arras claimed to have found an Ethiopian version of it which he published in 1973; its similarity to the Irish text gave the latter new

status. In the same year M. van Esbroeck brought out a Georgian version, which he had located in Tiflis, and another, a Pseudo-Basil, in the following year, found in Mount Athos.

Much still remains to be explored. The Syriac fragments have increased importance, being put as far back as the third century by one commentator. The whole story will eventually be placed earlier, probably in the second century—possibly, if research can be linked with archaeological findings on Mary's tomb in Gethsemani, in the first—a daunting task. All the earliest versions concur on the fact of Mary's bodily Assumption.

Contents: M. van Esbroeck, in a survey of all literary testimonies on the Assumption prior to the tenth century, lists compositions in nine languages.[3] Ten of these compositions are homiletic in character and at some distance from the *Transitus* type. This is distinguishable into two manuscript families. The first, with twenty-nine members, features the palm of the tree of life from the beginning of the story. The Virgin goes to Mount Olivet and receives the palm from the angel; the palm is placed in a shroud. After the arrival of the Apostles, the palm is given by the Virgin to St. John; Peter prays and speaks. At dawn, the archangels, Gabriel and Michael, arrive, and Mary's soul is given to Michael. The body is buried. Jews attack the bier. The high priest, their leader, is punished, his arms being mutilated. But he is miraculously healed and sent with the palm to touch and heal those who had been stricken blind. Peter and Paul engage in discussion. Seraphim arrive on the scene with Gabriel and Michael. Michael takes Mary's body and places it near the tree of life.

The distinguishing characteristic of the second group of manuscripts is the journey of the Blessed Virgin to Bethlehem where the Apostles assemble, and where she is pursued by the Jews. She and the Apostles are delivered by being miraculously borne to Jerusalem. She is borne to the tomb of Gethsemani. Again there is trouble caused by Jews. Their leader bears the same name, Jephonias, as in the first version of the legend, but he is not the high priest. The same miraculous outcome takes place. Many of the texts speak of Thomas as absent from the funeral, returning three days later, whereon the tomb is opened and seen to be empty.

Some versions of the legend are influenced by the Jewish-Christian concept of the hereafter. Whereas a delay of three days between the death and bodily resurrection is generally spoken of, this delay is, with the Copts, stretched to 206 days, an artificial contrivance used to justify two feasts, one of the Dormition in the Christmas season, the other of the Assumption on 15 August. 206 days separated them.

Theology: The emphasis on the Apostles as witnesses of the death and Assumption of Mary may suggest that the belief was of apostolic origin. In the immense scholarly research which preceded the promulgation of the dogma, attempts to trace such a link were not successful; this approach was abandoned. True, in a passage in Pseudo-Melito, XVI, 2-XVII, the Lord is depicted asking the apostles what he should do with Mary who had died. Peter significantly replied with and for all: "If therefore it might come to pass before the power of thy grace, it hath appeared right to us thy servants that, as thou, having overcome death dost reign in glory, so thou shouldst raise up the body of thy mother and take her with thee rejoicing into heaven. Then said the Saviour: Be it done according to your will."[4] Here it is not so much apostolic origin but apostolic authority that is invoked for the truth, a fact of importance in the development of the doctrine. In general, as R. Laurentin has shown, the Assumption Apocryha represent the exercise of the imaginative faculty in the domain of theology, akin, though also very different, to the parallel between the myths of Greek tragedy and Greek philosophy.[5]

Restraint must be used in interpretation of these stories which are evidence of the curiosity, the questioning, which may have begun in the second century, about the fate of Mary's body. The analogy with the martyrs must not be over-looked nor over-stressed. Implicit already, at times explicit, in the narratives is Mary's intercessory, even mediatorial, power. In the Georgian Pseudo-Basil text, we read: "O beloved faithful of Christ, what can be sweeter than glory in the memory of the holy Mother of God? For she is the Mediatress between God and men. And again the tomb of the holy Mother of God works cures and miracles as her body was made living at Gethsemani."[6]

---

[1]EARLY EDITIONS. Greek texts: C. Tischendorf, "Pseudo-John the Divine," in *Apocalypses Apocrypha*, (Leipzig, 1866), 95-112; A. de Santos Otero, *Los Evangelios apocrifos*, BAC, (Madrid, 1956), 619-644. Syriac texts: W. Wright, "The Obsequies of the holy Virgin," in *Contributions to the apocryphal Literature of the New Testament*, (London, 1865), 42-51; E A. Wallis Budge, *History of the Blessed Virgin Mary*, Luzac's Semitic Text and Translation Series, V, (1899), 97-153; Agnes Smith Lewis, "Apocrypha Syriaca," in *Studia Sinaitica*, XI, (1902).

Coptic texts: Forbes, "The departure of my Lady Mary from the world," in *The Journal of Sacred Literature and Biblical Records*, (1865), 127-135; Robertson, "Coptic Apocryphal Gospels," in *Texts and Studies*, IV, 2, (Cambridge, 1896).

Ethiopian texts: E. A. Wallis Budge, *Legends of Our Lady Mary*, (London, 1922), 152-167; id., *The Book of the Saints of the Ethiopian Church*, (London, 1928), IV, 1222-1224; M. Chaine, "Apocrypha de Beata Maria Virgine," in CSCO, (1909), 39-40.

Arabic texts: M. Enger, *Pseudo-Johannes Apostolus, Liber de Transitu, B. M. V.*, (Elberfeld, 1854). French tr. in Migne, *Dict. des Apocryphes*, II, 503-532.

Armenian text, ed. by P. I. Dayetsi, (1898). German tr. in *Theol. Quartalschrift.*, 84, (1902), 321-349.

Latin texts: C. Tischendorf, "Pseudo-Melito," in *Apocalypses Apocrypha*, (Leipzig, 1866), 124-136; D. Vetter, "Pseudo-Joseph of Arimathea," in *op. cit.*, 113-123.

RECENT EDITIONS. M. Jugie, A.A., "Discourse of John of Thessalonica," in PO, 19, 344-438; A. Wilmart, O.S.B., "L'ancien récit de l'Assomption," in *Analecta Reginensia*, ST, 59 (Rome, 1933), 323-362, (reprint in CMP, III, 440-448). C. Donahue, *The Testament of Mary. The Gaelic version of the Dormitio Mariae, together with an Irish Latin version*, (New York, 1942); A. Wenger, A.A., *L'Assomption*, (Paris, 1955), 210-240 and 245-256; M. Haibach-Reinisch, *Ein neuer Transitus Mariae des Pseudo-Melito*, (Rome, Academia Mariana, 1962). V. Arras, *De Transitu Mariae Apocrypha Aethiopice*, (text and Latin tr.), in CSCO, 342 and 343, (1973). M. van Esbroeck, "Apocryphes géorgiens de la Dormition," in AB, 91(1973), 55-75; id., "L'Assomption de la Vierge dans un Transitus pseudo-basilien," in AB, 92(1974), 125-163.

On many problems, cf. esp. E. Cothenet, in *Maria*, VI, 117-148; M. Jugie, A.A., *L'Assomption* . . . in ST, 114, (Rome, 1944), 103-171; P. Faller, "De priorum saeculorum silentio circa Assumptionem B. Mariae Virginis," in *Analecta Gregoriana*, 36(1946), 44-59; A. van Lantschoot, "L'Assomption de la Sainte Vierge chez les Coptes," in Gregor, 27(1946), 493-526; C. Balic, O.F.M., *Testimonia de Assumptione*, (Rome, 1948), I, 14-65; D. Baldi and A. Mosconi, *L'Assunzione di Maria negli apocrifa* in *Studia Mariana*, (Rome, 1948), I, 73-125; B Capelle O.S.B., "Vestiges grecs et latins d'un antique 'Transitus de la Vierge'," in AB, 67(1949), 21-48; H. Lausberg, "Zur literarischen Gestaltung des Transitus Beatae Mariae," in *Historisches Jahrbuch*, (1953), 25-49; A. Rivera, "La Mediación de Maria en los Apocrifos Asuncionistas," in EphMar, 8(1957), 329-336; B. Bagatti, O.F.M., "Le due redazioni del 'Transitus Mariae'," in MM, 32(1970), 279-287; id., "Ricerche sulle tradizioni della morte della Vergine," in *SacraDoc.*, 18(1973); *ibid.*, "S. Pietro nella 'Dormitio Mariae'," in *Bib. Or.*, 13(1971), 42-48; M. Vallecillo, O.F.M., "El 'Transitus Mariae' según el Manuscrito Vaticano Gr. 1982," in *Verdad Vita*, 30(1970), 187-260; M. MacNamara, *The Apocrypha in the Irish Church*, (Dublin, Inst. Higher Studies, 1975). [2]M. R.

James, *Apocryphal New Testament*, 194-227. Cf. A. Wenger, A.A., in *Maria*, V, 932-935. [3]Manuscript which will appear in Fribourg, communicated by the author to whom profound thanks. [4]M. R. James, *Apocryphal New Testament*, 215. [5]R. Laurentin, *Traité*, V, 61. [6]M. van Esbroeck, *Georgian Pseudo-Basil*, 162.

ASTERIUS (d. after 341)

A moderate Arian, A. shows in the homilies published in the present century (in a critical edition by M. Richard) that he adheres to traditional doctrine on the virginal conception, is aware of the Eve (*qv*)-Mary doctrine, and accepts, like so many of the early Greek Fathers, Origen's interpretation of Simeon's sword. "Peter denies, the disciples flee; the sword of doubt pierces Mary's soul."[1] His succinct comment on the Visitation (*qv*) notably contains the title *Theotokos* (*qv*), almost a century before Ephesus (*qv*): "Elizabeth, mother of the servant, in admiration of the Mother of God [*Theotokos*] cried out: 'And whence is this to me that the Mother of my Lord should come to me?' Christ has as yet no precursor and the latter's mother already announces the Mother of the Lord."[2]

---

[1]*Symbolae Osloenses; fasc. suppl., XVI, (1956); CMP, II, 52-54; Ps 13 also PG 55, 550-558; Hom. 25, 25 in PS, 13 (Richard), 198; PG 55, 555.* [2]*Hom. 29, 14 in Ps 18,* (Richard), 235.

ATHANASIUS OF ALEXANDRIA, ST., DOCTOR OF THE CHURCH (c. 295-373)

The essential contribution of A. to the development of Christology gives importance to his theology of Mary. This is found principally in the treatise on the Incarnation and the writings on virginity, all objects of much critical research, and in the *Letter to Epictetus* which raises no critical problem. The rich Marian texts, the Coptic sermons, do.[1] Alexandria was, in the fourth and fifth centuries, the home of orthodoxy. Within sixty years of A.'s death, his authority would count in the defence of Mary's title, *Theotokos*. It had been used by Alexander of Alexandria, but A. gave it currency.[2] It matched his Christology. Dealing with errors in this domain for Epictetus, bishop of Corinth, he insisted too on the physical reality of Mary's motherhood. The *Letter*, which occupies ten columns in Migne refers to Christ as Son of Mary six times, calling him also Son of the Father; it mentions Mary thirty-three times, twice as the Virgin. The "Word was not consubstantial with his body," for then "the mention

and ministry of Mary would be superfluous." Everything shows that she was truly human: her spouse; the manner of the birth of Jesus. Here A. uses language which has been difficult to reconcile with the virginity *in partu*.[3] His general conclusion is, "Therefore what came forth from Mary, according to the divine Scriptures, was human and the Lord's body was real; real I say, since it was the same as ours. For Mary is our sister, in that we are all sprung from Adam."[4]

A., as some of the Fathers before him, saw Lk 1:35 as a reference to the Son of God himself. He saw the virginal conception as a sign of the divinity: "Therefore also in the beginning, when he came down to us, he fashioned for himself the body from a virgin, in order to give no small indication of his divinity; for he who fashioned this is himself the Maker of these others. For who seeing that the body came forth from a virgin alone, without a man, would not think that he who was revealed in it was the Creator and Lord of other bodies?"[5]

A. used the patristic metaphor of the "unploughed earth"[6] for the virginal conception, as, like most of the Fathers, he interpreted Is 7:14 (see EMMANUEL) in this sense. He continued the title *aieparthenos* first used by Peter of Alexandria (*qv*).[7] He was probably first among the Fathers to use Jn 19:25-27 (see WOMAN IN) as an argument for the perpetual virginity: "By saying that, he teaches us that Mary had no other sons but the Saviour. If, in fact, she had another son, the Saviour would not have neglected him to entrust her to others . . . But because she was a virgin after having been his Mother, he gave her to the disciple as mother."[8]

The theme of the *Letter to the Virgins*, where this idea is expressed, is Mary as model of virgins, an idea already taught by A.'s predecessor, Alexander. This occasions a famous portrait of Mary taken over literally by St. Ambrose (*qv*) in the West, its origin linked with the *gnomai* or proverbs of the Council of Nicaea: "Mary was then a pure virgin, serene in her state of soul, doubly enriched. In fact she liked good works while fulfilling her duties, and holding upright thoughts on faith and purity. She did not like to be seen by men but prayed to God to be her judge. She was in no haste to leave her home, had no acquaintance with public places, remained constantly indoors living a withdrawn life, like the honey bee. She gave generously to the poor whatever in her housework was left over . . . Her words were discreet and her voice measured; she did not shout and was watchful in her heart to speak no wrong of another, not even willingly to listen to wrong spoken . . ."[9] So for over 800 words A. centers on Mary's personality his programme for Christian perfection, especially in the virginal way. A. thought that St. Paul (qv) had got his ideas about virginity from Mary's example. The slight blemishes which St. Ambrose removed from the portrait were Mary's need to struggle against bad thoughts and to control her anger—A. scarcely meant them as faults.

Mary, in the Annunciation, is lifted to the Holy Trinity (qv): "As the grace of the Trinity is one, the Trinity is undivided; which is to be seen in holy Mary. For the angel Gabriel sent to announce the forthcoming descent of the Word upon her said 'the Holy Spirit will come upon you' knowing that the Spirit was in the Word, and consequently he immediately added: 'And the power of the most high will overshadow you'. For Christ is the power and wisdom of God."[10]

If the Coptic sermons were authentic, we should have in A. as great a figure in Marian theology as he was in Christology. He would be prior to St. Epiphanius (qv) with the key concept of Mary as Mother of the living; he would see the Eve-Mary contrast in terms of death and life—as he also would have drawn it out in the context of purity, and he would have clearly seen the typology of the Ark of the Covenant. The glory of angels, to come to us, would come through Mary, the Mother of life.[11] But the question mark remains on authenticity.

[1]Works: PG, 25-28; H. G. Opitz and others, *Athanasius' Werke*, Berlin, 1934, ClavisG, II, 12-60; CMP, II, 55-87; EMBP, 169-191. "Contra Gentes et De Incarnatione," ed. R. W. Thomson, in *Oxford Early Christian Texts*, (1971); "De Incarnatione," ed. C. Kannengiesser, in SC, 199 "De Virginitate," in PG, 28, 252-281, and ed. E. von der Goltz, in TU, 29, 2; R. P. Casey, "The text of De Virginitate of Athanasius," in *Harvard Theol. Rev.*, 18(1925), 173-190 Armenian version, in *Sitzungsberichte des Preuss, Akad.*, 33(1935) Syriac version, "Athanasiana Syriaca," I, in Mus, 40(1927), 205-248; II, in Mus, 41(1928), 169-216. Coptic version, L. Th. Lefort, "Le De Virginitate de S. Clément ou de S. Athanase?", in Mus, 40(1927), 249-264; cf. esp. ed. of text with French tr. in Mus, 42(1929), 197-275; see also CSCO, 150, 151; "Un nouveau De Virginitate attribué à S. Athanase," in AB, 67(1949), 142-152; "Encore un De Virginitate de S.

Athanase," in *Mélanges de Ghellinck*, I, Jembloux, 215-221. "Lettres à Serapion," ed. and tr., J. Lebon, in SC, 15. Coptic sermons: F. Rossi, *I Papiri copti del museo di Torino*, vol. 2, fasc. I, 2; L. Th. Lefort, "Athanasiana Coptica," in Mus, 69(1956), 233-241; *ibid.*, ed. with French tr., "De sancta Virgine Dei Matre et de Elizabeth Joannis matre," in Mus, 71(1958), 5-50, 209-239. On authenticity of latter: for, see M. Starowieyski, in MM, 34(1972), 339-349; against, see R. Caro, *La Homilética, II*, 554-567. On spurious homilies, cf. R. Caro, *La Homilética, II*, in BHG 866, 1147t, 1161k, 1904; G. Mueller, *Lexicon Athanasianum*, (Berlin, 1952); cf. *Clavis PG*, 12-60; R. Laurentin, *Traité*, I, 158-159; G. Soll, in LexMar, 388-389; M. Aubineau, S.J., "Les écrits de S. Athanase sur la Virginité," in RAM, 31(1955), 140-171; G. Giamberardini, O.F.M., *Il culto mariano in Egitto nei primi sei secoli*, (Cairo, 1967); id., "Nomi e Titoli mariani nella filologia e nell' esegesi degli Egiziani," in EphMar, 23(1973), 205-230; G. Bardy, in DSp, I, 1047-1052. [2]*Or. III c. Arianos, 14, 29, 33*, in PG, 26, 349C, 385A, 393B; *Vita Antonii, 36*, in PG, 26, 897A. [3]PG, 26, 1057C. [4]PG, 26, 1061B. [5]"Contra Gentes et De Incarnatione," tr. and ed. by R. W. Thomson, in *Oxford Early Christian Texts*, (1971), 178; SC, 199, 333. [6]*Or. II c. Arianos, 7*, in PG, 26, 161B. [7]*Or. II c. Arianos, 70*, in PG, 26, 296B; *Exp. in Ps. 84, 11*, in PG, 27, 373A (work of somewhat dubious authenticity). [8]CSCO, 59. [9]CSCO, 60-61. [10]*Ep. ad Serapionem, III, 6*, in PG, 26, 633B; *op. cit.*, in SC, 15, 171. [11]Mus, (1958), 216, 218.

ATTICUS OF CONSTANTINOPLE (d. 425)

A. was second successor of St. John Chrysostom in the patriarchate of Constantinople (406-425).[1] One homily which deals with Our Lady is associated with him. It was published in two simultaneous translations from a ninth century Syriac manuscript in the present century.[2] Questions of authenticity were inevitable since half the homily already existed in PG, attributed to Proclus.[3] As a young man the latter was secretary to Atticus, who was not a great orator. The matter is complicated by quotations from St. Cyril of Alexandria (qv) in which he asserts that Atticus uses the word *Theotokos*, which title is not found in the part of the homily which most experts would link with the patriarch's name. R. Caro sums up a lengthy analysis of all the evidence thus: the Syriac manuscript is a combination of two homilies. One is on the feast of the *Theotokos*, composed after 431, attributed to Proclus; the other is on the birth of Christ, from the first quarter of the fourth century, looking to Atticus as its principal author, whom his secretary, Proclus, probably helped.[4]

In the Atticus section, the following points should be noted. Insistence on the virginity in words which recall Augustine (qv): "A virgin conceived, a virgin bore a child, a virgin brought him forth, a virgin begot him."[5] The motherhood was divine (though *Theotokos* is not used). This motherhood was salvific: "She bore the burden of the world," "the devil was silenced when the Virgin gave birth . . . she removed all weakness."[6]

[1]Cf. C. Verschaffel, in DTC, I, 2221; M. T. Didier, in DHGE, 5, 161-166; ClavisG, III, 105-107. [2]J. Lebon, "Le Discours d'Atticus de Constantinople sur la sainte Mère de Dieu," in Mus, 46(1933), 186-195; M. Brière, "Une homélie inédite d'Atticus, Patriarche de Constantinople," in *Rev. de l'Orient Chret.*, 29(1933-1934), 177-186. [3]R. Laurentin, *Traité*, I, 164-165. [4]R. Caro, *La Homiletica*, I, 71. [5]*ibid.*, op. cit., 74. [6]*ibid., op. cit.,* 75.

AUGUSTINE, ST., DOCTOR OF THE CHURCH (354-430)

A.'s views on Our Lady are found in his sermons, mostly those preached at Christmas, and in polemical and exegetical works.[1] His doctrine, subtle and profound if not far-reaching, gains from his Christo-centric outlook and from his lively sense of the Church (*qv*). Regarding one question, the virginal marriage, he fixed a milestone, an open path to understand St. Joseph's fatherhood.[2]

A., like St. Ambrose, his master, spoke of Mary as holy[3] (*sancta*) and he was explicit on her personal sinlessness: "Except, therefore, the holy Virgin Mary, concerning whom, for the honour of the Lord, I will have no question of sin; for we know how much to conquer sin in every way was given to her who merited to conceive and bring forth him who certainly had no sin."[4]

Was Mary free not only of personal, but of the original sin? The sentence just quoted occurs in Augustine's critique of Pelagianism. He was pressed to take a firm stand in his controversy with Julian of Eclanum, who forcibly accused him thus: "He [Jovianian] undermined the virginity of Mary by the condition of her childbearing; you deliver her to the devil by the condition of her birth."[5] The reply, which lacks the author's customary clarity, has occasioned a vast literature: "We do not deliver Mary to the devil by the condition of her birth; but for this reason, that this very condition finds a solution in the grace of rebirth."[6] The saint's theology of original sin, which explained the transmission through concupiscence, inherent in conjugal relations, blocked his thinking. "And thus it appears that the concupiscence through which

Christ did not wish to be conceived, has propagated evil in the human race, for the body of Mary, though it came from this, nevertheless did not transmit it for she did not conceive in this way."[7]

A. has but a fleeting vague reference to the favourite patristic Old Testament text (Is 7:14) on Mary's virginity (*qv*). (see EMMANUEL). He speaks of Christ "who deigned to come through Israel, and to become Emmanuel, God with us in the weakness of the flesh, not with us in the iniquity of the heart."[8] But he emphasized Mary's virginity again and again, before, in and after childbirth: "As a virgin she conceived, as a virgin she brought forth, a virgin she remained."[9] St. Gregory of Nyssa (*qv*) had already put forward the opinion that Mary had, prior to the Annunciation (*qv*), specially consecrated her flesh to the Lord, bound herself in some way to virginity. It was A. who formulated this doctrine in terms of a vow. Commenting on her answer to the angel, "How shall this be done . . ." he says: "This she certainly would not have said if she had not vowed [*vovisset*] herself as a virgin to God"[10] and "mindful of her resolve [*propositi*] and conscious of the sacred vow, for she knew what she had vowed . . ."[11] In support of the *virginitas in partu*, the argument is not drawn from Ez 44:2, but from the power of the risen Christ to pass through closed doors: "Why, therefore, could he who was able as a grown man to enter through closed doors, not be able as an infant to go out through an incorrupt body?"[12]

A. was the first of the Latin Fathers to outline a theology of St. Joseph (*qv*). St. Ambrose (*qv*), and more so St. Jerome (*qv*), had considered some of the biblical problems. On the saint's doubt (*qv*), A., just as St. Ambrose, inclined to a suspicion of adultery: "Since he knew that she was not pregnant by him, he thought as a consequence that she had committed adultery."[13] Others of the Fathers had been similarly misled, puzzled to find another solution to this problem. A.'s opinion did not impede his progress in thinking about the marriage. Invoking the fact of virginal marriages among Christians of his time, he showed by analysis of the bond that virginity, so far from weakening it, could bring a kind of perfection, and concludes: "Every good of marriage was fulfilled in the parents of Christ: offspring, loyalty and the sacrament. We recognize the offspring in Our Lord Jesus Christ himself; the loyalty in that no adultery occurred, and the sacrament (that is the indissolubility) because of no divorce. Only conjugal intercourse did not take place."[14] It is not conjugal sexual desire (*libido*), he says elsewhere, which makes marriage, but conjugal love.[15] The whole theory of the sacrament of Matrimony was to gain from this position, clarified by A. in the context of Mary and Joseph.

Christ, as the new Adam, is central to the whole Augustinian synthesis.[16] But when he sets the new Eve in opposition, it is the Church he thinks of: "Two parents have begotten us to death, two to life. The parents who have begotten us to death, Adam and Eve, the parents who have begotten us to life, Christ and the Church."[17] An examination of the *Enarrationes in Psalmos* shows that this typology, rather than the Eve-Mary parallel, occurs spontaneously to A.[18] There are brief allusions to the latter theme, but the context differs from the Annunciation setting favoured by so many of the Fathers (see EVE AND MARY), after St. Irenaeus, with, in A.'s case, some allusion to the restored dignity of woman. This has been seen in the passage already quoted. Thus in *Serm. LI*, he concludes an explanation of how each sex was restored, and given recognition and a role in the order of salvation, with the words: "Let the woman compensate for the sin of man deceived by her by giving birth to Christ."[19] But he goes on to show how women played an important role in the events of the Resurrection. The Apostles were to announce the miracle to the nations, but it was women who announced it to the Apostles. It ends with a glorification of the sex from which the Liberator was born without stain, which, as Creator, he wished to commend. There is another approach in the *De Doctrina Christiana* where he speaks of "the disease which entered the corrupt soul of woman" and the "salvation which came forth from the intact body of a woman." Similar or parallel links are discernible in the deception of man and his liberation.[20] Once he does use the patristic aphorism, "Death through a woman, life through a woman," but the context includes the witnesses of the Resurrection, as well as Eve.[21] The sermon was for Paschal time.

A. did not have to enter into the theological subtleties which marked the *Theotokos* debate

in the East. The basic reality was clear to him. He spoke of "God born of a woman"[22] and "How could we confess in the Rule of faith that we believe in the Son of God born of the Virgin Mary, if it was not the Son of God, but the Son of man who was born of the Virgin Mary?"[23] "Christ was born, God of the Father, man of a mother. From the immortality of the Father, from the virginity of the mother. Of the Father without a mother, of the mother without a father."[24] "Elizabeth conceived only a man, Mary, God and man. It is a wonderful thing how a creature could conceive the Creator."[25]

In many such statements the transcendence of Christ stands out clearly: "He was created from her whom he had created."[26] "He is made in thee who made thee, he is made in thee through whom you were made; indeed through whom were made heaven and earth, through whom all things were made, the Word is made flesh in thee receiving flesh and not losing divinity."[27]

There is insistence too on Christ's choice of his Mother, which never led the author to speak of a bridal relationship—for him Christ is the Spouse of the Church. "And he himself established what he chose so that he should go forth as a Spouse from his bridal chamber, that he should be seen by mortal eyes."[28] "Her omnipotent Son in no way removed his Mother's virginity, from whom he had chosen to be born."[29]

In this strictly theological position, one very human detail will find a place: "Give milk, O mother to [him who is] our food; give milk to the bread that comes from heaven."[30] "She ruled our king; she bore him in whom we are; she gave milk to [him who is] our bread."[31]

Mary's personal response to the divine plan prompted in the mind of the one who had struggled so arduously to reach faith himself, a distinctive piece of analysis, and a memorable phrase. Irenaeus's (qv) emphasis on faith and obedience and the notion of free consent (qv) are not as central to A.'s theory as the idea of conception in the mind which preceded that in the body, within which Mary's faith assumes vast significance for herself and for all mankind.[32] It is all put in a remarkable passage in *Serm. CCXV*: "When the angel had said this, she full of faith and conceiving Christ first in her mind and then in her body, 'Behold,' she said, 'the handmaid of the Lord, let it be done to me according to your word.' Let there, she said, be a virginal conception without male seed; let him be born of the Holy Spirit and an intact woman, in whom the intact Church will be born of the Holy Spirit . . . Mary believed and what she believed was done in her. Let us believe, so that what was done may benefit us."[33]

A. insists on Mary's faith in striking language: "Mary is more blessed in that she grasped faith in Christ, than in that she conceived his flesh, . . . and the maternal relationship would have been of no profit to Mary, if she had not more happily borne Christ in her heart than in her womb."[34] He has in this theory a ready answer to problems raised on Mt 12:46-50: "For whoever does the will of my Father in heaven is my brother and sister and mother." (Mt 12:50). "Should the Virgin Mary not have done the will of the Father," A. says, "she who by faith believed, by faith conceived, who was the chosen one from whom our salvation should be born among men, who was created by Christ before Christ was created in her."[35]

In what way was Our Lady involved in salvation according to A.? Referring by name to Ambrose, he says that Christ was "the only man who was a Mediator of God and men, because he was born of a virgin, did not encounter sin in his birth, was not held by the bonds of harmful generation."[36] Thus, in his polemic against Julian the Pelagian. In *Serm. CXCV* he develops the idea somewhat: "This is the Lord our God, this is the Mediator of God and men, a man who is our Saviour, who born of the Father created his Mother; born of a Mother glorified the Father: the only Son of the Father without female bringing forth, the only Son of his Mother without male embrace."[37] A. has elsewhere an allusion to the womb of the Virgin as the bridal chamber where a marriage took place, a union was effected between the Word and flesh. He speaks too of the salvation of mankind wrought when "a woman conceived in her womb the flesh of the Omnipotent one."[38] Yet if we are to get a theory of Mary's public role, it is rather in the typology of the Church that we shall most explicitly find it.

The passage on the Mediator, just quoted, leads on to a characteristic theme: "This is the fairest of the sons of men, [Ps.44.3], son of Holy Mary, Spouse of holy Church, which he made to resemble his mother: for he made it a mother for us and keeps it a virgin for himself . . . The

Church, therefore, like Mary, possesses perpetual integrity and incorrupt fruitfulness. For what she merited in the flesh, it has kept in the mind; save that she brought forth one, it brings forth many to be gathered into one through one."[39]

Frequently, as if speaking aloud a fixed pattern of personal thought, A. will couple Mary with the Church: "The whole Church should without error confess [the Mediator] born of the Virgin Mary and imitating his Mother it daily brings forth members and is a virgin"[40] and "The Virgin holy Church therefore celebrates today the offspring of the Virgin . . . Christ accordingly intending to make virginity for the Church in its heart first preserved it in Mary's body."[41] Mary alone is a mother and virgin in spirit and body, the Church is wholly mother and virgin in spirit, but in some members is a virgin of Christ, in others a mother, but not of Christ.[42]

The perspective is widened in one famous passage to convey some notion, which A. never fully developed, of the spiritual motherhood (qv) of Mary. Words italicized are quoted in LG, 53; the final words have an echo in LG, 65: "She [Mary] is not the spiritual mother of our Head, that is of the Saviour himself; spiritually it is she who is born of him. All believers, and she is one of them, are rightly called sons of the Spouse. [Mt 9:15]. *But she is truly the Mother of the members who we are, for she has cooperated in the birth of the faithful who are members of his Head.* Bodily, on the contrary, she is the Mother of the Head. For it was fitting that our Head, so as to give an outstanding sign, should be born of a virgin according to the flesh to signify that his members should be born of the virgin Church."[43] It is put more strongly elsewhere: "Truly the Church could not have been a virgin, if it had not found as its Spouse to whom it would be given, the Son of a virgin."[44] The same ideas are elaborated vividly by the saint in the *Sermo Denis* in which he proclaimed Mary as type of the Church.[45]

In the same sermon he manifests some caution: "Mary is holy, Mary is blessed, but the Church is better than the Virgin Mary. Mary is part of the Church [portio Ecclesiae], a holy member, an excellent member, a supereminent member, but always a member of the whole body. If she belongs to this whole body it is clear that the body is more than the member."[46]

The thinking of medieval theologians, starting or moving forward from the position of Ephesus, would remove a certain restrictive note in this formulation. Note that Vatican II, which summarized much of the thinking since A., adopted his words to define the Church's virginity, "integral faith, firm hope and genuine charity."[47]

A more difficult problem is that of devotion to Mary. No feasts of Our Lady were celebrated in Africa in A.'s time, so one can speak of liturgical piety only in the context of Christmas, which prompted so much of his praise of Mary. Was this praise a form of devotion? Was A.'s urge to imitation similar? These are subjects much debated, in which the whole outlook of the author's age must be borne in mind.

[1]Works in PL, 31-46, and volumes of CSEL and CCL. On the vast critical work acomplished on spurious Augustinian texts, cf. R. Laurentin, Traité, I, 126-130; CMP, 266-437; EMBP, 562-635; G. Morin in Miscellanea Agostiniana, (Rome, 1930). [2]Cf. P. Friedrich, Die Mariologie des Hl. Augustinus, (Cologne, 1907); D. Fernandez, C.M.F., "Un pensamiento de San Agustín sobre la Inmaculada," in Analecta Baetica, (1954), 13-63; V. Capagna, O.R.S.A., La Virgen Maria segun San Agustín, (Rome, 1956); P. Frua, O.S.M., L'Immacolata Concezione e S. Agostino, (Saluzzo, 1960); T. Janez Barrio, O.S.A., "Maria y La Iglesia según el pensamiento agustiniano," in Rev. Augustin. de Espiritualidad, 3 (1962), 22-46; S. Folgado Florez, O.S.A., "San Agustín y su eclesiológia mariana," in Cuid. Dios, 176(1963), 444-463; E. de Roover, O. Praem., "Augustin d'Hippone et l'interprétation de Luc 1:35," in Analecta praem., 45(1969), 24-45, 149-169; G. Jouassard, in Maria, I, 114-120; F. Hoffmann, in LexMar, I, 456-464; C. Boyer, S.J., "La controverse sur l'opinion de S. Augustin touchant la conception de la Vierge," in V.I., IV, 48-60; I.M. Dietz, O.E.S.A., "Ist die hl. Jungfrau nach Augustinus 'Immaculata ab initio'?", in V.I., IV, 61-112; id., "Maria und Kirche nach dem hl. Augustinus," in ME, III, 201-241; J. Huhn, "Maria est typus Ecclesiae secundum Patres, imprimis secundum S. Ambrosium et S. Augustinum," in ME, III, 163-200; E. Lamirande, "En quel sens peut-on parler de dévotion chez S. Augustin," in PCM, III, 17-35; J. Moran, O.S.A., "Puede hablarse de culto a Maria en San Agustín," in PCM, III, 37-47; J. I. Alcorta, "Munus ministeriale Mariae ejusque cultualis significatio apud S. Augustinum," in PCM, III, 49-61; N. Garcia Garces, C.M.F., "Fundamentos de la devoción a la Virgen en San Agustín," in PCM, III, 63-98. [3]Serm. CCXIII, in PL, 38, 1064. [4]De Nat. et Grat. XXXVI, 42, in PL, 44, 267. [5]Op. Imperf. c. Jul. IV, 22, in PL, 45, 1417. [6]op. cit., in PL, 45, 1418. [7]Contra Julianum, V, 15, 52, in PL, 44, 813. [8]Serm. CCCLXIX, 3, in PL, 39, 1656. For authenticity, cf. R. Laurentin, Traité, I, 127. [9]Serm. LI, 11, 18, in PL, 38 343 and elsewhere. [10]De Sanct. Virg. IV, 4, in PL, 40, 398. [11]Serm. CCXCI, 5, in PL, 38, 1318. [12]Serm. CXCI, 2, in PL, 38, 1010. Cf. Serm. CCXV, 4, in PL, 38, 1074. [13]Serm. LI, 9, in PL, 38, 338. Cf. Serm. CCCXLIII, 3, in PL, 39, 1507. [14]De nupt. et concup. I, 11,13, in PL, 44, 421. [15]Serm. LI, 13,21, in PL, 38, 344-345. [16]Cf. H. Rondet, S.J., "Le Christ, nouvel Adam dans St. Augustin," in BSFEM, 13(1955), 25-41. [17]Serm. XXII, 10, in PL, 38, 154. [18]Cf. B. Capelle, O.S.B., "La Nouvelle Eve chez les anciens docteurs Latins," in BSFEM, 12(1954), 64-66. [19]Serm. LI, 2, 3, in PL, 38, 335. [20]De Doctrina Christiana, I, 13, in PL, 34, 24. [21]Serm. CCXXXII, 2, in PL, 38, 1108. Cf. LG, 55, and notes. [22]De Trin., bk. VIII, 5,7 in PL, 42, 952. [23]Serm. CLXXXVI, 2, in PL, 38, 1000. [24]Serm. CXCIV, 1, in PL, 38, 1015. [25]Serm. CCLXXXIX, 2, in PL, 38, 1308. [26]Serm. CLXXXIX, 2, in PL, 38, 1005. [27]Serm. CCXCI, 6, in PL, 38, 1319. [28]Serm. CCCLXIX, 1, in PL, 39, 1655. [29]Serm. CLXXXVIII, 3, 4, in PL, 38, 1004. [30]Serm. CCCLXIX, 1, in PL, 39, 1655. [31]Serm. CLXXXIV, 2, 3, in PL, 38, 997. [32]Cf. J. Pintard, "Le principe 'prius mente quam corpore'," in BSFEM, 27(1970), 26-36. [33]Serm. CCXV, 4, in PL, 38, 1074. [34]De Sanct. Virg. III, 3, in PL, 40, 398. [35]Sermo Denis, (ed. G. Morin), XXV, 7, and passage cited in previous note. [36]Contr. Jul. Pelag., bk. II, 9, 32, in PL, 44, 695. [37]Serm. CXCV, 2, in PL, 38, 1018. [38]Serm. CCLXXXIX, 2, in PL, 38, 1308. [39]Serm. CXCV,2, in PL, 38, 1018. [40]Enchiridion, bk I, XXXIV, in PL, 40, 249. [41]Serm. CLXXXVIII, 3, 4, in PL, 38, 1005. [42]De Sanct. Virg., VI, in PL, 40, 399. [43]op. cit., in PL, 40, 399. [44]Serm. CLXXXVIII, 4, in PL, 38, 1005. [45]Sermo Denis, XXV, 8. [46]Sermo Denis, XXV, 7. [47]In Jo. Tr. XIII, 12, in PL, 35, 1499. Cf. LG, 64.

AVE MARIS STELLA — See Supplement, p. 379.

AVIS SALUTAIRES, LES

These are the significant words in the title of a controversial tract on devotion to Our Lady published before the last quarter of the seventeenth century (qv). It appeared in Latin, anonymously, in Ghent, in the first days of November, 1673, with the title Monita salutaria B. V. Mariae ad cultores suos indiscretos. It carried an Imprimatur dated October 31, from Ignace Gillemans, Canon and Archpriest of Ghent. He, himself a controversial figure, was able to perform such a canonical act in a diocese rendered vacant by the recent death of its bishop.

The tract ran to sixteen pages and to about 2,000 words, including the final prayer. There were a number of references to the Fathers, and a large number of scriptural quotations—fifty-seven in all. The fact that Gillemans had approved a theological work by a Canon Peter Van Buscum, which had denied the definability of the Immaculate Conception, was a bad omen. It was the theses of the tract, rendered aggressive by their succinctness, and the preposterous device of putting the entire composition in Our Lady's own mouth, that provoked wrath. The ensuing war of pamphlets (of which fifty appeared in one year) and of demonstrations was between secular and religious clergy, the latter Our Lady's defenders. The little book was labelled Jansenistic, then an emotive and costly stigma. The following quotations will illustrate the author's approach:

"They love me in vain who persevere in sins; for they who do not please God do not please me. Those whom I want to be my lovers, I desire to be my imitators. Do not think me the refuge of impenitent sinners. If you love me, do what I especially desire, namely love the Lord your God with your whole heart and your whole soul and your whole strength . . . Do not lightly receive every petty tale and any which is put in circulation about my apparitions, revelations, benefits, privileges . . . Nor is it to be thought that I shall feel for or weep over those who are damned by my Son. His will is my will . . . My Son says to you 'Not every one who says to me, Lord, Lord, shall enter the kingdom of heaven, but he who does the will of my Father who is in heaven' (Mt 7:21). Do you think it will be any greater advantage to them to say to me: Our Lady, Our Lady? . . . Praise given to me in my own right is vain; given to me as Mother and handmaid of the Lord it is holy . . . Do not honour me as if no approach is open to God through Christ without me . . . Let those who call me Mediatress and Advocate not do so in the sense in which my Son is strictly Mediator and Advocate. He is the Mediator of the New Testament . . . For I was not pleasing to the Almighty save in Christ and through Christ my Saviour and Redeemer . . . Do not call me Saviouress and Coredemptress . . . Do not say that whereas Christ is a severe Judge, I am the Mother of Mercy, that he has reserved justice to himself and entrusted mercy to me. God is most simple and without division in his being . . . Do not have more confidence in me than in God . . . Do not call yourself my slave . . . Do not think that the love one has for me is praiseworthy when my images are decked with stones and precious ornaments while Jesus Christ suffers in his poor, if he dies of hunger, of cold, in his members?"[1]

These opinions are in no wise heretical. The fury aroused by the pamphlet came from its generally negative approach, its undue emphasis on abuses. The confraternities, run by the religious, felt the sting. Apostles of Our Lady must have found the tone scathing: "dry little devotions"; "formulas and petty prayers"; "easy and convenient piety"; "for they boast of me as the patroness of their unjust and impious cause and the instigator of their impenitence." A certain praise of her was not "praise but vituperation." "Why compare nothing [any creature] to the infinite majesty?"[2] Certain phrases taken from their context were like stark abuse, and the general impression was that much, if not most, devotion to Mary was ill-conceived and unworthy. The author may have meant well; he was obviously ready to hurt. His identity was not revealed in further pamphlets which he published in defence of the *Avis*.[3] It was made known when, despite the support of bishops—one of whom, Choiseul of Tournai, sponsored the first French translation—and Cardinal Bona, his tract was put on the Roman Index. The condemnation was partial in 1674, absolute in 1676. The author was Adam Widenfeld, a Cologne lawyer, who devoted his free time to explaining Catholic doctrine to Protestants. Opinions of recent commentators on his significance vary.[4] P. Hoffer's judgment is comprehensive, not unfavourable.

[1]Tr. from text published with chapter division and headings, (Liege, 1674). Printed in M. Leydecker, *De historia Jansenismi, libri VI, quibus de Cornelii Jansenii vita et morte necnon de ipsius sequacium dogmatibus disseritur*, (Utrecht, 1695), 631-640. For quotations, cf. Paul Hoffer's definitive monograph, *La Dévotion à Marie au déclin du XVIIe siècle*, (Paris, 1938), 266-309. English tr., *Wholsome Advices from the Blessed Virgin to her indiscreet worshippers*, (London, 1687). [2]M. Leydecker, *De historia Jansenismi*, etc., (Utrecht, 1695), *passim*. [3]*Approbationes libelli cui titulus Monita salutaria B. V. Mariae ad cultores suos indiscretos*, (Ghent, 1674); *Epistola apologetica quam auctor libelli cui titulus Monita salutaria B. V. Mariae ad cultores indiscretos, scripsit ad ejusdem consorem*, (Malines, 1674). [4]For opposite view, cf. P. Hoffer, *op. cit.*; Cl. Dillenschneider, C.SS.R., *La Mariologie de St. Alphonse de Liguori*, I, (Fribourg, 1931), 33-43; G. M. Roschini, O.S.M., *Maria Santissima*, I, 512-513.

B

BALIC, KARL, O.F.M. (1899-1977)

Born in Croatia, this Franciscan has been a key figure in the development of Marian theology through international collaboration. Trained in Louvain in the days of Cardinal Mercier, a teacher in the Antonianum since 1933, B. organized Franciscan congresses to prepare for the dogma of the Assumption. He founded the *Academia Mariana* which became international in 1950, and pontifical in 1959. As president, he organized the international Mariological congresses from 1950 to 1975, and edited the proceedings down to the Zagreb Congress. He also edited several important collections of books on Our Lady. For the Fathers of Vatican II he edited *De Maria et Oecumenismo* and *De Scriptura et Traditione*.

He has written two volumes on the Assumption through the ages (a substantial work), and several lesser studies on the Marian theology of Scotus; also over 200 articles and prefaces of interest to the theology of Our Lady.

B. served on the advisory committee on *Munificentissimus Deus* (*qv*). His contribution to Vatican II was capital. He drafted the first schema, collaborated with Mgr. G. Philips on the second, issued various documents and assessments of reactions, and was consulted on the final draft which was to be accepted by the Fathers. Along with these multiple tasks, he carried on for years the critical edition of Scotus' works, a model of its kind, and helped organize the seventh Scotist centenary congress in 1966. He has received many awards for services to Marian theology.[1]

---

[1]Cf. P. Capkun-Delic, O.F.M., *Fray Carlos Balic, Escotista y Mariologo*, (with bibliography), (Buenos Aires, Studia Croatica, 1966); *ibid.*, in *Studia Mediaevalia et mariologica P. Carolo Balic, O.F.M., septuagesimum explenti annum dicata*, (Rome, 1971), 9-36 (bibliography by B. Hechich, O.F.M., 37-63). Bibliography by the same author in *Antonianum*, 45(1970), 14-22. Cf. J. M. Alonso, C.M.F., in EphMar, 20(1970), 227-235. Cf. esp. P. Melada, O.F.M. and D. Aracic, O.F.M., *P. Carlo Balic*, (Rome Pontifical Marian Academy, 1978), with complete bibliography.

BARRÉ, HENRI, C.S.SP. (1905-1968)

B., a Norman, was seminary professor and rector of French Seminary, Rome, 1953-1963. He fought in the Second World War, was imprisoned, and plunged thereafter into research on Marian theology in the Latin Middle Ages. As secretary of the French Marian Society in its great years, he contributed over eighty articles, several seminal, many very substantial, to proceedings, to *Marianum, Ephemerides Mariologicae*, and other reviews. Among his books are *Priéres Anciennes* (1963), and *Trinité que j'adore* (1965), and a monograph on Carolingian *Homiliaria* of Auxerre (1962).[1] B. had completed research on a monumental work dealing with the Marian Saturday. His studies on the Assumption, the queenship and the Mary-Church theme were distinctive. His assets were massive documentation, much of it unpublished manuscripts, rigorous precision, and balanced judgment.

---

[1]For obituary articles, cf. J. M. Canal, C.M.F., in EphMar, 19(1969), 359-365; G. Jouassard, in REA, 15(1969), (with bibliography), 3-8; C. Larnicol, C.S.Sp., in MM, 32(1970), 357-362.

BARTH, KARL (1886-1968)

B., a towering figure in Calvinist theology, expresses the Protestant theory about Our Lady, and he offers a critique of Catholic Marian theology with logical fidelity to his own basic position. He deals with the subject in early works, *The Great Promise*[1] and *Credo*[2], in occasional passages elsewhere in his works, but principally in the *Church Dogmatics* (part 2, vol. I).[3]

"God's revelation in its objective reality is the person of Jesus Christ."[4] This resembles Vatican II: "Christ, who is at the same time the Mediator and the fullness of all revelation." (*Verbum Dei*, 2). B. draws a narrow conclusion: "Revelation and therefore the Word of God and God himself is not to be sought anywhere else save in him who was born of the Virgin Mary, and again, that in him who was born of the Virgin Mary nothing else is to be sought other than God's revelation, God's word and God himself." "Revelation and reconciliation are irreversibly, indivisibly and exclusively God's work . . . Faith is not an act of reciprocity, but the act of renouncing all reciprocity, the act of acknowledging the one Mediator, besides whom there is no other."[5]

This general position will permit B. to defend the divine motherhood, which he will support with a quotation from Luther (*qv*): "She brought forth not a separate man, as if she on her side would have a son and God on his side would have his Son. But the same one whom God begot from eternity she herself brought forth in time."[6] Welcome too is his unequivocal stand on the virgin birth. He is almost scathing on his former disciple, Emil Brunner, who denied the privilege. *The Mediator*, Brunner's work, is "bad business" and *Man in Revolt* is "so bad that my only positive attitude to it is silence." The virgin birth at the outset of Christ's existence and the empty tomb at the end are signs. The first is "a denial not of man in the presence of God but of any power, attribute or capacity in him for God"; "*ex virgine*" is a judgment on man, for in the act of the Son of God assuming flesh "willing, achieving, creative, sovereign man as such cannot be considered a participator in God's work."[7] This is certainly Calvinist logic, not the best way to establish the particular truth.

With the same logic he advances his blunt critique of Catholic Mariology. He registers an "evangelical protest" against it; it appears to him an "excrescence" to be excised. His excursus draws on Catholic writers—Scheeben (*qv*), Diekamp, Karl Adam, and Gertrud von le Fort (from her work *Die Ewige Frau*). He adduces papal texts, and he recalls the dictum of St. Thomas that, because of the divine motherhood, Mary had *quaedam infinita dignitas*. The exegesis of the awkward synoptic texts is severely restrictive. Luther's interpretation of the Magnificat, especially the emphasis on Our Lady's lowliness, is welcomed. Mary's greatness "consists in the fact that all the interest is directed away from herself to the Lord." B. dismisses the new Eve concept as an early aberration. He quotes St. Ambrose on Mary as the temple of God. The first four centuries, he thinks, know nothing of the "later dogma, the later worship."

B. did not waste his time trying to prove that Marian cult arose from the pagan mother goddess, for "you can establish everything and nothing from the history of religion." Seeing a logical link between the dogmas of the Immaculate Conception (*qv*) and papal infallibility, he thought that Catholic dogma on Mary, grace, and the Church was all of a piece, paying a kind of left-handed tribute to the Mary-Church (*qv*) typology. "The 'Mother of God' of the Roman Catholic dogma is quite simply the principle, type and essence of the human creature co-operating servant-like [*ministerialiter*] in its own redemption on the basis of prevenient grace, and to that extent the principle, type and essence of the Catholic Church."[8]

B. can say, however, that Mary "is a figure absolutely raised above all the other figures of the Advent," i.e. Old Testament figures; that she is "an indispensable factor in biblical proclamation." He even says that "the operation of the Holy Spirit at the conception of Jesus is one mediated through Mary's faith."[9] His patrology is defective, as is his biblical exegesis. Yet it is the assumption or principle on which his critique rests which the Catholic theologian will reject. The creature cannot cooperate in any way in his own salvation.

B. takes no account of the eastern tradition, which, in his own great creative years, was powerfully stated by Sergius Bulgakov (*qv*). Commenting on Vatican II, he showed no sign of altering his views. He spoke of the "Mariological dogma with its so disagreeable development," "with its uncanny relationship to the essence and function of the Church," and regretted that there was no sign of its "even partial revocation." But he welcomed the honour shown by John XXIII to St. Joseph—putting his name in the Canon of the Mass. Joseph's role he saw as one "constant and unambiguous as a witness," and he thought that the Church should see herself as a guardian figure, a servant, in the example of the saint.[10]

This was an idea already expressed forcibly by the great Protestant theologian: "If I were a

Roman Catholic theologian I would lift St. Joseph up. He took care of the Child; he takes care of the Church ... Since Rome admits the mediation of the saints, why should it keep St. Joseph in the background? Personally I love St. Joseph greatly. I am just as much in favour of Josephology as I am hostile to Mariology, because I think that Joseph's role in relation to Christ is the role which the Church should play."[11]

[1]K. Barth, *The Great Promise*, tr. by H. Freund, (New York, 1963). [2]id., *Credo*, tr. by J. Strathearn McNab, (New York, 1936). [3]id., *Church Dogmatics*, tr. by G. T. Thompson and H. Knight, ed. by G. W. Romiley and T. F. Torrence, (Edinburgh, 1963), 132-202. Cf. also K. Barth, "Thoughts on the Second Vatican Council," in *The Ecum. Review*, 15(1963), 356-367. On Barth's Marian theology, cf. T. A. O'Meara, O.P., *Mary in Protestant and Catholic Theology*, (New York, 1966), 206-224; L. G. Tait, "Karl Barth and the Virgin Mary," in *Journal of Ecum. St.*, 4(1967), 416-425; C. O'Grady, M.S.C., *The Church in Catholic Theology: dialogue with Karl Barth*, II, (London, Dublin, 1969), 79-86; K. Algermissen, in LexMar, 604-611. For Barth on St. Joseph, cf. F. Filas, S.J., *St. Joseph after Vatican II*, (New York, 1967). [4]K. Barth, *Church Dogmatics*, 172. [5]ibid., *op. cit.*, 146. Cf. H. Küng, *Justification*, (New York, London, 1964). [6]Luther quotation, *Enarratio cap. 53, Isaiae, 1550*, in EA (Erlanger Ausgabe), Op. lat., 23, 476. [7]Karl Barth, *Church Dogmatics*, 194. [8]ibid., *op. cit.*, 143. [9]Cf. L. G. Tait, "Karl Barth and the Virgin Mary," in *Journal of Ecum. St.*, 4(1967); K. Barth, *Church Dogmatics*, 201. [10]ibid., "Thoughts on the Second Vatican Council," in *The Ecum. Review*, 15(1963), 361-362. [11]K. Barth, in *Una Sancta*, 18(1963), 308.

BARTHOLOMEW DE LOS RIOS, O.E.S.A.
(1580-1652)

Greatest Marian authority among the Hermits of St. Augustine, B. studied at the universities of Alcalá and Douai, worked in the Spanish Netherlands to found the Confraternity of the Slaves of Mary, and preached at the royal court in Brussels. His Marian works are: *Phoenix Thenensis e cineribus redivivus*, (Antwerp, 1637), a manual of devotion for the Confraternity of Slaves of Mary; *De Hierarchia Mariana libri sex: in quibus imperium, virtus et nomen B. V. M. declaratur, et Mancipiorum ejus dignitas ostenditur*, (Antwerp, 1641), his main work, over 800 pages. Also, *Historia B. M. V. de Bono successu, sive orationes piae et devotae, cum regulis et indulgentiis praefatae Sodalitatis*, (Antwerp, 1641); *Sermon de la Expectación*, (Brussels, 1644); *Horizon Marianus sive de excellentia et virtutibus B. Mariae Virginis tractatus novem: super totidem ejus festa infra anni circulum ab Ecclesia celebrari solita*, (Antwerp, 1647), 478 pages.[1]

B. aimed at establishing Marian devotion on a solid foundation. Mary's predestination (qv), he thought, is the cause of ours. "When she freely consented she can truly be called the cause of predestination and of all our filiation." He found evidence for the Immaculate Conception (qv) in Genesis, Song of Songs, and Luke, and he appealed to the Doctors and to the Church's teaching. He thought that not only Mary's divine motherhood but her role in our regard demanded it. How could she destroy the reign of sin if she herself had first felt its yoke disgracefully? Mary's privilege does not take from Christ's dignity as Redeemer. It enhances this, for the Virgin owes more to the Passion of Christ for being preserved from sin than we do for being delivered from it. Her initial grace surpassed all the graces of angels and saints collectively.

B. related Mary's person to each of the three divine Persons; she was the spouse of the Holy Ghost. He elaborates her part in the Redemption, calling her a helper like Christ in all things, but saving his uniqueness by the contrast of merit—*de condigno* and *de congruo*—and by defining his essential redemptive act as satisfaction, hers as impetration. The fullness of this act, by which she redeemed us, comprises her consent at the Annunciation, provision of the matter of sacrifice, renunciation on Calvary of her maternal rights, and perfect acceptance of the death of her Son. He goes so far as to say that Mary's will that he be given up would have sufficed for him to will it "without any eternal decree of the Father." Mary is *"Sacerdos nostrae propitiationis."*

After Mary's death and resurrection she was established in the queenship (qv), for which privilege B. argues very fully. Her power is universally as great as could be shared by God with a creature. She is placed over all goods, spiritual and temporal. The saints can only obtain what passes through her hands. Her prayer is all-powerful: "Others ask, you order; they seek, you prescribe; they obtain their request, you command."[2]

[1]Cf. A. C. Buron, "Causalidad de Maria en nuestra predestinación según el P. B. de los Rios," in EstM, 1(1942), 287-324; A. Musters, *La Souveraineté de la Vierge d'après les écrits mariologiques de Barthélemy de los Rios*, (Gand, 1946); Fl. Agudelo, *Naturaleza de la Esclavitud mariana*

según el padre Bartolome' de los Rios y San Luis Maria de Montfort, (Bogota, 1958); S. Folgado Florez, "La corredención mariana en el P. B. de los Rios," in *Ciudad de Dios*, 175(1962), 36-59, 229-250; *Ciudad de Dios*, 176(1965), 35-62; A. Sage, in *Maria*, II, 699-707; S. Garcia Casado, *Maria esposa del Verbo en Bartholomew de los Rios*, (Burgos, University Dissertation, 1975). [2]For texts and references supporting every assertion, cf. A. Sage, in *Maria*, II, 699-707; esp. DSp., s.v.

BASIL THE GREAT, ST., DOCTOR OF THE CHURCH (c. 330-379)

Born into a family of saints, enriched with the culture of Constantinople, and of Athens where his friendship with St. Gregory of Nazianzus (*qv*) was begun, B. became bishop of Caeserea in 370. He was the wise lawmaker of eastern monasticism. With Gregory, and Gregory of Nyssa, his own brother, he formed the trio of Cappadocians whose influence on behalf of the Nicene teaching was capital. His Marian teaching is found principally in the sermon on the birth of Christ, which is now admitted as genuine.[1] There are other significant passages in his works. Origen influenced his thinking.

In the *Hexaemeron*, homilies on the creation, B. appeals to the example of birds having fertile eggs without copulation, part of God's plan to help our faith, to show that "a virgin, keeping her virginity intact, should give birth,"[2] which is a statement of the *virginitas in partu*.

In the homily on the birth of Christ, he gives the reasons why Mary and Joseph were betrothed. Virginity should be honoured and marriage not despised. Joseph should be a witness to her purity, preserving her from calumny. The fullness of time for the Incarnation had come, and none in the world equalled Mary in purity before the Spirit who was to fashion that flesh which would bear God. "The virginity of Mary would be hidden from the prince of this world"[3]—an opinion derived by Origen (*qv*) from St. Ignatius of Antioch (*qv*).

B. defended the application of Is 7:14 to Mary (see EMMANUEL), arguing that if it did not apply to a virgin there would be no sign. He was aware that some proposed the translation *neanis* instead of *parthenos* for *almah*, but he appealed to Deut 20:25-28 to justify his interpretation, which was that of all the Fathers. He also rejects arguments against Mary's perpetual virginity based on Mt 1:25, "he knew her not until she had borne a son," claiming that "until" could be used indefinitely. "Lovers of

Christ cannot hear that the *Theotokos* ever ceased to be a virgin."[4] B. repeats Origen's story from the Commentary *In Mt*[5] that Zechariah was killed between the Temple and the altar because he brought Mary to the place reserved for virgins—after she had given birth to Jesus.[6]

B. also follows Origen in his exegesis of the "sword" (*qv*) foretold by Simeon, as did other eastern Fathers. It referred, he thought, to the *salos* and especially the *diakrisis*, which would afflict her soul in the moment of the Passion "as she stood by the Cross and saw what was done and heard the voices."[7] B. then thought of some kind of swaying in the mind and even doubting, as these words would respectively signify.

The use of *Theotokos* is noteworthy; elsewhere he refers to "the incarnate God, Emmanuel born of the holy Virgin."[8] In the Commentary on Is., if it be accepted as genuine, B. repeats his interpretation of 7:14. He recalls the typology of Adam created from the earth in regard to Christ, the final Adam, who assumed a body formed in a virginal womb—a recurring theme with the Fathers. Like Origen he considers Mary a "prophetess," because of the *Magnificat*.[9]

[1]Cf. R. Laurentin, *Traité*, I, 160; Sermon, in CMP, II, 234-246; in EMBP, 269-283; in ClavisG, II, 140-178. [2]*Hexaemeron*, in PG 29, 180B. [3]Homilies, in PG, 31, 1464B. Cf. G. Söll, "Die Mariologie der Kappadozier im Licht der Dogmengeschichte," in *Theol. Quartalschrift*, 131(1951), 163-188, 288-319, 426-457; *id.* in ASC, V, 2, 129-143. Cf. also S. S. Fedyniak, *Mariologia apud Patres Cappadoces*, (Rome, 1958). [4]PG, 31, 1468A. [5]Commentary *In Mt.*, in GCS, 38, 42-43. [6]PG, 31, 1469A. [7]*Ep. 260, 9*, in PG, 32, 968A. [8]*In Ps., 45, 6*, in PG, 29, 425C. [9]PG, 30, 464A-465B, 477B.

BASIL OF SELEUCIA (Fifth Century)

Little is known of B. save that he was bishop of Seleucia in Isauria at the time of the Council of Chalcedon, and until 458, when a letter was sent to him by the emperor Leo I. He may have lived longer after this date than was thought by his earlier biographers.[1] He took part in the *latrocinium* at Ephesus in 449, but returned to orthodoxy at Chalcedon. He is almost certainly the author of a remarkable homily entitled *On the Annunciation of the most holy Mother of God*. Authenticity was for a while rejected following the study by B. Marx[2], but R. Caro (see FATHERS OF THE CHURCH) accepts the work as Basil's[3], after a thorough review of all the arguments. The time and place of the homily were probably 449 and Constantinople. The elements of similarity with the work of Proclus (*qv*), which led Marx to attribute the sermon to him, point to literary dependence.

B. uses the title virgin (*parthenos*) frequently, at times with *Theotokos* (*qv*). He is evasive on the virginity *in partu*, which Proclus cherished. On the theme of the divine motherhood he strikes an awesome note; he cannot praise the *Theotokos* fittingly. How shall worthy things be composed of her, whose dignity surpasses all that is in the world: "What shall we say of the *Theotokos*, who shines above all the martyrs as the sun outshines the stars?"[4] ". . . the great mystery of the *Theotokos* is above every reason, loftier than speech."[5]

Mary's motherhood was related to the mystery of the Incarnation. "It was not a mere man who was begotten; but God the Word was incarnate of the Virgin, clothed with flesh the same as mine, so that he should save like by like . . . if he did not share in my flesh, he would not have given me life; if he had not truly taken my nature, I should not have been enriched by the kingdom of God."[6] Again he is seized by the mystery which is beyond all language or thought.

Mary's holiness (*qv*) is seen in the context of her virginity and motherhood: the sun of justice shone on her; she is the temple truly worthy of God.[7]

B. marks an advance especially by his insistence on Mary's mediation (*qv*) as linked with her divine motherhood. "Set as mediatress of God and men that the dividing element of hatred be taken away and heavenly and earthly [things] be made one . . ."[7] Hence too his conviction of her power, greater, as he explains, than that of Peter or Paul. The road is open for a doctrine of intercession rooted in the office of the *Theotokos*.

[1]Cf. E. Honigmann, *Theodoret of Cyrrhus and Basil of Seleucia*, in *Patristic Studies*, ST, 173, 174-184; ClavisG, III, 278-283.   [2]Homily, in PG, 85, 425-452; in CMP IV, 540-556; in EMBP, 943-955. Cf. B. Marx, *Procliana*, (Munster, 1940), 84-89; *id.*, "Der homiletische Nachlass des Basileios von Seleucia," in OCP, 7(1941), 329-369; R. Laurentin, *Traité*, I, 167; D. Del Fabro, "Le omelie mariane dei Padri Greci del V secolo," in MM, 8(1946), 212.   [3]*La Homiletica*, II, 288-305.   [4]PG, 85, 5, 441C.   [5]PG, 85, 2, 429B.   [6]PG, 85, 5, 445C.   [7]PG, 85, 5, 444A.

BASLE, COUNCIL OF (1439)

After the Council was repudiated by the Pope, it had no status as a teaching authority but it possesses interest in the development of the doctrine of the Immaculate Conception (*qv*) since it reveals what opinion was current in the Church at the time. Though most of the thirteenth-century Doctors had opposed the idea, the Franciscans, and others who supported it, hoped for a favourable decision by the Council, which they got. The debate was conducted by John de Romiroy and John de Segovia for the privilege, and John de Torquemada against. On 15 September, 1439, in the thirty-sixth session of the Council, the doctrine was defined and the feast established for the whole Church. The decree ran as follows: "We define and we declare that the doctrine according to which the glorious Virgin Mary, Mother of God, in virtue of a singular prevenient and operative divine grace was never really subject to original sin, was always exempt from all original and actual fault and accordingly holy and immaculate, is a pious doctrine in conformity with the Church's worship, the Catholic faith, right reason and Sacred Scripture, that it must be approved, held and professed by all Catholics and henceforth no one is allowed to preach or teach the contrary."[1] Earlier in the document, it was stated that God gave Mary a grace "by which liberating and preserving the most blessed person from the original stain, he redeemed her by a more sublime kind of sanctification" as it was made clear that "whatever is manifested about the dignity and sublime character of the Virgin Mary pertains to the praise and honour of her Son."

[1]E. Birk, *Monumenta Conciliorum Generalium saeculi XIV*; III, 364ff; Mansi, *Sacrorum Conciliorum etc.*, XXIX, 183. Cf. P. H. Ameri, *Doctrina theologorum de Immaculata B. V. M. Conceptione tempore Concilii Basileensis*, (Rome, 1954); J. Galot, S. J., in *Maria*, VII, 71-79; G. M. Roschini, *Maria Santissima*, 3, 176-186.

BEDE, THE VENERABLE (*c.* 673-735)

Bede, a Benedictine of Wearmouth and Jarrow monasteries, a great monastic historian, treats of Our Lady frequently in his gospel commentaries, and in his homilies, which are commentaries on biblical texts.[1] The *Hymnus XI in natali sanctae Dei genitricis* is genuine.[2] Bede continued patristic themes, at times achieving succinct summaries of previous opinions. He was insistent on the divine maternity. He thought that Mary's name in Hebrew meant Star of the sea and in Syriac, Mistress. Mary was the first woman to take the vow of virginity: "Since she was the first who surrendered herself to such great virtue, she deserved by special right to surpass other women in happiness."[3]

B. summarized patristic teaching on the marriage (qv): "Blessed Mary had then to have a husband who would be the most reliable witness of her integrity and the most faithful custodian of our Lord and Saviour; for this Child he [Joseph] would bring to the Temple the victims prescribed by the law; in the hour of persecution he would take him to Egypt with his Mother and bring him back, finally he would provide many other services called for by the fragility of the nature assumed."[4] B. elsewhere lists such reasons as: the guarantee afforded by Joseph's genealogy: the protection to Mary against stoning as an adulteress, which would be exploited by wayward women; and concealment of the virginal birth from the evil one.[5]

Mary by her humility—as well as her obedience—was in contrast with Eve (qv). Humility, too, she exemplified in the Purification, for "by a singular privilege she was above the law." There is no trace of Origen (qv) in his interpretation of the Sword of Simeon; he thinks of pain and grief. "She could not see without bitter pain, crucified and dying, him, for whom, though she in no way doubted that as God he would rise from the dead, she grieved stricken by the death of one taken from her flesh."[6]

B. interpreted the words "Mary kept these things in her heart" as a historian would. "She wished to disclose to no one the secrets of Christ which she knew, but she waited reverently for the time and the manner to disclose them."[7]

An official report of Vatican II quoted B. at length on Mary and the Church (qv). The mysteries of the Virgin's life are daily renewed in the Church—"which, following the example of the blessed, ever Virgin Mary as one wedded and at the same time immaculate, as a virgin conceives us of the Spirit, as a virgin brings us forth without pain, and as one espoused to one person and rendered fruitful by another, throughout its separate parts which make it one and catholic, is visibly joined to its ruling pontiff, and by the invisible power of the Holy spirit is given increase."[8] The influence of St. Ambrose (qv) is here evident.

Cana (qv) is set by B. in the context of the Church as the spouse of Christ: "It was not by chance, therefore, but by the grace of a certain mystery that he came to the marriage celebrated on earth in the manner of the flesh who had come down from heaven to earth to join the Church to himself with spiritual love, of which the bridal chamber was the womb of the incorrupt Mother of God, in which God was joined with human nature, from which he went forth as a bridegroom to associate the Church with himself."[9] B. could truly say that Christ associated the Church with himself through the mystery of the Incarnation. The idea and the word *sociare* are found in St. Augustine. Soon after, Ambrose Autpert (qv) will apply it to Mary's union with Christ, and then *socia*, the noun, will appear (see ASSOCIATE). B. has a suggestive passage on Christ as the "firstborn," linking the use in the infancy narrative with Rev 1:5 and Rom 8:29. The latter Pauline text is used by Vatican II (LG, 63) in the context of Mary's spiritual Motherhood.

---

[1]PL, 91, 92, 94; Homilies, crit. ed. by D. Hurst, O.S.B., in CCSL, 120, 122. Cf. G. Morin, O.S.B., "Le recueil primitif des homélies de Bède," in RevBen, 9(1892), 316-326; R. Laurentin, *Traité*, I, 137-138; F. Vernet, in DSp, I, 1322-1329; H. Graef, *Mary*, I, 162-165. [2]*Hymnus XI in natali sanctae Dei Genitricis*, in CCSL, 122, 433-434. [3]*In Lucan I*, in CCSL, 120, 33. [4]*Hom. 3 in Advent.*, in CCSL, 122,15. [5]*In Lucan I*, in CCSL, 120, 30-31. [6]*Hom. in Purif., 18*, in CCSL, 122, 132. [7]*Hom. in Nativ. Dni.*, in CCSL, 122, 49. [8]*In Lucan II*, in CCSL, 120,48-49. [9]*Hom. 14 Post Epiph.*, in CCSL, 122, 96.

BELLARMINE, ROBERT, ST., DOCTOR OF THE CHURCH (1542-1621)

Jesuit Provincial in Naples and Archbishop of Capua, Cardinal B. was a foremost theologian of the Counter-Reformation and involved in its controversies. His Marian doctrine is found in ascetical works such as *De septem verbis Domini in cruce*; in his famous Catechism which was approved by Pope Clement VIII; in occasional passages in the controversial works; especially in his sermons, those in the collected works, and many more in the *Opera oratoria postuma*, edited by S. Tromp, S.J.[1]

B.'s opinions are, in general, soberly formulated from a background of learning. Thus the reason given for Mary's marriage (qv) are those put forward at one time or another by the Fathers (qv).[2] When he asserts that Mary was the first to take a vow of virginity, he cites St.

Gregory of Nyssa (qv), St. Augustine (qv), St. Bernard (qv), St. Anselm (qv) and Venerable Bede (qv).[3] At a meeting of the Holy Office, 31 August, 1617, he expressed a reservation on the Immaculate Conception. The truth could be held as a pious opinion or a theological conclusion, but was not sufficiently founded in Scripture and Tradition to be defined *de fide*.[4] Yet he affirmed the truth in his Catechism, and developed it at length in his sermons. He linked it with an idea dear to him, Mary's election by God. Choosing her before all others, by his grace "preserving her from falling under original sin,"; "he adorns her with gifts and remains with her to preserve his treasure."[5] Mary, he says elsewhere, would have had original sin if God had not averted it by his grace—grace of the greatest kind, which she got from the merit of Christ's Passion, "therefore she was truly redeemed and liberated by the Mediator (2 Cor, 5:14; 1 Tim 2:5; Eph 5:25). And she is indebted to Christ no less than we are, indeed more than us, because she was freed in a nobler manner." He could then express a different opinion later on the definability: "It is expedient even necessary to define it."[6]

Commenting on Mary's presence on Calvary, B. emphasizes her union with her Son by the most perfect maternal love, and her unique sorrow (*ejus passionem et mortem plus omnibus defleverit*). "She loved greatly the flesh of her Son, but she loved more the honour of the Father and the salvation of the world."[7] He frequently speaks of Mary's choice as a factor in her lifework and this gives force to his strongest statement on her saving role: "She alone co-operated in the mystery of the passion, standing before the Cross and offering her Son for the salvation of the world. She was, after the Ascension, the teacher of the apostles and of all the saints. She, now in heaven as advocate and Mother of all, cooperates in the salvation of all the saved."[8] She taught, instructed and consoled the faithful; she was the "nurse of the Church."[9] He uses of Mary the title so favoured by modern theologians, associate (*socia*).[10]

Mary's Assumption was for him entirely certain. It flowed from the many special graces and privileges of her life. In heaven, she is above all others, angels and men. Though the intercession of the saints, and therefore of Mary, is always through Christ, B. has no doubt that Mary's intercession is, after Christ's unique: "Blessed Virgin who can obtain whatever you

wish"; "Miracles in the whole world show how useful it is to invoke her."[11] There is no place in the world without memory of her benefits. More profoundly, to explain this influence he takes up the medieval image of Mary as the neck of the Mystical Body of which Christ is the head: "Through her the influence of the Head descends on the body."[12]

---

[1]St. Robert Bellarmine's Louvain sermons *Super Missus est* (5), *In festo Annunt., De partu B. M. V., De Nativ. B. M. V.*, in vol. IX of his collected works, (Paris, 1870-1874). Advent and festive sermons, ed. by S. Tromp. S.J., (Rome, 1942-1946), vols. I, 266-307; II, 55-100; VI, 111-121, 289-295; VII, 302-324. Cf. S. Tromp, S.J., "Robertus Bellarminus et Beata Virgo," in Gregor, 21(1940), 162-182; *ibid.*, "Doctrina S. Roberti Bellarmini de Assumptione B. M. V. in caelum," in MM, 13(1951), 133-147; J. A. Hardon, S.J., "Bellarmine and the Queen of Virgins," in *Rev. for Religious*, 12(1953), 113-121; S. Alemany, C. O., "Prerogativas del alma de Maria en San Roberto Bellarmino," in EstEcl, 28(1954), 473-500; B. de Margerie, S.J., "La mariologie existentielle de S. Robert Bellarmin," in MM, 26(1964), 344-389; H. Graef, *Mary*, II, 24-26. [2]*Super Missus est*, I, in collected works (Paris, 1870-1874), IX, 476. [3]*De Assumpt.*, in *Opera oratoria postuma*, II, 87. [4]X. M. Le Bachelet, in DTC, VII, 1153, but cf. infra.[5]*Super Missus est.*, III, in *Opera oratoria postuma*, I, 267. [6]*In Concep.*, in *op. cit.*, 62. [7]*De septem verbis*, edn. Eger, Hungary, 92. [8]*In Nativ. B. V.*, in *Opera oratoria postuma*, VI, 295. [9]*In Assumpt.*, in *Opera oratoria postuma*, II, 99. [10]*De Assumpt.*, in collected works (Paris, 1870-1874), IX, 355. Cf. J. Brodrick, S.J., *St. Robert Bellarmine*, (London, 1928), I, 512-521. [11]*De Nativit. B. M. V.*, in collected works (Paris, 1870-1874), IX, 382. [12]*op. cit.*, IX, 378.

BENEDICT XIV (1675-1758; Pope, 1740)

A great canonist and a Pope called on to deal with difficult problems. B. in his "Profession of Faith for the Orientals" (1743) recalled briefly the Councils of Ephesus, Chalcedon and Nicaea II. His Apostolic Letter *Gloriosae Dominae Dei Genitricis Mariae*, 27 September, 1748, on the first Marian Congregation, praised devotion to Our Lady as based on the manifest will of God; it recalled Old Testament figures—Esther and Judith—and the Ark of the Covenant, and praised the work of the Jesuits, who, after the example of their founder, saw in Mary their intercessor, their refuge and their protection. An important passage, part of which was written into LG 53, is: "Because of all this, the Catholic Church, formed and nourished in the school of the Holy Spirit, has always professed to render humble tribute to her as Mother of her Lord and Redeemer, as Queen of heaven and earth. The Church has encompassed this most loving of Mothers. entrusted to her by the last words of her dying Spouse, with expressions of filial homage and devotion."[1]

---

[1]*Gloriosae Dominae Dei Genitricis Mariae*, in OL, 26.

BERNARD, ST., DOCTOR OF THE CHURCH (1090-1153)

B. is sometimes considered the special medieval doctor of Our Lady. Dante and Filippo Lippi in their different ways helped to foster the idea, as did writers of different schools down to recent times. Some of the recent Popes quote his best known maxim. A mass of writing has been spuriously ascribed to him, including the *Memorare* and the *Salve Regina* (*qv*).[1] A recent critical approach leads to such judgments as the following. B.'s output on Marian subjects was comparatively slight, about three-and-a-half per cent of the total corpus (sixty columns out of 2,200 in PL). He did not further the theology of Mary, not only by his opposition to the Immaculate Conception, but by restricting his interest to homiletics, with no thought of a formal treatise such as Eadmer composed. Save for the image of the aqueduct, and the idea of an act of oblation by Mary (and Joseph) in the Presentation of the Lord, B. did not add to the stock of ideas, images and biblical types already current. He was silent on the spiritual motherhood, sparing in what he said of the bodily Assumption, more restrained than his contemporaries on the Marian sense of the Song of Songs. Authors of such criticism—H. Barré and J. Leclercq notably—do not question B.'s immense influence. All must allow that, despite these limitations, his rhetoric and his noble enthusiasm, as well as his gift of the telling phrase and formula, were distinctive. He felt all language inadequate before this "incomprehensible glory."

The relevant writings are: four sermons (*Super missus est*) collectively entitled, "In Praise of the Virgin Mother"; sermons for liturgical feasts—three for the Purification, three for the Annunciation, four for the Assumption (to which recently a fifth, once of doubtful authenticity, has been added[2], that for the Octave of the same feast); *In Signum magnum* on the "Twelve Stars"; and the great sermon on the "Aqueduct" for the feast of Mary's Nativity.

The "Letter to the Canons of Lyons," the most strictly theological part of the corpus, is on the Immaculate Conception (*qv*). Attempts to reject the letter as spurious have failed. It contains a summary of Mary's excellence, as B. saw it: "The royal Virgin needs no spurious honour, endowed abundantly as she is with true titles to glory, marks of dignity. Honour becomingly the integrity of her flesh, the holiness of her life; admire the fruitfulness of a virgin, offer veneration to her divine offspring. Extoll the one unacquainted with concupiscence in conception or pain in giving birth. Preach that she is revered by angels, the desired of the nations, foreknown by patriarchs and prophets, chosen from among all, placed before all. Glorify the one who found grace, the mediatress of salvation, the restorer of the ages; exalt finally her who was exalted above the choirs of angels to the heavenly realms. These things the Church sings of her to me and it has taught me to sing also these same things."[3]

B. accepted the Augustinian idea that Original Sin was transmitted by concupiscence inherent in sexual intercourse. In the "Letter to the Canons of Lyons," a letter protesting against the celebration of the feast of the Immaculate Conception, he maintained that sin ". . . could not but be present where concupiscence was not absent." Defense of the privilege might imply that Mary was conceived virginally of the Spirit, "something unheard of thus far." Psalm 50, "in sin did my mother conceive me," and Tradition were, he erroneously thought, on his side. He tried to meet the arguments from the other side and finally announced that he would submit to any future decision of the Church.[4]

He was emphatic on the divine motherhood: "God from his own substance and that of the Virgin has made one only Christ, or rather has become one only Christ."[5] Mary is one to whom all look as "to the centre, the secret of God, the cause of things, the great business of the ages." She gave a unique example of virginity, was betrothed to one who, as B. shows, was foreshadowed in the Old Testament Joseph. St. Joseph's doubt (*qv*) he interprets favourably. The universal import of Mary's fiat in the Annunciation (*qv*) inspires a grandiose vision: "The whole world awaits prostrate at your feet. Not without reason, since on your word depend the consolation of the unfortunate, the redemption of slaves, the deliverance of the condemned, in a word, the salvation of all the sons of Adam, of your entire race."[6]

The sermon *In signum magnum* on Rev 12:1 (see WOMAN IN) shows Mary's place in the plan of salvation beginning with the antithesis Adam-Eve and Christ-Mary, leading to the well-known sentence, "We need a mediator to the Mediator and there is none more beneficial to us than Mary. Eve was cruel and through her the ancient serpent gave baneful poison to the man; but Mary is faithful who provided the remedy of salvation to men and women."[7] The critical edition does not have the word mediatress before Eve and Mary, but later in the passage the reader is urged to "give thanks to the one who has, in his most kind mercy, such a Mediatress." Her mercy is in turn open to the benefit of all.

B. admits that the woman of Revelations is the Church, but the vision can, he thinks, "with no inconvenience" be applied also to Mary. She fulfilled the ancient prophecy of Gen 3:15 (see WOMAN IN). Adjusting the biblical imagery a little, B. says that "the woman placed between the sun and the moon is Mary set between Christ and his Church."[8] B. then treats of the twelve great privileges—corresponding to the twelve stars—which he sees in Mary and ends with a prayer to her as the Mediatress of the Church.

In the sermon on the Aqueduct having firmly asserted that Christ the Lord is the fountain of life and that Mary is but the aqueduct or channel, "reaching to the most living source of waters beyond the heavens," he goes on to state the universality of her mediation: "God has placed in Mary the fullness of all good so that we should know that whatever hope we have, whatever grace, whatever salvation, flows from her who goes up streaming with delights." A little later comes the much-quoted sentence, favourite of Popes: "Let us venerate Mary with every fibre of our hearts, with our most intimate sentiments and desires, since this is his will who willed that we have everything through Mary."[9]

B. uses many similar phrases. Speaking of Mary's mercy, he has words which evoke the *Memorare*: "O Blessed Virgin should there exist anyone who has called on you in his necessities and remembers that you have failed him, let him be silent on your mercy."[10] Mary is our Advocate, the way, "the treasury of God." There is no cleavage between honour to the Son and Mother. She has given us a brother, she is the Mother of mercy. Does this mean merely Mother of Christ (who is mercy) or our merciful mother? B. is discreet. On the Assumption, we know his view from one sentence: the joy of those in heaven "who were enabled to hear her [Mary's] voice and to behold her face and to enjoy her blessed presence."[10]

In heaven, Mary intercedes for us. Rarely if ever has B.'s appeal *Respice stellam* been surpassed as a statement of hope in her clemency and power: "O whoever you may be who feel yourself on the tide of this world drifting in storms and tempests rather than treading firm ground, turn not your eyes from the effulgence of this star, unless you wish to be submerged . . . if she holds you, you do not fall; if she protects you, you have no fear; with her to lead you, you tire not; with her favour, you will reach the goal, conscious thus within yourself how rightly the word was spoken: 'And the Virgin's name was Mary'."[11]

[1]Works: PL, 183, 184, 187; P. Bernard, O. Cist., *St. B. et Notre Dame, étude d'âme, textes originaux et traduction*, (Paris, 1953); *Obras completas de St. B.*, BAC, (Madrid, 1955); critical ed. by J. Leclercq, O.S.B. and H. Rochais, *St. B. Opera Omnia*, (Rome, 1966). Cf. R. Laurentin, *Traité*, I, 153-154; F. Cavallera, "Bernard (Apocryphes attribués à Saint)," in DSp, I, 1499; F. de P. Sola, "Fuentes patrísticas de la Mariologia de St. B., " in EstEcl, 23(1949), 209-226; J. M. Humeres, "Quanta polleat auctoritate St. B. in doctrina de Mediatione B. M. V. declaranda," in EphMar, 2(1952), 325-350; C. Garcia, *St. B. Cantore de Maria; Las doce prerogativas de Maria según St. B.*, (Barcelona, 1953). Cf. esp. H. Barré, C.S.Sp., "St. B. Docteur Marial," in *Anal. S. O. Cist.*, 9 (1953), 92-113; G. M. Roschini, O.S.M., *Il Dottore Mariano*, (Rome, 1953); J. B. Bauer, "Lo pseudo-Origene, fonte di St. B. nel sermone 'De Aquaeductu'," in MM, 22(1960), 370-372; A. Wilmart, O.S.B., *Auteurs spirituels et textes dévots du moyen âge latin*, (Paris, 1932), 111; R. Laurentin, "'Verbum . . . non capiebatur in se'. Divinité du Christ et foi de Marie selon St. B.," in MM, 27(1965), 426-431; J. Leclercq, O.S.B., "'Marie Reine', dans les sermons de St. B.," in *Coll. Cist. Ref.*, 26(1964), 266-276; id., in *Maria*, II, 568-574; J. B. Auniord, O. Cist., in *Maria*, II, 581-613; H. Graef, *Mary*, I, 235-241; A. O. Le Bail, in DSp, I, 1485-1490; O. Stegmüller and D. Lauffs, in LexMar, 710-720. [2]Cf. J. Leclercq, O.S.B., in *Rech. de Théol. anc. méd.*, 29(1953), 5-12. [3]*Ep. 174 and Canon, Lugdun, 2*, in PL, 182, 333. [4]*Ep. 174 ad Canon, Lugdun; 7, 9*, in PL, 182, 335-336. English tr. of the letter in Bruno Scott James, *The Letters of St. Bernard*, (London, 1953), 289-293. [5]*In Laudibus V. M., Hom. 3, 4*, in *St. B. Opera Omnia*, (ed. by J. Leclercq, O.S.B. and H. Rochais), IV, 38. [6]*Hom. 4, 8* in *op. cit.*, IV, 53. [7]*In signum magnum*, in *op. cit.*, V, 263. [8]*In signum magnum, 5*, in *op. cit.*, V, 265. [9]*Serm. de Aqued., 7*, in *op. cit.*, V, 279. [10]*Serm. I in Assumpt., 1*, in *op. cit.*, V, 228. [11]*In Laud. V. M., Hom. 2, 17*, in *op. cit.*, IV, 35; quoted in letter on 8th Centenary (*Doctor Mellifluus*), 24 May, 1953. See OL, 344-345.

BERNARDINE OF BUSTI (1440-1513)

B. was author of the last substantial works on Our Lady on the eve of the Protestant Reformation. He gave up legal studies to enter the Franciscans and made preaching his lifework. His themes were the Holy Name, Our Lady, and St. Joseph. His Marian works include: Office and

Mass of the Conception of the Blessed Virgin, using elaborate arguments from the sources to prove the Immaculate Conception, *Elucidarium de I. C. cum Officio et Missa*; and, major and best known, *Mariale*, the name commonly given to his *Sermonarium de excellentiis gloriosae V. M.*, sixty-three sermons taking up twelve books. The first part appeared in 1492 in Milan, the whole work the following year. Before 1515, editions had come out in Strasbourg (3), Lyons (2), and Cologne. It was a widely used sermon source book. It is a huge and uneven composition (over 1,000 double-column pages in the 1588 edition of the works), in which interesting insights are accompanied by much uncritical, extravagant material, some obviously inherited from Pseudo-Albert (*qv*).

Nine sermons in the first book deal at length with the Immaculate Conception, and the Office is added. B. argues strongly from the quasi-universality of the feast, and adduces much more by way of arguments from history—some disparate, and some apocryphal. The book attributes everything possible to Mary. She merited (*qv*) to be Mother of God before the Incarnation *de congruo*, after her fiat *merito digni*; she then surpassed in merit all the elect.[1] As some of the medievals had said, she was the helper of our redemption (*adjutrix sive auxiliatrix nostrae redemptionis*), so she is a helper of our justification.[2] She is the "mediatress of salvation, of binding and uniting, of justification, reconciliation, intercession, communication."[3] She is appointed by God to dispense all "alms and graces." In this line of thought B. gives her titles such as "restorer," "reparatrix," and "reconciler." She is not only Queen, but "Empress of the world," with sovereignty in heaven, in hell, in purgatory, and in the world.[4] The idea of two kingdoms appeals to B., justice to God, mercy to Mary; though he does make it clear that God possesses both attributes and it is God who assigns the role of Mary. One who is weighed down in the forum of God's justice, may "call on his Mother's forum of mercy."[5]

On the question of Mary's knowledge, B. follows his master, Pseudo-Albert: she possessed all science, mechanical and liberal arts, Law, Philosophy, Medicine, Mathematics, Music, and Theology.[6] Mary, he held, had the dignity and grace of the sacrament of Orders, though she did not receive the sacrament. She had equivalently and excellently all that went with the priesthood.[7]

B. insisted on the fact of Mary's death (*qv*). Since she was "redeemed by her Son from original sin," God could, to show this, remit the guilt and retain the penalty. B. also thought that without death Mary would not be fully human, and Christ would not be of the race of Adam.[8]

The Assumption (*qv*) is defended enthusiastically and at length. B. thought that Pseudo-Augustine was in fact the great African.[9] But his real basis was the faith of the Church.

---

[1]*Mariale*, VII, 4, 2 (editions are not paged). [2]*op. cit.*, III, 1, 3. [3]*op. cit.*, III, 1. [4]*op. cit.*, III, 2, 3. [5]*op. cit.*, III, 3, 4. [6]*op. cit.*, IV, 9. [7]*op. cit.*, IV, 11. [8]*op. cit.*, I, 2, 2; *op. cit.*, XI, 1, 5. [9]*op. cit.*, XI, 1, 6 and *passim*. Cf. F. Cucchi, *La mediazione universale della santa Vergine negli scritti di B. de B.*, (Milan, 1942); O. Stegmüller, in LexMar, 721-725; H. Graef, *Mary*, I, 320-322.

BERNARDINE OF SIENA, ST. (1380-1444)

Apostle of the Holy Name of Jesus, Franciscan reformer, and tireless preacher, B. was an enthusiast for Our Lady. Most of his Marian sermons are grouped to make a "Treatise on the Blessed Virgin."[1] He also left an important sermon on St. Joseph (*qv*).[2] This homiletic material takes up about 200 pages in nine volumes which total over 4,500 pages. B. reproduced, often textually, much of the work of others: notably Peter John Olivi (*qv*), from whose *Quaestiones quatuor de Domina* he took over the first question on the Virgin's consent at the Incarnation, making two sermons therefrom; and Ubertino of Casale (*qv*) whose *Arbor Vitae Crucifixae Jesu* was his favourite quarry. Of its 101 chapters he took over forty-seven, with slight changes.[3] B. abounds in superlatives; he generally sees Mary's dignity and privileges at the limit of the possible. Certain phrases and some short passages need to be seen in context and in the entire context of his thought; occasionally he does exceed in somewhat daring rhetoric.

"The whole world after the fault of our first parents, was preserved by God through love for the Blessed Virgin" . . . "I do not doubt that God wrought all the deliverances and mercies in the Old Testament solely out of respect for this blessed maiden, on account of which he decreed in his predestination from eternity that she should be honoured above all his works."[4] God, he tells use in the same sermon, had from all eternity loved her beyond excess (*superexcessive dilexit*). In one of his sermons on the name of Mary he says that she is the highest of all creatures, that in glory she exceeds all other creatures; she is the nearest to Christ. She is the spouse (*qv*) of God, the spouse of God the Father.

Surprisingly in the case of a Franciscan, B. is a subject of controversy as to the Immaculate Conception. He wished to ignore the "scholastic warfare" on the subject. He believed in the privilege, some commentators think, but did not teach or defend it. Phrases like "a purity than which none greater under God can be thought of," or "through a special grace no sin had place in her," support this interpretation. But he speaks of a progress in sanctification which culminated in the moment of Mary's conception of the Son of God when she was impeccable "filled with new and incomprehensible virtues and graces." There is no analysis of the problem faced by Scotus, nor of the Augustinian legacy.[5] As to Mary's perfection in her mother's womb, the saint is most generous: "In her mother's womb she had the use of free will and perfect light in her intellect and reason . . . According to some she was in a more sublime state of contemplation than was ever any human creature in the fullness of age."[6]

On Mary's virginal consent, B. says that through her consent she reached a higher degree of union with God than would have been achieved by all others gathered in one. "Her merit in conceiving the Son of God exceeded the merits of all pure creatures."[7]

In a sermon entitled characteristically "The superadmirable grace and glory of the Mother of God," B. expounds Mary's unique position and power. A heading says, "What the Blessed Virgin could do for God which God could not do for himself." The bold idea and the series of paradoxes may surprise, even shock, as they did Miss Graef. "God could not beget anyone of himself but God; and nevertheless the Virgin made a Godman. God could only beget what was infinite, immortal, eternal, not sensible not touchable, invisible under the form of God; but the Virgin made him finite, mortal, dependent, temporal, touchable, open to the senses, visible under the form of a servant, his personality under created form." . . . "From the flesh of the Virgin, God, I say it weeping, clothed the loftiest height with lowliness, the sheerest delight with penalty, the greatest wealth with poverty, the purest light with darkness, the greatest honour with insult, what was most lovable with scourging . . . In truth it was in

every way impossible to God the Father to do such a thing from himself. Therefore in this lies the Virgin's prerogative that since God could not do it, he did not concede this to any other creature."[8] The initiative lay with God as the last sentence makes clear. For the apostle of the holy Name of Jesus, all spirituality was essentially Christocentric.

In the sermon on the Purification, B. interprets Mary's act of oblation thus: "For my beloved sons I offer him, that they may be redeemed, expiated, enlightened, instructed, remade, given grace and glorified; I manifest him, for he is the true Lamb who takes away the sins of the world."[9] The logical sequel appears in the account of the Passion of Christ and the compassion of Mary.

Munificentissimus Deus (*qv*) refers to B.'s teaching on the Assumption (*qv*). Therein he was influenced by Pseudo-Augustine (*qv*): "As the flesh of the Son was not subject to corruption . . . Thus the most holy flesh of the Mother, from which the Son's flesh was taken, should not suffer corruption, be burned or reduced to dust." Mary is queen, is above all rulers and powers. Analysing the concept expressed by "Domina," B. shows that her sway extends over the blessed, the demons, those in purgatory and those on earth. For the latter she is especially a queen of mercy.[10]

Mary is the universal Mediatress (*qv*). In this domain B.'s influence is great, as the true heir of St. Bernard whom he likes to quote, as he will be quoted by many subsequent theologians himself. "From the time that she conceived God in her womb, she has had, if I may so express it, a certain jurisdiction or authority in every temporal procession of the Holy Spirit, so that no creature receives any grace of virtue save through the distribution of the same Virgin Mary."[11] From Mary's womb, "as from a kind of ocean of the divinity have flowed the streams and rivers of all graces."[12] Elsewhere, after an analysis of the respective roles of the Son and the Holy Spirit, he concludes: "And since the Mother of the Son of God who produces the Holy Spirit is such, therefore all the gifts, virtues and graces of the Holy Spirit are bestowed through her hands on whom she wills, when she wills, how she wills and as much as she wills."[13] She is our Mother in the truest sense; she stands between us and the wrath of the judge, excusing our frailty, coming to our assistance, as she receives fully on our behalf the influence of the divinity.[14]

[1]*S. Bernardini Sen. opera omnia*, (Quaracchi, ed., 1950), VI, 65-180. For other Marian sermons, see *op. cit.*, II, 153-162, 371-397; IV, 464-484, 537-561. Cf. G. Folgarait, *La Vergine bella in S. Bernardino da Siena*, (Milan, 1939); L. Di Fonzo, O.F.M. Conv., *La Mariologia di S. Bernardino da Siena*, (Rome, 1947), F. Affelt, O.F.M., "The Marian doctrine of Bernardine of Siena," in *Franc. Educ. Conf.*, 35(1954), 196-222; A. Emmen, O.F.M., "San Bernardino e l'Immacolata Concezione di Maria," in *Studi Franc.*, 61(1964), 300-325. [2]*Serm., in Vigilia Nativit. Christi*, in *S. Bernardini Sen. opera omnia*, VII, 16-30. [3]Cf. Emmerich Blondeel d'Izegem, "L'Influence d'Ubertin de Casale sur S. Bernardin," in *Collect. Franciscana*, 5(1935), 5-44. For Marian sermons, cf. *ibid.*, 27-39; for sermon on St. Joseph, cf. *ibid.*, 39ff. [4]*Serm. 61, 1,4*, in *S. Bernardini Sen. opera omnia*, II, 373-374. [5]Cf. A. Emmen, O.F.M., "San Bernardino e l'Immacolata Concezione di Maria," in *Studi Franc.*, 61(1964). On the influence of Ubertino, cf. E. B. d'Izegem, in *Collect. Franciscana*, 5(1935), 30, 37-38; G. Abate, O.F.M., in V.I., VII, 2, 1-13. [6]*Serm. 51, 1, 2*, in *S. Bernardini Sen. opera omnia*, IV, 540. [7]*Serm. 51, 1, 2*, in *S. Bernardini Sen. opera omnia*, IV, 552. [8]*Serm. 61, 1, 4*, in *S. Bernardini Sen. opera omnia*, II, 375-376. [9]Sermon on the Purification, in *S. Bernardini, Sen. opera omnia*, VI, 155-156. [10]*Serm. de glorioso nomine Mariae, 2, 1*, in *S. Bernardini Sen. opera omnia*, VI, 91ff. [11]*Serm. 52 De salut. angel., 1, 2*, in *S. Bernardini Sen. opera omnia*, II, 157. [12]*S. Bernardini Sen. opera omnia*, II, 378. [13]*S. Bernardini Sen. opera omnia*, II, 379. [14]*S. Bernardini Sen. opera omnia*, II, 162.

BERNO OF REICHENAU (d. 1048)

Abbot of the monastery of Reichenau, B. liked to describe himself as the slave or bondsman of Mary. He composed four sermons of interest to Marian theology: on the Nativity of the Lord, and for the Nativity, Purification and Assumption of Our Lady.[1] He has also left a hymn for the Purification. In a letter to the king of Hungary, he exhorted him to have recourse confidently to Mary, "knowing certainly that if you are assiduous in entreaty to her you will be all the more speedily delivered from all difficulty."

[1]Sermons, ed. H. Barré, C.S.Sp., in EphMar, 14(1964), 39-62.

BÉRULLE, PIERRE DE (1575-1629)

Founder of the French Oratory, B. brought the reformed Carmelites to France and through his writings and personal influence began the French school of spirituality. It coincided with a great age of French civilization and with a wide European flowering of Marian doctrine and devotion. It was largely due to B. that French culture in the seventeenth century was not lacking in this distinctive element. In his major works, *Discours de l'état et des grandeurs de Jésus* (1623) and *La Vie de Jésus* (1629), and in other writings, his spiritual ideal of assimilation by the Christian to the "interior states" of Jesus is shown to imply constant advertence to Mary and an attitude of close dependence on her. The essential passages have been assembled in *Les Mystères de Marie* by M. Rigal,[1] which is here followed.

If B. is rightly styled the "apostle of the Word Incarnate," he is also the apostle of the Mother. "Your vocation is to be the Mother of God; to that God called you; with that, without knowing it, you have cooperated from the moment of your birth to the present hour."[2] B. is writing of the Annunciation (*qv*), a mystery he pondered much as it was central to his spiritual outlook. He analyzes the mental state of Mary at the moment of her *fiat*. B. recalls the Eve-Mary parallel. He tells us that "one of the first words of God himself after the sin, concerns the woman and the blessed seed which is to crush the serpent's head, that is Jesus and Mary."[3] He considers *Almah* (see EMMANUEL) a special title of Mary, its meaning being "hidden."[4] She was, he thinks, the first to "raise the standard of virginity."

Yet it is to the Incarnation that he returns preferably, making it the center of his thought. Jesus is living in the Virgin; she is the first soul in which he has established his life. "The Virgin is too linked to her Son not to be conformed and like to him; she is too near and familiar to be ignorant of his state and his secrets."[5]

B.'s view is, in fact, Trinitarian: "Since the most holy Trinity chooses you, O holy Virgin, and associates you with itself in this admirable operation, I cannot forget you in the mystery. I cannot separate what God has joined together in his work, a work in which he deigns to give you a part so great, so honourable, so proper to yourself alone among all creatures."[6] He says again that, in this masterpiece of their power and goodness, they wish to associate the Virgin with themselves, in the greatest of their operations: "As the crown of their glory, love and power wishing to join created being with uncreated being in one of their persons and to give him a new nature, they willed to share the glory of this work between the Virgin and themselves."[7]

Of the Holy Spirit Mary is the sanctuary, of the Son she is the Mother and handmaid. B., like some medievals, sees her as the spouse of the Father (see BRIDE): "He attracts her, he raises her up, he possesses her, he gives her thoughts, movements, disposition suited to the work which must be accomplished."[8] B. then adds some analyses which need to be taken in the entire context of his theology. He says that Mary's *fiat* had a more powerful issue than the divine *fiat* of creation, since this produced the universe, while hers produces the author of the universe. He says that Mary put the Son in a position wherein the Father exercises power over him: "If he is through all eternity the Son of the Father before becoming the Son of the Mother, he is not the Son subject to the Father before being the Son of Mary."[9]

B. believed that Mary being a "universe within the universe" belonged to a separate order from others, "an order related to the hypostatic union, which was a relationship with the divine persons."[10] He believed in the Immaculate Conception (*qv*): "The same moment gave her natural existence, the state of grace and life and movement of grace towards God."[11] Before the Annunciation, God had given her so much grace that "he seems to have exhausted in you his treasures, his favours, his wonders. But he is only beginning if we glance at the graces that followed."[12] She was in a state of "perpetual rapture," her senses, powers, and mind seized by eminent, exalted grace.

Logically B. urged devotion to Mary on those whom he directed spiritually, devotion which he wished to be "interior and spiritual, in no way external and sensible." He counselled his disciples not to separate what God had so divinely joined together, Jesus and Mary. He supported the vow of servitude, which was then current in the Confraternities of Slaves of Mary in Spain—whence B. may have brought it. "To the perpetual honour of the Mother and the Son, I wish to be in the state and quality of servitude with regard to her who has the state and quality of the Mother of my God . . . I give myself to her in the quality of a slave in honour of the gift which the eternal Word made of himself to her in the quality of Son."[13] "In this spirit and to this intention I turn to you, O most holy Virgin and I make to you the entire oblation, absolute and irrevocable of all that I am by the mercy of God, in existence and in the order of nature and of grace, of all that depends on them, of all the actions I shall ever perform."[14]

This practice is based on orthodox doctrine. The same orthodoxy governs B.'s teaching on the relationship between Mary and the priesthood of Christ.[15]

[1]M. Rigal, *Les Mystères de Marie*, in *Coll. Les Lettres Chrétiennes*, (Paris, 1961). Pierre de Bérulle's works ed. by P. Gibieuf with preface by P. Bourgoing, (Paris, 1644), photostat ed. (Paris, 1960), also ed. by Migne (1856). Cf. M. J. Nicolas, "La doctrine mariale du Cardinal de Bérulle," in *Rev. Thom.*, 43(1937), 81-100; Cl. Dillenschneider, C.SS.R., *La Mariologie de St. Alphonse de Liguori*, I, (Fribourg, 1931), 230-234; A. Molien, "Bérulle," in DSp, I, esp. 1559-1561; A. Rayez, S.J., "La dévotion mariale chez Bérulle et ses premiers disciples," in *Maria* III, 31-72; J. Lecuyer, "La Vierge Marie et la formation sacerdotale dans la tradition de l'école Bérullienne," in *Maria*, III, 73-93; Th. Koehler, S.M., "Possibilités de synthèse théologique contenues dans la doctrine mariale de Bérulle et de Gibieuf," in *Apôtre de Marie*, 35(1953), 125-143. On seventeenth century French Marian piety, cf. texts in *Les Grandeurs de Marie d'après les écrivains de l'école française*, ed. A. Molien, (Paris, 1936); C. Flachaire, *La dévotion à la Vierge dans la littérature catholique au commencement du XVIIe siècle*, (Paris, 1916). [2]M. Rigal, *Les Mystères de Marie*, in *Coll. Les Lettres Chrétiennes*, (Paris, 1961), 61. [3]*ibid., op. cit.*, 35. [4]*ibid., op. cit.*, 57. [5]*ibid., op. cit.*, 172. [6]*ibid., op. cit.*, 188. [7]*ibid., op. cit.*, 199. [8]*Vie de Jésus*, in Migne's ed. of Bérulle's works, ch. 7, 437. [9]*Grandeurs de Jésus*, in Migne's ed. of Bérulle's works, XI, 12, 386-387. [10]M. Rigal, *Les Mystères de Marie*, in *Coll. Les Lettres Chrétiennes*, (Paris, 1961), 200. [11]*ibid., op. cit.* [12]*ibid., op cit.* [13]M. Rigal, *Les Mystères de Marie*, in *Coll. Les Lettres Chrétiennes*, 204. [14]*ibid., op. cit.*, 205. [15]Cf. M. Dupuy, *Bérulle et le Sacerdoce*, (Paris, 1960), 113.

BIBLE, THE, AND MARY.

History: Mary lived in a society moulded and informed by the Old Testament; the New Testament was written while witnesses of her life were still living. Both testaments derive their importance from her Son. Within the Church founded by him, Scripture was the basis of reflection on his message and lifework and it was gradually given value as an element in worship. It was a quarry for arguments in the debates among Christians, and between Christians and pagans. The passages referring to Mary occur in the literature of apologetics from the second century (see JUSTIN, ST AND IRENAEUS, ST), in the formal commentaries from the third century (see ORIGEN), and in the homiletics from the fourth century. Treatment of Marian themes would continue in this manifold approach to the Bible, as the volume of patristic publication increased. In the East, the Apocrypha (*qv*) competed for attention since they had a continuing status denied them in the West after St. Jerome's (*qv*) outburst. Hence the investigation of patristic witness to Our Lady turns largely on the Fathers' interpretation of the well-known biblical passages, on concepts like the new Eve (which they drew from reflection on the Bible), and on moral ideals like virginity which they supported from study of Sacred Scripture. Certain feasts like the Conception of St. Anne (see IMMACULATE CONCEPTION), the Nativity of Mary (*qv*), the Presentation of Our Lady (*qv*), and the Dormition were prompted by the Apocrypha, but the *Hypapante* (Presentation of the Lord, *qv*), the Christmas cycle, and the Annunciation of the Lord dictated attention to the gospel texts. We have, therefore, abundant material thus inspired—witness St. Augustine's many Christmas sermons. Not all of the Fathers would go so far as St. Andrew of Crete (*qv*), who saw Mary everywhere in Scripture, or St. Jerome (*qv*) and St. Ambrose (*qv*), who, though more moderate, still showed some freedom in applying Old Testament images to Our Lady.

Use of the Bible in theological speculation went on through the Middle Ages with the differences of approach to be expected from different schools: Palamite in the East; at first monastic, and then scholastic, in the West. Here one major contribution was the twelfth century Marian interpretation of the Song of Songs (*qv*). There were excesses in the age of decline, with a new irruption of the Apocrypha. Controversy would come later, with the Protestant Reformation in fact. The Tridentine decree on Scripture and Tradition, a response to *Scriptura Sola*, a first principle of Protestantism, was hardened with time and possibly misunderstood.[1] But widely divergent assumptions and method marked the opposing theologians.

A new factor appeared in the nineteenth century—papal infallibility, which to Catholics offered a reliable guide in the understanding of the sacred text, but to Protestants seemed one more obstacle to the hearing of God's word. Each side reacted characteristically to the revolution in the historical sciences which broke out about the same time. Modernism within the Catholic body was an offshoot of this revolution—and more. It was dealt with in the centralized way which papal infallibility favoured. An indirect result of this condemnatory and punitive policy was restriction of the area in which Catholic biblical scholars could work. The great Père Lagrange was a near casualty.

Teaching Authority: Since interventions of the highest moment in Marian theology came from the modern Papacy—dated for convenience from Pius IX—and since the Papacy has been constantly active in Marian teaching at every level, we have here a kind of test case of the Bible and the Catholic teaching authority. The manipulation of isolated texts used by authors is absent from *Ineffabilis Deus*, of which the historical section, preliminary to the dogmatic formula, was not rigorously scientific. But the path of Scripture taken in conjunction with Tradition was already indicated.

When, after the Second World War, Catholic biblical scholars began to claim the rights of their trade, it was the Pope of the day, Pius XII, intensely Marian, who gave them their warrant in *Divino Afflante Spiritu* (1943). Seven years later, *Munificentissimus Deus* showed the same caution in the use of biblical texts, a still stronger tendency to interpret Scripture and Tradition as inter-related, not two separate "sources," and a generally more scientific character. Despite minor upheavals, this position was ratified in the teaching of Vatican II, *Constitution on Divine Revelation* (1965). The Council taught, and, in its Marian teaching practised, a doctrine on the supreme value of Sacred Scripture. It incorporated the ideas of the document issued by the Pontifical Biblical Commission, *On the Historical Truth of the Gospels* (1964). Biblical criticism is fully recognized.

Recent Trends: Within the world of Catholic scholarship certain problems and tensions were the background to these acts aforementioned. From decade to decade publications reflect the changed attitude. Exegesis and interpretation of Marian biblical texts are part of the pattern. Thus, contributors to the two conspicuous examples of Catholic biblical scholarship, the *Bible de Jérusalem* and the *Jerome Biblical Commentary* (1968), included writers on biblical Marian texts or themes. The Catholic biblical reviews, *Révue Biblique*, *Biblica*, *Estudios Biblicos*, *Rivista Biblica*, *Catholic Biblical Quarterly*, have carried work on these subjects. On the other hand, the scientific Marian reviews, *Marianum* and *Ephemerides Mariologicae*, have not neglected Old Testament or New Testament problems.

Chapter VIII in *Lumen Gentium* marked a change in presentation of Marian theology by its deliberate initial treatment of biblical topics. R. Laurentin (*qv*) had pioneered this break with the traditional doctrinal presentation in his *Court Traité de théologie mariale* (1953), which appeared simultaneously as a book and as part of the collective work of the new theology, *Initiation Théologique*. As in all such productions, a vast background of academic exercises such as dissertations and the like of library facilities and of scholarly exchange is rightly assumed. From an early date, the French Society for Marian Studies invited biblical scholars to its annual session. These communications were in some cases the seeds of important monographs.

Vatican Council II brought to a head, in Marian as in other departments of theology, the conflict between dogmatic and biblical theologians. A solution was sought resolutely and immediately in the first International Mariological Congress held after the Council, at San Domingo. The theme was *Mary in Sacred Scripture*, and several papers by well-known scholars dealt with the dual approach.[2] A formal statement of agreement by those following both disciplines was issued.[3]

With respect to the Old Testament, each relevant passage is dealt with separately. Literature on some is very abundant. The following division has been suggested: texts applicable to Mary only by accommodation, Jud 15:9, Prov 8, Sir 24; texts of debatable relevance, Jer 31:22, Ps 45, the Song of Songs; texts certainly relevant, Gen 3:15, Is 7:14, Mic 5:2.[4] Study of these different texts enables us to avoid the extremes of those who deny any reference to Mary in the Old Tesament and advocates of a universal Marian presence. Vatican II also pointed to the strong moral link between Old Testament concept of the "Poor of the Lord," the *anawim*, and Mary (LG 55); it also approved typology of **recent interest, describing emphatically the ancient Mary-Eve typology. (See EVE-MARY.)**[5]

With respect to the New Testament, each passage is dealt with and an attempt is made to make a fair selection from the immense bibliographies. Here, as in Old Testament subjects, confessional divisions no longer impede research. Protestants as well as Catholics investigate the subject.[6] With a few exceptions, there has been little Jewish or Jewish-Christian writing on Mary.[7] And little to offset the immense quasi-monopoly of western thinking, which itself has possibly suffered from conceit in its own mental categories because of lack of competition. One has only to recall the unhealthy cult of R. Bultmann before the critical attack of the Swedes.

Extra-biblical sources have been used, and will probably be increasingly used, in study of the New Testament as of the Old Testament— the Targums and Qumran notably. Apart from a few texts, the question whether there may be unanimous solutions of the critical and exegetical problems seems itself unanswerable. For even results on which unanimity now may exist have no guarantee of enduring acceptance.[8] We have also to await agreement among exegetes on the senses of Scripture, especially on the *sensus plenior*, which has relevance for the Marian texts.[9] But all texts are being dealt with—those referring, for example, to the "Brothers of the Lord," or those used polemically against Our Lady (see articles on *Matthew, Mark, Luke*). It will remain a subject for speculation why all that the Old Testament and New Testament contain on Mary should be, by quantitative standards, so slight in proportion to the entire contents of the Bible.[10]

---

[1]Cf. J. McHugh, The Mother of Jesus in the New Testament, (London, 1975); *Schrift und Tradition*, in *Mariologische Studien*, I, (Essen, 1962); *De Scriptura et Traditione*, ed. C. Balic, (Rome, 1963). [2]MSS, I-V. [3]On Mary in the Bible, cf. F. Ceuppens, *De Mariologia Biblica*, 2nd ed., (Rome, 1951); L. Deiss, C.S.Sp., *Marie, Fille de Sion*, (Bruges, 1959); M. Peinador, *Los temas de la Mariologia Bíblica*, (Madrid, 1963); Ortensio da Spinetoli, *Maria nella Tradizione Biblica*, 3rd ed., (Bologna, 1967); MSS, I, 119-120; DCath, (1965), 713. [4]Cf. C. Pozzo, S.J., *Maria en la obra de la Salvación*, (Madrid, BAC, 1974), 126-201. [5]On Old Testament, cf. Pozzo, *Maria*, as in Note 4; A. Robert, "La Sainte Vierge dans l'Ancien Testament," in *Maria*, I, 21-39; E. May, "Mary in the Old Testament," in J. Carol, *Mariology*, I, 51-79; J. Coppens, "La Mère du Sauveur a la Lumière de la Théologie vétero-testamentaire," in ETL, 31(1955), 7-20; A. Feuillet, "De fundamento Mariologiae in prophetis Veteris Testamenti," in MOE, 33-48; R. Laurentin, *Traité*, V, 161-167; P. Franquesa, "Estudios exegéticos sobre los textos bíblicos de Antiguo Testamento en el capitulo VIII de la 'Lumen Gentium'," in EstMar, 32(1969), 51-79. [6]Cf. Max Thurian, *Mary, Mother of the Lord, Figure of the Church*, (London, 1963); H. A. Oberman, "The Virgin Mary in Evangelical Perspective," in *Journ. Ec. St.*, 1(1964), 271-298; B. Roux, "Bilan de l'Ecriture au point de vue protestant," in BSFEM, 20(1963), 39-63; H. Räisänen, *Die Mutter Jesu im Neuen Testament*, (Helsinki, 1969). [7]See article JEWS, THE; cf. Robert Aron, *Les Années obscures de Jésus*, (Paris, 1960). [8]On the New Testament, cf. P. Gaechter, *Maria im Erdenleben*, 2nd ed., (Innsbruck, 1954); J. J. Weber, *La Vierge Marie dans le Nouveau Testament*, (Paris, 1951); J. Galot, *Marie dans l'Evangile*, (Paris, 1958, tr. *Mary in the Gospel*, Westminster, Maryland, 1965); A. Feuillet, "La Vierge Marie dans le Nouveau Testament," in *Maria*, VI, 15-69; C. Pozzo, S.J., *Maria en la obra de la Salvación*, (Madrid, BAC, 1974), 202-246; J. McHugh, *The Mother of Jesus in the New Testament*, (London, 1975); R. Laurentin, *Traité*, V, 18-40; *Mary in the New Testament*, (London, 1978); MM, 40(1978), I-II (entire issue), III-IV (several articles). MM, 41(1979), I-IV (several articles). [9]On the *sensus plenior*, cf. R. E. Brown, *The sensus plenior of Sacred Scripture*, (Baltimore, 1955); Jerome Comm., II, 615-618. [10]Cf. J. H. Newman, *Parochial and Plain Sermons*, II, (London, 1840), 135; Francisco Suarez, *De mysteriis vitae Christi* in *Opera Omnia*, 19, 1-3.

BIBLIOGRAPHY
Down to the present century, bibliographies of Marian literature have been attempted, and collections made of writings which approximate to bibliography—for example the works of I. Marracci, P. Alva y Astorga, and Agoston Roskovany whose nine-volume work on the Immaculate Conception quoted 30,000 Marian writings.[1] In 1891, M. Tavagnutti published in Vienna *Mariologische Bibliographie*, an ordered account of publications between the years 1837 and 1890. The *Marianum* Institute prompted, soon after its inception, a beginning in scientific bibliography. This was brought to an admirable issue in the successive volumes compiled and edited by G. M. Besutti, O.S.M.,[2] who was for many years simultaneously editor of the review. Besutti has given shorter selected bibliographies in different publications, each marked by the same excellence as his major work.[3]

Very many Marian publications have adopted the most rigorously scientific standards in bibliography. All those most frequently cited in the present work do so. Interest in Marian literature has also led to the establishment of specialized libraries on the subject in all its ramifications, at Louvain (removed from its original site at Banneux); at Dayton, Ohio (40,000 items); at the *Marianum* Institute, Rome (20,000 items); and at Lerida in Spain. Those in charge of these libraries and of other public and private Marian collections are well served by reviews of Marian literature in the specifically Marian reviews—*Marianum* and *Ephemerides Mariologicae* and in *La Revue des Sciences Philosophiques et Théologiques*.

[1]Cf. G. M. Roschini, O.S.M., *Maria Santissima*, I, 204-232.
[2]*Bibliografia Mariana*, I, 1948-1950, II, 1950-1951, III, 1952-1957, IV, 1958-1966, V, 1967-1972. [3]"Panorama Bibliografico," in *Theotocos, Enciclopedia Mariana*, 2nd ed., (Genoa-Milan, 1958), 883-918; "Panorama Bibliografico," in *Maria Mistero di Grazia*, (Rome, Teresianum, 1975), 304-334; "Saggio di introduzione alla bibliografia mariana dei secoli," I-V, in PCM, V, 247-287.

BIEL, GABRIEL (*c.* 1410-1495)
One of the last of the scholastics, a nominalist, B. treated extensively of Our Lady in his writings.[1] He defended the Immaculate Conception, and other established truths about Mary, whom he thought the Queen of Heaven, the "gate of heaven," the hope of all. Mary, he thought, cooperated in the passion of Christ. He was under the influence of Gerson, and echoed a famous phrase of St. Bernard in one passage:

"God did not wish us to have anything which would not pass through the hands of Mary . . . through whom all grace flows upon us; all salvation and redemption is consummated through her."[2]

[1]Cf. H. A. Oberman, "Mariology," in *The Harvest of Medieval Theology*, (Harvard University Press, 1963), ch. IX, 281-322.

BIRTH OF JESUS, THE
Mt 2:1 and Lk 2:4,6-7 state that Jesus was born in Bethlehem. Each evangelist also places the infancy in the days of king Herod, Mt 2:1,19; Lk 1:5 and since he died in 4 B.C. Jesus must have been born before that date. From the second century tradition in the Apocrypha (*qv*) mentions Bethlehem; St. Justin Martyr, a Palestinian (*qv*) in the same age refers to a "certain cave nigh the village."

Scholars debate the text in Lk 2:1-2: "In those days a decree went out from Caesar Augustus that all the world should be enrolled. This was the first enrolment, when Quirinius was governor of Syria." The details of this debate do not concern us here and the reader is referred to the most recent literature.[1] The significance of the birth story for a theology of the Blessed Virgin Mary lies in the stress it places on Mary's authentic human motherhood, and, through the presence of Joseph, the legal father, on the guarantee of Jesus' incorporation in the Davidic line, on his right to the kingly inheritance promised to the descendant of David.

[1]For discussion and bibliographies cf. R. E. Brown, *The Birth*, pp. 393-431; 513-516; 547-556; *Mary in NT*, pp. 143-152.

BLATHMAC (eighth century)
In 1964, Professor James Carney published for the Irish Texts Society poems by Blathmac, son of Cu Brettan, a Gaelic poet; the editor had discovered them in a seventeenth-century manuscript in the National Library of Ireland.[1] The poet was an eight-century monk with sound knowledge of the Scriptures and of the apocryphal material current in Ireland at the time. The first poem is of 149 stanzas—it may once have contained the mystic 150; the second has 109, again possibly out of 150. The theme of the first poem is lamentation with Mary for the suffering and death of her Son. In the second, the thought is of the victorious Christ, his judgment and his avenging of innocent blood.

The lamentation reveals striking personal relationship between Mary and the poet: "Come

BONAVENTURE

to me, loving Mary, that I may lament with you your very dear one. Alas that your Son should go to the cross, he who was a great diadem, a beautiful hero." B. wishes that "as far as every sea they would come with you and me to lament your royal Son . . . that they might lament on every hill-top the King who created every star." "Come to me, loving Mary, head of pure faith that we may hold converse with the compassion of unblemished heart. Come." The poet relies on Mary's intercession for himself and for others, and the *Lorica*, or protection note, appears. The judgment theme in the second poem is directed to Christ as Mary's Son: "It is by your Son—enduring deed—that many thousands will be struck down into the great fire before the Lord passes judgment on the deeds of all."[2]

---

[1]J. Carney, *The Poems of Blathmac, Son of Cu Brettan*, Irish Texts Society, 47. Cf. D. Flanagan, in Zagreb Congress, III, 265-275. [2]Excerpts *apud* D. Flanagan, in Zagreb Congress, III.

BONAVENTURE, ST. (1221-1274)

The Marian teaching of the great Franciscan, the Seraphic Doctor, was the product of a rich personality, professor of theology in the University of Paris, an authority on the contemplative life, and Master General of his order for seventeen years. Theology of Our Lady is found in: the commentary on the *Sentences* of Peter Lombard; commentaries on gospels of St. Luke and St. John; the *Collationes de donis Spiritus Sancti*; in various other works, and particularly in twenty-four sermons on Our Lady.[1] One of the latter, the sixth sermon on the Assumption[2], is probably spurious and so is a passage in the fourth on the Annunciation. Further critical research may eliminate more material. Among the recognized apocrypha of the saint, there are several Marian pieces. For centuries the *Speculum beatae Mariae Virginis* of Conrad of Saxony was attributed to him.

B. was much influenced by St. Bernard, to whom there are hundreds of references in B.'s works. Thus B. denied the Immaculate Conception (qv), thinking the opposite view "more commonly held, more reasonable and safer." He did not think it impossible, but thought it was fitting only to the "One through whom was wrought the salvation of all."[3] He feared that "while the excellence of the Mother was being

magnified, the glory of the Son might be diminished."[4] Caught in the web of Augustine's theory about the transmission, and thinking that only the Son, conceived by the Holy Ghost and born of the Virgin, could escape the original contagion, B. was at pains to attribute every other kind of perfection to Mary. She was the temple of God, made by divine power, adorned by divine wisdom, consecrated by divine grace, and filled with the divine presence. She exceeds all praise and devotion—even Scripture is inadequate in her praise. Sanctified in the womb, "she had all virtues most perfectly."[5] Whatever dignity or glory was partially given to the saints, was granted in its fullness to her.[6]

B. like his contemporaries dealt with the problem of Mary's merit (qv) in becoming Mother of God (qv), with some refinements of his own. Before the Annunciation (qv), she merited it with the merit of suitability, but with condign merit after the Annunciation and the descent of the Spirit upon her. In the latter way also she merited the remote preparation for the conception of Christ. But her greatness depended on Christ: "The Creator of all things rested, therefore, in the tabernacle of the virginal womb, since there he settled his bridal chamber that he might become our brother, he prepared a royal throne that he might become our prince, he assumed priestly ornament that he might become our pontiff. Because of the marriage union she is the Mother of God; because of the royal seat the Queen of heaven; because of the priestly ornament, advocate of the human race."[7] Mary, he adds, was suited to all this since she was of the race of men, of the race of kings, of the race of priests.

B. recalls the Eve-Mary parallel: "That woman namely Eve, drives us out of paradise and sells us, this one leads us back and buys us."[8] He recalls too the Eve-Church parallel—Eve from the side of Adam, the Church from the dying Christ on the Cross—and ends: "And as Abel and his successors were formed from Adam and Eve, so from Christ and his Church was formed the whole Christian people. And as Eve is the mother of Abel and of all of us, so the Christian people has the Virgin for mother."[9]

Mary liberates the whole human race. Christ, the price of our redemption, was taken from her, paid by her and is now possessed by her. She was present on Calvary when the price was being paid, "and she agreed that the price from her womb should be offered on the Cross for us,"... "accepting and agreeing with the divine will."[10] Understandably then, B. quotes liberally from St. Bernard: "All graces pass through the hands of Mary";[11] "she was as the aqueduct by which the incarnate Son of God came down to us"[12]; "Mary, this star of the sea"; "Mediatress between us and Christ." "For she," B. said, "found glory for herself and for others, because through her the gate of heaven was opened to us; for as through her, God came down to us, so it is right that through her we should ascend to God."[13]

As devotion, B. recommends praise of Mary, in whose bodily Assumption he believed. He appeals to the experience of those who practiced devotion to Mary: "I have never read of any saint who did not have a special devotion to the glorious Virgin . . . Those who are rooted in the Virgin Mother by love and devotion are sanctified, because she obtains their sanctification from her Son."[14] He associated Mary with Eucharistic piety: "Since through her this most sacred body has been given to us, so through her hands it should be offered and received in the sacrament, which is presented to us, and was born of her womb."[15]

[1]For bibliography, cf. *S. Bonaventura*, (Rome, 1974— seventh centenary volumes), V, 686; V. Plesser, O.F.M., "Die Lehre des hl. B. uber die Mittleschaft Mariens," in FranzSt, 23(1936), 353-389; L. di Fonzo, O.F.M.Conv., *Doctrina S. B. de universali mediatione Beatae Virginis Mariae*, (Rome, 1938); id., "De corporea Assumpt. B.V.M. ejusque gloria caelesti juxta S.B.," in MM, 1(1939), 327-350; E. Chiettinin, O.F.M., *Mariologia S. Bonaventurae*, (Sibenici-Rome, 1941); S. P. Titus, "Doctrina S. B. de mediatione B.V.M. quoad omnes gratias," in ASC, II, 293-318. Sermons, *Opera Omnia*, Quaracchi ed., vol. IX, 633-727. [2]Cf. J. Beumer, S.J., "Eine dem hl. Bonaventura zu Unrecht zugeschriebene Marienpredigt? Literarkritische Untersuchung des Sermo VI, 'De assumptione B. Virginis Mariae'," in FranzSt, 42(1960); ibid., "Die literarischen Beziehungen zwischen dem Sermo VI de Assumptione B.M.V. (Pseudo-Bonaventura) und dem Mariale oder Laus Virginis (Pseudo-Albertus)," in FranzSt, 44(1962), 455-460. [3]In Sent. III, d. 3, pt. 1, q. 2, Opera Omnia, III, 69. [4]op. cit., d. 3, pt. 1, q. 2, Opera Omnia, III, 68. [5]Serm. I, in Purif., Opera Omnia, IX, 638a. [6]Serm. II de Assumpt., Opera Omnia, IX, 692b. [7]Serm. IV de Annunt., Opera Omnia, IX, 672a. [8]Coll. de Donis Sp. S., 6, 14, Opera Omnia, V, 486. [9]op. cit., 20, V, 487. [10]op. cit., 15, V, 486. [11]Serm. IV de Annunt., Opera Omnia, IX, 672a-673b. [12]Serm. VIII in Pent., Opera Omnia, IX, 340b. [13]De Nativit. III, Opera Omnia, IX, 713b. [14]Serm. II de Purif., Opera Omnia, IX, 642a. [15]Serm. III de Corp. Christi, Opera Omnia, V, 559b.

BOSSUET, JACQUES BÉNIGNE (1627-1704) Sacred orator and outstanding prelate of the French "great century," B. put his own personal stamp on the Marian thought so prominent in his age and country: sobriety in conception; broad humanism; and theological expansiveness. His Marian doctrine is found in twenty-three sermons, in passages of the *Elévations sur les Mystéres*, in two works of controversy on the Emmanuel (qv) prophecy in Isaiah and on the Apocalypse, and in certain draft compositions and fragments. His two sermons on St. Joseph (qv) rank with other important texts of the century on the saint.[1]

B. wished his devotion to Our Lady free of doubtful narratives, apocryphal revelations, and uncertain argument or exaggeration. His basic principle was: "Let us accustom ourselves to judge her not by what a creature can claim, but by the dignity of her Son."[2] The great preacher spoke of her as an advance sketch of the future Christ. She was conceived immaculate, through the grace of Christ's redemption. Her union with Christ is entirely singular: "Jesus Christ gives himself so much to her that one can say that the common treasure of all men becomes her particular possession."[3] Hence too his idea of the special relationship between Mary and the Father: "His generaton in time must be a very pure image of his chaste generation in eternity. Only the Father could render Mary fruitful with his own Son; since this Son would be common to her and to God, God had to bestow upon her his own fruitfulness."[4] Bérulle (qv) and Olier (qv) would extend this idea and call Mary spouse of the Father, as did some medieval writers (see BRIDE, MARY AS). B. does use the bridal metaphor and the language of the Song of Songs in one of the passages wherein he seeks, with acknowledged sense of the mystery, to describe the relations of love between Mary and Jesus. On her life after the Ascension he writes: "The continual miracle was that Mary could live separated from her beloved."[5] When she did join him, it was in the glory of body and soul: "She was then raised up, most innocent Mary. No, the corruption did not dare touch this virginal body from which the conqueror of death was drawn."[6]

In the *Elévations*, B. points to the ancient doctrine of the new Eve as the foundation of the Church's devotion to Mary.[7] He draws out the parallel in detail in, among other sermons, that on the compassion of the holy Virgin.[8] Her saving role and her spiritual motherhood he bases both on the consent (qv) and on her presence on Calvary. "It was necessary to men that Mary should desire their salvation."[9] "We are those to whose salvation she consented when she said 'Let it be done to me according to your word'. She carried all of us in her womb with Jesus Christ, in whom we were."[10] The latter idea, implicit in St. Ambrose's (qv) writings, appears through the ages, and is found in Ad diem illum (qv).

These separate elements B. gathered together in one passage often quoted: "God having once willed to give us Jesus Christ through the Blessed Virgin, the gifts of God are without repentance and this his order does not change. It is and always will be true that having received through her charity the universal principle of grace, we should still receive through her intervention [entremise] the different applications in all the different states which make up the Christian life. Her maternal charity having contributed so much to our salvation in the mystery of the Incarnation, which is the universal principle of grace, she will contribute to it eternally in all the other operations which are but the consequences of it."[11]

---

[1] Bossuet's works, Oeuvres complètes, in ed. by F. Lachat, (Paris, 1862); also Oeuvres Oratoires de Bossuet, ed. by J. Lebarcq, later by Urbain and Levesque, (this ed. here quoted). Cf. P. Angers, S.J., "La Doctrine mariale de Bossuet," in Maria, III, 235-250; E. Janssens, La dévotion mariale de Bossuet, (Liège, 1946) [2] "Premier sermon pour la fête de la Nativité de la Sainte Vierge," in Oeuvres Oratories, III, 68. [3] "Deuxième sermon pour la fête de la Conception de la Sainte Vierge," in Oeuvres Oratoies, II, 256. [4] "Deuxième sermon pour la fête de la Visitation," in Oeuvres Oratoires, II, 207. [5] "Deuxième sermon pour la fête de l'Assumption," in Oeuvres Oratoires, IV, 507. [6] "Address for the vigil of the Assumption," in Oeuvres Oratoires, I, 66. [7] Elévations, 5, in Oeuvres complètes, ed. by F. Lachat, VII, 205. [8] Oeuvres Oratoires, II, 6. For other references, cf. op. cit., vol. I, 385-388, vol. III, 445-447, vol. I, 89, 183, vol. II, 300, 302, 309. [9] "Troisième sermon pour la fête de la Conception de la Sainte Vierge," in Oeuvres Oratoires, V, 603. [10] Elévations, 14, 8, in Oeuvres complètes. [11] "Troisième sermon pour la fête de la Conception de la Sainte Vierge," V, 604.

BOUDON, HENRI-MARIE (1624-1702)

Archdeacon of Evreux, B. contributed to the literature of his age on Mary. The influence of Bérulle (qv) is seen in his works. Those relevant to Marian theology are: Dieu seul ou le saint esclavage de l'admirable Mère de Dieu[1], an apologia for the slavery of love towards the Blessed Virgin; Les grands secours de la divine providence par la très Sainte Vierge, Mère de Dieu, invoquée sous le titre de Notre Dame du Remède[2], an aspect of Mary's universal mediation; and Avis catholiques touchant la véritable dévotion de la bienheureuse Vierge[3], an item in the controversy started by Les Avis Salutaries (qv). Here, B. was replying to La dévotion à la Vierge et le culte qui lui est dû (1693), a book by A. Baillet written in answer to sermons by Bourdaloue. B. was moderate and charitable; he used the ideas of Les Avis Salutaires, adding the modifications and nuances which Adam Widenfeld had omitted.

---

[1] Oeuvres Complètes, ed. by Migne, (Paris, 1856), II, 370-586. Cf. Cl. Dillenschneider, C.SS.R., La Mariologie de St. Alphonse de Liguori, I, (Fribourg, 1931), 242-246; P. Hoffer, La Dévotion à Marie au déclin du XVIIe siècle, (Paris, 1938), 259. [2] Oeuvres Complètes, II, 755ff. [3] Oeuvres Complètes, I, 327-377.

BOURASSÉ, J. J. (1813-1870)

A professor of dogmatic theology and an archaeologist, J. J. Bourassé published, in 1862, in collaboration with J. P. Migne (qv), thirteen large volumes entitled Summa aurea de laudibus B.M.V. It was a collection of works by different authors on every aspect of Marian history, liturgy, patrology, biography, "relics," iconography, scholastic theology, controversy, and ecclesiastical teaching. It is principally consulted for the works of St. Peter Canisius (qv), some of those by I. Marracci (qv), and one by Peter Alva y Astorga (qv), which are reproduced. In general the compilation is marred by a lack of critical standards and by injudicious selection of materials.

BOURLDAOUE, LOUIS, S.J. (1632-1704)

A sacred orator highly esteemed in France of his day, B. preached on the feasts of the Annunciation, the Assumption, and the Immaculate Conception. He sought a middle course in the contemporary controversies. In 1691, late in the day, in sermons on the Assumption and the Immaculate Conception (qqv) he defended Catholic doctrine against Les Avis Salutaires (qv).[1] He shows how the titles of Mediatress (qv) and Restorer (Réparatrice) are compatible with the dignity of the unique Mediator. Recalling that we were saved by the blood of Christ, he goes on "but we cannot overlook the fact that Mary provided, offered, delivered for us the blood which served as our ransom, for it is on this that the whole Church has taken its stand to qualify her as Mediatress and Restorer of men." Also, "God's helper in the achievement of our salvation is Mary and as salvation began through her and through her consent to God's word, it is through her cooperation that it must be fulfilled."[2] B. likewise shows the sound theological sense of accepting the doctrines of the Immaculate Conception and the Assumption. He dealt skillfully with a problem sometimes presented in a loaded manner: should sinners be encouraged to pray to Our Lady? Yes, for through prayer to her they may acquire repentance; they should not be told that prayer to her will benefit them if they remain in sin.

[1]*Oeuvres Complètes*, (Paris, Vivès, 1876), III, 238-244; IV, 209-231. Cf. Cl. Dillenschneider, C.SS.R., *La Mariologie de St. Alphonse de Liguori*, I, (Fribourg, 1931), 139-145; P. Hoffer, S.M., *La Dévotion à Marie au déclin du XVIIe siècle*, (Paris, 1938), 254-256; E. Griselle, *Bourdaloue: Histoire critique de sa prédication*, (Paris, 1901). [2]*Oeuvres Complètes*, (Paris, Vivès, 1876), III, 240, 243.

BRIDGET OF SWEDEN, ST. (1303-1373)

Widow of a Swedish nobleman, foundress of a religious order of the Most Holy Saviour, B. was known for her revelations.[1] She also composed the *Sermo Angelicus de Virginis Excellentia*, twenty-one readings covering the life of Mary, with theology interwoven and intended for the Office of her religious. A Franciscan tertiary, B. had the ideas of the Franciscan school on Mary's place in the divine plan, and on the Immaculate Conception (*qv*) (which Mary herself reveals).[2] B. had her own idea on Mary's six sorrows: of knowledge, because Mary foreknew the Passion; of hearing, when she heard Jesus insulted; of sight, when she saw him crucified (she swooned, B. thought); of touch, when she wound him in burial cloths; of desire, when she wished to accompany him to heaven at the Ascension; and of compassion in the sufferings of the Apostles.[3] Mary's importance in the Redemption appears in one revelation: "I dare to say that the sorrow of my Son was my sorrow, all the more as his heart was my heart, for as Adam and Eve sold the world for an apple, in like manner my dear Son and I bought back the world, as it were, with one

heart."[4] B. believed that the risen Jesus appeared first to his Mother; that she remained on for fifteen years to help the infant Church; and when she died (some days, or fifteen days after), she was assumed bodily into heaven. She is Queen of Heaven, Mother of the elect and of those in Purgatory, Mother of Mercy. B. calls her *salvatrix*.[5] Her intercession is powerful; all graces come to us through her. The revelations were widely read. They influenced such writers as Luke Wadding (*qv*), who mentions B.'s revelation on the Immaculate Conception in his memorandum to the Pope, Denis the Carthusian (*qv*), and St. Alphonsus Liguori (*qv*), who frequently refers to her.

[1]Cf. H. Redpath, *God's Ambassadress*, (Milwaukee, 1947); *Revelationes*, ed. by G. Durante, 2 vols., (Rome, 1628); *Revelaciones Extravagantes*, ed. by L. Hollman, (Uppsala, 1956); *Sermo Angelicus, Opera minora II*, ed. by Sten Eklund, (Uppsala, 1972). Cf. F. Vernet, in DSp, I, (1943); B. Thierry d'Argenlieu, O.P., in *Maria*, IV, 401-414; H. Graef, *Mary*, I, 309-310. [2]*Revel.*, 6, 49. [3]*Revel.*, 6, 57. [4]*Revel.*, 1, 35. [5]*Revelaciones Extravagantes*, ed. by L. Hollman, (Uppsala, 1956), 56, 14.

BROTHERS OF JESUS

The New Testament texts which refer to brothers or a brother of Jesus or the Lord are: (a) Mt 12:46-50, Mk 3:31-35, Lk 8:19-21; (b) Mt 13:55-56, Mk 6:3; (c) Jn 2:12, 7:3,5,10; (d) Mt 28:10, Jn 20:17; (e) Acts 1:14; (f) 1 Cor 9:5; (g) Gal 1:19.

Interpretation of these passages is relevant to the fact of Mary's virginity.

The (a) texts report the incident of Jesus' Mother and "brothers" asking for him as he preached. The (b) texts related the sequel to Jesus' preaching in the synagogue in his own district. Luke (who specifies Nazareth) has at this point no mention of the brothers named by Matthew (13:55) and Mark (6:3) as James and Joseph (Joses in Mark), Simon and Juda but reports the question: "Is not this the son of Joseph?" This is to be understood in relation to the infancy narrative, and to "the son of Joseph, as was supposed," at the beginning of Lk 3. In the (c) texts come the mentions found in John of the brothers of Jesus who went to Capharnaum with him after the Cana (*qv*) episode, and appear again urging him to go up to Jerusalem "so that your disciples will see the works you do." "For even his brothers did not believe in him," we read. What is said of "my brothers" by the risen Lord, as recorded in the (d) texts is not generally considered when this queston is being discussed; there may be a link with Jn 7:5 and the same word, *adelphos*, is used as in all other texts. In Acts, there is a brief account of the disciples persevering together in prayer, "with Mary, the mother of Jesus and his brothers." Paul speaks of the "brothers of the Lord" in 1 Cor and of "James, the Lord's brother," in Gal.

How to interpret these texts is a problem debated since patristic times. *Adelphos* (found in every instance) means a blood brother, but its usage in the New Testament is vastly extended. Acts 1:15 says that Peter stood up in the midst of the "brothers." He addressed them as "Men brothers," a very common form of address. *Adelphos* occurs in the epistles and in Revelation with the same general sense—in such striking phrases as "he [Christ] appeared to more than 500 brothers at one time" (1 Cor 15:6) and "that he might be the first-born among many brothers" (Rom 8:29). Silvanus is described as "a faithful brother" (1 Pet 5:2); Paul speaks of a Christian as "one who bears the name of brother" (1 Cor 5:11).

Hebrew and Aramaic have no word for cousin, and the Hebrew word *'ah* (brother) is used in the Old Testament for kinsman, translated by the Septuagint as *adelphos*. Greek had the word *anepsios* for cousin (Col 4:10) but the influence of the Septuagint would dictate use of the other word. Papyri from contemporary Egypt show similar use.

Some of the gospels were written while the "brothers of the Lord" were still living; so were Acts and other New Testament works. Precise relationship of these "brothers" to Jesus is difficult to establish with certainty. They could not have been children of Mary born before Jesus, for at the time she was a virgin (see VIRGINITY OF MARY); he was her first-born (Mt 1:25 and Lk 2:7). Tertullian (*qv*), Helvidius, Jovinian and Bonosus in the third and fourth century held that they were children of Mary born after Jesus. She is never called their mother, however, nor is there mention of them in the episode of the Passover feast when Jesus was twelve years old. It would be unthinkable for a Jewish mother to leave her children at home so that she might travel. In Mk 3:20-21 and Jn 7:2-5, the relatives or brothers of Jesus, are shown telling him what to do. This would be impossible if they were younger brothers of the same family; nor would there be any sense, on this assumption, in the commendation of Mary to John (Jn 19:27). Mt 27:56 and Mk 15:40 name the mother of two of the "brothers" James and Joseph in Matthew, James the Younger and Joses in Mark. She is certainly not Mary, the Mother of Jesus. Significantly too, Mark (who has no infancy narrative) felt it proper before naming the "brothers" to describe Jesus as "the Son of Mary" (6:3). Whenever he and the other evangelists speak of the "brothers" in Mary's company, none, directly or indirectly, relates their birth to her. The association is during the public ministry.

Of the four ancient writers who thought that the "brothers" were Mary's sons, Tertullian eventually left the Church and the other three were repudiated officially in their time.[1] Jovinian is remembered because he entered the life of St. Ambrose (*qv*); Helvidius, because his short work—now lost—prompted a reply by St. Jerome (*qv*).[2] Jerome did not cling fast to all the details of his theory,[3] but certain points which he made remain valid; e.g., his explanation of the text "[Joseph] knew her not until she had borne a son" (Mt 1:25). On the analogy of many similar texts, he showed that this did not mean that Joseph knew her afterwards.

Another opinion which originated in the Apocrypha (*qv*), appealed to some early writers, notably Origen (*qv*), and was taken up by St. Epiphanius (*qv*). It was that the "Brothers of the Lord" were sons of Joseph by a former marriage. In the West this view was supported by St. Hilary of Poitiers (*qv*) and Ambrosiaster (*qv*). Its foremost defender in modern times is J. B. Lightfoot.[4] There is no evidence whatsoever for it in the gospels. Nowhere, directly or indirectly, are the "Brothers of Jesus" called the sons of Joseph. The authors of the infancy narratives were insistent on his Davidic ancestry. Any sons of his, therefore, were Davidides, who could not be casually overlooked—who could, in fact, compromise the succession of Jesus to Joseph's Davidic rights. Failure to mention Jews of such religious, political and social importance in such a context would be highly improbable. Rarely if ever, moreover, did a son take his father's name among the Jews—a fact which excludes one of the "Brothers."[5]

The way in which the theory developed excludes them all. Origen noted that the apocryphal *The Gospel according to Peter* (of which the relevant part is still lost) and *The Book of James* (the *Protevangelium*), prompted the theory, since they spoke of a former marriage. The only one of the two works available to us does indeed speak of this marriage but does not identify the sons. In a subsequent apocryphon, *The Infancy Story of Thomas* (c.200, but not earlier), an identification is made in an incident involving an alleged son of Joseph—James. *The History of Joseph the Carpenter*, later still (c. 400), cites four names—Jude, Joset, James and Simon in the Coptic version; Jude, Justus, James and Simon in the Arabic. Names of two sisters are also given, Lysia and Lydia (Coptic), Assia and Lydia (Arabic).[6] It is a typical example of accretions to a legend.

When St. Epiphanius undertook to organize such dubious material, he gave Joseph eighty years of age at the time of his marriage to Mary. If his first marriage had taken place when he was under thirty, his sons would be, during the public ministry of Jesus, about eighty.[7]

The problem of the "brothers'" relationship to Jesus still remains. St. Jerome's theory of cousins through their mother has prevailed for a long time. With reassessment of the evidence, especially from Hegesippus (a second century Palestinian Christian whose Memoirs are partially found in the *Historia Ecclesiastica* of Eusebius of Caeserea),[8] Fr. Blinzler concludes his patient, exhaustive account with this judgment: "The so-called brothers and sisters of Jesus were male and female cousins. The relationship of Simon and Jude with Jesus occurs through their father Klopas and thus these were Davidides; their mother's name is unknown. The mother of the Lord's brothers, James and Joses, was a different Mary from the Lord's Mother. Either she or her husband was related to the family of Jesus, but the nature of this relationship cannot be ascertained."[9]

[1]Cf. J. McHugh, *The Mother of Jesus in the New Testament*, (London, 1975), 206. [2]*Adversus Helvidium de Perpetua virginitate beatae Mariae*; PL 23, 193-216. [3]Cf. J. McHugh, *The Mother of Jesus in the New Testament*, (London, 1975), 223-233, 246. [4]"The Brethren of the Lord," in *The Epistle to the Galatians*, (London, 1896), 252-291. [5]Cf. W. F. Albright and C. S. Mann, *The Gospel according to Matthew*, in *Anchor Bible*. [6]Cf. Bodmer ed., IX, 2, 19, also XVII, 35. [7]*Haereses*, n. 78, in PG, 42, 699-740. [8]*Historia Ecclesiastica*, 2:23, 3:20, 3:32, in PL, 20, 196-197, 252-253, 284B. [9]J. Blinzler, *Die Brüder und Schwestern Jesu*, (Stuttgart, 1967), 138.

BROWN, RAYMOND E. (1928-   )

A very well-known biblical scholar, B. has written on Our Lady in several works.[1] In his commentary on St. John (Anchor Bible), he deals at length with the Cana (*qv*) and Calvary episodes (see WOMAN IN Jn 19:25-27). His inaugural lecture in Union Theological Seminary on the virginal conception, first published in *Theological Studies* (1972) was reproduced with some alteration in *The Virginal Conception and Bodily Resurrection of Jesus*.[2] His interest here manifest in the infancy narratives (*qv*) was further expressed in "Luke's Method in the Annunciation Narratives of Chapter One" which he contributed to *Famine in the Land*, essays in honour of Fr. J. L. McKenzie.[3] In "The Meaning of Modern New Testament for an Ecumenical Understanding of Mary,"[4] B. developed a personal biblical theology of Mary. In his large work, *The Birth of the Messiah*, on the infancy narratives, he expands his ideas on many of the problems of Marian theology. In the combined work, *Mary in the New Testament* (London, 1978), which with eleven other scholars, Catholic and Protestant, he helped to produce, and in which he had in places dominant influence, he adds an ecumenical statement on Our Lady, expressive of a "least common denominator." References to the last two works are given throughout this dictionary, which does not imply agreement with B.'s conclusions.

[1]For a general assessment, cf. R. Laurentin, "Exegèses réductrices des évangiles de l'enfance," in MM, 41(1979), 76-100; M. O'Carroll, C.S.Sp., in ITQ, 45(1978), 282-283 and ITQ, 46(1979), 297-299; M. O'Carroll, C.S.Sp., in MM, 37(1975), 441ff and in RSPT, 60(1976), 311-315. [2]*The Virginal Conception and Bodily Resurrection of Jesus*, (London, Dublin, 1973), 21-68. [3]*Famine in the Land*, ed. by J. W. Flanagan, A. Robinson, (Roanoke, Virginia, 1976). [4]*Biblical Reflections on Crises Facing the Church*, (New York, 1975), 84-104.

BRUNO OF ASTI (d. 1123)

A Benedictine, some time abbot of Monte Cassino, and a supporter of St. Gregory VII's (*qv*) reforms, B. was chosen by the Pope as bishop of Segni. B. was a noted exegete. He treats of Mary's privileges and power in his biblical commentaries, sermons, and in reflections for feasts or Marian titles called *"Sententiae."* Mary was "a virgin before childbirth, in childbirth and she remains a virgin after childbirth."[1] Thus B. in his *Sententiae* on the Purification, wherein he also sees the turtle doves and young pigeons as symbols of chastity and innocence, and points to Mary's oblation as specially significant—an idea St. Bernard (*qv*) had in the same age—and one to be imitated. More than once, B. explains Mary's conception of her divine Son through her faith: "She heard and believed and believing conceived."[2] He continues the Eve (*qv*)-Mary contrast. The rod of Aaron, which he thought to be in the Ark of the Covenant was the symbol of Mary bringing forth a Son without seed.[3]

B. identified Mary and the Church (*qv*): "For what is understood by Mary save the holy Church?" This remark in the commentary on Exodus is amplified in his explanation of Ps 44(45): "There are many daughters of the kings, but only one who is queen, by which we understand the Catholic Church or the Virgin Mary, who of the whole Church itself is queen and mistress. She stands at the right hand of God, for more than any mere creature she is honoured by God." On verse 10 he adds, "Although this can be suitably understood of the whole Catholic and universal Church, I shall nevertheless expound it of the Blessed Virgin Mary, who, as I have already said, is the mistress of the whole Church."[4] B. says explicitly that the woman in Rev 12 (*qv*) is the Church, but he has a Marian interpretation of 14:17. On Ps 84, he has an allegorical comment on the earth and heaven as representing Mary.

Mary's power on our behalf is affirmed by B.: "Consider for a moment what great graces we owe to the most blessed Mother of God."[5] Thus too he can call for preaching and praise of Mary "that we should feel that she is praying to her Son for us and know that the Son himself is agreeing with her on our behalf."[6]

---

[1] PL, 165, 1027D. On Bruno, cf. A. des Mazis, in DHGE, 10, 968-970. [2] *De Annunt.*, in PL, 165, 1030A; cp. PL, 164, 858C. [3] *Exp. in Exod., 25*, in PL, 164, 310B. [4] *In Ps 44*, in PL, 164, 857D. [5] *De Nativit.*, in PL, 165, 1025C. [6] *De laude B. M. Civitatis Dei*, in PL, 165, 1022C.

BUDGE, E. A. W. (1857-1934)

An eminent Orientalist, archaeologist and expert at the British Museum, B., author of very many scholarly publications, rendered signal service to Marian theology by his translations from manuscript Syriac, Coptic and Ethiopian material.[1] In 1899 he published *The History of the Blessed Virgin Mary*, based on a thirteenth/fourteenth century manuscript found at Alkos compared with another of the Royal Asiatic Society. The work is heterogeneous, composed of a summary of the *Protevangelium*, a gospel of the infancy, incidents from the public life of Christ, a Tansitus (see ASSUMPTION APOCRYPHA), and a Syriac collection of miracles by Our Lady. B.'s Coptic translations were: *Coptic Apocrypha in the Dialect of Upper Egypt* (1913), a section of which is *Mysteries of St. John the Apostle and the Holy Virgin*; and *Miscellaneous Coptic Texts in the Dialect of Upper Egypt*, (1915), from a tenth/eleventh century manuscript. This contained discourses attributed to St. Cyril of Jerusalem, St. Epiphanius, St. Cyril of Alexandria, and Demetrius of Antioch, spurious but of interest. In 1928, B. brought out *The Book of Saints of the Ethiopian Church* (four volumes). *The Miracles of the Virgin and the Life of Hanna*, from manuscripts owned by Lady Meux, was published in a limited deluxe edition. Pope Leo XIII (*qv*) in thanks for a presentation copy sent Lady Meux a silver bust of himself and a letter from Cardinal Rampolla, Secretary of State. *One hundred and ten Miracles of Our Lady Mary* (1923) was a popular work. B. had published the companion volume the previous year, *Legends of Our Lady Mary the Perpetual Virgin*. The introduction is informative on Ethiopian Marian ideas.

---

[1] *By Nile and Tigris*, ed. by E. A. Wallis Budge, (London, 1920); 'Aethiopica," in *Revue Philologique*, (July, 1935), 134; P. Peeters, *Evangiles Apocryphes*, (Paris, 1914), cf. Introduction; R. Caro, *La Homilética*, II, 557, n. 1; V. Arras, *De Transitu Mariae Apocrypha Aethiopice*, I, in CSCO, 343, cf. Introduction; M. R. James, *The Apocryphal New Testament*, (Oxford, 1960), *passim*.

BULGAKOV, SERGIUS (1871-1944)

A great, possibly the greatest, modern Russian writer on Our Lady, B., son of an Orthodox priest, was converted from Marxism and recovered his lost faith through the impact of the Sistine Madonna. Later, he was to turn to the Icon as the most congenial religious symbol, writing a dogmatic essay on the subject. Ordained a priest in 1918, he was exiled and eventually settled in Paris as professor and dean of theology in the St. Serge Institute (1923). The core of his thought is "sophiological" theology, an elaborate doctrine of *Sophia* or divine wisdom as the living source and explanation of all things. He had an intuition of it, he claimed, in a moment of ecstasy in the church of Santa Sophia in Constantinople. This was in January, 1923, as he was thinking of becoming a Catholic. Sophia, in the Ikon of Novgorod, is for him inspiring. His chief Marian work, *The Burning Bush*, (1927), is in Russian. His ideas are fully expressed in: *L'Orthodoxie*,[1] which appeared in French; *The Wisdom of God*, published in London, (1937); and *Le Paraclet*, French translation, (1946), of his work on the Holy Spirit, issued in Russian in 1936. B. took an active part in the ecumenical movement as a member of *Faith and Order*, and insisted on the importance of thinking on Our Lady.

"Protestantism," B. thought in its lack of veneration for the Virgin "differs in almost equal measure from both Orthodoxy and Catholicism." "Love and veneration for the Virgin is the soul of Orthodox piety, its heart, that which warms and animates its entire body. A faith in Christ which does not include his virgin birth and the veneration of his Mother is another faith, another Christianity from that of the Orthodox Church." She was the summit of Old Testament sanctity: "Thus the Church of the Old Testament had for its purpose the elevation, the conservation and the preparation of a holy humanity worthy to receive the Holy Spirit, that is, worthy of the Annunciation, in the person of the Virgin."[2]

B. recalls that the Orthodox Church does not accept the Catholic dogma of 1854, the Immaculate Conception. He rules out personal sin, and then he states: "However the force of original sin, which varies greatly from man to man, is in her reduced to the point of a mere possibility never actualized. In other words, the Blessed Virgin knows no personal sin, she was manifestly sanctified by the Holy Ghost from the very moment of her conception."[3] In *The Burning Bush* (more accurately *The Unconsumed or Unburned Bush*), while again lauding Mary's dignity and holiness, he sees stages in her liberation from the effects of Original Sin: the Annunciation and Pentecost.[4]

Mary shared in the Passion of Christ. She was the first to participate in his resurrection, the center, after the Ascension of the apostolic community. She was assumed bodily into heaven after death.

Some special points are noteworthy in B.'s synthesis. "In her is realized the idea of divine Wisdom in the creation of the world, she is Divine Wisdom in the created world. It is in her that Divine Wisdom is justified, and thus the veneration of the Virgin blends with that of Divine Wisdom . . . She is the justification, the end and the meaning of creation."[5]

This view of Mary in the sophiological plan is linked with her special relationship with the Holy Spirit. B. anticipated Vatican II in teaching a visible descent of the Spirit on Mary at the Annunciation: "The Annunciation was a complete and therefore hypostatic descent of the Holy Spirit and his entry to the Virgin Mary . . . By his coming into the Virgin Mary the Holy Spirit identifies himself in a way with her through her God-motherhood . . . He does not at all leave her after the birth of Christ, but remains forever with her in the full force of the Annunciation."[6]

In one work he is almost carried away and thinks that the limits of the creature are passed in the deification of Mary. Her life of grace is the hypostatic life of the Holy Spirit. But he withdraws from this extreme position and qualifies the statement.[7] In *The Wisdom of God*, he rejects the idea of an incarnation of the Spirit and says: "He abides, however, in the ever-virgin Mary as in a holy temple while her human personality seems to become transparent to him and to provide him with a human countenance."[8]

In a commemoration volume for Ephesus (1931), B. asserted that "as long as there exists this mysterious antipathy against any Marian devotion on the part of Protestantism, a true reunion of the churches is impossible—a correct doctrine of the Church is impossible without a Mariology. The Mother of God is the personal head of the Church (though certainly in a different sense from Jesus Christ himself), namely as head of mankind, as the creaturely centre."[9] For B., Mary "as the personification of the Church is raised above all sin." She is the heart of the Church; in her is centered the spirit proper to the Church, the principle of its realization. She is the heart of the world and the spiritual center of all mankind.

Mary is our Mediatress, leading us to her Son: "Living in heaven in a state of glory the Virgin remains the mother of the human race for which she prays and intercedes . . . She covers the world with her veil praying, weeping for the sins of the world; at the Last Judgment she will intercede before her Son and ask pardon from him."[10] All this derives its value from her *fiat* repeated on Calvary and from her unique relationship with the Spirit. Indeed through him, B. would contend, Mary's virginity was a recovery of the power given to our first parents before the Fall, to conceive spiritually, suprasexually. She was, he thought, essentially virgin.

---

[1]Sergius Bulgakov, *L'Orthodoxie* (Paris, 1932, English tr. *The Orthodox Church*, London, 1935). Cf. ch. 8. Cf. ch. VI, "The veneration of Our Lady," in *The Wisdom of God*, (London, 1937), 173-196. On Mary and the Spirit, see *Le Paraclet* (1946), 237-239. On Bulgakov's Marian teaching, cf. L. A. Zander (author of a two-volume work on B. in Russian, Paris, 1948), in LexMar, 992-995; A. Legisa, *Divina maternitas Mariae in Sergio Bulgakov*, (Madrid, 1953); A. Wenger, A.A., in *Maria*, V, 974-979; *ibid.*, "Expérience et Theologie dans la doctrine de Serge Boulgakov," in NRT, 77(1955), 939-962. Cf. esp. B. Schultze, S.J., in *Maria*, VI, 229-235. For Bulgakov in the ecumenical movement, cf. E. Lamirande, "La Théotokos et les travaux du mouvement oecuménique 'Foi et Constitution'," in EphMar, 13(1963), 77-105. On Mary and the Spirit, cf. C. L. Graves, *The Holy Spirit in the Theology of Sergius Bulgakov*, Doctoral Dissertation, Basle University, World Council of Churches, (Geneva, 1972); also in EphMar, 3(1953), 393-446. [2]*The Orthodox Church* (London, 1935). 137-138. [3]*The Wisdom of God* (London, 1937), 174. [4]Cf. B. Schultze, S.J., in *Maria*, VI, 231-232. [5]*The Orthodox Church* (London, 1935), 139. [6]*Le Paraclet* (1946), 238-239.

[7]B. Schultze, S.J., in *Maria*, IV, 231. [8]*The Wisdom of God* (London, 1937), 176. [9]*Die Hochkirche*, ed. by Friedrich Heiler, (1931), 244. [10]*The Orthodox Church* (London, 1935), 139.

BULLINGER, HEINRICH (1504-1575)

Zwingli's successor at Zurich, B. showed that Marian doctrine and piety did not disappear with the advance of the Reformation. Many of his ideas on the subject are Catholic. He composed a *Marienpredigt*, and treated of Our Lady also in a commentary on Luke, and *De origine erroris*.[1] B. believed that Mary was the Mother of God, a Virgin, before, in, and after childbirth. He saw her as a unique being, her life directed by pure faith and burning love of God. He says in one passage that he did not wish to take a stand on the Immaculate Conception (*qv*) and the Assumption (*qv*), save to emphasize her great sanctity and her eternal happiness in heaven. Elsewhere he writes: "For this reason we believe that the most pure bridal-chamber of the Virgin Mary Mother of God (*Deiparae*) and temple of the Holy Spirit, that is her most holy body, was borne to heaven by the angels."[2] Though making it clear that he is not hostile to Mary, i.e. not an enemy of Christ, B. rejects invocation to her and her mediation. B. tried to alter Calvin's ideas of Zwingli, whom the Frenchman had at first thought little of, then raised to the level of second-class theologian.

---

[1]Marian texts, W. Tappolet, *Das Marienlob der Reformatoren*, (Tübingen, 1962), 263-338. [2]*De origine erroris libri duo*, cap. 16, *apud* Tappolet, 327.

C

CABASILAS, NICHOLAS (Fourteenth Century)

Little is known of the life of this important Byzantine theologian. He was born about 1320 in Thessalonica, and died after 1380, possibly about 1396. He assumed the central tenets of the Palamite theologians: all creation is centered on the Incarnation (see PALAMAS, GREGORY). C. was author of three Marian homilies, published by M. Jugie (*qv*) in 1926: on the Nativity of Mary (BHG 1107n); on the Annunciation (BHG 1092c); and on the Dormition (BHG 1147n).[1] The first homily deals largely with Mary's holiness; in the second, her role in salvation is a theme. The third homily shows her at the summit of creation with her divine Son.

For C., Mary was the "new man," the accomplished ideal of mankind as God planned it. "For the Virgin was alone and truly the work of pious prayer, in which there was nothing wayward, and the only gift of God worthy to be given to those who asked for it, and to be received by them."[2] Nature could contribute nothing to the making of the Immaculate one. God did everything, "thrusting nature aside, so to speak, to create the blessed one, as he did the first man. And truly in the most special and proper sense, the Virgin is the first man, who first and alone manifested nature."[3]

"The dividing wall and barrier of enmity did not exist for her and everything that separated the human race from God was, in her case, taken away."[4] This looks like a statement of the Immacualte Conception (qv), but C. attributes so much to Our Lady's own action that he has been blamed for Pelagian or semi-Pelagian views. Her own action could not affect the initial moment of her holiness. "For, in her, man superbly showed by his deeds the strength which he has against sin, and she, by moderation of mind, singleness of purpose and greatness of soul, avoided all misconduct."[5] True, the author had earlier stated that God had chosen Mary "as a kind of sanctuary for himself and had preferred her before all the earth."[6] The idea of Mary manifesting nature as God intended it is common to C. His anthropology is complex. Someone had to show man as God meant man to be, and this had to be done by overcoming all sin "from within man himself, by diligence and strength."[7] C. repeats in different phrases his conviction of Mary's surpassing holiness.

Linked therewith is her role in our regard: "For there was no saint before the Blessed one was; first and alone really free from sin, she showed herself holy, the saint of saints and whatever may be said more, and she opened the door of holiness to others, being excellently prepared to receive the Saviour, from whom all the saints and prophets and priests, whoever were found worthy of the divine mysteries, have had their being."[8] Again, C. puts his ideas forcibly: "The incarnation of the Word was not only the work of the Father, of his power and of his Spirit, but was also the work of the will and the faith of the Virgin; without the consent of the Immaculate one, without the contribution of her faith, this plan was as unrealisable as without the intervention of the three divine persons themselves."[9]

Eve helped Adam, but Mary helped God. She was his most suitable cooperator. "Being assumed as a helper not simply to contribute something as one of those moved by another, but

that she should give herself and become the fellow-worker [sunergos] of God in providing for the human race, so that with him she should be an associate and sharer in the glory which would come from it."[10] C. makes it clear that the partnership should be "in all the sufferings and affliction. He, bound on the Cross, received the lance in his side; the sword, as divinely inspired Symeon foretold, pierced her heart."[11]

C. says that Mary was our advocate with God before the Paraclete came. In the third homily, he shows Mary's excellence over all on high, over all the angels. He ends with an epilogue which glorifies her as salvation of men, light of the world, way to the Redeemer, co-cause [sunaitios] with Christ, the cause of our sanctification.[12]

[1]PO, 19, 456-510 (introduction 456-465). Cf. M Jugie, "La doctrine mariale de Nicolas Cabasilas," in Echos d'Orient, 18(1919), 373-388; L'Immaculée Conception, by M. Jugie, 246-263; L'Assomption, by M. Jugie, 332-333; D. T. Strottman, "La Théotokos, Prémices des justifiés," in Irenikon, 27(1954), 131ff; L. Maggini, "L'Assunzione di Maria secondo tre teologi bizantini (Palamas, Cabasilas, Glabras)," in Sapienza, 3(1950), 441-445; E. Toniolo, O.S.M., La Mariologia di Nicoló Cabasilas, (Vicenza, 1955); A. Wenger, A.A., in BSFEM, 13(1955), 49-52; Or. Kalogerou, Maria he Aeiparthenos Theotokos kata ten orthodoxon pistin, (Thessalonica, 1957), 85-93; M. Lot-Borodine, Un Maître de la spiritualité byzantine, N. C., au XIVe siècle,(Paris, 1958); P. Nellas, "Essai sur la Mère de Dieu et l'humanisme théocentrique," in Le Messager orthodoxe, (1970), n.51, 4-14; S. Salaville, in DSp, 2, 1-9; H. Graef, in Mary, I, 339-342. Cf. esp. B Schultze, S.J., in MO, 368-389. [2]In Nativ., 4, in PO, 19, 469. [3]ibid. [4]In Annunt., 3, in PO, 19, 486. [5]In Nativ., 15, in PO, 19, 481. [6]ibid. [7]In Nativ., 14, in PO, 19, 480. [8]In Dorm., 8, in PO, 19, 504. [9]In Annunt., 4, PO, 19, 488. [10]ibid. [11]In Dorm., 12, in PO, 19, 508. [12]In Dorm., 13, in PO, 19, 509-510.

CAESAR OF HEISTERBACH (Thirteenth Century)
A Cistercian monk of the diocese of Cologne, C. wrote Dialogue . . . miraculorum[1] between 1220 and 1230. He expressed the idea that Mary protects Cistercian monks with her mantle-an idea known to iconography as the Madonna of the Mantle, the Russian Pokrov. C. also composed: De solemnitatibus B. M. V. octo sermones;[2] Tractatus super 'Quae est ista';[3] Expositio super sequentiam 'Ave praeclara maris stella'; XXII homiliae ad honorem Dei Genitricis, explicatio cantici Salomonis; and Libri duo super verba 'Signum Magnum'.[4]

[1]Ed. J Strange, (Cologne, 1851). C.'s *Volumen . . . Miraculorum*, ed. by A. Meister, is in *Römischen Quartalschr.*, 13, *supplementband*, (1901). Cf. *Bibliotheca Hagiographica Latina*. [2]Ed. by v. Hilka, *Die Wundergeschichten des C. v. H.*, (Bonn, 1933), I, 2-60. [3]Ed. by Schutz, in *Summa Mariana* (Paderborn, 1908), 687-716. [4]Ed. by Tissier, in *Bibliotheca Patrum Cistercensium*, (1660).

CALVIN, JOHN (1509-1564)

C.'s ideas about Mary were related to his theology of predestination, grace and faith. His writings, specifically on Mary, are much fewer in number than those left us by Luther (*qv*). In content he is also restricted.[1] Though his theory was thought out in a positive way, there is an element of reaction against Catholic ideas and practice: "How necessary this warning became, in consequence of the gross and abominable superstitions which followed, is known well enough. For Mary has been made Queen of Heaven, the Hope, the Life and the Salvation of the world, and, in fact, their insane raving went so far that they just about stripped Christ and adorned her with the spoils. And when we condemn these accursed blasphemies against the Son of God, the Papists call us malicious and envious. Nay they spread the wicked slander that we are deadly foes to the honour of the holy Virgin. As if she had not all the honour that belongs to her without being made a goddess. As if it were honouring her to adorn her with sacrilegious titles and put her in Christ's place. It is they who do Mary a cruel injury when they snatch from God what belongs to him, that they may deform her with false praise."[2] Again he specifies: "For many prayers have been forged full of horrible blasphemies, such as those which request the Virgin Mary to command her Son, and exert her authority over him—and which style her the haven of salvation, the life and hope of those who trust in her." Elsewhere he attacks the practice of using relics.[3]

With these sentiments must be taken some of the touching things C. says about Mary in his gospel commentaries: "Let us act as did the Virgin Mary and say, 'Lord let it be done unto me according to your word'. . . . We see then the instruction that is given to us here by the Virgin Mary, who will be to us a good teacher, providing that we take advantage of her lessons as it becomes us . . . ." "But Elizabeth holds here the means which we ought to use, that is to say, that she honours the Virgin in as much as she is honoured by God . . . . She does not stop at her, and she does not lessen or obscure in any way the honour due to God."[4] Why, he asks, does Elizabeth call her blessed? and answers from his own basic principles: "We are all accursed in Adam and blessing comes to us from the sheer gratuitous favour of God."[5]

It is in the light of this view that he can say that Mary will take her revenge, on the last day, on those of whom she is the "mortal enemy," the Papists, for it is oppobrium and insult to say that "she snatches honour from God, her God." "We are nothing, we are worth nothing and we hold all from the pure bounty of our God."[6]

This whole outlook determines understanding of C.'s ideas on Mary. He accepted the four first Councils and the three Creeds, but subject to the norm of Scripture. He therefore held that Mary was the Mother of God: "It cannot be denied that God in choosing and destining Mary to be the Mother of his Son, granted her the highest honour." "Elizabeth called Mary Mother of the Lord, because the unity of the person in the two natures of Christ was such that she could have said that the mortal man engendered in the womb of Mary was at the same time the eternal God."[7] Yet he scarcely used the title Mother of God and, in a letter to the Calvinist community of London, he discouraged its use. "To speak of the Mother of God instead of the Virgin Mary can only serve to harden the ignorant in their superstition."[8]

On the virgin birth and cognate matters, he was entirely Catholic. He thought the marriage (*qv*) had taken place to preserve the secret of Jesus' origin. Mary and Joseph knew that her Son was divine. The words of Is 7:14 refer to a virginal conception. C. castigates the Rabbis, who identify Emmanuel with Hezekiah. He brushes aside the difficulties sometimes raised from "first born" and "brothers of the Lord" against the perpetual virginity of Mary. But he will not hear of a vow on Mary's part; this he thinks a "weak," even an "absurd" opinion, implying monasticism among the Jews.

As to Mary's privileges, C. rejects totally the Immaculate Conception (*qv*) as he does the Assumption (*qv*). He thought that the latter feast had one advantage—Catholics thinking that Mary had been assumed bodily could not worship her relics. From his whole theory of justification, he was led to interpret the word *Kecharitomene* (Lk 1:28) as a sign of God's external favour. Here he was far more rigid than Luther or Zwingli.

The virtue which C. especially admired in Mary was her faith. He praised too her prompt obedience in the *Fiat* (see CONSENT). She gives herself entirely to God. She not only expects the result, but eagerly seeks it. Using the title treasurer of grace (*trésorière de la grâce*), he first repudiates the meaning given it by the "Papists," making Mary the dispenser of graces, and then offers his own. "For she kept the doctrine which today opens to us the kingdom of heaven and which leads us to our Lord Jesus Christ: she kept this as a deposit and through her we received this and today we are edified therefrom. This is therefore the honour God gave her; let us consider her in this way: not that we should remain with her or make an idol of her, but that we should be led to our Lord Jesus Christ, for she sends us to him."[9] He also says that Mary, taking God's promise into her heart, conceived and brought forth salvation for herself and the whole world.[10]

Mary can, in Calvin's theological system, have this role as she exemplifies the characteristic Calvinist virtues. Invocation of Mary he forbids. Not only does he complain that the "Papists have changed this greeting [the Hail Mary] by a magic exorcism into a petition." He brands all invocation of the Virgin execrable blasphemy. He attacks, too, holy images of any kind, therefore of Our Lady, calling them idols and pours scorn on the decrees of the Second Council of Nicaea. These he seems to have learned at second hand and did not understand.

[1]Works in *Calvini Opera* (CR), (Braunschweig-Berlin, 1863-1900), 59 vols. On the infancy narratives, cf. CR, 45, 5-107; 39 sermons, in CR, 46, 1-488. Texts in W. Tappolet, *Das Marienlob des Reformatoren*, (Tübingen, 1962), 163-218; *Opera Selecta*, (Munich, 1926-1952, 5 vols.); English tr. of *Calvin's Commentaries*, ed. by D. W. Torrance and T. F. Torrance, (Edinburgh, 1959); *Tracts and The Gospel according to St. John*, tr. by T. H. L. Parker; *Treatises*, tr. by H. Beveridge, (Edinburgh, 1958). Cf. D. B. Dupuy, O.P., "La Mariologie de Calvin," in *Istina*, 5(1958), 479-490; J. Cadier, "La Vierge Marie dans la dogmatique réformée au XVI et au XVII siècles," in *La Rev. réformée*, (1958), 46-58; K. Algermissen, in LexMar, 1040-1046; E. Stakemeier, in MO, 459-473; T. A. O'Meara, O.P., *Mary in Protestant and Catholic Theology*, (New York, 1966), 125-135; J. Bosc, in BSFEM, 20(1963), 18-25. [2]*Tracts and the Gospel according to St. John*, tr. by T. H. L. Parker, 47. [3]*Treatises*, 2, 146. [4]*op. cit.*, 1, 320ff. [5]CR, 46, 95 and 107. [6]CR, 46, 122. [7]CR, 45, 348 and 35. [8]*Lettres Anglaises*, (Paris, 1959), 181. [9]CR, 46, 310. [10]CR, 45, 36.

CANA, THE WEDDING AT

The episode is narrated by St. John (*qv*) only.[1] It reveals the human character of the Saviour in an attractive way. A guest at a wedding party, he draws on his divine power to rescue his host from an embarrassing situation. He does so with delicacy and generosity and the whole incident is coloured by the presence of his Mother, thoughtful and discreet. Wine is hallowed at the beginning of Christ's public ministry, as it will be divinized to perpetuate that ministry.

Sources and literary form: Since the miracle is not narrated in the Synoptic Gospels, R. Bultmann, C. K. Barrett and others explain the story as an effect of Hellenistic Dionysus worship. Dionysus was the god of vintage, whose festival on 6 January was marked by fountains spouting wine from the temples of Andros. The feast of the Epiphany is on the same day and the gospel reading for that day is the Cana story—an example of the "baptism" of a pagan festival, not the only one, and no more than that.

The problem of the dialogue is different. Were these the only words recorded in the primitive tradition of the miracle? If not, why were they chosen? The miracle opens the Johannine book of signs. M. E. Boismard, following E. B. Allo, O.P., sees in Jn 1:19-2:11 a pattern which emphasizes the sequence of events in seven days, the Cana episode on the last day. It is a hint of the new creation in the opening of Christ's ministry. John opens the story by saying that Cana was "on the third day," however, and Gen 2:2, though saying that on the seventh day God "finished his work," adds that he rested. A. M. Serra, using the Targum of Pseudo-Jonathan, on Ex 19:4, contends that John identifies Cana as the new Sinai, as the Synoptics understood the Transfiguration. There are points of literary contact between Ex 19 developed in the Targum, and the narrative of John. "All that the Lord has spoken we will do." (Ex 19:8). "Do whatever he tells you." (Jn 2:5). Pharaoh's words (Gen 41:55) are also parallel: "Go to Joseph; what he says to you, do." Serra's theory would support an interesting idea on the role which John gives to Mary. This will be mentioned later.

Interpretation of the text: There is a nuance between "the Mother of Jesus was there" and "Jesus also was invited," which would support the conjecture that Mary was helping the family with the festivities. This would explain her knowledge of the embarrassing shortage of wine.

Were her words "They have no wine" a request for a miracle? Braun with others thinks it impossible, as Cana was the first miracle and she had no previous experience of the kind. Feuillet defends the view of older authorities (Chrysostom, Augustine, Maldonatus, Knabenbauer): Mary sought a messianic miracle.

"Woman" as a form of address was not unusual or disrespectful (Mt 15:28; Lk 13:12; Jn 4:21; 8:10, 20:13), but it was unusual to use to a mother. Jesus also used it in addressing his Mother in the Calvary scene (Jn 19:26). "What have you to do with me? My hour has not yet come." The first part of the reply was seen as a rebuke by some of the Fathers, and from Augustine (qv) on, as a refusal accompanied by a decision to separate Mary from the Lord's ministry. Rupert of Deutz (qv), Newman (qv), and F. M. Braun put this view cogently, adding that when Jesus' "hour" will have come the Mother will be reinstated. John does not support this interpretation, for immediately after the miracle he records that Mary accompanied Jesus to Capernaum (2:12). If there was to be separation surely silence, as in the case of St. Joseph (qv), would have been the obvious means to ensure it. It would be very clumsy to signify a kind of dismissal by working a miracle solely at the request of the one being dismissed—a self-defeating method.

The principal difficulty to the view is that Mary did not so understand her Son's reply. Her words, "Do whatever he tells you," would be very difficult to understand if she had felt either rebuffed or thrust aside. Moreover, the working of the miracle would be a very striking *volte face* on Jesus' part.

The "hour" has been taken to mean the hour of the first miracle. Since St. Augustine, however, who was followed by St. Thomas Aquinas (qv), another meaning has been attached to the word. It is the hour of Christ's death and glorification. Very many moderns, notably F. M. Braun and R. E. Brown, press this interpretation. For them, it follows from Johannine usage throughout the gospel. Everywhere "hour" refers to the death and glorification. These for John are one, except for 16:21, where the analogy may be said to imply it.

But some problems remain. The Greek Fathers thought mostly of the "hour" as the beginning of miracles. If "hour" has a unitary sense in John, why, when it was imminent,

is a descriptive phrase added in 13:1, "his hour to depart out of this world to the Father"? John does not indicate any lack of understanding on Mary's part (as did Luke in 2:50). If she then understood the word "hour" in reference to his death, how could she have continued the thread of her dialogue with no apparent heed to this meaning? Her words to the waiters are in keeping with her own previous request. It bears no relationship to the death of Christ. Lagrange contended that to adopt this interpretation is to disrupt the whole story for the sake of verbal agreement. For there is nothing whatever within the story which suggests a thought of Christ's death. This meaning must rest for its validity on the meaning of the word elsewhere in the gospel after the Cana incident.

The episode is given a completeness and is cut off from other events preceding it by the words, "Jesus manifested his glory; and his disciples believed in him." (2:11). Since John does not say that Mary believed in him as a consequence of the sign, the clear implication is that she already did so. Does the evangelist also imply that to her the glory of which he spoke in 1:14 had already been manifested? Here we are merging on theology. Note that some of the problems here raised are avoided by those who either interpret the hour as both the beginning of miracles and the moment of death or see Christ's reply to his Mother as a question: Has not my hour come?

Theological implications: The central truth is Christological. The wedding which symbolizes messianic times (Is 54:4-8; 62:4-5) and the abundance of wine in the time of fulfillment (Jer 31:12; Hos 14:7; Amos 9:13-14) constitute the Old Testament background. There is a pointed contrast between the rites of the Old Law, of which the water is a figure, and Christ's gift of the Spirit, symbolized by the excellent wine. The word "woman" has an echo of Gen 3:15 (see WOMAN IN), placing Mary as the new Eve (qv) at the beginning of the new creation. A. M. Serra sees an implicit identification between Mary and the Israel of old, John's version of the Daughter of Zion theme, which in no way clashes with the new Eve typology. On this level one may see continuity in the words spoken on Calvary, when Mary is also addressed as "woman." In both narratives she has shed her own name for that which she was given within the community of messianic believers: Mother of Jesus; the

Great Lady of the ancient Jewish kingdom; the Mother of the king; the first woman in the land. Her role at Cana is subordinate but indispensable. She took the initiative. She alone mentioned the word wine. She was the intermediary between Jesus and the bridegroom and, bypassing the chief steward, the waiters. Only in his commentary on Cana does St. Thomas give her the title Mediatress.

The Cana episode has been studied for indications of sacramental theology, especially on the Eucharist. The similarlity between the change of water into wine and multiplication of bread in Jn 6 prompts such an interpretation. It cannot be pressed too far. Let us finally note the view which discerns effects of Old Testament Wisdom tradition in the miracle, compared with the call of the disciple in Jn 1 and the "banquet" in which the miraculous bread is eaten.

Teaching Authority: Since Leo XIII, the Popes have taught, from time to time, that Cana exemplifies Mary's intercession, her maternal care for her children. They have adapted Mary's words to the waiters in referring to the essential precepts of the Master. Pius XII related Cana to Mary's mediation: "The grace of Christ comes to us through the Mother of Christ. She in fact 'Sumens illud Ave Gabrielis ore', who greeted her as full of grace, became at the same time Mother of Christ and Mother of divine grace. The maternal office of 'Mediatress' really began at the very moment of her consent to the Incarnation; it was manifested for the first time by the first sign of Christ's grace, at Cana in Galilee; from that moment it rapidly spread down through the ages with the growth of the Church."[2]

The first Marian schema prepared for Vatican II in the section on Mary and Christian unity spoke of her as one "who interceded that the Word incarnate would, in Cana of Galilee, work the first sign from which his disciples believed in him." (Jn 2:3; 2:11). The second schema had in its first three drafts these words in the section on Mary during the public ministry: "In the public life of Jesus his Mother appears prominently, even at the beginning when in Cana of Galilee, moved by pity she brought about by her intercession the first sign of the outpouring of messianic grace." (Jn 2:1-11). Alterations were suggested at the *Modi* stage. "Prominently"

should be dropped, since Mary appeared only once in the Synoptic Gospels; "moved by pity" should go, as it was gratuitous. There had been "messianic graces" in the Saviour's infancy. "By her intercession" should be deleted lest the Council decide a matter freely debated by exegetes. One of these *Modi* was accepted: "The beginning of the signs of Jesus the Messiah" replaced the earlier formulation.[3]

---

[1]Bibliography (1920-1965) in E. Malatesta, *St. John's Gospel, Analecta Bibl.*, (Rome, 1967), nn. 1321-1428; B. M. Metzger, *Index to Periodical Literature on Christ and the Gospels*, nn. 6181-6222. Besides Jerome Comm. and New Cath. Com., works on St. John's Gospel by Lagrange, Hoskyns, Dodd, Bultmann, C. K. Barrett, R. Schnackenburg (1965) and R. E. Brown (1966). Cf. also R. Schnackenburg, *Das erste Wunder Jesu*, (Freiburg, 1951); O. Cullmann, *Les sacrements dans l'Évangile johannique. La vie de Jésus et le culte de l'Église primitive*, (Paris, 1951), 36ff. P. Gaechter, S.J., *Maria im Erdenleben*, 2nd ed., (Innsbruck, 1953), 155-200; F.-M. Braun, O.P., *La Mère des Fidèles*, 2nd ed., (Paris, 1954), 49-74; J. Michl, "Bemerkungen zu Joh. 2:4," in BB, 36(1955), 492-509; M. E. Boismard, O.P., *Du Baptême à Cana*, (Paris, 1956), 133-159; J. P. Charlier, *Le Signe de Cana*, (Brussels, 1959); A. Feuillet, "L'Heure de Jésus et le signe de Cana," in ETL, 36(1960), 5-22; *ibid.*, "La signification fondamentale du premier miracle de Cana (Jn 2:1-11) et le symbolisme johannique," in *Rev. Thomiste*, 65(1965), 517-535; S. Hartdegen, "The Marian significance of Cana," in MSt, 11(1960), 85-103; A. Bresolin, "L'esegesi di Giov. 2:4 nei Padri Latini," in REA, 8(1962), 243-273; R. J. Dillon, "Wisdom Tradition and Sacramental Retrospect in the Cana Account (Jn 2:1-11)," in CBQ, 24(1962), 268-296; M. Thurian, *Mary, Mother of the Lord, Figure of the Church*, (London, 1963), 117-144; E. J. Kilmartin, "The Mother of Jesus was there," in ScEccl, 15(1963), 257-283; J. Reuss, *Joh. 2:3-4 in Johannes-Kommentaren der griechischen Kirche, Neutestament. Aufsätze*, (Regensburg, 1963), 207-213; J. Hanniman, "L'Heure de Jésus et les noces de Cana," in *Rev. Thomiste*, 64(1964), 569-583; J. Galot, S.J., *Mary in the Gospel*, (Westminster, Maryland, 1964), 104-178; J. P. Michaud, *Le Signe de Cana dans le contexte johannique*, (Montréal, 1964); id., in MSS, V, 37-97; A. Smitans, *Das Weinwunder von Kana, Die Auslegung von Joh. 2:1-11 bei den Vätern und heute*, (Tübingen, 1966); J. D. M. Derrett, "Water into Wine," in *Law in the New Testament*, (London, 1970), 228-246; A. M. Serra, O.S.M., "Le tradizioni della teofania sinaitica nel Targum dello pseudo-Jonathan Es 19, 24, e in Giov. 1:19-2:12," in MM, 33(1971), 1-39; id., *Contributi dell'Antica letterature giudaica per l'egesi di Giovanni 2:1-12 e 19:25-27*, (Rome, Herder, 1977); J. M. Goicoechea, O.F.M., "Maria, la madre de Jesus en las bodas de Cana," in MSS, V, 3-35; M. A. Poulin, "Origine de l'appelation 'femme' dans Jean 2:4," in MSS, V, 139-149; *Mary in NT*, 182-194; J. McHugh, *The Mother of Jesus in the New Testament*, (London, 1975), 361ff. [2]Apost. Letter, "Per Christi Matrem," (15 May, 1947), in OL, 276. [3]*Modi*, in LG, (Vatican Press, 1964), ch. VIII, 12-13.

CAROL, JUNIPER B., O.F.M. (1911-   )

C., a Cuban, is a key figure in the upsurge of Marian studies in the United States. He has pursued studies in Washington and Rome, served on the Duns Scotus Commission, and taught Dogmatic Theology. In 1949, C. founded *The Mariological Society of America*, of which he was president until 1954, and has been secretary since then. He has been editor since 1950 of *Marian Studies*, the only review of its kind in English. C. was editor of three volumes of *Mariology*, and contributed some fifty articles to scholarly reviews. He specialized in Coredemption.[1] C. has received several honors, notably from Dayton University and St. John's University, Brooklyn, New York.

[1] *The Blessed Virgin's Coredemption Vindicated*, (Quaracchi, 1937). Cf. esp. *De Corredemptione B.V.M.*, (Vatican City, 1950); *Fundamentals of Mariology*, (New York, 1956, Spanish tr. Madrid, 1964).

CARPENTER OF NAZARETH, THE

Mary of Nazareth was the wife of the village carpenter. When he died, his place was taken by his son, as was the Jewish custom in such crafts (Mk 6:3; Mt 13:55). Most of her life was a partnership, within a small social unit, with one who worked with his hands to make the simple articles of household furniture or for house-building needed in those days. St. Justin (*qv*), who was a native of the area, said that the carpenter of Nazareth also made "ploughs and yokes." The *techton* was a worker in wood. None were demeaned by the occupation.[1] Some thirty Old Testament texts teach the necessity and the dignity of manual work; more than a hundred could be drawn from the Talmud with the same lessons. Acceptance of the ideal was exemplified by the historic leaders of Israel, by prominent Rabbis and jurists, and by St. Paul in New Testament times.

Though St. Joseph was a descendant of the royal house of Israel, his status in the community was limited by his calling. He could have owned a small plot of ground to keep a few beasts, perhaps for a little tillage. Household tasks and chores fell largely to Mary. That was the pattern of her life and her holiness until the events of the public ministry of Jesus.

[1] Cf. D. O'Shea, *Mary and Joseph*, (Milwaukee, 1949), 70-72; esp. R. de Vaux, *Ancient Israel; its Life and Institutions*, (London, 1961), 76-78; H. Daniel-Rops, *Daily Life in Palestine in the time of Christ*, (London, 1962), 146-149; articles on "Work" in dictionaries of the Bible, Léon-Dufour, Bauer, McKenzie.

CARROLL, EAMON R., O. CARM. (1921-   )

Graduate of the Gregorian University, and Professor in Catholic University, Washington, C. has published a monograph on Arnold Bostius, *Understanding Mary* (1979), and many articles on Marian theology.[1] He has been a contributor to *Mariology*, edited by J. B. Carol, O.F.M., and to *Marian Studies*. C. is widely known as lecturer on current Marian problems, especially in the ecumenical field.

[1] Cf. EphMar, 20(1970), 137-138.

CARTHAGENA, JOHN DE, O.F.M. (1563-1617)

A Spanish theologian, C. had been a Jesuit before entering the Franciscan order. His books remain in seventeenth century editions except the one most relevant to Marian theology: *Homiliae catholicae de sacris arcanis Deiparae Mariae et Josephi, libri XIX*.[1] The nineteen books contain 244 essays rich with patristic and scholastic erudition. The plan is the life of Mary from the Immaculate Conception to the Assumpton (*qv*), with concluding books on devotional subjects.

Though C. thought the Immaculate Conception conformable to all the sources and interpreters of Revelation, he insisted that Mary had the "Debt of sin" (*qv*). Thus her privilege was from the "preserving grace of Christ" and she received the "benefit of the Redemption." He analyzes the fullness of grace lengthily. He thought that "through no pure creature, not even through all taken together, can we come to know the divine attributes more than through the Blessed Virgin alone."[2] He has the necessary refinements and distinctions to safeguard Christ's uniqueness and transcendence, while defending a role of immense importance attributable to Mary in the Redemption and all its effects. "She was chosen and predestined that she could be not only Christ's Mother but his helper [*coadjutrix*] and single companion in the redemption and restoration of the human race . . ."[3] He applies the distinction *de condigno* and *de congruo* to characterize the distinct contributions of Christ and Mary. He thought that doubt attributed (falsely as we know) to some Latin Doctors, did not prevent the Church from "giving all the certainty which it can supply to this truth save what a definition brings with it."[4] Mary is the Mediatress (*qv*) of all graces: "Whatever graces and helps are communicated to men are poured on them from Christ the Head, through the Virgin as through a mystical neck." "As God made her the treasurer of grace, so he also made her the dispenser of all spiritual goods, even of glory itself." "I do not doubt that all the predestined reach eternal blessing through her prayers."[5] Mary shares the dignity of the Head in a wonderful way. She was loved by God more than the Church; hence "he decreed that conceiving and bringing forth a Redeemer she should bring healing to the Church."[6]

---

[1]*Homiliae catholicae de sacris arcanis Deiparae Mariae et Josephi, libri XIX,* (Napes, 1859). Cf. also *De sacra antiquitate ordinis B. M. de Carmelo,* (Antwerp, 1620; Cologne, 1645; Spanish tr., Seville, 1623). Cf. F. Stegmüller, in LexMar, 1067-1072; M. de Castro, in DSp 8, 323-324; J. Vasquez, "Juan de Cartagena, Vida y obras," in Anton., 39(1964), 243-301 and 40(1965), 320-325; P. Martinez, "La Inmaculada Concepción según las doctrinas de Juan de Cartagena y Juan Serrano," in V. I., VII, 2, 209-241; K. Balic, *Testimonia de Assumptione,* II, (Rome, 1950), 153-155. [2]*Homiliae* XV, 8, 1-2. [3]*Homiliae* I, 3, 4. [4]*Homiliae* XIV, 13, 21. [5]*Homiliae* XIV, 17, 4; *Homiliae* XIV, 17, 2; and *ibid.* [6]*Homiliae* V, 7, 20.

CASSIAN, JOHN (*c.* 360-*c.* 435) — See Supplement, pp. 379-80.

CATECHETICS

The problems facing the teacher of religious knowledge in Catholic schools, in the domain of Marian doctrine as in others, are twofold: how to convey the essentials without dilution and how to ensure maximum acceptance for them.[1] The second problem is pedagogic largely, including therein the important factor of the teacher's personal conviction. The first question is one which touches the body of teaching transmitted through authentic channels within the Church, growing according to the proper laws of doctrinal development renewed in the spirit and directives of Vatican II. Recent experience has encouraging results to show, as it has mistakes and bad decisions to regret. The question of Marian catechetics was raised by Cardinal Wojtyla at the Episcopal Synod in 1977 on catechetics in general. John Paul II in the Apostolic Exhortation, *Catechesi Tradendae* (16 October, 1979) dealt with the subject as with the many others raised in the Synod.

---

[1]Cf. F. M. Jelly, O.P., "Mary and the renewal of Catechetics in our time," in MSt, 28(1977), 10-21; J. A. Hardon, S.J., "The Blessed Virgin in Modern Catechetics," in MSt, 29(1978), 79-92; symposium, *La Madonna nella catechesi.* (Naples, Edizioni Domenicane Italiane, 1971); B. Trutter, *Marienlehre und religiöse Unterweisung,* (Dayton, 1975); EphMar, 30(1980), special issue, "Maria en la Catequesis y en la piedad popular."

CATHERINE OF SIENA, ST., DOCTOR OF THE CHURCH
(1347-1380)

The great Dominican mystic has, in her Dialogue, Letters and Prayers, important suggestive points on Our Lady. Her method was intuitive. Characteristic is her *Elevation on the feast of the Annunciation.*[1] Mary is a treasury of mercy. She is the "temple of the Trinity, the bearer of the fires [of love], the presenter of mercy, for by the giving of your flesh to the Word, the world was reconquered." C. expresses her love for Mary strongly. In her was written the Word from whom we have received the doctrine of life. C. offers Mary prayers for the sweet spouse of her divine Son [the Church] and for its Vicar on earth that he may have light and judgment to reform the holy Church. On the Annunciation feast C. prays with boldness, "for on this day of graces nothing can be refused to her."

---

[1]Cf. G. Agresti, O.P., "Aspetti mariano-mariologici in S. Caterina da Siena," in *Bull. Sienese stor. pat.,* 69(1962), 220-223; L. Grassototo, "Aspetti mariani della vita e dottrina di S. Caterina da Siena, dottore della Chiesa," in *Mater Ecclesiae,* 6(1970), 170-174; Luis Lopez de las Heras, "La imagen de Maria en S. Catalina de Siena," in *Studium,* 13(1973), 249-279, (*Elevation on the feast of the Annunciation,* 252-256, quoted here).

CHAMINADE, WILLIAM JOSEPH
(1761-1850)

A French priest whose life spanned the French Revolution and the Bourbon Restoration, C. had a key role in the Bordeaux region in the revival of Catholic life, and the rehabilitation of priests who had taken the oath to the Constitution. His varied continuous apostolate was centered on Our Lady.[1] He founded the Congregation of the Daughters of Mary Immaculate in 1816 and the Society of Mary (Marianists) in 1817. His idea that Mary, the Woman of Gen 3:15 (*qv*), would show her special power in overcoming the evils of these latter days, recalls St. Louis Marie de Montfort (*qv*), whose book was unknown to him. The Legion of Mary would accept these words fully: "We have understood this heavenly thought (that Mary is the hope, the joy, the life of the Church) and we have hastened to offer our feeble service to Mary to work under her command and fight beside her. We have enrolled ourselves beneath her banner as her soldiers and ministers and we have bound ourselves by a special vow of stability to support her with all our strength to the end of our lives, in the struggle against hell."[2] This is a concept of the apostolate (qv) in reference to Mary. The Marianists have well served the apostolate of the school and university, and of the written word.[3] Conspicuous Marian theologians have been E. Neubert, P. Hoffer and Th. Koehler. The Marian library at Dayton is now known as the largest in the world.

[1]Critical ed. of works, *Ecrits marials*, ed. by J. B. Armbruster, S.M., 2 vols., (Fribourg, 1966). Cf. E Neubert, *La doctrine mariale de M. Chaminade, Cahiers de la Vierge* (Paris, 1937); *ibid.*, in *Maria*, III, 345-349; J. B. Armbruster, *Maria nella vita del P. Chaminade* (papers of Mariological Congress of 1968, Brusasco, 1969); P. Hoffer, S.M., *La Vie Spirituelle d'après les écrits du P. Chaminade*, (Rome, Marianist Generalate, 1968); J. Samaha, S.M., "Chaminade's contribution to Mariology," in EphMar, 27(1977), 5-28. [2]*Maria*, III, 346-347. [3]1,500 titles of books and articles with other items, in B. Wyder, *Bibliographie mariale marianiste*, (Brusasco, 1969); H. Lebon, S.M., in DSp, II, 454-459.

CHARISMATIC RENEWAL, THE — See Supplement, p. 380.

CHRISTOLOGY, RECENT — See Supplement, p. 380.

CHRIST-TYPE, CHURCH-TYPE THEORIES

Between the dogma of the Assumption (qv) and the Lourdes Mariological Congress in 1958, the Mary-Church (qv) theme had come into prominence in Marian theology. With so much writing on the subject, a cleavage of thought began to appear between two systems or general theories about Our Lady, each assembling and unifying ideas about her in its own way.[1] It was a matter of intellectual approach and tendency, and, since all Catholics must hold certain truths about Our Lady, there was not on each side a totally closed system. Those who retained the traditional emphasis on the divine motherhood, on Mary's similarity with her divine Son and on the close union between them, were committed to a Christ-type theology of Mary. The Church-type doctrine was defended and elaborated by those who stressed the importance of Mary as type of the Church, who analyzed the analogy and parallel between them.

The theme of the Lourdes Congress was "Mary and the Church." This did not signify victory for the Church-type theologians. Both sides were well represented. For many not conversant with the movement of ideas, the Congress was at least informative. Mary's part in the Redemption was still acutely debated, and Fr. H. M. Koester's paper showed how the debate was influenced by the divergent viewpoints on Marian theology in general.

Since the Church was a central theme of Vatican II, it could be expected that its teaching would lean towards, even favour, Church-type Marian doctrine. An early initiative by some Council Fathers seemed to justify this hope. They objected to an independent schema on Our Lady and asked that teaching about her form part of the schema on the Church. Whatever was thought or said by experts, or Observers or in the lobbies, the only firm evidence is in the statements by Cardinals Santos and Koenig in the session of 24 October, 1963. Cardinal Santos said: "Finally it seems better to have the Constitution on the Blessed Virgin Mary separate from the Constitution on the Church lest the Council appear to wish to decide the controversy between Catholics about Mariology called 'Christ-type' and that called 'Church-type'."[2] Cardinal Koenig, as if aware of such a fear, was conciliatory: "And let it not be said that such a schema or a chapter so integrated could only show Mariology in a manner that is called Church-type, in which the Blessed Virgin is shown only as a member among other members of the Church passively receiving the benefits of the Redeemer. Since the Church is not a mere fruit of the Redemption but an instrument in the hand of Christ actively cooperating towards salvation, the Blessed Virgin in such a chapter or integrated schema can be excellently proposed as the most sublime cooperator with Christ through his grace in accomplishing and spreading the work of salvation. It is clear that such a chapter greatly exalts the dignity of the Mother of God."[3]

One result of the vote, following the presentation of the two reports, was the decision to draft a new schema. The experts to whom this task was given represented the two trends. K. Balic, O.F.M., mostly responsible for the earlier schema, had, in this text, taken the

Christ-type viewpoint, while Mgr. Philips had published important studies which showed him particularly sensitive to the Church-Mary theme[4]—though not necessarily committed to all that the Church-type theory implies. The title of the new schema, which would be chapter VIII of the Church Constitution, manifested a wish to reconcile the two theories: *The Blessed Virgin Mary Mother of God in the mystery of Christ and of the Church.*

An introductory report to the Council Fathers first conceded an important point: "But from the other viewpoint, to explain this link between Mary and the Church it is necessary to consider the office of the Mother of God in the very mystery of the Word Incarnate. But from this aspect, an exposition of Mariology exceeds a treatise on the Church. For which reason it could not be placed at the end of the schema and had to be prolonged beyond its strict limits so that a general view, sufficiently founded in faith, would be had of the Blessed Virgin." Later the report dealt with the contrasting theories: "From this it does not at all follow that the Council is imposing a fixed solution to the controversy between the so-called Christ-type and Church-type tendencies about Mary's person. In the absolute sense Christ is the type of all perfection, whom Mary resembles in a singular way, so that, following an ancient tradition, she can be called the type of the Church. The Christ-type and the Church-type interpretations do not exclude each other; they complete each other."[5]

[1]Cf. esp. C. Pozzo, S.J., "Las tendencias existentes en la mariologia católica contemporanea," ch. I, in *Maria en la obra de la salvación*, (Madrid, BAC, 1974), 20-64. Representing Christ-type theory, cf. J. de Aldama, S.J., *Temas de teologia mariana*, (Madrid, 1966); M. J. Nicolas, O.P., *Théotokos. Le mystère de Maria*,(Tournai, 1965); C. Vollert, S.J., "The structure of Marian theology," ch. I, in *A Theology of Mary*, (New York, 1965). Representing Church-type theory, cf. H. M. Koester, *Unus Mediator*, (Limburg, 1950); id. *Die Magd des Herrn*, 2nd ed., (Limburg, 1954); O. Semmelroth, *Mary, Archetype of the Church*, (New York, 1964; English tr. of *Urbild der Kirche*); H. M. Koester, in ME, II, 21-49. [2]*Relationes circa schema Constitutionis dogmaticae de B. V.*, (Vatican Press, 1963). [3]*op. cit.,* [4]Cf. "Perspectives mariologiques; Marie et l'Église, Essai bibliographique," in MM, 15(1953), 436-511; "Marie et l'Église, un thème théologique renouvelé," in *Maria*, VII, 365-419. [5]Official *Relatio* presented by Archbishop (later Cardinal) Roy, ch. VIII, in LG, (Vatican Press, 1964).

CHRONOLOGY

The chronology of Mary's life is known to us through that of her divine Son.[1] The results of recent research vary somewhat, as can be seen by comparing New Testament Chronological tables given by T. Corbishley, S.J.[2] and H. Daniel-Rops[3], each summarizing the findings of scholars. Some points in the time sequence are fixed. Mary gave birth to Jesus before the death of Herod which took place in 4 B.C. She was present at the crucifixion some time between 30 A.D. and 33 A.D. Taking Jewish custom as a basis of conjecture, she would have been between twelve and a half and fourteen years at the time of her betrothal, and the Annunciation would have taken place within a year of this ceremony. We have no firm evidence or even reliable indication of the time of Mary's passing from this world. The variables within that framework depend on different estimates on the date of Christ's birth, put as early as 8 B.C. by some scholars, on differences of opinion on the length of his public ministry and, consequently, on the year of his death, put at 30 A.D. by some, 33 A.D. by others.

[1]Cf. U. Holzmeister, *Chronologia Vitae Christi*, (Rome, 1933); L. Girard, *Cadre chronologique du ministère de Jésus*, (Paris, 1953); T. Corbishley, S.J., "The Chronology of New Testament Times," in NewCathComm, 898-901. Also P. Gaechter, S.J., "The Chronology from Mary's Betrothal to the Birth of Christ," in TheolSt, 2(1941), 147-170, 347-368; id., in *Maria im Erdenleben*, 2nd ed., (Innsbruck, 1954), II, 78-126. [2]T. Corbishley, S.J., "The Chronology of New Testament Times," in NewCathComm, 899. [3]*Daily Life in Palestine at the time of Christ*, (London, 1962), 450-451.

CHRYSIPPUS OF JERUSALEM (399-479)

Born in Cappadocia, C. was a monk in the monastery of St. Euthymius in Jerusalem. He was ordained a priest about 455, and left many writings. Among the few which have survived is the *Oratio in Sanctam Mariam Deiparam* (BHG 1144n), a sermon on Our Lady, important because of its contents and its relevance to the origins of Marian Liturgy (see LITURGY).[1] Mary is also briefly referred to in a homily on St. John the Baptist.

The sermon is (with an introduction and conclusion on "Ave, gratia plena, Dominus tecum") mostly a commentary on biblical texts used for a feast of Our Lady—Ps 131:8; Ps 44:11; Is 7:14; Gal 4:4 Lk 2:4-8. In the *chairetismoi*, modelled on the *Ave*, C. recalls other biblical images: the burning bush (Ex 3:2); the closed door (Ezek 44:2); and the stone cut by no human hands (Dan 2:34). Ps 131:8 is applied to the

Incarnation, and when God has arisen and come to the ark of his sanctification (RSV "might"), "the ark, which he has sealed i.e. Mary will with all rise from the Fall, in which her relationship with Eve has involved her."[2]

All are here shown to benefit by Mary's role; in the opening lines she is said to "bring forth as fruit life for the entire human race." Mary is for C. the "root of all good things." To show her role, he uses the Eve-Mary (qv) parallel and antithesis, but in an original way. The devil, seeing us "recalled to the primal adoption of sons through a woman," speaks thus: "How does it happen that the instrument which became my helper in the beginning is now opposed to me? A woman brought it about that I should take the human race into tyranny and a woman has thrown me out from tyranny. The ancient Eve exalted me, the new one 'threw me down."[3] The monologue continues (with a curious item concerning the devil's attempt to sow doubt in St. Joseph's mind) to end on the idea of human freedom regained and heirship to the kingdom of heaven established. Satan feels doubly cheated.

C. took the virginal conception as a sign of the divinity.[4] He believed in the *virginitas in partu*. The Annunciation is a message of future espousal (see SPOUSE) to the Father and in its accomplishment the Trinity is involved: "The Father himself will espouse you, the Spirit will achieve those things needed to the espousal and the Son will also share the beauty of your temple."[5]

Did C. think Mary subject to original sin? The reference to her relationship with Eve which involved her in the Fall seems to imply this, as does the fact that C. was at pains to stress Jesus' exemption from all sin.[6] His idea of Mary's immense role follows from the theory then common among the Greek Fathers, that the Incarnation itself was redemption for all, and looked to, and in a sense included, the later mysteries.

[1]*Oratio in sanctam Mariam Deiparam*, ed. by M. Jugie, A.A., in PO, 19, 336-343; CMP, 576-587; EMBP, 1013-1023; ClavisG, III, 287-288. Cf. R. Caro, *La Homiletica*, I, 211-226; M. Jugie, A.A., "Oratio in sanctam Mariam Deiparam," in *Le culte de la Sainte Vierge en Orient au Ve Siècle*, 297ff; J. Crehan, S.J., "The Assumption and the Jerusalem Liturgy," in TheolSt, 30(1969), 312-325; Ch. Martin, S.J., "Mélanges d'homilétique byzantine, I, Hesychius et Chrysippe de Jérusalem," in RHE, 35(1939), 54-60;

B. Capelle, O.S.B., "La fête de la Vierge à Jérusalem au Ve siècle," in Mus, 56(1943), 1-33; T. Gallus, S.J., "Antithesis 'Eva Maria' cum Gen 3:15 conjuncta apud Chrysippum," in *Div. Thomas* (Plac.), 59(1956), 71-74. [2]*Oratio in sanctam Mariam Deiparam*, in PO, 19, 338. [3]PO, 19, 340-341. [4]PO, 19, 339. [5]*op. cit.* [6]*op. cit.*

CHRYSOGONUS, LAURENTIUS, S.J. (1590-1650)

C. was the greatest Croatian Mariologist (Lovro Grizogon), and author of an encyclopaedic work, *Mundus Marianus*, which contains over 3,000 folio pages in all. Part I, published in Vienna, 1646, treated of Mary as a mirror reflecting God and his perfections. Part II, published in Padua in 1651, dealt with Mary as a mirror reflecting the heavenly world and its perfections. Part III, published in Augsburg in 1712, showed Mary as a mirror reflecting the earthly world and its perfections.[1] Mary has for the author a cosmic role. She was the summit of creation and the meaning and purpose of all things under her divine Son, for, through her, the whole of creation was in a way associated with the person of the Word. This thought is similar to that of Theophanes of Nicaea (qv), whose work C. did not know. His own work is uneven; the best Marian theology is found in Part I. His erudition was enormous and is evident in the quotations from a vast army of patristic and medieval writers. His basic principles are sound: Mary's divine motherhood, and her cooperation in the work of our Redemption. He was mostly influenced by Richard of St. Laurent (qv), and to a lesser extent by the Victorines, Ubertino of Casale (qv), Bernardine of Siena (qv) and Pelbart of Temesvar.

[1]Cf. A. Katalinic, S.J., "'Mundus Marianus' a Laurentio Chrysogono S.J. conscriptus," in MM, 24(1962), 544-560; *ibid.*, "De cultu mariano a saeculo VI ad saeculum XI in prima encyclopaedia mariana a Laurentio Chrysogono, Croata, conscripta," in Zagreb Congress, II, 197-205.

CIRILLONAS (d. Early Fifth Century)

C., a Syrian poet, treated Marian themes in passages found in his slight corpus of writing.[1] He insists on the virginal conception, expounding it with varied imagery. Mary's Son was the "bread come from heaven, not sown or rooted in the earth."[2] Echoes of Ex 12:34 (the leaven wrapped in a linen cloth), or possibly of Prov 30:4, are found in C.,[3] to express the virginal motherhood. A disputed text may refer to the Immaculate Conception (qv), though another rendering would be to the Eucharist.[4] The Eve-Mary (qv) parallel and contrast are filled out with original imagery.[5]

[1]CMP, II, 538-539; Cf. C. Vona, I Carmi di Cirillona, (Rome, 1963); I. Ortiz de Urbina, S.J., "La Mariologia nei Padri Siriaci," in OCP, 1(1935), 110-111. [2]C. Vona, op. cit., ch. II, 75. [3]ibid., op. cit., ch. II, 76. [4]ibid., op. cit., for different opinions, 50-52. [5]C. Vona, op. cit., ch. V, 126-128.

CLARET, ST. ANTHONY MARY
(1807-1870)

C., missionary apostolic in Catalonia and the Canaries, archbishop of Santiago de Cuba, confessor to the queen of Spain and restorer of the Escorial monastery, was attacked, even physically, by the anticlerics of the day. He was exiled by the First Republic and, having attended Vatican I, died in France. Through the Congregation of the Sons of the Immaculate Heart of Mary which he founded in 1849, he has powerfully affected Marian theology in Spain.[1] His writings were pastoral and devotional: La Archicofradia del Corazon de Maria; Balsamo eficaz; La Escalera de Jacob; El Escapulario azul-celeste; La Devocion al Santisimo Rosario; El Rosario explicado; Novena al Corazon de Maria; La Virgen del Pilar y los Francmasones. He wrote of Mary in many of his other educational or catechetical works.

In the present age, Claretians have contributed in many ways to Marian studies and scientific research. In 1941, N. Garcia-Garces (qv) founded the Spanish Mariological Society which has been ably supported by the Claretians as by other Spanish theologians. In 1951, he launched the review Ephemerides Mariologicae. Claretians since then have been among its regular contributors, assisting adjustment to post-conciliar trends. Since 1975, the Marian Center, Cor Mariae Centrum, has been an official work of the Congregation, directed by a Claretian, designed to provide specialist services. Among distinguished Marian scholars of the religious institute are J. M. Alonso (qv), J. M. Canal, D. Fernandez, N. Garcia-Garces, M. Peinador, and A. Rivera.

[1]Escritos autobiográficos y espirituales, (Madrid, 1959); Cf. N. Garcia-Garces, C.M.F., in Maria, III, 405-427; J. Aramendia, C.M.F., in DSp, II, 932-937; J. M. Canal, "La

oracion 'Oh Virgen y Madre de Dios'" in St. Claret., 5(1966), 105-116.

CLEMENT OF ALEXANDRIA
(d. before 215)

C. followed Pantaenus as head of the Catechetical School of Alexandria. In a few brief passages on Mary, he expresses ideas not then as yet prominent among the Fathers.[1] He speaks of the virginity in partu thus: "For certain people say that Mary examined by the midwife after she had given birth was found to be a virgin."[2] The source is evidently the Protoevangelium of James (see APOCRYPHA). C. speaks of the Scriptures, like Mary, bringing forth truth. He points to the Mary-Church parallel in the following words: "O mysterious wonder! There is only one Father of all, only one Word of all, and the Holy Spirit is also one and he is everywhere. There is but one Virgin Mother. I like to call her the Church. Alone this mother has not had milk, for she alone is not a woman but a virgin and a mother, immaculate as a virgin, loving as a mother; and she calls her children and feeds them with holy milk: the Word a child."[3] C. taught the virginal conception. He attributed the making of Christ's human body to the Holy Spirit.[4] Some of the early Fathers thought of the Word himself. "But the Lord Christ, fruit of the Virgin, did not seek the sweet breast of a woman, did not ask her for his food. When the Father, full of kindness, rained down his Word, the latter became for men a spiritual food."

[1]Works, in GCS, 12, 15, 17, PG, 8-9; CMP, I, 57-59; EMBP, 53-55. Cf. H. Holstein, S.J., in BSFEM, 9(1951), 20-21; A. Muller, Ecclesia-Maria, Die Einheit Marias und der Kirche, (Fribourg, 1951), 103-105. [2]Stromata VII, 16, in GCS, 17, 66; PG, 9, 529, 30. [3]Paedag. I, 6, 21, in GCS, 12, 115; PG, 8, 300-301. [4]Excerpt from Theodotus 60, in GCS, 17, 12, also in SC, 23, 178; PG, 9, 688B.

CLORIVIERE, PIERRE-JOSEPH PICOT DE
(1735-1820)

A French Jesuit, C. was a victim of the French Revolution and of the suppression of his society, which eventually he helped to restore. He is known principally through the documents of two societies which he founded in the days of the Revolution, the Priests of the Heart of Jesus and the Daughters of the Heart of Mary.[1] Much of his written work is unpublished. He had an authentic mystical gift, and strove to maintain Marian ideas and devotion in an age when they had in many places declined. In piety, he continued the ideas of the French school of the seventeenth century. He wrote a life of St. Louis Marie de Montfort (*qv*), but could not have known that Saint's book on true devotion. In doctrine he insisted on the close union, partnership of a kind, between Jesus and Mary. He resisted firmly the objections against Marian cult, and was of the opinion that the Church believed in the Immaculate Conception and the Assumption. C. had intuitions on the evils that were to come in his time.

---

[1]Works: *Pierre de Clorivière, d'après ses notes intimes de 1763 a 1773*, 2 vols., ed. by H. Monier-Vinart, (Paris, 1935); *Lettres du Pierre Clorivière*, 2 vols., (Paris, 1948); *Documents constitutifs des Sociétés, 1790-1820*, (Paris 1935); *Voila votre Mère. Extraits des oeuvres du Pierre Clorivière*, (Paris, 1935), devotional anthology. Cf. H. Monier-Vinard, in DSp, II, 974-979; Cl. Dillenschneider, C.SS.R., in *Marie au service de notre Rédemption*, (Hagenau, 1947), 130-138; A. Rayez, S.J., in *Maria*, III, 309-328.

COMMUNION OF SAINTS — See Supplement, p. 380.

COMPASSION, OUR LADY'S

Mary's compassion in the theological sense is her participation in the Passion of her divine Son.[1] Early patristic thinking on this subject was deflected from the truth by Origen's (*qv*) interpretation of the sword (*qv*) in Simeon's prophecy. Already in the East this opinion was losing ground by the sixth century, and with Jacob of Sarug (*qv*) we have the image of the sorrowing Mother: "Your Mother bore many sufferings on your account; every affliction surrounded her at your crucifixion. How many mournful weepings and tears of suffering did her eyes not shed when they were carrying out your funeral and when they bore you into the sepulchre and placed you there. How many terrors did the Mother of mercy not experience when the guards of the sepulchre turned her away so that she should not approach you. She endured pains when she saw you hanging on the Cross and there with a lance they pierced your side on Golgotha, when the Jews had sealed the tomb in which had been placed your body living, giving life and remitting offences."[2] Strangely Jacob has nothing on this theme in his homily on Mary and Golgotha. George of Nicomedia (*qv*) speaks of "the Mother stricken by the most poignant of natural sorrows"[3] on Calvary and goes on to interpret

Jn 19:25-27 in the sense of Mary's motherhood of the apostles while she remains with them—the limited beginnings of a doctrine of spiritual motherhood from this text.

Among the Latins, St. Ambrose (*qv*) gave much thought to this moment in Mary's life. He admired her fortitude: "I read that she stood [by the Cross]; I do not read that she wept."[4] In three other passages Ambrose, repeating himself a good deal as to phrasing, expresses on the Calvary incident a core of thought which has theological and spiritual relevance. "But Mary was not less than it was fitting that the Mother of Christ should be; as the Apostles fled, she stood before the Cross gazing tenderly on her Son's wounds, because she was awaiting not so much the death of her Child as the salvation of the world. But perhaps she, the royal palace, since she knew that the Redemption of the world would be through the death of her Son, thought that she by her death would add to the public gift. But Jesus did not need a helper for the Redemption of all, he who said: 'I am become like a man without help, free among the dead.' He welcomed his mother's affection, but did not seek human help. We have, therefore, instruction on duty. The reading teaches what maternal affection ought to imitate, what filial respect should follow; mothers ought to expose themselves in moments of danger for their sons, sons should be pained more by care for their mothers than by sadness at their own lot."[5] Thus, in the commentary on St. Luke. In Epistle 63, the saint emphasizes more strongly the recommendation to imitation of Mary.[6] In the *De institutione Virginis* the portrait is more complete: "The Mother stood, no ignoble sight, for she did not fear the slayer. The Son hung on the Cross, the Mother offered herself to the persecutors." Mary may have hoped to die with Christ and rise with him, "for she was not igorant of the fact that the one whom she had brought forth would rise from the dead."[7] The whole picture is related to the theme of admiration central to the treatise.

Milo of St. Amand (*qv*) had another intuition. He spoke of Mary's tears on Calvary "by which joy came into the world."[8] Two hundred years later, St. Peter Damian (*qv*) interpreted the sword of Simeon in the sense of compassion: "As if he were saying that while your Son felt the passion in his body, a sword of compassion pierced your soul."[9] Arnold of Bonneval (*qv*), very conscious of the opinion of St. Ambrose, could nevertheless write: "Both equally offered the one holocaust."[10] Meanwhile popular compositions, the *Planctus* and *Marienklagen*, laments for Mary's sorrow, attempted to describe the sufferings of Our Lady in elaborate detail. The feast of the Dolours of Mary signified the liturgical expression of the idea.

In modern times, theologians, prominent among them Quirino de Salazar (*qv*), have sought to integrate a theory about Mary's compassion into a theology of the Redemption. Some papal opinions are often quoted. Thus, Benedict XV: "Mary suffered and, as it were, nearly died with her suffering Son; for the salvation of mankind she renounced her mother's rights and, as far as it depended on her, offered her Son to placate divine justice; so that we may well say that she with Christ redeemed mankind."[11]

Pius XII achieved a synthesis of this idea and the new Eve (*qv*) typology: "She it was who immune from all sin, personal or inherited, and ever more closely united with her Son, offered him on Golgotha to the Eternal Father together with the holocaust of her maternal rights and motherly love, like a new Eve for all the children of Adam contaminated through his unhappy fall, and thus she, who was the Mother of our Head according to the flesh, became by a new title of sorrow and glory the spiritual Mother of all his members."[12]

The phrase "holocaust of her maternal rights" raises the problem of Mary's part in the Redemption (*qv*). Vatican II (*qv*) put the reality otherwise: "There she stood, in keeping with the divine plan [cf. Jn 19:25], suffering grievously with her only-begotten Son. There she united herself with a maternal heart to his sacrifice, and lovingly consented to the immolation of this Victim which she herself had brought forth." (LG 58).

[1]Cf. R. Bernard, "La compassion et la maternité spirituelle de Marie," in *La Vie Spirit.*, 27(1931), 20-31; "Notre Dame des Sept Douleurs," in *La Vie Spirit.*, 28(1931), 125-138; A. Wilmart, O.S.B., *Auteurs spirituels et textes dévots du moyen âge latin*, (Paris, 1932), 505-536; W Lipphardt, "Studien zu den Marienklagen," in *Beiträge zur Geschichte der deutschen Sprache und Literatur*, 58(1934), 390-444; G. Journet, "Notre Dame des Sept Douleurs," in *Cahiers de la Vierge*, 2nd ed., (Paris, 1934); F. Mugnier, *La Compassion de Marie*, (Paris, 1935); A. Luis, "Evolutio historica doctrinae de Compassione B.M.V.," in MM, 5(1943), 261-285; P. Regamey, "La Compassion de la Sainte Vierge," in *La Vie Spirit.*, 73(1945), 151-165; A. M. Lépicier, *Mater Dolorosa, Notes d'histoire, de liturgie et d'iconographie sur le culte de Notre Dame des Douleurs*, (Spa, 1948); H. Barré, C.S.Sp., "Le 'Planctus Mariae' attribué à S. Bernard," in RAM, 28(1952), 243-266. [2]"Serm. de Transitu Dei Genitricis Mariae," in *Oriens Christ.*, 5(1965), 92. [3]*Hom. 8 on Jn 19:25-27*, in PG, 100, 1475C. [4]*De obitu Valentiniani 39*, in CSEL, 73, 348; PL, 16, 1371B. [5]*In Luc., 10, 132*, in CCL, 14, 383; CSEL, 32, 4, 505; PL, 15, 1837. [6]*Epist. 63, 110*, in PL, 16, 1218BC. [7]PL, 16, 49, 318. [8]MGH, III, 645. [9]*Serm. 46 In Nativ. B. M.*, in PL, 144. [10]*De Laudibus*, in PL, 189, 1727A. [11]*Inter Sodalicia*, in OL, 194. [12]*Mystici Corporis*, in OL, 253.

CONGRESSES, MARIAN AND MARIOLOGICAL

Since the first Italian congress held in Livorno in 1895, there have been over 150 noteworthy national, regional, or international congresses in honour of Our Lady. There were others of less significance.[1] Between 1947 and 1958 inclusive, 129 took place (counting only those with published records), forty-three in 1954 alone. Early in the century, six congresses were held in Brittany between 1904 and 1933. About the time of the dogma of the Assumption, the Franciscan Order undertook the organization of a number on this theme.[2]

The first important congress in France had been in Lyons in 1900. After one held in Chartres in 1927, a permanent national committee was set up, with papal and episcopal encouragement, to ensure planning of future similar events. It was agreed that the Chartres congress would be considered first in the series. It was followed by others in Lourdes (1930), Laons-Liesse (1934), Boulogne sur Mer (1938), Grenoble-La Salette (1946, attended by Archbishop Roncalli, later John XXIII, then Nuncio in Paris), Rennes (1950), Lyons (1954), and Lisieux (1961).

Prior to 1950, international Marian congresses had been held in Fribourg (1902), Rome (1904), Einsiedeln (1906), Saragossa (1908), Salzburg (1910), and Trier (1912). The Marian congress which coincided in Rome with the 1950 Holy Year and the dogma of the Assumption was, for the first time in the series, accompanied by an international Mariological Congress devoted to the theme *Alma Socia Christi*. This whole gathering had been organized by the Franciscan Marian Commission which had been founded by Fr. K. Balic, O.F.M. (*qv*) in 1946 to plan the Franciscan congresses. After the Rome congresses, the International Marian Academy, with Fr. Balic as president, was established to assume responsibility for future congresses. Though the proceedings of the

Saragossa, Salzburg and Trier congresses have the words fourth, fifth and sixth in their titles, it was decided to consider Lyons in 1900 as first in the series, those just held in Rome being, therefore, eight Marian and the first Mariological. The subsequent Mariological congresses which, on each occasion, were immediately followed by a Marian congress, were on the following themes: Rome, (1954), *Virgo Immaculata*; Lourdes (1958), *Maria et Ecclesia;* Santo Domingo (1965), *Maria in Sacra Scriptura;* Lisbon (1967) (Marian assembly at Fatima), *De primordiis cultus mariani;* Zagreb (with Marian assembly at Maria Bistrica) (1971), *De cultu mariano saeculis VI-XI;* Rome (1975), *De cultu mariano saeculis XII-XV;* and Saragossa (1979), *De cultu mariano saeculo XVI.* Regional and international gatherings have also been held through the century by the Marian Congregations.

In all such assemblies, the place chosen, as can be seen from the lists given, will generally commend itself by reason of some centenary or similar commemoration. Papal support has been generous with the appointment of Legates for the large congresses, and very often a special doctrinal or devotional message. Pius XII's address to the 1954 congress on method in Mariology, and Paul VI's to the 1975 one on the *Via pulchritudinis*, rise above conventional greetings.

---

[1]Cf. A. Boucher, "L'Oeuvre du comité national français des congrès marials," in *Maria*, III, 617-625; Lorenzo M. di Fonzo, O.F.M.Cap., in *Théotocos*, 646-648; R. Laurentin, *La Question mariale*, (Paris, 1963), 17. Cf. esp. G. M. Roschini, O.S.M., *Maria Santissima*, IV, 393, 452-468 (list of 147 important congresses from 1900-1967).

CONRAD OF SAXONY (d. 1279)

A Franciscan, of Hildesheim and Provincial of Saxony, C. wrote the *Speculum Beatae Mariae Virginis seu Expositio salutationis angelicae*,[1] a commentary on the *Ave Maria* in eighteen lessons. He used many quotations from Venerable Bede (*qv*), St. Anselm (*qv*), St. Peter Damian (*qv*) whose writings he sometimes attributed to St. Bernard (*qv*) (whom he also quotes frequently); also from Ambrose Autpert's (*qv*) sermon on the Assumption which he attributed to St. Augustine (*qv*), and from Pseudo-Jerome (*qv*) and Pseudo-Augustine (*qv*), taking each work as genuine. His own work was for long attributed to St. Bonaventure (*qv*).

C. did not hold the Immaculate Conception (*qv*). As did his contemporaries, he expounded the fourfold meaning of *Maria*: bitter sea; star; illuminatress; and lady. C. concluded his work with a prayer: "O Mary . . . bitter sea, help us that we may be totally consumed in the bitterness of true penance. O Mary, star of the sea, help us that through the sea of this world we may find the true way spiritually. O Mary, illuminatress, help us that we may be eternally illumined in glory. O Mary, Lady, help us that under your sway we may be filially ruled, through Our Lord."[2]

C. not only thinks of Mary as helper, but as Advocate (*qv*): "O Mary, our advocate. Behold we still need that you should make representation on our behalf."[3] As Mediatress too: "First give heed, dearest ones, to the fact that Mary our dawn is for us a Mediatress to God."[4] In Ambrose Autpert's words, C. speaks of Mary as associate of Christ: "The king of kings himself associates you with him with the embrace of love, loving you before all others as a true mother and fair spouse."[5] Mary transcends all angels and is the mistress of heaven and earth, ordering the angels. But she is, for C. too, the "universal Mother of all the faithful."[6]

---

[1]*Speculum Beatae Mariae Virginis seu Expositio salutationis angelicae*, in *Bibl. Franc. Ascet. Med. Aevi*, 2, (Quaracchi ed., 1904). Cf. L. di Fonzo, O.F.M.Conv., "La regalità di Maria in una celebre opera mariana di Fra Corrado di Sassonia," in *Luce Serafica*, 19(1943), 69-71; S. Girotto, O.F.M., *Corrado di Sassonia, predicatore e mariologo del sec. XIII*, (Florence, 1952). [2]*Speculum Beatae Mariae Virginis seu Expositio salutationis angelicae*, in *Bibl. Franc. Ascet. Med. Aevi*, (Quaracchi ed., 1904), 43. [3]*op. cit.*, 80. [4]*op. cit.*, 155. [5]*op. cit.*, 90. [6]*op. cit.*, 135.

CONSENT, MARY'S, AT THE ANNUNCIATION

Mary's response to the message of the angel: "Behold I am the handmaid [*qv*] of the Lord; let it be to me according to your word." (Lk 1:38). The biblical background is sketched in other articles. Here the theological meaning of Mary's consent is considered.[1] The patristic doctrine of the new Eve (*qv*) emphasized Mary's obedience and faith in contrast to Eve's disobedience and unbelief. This is really the theory of her consent, which would be later made more explicit. St. Bernard (*qv*), in the fourth homily *Super missus est* imagines "the whole world on bended knees" awaiting Mary's response to the angel, for on it will depend in a word "the salvation of all the children of Adam, of your whole race." A century and a half later, Peter John Olivi (qv) devoted one of his *Four Questions on Our Lady* to Mary's consent, and in the fifteenth century St. Bernardine took over the entire text as Sermons V and VI of his treatise on Our Lady. This time the emphasis is on the perfection, the immensity of the merit won by Mary's word. St. Thomas Aquinas (qv) saw Mary's consent "awaited in the place of all mankind."

Modern theories of Mary's share in the redemptive work of her divine Son are based on the meaning and effect of the consent. Support for such a view is forthcoming from the Teaching Authority (qv). Thus Leo XIII (qv) writes: "The eternal Son of God, when, for the redemption and honour of man, he wished to take the nature of man and was, in so doing, about to enter a mystical marriage with the whole human race, did not do so until the utterly free consent of the appointed Mother was forthcoming; she took the place of the human race."[2]

The doctrine is given prominence by Vatican II. The first schema had these words: "By this consent Mary, a daughter of Adam became not only Mother of Jesus, the unique divine Mediator and Redeemer, but also with him and under him she associated her work in accomplishing the Redemption of mankind. But this saving consent of the Mother of God and her partnership in accomplishing the work of Redemption persevered from the time of the virginal conception of Jesus Christ until his death, was indeed conspicuous when she took her stand by the Cross, in keeping with the divine plan." The final text of *Lumen Gentium* reads as follows: "By thus consenting to the divine utterance Mary, a daughter of Adam, became the Mother of Jesus." This had been preceded by the more comprehensive statement which linked Mary's consent to the divine motherhood: "The Father of mercies willed that the consent of the Mother should precede the Incarnation, so that as a woman had contributed to death, so also a woman should contribute to life." (LG 56).

H. Barré raised the important question related to Mary's consent. How was it related to that of Christ which was necessary to the Incarnation? It was consideration of such a problem which led Scheeben (qv) to his theory of the bridal motherhood. Pius IX and Pius XII

taught that Jesus and Mary were included in one and the same eternal divine decree, i.e. of predestination.

[1]Cf. J. M. Bover, S.J., *Deiparae Virginis Consensus. Corredemptionis ac Mediationis Fundamentum*, (Madrid, 1942), 36-140, but with some caution as patristic studies have notably advanced since then, esp. on St. Ephraem; H. Barré, C.S.Sp., "Le consentement à l'Incarnation rédemptrice. La Vierge seule ou le Christ d'abord," in MM, (1952), 233-266; R. Laurentin, *Traité V*, 141-142. [2]*Octobri mense*, (22 September, 1891); *Leonis P. M. Acta XI*, 303; OL, 108-109.

CONSECRATION

History:[1] Suggestions of a personal attitude towards Mary resembling consecration or self-donation are found before St. Ildefonsus of Toledo (qv). It was at one time thought that he first used the devotional phrase *servus Mariae* (servant, slave of Mary), but H. Barré (qv) found evidence in African sermons from the fifth and sixth centuries for the existence of the title. The word occurs in the literature of the Middle Ages. The formulation of Ildefonsus remains notable: "Therefore I am your servant [*servus*] because your Son is my Lord. Therefore you are my Lady because you are the handmaid of my Lord. Therefore I am the servant of the handmaid of my Lord because you, my Lady, have become the mother of my Lord. Therefore I have become a servant because you have become the mother of my maker."[2] In the East, St. John of Damascus (qv) came nearer to the idea of consecration: "O Lady, before you today we take our stand. Lady, I call you Virgin Mother of God and to your hope, as to the surest and strongest anchor we bind ourselves; to you we consecrate our mind, our soul, our body, all that we are, we honour you as much as we can with psalms and hymns and spiritual canticles."[3]

Two prayers to Mary in the Spanish liturgy link the idea of *servitus* with her spiritual motherhood.[4] The word with the verb *servire* continues to appear in prayers. Pope John VII (d. 707) claimed to be *Servus Sanctae Mariae*. The correlative title of Our Lady, *Domina*, of ancient origin, was given special status by St. Anselm (qv). St. Bernard (qv) saw a special commendation to Mary, if not explicit consecration, as a practice in keeping with her universal mediation: "Whatever you are about to offer, remember to commend it to Mary, so that through the same channel whence grace flowed, it may return to the giver of grace."

Post-Reformation Marian piety was to favour more explicit forms. The sixteenth century Marian Congregations included in their programme of holiness a formal engagement to Our Lady, called *Oratio sodalitatis*. The seventeenth century saw the appearance in Spain of the confraternities of "Slaves of the Virgin." The idea was taken up in France, and it was developed into a regular practice of personal consecration to Our Lady by Cardinal de Bérulle (*qv*), St. John Eudes (*qv*), Francois Poiré, S.J., and St. Louis Marie Grignion de Montfort (*qv*). The latter emphasized a Christocentric aspect of the devotion as he recommended it. "This devotion consists then in giving oneself entirely to the Blessed Virgin in order to belong entirely to Jesus Christ through her." There was a personal element also in the acts of consecration by kings during the same century: of France, by Louis XIII; of Poland, by John Casimir; of Portugal, by John IV; and the Austrian dominions, by Ferdinand III.

Thereafter the practice was taken up widely. The prayer of the Marian Congregations now became an act of consecration. St. Alphonsus Liquori (*qv*) offered his readers a special formula of the kind. A fresh impetus came in the nineteenth century with the revival of Marian devotion in France. About the time of the Miraculous Medal, a Parish Priest, Abbé Desgenettes of Notre Dame des Victoires, acting on what he thought was a heavenly command, consecrated his parish to the Immaculate Heart of Mary. Religious practice was almost instantaneously transformed and an indifferent urban area became a center of religious fervour. A number of the religious founders of the time, Francis Libermann (*qv*), William Chaminade (*qv*), and St. Anthony Mary Claret (*qv*), gave prominence to the practice of consecration in the official written rules of their societies. Such recommendation is conventional in the religious foundations since then.

Teaching Authority: In 1899, Leo XIII (*qv*) influenced by the suggestion of a Good Shepherd nun in Portugal, Maria Droste zu Vischering, consecrated the human race to the Sacred Heart of Jesus. This event gave a certain stimulus to the practice of consecration to the Immaculate Heart. The official collection, *Preces et Pia Opera*, published with the approval of Pius XI in 1938, gives the texts of acts of consecration indulgenced by the Church. They include St.

Louis Marie de Montfort's lengthy prayer and an act of consecration to the Immaculate Heart of Mary for use by groups, each approved with Indulgences in 1907 by St. Pius X (*qv*).

Marian Congresses (*qv*), in France particularly, began to support the idea of consecration of mankind to the Heart of Mary, similar to that made to the Sacred Heart of Jesus. Thus at the national Marian congress held at Boulogne-sur-mer in 1938 the wish was expressed "that the Holy Father would deign to make the official consecration of the human race to the Immaculate Heart of Mary as had been asked at the congresses of Lourdes in 1930 and Liesse in 1934, that the Holy Father would deign to sanction the addition throughout the world of *Regina Mundi* to the Litany of Loreto." Fr. Garrigou-Lagrange, O.P., then internationally esteemed, defended the idea in his work, *La Mère du Sauveur*, in 1941.

On 31 October of the following year, Pius XII (*qv*), speaking by radio to pilgrims gathered at Fatima for the Silver Jubilee of the Apparitions, concluded his address with a lengthy prayer of consecration: "To you and to your Immaculate Heart in this tragic hour of human history, we commit, we entrust, we consecrate not only holy Church, the mystical body of your Jesus, which suffers and bleeds in so many places and is afflicted in so many ways, but also the entire world torn by violent discord, scorched in a fire of hate, victim of its own iniquities . . . Finally, just as the Church and the entire human race were consecrated to the Heart of your Jesus, because by placing in him every hope it may be for them a token and pledge of victory and salvation; so, henceforth, they are perpetually consecrated to you, to your Immaculate Heart, O our Mother and Queen of the world, in order that your love and protection may hasten the triumph of the kingdom of God."[5]

The Pope repeated the consecration in St. Peter's Basilica on 8 December following. He had made an allusion to Russia in the text. In the Encyclical *Sacro vergente anno*, 7 July, 1952, to the peoples of Russia, he dedicated and consecrated "all the peoples of Russia to that same Immaculate Heart."[6] In the years after the Pope's initiative, especially during the Marian Year (1953-1954), the practice of consecration was widely taken up. Dioceses, institutes, houses, and countries were consecrated to the Heart of Mary.

John XXIII (qv), in his first Encyclical, *Ad Petri cathedram*, recalled the important act of 1942 in Pius XII's pontificate and he later supported similar acts of piety comprising Italy, Honduras, and Nicaragua. During Vatican II, Paul VI (qv) had been asked to renew, in union with the whole Hierarchy, the official act of Pius. In the concluding address to the third session of the Council, in which he proclaimed Mary Mother of the Church, he recalled the event in these words: ". . . the whole world which this Ecumenical Council thinks of with intense and loving care, which our predecessor, Pius XII, not without heavenly inspiration, solemnly consecrated to the Immaculate Heart of the Virgin Mary. We have thought it right that today this act of religious fealty should be commemorated [*commemorari*] by us." The Pope then announced that he was sending the Golden Rose to Fatima. "For this reason," he went on, "we also entrust [*committimus*] the whole human race for its protection, its difficulties and anxieties, its legitimate aspirations and ardent hopes to the guardianship of the heavenly Mother."[7]

In the Apostolic Exhortation, *Signum Magnum*, 13 May, 1967, coinciding with the papal visit to Fatima for its Golden Jubilee, we read: "Since the twenty-fifth anniversary is recalled this year of the solemn consecration of the Church and of mankind to Mary, the Mother of God and to her Immaculate Heart, by our predecessor of venerated memory, Pius XII, on 31 October, 1942, on the occasion of the broadcast message to the Portuguese nation, a consecration which we ourself have renewed on 21 November, 1964, we exhort all the sons of the Church to renew personally their consecration to the Immaculate Heart of the Mother of the Church and to bring alive this most noble act of veneration through a life ever more consonant with the divine will and in a spirit of filial service to, and of devout imitation of, their heavenly Queen."[8]

Theology: Pius XII spoke of "consecration to the Mother of God in the Marian Congregation as a total gift of oneself, for life and eternity." Recent attempts to rethink consecration to Mary appear to minimize it, if not to question its validity. The weight of the tradition outlined above is against such questioning. It is because of her unique participation in the divine, through her motherhood of the Word Incarnate,

and her unique role in our regard, through her mediation of grace, because too of a mysterious participation in the priesthood of Christ and his Church, that she is empowered to receive our gift of ourselves and establish it in God.

[1]Cf. R. P. Poupon, *Le Poème de la parfaite consécration à Marie suivant S. Louis Marie Grignion de Montfort et les spirituels de son temps*, (Lyons, 1947); E. Neubert, S.M., *La vie d'union à Marie*, 5th ed., (Paris, 1954); L. J. (Cardinal) Suenens, *The Theology of the Apostolate*, (Cork, 1953, Chicago, 1955); A. Menningen, S.A.C., *Die Marienweihe. Eine theologische Studie*, (Limburg, 1955); Basilio de San Pablo, "Valor ascético de la consagración a Maria," in EstM, 17(1956), 415-451; J. M. Canal, C.M.F., *Consecratio Marialis, De consecratione facta B. V. ejusque Cordi immaculato*, (Madrid, 1960); J. M. ALonso, C.M.F., "La consagracion al Corazón de Maria acto perfecto de la virtud de la Religión," in *Teología de Fatima*, (Madrid, 1961), 49-98; K. Rahner, S.J., "Die Weihe an Maria in den Marianischen Kongregationen; ihr theologischer aspekt und ihr Reflex in Leben," in *Quatrième centenaire des congrégations mariales. Documents du congrès européen*, Rome, 8th-12th September, 1963, (Rome, 1963); H. Barré, C.S.Sp., "Le culte marial en Afrique après S. Augustin," in REA, 13(1967), 57-80, 285-317; R. Laurentin, in *Vie Spirit.*, (1966), 741; *Consécration à Notre Dame*, (110 papal documents from Benedict XIV to Paul VI), ed. by L. Paulussen, in *Congrégations et Associations Mariales*, (Paris, 1967); L. Vandergheynst, *Le Pape et la consecration du monde à Marie*, (Brussels, 1968); *Teologia e pastorale della consacrazione a Maria. Aggiornamento teologico-pastorale alla luce del Vaticano II*, Rome, 8th-12th July, 1968, ed. by Collegamento Mariano Nazionale, (Rome, 1969); G. Geenen O.P., "Les antécédents doctrinaux et historiques de la consécration du monde au coeur immaculé de Marie," in *Maria*, I, 827-873; E. Cardinal Tisserant, "La consécration à Marie, moyen efficace d'assurer le triomphe du royaume de Dieu," in ME, XVI, 113-121; J. de Finance, "Consécration," in DSp, II, 1576-1583; J. de Aldama, S.J., "Cultus marianus servitutis a primordiis usque ad S. Anselmum Cantuariensem," in Zagreb Congress, IV, 403-426; L. Herran, "Proceso evolutivo del 'servicio amoroso' a Nuestra Señora la Virgen Maria: de S. Ildefonso a S. Anselmo," in Zagreb Congress, IV, 427-472; A. Rum, S.M.M., "Papa Giovanni VII (705-707): 'Servus Sanctae Mariae'," in Zagreb Congress, III, 249-263. [2]*De virginitate sanctae Mariae*, ed. by V. G. Blanco, (Madrid, 1937); BAC, 320, 12, (1937 ed.) 163; BAC, 148; PL, 96, 106. Cf. also psqq. in each case. [3]*Hom. I in Dorm.*, in PG, 96, 720A. [4]"Oracional Visigótico," ed. by J. Vives in *Monumenta Hispaniae Sacra*, (Barcelona, 1946), 75, 78. [5]AAS, 34(1942); OL, 251-252. [6]AAS, 44(1952); OL, 343. [7]AAS, 56(1964), 1017. [8]AAS, 59(1967), 475.

CONTENSON, VINCENT , O.P. (1641-1674)

C. deals with Marian questions in his *Theologia Mentis et Cordis*.[1] He is principally interested in the sublime spiritual perfection of Mary. He deals with her prerogatives in the order of nature, of grace, of glory, and of the hypostatic union. He deduces from the transcendence of the divine maternity far-reaching conclusions on Mary's fullness of grace, holding that the initial grace she received was superior to that possessed by all the just assembled. This, though he did not write of the Immaculate Conception (qv), "because of the respect due to the apostolic constitutions of the Holy See." Mary advanced to still higher degrees of grace through her merits until she was crowned with the "fullness of supreme excellence." We are to benefit by this abundance. Mary shares with us the love she has for her Son, who proclaimed her our mother from the Cross. She is the Mediatress. "Through the Word all things were made, without the Mother of the Word they were not remade." "Mary is the life through whom Christ the Life came to us, through whom Christians have access to life." Mary, C. thought, was "the complement of the Trinity, because through her the Trinity, hitherto unknown, was made manifest." C. insisted on the need for Marian devotion. To be a Christian, certainly a Catholic, one must be a "Marian." But one must also practice charity and solid virtue.

[1]Vol. III, Dissertation 6, *Mariologia seu de incomparabilibus Deiparae Mariae Virginis dotibus*, ed. by Vives, (1875), 259-300. Cf. Cl. Dillenschneider, C.SS.R., *La Mariologie de St. Alphonse de Liguori*, (Fribourg, 1931), 182-184; H. Graef, *Mary*, II, 45-46.

COSMAS VESTITOR (Eighth-Ninth Centuries)
Not much is known of C. save that he lived during part of the second half of the eighth century and the first half of the ninth, and that he wrote in Greek. His four homilies on the Assumption (qv) are contained (in Latin translation) in a tenth century manuscript.[1] They were to influence western thinking by being used in a famous composite manuscript on the Assumption, which also drew on material from the sermons of St. Germanus (qv) and St. Andrew of Crete (qv) (see EASTERN INFLUENCE).

C. uses the apocryphal traditions and the *Euthymiac History*. In the first homily, he shows the influence of St. Germanus. In the later ones, there are occasional flashes of theology, anticipating Pseudo-Augustine (qv). "From the one body [of Mary and Christ] there has been one deposition and one elevation to immortality, since the flesh of the Mother and the Son is known to be the same. And because the Son sits at the right hand of the Father, the Mother, too, has received incorruption in her passing and

is lawfully in heaven, dwelling with the Father together with her Son before the promised [general] resurrection."[2]

C., true to the Byzantine tradition, sees the effect of Mary's Assumption: "Because we knew that you were to be taken away, we had comfort [coolness] also with our sorrow, having you as a Mediatress with God."[3]

[1]*L'Assomption*, ed. by A. Wenger, 315-333; *ibid.*, "Les Homélies inédites de Cosmas Vestitor sur la Dormition," in REB, 11(1953), 284-300; ClavisG, III, 538-541. [2]IV, 12, *L'Assomption*, 330. [3]III, 4, *L'Assomption*, 324.

CRASSET, JEAN, S.J. (1618-1692)
C. was a preacher and spiritual director who was drawn into the *Avis Salutaires* (qv) controversy. His contribution was one of the best books on Marian theology of the age: *La Véritable dévotion envers la Sainte Vierge établie et défendue*.[1] C. tried to be fair, but was occasionally too severe on the *Avis*. He points out that mere devotion without reform of conduct—penance and keeping the commandments—is useless. C. proceeds from the basic truth that Mary's will is the will of God, and he rejects the contrast between divine wrath and Mary's mercy. He feels it necessary to affirm such a common-sense idea as "it is not reasonable to believe that devotion to the holy Virgin is a more powerful means of salvation than that to her Son . . . It is certain that the love of Jesus Christ is more powerful to save us than the love of Mary." In the heated atmosphere of the time, attempts were made to have the book condemned and an extremist tried to set C. in opposition to Bossuet. The latter had no part in this, and C., in the preface to the second edition, claimed that he and Bossuet were in agreement, though differing in the manner of expression. The book was unfairly attacked in England by a "Mr. Fleetwood," author of *An Account of the Life and Death of the Blessed Virgin according to Romish Writers*.[2]

[1](Paris, 1679, 2nd ed. 1687). Cf. P. Hoffer, S.M., *La dévotion à Marie au déclin du XVIIe siècle*, (Paris, 1938), 241-250; Cl. Dillenschneider, *La Mariologie de St. Alphonse de Liguori* (Fribourg, 1931), 209-218; H. M. Baron, "Le Père Jean Crasset, les jansénistes et la dévotion à la Sainte Vierge," in BSFEM, 4(1938), 137-184; H. Graef, *Mary*, II, 51-53.

CU CUIMHE THE WISE (d. before 747)
C. was an Irish poet who composed a hymn in praise of Mary, *Cantemus in omni die*, which

contains some interesting theology.[1] "Mary," he says, "Mother of the Lord most high, gave the appropriate remedy to sick mankind." She is "the highest, the venerable holy Virgin who did not withdraw from faith (qv) but remained steadfast." She was unique among mothers. The Eve-Mary contrast is thus expressed: "Through a woman and a tree the world first perished, through the virtue of a woman it returned to salvation." C. uses the Pauline word *Lorica*, "the breastplate of righteousness" (Eph 6:16; "the breastplate of faith," 1 Thess 5:8), which gave its name to a whole series of protection prayers. "Let us put on the arms of light, the breastplate and shield that we may be perfect to God, welcomed through Mary." We must intercede to Mary for our eternal salvation, to escape the flame and to dwell on high—relying on Mary's merit, twice mentioned by C. in his short poem.

[1] J. H. Bernard, and R. Atkinson, *The Irish Liber Hymnorum*, (London, 1898), 33-34. Cf. G. M. Dreves, in AH, 51, 305-306; F. J. Mone, *Lateinische Hymnen*, II, 383. Cf. P. F. Moran, *Essays on the origin, doctrine and discipline of the early Irish Church*, (Dublin, 1864), 225-226.

CYRIL OF ALEXANDRIA, ST., DOCTOR OF THE CHURCH (d. 444)

In the doctrinal crisis which was resolved at the Council of Ephesus, C. was always a central, mostly a dominant figure. From his uncle, Theophilus, whom he succeeded in the see of Alexandria in 412, he inherited hostility towards Constantinople. His literary output was vast— ten volumes of *Patrologia Graeca*, though not all is authentic.[1] Of interest to Marian theology, besides the letters on the *Theotokos* controversy and the great Ephesus homily (BHG 1151), are homilies such as that on the Presentation of the Lord (BHG 1963) and exegetical passages.

The Theotokos controversy: Nestorius, an eloquent monk from Antioch, was appointed to the see of Constantinople in 428 by the Emperor Theodosius. He was soon entangled in a theological debate about the Incarnation. Though clearly Christological, the debate came to a head on the word *Theotokos* as a true title for Our Lady. The term had been in use for over a century, and among its defenders in Constantinople was a great orator, Proclus (qv), who preached a sermon justifying it in presence of Nestorius.[2]

The latter preferred the word *Christotokos*. He thought Mary worthy of all praise, but his Antiochene outlook led him to insist on Christ's manhood. His real difficulty was with the communication of idioms, by which what the human Christ did and suffered may be attributed to the divine person. Nestorius feared a recurrence of Apollinarianism, which had been condemned at the Council of Constantinople. The Word of God was, he thought, conjoined rather than united to him who was born of Mary, and this seemed to imply division in Christ.[3]

From those in Constantinople offended by these views, an appeal for help went to the bishop of Alexandria. He had not been explicit on the term *Theotokos*; it is doubtful if he had even used it.[4] But his Alexandrian theological outlook, his immense learning, his sensitivity towards Constantinople's rising power, all impelled him to intervene. In 429, he published a paschal letter[5] and a special letter to the Egyptian monks[6] refuting Nestorius' arguments; he also wrote to Nestorius, who objected to his interference. Having written to Acacius of Beroea, at one time his uncle's ally, C. sent a second letter to Nestorius, courteous in tone, clearing up misunderstandings and conceding as much as possible.[7] This letter, *Kataphluarousi*, was later solemnly approved at Ephesus. Nestorius, in his reply, did not yield; he insisted on the difference between the divinity and humanity in Christ, and maintained that the exact title for Mary was *Christotokos* and not *Theotokos*.[8] C. redoubled his efforts, despatching three theological documents on the matter to the Emperor Theodosius, to Pulcheria and Eudoxia, queens, and to Arcadia and Marina, princesses.[9]

Rome had apparently manifested curiosity, and it was now apparent to the Alexandrian that he could not settle the dispute locally. So he forwarded a large dossier on the case to Pope Celestine. Nestorius had already reported the debate from his side, and an unfavourable reply to his sermons had been sponsored by Rome, from the great monastic author, Cassian.[10] C., in this dossier, continued the practice he had begun in his letters to the imperial court, the compilation of patristic texts. It has won him the honour of being the first to use the "patristic argument" and the pioneer in such anthologies, which appeared from time to time—whence his title *Sigillum Patrum*.

Henceforth Rome and Alexandria were hand in glove. A synod in the eternal city in August (430) decreed that Nestorius must retract his errors within ten days of notification. Letters in this sense were sent to him and to the church at Constantinople; notabilities of the East were also informed.[11] The letters were entrusted to C. for delivery.

The victory was almost imperilled by a new turn in events. C., before fulfilling his commission, summoned a synod in Alexandria in November, 430. It was the occasion of a famous, much controverted document, the letter with the twelve anathemas, or "Twelve Chapters." Therein C. pronounced anyone refusing to call Mary *Theotokos* anathema, but he went much further. Sensitive points of Christology were treated, and the insistence on Christ's unity came dangerously near to Apollinarianism. Further complications followed. When the four bishops, named to deliver the papal documents to Nestorius, arrived in his city, they found that some time before, on November 19, Theodosius, urged by Nestorius, had summoned a General Council to meet at Pentecost in the following year in Ephesus.

Things seemed to have swung in Nestorius' favour. He claimed that the papal ultimatum lapsed by reason of the Council, and Rome later replied to C.'s pleas for action, that time be allowed. Moreover, Nestorius sent the "Twelve Chapters" to John, the young bishop of Antioch, who took offense at what he considered their Apollinaristic trend. Whereas he had first counselled Nestorius to submit to Rome, now he supported him and had two of his suffragans prepare written refutations of C.'s latest compositions—to which the latter replied.[12] During the Council, he returned to the subject, providing an explanation of the "Twelve Chapters."[13] Nestorius had written to the Pope saying that he had no objection to the title *Theotokos*, if it were free of Arian and Apollinarian connotations. The Pope, for his part, made it clear to the three legates whom he sent to the Council, that they were to secure the same result as in the Rome synod, to which purpose they were to act in concert with C.[14]

C. acted without them. They had not arrived by June 7, date fixed for the Council by the emperor and accepted by the Pope. Nor had John of Antioch and his party. C. and a contingent of Egyptian bishops were at work, as well as Nestorius with his less numerous supporters. Memnon, bishop of Ephesus, supported C. On 21 June, the latter announced a surprising decision. He would hold the first session of the Council next day. Despite a signed protest by sixty-eight bishops, he persisted.

Between 130 and 150 bishops assembled on 22 June in the church of St. Mary. Candidianus, the imperial representative, ordered them to leave. His sole warrant was the letter from the Emperor officially opening the Council. He read this on request, and was then put out. Those present considered the Council inaugurated.

C. assumed the presidency. Things were made easier for him by Nestorius' refusal to attend. The procedure was thereon simple and swift. The Nicene Creed was read and then C.'s letter, *Kataphluarousi*. The assembly was asked if the doctrine therein was in agreement with the faith of Nicaea. The Fathers approved unanimously. When Nestorius' letter in reply to that of C. was read, there were cries of "Anathema." A number of other documents were then read, notably the anathemas, or "Twelve Chapters," on which no judgment was sought. A report was given on Nestorius' present sentiments by two archbishops who had been in contact with him. Then the bishops heard a series of extracts from the Fathers and from Nestorius' writings. He was deposed. That evening the crowd were jubilant, chanting "Praised be the Theotokos! Long live Cyril!" as they accompanied him and his bishops to their lodgings. Confusion and turmoil soon followed, but what was done that day was never undone.

The pertinent passage was: "Now the Word's being made flesh is nothing else than that he partook of flesh and blood in like manner with us, and made our body his own, and proceeded man of a woman without having cast away his divinity . . . . That is what the expression of the exact faith everywhere preaches; this is the mind we shall find in the holy Fathers. In this sense they did not hesitate to call the holy Virgin God's Mother [*Theotokos*]—not as though the nature of the Word or his divinity took beginning of being from the holy Virgin, but that of her was begotten the holy body animated with a rational soul; to this body the Word was united personally, and so he is said to have been according to the flesh." The words are C.'s.

Strange things happened within the weeks following 22 June. John of Antioch with his bishops arrived on 26 June, and staged a council of their own, attended by Nestorius. Candidianus and some dissident bishops deposed C. and Memnon, and excommunicated their associates. The papal legates arrived early in July, sought from C. a record of proceedings, and formally approved the decisions of 22 June. A special envoy was sent by the emperor who had been informed by all parties, and he imprisoned C., Nestorius, and Memnon. They emerged eventually. The Council was dissolved by the emperor in September and C. was back in his diocese in October. Nestorius returned to his monastery in Antioch, and died in upper Egypt (c.451). In the Creed of reunion (433), the eastern bishops accepted the title *Theotokos*.

Abundant Marian oratory was an immediate side effect of the Council. One item, rightly called "the most famous Marian sermon of antiquity," has now, after some recent doubt, been again fully restored to C. as its author.[15] A series of glowing titles hymn the praise of Mary. Through her are wrought all the glories of salvation and sanctification (see MEDIATRESS): "Through thee, the Trinity is glorified; through thee, the Cross is venerated in the whole world . . . through thee, angels and archangels rejoice, through thee, demons are chased . . . through thee, the fallen creature is raised to heaven . . . through thee, churches are founded in the whole world, through thee, peoples are led to conversion."[16]

This is a statement of Mary's mediation, an inspired utterance by a man privileged to unite his personal intuition with the revealed truth of God—scarcely equalled save by his predecessor in Alexandria on another similar occasion. In the commentary on the miracle of Cana, C., earlier in his career, had analyzed the interplay of petition and response between Mother and Son. Jesus showed his respect for his Mother: "Besides, Christ shows that the greatest honour is due to parents when, through reverence for his Mother, he undertakes to do that which he did not wish to do."[17] Though questions, recently much debated, do not occur to C., his own favourite themes intermingle with the commentary, the removal of the curse on women for example: "Many noteworthy things were achieved by this one first sign. Honourable marriage is sanctified and the curse against women is lifted; no longer will they give birth

to children in pain, since Christ has blessed the very beginning of our coming to life."[18]

Thoughtfulness for the Mother is seen by C. also in the scene on Calvary, when the dying Jesus provided a guardian for her: "What useful lesson did Christ here teach? First of all, we would say that he wished to confirm the precept of the law: Honour thy father and thy mother."[19] In this commentary, C. uses phrases about Mary which seem to continue the opinions of Origen (*qv*) and St. Basil (*qv*) on imperfection in her faith: "In all likelihood, even the Lord's Mother was scandalised by the unexpected passion, and the intensely bitter death on the Cross . . . all but deprived her of right reason."[20] He tries to imagine the thoughts that passed through Mary's mind. Had Jesus been mistaken when he said he was the Son of Almighty God? Why was he crucified who said he was the life? Why did he who had brought Lazarus back to life not come down from the Cross? Then he recalls what had been written of the Lord's Mother: Simeon's sword, "the sharp force of the Passion which could turn a woman's mind to strange thoughts."[21] The word woman is significant, for C. thought that the frailty of the female sex was a factor in what he then thought was collapse.

It has been assumed that the same view was expressed by C. in a commentary on Zech 13:7,[22] and in his homily on the Presentation as it is recorded by St. Luke. In face of the detailed study by R. Caro of the latter text and of the literary chronology of C., this continuity can no longer be assumed.[23] The Lucan homily coming within the period of C.'s reflection on the mystery of the *Theotokos* shows a shift in emphasis towards the opinion which would later prevail, which already in the West, Augustine (*qv*), C.'s contemporary would favour.

C. frequently writes of the virginity (*qv*) of Mary. He applies Is 7:14 to Mary as a virgin mother, and even thinks that the fact that Moses' father is not named in Ex 2 points in typology to the absence of a father of the true Saviour.[24] Joseph was given a special role as father of the Child, with whose conception he had no part. As to the actual wonder of the birth, C. uses the image of Ezek 44:2, the "closed door," and that of the burning bush in Ex 3. The Virgin gives birth without damage to her virginity.[25]

Mary's perpetual virginity, C. frequently taught. Mary is the ornament of virginity, the

CYRIL OF JERUSALEM

queen of virgins. The term "first-born" does not imply other sons or children. The "Brothers of the Lord" were, C. thought, children of an earlier marriage of St. Joseph—therein he followed the Apocrypha (qv), as did others of the eastern Fathers.[26]

C. seems to have had some intuition of the Mary-Church (qv) typology, for his famous litany of praise, spoken after Ephesus, ends with the words, "let us give glory to Mary, ever virgin, that is to the holy Church, and her son and immaculate spouse. To him glory for ever and ever."[27]

[1]St. Cyril's works, ed. by J. Aubert (Paris, 1638, repr. in PG 68-77 with additions); C.'s works in part, ed. by E. Pusey (Oxford, 1868-1877). For controversy with Nestorius, cf. critical ed. by E. Schwartz, in ACO, I, 1-8; CMP, IV, i, 143-293; EMBP, 697-811. Cf. R. Laurentin, Traité, I, 166; R. Caro, S.J., La Homilética, I, 76-94; II (on BHG 1151), 269-283; ClavisG, III, 1-57; A. Eberle, Die Mariologie des Hl. Cyrillus von Alexandrien, (Freiburg, 1921); Cl. Dillenschneider, Le sens chrétien et la Maternité divine de Marie au IVe et Ve siècles de l'Église, (Bruges, 1929); Pius XI, Encyclical, "Lux Veritatis," in AAS, 23(1931), 493-517; A. d'Alès, "S. Cyrille d'Alexandrie et les Sept à Sainte-Marie d'Ephèse," in RSR, 22(1932), 62-70; J. Puig de la Belcassa, "Los doce anatematismos de San Circilo. Fueron aprobados por el Conclio de Efeso?," in EstEcl, 11(1932), 5-25; H. du Manoir, S.J., Dogme et spiritualité chez S. Cyrille, (Paris, 1944); ibid., in DSp, II, 2672-2683; ibid., in LexMar, 1224-1233; ibid., "La scène de Cana commentée par S. C.," in PCM, III, 135-162; Pius XII, Encyclical, "Orientalis Ecclesiae," in AAS, 36(1944), 129-144; Nilus a S. Brocardo, O.C.D., De maternitate divina beatae Mariae semper Virginis Nestorii Constantinopolitani et Cyrilli Alexandrini sententia, (Rome, 1944); G. Joussard, "L'activité littéraire de S. C. d'A. jusqu'à 428," in Mélanges E. Podéchard, (Lyons, 1945), 159-174; ibid., in Maria, I, 122-135; ibid., "L'interprétation par S. C. d'A.de la scène de Marie au pied de la croix," in V.I., IV, 28-47; B. Lavaud, O.P. and H. Diepen, O.S.B., "S. C. d'A. Court traité contre ceux qui ne veulent pas reconnaître Marie Mère de Dieu," in Rev. Thomiste, 56(1956), 688-712; J. Liebaert, "L'évolution de la Christologie de S. C. d'A. à partir de la controverse Nestorienne," in Mélanges de Sc. Rel., 27(1970), 27-48; M. Aubineau, S.J., "Deux homélies de C. d'A. De hypapante," (BHG 1958 and 1963)?, in AB, 90(1972), 100; A. Luis, C.SS.R., "S. Cirilo y Nestorio. Enciclica 'Lux Veritatis'," in EstM, VIII, 325-344; G. Söll, S.D.B., "Maria und die Kirche bei den Griechischen Vätern seit C. v. A.," in ME, III, 137-162; G. Vassalli, S.S.S., "Accenni e motivi per il culto mariano in San Cirillo d'Alessandria," in PCM, III, 163-204.

On Nestorius, cf. F. Loofs, Nestoriana, (Halle a. Salle, 1905); Livre d'Héraclide, tr. Nau, (Paris, 1910). [2]PG 65, 680-692; ACO I, 1, 1, 103-107. [3]F. Loofs, Nestoriana, (Halle a. Salle, 1905), 338ff. [4]G. Jouassard, in Maria, p. 99, n. 59; G. Vassalli, S.S.S., "Accenni e motivi per il culto mariano in San Cirillo d'Alessandria," in PCM, III, 165. [5]PG 77, 768-800. [6]ibid., 9-40; ACO I, 1, 1, 10-23. [7]PG 77, 44-49; ACO I, 1, 1, 25-28. [8]PG 77, 49-57; ACO I, 1, 1, 29-32. [9]"De recta fide ad Theodosium, De recta fide ad Augustas, De recta fide ad Dominas," in ACO I, 1, 1, 42-72; ACO I, 1, 5, 26-61, 62-118. [10]Cf. letter of Nestorius, one of a series, Saepe scripsi, in ACO, 1, 2, 14-15; F. Loofs, Nestoriana, (Halle a. Salle, 1905), 169-172. [11]ACO I, 1, 75-91; PL 50, 458-500; PG 77, 89-93. [12]"Against Theodoret of Syrus," cf. PG 76, 385-452; ACO I, 6, 107-146. "Against Andrew of Samosata," cf. PG 76, 316-385; ACO I, 7, 33-65. [13]PG 76, 293-312; ACO I, 5, 15-25. [14]Texts of May 8th, 431, in PL 50, 503, 505-512; ACO, II, 22-26. [15]R. Caro, La Homiletica, II, 269-278. [16]PG 77, 992BC; ACO I, 1, 2, 102-103. [17]PG 73, 225C. Cf. H. du Manoir, "La scene de Cana commentée par St. Cyrille d'Alexandrie," in PCM, III, 135-162. [18]PG 73, 228B. [19]PG 74, 664C. [20]PG 74, 661B. [21]PG 74, 661C-664A. [22]Cf. G. Joussard, "L'interpretation par S. Cyrille de la scène de Marie au pied de la Croix," in V.I., IV, 28-47. [23]La Homiletica, 1, 137ff, esp. 147. [24]In Is., in PG 70, 204C; In Exod. in PG 69, 396A. [25]Apol pro XII cap., contra Orient., in PG 76, 317C, 321AB; In Luc., in PG 72, 485AB. [26]In Gen:, in PG 69, 325C. [27]PG 77 996C.

CYRIL OF JERUSALEM, ST. (d.387)

C. was bishop of Jerusalem from early in 349 to 387. He was involved in the Christological controversies of his time, being disturbed in his tenure of office. He was present at the first Council of Constantinople. Scholars agree that he is the author of the first series of Catecheses associated with his name (I to XVIII), but probably not of the Mystagogical Catecheses, which have no interest for Marian doctrine. His orthodoxy is sure; Leo XIII proclaimed him a Doctor of the Church.

There are occasional passages referring to Mary in the Catecheses, but most of the saint's Marian doctrine is in XII.[1] Mary was descended from David.[2] The one fact in her life which C. treated at length was the virginal conception. He has a polemical approach against the Greeks and the Jews. The former he refuted from their own "fables";[3] the latter from the miracles of the Old Testament.[4] Like St. Justin Martyr (qv), he deals in some detail with Is 7:14, on the translation of almah and the impossibility of Hezechiah being Emmanuel—for chronological reasons.[5] He sees a Marian sense in Ps 22:9.[6] Attention is given also to New Testament texts, and C. shows, at some length, that the word "father," applied to St. Joseph (qv), does not mean physical paternity.[7]

As a pre-Ephesus Father, his opinion on the divine motherhood will be closely scrutinized. He uses Theotokos (qv) once only,[8] but his affirmation of the truth is quite firm: "The only-begotten Son of God, . . . seeing Mary his own mother according to the flesh . . . ."[9] "The Virgin-born God"[10] . . . "God the Word made man in truth . . . of the Virgin and the Holy Spirit . . . ."[11]

C. speaks of the Holy Spirit (qv), but his insistence is on the sanctification of Mary and the pure birth of Christ: "The Holy Spirit, coming upon her, sanctified her to receive him 'through whom all things are made'."[12] "His generation was pure and undefiled; for where the Holy Spirit is, there all defilement has been taken away."[13] The problem of the Purification (qv) is not faced directly here, but it seems to be implicit.

C. continues the Eve (qv)-Mary parallel: "Through Eve, yet a virgin, came death, there was need that through a virgin, or rather from a virgin, life should appear; that as the serpent deceived the one, so Gabriel should bring the good news to the other."[14] There is a hint of a theology of woman elsewhere: "A debt of gratitude was due from womankind; for Eve was begotten of Adam, not conceived of a mother, but, as it were, brought forth from man alone. Mary then paid the debt of gratitude when, not of man, but immaculately of her own self, she conceived of the Holy Spirit by the power of God."[15]

[1]Texts: Maurists, 1720, in PG 33, 33-1180; improved by W. K. Reischl and J. Rupp, 2 vols. (Munich, 1848, 1860, repr. Hildesheim, 1967). French tr. by J. Bouvet, *Cyrillus Hierosolymitanus, Catechèses baptismales et mystagogiques (Les Écrits des Saints)*, (Namur, 1962). Eng. tr. by E. Telfer, *Cyril of Jerusalem and Nemesius of Emesa* (Library of Christian Classics), (London, 1955); Leo McCauley and A. A. Stephenson, *The Works of St. Cyril of Jerusalem*, 2 vols., (Washington, 1969, 1970). ClavisG, II, 289-296; ClavisG, III, 1-57. [2]*Works*, vol. 1, XII, 23, 24, pp. 241-243. [3]*op. cit.*, XII, 27, 244. [4]*op. cit.*, XII, 28-30, pp. 244-246. [5]*op. cit.*, XII, 21, 22, p. 240. [6]*op. cit.*, XII, 25, p. 243. [7]*op. cit.*, VII, 9, pp. 174-175. [8]*op. cit.*, X, 19, p. 208, n. 109. [9]*op. cit.*, VII, 9, p. 175. [10]*op. cit.*, XII, 1, p. 227. [11]*op. cit.*, XII, 3, p. 228. [12]*op. cit.*, vol. 2, XVII, 6, p. 100. [13]*op. cit.*, vol. 1, XII, 32, p. 247. [14]*op. cit.*, XII, 15, p. 235. [15]*op. cit.*, XII, 29, p. 246. On St. Cyril's Marian theology cf. D. Fernandez, C.M.F., "Maria en las Catequesis de S. Cirilo de Jerusalem," in EphMar, 25(1975), 143-171.

D

DANTE ALIGHIERI (1265-1321)

The supreme poet of Christendom, D. has been called the supreme poet of Mary also.[1] He expressed the Marian ideal of the twelfth and thirteenth centuries, an ideal which clergy and laity, theologians, preachers, mystics, painters, musicians, sculptors, builders, stained-glass workers, popular dramatists, all in their different ways, tried to serve. D. names Mary more than sixty times in the *Divine Comedy*. In the many passages wherein he speaks of her, there is implicit or explicit a theology of Mary proportioned to the theme of the work. This theology includes the great traditional truths—the divine maternity, Mary's glorification, her queenly position, especially her mediatorial office. One passage in the *Paradiso*, Canto 33, most frequently quoted (St. Bernard's prayer) summarizes the poet's ideas on Mary. Mgr. R. A. Knox's translation appears among the hymns to Our Lady in the reformed Breviary: "Maiden, yet a Mother, daughter of thy Son, high beyond all others, lowlier is none; thou the consummation planned by God's decree, when our lost creation nobler rose in thee . . . Nor alone thou hearest when thy name we hail; often thou art nearest when our voices fail; mirrored in thy fashion all creation's good, mercy, might, compassion grace thy womanhood." D., as a Marian theologian and devotee, has been the subject of a considerable literature, most of it, understandably, in Italian.[2]

[1]Cf. D. Charbonneau, O.S.M., "Some Mariological Concepts in Dante's Divine Comedy," in MM, 18(1956), 282-294; D. Franchetti, *Maria nel pensiero di Dante*, (Turin, Torino Grafica, 1958); P. Boncompagni, *La Madre di Dio nella Divina Commedia*, (Rome, 1958); L. Ferroni, *La Vergine Madre, regina della gloria e mediatrice di grazia*

nel poema di Dante, (Macerata, tip. S. Giuseppe, 1960); G. Palmenta, *La Vergine Madre nella Divina Commedia*, (Catania, 1971); S. Ragazzini, O.F.M.Conv., "La Madonna nells Divina Commedia," in ME, XV, 279-301. ²Cf. G. M. Roschini, O.S.M., *Maria Santissima*, I, 456.

DAUGHTER OF ZION

In the Old Testament, the title Daughter of Zion was applied first to a section of the city of Jerusalem. It came to be used, in a symbolic way, for the city itself and eventually given a spiritual meaning—a female title found most apt to express the corporate personality of Israel, the Bride of God.¹ The Daughter of Zion is portrayed as one suffering, who awaits the coming of the Lord, virgin Israel oppressed and sometimes unfaithful, a poor one, a mother in travail until her children are born.

Nowhere in the New Testament is Mary called the Daughter of Zion. The title is found only twice in these books. Matthew and John, in their accounts of Christ's last entry to Jerusalem, recall, with variations, Zechariah's words to the Daughter of Zion, that her king comes to her "riding on an ass, on a colt, the foal of an ass." (Zech 9:9; Mt 21:5; Jn 12:15).

The idea that Mary was the Daughter of Zion has come from study of the Lucan infancy narrative, an interpretation defended by Catholics and Protestants. In 1939, S. Lyonnet argued that *Chaire* in Lk 1:28 should be translated "Rejoice," thus prompting comparison with the Old Testament Daughter of Zion texts. Some years later, H. Sahlin, a Swedish Lutheran, argued that Luke's Hebrew source identified Mary with the Daughter of Zion; Sahlin thought that Luke himself did not see the identification. Sahlin looked also for support for the interpretation in John. A. G. Hebert, who spread the idea to the English and French-speaking world, thought that Luke himself knew it and that it was perceived by other New Testament writers. These Protestant writers were supported in the interpretation by others (G. A. F. Knight, R. Leaney and especially Max Thurian of Taizé), whose book appeared during Vatican II (*qv*). Catholic writers, who early lent their authority to the thesis, included R. Laurentin, P. Benoit, O.P., and L. Deiss, C.S.Sp. On the interpretation of Luke, there have been dissenting Protestant and doubting Catholic voices in very recent years; some of the latter would still see some foundation for the title.

Of three Old Testament passages—Joel 2:21-23, Zech 9:9, and Zeph 3:14-17—it is Zeph 3:14-17 that is frequently set in parallel with Lk 1:28, 30, 31. "Rejoice, [*chaire*] O Daughter of Zion . . . The King of Israel, the Lord, is in your midst . . . Do not fear, O Zion [LXX has Take heart Zion] . . . The Lord your God is in your midst, a warrior who gives victory." (Zeph 3:14-17). "Rejoice [*chaire*], O favoured one, the Lord is with you . . . Do not be afraid, Mary, for you have found favour with God. And behold you will conceive in your womb and bear a son and you shall call his name Jesus." (Lk 1:28, 30, 31). B. Rigaux does not find the dependence here certain, and R. E. Brown finds the argument from the similarity of *Chaire* (with this given a theological meaning) forced. Rigaux sees a parallel emphasis in Luke on Jerusalem as the "privileged place chosen by God for the mystery of salvation," and on the link between Mary and Jerusalem. Daughter of Zion by metonomy would refer to the inhabitants of Jerusalem, and among them Mary, in the divine economy, has the first place. She is the Daughter of Zion *par excellence*, uniting the two Testaments.

A figurative or symbolic reference to the Daughter of Zion giving birth to a new people in the messianic age has been seen in the Woman in Jn 19:25-27 (*qv*).

After the debate in the Council on *Lumen Gentium*, chapter VIII, forty Fathers asked that reference be made in the text to Our Lady as Daughter of Zion. The suggestion was accepted, but the commission refused to add a reference to Sacred Scripture. In the section on the Old Testament, after the reference to Mary as preeminent among the Poor of the Lord (*qv*), the words, "the exalted Daughter of Zion," were added to go with "with her and after a long expectation of the promise, the times were at length fulfilled and the new dispensation established." (LG 55)

¹Cf. S. Lyonnet, S.J., "Chaire Kecharitomene," in BB, 20(1939), 131-141; H. Sahlin, *Der Messias und das Gottesvolk. Studien zur protolukanischen Theologie*, (Uppsala, 1945), and "Jungfru Maria-Dottern Zion," in *Ny Kyrklig Tidschrift*, 8(1949), 102-125; A. G. Herbert, "The Virgin Mary Daughter of Zion," in *Theology*, 53(1950), 403-410, tr. in *Vie Spirituelle*, 85(1951), 127-139; G. A. F. Knight, "The Virgin and the Old Testament," in *Reformed Theol. Rev.*, (Australia), 12(1953), 1-13; R. Laurentin, "Traces d'allusions étymologiques en Luc 1-2," in BB, 37(1956), 435-456; *Structure et Théologie de Luc I-II*, (Paris, 1957), 148-161; L. Deiss, C.S.Sp., *Marie Fille de Sion*, (Paris,

1958), and "Le thème biblique de Marie, Fille de Sion (dans la fête de l'Immaculée Conception)," in *Assemblées du Seigneur*, 80(1966), 29-51; S. Zimmer, *Zion als Tochter, Frau und Mutter. Personifikation von Land, Stadt und Volk in weiblicher Gestalt*, Dissertation, (Munich, 1959); A. Strobel, "Der Gruss an Maria (Lk 1:28). Eine philologische Betrachtung zu seinem Sinngehalt," in *Zeitsch. f. d. Neutest. Wissensch.*, 53(1962), 86-110; M. Thurian, *Mary, Mother of the Lord, Figure of the Church*, (London, 1963), 13-19; J. Schreiner, *Sion-Jerusalem, Jahwehs Königssitz*, (Munich, 1963); P. Benoit, "Et toi-même, un glaive te transpercera l'âme," in CBQ, 25(1963), 251-261; H. Cazelles, "Fille de Sion et théologie mariale dans la Bible," in BSFEM, 21(1964), 51-71; "La fonction maternelle de Sion et de Marie," in MSS, VI, 165-178; J. A. de Aldama, S. J., "El tema mariano 'la Hija de Sion' en la liturgia visigótica," in *La Ciudad de Dios*, (1968), 863-881; C. F. Correia, "Maria filha de Siao. Alcance eclesiomariologico e dimensao ecumenica do titulo," in *Theologica*, (Braga), 4(1969), 437-455; H. Raisänen, *Die Mutter Jesu im Neuen Testament*, (Helsinki, 1969), 86-92; Mary in NT, 128-134; B. Rigaux, O.F.M., "Fille de Sion," in *Studia mediaevalia et mariologica P. C. Balic, O.F.M., 70um explenti annum dicata*, (Rome, 1971), 405-422; J. McHugh, *The Mother of Jesus in the New Testament*, (London, 1975), 37-52, 150-153; R. E. Brown, *The Birth of the Messiah*, (London, 1977), 320-328, 353, 465.

DEATH OF MARY, THE

In the Apostolic Constitution, *Munificentissimus Deus* (*qv*), Pius XII used the phrase, "having completed the course of her earthly life," in regard to the end of Mary's life. He did not say that she died. His words are borrowed exactly by LG 59. In the years between the two documents, a considerable literature grew up on the question whether Mary did die.[1] Very little has appeared since Vatican Council II.

Evidence from Sacred Scripture does not exist, testimony from the Fathers is slight. Origen (*qv*) speaks of Mary's death, but the text is of doubtful authenticity. St. Gregory of Nyssa (*qv*) says death came near her, "and was shattered on her." "It first stumbled on the fruit of her virginity as on some rock." This may be more relevant to Christ's resurrection than to Mary's possible immortality. St. Epiphanius (*qv*), a Palestinian, has most to say on the subject, which stirred his curiosity, but his final judgment is inconclusive. He notes that Scripture does not speak of Mary as having died or not having died, nor of her accompanying John to Asia, and he goes on: "Rather Scripture is absolutely silent, because of the extraordinary nature of the prodigy, in order not to shock the minds of men. For my part I kept my own thoughts and I practise silence. For it may be that somewhere we have found hints that it is impossible to discover the death of the holy, blessed one." Epiphanius then refers to Rev 12:14: "The woman was given an eagle's wings and she was carried off into the wilderness that the dragon might not seize her," adding, "it may be that this is fulfilled in her." "However," he says, "I do not assert this absolutely, and I do not maintain firmly either that she died . . . Did she die? We do not know."[2] Later he returns to the subject: "Either the holy Virgin died and was buried; then her falling asleep was with honour, her death chaste, her crown that of virginity. Or she was killed, as it is written: 'And your own soul a sword shall pierce'; then her glory is among the martyrs and her holy body amid blessings, she through whom light rose over the world. Or she remained alive, since nothing is impossible with God and he can do whatever he desires; for her end no one knows."[3]

Timothy of Jerusalem, in a homily on Simeon and Anna, was explicit: "Therefore the Virgin is immortal to this day, seeing that he who had dwelt in her transported her to the regions of her assumption."[4] Timothy was assigned a date between the fourth and fifth centuries by Fr. M. Jugie (*qv*), between the sixth and eighth by Dom Capelle.

Thereafter Mary's death was not a subject of dispute; it was taken for granted. But as reflection on the Immaculate Conception (*qv*) advanced, ideas emerged which were favourable to Mary's freedom from death. She was, some argued, exempted from the fourfold sting of the serpent, which included the return of the body to dust through death. The positive opinion on her immortality, found in two isolated works in the seventeenth and eighteenth centuries, was more frequently expressed after the dogma of the Immaculate Conception, and with still greater assurance after the dogma of the Assumption—notably by Fr. T. Gallus, S.J. and Fr. G. M. Roschini, O.S.M. (*qv*). The latter had taught Mary's death in his early work. Fr. Balic, O.F.M. (*qv*) opposed the thesis of immortality; he referred to it unfavourably in notes to the first schema drafted for Vatican II (*qv*).

Fr. M. Jugie, A.A., a member of the drafting committee of the text on the Assumption, had persuaded the Pope that the question of Mary's death should be separated from the fact of bodily Assumption. The immortalists saw the Pope's phrase as at least indirectly encouraging their view. They were not deterred by references in the Apostolic Constitution to Mary's death in a general way, or in quotations from ecclesiastical writers, notably St. John of Damascus and St. Francis de Sales, and in the prayer *Veneranda* from the Gregorian Sacramentary.

Arguments cannot be drawn from the faith of the Church as Pius XII did for the Assumption. Reasoning is deductive and seeks to establish the fact of death or preservation from it from theological principles. Some argue that immortality follows from the Immaculate Conception, and they think that their argument is strengthened by a phrase in *Munificentissimus Deus* linking this privilege with the Assumption. Mary, sinless in a sinful world, was exempted from certain effects of sin, disorder in her affective nature, pains of childbirth. Would the final exemption not be logical? Some will escape death on the last day. Can anyone enjoy a privilege denied to Mary?

On the other side, it is urged that, as Mary was made like to Christ in her bodily resurrection, she must have been so too in death preceding it. But death was inflicted on him by evil men so that this argument cannot be fully pressed. Again some, at the end of time, will gather the fruits of his resurrection without tasting death.

[1]For bibliography, cf. F. Maggioni, "La morte della Madonna negli scritti recenti," in *Scuola cattolica*, 81(1953), 33-50; J. Galot, S.J., in *Maria*, VII, 234-237; G. M. Roschini, O.S.M., in *Maria Santissima*, III, 624-632. For general studies, cf. T. Gallus, *La Vergine immortale*, (Rome, 1949); G. M. Roschini, *La Madonna secondo la Fede e la Teologia*, III, (Rome, 1953), 255-295; R. Laurentin, *Traite'*, V, 182-185. Cf. MSt, (1957), esp. "The Testimony of the Patristic Age concerning Mary's death," by W. J. Burghardt, S.J., pp. 58-99, separately issued in *Woodstock Papers*, 2; E. Castonguay, O.F.M., *La fin terrestre de la Mère de Dieu*, (Montreal, 1957). Cf. also K. Balic, O.F.M., "La controversia acerca de la muerte de Maria Santísima desde la Edad Media hasta nuestros dias," in EstM, 9(1950), 101-123; A. Rivera, C.M.F., "La muerte de Maria en la tradición hasta la Edad Media (Siglos I al VIII)," in EstM, 9(1950), 175-212. T. Gallus, S.J., "'Ad immortalitatem' B. M. Virginis," in MM, 12(1950), 26-53, and "Ad quaestionem mortis post Bullam 'Munificentissimus Deus'," in MM, 15(1953), 265-269; G. M. Roschini, "Il problema della morte di Maria SS. dopo la Costituzione dogmatica," in MM, 13(1951), 148-163; "Did Our Lady die? Some reflections on Munificentissimus Deus," in IER, 80(1953), 73-88; G. Corr, O.S.M., "Did Our Lady die?," in CRev, 37(1951), 12-20; E. Suaras, O.P., "En torno a la teologia de la muerte de la Santísima Virgen. Contestación al P. Roschini," in EphMar, 2(1952), 247-282; M. Quera, S.J., "El privilegio de la Inmaculada Concepción de Maria 'exige' su immortalidad?," in EstEcl, 28(1954), 581-602; B. Farrel, "The Immortality of the Blessed Virgin Mary," in TheolSt, 16(1955), 591-606; W. M. G. Most, "The Evidence of the Postridentine Theologians on Mary's death," in EphMar, 9(1959), 493-496; G. Scelzi, "La morte della Vergine in conformità con Cristo nel pensiero della Chiesa Greca," in MM, 19(1957), 90-114; T. Bartolomei, O.S.M., "La mortalità di Maria," in EphMar, 10(1960), 385-420; C. di Marco, "Sublimiori modo redempta," in *Nuovo argomento teologico sulla immortalità della Vergine*, (Isola del Liri, 1962); B Bagatti, O.F.M., "Ricerche sulle tradizioni della morte della Vergine," in *Sacra Doctrina*, 18(1973), 185-214. [2]*Panarion 78, 10-11*, in GCS 37, 461-462. [3]*Panarion 78, 23*, in GCS 37, 474. [4]PG 86, 245C.

DEBT OF SIN, THE

The debt of sin, *debitum peccati*, is the necessity which lies on all men to contract original sin. The necessity arises from being conceived in the normal way of human generation, and incurring loss of grace through descent from Adam. A remote necessity, *debitum remotum*, comes from the fact of generation; a proximate necessity, *debitum proximum*, from descent from Adam. For centuries, a keen debate was carried on as to whether Our Lady incurred the debt of sin.[1] Some contended that she contracted the debt of sin remotely through being conceived in a normal way, others that she did so proximately because of her descent from Adam. But a third opinion maintains that, because of the Immaculate Conception (*qv*), there can be no question of any kind of debt of sin. Since Mary was indissolubly one with Christ in the eternal decree of divine predestination, since she was raised to the ineffable dignity of the divine motherhood, endowed with sublime grace with which she at all times fully cooperated, she was immune from every debt of sin. Though opinion at one time or another may appear to favour the *debitum remotum* or the *debitum proximum*, Fr. Carol's survey has shown that "the majority by far since the fifteenth century, but especially at the present time, favours Mary's immunity from every debt of sin . . . ." This is not to reduce theology to statistics. It does show that the view here taken has by many been fully considered and thought acceptable.

[1]For an exhaustive bibliography covering over 660 authors, cf. J. B. Carol, O.F.M., "The Blessed Virgin and the 'Debitum Peccati'. A bibliographical conspectus," in MSt, 28(1977), 181-256. Cf. "De debito contrahendi peccatum originale in B. V. Maria," in V. I. XI, and record of debate during the same Congresses, *ibid.*, 456-491. On which, cf. J. M. Alonso, C.M.F., "Num B. Virgo peccati debito fuerit

obnoxia? Annotationes quaedam in publicam disputationem in Mariologico Congressu Internationali Romae habitam," in EphMar, 5(1955), 33-46; *ibid.*, "De quolibet debito a B. M. V. prorsus excludendo," in EphMar, 4(1954), 201-242. Cf. also K. Balic, O.F.M., *De debito peccati originalis in B. Virgine Maria investigationes de doctrina quam tenuit Joannes Duns Scotus*, (Rome, 1941); J. F. Bonnefoy, O.F.M., "La negación del 'debitum peccati' en Maria," in *Verdad y Vita*, 12(1954), 102-171; *id., Quelques théories modernes du "debitum peccati"*, (Rome, 1954), also in EphMar, 4(1954), 269-331; J. B. Carol, O.F.M., "Our Lady's immunity from the Debt of Sin," in MSt, 6(1955), 164-168, also *Fundamentals of Mariology*, (New York, 1956), 113-119; J. Alfaro, S.J., "La formula definitiora de la Inmaculada Concepción," in V. I., II, 201-275.

DEMETRIUS CHRYSOLORAS (d. c. 1430)

A native of Thessalonica, and a friend of Manuel Palaeologus, D. was the author of two homilies on Our Lady, on the Annunciation and the Dormition (BHG 1117p, 1141n),[1] unpublished until the present century, as were all his works. D. follows certain traditions from the Apocrypha, such as that Joachim an Anne were sterile and Mary was a child of prayer. He excludes all sin from Mary's life and he also teaches the bodily Assumption. Mary had no tendency towards sin such as is found in all men. She was the perfect man, i.e. human being. In body and soul she surpassed every wonder. D. outlines the parallel between Jesus and Mary, but he attributes so much to Mary that his phrasing sometimes borders on Pelagianism.

[1]Cf. I. Roca Melia, "Demetrio Crisoloras y su homilia inedita sobre la Dormición de Maria," in *Helmantica*, 35(1960), 5-60; *id., La Asunción de Maria en Demetrio Crisoloras*, (Salamanca, Ecclesiastical University Press, 1961); *ibid.*, "La anunciación del Angelo a Maria en Demetrio Crisoloras," in EphMar, 14(1964), 378-394; *ibid.*, "Discurso de acción de gracias a Maria por Demetrio Crisoloras," in *Humanidades*, 16(1964), 135-146. Cf. also M. Jugie, A.A., *L'Immaculée Conception*, 298-301; *id., L'Assomption*, 336-337; P. Gautier, "Action de Grâces de Démétrius à la Théotocos pour l'Anniversaire de la bataille d'Ankara (28 Juillet, 1403)," in REB, 19(1961), 340-357.

DEMETRIUS CYDONES (d. 1397/1398)

A state official in the Byzantine empire, D. had read St. Thomas Aquinas (*qv*) and accepted the Catholic Church. He had translated part of St. Thomas' *Summa* into Greek. Among his writings, all unpublished, is a long discourse on the Annunciation (BHG 1121p and Auctarium).[1] Though he speaks of God purifying and sanctifying Mary to free her from all temptation, the idea may not have included Original Sin (see PURIFICATION). For he has passages which

seem to imply the Immaculate Conception (*qv*): "The Word of God found in Mary the worthy abode of his divinity. To this Virgin without delay and before her birth he gave the Holy Spirit; he beautified her with the gift of holiness, thus preparing for himself beforehand a palace worthy of his royalty." "But it is clear that God kept the Virgin in every way in immaculate purity."[2]

[1]Cf. M. Jugie, A.A., "Le discours de Demetrius Cydones sur l'Annontiation et sa doctrine sur l'Immaculée Conception," in *Echos d'Orient*, 17(1915), 97-106; *id., L'Immaculée Conception*, 275-281. [2]M. Jugie, A.A., *op. cit.*, 278-279.

DENIS THE CARTHUSIAN (1402/3-1471)

Born in Rijkel, Belgian Limburg, D. entered the Carthusian order in 1423. He had studied at Cologne University, where he received a Thomist training. He is the most prolific writer of his order known to the public. D. was known as *Doctor Ecstaticus* because of his visions and mystical experience. His devotion to Our Lady, on which we have his own testimony,[1] was profound. His doctrine on Our Lady can be found in numerous passages throughout his works: especially in the two treatises, *De Praeconio et dignitate Mariae*[2] (1432/34) and *De dignitate et laudibus Virginis Mariae*[3] (c. 1458); in the course of the *Enarratio in Canticum Canticorum*;[4] in commentaries on well known Old Testament passages (Prov 31, Sir 24)[5], on the Magnificat (*qv*), and on Marian hymns;[6] as well as in some thirty-five sermons on the feasts of the Conception of the Blessed Virgin Mary, of her Nativity, Purification, Annunciation, Visitation, and Assumption.[7]

D. continues the medieval themes on Our Lady, but not in any very systematic way. He leans on St. Bernard (*qv*) and invokes the Fathers—especially St. Augustine (*qv*), not excluding the *spuria* (especially the sermon of Ambrose Autpert *qv*). He uses Pseudo-Albert (*qv*) as if he were Albert the Great (*qv*). He quotes St. Bridget of Sweden (*qv*), as did other theologians, even Luke Wadding, O.F.M. (*qv*), and takes respectful note of the Council of Basle (*qv*).

D.'s method is distinguished by abundant use of titles (*qv*) for Mary, many of them related to her lifework: e.g. enlightener (illuminatrix); saviour (*salvatrix*); principal cooperator (*cooperatrix*) in salvation; helper in the redemption (*adjutrix redemptionis*); as well as mediatress, advocate, and other customary titles. In relation to the Holy Trinity and to each of its persons, D. uses words like associate (*consocia*), partner (*consors*), or spouse. He frequently writes of Mary's relationship with the Trinity, saying that as the Son of God was her Son, the Father would make her his spouse or associate parent (*parentela*). The Holy Spirit would take her as his sanctuary, his bridal chamber, his throne, his couch, his high and only temple, his friend, his secretary, his adviser.[8] Mary, he asserted, was raised to partnership with the most essential and most holy Trinity.

On the Immaculate Conception, D.'s thought evolved. In his earlier works he contrasted Mary, free from personal sin, with Christ, who was free from original sin as well; or, in commenting on Rom 5:12, "in whom all men sinned," he excepted Christ but not Mary. He wrote explicitly: "Christ preserved most pure from all guilt the Mother whom he had chosen for himself and created, and he sanctified her in the womb of her mother."[9] After the Council of Basle he changed his approach: "We must inquire according to the decision of the Church, which we are obliged to obey."[10] He expounds the Immaculate Conception at length, following the Franciscan school.[11]

D., as an authentic mystic, probed deeply Mary's mystical knowledge, discussed the gift of wisdom as she enjoyed it, the mode of her contemplation. He thought that she had occasionally a direct vision of God.[12] He taught that she was assumed, body and soul, into heaven.

He thought of Mary's saving role in comprehensive terms. Both sexes were honoured in the work of our restoration, human nature in the male sex immediately united with the Saviour through the hypostatic union, "a human person also in the female sex, making her his own mother so that thus he should save and unite with him the whole human race."[13] As our perdition was due to a woman who, "prompting and cooperating, led the man to eat the forbidden fruit, thus our redemption was effected through a woman." "In truth you wished her to be a cooperator in the whole of our salvation, and you set her up as the advocate of the Church, and decreed to save many through her . . ."[14] D. saw her compassion as the special means

whereby she joined in the work of salvation— "its eminent character, its power and merit." After God, she is the origin, Mother and dispenser of all charisms conferred on us. She has the kingdom of mercy, and whatever grace God gives passes through her hands.[15] Mary he calls explicitly Mother of the Church (*qv*).[16]

In D.'s interpretation of the Song of Songs (*qv*), the Church is the universal spouse of Christ, each faithful soul the particular spouse, the Blessed Virgin the singular spouse. He elaborates different relations between Mary and the Church as he comments on the Song.

---

[1]*Opera Omnia*, (Montreuil, Tournai, 1896-1935. 42 vols.), 35, 484; 36, 133-136. [2]*op. cit.*, 35, 479-574. [3]*op. cit.*, 36, 11-174. [4]*op. cit.*, 7, 291-447. [5]*op. cit.*, 7, 204-207; 8, 153-156. [6]*op. cit.*, 35, 82-92. [7]*op. cit.*, 31 and 32. Cf. A. Stoelen, in DS, III, 430-449; B. Tonutti, *Mariologia Dionysii Carthusiani*, (Rome, 1953); F. M. Bauducco, "L'Illuminatrice nelle opere di Dionigi il Certosinio," in MM, 10(1948), 191-210; *ibid.*, "Due Mariologie di Dionigi il Certosino," in MM, 13(1951), 453-470; *ibid.*, "De Maria et Ecclesia apud Dionysium Carthusianum," in ME, III, 375-388; *ibid.*, "Fonti della mediazione nella mariologia di Dionigi il Certosino," in MM, 33(1971), 457-501; *ibid.*, "Influssi di Dionigi il Certosino sulla mediazione Mariologica in S. Pietro Canisio e S. Alfonso Maria de Liguori," in Palaestra del Clero, 50(1971), 1366-1379. [8]*Opera Omnia*, (Montreuil, Tournai, 1896-1935), 36, IV, 9, 10, 160-163. [9]*In Ps. 45*, in *Opera Omnia*, 6, 15a. [10]*In Sent. III*, dist. 3, q. 1, in *Opera Omnia*, 23, 98. [11]*De praeconio et dignitate Mariae*, Bk. 2; *De dignitate et laudibus Virginis Mariae*, Bk. 2, 3, 9, 10. [12]*op. cit.*, I, 26, p. 53. [13]*op. cit.*, II, 23, p. 99; *De praeconio et dignitate Mariae*, III, 25, p. 563. [14]*Opera Omnia*, (Montreuil, Tournai, 1896-1935), 7, 415. [15]*De praeconio et dignitate Mariae*, III, 5, p. 538.

DEVELOPMENT OF DOCTRINE, THE

The development of doctrine in regard to the theology of Our Lady, particularly the dogmas of the divine motherhood, of the Immaculate Conception (*qv*) and the Assumption (*qv*), has involved many factors which have to be studied in each separate truth or proposition. In the present century, considerable attention has been given to the dogma of the Assumption (*qv*) and an extensive literature made available.[1] Reflection on the privilege, as on that of the Immaculate Conception, may stimulate a fresh theology of development, as of revelation and tradition.

Theories of development heretofore followed a theology of revelation which was heavily propositional. The emphasis was changed by Vatican II to personal manifestation of Jesus Christ, "the Mediator and fullness of all revelation." (*Verbum Dei*, 2). The history of the great

Marian truths is summarized in the relevant articles in the present work. There is now room for study and analysis of the factors which influenced the faith of the Church in each case, study which would show how the Church "moves forward towards the fullness of divine truth until the words of God reach their fulfilment in her." (*Verbum Dei*, 8). The problem in each case is to show how "the growth in the understanding of the realities and the words which have been handed down" (*Verbum Dei*, 8) was successfully accomplished, how, despite apparent lack of implicit or explicit links, what has been taught by the Church either with its solemn or ordinary authority is part of the initial deposit of faith.

[1]Cf., on development in general, the important works of J. A. Möhler, *Symbolism*, (Eng. tr., London, 1843 and subsequent edns.); J. H. (Cardinal) Newman, *Essay on the Development of Christian Doctrine*, (London, 1845, 2nd ed., 1878) and *On Consulting the Faithful in Matters of Doctrine*, ed. by J. Coulson, (London, 1961); F. Marin-Sola, O.P., *L'évolution homogène du dogme catholique*, (Fribourg, 1924); L. de Grandmaison, S.J., *Le dogme chrétien, sa nature, ses formules, son développement*, (Paris, 1928); E. Dhanis, S.J., "Révélations explicite et implicite," in Gregor, 34(1953), 187-237; a symposium, *Lo sviluppo del dogma secondo la dottrina cattolica. Relazione lette nella seconda settimana teologica 24-28 settembre, 1951*, (Rome, 1953); C. (Cardinal) Journet, *Le Message Révélé, sa transmission, son développement, ses dépendances*, (Paris, 1963); K. Rahner, S.J., "The Development of Dogma," in *Theol. Investigations*, I, (London, 1965), 2nd ed., 39-77. For Development of Marian doctrine, cf. E. Neubert, S.M., *Marie dans le dogme*, (Paris, 1933); Cl. Dillenschneider, C.SS.R., *Le sens de la foi et le progrès dogmatique du mystère marial*, (Rome, Pontifical Marian Academy, 1954); C. Journet, *Esquisse du développement du dogme marial*, (Paris, 1954); G. Filograssi, S.J., "Lo sviluppo del dogma nel congresso mariologico del 1954," in Gregor, 41(1960), 80-106; K. Balic, O.F.M. (ed.), *De Scriptura et Traditione*, (Rome, Pontifical Marian Academy, 1963), 591-649; H. Holstein, S.J., "Le développement du dogme marial," in *Maria*, VI, 243-293; C. Vollert, "Development in Marian dogma," in *A Theology of Mary*, (New York, 1965), 223-250; R. Laurentin, *Traité*, V, 15-100, esp. 82-100; J. McHugh, *The Mother of Jesus in the New Testament*, (London, 1975), Introduction, xxiii-xlvii; W. H. Marshner, "Criteria for doctrinal development in Marian dogmas," in MSt, 28(1977), 47-100.

DEVOTIONS

Devotion to Mary was, from early times, in the framework of the Liturgy (*qv*). With this development, there went also, in the East and West, manifestations of popular piety, evidence that Mary's intercession (*qv*) was part of traditional belief.[1] Such evidence from the East would be the vision of Mary to Gregory the Wonderworker (*qv*), related by Gregory of Nyssa (*qv*) and the *Sub tuum* (*qv*). Such too would be the legends of Theophilus and of Mary of Egypt, and the hymns which culminate in the sublime *Akathistos*. These devotions passed to the West where, in medieval times, others were designed and accepted: the *Ave Maria* (*qv*), the *Angelus* (*qv*), the *Rosary* (*qv*), Litanies, commemorative of the joys and the sorrows of Mary, and with time a vast flowering of pious practices associated with icons, images like the Miraculous Medal, shrines, Marian titles expressing Christian hope, holding memories of past benefaction such as Mother of mercy, Help of Christians, even the very name of Mary. From early times, consecration was a mode of piety found satisfying by Christian faith and sentiment. In modern times, the Heart of Mary (*qv*) has been the object of such consecration as of petition, praise, thanksgiving and atonement. No one can measure the extent or depth of personal, intensely private devotion which through the centuries has been directed to Our Lady all over the world. "The Church," says Vatican II, "has approved various forms of piety towards the Mother of God within the limits of sound and orthodox doctrine, in keeping with circumstances of time and place and with the character and genius of the faithful." (LG 67).

[1]Cf. *Maria*, vols. II, III, bk 6, L'Histoire due culte et de la spiritualite' marials; G. G. Meersseman, O.P., *Der Hymnos Akathistos im Abendland*, 2 vols., (Fribourg, 1958, 1960); H. Graef, *Mary*, I and II; H. Barre, C.SS.Sp., *Prières Anciennes*.

DEVOTIONS FORBIDDEN

The Church has tolerated a wide diversity in the forms of piety inspired by Our Lady. But there are limits beyond which the devout must not go.[1] On 28 January, 1875, the Roman authorities, i.e. the Holy Office, condemned any devotion to the most pure blood of the Blessed Virgin. Two books on the subject were put on the Index of Forbidden Books: *Del sangue purissimo e verginale della Madre di Dio Maria*, which had appeared in Naples in 1863; and *Del sangue sacratissimo di Maria. Studi per ottenere la festivita del medesimo*, which had been published in Perugia in 1874.[2] Instructions were issued from time to time by the Roman authorities also to restrain certain excesses in the devotion, in itself approved, to Our Lady of the Sacred Heart. The title *Queen of the Sacred Heart* or *Mother of the Sacred Heart* was not permitted, nor was any writing which would convey the idea that Mary exercised rule or sway over her divine Son. The devotion to Our Lady of the Cross has also been forbidden.

A more complicated sequence of events followed the cult of the Virgin Priest. It originated in a French religious congregation, the Daughters of the Heart of Jesus, influenced in this by their foundress, Marie Deluil-Martiny, herself instructed by Fr. Giraud. About the time of the foundation, there appeared a book entitled *Marie et le Sacerdoce* by Mgr. O. van den Berghe, which was praised in an apostolic brief by Pius IX, who even wrote that Mary "had been called Virgin Priest by the Fathers of the Church." St. Pius X commissioned two Cardinals to compose a prayer to *Virgo Sacerdos* and then indulgenced it for the universal Church (9 May, 1906).[3]

Within seven years (15 January, 1913), the Roman attitude had changed. A decree of the Holy Office forbade images of the Virgin Mary wearing priestly vestments. A stricter ruling came on 10 March, 1927 when, in the name of the Holy Office, Cardinal Merry del Val wrote to the bishop of Adria in Italy on the occasion of an article which had appeared in *Palestra del Clero* entitled *La vera Divozione alla Vergine Sacerdote*. "The devotion," said the official document, "in accordance with the decree . . . is not approved and cannot be spread."[4] It was not merely the image but the devotion which was now banned. Fr. E. Hugon, O.P. learned from the Holy Office "that it did not wish there to be any further question of devotion to the Virgin Priest. It will meet the intentions of the Holy Office if there is complete silence on this question which inadequately instructed souls could not understand exactly."[5]

No patristic text has been found to justify Pius IX's assertion which was made in a letter to a private individual. The later condemnatory documents did not deal with the strictly theological question of Mary's participation in the priesthood of Christ. A devotion which could, at the time, have led to confusion, was halted. The Holy Office (8 March, 1941) censured the practice spread by *La Crociata Mariana*, promising graces to those who wore a medal without any obligation to do good works.[6]

[1]Cf. R. Laurentin, *Marie, l'Église et le Sacerdoce*, I, (Paris, 1952), 437ff, 509ff; *ibid.*, "Le problème du sacerdoce marial devant le Magistère," in MM, 10(1948), 160-178; P. Galtier, "La dévotion à Marie 'Vierge-Prêtre'," in *Prêtre et Apôtre*, 11(1929), 203-205. [2]A. de Bonhome, "Dévotions Prohibées, Dévotions à la sainte Vierge," in DSp, III, 784-787; DCath, 19(1928), 809-810. [3]ASS 40, 109. [4]DCath, 19(1928), 809. [5]*Palestra del Clero*, 6(1927), 611. [6]AAS, 33(1941), 69.

DIDYMUS OF ALEXANDRIA, THE BLIND
(d. 398)

A blind layman placed at the head of the Alexandria Catechetical School of St. Athanasius (*qv*), D. had among his pupils St. Gregory of Nazianzus (*qv*), St. Jerome (*qv*), and Rufinus. Many of his works have been lost; some were recovered in the Papyrus finds at Toura, south of Cairo in 1941. His best-known work *De Trinitate* is not universally accepted as genuine; the treatise *De Spiritu Sancto* exists only in St. Jerome's Latin translation.[1] D.'s high esteem for Mary, whom he calls *Theotokos*[2] and ever-Virgin[3] is seen also in occasional passages in his controversial works against the Manichees and Eunomius in his Old Testament commentaries, and his brief works on New Testament epistles. His views are orthodox, without originality.

While insisting on the virginal motherhood, D. is equally emphatic on the reality of the human nature assumed by the Word: "He is called a son of man to confound the Docetists. Although he has not his existence from a father, he is nevertheless from a mother. Thus therefore he is said to be 'made from a woman'."[4] The Old Testament image from Dan 2:34, "the stone cut by no human hands," is applied to the Virgin's Son, and D. follows the patristic tradition on the Marian sense of Is 7:14. D. taught the virginity *in partu* and also Mary's perpetual virginity: "For the Virgin in the highest degree more honourable and renowned than all others was not married to anyone; nor did she become the mother of any other, but after childbirth remained ever and always an undefiled Virgin; nevertheless her firstborn is rightly so called, he who fashioned her and all."[5] It was the creative power of the most high which, "as the Holy Spirit came upon the Virgin Mary, made the body of Christ."

[1]Works: PG 39; SC 83, 85 (L. Doutreleau); *Didymi Alexandrini in Epistulas brevis enarratio*, ed. by F. Zoepel, (Munster, 1914); *Didymus der Blinde Kommentar zu Hiob*, ed. by A. Heinrichs and others with German tr., *Didymus der Blinde Psalmen-kommentar*, ed. by M. Grönewald and

others with German tr. (both in *Papyrologische Texte und Abhandlungen*); CMP, II, 318-333; EMBP, 386-392. Cf. G. Bardy, *Didyme l'Aveugle*, (Paris, 1910); *id.* in DSp, III, 868-871; J. Lebon, "Le Ps.-Basile (Adv. Eunomium IV-V) est bien Didyme d'Alexandrie," in Mus, I(1937), 61-83; L. Doutreleau, S.J., "Le De Trinitate, est-il l'oeuvre de Didyme l'Aveugle," in RSR, 45(1947), 514-557; L. Beranger, "Sur deux énigmes du De Trinitate de Didyme l'Aveugle," in RSR, 51(1963), 255-267; A. van Roey, in DHGE, 14(1960), 416-427; O. Stegmüller, in LexMar, 1385; ClavisG, II, 104-111. ²*De Trin.*, 2, 4, in PG 39, 481C. ³*De Trin.*, 1, 27, in PG 39, 404C. ⁴*Comment. in Ps*, 30, 21, Grönewald, et al., 3, 120. ⁵*De Trin.*, 3, 4, in PG 39, 832D.

DILLENSCHNEIDER, CLEMENT, C.SS.R.
(1890-1969) — See Supplement, pp. 380-381.

DOCTORS OF THE CHURCH, MARIAN
Most of the thirty-two Doctors of the Universal Church, officially recognized between the tenth century and 1970, have dealt with Our Lady in their writings or sermons. Devotion to her was a feature of their holiness, in some cases strikingly so. Those most prominent or influential in the history of Marian theology are dealt with separately: St. Ephraem, St. Ambrose, St. Jerome, St. Augustine, St. Cyril of Alexandria, and St. John of Damascus among the Fathers; St. Anselm, St. Bernard, St. Albert the Great and St. Thomas in medieval times; St. Peter Canisius, St. Lawrence of Brindisi, and St. Alphonsus Liguori in the post-Reformation period. Though John Duns Scotus is not in the universal calendar of saints or *Beati*, he is venerated by Franciscans as a Marian Doctor. St. Irenaeus, father of Marian theology, is not included in the list of Doctors because he was a martyr, more highly honoured therefore. Francis Suarez (*qv*) is sometimes styled *Doctor Eximius*.

Most of these saintly men were active in the government of the Church or in its pastoral activity. None of them were restricted in their theological interest to the theology of Our Lady. Two who may pass for special Marian Doctors, because of the wide popularity of their works, or the common currency of their sayings—St. Bernard, for example, or St. Alphonsus—were authors of a vast corpus in which Marian writing is quantitatively slight. Careful reading of the works of all the Marian Doctors will show that the general Christian perspective was not distorted by their theology of Our Lady. The doctrine of Christ's universal and absolute primacy has been vigorously argued by some who were particularly full on the vocation and privileges of Our Lady: Duns Scotus and St. Lawrence of Brindisi pre-eminently so.

DOUBT, ST. JOSEPH'S
"Now the birth of Jesus Christ took place in this way. When his mother Mary had been betrothed to Joseph, before they came together she was found with child of the Holy Spirit; and her husband Joseph being a just man and unwilling to put her to shame, resolved to send her away quietly. But as he considered this, behold an angel of the Lord appeared to him in a dream, saying 'Joseph, son of David, do not fear to take Mary, your wife, for that which is conceived in her is of the Holy Spirit; she will bear a son, and you shall call his name Jesus, for he will save his people from their sins.'" (Mt 1:18-21).

The general opinion held about the infancy narrative of Matthew will determine interpretation of this passage.[1] Three theories have been proposed to explain Joseph's hesitation, or "doubt" to use a word that begs the question. He suspected Mary of adultery; he was in a state of perplexity, "a kind of stupefaction and great wonder" (Suarez) in which certain things, above all Mary's innocence, were clear to him and others unknown or uncertain; he thought she had become pregnant by a divine intervention. The first opinion was held by some of the Fathers, St. Justin Martyr (*qv*) and St. John Chrysostom (*qv*) in the East, St. Ambrose (*qv*) and St. Augustine (*qv*) in the West. It is first found in the *Protevangelium* of James (see *Apocrypha*): "If I hide her sin I am fighting the law of the Lord."[2] The writers who reject it appeal to Matthew's description of Joseph as *dikaios*, just, upright. "It is not the mark of a just man," says St. Basil (*qv*), "to hide crimes by silence." The second theory was suggested by St. Jerome (*qv*), clarified by Suarez (*qv*), and until recently defended by many Catholic writers. The idea that Joseph knew that Mary's conception was divine was first proposed by eastern Fathers, and eventually found its way westward.

Eusebius (*qv*) says that "Joseph knew that the pregnancy of the Virgin was from God"; St. Basil says "Joseph discovered the pregnancy and its cause, namely that it was by the Holy Spirit"; St. Ephraem (*qv*) says that "Joseph understood that this was an admirable work of God." All depict Joseph in a state of fear or awe. E. says: "But he thought especially of sending her away so as not to commit a sin in allowing himself to be called father of the Saviour. He feared to live with her lest he dishonour the name of the Virgin's Son. That is why the angel said to him,

'Do not fear to take Mary to your home.'"[3] St. Romanos the Singer (*qv*) speaks of Joseph as "terrified." Mary's womb has become to him a "furnace filled with fire"; should he, like Moses of old, take off his shoes and approach to listen to Mary and be instructed?

A homily in Paul the Deacon's (*qv*) *Homilarium*, attributed to Origen (*qv*), put the idea in circulation in the West: "Accordingly he [Joseph] wished to dismiss her since he knew that the power of mystery and some marvellous sacrament was in her, which he thought himself unworthy to approach."[4] The saint's attitude is compared to that of Elizabeth, amazed that the Mother of her Lord should come to her, or to Peter's, as he bade the Lord to withdraw from him. The author of the homily may have been a sixth century bishop. A more influential voice was added, that of St. Bernard (*qv*): "Thus, therefore, Joseph, thinking himself unworthy and a sinner, said to himself that he ought not to share his dwelling with one before whose marvellous dignity he stood in awe. He saw and shrank from one pregnant who gave a certain sign of the divine presence and because he could not grasp the mystery he wished to send her away."[5] St. Bernard develops the parallels with Peter (Lk 5:8), the centurion (Mt 8:8), and Elizabeth (Lk 1:43). St. Antoninus of Florence (*qv*) took up his words and adds his own comment: "O inestimable praise of Mary, he rather thought that a virgin could conceive than that Mary could sin." Since she was the Mother of God, Joseph thought himself "unworthy to remain along with such great sanctity."[6]

Recent biblical studies occasionally interpret "she was found with child of the Holy Spirit" as knowledge possessed by Joseph. Fr. Léon-Dufour then translates the particle *gar* (v.20) not as "*for* that which is conceived in her" but, after a pause, "true, that which is conceived in her"; again, others translate just by the word "because." Attempts are made to support a fragile linguistic argument by reconstruction of the Aramaic text on which there cannot be certainty.

The word *dikaios* presents difficulty for each of the first two theories on the doubt. It undermines the suggestion that Joseph suspected Mary for, as an upright or law-abiding man, he must in that case denounce her. If, as the second theory maintains, he was in a state of perplexity, his action in sending Mary away quietly would appear irresponsible; for he was making a positive decision which must have immense effects on her life, without knowledge of the facts. If he knew that the Child was of divine origin and feared with a holy fear, he would logically conclude that God would provide for the future of his own work. The point of the angelic message then would be that it was through him that God would so provide. He would be legal father of Mary's Child ("you shall call his name Jesus") and this fatherhood was linked with salvation history ("for he will save his people from their sins"). That Joseph needed but this enlightenment may be seen from the fact that he obeyed immediately. Even if it be held that the dream pattern excluded questioning on his side, there is no sign of hesitation in understanding or conduct.

---

[1]Cf. J. Seitz, *Die Verehrung des hl. Joseph in ihrer geschichtlichen Entwicklung bis zum Konzil von Trient dargestellt*, (Freiburg in Breisgau, 1908), 49ff; U. Holzmeister, S.J., *De Sancto Joseph Quaestiones Biblicae*, (Rome, 1945), 74; R. Bulbeck, S.J., "The Doubt of Joseph," in CBQ, 10(1948), 296-309; X, Léon-Dufour, S.J., "L'Annonce à Joseph" in *Mélanges André Robert*, (Paris, 1957), 39-97; id., "Le juste Joseph," in NRT, 81(1959), 225-231; and "L'Annonce à Joseph," in *Etudes d'Évangile*, (Paris, 1965), 65-81; K. Rahner, S.J., "Nimm das Kind und seine Mutter," in *Geist und Leben*, 30(1957), 14-22; F. Filas, S.J., "St. Joseph's Doubt," in *The Man closest to Jesus*, (Boston, 1962), 134-152; C. Spicq, O.P., "Joseph son mari étant juste (Mt 1:19)," in RB, 71(1964), 206-214; M. Kramer, "Die Menschwerdung Jesu Christi nach Matthäus (Mt 1), in BB, 45(1964), 1-50; A. Pelletier, "L'Annonce à Joseph," in RSR, 54(1966), 67-68, A. Sicari, "Joseph justus' (Mt 1:19): La storia dell'interpretazione e le nuove prospettive," in *Cahiers de Josephologie*, 19, (Montreal, Valladolid, Rome, 1971), 62-83; G. Danieli, "Storicità di Mt I-II, Stato presente della discussione," in *op. cit.*, 53-61; E. Rasco, "El anuncio a José (Mt 1:18-25)," in *op. cit.*, 84-103; T Stramare, "I sogni di S. Giuseppe," in *op. cit.*, 104-122. R. Pesch, "Eine alttestamentliche Ausführungsformel in Matthäus-Evangelium," ion *Biblische Zeitschrift*, 11(1967), 79-91; J. M. Germano, "Nova et vetera in pericopam de sancto Joseph (Mt 1:18-25)," in *Verbum Domini*, 46(1969), 351-360; P. Barbagli, O.C.D., "Joseph, fili David noli timere accipere Mariam conjugem tuam (Mt 1:20)," in MSS, IV, 445-463; T. Stramare, "'Giuseppe Uomo Giusto' in Mt 1:18-25," in *Rivista Biblica*, 21(1973), 287-300; R. E. Brown, *The Birth of the Messiah*, (London, 1977), 125-132. [2]*Protevangelium*, XIV:1. [3]"Commentaire de l'Evangile Concordant," ed. by L. Leloir, O.S.B., in SC 121, II, 5, 68. [4]PL 95, 1164C. [5]*In Laud. Virg. Matr., Hom. 2*, ed. by J. Leclercq, O.S.B., (Rome, 1966), IV, 31-32. [6]*Summa Theol.*, IV, Tit. XV, 7, (photolithograph ed., Graz, 1959), 957.

DUFF, FRANK (1889-1980)

He was a higher government servant with long experience in St. Vincent de Paul Conference work when, in Dublin on 7 September, 1921 with a number of others, he founded the Legion of Mary.[1] The association spread throughout the world, beginning with Scotland in 1927; it presently exists in 1,500 dioceses in all the continents. It has been encouraged by every Pope since Pius XI, and enjoys the patronage of many episcopal conferences. The Cause of beatification of Edel Quinn, a legionary envoy to Africa, has been introduced in Rome. F.D.'s Marian idealism and outlook, inspired by de Montfort, are to be found in the *Handbook of the Legion of Mary* (several editions translated into principal langauges of the world), in very many articles published in *Maria Legionis*, in books which assemble these articles with other essays, and in lectures and a voluminous correspondence sent all over the world through sixty years—the latter numbering certainly over a hundred thousand items. Mary for him "is the spouse of the Holy Ghost; she is the channel of every grace which Jesus Christ has won. We receive nothing which we do not owe to a positive intervention on her part." The genius of the Legion has been to link a keen sense of the apostolate with devotion to Mary, to assure vision and perseverance—an example of pastoral Marian theology, to which D.'s contribution has been significant. He was a lay Auditor at Vatican II (*qv*).

[1]Cf. C. Hallack, *The Legion of Mary*, 5th ed. with additional ch. by M. O'Carroll, C.S.Sp. (London, 1950); L. J. Cardinal Suenens, *Theology of the Apostolate*, (Westminster, Maryland, 1954), a commentary on the legionary promise; Francis Ripley and F. S. Mitchell (F. Duff), *Souls at Stake*, (Dublin, 1948); F. Duff, *The Spirit of the Legion of Mary*, (Glasgow, 1956); *Miracles on Tap*, (Bay Shore, 1962); also *Walk with Mary, Virgo Praedicanda*, (Dublin, 1967); and *The Woman in Genesis*, (Dublin, 1976).

E

EADMER (1060/64-1130)

E. was a close associate of St. Anselm of Canterbury (*qv*), whom he accompanied into exile. He was the author of two important works on Our Lady: *Tractatus de Conceptione sanctae Mariae*; and *De Excellentia Virginis Mariae*. The former was for a long time spuriously attributed to St. Anselm. The *De IV virtutibus Mariae* (PL 159, 579-586), printed among E.'s works in Migne, is by William of Malmesbury (*qv*)[1]

The treatise on Our Lady's conception offset St. Bermard's (*qv*) letter to the Canons of Lyons. Whether it was written deliberately to do so is difficult to establish, for chronological reasons. E., in the midst of much confusion of thought, with progress still hindered by the Augustinian legacy concerning concupiscence, got at the essential truth. Mary was preserved from sin by a special divine grace. He used phrases which would not look irrelevant centuries later: "the beginning [outset] of her conception"; and "a singular power and operation of the Godhead."

E. thought the devotion of the faithful a better guide than the learned who opposed the feast of the Conception. If Jeremiah and John the Baptist were sanctified in the womb, "who," he asks, "would dare to say that the unique propitiation of the whole world and the unique and sweetest resting-place of the only Son of almighty God was in the beginning of her conception deprived of the grace and illumination of the Holy Spirit."[2]

E. had to counter a view that original sin was transmitted by concupiscence inherent in sexual intercourse. To do so he borrowed an image from plant life, the chestnut "conceived, nourished and formed under thorns but remote from them." Could Mary, conceived among the thorns of sin, not be rendered completely immune from any hurt by them? "He [God] certainly could do it; if, therefore, he willed it, he did it."[3]

This is the distinction between active and passive conception. There were other difficulties. E. in his other work states that Mary was redeemed by Christ: "But God who assumed a man from your most chaste flesh did this for your and our common salvation."[4] What of the text "All have sinned in Adam" (Rom 5:12)? E. did not have Scotus' answer. He appealed to the eminent grace of God which placed Mary above all save her Son. She could not in her conception be bound by the ordinary law, "but was kept utterly free from all contact with sin by a power and operation of the Godhead singular and beyond the grasp of the human intellect." Mary's majesty dominated E.'s thinking. God alone was above her; for she was the Mother of God. She must then be spotless and without any sin. But he linked very closely with her maternal dignity, her universal queenly office as a basis for the privilege. "He made you his unique Mother and at the same time constituted you mistress and empress of all things . . . that you might be thus you were created from the initial moment of your conception in your mother's womb by the operation of the Holy Spirit."[5] Was God, who kept some angels sinless as others sinned, not able to preserve from sin the woman who was to be his mother? God, in his eternal plan, destined Mary as ruler and queen of angels. Shall we believe that with grace inferior to the angels she was conceived as are sinful men? Am I, he exclaims, to believe that she, whose destiny was the object of divine power, whose gifts flowed from divine wisdom, who was chosen by Mercy himself for a part in the salvation of all, could in her conception, be stricken with the death caused by sin, that which came from the devil's hatred?

From the sight of Mary "presiding over angels and archangels, disposing all things with her Son," E. turns to our need. "He is our mercy and you are Mother of the same mercy . . . do not fail us for he, who, that we might be saved, became through you our brother, will not disregard your will as to our salvation."[6]

E. elaborates his views on Mary's queenly power and intercession in his other treatise. The influence of Anselm is apparent: "As God, through creating everything by his power, is the Father and Lord of all, so blessed Mary, re-creating all things by her merits, is the Mother and mistress of things; for God is the Lord of all, constituting the individual things in their nature by his own command; and Mary is the mistress

of things, . . . restoring the individual things to their congenital dignity through the grace she merited."[7] E. does not speak of two kingdoms, justice ruled by Jesus and mercy by Mary. But in presence of the just Judge he thinks that "if the name of his Mother be invoked, her merits intercede so that he [who prays] is answered even if the merits of him who invokes her do not deserve it."[8] He tries to express the mysterious interventions of the Mother of Mercy. He must be read entirely on the subject and due allowance made for rhetoric: "If you, who are the Mother of God, and therefore the true Mother of Mercy, deny us the effect of the mercy of him whose mother you have been made so marvellously, what shall we do when your Son comes to judge all men with a just judgment?"[9]

[1]Works, in PL 159; critical ed., by H. Thurston and Th. Slater, of *Tractatus de Conceptione sanctae Mariae*, (Freiburg in Breisgau, 1904); *Eadmero*, ed. by P. M. Pennoni, (Rome, Libreria Mariana Editrice, 1959). Cf. R. Laurentin, *Traité*, I, 149; A. W. Burridge, "L'Immaculée Conception dans la théologie mariale d'Angleterre," in RHE, 32(1936), 570-597; G. Geenen, O.P., "Eadmer, le premier théologien de l'Immaculée Conception," in V.I., V, 90-136; H. Barré, S.C.Sp., "Le 'de quattuor virtutibus' et son auteur," in EphMar, 3(1953), 231-244; A. Bonnar, O.F.M., "Eadmer 'De Conceptione sanctae Mariae'," in IER, 90(1958), 378-391; J. de Aldama, S.J., "Eadmero y S. Bernardo," in EphMar, 10(1960), 489-498; M. Lamy de la Chapelle, O.S.B., "Le mystère de la pureté de Marie selon Eadmer," in RAM, 38(1962)), 5-36; D. White, O.S.M., "Marian Servitude according to Eadmer of Canterbury," in *Studi Storici O.S.M.*, 14(1964), 5-36; I. Riudor, S.J., "La realeza de Maria en Eadmero," in EstM, 17; A. Gabassut, in DSp, IV, 1-5. Articles at Zagreb Congress: K. Binder, "Marienkult und Marienverehrung beim Eadmer von Canterbury," III, 665-710; H. J. Brosch, "Die Anrufung Marias als Mutter der Barmherzigkeit," IV, 499-514. [2]*Tractatus de Conceptione sanctae Mariae*, (Freiburg im Breisgau, 1904), 9, p. 9. [3]*op. cit.*, 10, p. 11. [4]*De Excellentia*, in PL 159, 580A. [5]*Tractatus de Conceptione sanctae Mariae*, (Freiburg im Breisgau, 1904), 11, p. 12. [6]*op. cit.*, 32, p. 41. [7]*De Excellentia*, in PL 159, 578A and B. [8]*op. cit.*, in PL 159, 570B. [9]*op. cit.*, in PL 159, 579A.

EASTERN INFLUENCE ON THE WEST
Eastern influence on western doctrine and devotion related to Our Lady was, in the first millennium, overwhelming and indispensable.[1] The first element in this continuing complex process was the Sacred Scriptures, which were composed in the East. On a different level was the influence of the Apocrypha (qv), which began to reach the West in the sixth century.

Slight traces are found as early as the fourth. *Pseudo-Matthew*, an adaptation of the *Protevangelium*, appeared about mid-sixth century and eclipsed any translations which may have appeared before that. The *Transitus* stories, which originated in the East in the fifth or sixth centuries, begin to infiltrate the West in the sixth and seventh.

A stimulus to theology as well as to devotion, the Liturgy was an area in which open borrowing from the Orient by the Latins enriched their capital. A decisive point was the introduction in Rome in the seventh century of the four great feasts. These were: 1. The Hypapante, Presentation of the Lord (*qv*), eventually, and up to Vatican II and its aftermath, celebrated as Purification of Our Lady (*qv*), which was begun in Jerusalem towards the end of the fourth century and brought West between 640 and 649; 2. The Dormition (*qv*), found in Jeruslaem about 430, celebrated in Rome about 650; 3. The Annunciation (*qv*), not easily traced to its origins in the East, adopted in Rome at mid-seventh century; 4. The Nativity of Mary (*qv*), which arose in the East about 650 and found its way to Rome a little before the end of the century. To these four, the Conception of Mary (*qv*) and the Presentation of Mary (*qv*) were later added. With the feasts came antiphons, special forms of invocation and prayers such as the *Sub Tuum* (*qv*). In the eighth century, Eastern legends depicting Mary as a powerful intercessor, attentive to sinners and the afflicted, found their way from Greek into Latin: the *Theophilus Legend* (*qv*); and the *Life of Mary of Egypt*, translated by Paul the Deacon (*qv*). At the end of the century, the *Akathistos* (*qv*) hymn was similarly imported. Eastern homilies by Proclus (*qv*) and Antipater of Bostra (*qv*) were taken into the Latin readings. Titles which contain and suggest an immense theology—*Despoina, Domina*, Lady, *Mesites, Mediatrix*, and Mediatress (*qv*) will become part of the western stock of ideas. The second title was used for centuries in the East before becoming current in the West. Iconography made the transition more quickly.

In the domain of theology, St. Ambrose (*qv*) was particularly indebted to the eastern Fathers he chose to study; his portrait of the Virgin Mary is closely modelled on that of St. Athanasius (*qv*). All western thinking was influenced by the Council of Ephesus. Previously, St. Ambrose had used *Mater Dei*; now with the acceptance of

Theotokos, Dei Genitrix would become widespread. In the development of the theology of the Assumption, the *Mariale* of Reichenau was to have considerable effect. Considered until recently to exist towards the end of the tenth century, it must now be dated in the second half of the ninth. It reproduced fourteen eastern homilies on Mary, ten of which deal with the Assumption. We now know that the *De Assumptione*, the composite product in Greek, a synthesis of the others, was the work of John, bishop of Arezzo, from the second half of the ninth century. Through the whole corpus, the great eastern Marian theology of the eighth century, in the works reproduced by St. Germanus of Constantinople, St. Andrew of Crete and St. John of Damascus, would influence western thinking.

[1]Cf. E. Wellesz, *Eastern Elements in Western Chant (Monumenta musicae byzantinae Subsidia*, II, 1), (Oxford, 1947); L. Brou, "Les chants en langue grecque dans les liturgies latines," in *Scaris Erudiri*, 1(1948), 165-180 and 4(1952), 226-238; A. Siegmund, O.S.B., *Die Überlieferung der griechischen christlichen Literatur in der lateinischen Kirche bis zum zwölften Jahrhundert*, (Munich-Pasing, 1949); G. G. Meersseman, O.P., *Der Hymnos Akathistos im Abendland*, (Fribourg, 1958, 1960), 2 vols.; A. Baumstark, *Comparative Liturgy*, revised by B. Botte, O.S.B., tr. by F. L. Cross, (London, 1958); H. Weisweiler, "Das frühe Marienbild der Westkirche unter dem Einfluss der dogma von Chalcedon," in *Scholastik*, 28(1953), 32-60, 504-525. Cf. esp. H. Barré, C.S.Sp., "L'Apport marial de l'Orient à l'Occident," in BSFEM, 19(1962), 27-89; J. de Mahuet, S.M., "Essai sur l'Orient et l'iconographie mariale de l'Occident," in BSFEM, 145-183; D. M. Montagna, O.S.M., "La liturgia Mariana primitiva (sec. IV-VI)," in MM, 24(1962), 84-128, also a separate issue; J. M. Sauget, *Bibliographie des Liturgies Orientales, (1900-1960), (Rome, Pont. Institute Orient., 1962)*, 29-30; H. Graef, *Mary*, I, 202; J. Lafontaine-Dosogne, *Iconographie de l'enfance de la Vierge dans l'empire byzantin et en Occident*, (Brussels, 1964); R. Laurentin, *Traité*, V, 70; *id.*, "Marie dans le culte. Ce que l'Occident doit à l'Orient du VIe au XIe siècle," in Zagreb Congress, II, 17-36; B. Capelle, O.S.B., "La liturgie mariale en Occident," in *Maria*, I, 215-245; *ibid.*, "La messe gallicane de l'Assomption son rayonnement, ses sources," in *Miscellanea Liturgica in honorem L. C. Mohlberg*, (Rome, 1949), vol. II, 33-59; G. Frénaud, O.S.B., "Le culte de Notre Dame dans l'ancienne liturgie latine," in *Marie*, VI, 157-211; G. Philippart, "Jean Évêque d'Arezzo (IXe Siècle) auteur du De Assumptione de Reichenau," in AB, 92(1974), 345-346.

EASTERN LITURGIES — See Supplement, pp. 381-382.

ECUMENISM

John XXIII (*qv*) made Christian Unity one of the ideals of his pontificate, and he hoped that Vatican II (*qv*) would promote it.[1] He set up the Secretariat for Christian Unity to facilitate the

Council's work to this end. The presence at the sessions of Observers, from the separated Christian communities, was a signal proof of this intention. So was the relaxation of rules and official practices, overt or hidden, which had hitherto impeded the efforts of Catholics desirous of working for Christian Unity. In the changed atmosphere, the Council manifested ecumenical concern in many of the texts which it approved. Its essential doctrine on the subject is laid down in the Decree on Ecumenism. This document gives, first, an outline of the theology of Christian unity; next, practical advice; and then a brief description of the two great bodies separated from the Roman Catholic Church. Each part of the decree has some relevance to Marian theology and devotion.

In the Council teaching, the exemplar and source of unity is the Most Holy Trinity. The Holy Spirit, by reason of his presence and activity, is "the principle of the Church's unity." In *Lumen Gentium*, which was promulgated on the same day as the Decree on Ecumenism, Our Lady's privileged position towards each person of the Most Holy Trinity is mentioned, and there is some indication of a doctrine on her special relationship with the Holy Spirit. The theme of Mary and the Church is treated more fully than in any previous document to come from the Teaching Authority. These are pointers. Account must be taken too of the theology of the Church and the Holy Spirit, suggested in the Decree on the Church's missionary activity. Theoretically then, and from the teaching of Vatican II, one can justify a special role for Our Lady in the work of Christian Unity.

The difficulty felt in the practical order is that Mary herself seems to be a subject of the disagreement which keeps Christians apart. Is she not then an obstacle to Christian unity? How will Catholics begin and sustain the dialogue which the Council prescribes as a means towards unity? "The manner and order in which Catholic belief is expressed should in no way become an obstacle to dialogue with out separated brethren. It is, of course, essential that doctrine be presented in its entirety." (Decree II, 11). Attention must be given to the "hierarchy of truths," since they vary "in their relationship to the foundation of the Christian faith." There is a firm directive in LG, 67: "Let them [theologians and preachers of the divine word] painstakingly guard against any word or deed which could lead separated brethren or anyone else into error regarding the true doctrine of the Church." Pope John's much-quoted opinion is here relevant: "The substance of the ancient doctrine of the deposit of the faith is one thing, and the way in which it is presented is another, *the sense and content being preserved intact*." The italicized words are often omitted.[2]

The Council distinguishes between the Orthodox and the western ecclesial communities which derive from the Reformation. The Marian ecumenist must carefully note the differences. The theology and cult of Our Lady began in the East and flourished there for centuries. In modern times, there has been greater theological development (*qv*) and devotional innovation about Our Lady among Catholic than among Orthodox. Nothing, however, can dim the glory of the Byzantine liturgy of Mary *Theotokos*, greatest of all such creations.

The Catholic dogmas of the Immaculate Conception (*qv*) and the Assumption (*qv*) presented a difficulty because they were papally pronounced, and this difficulty was increased by doctrinal traditions. Original sin was not understood in the East as in the West, where St. Augustine's idea was dominant. That the great Easterners in speaking of Mary as all-holy included in this praise exemption from the initial guilt is certain. Regrettably, *Ineffabilis Deus* (*qv*) does not, in its historical section, mention them. The Assumption as a belief arose and was developed in the East, and the essential testimonies in *Munificentissimus Deus* (*qv*) from the first millennium are, except for references to the Popes and the Liturgy (*qv*), all from the Orient. But not all Orthodox theologians were happy that the question of Mary's death (*qv*) was left open. The brief general descriptions of eastern Marian traditions, theological and devotional, in the papal and Council documents, do not touch such controversial points. On the other hand, there is continuity down to the present time in the eastern traditions, which as Bulgakov pointed out, makes Protestants and Orthodox look so unlike each other. "It is in the absence of the Virgin in belief and in life that Protestantism differs most from Orthodoxy." He felt that this "antipathy" would make Christian unity impossible.

Catholics in dialogue with Protestants have to deal with: 1. historical study of the sixteenth century ideas and practice about Our Lady which prompted the Protestant reaction, which would be repudiated by enlightened Catholics; 2. the Marian teaching and devotional practice of the founding fathers of the Reformation; 3. recent Protestant writing on Our Lady and any possible relationship between this and the body of the faithful; and 4. the changing climate of opinion in related areas, either ideological, such as the dignity and status of women, or methodological, such as the "return to the sources"—that is, the scientific study of the Fathers and of Sacred Scripture. Catholics and Protestants, it should be noted, have worked together in interpretation of Sacred Scripture from the days of Pius XI.

A still more profound question remains. How are two conflicting theories of divine grace to be reconciled—the Catholic calling for cooperation on the part of the saved, the Protestant rejecting any such participation. That dialogue can replace confrontation has been shown in recent times: in such encounters, for example, as those organized by the French Society for Marian Studies, and in the English Ecumenical Society of Our Lady, founded in 1967.

A more difficult subject in the area of method is the determination of the order or "hierarchy of truths" and the degree of assent demanded at each level. Attempts thus far have not been too happy. In this as in other aspects of the ecumenical movement, Catholics have not been helped by the crisis of faith and authority within their own body. At the International Mariological Congresses in Rome (1975) and Saragossa (1979), agreed statements were signed by theologians of different confessions.

---

[1]Cf. collective works: "Maria et Christiani ab Ecclesia separati," in ME, X, (Rome, 1960); EstM, 22(1961); De Mariologia et Oecumenismo, ed. by K. Balic, O.F.M., (Rome, Pontifical Marian Academy); "De beata Virgine Maria et hodierno motu oecuménico," in MSS, VI, (Rome, 1967); "Mariologie et oecumenisme," in BSFEM, 19, 20, 21(1962, 1963, 1964); Publications of the Ecumenical Society of the Blessed Virgin Mary, (London); La Madonna e l'ecumenismo, (Rome, Opera Madonna Divino Amore, 1966); La Madonna e l'Ecumene, (First Marian Symposium for Umbria, 1971. San Gabriele, ed. "Eco," 1972); P. Zobel, M. Caplain, H. Roux, A. Kniazeff, La Vierge Marie, l'Église en Dialogue, 8, (Tours, Mame, 1968); "Marialis Cultus," comment by Y. M. Congar, O. P., M. Thurian, A. Kniazeff, in La Maison Dieu, 121(1975), 98-121; Oekumenisches Gespraech, Die Mittlerschaft Mariens, basic text by H. Chavannes, with comments in EphMar, 24(1974), 5-229, 265-470 and 26(1976), 125-199; C. Crivelli, "Marie et les protestants," in Maria, 1, 675-695; S. Tyskiewicz, "La dévotion

des saints russes à Marie," in Maria, III, 697-710; G. M. Corr, O.S.M., "La doctrine mariale et la pensée anglicane contemporaine," in Maria, III, 711-731; A. Wenger, A.A., "Foi et piété mariales à Byzance," in Maria, V, 923-982; J. Hamer, O.P., "Marie et le protestantisme," in Maria, V, 983-1006; B. Schultze, S.J., "Marie et l'Église dans la sophiologie russe," in Maria, VI, 213-240. Cf. esp. A. Cardinal Bea, S.J., "Accord de la doctrine et de la piété mariales avec l'ésprit oecuménique," in Maria, VII, iii-xiii, D. Stiernon, A.A., "Marie dans la théologie orthodoxe gréco-russe," in Maria, VII, 239-336.

Catholic works: D. Bertetto, S.D.B., Maria e i protestanti, (Rome, 1957); A. Algermissen, "Mariologie und Marienverehrung der Reformation," in TheolGlaube, 49(1959), 1-24; Y. M. Congar, O.P., "Marie et l'Église chez les Protestants," in Chrétiens en dialogue, (Paris, 1964), 675-693; T. A. O'Meara, O.P., Mary in Catholic and Protestant Theology, (New York, 1966); E. Carroll, O.Carm., "Protestant reaction to the role of Mary in Vatican II," in AER, 154(1966), 289-301; T. Cranny, S.A., "Marie, Madre del'Unita," in Unitas, 22(1967), 248-259; J. Pintard, Marie dans l'Église divisée. Mère de la Réconciliation, (Paris, 1968); G. Söll, S.D.B., "La devozione mariana e un ostacolo per l'unità dei cristiani?," in MM, 31(1969), 363-384; M. Gonzalez Bueno, O.P., Marchas marianas de unidad, (Villava-Pamplona, Ed. Ope, 1969); S. C. Napiorkowski, O.F.M.Conv., "Le mariologue peut-il être oecuméniste? Du rôle de la mariologie contemporaine dans le dialogue oecuménique des protestants et des catholiques," in EphMar, 22(1972), 15-76; J. Alfaro, S.J., "Maria y l'union de los Cristianos," in EclXaver, 18(1968), 275-318; G. M. Papini, O.S.M., "Teologia ecumenico-mariana in occidente," in MM, 35(1973), 184-240; C. Pozo, S.J., Problemas ecumenicos de la Mariologia, in Maria en la obra de la salvación, (Madrid, BAC, 1974).

Protestant works: The Mother of God, ed. by E. I. Mascall, (London, 1949), with Orthodox participation; Zagreb Congress, II, 125-136; G. Miegge, La Vergine Maria, (Torre Pellice, 1950); R. Schimmelpfennig, Die Geschichte des Marienverehrung im deutschen Protestantismus, (Paderborn, 1952); W. Tappolet, Das Marienlob der Reformatoren: Luther, Calvin, Zwingli, Bullinger, (Tübingen, 1963), Max Thurian, Mary, Mother of the Lord, Figure of the Church, (London, 1963); H. Asmussen, Maria, die Mutter Gottes, 2nd ed., (Stuttgart, 1957); W. Delius, Geschichte der Marienverehrung, (Munich, Basle, 1963); S. Benko, Protestants, Catholics and Mary, (Valley Forge, Judson Press, 1968); A. M. Allchin, "Mary, Virgin and Mother, an Anglican approach," in One in Christ, 5(1969), 275-290; G. S. Wakefield, 'The Virgin Mary in Methodism," in One in Christ, 4(1968), 156-164; C. A. Ridder, Maria als Miterlöserin, (Göttingen, 1965); H. Räisanen, Die Mutter Jesu im Neuen Testament, (Helsinki, 1969); J. de Satge, Mary in the Christian Gospel, (London, SPCK, 1976); F. W. Kunneth, "Um eine dogmatische Begründung evangelischer Marienverehrung," in Zagreb Congress, II, 169-182. Meletios, "Postura actual de la Iglesia orthodoxa acerca de la doctrina y del culto a la Madre de Dios," in EstM, 32(1969), 275-288; I. C. Gheorghescu, "La doctrine sur la Sainte Vierge dans l'Orthodoxie et le Catholicisme," in Orthodoxia, 22(1970), 382-399; A. Stawrowsky, "La Sainte Vierge Marie. La doctrine de l'Immaculée Conception des Églises Catholique et Orthodoxe, Etude comparée par un théologien orthodoxe," in MM, 35(1973), 36-112; B. de Margerie, S. J., "Ecumenical Problems in Mariology," in MSt, 26(1975), 180-203; A. Ross

Mackenzie, "Mariology as an ecumenical problem," in MSt, 26(1975), 204-220; D. Dietz, O.M.I., "The Hierarchy of Truths about Mary," in MSt, 27(1976), 41-63.

EKBERT OF SCHONAU (d. 1184)

Brother of the mystic, St. Elizabeth of Schönau, E. studied at the school of St. Victor's in Paris. He was abbot of Schonau from *c.* 1166. Some of his writings have been published.[1] They include a treatise on the Magnificat, a commentary on *Missus est*, meditations, prayers, and fragments of sermons. A prayer to the Holy Heart of Mary by E. is the first known of its kind.[2] A homily among the items of Paul the Deacon's *Homiliarium* (in curtailed form among the spuria of St. Bernard (qv)), is by E. He shows the influence of St. Bernard.

[1]F. W. E. Roth, *Die Visionen der hl. Elisabeth und die Schriften der Abte, und Emenco*, (Bruen, 1884)—on the Magnificat, 230-247, on *Missus est*, 248-263; PL 95, 1514-1519; PL 184, 1009-1014. R. Laurentin, *Traité*, I, 140, 153. [2]H. Barré, C.S.Sp., "Une prière d'Ekbert de Schönau au Coeur de Marie," in EphMar, 2(1952), 409-423. Cf. K. Koster, "Ekbert de Schönau, écrivain mystique et prédicateur," in DSp, IV, 584-585; A. Wilmart, O.S.B., *Auteurs spirituels et textes du moyen âge latin*, (Paris, 1932), p. 421, n. 4.

EMMANUEL (ISAIAH 7:14)

"Therefore the Lord himself will give you a sign. Behold a young woman [virgin] will conceive and bear a son, and shall call his name Emmanuel."[1]

It is probable that from the second century to the twentieth more has been written on this verse from the Old Testament than on any other from that source. In 1905, E. Condamin, in his commentary on Isaiah, referred to the constant appearance of monographs and articles on the text. This flow continues without agreement among scholars.

Origin: Some striking extra-biblical parallels have been brought to light, from the writings discovered at Ras Shamra, ancient Ugarit. Of the marriage of Nikkal and Yarih it is said: "A virgin will give birth . . . a damsel will bear a son." But the textual reading, when closely examined, shows that Is 7:14 cannot be regarded as a quotation from Ras Shamra. The appeal to the Legend of Karit is likewise inconclusive. The Isaian origin of v. 14 is accepted by critics; that of the following verses is variously questioned.

History: The important word *almah*, translated above as "a young woman" was translated by the *Septuagint* as *parthenos*, which usually but not invariably means virgin. From the *Septuagint*, Matthew took the quotation which he used in the infancy narrative. (Mt 1:23). This textual use may have influenced the Fathers. The massive patristic witness remains impressive. The first theologians of Our Lady, St. Justin Martyr (qv) and St. Irenaeus (qv), followed by Tertullian (qv) and Origen (qv), interpreted the oracle explicitly and often at length in terms of the virginal conception. They were followed by practically every Father of the Church in the East and West, certainly by everyone who had any occasion to consider the text. St. Augustine (qv) was no exception, as a sermon restored to him in recent times makes clear. This unanimity affected writers and preachers for centuries; Calvin and Luther accepted the interpretation.

Teaching Authority: With such unanimity, the teaching authority did not intervene until the eighteenth century when I. L. Isenbiehl denied the reference to the virginal conception and the true Emmanuel, and was severely condemned by Pius VI.[2] The oracle is mentioned only once in papal teaching before Vatican Council II in an address by Pius XII.[3]

Vatican II was restrained in dealing with the oracle: "Likewise this is the Virgin who will conceive and bring forth a Son, who will be called Emmanuel." (Is 7:14; Mic 5:2,3; Mt 1:22, 23; LG 55). "Likewise" (*similiter*) refers to the qualification already expressed in the same paragraph on the interpretation of Gen 3:15 (see WOMAN IN), "as they [early documents of the Old Testament] are read in the Church and are understood in the light of a further and full revelation." "Likewise" was maintained in the final draft despite a request by thirty-four Fathers that the text on the Old Testament be strengthened, and by three Fathers that the word itself be deleted. The report commented: "There is no doubt about the meaning of the quotation in Mt 1:22,23. But exegetes do not fully agree on the *literal* meaning of the Old Testament text."[4]

Recent Studies: Little has been left unexplored. Modern critical scholarship sees the oracle as related rigidly to the person and situation described by Isaiah. Ahaz, threatened by Rezin of Damascus and Pekah of Israel who had surrounded Jerusalem because he would not join them against Assyria, thought of an alliance with Assyria. Isaiah opposed this as it would reduce Judah to vassalage to Assyria. Since 734 was the year of crisis, scholars think that the oracle must be fulfilled then or soon afterwards. Pressed by the prophet to ask God for a sign of his protection, Ahaz, faithless, with specious talk about not tempting the Lord, rejected the offer. Whereupon Isaiah announced the oracle. A child, probably of the Davidic line, would be born within a short time. He would assist the House of David and would thereby deserve the title "God with us." The mother, the *almah*, would be a marriageable woman, probably a virgin. She could not be Isaiah's own wife, probably not the mother of Hezekiah (a view held in ancient Jewish times). *Almah* is used nine times in the Old Testament, never for a married woman, but not on the highest level of chastity in Song 6:8 and Prov 30:19. According to these recent scholars, there is no question of a future virginal conception as in Matthew. *Bethulah* is the Hebrew word for a virgin. The participial construction in Hebrew is, in regard to the conception, vague on the precise moment of time. The *Septuagint* uses the future and changes "she will call" to "you will call"; Matthew makes a further change, "they will call." *Lumen Gentium* follows Mt. Aq, Sym, and Theod, translating *almah* by *neanis*, a young woman. Trypho and St. Justin debated the point.

This analysis gives no final solution to the Emmanuel problem. What value as a sign would an ordinary birth have? There is no resemblance, on this theory, between the birth of the Emmanuel and the series of miraculous births in the Old Testament and the New Testament. It is maintained that messianism was not at this time understood to refer to a single future king. But, since the plan of salvation, which was assured by Yahweh (Gen 3:15), comprised a woman in an important role, the opinion of those who see in Is 7:14 an echo of Gen 3:15 cannot be dismissed lightly.

[1]For bibliography from 1883 to 1951, cf. J. Coppens, "La Prophétie d'Emmanuel," in *L'Attente du Messie (Recherches Bibliques)*, (Bruges, 1954), 39-41; to 1972, cf. G. Del Olmo Lete, "La Profecia del Emmanuel. Estado actual de la Interpretacion," in EphMar, 22(1972), 357-385. For general commentaries, cf. P. Auvray and J. Steinmann, *Isaie*, 2nd ed., (Paris, 1957); E. J. Kissane, *The Book of Isaiah*, 2nd ed., (Dublin, 1962); F. Montagnini, *Il libro di Isaia. Parte prima.*, (Brescia, 1966). Cf. also A. Schulz, "Alma," in *Bibl. Zeitschr.*, 23(1935-1936), 229-241; E. J. Young, "The Immanuel Prophecy," in *Studies in Isaiah*, (London, 1955), 160-172; S. Mowinckel, *He That Cometh*, (Oxford, 1956), 114-118; J. J. Stamm, "Neuere Arteiten zum Immanuel-Problem," in *Zeitschr. Altt. Wiss.*, 68(1956), 46-53; R. G. Bratcher, "A Study of Isaiah 7:14," in *Biblical Translator*, 9(1958), 97-126; H. Wildberger, *Jesaja (Biblischer Kommentar, Altes Testament X)*, (Neukirchen-Vluyn, 1969); id., "Die Immanuel-Weissagung und die Eschatologie des Jesaja," in *Theol. Zeitschr.*, 16(1960), 439-455; ibid., "Die Immanuel-Perikope im lichte neuerer Deutungen," in *Zeitschr. der deutschen morgenländischen Gesellschaft*, Suppl. 1(1969), 281-290; F. L. Moriarty, "The Immanuel Prophecies," in CBQ, 19(1957), 226-233; R. Criado, "El valor de 'laken' (Vg propter) en Is 7:14. Contribución al estudio del Emmanuel," in Est Ecl, 34(1960), 741-751; E. F. Sutcliffe, "The Emmanuel Prophecy of Isaias," in EstEcl, 34(1960), 753-765; J. Coppens, "L'Interprétation d'Is 7:14 à la lumière des études les plus recéntes," in *Lex tua Veritas*, ed. H. Gross-F. Mussner, (Trier, 1961), 31-45; id., *Le messianisme royal*, (Paris, 1968), 67-85; J. Prado, C.SS.R., "La madre de Emmanuel: Is 7:14. Resena del estado de las questiones," in *Sefarad*, 21(1961), 85-114; F. Montagnini, "L'Interpretazione di Is 7:14 di I. L. Isenbiehl," in *Il Messianismo* (7th biblical week), (Brescia, 1966), 95-104. Cf. esp. R. Kilian, *Die Verheissung Immanuels Jes 7:14 (Stuttgarter Bibelstudien 35)*. (Stuttgart, 1968); id., "Die Geburt des Immanuel aus der Jungfrau Jes 7:14," in *Zum thema Jungfrauengeburt*, ed. by K. S. Frank and others, (Stuttgart, 1970), 9-35; J. J. Scullion, "An approach to the understanding of Isaiah 7:10-17," in *Jour. Bibl. Lit.*, 87(1968), 288-300; M. Rehm, *Der Königliche Messias im Licht der Immanuel-Weissagungen des Buches Jesaja*, (Kevalaer, 1968); J. Lust, "The Immanuel Figure: a Charismatic Judge-Leader," in ETL, (1971), 464-470; J. Carreira des Neves, "Isaias 7:14 no texto Massoretico e no texto grego. A obra de Joachim Becker," in *Didascalia*, 2(1972), 79-112, 79-112; G. Del Olmo Lete, "El Emmanuel. Ensayo de Interpretación formal," in EphMar, 23(1973), 345-361; F. M. Braun, O.P., in BSFEM, 12(1954), 19; H. Cazelles, in ME, V, 51ff; R. E. Brown, *The Birth of the Messiah*, (London, 1977), 143-153. [2]*Enchiridion Biblicum*, 5th ed., (Rome, 1961), 315. [3]October 18th, 1954, in OL, 404. [4]*Modi*, ch. VIII, in LG, (Vatican Press, 1964), 9.

ENGELBERT OF ADMONT (c. 1250-1331)

A Benedictine abbot who studied in Prague and Padua, E. was a man of wide culture.[1] His Marian theology is more akin to that of Richard of St. Laurent (*qv*) and Pseudo-Albert than to the thinking of St. Thomas Aquinas (*qv*) and St. Albert the Great (*qv*). It is contained in the *De gratiis et virtutibus B. V. M.*,[2] the *De officio ancillari B. V. M.*,[3] the *Psalterium B. M. V.*,[4] a lengthy work in verse, and in two parts of an unpublished work, *Super duodecim antiphonas*, i.e. *Virgo virginum* and *Mundi domina*.

The first treatise ranges widely over Marian questions. It is in four parts: the life and virtues of Mary in the gospels; her active life; her contemplative life; and her death and glorification. The order of ideas is not strict. Mary underwent a threefold purification: in the womb; at the Annunciation; and when Christ was in her womb. Like Pseudo-Albert, E. tends to attribute graces and powers to Mary by way of deduction —the graces of the seven sacraments, of the priesthood therefore, and vast knowledge. On the Assumption (qv), he follows Pseudo-Augustine (qv). He extols Mary's queenly power and sees her in a special "hierarchy" beneath God but above angels and men. She intervenes in human affairs in every moment of need, and is a faithful mediatress of grace.[5]

E. may, in this work, show influence by Pseudo-Denis the Areopagite and Hugh of St. Victor. He can also pen a concise passage replete with theology acceptable today: "She [Mary] stood therefore fixed in faith, joined in the passion and attached to the crucified One in communion and association with his passion and the salvation of men, the individual associate of the passion, to which she had been predestined and chosen as minister of the Incarnation, of the whole work of our redemption, partner [consors] of the supreme consolation to come through Christ."[6]

The same idea of participation in the work of redemption and association is found in the De officio ancillari, first published in 1954: "Since therefore among the privileges of the blessed Virgin, one of the principal was supreme communion in the passion of Christ and consequently in the work of human redemption . . ."[7] "Joy at the resurrection and ascension followed the passion and the joy mixed with sorrow in the passion fittingly and justly [de congruo et condigno], as she had been the inseparable associate of the passion, sorrow and labour of Christ from his youth as has been already shown in each case."[8] This short work shows how Mary was the handmaid, ancilla, of the Lord in the successive mysteries of his life. Then after a lengthy explanation of the assertion that his sorrow was mingled with joy in the passion, it applies the same idea to Mary and proceeds to consider her five other joys: the Annunciation; the birth of Christ; the Resurrection; the Ascension; and Mary's Assumption.

[1]Cf. G. B. Fowler, in DSp, IV, 745-747. [2]B. Pez, Thesaurus anecdotum novissimus, (Augsburg, 1721), vol. 1, pt. 1, 505-761. [3]"De officio ancillari B. V. M.," ed. by G. B. Fowler, in Mitteilungen des Instituts fur Oesterreichische Geschichtsforschung, 92(1954), 381-389, intr. 378-381. [4]C. Blume and G. M. Dreves, An. Hymn., 35, 79-90; G. G. Meersseman, Der Hymnos Akathistos im Abendland, (Fribourg, 1960), II, 133-145. [5]B. Pez, Thesaurus anecdotum novissimus, (Augsburg, 1721), vol. 1, pt. 2, 579ff. [6]op. cit., vol. 1, pt. 1, 33, 556. [7]"De officio ancillari B. V. M.," ed. by G. B. Fowler, in Mitteilungen des Instituts fur Oesterreichische Geschichtsforschung, 92(1954), 385. [8]op. cit., 389.

EPHESUS
(See St. Cyril of Alexandria)

EPHRAEM OF SYRIA, ST. (c. 306-373)
E., the "Lyre of the Holy Spirit," deserves the title Marian Doctor also. It now rests on a sure foundation with the completion of the critical edition of his works. This eliminates the Hymns to the Virgin, and establishes the commentary of Tatian's Diatessaron as authentic. Thus much of the previous bibliography becomes irrelevant but already authoritative monographs have examined the authentic corpus.[1] In quality and quantity, it surpasses St. Athanasius and the Cappadocians.

E. was fortunate in his training by James, bishop of Nisibis (303-338) and his second successor, Vologesus (346-361). He taught first in Nisibis, but left for Edessa after the advent of the Persians in 363. He was immensely prolific in sacred poetry, with a vivid sense of persons and imaginative skill disciplined by sound theology. He insists so much on Mary's sinlessness that he is invoked as a supporter of the Immaculate Conception (qv). In the Nisibene Hymns, he writes: "Thou alone and thy Mother are in all things fair; for there is no flaw in thee and no stain in thy Mother. Of these two fair ones, to whom are my children similar?"[2] There are other texts which call for subtle interpretation in support of the theory. Mary is spoken of as one baptized: "And I am a spouse. For thou art chaste. I am handmaid and daughter; of blood and water; for thou hast purchased and baptised me. The Son of the heavenly one who came and took up his abode in me and I became his Mother."[3] Again he speaks of the eye as cleansed by the light of the sun, and he goes on: "In Mary, as in the eye, the Light came to dwell and it cleansed her spirit, refined her thoughts, sanctified her mind and purified her virginity."[4] These texts are no contradiction of Mary's initial holiness; nor are others found in the

Armenian version of the commentary on the *Diatessaron* which seem to imply fault—doubt, for example, on the Resurrection. Here E. confused Mary with Mary Magdalene. Again the absence of a doctrine of Original Sin cannot be invoked.

E. thought that Mary, as well as Joseph, was of the house of David. She was married because the guarantee of royal descent from David had to be given through a man (women's names were not found in the genealogies), and to have a witness against a possible charge of adultery. On Joseph's doubt (*qv*), the Armenian version of *the commentary on the Diatessaron* gives the interpretation that the saint knew of the divine intervention: "All these signs led him to believe that the thing had come from God."[5] "If he had known that this conception had not come from the Spirit, it would have been dishonourable on his part not to denounce her publicly."[6] But the Syrian version records suspicion on Joseph's part of violation suffered by Mary, an idea absent from the Armenian. The father-child relationship between Joseph and Jesus is described in the Hymns for the Nativity. Joseph, conscious of his kingly ancestry and his present lowliness, is filled with wonder "that the Son of the Most High should be my son"; "Joseph caressed the Son as a little child; he served him as God."[7] The Armenian version notes such compliments to the saint as Luke's genealogy which goes back to Adam "who was of God"—"to display the value of this man who was found worthy to minister to the divine economy and to be called spouse of Mary." Also the choice of Joseph of Arimathea for the burial of Christ "so that full honour should be given to the name of Joseph, which presided at his burial as at his birth in the cave."[8]

In all that E. says about St. Joseph, the virginal conception is emphasized. He is equally explicit on the *virginitas post partum*. On the *virginitas in partu*, particularly on the painless birth, he is not altogether consistent—mostly favourable, with a few ambiguous texts.

E. abounds in the Mary-Eve (*qv*) parallel and contrast. "Behold the world; two eyes are placed in it; Eve was the blind, left eye; the right, shining eye is Mary."[9] It is basically the contrast of death and life. Eve gave birth to Cain the murderer, Mary to the Lifegiver. "But Eve, mother of all the living, became the source of death to all living. But Mary, the new branch, took growth from Eve, the old vine and Christ, the new Life, dwelt in her."[10] That this theory contained more than a hint of Mary's saving role, which is seen in E.'s application of Gen 3:15 (see WOMAN IN) to her, is clear when he speaks of Mary opening "the closed mouth of death, the bolted door of Scheol, to display a new way to the grave." Adam, we read elsewhere, received from Eve a garment of wretchedness and, hideous, was driven out of the garden. Mary fashioned for him a new garment, and the garden welcomed him, splendid, in it. E. had a premonition of the title St. Epiphanius (*qv*) would use, "Mother of the living," when he told the children of Eve that through Mary they were taken from their "old mother." A cosmic role is intimated: "Mary gave birth to the lamp which with the seven blessed lights enlightens all creation."[11]

The patristic idea of conception through the ear and the image of the virgin earth are familiar to E.: "Death entered by Eve's ear; that is why life entered by Mary's ear." "For as from the small womb of that ear death entered and spread about, so through the new ear of Mary life entered and spread about." "The virgin earth gave birth to that Adam, head of the earth, today the virgin gave birth to Adam, head of heaven."[12]

The controversy on *Theotokos* (*qv*) was to flare up within sixth years of E.'s death. His thought is in harmony with Ephesus (*qv*) and Chalcedon. "For I am servant of your Godhead, though also mother of your humanity, O Lord and Son." "As God he was the hope of his Mother, as man her beloved Child and Son." "For thou art the Son of God and son of man, Son of Joseph, David's son and Son of Mary." "What Mother has ever called her son Son of the Most High?"[13] Here surely is the doctrine of the two natures and one person, of the motherhood related to the person.

E. is probably the first writer to call Mary bride of Christ (see SPOUSE). "Thy Mother she is, she alone, and thy sister along with all; she became thy Mother, she became thy sister. She is also thy Bride, along with the chaste [virgins]."[14]

Vatican II (*qv*), summing up a long tradition, compared baptism and preaching in the Church with the virgin birth, thus showing the basis of the Mary-Church (*qv*) typology. E., dealing with the parallel between the virgin birth and baptism, takes the Lord as the minister. He does speak of Mary as "the symbol of the Church."[15]

and in the commentary on the *Diatessaron* he identifies them thus: "He freed his Church from circumcision and replaced Josuah, son of Nun, by John who was a virgin to whom he entrusted Mary, his Church, as Moses entrusted his flock to Josuah."[16] E. also links Mary with the Eucharist: "He, the only one who came forth from Mary, took and broke the bread, the unique one, the symbol of that body." "The Church gave us the living bread in the place of those *azymi* which Egypt had given. Mary gave us the bread of life instead of the bread of weariness which Eve gave."[17]

E.'s exlated ideal and theology of virginity came ultimately from his reflection on Mary: "Mary the thirsting field, has in Nazareth conceived Our Lord through her hearing. You also, O woman, thirsting for water, have conceived the Son through your hearing."[18] Christ is all in all, and E. applies this to the relationship between Mary and John. Each saw Christ in the other. Speaking of Mary's consciousness of the living fruit she had brought forth, he adds, "It was the Church and the Son in her,"[19] a suggestion of that dependence of the Church on Mary explained by Pope Paul's proclamation of the title "Mother of the Church."

[1]Critical ed., by E. Beck, O.S.B. for CSCO; refs. to German tr. CMP, II, 476-537. For commentary on the *Diatessaron*, Syrian, cf. L. Leloir, O.S.B., Chester Beatty Monographs, VIII, (Dublin, 1963); Armenian (using Syrian), in SC 121. For Syrian, cf. also P. Ortiz de Valdivielso, *Studia Papyr.*, 5(1966); CMP, II, 476-537. Cf. esp. I. Ortiz de Urbina, S.J., "La Vergine nella teologia di S. Efrem," in *Orient. Christ. Analecta*, 197, (Rome, 1974); E. Beck, O.S.B., "Die Mariologie der echten Schriften Ephraems," in *Oriens Christianus*, 40(1956), 22-39; *id.*, in DSp, IV, 788-800. For previous bibliography, cf. G. M. Besutti, O.S.M., in PCM, V, 264-265. Cf. Leloir, O.S.B., "Divergences entre l'original syriaque et la version arménienne du commentaire d'Ephrem sur le Diatessaron," in ST, 232, (Vatican, 1964), 303-331; H. Graef, *Mary*, I, 57-62. [2]*Hymn 27, v. 8*, in CSCO 219, 76. [3]*Nativity Hymns, 16, 10-11*, in CSCO 187, 76. [4]*Church Hymns, 36, 2*, in CSCO 199, 88. Cf. I. Ortiz de Urbina, S.J., "Vale el testimonio de San Efren en favor de la Inmaculada?," in EstEcl, 28(1954), 417-422; for opinion against, cf. L. Hammersberger, *Die Mariologie der ephremischen Schriften*, (Innsbruck, 1938). [5]L. Leloir, O.S.B., in SC 121, 67. [6]*ibid.*, in SC 121, 11, 4, p. 68. [7]SC 121, 5, 17, p. 41. [8]SC 121, 1, 26, p. 26; and 21, 20, p. 385. [9]*Hymns on the Church*, in CSCO 199, 37, 5, p. 90. [10]*Sermon on Our Lord, 3*, in CSCO 271, 4. [11]*Hymns on Virginity*, in CSCO 224, 5, 3, p. 18. [12]SC 121, 20, 32, pp. 366-367; *Hymns on the Church*, in CSCO 199, 49, 7, p. 122; *Nativity Hymns, 1, 16*, in CSCO 187, 3. [13]*ibid., 5, 20*, in CSCO 187, 42; *ibid., 9, 1*, in CSCO 187, 55; *ibid., 6, 2*, in CSCO 187, 43; *ibid., 8, 17*, in CSCO 187, 53. [14]*ibid., 11, 2*, in CSCO 187, 61. [15]*Hymn on the Crucifixion, 4, 17*, in CSCO 249, 43. [16]SC 121, 12, 5, p. 216. [17]*Nisibene Hymns*, II, 46, 11, p. 46; *Hymns de Azymis, 6, 7*, in CSCO 249, 11. [18]*Hymns on Virginity*, in CSCO 224, 23, 5, p. 74. [19]*Hymns on the Faith, 81, 4*, in CSCO 155, 212.

EPIPHANIUS, ST. (*c.* 315-403)

A Palestinian, a remarkable linguist, E. was for many years a monk before he was elected bishop of Salamis in Cyprus in 367. Resolute in the Nicene faith, he treated of Marian questions in the *Ancoratus*, a doctrinal work, but especially in the *Panarion*, a refutation of eighty heresies. In heresy seventy-eight, he dealt with the Antidicomarianites, who taught that, after the birth of Jesus, Joseph lived with Mary as his wife in an ordinary way, and the Collyridians, a mostly female sect in Thracia and Upper Scythia, who offered quasi-divine honours to Mary.[1] E. was also the author of an unpublished sermon on the *Hypapante*, the Purification (BHG 1956s). The sermon *De Annuntiatione* (PG 43, 485-501; BHG 1143) is spurious, as is the Syriac sermon published by E. A. Wallis Budge (*qv*) in *Miscellaneous Coptic Texts* (pp. 120-145).

E. established Mary's perpetual virginity and had an intuition of her perfect holiness. He furthered reflection on the Eve (*qv*)-Mary parallel and contrast by applying to Mary the title "Mother of the living" (Gen 3:20), and he showed, within the same context of the new Eve, a relationship between Mary and the Church (*qv*). He clarified the nature of cult to Our Lady and, finally, he raised, in terms clear and compelling, the problem of the Assumption, and also showed its complexity.

E. saw the fulfillment of Gen 3:15 (see WOMAN IN) in the Son of Mary, with some insistence on Mary's virginal conception, so that it is almost a Marian interpretation.[2] Like the Fathers prior to him and so many after, he applied Is 7:14 (see EMMANUEL) to Mary. In common with a number of second and third century writers, he understood Lk 1:35 as a reference to the Son, though he did not exclude the Holy Spirit from the Incarnation: "Without male intercourse he fashioned for himself a most holy body from Mary *Theotokos*."[3]

E. referred so explicitly to the Only-begotten "opening the womb"—though in a context of Christ as the spouse of the Church—that he does not appear to have held the *virginitas in partu* (*qv*).[4] On the virginal conception which was the explicit faith of the Church, he was emphatic: "She is not spoken of as a woman united with a man and married, but in the proper sense she is called a virgin who in herself, without male cooperation, brought forth the Word of God."[5] His decisive contribution was to rebut the heretics who denied Mary's perpetual virginity. Following the Apocrypha, as he did in regard to the marriage (qv), he held that Joseph's great age forbade normal married life, as did the impropriety of dishonouring Mary, the holy vessel; this would be to dishonour the Lord himself. E. invoked Jn 19:25-27 (see WOMAN IN) as proof that Mary had no other children than Jesus, and he cited a fable that the lioness gives birth only once. He appealed to the example of the prophets and of St. Paul, and dealt with the difficult texts such as "before they came together" and "he did not know her" (Mt 1:18, 25), and those speaking of the "Brothers of the Lord" (qv). E., again following the Apocrypha, took these to be children of Joseph by an earlier marriage.

The passage on the new Eve is involved and difficult, if rich in content. On appearances, says E., Eve is the mother of the living, but in truth it is "from Mary that life itself has been begotten for the world, that she should bring forth a living being, become his mother. Figuratively then (di ainigmatos) Mary has been called Mother of the living." Recalling Job 38:36, he then contrasts Eve weaving garments for Adam naked through her fault, with the "garment of immortality" we have through the one born of Mary. He goes on: "But here another wonder must be considered about Eve and Mary. Eve was for men an occasion of death and through her death entered the world; Mary was an occasion of life and through her life has been begotten for us. That is why the Son of God came into the world, and where sin has abounded grace has abounded all the more [Rom 5:20]. From where death came life came forward, so that life should come in the place of death, shutting out death which had come through the woman, and it was he who through a woman became life for us. And as Eve still a virgin sinned by disobedience, the obedience of grace came anew through the Virgin when the announcement was made of the descent from heaven and the appearance of eternal life."[6]

E.'s opinion on the end of Mary's life is enigmatic: "How," he says in a somewhat neglected passage, "shall Mary, the holy one, not possess the kingdom of heaven in the flesh [meta sarkos], she who was not lewd or wanton, who did not commit adultery, was in no way at fault in what concerned the flesh, but remained unsullied?"[7] In a better known passage, he remarks first on the silence of Scripture about Mary's death and burial, on the absence of any record of her journey to Asia Minor with John. The silence of Scripture he explains by "the extraordinary nature of the prodigy, in order not to shock the minds of men." He himself keeps silence: "On the one hand, you see Simeon say of her, 'And your own soul a sword shall pierce, that the thoughts of many hearts may be revealed' [Lk 2:35]. On the other hand, when the Apocalypse of John says 'And the dragon hastened against the woman who had brought forth the male child, and there were given to her an eagle's wings, and she was carried off into the wilderness, that the dragon might not seize her' [Rev 12:13-14], it may be that this is fulfilled in her."[8] He will not say this absolutely, nor maintain that she died. Scripture has left the matter uncertain. In a later passage, he says that she may have died and been buried, or been killed—as a martyr. "Or she remained alive, since nothing is impossible with God and he can do whatever he desires; for her end no one knows."[9] The allusion to Rev 12 (see WOMAN IN) may be the first Marian interpretation of that text.

A Palestinian with opportunity for some research, E. does not speak of a bodily resurrection and remains noncommittal on the way Mary's life ended. He nowhere denies the Assumption, or admits the possibility of Assumption without death, for he has found no sign of death or burial. He suggests several different hypotheses and draws no firm conclusion.[10]

His critique of the Collyridians, who ceremonially offered and ate bread in honour of Our Lady, allows him to distinguish devotion to Mary from worship of God. He also rejects a priesthood (qv) of women, stating that if any woman in the New Testament could have the priesthood, "to none rather than Mary should the priesthood have been entrusted, she who was so honoured that she received in her womb the king of all, the God of heaven, the Son of God. Through the singular kindness of God, her womb by a mighty and stupendous mystery was prepared as a temple and dwelling for the incarnation of the divine Word."[11] E. extolls Mary's greatness, likes to speak of her as *Hagia Maria*, and applies to her twice the title *Theotokos*.

[1]Works in PG 41-44; GCS 25,31, 37. Cf., CMP, 126-209; EMBP, 398-445; ClavisG, II, 324-341. Cf. also R. Laurentin, *Traité*, I, 160--161; RSPT, 52(1968), 542; F. J. Dolger, "Die einartige Marienverehrung der Philomarianiten oder Kolliridianen in Arabien," in *Antike und Christentum*, I(1929), 118; E. Smothers, "St. Epiphanius and the Assumption," in AER, 125(1951), 355-372; T. Gallus, S.J., "Ad Epiphanii interpretationem mariologicam in Gen 3:15," in *Verbum Domini*, 14(1956), 272-279; G. Jouassard, in *Maria*, I, 88-92; *ibid.*, "Deux chefs de file en théologie mariale dans la seconde moitié du IVe siècle: S. Épiphane et S. Ambroise," in Gregor, 42(1961), 5-36; D. Fernandez, C.M.F., "De Mariologia S. Epiphanii," (*Pont. Academia Mar. Intern.*, Rome, 1968); J. Galot, S.J., *Déviation du culte marial et saine tradition: S. Épiphane et les Collyridiens*, in PCM, III, 291-301; E. Megyer, *Mariologia S. Epiphanii*, (Rome, Gregorian University, 1969); H. Graef, *Mary*, I, 70-73. [2]*Haer. 78, 18, 19*, in GCS 37, 469-470; PG 42, 729-732. [3]*Ancoratus, 30*, in GCS 25, 38, 39; PG 43, 69, 72B (cp. *Haer. 24, 9*, in GCS 25, 26; PG 41, 317. *Haer 77, 26*, in GCS 37, 438; PG 42, 677C). [4]*Haer. 78, 19*, in GCS 37. Cf. D. Fernandez, C.M.F., "De Mariologia S. Epiphanii," (*Pont. Academia Mar. Intern.*, Rome, 1968), 100-101. [5]*Haer. 30, 20*, in GCS 25, 360; PG 41, 437. [6]*Haer. 78, 18*, in GCS 37, 468-469; PG 42, 728-729. Cf. esp. Th. Camelot, O.P., in BSFEM, 12(1954), 160-163; A. Muller, *Ecclesia-Maria, Die Einheit Marias und der Kirche*, (Fribourg, 1951), 140-144. [7]*Haer. 42, 12*, in GCS 31, 158; PG 41, 777B. [8]*Haer. 78, 11*, in GCS 37, 461-462; PG 42, 716. [9]*Haer. 78, 23*, in GCS 37, 474; PG 42, 737. [10]For a somewhat different view, cf. O. Faller, *De priorum saeculorum silentio circa Assumptionem B. M. V.*, (Rome, 1946), 33-43. [11]*Haer. 79, 3*, in GCS 37, 477; PG 42, 744AB.

EPIPHANIUS THE MONK
(Early Ninth Century)
A monk of Constantinople, about whom little is known, E. was the author of a life of Mary (BHG 1049; Auctarium 1049). Much of the contents are apocryphal.[1] E. describes Mary's physical appearance. He thought that her life lasted seventy-two years. Of these, six-and-a-half were spent in the Temple, where she had been offered to the Lord by her parents at the age of seven. When she was twelve years old, she heard a miraculous voice saying to her: "You will give birth to my Son."[2] She was fourteen when she was married to St. Joseph, a widower about seventy years of age with many sons and daughters: the purpose being to give her "protection and the preservation of her undefiled virginity."[3] Joseph took her, the *Theotokos*, and Jesus to Egypt, with his family, where they spent five years. Mary's purity was exalted above that of all other women—"it was alien to human nature." In her great sorrow, she did not go to the tomb after her Son's death. After the Ascension, St. John took her to holy Sion which he had purchased.[4] "She healed many sick people and freed those overcome by impure spirits; she gave alms and sympathy to the poor and to widows."[5] The Apostles remained near her until her death. When she was laid in the tomb, "all present looked on, her body became invisible before their eyes."[6] The event was wonderful, but the bodily Assumption (*qv*) is not explicitly affirmed.

[1]Pg 120, 185-216 (version of J. A. Mingarelli, here followed). For a somewhat different text, cf. A. Dressel, *Epiphanii monachi et presbyteri scripta edita et inedita*, (Paris-Leipzig, 1843). See J. Darrouzes, in DSp, IV, 862-863; H. Graef, *Mary*, I, 182-183. [2]Pg 120, VI, 193B. [3]PG 120, VIII, 196B. [4]PG 120, XXI, 209A. [5]PG 120, XXII, 212A. [6]PG 120, XXV, 216A.

ERASMUS OF ROTTERDAM (d. 1536)
E. is controversial in Marian doctrine and devotion as in other problems of his day. He refused to join the Reformers, yet his criticism of Catholic practice and of traditional Catholic doctrine, though not heretical, was to "prepare and open the way to all the Lutheran errors" (the conclusion of J. M. Alonso, C.M.F.).[1] The abuses in Marian piety which irked E.'s friend, St. Thomas More, did not merit the caricatures in his best-known work, the *Familiar Colloquies*. He deals with Marian questions also in his commentaries on the Bible and in other works, with passing remarks in his correspondence.

E. composed a *Carmen Votivum* in Greek to Our Lady of Walsingham after visiting the shrine; he wrote a *Paean Virgini Matri dicendus* in 1523, glorifying Mary and extolling her intercession. In the same year, he published a Mass and Office in honour of Our Lady of Loreto, *Virginis Matris apud Laurentum cultae Liturgia*, which he reissued two years later with a homily as *Liturgia Virginis Lauretanae*. His prayer to Our Lady, *Obsecratio ad Virginem Matrem in rebus adversis*, invokes her as our only hope in crises.

The humanist's attitude changed with the years. In his translation and commentaries, *Adnotationes*, on Sacred Scripture, he seemed to take every opportunity to lessen not only devotion to Our Lady, but her person. He changed the Latin translation *gratia plena* to *gratiosa* (see FULL OF GRACE), and *humilitatem*, humility, to *abjectionem*, lowliness, in the *Magnificat*. Therein modern usage confirms him. But in exegesis of the "awkward" texts (Mt 12:46-50; Mk 3:31; Lk 8:19-21, as well as Lk 2:35 on the sword of Simeon (qv), and Lk 2:50 "they did not understand the word he spoke to them"), he took a minimalist position. He maintained that Mary did not know the divinity of her Son in his infancy. The satires in the *Colloquies* attacked not only excesses but established Marian titles (Star of the Sea, Queen of Heaven, Mistress of the world, Port of salvation); he also makes fun of the *Salve Regina*.

True, E. recommended imitation of Mary and the saints, and prayer to the Holy Spirit. He wished Marian devotion to be biblical, interior and Christo-centric, but he lacked appreciation of tradition and the life of the Church, and he could not resist his facility for irony. He met very considerable criticism in his day from Alcalá and Salamanca and the universities of Louvain and Paris, and spent time defending himself against his critics. Later, St. Peter Canisius (qv) undertook to refute him, coining a memorable phrase: *Aut Erasmus lutherizat aut Lutherus erasmizat.*

[1]In the Leyden ed. of Erasmus' works (1703-1706), passages of interest are in vols. I, V,. VI. English tr., *Colloquies of Erasmus*, by Craig R. Thompson, (Chicago, 1965), 133-146, 287-311, 314-355, 464-477. Cf. St. Thomas More, "Letter to a Monk," in *Selected Letters*, ed. by E. F. Rogers, (Yale University Press, 1967), 114-144 (a "defense" of Erasmus in general matters and an account of excess in Marian piety). For St. Peter Canisius on Erasmus, cf. his *De Maria Virgine incomparabili . . . .*, (Ingolstadt, 1577), in *Epistulae et Acta*, ed. Braunsberger. Cf. Cl. Dillenschneider, *La Mariologie de St. Alphonse de Liguori*, (Fribourg, 1931), I, 15ff; J. Coppens, "Érasme exègete et théologien," in ETL, 44(1968), 191-204; A .Licari, O.F.M., *Some Writings of Desiderius Erasmus of Rotterdam concerning the Mother of God*, (Rome, Antonianum, 1966). Cf. esp. J. M. Alonso, C.M.F., "Erasmo, Hombre-Puente en la Historia de la Devoción Mariana," in EstM, 36(1972), 235-264; H. Graef, *Mary*, II, 2-6; esp., J. A. Alonso, *Erasmus, Corpus Mariologicum*, Dayton, 1980.

ETHERIA (Fourth Century)
Authoress of a diary of a famous pilgrimage or journey to Egypt, the Holy Land, Edessa, Asia Minor, and Constantinople, Etheria or Egeria (at one time St. Silvia) gives the earliest known eye-witness account of the feast of the Purification: solemn procession, homily on Luke's narrative, and Mass, all with the bishop presiding.

Texts: Geyer, in CSEL; A. Francheschini and R. Weber, O.S.B., in CCSL, 175; H. Pétre, in SC 21; English tr. by J. Wilkinson (London, 1971). Cf. J. G. Davies, "The 'Peregrinatio Egeriae' and the Ascension," in *Vig. Chr.*, 8(1954), 93-100; P. Devos, S.J., "La date du voyage d'Egerie," in AB, 85(1967), 165-194; *ibid.*, "Egerie à Béthlehem, Le 40e jour après Pâques à Jérusalem en 383," in AB, 86(1968), 87-108; J. Crehan, S.J., "The Assumption and the Jerusalem Liturgy," in TheolSt, 39(1969), 312-325; G. M. Roschini, O.S.M., *Maria Santissima*, IV, 44; E. D. Hunt, "St. Silvia of Aquitaine, The role of a Theodosian Pilgrim in the Society of East and West," J.T.S., N.S., 32(1972), 351-373.

EUCHARIST, THE, AND OUR LADY
The basis of a relationship between Mary and the Eucharist was expressed by St. Thomas Aquinas (qv): *Ave verum corpus natum de Maria Virgine*. The body of Christ came from Mary; bread is changed into his body and in the same mystery the Precious Blood is included.[1] Mother and Son are united in an indissoluble bond (LG 53), and this union persists eternally. Exemplary Christians and saints, the good faithful, have reached such truth intuitively and practiced it in manifest fashion.

Particular questions arise. What is the mode and degree of Mary's participation in the priesthood of Christ, which is directly related to the Eucharist and to the Mass? Is there a sacramental meaning in the episode of Cana? What was Mary's own Eucharistic practice? Was there a significance in the appointment of St. John as her companion and guardian, her son in place of Jesus, since John had a role of special intimacy at the Last Supper?

We have been told nothing about Mary's own Eucharistic practice. Medieval writers and others since have followed the way of invention or reasonable guesswork. For us, Eucharistic practice is an infallible means of increase in God's grace. Mary's mediation of grace, of all graces in the view of many theologians, is relevant to sacramental encounter with God in Christ. In this encounter, the Eucharist holds total primacy, for in it we not only encounter Christ, but receive him directly into our bodies and souls—grace with the author of grace: his flesh and blood, so received, having taken their origin in the flesh and blood of Mary.

EUSEBIUS

[1]Cf. S. J. Bonanao, C.M.F., "The divine maternity and the Eucharistic body in the doctrine of Paschasius Radbertus," in EphMar, 1(1951), 379-394; N. Garcia Garces, C.M.F., "La Virgen y la Eucaristia en la himnografia medieval," in EphMar, 2(1952), 205-245; and "La santisima Virgen y la sagrada Eucaristia," in *Ecclesia a Spiritu Sancto edocta*, (Fest. G. Philips, Gembloux, 1970), 547-570; O. Fidel de Benisa, C.M.F., "El Corazon Eucaristico de Maria y Eucaristia," in EphMar, 7(1957), 125-140; T. Urquiri, C.M.F., "De devotione erga Cor Eucharisticum B.M.V.," in EphMar. 7(1957), 98-125; E. Boularand, S.J., "La Vierge et l'Eucharistie," in RAM, 34(1958), 3-27, 361-392; G. Frénaud, O.S.B., "Marie et l'Eucharistie dans la Liturgie," in CM, 4(1960); R. Laurentin, "The Eucharist and Mary," in *Marian Library Studies*, (Dayton, 1965); K. Balic, O.F.M., "Maria und die Eucharistie," in *Mar. Jahrbuch*, 1, 97-105; Ch. de Keyser, S.S.S., "La Vierge et l'Eucharistie: l'Eucharistie, don de Marie," in *Rev. Eucharist, du Clergé*, 69(1966), 279-287; T. M. Bartolomei, O.S.M., "Le relazioni di Maria alla Eucaristia considerata come sacramento e come sacrificio," in EphMar, 17(1967), 313-336; P. Balaguer, "Ante el Congreso Eucaristico Nacional. Maria y la Eucarista," in *Il Clero*, 61(1968), 348-356; L. Ligier, S. J., *La Vierge dans l'Eucaristie de l'Église*, (Tours, 1968), 52-69; U. Rocco, S.J., "Culto eucaristico e devozione alla Madonna," in *Pal. Clero*, 47(1968), 521-531; V. Ca Render Vivacqua, O.F.M.Cap., *La dottrina eucaristico-mariana nel primo teologo di "S. Maria del SS Sacramento"—P. Michele da Cosenga (1598-1650/56)*, (Rome, 1969); also *id.*, in *Italia Francescana*, 44(1969), 174-195, 252-282; H. Cazelles, "La Bible, Marie et l'Eucharistie," in CM, 16(1972), 17-24; A. Kniazeff, "Marie et l'Eucharistie d'àpes la liturgie orthodoxe," in CM, 16(1972), 25-34; P. (Cardinal) Parente, "De cooperatione B.V.M. in SS. Eucharistia sacramento Ecclesiae unitatis," in ME, II, 207-222. Cf. esp. R. Spiazzi, O.P., "L'Eucaristia e Maria SS foundamento e corona dell'ordine soprannaturale," in ME, VIII, 35-51; G. Vassalli, S.S.S., "La communione di Maria presso i teologi medievali dei secoli XII-XIV," in ME, VIII, 65-131; J. Solana, S.J., "Cultus erga B.V.M. et Eucharistia," in PCM, 407-413.

EUSEBIUS OF CAESEREA (c. 260-c. 340)

The father of Church history, confidant and associate of the emperor Constantine, and an important figure at the Council at Nicaea, E. came under the influence of Origen through his tutor, Pamphilus. He deals with Marian themes in a number of his works, principally in the *Demonstratio Evangelica* and the *Quaestiones Evangelicae ad Stephanum*.[1] The main work from his pen, the church history, serves us also by recording the text of a writer important in one area. Hegesippus (see BROTHERS OF THE LORD).

For E., Mary was *Theotokos*, and the use of the word was, at the time, the touchstone of orthodoxy.[2] E. also, of course, believed in the virgin birth, which for him as for others of the Fathers, was linked with the divinity. Christ took on the habit of mortal man, "but not as a man, rather as God from a Virgin most pure and not experiencing wedlock."[3] There was no question of intercourse or corruption. E. was particularly attracted by the Is 7:14 text (see EMMANUEL); he comments on it at length in his work on Isaiah.[4] He also applied Is 8:3, "And I went to the prophetess, and she conceived and bore a son," to Mary for the original reason which follows: "He calls her who is to give birth to Emmanuel the prophetess, because she will have a share in the Holy Spirit, according to this saying, 'The Holy Ghost will come upon you and the power of the Most-High will overshadow you'. Therefore this power of the Most-High which says through prophecy, 'And I went to the prophetess' relates future things as if they were past, in prophetic manner."[5]

Though E. thinks this interpretation important, setting it forth twice, it is on the first text, Is 7:14, that he delays. He knows, of course, the problems of translation, quotes Symmachus, and clings to the *Septuagint*. Curiously, the other accepted datum of patrology—the Eve (qv)-Mary parallel and contrast—does not interest him. In explaining St. Joseph's position, he recalls the view of St. Ignatius of Antioch (qv) that the Child's virginal birth must be hidden from the "prince of this world." He defends lengthily the interpretation of Mt 1:18 that Joseph knew the divine origin of the Child: "Why and how the matter was made known to Joseph, Scripture tells us that to Joseph the just man it was revealed by the Holy Spirit . . . But since he knew that the conception by the Virgin was divinely from the Holy Spirit and deemed her too exalted to allow him to dwell longer with her, the evangelist rightly says that Joseph's decision was to put his spouse away quietly, not to defame her and not to expose her to common talk."[6] (See DOUBT OF ST. JOSEPH). E. analyzes at length the Davidic question which involved Joseph, defending Mary's descent from the king.[7] He also discusses the "Brothers of the Lord" (qv)[8]. E. makes no mention of an earlier marriage by the saint, an idea held by some of the eastern Fathers.

E. applies the meaningful epithet *panagia* (all-holy) to the Virgin. It had been used of God, the Word and the Trinity, and was probably first applied to Mary by Origen (qv).[9]

[1]EMBP, 113-152; CMP, 10-52; ClavisG, II, 262-275. [2]*In Ps. 109,4*, in PG 23, 1344A. [3]*Demonstr. Evang. 4, 10, 20*, in PG 22, 281A-B; GCS 23, 169. [4]Cf. In Is 7:14 in PG 24,

133C-136D. Cf. also *Eclogae prphet.*, *4*, *4*, in PG 22, 1201C-1204B; *Demonstr. Evang.*, *3*, *2*, *51*, in PG 22, 180-181; *Demonstr. Evang. 7*, *1*, *26-56*, in PG 22, 496B-504C. [5]*In Is 8:1*, in PG 24, 141A. [6]*Quaestiones Evang. ad Stephanum*, *I*, *3*, in PG 22, 884B-884D. [7]*Quaestiones Evang. ad Stephanum*, *I*, *7-9*, in PG 22, 888-889. [8]*In Ps. 68*, in PG 23, 737A-740A. [9]*De Eccles. Theol.*, *3*, *16*, in GCS 14, 174; PG 24, 1033B; *Origen, In Luc. 6*, in PG 17, 329.

EUTHYMIUS OF CONSTANTINOPLE
(*c.* 834-917)
E. was a monk who became Patriarch of Constantinople and confessor to Leo VI (*qv*) "the Wise." He lived through difficulties, and was eventually displaced by a rival. E. was a charitable, firm ruler. His Marian theology is contained in three homilies on the conception of St. Anne and one on Our Lady's girdle.[1] He may be the author of a homily on the Presentation.[2]

E. held the view that Mary was born of a sterile parent and may have been led from the belief in a miraculous origin to a doctrine of total sanctity. This he held: "You surpass the Cherubim and the Seraphim, and all that is save God, you who are wholly good."[3] Mary is the most splendid dwelling place of God, "most brilliant, most holy, from pure, immaculate and distinguished blood";[4] "the pure, unsullied, untouched most immaculate and most beautiful spouse (*qv*) of the invisible and unfathomable God."[5] Though original sin is not mentioned, there is no place for it in this radiant picture.

E. thought that Mary was involved at the center of salvation: "Today the daughter of Adam and Eve, who brought them back from the infernal regions of the earth and reconciled them to God."[6] "She is the cause of our salvation, the beginning of our consolation, having no end, the root of all good things, the author of indescribable gifts."[7] From that basic position, he goes on to sweeping, all-inclusive affirmation of Mary's mediatorial, compassionate and intercessory power, to a degree which must be compared with the doctrine of St. Germanus (*qv*) and the Palamites, especially Theophanes of Nicaea (*qv*). Mary is the virgin "who will manifest the great and hidden mystery, bringing into one those separated, and removing the wall of hostility [Eph 2:14], who will call back our forefathers and every just soul from the lower region, who will purify us from our uncleanness, providing us with the adoption of sons, will show us to be children of light, sanctify the whole world . . . destroy all heresies and cover with

ignominy their baneful wicked leaders and teachers."[8] Mary "encourages and comes to the aid of those eager to live in the fear [of God], she restores the broken, invites and consoles those despairing because of the multitude of their transgressions of God's commandments, she lifts up and helps the sad, the afflicted, those a prey to adversity and snatches them from the hand of the deceitful; she visits and raises up those held by grave disease, whose soul is scarcely stirring."[9]

E. then lists the public, political, and social evils from which Mary delivers us, for her intercession is unwearying, her supplications ceaseless. A long prayer which ends one homily stresses Mary's power while calling on her mercy: "May you be compassionate because of our sins and reduce them to nothingness. As Mother of the creator you can do whatsoever you will . . . After God you can do all things and in all things your Son and God and the Lord of all of us yields to you as his Mother."[10] E. also praises the power of Mary's girdle as a relic in terms equally strong.[11]

[1]On the conception, cf. PO 16, 499-505; PO 19, 441-447, 448-455. On the girdle, cf. PO 16, 505-514. Cf. Beck, 549-550; M. Jugie, in PO 16, 463-487; *id., L'Assomption*, 695-696, 705-707; *id., L'Immaculée Conception*, 181-183. [2]BHG, 1112q. [3]PO 19, 5, p. 453. [4]PO 19, 5, p. 501. [5]PO 16, 3, pp. 508-509. [6]PO 19, 4, p. 452. [7]PO 19, 1, p. 442. [8]PO 16, 5, p. 502. [9]*op. cit.* [10]PO 19, 5, p. 447. [11]PO 16, 4, p. 510.

EVE AND MARY
Scripture: The idea of Mary as the new or second Eve has prompted much discussion in recent times.[1] The early Christian writers who taught it, St. Justin Martyr (*qv*), St. Irenaeus (*qv*) and Tertullian (*qv*), wrote in a biblical context—the Annunciation compared with the temptation of Eve. After the narrative of the human origins, Eve is rarely mentioned in the sacred text, twice only in the New Testament (1 Tim 2:15; 2 Cor 11:2-3). Abraham and Moses are each mentioned over sixty times in the New Testament. Abraham is the only Old Testament figure named by Mary (Lk 1:55). The classic Pauline passages on Christ as the new Adam (Rome 5:12-21; 1 Cor 15:21-22, 45-49) do not mention Mary. The 2 Cor 11 text on the faithful, "betrothed to Christ as a pure bride to her one husband," continues, "But I am afraid that, as the serpent deceived Eve by his cunning, your thoughts

will be led astray from a sincere and pure devotion to Christ." This could provide a basis perhaps for the Eve-Church typology which appealed to St. Augustine and before him had been perceived by Tertullian.

If Mary is not explicitly called new Eve, there are elements which, taken cumulatively, give a biblical foundation for the title. The emphasis on a woman as partner of the man called to a saving role recurs in Old Testament writings, and is given prominence in the great oracles, Gen 3:15 (see WOMAN IN) and Is 7:14 (see EMMANUEL), between which there may be continuity. There is the manifold insinuation of a new creation in the infancy narratives and in St. John's Gospel. There is the remarkable parallel, noted by the early Fathers, between the dialogue of Eve and the serpent (Gen 3:1-7) and that of Mary and Gabriel (Lk 1:28-35). Exegetes are not agreed on all the particulars within these patterns, or on whether Jn 19:25-27 (see WOMAN IN) is the fulfillment of Gen 3:15 or even of Gen 3:20, where Eve is named "mother of all living."

History: The origin of the idea that Mary was a new or second Eve is difficult to establish. The three writers mentioned represent wide areas within which the idea was firmly held, a fact which was not altered by mutual borrowing, if this took place. Was the idea current in the time of the Apostles, as J. H. Cardinal Newman (*qv*) and Mgr. J. Lebon (*qv*) suggested? Did it belong to the early catechesis as others contend? Already supported by the important triple testimony in the second and early third centuries, the theory would persist. In the subsequent *literary* development, it is independent of a Marian interpretation of Gen 3:15, though the *objective* convergence on one reality remains true. Among the pioneers, St. Irenaeus had the most profound insight. He it was who stamped the idea on the mind of Christendom.

The Greek Fathers of the next centuries carry forward the tradition with occasional development. St. Gregory of Nyssa (*qv*) contrasts Mary's joy in childbirth with Eve's sorrow and pain. St. John Chrysostom (*qv*) crystallized the saving aspect, "a virgin [Eve] had cast us out from paradise, through a virgin [Mary] we have found eternal life." The Syrians were not lacking in acceptance of the tradition. With St. Epiphanius (*qv*), we have an extension of the parallel. Unless it be true that St. Athanasius (*qv*)

was ahead of him, Gen 3:20 is applied to Mary, the "Mother of the living."

The great Latin doctors, each in his own manner, handle the theme. St. Ambrose (*qv*), apostle of perfection in the female sex, was intellectually absorbed in the virginal privilege of Mary: "Come then Eve, now Mary, who brought us not only virginity but God." St. Jerome was attracted by the Eve-Church typology, using the lapidary phrase: "Death through Eve, life through Mary" (for which he appears in the annotation to LG 56), and again "The former drove us from paradise, the latter leads us to heaven." St. Augustine (*qv*) is discreet. Reflecting constantly on the Church and Christ its head, he saw Eve as the figure of the Church, which he also called "mother of the living." Mary is the model of her sex. The death-life antithesis is for him "through a *woman* death, through a *woman* life."

The Eve-Mary parallel and contrast will continue to figure in medieval writing. H. Barré (*qv*) locates 200 texts between the fifth and early thirteenth centuries. A distinctive Latin contribution was the adaptation of Gen 2:18, "a helper like unto himself" to Mary, an enlargement of the basic concept which would influence theories of the Redemption. Hermann of Tournai (*qv*) seems to have been the pioneer. The general idea has a prominent place in the thinking of St. Bernard (*qv*).

In later times, Bossuet (*qv*) excelled in expounding the theme. Scheeben (*qv*) used it to support his theory of the bridal motherhood. Newman, in his vindication of Catholic belief and practice against Pusey (*qv*), appealed to it as the great "rudimental teaching" of the Fathers. Already in 1845, in the *Essay on Development*, he had fashioned around it a remarkable synthesis. Louis Billot, S.J., a great dogmatic theologian, stated the parallel almost in the terms of a fundamental principle: "It is generally to be held about the Virgin Mother that in the order of restoration she holds the place that Eve held in the order of perdition."[2]

Teaching Authority: St. Leo the Great (*qv*) is notably absent from H. Barré's lists. Innocent III did refer to the subject in two sermons.[3] Pius IX (*qv*) in the Bull *Ineffabilis Deus* (*qv*) does so to show that the Fathers compared Mary with Eve "to demonstrate the original innocence and sanctity of the Mother of God" and recalls that "they have also exalted her above Eve with a wonderful variety of expressions."[4]

The principal papal contribution to teaching was made by Pius XII (qv). The passages are in important doctrinal works: "[Mary] offered him on Golgotha to the eternal Father together with the holocaust of her maternal rights and motherly love, like a new Eve, for all the children of Adam contaminated through his unhappy fall."[5] "We must remember especially that, since the second century the Virgin Mary has been designated by the holy Fathers as the new Eve, who, although subject to the new Adam, is most intimately associated with him in that struggle against the infernal foe which, as foretold in the *Protoevangelium*, would finally result in that most complete victory over sin and death which are always mentioned together in the writings of the Apostle of the Gentiles."[6] "Mary, in the work of redemption was by God's will joined with Jesus Christ, the cause of salvation, in much the same way as Eve was joined with Adam, the cause of death . . .";[7] "the Blessed Virgin is Queen not only as Mother of God, but also because she was associated as the second Eve with the new Adam."[8] Thus Pius brought together the two traditions, Mary as new Eve, and the Woman in Gen 3:15. He set the Eve-Mary parallel not in the Annunciation but in Calvary, and he saw it as a basis for Mary's part in our salvation.

Vatican II recalled the theme. It did not appear in the first schema drawn up by Fr. Balic (qv) and his associates. It was mentioned in some of the proposed drafts submitted to the theological commission. In the promulgated text, the biblical setting chosen is the Annunciation: "For she, as St. Irenaeus says, 'being obedient became a cause of salvation to herself and to the whole human race.' Hence in their preaching not a few of the early Fathers gladly assert with him: 'The knot of Eve's disobedience was untied by Mary's obedience. What the virgin Eve bound through her unbelief, Mary loosened by her faith.' Comparing Mary with Eve, they call her 'the mother of the living' and still more often they say: 'death through Eve, life through Mary'." (LG 56). The Fathers mentioned in the annotation, besides St. Jerome, are St. Epiphanius, St. Augustine, St. Cyril of Jerusalem, St. John Chrysostom and St. John of Damascus (qqv). Later the Eve-Mary theme is mentioned in the context of the Mary-Church typology: "For believing and obeying, Mary brought forth on earth the Father's Son. This she did, knowing not man but overshadowed by the Holy Spirit, as the New Eve, who put her trust, which was weakened by no doubt, not in the ancient serpent but in the messenger of God." (LG 63).

[1]Cf. esp. "La Nouvelle Éve," in BSFEM, 12, 13, 14(1954, 1955, 1956); E. Hoskyns, "Genesis I-III and St. John's Gospel," in *Journal of Theol. St.*, 31(1920), 210-218; A. Feuillet, "Marie et la nouvelle création," in VieSp, 81(1949), 467-478; A. M. Dubarle, O.P., "Les fondements bibliques du titre marial de nouvelle Eve," in RSR, 39(1951), 49-64; H. Coathalem, S.J., *Le parellélisme entre la Sainte Vierge et l'Église dans la tradition latine jusqu'à la fin du XIIe siècle*, (Rome, 1954), 28-29; E. Guldan, *Eva und Maria Eine Antithese als Bildmotiv*, (Graz-Cologne, 1966); L. Cignelli, *Maria nuova Eva nella patristica greca*, (Assisi, 1966); P. Andriessen, O.S.B., "Die neue Eva des neuen Adam," in *Von Christus zur Kirche*, (1966), 109-137; D. Barsotti, *Le donne dell'alleanza da Eva a Maria e alla Chiesa sposa di Cristo*, (Turin, 1967); K. N. Nyberg, *The new Eve*, (Nashville, Abingdon Press, 1967); R. Murray, "Mary, the second Eve in the early Syrian Fathers," in *Eastern Churches Quart.*, 3(1970, 1971), 372-395; M. Starowieyski, "Maria nuova Eva in traditione Alexandrina et Antiochena (saeculo V)," in MM, 36(1972), 329-385; M. Jourjon, "Marie avocate d'Eve selon S. Irénée," in PCM, II, 143-148; M. Planque, in DSp, IV, 1779-1783. [2]*De Verbo Incarnato*, 6th ed., (Rome, 1922), 380. Cf. quotation from Bossuet, in *op. cit.*, p. 386, n. 1. [3]*In Purif.*, *In Assumpt. 2*, in PL 217, 506B, 581-582. [4]OL, 74. [5]*Mystici Corporis Christi*, (29th June, 1943), in OL, 253. [6]*Munificentissimus Deus*, (1st November, 1950), in OL, 317. [7]*Ad caeli Reginam*, (11th October, 1954), in OL, 393. [8]*op. cit.*, in OL, 394.

EXEMPLAR

Vatican II speaks twice of Our Lady as exemplar (Latin *exemplar*). "She is hailed . . . as the Church's type and most conspicuous exemplar in faith and charity." (LG 53). "In the mystery of the Church . . . the Blessed Virgin Mary has gone before, affording in eminent and singular manner the exemplar of a virgin and mother." (LG 63).

This idea is larger than that of model, which connotes freedom of choice, and type, which connotes a process of the mind, though one that must have some objective validity. Exemplar is essentially and totally objective, that which exists prior to another entity which will be designed on it as a basis. It thus suggests strongly the primacy (qv) of Mary, without going as far as Suarez, St. Bernardine of Siena, or St. Lawrence of Brindisi (qqv), who in different ways thought of Mary as the cause—after Christ—of the universe.

F

FAITH, OUR LADY'S

Mary, as preeminent among the Poor of the Lord (qv), possessed in full the faith of Israel; as Daughter of Zion (qv), she embodied believing faithful Israel.[1] The Lucan infancy narrative (qv) tells, in the episode of the Annunciation, of Mary's act of faith in response to Gabriel's message. Later the biblical text interprets her words as an act of faith: "Blessed is she who has believed, that there would be a fulfillment of what was spoken to her from the Lord."(Lk 1:4). The faith of the Annunciation (qv), singled out for praise by the early patristic theologians of the Eve (qv)-Mary parallel and contrast, in fact presupposed Mary's Jewish faith. She was committed to the revealed message as Israel embodied it—the election, the covenant, the promises, the law, a divine message transmitted in writing and tradition, enriched at certain great moments by the prophets. We are given no details of this life of faith, no basis on which to build a psychology of Mary's faith. Her motive of credibility, in the initial and early stages, was the general one of a believing community around her, the instruction and example of her parents and teachers. This was gradually replaced by the inherent force of divine truth.

The Annunciation was a private revelation (qv), the starting-point of a later public revelation. The Mediator and fullness of this and all divine revelation is Jesus Christ. Mary's faith was in time prior to the existence of Jesus Christ. By her faith she mediated the Incarnation, God's supreme self-disclosure to man. That it became an object of her own immediate belief is the view defended in this work. (see KNOWLEDGE MARY'S).

Controversies about alleged temptations against faith met by Mary are dealt with separately (see SWORD OF SIMEON (qv) and FAITH OF MARY IN THE PASSION (qv). Certain of the Fathers and Doctors extolled Mary's faith. St. Ambrose (qv) showed the singular way in which it enlivens the believing community. "You see that Mary had not doubted, but believed: and therefore she attained the fruit of faith .... But you who have heard and believed are happy; for whatever soul has believed conceives and engenders the Word of God and recognizes his works. Let the soul of Mary be in each that she may glorify God. If according to the flesh there is one mother of Christ, according to faith, none the less, Christ is the fruit of all. For every soul receives the Word of God, provided it is immaculate and free from vices, keeping chastity with unblemished purity."[2]

For St. Augustine, virginity, faith, and the Church were a frame of reference for thought about Mary. Repeatedly he says that Mary "conceived by faith." "Mary is more blessed for perceiving the faith of Christ than for conceiving the flesh of Christ, for to one who said 'Blessed is the womb that bore thee' he replied 'Yea, rather, blessed are they who hear the word of God and keep it' [Lk 11:27, 28]. Finally, what did his brethren, that is his relations in the flesh who did not believe in him, benefit by that relationship? Thus the maternal proximity of Mary [to him] would have been of no avail if she were not more fortunate to bear Christ in her heart than in her flesh."[3] The corporate effect of faith was in Augustine's mind also and he developed Ambrose's idea of faith as the basis of the Mary-Church typology (see TYPE OF THE CHURCH).

Great doctors and preachers of later ages continue the praise of Mary's faith, none perhaps in such vivid detail as St. Alphonsus Liguori (qv): "She saw her Son in the crib at Bethlehem and believed that he was the Creator of the world. She saw him flee from Herod and believed that he was the King of kings. She saw him born yet believed him to be eternal. She saw him poor and in need of food and believed that he was the Lord of the universe. She saw him lying on the straw and believed that he was omnipotent. She observed that he did not speak, and yet believed that he was filled with infinite wisdom. She heard him cry and believed that he was the joy of paradise. Finally she saw him in death, despised and crucified, and even though faith wavered in others, she remained firm in her conviction that he was God."[4]

Teaching Authority: The Popes generally speak of Mary as one who helps the faithful to preserve and deepen their faith. St. Pius X (*qv*) expressed a more profound thought which recalls the teaching of St. Ambrose and St. Augustine: "The Son of God made man being the 'author and finisher of faith', it surely follows that his Mother most holy should be recognized as participating in the divine mysteries and as being a guardian of them, and that upon her as a foundation, the noblest after Christ, rises the edifice of the faith of all the centuries."[5]

Vatican II (*qv*) recalls the Patristic doctrine of Mary's cooperation "in the work of salvation through free faith and obedience." (LG 56). It tells us that "she advanced in her pilgrimage of faith and loyally persevered in her union with her Son unto the Cross." (LG 58). Mary's faith is later made the basis of the Mary-Church typology: "As St. Ambrose taught, the Mother of God is a type of the Church in the context of faith, charity and perfect union with Christ." (LG 63). "[The Church] imitating the Mother of her Lord, and by the power of the Holy Spirit, preserves with virginal purity an integral faith, a firm hope and a sincere charity." (LG 64). Later we are told that Mary "unites and mirrors within herself the central imperatives of the faith." (LG 65).

[1]J. B. Terrien, *La Mère de Dieu*, (Paris, 1900), II, 222-225; R. Garrigou-Lagrange, O.P., *La Mère de Dieu et notre vie intérieure*, (Lyons, 1941), 132; J. Weiger, *Mary, Mother of Faith*, (New York, 1959); M. O'Carroll, C.S.Sp., "Our Lady's Faith," in *Mediatress of All Graces*, (Dublin, 1959), 106-117; G. Alastruey, *The Blessed Virgin Mary*, (St. Louis, 1963), I, 180-184; J. Cascante, "Singularidad y ejemplaridad de la fé en Maria," in EstM, (1966, ed. 1967), 13-41; M. B. Eyquem, O.P., "La foi de Marie et les noces de Cana," in VieSp, 117(1967), 169-181; D. Bertetto, S.D.B., "Maria, modello di fede," in *Perfice munus* (Turin), 44(1969), 194-203; G. Marafini, "La fede di Maria negli anni della vita nascosta a Nazareth," in *Teologia e pastorale della consacrazione a Maria*, (Collegamento Mariano Nazionale, Padua, 1969), 203-209; J. Pintard, "Le principe 'prius mente quam corpore' dans la patristique et la théologie latines,' in BSFEM, 27(1970), 25-58; L. (Cardinal) Shehan, *Woman of Faith*, (Baltimore, 1971); G. Philips, "Un thème théologique ravivé: la foi de la Sainte Vierge," in *Studia mediaevalia et mariologica P. C. Balic, O.F.M., 70um explenti annum dicata*, (Rome, 1971), 575-588; J. J. Cardinal Carberry, *Mary's Pilgrimage of Faith*, (Boston, 1972); American Hierarchy, *Behold your Mother, Woman of Faith*, (Washington, 1973); J. Galot, S.J., *La fede di Maria e la nostra*, (Assisi, 1973); J. Auer, "De fide B.M.V. a Deo data, a Christo probata, purgata, gratificata," in MSS, IV, 421-430; M. B. Schepers, O.P., "Mary and the Pauline Doctrine of Justification by Faith and the Law of Sin," in MSS, IV, 501-518; F. Mussner, "Der Glaube Mariens im Lichte des Römerbriefs," in MariolSt, 3(1964), 11-21. [2]*In Luc. II, 26*, in CSEL, 32/4, 55. [3]*Sermo Denis*, XXV, 7, ed. by G. Morin. [4]*The Glories of Mary*, (tr. Baltimore, Dublin, Helicon, 1963), II, 3, p. 161. [5]*Ad diem illum*, in OL, 168-169.

FAITH OF MARY IN THE PASSION, THE

In Christian literature, there are two different interpretations of Mary's attitude in the moment of Christ's death. A number of Fathers of the Church saw the sword of Simeon's (*qv*) prophecy as a prediction of Mary's failure in faith on Calvary. The Origen (*qv*) interpretation of Lk 2:35 lapsed. Another tradition directly opposed to it arose and remained: Mary was the sole faithful one on Calvary, unshaken by events. She then stood for the whole Church.[1]

The first clear testimony is from Odo of Ourscamp (d. 1171, wrote *c.* 1160): "Mary Magdalen . . . shaken by the Passion lost her faith [in Christ's divinity], as did the disciples; we believe that the Mother of the Lord alone was immune from this unbelief."[2] Alan of Lille (*qv*) took up the idea a lifetime later: "When the disciples fell from faith at the time of the Passion, while the Virgin did not fall from the state of faith . . . . The Apostles having failed in faith were not in the Church or of the Church but, as it were, wandered near to the Church because of their unbelief . . . Mary through her faith represented reality to others."[3] It was Philip the Chancellor (d. 1236) who expressed the full idea: "Whence they say that the Church existed in the Virgin alone, for her faith alone remained in the Passion; for which reason they say that her memory is recalled on Saturday."[4] About the same time, Caesar of Heisterbach (*qv*) (d. 1240) develops the idea. Recalling that, as the Lord had predicted, the Apostles fell away from constancy in the faith and remained thus until their faith was restored by the Resurrection, he goes on: "During this time the Virgin, the only one grounded in faith, persevered; indeed she alone was then the Church. For which reason, on Saturday, a cult deservedly special is to be rendered to her by children of the Church, in fastings, celebration of Masses and in other divine offices."[5] Alexander of Hales repeats that the Church existed in the Virgin alone. Hugh of St. Cher, Richard of St. Laurent (qv), and others hold the same view. St Bonaventure (qv) writes: "It must be believed indubitably that the Virgin Mary always persisted in the faith; hence faith found in her a solid basis. Hence while the disciples did not believe and doubted, she was the one in whom the faith of the Church remained solid and unshaken; and therefore, on Saturday, the whole Church holds solemnities in her honour."[6] Another writer of the time speaks of Mary supporting and bearing "the whole fabric of the Church." Thereafter the general opinion would be that of St. Thomas (qv): Mary's faith was entirely sure, (firmissima). Engelbert of Admont (qv) would bring the idea into his synthesis on Mary's association (see ASSOCIATE) with Christ.

[1]Cf. Y. M. Congar, O.P., "Incidence ecclésiologique d'un thème de dévotion mariale," in Mélanges de Sc. Rel., 7(1950), 277-291; H. Barré, C.S.Sp., in BSFEM, 9(1951), 83-84; R. Laurentin, Marie l'Église et le Sacerdoce, I, (Paris, 1953), 138-139. Cf. esp. C. Binder, O.S.B., "Thesis in passione Domini fidem Ecclesiae in Beatissima Virgine sola remansisse," in ME, III, 389-488. [2]"Quaestiones," II, 56, ed. by J. B. Pitra, in Analecta novissima spicilegii Solesmensis, vol. II, (1878), 53. [3]Elucid. in Cant. Canti, 1, in PL 210, 58B, 59C. [4]Summa de Bono, apud Congar, p. 279, n. 4. (Paris Bibl. Nat. Latin 15749 fol88 ra, rb). [5]Apud Binder, in ME, III, 419. [6]In III Sent. D. III, p. 1, a.2, q.iii, ad 2, Quarrachi ed., vol. 3, 78.

FATHER, GOD THE, AND OUR LADY

The existential purpose of the Christian economy stated by St. Paul (qv) is "that we might receive the adoption of sons" (Gal 4:5). In this very context the Apostle speaks of Mary: "God sent his Son, born of a woman." (Gal 4:4). Mary's relationship with God the Father was seen by the Fathers of the Church in terms of the Son who came from each. The distinction was put succinctly by the Council of Chalcedon: ". . . indeed born of the Father before the ages according to divine nature, but in the last days the same born of the Virgin Mary Mother of God according to human nature."[1]

The same Christ was Son of the Eternal Father and of the Virgin Mary. St. Thomas Aquinas (qv) argued subtly to establish the one sonship,

despite the two generations and births. Other writers have striven to express Mary's position vis a vis the Father by the bridal concept (see SPOUSE), but without gaining unqualified acceptance. The Second Vatican Council has sanctioned the term "daughter," used by (among others) Newman (qv) and Pius XII (qv), giving it an added richness. "Therefore she is also the well-beloved [praedilecta, favourite] daughter of the Father." (LG 53). This comes after the affirmation of her special redemption and indissoluble union with Christ, so that she should be Mother of the Son of God.

Thus Paul VI (qv), as others before him, could speak of Mary as our sister, as well as Mother of the Church—different facets of the same mystery, which no image or idea can exhaust, and to which all must be applied with awareness of this limitation.

[1]DS, 61.

FATHERHOOD, ST. JOSEPH'S

In the gospels, St. Joseph is spoken of as the father of Jesus and Jesus is called his son.[1] "Is not this the carpenter's son?" (Mt 13:55); "And his father and his mother marvelled at what was said about him" (Lk 2:33); "Behold, your father and I have been looking for you anxiously" (Lk 2:48); "Jesus, when he began his ministry, was about thirty years of age, being the son (as was supposed) of Joseph . . ."(Lk 3:23); "And they said: 'Is not this the son of Joseph?'" (Lk 4:22); "They said 'Is not this Jesus, the son of Joseph, whose father and mother we know?" (Jn 6:42). Joseph and Mary are called the parents of Jesus (Lk 2:27, 41). Joseph was told by the angel to name Jesus (Mt 1:21) and "he called his name Jesus" (Mt 1:25). Naming was a parental prerogative. He was told by a divine messenger to transfer the family from one domicile to another (Mt 2:14, 21). Jesus was obedient to him (Lk 2:51).

These facts have customarily been expressed in the title "foster father." Theological research, however, has sought to advance beyond this concept and give a more satisfactory explanation of Joseph's fatherhood. Attempts to show the saint miraculously involved in the procreation of Jesus, that is without violating Mary's virginity, have been condemned: there was no physical basis for the fatherhood. But the relationship was not that of a man caring for a child who has no relation at all with the man's marriage. St.

Augustine prepared the way for a solution by fully clarifying the doctrine of Our Lady's marriage. Through the marriage, of which Jesus was, miraculously, the fruit, Joseph shared in Mary's parenthood. St. Thomas took up this view, stating that "the marriage [of Mary and Joseph] was especially ordained for this purpose, that the Child should be received and brought up within it."

With variations and additions, the idea persists in literature on St. Joseph. The saint is sometimes seen as the image of the Eternal Father, who gave him something of his own infinite love for his eternal Son. Bossuet enlarges on this opinion, which must be expressed with accuracy.

There has been much discussion about the title which would properly express the fatherhood. St. Joseph was more than either a "foster" or "adoptive" father since the Child belonged to his marriage, and was not brought into it from an outside parentage. He was more than a "legal" father, though in the infancy of the Saviour he fulfilled the duties of a legal father and, within the community, was accepted as such. That he was thought of as the true father (Lk 3:23) is the justification for the title "putative" father; yet a deeper reality is implied in the message of angel (Mt 1:20-21). The epithets "matrimonial," "vicarious," and "eminent spiritual" have also been rejected despite plausible argument in support of each.

A number of recent writers accept "virgin father," but it too is open to objection, since it was not merely as a virgin but as the husband of Mary that Joseph entered the mystery. The title does emphasize a distinctive feature of his vocation to serve the Incarnate Word.

[1]J. Reimsbach, S.J., "Le Patronage de S. Joseph," in Gregor, 2(1921), 337-351; P. Hormaeche, S.J., "Derecho de San José a la protodulia," in EstEcl, 6(1927), 21ff; J. Mueller, S.J., Der Heilige Joseph: Die dogmatischen Grundlagen seiner besonderen Verehrung, (Innsbruck, 1937. English tr. The Fatherhood of St. Joseph, St. Louis, 1952); G. (Archbishop) Breynat, O.M.I., S. Joseph, Père Vierge de Jésus, (Montréal, 1944. Based on articles, in Rev. de l'Université d'Ottawa, 5(1936), 73-80, 8(1938), 81-111); C. Macabiau, S.J., Primauté de S. Joseph d'après l'épiscopat catholique et la théologie, (Montreal, 1945); U. Holzmeister, S.J., De S. Joseph Quaestiones biblicae, (Rome, 1945), 84-89; R. Garrigou-Lagrange, O.P., "De paternitate S. Josephi," in Angelicum, (1945), 105-109; J. M. Parent, O.P., La paternité de S. Joseph, (Ottawa, 1958); B. Llamera, O.P., "La paternidad de San José en la teologia católica," in EstJos, 5(1951), 205-235; ibid., "Teologia de San José," in La Editorial Católica, (Madrid, 1953); F. Filas, S.J., Joseph and Jesus, (Milwaukee, 1952); id., The Man Closest to Jesus, (Boston, 1962), 155-336; R. Gauthier, La paternité de S. Joseph, (Montreal, 1948, from CahJos, 1-6); M. O'Carroll, C.S.Sp., Joseph, Son of David, (Dublin, Gill, 1963), 139-153.

FATHERS OF THE CHURCH

Ecclesiastical writers of the early centuries, noted for holiness, purity of doctrine and approved by the Church, form collectively a monument of Sacred Tradition. With the whole of Tradition, then, and Sacred Scripture (see BIBLE, THE), they give us access to divine revelation. Both are interpreted by the teaching authority of the Church.[1]

History: The Fathers of the Church influenced one another in their Marian doctrine. Sometimes they did so by controversial exchanges, sometimes by direct borrowing (as St. Ambrose (*qv*) from the easterns) or again by compilation of texts (such as that made by St. Cyril of Alexandria (*qv*) in the Theotokos (*qv*) controversy). Medieval and later writers were dependent on the Fathers. This explains the persistence of certain ideas—Origen's (*qv*) interpretation of the sword of Simeon (*qv*) in the East; St. Augustine's (*qv*) idea of Original Sin, which impeded development of the doctrine of the Immaculate Conception, in the West; or, again, in the East, the approval given by St. Epiphanius to the legend of Joseph's early marriage.

The doctrine of the Assumption was blocked and then furthered by documents spuriously attributed to St. Jerome (*qv*) and St. Augustine respectively (see PSEUDO-JEROME AND PSEUDO-AUGUSTINE). The arrival in the West of eastern patristic homilies, affirming the doctrine, had an important effect on its acceptance. From the twelfth century, the writings of a Marian doctor, St. John of Damascus (*qv*), were circulating in the Latin world. Among the Scholastics, St. Thomas was noted for his patristic learning.

At the outset of systematic Marian theology, Suarez (*qv*) and Petavius (*qv*) adduced patristic quotations in support of their theses. The indefatigable I. Marracci (*qv*) quarried the writings of the Fathers. A hardening and narrowing of the thesis mode of treatment eventually led to a certain decadence, especially in the composition of manuals and other academic works. The temptation, not always resisted, was to use, even to force patristic texts (which generally meant excerpts) as proof of a thesis, even when it expressed a truth to which the Fathers had not adverted. This defect of method undermined confidence in the presentation of patristic teaching. The attribution to the Fathers of truths which had emerged as a result of much reflection since their time, was a failure to recognize true development of doctrine (*qv*). The truth reached would be a valid development from their theology, in which case a certain delicacy was required in handling their texts, a nuanced account of what they held in comparison with what later reflection on the whole deposit of faith produced.

Account must be taken of the nineteenth and twentieth century prelude to the recent scientific study of patristic Marian themes. J. J. Bourassé devoted volumes V and VI of his collection to patrology. Cardinal Newman (*qv*) discovered Marian doctrine in the Fathers. Scheeben (*qv*) and Terrien (*qv*) gave them considerable attention. In 1893, an English Redemptorist, Thomas Livius, brought out a 480-page book on *The Blessed Virgin in the Fathers of the First Six Centuries*, then not fully valued, now, understandably, needing emendation. Noteworthy also are H. Hurter's edition of selected Marian homilies,[2] and O. Bardenhewer's *Marienpredigten aus der Vaterzeit* (Munich, 1934).

Where the nineteenth century really opened the way to renewal was in the edition of texts. Migne's vast collections (PL, 1844-1864; PG, 1857-1866) were—and still are—of incalculable benefit to Marian theologians. GCS (1897) and CSEL (Vienna, 1866) linked Migne to the presentday critical age. PO (1907) and CSCO (1903) swell the volume of available textual material.

Teaching Authority: In Marian theology, as in other areas, the teaching authority acts as interpreter of the Fathers. The important statement at Ephesus was prefaced by the clause "thus the holy Fathers did not hesitate . . . ." Pius IX, in the Bull *Ineffabilis Deus* (*qv*), referred frequently to the "Fathers" or to the "Fathers and writers of the Church." No one is named. Three are named by Pius XII (*qv*) in the Apostolic Constitution, *Munificentissimus Deus*. They are St. John Damascus, St. Germanus of Constantinople (*qv*), and the author of a debated text, Modestus of Jerusalem (*qv*), who is named in a note, but the textual authenticity is left open. Pius XII in *Ad Caeli Reginam* (*qv*)

quotes ten writers of the patristic era. In the same year (1954), the Pope gave an address to Marian theologians, in which he spoke of the need for taking "Catholic Tradition and the sacred teaching authority" into account when interpreting sacred Scripture. He did not mention the Fathers, but they were implied.

The notes to chapter VIII in *Lumen Gentium* mention some fourteen Fathers of the eastern and western Church. The instructions to theologians and preachers was that they should pursue "the study of sacred Scripture, the holy Fathers, the doctors and liturgies of the Church," and explain them under the guidance of the Church's teaching authority (LG 67). There are six patristic references in Paul VI's *Signum Magnum* (*qv*) and twenty in *Marialis Cultus* (*qv*). The section in the latter document, most heavily indebted to patristic inspiration, is that which deals with Mary and the Holy Spirit (*qv*).

Recent Studies: After the Second World War, before the Council, an impetus was given to study of Marian themes in the Fathers by the "new theology," which sought renewal in a "return to the sources"—a truly scientific study of all early sacred documents. This required extensive research which had three objectives. First, the preparation of thoroughly critical editions, which led to expansion of the collections already in being and the inception of new ones (SC, 1942 and CCSL, 1953); secondly, and closely linked with the first, the search for unpublished texts; thirdly, interpretation of the Fathers which would be true to their intellectual outlook and background, not selective or forced reading of their texts in the light of our contemporary problems.

There has been progress towards all three objectives. M. Jugie (*qv*), in his articles and two major works, faced the critical difficulties. A. Wilmart, O.S.B. (*qv*), H. Barré, C.S.Sp. (*qv*) and others attacked the vast mass of Latin *spuria*, many of them clustering about the name of Augustine. Until recently, eastern texts of the patristic period had not been so completely investigated. A vast survey of material associated with St. John Chrysostom has been begun. An admirable critical study of Greek Marian homiletics of the fifth century has come from R. Caro, S.J. The articles in this work dealing with each author of the period list the works and manuscripts, if any, which have been recently discovered and published. F. Halkin's excellent guides map the field accurately.[3] R. Laurentin (qv), in the first edition of his *Court Traité*, gave a detailed account of the critical position for Migne's (qv) two collections.[4] E. Dekker's *Clavis Patrum Latinorum* and the *Clavis Patrum Graecorum*, of which volumes II and III have appeared, serve Marian as well as other theologians; all benefit too by Lampe's *Patristic Greek Lexicon* and Hamman's Supplement to the *Patrologia Latina*. Among the Syrian Fathers, St. Ephraem has benefitted by a complete critical edition at the hands of E. Beck, O.S.B.

Interpretation of the doctrine, contained in texts amended or supplemented, is the real task of the patrologist. A seminal essay, which set the tone for the age, was Mgr. G. Jouassard's contribution to the first volume of *Maria*. Another work which had considerable influence was A. Mueller's *Ecclesia-Maria*. The French Society for Marian Studies assigned a place to Patrology in its annual sessions, as did the International Mariological Congresses. Monographs on individual Fathers, either by way of introduction to edited texts (as in *Sources Chretiénnes*) or as independent works, and general studies of patristic themes, have increased in number. Research into early Liturgy, or into Marian archaeology, has occasionally joined with reflection on writings or sermons of the time. Whole areas have been described, such as early Egypt by G. Giamberardini, O.F.M.[5]

Two collections of texts are noteworthy and promising. D. Casagrande, has, in *Enchiridion Marianum Biblicum Patristicum*, given the first single-volume corpus of the principal patristic texts on Our Lady to appear in the present age. For the most part, the text is Migne's, as the cost of employing the text of later critical editions proved prohibitive. Essential material is taken from *Patrologia Orientalis* and account is taken of PLS. The more ambitious work by S. Alvarez Campos, *Corpus Marianum Patristicum*, will have six volumes, bringing the compilation down to the end of the seventh century. Critical editions are used. Latin texts are simply reproduced. Greek texts are provided with Latin translations for the Greek Fathers; Latin only for the Syrian.

currently appearing (esp. DSp and the successive issues of G. M. Besutti's *Bibliografia Mariana*), cf. A. d'Alès, S.J., "Marie dans l'ancienne tradition patristique," in *Dict. Apol.*, III, 155-209; I. Pate, *Patristicum Praeconium, seu selecti textus in quibus Sancti Patres beatam Mariam Dei Matrem venerantur et concelebrant*, (Paris, 1886); I. Ortiz de Urbina, S.J., "La Mariologia nei Padri Siraici," in OCP, 1(1935), 100-113; id., "Lo sviluppo della Mariologia nella Patrologia Orientale," in OCP, 6(1940), 40-82; A. Ehrard, *Üeberlieferung und Bestand der hagiographischen und homiletischen Literatur der grieschen Kirche*, 3 vols., Leipsiz, 1937-1952). Cf. esp. G. Jouassard, "Marie à travers la patristique," in *Maria*, 1(1947), 71-157; G. M. Roschini, O.S.M., *Mariologia*, I, (Rome, 1947), 77-191; id., *Maria Santissima*, 1, (1969), 284-340; M. Gordillo, *Mariologia Orientalis*, (Rome, 1954); A. Mueller, *Ecclesia-Maria. Die Einheit Marias und der Kirche*, 2nd ed., (Fribourg, University Press, 1955); W. Burghardt, S.J., "Mary in Western Patristic Thought," in *Mariology*, I, (1955), 109-155; id., "Mary in Eastern Patristic Thought," in *Mariology*, II, (1957), 88-153; id., "Patristic Studies—Mariology," in *Theology in Transition*, ed. by E. O'Brien, S.J., (New York, 1965), 149-155; R. Laurentin, *Traité*, I, 118-173; id., *Traité*, V, 42-66, ibid., "Bulletin marial," twice yearly in RSPT, (1962 et seq.), esp. "Datation, attributions, réeditions en Patristique grecque," 52(1968), 539-551; F. Spedalieri, S.J., *Maria nella Scrittura e nella Tradizione della Chiesa primitiva*, I, (Messina, 1961); id., *op. cit.*, II, (Rome, Herder, 1968); D. Montagna, *La lode alla Theotokos nei testi greci dei secoli IV-VII*, (Rome, Marianum, 1963); H. Graef, *Mary*, I, 32-159; E. Toniolo, O.S.M., "Omelie mariane bizantine. Testi scelti e tradotti. I Authentiche del IV-V secolo," in MM, (Rome, 1968); J. de Aldama, S.J., *Maria en la patrística de los siglos I y II*, (Madrid, BAC, 1970), xv; Th. Koehler, S.M., *Maria nei primi secoli*, (Centro Mariano Chaminade [Fons signatus 10], 1971); R. Caro, S.J., *La Homilética*; D. Fernandez, C.M.F., "Mariologia Patrística postconciliar," in EphMar, 27(1977), 49-80; G. M. Bessuti, O.S.M., "Saggio di introduzione alla bibliografia mariana dei secoli I-V," in PCM, V, 247-287; Beck. [2]*Sanctorum Patrum de Sanctissima Dei Genitrice Maria; Sermones selecti*, ed. by H. Hurter, (Paris, 1913). [3]BHG; Auctarium. [4]R. Laurentin, "Table rectificative des pièces mariales inauthentiques ou discutées contenues dans les deux patrologies de Migne," in *Traité*, I, 121-173. [5]G. Giamberardini, O.F.M., *La Mediazione di Maria nella Chiesa egiziana*, (Cairo, 1952).

FATIMA

Like Lourdes (qv), Fatima has interest for the theologian as a focus or meeting-point of the sentiment of the faithful (qv), and as a Marian center which has prompted significant papal pronouncements. It was at the end of an address to a gathering at Fatima, on the occasion of the Silver Jubilee of the Apparitions (31 October, 1942), that Pius XII first pronounced the act of consecration of the world to the Immaculate Heart (qv) of Mary.[1] On 13 May, 1946, the same Pope delivered a lengthy address to pilgrims at the shrine on the theme of Mary's royalty.[2] Paul VI's Apostolic Constitution, *Signum Magnum*

---

[1]Besides works mentioned in the text and standard works on Patrology (e.g. Altaner and Quansten) and dictionaries

(qv) (13 May, 1967), was issued on the Golden Jubilee of the Apparitions, when the Pope visited Fatima. An expert in Marian theology, J. M. Alonso, C.M.F. (qv), has undertaken a critical study of the history and theology of Fatima.[3] Officially chosen and with access to all documents, he has completed a seventeen-volume work on the subject.

[1]OL, 250-252. [2]OL, 264-270. [3]Cf. J. M. Alonso, C.M.F., *Historia critica de Literatura sobre Fatima*, (Fatima, 1967); *id.*, "El Corazón Inmaculado de Maria alma del mensaje de Fatima," I, in EphMar, 22(1972), 240-303; *id., op. cit.*, II, in EphMar, 23(1973), 19-75; *id., Fatima, Historia y Mensaje*, 3rd ed., (Madrid, Centro Mariano, 1977); *id., La gran promesa del Corazón de Maria en Pontevedra*, 3rd ed., (Madrid, Centro Mariano, 1977); *id., Fatima y Russia, el mensaje escatalogico de Tuy*, (Madrid, Centro Mariano, 1976); *id., La verdad sobre el secreto de Fatima. Fatima sin mitos*, (Madrid, Centro Mariano, 1976).

FINDING IN THE TEMPLE, THE

The passage which ends Luke's infancy narrative (2:41-52) gives us our only direct information on the life of Jesus between his infancy and his entry into public life—on the hidden years.[1] It records his first spoken words, and the first of the two sentences spoken to him by Mary in the New Testament—the second being "They have no wine" (Jn 2:3). The story would appear out of place in the infancy narrative and may have been taken by Luke elsewhere, but it is, in its present state, worked into his composition. It makes a kind of Temple diptych with the Presentation, just as there is an Annunciation and a birth diptych. It is in tune with a Hellenistic custom, known in Luke's world, of narrating a childhood story which foreshadows future greatness. The historian Josephus tells us that, at the time of his own religious initiation, the chief priest and leading men of Jerusalem used to have talks with him. The apocryphal infancy gospel of Thomas borrows the story and makes an addition. When the Child Jesus has made his reply to his mother, the scribes and Pharisees ask Mary if she is the mother. When she answers that she is, "They said unto her: Blessed art thou among women, because God hath blessed the fruit of thy womb. For such glory and such excellence and wisdom we have neither seen nor heard at any time."[2]

Certain problems raised about the passage are relevant to Christology, such as the eschatological fulfillment of Is 11:2, the messianic portrait emphasizing wisdom and intelligence.

Mary is given prominence by the evangelist. Though Joseph is present, she it is who questions Jesus on the motive of his stay in the Temple. She it is who keeps these things "in her heart." This concluding reflection, taken with Luke's declared intention of setting down what had been delivered by "those who from the beginning were eyewitnesses and ministers of the word" (1:2), lends probability to the opinion that in some way the story came from Mary—a suggestion vigorously rejected by some modern exegetes.

Jesus' reply has puzzled many and commentators are not agreed on the solution. There is an ancient debate on the final words in v.49, "in my Father's house," or "about my Father's business" or "in the household [relatives] of my Father." Some seem to overlook the first question Jesus asked, which has its own difficulty. Why should a child of twelve express surprise that his parents look for him when he is lost? And what intention were they to see in his absence? That he would stay indefinitely in the Temple? Hence the suggestion that the following sentence be translated "they *had* not understood the word he *had* spoken to them," which is not grammatically easily accepted.

It has been argued that the "they" referred to the bystanders, not Mary and Joseph—this to show that Mary did not lack understanding.

The source of Mary's pain in the separation from Jesus, pain for which Luke uses the same word, *hodunao*, as he does for the pain of hell (16:24-25), was not related to who Jesus was but to what he had done. From Lk 1:32, 35, it is clear that she knew who he was. What she did not understand then had nothing to do with his relationship to the Father, his divine sonship, but with duty laid on him by the Father. If the incident forms a diptych with the Presentation, we should look for a meaning that later events would manifest, as in Simeon's prophecy of the sword. The Passover setting and the three days which prefigure the three days of the final Passover in the life of Christ, the echo of "my Father's house" in Jesus' last words according to Luke, "Father into thy hands I commit my spirit" (23:46), render R. Laurentin's opinion worthy of consideration. He says, "What Mary did not understand according to the evangelist, what she pondered in her heart, (2:51), and understood only later, was the mystery of the Passover, the fulfilment of the Annunciation promises. From the infancy of Jesus, Mary knew the first and very obscure foreshadowing of it, a foreshadowing already sensibly marked with the sign of pain."[3] This opinion has been challenged. It does accord with a solemn moment in life, the moment when a boy announces to his parents, as a Jewish boy of twelve would do, his lifework and its possible outcome—in this case the final Passover, what John will call the hour of Jesus.

---

[1]Cf. R. Winterbotham, "The Story of the Lost and Found," in *Expositor*, ser. 8, 3(1911), 255-261; M. A. Power, S.J., "Who were they who 'understood not'?," in ITQ, 7(1912), 261-281, 444-459; C. Guignebert, *La vie cachée de Jésus*, (Paris, Flammarion, 1921); P. J. Temple, "What is to be understood by *en tois* (Lk 2:49)," in ITQ, 17(1922), 248-263; *id., The boyhood consciousness of Christ*, (New York, Macmillan, 1922); *id.*, "Christ's holy youth according to Lk 2:52," in CBQ, 3(1941), 243-250; *id., Pattern Divine*, (St. Louis-London, Herder, 1950), 193-245, 357-364; *id.*, "Origen and the Ellypsis in Lk 2:49," in ITQ, 21(1954), 367-375; E. Burrows, S.J., *The Gospel of the Infancy*, (London, Burns, Oates and Washborne (Bellarmine Series VI), 1940), first essay; D. O'Shea, *The Holy Family*, (Dublin, Gill, 1944), 182-221; T. Watkin, "Why hast thou done so to us? (Lk 2:48)," in CRev, 27(1947), 304-306; J. M. Bover, S.J., "Una nueva interpretación de Luc 2:50," in EstBib, 10(1951), 205-215; J. E. Renie, "'Et Jesus proficiebat sapientia et aetate et gratia apud Deum et homines' (Lk 2:52)," in *Miscell. Biblica. et Orient.* ed. by A. Metzinger, (Rome, Herder, 1961), 340-350; P. Winter, "Lk 2:49 and Targum Yerushalmi," in *Zeitsch. Neut. Wiss.*, 45(1954), 145-179 and 46(1955), 140; R. Laurentin, *Structure et Théologie de Luc I-II*, (Paris, Gabalda, 1957), 141-146, 168-173; *id., Jésus au Temple: Mystère de Pâques et foi de Marie en Luc 2:48-50*. (Paris, Gabalda, 1966); *id.*, "Non intellexerunt verbum quod locutus est ad eos' (Lc 2:50)," in MSS, IV, 299-314; B. van Iersel, "The Finding of Jesus in the Temple. Some Observations on the Original Form of Lk 2:41-51a," in NovT, 4(1960), 161-173; R. Aron, *Les années obscures de Jésus*, (Paris, Grasset, 1960, 119-200 and English tr., *Jesus of Nazareth: The Hidden Years*, London, Hamish Hamilton, 1962, 83-139); J. Dupont, "Luc 2:41-52: Jésus à douze ans," in *Assemblées du Seigneur*, Bruges, 14(1961), 25-41; J. Galot, S.J., *Mary in the Gospel*, (Westminster, Maryland, 1965), 98-103; F. Spadafora, "'Et ipsi non intellexerunt' (Lc 2:50)," in *Divinitas*, 11(1967), 55-70; A. Martinelli, O.F.M., "Essi non compresero' (Lc 2:50)," in *Miscell. Francesc.*, 67(1967), 246-320; J. B. Cortes, S.J. and F. Gatti, "Jesus' first recorded words (Lk 2:49-50)," in MM, 32(1970), 404-418; J. K Elliott, "Does Luke 2:41-52 anticipate the Resurrection?," in *Expository Times*, 83(1971-1972), 87-89; E. Pax, "Jüdische Familienliturgie in biblisch-christlicher Sicht," in *Bibel und Leben*, 13(1972), 248-261; A. Feuillet, *Jésus et sa Mère*, (Paris, Gabalda, 1974), 69-79; G. Schmahl, "Lk 2:41-52 und die Kindheitserzählung des Thomas, 19:1-5," in *Bibel und Leben*, 15(1974), 249-258; J. McHugh, *The Mother of Jesus in the New Testament*, (London, 1974), 113-124. R. E. Brown, *The Birth*, 471-496; H. J. de Jonge, "Sonship, Wisdom, Infancy," in NTS, 24(1978), 317-354; *Mary in the New Testament*, 157-162. [2]M. R. James, *The Apocryphal New Testament*, (London, 1960), 54; E. Hennecke, *New Testament Apocrypha*, I, (London, 1963, 1965). [3]R. Laurentin, *Jésus au Temple: Mystere de Pâques et foi de Marie en Luc 2:48-50*, (Paris, Gabalda, 1966), 108-109.

FRANCIS OF MEYRONNES (MAYRONIS)
(c. 1285-after 1328)

F., a Franciscan philosopher and theologian, was important in the movement of thought in favour of the Immaculate Conception (*qv*). He taught at Paris. His ideas are found in: a) his commentary on book III of the *Sentences*;[1] and b) in two sermons, *Absit istam rem facere* and *Candor est lucis aeternae*.[2] Another sermon associated with his name is doubtfully genuine.[3] F. intergrates his opinion in the Scotist conception of Christ as the predestined Son of God independently of Adam's sin. Mary was also so predestined. If Mary had not been freed of original sin, he thinks, she would have suffered a greater loss than the pains of hell. The angels would have been purer than she; Christ would not have been the perfect Mediator. As his Mother, she had this claim on him and it is better to believe too much about her than too little. F. also believed in the Assumption (*qv*).

---

[1](Venice, 1506, 1519, 1520). Cf. J. Juric, O.F.M., "Franciscus de Mayronis Immaculatae Conceptionis eximius vindex," in *Studi Franc.*, 51(1954), 224-263. [2]ed. by Alva y Astorga, in *Monumenta antiqua seraphica pro Immaculata Conceptione V. Mariae*, (Brussels, 1665), 317-322, 322-326. Cf. J. Juric, "De redactione inedita sermonis 'Absit' Francisci de Mayronis in festo Conceptionis B.M.V.," in *Studi Franc.*, 53(1956), 3-54. [3]Cf. P. A. Pompeii, O.F.M.Cap., for text and critical position, in *Miscellanea Franc.*, 55(1955), 545-557.

FRANCIS DE SALES, ST., DOCTOR OF THE CHURCH,
(1567-1622)

The views of F. on Our Lady are significant because of his achievement as a spiritual director, religious founder, and as a bishop in a crucial age. His devotion to Mary was deep and sensitive. His theological opinions on the subject are found in passages in his best-known works, *Introduction to the Devout Life* and the *Treatise on the Love of God*, and in over twenty of his 240 published sermons; also in occasional brief passages and notes. His Marian sermons were given on the feasts of Our Lady, six of them on the Assumption; his sermon on St. Joseph (*qv*) matches other seventeenth century documents concerning the saint.[1]

F. saw the advantage of a middle way, "the royal way," between excesses of opinion. "To some, she [the Church] points out that the Virgin is a creature, but so holy, so perfect, so perfectly allied, joined and united with her Son, so loved and cherished by God, that one cannot love the Son without loving the Mother intensely for love of him, without honouring the Mother for the honour of the Son. But to others she [the Church] says: 'Sacrifice is the supreme honour of *latria* which can be offered only to the Creator and do you not see that the Virgin is not the creator, but a creature, though most excellent?' For myself, I have been accustomed to say that in a way the Virgin is more a creature of God and of his Son than the rest of the world, in so far as God created in her much more perfection than in his other creatures; that she is more redeemed than the rest of men, because she was redeemed not only from sin but from the power and the very inclination to sin."[2]

F. had the Reformers in mind in some passages which he wrote on Our Lady— once he dealt with Calvin by name. The saint included the Immaculate Conception (*qv*) in the benefits Mary drew from the Redemption: "The most holy Virgin ought to have had this particular privilege, for it would not be right that the devil could reproach Our Lord with the fact that the one who bore him in her womb had been subject to himself."[3] F. teaches the traditional doctrine of Mary's holiness, mentioning that she was free from venial sin. Her life was a continual progress from love to love. In love, she joined her Son on Calvary and suffered with him, sharing "his misery through her pity, his sufferings through her sympathy, his Passion through her compassion (*qv*)."[4] She accepted her suffering for "our salvation and that of the whole world." The love with which she loved St. John extends far beyond him, "for she saw well that Our Lord gave her St. John as a son, and gave her also consequently all Christians to whom as children of grace he wished her to be a mother."[5]

F. insists, more than many writers, that Mary's death was a death of love. He held, as *Munificentissimus Deus* (*qv*) recalls, that she was bodily assumed into heaven. F. draws attention to the ancient symbolism of the Ark (*qv*). He relates the privilege to Our Lord's filial love and duty to his Mother. In heaven, Mary is queen. In heaven, she prays for us. Knowing that Calvin had objected to a certain interpretation of the title "treasurer of graces" used now by F. himself, he phrased his ideas carefully. He recalls that he

has said "a hundred times" that the Saviour and Mary are advocates in different ways, he an advocate of justice, she of grace. "If Jesus Christ prays in heaven, he prays in his own right; but Our Lady prays only as we do by right of her Son, but with more credit and favour than us. Do you not see that all that redounds to the honour of her Son and magnifies his glory?"[6] In this passage, F. appears almost to put Mary's intercession on the same level as that of the saints. Elsewhere he makes it clear that the divine motherhood puts her inestimably higher than the saints. He urged devotion to her as he practiced it faithfully himself.

---

[1] *Oeuvres complétes*, 26 vols. (Annecy, 1892). Cf. Ch. Flachaire, *La dévotion à la Vierge dans la littérature catholique au commencement du XVIIe siècle*, (Paris, 1916, reissue, 1957), ch. II, 34-43; E. Campana, "La Mariologia di S. Francesco di Sales," in *Riv. Mater Dei*, (1936), 82ff; H. Barré, "Le témoignage de S. François de Sales sur l'Assomption corporelle de Marie," in MM, 13(1951), 292-305; E. J. Carney, O.S.F.S., *The Mariology of St. Francis de Sales*, (Eichstatt-Vienna, 1964); L. M. Comte, *Marie, mère et éducatrice selon S. François de Sales, Vatican II et Paul VI*, (Paris, 1970); V. Viguera, "Essai sur une mariologie dans l'oeuvre de S. Francois de Sales," in EphMar, 23(1973), 231-251; Mgr. F. Vincent, "S. François de Sales," in *Maria*, II, 991-1004. [2]"Serm. pour l'Assomption," 1602, in *Oeuvres complètes*, (Annecy, 1892), VII, 458. [3]*op. cit.*, X, 404. [4]*op. cit.*, IV, 269. [5]*op. cit.*, IV, 442. [6]*op. cit.*, VII, 459.

FULBERT OF CHARTRES, ST. (d. 1028)

F., an Italian educated at Rheime, was bishop of Chartres from 1006 until his death. He restored the famous cathedral of Our Lady. He loved to celebrate the feast of her Nativity and his devotion to her passed into legend. His fame and his reputation for holiness were widespread. His Marian theology, the most important of his age, is found in: a) his sermon on the Purification, b) his sermons on the Nativity, c) rhymed *responsoria*, d) *De beata Virgine*, e) in this great prayer to Our Lady,[1] and in another shorter prayer. Questions of authenticity have been debated by two scholars, J. M. Canal and H. Barré (*qv*). Not only sermons IV and V (PL 141, 320B-325C)[2] but sermon VI is to be considered genuine. Two further sermons on the Nativity (*Gloriosam solemnitatem* and *Nativitatis gloriosae*) are spurious.

F. does not deal with the problem of the Immaculate Conception (*qv*). He writes: "In this necessary conception there is no doubt that a vivifying and ardent spirit filled each parent with singular power and that the custody or the visitation of holy angels was never lacking."[4] "O exceedingly blessed Virgin who in merit is to be compared with no other nor thought equal in regard to chastity."[5]

In the history of interpretation of Gen 3:15, F. was an innovator. He identified the victory with Mary personally, in her own life, not with her offspring. "And if anyone asks in what way she crushed the serpent's head, it was certainly in this—that she offered a sacrifice to God at once of her virginity and humility. By preserving her virginity she is shown to have vanquished the concupiscence of the flesh; by her humility, which renders one poor in spirit, the concupiscence of the mind."[6]

F. defended the Assumption as a pious belief, linking Mary's intercession with it: "Christian piety therefore believes that Christ, God, the Son of God, gloriously raised up [resuscitaverit] his Mother and exalted her above the heavens, and that John, the virgin and evangelist, who ministered to her on earth, merits to share her glory in heaven. The grace and glory the Lord gave to his Mother are incalculable. But this we know for certain, that the just more swiftly obtain through his Mother's intercession whatever they ask of him whereas sinners have received mercy beyond all hope."[7]

F. continues the Is 7:14 Marian interpretation (see EMMANUEL). He bids Eve (qv) rejoice in her descendant who "mercifully releases her and her race from the fetter of death."[8] He likes to associate mercy with Mary; she is "full of mercy," "Mother of mercy." But in his great prayer he also recalls her exalted privilege: "Holy Virgin Mary, Queen of angels, ruler of masters, be for me a merciful intermediary [interventrix] with the King of all kings . . . ."[9] "The Mother of the Lord holds sway everywhere and is everywhere munificent, enabled certainly to send holy angels on her ministry and, when she wills, to destroy the schemes of the lower powers."[10]

[1]Texts in PL 141, 319-331, 345; J. M. Canal, C.M.F. infra. Cf. P. de Puniet, La vie et les arts liturgiques, 12(1925-1926), 488, on the responsoria; Y. Delaporte, Une prière de saint Fulbert de Notre Dame, (Chartres, 1928); ibid., "Une prière de saint Fulbert de Chartres à Notre Dame," in VieSp, 86(1952), 467-476; H. Barré, C.S.Sp., "Fulbert de Chartres," in Prières Anciennes, 150-162; "Pro Fulberto," in RTAM, 31(1964), 324-330; J. M. Canal, C.M.F., "Los sermones marianos de San Fulberto de Chartres," in RTAM, 29(1962), 33-51; id., "Texto critico de algunos sermones marianos de San Fulberto de Chartres etc.," in RTAM, 30(1963), 55-87; id., "Los sermones marianos de San Fulberto de Chartres. Conclusión," in RTAM, 33(1966), 138-147; id., "En torno a San Fulberto de Chartres," in EphLit, 80(1966), 211-225; R. Laurentin, in RSPT, 50(1966), 544-545; id., in BSFEM, 12(1954), 101-103, 125; J. Pintard, "S. Fulbert à l'origine du culte chartrain de la Nativité de Notre Dame," in Zagreb Congress, III, 551-569. [2]Critical ed. by J. M. Canal, C.M.F., in RTAM, 30(1963), 56-61, 331-333. [3]"Gloriosam solemnitatem," and "Nativitatis gloriosae," ed. with reservation, by J. M. Canal, in RTAM, 30(1963), 69-83. [4]Serm. VI in Nativ., ed. by J. M. Canal, in RTAM, 30(1963), 63. [5]op. cit. [6]Serm. IV, in PL 141, 320D, and also in RTAM, 30(1963), 57. Cf. R. Laurentin, in BSFEM, 12(1954), 103 and 125. [7]Serm. V, in PL 141, 325B, and also in RTAM, 30(1963), 332. [8]Serm. VI, in RTAM, 30(1963), 67. [9]RTAM, 30(1963), 85. [10]Serm. IV, in PL 141, 324, and also in RTAM, 30(1963), 61.

FULGENS CORONA (September 8th, 1953)

This is the Encyclical Letter published by Pius XII (qv) on the centenary of the dogma of the Immaculate Conception (qv), for the special Marian year proclaimed thereon.[1] The papal text falls into the following parts: introduction on the dogmatic event and the occurrence of the Lourdes apparitions soon after; scriptural, patristic and theological aspects; the belief in the life of the Church; relationship between the two papal dogmas; and the proper manner of celebrating the Marian year, in private and in public.

[1]AAS, 45(1953), 577-592; OL, 346-357.

FULGENTIUS OF RUSPE (d. 533)

Bishop of Ruspe in North Africa, F., a disciple of St. Augustine (qv), was vigorous against Arianism and Pelagianism. He deals with Marian themes in many passages of his works, particularly in his letters to Thrasamund, king of the Vandals, and to Peter the Deacon (Letter XVII).[1] F. elaborates the doctrine of the Incarnation, in which Mary's part is fully clarified, stressing the identity of the Son of the Father and of the virgin. He repeats the Eve (qv)-Mary parallel and contrast: "Thus sin and the penalty of sin which, through the crime of a corrupt woman, entered the world is removed from the world by the offspring of an inviolate woman. And as in the condition of the human race it happened that we were bound by the bond of death through a woman made from man alone, divine goodness arranged that, in the redemption of the human race, life should be restored to men through a man born of a woman alone. In the former case, the devil by vilest deceit associated human nature with him in the likeness of sin; in the second, God took human nature into the unity of a person. There, a woman was deceived that she should become the devil's daughter; here, a virgin was filled with grace that she should become mother of the most high and unchanging only-begotten Son of God. There, an angel cast down by pride took control of the mind of the woman he seduced; here, God lowering himself through mercy filled the womb of the incorrupt virgin from whom he would be born."[2]

F. has a stimulating thought (which he does not develop at length) on the Holy Spirit (qv): "We are re-born of the same Spirit, from whom Christ was born. Christ is formed according to faith in the heart of each believer by the same Spirit by whom according to the flesh he was formed in the womb of the Virgin."[3] He turns from this thought to an anti-Pelagian idea on the necessity of grace in Mary's case and in that of the believer.

[1]Works in PL 65; EMBP, 1069-1077. Cf. J. B. Bauer, "De S. Fulgentii Mariologia," in MM, 17(1955), 531-535. [2]De Fide . . . ad Petrum, in PL 65, 680B. Cp. Serm. II in Natali Dni, in PL 65, 728D. [3]Letter XVII to Peter the Deacon, in PL 65, 476C.

FULL OF GRACE

This is the English translation for *gratia plena*, which is the Vulgate rendering of *Kecharitomene* (Lk 1:28). This Greek term means favoured one: it is from *charitoun*, a factitive verb, "to make one favoured, to give one grace." Full of grace became a key description of Mary in western tradition. Until very recently, it was used by every writer in the Latin Church, in all official documents of the teaching authority down to Vatican II. The Council would not alter it despite requests from Council Fathers to do so.[1]

Mary's fullness of grace became a basic concept about her in theology. It was expounded in relation to her vocation as Mother of God; views have been expressed on the one hand that it was separable, and on the other inseparable, from this office. It has been seen as the foundation of Mary's unique holiness and consequent sinlessness, and it has been proposed as the fundamental principle of all Marian theology. Scholastic theologians have deduced from it the

entire grouping of the theological and moral virtues, the Gifts of the Holy Spirit, and extraordinary graces and charisms. In medieval times, Pseudo-Albert had made a still wider series of deductions. Mary's merit is proportionate to her grace.

Vatican II speaks thus of Mary's eminent grace: "Because of this gift of sublime grace, she far surpasses all other creatures, both in heaven and on earth." Adorned from the first instant of her conception with the splendours of an entirely unique holiness, the Virgin of Nazareth is, on God's command, greeted by an angel messenger as "full of grace." (Lk 1:28, LG 53, 56).

Prior to the Vulgate, *Kecharitomene* was not uniformly rendered by *Gratia plena*; *gratificata* or *benedicta* occur in some manuscript versions. Erasmus used *gratiosa*, and in this was followed by the Reformers. St. Peter Canisius protested against this.

[1]Cf. A. Julischer, *Das Neue Testament in Altlateinischer Überlieferung nach den Handschriften*, (Berlin, 1954), 6; S. Lyonnet, S.J., "Chaire Kecharitomene," in BB, 20(1939), 131-141; R. Laurentin, *Structure et Théologie de Luc I-II*, (Paris, Gabalda, 1957); B. Bourassa, "Kecharitomene, Lc. 1:28," in ScEcl, 9(1957), 313-316; E. R. Cole, "What did St. Luke mean by Kecharitomene," in AER, 139(1958), 228-239; A. Strobel, "Der Gruss an Maria (Lc 1:28)," in ZNW, 53(1962), 86-110; M. Cambe, "La Charis chez S. Luc. Remarques sur quelques textes, notamment le Kecharitomene," in RB, 70(1963), 193-207; G. M. Verd, "Gratia plena. Sentido de una traducción," in EstEcl, 50(1975), 357-389; F. Marchisiano, *L'interpretazione di Kecharitomene (Lc 1:28) fino alla metà del secolo XIII. Contributo alla mariologia biblica*, (Rome, 1968).

FUNDAMENTAL PRINCIPLE IN MARIOLOGY, THE

Since the theology of Our Lady comprises inter-related truths (as does any body of knowledge), coherence and progress would seem to demand agreement on a basic or primary truth. Suarez (qv), the first exponent of systematic Mariology, felt this need. St. Lawrence of Brindisi (qv) stated it clearly.[1] Since the thirties of the present century, the problem has been frequently discussed. It has lapsed somewhat since Vatican Council II (qv). The results of discussion, however, remain impressive. K. Rahner, in 1954, proposing his own answer to the problem, listed ten others. R. Laurentin, in 1968, estimated that the number of answers had risen to thirty.

Some theories are based on analogy of one kind or another between Mary and Christ, others on a relationship between them. Christ-type and Church-type ideas affect the first group of theories differently. Thus Mary is seen as the new Eve, and for Louis Billot this would appear the basic principle. Mary as archetype of the Church was the central idea of O. Semmelroth's book. K. Rahner proposed the idea of Mary as the highest instance of the Redemption, an opinion which had some effect on the speech made by Cardinal Koenig at Vatican II (24 October, 1963). A. Mueller, author of a seminal work on Mary and the Church, concluded that Mary's fullness of grace, rightly understood, was the key to her whole life.

Those who proceed from a relationship, that of motherhood, differ in the application of their thought. M. J. Scheeben defended the concept of the bridal motherhood. J. M. Bover, S.J., chose the divine maternity seen in its full, concrete, historical significance. N. Garcia Garces, C.M.F., thought of Mary as "Mother of the whole Church, head and members"; G.M. Roschini, O.S.M., thought of Mary as the universal mother. Cl. Dillenschneider, C.SS.R., concluded a work devoted entirely to the subject with this elaborate formula: Mary's divine, messianic maternity in its personal, soteriological and ecumenical dimensions. G. de Broglie, S.J., also framed a comprehensive statement: Mother of the Word divine, incarnate among us to save mankind by his expiatory renunciation and by the association of redeemed souls to this way of life.

There is no direct official teaching on the subject. There has been, however, a repeated emphasis in Council and papal pronouncements on the divine motherhood. The essential title is used by Ephesus which proclaimed it, by Trent which referred to Mary in its teaching on Original Sin, and by Pius IX in the dogma of the Immaculate Conception and Pius XII in that of the Assumption. Vatican II devoted some 200 words of chapter VIII in *Lumen Gentium* to titles of Mary. She is styled Mother in sixteen different ways, Mother of God most frequently. The Council expressed two other ideas of some relevance, the indissoluble union between Jesus and Mary and the Mary-Church typology. No principle emerges with absolute explicitness.

The debate has helped to enlarge the theological vision of Mary and can still do so, provided the deductive method, which it favours, does not become detached from the sources of Marian theology.

[1]Cf. L. Billot, S.J., *De Verbo incarnato*, (Rome, 1927), 386; J. Bover, S.J., "Sintesis organica de la Mariologia en function de la associación de Maria a la obra rendentora de Jesucristo," in EstEcl, (Madrid, Pozas, 1929); J. Bittremieux, "De principio supremo Mariologiae," in ETL, 8(1931), 249-251; *id., Marialia*, (Brussels, 1936), 16-29; *id.*, in ETL, 12(1935), 607-609; E. Druwé, S.J., "Position et structure du traité marial," in BSFEM, (1936), 16-29; C. Feckes, "Das Fundamental-Prinzip der Mariologie," in *Scientia Sacra*, (1935), 252-276; "M. J. Scheeben, théologien de la mariologie moderne," in *Maria*, III, 555-571; N. Garcia Garces, C.M.F., *Maria coredemptrix*, (Rome, 1940); S. Alameda, "El primer principio mariologico segun los Padres," in EstM, 3(1944), 163-186; G. M. Roschini, O.S.M., *Mariologia*, (1946), I, 323-379; *id., La Madonna secondo la Fede e la Teologia*, (Rome, 1953), 97-115; *id., Maria Santissima*, I, 103-199; O. Semmelroth, *Urbild der Kirche*, (Wurzburg, Echter Verlag, 1949. English tr. *Mary, Archetype of the Church*, London, Sheed and Ward, 1963); A. Mueller, "Um die Grundlagen der Mariologie," in *Divus Thomas*, (Fribourg), 29(1951), 385-401; H. Mühlen, "Der 'Personalcharakter' Mariens nach J. M. Scheeben: Zur Frage nach dem Grundprinzip der Mariologie," in *Wissenschaft und Weisheit*, 17(1954), 191-213; K. Rahner, S.J., "Le principe fondamental de la théologie mariale," in RSR, 42(1954), 481-522; Cl. Dillenschneider, C.SS.R., *Le principe premier d'une théologie mariale organique. Orientations*, (Paris, Alsatia, 1955); C. Vollert, S.J., "The Fundamental Principle of Mariology," in *Mariology*, II, 30-87; *id.*, "The Fundamental Principle of Marian Theology," in *A Theology of Mary*, (New York, Herder, 1965), 49-112; A. Patfoort, "Le principe premier de la mariologie," in RSPT, 41(1957), 445-454; G. Girones, "Ensayo sobre el problema fundamental de la mariologia," in *Anales del seminario de Valencia*, 4(1964), no. 8, 31-73; R. Laurentin, *Traité*, V, 103-108; G. de Broglie, S.J., "Le 'principe fondamental' de la théologie mariale," in *Maria*, VI, 299-365; *id.*, in MSt, 10(1959), several articles.

G

GALOT, JEAN, S.J. (1919-) — See Supplement, p. 382.
GARCIA GARCES, NARCISO, C.M.F. (1904-) — See Supplement, p. 382.

GEOFFREY OF VENDOME (*c.* 1070-1132) Abbot of the Benedictine monastery of the Trinity at Vendome, G. had a public role in the life of the Church, was a supporter of the reforms of Gregory VII, and was named a Cardinal. He was the author of two Marian sermons rich in doctrine.[1] In the first sermon on the Purification (qv), he has a rare tribute to the Jewish people (see JEWS AND MARY): "Beyond and above everything else which he had given them, from them he chose his Mother and from their flesh he took flesh . . . . Jesus preferred to take flesh in the people of Israel, rather than in any other race, to their greater glory. In this flesh therefore his noble Mother conceived and brought him forth and for [our] salvation and as an example of humility, she offered him in the temple a living and vivifying victim in the odour of sweetness."[2] The offering of Jesus in the Temple by Mary and Joseph (qv) was taught in the same age by St. Bernard (qv).

Mary's Son is her father and her spouse (qv), for she was created by him and is united with him in charity.[3] She holds the primacy over all creatures, and is the "empress of angels and of men." She is the Mother of Christians because she is the Mother of Christ, and Christians are Christ's brothers.[4] He wished his Mother to be ours so that she should help us in our need; we should then run to her and to him through her. "Let her not remember our wrongs but be overcome by the love with which she brought us forth."[5] G. is very strong on Mary's intercession, her motherly mercy. She can obtain what she wants by her motherly command; no one for whom she has prayed even once will perish. Witness Cana (qv), the Theophilus (qv) legend, and let us recall the meaning of her saving motherhood, the range of her merits.[6]

[1] Serm. VII in Purif. S. M., in PL 157, 262-266; Serm. VIII in omni fest. B. M. Matris Domini, in PL 157, 266-270. [2] PL 157, 265D-266A. [3] PL 157, 267B. [4] PL 157, 266A. [5] PL 157, 266B. [6] PL 157, 268B-269C.

GEORGE OF NICOMEDIA (d. after 880)

Metropolitan of Nicomedia, G. was a friend of Photius (qv). Of his 170 homilies, only a fraction have been published, most of them on Our Lady as follows: two on the Conception of Mary (BHG 1102, 1111);[1] one on the Conception and Nativity (BHG 1125z);[2] three on the Presentation (BHG 1152, 1108, 1078);[3] one on Our Lady by the Cross (BHG 1139); and one on the Mother of God and the risen Christ (BHG 1156).[4] One homily on the Presentation has not been published (BHG 1144k), nor has one on Joseph and Mary (BHG 1109g). There is much about Mary's parents in the sermons on

the Conception. G. insists on Mary's initial holiness: "She is the magnificent first-fruits which human nature offered to the Creator . . . holier than the purest in us." There was no stain in her. The angelic food she ate in the Temple (here as elsewhere the influence of the Apocrypha is felt) did not purify her from sin as the Bread of Life does us, "for she who ate it had no sins; she was pure and free from all sins."[5]

G.'s prolix style covers important insights: "Through you the exiled human race returns to its abode . . . through you we have the true signs of the resurrection; through you we hope that we shall reach the kingdom of heaven, we have a helper of our salvation, a benefactress."[6] Mary is the mediatress (qv) of our regeneration, the one who obtains our future joy. She is the living temple, higher than the heavens, wider and more spacious than the whole creation.

Dealing with Mary's intercession, G. yields nothing to Germanus (qv): "You have power unconquerable, force that cannot be reduced, nothing resists your power." This is because her Son has so exalted her. When G. deals with Mary's mercy, he does not, like some of the medieval Latin writers, set up two kingdoms, justice ruled by Christ and mercy by his Mother. Saying that we tend to attribute the Son's power and benefaction to her, he goes on: "When we constantly offend him we remain despicable, unworthy that he should care for us. Therefore you as our mediatress, approaching him, reconcile us as if all the more lenient in imitation of him. You bend his immense clemency to mercy on us; watchfully you intercede for us, which is clearly suited to his clemency and your protection."[7]

On one point, G. is something of a landmark. During and after medieval times, and by the modern Popes, Jn 19:25-27 (see WOMAN IN) was understood in the context of the spiritual motherhood (qv), but not so by the Fathers of the Church. G., coming at the end of the patristic age, does have this insight, though in a limited way: "For through him," [says Christ to his Mother], "I bequeath also the rest of my disciples. And as long as you will live with them and stay with them, as it shall be my will, you will give them your bodily presence in place of mine. Be for them all that mothers are naturally for their children, or rather all that I should be by my presence; all that sons are, they will be for you."[8] Thus he interprets his words to John: "It is not only for you, but also for the other disciples that I have made her mother and guide, and it is my wish that she should be honoured in the fullest sense with the dignity of mother. Though I have forbidden you to call anyone on earth father, I wish nonetheless that you call her mother and honour her as such, she who was for me an abode more than heavenly and showed me a resolve with which nature is unacquainted."[9]

This is a motherhood of the disciples only and apparently for the lifetime of the Mother; still a development had taken place. The text had been given a meaning wider than physical care for the mother by a disciple especially trusted. The spiritual aspect is not yet explicit, but the mystery commemorated invites such reflection—eventually at least.

G. devotes a homily to Mary at the sepulchre of the dead Christ in which he adheres to a tradition already established in the East, that Christ appeared first after the Resurrection to Mary. "Thus accordingly with none between, on her first the clear light and joy of the Resurrection shone."[10]

[1]A. Mai, *Nova Patrum Bibliotheca*, (ed. 1905), 163-166; PG 100, 1336-1354. [2]PG 100, 1376-1400. [3]PG 100, 1401-1420, 1420-1440, 1440-1456. [4]PG 100, 1457-1489, 1489-1504. Cf. Beck, 543; M. Jugie, *L'Immaculée Conception*, 173-177; R. Laurentin, *Traité*, 1, 159; *VIIIe Congrès Marial national, Rapports doctrinaux*, (Paris, 1962, for congress of 1961), 3-4; Th. Koehler, S.M., in BSFEM, 16(1959), 141-144. [5]PG 100, 1448B. [6]PG 100, 1437C. [7]PG 100, 1455A. [8]*Hom. in "Stabant autem"*, in PG 100, 1476D. [9]*op. cit.*, in PG 100, 1477B. [10]*In SS. Mariam assistentem in sepulchro*, in PG 100, 1497A.

GERARD OF CSANAD, O.S.B., ST. (d. 1047)

Bishop and martyr, and apostle of Hungary, G. composed sermons on Our Lady, which have not survived save in extracts in works by other writers.

H. Barré, "L'Oeuvre mariale de Saint G. de Csanad," in MM, 25(1963), 262-296; G. Morian, "Un théologien ignoré du XIe siècle, l'évêque-martyr Gerard de Csanad, O.S.B.," in RevBen, 27(1910), 516-521.

GERHOH OF REICHERSBERG (1093-1169)

G. was a reformer, in the spirit of Pope St. Gregory VII. He was present at the first Lateran Council, and involved in the public controversies of his day. G. was abbot of the Reichersberg monastery of the Canons Regular of St. Augustine. He treats of Our Lady in his work on the glory and honour of the Son of Man, in commentaries on the Psalms, and in the prologue which he wrote to the important homily on the Assumption by John of Arezzo. The homily, published by A. Wenger, was considered until some years ago anonymous.[1] It is a composite of eastern homilies affirming the truth.

G. thought that, as smoke before the brightness of the sun and wax before the fire, "the original guilt ceased and was consumed [in Mary] by the Holy Spirit giving her light and warmth, that is by divine love . . . ."[2] This implies original sin in Mary. G. believed in her bodily Assumption. Passing references to it are found in his works. Many are already risen with Christ.[3] The power of God is exalted—"you are thought faithfully to have raised the virginal body of your Mother."[4] In the prologue to the famous homily, giving permisson to nuns to read it, not only privately but in church, he presents an apology for its contents.

In praising the apostles, G. takes the opportunity to point to Mary's excellence: ". . . except the privilege of the incomparable dignity of the most blessed Virgin Mary who also, when the apostles fled, remained with her Son in his trials." G. recalls the Nestorian controversy and the title *Theotokos* (qv): Christ was born in heaven without a mother, on earth without a father.

Mary was the centerpiece of salvation history: "But the Blessed Virgin Mary was the choicest part of the ancient synagogue, so loved by God the Father that he inflamed her with his love beyond all others, made her pregnant with the Word his Son who was uttered in her and—conceived in mind before in the body—came forth from her as a bridegroom from his bridal chamber, loving the new church and every faithful individual within it as a bride adorned for her husband. Among all these brides, the blessed Virgin Mary was adorned beyond all others and remains so, the fulfilment of the synagogue as the choicest daughter of the patriarchs and, after her Son, the new beginning of the holy Church as Mother of Apostles, to one of whom was said, 'Behold your mother'."[5] Elsewhere G. widens the range of Mary's spiritual motherhood to "every one who is my brother." These she brought forth as a mother when, "knowing that her only Son was suffering to free and save them, she was tormented by the sword of suffering which pierced her soul that she might give [spiritual] birth to them."

---

[1] Works in PL 193, 194. For prologue to the Assumption homily, cf. A. Wenger, A.A., *L'Assomption*, 337-340. Cf. A. Sage, in *Maria*, II, 686-693. [2] *In Ps. 1*, in PL 193, 639A. [3] PL 193, 979C. [4] PL 194, 126B. [5] *Lib. de gloria et honore filii hominis, X*, in PL 194, 1105A.

GERMANUS II — See Supplement, p. 382.

GERMANUS OF CONSTANTINOPLE, ST.
(c. 635-733)

With St. Andrew of Crete and St. John of Damascus, G. forms the great trio of eighth century Byzantine Marian theologians. He was an opponent of the iconoclasts. His ideas on the Assumption (qv) found their way to the West through translation and borrowing in the tenth century (see EASTERN INFLUENCE). He is quoted in *Munificentissimus Deus* and *Ad Caeli Reginam*, and referred to in annotations to LG 56, 59, and 62.[1] His Marian doctrine is found in a homily on the Presentation (BHG 1103), three on the Dormition (BHG 1119, 1135, 1155), one on Our Lady's Girdle, a relic preserved at Constantinople (BHG 1086), and in a sermon recently published on the protection of Constantinople from enemy attack (BHG 1130s).

The homily on the Annunciation (PG 98, 320-340) is of doubtful authenticity (BHG 1145n); St. John Chrysostom and St. John of Damascus are mentioned as its possible authors. St. John Chrysostom is also mentioned for the second sermon on the Presentation (BHG 1104; PG 98, 309-320). A second homily on the Girdle (BHG 1123g) is questionably genuine. G.'s name is mentioned with others for a third, on the deposition of the Girdle (BHG 1147), and with St. Andrew of Crete and St. John of Damascus for a homily on the Nativity (BHG 1092; PG 97, 861-881).

The authentic sermon on the Presentation (PG 98, 292-309) contains a rich eulogy of Mary. She is "most pure"; "surrounded by untouched and immaculate virginity"; "fed by angels . . . the child grew and became strong, and the whole force of the curse by which we were struck in Eden was foiled"; "wholly without stain." As image succeeds image and superlatives pile up—"holier than the saints, higher than the heavens, more glorious than the Cherubim, more honourable than the Seraphim, and venerable beyond every creature"—it would seem that G. saw no sin in Mary, not even original.

The passage quoted by Pius XII speaks of Mary's body as "virginal, all holy, all chaste, entirely God's dwelling," incompatible with corruption.[2] G. is influenced by the Apocrypha. He imagines a lengthy address to Mary by her divine Son, which puts the emphasis on their union as the basis of the Assumption: "Where, therefore, I am you must be, Mother inseparable from your Son never taken from you."[3] Gethsemane is to be the place of burial so that, from where Christ went "to the death of my cross, life-giving and freely accepted, it having laid down your body it should be swiftly borne to life." The body was taken instantaneously from the hands of the Apostles, as all looked on.

Mary, "transported to God, is a Mediatress to us." G. has a much quoted passage on the universal role of her mediation: "No one is saved save through you, most holy one; no one is delivered from misfortune save through you, most pure one; there is no one to whom a gift is given save through you, most chaste one; there is none to whom in mercy the gift of grace is granted save through you, who are most venerable. Who in return would not bless you? Who would not exalt you, if not as you really deserve, at least with his whole heart, you who have been glorified, beatified, who have been the object of great things from your Son and God. This is why all generations will proclaim you blessed."[4] Elsewhere, Mary is exalted as our "unchangeable hope, imperturbable protection, fixed refuge, ever-watchful intercessor, . . . sure help . . . rampart secured on all sides, strong tower of help." Those Mary helps, include even the damned and accursed. "To whom else will we go?," he exclaims. "You have the words of eternal life. These words are the prayers by which you intervene on our behalf before God. In fact you never cease to work wonders for us, holy is your name; it is blessed by angels and men, for all generations."[5]

In the recently published homily (BHG 1130s) the saint describes in detail how the *Theotokos* worked a miracle to save the city of Constantinople in a desperate moment. He was at pains to attribute the victory to her, making no mention of the emperor, Leo III. Did he foresee the support the latter would give to the iconoclasts?

G. called himself Our Lady's slave, *doulos*, and spoke thus of others also.[6]

¹Works in PG 98; recent ed. V. Grumel, "Homélie de S. Germain sur la délivrance de Constantinople," in REB, 16(1958), 183-205; EMBP, 1365-1432. Cf. R. Laurentin, *Traité*, I, 172; M. Jugie *L'Immaculée Conception*, 114-119; id., *L'Assomption*, 226-233; I. Carli, *La dottrina sull' Asunzione di Maria di S. Germano di Constantinopoli*, (Rome, 1944); Melchior a S. Maria, O.C.D., "Doctrina S. Germani C. de morte et assumptione B.V.M.," in MM, 15(1953), 195-213; E. Perniola, *La Mariologia di S. Germano*, (Rome, 1954); T. Horvath, S.J., "Germanus of Constantinople and the Cult of the Virgin Mary, Mediatrix of all Men," in Zagreb Congress, IV, 285-299; J. Darrouzès, in DSp, VI, 309-311; H. Graef, *Mary*, I, 145-150; ClavisG, III, 503-510. ²PG 98, 345B; AAS (1950), 761. ³In Dorm. Deiparae, III, in PG 98, 361A. ⁴In SS. Deiparam Zonam, in PG 98, 380BC. ⁵PG 98, 372C. ⁶PG 98, 381B.

GERSON, JOHN (1363-1429)

Born near Rethel in the Ardennes, educated in Navarre College, Paris, G. became Chancellor of the University of Paris in 1395. He was an influential figure involved in public church events, especially the Council of Constance (qv), and was noted as a writer on mysticism.[1] Marian theology is found in a letter-treatise, *De susceptione humanitatis Christi*, on the Incarnation;[2] in a lengthy work in twelve parts, entitled *Collectorium super Magnificat*,[3] wherein many other topics are treated; in some remarkable sermons on feasts of Our Lady, and in other sermons. G. notably furthered the cult of St. Joseph (qv). He treated of the saint in sermons and poems, one of these containing 2957 verses in twelve books.[4]

The letter-treatise (in reply to excesses) enuntiates twenty-four "truths," and ten directive principles. Some concern Our Lady. The Immaculate Conception (qv) is affirmed as "probable and pious." G. was bound by his university office to defend it: "If Christ was the most perfect redeemer of all, enduring death for all, it was fitting that he should redeem his Mother most perfectly; this could not be more suitably done than by preserving her lest she fall rather than raising her when she had fallen."[5] This was the solution proposed by Scotus (qv).

Christ gave to his Mother all the graces deemed suitable in his wisdom. G. criticizes the excesses produced by the argument of suitability, *potuit, decuit ergo fuit*, such as that Mary enjoyed the use of reason from her conception or birth, that she never slept or that she contemplated God in her sleep. It would also be rash and against the holy Doctors, he thought, to assert that Christ revealed to her the whole course of his or her life.

In the sermon on the Immaculate Conception, G. deals with objections drawn from the Latin Doctors.[6] In the *Collectorium super Magnificat*, he analyzes the spousal relationship between Mary and God (see SPOUSE). "No pure creature not united with the divinity, with the exception of the soul of Christ, was more worthy to be named the spouse of God." This was at three moments, in the instant of her creation, in her conception of the Son of God, and in the consummation when she was assumed body and soul into heaven.[7] G. continues the medieval theme of the kingdoms of justice and mercy, saying that Mary is *quodammodo* queen of the second.

In the same work Mary and the priesthood is discussed. G. knew that Mary did not have the priestly character as priests have it, but she was so endowed in a more eminent manner for the reconciliation of sinners, the opening of Paradise. "Mary, on the night of Holy Thursday, though she did not receive the character of the priestly order—though Judas was marked by this seal—bore, more than her life companions, the anointing of a royal priesthood."[8] It was not that she had the power to consecrate, but to offer the pure, full, and perfect host on the altar of her heart, where the fire of the holocaust burned ceaselessly. Likewise he thought of Mary and the Eucharist (qv): "You are the Mother of the Eucharist, because you are the Mother of good grace. You, more than all others after your Son, were aware of this sacrament hidden from the ages."[9] Again he turns to a consideration of the angels of whom Mary is queen, elaborating the role of the nine choirs.

G. adopted St. Bernard's axiom that through Mary's hands God wishes us to have all things. He prayed to her as Queen of heaven, mistress of the angels, advocate (qv), mediatress (qv) of our prayer, Virgin most merciful, Mother of mercy. He can think of her in any context, in preaching for example on the Last Supper,[10] and in preaching before the Council on the Fathers, that she would pour upon them something of the superabundant grace with which the Spirit had filled her.

It was in the close bond with Mary that G saw the greatness of St. Joseph. Preaching on her Purification, he turned naturally to a favourite theme, the feast of the Espousals

GIAMBERARDINI — GOTTSCHALK

which he was promoting: "Say why there is no feast among the Latins of Joseph, the virginal husband of Mary, the most faithful foster-father and guardian of the boy Jesus?"[11] In the great sermon *Jacob autem* on the saint, preached before the Council Fathers, he mentions, without committing himself, the pious belief that Joseph was bodily assumed into heaven.[12] He thought that Joseph knew that Mary's pregnancy was of the Holy Spirit.

---

[1]Works, *Opera Omnia*, ed. by Ellies-Dupin, (Antwerp, 1706); critical ed. by P. Glorieux. Cf. J. M. Bover, S.J., "Universalis B. Mariae Virginis mediatio in scriptis Johannis Gerson," in Gregor, 9(1928), 242-268; L. Mourin, "Jean Gerson, prédicateur français pour les fêtes de l'Annonciation et de la Purification," in *Rev. belge de Philologie et de l'Histoire*, 27(1949), 361-598; A. Combes, "La doctrine mariale de Jean Gerson," in *Maria*, II, 865-882; H. Graef, *Mary*, I, 311-314. On St. Joseph, cf. I. N. Maegawa, "La Doctrine de Jean Gerson sur St. Joseph," in CahJos, 7(1959), 181-194, and 8(1960), 9-39, 251-292 (also separate issue in Anton, Rome, 1961); P. Glorieux, *St. Joseph dans l'oeuvre de Gerson* in *St. Joseph durant les quinze premiers siècles de l'Eglise, Actes du Symposium international sur St. Joseph*, (Rome, 1970, Montreal, 1971). [2]"De susceptione humanitatis Christi," in *Opera Omnia*, ed. by P. Glorieux, II, 263-274. [3]"Collectorium super Magnificat," in *Opera Omnia*, IV, ed. by Ellies-Dupin, (Antwerp, 1706), 229-512; *op. cit.*, in *Opera Omnia*, ed. by P. Glorieux, VIII, 163-534, here quoted. [4]Josephina, in *Opera Omnia*, ed. by P. Glorieux, IV, 31-100. [5]"Letter 56," in *Opera Omnia*, ed. by P. Glorieux, II, 266. [6]"L'Oeuvre oratoire en français," in *Opera Omnia* (ed. P. Glorieux, VII, 1076-1077. [7]*Opera Omnia* (ed. P. Glorieux), IV 224-225. [8]*op. cit.*, IX, 384. [9]*op. cit.*, IX, 413. Also cf. IX, 376ff. [10]*op. cit.*, V, 546-547. [11]*op. cit.*, V, 356. Cf. also, "Pour la fête de la Desponsation de Notre Dame," in *op. cit.*, VII, 11-15; "Considérations sur St. Joseph," in *op. cit.*, VII, 63-94; "Autres Considérations sur St. Joseph," in *op. cit.*, VII, 94-99.

GIAMBERARDINI, GABRIELLE, O.F.M. — See Supplement, p. 382.

GILLETT, MARTIN (1902-1980) — See Supplement, pp. 382-383.

GODFREY OF ADMONT (d. 1165)

First a monk in the Benedictine monastery of St. George in the Black Forest, a friend of Gerhoh of Reichersberg (*qv*), G. became Abbot of Admont in Styria in 1138. In the course of his twenty homilies on Marian feasts of the time, he suggests or develops ideas on Our Lady mostly characteristic of his age.[1] Mary's purification took place at the descent of the Spirit upon her at the Annunciation (*qv*). Here G. was singular among his contemporaries. Mary is the Spouse (*qv*) of Christ; the Song of Songs must be so interpreted.

The principal emphasis, however, is on Mary's part in our salvation. She is the "cause of our

redemption," "the matter of redemption," "the quasi-reparatrix of the human race." Mary was predestined as the helper of Christ the Redeemer, as Eve was Adam's helper. Her compassion was a contribution.

Mary's mediation is described by G. in comprehensive terms. She is the foundation on which God has built the Church, the foundation of our faith; for the first fruits of our faith are belief that she is the Mother of our Creator and Redeemer. She is the source of all the means of salvation—of the Sacraments, which prolong the humanity of Christ. In heaven where she is mistress of all, all the prayers of the saints must pass through her; through her all are sanctified and predestined. She is the universal Mediatress (*qv*). Each person of the Holy Trinity is her lover.

---

[1]Cf. J. Beumer, "Der mariologische gehalt der Predigten Gottfrieds von Admont," in SK, 35(1960), 40-56; U. Faust, O.S.B., "Gottfrieds (von Admont) Mariologie und ihre Quellen," in *Studien und Mitteilungen zur Geschichte des Benediktiner-Ordens*, 75(1964), 340-349.

GOTTSCHALK OF LIMBURG (d. 1098)

Fr. H. Barré (*qv*) thought that G., a Benedictine monk, was "the most remarkable Marian author of his time."[1] With St. Anselm of Lucca (*qv*) and St. Peter Damian (*qv*), he ushers in the age of St. Anselm of Canterbury (*qv*). He was chaplain to the German emperor Henry IV and provost of the church of Our Lady at Aix la Chapelle. He is the author of sequences in honour of Our Lady, and of two *opuscula*, one on the Assumption, the other, a sermon on the Blessed Virgin.[2] The latter item enjoyed much favour in the past. Some manuscripts attribute it to St. Augustine (*qv*); Engelbert of Admont (*qv*) quotes it as from St. Anselm.

The first *opusculum* is an explanation and defense of the author's own sequence on the Assumption, particularly on the words: "The faithful people of God wish [*optat*] that your body should neither be corrupt or dissolved by decay, and that you should now rejoice in the crown of those risen." Objection is made, he suggests, to the fact that he said that it was a wish: ". . . in their judgment I ought to have positively affirmed that in her, that is Our Lady, the resurrection is already complete, that she is in heaven body and soul."[3] G. strives to reconcile his mere wish for Our Lady's resurrection with his exalted idea of her sanctity and proximity to God, and her sinlessness, "except original sin." He speaks of the Spirit's care of her being so entire that "she was never touched by a cloud of sin in either her heart or her body."[4] Though he sees that Mary's sinless character did, in one respect, make her a total exception, he would go no further than the wish. "Who would not wish it, who loves God or the Mother of God? But no one can dare affirm it, who reads the writings of the holy fathers on the resurrection of the dead."[5] Thereon G. adduces texts from St. Augustine (*qv*) and Pseudo-Jerome (*qv*) to continue his apologia.

The sermon on the Blessed Virgin is a development of the theme of Mary's universal mediation (*qv*): "There is nothing between us and God save with you mediating [*te mediante*], mother and virgin."[6] She and she alone was chosen as the means [*materia*] of our saving reconciliation, of the elimination and condemnation of the evil one. Mary, whom G. loves to call Lady, is the door "by which God [came] to us and we must go to him." She is the Mother and Lady of mercy (*qv*). The saints need her help; St. Michael and his angels obey her.

Mary suffered with Christ, "for there were as many wounds inflicted in her heart as outrages which he had to endure."[7] Finally, we are given his statement of the essential doctrine of Mary's universal mediation in regard to grace: "The manifold fullness of that grace, of which we have all received, was wholly poured on you and through you by many streams transmitted . . . all the saints by One alone through you alone were made holy . . . your merit surpasses the prayers of all the saints, indeed the prayer of all the saints is directed to God through you alone."[8] "Mediatress of the Mediator," he writes in his sequence *Fecunda Verbo*, "you are the Mother in whom man is joined to God, God to man."[9] Even in his enthusiastic homily, G. must say that though exalted above the angels, only God knows whether Mary is so "in the body or outside the body." "We want to believe it," he says.

[1]H. Barré, *Prières Anciennes*, 259. [2]G. M. Dreves, "Godescalcus Lintpurgensis. Gottschalk, Mönch von Limburg und Hardt, und Propst von Aachen, ein Prosator des XI Jahr.," in *Hymnologische Beiträge*, 1, (Leipzig, 1897), 91-107, 159-166; AH, 50, 339-369. Cf. H. Barré, *loc. cit.* [3]G. M. Dreves, *op. cit.*, in *Hymnologische Beiträge*, 1, (Leipzig, 1897), 94. [4]G. M. Dreves, *op. cit.*, 97; *id.*, in BSFEM, 7(1949), 77-80; H. Graef, *Mary*, 1, 208-209. [5]G. M. Dreves, *op. cit.*, 99. [6]*ibid.*, *op. cit.*, 159. [7]*ibid.*, *op. cit.*, 164. [8]*ibid.*, *op. cit.*, 165. [9]"Fecunda Verbo," ed. by G. M. Dreves, in *Hymnologische Beiträge*, 1, (Leipzig, 1897), 170.

GREGORY THE GREAT, ST., DOCTOR OF THE CHURCH
(c. 540-604)

This great Pope gives occasional comments on Marian themes or Marian biblical texts.[1] On the *Unus Mediator* Pauline text (1 Tim 2:5), he shows at length that it was as Son of the Father and of the Virgin that Christ was set in this unique position. "He was from the Father without a mother before the ages, the same at the end of the ages from a mother without a father."[2] On Mt 12:48-50, G. thinks that Mary momentarily represented the Synagogue, which Christ no longer recognized. Commenting on the Cana (*qv*) passage he interprets 2:4: "That I can work a miracle comes to me from my Father, not from my mother" . . . "I do not recognize you in [working] the miracle which I do not do from the nature I got from you. When the hour of death will have come I shall recognize you as my Mother for it is from you that I have the power to die."[3] G. illustrates the *virginitas in partu* (*qv*) from the risen Christ's power to pass through closed doors. A passage in the commentary on the first Book of Kings, in which Mary is compared to a mountain to show her superiority to the angels, is probably authentic, but it is part of a book which may have been retouched by another after leaving G.'s hand.[4] G. saw the Incarnation as an espousal by the Father of the eternal Son with human nature in the womb of the Virgin.

[1]EMBP, 1242-1250. Cf. R. Laurentin, *Traité*, 1, 136; B. Capelle, O.S.B., in RevBen, 41(1929), 205; *Clavis Patrum Latinorum*, 1719. [2]*Moralium Libri*, 52, 85, in PL 76, 90. [3]*Epistolae, Lib. X, Ep. 39*, in PL 77, 1098. [4]*In I Regum, Lib. 1, cap. 1, 5*, in PL 79, 25C-26B.

GREGORY NAREK, ST. (c. 944-1010)

An Armenian sacred writer, known because of his sacred verse as the Pindar of the Armenians, G. was the author of an apologetic work against a sect of the times, a commentary on the Song of Songs (*qv*), and panegyrics and hymns for the principal feasts, many of which have passed into the Armenian Liturgy.[1] His principal work is *Mystical Elegies*, ninety-five lyrical compositions entitled "Colloquies with God springing from the depth of the heart." Number eighty deals with Mary. He devotes one lengthy panegyric, *Kommark Khempita*, entirely to her. G.'s dominant idea was the divine motherhood, source of all Mary's glory. He extolled her singular holiness (*qv*), and believed in her bodily Assumption (*qv*).

[1]Italian tr. of *Kommark Khempita, Discorso panegirico sulla Beatissima Vergine*, (Venice, San Lazaro, 1904); J. Bover, S.J., "Un notable mariologo armeno: S. Gregorio de Narek," in *Rev. Espan. de Teologia*, (1941), 409-417; G. Amadonni, O.P.Mech., "Il piu grande dottore mariano della Chiesa Armena: S. Gregorio di Narek," in ASC, V, 80-95; J. Mécénian, S.J., *La Vierge Marie dans la litterature mediévale de l'Arménie, Grégoire de Narek et Nerses de Lambron*, (Beyrouth, Institut de Lettres Orientales (Armenian Collection), 1954).

GREGORY OF NAZIANZUS, ST.
(*c.* 329-*c.* 390)

Like his fellow Cappadocians, St. Basil (*qv*), his great friend, and St. Gregory of Nyssa (*qv*), Basil's brother, a champion of Nicene doctrine, G. deals with Our Lady in slight passages scattered through his works. Two generations before Ephesus (*qv*), he was using the title *Theotokos* (*qv*).[1] After an explanation of the unity of the incarnate Son of God, which ends "so that by the same whole man who was God, the whole man who had fallen into sin should be remade," he stated: "If anyone does not believe the holy Mary to be *Theotokos*, he is without the Godhead. If anyone should say that Christ passed through the Virgin as through a channel, and was not formed in her at once in a divine and human way, divine because without the work of man, human because subject to the law of human conception, he is equally atheistic."[2] This is a rejection of Appolinarianism and also an anticipation of Ephesus. In another passage, G. showed how the latter Council would bring doctrinal completion to Nicaea: "For the whole Adam fell by the fatal taste. Accordingly, in a human manner and beyond the human manner in a venerable womb of the Virgin incarnate (O miracle unbelievable to weak minds), he came a God and mortal, uniting the two natures in one, one hidden, the other manifest to men."[3] "The God man was sprung from the Virgin's womb, joined together by the Spirit of the high God." ... "The Mother was the temple of Christ, Christ [the temple] of the Word."[4] In the same passage, he seems to teach the *virginitas in partu*—"the virgin untouched gave birth to him."

For G., Mary was the beginning of virginity in its fullest and most honoured sense; women should practice virginity to become "mothers of Christ."[5] Mary herself was "undefiled" (*achrantos*). G., who was careful to eliminate all sin from Christ in his birth, used of Mary a word which was destined to influence subsequent thinking in the East. "He took all things human save sin: conceived of a Virgin who had been purified previously [*prokathartheise*] by the Spirit in soul and body (for it was becoming to honour child-bearing and show preference for virginity)."[6] The strongest word used before G. was by Cyril of Jerusalem (*qv*), who spoke of *hagiasmos* in the same context. The theory has been invoked in discussion about eastern opinions on the Immaculate Conception (*qv*, and see also PURIFICATION).

In the development of a doctrine of Mary's intercession, a text from G. is quoted. Thecla, a virgin tempted by the devil, thinks of the Virgin Mary, as a "suppliant beseeching her to give assistance to a virgin in danger."[7]

[1]Cf. *Or. 29, 4*, in PG 36, 79A. Cf. bibliography to article on "Basil, St. Doctor of the Church"; CMP, II, 246-259; EMBP, 306-310; DSp, VI, 932-972; ClavisG, II, 179-209. [2]*Ep.101*, in PG 37, 177C. [3]*Poemata dogmatica, 9*, in PG 37, 460A. [4]*Poemata ad alios*, in PG 37, 1565. [5]*Or. 38, 1*, in PG 36, 313A. [6]*Or. 38, 13*, in PG 36, 325B; *Or. 45, 9*, in PG 36, 633D. [7]*Or. 24, 11*, in PG 35, 1181A.

GREGORY OF NYSSA, ST., DOCTOR OF THE CHURCH
(*c.* 335-394)

The mystical theologian among the great Cappadocian Fathers, influenced by Origen and the Alexandrian school, G. quantitatively exceeded either Basil (*qv*) or Gregory of Nazianzus (*qv*) on Marian themes. His contribution was significant on two points. Questions of authenticity, however, arise. Despite the query by Mgr. Jouassard (see FATHERS OF THE CHURCH). G.'s authorship of the Life of St. Gregory the Wonderworker (BHG 715), is tentatively accepted by many. So is the sermon on the Birth of Christ (BHG 1915) and that on the Annunciation (BHG 1144h), found in the *Patrologia Graeca* among the spurious works of St. John Chrysostom (*qv*).[1] A number of homilies of doubtful authorship await verification: BHG 1077n, 1139n, 1148n; and Auctarium 1122x.

Much of G.'s thinking about Mary centers on her virginity. He uses the image of the "virgin earth." "Wisdom [i.e. Christ] according to what is said built himself a house, forming into a man the earth taken from the Virgin, through whom he was mingled with humanity."[2] He applies Old Testament texts to Mary: e.g. Is 7:14 (see EMMANUEL); an unidentified passage on the "young woman or heifer who has given birth and has not given birth"; and Is 8:3, on the prophetess.[3] He sees Miryam, Moses' sister as a type of Mary, the tympanum which she played after crossing the Red Sea being a type of Our Lady's virginity.[4]

In the sermon on the Birth of Christ, G. gives an account of Mary's birth in answer to her mother's prayer in imitation of the mother of Samuel. She also would dedicate her child to God. Mary was duly brought up in the Temple, and it is in this context that G. expressed his opinion that Mary had bound herself to virginity before the Annunciation (see VOW OF VIRGINITY). It would seem absurd to the priests that she should be married: "It would be akin to sacrilege if a man were to become master of a gift sacred to God."[5] They then thought of espousing Mary to someone who would ensure the custody of her virginity, for which misson Joseph seemed most suited. Mary's reply to Gabriel, "How shall this be since I do not know man?," is taken to indicate her purpose of virginity. For she felt obliged "to maintain untouched and as a sacred offering entire the flesh consecrated to God."[6] He enlarges on the descent of the Holy Spirit and on the "Power of the most high."

G. is more insistent on the *virginitas in partu*, than any of his contemporaries. Some of the images he used to expound it have been mentioned. Another was the burning bush seen by Moses on Mount Horeb. As the bush kindles, and is not burned, "so this is the Virgin who brings forth the light and is not corrupted."[7] Among the mysteries of Bethlehem is: "The Child [is] wrapped in swaddling clothes and laid in a manger and the mother, an incorrupt virgin after childbirth, embraces her Son."[8] G. relates the apocryphal story of the slaying of Zechariah between the Temple and the altar, because he allowed Mary after childbirth to take her place among the virgins. Against Apollinarius (qv), he proclaims fully the real physical motherhood of Mary.

G. almost anticipates the exuberant effusions of the great Byzantines: "You are adorned beyond every creature, beautified above the heavens, you shine more than the sun, are exalted above the angels; you were not taken away to the heavens, but remaining on earth you drew to yourself the Lord of heaven and the King of the universe."[9] Mary was always a virgin, undefiled, "pious and dutiful, the honour of our nature, the gate of our life, the one who won salvation for us."[10]

This eastern doctor expresses an idea which would be more amply developed in the West by St. Augustine (qv): "What was achieved in the body of Mary, the inviolate Virgin, by the perfect divinity of Christ, which shone forth in that Virgin, the same will happen in the soul of everyone who is adorned with chastity and in the virginal way follows reason as a guide."[11] This is already an intuition of the relationship between the virgin motherhood and grace in the souls of the just. With G., it is limited to those with the virginal engagement, but extension will be logical and the final formula will occur in LG 65.

G. also takes up the Eve (qv)-Mary theme: "Woman was defended by woman; the first opened the way to sin; the present one served to open the way to justice. The former followed the advice of the serpent, the latter brought forth the slayer of the serpent and brought to light the author of light. The former introduced sin through the tree, the latter brings in grace through the tree"[12]—i.e. the tree of the Cross.

G. gives Mary the title *Theotokos* (qv), which accords with his theology of the Incarnation.[13] His insight on Mary's vow of virginity remains a starting-point in thought on the subject. His other novelty in patristic writing occurs in his life of St. Gregory the Wonderworker (qv). It is an account of a vision of the Blessed Virgin to this saint. She was accompanied by St. John the Evangelist (qv), and she exhorts him to make known to Gregory "the mystery of true piety," which John said he was ready to do, for "such was her wish."[14]

G. accentuates the note of joy in his writing about Mary. As Eve introduced death through sin and gave birth in sorrow and pain, "it was fitting that the Mother of life should begin her pregnancy with joy and complete her giving birth in joy"[15]—an interesting addition to the Eve-Mary theme. Since Mary is "the root of joy" and should fittingly spread the news of joy manifest in the Resurrection, G. thought that she was "the other Mary" who, according to Mt 28:1, came to the tomb on Easter morning with Mary Magdalen.[16] Accepting the eastern view that the Brothers of the Lord (qv) were sons of Joseph by an earlier marriage, G. suggested clumsily that Mary, "the mother of James and Joseph" (Mt 27:56) was really the *Theotokos* (qv), and that the device was used by the evangelists to conceal the virgin motherhood from the Jews. These, he thought, would have killed her had they known it.[17]

[1]R. Laurentin, *Traité*, I, 161, 163. Cf. J. Rousse, in DSp, 6, 972-1011, and bibliography in article on St. Basil; G. Jouassard, *Maria*, I, 88, n.22; ClavisG, II, 209-230. [2]*Contra Apollin.*, 9, in PG 45, 1141C. [3]*Testimonia contra Judaeos, 3*, in PG 46, 208ff. [4]*De Virginitate, XIX*, in PG 46, 395A-398A. [5]*Sermo in nat. Dni*, in PG 46, 1140A. [6]PG 46, 1140D. [7]PG 46, 1136B. [8]PG 46, 1141B. [9]*Sermo de Annunt.*, in PG, 765. [10]*op. cit.*, in PG 62, 767. [11]*De Virginitate, II*, in PG 46, 324B. Cf. M. Aubineau, in SC 119, 268. [12]PG 46, 1148AB. [13]*De Virginitate, XIII*, in PG 46, 377D; *Epist. 3, 24*, in PG 46, 1022A. [14]*Vita S. Greg. Thaum.*, in PG 46, 912C. Cf. M. Jugie, A.A., "Les Homélies mariales attribuées à Gregoire le Thaumaturge," in AB, 43(1925), 95. [15]*In Cant. Canticorum, 13*, in PG 44, 1053C. [16]*De Resurrectione, 2*, in PG 46, 633B. [17]*op. cit.*, in PG 46, 648A.

GREGORY PALAMAS, (d. 1359)

The great teacher of Hesychasm, G., like the others of the school named from him (Palamites) has a rich Marian doctrine. The emphasis is on Mary's mediation, which is related to the absolute, universal primacy of Christ. The Marian doctrine is found in his homilies: on the Nativity of Mary (BHG 1130); two on the Presentation (BHG 1091, 1095); on the Annunciation (BHG 1118g); on the vision of the risen Christ, *In Dominica Unguentiferarum* (BHG 1100); on the Dormition (BHG 1145); and on the genealogy of Christ. Some of these homilies are printed in PG 151, others must be sought in the rare edition by Sophocles Oikonomos.[1]

Through the divine maternity, Mary's destiny has for G. a vastness which includes all creatures in its influence, and calls for the highest gifts in her person. "Mary is the cause of what had gone before her, the pioneer of what has come after her, she distributes eternal goods; she is the thought of the prophets, the head of the Apostles, the support of martyrs, the certainty of doctors. She is the glory of earth, the joy of heaven, the ornament of all creation. She is the principle, the source, and the root of ineffable good things. She is the summit and the fulfillment of all that is holy."[2] Mary, G. thought, was on the confines of the created and uncreated; she stands alone between God and the whole human race. She made God the Son of man, and makes men the sons of God. He thought that "all the divinely inspired Scripture was written because of the Virgin, who brought forth God."

Like many Easterns, G. thought that Mary was born of sterile parents. He also thought that during her stay in the Temple she practised Hesychasm, thus preparing herself for her future mission. Again and again, his praise of Mary is in superlative terms: "Today a new world and a wonderful paradise have appeared. In it and from it a new Adam is born to reform the old Adam and renew the whole world . . . . God has kept this Virgin for himself from before all ages. He chose her from among all generations and bestowed on her grace higher than that [given] to all others, making of her, before her wondrous childbirth, the saint of saints, giving her the honours of his own house in the Holy of Holies . . . . Wishing to create an image of absolute beauty and to manifest clearly to angels and to men the power of his art, God made Mary truly all beautiful . . . he made of her a blend of all divine, angelic and human perfections, a sublime beauty embellishing the two worlds, rising from earth to heaven and surpassing even this latter." . . . "Must not the one who was to give birth to the fairest among the sons of men have been comparable to him in everything and been clothed by her Son with marvellous beauty? This Son was, in fact, to resemble her in every aspect so that whoever would see Jesus would at once recognize, because of this perfect resemblance, the Virgin his Mother."[3]

M. Jugie argues from such passages that G. was expressing a doctrine of Immaculate Conception. G. also speaks of the Holy Spirit choosing and purifying the series of Mary's ancestors. J. Meyendorff thinks that Christ was the only exception to Original Sin in the thought of G.: "He alone was not conceived in iniquity . . . . If he had come from [male] seed, he would not have been a new man; belonging to the old race and heir to Adam's error, he would not have been able to receive within him the fullness of the divinity."[4] G. thought that Mary was purified (see PURIFICATION), and he spoke of the sentence against Adam and Eve changing into a blessing at the moment of the Annunciation. Meyendorff thinks that he would have held the doctrine of the Immaculate Conception if he had had the western idea of original sin.

G.'s idea of Mary's mediation is not open to doubt or question. It is implicit in his theory of her destiny, her place in creation. It is made explicit: "No divine gifts can reach either angels or men, save through her mediation . As one cannot enjoy the light of a lamp . . . save through the medium of this lamp so every movement towards God, every impulse towards good coming from him is unrealizable save through the mediation of the Virgin." She does not cease to spread benefits on all creatures, not only on us men, but on the celestial incorporeal ranks."[5]

Mary, says G., received gifts of knowledge precociously. The mutual love between her and Jesus was perfect. She was the first to see the risen Jesus, and was herself bodily assumed with but slight delay after death.[6]

---

[1]*In Annunt.*, in PG 151, 165-178; *In Dominica Unguentiferarum*, in PG 151, 235-248; *In Dorm.*, in PG 151, 459-474; *In Christi genealogiam*, ed. of Sophocles Oikonomos, (Athens, 1861, copy in Bollandist Library), 212-224; *In Nativit.*, ibid., 1-16; *In Praesent.*, I, II, ibid., 120-130, 131-180. Cf. Beck, 712-715; M. Jugie, *L'Immaculée Conception*, 225-240; id., *L'Assomption*, 331-332; M. Gordillo, S.J., "L'Immacolata Concezione . . . nella Mariologia dei Palamiti," in V.I., 170-195; ibid., in DTC, XI, 1735-1776; S. de Simio, *La Mariologia nelle omelie di Gregorio Palamas*, (Vieste, La Viestiana, 1958); J. Meyendorff, *Introduction a l'étude de Grégoire Palamas*, (Paris, 1959), 317-322; M. J. Le Guillou, *The Tradition of Eastern Orthodoxy*, (Faith and Fact, London, 1962), 100ff. Cf. esp. B. Schultze, in MO, 358-367; H. Graef, *Mary*, I. [2]177B [3]Ed. of Sophocles Oikonomos, (Athens, 1861), 6; ibid., 214. [4]ibid., 230; PG 151, 192C. [5]Ed. of Sophocles Oikonomos, (Athens, 1861), 159; PG 151, 472A. [6]*In Dorm.*, in PG 151, 468A.

GREGORY VII, ST., POPE (d. 1085)

The great reforming Pope of the eleventh century reveals in his letters and in public statements a strong sense of Mary's power and sensitive devotion to her.[1] Mathilda of Tuscany, a supporter of the Papacy, was also his spiritual disciple, and since he dissuaded her from taking the veil as a nun, he entrusted her to a wise tutor, St. Anselm of Lucca (qv). Prayers composed for the Countess reflect G.'s thinking. Thus, G. in his own letter to Mathilda: "Of the Mother of the Lord, to whom I have entrusted, do entrust, and shall not cease to entrust you, whom heaven and earth do not cease to praise, though they cannot do so as she deserves, what shall I say to you?"[2] Again: "Hold to this without

doubt that since she is higher, better and holier than any other mother, she is all the more clement and gentle towards converted sinners . . . . Put away, therefore, the wish to sin and, prostrate before her, shed tears from a contrite and humble heart. You will, I promise without doubt, find her readier than a mother in the flesh and meeker in love for you."[3]

The Pope, in official acts, liked to mention Mary in an important role. Thus in the formula of excommunication against Henry IV occur the words, "confident in the judgment and mercy of God and of his most merciful Mother, the ever Virgin Mary."

Other formulas reveal G.'s profound theology of Mary: "May Almighty God, from whom all good things come, by the merits of Our Lady, the heavenly queen, and by the intercesson of the blessed Apostles Peter and Paul strengthen and keep your hearts . . . ."[4] "May Almighty God by the merits of the Lady on high and by the prayers of the blessed Apostles Peter and Paul and of blessed Ambrose enlighten your minds and establish them in his law . . . ."[5] The difference between reference to Mary's merits and the saints' prayers is significant and needs no great explanation.

---

[1]Cf. J. M. Salgado, O.M.I., "La dévotion mariale de S. Grégoire VII, son rayonnement et sa source," in Zagreb Congress, III, 583-595. [2]PL 148, 328AB. [3]PL 148, 328B. [4]*Letters*, in PL 148, 453C. [5]op. cit., in PL 148, 446C.

GREGORY OF TOURS, ST. (538-594)

A zealous pastor in an age of transition, G.'s principal interest was in historical matters. What he says about Mary is brief but in one instance is an important testimony to belief.[1] In the prologue to his *History of the Franks*, he inserts an act of faith in Mary's perpetual virginity. In the *Books of Miracles*, he speaks of miracles at a well at Bethlehem, or due to "relics" of Our Lady, and he mentions the Basilica built by the Emperor Constantine in honour of Our Lady. It is his testimony to belief in the Assumption, the first of its kind in the West, that is noteworthy: "Finally when blessed Mary having completed the course of this life, was to be called from the world, all the apostles gathered to her house from their different regions. And when they had heard that she was to be taken from the world, together they kept watch with her; and lo, the Lord Jesus came with his angels and taking her soul, he gave it to the archangel Michael and withdrew. At dawn the apostles raised her body with a pallet and they placed it in a vault and they guarded it awaiting the coming of the Lord. And lo, a second time the Lord stood by them and he ordered the holy body to be taken and borne to paradise; there having rejoined the soul exultant with his elect, it enjoys the good things of eternity which shall know no end."[2]

[1]EMBP, 1135-1136. [2]*Libri Miraculorum*, in PL 71, 708.

GREGORY THE WONDER-WORKER, St.
(d. *c.* 270)

Three Marian homilies attributed to this author are almost certainly spurious.[1] He is of interest to the history of devotion to Our Lady because St. Gregory of Nyssa (*qv*) narrates an apparition of Our Lady to him. The story occurs in the *Vita Gregorii Thaumaturgi*,[2] which is probably genuine, though one patristic scholar, Mgr. G. Jouassard, thought it spurious. Mary, accompanied by St. John the Apostle, appears in the night, more than life-size, surrounded by light, "as if a brilliant torch had been lit." She tells John to make known to the young man, that is Gregory, the mystery of piety (the true faith). He said that he was ready to do this for the Mother of the Lord, because such was her wish.

[1]PG 10, 1145C-1178B. Cf. R. Laurentin, *Traité*, I, 156-157; M. Jugie, A.A., "Les Homélies mariales attribuées a Grégoire le Thaumaturge," in AB, 43(1925), 86-95. [2]PG 46, 893A-957D, (apparition, 909-913A); G. Jouassard, *Maria*, I, 84, n.22

GROSSETESTE, ROBERT (*c.* 1168-1253)

Philosopher and theologian, founder of the Franciscan school at Oxford, of which university he was probably the first chancellor. According to William of Ware (*qv*), he had defended the Immaculate Conception (*qv*).[1] Recent scholarship indicates that in an early sermon he admitted the possibility of the privilege and in a sermon given at the end of his life, he affirmed the fact. "We believe," he says in the first, "that she was purified of the original [sin] in her mother's womb."[2] He first speaks of purification and sanctification after the infusion of the soul as a possibility, and then goes on, "in another way she could have been cleansed and sanctified in the very infusion of the rational soul, and in this way it would have been purification not from sin which was in her at any time, but that would have been in her if she had not been sanctified in the very infusion of the rational soul."[3] G's final opinion, however, was given thus: "It was more fitting that the God man . . . should be conceived and born of a woman who was free of the movements of concupiscence of the flesh and to be free of them, never in any way contaminated or stained by sin . . . It is fitting, therefore, that the Mother of God and man should be purified from the *fomes* of concupiscence and the stain of sin in the first moment of her life in the womb."[4] The author had the idea of preventive redemption: "It is likewise said that she was redeemed not from a fault that was in her, but that would have been in her if she was not preserved by grace."[5]

[1]*Bibl. Franc. Scholastica Medii Aevii*, 3, Quaracchi, 1904, p. 6. Cf. E. Longpré, "Robert Grosseteste et l'Immaculée Conception," *Arch. Franc. Hist.*, 26(1933), 550-51; Servus of St. Anthony's, O.F.M.Cap., "Robert Grosseteste and the Immaculate Conception," in *Collect. Franc.*, 28(1958), 211-227. [2]Servus of St. Anthony's, *art. cit.*, pp. 221-222. [3]*Ibid.* [4]*Ibid.* p. 220. [5]E. Longpré, *art. cit., ibid.*

GUERRIC OF IGNY, BL. (d. 1157)

A Cistercian, who may be included in the circle of St. Bernard (*qv*), G. spent some time at Clairvaux after abandoning the eremitical life at Bernard's suggestion, but before becoming the second abbot of the monastery of Igny in the diocese of Rheims. His Marian doctrine is contained in thirteen sermons, of which four are on the Purification, three on the Annunciation, four on the Assumption, and two on the Nativity of Mary.[1]

G.'s fundamental interest in Marian theology is the spiritual motherhood (*qv*), and his most important passage on this topic is quoted in the reformed Roman Breviary. "The first Eve is not so much a mother as a stepmother, since she handed on to her children an inheritance of certain death rather than the beginning of light. She is indeed called the mother of all the living, but she turned out to be more precisely the murderer of the living, or mother of the dead, since the only fruit of her child-bearing was death. And as Eve was incapable of fulfilling the vocation of her title, Mary consummated the mystery. She herself, like the Church of which she is the type, is a mother of all who are reborn to life. She is in fact the mother of the Life by which everyone lives, and when she brought it forth from herself she in some way brought to rebirth all those who were to live that life."[2] The word *forma*, translated type in this passage, is basic to G.'s thought and implies a certain causality, first on the part of Christ, whose life is the *forma* of the believer's life, and then on the part of Mary, who participates in the causality implied. G. urged his hearers to give practical meaning to this typology: "Let him take in his hands [as Simeon did] the Child whom Mary, his Mother brings, that is let him grasp with love the Word of God, which the Church his mother offers him."[3] The soul becomes, in a way, a mother to Christ within it.

Mary's holiness was assured before the Incarnation, and G. uses the word "purified," but "the conception of the Saint of saints is the supreme sanctification, and none is holier than she who became Mother of holiness itself."[4] "O Son of God, nothing, nothing certainly displeased you in this abode which was yours, which you deigned to gaze upon so willingly and reward so generously."[5]

For G., Mary is the Mediatress (*qv*); the contrast with Eve is touched on in the sermons.[6]

He hints at the bodily Assumption (*qv*), but does not affirm it explicitly. Through Mary we have had a share in the Fruit of life. Her position is unique: "Mary, I say, has been exalted above the choirs of angels, so that the Mother contemplates nothing above her save the Son, the Queen admires nothing above her save the King, our Mediatress venerates nothing above her save the Mediator."[7]

[1]PL 185; critical ed. by J. Morson and H. Costello, SC 166, sermons on the Purification, p. 306-383; SC 202, on the Annunciation, p. 108-163, on the Assumption, p. 414-471, on the Nativity, p. 472-497; intr.esp. p. 36-41; cf. J. Morson and H. Costello, in DSp, VI, 1113-1121; cf. Cl. Bodard, *Le Christ, Marie et l'Eglise dans la prédication du Bx. Guerric*, Coll. Ordinis Cist. Reform., 19(1957), p. 273-299; B. Pennington O.C.S.O., *Guerric of Igny and his Sermons for the feast of the Assumption*, St. Monastica, 12(1970), p. 87-95. [2]*Serm. 1 in Assumpt.* SC 202, p. 416-18; cp. Roman Breviary, second reading for Our Lady *in sabbato.* [3]*Serm. 3 in Purif.* SC 166, 344. [4]*Serm. 4 in Purif.* 360. [5]*Serm. 1 in Assumpt.*, 424. [6]SC 202, 416; 472. [7]*Serm. 1 in Assumpt.* 7, 426; cp. SC 166, 334.

H

HAIL MARY, THE

One of the prayers to Our Lady most frequently recited, essential to the Rosary and the Angelus (*qqv*), it has taken permanence because of the importance which the Church attaches to these devotions. It is in two parts, each with its own history. The first part is made up of two salutations in Luke (1:28, 1:42, by Gabriel and Elizabeth). The union of the two in one formula is found in the Liturgies of St. James of Antioch and St. Mark of Alexandria, which may go back to the fifth or even fourth century—likewise, in the Liturgy of the Abyssinian Jacobites, and in the ritual of St. Severus (538). Egyptian *ostraca* of the sixth or seventh century have an addition: "Because you have conceived Christ, the Son of God, redeemer of our souls." *Maria* is added in some copies of the Liturgy of St. James; *Maria, Theotokos Parthenos* in some Greek churches.

The two greetings (Lk 1:28, 42) are both attributed to Gabriel in the gospel of Pseudo-Matthew (see APOCRYPHA), and in a ninth century hymn, *Deus qui mundum crimine jacentem.*[2] A mutilated inscription in the Roman church of Santa Maria Antiqua has the same reading.

In the western Liturgy, the prayer formula is assigned from the seventh century as an Offertory antiphon for the feast of the Annunciation, Wednesday in December Quarter Tense, and the fourth Sunday in Advent. The Hail Mary was undoubtedly made popular by the Little Office of Our Lady. Stories related by St. Peter Damian,[3] Hermann of Tournai,[4] and of a Polish princess, daughter of Mesko II, and wife of King Iziaslaw of Kiev,[5] show that the prayer was in private use in monastic and lay circles in the eleventh century. It was associated with the joy of the Annunciation. The name Jesus is sometimes said to have been added by Urban IV (1261-1264). It was certainly part of the prayer before the fourteenth century. An official ruling about the Hail Mary occurs for the first time in the statutes of Odo of Silliac, bishop of Paris, dated 1198: "Let priests ceaselessly exhort the people to say the Lord's prayer, the 'I believe in God' and the salutation of the Blessed Virgin."[6]

The second part of the prayer, prompted by the need to join petition to praise, may have been influenced by the Litanies of the Saints, introduced towards the end of the seventh century with the invocation to Mary, *Sancta Maria, ora pro nobis*. By the fifteenth century, two endings are found: *Sancta Maria, Mater Dei, ora pro nobis peccatoribus*, (by St. Bernardine of Siena, the Carthusians, and in Synodal Constitutions of Augsburg and Constance); *Sancta Maria, Mater Dei, ora pro nobis nunc et in hora mortis nostrae, Amen*, (by the Servites, in a Roman Breviary, and, with variations, in some German dioceses).[7] The current form was fixed in the sixteenth century, adopted by the Mercedarians, Camaldolese and Franciscans early in the century. It was included in the reformed Breviary (1568) by St. Pius V until, by the decree *Cum nostra* (23 March, 1955), it was omitted.

---

[1]Cf. H. Leclercq, "Marie (Je vous salue)," in DACL, X, 2043-2062; H. Thurston, S.J., *Familiar Prayers*, ed. by P. Grosjean, S.J., (London, 1953), 90-114; *ibid.*, "Ave Maria," in DSp, I, 1161-1164; J. Laurenceau, O.P., "Les débuts de la récitation privée de l'antienne 'Ave Maria' en occident avant la fin du XIe siècle," in Zagreb Congress, II, 231-246; D. Montagna, O.S.M., "La formula dell Ave Maria a Vicenza in un documento del 1423," in MM, 26(1964), 234-236; G. M. Roschini, O.S.M., *Maria Santissima*, IV, 60, 163, 232-236; R. Schnackenburg and H. Dünninger, "Ave Maria," in LexMar, 477-486. [2]AH 51, 143. [3]*De bono suffragiorum*, in PL 145, 564BC. [4]MGH, Scriptores XIV 298-299. [5]H. Barré, C.S.Sp., *Prières Anciennes*, 278-286. [6]"Statuta Odonis," in Mansi, 22, 681. [7]R. Schnackenburg and H. Dünninger, "Ave Maria," in LexMar, 481.

HANDMAID OF THE LORD

Of the many titles of Our Lady found in Christian literature, this is the one she herself chose (Lk 1:38). *Doule Kuriou* is translated *Ancilla Domini* in the Vulgate. *Ebed* (a servant) occurs 807 times in MT and *Doulos* (of which Luke here uses the feminine) is used by the Septuagint to render the title slightly less often than *Pais* (327 to 340 times). Other renderings are much less frequent. Mary repeats the title in the *Magnificat* (Lk 1:48). It is used in the plural (Acts 2:18), but not anywhere applied to an individual save Mary.[1]

The word, which is somewhat clouded by the English rendering "handmaid," when understood in Old Testament servant theology, is a high compliment. It implies certainty on the transcendence of God and submission to his design. God's might and sovereignty, which evoke and answer "service," is a theme of the *Magnificat* which insinuates that Mary is a type of Israel, God's servant, *pais*. It pays honour to Abraham, God's servant (see Gen 18:3). The

Magnificat points to the "servant's" characteristic quality, *tapeinosis* (Lk 1:48), which may be linked with Christ's description of himself as *tapeinos te cardia*, a lowly of heart. The lowly were God's favourites, the Poor of Yahweh.

The Lucan titles form a striking parallel with the Christological hymn (see Phil 2:6-11). Mary is the *doule* for whom God has done great things, whom all generations will call blessed. Christ "emptied himself, taking the form of a servant [*morphen doulou*] being born in the likeness of men." He humbled himself, becoming obedient unto death, death on a cross. "Therefore God has highly exalted him and bestowed on him the name which is above every name."

---

[1]Cf. W. Zimmerli and J. Jeremias, *The Servant of God*, (London, SCM, 1957); A. Blanco Ruiz, C.M.F., *Sierva de Yave*, (Madrid, Coculsa, 1966); J. Vogt, "Ecce Ancilla Domini, Eine Untersuchung zum sozialen Motiv des antiken Marienbildes," in *Vigiliae Christianae*, 23(1969), 241-263; M. Miguens, O.F.M., "Servidora del Senor," in MSS, IV, 73-110; A. Spindeler, "Knecht Gottes und Madg des Herrn," in MSS, IV, 111-121; H. B. Beverly, "The Handmaid of the Lord," in *Interpretation*, 30(1976), 397.

HEART OF MARY, THE

In western Europe, from medieval times, the Heart of Mary begins to appear within the complex of devotional ideals and symbols which are distinctive of Latin Christian, later Catholic culture. With the full emergence of devotion to the Sacred Heart of Jesus in the seventeenth century, the idea became more explicit, was more widely adopted. To this development, St. John Eudes made an important contribution. After the decadence in Marian piety which marked the eighteenth century, the revival in the nineteenth was in places associated with devotion to the Heart of Mary. In the present century, Fatima has been an important factor in the cult.[1]

Sacred Scripture: Heart in Sacred Scripture is the focal point of spirit and courage, of interior insight, of man's planning and volition, of the ethical decisions of the whole, undivided man.[2] There are two explicit references to the heart of Mary in the New Testament, Lk 2:19, and Lk 2:51. "Mary kept all these things pondering them in her heart." Here there is question of knowledge, a certain kind of experiential knowledge, more than the love which in later times will be attributed to the heart; one does not exclude the other. Simeon's oracle on the sword, as interpreted by Fr. Benoit, signifies

Mary bearing the drama of her people, "in her living person, in her heart of flesh." Theologians of the Heart of Jesus see in certain Old Testament messianic texts a foreshadowing of the later revelation, Ps 40:8 for example, "I delight to do thy will, O my God, thy law is within my heart." (cp. Heb 10:5-9). The prophetic announcements in Jeremiah and Ezek referring to Israel may be interpreted typologically of Mary, the embodiment of her people. "But this is the covenant which I will make with the house of Israel after those days, says the Lord: I will put my law within them and I will write it upon their hearts; and I will be their God and they will be my people." (Jer 31:33). "A new heart I will give you, and a new spirit I will put within you; and I will take out of your flesh the heart of stone and give you a heart of flesh." (Ez 36:26).

History: In patristic and medieval writings, many texts have been found which use the heart in Mary's case to designate her spirit, the center of her personality, from which response to divine things came, where the Holy Spirit works, wherein she cooperated in salvation, wherein lie treasures of grace for men. Thus Richard of St. Laurent (*qv*) writes: "From the heart of the Virgin went forth faith and consent, the two things by which the salvation of the world was begun."[3] "The Holy Spirit," says Godfrey of Admont (*qv*), "has placed and gathered in the Heart, without stain, of the Virgin Mary, all the elements of healing grace, that is, all the gifts of compassion and reconciliation. Thus as there are in the human race illnesses of great variety, springing from weaknesses, this Heart contains also numerous and varied remedies to bring health and healing to souls that are sick."[4]

In the East, Symeon Metaphrastes had expressed the idea of Mary's compassion in relation to her heart. "Your side has been pierced, but my heart has been pierced also." Arnold of Bonneval related the compassion to Christ's sacrifice. "Christ and his Mother had both but one will, and offered but one holocaust to God; she by the blood of her heart, he by the blood of his body."[5]

All of the quotations of this kind are taken from treatises on other subjects, where they occur transiently, as it were. The first known prayer to the Heart of Mary, composed about 1184 by Ekbert of Schönau (*qv*), is devoted entirely to the theme. It opens thus: "I shall speak to your Heart O Mary, I shall speak to your pure Heart, Mistress of the world, and I shall adore at the holy temple of God, from the most profound depths of my soul. From deep within me I shall salute your Immaculate Heart which first beneath the sun was found worthy to welcome the Son of God, coming forth from the bosom of the Father." Ekbert continues figuratively, recalling the Ark of Sanctification and ends on this note: "Let every soul magnify you, O Mother of sweetness, and the tongues of all the devout praise the happiness of your Heart whence our salvation flowed."[6]

St. Mechtild of Hackeborn (1240-1298) and St. Gertrude the Great (1256-1302) greatly influenced the spirit of their Cistercian monastery at Helfta, a high center of feminine culture, to interest in devotion to Mary's heart. In the next century, St. Bridget of Sweden (*qv*) has a somewhat similar thought to that of Arnold of Bonneval. Medieval theologians, especially the great Franciscans, return to the theme, as do the Jesuits later. We find St. Francis de Sales dedicating his *Treatise on the Love of God* to "the most amiable Heart of the well-beloved of Jesus." The notable advance made by St. John Eudes was due to his success in having Mass in honour of the Heart of Mary accepted (celebrated for the first time on 8 May, 1648), to the stimulus he gave to prayers, litanies and acts of consecration, and to the substantial treatise he had composed on the subject before death. He had also dedicated, at Coutances in 1655 and Caen in 1664, the first churches in the world dedicated to Mary's Heart.

Church Authority: Fr. Joseph Gallifet, S.J., had added to his important work on the Sacred Heart of Jesus, which first appeared in French in 1733, some sections on the Sacred Heart of Mary. It was this author's wish that the Mass of the Heart of Mary would be approved by Rome. His efforts came to naught. Already, on 8 June, 1669, the Congregation of Rites had refused a similar request. Things changed with the authorization of the feast of the Sacred Heart of Jesus in 1765. In due course, in 1799, the parallel feast of the Heart of Mary was permitted by Pius VI for certain religious societies and the diocese of Palermo. In 1805, Pius VII extended the permission to all institutes and dioceses requesting it. For the present, there would be no special Mass and office; those of the Nativity of Our Lady must suffice.

167

New factors would affect the development of ideas in the nineteenth century. A number of religious congregations and societies were founded under the formal patronage of the Heart of Mary. The Daughters of the Heart of Mary were founded by Fr. de Clorivière, S.J. (qv); this first was followed by more than forty others. Popular preachers or zealous pastoral figures—Abbé MacCarthy and Abbé Desgenettes in early nineteenth century France, Fr. Henry Young later in Dublin—proposed the devotion with success. The practice of consecration (qv) already established would be, with official encouragement, directed to Mary's heart. Formulas of consecration were approved and indulgenced at intervals from 1807 on. The great movement of national congresses brought an impetus in the way of requests to church authorities to make a public act of consecration to Mary's Heart, similar to that made by Leo XIII to the Sacred Heart of Jesus. The French National Congress of 1938, which recalled Louis XIII's dedication of the realm to Our Lady in 1638, requested "the official consecration of the human race to the Immaculate Heart of Mary." The Portuguese bishops had taken the initiative in the matter for their dioceses and country on 13 May, 1931. In the early years of the second World War, reports were circulated that during the Apparitions at Fatima Our Lady had asked that mankind—and in particular Russia—be consecrated to her Immaculate Heart.

Pius XII, broadcasting to Portugal for the twenty-fifth anniversary of the Apparitions, concluded his address with a lengthy formula which contained these words: "To you and to your Immaculate Heart in this tragic hour of human history, we commit, we entrust, we consecrate, not only the whole Church, the Mystical Body of your Jesus which suffers and bleeds in so many places and is afflicted in so many ways, but also the entire world torn by discord, scorched in a fire of hate, victim of its own iniquities."[7] In 1952, the Pope repeated the act for the peoples of Russia.

There was no Encyclical on the devotion as there had been on the Sacred Heart of Jesus, notably *Haurietis Aquas*. But the decree of the Sacred Congregation of Rites, extending the feast of the Immaculate Heart, with a new Mass and office, to the whole Church, did contain some doctrine. It recalled the antiquity of the devotion, referring to commentaries on the Song of Songs, to medieval and recent holy people, men and women, who "had opened the way" to it. "Under the symbol of the Heart of the Mother of God, her eminent holiness and especially her most ardent love for God and her Son Jesus are venerated with piety, as well as her maternal devotion to men ransomed by the divine blood."[8]

[1]Cf. article in this work on John Eudes, St.; cf. also C. di Targiani and R. Hauser, *The Admirable Heart of Mary*, (New York, 1948); Fr. Pinamonti, S.J., *Il sacro cuore di Maria*, (Florence, 1699); H. Hachette-Desportes, *La dévotion au Coeur de Maria*, 2nd ed., (Paris, Decoutiere, 1825); Fr. MacCarthy, S.J., "La dévotion au Saint Coeur de Marie," in *Sermons du R. P. MacCarthy*, (Paris, Poussielgue-Rusand, 1840), 83-121; St. Antony M. Claret, *El Corazón de Maria*, (Madrid, 1863); Abbé Boiteux, *Le Saint Coeur de Marie*, (Paris, 1876); A. Le Doré, C.J.M., *Les Sacrés Coeurs et le Ven. Jean Eudes, premier apôtre de leur culte*, (Paris, Lamulle et Poisson, 1891), 2 vols.; J. V. Bainvel, S.J., *Le Saint Coeur de Marie*, (Paris, Beauchesne, 1918); P. Lebrun, C.J.M., *La dévotion au Coeur de Marie, étude historique et doctrinale*, (Paris, Lethellieux, 1918); Fr. Pujolras, C.M.F., *Cultus purissimi Cordis B. Mariae Virginis, Natura et fundamenta*, (Milan, Editrice Ancora, 1943). Cf. esp. J. M. Bover, S.J., "Origen y desenvolvimiento de la devoción al Corazón de Maria en los Santos Padres," in EstM, (1944, ed. 1945), 59-171; "Teses apresentadas ao congresso mariologico Luso-Espanhol, na Fatima," in EstM, (1944, ed. Fatima, 1945); E. Pichery, O.S.B., *Le Coeur de Marie, Mère du Dieu Sauveur*, (Paris, Spés, 1947); J. Calveras, S.J., *El Ojeto de culto al Corazón Inmaculado de Maria*, (Barcelona, Libreria religiosa, 1948); N. Garcia Garces, C.M.F., *Cordis Mariae Filius*, (Barcelona, 1949); H. Barré, C.S.Sp., "Une prière d'Ekbert de Schönau au Saint Coeur de Marie," in EphMar, 2(1952), 409-423; J. Galot, S.J., *Le Coeur de Marie*, (Museum Lessianum Section asc. et myst. 48, Desclée et Brouwer, 1955); J. M. Alonso, C.M.F., "Virgo Corde," in EphMar, 9(1959), 175-228; *ibid.*, "El Corazón Inmaculado de Maria, alma del mensaje de Fatima," I and II, in EphMar 22(1972), 240-303, and 23(1973), 19-75; "Fatima et le Coeur Immaculé de Marie," in EphMar, 22(1972), 421-442; G. de Becker, SS CC, *Les Sacrés Coeurs de Jésus et de Marie*, in *Etudes Picpussiennes*, 5(1959); L. M. Faccenda, O.F.M.Conv., *Il Cuore Immacolato di Maria*, 2nd ed., (Bologna Editrice Milizia Mariana, 1965); G. M. Morreale, S.J., "La dottrina di tre papi nella Consacrazione al Cuore Immacolato di Maria," in *Teologia e pastorale della consacrazione a Maria*, (Collegamento Mariano Nazionale, Padua, 1969), 63-81; H. Chavannes, "La Vierge Marie et le don du coeur nouveau," in BSFEM, 27(1971), 225-236; B. de Margerie, S.J., *Le Coeur de Marie, Coeur de l'Église*, (Paris, 1967). [2]TDNT, III, 612. [3]*De Laudibus S. M.*, (Inter op. Alberti Magni, ed. Borgnet, 36), 2, 2, 2, p. 82. [4]*Hom. in Assumpt.*, 7, in PL 174, 986. [5]*De laud, B.M.V.*, in PL 189, 1727. [6]H. Barré, C.S.Sp., "Une prière d'Ekbert de Schönau au Saint Coeur de Marie," in EphMar, 2(1952), 412. [7]OL, 343. [8]AAS, 37(1945), 50-51.

HELINAND OF FROIDMONT (d. 1212)

A Cistercian preacher and chronicler, H., besides other sermons in which Mary is mentioned, such as those for the Christmas cycle and one for the feast of All Saints, preached two for each of the following feasts: the Purification; the Assumption; and the Nativity.[1] Though he held that Mary was sanctified in the womb, he was emphatic on her personal sinlessness. Her destiny he saw in a Trinitarian setting: ". . . she who was from eternity predestined as the wife [*conjugem*] of the Father of spirits to have a common Son with him and be the Mother of God, the sanctuary of the Holy Spirit, the temple of the whole Trinity, the rightful house of wisdom."[2] Mary was filled with the Holy Spirit and H. singled out for praise the theological virtues: "Truly Mary was strong in faith believing the impossible, strong in hope, expecting unheard of things, strong in charity, wanting only heavenly promises, despising all things earthly."[3]

As with all twelfth century writers, H. is conscious of Mary's special role in human lives: "Today a cause of joy is proposed more especially to men than to angels for in Mary was born to us the exemplar of most perfect holiness, the help of most powerful intercession."[4] To signify Mary's place in the Church, H. uses the metaphor of the neck, first used by Hermann of Tournai: "For what is then meant by the neck save our Mediatress, the Blessed Virgin, who is singularly eminent in the Body which is the Church, through whom we merited to receive the author of life, that is the Bread of life which comes down from heaven and gives life to the world."[5] He goes on to say that through Mary Christ became the Head and Spouse of the Church, as in a parallel text on the metaphor of the neck and the Mediatress, he says significantly that it was through her that he became the Mediator of God and men. H. knows the stories of Mary of Egypt (*qv*) and of Theophilus (*qv*). In the mentality of the age, he prays: "For she is the Mother of mercy . . . and the Mother of grace and therefore powerful quickly to soothe the sinner, quickly to sway the judge, quickly too, when necessary, to punish the insolent."[6]

[1]PL 212, 529-544, 636-652, 652-668. [2]PL 212, 638C. [3]PL 212, 650A. [4]PL 212, 653A. [5]PL 212, 667B. Cp. PL 212, 640. [6]PL 212, 648D.

HENRY OF GHENT (1217-1293)

Philosopher and theologian of the University of Paris, and Archdeacon of Tournai, H. was called *Doctor Sollemnis* because of his varied genius.[1] Marian doctrine is contained in different *Quodlibeta*: IV, on the relation of sonship between Jesus and his Mother; IX, Question 11, on the marriage with St. Joseph and the vow of virginity; XIV, Question 2, in defense of the view that Mary's soul in the very moment in which it was united to the body was both contaminated by sin and sanctified. His principle was that we ought to affirm about Mary what was most conformable to her most high dignity as Mother of God; to the supreme love God bears towards her; to the devotion we owe her; and to the teaching of the holy Fathers—provided it does not conflict with right reason and our view of what is perfect.

[1]J. M. de Goicoechea y Viteri, O.F.M., *Doctrina mariana de Enrique de Gante*, (Lima, 1944); A. Schulter, "Die Bedeutung Henrichs von Gent für die Enfaltung der Lehre von die unblecten Empfängnis," in *Theol. Quartalschr.*, 118(1937), 312-340, 437-455. Cf. also MM, 16(1954), 290-316.

HERMANN THE CRIPPLE (d. 1054)

Benedictine monk of Reichenau, H. was given his name because he was partially paralyzed. It is not certain that he was the author of the *Alma Redemptoris Mater* and the *Salve Regina* (*qv*). It does not appear possible to deny him authorship of the Sequence, *Ave praeclara maris stella*.[1] Fr. J. M. Canal, C.M.F. denies the authenticity of all the Marian work of H.

[1]PL 143, 443A-444A. Cf. H. Barré, C.S.Sp., *Prières Anciennes*, 260; M. Manitius, *Geschichte der lateinischen Literatur im Mittelalter*, (Munich, 1911-1931), II, 775-776; J. M. Canal, C.M.F., "Hermannus Contractus ejusque Mariana Carmina," in *Sacris Erudiri*, 10(1958), 170-185.

HERMANN OF TOURNAI (d.c. 1147) — See
Supplement, p. 383.

HESYCHIUS (d. after 451)

A monk and priest in Jerusalem known and esteemed as a teacher and exegete of Sacred Scripture, H. made a contribution to Marian theology of capital importance. He was contemporary with Ephesus, and outlived Chalcedon. Especially important are his two homilies on the holy *Theotokos* (BHG 1132, 1133) and three on the Presentation (*Hypapante*) of the Lord (BHG 1956, 1957, the third in Georgian).[1] Three homilies are in *Patrologia Graeca*. Four appear in the recent critical edition by M. Aubineau. The editor of the Georgian text thinks its authenticity "not less plausible than that of the others on the Presentation."

H. contrasts Mary—the "second virgin"—with Eve, the first virgin. Mary reversed all the misery of the female sex, all the sadness in child-bearing; she "dispelled the cloud of anxiousness which hangs over all women in childbirth." The first parents are twice mentioned: "The only-begotten Son of God, creator of the world, was borne by her as an infant, he who refashioned Adam, sanctified Eve, destroyed the dragon and opened paradise, keeping firm the virginal seal."[2] Mary herself is given the chief role in another passage. H. asks who is the virgin of Is 7:14 (see EMMANUEL), and replies: "Conspicuous among women, chosen from virgins, outstanding ornament of our nature, pride of our clay, who freed Eve from her disgrace, Adam from the penalty threatening him, cut down the dragon's insolence, she whom the smoke of our desire never reached, whom the worm of sensual pleasure has not spoiled either."[3]

H. uses many images and titles for Mary, offering one of the first litanies: Star of life; Pure Turtle-dove; Dove without stain; Throne; Temple; Seat; Jewel-case; Ark of the Word Incarnate; Casket holding the pearl; Sky wherein shines the Sun; Plant of incorruptibility; Paradise of immortality. He calls Mary *Theotokos* (qv), twice in the first homily on the *Hypapante*, seven times in all: "She bore in her womb God whom creation cannot contain."

Related to the godhead of the Son is the virginal conception (see VIRGINITY). He insists that "Joseph was not the father," and [Mary's] womb did not receive seed of man." He likewise, as is clear from an earlier quotation, insists on the "*virginitas in partu*" (qv): "Christ did not open but left closed the door of the Virgin; he did not violate nature's seal, did not harm the one giving birth; for her, in reality, he left intact the sign of virginity." (*Hom. I in Praesent.* 3, 6-9); the text of Ez 44:2 is used on this subject. H. uses many Old Testament images: the rod of Jesse; the burning bush; the uncut stone of Daniel.[4]

The Georgian homily introduces the Presentation as the "mother of all feasts," contrasts Eve from whom came the curse with her daughter "who bears the fountain of life"; it lengthily

paraphrases Simeon's prophecy to end thus: "Then you will be astounded and made to tremble and a sword, as it were, will pierce your soul, when you see the veil of the Temple rent but not by human hand."[5] In the Greek homilies the sword is more explicitly interpreted as doubt: "Doubt is called the sword because as the sword divides and separates bodies so doubt also divides souls and causes them to hesitate. In fact, though Mary was a virgin, she was a woman, though she was the Mother of God, she was of our stuff [paste]."[6] In the second homily, H. speaking to Mary (that is, paraphrasing Simeon) tells her that a sword, *viz.* doubt, will pierce her soul and she will be astonished when she sees hanging on a cross the one conceived and born miraculously.

H. saw the Magi as exemplars of faith. He thought, as did other Fathers, that Mary was the first to see the risen Jesus: "She first welcomed Jesus coming from the dead, first began to proclaim the resurrection, first revealed joy for the disciples."[7]

Mary is seen in relationship with the persons of the Most Holy Trinity: "The Holy Spirit came to you, the Father overshadowed you, the Son dwelt as one borne in the womb." "The Father comes, the Holy Spirit overshadows you and the only-begotten having taken flesh is born of you."[8]

Taken with the information supplied by the Armenian and Georgian lectionaries, the homilies of H. help considerably to further research, which has been conducted by several scholars over the last fifty years, on the origin and early development of Marian feasts.[9] *Hom. V*, one of the earliest "witnesses" to a feast of the divine motherhood, strengthens the case for a feast on 15 August. It would later become a feast of the Dormition, eventually of the Assumption (qv). This undermines the thesis advanced by M. Jugie (qv) that this feast belonged to the Nativity cycle, an opinion opposed by B. Capelle, but lately supported by R. Caro. *Hom. VI* seems to have been preached for a feast within the Octave of the Epiphany, a feast of the Incarnation which may have been the first form of a feast of the Annunciation (qv). H.'s homilies for the *Hypapante* were probably the first preached for that feast. These conclusions cannot, however, be put forward as entirely certain.

[1]Works: PG 93, 1453-1477; critical ed., M. Aubineau, S.J., *Les Homélies Festales d'Hesychius de Jérusalem*, (Brussels, Les Bollandistes, Subsidia Hagiographica 59, 1979). Cf. M. Aubineau's ed. for the following: *Hom. I in Praesent.*, in M. Aubineau ed., 24-42; *Hom. II in Praesent.*, in M. Aubineau ed., 61-74; *Hom. V in SS. Deip.*, in M. Aubineau ed., 158-168; *Hom. VI in SS. Deip.*, in M. Aubineau ed., 194-204. For Georgian homily, cf. G. Garitte, "L'Homélie georgienne d'Hesychius de Jérusalem sur l'Hypapante," in Mus, 84(1971), 353-372; ClavisG, III, 257-269; cf. also R. Caro, *La Homilética*, I, 39-58; Ch. Martin, S.J., "Fragments en onciale d'homélies grecques sur la Vierge attribuées à Hesychius de Jérusalem," in RHE, 31(1935), 356-359; K. Jussen, "Die Mariologie des Hesychius v. Jerusalem," in *Theol. in Gesch. u. Gegenwart*, (1957), 651-670. Cf. esp. J. Kirchmeyer, in DSp, s.v., VII, 399-408; J. M. Alonso, C.M.F., "La espada de Simeon (Lc 2:35a) en la exegesis de los Padres," in MSS, IV, 247-248; R. S. Pitmann, *The Marian Homilies of Hesychius of Jerusalem*, (Washington, D.C. Doctoral dissertation, Catholic University, 1974, publ. in Xerox ed. Ann Arbor). [2] *Hom. V de SS. Deip. 1*, in PG 93, 1461; *Hom. V in SS. Deip.*, in M. Aubineau ed., 158. [3]*Hom. V de SS. Deip. 4*, in PG 93, 1465; *Hom. V in SS. Deip.*, in M. Aubineau ed., 164. [4]*Hom. V in SS. Deip. 1*, in M. Aubineau ed., 158; *Hom. V in SS. Deip. 5*, in M. Aubineau ed., 166. [5]Mus, 84(1971), 370-371. [6]*Hom. I in Praesent.*, 8, in M. Aubineau ed., 41. [7]*op. cit.*, 2, in M. Aubineau ed., 29. [8]*Hom. V de SS. Deip. 1*, in PG 93, 1461; *Hom. V in SS. Deip.*, in M. Aubineau ed., 158; *Hom. V de SS. Deip. 5*, in PG 93, 1465; *Hom. V in SS. Deip.*, in M. Aubineau ed., 166. [9]For bibliography, see article on Liturgy in the present work; *Armenian Lectionary*, ed. by Renoux, in PO 35-36; *Georgian Lectionary*, ed. by Tarchnischvili, in CSCO 204. For relevance of Hesychius' homilies, cf. M. Aubineau, S.J., *Les Homélies Festales d'Hesychius de Jérusalem*, (Brussels, Les Bollandistes, Subsidia Hagiographica 59, 1979), lxiv-lxv, 132-146, 184-189.

HILARY OF POITIERS, ST. (*c.* 315-367)

A noted opponent of the Arian heresy and the most prominent Latin theologian of his time, H. deals with Marian questions in occasional passages of his works, but does not directly confront the problems which would arise for the great Latin doctors of the next generation.[1] In his commentary on Matthew, he writes of Joseph's role as a witness to the conception by the Holy Spirit, and then makes a subtle point that, when Mary and Joseph are mentioned, she is spoken of as the Mother of Christ, not as the wife of Joseph.[2] H. followed the Greek Fathers in thinking that the "Brothers of the Lord" (*qv*) were sons of Joseph by an early marriage: "If they had been Mary's sons and not those taken from Joseph's former marriage, she would never have been given over in the moment of the Passion to the apostle John as his mother, the Lord saying to each: 'Woman, behold your son' and to John 'behold your mother' (Jn 19:26-27), as he bequeathed filial love to a disciple as a consolation to the one desolate."[3] On the incident of Mary and the brothers waiting outside for Jesus, H. proposes a novel exegesis: "But since he came unto his own and his own did not receive him, in his mother and brothers the Synagogue and the Israelites are foreshadowed, refraining from entry and approach to him."[4] Though influenced by Origen (*qv*), H. does not follow his interpretation of the sword of Simeon (*qv*), but thinks that it signifies Mary's accountability in judgment: "A sword will pierce blessed Mary's soul that thoughts may be revealed from many hearts. If this Virgin who was capable [of bearing] God, is to come to the severity of judgment, who will dare to wish to be judged by God?"[5]

H.'s approach to the divine motherhood is through the identity of the Son of God and the Son of the Virgin. "God the Son of God abiding before all ages, in the habit of human nature, that is, a man of our body and soul, was born from the child-bearing of the Virgin."[6] "The only-begotten Son of God taking the body of our nature from the Virgin . . ."[7] In his main work on the Trinity, H. especially insists on the virginity in the conception, but not on *virginitas in partu* (*qv*): "I do not inquire how he was born of a Virgin: whether her flesh suffered any loss as it gave birth to perfect flesh."[8]

In the *De Trinitate* there is also some emphasis on the role of the Holy Spirit in the virginal conception. H. applies 1 Cor 15:47, "the first man is from the earth, a thing of dust, the second man is from heaven," to the Spirit's action. "And when he says that the second man is from heaven, he bears witness to his origin from the approach of the Holy Spirit coming down upon the Virgin; and therefore since the man is and is from heaven, the child-bearing is from the Virgin and the conception from the Spirit."[9]

[1]EMBP, 156-165; CMP, 29-49. [2]*In Mt. 1, 3*, in PL 9, 922A. [3]*In Mt. 1, 4*, in PL 9, 922B. [4]PL 9, 12, 24, 933B. [5]*In Ps. 118, 3, 12*, in CSEL 22, 384, also in PL 9, 523A. [6]*In Ps. 53, 8*, in CSEL 22, 141, also in PL 9, 342B. [7]*In Ps. 118, 14, 8*, in CSEL 22, 478, also in PL 9, 592C. [8]*De Trinit. 3, 19*, in PL 10, 87A. [9]*De Trinit. 10, 17*, in PL 10, 356A.

HILDEBERT OF LAVARDIN (d. 1133)

H. was bishop of Le Mans and afterwards archbishop of Tours. PL 171 attributes 143 sermons to him, of which nine at most are authentic.[1] His alleged Marian works have been restored by scholarship to the authorship of Peter Lombard (*qv*), Geoffrey Babion, Peter Comestor, Maurice de Sully, bishop of Paris and Peter the Painter. He wrote a life of Mary of Egypt[2] (*qv*) and a hymn to Our Lady.[3]

[1]Cf. R. Laurentin, *Traité*, I, 149-150; A. Wilmart, "Les sermons d'Hildebert," in RevBen, 47(1935), 15-21. [2]PL 171, 1321-1340. [3]"L'Inno alla Vergine di Ildeberto di Lavardin," in *Città di Vita*, 6(1951), 292-294.

HINCMAR (d. 882)

It is said that a church "in honour of the ever-Virgin Mary, Mother of God" was built by Nicaise, archbishop of Rheims in the fifth century. Hincmar, a ninth century archbishop, restored the building, and , for the occasion of its inauguration, composed inscriptions for the Virgin's altar, its statue, and a gospel lectionary. Further, he had copies made of the Pseudo-Jerome (*qv*) letter (which he thought authentic) and of the *De Ortu sanctae Dei genitricis Mariae* of Ratramnus (*qv*). For a splendidly produced copy of the latter he composed a preface, his long dogmatic poem on the Virgin Mary.[1] She "suffered no pain" in her virginal childbirth. More interestingly perhaps, he expresses the Mary-Church (*qv*) parallel: "One is the person and twofold the substance [nature] of Christ, whom your loving virginity brought forth as God. As the Church from the Holy Spirit by her virginity brings forth children from the depth of the [baptismal] font."[2]

H. has an enigmatic passage on Mary's incorruption after death. "The sacred flesh of God was not corrupt in the grave, nor was yours from which God himself took his body; with whom, as the Star of the sea, you now dwell in the high heavens, jointly honoured [*concelebrata*] by devout angelic praise."[3] He does not say that Mary was assumed corporeally, but the parallel with the risen Christ seems to imply it. H. recalls the words of the dying Christ to strengthen his own plea for help: "When I come to die, O you who are placed over heaven's famous ministers, reigning with Christ, be merciful, I beg you, to me, that I may merit a share with those whom grace saves in a destiny of light, peace and rest."[4]

H., in his inscription for Our Lady's altar, speaks of himself as her constant client, servant, "*cultor ubique suus.*"[5] His own epitaph read: "Be merciful, holy Mary, to your client" (*Sis pia cultori, sancta Maria, tuo*).[6]

[1]*Poet. Lat.*, 3, in MGH, 410-412. Cf. H. Barré, *Prières Anciennes*, 80-81; G. G. Meersseman, *Der Hymnos Akathistos im Abendland*, I, (Fribourg, 1958), 145-147; L. Scheffczyk, *Mariengeheimnis*, 103-109. [2]*Poet. Lat.*, 3, in MGH, 410. [3]*op. cit.*, in MGH, 412. [4]*op. cit.* [5]*op. cit.*, in MGH, 409. [6]H. Barré, *Prières Anciennes*, 81.

HIPPOLYTUS OF ROME, ST. (d. 235)

Photius (*qv*) thought that H. might have been a disciple of St. Irenaeus (*qv*) and Origen's (*qv*) teacher. There are references to Mary in several of the fragments of his works which have survived.[1] He taught Mary's motherhood of the Word Incarnate, the virginal conception, and he seems to have had an intuition of the relationship between the only-begotten who became man and who was the first-born (of many brethren). "Tell me, O blessed Mary, what was conceived in your womb; and what was borne in your virginal womb? For it was the first-born Word of God, [come] from heaven to you, and formed in the womb as the first-born man; so that the first-born Word of God should be shown united to the first-born man."[2] H. applied Is 11:1 to Mary's motherhood of Christ.

Attempts have been made to attribute the first use of the title *Theotokos* (*qv*) to H. It is found in the Greek text of the *De benedictionibus patriarcharum* (ed. TU, 38a, p. 13, l. 7). and appears to lie behind the Syrian version of the *In Canticum*, (GCS Hippolytus, 1a, p. 359). The Armenian text of the *De benedictionibus patriarcharum* shows that the title *Theotokos* was an interpolation.[3]

[1]CMP, 60-72; EMBP, 69-79. Cf. G. Jouassard, "Le prémier-né de la Vierge chez saint Irénée et saint Hippolyte," in *Rev. Sc. Rel.*, 12(1932), 509-532, and 13(1933), 25-37. [2]*In Elcana et Anna, apud* Theodoret of Cyrus; *Dial. I*, in GCS 1, 2, 121, PG 10, 863B. [3]Cf. R. Laurentin, *Traité*, V, 171.

HOLINESS OF MARY, THE[1]

Holiness implies absence of sin and godliness in personal behaviour—the direction of man's whole being and activity to God. The principle of holiness is the grace of Christ which makes us "sharers in the divine nature," conformed to Christ as the sons of Christ as the sons of God, temples of his Spirit, heirs to his everlasting kingdom.

Sacred Scripture: The portrait of Mary given by Luke is one of perfection directly related to God. The word *Kecharitomene* (Lk 1:28) immediately places her on a higher level than Zechariah and Elizabeth, righteous in the Old Testament sense. She is God's favoured one. She has found favour with the Lord (Lk 1:30); her Child will be called holy (Lk 1:35); she is blessed among women, blessed because she has believed (Lk 1:42, 45); all ages will recognize her blessing (Lk 1:48); God has done mighty things for her (Lk 1:49); she is a contemplative soul (Lk 2:19, 51). In the Lucan typology, she is God's people at prayer, pilgrimage to the Temple, pre-eminent among the Poor of the Lord, capable of sanctifying others (Lk 1:44), inspiring awe in her elders, Simeon and Elizabeth. The later synoptic texts and the Johannine passages do nothing to lessen this praise.

History: The early Fathers, especially the Easterns, did not grasp the truth of Mary's sinlessness, of her personal excellence. There are occasional references to flaws in her conduct. Thus St. Irenaeus (*qv*) thought that there was untimely haste on her part at Cana, that the Lord appeared to repel her. Origen (*qv*) began the tradition of associating doubt with the oracle of Simeon (see SWORD OF SIMEON). The picture of Mary, model of virgins, composed by St. Athanasius, is not entirely flawless. St. John Chrysostom, in sermons to the people, spoke of Mary's failings. St. Cyril of Alexandria is a subject of debate. Cardinal Newman, followed recently by Fr. H. du Manoir, S.J., would not accept that the doctor of the divine motherhood "attributed sin in any way, even venial, to Mary." Mgr. G. Jouassard wrote of the "shipwreck of her faith," as St. Cyril described her on Calvary. Tertullian, among the Latins, thought that Christ—in the "difficult" synoptic texts—rejected his Mother, whom Tertullian compares to the unbelieving synagogue.

St. Ambrose, in adopting the portrait of St. Athanasius, eliminated all imperfection from it. He first spoke of Mary in the West as *sancta*, holy, and the doctrine of her personal sinlessness was still more emphatically taught by St. Augustine. In the East, similarly, the title *panagia*, all holy, became more and more the accepted description of Mary. Byzantine theology, from the sixth century on, exalts Mary's perfection and eminence with an endless flow of metaphor. The idea also strongly influenced Byzantine liturgy.

In the West, the debate on the Immaculate Conception was to continue for centuries; Mary's freedom from concupiscence was accepted much earlier. From Suarez on, a different aspect of her sanctity was discussed—the comparison between her degree of grace, even in the initial moment of her life, with the grace of the saints, even with that of all other creatures combined. Another subject of contention, to arise at the same time, was the relationship between Mary's holiness and the divine motherhood (see MOTHER OF GOD).

Teaching Authority: The Council of Trent taught that Mary, by a special privilege, was preserved from all sin, even venial.[2] The modern Popes frequently praise her surpassing excellence, not only in occasional pronouncements but in documents of a doctrinal character. Thus St. Pius X in *Ad diem illum* declared that she "excels all in sanctity." Pius XII in *Munificentissimus Deus* wrote of her as "the noble associate of the divine Redeemer who has won a complete triumph over sin and its consequences." The same Pope in *Ad Caeli Reginam* joined with his own praise the words of Pius IX in *Ineffabilis Deus*: "To understand this supreme degree of excellence which raises the Mother of God above all creation, it is a help to note that, from the first moment of her conception, she was filled with an abundance of grace far beyond that of all the saints. Hence Pope Pius IX wrote that Almighty God 'placed her far above all the angels and all the saints, and so filled her with every heavenly grace taken from his own divine treasury, that she was always free from all stain of sin, all beautiful and perfect, possessing such a fullness of innocence and holiness to be found nowhere outside of God, and which no one but God can comprehend.'"

Vatican II proclaims Mary's holiness clearly: "Because of this gift of sublime grace [the divine motherhood], she far surpasses all other creatures both in heaven and on earth." Also, "... the usage prevailed among the holy Fathers whereby they called the Mother of God entirely holy and free from all stain of sin, fashioned by the Holy Spirit into a kind of new substance and a new creature. Adorned from the first instant of her conception with the splendours of an entirely unique holiness, the Virgin of Nazareth is, on God's command, greeted by an angel messenger as 'full of grace'." (Lk 1:28). "And so they [the followers of Christ] raise their eyes to Mary who shines forth to the whole community of the elect as a model of the virtues." (LG 53, 56, 65).

[1]Cf. M. J. Scheeben, *Mariology*, II, 3-31, 112-139; J. B. Terrien, *La Mère de Dieu*, (Paris, Lethielleux, 1900), Pt. I, vol. II, bk. VII, 191-314; B. Ravagnan, "De Mariae plenitudine gratiae," in MM, 3(1941), 102-123; G. Rozo, *Sancta Maria Mater Dei, seu de sanctificatione B. M. V. vi divinae maternitatis*, (Milan, 1943); G. R. de Yurre, "La teoria de la maternidada divina formalmente sanctificante en Ripalda y Scheeben," in EstM, 3(1944), 255-286; J. A. de Aldama, S.J., "El valor dogmático de la doctrina sobre la immunidad de pecado venial en Nuestra Señora," in *Archivo Teológico Grandadino*, 9(1946), 53-67; C. Feckes, "Die Gnadenausstattung Mariens," in *Katholische Marienkunde*, ed. by P. Straeter, (Paderborn, 1947), II, 101-179; G. Jouassard, *Maria*, I, 114-122; id., "Le probleme de la sainteté de Marie chez les Peres depuis les origines de la patristique jusqu'au Concile d'Ephèse," in BSFEM, 5(1947), 13-31; G. M. Roschini, O.S.M., *Mariologia*, II, (1948), 105-196; id., *La Madonna secondo la fede e la teologia*, III, (Rome, 1953), 91-162; id., *Maria Santissima*, III, 269-336; J. M. Delgado Varela, "Maternidad formalmente santificante: Origen y desenvolvimiento de la controversia," in EstM, 8(1949), 132-184; R. Laurentin, "Sainteté de Marie et de l'Eglise," in BSFEM, 11(1953), 1-27; id., *Traité*, V, 119-122; G. van Ackeren, "Does the Divine Maternity formally sanctify Mary's soul?," in MSt, 6(1955), 63-101; M. de Tuya, "Valoración exegético-teológica del 'Ave gratia plena'," in *Ciencia Tomista*, 43(1956), 9-27; F. P. Calkins, "Mary's fullness of grace," in *Mariology*, 297-312; G. Alastruey, *The Blessed Virgin Mary*, (St. Louis, Herder, 1963), 147-178; J. Galot, S.J., "La Sainteté de Marie," in *Maria*, VI, 419-448; C. Vollert, "The Holiness of Mary," in *A Theology of Mary*, (New York, Herder, 1965), 191-208; Anastasio del SS. Rosario, O.C.D., *La santità di Maria e la santità della Chiesa, La santità nella Costituzione conciliare sulla Chiesa*, (Rome, Teresianum, 1966), 219-241; E. Carroll, O.Carm., "Theological reflections on Our Blessed Lady's 'impeccabilitas'," in PCM, II, 371-385; L. M. Herran, "Lo social y lo personal en la gracia de Maria," in EstM, 29(1967), 91-144; J. Gummersbach and M. Viller, "Confirmation en grâce," in DSp, II, 1428. [2]DS, 1573. [3]OL, 395.

HONORIUS AUGUSTODUNENSIS
(*fl.* 1106-1135)

Less is known about H. than about any other writer of the age. He may have been a Benedictine and may have lived in Bavaria and England.[1] His Marian theology is found in the *Sigillum B. Mariae ubi exponuntur Cantica Canticorum*[2] a commentary on the Song of Songs (*qv*); in his liturgical works, *Gemma Animae* and *Sacramentarium*; and in sermons

on the Purification, the Annunciation, the Assumption and the Nativity.[3]

H. thought himself unworthy "with soiled lips" to praise the Mother of the Creator. Christ, sanctifier and lover of sanctity, showed what praise she deserves when he judged her worthy of his own vesture. "Since he preferred to be born of a virgin, the reason was clear to all that, as death entered by a woman who was a virgin, so life should enter through a woman who was a virgin." [4] With this reference to the Eve (*qv*)—Mary parallel and contrast, H. did not exhaust his Old Testament study. He thought that Mary was prefigured in many ways in ancient times and announced in the burning bush, the bedewed fleece of Gideon—"the Virgin pregnant with sacred offspring"—the rod of Is 11, the closed door of Ez 44:2, and the stone "cut by no human hands" in Dan 2:34.

H., suffering the limitation of his age, did not hold the Immaculate Conception, but he taught the sinlessness of Mary. "And since there is no stain of sin in thee, come from Lebanon, that is from the brightness of chastity to the joys of heaven."[5] Mary's death (*qv*) was followed by two processions. One bore her body to the tomb; the other was occasioned "because her most blessed spirit was borne to the heavenly places, while angels advanced with the Son of God." "Her body," he adds, "is believed to have been raised afterwards and placed in heavenly glory."[6]

H. is admirable on the Mary-Church (*qv*) typology. "The glorious Virgin Mary was a type of the Church, as a virgin and mother . . . . [the Church is] proclaimed a mother, because being fertile by the Holy Spirit, though her, children are brought forth daily to God in baptism. She is said to be a virgin because, keeping the integrity of faith inviolate, she is not corrupted by heretical perversion. Thus Mary was a mother bringing forth Christ and remaining wholly a virgin after childbirth. Accordingly all that is written of the Church is appropriately read also of her."[7]

H. uses characteristic Marian titles (*qv*) of the time, "consolation of the wretched, refuge of sinners, restoration of the fallen." When he speaks of her as Queen of the angels, however, it is to urge imitation of her humility and chastity. "Christ," he says, "came from the heights to the depths that he might raise his

Mother to the heights; the Church, through the merits of the Virgin, ascends ever higher."8

[1]Cf. E. Aman, in DTC, 7, 139-178; Y. Lefevre, in DSp, VII, 730-734; G. Marocco, S.D.B., "Nuovi elementi sull'Assunzione nel Medio Evo Latino," in MM, 12(1950), 419-420. [2]PL 172, 495-518. [3]PL 172, 849-852, 901-908, 991-994, 999-1002. [4]PL 172, VIII, 517B. [5]PL 172, IV, 506D. [6]PL 172, VIII, 517-518. [7]PL 172, 499D. [8]PL 172, VII, 513D.

HUGH OF NEWCASTLE
H. was a Franciscan teacher in Paris, whose *Reportatio*, lectures on the Sentences, inform us that the opinion opposed to the Immaculate Conception was "fairly common."[1] He does not commit himself to either view. H. sets out the arguments of the opponents, and, with sympathy, those of the defenders, as well as their replies to the former.

[1]A. Emmen, O.F.M., "Hugo de Novo Castro ejusque doctrina de Immaculata Conceptione," in *Studi. Franc.*, 16(1944); F. de Guimaraens, O.F.M.Cap., "La doctrine des théologiens sur l'Immaculée Conception de 1250-1350," in *Études franc.*, 4(1954), 49-50.

HUGH OF ST. VICTOR (1096-1141)
H. was a theologian and mystical writer, one of the Victorines, named for their Paris monastery of St. Victor, of the Canons Regular of St. Augustine. He dealt with Marian themes in his commentary on the *Magnificat*; a treatise on Mary's virginity; part three of his short work on the Incarnation; a sermon on the Assumption; and two other brief items.[1] In these pieces, we get the Marian insights of the age, with occasional flashes of mystic intensity. Thus on the parallel between Mary and the Church: "First your friend, Mary the virgin and mother, brought you forth; afterwards your friend, the Church, virgin and mother, was brought forth from you. Coming in the flesh, you became the Son of your spouse, a mother and virgin in body. Dying, you became the parent of your spouse who is a virgin in faith. By being born from your spouse, you received the substance of infirmity; by dying, you gave your spouse the sacrament of incorruption."[2]

H. insisted on each phase of the virginity. He was as near to holding the Immaculate Conception (*qv*) as he could be from principles opposed to it. Mary received the fullness of grace, especially in the coming of the Spirit; she was beloved of the Trinity. "Therefore your grace is above all grace, your excellence above all merit, you are supreme before all, holier than everyone."[3] The reason given is the virginal motherhood. H. understood her marriage (*qv*) with Joseph (*qv*) as a type of the union of God and the soul, *societas*. This association (see ASSOCIATE) is more profound and spiritual between Mary, "spouse of the eternal King," and her beloved, with whom she hastens to be associated (*sociari*). "I call her [H. attributes the words to Christ] because she is pure, I invite her as one faithful, I desire her as all fair. 'Thou art all fair, my love.' O what association! The all fair one associates with himself one who is all fair.... I [again Jesus speaks] by nature, thou by grace."[4]

H. employed the Eve-Mary contrast. Eve, in her pride, wished to be equal to God and was rebuffed; Mary, in her humility, chose to be the handmaid of the Lord and was the chosen one. "And since the beginner of the fault was brought down by a woman, a woman with no male help conceived and brought forth the beginner of grace."[5] Mediation of grace follows. "Mary was full of grace, for, through her, grace came down on all the children of men."[6] "Through Mary, Christ is given and through Christ, salvation."[7] The conclusion is a human one, quite medieval: "Hence if in your supplication you fear to approach Christ, turn your gaze to Mary."[8]

H. does not openly teach the bodily Assumption; he insinuates it in a passage which echoes Song of Songs.[9] But it is Mary's mystical ascension that interests him rather than her bodily glorification.

[1]PL 175, 414-432; PL 176, 857-876; PL 177, 320-324, 1209-1222; RAM, 31(1955), 269-271. Cf. R. Baron, *La pensée mariale de Hughues de S. Victor*, 248-268 (followed by unpublished items); *id.*, in DSp, II, 902-939. [2]PL 177, 1211A. [3]PL 177, 1213D-1214A. [4]PL 177, 1211B. [5]PL 177, 321D. [6]*op. cit.* [7]RAM, 31(1955), 269-271. [8]*op. cit.*, [9]PL 177, 1216B.

HYMNS
It has been calculated that there exist altogether 15,000 hymns in honour of Our Lady. Some 4,000 are original, the others derivative in one way or another.[1] Fr. U. Chevalier's basic work, *Repertorium Hymnologicum* (under words like *Ave, Maria, Virgo*) gives an idea of the manner; the standard collections by Mone and Dreeves show the contents. Two hymns are of such importance as to call for separate treatment

in the present work, the *Akathistos* and the *Salve Regina*. The hymn form was used as a vehicle for theological thought in the East, by the Syrians St. Ephraem (*qv*), Jacob of Sarug (*qv*), and Romanos the Singer (*qv*) who wrote in Greek. In the West, Fathers and ecclesiastical writers refer to Mary in their hymns. The poets of the fifth and sixth centuries, Sedulius and Venantius Fortunatus, made striking contributions. Sedulius was author of the *Carmen Paschale*, from which the Introit of Masses in honour of Our Lady, *Salve sancta parens*, was taken by the Roman rite. Venantius was not the author of the *Ave Maris stella*, which is not found in manuscripts before the ninth century. He may have been the author of the other well-known composition, *Quem terra, pontus aethera*. Authorship and dating of the great hymns is still a matter of research. The *Alma Redemptoris Mater* may have been written by

Hermann the Cripple of Reichenau Abbey. The *Stabat Mater*, which has challenged so many great musicians, was probably the work of Jacopone da Todi (d. 1306).

Hymns used in the Liturgy have a bearing on Tradition and are therefore closely studied. An admirable example of such analysis is the paper by Dom G. Frénaud, O.S.B., presented to the Lourdes Congress in 1958 on Mary's queenship in the Liturgy. Cardinal Goma, a member of the Spanish commission established by Pius XI to study the definability of Mary's universal mediation, used popular hymns to show the sentiment of the faithful supporting this truth.[2]

[1]Cf. Isidore Cardinal Goma, *Maria Santísima*, II (Barcelona, 1942); H. Barré, C.S.Sp., *Prières Anciennes*, 242-26.
[2]Isidore Cardinal Goma, "Los 'Gozos' populares y la Mediación," in *Maria Santísima*, II, 381-441; Dom Frénaud, in ME, V, 75ff.

I

ICONS

Icons have an immense importance in the devotional, spiritual and theological life of the eastern Orthodox Church.[1] The theological interest is, in recent times, particularly strong among Russian writers, Soloviev, Florenskij and the greatest of them, Sergius Bulgakov (*qv*) in whose work the Icon of Novgorod was especially inspiring. The icon is not like works of western religious art (*qv*), the result of personal fulfillment, individual choice, or the arbitrary will of a patron. It must be made in obedience to religious rules which are strict, and to traditions which seek to present a prototype of the heavenly humanity that is to come. The absence of perspective, of movement, and of shade, illustrate this quest for an image that will be free of everything that would prevent communion with the divine. The icon is a sacramental, occasionally the instrument of miraculous power, itself allegedly manifesting sometimes the miraculous by sudden illumination.

Our Lady—the *Theotokos*—is, after Jesus Christ, the most important theme in icons. Icons exist for the great feasts of Mary: the Nativity; the Annunciation (*qqv*); the Presentation in the Temple; the Birth of Christ (*qqv*); the Purification (*qv*); and especially the Dormition. Mary prominently appears in the Iconostasis. Different types of Marian icons have been classified: a) the *Kyriotissa*, or Virgin in majesty, with which is linked the *Nicopea*, the one who gives victory; b) the *Blachernitissa*, the Virgin praying, deriving from the ancient shrine of the Blakhernae, in Constantinople; c) the *Haghiosoritissa*, originating in the shrine of Our Lady's Girdle or *Zona*, a relic venerated by Byzantines and glorified by preachers and poets; d) the *Hodegetria*, Guide of the Way, which name is of unknown origin, but the icons so grouped are many, and widespread, even so far as Italy; e) the *Eleousa*, the Mother of the tenderness, the type exemplified in the supreme instance of the icon, Our Lady of Vladimir, still honourably placed in the Tretiakov Museum in Moscow and widely reproduced. Associated with this last type is the *Strastnaia*, the Sorrowing Virgin, exemplified in Our Lady of Perpetual Help; the *Glycophilousa*, the Virgin kissing the Child's hand; the *Galactotrephousa*, the Virgin giving milk to the divine Child; the *Virgin Source of Life*, and the *Pokrov*, the Protectress, a favourite icon of the Russians.

[1]Cf. W. Felicetti-Liebenfels, *Geschichte der Byzantinische Ikonenmalerei*, (Lausanne, 1956); L. Ouspensky and V. Lossky, *The Meaning of Icons*, (Boston, 1956); L. Ouspensky, "Essai sur la théologie de l'Icône dans l'Église orthodoxe," in *Recueil d'Etudes orthodoxes*, 2, (Paris, 1960); id., in NCE, VII, 324-326; P. Evdokimov, *L'Art de l'Icône. Théologie de la beauté*, (Bruges-Paris, 1970); T. Spidlik, "Icône," in DSp, VII, 1224-1229; P. Miquel, "Théologie de l'Icône," in DSp, VII, 1229-1239. On Marian icons, cf. G. A. Wellen, *Theotokos. Eine ikonographische Abhandlung über das Gottesmutterbild in frühchristlicher Zeit*, (Utrecht-Antwerp, 1960); W. Sas-Zaloziecky, "Byzantinische Madonnen," in LexMar, 1011-1019; J. E. Basterra, C.SS.R., "Mariologia Oriental ensenada en los Iconos," in EstM, 21(1961), 71-86; M. Vloberg, O.S.B., "Les types iconographiques de la Mère de Dieu dans l'art byzantin," in *Maria*, II, 403-443; R. de Journel, S.J., "Marie et l'iconographie russe," in *Maria*, II, 445-481. Cf. esp. D. Stiernon, A.A., "Iconodulie et Iconographie," in NCE, VII, 327-332.

IGNATIUS OF ANTIOCH, ST. (d. *c.* 110)

Third bishop of Antioch, and second successor to St. Peter, Ignatius the martyr is author of the first written testimony on Mary after the gospels. The Marian passages in his Letters are here given, leaving the reader to consult the recent works cited in the notes to this article in regard to their authenticity. "There is but one physician, bodily and spiritual, born and unborn, God who became flesh, true life in death, from Mary, from God, first suffering and then impassible, Jesus Christ, Our Lord." (Ephesians, 7:2). "Because our God, Jesus Christ, was borne in the womb by Mary according to the divine plan; [he was] of Davidic descent and was also of the Holy Spirit. He was born and baptized that by his passion he might purify the water." (Ephesians, 18:2). "The virginity of Mary and her child-bearing were hidden from the Prince of this world, as was likewise the death of the Lord: three mysteries noised about but accomplished in the stillness of God." (Ephesians, 19:1). "Be deaf whenever one speaks to you apart from Jesus Christ who was of the race of David, of Mary, who was really born, ate and drank, was really persecuted under Pontius Pilate . . . who

really rose from the dead, since his Father raised him up; his Father will likewise raise up in Christ Jesus, apart from whom we have no real life, all who believe in him." (Trallians, 9:1-2). "I extol Jesus Christ, God, who has made you so wise . . . He is really of the race of David according to the flesh, the Son of God by the will and power of God, was born of a virgin and baptized by John to fulfill all righteousness upon him." (Smyrnaeans, 1:1). The importance of these texts for Marian theology lies in the affirmation of Mary's virginity (*qv*), in the tendency to include her in the whole plan of salvation, and in the idea which was taken up and developed later, through the influence of Origen (*qv*), that the virginal conception was concealed from Satan. This would become a classic motive given by the Fathers for the marriage of Mary and Joseph.

[1]Works in PG 5; Funck-Bihlmeyer, *Die Apostolischen Väter*, I, (Tübingen, 1956); Th. Camelot, O.P. and J. A. Fischer, "Die Apostolischen Väter, Griechisch-Deutsch," in SC 10, (Munich, 1956). Cf. R. Weijenborg, O.F.M., *Les Lettres d'Ignace d'Antioche. Étude de critique littéraire et de théologie*, (Leiden, E. J. Brill, 1969). On Ignatius' Marian theology, cf. A. M. Cecchini, O.S.M., "Maria nell'Economia di Dio secondo Ignazio di Antiochia," in MM, 14(1952), 373-383; F. Spedalieri, *Maria nella Scrittura e nella Tradizione primitiva*, (Messina, 1961), 133-136; A. Gila and G. M. Grinza, O.S.M., *La Vergine nelle lettere di S. Ignazio di Antiochia*, (Turin, S. Maria di Superga, 1968); J. de Aldama, S.J., *Maria en la patrística de los siglos I y II*, (Madrid, BAC, 1970), 63-64, 81-82, 189-211, 230-233, 248-249; P. Meinhold, "Christologie und Jungfrauengeburt bei Ignatius von Antiochien," in *Studia mediaevalia et mariologica K. Balic etc.*, (Rome, 1971), 465-476; J. M. Alonso, C.M.F., "Las cartas de S. Ignacio de Antioquia. Estado actual de las cuestiones. El 'Corpus Mariologicum'," in EphMar, 22(1972), 113-124.

ILDEFONSUS OF TOLEDO, ST. (d. 667)

A Benedictine abbot who became archbishop of Toledo, I. was the author of *De Virginitate B. Mariae*, a treatise which gave the doctrine already well established on Mary's virginity (*qv*), and was addressed to two heretics, Jovinian and Helvidius, and an unnamed Jew.[1] The work is in twelve chapters, includes a good deal about the mystery of the Incarnation, and is rhetorical and repetitive. I. liked to multiply synonyms and to return to the same themes. He abounded in rich titles of Mary. To Jovinian, he opposed Mary's virginity in conception and *in partu* (see VIRGINITAS IN PARTU); to Helvidius, the perpetual virginity; and to the Jew, considerations on the virginal motherhood and a warning that to lessen the glory of the Virgin Mother would bring disrespect on the Son.

The core of his thought is on the virginity. "Behold a virgin from God, a virgin from man, a virgin by the angel witnessing, a virgin with her spouse her judge, a virgin before she had a spouse, a virgin with her spouse, an undoubted virgin, though her spouse was doubting. A virgin before the advent of her Son, a virgin after her Son was begotten, a virgin with the birth of her Son, a virgin after her Son was born."[2]

Mary's destiny was theocentric—"chosen by God, assumed by God, called by God, near to God, adhering to God, united with God."[3] Her virginity, preserved in childbirth, puts her above the angels: "I place above the status of angels, which can be disturbed, the wonderfully singular virginity, which the nativity of the Son of God left so much increased by the glory of incorruption . . . ."[4]

I. insists strongly on Mary's role in our redemption. "Behold, through this Virgin, the whole earth is filled with the glory of God. All, from small to great, have known the great God through this Virgin. Through this Virgin, all have seen the salvation of God."[5] "Because he was my Redeemer, he was your Son. Because he was the price of my ransom, his Incarnation took place from your flesh, and thus he healed my wounds . . . he drew a mortal body from the body of your mortality and therein he wiped out my sins which he bore."[6] I. saw the great fact of the virginal motherhood, surrounded as it is with wonders directed "to my salvation and that of the world, my redemption and that of the world, my justification and that of the world, my liberation and that of the world."

I. is particularly appreciated for his profound intercessory passages: "My lady, my sovereign, my ruler, Mother of my Lord, handmaid of your Son, Mother of the maker of the world, I ask you, I beg you, I beseech you, let me have the Spirit of your Lord, let me have the Spirit of your Son, let me have the Spirit of my Redeemer, that I may know true and worthy things about you, speak true and worthy things about you, that I may love whatever is true and worthy of you."[7]

Chapter XII of his work is one of the greatest prayerful compositions of early centuries. It loses by quotation, but one passage reveals two ideas that recur through the ages, consecration to Mary—and thereby acceptance of her royalty—and union between her and the Spirit.

"I am therefore your servant [servus, possibly slave], because my Lord is your Son. You are therefore my mistress, because you are the handmaid of my Lord. I am therefore the servant of the handmaid of my Lord, because you my mistress have become the Mother of my Lord . . . . I ask you, I ask you, holy Virgin, that I should have Jesus from that Spirit (qv) from whom you conceived Jesus. Through that Spirit, may my soul receive Jesus, through whom your flesh conceived the same Jesus. May I know Jesus from that Spirit, from whom it was given to you to know, to have and to bring forth Jesus."[8]

Similarity between some Marian prayers in the great *Oracional Visigótico* and those of I. has suggested his influence in their composition."[9]

---

[1]PL 96, 51-110. Critical ed. of *De Virginitate B. Mariae*, by V. Blanco Garcia, (Madrid, 1937; 2nd ed. Saragossa, 1954). On Ildefonsus, cf. A. Braegelmann, *The Life and Writings of St. Ildefonsus*, (Washington, 1942); for authenticity, R. Laurentin, *Traité*, I, 140-142. Cf. J. M. Cascante Davila, *Doctrina mariana de S. Ildefonso de Toledo*, (Barcelona, 1958); J. M. Canal, C.M.F., "Fuentes del 'De virginitate sanctae Mariae' de San Ildefonso de Toledo," in *Claretianum*, 6(1966), 115-130; id., "San Hildefonso de Toledo; Historia y Legenda," in EphMar, 17(1967), 437-462; P. H. Koster, S.A.C., "Ildefons von Toledo . . ." in Zagreb Congress, III, 197-222; J. M. Cascante Davila, "La devoción y el culto a Maria en los escritos de S. Ildefonso de Toledo," in Zagreb Congress, III, 223-248. [2]*De Virginitate B. Mariae*, ed. by V. Blanco Garcia, (Madrid, 1937, 2nd ed. Saragossa, 1954), I, 65. [3]*op. cit.*, I, 61. [4]*op. cit.*, XI, 156. [5]*op. cit.*,IV. [6]*op. cit.*, XII, 163. [7]*op. cit.*, I, 61. [8]*op. cit.*, XII, 164. [9]H. Barré, *Prières Anciennes*, 32-33.

IMITATION OF MARY

Imitation of Mary has been frequently proposed as a means of attaining Christian perfection.[1] The idea was first related to Mary's virginity (qv) by Alexander of Alexandria, as we learn from his successor, St. Athanasius, and by the *gnomai* or proverbs of the Council of Nicaea. "You have the conduct of Mary, who is the type and image of the life that is proper to heaven," says Alexander; "if, therefore," say the *gnomai*, "a girl wants to be called a virgin, she should resemble Mary." In the West, St. Ambrose set the pattern with the words, "Mary's life is a rule of life for all."[2]

The ideal persisted and was interpreted in each age and culture according to its mentality: in medieval times, with Mary's compassion (qv) in mind; in the time of the Reformation, with insistence on divine transcendence by the

Reformers; on the necessity for sincere Christian conduct, by the doctors of the Counter-Reformation, notably by St. Robert Bellarmine (*qv*). The French school aimed at some kind of identification with Mary in her interior dispositions. Nineteenth and twentieth century religious founders point to Mary as the model of apostolic activity. Contemplatives have seen her as the model of perfect prayer.

Papal teaching has often turned on the importance and benefits of imitating Mary in the manifold perfections of her life. Leo XIII wrote a sentence which would serve as a summary of so much that followed: "But see how a kindly and provident God has established for us in Mary a most fitting exemplar of every virtue."[3]

Vatican II, which emphasized the theme of imitation, might be said to illustrate it from the gospel: "In the course of her Son's preaching, she received his praise when, extolling a kingdom beyond the claims and ties of flesh and blood, he declared that blessed were those who heard and kept the word of God as she was faithfully doing." (cf. Lk 2:19, 51; Mk 3:35; Lk 11:27-28). The whole Church was brought under the idea: "Imitating the Mother of her Lord, and by power of the Holy Spirit, she [the Church] preserves with virginal purity and integral faith, a firm hope and sincere charity." (LG 64). In the personal context, we have such words as these: "The Virgin Mary, in her own life, lived an example of that maternal love by which all should be fittingly animated who cooperate in the apostolic mission of the Church on behalf of the rebirth of man." (LG 65). Here imitation is related to the profound life of the spirit. Application is made to the apostolate: "The perfect example of this type of spiritual and apostolic life is the most Blessed Virgin Mary, Queen of Apostles." (Decree on the Laity, 4) "They [priests] can always find a wondrous model of such docility [to the Holy Spirit] in the Blessed Virgin Mary. Led by the Holy Spirit, she devoted herself entirely to the mystery of man's redemption." (Decree on Priests, 18). The Decree on Religious quotes the words of St. Ambrose already given.

In *Marialis Cultus* (*qv*), Paul VI dealt with a difficulty raised by those who "find it difficult to take as an example Mary of Nazareth because the horizons of her life, so they say, seem rather restricted in comparison with the vast spheres of activity open to mankind today." The Pope had in mind the feminist revolution. He urged theologians, Christian leaders, and the faithful to consider these difficulties carefully and offered his own suggestions: "First, the Virgin Mary has always been proposed to the faithful by the Church as an example to be imitated, not precisely in the type of life she led, and much less for the socio-cultural background in which she lived and which today scarcely exists anywhere. She is held up as an example to the faithful rather for the way in which, in her own particular life, she fully and responsibly accepted the will of God." (cf. Lk 1:38). Paul VI adds that the Church is not tied to any particular image of Mary created for popular instruction in a particular cultural setting, in one generation after another. Each age, this age, must approach the figure of Mary in the gospel with its own anthropological ideas and needs.

The Pope, in a later passage, analyzes in detail, with a wealth of gospel reference, Mary's exemplary holiness, manifest in solid, evangelical virtues. Thus encouraged, the disciple of Mary will seek through the Spirit, who brings such things to fulfillment, to draw on the perfection of Mary for that magnetic impulse which touches the spirit and renders it truly dynamic.

[1]Cf. H. Graef, *Mary*, I, 50-51; D. Bertetto, S.D.B., "De cultu imitationis B. M. V. apud Patres Latinos," in PCM, III, 99-118. [2]*De Virginibus, II, 2, 15.* [3]*Magnae Dei Matris* (8th September, 1892), in OL, 121.

IMMACULATE CONCEPTION, THE

Dogma: The Papal Bull, *Ineffabilis Deus* (*qv*), defined the Immaculate Conception as a dogma of faith. The dogmatic formula was that "the most Blessed Virgin Mary, in the first instant of her Conception, by a singular grace and privilege granted by Almighty God, in view of the merits of Jesus Christ, the Saviour of the human race, was preserved free from all stain of original sin."[1] The relevant article gives the stages by which this text was reached. The person of Mary, not merely her soul, was the subject of the immunity from original sin. The phrase, "in the first instant of her Conception," avoided debates which belong more properly to biology. There is a nuance between grace and privilege and each was singular; therefore there can be no question of another enjoying this particular divine favour. The phrase, "in view of the merits of Jesus Christ, the Saviour of the human race," resolved the centuries-old problem of Mary's redemption by Jesus Christ. The universality and efficacy of his work were not affected by the Immaculate Conception. "All stain" covered every kind of effect that the sin of Adam could have in the human person.

The dogma was recalled in the Golden Jubilee Encyclical *Ad diem illum* (*qv*); the full dogmatic formula was repeated by Pius XII in *Fulgens Corona* (*qv*) for the Centenary. The phrase, "preserved free from all stain of original sin," was written into LG 59.

The Bible: Nowhere in the sacred books do we read, in explicit terms, that Our Lady was conceived immaculate. The question then is how it is implied. The texts used to show this are: Gen 3:15 (see WOMAN IN); Lk 1:28 ("Full of grace") and Lk 1:42 ("Blessed art thou among women") (see ANNUNCIATION). These texts are now studied with the methods of critical exegesis and are more fully understood than in times past. "Full of grace" is a mistranslation, but in the Latin tradition it influenced thinking on this subject. Pius IX, moreover, drew on Sacred Scripture in combination with the teaching of the Fathers.

Tradition: The clear emergence of the idea in Tradition dates from the fourth century.[2] Cardinal Newman did write that he drew the doctrine from the patristic teaching on Mary as the new Eve (*qv*), but few others would go beyond saying that there is implicit harmony between the two ideas.

The first apparently explicit testimony is from St. Ephraem (*qv*), but his opinion is controverted. In the *Nisibene Hymns*, he says: "Certainly you alone and your Mother are from every aspect completely beautiful, for there is no blemish in thee, my Lord, and no stain in thy Mother."[3] St. Ambrose's opinion is also controverted: "Adopt me, however, not from Sarah but from Mary, so that it might be an incorrupt virgin, virgin by grace free from all stain of sin." This is clear witness to Our Lady's holiness and sinlessness, but not directly relevant to the Immaculate Conception.

On St. Augustine's opinion, there is greater debate and a vast literature. In answer to Pelagius, he used the phrase, "except the holy Virgin Mary, about whom, for the honour of the Lord, I want there to be no question where sin is mentioned."[4] But when, in another controversy,

Julian of Eclanum dealing with Augustine's view of original sin, said to him, "you deliver Mary herself to the devil through the condition of her birth"; his reply was, "We do not deliver Mary to the devil by the condition of her birth; but for this reason, because this very condition is resolved by the grace of rebirth."[5] Whatever this text means, its author's negative influence on development of doctrine (*qv*) is undeniable. He thought that original sin was transmitted by conjugal intercourse through inherent concupiscence. Christ was immune because he was conceived virginally—the conclusion was drawn that Mary was not.

In the fifth century, St. Maximus of Turin spoke of "the original grace" which would make Mary a suitable dwelling for Christ, but with no adequate explanation. Progress from the idea of special holiness to complete holiness continued in the East. Theoteknos of Livias (*qv*), in the celebrated homily on the Assumption, spoke of Mary as "all fair," "pure and without stain," "from pure and immaculate clay."[6] St. Andrew of Crete (*qv*), preaching on the Nativity of Mary, used words compatible with the privilege, but did not specify the moment of initial holiness as the conception: "Today the pure nobility of men receives the grace of the first creation by God and thus returns to itself."[7] Likewise St. Germanus of Constantinople (*qv*) addresses Mary as "most immaculate" (*panachrante*), but in a context which refers only to personal sins.[8] In the next century, Paschasius Radbert (*qv*) in the West wrote that the veneration of Mary's birth throughout the whole Church showed that she was immune from original sin.[9] But he did not specify the moment of sanctification.

Liturgy: The feast of Mary's Nativity was certainly celebrated in the Orient in the second half of the sixth century. Towards the end of the seventh century, the feast of the Conception came into being.[10] It had its origin in the apocryphal story of the miraculous conception of Mary. Thus the story is told in the *Protevangelium*, as *Papyrus Bodmer V* gives the text, now the true one. Joachim hears that his wife had conceived at a time when he could not have been the father.[11]

The history of the feast in the West, for instance its early appearance in Ireland, is controverted.[12] It existed in England, possibly brought by some eastern monk, towards 1060, disappeared after the Norman conquest in 1066, was revived about 1127/28, and passed thereafter into Normandy, France, Belgium, Spain, and Germany.[13] The importance of the feast in the development of doctrine was immense. It ensured a foundation which is always indispensable to doctrine, the *sensus fidei*, the conviction of the faithful.

Yet doctrinal progress was to be impeded for centuries as theologians sought to explain what precisely was the object of the feast.

Medieval Controversy: On a superficial view, one may ask how did the doctrine survive against the great theologians and Doctors who in the twelfth and thirteenth centuries opposed it? Occasionally, however, in so doing, they expressed ideas which would help in its final formulation. St. Anselm (*qv*) denied the doctrine, but it could find a place within his general description of Mary's holiness—"a degree of purity than which no greater can be imagined apart from God."[14] He also taught that original sin was an absence of original justice, which would minimize the factor of concupiscence in transmission. St. Bernard (*qv*) still clung to the Augustinian idea; so did Peter Lombard (*qv*).[15]

St. Albert the Great (*qv*), though denying the Immaculate Conception, thought that Mary was sanctified in her mother's womb. St. Bonaventure (*qv*) shared this view, but he did admit that God could have granted Mary the privilege. St. Thomas Aquinas (*qv*) also held the doctrine of sanctification in the womb, but he rendered a service to development of doctrine by his insistence on the universality of the redemption, which must include Mary. In this, he was joined by Alexander of Hales.[16]

It was Duns Scotus (*qv*) who broke out of this impasse. His contribution to the development of doctrine has been the object of controversy quite recently. But his insistence on the fact that the privilege came from the perfect Mediator was important, and he clarified the idea.

The decision of the Council of Basle (*qv*) to define the doctrine was taken unfortunately after the assembly had broken with the Pope. The terms of the decree differ in points from the final formula adopted by Pius IX. The phrase, "pious doctrine," is used instead of "revealed doctrine." The words, "in view of the merits of Jesus Christ, the Saviour of the human race," are not found; nor are "in the first instant of

her conception." But the Council took a position on the substance of the truth. Debate hardened thereafter.

The Papacy would be prompted to intervene from time to time. Sixtus IV was the first to do so. By his Constitutions, *Cum praexcelsa* (1477), and *Grave nimis*, issued in the midst of violent polemics against the doctrine conducted by Vincenzo Bandelli, O.P., he approved the Mass in its honor for use in Rome and forbade either side in the controversy to call the other heretical.[17] Many of the European universities, influential centers at the time, followed the example of Paris, which in 1497 decreed that henceforth those admitted to degrees must take an oath to defend the Immaculate Conception.

The Constitutions of Sixtus IV were recalled by the Council of Trent (*qv*) in its brief mention of the question—a discreet pointer to the ultimate solution. In the seventeenth century, the controversy blazed anew. Extreme measures were adopted such as the vow (*qv*) taken by some to defend the "pious opinion," even to the shedding of their blood, or the repressive action of the Roman Inquisition, controlled by the opponents. It decreed between 1627 and 1644 that the phrase "Immaculate Conception" could not be used; supporters must speak of the conception of the immaculate Virgin. Authors such as H. Maracci (*qv*) were penalized for contravention.

Defenders of the privilege produced, none the less, an enormous literature, uneven in quality. Between 1600 and 1800, the Jesuits alone brought out 300 works on the Immaculate Conception. Ruling princes supported the doctrine, and the royal house of Spain sent several delegations to Rome to request a definition of it. (see WADDING, LUKE). It was an age in which many kingly gestures of devotion to Mary were made.

Through the pressure exerted by the kings of Spain, the Papacy increasingly lent its authority to the doctrine. St. Pius V had by the Bull *Super speculam* (1570) renewed the decrees of Sixtus IV. Paul V, by the Constitution *Regis Pacifici* (July 6, 1616), did likewise. But by the Bull *Sanctissimus* (September 12, 1617), he forbade public action against the doctrine, conceding, however, that he was not condemning the opposing view, which must not be attacked. Gregory XV, by the Bull *Sanctissimus* (May 24, 1622), extended the prohibition to private acts, with the same clause. The Dominicans were exempted by an indult of July 28 in the same year, but they could only discuss the opinion among themselves.[18]

With the Bull *Sollicitudo omnium Ecclesiarum* (December 8, 1661), issued by Alexander VII in reply to the request of Philip IV of Spain, a turning-point was reached.[19] Without condemning the opposing opinion, the Pope manifested the preference of the Holy See for the doctrine and protected it. *Ineffabilis Deus* brought some amendments to this text, but the parallel, at a distance of almost 200 years, is noteworthy. Opposition declined thereafter. The Liturgy was to be a factor in achieving peace after the passion of debate, as was popular devotion. The Constitution *In Excelsa*, issued by Innocent XII (May 15, 1695), imposed on the whole Church the Office and Mass of the Conception of the Immaculate Virgin Mary, with Octave. On December 6, 1708, Clement XI, by the Constitution *Commissi nobis*, established the feast as a holyday of obligation.

Marian theology and piety deteriorated during the age of the Enlightenment and the Revolution which followed it. The revival came from an unexpected source, the Apparition (*qv*) of the Miraculous Medal in 1830. The final stage of the development of the dogma of the Immaculate Conception was thus effected to the accompaniment of a spreading movement of prayer, whose formula was "O Mary conceived without sin, pray for us who have recourse to thee."

[1]DS. On the Immaculate Conception, cf. V.I.; M. Jugie, A.A., *L'Immaculée Conception*; E. D. O'Connor (ed.), *The Dogma of the Immaculate Conception*, (Notre Dame, 1958); J. Galot, S.J., L'Immaculée Conception," in *Maria*, VII, 9-116; G. M. Roschini, *Maria Santissima*, III, 9-267; J. B. Carol, O.F.M., "Reflections on the Problem of Mary's Preservative Redemption," in MSt, 30(1979), 19-88. [2]Cf. G. Jouassard, "The Fathers of the Church and the Immaculate Conception," in *The Dogma of Immaculate Conception*, ed. by E. D. O'Connor, (Notre Dame, 1958), 51-86. [3]*Script. Syri*, in CSCO, 218, 161; CSCO, 219, 76, ed. E. Beck. [4]*De natura et gratia, 36, 42*, in PL 44, 267. Cf. C. Boyer, "La Controverse sur l'opinion touchant la conception de la Vierge," in V.I., IV, 48-60; I. M. Dietz, "Ist die Hl. Jungfrau nach Augustinus 'Immaculata ab initio'?," in V.I., IV, 61-112; further bibliography in *Enchiridion theologicum Sancti Augustini*, (Madrid, 1961), 349ff., n. 4. [6]A. Wenger, A.A., *L'Assomption*, 275-276. [7]PG 97, 812A. [8]*Orat. 2 in dorm. B. Mariae*, in PG 98, 357. [9]*De partu Virginis, I*, in PL 120, 1372. [10]Cf. J. A. de Aldama, S.J., "La fiesta de la Concepción de María," in EstEcl, 36(1961),

427-459. [11]*Papyrus Bodmer V*, ed. M. Testuz, (Cologny, Geneva, 1958), IV, 1, p. 7. [12]Cf. P. Grosjean, "La prétendue fête de la Conception dans les églises celtiques," in AB, 61(1943), 91-95; F. O'Briain, O.F.M., "The Feast of Our Lady's Conception in the Medieval Irish Church," in IER, 70(1948), 687-704. [13]A. W. Burridge, "L'Immaculée Conception dans la théologie mariale de l'Angleterre du Moyen-Âge," in RHE 32(1936), 570-597; A. M. Cecchin, "L'Immacolata nella liturgia occidentale anteriore al secolo XIII," in MM, 5(1943), 58-114. [14]*De conceptu virg., 18*, ed. by Schmitt, II, 159. [15]*Sent. 2, dist. 31, c. 3*, in PL 192, 724. Cf. PL 192, 760ff. [16]*Summa Theologiae*, 3 p. tr. 2 q. 2 m.2 c. 1 a.2. [17]Cf. C. Sericoli, *Immaculata B. M. Virginis Conceptio juxta Xysti IV Constitutiones*, (Rome, 1945). [18]Cf. R. Laurentin, "Le Magistère et le développement du dogme de l'Immaculée Conception," in V.I., II, 65-78. [19]Cf. C. Gutierrez, "España por el dogma de la Inmaculada: La ambajada a Roma de 1659 y la Bula 'Sollicitudo' de Alejandro VII," in *Miscellanea Comilas*, 24(1955).

IMMACULATE HEART OF MARY
See HEART OF MARY

INEFFABILIS DEUS (8 December, 1854)
This is the Bull which solemnly defined the Immaculate Conception (*qv*). Its author, Pius IX (*qv*), took note of the increasing demand during the pontificate of his immediate predecessor, Gregory XVI, and the early years of his own, for a dogmatic definition of the Marian privilege. It had come from "bishops, the secular clergy, religious orders, sovereign rulers and the faithful."[1] That he might "proceed with great prudence," he established a special congregation of cardinals and also selected "priests, both secular and regular, well trained in the theological sciences," bidding them consider the matter and report to him.

Pius IX, in 1847, had congratulated Fr. Giovanni Perrone on his book dealing with the Immaculate Conception, which had as a second title "Can it be defined by dogmatic decree?" Of twenty theologians whom the Pope consulted in 1848, seventeen gave a favourable reply. To a preliminary meeting of the Congregation of Cardinals, he put two questions: Should he define the privilege? How? To the first, they answered affirmatively, and advised consultation of the bishops as to the second. Thereupon Pius XII decided to send an Encyclical Letter to the world's episcopate, stating the position and requesting their views.

The letter, *Ubi Primum*, was sent from Gaeta, dated 2 February, 1849. It bore the influence of Fr. Perrone and delighted Cardinal Newman (*qv*), then in Rome, because it asked the bishops to inform the Pope about the devotion of the faithful as well as the clergy regarding the Immaculate Conception, and the desire for a papal definition. The bishops were also to give their own thoughts.

Of 603 bishops consulted, 546 favoured definition; four opposed the definability. The remainder were undecided either as to its opportuneness or the manner of presenting the doctrine. In 1850, the Pope consulted three theologians on the project; one disagreed. In the following year, Fr. Perrone, on a secret papal order, drafted a first *schema, Deus Omnipotens.* Pius had, meanwhile, been very impressed by an essay on the subject published by Dom Guéranger. He thought it "the best thing he had seen on the subject." He heard the Benedictine in audiences in 1851-1852 and entrusted him with Fr. Perrone's (*qv*) schema. Dom Guéranger made a second draft, which was translated (*Quemadmodum Deus*) by the other theologian of the Immaculate Conception then in Rome, Carlo Passaglia (*qv*). A third draft was composed by a commission largely dominated by Passaglia, *In Mysterio.* On 22 March, 1854, Pius named a consultative assembly, composed of twenty-one Cardinals and many theologians. Between early September and the end of November, five further draft Bulls were considered.

Bishops arriving in Rome added to the difficulties of textual composition. Important decisions were taken. Passaglia's *schema* had a heavy patristic apparatus, which was fortunately dropped. He had shown little critical sense in his massive three-volume work, *De immaculato Deiparae semper Virginis conceptu.* Footnotes were ruled out in the final text. Cardinal Pecci intervened to change the reference to Our Lady's soul (given prominence in the Bull of Alexander VII) and so center the privilege on her person, object of the feast.

The age was not one of critical bibilical and patristic scholarship. The document was saved from undue effects of this deficiency by the Pope's decision to present the teaching of the Fathers and the belief of the Church *in globo.* He gave this directive to his private secretary, Mgr. Pacifici, who was charged with the composition of the final text after the Cardinals in Consistory had, on 1 December, 1854, approved the second last *schema.* The Pope then announced 8 December as the date of promulgation. He took four Cardinals (Wiseman, Brunelli, Caterini and Santucci) into consultation who sent suggestions to him. The decree, that is the strictly dogmatic passage, was ready on the day announced. The complete Bull was ready for distribution in mid-January of the following year. The defining formula was: "Accordingly, by the inspiration of the Holy Spirit, for the honour of the holy and undivided Trinity, for the glory and adornment of the Virgin Mother of God, for the exaltation of the Catholic faith and for the furtherance of the Catholic religion, by the authority of Jesus Christ Our Lord, of the Blessed Apostles Peter and Paul and our own, We declare, pronounce, and define that the doctrine which holds that the most Blessed Virgin Mary, in the first instant of her Conception, by a singular grace and privilege granted by Almighty God, in view of the merits of Jesus Christ the Saviour of the human race, was preserved free from all stain of original sin, is a doctrine revealed by God and therefore to be believed firmly and constantly by all the faithful."

The general historical review which, in the Bull, preceded this statement, reflects the state of theological science at the time. Though the biblical texts were interpreted in the light of patristic and Church teaching, which left scientific exegesis open, the Pope, in summary statements, used a form of confident generalization which would not be acceptable to Patrologists: ". . . it is the clear and unanimous opinion of the Fathers" . . . and ". . . they declared that she was foretold by God when he said to the serpent . . . ." On the precise point of Gen 3:15 (see WOMAN IN), Vatican II differed from Pius IX using "foreshadowed" instead of "indicated" (*adumbratur* for *designatur*). The word was upheld at the *Modi* stage against an express request by 144 Fathers for the word of Pius IX.

The lyrical note in the text was personal, Italian. The use of superlatives was lavish (ninety-six compared with forty-five in *Munificentissimus Deus*, less than a dozen in LG 8). In contrast too with these texts, *Ineffabilis Deus* refers to no Doctor by name, and to no Pope save Alexander VII (whose words name his own predecessors). The reference to Philip of Spain, in the quotation from Alexander VII is justified.

INFANCY

In this development of doctrine, Catholic Spain had fulfilled a historic role.

[1]OL, 78. Latin text of the Bull, *Pii IX Pontificis Maximi Acta*, (Rome, Vatican Press), I, 1, 597-619; OL, 61-82. Replies by the bishops, *Pareri sulla definizione dogmatica dell'Immacolato Concepimento della beata Vergine Maria*, (Rome, 1851-1854), 10 vols.; full documentation in V. Sardi, *La solenne definizione del dogma dell'immacolato conceptimento di Maria Santissima, Atti et documenti*, (Rome, Vatican Press, 1904, 1905), 2 vols. Cf. J. Perrone, *De Immaculato conceptu. An dogmatico decreto definiri possit?*, (Avenione, 1848); P. Guéranger, O.S.B. (noted liturgist), *Mémoire sur la question de l'Immaculée Conception*, (Paris, 1850); G. Marocco, *La Bolla "Ineffabilis Deus" di Pio IX Studio storicodogmatico del suo processo formativo*, (Alba, 1953); J. Alfaro, "La formula definitoria de la Immaculada Concepcion," in V.I., II, 201-275.

INFANCY NARRATIVES, THE

The name refers now by almost general agreement to the first two chapters of Matthew and Luke.[1] These chapters have contributed enormously to Christianity. Iconography has repeatedly drawn inspiration from them. Popular piety has taken the *Ave Maria* (see HAIL MARY) and the *Angelus* (qv) from Luke; the Liturgy has taken from it the *Magnificat, Benedictus*, and *Nunc Dimittis*, and, as well as the feasts of the Christmas cycle, those of the Annunciation, the Visitation (qqv), and the Presentation of the Lord (qv). The first chapters of Matthew and Luke were the subject from early times of homiletics and commentaries which furthered the theology of Our Lady and St. Joseph. Christian doctrine is thus indebted to them.

Critical study of biblical texts has in the present age been directed to these first two chapters of Matthew and Luke. If English-speaking Catholic scholars have not notably contributed to this research and reflection, the work of R. E. Brown by its size and intention restores the balance. Scholars of different outlook and relying on different techniques have conducted the textual analysis. Source, form, and redaction criticism have been at work, as has the history of religions. What results from such study must be related to fundamental truths concerning revelation, inspiration, sacred tradition, and the teaching authority.

Each author arranges his material according to a fixed pattern: Matthew in a series of incidents each of which ends in an Old Testament quotation; Luke in a double diptych composed of annunciation and birth stories of John the Baptist and Jesus. In Matthew's account, Joseph dominates. Mary dominates in Luke's narrative. Two questions have been much debated in regard to the contribution of each evangelist—historicity and theology, or in the latter case, to be more precise, Christology.

There are many discrepancies. Yet despite the difference in topics, approach and treatment, they have the following factual points in common: a) Mary, Mother of Jesus, was at the time of her conception, betrothed to Joseph (Mt 1:18; Lk 1:27); b) an angel foretells the birth of Mary's son (Mt 1:20-23; Lk 1:30-35); c) Joseph was a decendant of David (Mt 1:20; Lk 1:27); d) the conception of Mary's child takes place or is decided independently of Joseph (Mt 1:18; Lk 1:38); e) the conception was the work of the Holy Spirit (Mt 1:18, 20; Lk 1:35); f) the Child's name, Jesus, was made known to the parents by an angel (Mt 1:21; Lk 1:31); g) an angel states that Jesus is to be Saviour (Mt 1:21; Lk 2:11); h) at the time of the birth, Mary and Joseph were a united pair (Mt 2:1; Lk 2:5); i) the birth took place in Bethlehem (Mt 2:1; Lk 2:6-7); j) after the early events of the infancy, the Holy Family settled in Nazareth (Mt 2:23; Lk 2:39); k) the infancy of Jesus is located in general history by explicit reference to Herod (Mt 2:1; Lk 1:5).

There are other points of similarity. The Old Testament influences each narrative considerably. Apart from theories which make each of the infancy narratives a gratuitous composition fashioned from Old Testament material, Matthew presents direct Old Testament quotations, and Luke's text has very many verbal similarities with the earlier inspired books (see DAUGHTER of ZION, MAGNIFICAT). Each evangelist recalls Is 7:14 in particular, Matthew quoting directly, Luke by a remarkable parallel in 1:32. The oracle is in the second person with Jesus instead of Emmanuel. Abraham, the father of believers, is at the origin of Matthew's genealogy, and named in the Lucan canticles, *Magnificat* and *Benedictus*.

Each evangelist evokes the Godhead, Matthew by applying the title Emmanuel to Jesus (1:23), Luke by giving him the title Son of God (1:32). Each records a heavenly sign at the birth of Jesus, Matthew, a star (2:2), Luke, an angelic choir (2:9-13).

Scholarly literature on the infancy narratives was for a while prone to see the key to the problems of these chapters as *midrash*. It is now seen that they do not correspond to this or any typical Jewish literary genre; they are perhaps suitably styled "fulfillment narratives." Nor does the theory of an imposed "high Christology" command universal assent—a reading back to the days of Jesus' concepton and infancy of the intuition granted to the disciples in his risen and exalted state. On the same theory, Mark would read this intuition back into the public ministry, and Paul and John to Jesus' pre-existence. The exegete must still explain why writers with a sense of the factual—Matthew by setting down a genealogy, Luke by declaring his intent in factual terms—felt compelled to use the details which we read in their books. Apart from the fact of divine inspiration, the very impact of the risen Christ and the descent of his Spirit sharpened their sensitivity to what concerned him.

---

[1]Besides commentaries on the two gospels, cf. P. A. Durand, S.J., *L'Enfance de Jésus Christ*, (Paris, 1908); F. Kattenbusch, "Die Geburtsgeschichte Jesu als Haggada der Urchristologie," in *Theologische Studien und Kritiken*, 102(1930), 454-474; P. Minear, "The Interpreter and the Birth Narratives," in *Symbolicae Bibl. Uppsalienses*, 13(1950), 1-22; F. W. Goodman, "Sources of the first two chapters in Mt. and Lk.," in *Church Quarterly Review*, 162(1961), 136-143; P. F. Thompson, "The Infancy Gospels of St. Matthew and St. Luke compared," in *Studia Evangelica, 1*, TU, 73(Berlin, 1959), 217-222; J. Delorme, "À propos des Evangiles de l'Enfance," *Ami du Clergé*, 71(1961), 760-764; R. Leaney, "The Birth Narratives in St. Luke and St. Matthew," in NTS, 8(1961-1962), 158-166; C. S. Mann "The Historicity of the Birth Narratives," in *Historicity and Chronology in the New Testament*, Theology Collection 6, (London, SPCK, 1965), 46-58; A. G. Wright, "The Literary Genre Midrash," in CBQ, 28(1966), 105-138, 417-457, (book form, Staten Island, 1967); K. H. Schelkle, *Die Kindheitsgeschichte Jesu, Wort und Schrift*, (Düsseldorf, 1966), 59-75; A. Vogtle, "Die Geburt des Erlösers," in *Bibel und Leben*, 7(1966), 235-242; id., *Das Evangelium und die Evangelien*, (Düsseldorf, 1971); J. Cardinal Daniélou, S.J., *Les Évangiles de l'Enfance*, (Paris, 1967); Ortensio da Spinetoli, O.F.M.,Cap., *Introduzione ai Vangeli dell' Infanzia*, Brescia, 1967); id., "Vangeli dell' Infanzia," in *Enciclopedia delle Religioni*, (Florence, Vallechi, 1971), II, 1388-1398; C. Perrot, "Les récits d'enfance dans la Haggada antérieure au IIe siècle de notre ère," in RSR, 55(1967), 481-518; ibid., "Les Évangiles de l'enfance: Mt. 1-2; Lc. 1-2," in *Cahiers Évangile* 18(Paris, Cerf, 1976); C. Cardinal Journet, "Les Évangiles de l'Énfance et la critique historique," in *Nova et Vetera*, 43(1968), 65-72; W. Knorzer, *Wir haben sein Stern gesehen. Die Kindheitsevangelien nach Lukas uns Matthäus*, (Stuttgart: Verlag Katholisches Bibelwerk, 1968); M. Laconi, O.P., 'Vangeli dell' Infanzia nella duplice presentazione di Matteo (cc. 1. 2) e di Luca (cc. 1. 2.)," in *Rivista di ascetica e mistica*, 13(1968), 31-43; A. Ibañez Arana, "Sobre los Evangelios de la Infancia de Jesus," in *Lumen (Vitoria)*, 17(1968), 128-140; J. Riedl, *Die Vorgeschichte Jesu. Die Heilsbotschaft von Mt. 1-2 und Lk. 1-2*, (Biblisches Forum 3; Stuttgart: Verlag Katholisches Bibelwerk, 1968); M. McNamara, "God's Living Word: Infancy Narratives and Midrash," in *Doctrine and Life*, 18(1968), 701-705 and 755-762; R. Le Déaut, C.S.Sp., "À propos d'une définition du Midrash," in BB, 50(1969), 395-413; L. Hermans, *L'Infanzia di Gesu nella Bibbia*, (Bari, 1969); C. Hughet, *Pour comprendre l'enfance de Jésus*, (Paris, 1969); E. Nellessen, "Zu den Kindheitsgeschichten bei Matthäus und Lukas," in *Theol. Zeitschr.*, 78(Trier, 1969). 305-309; R. Schnackenburg, *Die Geburt Christi ohne Mythos und Legende*, (Mainz, 1969); C. Gancho, "Infanzia. Vangelo dell'," in *Enciclopedia della Bibbia*, IV, (1970), 300-314; J. Winandy, O.S.B., *Autour de la naissance de Jésus. Accomplissement et prophétie*, (Paris, 1970); H. Wansbrough, "The Childhood of Jesus," in CRev, 55(1970), 112-118; J. Kosnetter, "Der Geschichtswert der Kindheitsgeschichte (Mt. 1-2; Lk. 1-2)," in *Festschrift Franz Loidl zum 65 Geburtstag*, (Wien, 1970), 73-93; S. Zedda, S.J., "Maria nel Vangelo dell' Infanzia," in *La Madonna nella professione di fede del popolo di Dio*, (Rome, Collegamento Mariano nazionale, 1970); J. D. M. Derrett, "Further Light on the Narratives of the Nativity," in NovT, 17(1975), 81-108; R. E. Brown, *The Birth of the Messiah*, (New York, London, 1977); *Mary in NT*, 74-97, 107-162; R. Laurentin, "Exégèses réductrices des Évangiles de l'Enfance," in MM, 41(1979), 76-100.

INNOCENT III, POPE (1161-1216)

The mighty Pontiff, a great preacher, dealt with Marian themes in his sermons for the Advent and Christmas cycles and for the four feasts, the Nativity, Purification, Annunciation, and Assumption. Occasional passages occur elsewhere in his works.[1]

I. Puts the Eve (*qv*)-Mary contrast with conciseness: "Hail, for through you the name of Eve will be changed [Eva, Ave]. She was full of sin, you are full of grace. She withdrew from God, the Lord is with you. She was accursed among women, but you are blessed among women. Cain, the fruit of her womb, was accursed, but blessed will be the fruit of your womb, Jesus. Through her, death entered the world, through you, life returned to the world."[2]

I. thought that Mary was "begotten [*producta*] in guilt." This was his personal opinion and did not commit his office. Nor did this passage: "These things completed, the Holy Spirit came immediately and prepared a threefold way before the face of the Lord. The first was virginal consent, the second cleansing of the flesh, the third formation of the body. The first was the mental consent in the virgin, the second was cleansing of the flesh from the root of sin, the third formation of the body from the most pure blood. For the author of faith could not be conceived of a faithless one, therefore the first way, the virgin's consent, had to be prepared. At once, the Holy Spirit came upon her; he had first come upon her when, in the womb of her mother, he had cleansed her of original sin, but now he descended in her to cleanse her flesh of the root of sin, so that she should be wholly without wrinkle, or stain."[3]

I. was seized with wonder at the constrasts in the Incarnation. "O truly new thing which the Lord has done today on the earth; for a star conceived the sun, a creature the Creator, a daughter the Father."[4] Reflecting on the Old Testament figure of Aaron's rod, he throws off a lengthy eulogy of Mary: "Straight through faith, upright through hope, noble through charity, delicate through modesty, graceful through contempt of the world, supple through compassion for the neighbour, leafy through the accomplishment of good works, flower-bearing through the glory of virginity, fruitful through the privilege of fecundity."[5] Elsewhere it is Mary's humility he praises.

Mary's intercession was congenial to one who sang of her as "Hope of the world" and who spoke of her as "the dawn" who was "the end of our condemnation and the origin of salvation."[6] Hence such a passage as this: "Who ever devoutly invoked her and was not heard by her? She is 'the mother of fair love and of holy hope' who prays for the miserable; pleads for the afflicted, intercedes for sinners." Whoever is assailed by the world, the flesh or the devil should look to the "army set in battle line, implore Mary that she, through her Son, 'may send help from the sanctuary and give support from Zion'."[7] On the bodily Assumption, I. was silent.

---

[1]Marian sermons in PL 217. *Encomium de B. V. M. et Filio ejus Jesus Christo*, PL 217, 915-916; *Hymnus de Christo et B. V. M. dignissima Matre ejus*, 917-920. [2]*Serm. 2, In solemn. Purific. gloriossissimae semper V. M.*, in PL 217, 506B. [3]PL 217, 506CD. [4]*In solemn. Annunt.*, in PL 217, 522. [5]*Encomium de B. V. M. et Filio ejus Jesus Christo*, 915. [6]*Serm. 2 de Assumpt.*, in PL 217, 581B. [7]*Serm. de Nativit. B. M.*, in PL 217, 586A.

INTERCESSION, MARY'S

Sacred Scripture: Our invocation of Mary presupposes her power and willingness to intercede on our behalf. This intercession is an aspect of her mediation (*qv*), and it is an exercise of her spiritual motherhood (*qv*).[1] The scriptural testimony on the subject may, at first sight, appear slight. Luke's infancy narrative does not refer explicitly to any intercession by Mary. A theme, however, of the tradition written down by Luke, is that Mary as Daughter of Zion, representative therefore of Israel, has a role between God and man. This would agree with implicit intercession in the *Fiat* of the Annunciation (*qv*). In the *Magnificat* and the Temple episode, she typifies Israel in prayer, and Israel in prayer was given to intercession.

The Cana episode is frequently chosen to illustrate Our Lady's intercession, and its import is deepened by Jn 19:25-27. Vatican II notes that Mary, "by her intercession, brought about the beginning of miracles by Jesus the Messiah (cf. Jn 19:1-11)." (LG 58). The Council also refers to Acts 1:14, which describes the Apostles "continuing in one mind in prayer with the women and Mary, the Mother of Jesus, and with his brethren," and adds: "We see Mary prayerfully imploring the gift of the Spirit, who had already overshadowed her in the Annunciation." (LG 59).

History: Slender threads of evidence from very early times tempt us to see belief in Mary's intercession—from the archaeology of the Holy Land, and from the Assumption Apocrypha. In the earliest known version of the latter, the Ethiopian "Book of Rest," two episodes strongly suggest Mary's intercession. The funeral procession, accompanying her body to the tomb, is interrupted by Jews who wished to desecrate the body. The leader, the High Priest, is dramatically punished—his hands remain stuck to the bier, severed from his body. When he cries out to Peter for mercy, Peter tests his faith and tells him: "Go then and kiss the body of Mary saying: I believe in you and in the fruit which came from you." When he had blessed Mary for three hours, and done as Peter bade him, he was cured."[2] Later, when Mary, now soul and body reunited, was allowed with the Apostles to see the souls in torment, these cried out to her: "Mary, we implore you, Mary, light and Mother of lights, Mary, life and the mother of Apostles, Mary, golden light, you who bear every true lamp, Mary, our mistress and Mother of our Lord, Mary, our Queen, beg of your Son that he should allow us a little rest." Mary's reply is not given, whereas that of the Apostles to a similar prayer is. The Lord, because of Michael's tears and his Apostles, "and Mary, my Mother," grants relief to those in torment.[3]

The first patristic testimony is a subject of controversy. St. Irenaeus (*qv*) first used the word *Advocata* of Mary,[4] in the *Adversus Haereses* and in the *Demonstration of the Apostolic*

Preaching. The debate centers on whether the word is used in the sense of intercessor for Eve or merely to designate her counterpart. In the fourth century, St. Gregory of Nazianzen describes an instance of prayer to the Blessed Virgin by a virgin Justina, whose virginity was threatened by a suitor.[5] In the same age, St. Gregory of Nyssa (*qv*) narrates an apparition of Our Lady to his namesake, Gregory the Wonderworker. She appeared with St. John and told him to make known to the young man (that is to Gregory) the mystery of piety, and John said that he was ready to do this.[6] Here Mary is not invoked, but grants a favour as if she were. The evidence from St. Ambrose (*qv*) is more subtle. He did perceive the power of some intervention by the dead on behalf of the living (see ADVOCATE), and speaking to virgins, he tells them that their souls resemble an altar whereon "Christ is each day immolated for the redemption of his body."[7] For St. Ambrose, Mary was the first and model of all virgins.

In his age, the Liturgy fully reflects growing awareness of Mary's heavenly power; it was then that her name was included in the *Communicantes* of the Mass. Still earlier, there is the most impressive piece of evidence from all the early centuries, the *Sub Tuum* (*qv*). The great Augustine (*qv*) could not bring himself to address Mary directly, save in a few exceptional moments—as when recalling the Mother and Child in the Christmas scene, "Give milk, Mother, to him who is our food, give milk to the bread coming down from heaven . . . give milk to him who made you such that he could be made from you, who brought to you the gift of fruitfulness in conception and in birth, did not take from you the ornament of virginity."[8] But that is praise not invocation, near as it may come to this.

There is no doubt at all about another testimony from the same century. Basil of Seleucia (*qv*) ends his sermon on the Annunciation with this prayer: "O Virgin all holy, he who has said of you all that is honourable and glorious has not sinned against the truth, but remains unequal to your merit. Look down on us from above and be propitious to us. Lead us in peace and having brought us without shame to the throne of judgment, grant us a place at the right hand of your Son, that we may be borne off to heaven and sing with the angels to the uncreated, consubstantial Trinity."[9] Here already one may note what so often is found in prayers to Mary

through the ages, the conviction that she herself can accomplish what she is asked for.

Mary's intercessory role is amply expressed in the sixth century by Romanos the Singer (*qv*). To Adam and Eve in prayer, Mary replies thus: "Cease lamentations, I shall become your advocate with my Son; do you put away sadness since I have brought joy into the world, for it is to overthrow the realm of sorrow that I have come, full of grace."[10] Mary, in the Magi scene, asks her Son, on their behalf, to "give three requests to her who brought you into the world." ". . . I pray to you for all men. You have made me the voice and honour of all my race; the earth which you have made has in me a sure protection, a rampart and support. Those whom you drove out of the paradise of delight turn their eyes towards me, for I bring them back there; let the universe realize that you were born of me, my little Child, God before time began."[11] Later in the same age, Theoteknos of Livias (*qv*) used a similar metaphor: "Raised to heaven, she remains for the human race an unconquerable rampart, interceding for us before her Son and God."[12]

Byzantium was filled with conviction on the power of Mary's prayer. Constantinople gloried in the title "City of the Theotokos" and claimed that in the seventh and eighth century, three times (in 619, 626, and 718), its Patroness had intervened miraculously to save it from its enemies. "God and the Theotokos" is the refrain of the discourses which mark these heavenly favours. St. Germanus of Constantinople (*qv*), recounting the victory on a feastday of the Assumption, went on: "The Word of God born of her . . . disposed things with reason and wisdom that it should appear to all most openly and most evidently that his own Mother herself interceded with him for our rescue, and that she should be unanimously recognized as the one who caused the repulse and rout of our enemies."[13] Well might the saint exclaim on another occasion: "Yes, all that touches you is truly enigmatic, surpassing nature, above speech and all power. For that reason your intercession is beyond our understanding."

John the Geometer (*qv*) continued this tradition. Mary, he thought, was an intercessor for all before her Assumption (*qv*). After that event, her power was amplified: "You scatter your favours with still greater abundance since you possess more fully him who is their source and who is entirely willing to give them to us, rather you possess almost everything by yourself and you show largesse to whom you will and to him who begs it of you."[14]

A first great name in the West is that of Ambrose Autpert (qv): "Let us entrust ourselves with all our soul's affection to the intercession of the Blessed Virgin; let us all, with all our strength, beg her patronage, that, at the moment when on earth we surround her with our suppliant homage, she herself may deign in heaven to commend us with a fervent prayer. For without any doubt she who merited to bring ransom for those who needed deliverance, can more than all the saints benefit by her favour those who have received deliverance."[15]

Ambrose linked intercession with the universal motherhood (see MOTHER OF GRACE). To him, we owe a prayer taken up by all, because it was falsely thought to be from St. Augustine: "Come to the help of the miserable, assist the faint-hearted, restore the weak; pray for the people, intervene on behalf of the clergy, intercede for the choir on monks, plead for the devout, female sex; may all feel your help who devoutly celebrate your birthday."[16]

Paul the Deacon (qv), urging all to approach Our Lady, concludes: "For she who brought forth the source of mercy, Jesus Christ, our God and Lord, receiving from him all things, will, through him, grant the wishes of all."[17] Commenting on the in primis of the Communicantes in the Mass, Paul based the superiority of Mary's intercession over that of the saints on the fact that "she alone merited to bring forth God and man."

In the next century, Paschasius Radbert (qv) linked prayer to Mary with a strong Christocentric sense: "Let us approach with confident spirit the throne of the high Priest, where he is our victim, priest, advocate and judge."[18] St. Peter Damian (qv) had an intuition of Mary's prayer flowing from her mediation: "May we deserve to have the help of your intercession in heaven, because as the Son of God has deigned to descend to us through you, so we also must come to him through you."[19]

With St. Anselm (qv), the accent is on the spiritual motherhood: "The Mother of God is our mother. May the good mother ask and beg for us, may she request and obtain what is good for us. Let her ask her Son for her sons, the only-begotten for the adopted, the master for the

servants. Let the good Son hear his Mother for his brothers, the only-begotten Son for those whom he adopted, the Master for those whom he freed."[20] The way was then open for the ample teaching of St. Bernard. Mary's intercession was henceforth a constant in doctrine, spirituality, homiletics and, as from early times, it also informed abundantly Liturgy and hymnography. It would take whole books to document this assertion; as much space would be needed to quote all that the modern Popes said on the subject.

The Councils: After the crisis of the Reformation, the Council of Trent repeated traditional Christian teaching on the intercession of the saints, which applies preeminently to Mary: "The saints who reign together with Christ, offer up their prayers to God for men; . . . it is good and useful to invoke them suppliantly and, in order to obtain favours from God through his Son Jesus Christ our Lord who alone is our Redeemer and Saviour, to have recourse to their prayers, assistance and support."[21]

The subject occasioned no controversy within Vatican II. The first *schema* spoke of Mary interceding with love for us constantly before God and Christ. The first draft of the new *schema* contained the words, "not even in the heavenly Jerusalem is she separated from her Son, since she does not cease by her intercession to win us gifts of eternal salvation." The rewritten passage, after the meeting in June, 1964, was stronger: "Taken up into heaven she did not lay aside this saving role but, by her manifold intercession, she continues wondrously to win for us gifts of eternal salvation. "Wondrously" (*mirum in modum*) was deleted at the next stage; otherwise there was no change. (LG 62). The Council urged prayer to Mary: "Let the entire body of the faithful pour forth persevering prayer to the Mother of God and Mother of men. Let them implore that she who aided the beginnings of the Church by her prayers may now, exalted as she is in heaven above all the saints and angels, intercede with her Son in the fellowship of all the saints." (LG 69).

[1] Cf. M. J. Nicolas, O.P., "Intercession," in DSp, 7, 1858-1870. On Mary's intercession, cf. J. Galot, S.J., "L'Intercession de' Marie," in *Maria*, VI, 515-550. Cf. esp. J. Galot, S.J., "Recherches sur l'intercession de Marie," in BSFEM, 23, 24, (1966), 67; E. Dublanchy, "Marie, gloire et puissance d'intercession de Marie au ciel," in DTC, IX, 2433-2439; G. Bardy, "La doctrine de l'intercession de Marie chez les Pères

greces," in VieSp, supplément, 56(1938), 1-37; J. Danzas, "L'intercession mariale dans la piété russe," in VieSp, supplément, 57(1938), 16-36; P. Hoffer, S.M., "L'intercession de la très Sainte Vierge chez les maîtres de l'Ecole française," in VieSp, supplément, 56(1938), 65-101; G. Frenaud and G. Oury, O.S.B., "La médiation d'intercession dans la liturgie mariale," in CM, 6(1962), 82-96; H. Barré, *Prières Anciennes*, *passim*; W. G. Most, "The Virgin Mary's Intercession," in MSt, 22(1971), 27-48; and see articles on MEDIATION, SPIRITUAL MOTHERHOOD, and REDEMPTION, MARY'S PART IN THE, in the present work. ²Latin tr. of text, V. Arras, *De Transitu Mariae Apocrypha Aethiopice*, (1973), in CSCO 343, 28ff. ³*op. cit.*, 38. ⁴*Adv. Haer.*, *V, 19, 1*, in PG 7, 1175A-1176A; *Demonstratio apost. praed.*, *32, 33*, in PO 12, 756; TU, 31, 1, 18-19; SC 62, 82-86. For debate, cf. M. Jourjon, in BSFEM, 23(1966), 38-42. ⁵*Or. 24, 11*, in PG 35, 1181A. ⁶PG 46, 912. ⁷*De Virginibus*, ed. by E. Cazzaniga, C.S.Lat. Parav., (1948), II, 18, p. 41. ⁸*Serm. 369, 1*, in PL 39, 1655. For authenticity, cf. H. Barré, *Prières Anciennes*, 23, n. 20. ⁹PG 85, 452AB. ¹⁰*2nd hymn for the Nativity*, in SC 110, 101. ¹¹*2nd hymn for the Nativity*, in SC 110, 107. ¹²A. Wenger, A.A., *L'Assomption*, 291. ¹³V. Grumel, "Homélie de S. Germain sur la délivrance de Constantinople," in REB, 16(1958), 205. ¹⁴A. Wenger, A.A., in BSFEM, 23(1966), 69. ¹⁵PL 39, 2134. ¹⁶Cf. H. Barré, in BSFEM, 23(1966), 86, n. 41. ¹⁷PL 95, 1574. ¹⁸Pseudo-Ildefonsus, *Serm. I in Assumpt.*, in PL 96, 249B. ¹⁹PL 144, 761B. ²⁰*Orat. VII, apud*, H. Barré, *Prières Anciennes*, 305. ²¹DS 1821.

IRENAEUS, ST. (d. after 193)

Brought up in the circle of Polycarp at Smyrna with memories of the apostolic age, I. was bishop of Lyons where he was martyred. His sense of tradition and his attention to biblical themes give him exceptional importance and explain the constant interest in his writings, particularly strong in the present century. His vast perspectives and synthesis have won him the title, Father of Christian Theology. In his age, the theology of Our Lady was truly born;[1] The creative intuition was the concept of Mary as the new Eve (qv). Whatever its origin, and allowing for the fact that St. Justin (qv) showed acquaintance with it, I. remains its greatest exponent and with him it suggests already immense possibilities of development. His doctrine is found in the *Adversus Haereses* and the *Demonstratio apostolicae praedicationis*.[2] Book III of *Adversus Haereses*, which contains most of the relevant texts, was critically edited by F. Sagnard for *Sources Chrétiennes* in 1952, an edition highly praised, although recent manuscript discoveries entail revision. Books I, IV (1965), and V (1969) have appeared in the same collection, which will provide a complete edition to supersede those of R. Massuet (used by the *Patrologia Graeca*), of W. W. Harvey

(1857), and of books I and II of U. Mannucci (1907). The *Demonstratio apostolicae praedictionis* was known to Eusebius. It was found in an Armenian translation in 1904, and has been translated into several languages since then.[3]

Beginning with the Pauline idea of Adam as the type of Christ who was to come, I. takes up at once Mary's role. Since the Saviour preexisted, he had to become that which would be saved, so that salvation would not be meaningless. "Consequently," I. goes on, "the Virgin Mary is found obedient, saying 'Behold your handmaid, Lord, let it be done to me according to your word'. But Eve was disobedient; though still a virgin she did not obey. For as she, though wedded to Adam, was still a virgin . . . being disobedient, she became a cause of death to herself and to all mankind. So Mary, having a predestined husband, but none the less a Virgin, was obedient and became to herself and to the whole human race a cause of salvation."[4]

There is a hint here, as Mgr. Jouassard pointed out, that, for I., Eve was a type of Mary, a previous sketch as it were, as Adam was of Christ.[5] Mary is part of God's masterplan, which is worked out, as I. explains it, through a *recirculatio*, an undoing along the same path of the original evil. This is a tied knot, and is unloosed at each stage by counterparts of those involved, Adam by Christ, the tree of Eden by the tree of the Cross, Eve by Mary. "Because of this, the Law calls her who was betrothed to a man, even though she was still a virgin, the wife of her betrothed, signifying the *recirculatio* from Mary to Eve; for what has been tied cannot be unloosed, save by undoing in reverse order the binding of the knots, so that the first bound together should be loosed by the second, in other words, that the second should free the first . . . . Because of this, Luke began his genealogy from the Lord, and brought it back to Adam, indicating that it was not they [the fathers] who had regenerated him [the Lord] in the gospel of life, but he them.

In the same manner, the knot of Eve's disobedience was untied by Mary's obedience; for what Eve bound by her unbelief, Mary loosed by her faith."[6]

This is a classic text. To the doctrine expressed in it, I. returned later in Book V of the same work, and after that in the *Demonstratio apostolicae praedicationis*. In the first, after recalling the "recapitulation" by Christ, he went on, "and to undo the seduction by which the virgin Eve, betrothed to a man, was wickedly misled, Mary, a virgin betrothed, was given good tidings of truth by an angel. For as the former was seduced by an angel's talk to turn from God betraying his word, so the latter was given good news by the angel's talk that she should bear God, being obedient to his word. The former had disobeyed God, and the latter was persuaded to obey God, so that the virgin Mary should become the advocate of the virgin Eve. And as the human race was bound to death by a virgin, by a virgin it was delivered: virginal disobedience is balanced by virginal obedience."[7]

The text of the *Demonstratio apostolicae praedicationis:* "And just as it was through a virgin who disobeyed that man was stricken and fell and died, so too it was through the Virgin who obeyed the word of God that man resuscitated by life received life. For the Lord came to seek back the lost sheep, and it was man who was lost and therefore he did not become some other formation, but he likewise, of her that was descended from Adam, preserved the likeness of formation; for Adam had necessarily to be restored in Christ, that mortality be absorbed in immortality, and Eve in Mary, that a virgin advocate of a virgin should undo and destroy virginal disobedience by virginal obedience."[8]

If the word "advocate"—which in the Greek original probably read *paracletos*—were to be read in its plenary Latin sense, we should have a doctrine of Mary's intercession (*qv*) already in the second century. The matter is highly controversial.[9] The phrase, "cause of salvation to herself and to the whole human race," in the earlier text, is likewise much discussed. It is quoted in LG 56 with I.'s name,[10] the only one with that of St. Ambrose (*qv*) to figure in the body of the text.

I. expressed his belief in the divine motherhood in terms which anticipated *Theotokos:* "The Son of God was born of the Virgin."[11] In dealing with the virginal conception, on which he insisted often, he invokes Old Testament texts and figures. Adam was fashioned from the "virgin earth,"[12] a type of the virgin birth. Is 7:14 was especially related to the Virgin Mary.[13] The stone cut by no human hands in Dan 2:34 was also a type of her motherhood, with which text I. linked Is 28:16.[14] On Gen 3:15

(see WOMAN IN), he is quoted as the first of the Fathers to interpret the oracle in a Marian sense, but he does so in the context of a collective meaning, with the conflict between the demon and the descendants of Eve, the triumph won by Christ, born of the Virgin Mary.[15]

I. is one of the early Fathers who read Jn 1:13 in the singular "he who was born . . .", which implies the virginal conception.[16] On the Cana episode, he appears to see some undue eagerness on Mary's part and almost a rebuke in the words of Christ. "When Mary hurried to the admirable sign of the wine, and before the time desired to participate of the mixed cup, the Lord restraining [*repellens*] this untimely haste said: 'What is it to me and to thee, woman; my hour has not yet come' awaiting the hour known beforehand to the Father."[17] The context is the complete foreknowledge of the Father and the accomplishment of all things by the Son at the proper time. It is not a discussion of Mary's holiness. On the subject, I. is not explicit, but a high degree of perfection is implied in the Eve-Mary contrast.

I. favoured the title "firstborn of the Virgin." Taken with two brief but significant passages, it would appear to imply an extension of the Virgin's motherhood to others spiritually. The first shows our regeneration in the faith as linked with that of the Son of God from the virgin, identical even with it.[18] The second speaks of the Word, Son of God, son of man, who, "a pure one purely opens the pure womb, which regenerates men in God, which he himself had made pure."[19] This text, as the previous one, has been intrepreted as of the Church, and remains a subject of controversy. The relationship between Mary and the Church is discernible in I., notably when, in regard to the *Magnificat* (*qv*), he says that "Mary cries out prophetically in the name of the Church."[20]

[1]Cf. G. Jouassard, "Le 'premier-né' de la Vierge, chez St. Irénée," in RevSR, 12(1932), 509-532; *ibid*., "La théologie mariale de St. Irénée," in *L'Immaculée Conception: Actes du VIIe Congrès marial national*, (Lyons, 1954), 265-276; J. Garçon, *La mariologie de St. Irénée*, (Lyons, 1932); B. Przbylski, *De Mariologia S. Irenaei Lugdunensis*, (Rome, 1937); N. F. Moholy, "St. Irenaeus, the Father of Mariology," in *Studia Mariana*, VII, (First Franciscan national congress, 1950. Burlington, Wisconsin, 1952), 129-187. [2]CMP, I, 34-54; EMBP, 33-53. [3]*Demonstratio apostolicae praedicationis*, Latin tr. by S. Weber, (Freiburg, 1917); French tr. by L. M. Froidevaux, in SC 62; English tr. by J. P. Smith, in *Ancient Christian Writers*. [4]*Adv. Haer*.,

III, 22, 4, in SC 34, 378-380; PG 7, 958-960; SC 211, 438-444. [5]*L'Immaculée Conception: Actes du VIIe Congrès marial national*, (Lyons, 1954), 268. [6]On this and following texts, Cf. G. Jouassard, in BSFEM, 12(1954), 37-39. [7]*Adv. Haer., V, 19, 1*, in SC 152, 248-250; PG 7, 1175-1176. [8]*Demonstratio apostolicae praedicationis, 33*, English tr. by J. P. Smith, in *Ancient Christian Writers*, 69. [9]Cf. G. Jouassard, in BSFEM, 12(1954), 40; M. Jourjon, in BSFEM, 23(1966), 38-42. [10]Cf. J. de Aldama, S.J., "Sibi causa facta est salutis," in EphMar, 16(1966), 34-39. [11]*Adv. Haer., III, 16, 2*, in SC 34, 280. [12]*Demonstratio apostolicae praedicationis, 32*, English tr. by J. P. Smith, in *Ancient Christian Writers*, 68. [13]*Adv. Haer., XXI*, in SC 34, 348. [14]*op. cit.*, in SC 34, 364. [15]Cf. R. Laurentin, in BSFEM, 12(1954), 93-97. [16]*Adv. Haer., III, 16, 2* in SC 34, 280; *Adv. Haer., III, 19, 2*, in SC 34, 334; *Adv. Haer., III, 21, 5*, i SC 34, 362-366. [17]*Adv. Haer., III, 16, 7*, in SC 34, 292-294. [18]*Adv. Haer., IV, 33, 4*, in SC 100, 810-812. Cf. G. Jouassard, "Le 'premier-né' de la Vierge' chez St. Irénée," in RevSR, 12(1932), and L. Regnault, in DS 7, 1954-1955. [19]*Adv. Haer., IV, 33, 11*, in SC 100, 830. [20]*Adv. Haer, III, 10*, in SC 34, 164.

ISAAC OF STELLA (d. *c.* 1178)

I. was a Cistercian abbot born in England, and a friend of St. Thomas Becket, who spent his monastic life in France. He was author of four sermons on Our Lady, three on the Assumption,[1] and one on the Nativity.[2] Due to the influence possibly of Usuard's Martyrology and Pseudo-Jerome (*qv*), I. was hesitant on the bodily Assumption (*qv*). He did not know whether Mary was assumed ("with the body or without the body, I do not know, God knows"),[3] but he believed that she was taken to the very highest heaven. He was insistent on Mary's dependence on Christ, "the father of her nature, the Lord of her life, the redeemer of her soul, the guardian of her state, the guide of her progress, today the one who receives her spirit."[4]

The most remarkable passage he wrote on Our Lady is on the Mary-Church parallel; it is mentioned in the annotation of *Lumen Gentium*.[5] Applying the rule of general and particular to the Church and to Mary, and concluding, "when mention is made of either, it is to be understood almost indifferently and conjointly of both," he says: "Each is mother, each is virgin; both conceive in holiness from the same Spirit; both bring forth a child without sin for God the Father. Mary gave birth to the absolutely sinless Head for the Body; the Church gave birth, in the forgiveness of every sin, to the Body for the Head. Each is the mother of Christ, but neither without the other gives birth to the whole Christ .... Christ abode for nine months in the tent of Mary's womb; he abides until the consummation of the ages in the tent of the Church's

faith. He will abide forever and ever in the knowledge and love of the faithful soul."[6]

[1]PL 194, 1862-1872. [2]PL 194, 1872-1876. Cf. G. Raciti, in DSp, VII, 2011-2038. [3]*In Assumpt. I*, in PL 194, 1862B. [4]*In Assumpt. III*, in PL 194, 1870D. [5]LG 64, n. 8. [6]*In Assumpt. I*, in PL 194, 1863A-1865C. Cf. G. Salet, on *Serm. in Quing. 8*, in SC 207, 342-343.

ISIDORE GLABAS (d. *c.* 1397)

Archbishop of Thessalonica, I. is one of the great quartete of fourteenth-century Byzantine Marian theologians, the Palamites. His ideas are found in four homilies: on the Nativity of Mary; on her Presentation in the Temple; on the Annunciation; and the Dormition.[1] The fourth homily may have suffered interpolation in the course of time; it is substantially genuine.

I. carried Byzantine praise of Mary to its loftiest peak—beyond the permissible limit, his critics would say. The essence of his position was that Mary was the center of the universe. God, in creating men, had her in mind. Because of her, the heavens and earth were created. All that was and is and will be came into being because of her. "All was made for us and we because of her."[2] Mary is the "new man,"[3] and the new creature is not like the old. She was born of parents, prayerful but sterile—a traditional Byzantine idea. But I. held that she is, in her origin, superior to the angels, not an angel or a man, but a superior nature. On the other hand, she died—in this most like her Son, though her body, given to the earth for the shortest time, was incorrupt. Mary was, in a sense, a co-creator with God: "And, if it be not too bold, the blessed Virgin is perhaps the co-creatress with God, even before she came into the world, who drew forth into being, together with him, both visible and invisible creatures."[4] Mary is the daughter and mother and spouse of God.

I. is disconcerting in his attribution of Christological texts to Mary (Jn 1:14, 14:6; Col 3:3; Eph 2:18; Lk 1:78). He thought it forbidden to speak of her purity. Yet he did relate it to Christ: "As to what concerns her freedom from sin, no one more than that most innocent one, bore resemblance to Christ; it was then fitting that the Mother should be made more conformable to the Son than any others."[5] Her origin had to be totally in an encounter with God, "so that, as far as it was possible, the all-immaculate one should escape the law of which the prophet speaks, and say of herself: 'I have not been conceived in iniquity."[6] She was truly a child of prayer and of the fear of the Lord. In another context I. can say that she alone, "in a new way beforehand, gave birth to her parents,"[7] a remark related to Mary's cosmic destiny, and clearly not to be taken literally.

If the passages on Mary's purity seem to exclude original sin, a problem arises out of the homily on the Dormition (n. 33), where I., speaking of original sin, says: "It was with this alone that she came to life and appeared to the human race."[8] From all other stain, she was free. The apparent contradiction is explainable on a change of mind by I.—development in his thought, or by interpolation due to a later writer or copyist.

Mary's part in salvation, her role as mediatress, follows directly from her unique position and holiness. "And truly the Virgin, without doubt, was for all a cause of restoration to a better state."[9] Because of her, God freed the human race from the sentence of condemnation, and man reached the likeness of God. Through her, our regeneration is accomplished. No one approaches the Father save by the new Offspring; no one approaches him save through his Mother.[10]

---

[1]PG 139, 12-164. Cf. M. Jugie, *L'Immaculée Conception*, 263-275; B. Schultze, S.J., in MO, 406-417; H. Graef, *Mary*, I, 342-346. [2]*In Annunt. 23*, in PG 139, 105B. [3]*In Annunt. 22*, in PG 139, 104B. [4]*In Annunt. 23*, in PG 139, 105A. [5]*In Nativ., 17*, in PG 139, 37A. [6]*In Present., 13*, in PG 139, 52C-53A. [7]*In Nativ., 3*, in PG 139, 16A. [8]*In Dorm., 33*, in PG 139, 161B. [9]PG 139, 13C. [10]Cf. B. Schultze, S.J., in MO, 413-416.

ISIDORE OF SEVILLE, ST., DOCTOR OF THE CHURCH (*c.* 560-636) — See Supplement, p. 383.

ISLAM

Interest in Moslem attitudes towards Our Lady has grown since the brief mention of the subject by Vatican II (*qv*): "Though they [Moslems] do not acknowledge Jesus as God, they revere him as a prophet. They also honour Mary, his virgin Mother; at times they call on her, too, with devotion." (The Church and the non-Christian Religions, art. 3). This devotion is manifest at shrines in Moslem lands, notably at Meryemana near Ephesus in Turkey.

The roots of Islamic teaching and practice are in the Koran which has much to say about Mary, principally in Sura III on *The family of Imran* (the name given to Mary's father) and Sura XIX

on *Mary*.[1] Mary is named thirty-four times in the whole book; twenty-four times she is linked with the name of Jesus. There is at times striking resemblance to the *Apocrypha*. The canonical gospels have had very little influence.

The family was among those chosen by God "above all human beings"; its special destiny is made explicit with these words: "O Mary, verily hath God chosen thee, and purified thee and chosen thee above the women of the worlds."[2] Mary's image is thus sketched: "And Mary, Imran's daughter, who kept her maidenhood [virginity] and into whose womb we breathed of our spirit and who believed in [confirmed] the words of her Lord and his Scriptures [books] and was one of the devout [obedient]."[3]

The circumstances of Mary's birth were special. "'O my Lord,' said her mother, 'I vow to thee what is in my womb, for thy special service [in dedication]. Accept it from me; for thou hearest, knowest.' And when she had given birth to it, she said, 'O my Lord. Verily I have brought forth a female'—God knew what she had brought forth; a male is not a female—'and I have named her Mary, and I take refuge with thee [commend her to thee] for her, and for her offspring, from Satan the stoned [accursed].'"[4] The last sentence—taken with a famous *Hadith*, "Every newlyborn son of Adam is touched by Satan, save the Son of Mary and his Mother"— appears to teach an immaculate birth. In succeeding ages, much thought was given by the commentators to the privilege. The child was in Zechariah's care in the Temple, and fed miraculously. We read of this also in the Apocrypha: "So oft as Zechariah went in to Mary at the sanctuary, he found her supplied with food. 'Oh, Mary!," said he, 'whence hast thou this?' She said, 'It is from God; for God supplies whom he will, without reckoning.'"[5]

The account of the Annunciation is thought to be the most ancient Marian text in the Koran: "And make mention in the book of Mary, when she went apart from her family, eastward, and took a veil to shroud herself from them: and we sent our spirit to her, and he took before her the form of a perfect man. She said, 'I fly for refuge from thee to the God of mercy! If thou fearest him, begone from me! He said: 'I am only a messenger of the Lord, that I may bestow on thee a holy son.' She said: 'How shall I have a son, when man hath never touched me? And I am not unchaste.' He said: 'So shall it be. The Lord hath said: 'Easy is this with me'; and we will make him a sign to mankind, and a mercy from us. For it is a thing decreed.'"[6]

Mary's birthpangs are mentioned—contrary to Christian tradition of the painless birth. When she came with the babe to her people, they criticized her: "O Mary, now thou has done a strange thing [thou hast surely committed a monstrous thing]."[7] Mary was miraculously defended by her new-born Son. "He said: 'Verily, I am the servant of God; he hath given me the Book and he hath made me a prophet; and he hath made me blessed wherever I may be, and hath enjoined me prayer and almsgiving so long as I shall live, and to be dutiful to her that bore me, and he hath not made me proud, depraved [unprosperous]. And the peace of God was on me the day I was born, and will be the day I shall die, and the day I shall be raised to life. This is Jesus the Son of Mary; this is a statement of the truth, concerning which they doubt."[8]

The Koran criticizes the Jews for their lack of belief, "and for having spoken against Mary a grievous calumny."[9] St. Joseph does not appear in the record, nor is there mention of the Visitation (qv), nor of the Matthaean episodes, the advent of the Magi, the massacre of the Innocents, or the Flight into Egypt. Intercession (qv) came later in Islamic theory and practice. The narrative of the Koran does not speak of it.

---

[1]Quotations are from translation of the Koran by J. M. Rodwell, in *Everyman's Library* series; where necessary, alternative renderings (in brackets) are from *The Koran Interpreted* by A. J. Arberry, (London, 1963). On Mary in Islam, cf. M. Vloberg, "L'Immaculée dans le Coran et dans l'Islam," in *Revue Notre Dame*, (February, 1912). Cf. esp. J. M. Abd-el-Jalil, O.F.M., in *Maria*, I, 185-211; Hussain Mones, "El capítulo de Maria en el Coran (Surat Maryam)," in *Unidad Cristiana*, 19(1969), 197-209; N. Geagea, O.C.D., "Maria nel messagio coranico," in *Eph. Carmeliticae*, 23(1972), 235-408; id., "Maria segno ed esempio secondo il Corano," in Zagreb Congress, V, 369-388; G. C. Anawati, O.P., "Maria nell'Islam," in *Sacra Doctrina*, 18(1973), 267-283; T. Jablanovic, "Les privilèges de Marie selon les sources de la foi islamique," in Zagreb Congress, V, 357-368; B. Krilic, O.F.M., "Maria die Mutter Jesu im Koran und in der islamischen Ueberlieferung," in Zagreb Congress, V, 389-401; E. Testa, O.F.M., "De mutua relatione inter mariologiam Mahumetis et mariologiam Judaeochristianorum," in Zagreb Congress, V, 403-432; H. A. R. Gibbs and J. H. Kranmers, article "Maryam," in *Shorter Encyclopaedia of Islam*, (Brill, Leiden, 1974), 327-330 (double column). [2]"Sura III, 37," from translation by J. M. Rodwell, in *Everyman's Library*, 390. [3]"Sura LXVI," from translation by J.M. Rodwell, in *Everyman's Library*, with alternative rendering (in brackets) from *The Koran Interpreted*, by A. J. Arberry, (London, 1963). [4]"Sura III, 31," translations as above, 389. [5]ibid. [6]"Sura XIX," from translation as above, 118. [7]"Sura III," from translations as above, 119. [8]"Sura III," from translations as above, 119. [9]"Sura IV," from translation by J. M. Rodwell, in *Everyman's Library* series, 427.

J

JAMES OF VORAGINE
(c. 1230-c. 1298)
A Dominican, born in Varazze, J. was Provincial of his order in Lombardy. In 1292 he became archbishop of Genoa. A *Mariale Aureum* is attributed to him.[1] In nineteen books, following the order of the letters of the alphabet except for K, U, W, X, Y, and Z, the author deals with titles of Mary, or words which in one way or another may be associated with her. Biblical and other figures and ascetical terms—the list begins with *Abstinentia* and ends with *Vulnera*—occur, but so do strictly theological words like *Adjutrix, Advocata, Assumptio,*

Mediatrix, Regina Coeli, and *Sponsa Dei*. The great Latin Fathers are known to the author, who likes to quote St. Bernard and Hugh of St. Victor—a compendium which fits the age.

J. is better known from the *Legenda Aurea*, a varied compilation on the saints and liturgical feasts, extant in five hundred manuscripts, which between 1470-1530 was the book most frequently printed and appeared in very many translations.[2] The author deals with Marian topics in his writings on the feasts of the Nativity of Our Lord, of the Purification, Annunciation, Nativity, and especially the Assumption (qv) of Our Lady.[3] In the last section, J. follows the famous homily of Reichenau on the Assumption, a composition long taken as anonymous, which is now known to be the work of John, bishop of Arezzo, who lived in the second half of the ninth century.

---

[1]*Mariale Aureum*, ed. by A. Figarol, (Paris, 1874). Cf. M. Grabmann, "Die Schönheit Marias nach dem Mariale des Jacob . . .," in *Divus Thomas*, (Fribourg), 27(1949), 87-102; P. Lorenzin, "Mariologia Jacobi a Voragine," in *Bibl. Mariana medii aevi*, (Rome), 6(1951). [2]*Legenda Aurea*, ed. by Th. Graesse, (Regensburg, 1891); French tr., *Jacques de Voragine, La Legénde Dorée*, by J. B. M. Roze, ed. by H. Savon, (Paris, 1967). [3]On the Assumption, cf. J. B. M. Roze, *Jacques de Voragine, La Legénde Dorée*, II, (Paris, 1967), 86-111; (see EASTERN INFLUENCE).

JAMES (JACOB) OF SERUGH (c. 451-521)

J., the greatest Syrian poet after St. Ephraem, has been called the "Flute of the Holy Spirit." He was a monk who became in his old age the bishop of Batnan, the chief town of Sarugh in Osrhoene. Some 300 of his metrical homilies have come down to us of which 212 have been published.[1] His Marian homilies are available[2] and several scholarly studies about him contain extracts from them.[3] A recently published homily by him entitled *Mary and Golgotha*,[4] expresses one idea of importance—that Mary is too sublime to be spoken of.[5] This is hyperbole since the poet says a good deal about her. He abounds in vivid titles and imagery. For example, Mary is "Mother of the Sun of justice," "Mother of the morning," "Splendid Rock in which the King dwells," "Palace of flesh," "Ark of the divinity," "Seat of the King of kings," "Port of mysteries," "Ship full of riches," "Virgin vine," "Daughter of the stars," etc.

J. writes at length on the divine motherhood. Mary's son is the Son of the Father: "The Only-begotten is one, in essence and in humanity, Son of the greatness and Son of Mary: one only Saviour, from the Most High and from the daughter of David: one only Lord of all."[6]

"At the beginning of your route [life] rises an unspeakable wonder, a Virgin giving birth and remaining in her virginity."[7] Almost all the *madrase*, composed by J. which are in manuscripts in the British Museum, deal with the virginity of Mary, as do many passages in the homilies. He exults in the one who is virgin and mother, in the beauty of the virgin: "She was exceedingly beautiful, splendid among women, who brought forth the Sun, and he did not corrupt, did not soil the beauty of her virginity."[8]

She was a virgin in the moment of childbirth. (J. uses the metaphor of the "unploughed earth"). To the one conceived and born of a virgin, J. applied Isaiah's title "Wonderful."[9]

We are given a lengthy account of Joseph's problem, his anxiety, and a very original passage on the saint's love and admiration once the doubt (*qv*) was removed.[10]

On Mary's holiness, J. spoke enthusiastically: "If there had been a stain or defect in her soul, God would have chosen another stainless soul."[11] He thought her sublime, and, especially in the first homily, developed this idea of moral beauty at length. "She was full of beauty both by nature and in her will, since she was never defiled by ignoble thoughts, walked on her way without faults, without sins."[12]

The poet gave special attention to the work of the Holy Spirit. "The Holy Spirit came on Mary to remove from her the ancient condemnation of Eve and Adam. He sanctified her, purified her and made her blessed among women.[13] "The Son sanctified her by the Spirit and made her pure, purified and blessed, as Eve was before the serpent spoke to her . . . ."[14] When this idea of purification by the Spirit is taken with certain passages in the homilies which seem ambiguous on the subject of the painless childbirth, and with J.'s generally exalted notion of Mary's holiness and purity, his attitude to the Immaculate Conception appears to some debatable, to others negative.[15] He did not see the problem as it was stated by Latin theologians.

Mary's role was seen in the parallel with Eve (*qv*), but widened. "The second Eve, who has given birth to life among mortals, and has paid and liquidated the debt of her mother Eve."[16] "Through her divine motherhood, Adam has been delivered from his servitude . . . . Through her, the heavenly powers have been reconciled with the mortals . . . . Through her, the closed way to paradise has again been made passable."[17]

The fifth homily, which deals with Mary's passing and burial, includes a passage on her compassion (*qv*) on Calvary, or rather at the moment of the burial, unusual in the East, anywhere at that time.[18] She is also given the title "Mother of Mercy." Recalling a legend about the burial of Moses, J. states that the Lord himself came to bury Mary on Mount Olivet.

---

[1]*Homiliae Selectae Mar-Jacobi Sarugensis*, ed. in Syrian, by P. Bedjan, 5 vols., (Paris, 1905-1910). Cf. J. B. Abbeloos,

De vita et scriptis sancti Jacobi Batnarum Sarugi in Mesopotamia episcopi, (Louvain, 1867). [2]C. Vona, *Omelie mariologische di S. Giacomo di Sarug*, (Rome, 1953), lengthy introduction; Italian tr., in EMBP, 1041-1065. [3]A. van Roey, "La Sainteté de Marie d'après Jacques de Saroug," in ETL, 31(1955), 46-62; V. I., IV, 113-132; H. Graef, *Mary*, I, 119-123; 5th Hom. "De Transitu Dei Genitricis Mariae," in *Oriens Christianus*, 5(1905), 91-99. [4]"Mary and Golgotha," ed. by P. Mouterde, in *Mélanges de l'Université de St. Joseph*, 26, (Beyrouth, 1944-1946), 9-14. Cf. F. Graffin, in DS, 8, 56-60. [5]"Mary and Golgotha," ed. by P. Mouterde, 10. [6]6th Hom., cited by number of the homily and the number of the lines in *Vona*, 849-851. [7]"Mary and Golgotha," ed. by P. Mouterde, 10. [8]4th Hom., in *Vona*, 171-172. [9]4th Hom., in *Vona*, 150ff. [10]2nd Hom., in *Vona*, 337-354. On Joseph's "doubt," cf. 6th Hom., in *Vona*, 555ff. [11]1st Hom., in *Vona*, 193-194. [12]1st Hom., in *Vona*, 143ff. [13]1st Hom., in *Vona*, 373-375. [14]1st Hom., in *Vona*, 400. [15]Cf. M. Jugie, *L'Immaculée Conception*, 15; P. Kruger, "Die Frage der Erbsundigkeit des Gottesmutter im Schriftum des Jacob. . . . ," in *Ostkirchliche Studien*, 1(1952), 187-207; C. Vona, *Omelie mariologische di S. Giacomo di Sarug*, (Rome, 1953), 81ff. [16]1st Hom., in *Vona*, 45. [17]1st Hom., in *Vona*, 447ff. [18]5th Hom., in *Vona*, 20ff.

JANSENISTS, THE

Jansenists have sometimes been criticized for hostility to Marian piety. In the controversy which the *Avis Salutaires* stirred up, some of Adam Widenfeld's supporters were Jansenists. There is plenty of evidence to show that, at the outset, Mary had an important place in the writings and practices of the leading spirits of Port Royal. In prayers used there, she was spoken of as one "through whom in some way God pours grace upon us, as through her he gave us the author of grace," or again, as "Queen, Mediatress, Advocate." As time passed, the inspiration of the movement waned, and a certain aridity settled on it. "One can leaf through the voluminous correspondence of the great Jansenistic spiritual directors without meeting anything but a brief and trivial allusion, and that rarely, to Our Lady. At times, nevertheless, they do let drop one or other fine text, but it merely repeats past formulas, and appears a museum piece." This was at the decline of what the same writer calls the "magnificent considerations with which Saint-Cyran had enriched piety."[1]

[1]Cf. L. Cognet, "Port Royal," in *Maria*, III, 121-151; quotations, 136, 149-150. Cf. C. Flachaire, *La dévotion à la Vierge dans la littérature au commencement du XVIIe siècle*, (Paris, 1916), 82-97; P. Hoffer S. M., *La dévotion à Marie au déclin du XVIIe siècle*, (Paris, 1938), 59-117; Cl. Dillenschneider, C.SS.R., *La Mariologie de St. Alphonse de Liguori*, I, (Fribourg, 1931), 37-39.

JEROME, ST., DOCTOR OF THE CHURCH
(*c.* 347-420)

An accomplished Latinist with a command of Greek and Hebrew, widely travelled, J. was secretary of Pope St. Damasus I in Rome, founder of monasteries with St. Paula and her daughter Eustochium in Bethlehem, and personally linked with the greatest minds of his time. He will always excite interest as a great biblical scholar, a unique translator of the Bible, and a tempestuous but highly erudite controversialist. His Marian doctrine is found in his essays against Helvidius and Jovinian, in his epistles, in a sermon on the Nativity of Christ, and in many of his biblical commentaries, more abundantly those on Matthew and Isaiah.[1]

The dominant theme of his Marian doctrine was Our Lady's virginity.[2] It was related to a debate current, especially in Roman circles, on the superiority of virginity over marriage, but J.'s intervention, based on the Bible, was more far-reaching than fourth-century Rome. It came in response to a work by Helvidius[3] which defended the equality of marriage and virginity. The author had supported his thesis from the life of Mary, asserting that after the virgin birth she had lived a normal married life with St. Joseph. Her children were the brothers and sisters of the Lord mentioned in the gospels and in other New Testament works.

Arguing from widely selected examples of biblical usage, J. showed, with more verve than usual, that the phrases picked out of the infancy narratives (*qv*) in support of Helvidius' thesis, were all compatible with the perpetual virginity. The virginal conception was not of course at issue. Helvidius insisted that Matthew, using the word "espoused" (*desponsatam*), not "entrusted" (*commendatam*), of Mary's relationship with Joseph, implies that, after the birth of Jesus, they lived as man and wife. "Before they came together" (Mt 1:18); "Take unto thee Mary thy wife" (Mt 1:20); "He knew her not until she brought forth her first-born son" (Mt 1:25).

J. was prompted to advance a new idea, which would be accepted in the West and influence the theology relative to St. Joseph. "But just as we do not deny what is written, we reject what is not written. That God was born of a virgin, we believe because we read it. That Mary consummated marriage after her childbirth, we do not believe because we do not read it. Nor do we say this in order to condemn marriage, for virginity is itself a fruit of marriage, but because there is no license to draw rash conclusions about holy men . . . . You say that Mary did not remain a virgin; even more do I claim that Joseph was also virginal through Mary, in order that from a virginal marriage a virginal son might be born . . . he who merited to be called the father of the Lord remained virginal with her."[4]

There are many pithy phrases in the work: "The first-born is not one after whom others came, but before whom there was none."[5] Against the idea that there must have been other children of Mary: "Was Joseph really his father? . . . . Was he thought so? Let the brothers be thought of in the same way as is the father?"[6] J. worked out a whole theory about the "Brothers of the Lord," which long prevailed. It drew a searching critique from Bishop Lightfoot in the nineteenth century.[7] J. held that the brothers were cousins. Tertullian (qv), cited against the perpetual virginity, was dismissed by J. thus: "I have nothing more to say of Tertullian than that he was not a man of the Church."[8]

On the precise moment of birth, he writes: "She [Mary] herself wrapped the infant in swaddling clothes, she was mother and midwife."[9] He went on to dismiss the story of the midwives found in the *Protoevangelium* of James (see APOCRYPHA) as "*deliramenta apocryphorum*," ravings of the apocrypha. This may have been his reason for not considering the *virginitas in partu*. Ezek 44:2 is by the Fathers generally applied to Mary a virgin *in partu*, but, though J. comments on it in a Marian sense, he pointedly says, "who remained a virgin before and after childbirth" only.

His position was rendered embarrassing by the condemnation of another heretic, Jovinian, at the Synod of Milan (*c.* 390) on this point explicitly. J. was almost involved in the condemnation. Pressed to take a stand or justify himself, he issued the *Adversus Jovinianum*,[10] in which he wrote much on virginity, little on Our Lady, still less on the *virginitas in partu*. Urged to withdraw this work by his former fellow student, the Roman senator Pammachius, he composed a letter to his friend by way of *apologia*,[11] without committing himself.

J. continued the Eve-Mary theme, though briefly: "Eve brought forth in pains. But after the Virgin conceived in the womb and brought forth a son to us . . . the curse was broken.

Death by Eve, life by Mary; thus the gift of virginity flowed more profusely into women, because it began with a woman."[12] The great biblical scholar follows the idea of Mary through the Old Testament. He wrote often and at length on the *Almah* prophecy in Is 7:14 (see EMMANUEL), which he applied to Mary, showing that he was fully aware of the linguistic problem, adding too a curious version of his own. *Almah* can mean not only a virgin, but one hidden. He knew well that *bethulah* was the Hebrew word for virgin.[13] Mary is the "light cloud" of Is 19:1;[14] the "rod" of Is 11:1;[15] the "garden enclosed" of Song 4:12;[16] the "king's daughter" of Ps 44:14;[17] in type, Abishag, given to David in his old age (1 Kings 1:3);[18] a symbol of wisdom; "the woman who shall compass a man" of Jer 31:22;[19] the desert of Hos 13:15, which symbolizes the womb of holy Mary, which germinated without any human seed;[20] the Daughter of Zion of Is 37:22.[21]

J. had no problems about Mary's holiness (qv), whom he called holy and described as "overflowing with the graces of the Holy Spirit,"[22] "of such great purity that she merited to be the Mother of the Lord." He thought she was of the house of David. Though he lived before the *Theotokos* controversy, he equivalently affirmed the orthodox doctrine—God was born of a virgin. "Nor do we call one Jesus Christ and another God, as a new heresy falsely says, but the same one before the ages and after the ages, before the world and after Mary, indeed from Mary, we call the "great God our Saviour Jesus Christ."

The notion of imitation, which would be so important as time advanced, is already found with J., though still in the context of virginity. "Let her [a virgin] imitate Mary, whom Gabriel found alone in her cell, and she perhaps was struck with fear, because, contrary to her custom, she was looking on a man. Let her imitate the one of whom it is said, 'All the glory of the king's daughter is from within.' Let her speak to her beloved as one wounded by the spear of love. 'The king has brought me to his cell'."[24] The perspective is enlarged in the commentary on Mt 12:46-50: "They are my mother who each day beget me in the souls of believers; they are my brothers who do the deeds of my Father."[25] To Eustochium, he says that she too "can be a mother of the Lord."[26]

[1]CMP, III, 212-258; EMBP, 513-550; DSp, VIII, 901-918 (J. Gribomont); H. Graef, *Mary*, I, 89-94; R. Lautentin, *Traité*, I, 124-125; J. Niessen, "Die Mariologie des heiligen Hieronymus," in *Ihre Quellen und ihre Kritik*, (Munster, i. W., 1913). [2]Cf. G. Jouasard, in *Maria*, I, 106ff; J. McHugh, *The Mother of Jesus in the New Testament*, (London, 1975), Pt. 2, ch. 8, 223-231. [3]*De beatae Mariae virginitate perpetua adversus Helvidium liber unus*, in PL 23, 183A-206B. [4]PL 23, 203AB. [5]PL 23, 192B. [6]PL 23, 201A. [7]J. B. Lightfoot, "The Brethren of the Lord," in *St. Paul's Epistle to the Galatians*, ed. 10, (London, 1896), 252-291. [8]PL 23, 201B. [9]PL 23, 192A. [10]PL 23, 211-338. [11]*Liber apologeticus ad Pammachium*, in PL 22, 493-511. [12]*Ep. 22:21*, in CSEL 54, 173. [13]*In Is. 3, 7, 14*, in CCSL 73, 102-105; *In Amos 1, 3, 12*, in CCSL 76, 252; *Adv. Jovin. 1, 32*, in PL 23, 254D-255A. [14]*In Is. 4, 11, 1-3*, in CCSL 73, 147-148. [15]*In Is. 5, 19, 1*, in CCSL 73, 192. [16]*Adv. Jovin. 1, 31*, in PL 23, 254. [17]*Ep. 107, 7*, in CSEL 55, 298. [18]*Ep. 52, 4*, in CSEL 54, 420. [19]*In Jer. 6, 31, 22*. [20]*In Oseam 3, 13, 15*, in CCSL 76, 150-151. [21]*Adv. Jovin. 1, 32*, in PL 23, 255B. [22]PL 22, 422, 700. [23]*In Ep. ad Titum, 2:12*, in PL 26, 587A; CCSL 74, 313. [24]*Ep. 107, 7*, in CSEL 55, 298. [25]*In Mt. 2, 12:46-50*, in CCSL 77, 100. [26]*Ep. 22:38*, in PL 22, 422.

JEWS, THE

Vatican II (*qv*) emphasized the continuity between ancient Israel and the Church: "Israel, according to the flesh, which wandered as an exile in the desert, was already called the Church of God (Esd 13:1; cf. Num 20:4; Deut 23:1ff.). Likewise, the new Israel, which while going forward in this present world, goes in search of a future and abiding city (cf. Heb 13:14), and is also called the Church of Christ (cf. Mt 16:18)." (LG 9). This succinct statement should be read against the background of the Council's teaching on the unity of the two Testaments, Old and New. The New is hidden in the Old, and the Old is made manifest in the New. "The books of the Old Testament, all of them caught up into the Gospel message, attain and show their full meaning in the New Testament (cf. Mt 5:17; Lk 24:27; Rom 16:25-26; 2 Cor 3:14-16), and, in their turn, shed light on it and explain it." (*Constitution on Divine Revelation, 16*).[1]

Vatican II, in its teaching on Our Lady, considered texts in the Old Testament in which Mary is foreshadowed. By applying to her the title "Daughter of Zion," and identifying her with the "Poor of the Lord," it sketched her role as the fulfillment of her people. She is a unifying bond and a symbol in Judaeo-Christian history and consciousness. The terrible tragedies of recent times were in some way the occasion, if not the cause, of the statement of Vatican II on the

Jews. The Lehmann brothers, Catholic priests, had appealed to Vatican I for such a pronouncement in vain. Relevant to our subject is the fact that at no time in the vicissitudes of discussion of the Jewish question during Vatican II was objection raised to mention of the Blessed Virgin, made by way of addition to the well-known Pauline text which ends, "from whom is Christ according to the flesh" (Rom 9:4-5), after which we read, "the son of the Virgin Mary" (*Declaration on the non-Christian religions, 4*).

Jewish and Catholic collaboration in Bible study is now accepted—witness the Anchor Bible and the Roman Bible. In 1947, at Seelisberg in Switzerland, sixty Catholic, Protestant, and Jewish theologians agreed on ten points as a guide to preaching and teaching matters affecting the Christian and Jewish religions and history. The second point obliged preachers and teachers to remember that Jesus was "born of a Jewish mother," belonging to the family of David and the house of Israel, and that his everlasting love and mercy embrace his own people and the whole world.[2]

With the exception of Schalom Ben-Chorin's work, which is a study of mythology, there has been little Jewish literature on Our Lady, in comparision with works on Jesus Christ—one of which, by G. Vermes, does consider Mary. Jews, who have entered the Catholic Church, have quickly assimilated the characteristic piety towards Mary. The brothers, Theodore and Alphonse Ratisbonne, in the nineteenth century, founded the religious societies of Our Lady of Zion for the conversion of the Jewish people. Alphonse's conversion was associated with the Miraculous Medal. Francis Libermann (*qv*), remarkable as a spiritual guide and missonary founder, placed his society under the patronage of the Holy Heart of Mary (*qv*), and felt that its eventual union with the older congregation of the Holy Spirit (*qv*) was appropriate from the devotional and apostolic aspects. The cause of his beatification has been introduced, as has that of another Jewish convert, Edith Stein, a woman of remarkable intellect, the philosopher Husserl's favourite pupil, who found her vocation in the Marian order of Carmel, and final glory in martyrdom at Auschwitz prison camp.

Thus, recent empirical evidence joins that of the first centuries to show Mary as a symbol of continuity between Israel and Christianity. Jews have to ponder the fact that one of their race is the supreme heroine of Christendom; in the unanimous judgment of Christians, the most perfect human being after her Son. Recent research into Jewish-Christian theology and liturgical forms in the first centuries have shown how much we are indebted to those who saw in Christ the deliverer of his people, and, in his Mother, the heiress to the *Gebirah* of old, the King's Mother, the most important woman in the messianic community.

[1]Cf. J. Cardinal Daniélou, S.J., *Théologie du Judéo-Christianisme*, (Tournai, Desclee, 1957); B. Bagatti, O.F.M., *L'Église de la Circoncision*, (Jerusalem, 1965); G. Baum, *The Jews and the Gospel*, (London, 1961); R. Le Déaut, C.S.Sp., "Miryam, soeur de Moise et Marie, Mère du Messie," in BB, 45(1964), 198-219; A. Cardinal Bea, S.J., *The Church and the Jewish People*, (London, 1966). Jewish writers include: J. Klausner, bk. 8, ch. 2, "The Jewishness of Jesus," in *Jesus of Nazareth*, (London, 1947); M. Goldstein, *Jesus in the Jewish Tradition*, (New York, 1950); R. Aron, *The Jewish Jesus*, (New York, 1971); G. Vermes, *Jesus the Jew*, (London, Fontana Books, 1973); S. Ben-Chorin, *Mutter Miryam, Maria in jüdischer Sicht*, (Munich, List-Verlag, 1971). [2]G. Baum, *The Jews and the Gospel*, (London, 1961), 287.

JOHN CHRYSOSTOM, ST., DOCTOR OF THE CHURCH
(354-407)

One of the greatest of the eastern Fathers, J., born in Antioch, was ordained a priest there, and for twelve years attained renown as a preacher. He became Patriarch of Constantinople in 397. His ideas were theologically Antiochene. He was a moralist. Among his published works is a very large number of spurious items, possibly one-third of the whole. Scholars have begun the immense task of assortment.[1] Passages relevant to Marian theology are found in his homilies, in his commentaries on the gospels of St. Matthew and St. John, and elsewhere.[2] They are quantitatively slight and express some views which have long since been discarded.

J. was not called upon to work out a theology of Mary's divine motherhood. But in his commentary on Is 7:14 (see EMMANUEL), he leaves no doubt that God was born of Mary. Quoting the verse, he insists that Emmanuel means "God with us;" he insists that he became truly man;[3] again, he says, "the prophet is here expressing wonder at the incarnation."[4] He says explicitly elsewhere that the ineffable, indescribable, incomprehensible Son of God, equal to the Father, "deigned to be born of a virgin."[5]

J. put the Eve-Mary parallel pithily. Christ triumphed by the very weapons that the devil had used. "A virgin, the wood, and death were the symbols of our defeat. The virgin was Eve, for she had not yet known her husband; the wood was the tree . . . . And behold, a second time, a virgin, the wood and death; the symbols of defeat have become the symbols of victory. For Mary is in the place of Eve."[6] A wider perspective is opened in another passage. "A virgin drove us from paradise; through a virgin, we have found eternal life."[7]

On the virginity, J. was vigorous and explicit. He used the image of the virgin earth and, dealing with the role of St. Joseph (*qv*), he turned especially to his virtue, and composed a tribute to him, unequalled in the first Christian millennium.[8] J. was also in advance of many of the Fathers in his opinion of the fatherhood of Joseph—the exception being St. Augustine (*qv*).

On the subject of Mary's holiness, J. has disconcerting passages. They may be partially explained by his preoccupations as a moralist. He thought that the idea of suicide entered her mind at the Annunciation (*qv*), when she felt that she would be exposed to shame. Yet, in the same passage, he wrote: "In fact, the Virgin was admirable, and Luke declared her virtue when he says that, when she received the [angel's] greeting, she was not filled with joy and she did not accept his words, but was troubled and sought what his greeting should be."[9] On the suggestion of suicide, one must recall J.'s view of the virtuous "suicide" of martyred women saints.[10]

J.'s intention to draw moral lessons from the gospel episodes, and the theological climate in which he lived, misled him in regard to certain words of the Saviour to, or about, his Mother. He thought that Mary at Cana "wished to confer a favour on the company, and also to make herself more conspicuous by means of her Son. Perhaps too, she suffered something human, as his brethren did who said, 'Show thyself to the world,' wishing to bring themselves glory from the miracles."[11] J. then developed extensively the idea that, though Jesus did not lack reverence for his Mother, he felt he must elevate her thoughts about him. The author brings in Mk 3:33 and expounds it in the same sense. So the reply, "What is it to me and to thee, woman," is explained. He also wished to show that miracles should be asked for, not by relatives, but by those who needed them. "For while he cared for the honour due to his Mother, he cared more for her salvation, and for the good of many, for which cause he had taken flesh."[12] Jesus worked the miracle, showing his freedom from any "hour," and also sparing his Mother embarrassment.[13]

J. returned to the synoptic text as Matthew gave it (12:46-50), asserting that Jesus was "not ashamed of his mother, nor denied that she had given him birth," but "that he should show that no advantage would be hers from this, unless she kept all the commandments."[14] He spoke of ambition on Mary's part. In his comment on Jesus' reply to the woman from the crowd who praised his Mother, he spoke similarly—no denial of physical relationship, but emphasis on the relationship based on virtue.

These minimalist remarks derive in part from J.'s view that Mary did not know of her Son's divinity.[15] But on Calvary, "he [Jesus] shows his great love and entrusts her to the disciple whom he loved."[16] The context is always moral exhortation and thus the comments seem to have been taken.

[1]Cf. R. Laurentin, *Traité*, I, 161-164; J. de Aldama, *Repertorium Pseudo-Chrysostomicum*, (Paris, 1905); M. Aubineau, "Une enquête dans les manuscrits chrysostomiens: Opportunité, difficultés, premier bilan," in RHE, 63(1968), 5-26; A. Wenger, A.A., in DS, fasc. 52-53, c. 332. [2]EMBP, 448-502; CMP, 374-439; ClavisG, 491-672. [3]*Contra Judaeos et Gentiles quod Christus sit Deus, 2*, in PG 48, 815. [4]*In Ps 117, 6*, in PG 55, 337. On tr. of *almah* in Is 7:14, cf. *In Matt., Hom. 5, 3*, in PG 57, 57. [5]*In Matt. II*, in PG 57, 25. [6]*De coemet. et de cruce, 2*, in PG 49, 396. [7]*In Ps. 44, 7*, in PG 55, 193. [8]*In Matt. 4, 3-5*, in PG 57, 43-46. [9]PG 57, 45. Cf. G. M. Ellero, O.S.M., *Maternità e virtù di Maria in S. Giovanni Crisostomo*, (Rome, 1964). [10]Cf. G. M. Ellero, O.S.M., *op. cit.*, (Rome, 1964), 20. [11]*In Jn 21, 2*, in PG 59, 130. [12]*In Jn 3*, in PG 59, 131-132. [13]*In Jn 22, 1*, in PG 59, 134. [14]In PG 57, 464. [15]*In Ps. 49, 1*, in PG 55, 242. [16]*In Jn. 85, 2*, in PG 59, 461.

JOHN OF THE CROSS, ST., DOCTOR OF THE CHURCH
(1542-1591)

Because of J.'s strong, integrated mystical personality and his scientific precision as an observer and narrator of spiritual phenomena, facts in his life take on a more than customary meaning.[1] In a life enriched with divine favours, J. attributed to Our Lady crucial instances of supernatural power. She saved him from drowning as a child, attracted him to Carmel, and delivered him from prison. He died happy at the thought that he would recite Our Lady's Matins in heaven. The memory of these favours and the sight of her picture, he once said, restored peace and clarity to his soul. In brief references to Mary, J. emphasized her consent at the Incarnation, her divine motherhood, the honour due to her, and the forms of piety appropriate to it— with words of caution on possible abuses.

[1]Elisée de la Nativitée, in *Maria*, II, 855-856; Otilio del Nino Jesus, "Mariologia de S. Juan de la Cruz," in EstM, 2(1943), 359-399; J. Mondel, S.J., *La Purification de la Sainte Vierge dans la perspective de S. Jean de la Croix, Carmelus*, (Petit Castelet, 1967), 32-46.

JOHN OF DAMASCUS, ST., DOCTOR OF THE CHURCH
(*c.* 675, died at some time between 749 and 753)

J. was the last and one of the greatest of the Greek Fathers. Little is known of his life, save that he came of a noble Damascus family, entered the monastery of St. Sabas near Jerusalem about 718, and devoted his life to study. The results of this study cover a wide range in theology, with special emphasis on the Incarnation. J., as is well known, opposed the iconoclasts. His Marian theology, which is wonderfully full, is found in his great work *De Fide Orthodoxa*, in homilies, a canon, and hymns.[1] His style is exuberant in the Byzantine manner, but superlatives and eulogy express doctrine, sound at every point.

J. was uninhibited in expressing his own devotion. "What is sweeter than the Mother of God? She holds my mind captive; she has seized my tongue; on her, I meditate day and night. Since she is Mother of the Word, she has words abundant."[2] "O daughter of Joachim and Anna and mistress, receive the prayer of a sinful servant, but one who, none the less, loves and cherishes you ardently, holds you as his only hope of joy, the guardian of his life, his interpreter with your Son, and sure pledge of salvation."[3] There is even a passage in which the practice of consecration is suggested: "O Lady [*Despoina*], Lady I say and again Lady, binding hope to you, as to a most secure and firm anchor, today we offer ourselves to you; to you we consecrate our mind, soul, body, in a word, ourselves, entirely, and with psalms, hymns, spiritual canticles, we honour you with all our power."[4] He was convinced of the utter inadequacy of human language to describe her.

J. thought that the word *Theotokos* expressed the whole mystery of the Incarnation.[5] In a classic passage in the *De Fide Orthodoxa*, he expounds the meaning of the title. "We preach that the holy Virgin is properly and truly the Mother of God. For as the true God was born of her, she accordingly is God's Mother, who gave birth to the true God incarnate of her. We say that God was born of her, not because the divinity drew the principle of its existence from her; but because the Word himself, who, before the ages beyond all time, was begotten, and, without beginning, is eternally one with the Father and the Holy Spirit, did, in these last days, for our salvation, dwell in her womb, and, having assumed flesh, was born of her, without any change."[6]

Attuned with this vocation was Mary's destiny: "She who was predestined before the ages in the plan of God's forekowledge, foreshadowed and foretold by the Holy Spirit in diverse images and words of the prophets, was, in the fullness of time, born of the race of David, as had been promised to him."[7] Elsewhere he listed the great Old Testament images or oracles which were customarily applied to Mary.[8] He repeated the Eve (qv)-Mary parallel, by now a constant in patristic thought, but tended to relate it to immortality or the Assumption.[9] He also used the symbolism of the Ark of the Covenant.

J. often spoke of Mary as a sublime being. Understandably he was invoked on behalf of the Immaculate Conception (qv). He related the privilege closely to the parents, whose names he always mentioned with veneration: "O most blessed loins of Joachim from which came forth a spotless seed! O glorious womb of Anne in which a most holy offspring grew and was formed by the increase gradually received from her! O womb in which a living heaven, vaster than the vastness of the heavens was conceived!

. . . . O miracles of miracles and of wonders the mightiest wonder! It was indeed right that by miracles the way should be made for the ineffable incarnation of God by which he bent down to us."[10] J. used the word "purify" of the Holy Spirit's action[11]—not to imply sin (for that would contradict not only the passage quoted, but many other descriptive phrases), but to signify elevation to the sphere where the virginal conception takes place. (See PURIFICATION).

Mary preserved her virginity in childbirth. "In birth, he kept her virginity safe . . . keeping her [body] closed."[12] J. believed in her perpetual virginity.

J. was a great doctor of the Assumption, as his three homilies on the feast fully show. "But even though, according to nature, your most holy and happy soul is separated from your most blessed and stainless body, and the body as usual is delivered to the tomb, it will not remain in the power of death and is not subject to decay. For just as her virginity remained inviolate while giving birth, when she departed from life her body was preserved from destruction and only taken to a better and divine tabernacle which is not subject to any death."[13] The passage quoted by Pius XII (qv) in *Munificentissimus Deus*, from the second homily, contains the same idea—that the Assumption was linked with the *virginitas in partu*. "It was fitting that she, who in childbirth had kept her virginity undamaged, should also, after death, keep her body free from all corruption."[14] The same Pope also appealed to J. in support of the queenship of Mary.

The bridal theme occurs in the second homily—but Mary is spoken of as spouse of the Father. "It was fitting that the bride whom the Father had espoused should dwell in the heavenly bridal chambers."[15]

Mary is called Mediatress, and J. introduces the concept with a favourite Old Testament image which he liked to apply to her, Jacob's ladder. "For you, acting as a mediatress [*mesiteusasa*] and becoming the ladder of God descending to us . . . you brought together what had been rent apart." . . . men following an angelic way of life are taken to heaven."[16] Mary is the fountain of life, the workshop [*ergasterion*] of our salvation. "Through her, our reconciliation with God has been consecrated, peace and grace bestowed; . . . she has won for us all good things."[17] "Thus you are also the fountain of true light, the inexhaustible treasury of life itself, the most fruitful source of blessing, who has won for us and brought us all good things, though for a while you are covered corporeally with death; none the less you pour out pure and inexhaustible streams of immense light, immortal life, and true happiness, rivers of grace, fountains of healing, everlasting blessing."[18] St. Bernard had little to add to this theory of universal mediation.

[1]EMBP, 1598-1719. Cf. R. Laurentin, *Traité*, I, 170-171; V. A. Mitchel, *The Mariology of St. John Damascene*, (Turnhout, 1930); V. Grumel, "La Mariologie de St. Jean Damascène," in *Echos d'Orient*, 40(1937), 318-346; J. M. Canal, "San Juan Damasceno, doctor de la muerte y de la Asunción de Maria," in EstM, 12(1952), 270-330; L. Ferroni, "La Vergine, nuova Eva, cooperatrice alla divina Economia e Mediatrice secondo il Damasceno," in MM, 17(1955), 1-36; B. M. Garrido, O.S.B., "Lugar de la Virgen en la Iglesia, según san Juan Damasceno," in EstM, 28(1966), 333-353; P. Voulet, S.J., "Joannes Damascenus, S., Homélies sur la Nativité et la Dormition," in SC, 80(1961), text, introduction, notes; D. Montagna, O.S.M., "Una nuova edizione delle Omelie di S. Giovanni Damasceno," in MM, 25(1963), 153-155; ClavisG, III, 511-536. [2]*Hom. III in Dorm., 1*, in PG 96, 753C. [3]*Hom. I in Nativ. B. V. M., 12*, in PG 96, 680B. [4]*Hom. I in Dorm., 14*, in PG 96, 720CD. [5]*De Fide Orthod., Bk. III, ch. XII*, in PG 94, 1029C. [6]*De Fide Orthod., Bk. III, ch. XII*, in PG 94, 1028BD. [7]*De Fide Orthod., Bk. IV, ch. XIV*, in PG 94, 1156A. Cf. *Hom. I in Nativ. B. V. M., 7*, in PG 96, 672C. [8]*Hom. I in Dorm., 9*, in PG 96, 713BC. [9]*Hom. I in Nativ. B. V. M., 7*, in PG 96, 672, 727, 734. [10]PG 96, 664B. [11]*De Fide Orthod., Bk. III, ch. II*, in PG 94, 985B; PG 96, 704A. [12]*De Fide Orthod., Bk. IV, ch. XIV*, in PG 94, 1161A. [13]PG 96, 716B, tr. by H. Graef. [14]PG 96, 741B. [15]*op. cit.* [16]PG 96, 713A. [17]PG 96, 744C. [18]PG 96, 716C.

JOHN OF EUBOEA (d.c. 750) — See Supplement, p. 383.

JOHN EUDES, ST. (1601-1680)

A Norman, born into a family of marked Marian piety, J. was educated by the Jesuits. To Mary's mediation he attributed many graces received from God. He was a member of the French Congregation of the Oratory, recently founded by Cardinal de Bérulle, from 1623 to 1643, when he founded his own Congregation of Jesus and Mary for the education of priests. J. had begun the sisterhood, the Congregation of Our Lady of Charity of Refuge, in 1641. A very successful pracher of missions and director of souls, J. had a strong mystical vein. His spirituality was centered on the Hearts of Jesus and Mary. It was due to his efforts that the first Mass of the Heart of Mary (qv) was celebrated in Autun on 8 February, 1648. In his personal life, he had taken the vow of slavery to Mary, then recommended by Bérulle, and he had written an elaborate "Contract of Marriage with the Most Blessed Virgin, the Mother of God." His thinking was characteristic of the French school, influenced by Fr. de Condren as well as by Bérulle. His principal Marian writings are *The Admirable Heart of Mary* (1680) and *The Admirable Infancy of the Most Holy Mother of God* (1676). But his works, *The Priest, his Dignity and Obligations* and *The Life and Kingdom of Jesus in Christian Souls* also contain relevant passages.[1]

The saint's advice to priests to cultivate devotion to Our Lady is profoundly based: "The salvation of immortal souls is also the great work of the Mother of God . . . . All the Fathers of the Church say clearly that she is co-redemptress with Christ in the work of our salvation . . . . Christ immolated himself upon the cross for the redemption of mankind, and Mary made a similar sacrifice in undergoing untold sufferings and sorrows."[2] The analogy between the priest and Mary is related to each of the three divine persons; the priest, like Mary, shares in the fatherhood of the First Person. As Mary is cooperator, he is coadjutor with Christ; each in different ways is associated with the Spirit. "Since all graces coming from God pass through Mary's hands, so, too, they are given to you by the ministry of his priests. Mary is the treasury of the Blessed Trinity; priests also share this prerogative."[3]

In *The Life and Kingdom of Jesus in Christian Souls*, J. stresses the very close bond between Jesus and Mary. "So closely are Jesus and Mary bound up with each other that whoever beholds Jesus, sees Mary; whoever loves Jesus, loves Mary; whoever has devotion to Jesus, has devotion to Mary . . . . You must see and adore her Son in her, and see and adore him alone."[4]

This union, a mystical reading of Vatican II's later teaching on the indissoluble bond between Jesus and Mary (LG 53), continues as a theme in J.'s principal work on Our Lady, the first full length book on the Heart of Mary. J. himself had already composed a brief work, and had finished *The Admirable Heart of Mary* just before he died. It was published posthumously.

The book approaches the whole mystery of Mary from many angles. J. analyzes different meanings of the word "heart" as applied to Our Lady, looks for a varied symbolism of its perfections in the physical world and in the Old Testament, relates the Heart of Mary to each of the divine persons, and looks for supporting evidence in Sacred Scripture, in the Fathers (qv), the Popes, bishops and saints. He delays over the merits of the Heart of Mary, turns to comment on the "canticle of the Heart of Mary" (the *Magnificat*), and gives abundant practical motivation and advice. The saint added a section on the Sacred Heart of Jesus.

The book is repetitive, and the author could not escape the critical deficiencies of his time.

At times, he achieves devotional writing of the best kind. His insights were mystical in the true sense, and he avoids doctrinal excess, largely through vast reading in the great theologians. Where he seems to exceed, he must be read entirely. Thus when he says that "her Heart is the origin of everything noble, rich and precious in all the holy souls which form the universal Church in Heaven and earth," or that "the Heart of the Mother of the Saviour is, in a certain sense, the fountain and source of all that is holy and admirable in the life and successive mysteries of our divine Redeemer himself," there is no need to fear a diminution of Christ. Ultimately, it is in her consent (qv) that he sees the justification for his view.

J. also composed a Mass and Office in honour of the Heart of Mary, as well as other prayers for private use.

[1]*Oeuvres Complétes*, (Vannes, 1905-1911, English tr. ed. by the Eudists, New York, 1946). Cf. C. Lebrun, C.J.M., *The Spiritual Teaching of St. John Eudes*, (London, 1934); P. Herambourg, C.J.M., *St. John Eudes, A Spiritual Portrait*, tr. by R. Hauser, (Westminster, Maryland-Dublin, 1960); P. Georges, *S. Jean Eudes, Modèle et Maître de vie mariale*, (Paris, 1946); V. Jurga, *La dévotion au Coeur Immaculée de Marie d'après et dans l'ouevre de S. J. Eudes et l'enseignement postérieur, de l'Église*, (Rome, Vatican City, 1956); Cl. Guillocheau, S.J., "Le coeur dans l'oeuvre de S. Jean Eudes," in RAM, 37(1961), 167-192; L. Barbe, C.J.M., in *Maria*, III, 165-179; P. Milcent, in DSp, VIII, 488-501. [2]*The Priest, his Dignity and Obligations*, tr. by W. L. Murphy, (New York, 1947), 134-135. [3]*op. cit.*, 202. [4]*The Life and Kingdom of Jesus in Christian Souls*, tr. by a Trappist Father, (New York, 1946), 271.

JOHN THE EVANGELIST, ST.

It is for biblical experts to settle the question of authenticity in regard to the different New Testament books traditionally attributed to St. John. In that *corpus*, these passages bear directly on Marian theology: Jn 2:1-11 (see CANA); Jn 19:25-27 (see WOMAN IN); Rev 12:1-17 (see WOMAN IN). Indirectly related to questions on Our Lady are Jn 1:13 and Jn 16:21-22. This text is dealt with in relation to Jn 19:25-27.[1]

Taking the first three of these texts, there is the obvious difference, between the gospel and Revelations, of incident and heavenly vision. In one incident, spoken words are recorded of Mary. Each incident can be viewed factually and symbolically.

The word "woman" occurs in all three passages, and the problem is whether it is a link word, revealing a common thought. This would be so if each passage could be related to Gen 3:15, if the word "woman" signifies that Mary is the new Eve (qv).[2] There are resemblances between the early chapters of Genesis and Jn 1-2.[3] The struggle foretold between Satan (the serpent) and the woman, between her seed and his, takes place on Calvary, and is a background to the words of Jn 19:25-27. The reference to the woman's "offspring" in Rev 12:17 recalls the "seed" of Gen 3:15.

The "Hour" of Jesus is mentioned in the Cana incident (Jn 2:4), and the Calvary episode concludes with the words, "And from that hour the disciple took her to his own home" (Jn 19:27).

Again the thread of discipleship runs through all three accounts. "His disciples believed in him" after the sign of Cana (Jn 2:11); John on Calvary is "the disciple whom he loved" (Jn 19:26). Rev 12 speaks of the woman's offspring as those who "keep the commandments of God and bear testimony to Jesus" (Rev 12:17), which echoes the words of the fourth gospel: "If you love me, you will keep my commandments" (Jn 14:15) and "You also are my witnesses, because you have been with me from the beginning." (Jn 15:27).

Motherhood in different contexts is a theme in each text: the Mother of Jesus (2:1) at Cana; the Mother of the disciple (19:26-27) on Calvary; the Mother of the Messiah in Rev 12 v.5, which quotes the strictly messianic Ps 2:9, and of "the rest of her offspring" (Rev 12:17). To relate these variations on a theme is a task for the Johannine theologian.

[1]Cf. F. M. Braun, O.P., *La Mère des Fidèles, Essai de théologie johannique*, (Paris-Tournai, 1953), 184-185; "De Beata Virgine Maria in Evangelio S. Joannis et in Apocalpysi," in MSS, V, (Rome, 1967); A. Feuillet, P.S.S., *Johannine Studies*, (New York, 1965); *id.*, *Jésus et sa Mère, d'après les récits lucaniens de l'Enfance et d'après St. Jean*, (Paris, 1974); J. McHugh, "Mother of the Word Incarnate, (Mary in the Theology of St. John)," in *The Mother of Jesus in the New Testament*, (London, 1975), Pt. II, ch. 10, Pt. III, ch. 1-6, 351-532; Mary in NT, 179-218. Cf. R. E. Brown, "The Gospel According to John," in the *Anchor Bible*, (New York, 1966). [2]Cf. E. Hoskyns, "Genesis 1-3 and St. John's Gospel," in *Journ. Theol.St.*, 31(1920), 210-218; T. Barrosse, "Seven Days of the New Creation in St. John's Gospel," in CBQ, 21(1959), 507-516.

JOHN DE LA ROCHELLE (d. 1245)

J., a Franciscan, was influenced by William of Auxerre and Philip the Chancellor, but especially by Alexander of Hales with whom he worked on the first and second books of the

Summa Theologica, inserting his own *"Quaestiones de sanctificatione B. Virginis."*[1] J. wrote twenty-eight sermons on the four feasts of Our Lady then celebrated in the West (the Purification, Annunciation, Assumption, and Nativity), and one on Is 11:1. Two of his sermons on the Purification of Our Lady contain little on Mary.

---

[1] Cf. V. Doucet in introduction to vol. IV of the *Summa Theologica* of Alexander of Hales, (Quaracchi, 1948), ccxi-ccxviii, ccclx-ccclxx, ccxcv; K. L. Lynch, O.F.M., ed, of *Eleven Marian Sermons: John de la Rochelle, O.F.M.,* (Louvain-Paderborn, 1961, Franciscan Institute Publications, Text Series 2); J. Beumer, S.J., "Die Marienpredigten des Johannes von Rupelle O.F.M. und ihr Verhältnis zu dem Sammelwerk Richards von Saint-Laurent De laudibus Beatae Mariae Virginis," in FranzSt, 47(1965), 44-64.

JOHN OF GARLAND (d.c. 1272) — See Supplement, p. 383.

JOHN THE GEOMETER (Tenth Century)
Little is known about J. beyond the fact that he was an officer in the imperial army who fell into disgrace and, after dismissal, lived piously in retirement. It is unlikely that he was a monk or priest or archibishop.[1] He brought to his writing on Our Lady a profound grasp of Byzantine theology and a refined literary style. The epigrams attributed to him and published by Migne under his name[2] are probably the work of a Nilus, who was not Nilus of Ancyra. In the *Patrologia Graeca*, the long, splendid *Oratio in Annuntiationem Deiparae*[3] and the poems in honour of Our Lady[4] are authentic. What has drawn attention to J. in the present age is the publication of extracts and of a substantial part of his greatest work, notable in the whole history of Byzantine Marian theology, the *Life of Mary.* Fr. M. Jugie (qv) gave some extracts,[5] and Fr. J. Galot, S.J., did so more generously.[6] Meanwhile, Fr. A. Wenger, A.A., has published fully the concluding section, one fifth of the whole work;[7] and he later gave further extracts to the French Society of Marian Studies' annual meeting and bulletin.[8] Integral publication of the manuscript will be a major event in the history of theology and literature. There are three manuscripts, one in the Vatican, one in Paris (both used by Fr. Wenger), and one in Genoa (a copy of which in the Bollandist library in Brussels was used by Fr. Galot).

The poems express, with typically Byzantine style and deep insight, the unique perfection of Mary. So much so that Fr. Jugie thought that certain phrases, taken with passages in the

Annunciation *Oratio*, taught the Immaculate Conception (qv): ". . . a shoot from the old stock planted from the beginning in the verdant and delightful garden [of paradise]";[9] "masterpiece of the divine artist who exhausted his art in fashioning you";[10] "she had already been, through the Holy Spirit, full of grace and made worthy of such espousals";[11] "unconquered, mighty ornament of each world"[12] "conceived in joy, borne in joy in the womb, and in joy also brought into the light."[13] The idea, in the last quotation, is strengthened by the close parallel which J. presents with the case of Christ himself, "and who [Mary] again conceived and bore in the womb in joy and brought forth the joy which equally transcends every word and thought."[14]

In the *Oratio in Annuntiationem Deiparae*, the contrast between Eve (qv) and Mary is drawn out to constitute more a portrait than to show a role, ending "because of her who evilly exchanged words with the devil, she [is chosen] who in her self-restraint addressed God and exercised her mind in constant meditation on divine oracles . . . the Virgin Mediatress of the Word . . ."[15] J. refers to the *virginitas in partu*, using many figures to illustrate it.[16] In the *Oratio*, J. elaborates the theme of Mary's divine espousal and of the Incarnation. He touches on Mary's general mediatorial role: "The Virgin was the mediatress of the Word, who was to be the mediator as well as a virgin, and thus the handmaid became the daughter, the daughter the bride and the bride, mother."[17] "The relief of pain, destruction of enmity, ransom from captivity, elevation of mortals to God and joining of flesh with God . . . ."[18] With these titles, he addresses Mary.

Yet here as in the poems, J., who liked to call Mary mediatress,[19] tends to manifest the range of her spiritual power, she who surpasses each order of angels. ". . . tireless companion of those journeying through life"; "light of those astray, lighting again the way in darkness"; "strongest leader of leaders, providing discreetly advice to souls"; "house of divine graces, royal bridal chamber of the Trinity, in which are hidden all good treasures." J. hopes especially for wisdom from Mary, and other intellectual gifts, science of every kind, especially of sacred things, literature; she is the health of the sick, the source of remedies. He writes at length of her sovereignty, and she is honoured or adorned by those who through her obtained salvation, a multitude who know that the new grace of their renewal binds them to her.[20]

If such be the manifestation of Mary's power, the source behind it is revealed in the *Life of Mary*, which is conceived as a discourse on the Assumption as the culmination of her life. The key passage states the inseparable bond between Mother and Son. "The Virgin, after giving birth to her Son, was never separated from him in his activity, his dispositions, his will, even if, contrary to Christ, she was separated as a person [he had spoken of the union of two natures in one person in Christ]. When he went away, she went with him, when he worked miracles, it was as if she worked them with him, sharing his glory and rejoicing with him. When he was betrayed, arrested, judged, when he suffered, not only was she everywhere present beside him and even realized especially then his presence, but she even suffered with him or rather, if it be not rash to say it, she suffered still more than him."[21] He goes on to attentuate this latter view, by pointing to the Son's divinity and the Mother's weakness as a woman. "Terribly sundered, she would have wished a thousand times to suffer the evils she saw her Son suffering."[22]

Reason cannot understand the sufferings of Mary, as it cannot understand the virgin birth. But these sufferings entered into the plan of redemption. "We give thee thanks for having suffered for us such great evils, and for having willed that your mother should suffer such great evils, for you and for us, so that not only should the honour of sharing your sufferings earn a participation in glory, but that the memory of the sufferings endured for us should lead her to work our salvation, and that she should keep her love for us . . . ."[23] Christ gave himself as ransom for us and gives his mother as ransom for us at every moment, "so that you should die for us once and she should die thousands of times in her will, her heart burning just as for you, so also for those for whom she, as the Father, has given her own Son, knowing him to be delivered to death."[24]

Like George of Nicomedia (*qv*), J. thought that Mary awaited the Resurrection at the tomb, and was its first witness. After the Ascension, Mary, he contended, had a central role in the Church in Christ's place, directing and sustaining the apostles. She suffered with and for the Church "as a universal mother," bearing in her heart the very sufferings of the apostles.

The long passage, wherein J. explains his opinion on the bodily Assumption, is a subject of controversy. He speaks of Mary being raised to the heavens, "first as spirit without the body," and "now it is the body which is raised without the spirit," which led Fr. Jugie to attribute to him a theory of "double assumption."[25] But he had previously spoken of "the Virgin borne wholly to her Son and to God, to live and reign with him, and thus it is not only through her Son but also through her that our nature is introduced to the heavens and reigns over all things visible and invisible."[26] The bodily resurrection of Mary is presupposed by J.'s whole doctrine.

Her mediation, as "second mediatress after the first Mediator, God-bearing human nature after the God who bore human nature," is now assured to us, "the ladder by which God descends and man ascends." Her intercession is universal and attested to by countless miracles, for she possesses almost everything by herself, and grants largesses to whom she will and to those who beseech her.[27] As queen, she seems to render the King still more merciful, and to the Spirit she is another Paraclete.[28]

Mary, J. teaches (and here he marks a clear advance on the Byzantine tradition), is our mother—, "mother of all, and of each more than our mothers, loving us more than one can express."[29]

---

[1]Cf. F. Scheidweiler, "Studien zu Johannes Geometra," in ByzZeitschr, 45(1952), 277-319; but also J. Darrouzes, in DS, 6, 265-266, with bibliography. [2]PG 106, 854-868. [3]PG 106, 811-848. [4]PG 106, 855-868. Cf. J. Sajdak, "Joannis Kyriotis Geometrae Hymni in SS. Deiparam," in *Analecta Byzantina*, (Poznan, 1931); V. Laurent, "Les poésies mariales de Jean Kyriote le Géomètre," in *Echos d'Orient*, 31(1932), 117-120. [5]M. Jugie, *L'Immaculée Conception*, 185-188; id., *L'Assomption*, 316-320. [6]J. Galot, S.J., "La plus ancienne affirmation de la corédemption mariale," in RSR, 45(1957), 187-208. [7]A. Wenger, A.A., *L'Assomption*, 363-425. [8]On Mary's intercession, cf. BSFEM, 23(1966), 66-70. [9]Poem 2, in PG 106, 857B. [10]Poem 3, in PG 106, 861A. [11]*Oratio in Annuntiationem Deiparae*, in PG 106, 820A. [12]Poem 4, in PG 106, 865C. [13]*Oratio...*, in PG 106, 845A. [14]*op. cit.*, in PG 106, 845A. [15]*op. cit.*, in PG 106, 817B. [16]*op. cit.*, in PG 106, 836B. [17]PG 106, 817B. [18]PG 106, 845A. [19]A. Wenger, A.A., *L'Assomption*, 407-415. [20]*Oratio . . .*, in PG 106, 840-845; Hymn IV, in PG 106, 865ABC. [21]*Apud* A. Wenger, A.A., in BSFEM, 23(1966), 66. [22]BSFEM, 23(1966), 66. [23]A. Wenger, A.A., *L'Assomption*, 406. [24]*ibid., op. cit.*, 406. [25]M. Jugie, *L'Assomption*, 316-320. [26]A. Wenger, A.A., *L'Assomption*, 393. [27]BSFEM, 23(1966), 70. [28]A. Wenger, A.A., *L'Assomption*, 408. [29]*L'Assomption*, 412.

JOHN MAUROPOUS (d. *c.* 1079)

J. was Metropolitan of Euchaites in Pontus, and author of a sermon on the Dormition and of some sixty-eight *Theotokia*, as well as of Marian passages in other works.[1] Some of the *Theotokia* have been published. In the Christological Canons published by Enrica Follieri, there are repeated prayers to the *Theotokos*, with Byzantine doctrine implied or explicit. For J., Mary is the spouse of God;[2] through her, he pours out blessing on the whole race.[3] She was foretold in the Old Testament in many signs—in Is 7:14, Dan 2:34, Ez 44:2, and in the Ark of the Covenant. Through her, the creature is restored and newly fashioned.[4] The Canon prayers emphasize this role and the power that it implies: "You raised up our nature fallen in the abyss of hell by giving birth to God, who lifts the poor from the ground and causes the miserable to rise from the dung-hill, O Virgin without fault."[5] "You manifested to us, Mother of God, Virgin all pure, the divine mystery unknown to all the incorporeal beings, known to God alone."[6] Mary is the queen, the helper, the one who mediates. Through God to her, even the impossible is possible, for she has thrown down the great wall of enmity and the ancient curse.[7] She is particularly invoked in dangers, the storms of life.

J. believed in an apparition of the risen Christ to Mary.[8] He described the dual Assumption of Mary not without some vagueness on the ultimate outcome—whether soul and body were united. Mary is above the angels and accompanied by thousands of them.[9]

[1]*Sermo in SS. Deip. Dorm.*, in PG 120, 1075-1114; E. Follieri, "Otto canoni paracletici a Nostro Signore Gesu Cristo, (Giovanni Mauropode)," in *Archivio italiano di storia della pietá*, 5, (Rome, 1968); S. Eustradiades, *Theotokarion*, (Paris, 1931).Cf. M. Jugie, *L'Assomption*, 321-322. [2]PG 120, 1081C. [3]PG 120, 1085. [4]PG 120, 1105A. [5]*Can. 3, 4,* apud E. Follieri, 89. [6]*Can. 6, 4,* apud E. Follieri, 141. [7]*Can. 8,7,* apud E. Follieri, 179; *Can. 7, 3,* apud E. Follieri, 155. [8]PG 120, 1092B. [9]*Can. 4, 5,* apud E. Follieri, 109.

JOHN PAUL II (Pope 1978-   ) — See Supplement, pp. 383-384.

JOHN OF ROMIROY (Fifteenth Century)

A Master in Theology, and treasurer of the church of Le Puy-en-Velay, J. was a promoter of the positive thesis on the Immaculate Conception (*qv*) at the Council of Basle. He urged the Council Fathers to extend the feast to the universal Church so as to win Our Lady's help for a successful outcome to their deliberations. J. thought they should end the controversy about Our Lady's privilege, relieving the Christian people of the scandal caused by doubts about what they celebrated in the feast. Though he referred to miracles, he also appealed to biblical texts—Gen 2:18, 3:15, and Rev 12. He also reproduced the argument of Duns Scotus on the perfect Mediator, and insisted on the superiority of redemption by preservation over restoration from a fallen state. J.'s memorandum was printed in Rome over a century later.[1] He was probably also the author of three lesser works on the Immaculate Conception.

[1]See the report *Tractatus de veritate Conceptionis Beatissimae Virginis pro facienda relatione coram Patribus Concilii Basileae, A. D., 1437,* (Rome, 1547). Cf. A. Emmen, O.F.M., "Joannes de Romiroy sollicitator causae Immaculatae Conceptionis in Concilio Basileensi," in Anton, 32(1957), 335-368; J. Galot, S.J., *Maria,* VII, 72-74.

JOHN OF SEGOVIA (d. 1456)

A Spanish theologian, Canon of Toledo, and Professor in Salamanca, J. represented the King of Castile and his own university at the Council of Basle. He was a defender of the Immaculate Conception (*qv*) thesis, which was adopted by the Council after it separated from the Pope. His ideas are developed in a lengthy treatise.[1] He based his argumentation on the divine maternity and on Mary's union with Christ in the Redemption, each in the context of Mary as the spotless bride of God and of Christ. Any infection by sin would have impaired this spotless character. In dealing with Mary's role in the Redemption, J. insisted that she acted as a secondary cause while Christ was the primary one. The secondary cause, he thought, derived its efficiency from the first.

[1]*Septem allegationes et totidem avisamenta pro informatione Patrum concilii Basileensis . . . circa sacratissimae virginis Mariae immaculatam conceptionem ejusque praeservationem a peccato originali in primo suae animationis instanti,* (Brussels, 1664). Cf. E. Amann, in DTC, VIII, 816-819; J. Galot S.J., in *Maria,* VII, 74-76; J. Martin Palma, "Maria y la Iglesia según Juan de Segovia y Juan de Torquemada," in EstM, 18(1957), 207-230; H. J. Garcia, "Juan de Segovia, defensor de la Inmaculada Concepción de Maria," in *Estudios Segovianos,* 10(1958), 179-195.

JOHN OF THESSALONICA (d. *c.* 630)

J., as Archbishop of Thessalonica, was popular as a preacher, and ready to mount the ramparts of the city when it was besieged to encourage the defenders. He was reputed by his successor to have saved the city from earthquake by his prayers. He introduced the feast of the Dormition to his church, judging that he should conform to universal practice.[1] His lengthy homily on the feast was an *apologia* for his action, a plea for attention to its meaning. Though trying to free the story of unjustifiable accretions, he broadly reproduces the apocryphal version of Mary's death. The manuscript tradition (BHG 1144-1144c, 1144d-1144g) is complicated and, though J. is apparently silent on the essential fact of bodily resurrection (though it is found in some interpolations) scholars agree that it would have been in the source he used. It may yet be found in one unpublished version of the homily (BHG, *Auctarium*, 1056g, 1056gb).

More remarkable is the doctrine of Mary's spiritual motherhood, not a characteristic Byzantine theory. "Then the thrice blessed apostles of the Lord, entering together Mary's house, greeted her, saying, 'Mary, Mistress of the universe, our Mother and mother of all who believe in Christ, the grace of God and the Father be with you'." Peter also pronounces a eulogy of those who enter the virginal state.

[1] Ed. by M. Jugie, A.A., in PO 19, 375-405; short version, in REB, 11(1953), 156-164. Cf. M. Jugie, A.A., in *Echos d'Orient*, 21(1922), 293-307; *ibid*., "Analyse du discours . . . sur la Dormition," in *Echos d'Orient*, 22(1923), 385-397; *id*., in DTC, VIII, 819-823; M. Jugie, A.A., *L'Assomption*, 139-154; M. L. Carli, "Le fonti del racconto della dormizione di Maria di G. T.," in MM, 2(1940), 308-313; MM, 4(1942), 1-9; B. Capelle, O.S.B., "Les anciens récits de l'Assomption de J. de T.," in RTAM, 12(1940), 209-235; *ibid*., "Vestiges grecs et latins d'un antique 'transitus' de la Vierge," in AB, 67(1949), 21-48; L. Brou, "Restes de l'ancienne homélie sur la dormition de l'archevêque Jean . . . dans le plus ancien antiphonaire connu," in *Archiv für Liturgie-wissenschaft*, 2(1952), 84-93; A. Wenger, A.A., *L'Assomption*, 240-241, 245-256; M. Candal, *Catholicisme*, VI, 575-577.

JOHN TORQUEMADA, O.P., CARDINAL
(1388-1468)

J. was a Spanish theologian who took part in the Council of Basle, and argued against the thesis of Mary's Immaculate Conception (*qv*). His report was printed in Rome over a century later, and was reprinted in the nineteenth century by E. B. Pusey (*qv*).[1]

[1] Joannes de Turrecremata, *Tractatus de veritate Conceptionis Beatissimae Virginis pro facienda relatione coram Patribus Concilii Basileae, A. D., 1437*, (Rome, 1547, ed.

by E. B. Pusey, London, 1869). Cf. K. Binder, "Kardinal Juan de Torquemada und die feierliche Verkündigung der Lehre von der unbefleckten Empfängnis auf dem Konzil von Basel," in V.I., VI, 146-163; J. Martin Palma, "Maria y la Iglesia según Juan de Segovia y Juan de Torquemada," in EstM, 18(1957), 207-230.

JOHN XXIII, POPE (Reigned, 1958-1963)
J. was intensely devoted to the Blessed Virgin Mary. He had visited many of her shrines, from Fatima to Czestochowa, preaching constantly on her privileges and her power on our behalf. This practice he maintained as Pope. His pronouncements on Our Lady, and all official acts of his pontificate related to her cult, provide 476 pages of texts. In quantity, this is larger than any equivalent period (four-and-a-half years) in the history of the Papacy, with the exception of the years in Pius XII's pontificate, from 1953 to 1958, which included the Marian and Lourdes centenary years.[1] J.'s favourite theme was the spiritual motherhood of Mary, and he insisted on her intercessory role. He issued four public letters on the Rosary (*qv*) and published a series of meditations on the different mysteries. J. particularly honoured the Immaculate Conception. He warned against excesses in Marian piety and against improper limitation. His campaign of prayer for Vatican II was overtly and constantly directed to Mary.

[1] *Acta Mariana Joannis PP. XXIII*, ed. by D. Bertetto, S.D.B., (Rome, 1964). Cf. *id., Il magistero mariano di Papa Giovanni*, (Turin, Piero Gribaudi, 1969); G. Ceruti, S.M.M., *L'anima mariana di Papa Giovanni*, (Rome, Centro Mariano Monfortano, 1969); A. Molina, "Doctrina espiritual mariana de Juan XXIII," in EstM, 35(1970), 115-161; A. Moreno, S.J., "El Papa Juan XXIII y la devoción a la Santisima Virgen Maria," in *Regina Mundi*, 33(1971), 53-72.

JOSEPH, ST.
Sacred Scripture: The infancy narratives (*qv*) of Matthew and Luke contain the only factual information on J. in the Bible. The other references to him in the gospels are by way of designation (Mt 13:55; Lk 3:23, 4:22; Jn 1:45, 6:42).[1] Matthew and Luke give genealogies of the saint, Matthew in the opening passage of the gospel, Luke after the story of the baptism. The two lists differ, and various explanations have been given of the discrepancies. Matthew's list descends from Abraham, father of believers, at the origin of the old covenant, to Jesus, author of the new covenant. Matthew follows at once with the story of the virgin birth, work of the

Spirit, sign of a wholly new world. Luke's longer list ascends to Adam, reflecting the universalism which is a feature of his gospel. Each genealogy contains the name of David, essential to Christ's place among his people.

Matthew says that Jacob begot J. (*egenessen ton Joseph*) (1:16). Luke describes Jesus as the son, as it was supposed, "of Joseph, the son of Heli" (3:23). Different solutions have been proposed to explain his double fatherhood. One theory appeals to the "levirate marriage" (Latin *levir*, brother-in-law) prescribed in Deuteronomy (25:5-7). If brothers live together and one of them dies without a son, the surviving brother should marry the widow. If this were so in J.'s case, he would have only one paternal grandfather. He is given Matthan by Matthew and Mathat by Luke, with a different ancestral line to David in each case. To solve this difficulty, Julianus Africanus (d. *c.* 250) suggested that Jacob and Heli were uterine brothers, born of the same mother but of different fathers. When Heli died after a childless marriage, his brother Jacob married the widow, who was mother of J. in her second marraige. U. Holzmeister opposed his view, contending that uterine brothers did not live together as Deuteronomy prescribed.

Holzmeister favoured the opinion that Luke gave J. an adoptive father, none other than Our Lady's own father.[2] A son-in-law could be virtually adopted if his wife were the only daughter, the heiress. Eusebius of Caeserea (*qv*) held that J. and Mary were of the same tribe. A view of the genealogy—which seems to have support in St. Justin (*qv*), is found also in Annius of Viterbo (*c.* 1490), and was defended by Suarez—makes it that of Mary. The words in Lk 3:23 should then read, "Jesus being, as was supposed, the son of Joseph [but really the grandson] of Heli." It is customary to object that genealogies of women were not given, but Judith's is recorded (Jud 8:1), and female lineage is elsewhere mentioned (Num 26:33, 1 Chr 2:16-17). It seems certain that Luke's choice was determined by regard for the legal fatherhood of Jesus, for he places the genealogy alongside the story of Jesus' assumption of his public activity.

No facts in J.'s life, prior to the betrothal, are given us save that he was a carpenter, *techton*. The word almost certainly refers to a worker in wood, maker of the articles needed in a Galilean village for domestic use or outdoor work. Ploughs have been traditionally mentioned, possibly small building frames. The Apocrypha (*qv*) speak of houses he was building. J. may have owned a plot of ground nearby. Timber was plentiful.

J. may have been born in Bethlehem or Nazareth, though Jerusalem is mentioned also. The Apocrypha represent him as an old man, a widower at the time of the marriage (*qv*). They add picturesque accounts of the miraculous sign by which he was chosen as Mary's fiancé from among several summoned by the High Priest—by a dove which flew from his staff and alighted on his head (or, in a later version, from his suddenly flowering staff) and flew to heaven. Old Testament elements—the choice of Aaron by Moses after his rod had blossomed (Num 17:1-5, 6-8; Is 11:1), or the shoot from the stump of Jesse—and the story of the dove in the baptism of Jesus influenced this composition. Underlying it is the belief that God must have manifested his will about this marriage in a special way.

J. was not the physical father of Jesus (see VIRGINITY OF MARY), and the virginal conception was the occasion for him of anxiety from which he was relieved by a mystical dream. (see DOUBT OF ST. JOSEPH). Since St. Jerome's exegesis, the eastern view of prior marriage has been abandoned in the West, and many have explicitly taught that the saint entered readily into Mary's idea of a virginal marriage (see BROTHERS OF THE LORD). Catholic scholars, like S. Lyonnet, R. Laurentin, and G. Graystone, have shown that Mary's vow or promise of virginity was not incompatible with the mentality of the time. J.'s virginity was exalted by the mystery of the Incarnation.

Luke mentions J. once in Chapter 1 of his gospel, as Mary's fiancé, "a man whose name was Joseph, of the house of David" (1:27). At the beginning of Chapter 2, he appears as her companion—again she is called his betrothed. It is in the Temple mysteries that he is first spoken of with Mary as a parent (v.27), father (v.33), and again parent (v.41), and by Mary, to Jesus, as "your father" (v.48). His fatherhood is restricted to a legal context, as the Presentation and the Passover were legal duties. He is significantly not called father until the Child is born, and the birth proclaimed by a heavenly sign. (see FATHERHOOD OF JOSEPH).

If the saint has a subdued role in Luke, he is a central figure in Matthew's infancy narrative. Apart from the virginal conception clearly taught in Chapter 1, there is a theology of J., in embryo, in the words and deeds reported. He was a just man, that is faithful to the Torah, and, by implication, to the traditions of the Old Testament. As Mary was given an idea of the saving role of her Son, to which her consent would commit her, J. was also briefly informed on the future plan of salvation. "She will bear a Son and you shall call his name Jesus, for he will save his people from their sins." (Mt 1:21). As Mary cooperated by faith and obedience, so did J., who "did as the angel of the Lord commanded him."

J.'s death is not mentioned in the New Testament. He may have been dead before Jesus began his public ministry. It is generally thought that he was so at the time of the Passion and death of Christ. Why otherwise should Mary be entrusted to John?

History: The Fathers of the Church spoke or wrote of J. in relation to Our Lady's virginity. They were curious as to the reasons why she should, though a virgin, have a husband. With St. Augustine, we have an incipient theology. He established the true nature of the marriage and explained the fatherhood.

Yet centuries would pass before substantial works could appear on J.—on his dignity, vocation, holiness, gifts, and intercession. A continuing thread is discernible in medieval times. St. Thomas gave the final synthesis on the marriage. Towards the end of the thirteenth century, Peter John Olivi and Ubertino of Casale (*qv*) gave thought to J. In the next century, Ludolph the Carthusian, Bartholomew of Pisa, and St. Bridget of Sweden (*qv*) had some interest. In the fifteenth century, so had Cardinal Peter d'Ailly (d. 1430), St. Bernardine of Siena (*qv*), who borrowed heavily from Peter John Olivi and Ubertino of Casale and, above all, John Gerson (*qv*) whose writing was valuable in quantity and quality. In the following century appeared the *Summa de donis sancti Josephi* of Isidore of Isolanis (1522); *Josephina* of Bernardine of Laredo (1535); *Libro de la vida y excelencias de el Bienaventurado S. Joseph* of Andrew de Soto (1593); and *Josephina* by Jerome Gracian (1597). In the *De Mysteriis vitae Christi* (1592), Suarez treated questions about the saint in his customary scientific manner. In the same age, a different kind of influence was felt—that of St. Teresa of Avila. Her enthusiasm for Saint Joseph was remarkable, vividly expressed in her writings, and perpetuated in the twelve convents founded in his honour.

The seventeenth century was a golden age. St. Francis de Sales (*qv*) and Bossuet (*qv*) were conspicuous among many preachers and writers on J. Fr. Sommervogel listed 130 works by Jesuits after 1600. A decline set in during the eighteenth century, with some notable exceptions like St. Alphonsus Liguori; but the nineteenth and twentieth centuries, under the stimulus of the Popes, saw a recovery.

Teaching Authority: In administrative Roman documents since the sixteenth century, occasional references to J. occur. More substantial teaching has come from the modern Popes. By the decree, *Quemadmodum Deus* of 8 December, 1870, Pius IX (*qv*) proclaimed the saint Patron of the Church, and, in the Apostolic Letter *Inclytum Patriarcham*, he explained the reasons for this act, sketching a theology of the saint. The sketch was filled in with *Quamquam Pluries* (15 August, 1889). Leo XIII's Encyclical on J., still the most important papal document on him. "For he, indeed," said the Pope, "was the husband of Mary, and the father, as was supposed, of Jesus Christ. From this arise all his dignity, grace, holiness, and glory." In the Brief, *Neminem fugit* (14 June, 1892), the Pope, encouraging devotion to the Holy Family, took occasion to speak of J. St. Pius X (*qv*) acted more on the pastoral level, approving a prayer to his personal patron, composed by himself, and likewise approving the Litany of the saint. Benedict XV issued a *Motu proprio* (25 July, 1920), to honour the Golden Jubilee of the proclamation of J.'s universal patronage of the Church. Pius XI (*qv*) spoke often in addresses of the merits, power, and dignity of the saint, a special protector against atheistic communism, he thought. Pius XII instituted the feast of J. the Workman (1 May, 1955), and composed a prayer to match this title. John XXIII (*qv*) published an Apostolic Letter, *Le voci* (19 March, 1961), summarizing the teaching of his predecessors in office, and naming J. "Protector of the Second Vatican Council." Pope John, on his own initiative, during the first session, decided that the saint's name would appear in the Roman Canon. A petition, sponsored by centers in

Montreal, Valladolid, and Viterbo, had been widely distributed, in the years before the Council, to obtain this inclusion of the saint's name, not only in the *Communicantes*, but in the *Confiteor*, the *Suscipe Sancta Trinitas*, and *Libera nos*. It was signed by 400 bishops, among others, and recalled similar requests to the Holy See since 1815. Pope John's decision was publicly welcomed by Karl Barth (*qv*).

Vatican II said nothing about J., for the only place where his name occurs is in a quotation from the Roman Canon altered by the Pope (LG 50). The account of the Annunciation, based on Luke, in effect deletes the saint's name. In early comments, in the *aula* and in the written submissions, requests were made that this unjustified error be corrected. This was a Council aiming at biblical presentation![3] The commission refused to listen. If their intention was to please the separated brethren, they were singularly misguided. Soon after the Council, a Swiss Protestant published a stinging criticism, profoundly enlightened, of their arbitrary mutilation of a biblical datum. It was bad exegetically, he maintained; for, by eliminating J., through whose genealogy Jesus was heir to the Davidic promise, the Saviour's Jewishness, his messianic character, and possibly his historicity, were compromised. It was also bad spiritually, for J. shows how men, incapable of accomplishing the divine promises of producing a Saviour, can receive the promised Saviour, give him a place of dignity, offer him a family, and protect him.[4] The commission may have found mention of J. too "pious." Some Fathers of Vatican I had a similar reaction to the statement: "The Church is the Mystical Body of Christ."

[1]Two reviews, EstJos, (1947) and CahJos, (1953), J. de Jesus Maria, "Bibliografia fundamental josefina," in EstJos, 20(1966), 41-139; A Trottier, *Essai de bibliographie sur S. Joseph*, 4th ed., (Montreal, 1968); *id., Le Patronage de S. Joseph*, proceedings of the 1955 Study Congress, (Montreal, 1956); *Saint Joseph durant les quinze premiers siècles de l'Eglise*, (Montreal, 1971). Cf. E. Rasco, *El anuncio a José (Mt 1:18-25)*, proceedings of the international Symposium on St. Joseph (Rome, 1970), 84-103; T. Stramare, "I Sogni di San Giuseppe," proceedings of the International Symposium on St. Joseph, (Rome, 1970), 104-122; J. M. Canal Sanchez, C.M.F., "San José en los libros apocrifos del Nuevo Testamento," proceedings of the international Symposium on St. Joseph, (Rome, 1970), 123-149; P. Grelot, G. M. Bertrand, C.S.C., R. Gauthier, C.S.C., A Solignac, in DSp, VIII, 1289-1323, separate issue, *Joseph et Jésus*, (Paris, 1975); U. Holzmeister, S.J., *De sancto Joseph quaestiones biblicae*, (Rome, 1945); L. M. Ramlot, "Les généalogies bibliques: un genre oriental," in *Bible et vie chrétienne*, (1964/6), n.60, 53-70; M. D. Johnson, *The Purpose of the Biblical Genealogies with Special Reference to the Setting of the Genealogies of Jesus*, (Cambridge, 1969). See articles on *Birth of Jesus, Brothers of the Lord, Doubt of Joseph, Infancy Narratives*, and *Marriage of Mary* in the present work. J. Seitz, *Die Verehrung des hl. Joseph in ihrer geschichtlichen Entwicklung bis zum Konzil von Trient dargestellt*, (Fribourg im Brisgau, 1908); R. Balmori, "Anuncio a José y Misterio Pascal," in EstJos, 21(1967), 187-201; J. C. Vives y Tuto, *Summa josephina ex patribus, doctoribus asceticis*, (Rome, 1907); J. Dusserre, "Les origines de la dévotion à S. Joseph," in CahJos, (1953, 1954); G. M. Bertrand and G. Ponton, *Textes patristiques sur S. Joseph*, (Montreal, 1966); G. Giamberardini, O.F.M., *San Giuseppe nella tradizione copta*, (Cairo, 1966); D. O'Shea, *Mary and Joseph*, (Milwaukee, 1949); J. Mueller, *The Fatherhood of St. Joseph*, (London, 1952); B. Llamera, O.P., *Teologia de San José*, (Madrid, 1953), English tr., *St. Joseph*, (St. Louis, 1962); F. L. Filas, S.J., *Joseph and Jesus*, (Milwaukee, 1956); *ibid., Joseph the Just*, (London, 1958); *id., The Man Closest to Jesus*, (Boston, 1962); *id., St. Joseph after Vatican II*, (New York, 1969); M. O'Carroll, C.S.Sp., *Joseph, Son of David*, (Dublin, 1963); T. Stramare, "Giuseppe, sposo di M. V.," in *Bibliotheca Sanctorum*, 6(1965), 1251-1287. [2]U. Holzmeister, S.J., *De sancto Joseph quaestiones biblicae*, (Rome, 1945), 12. [3]For the speech in the *aula* of Bishop Juan Ambrosio Abasolo y Lecue, O.Carm., cf. G. M. Besutti, O.S.M., in MM, 28(1966), 79, and esp. "Acta synodalia Conc. Oecum. Vatican II," Vol. III, Periodus IIIa, Pars 1a, 473-474. For the written submission of Bishop Ceocchi, supported by eight others, cf. *op. cit.*, Vol. III, Periodus IIIa, Pars 2a, in MM, 28(1966), 107. Cf. *Modi*, (Vatican City, 1964), 12. [4]J. J. von Allmen, "Remarques sur la Constitution Dogmatique, Lumen Gentium," in *Irenikon*, 39(1966), 22-23.

JOSEPH BRYENNIOS (d. 1436/38)

A Byzantine theologian and preacher who lived in Crete, Constantinople, and Cyprus, J. was involved in discussion on reunion between East and West, ending in opposition thereto. He had some knowledge of Latin theology.[1] His Marian homilies are not very well known: three on the Annunciation (BHG 1092i, 1099k, 1116s); two on the Nativity of Mary (BHG 1099i, 1127i); and a thanksgiving sermon when the Hodegetria icon (*qv*), taken to the city walls during a blockade, was being brought back to its shrine in 1422 (BHG 1102q). An unpublished sermon by J. is a panegyric for every feast of the *Theotokos*.

Fr. M. Jugie (*qv*) argues strongly that, though J. used the phrase "sanctified in the womb," his strong statements on Mary's initial holiness amount to a doctrine of the Immaculate Conception. In the homilies on the Nativity and the Annunciation (*qv*), J. taught the greatness of the *Theotokos*, the new Eve, and the ever-Virgin, and he showed her place in the economy of salvation. In the thanksgiving homily, he praised Mary, in litany form, as the triumphant Mediatress (qv), reconciler, and Queen of the world. On the bodily Assumption, he remained an ambiguous witness. In the second Nativity sermon, he praised Mary in terms which imply a positive view; in his correspondence, he expressed doubt. Mary, J. thought, was also Mediatress of grace to the angels.

[1]*Works* of Joseph Bryennios, ed. in Leipzig (I, II in 1768, III in 1784). Cf. M. Jugie, A.A. *L'Immaculée Conception*, 292-298; *ibid.*, *L'Assomption*, 336; A Palmieri, in DTC, XI, 1156-1161; L Brehier, in DHGE, X, 993-996; D. Stiernon, A.A., in DSp, VIII, 1323-1330.

JOSEPH THE HYMNOGRAPHER
(*c.* 816-886)

A liturgical poet born in Syracuse, J. was a refugee in Greece from the Saracen invaders. Over 400 compositions have been identified as his, and there are probably more. The Marian poems, Canons, and *Theotokia* were published by H. Marracci[1] (qv) and are reproduced by Migne[2] (qv). The core of doctrine expressed in these poems truly represents Byzantine Marian theology. Mary's initial holiness is stressed. "Unusual is your conception . . . everything about you, O immaculate one, is exceptional and wonderful above all language and thought."[3] "A daughter exalted above the angels is born on earth in incomparable sanctity and purity."[4] She is all holy and all immaculate. The spiritual Spouse found her alone, a lily among thorns and flower of the valleys. J. liked to recall that Mary was born of a sterile parent, and repeatedly spoke of her as the spouse (qv) of God. "The Holy Spirit wholly sanctified you [in the temple], wherefore you have become the most fair spouse of the Father and mother of the Son."[5] Mary died in accordance with the law of nature which was not really binding on her, she who had given birth not in the ordinary way; but she was bodily assumed. "Your tomb declares that you were buried, and it now openly shows that you have been bodily borne to the heavens."[6] In heaven, Mary is queen of all creatures.

Mary's role is sketched: "Through your incorrupt birth-giving, O august one, you clothed with the garment of incorruption all those denuded through corruption."[7] She is the heavenly ladder by which God the Word communicated with men; she is the wound inflicted on demons, the salvation of men, the ornament of angels.

From such views come his prayers, some echoing the *Sub tuum* (qv). "Strengthen, O Lady most unsullied, my weakness, you who brought forth the power of the Almighty . . . ."[8] "O unique hope and help of the faithful, Mother of God, hasten to help those immersed in troubles . . . fleeing to thee, O Virgin . . . .Refuge of Christians, helper of those who are held in difficulties, O most holy Virgin, do not despise us who are in incessant dangers."[9] She is the one who obtains all good things for us. J. regarded himself as her slave. She was made the source of remedies, and he asked her to heal his soul.

[1]H. Marracci, *Sancti Josephi Hymnographi Mariale*, (Rome, 1661). [2]PG 105, 978-1414. Cf. D. Stiernon, s.v., in DSp. VIII, 1349-1354; *id.*, in REB, 31(1973), 243-266 (review of Greek work by E. I. Tomadakes). [3]Canon 1, *In pervigilio ingress. SS. Deiparae in templum* 4, in PG 105, 993C. [4]*In pervigilio Nativ. B. Deiparae* 4, in PG 105, 985B. [5]PG 105, 993D. [6]*In pervigilio obdormitionis . . . .*, in PG 105, 1001A. [7]Canon 4, *In depositione pretiosae vestis SS. Deiparae in Blachernis*, in PG 105, 1005B. [8]*In sancta matre nostra Domnica*, in PG 105, 1045C. [9]*Ex canone in Sanctum Basilium episcopum Amaseae*, in PG 105, 1109B.

JOUASSARD, GEORGES (1895-1982) — See
Supplement, p. 384.

JUGIE, MARTIN, A. A. (1878-1954)

J. lived for six years in Jerusalem, and for twelve years in Constantinople; he taught in Roman universities.[1] Through his immense erudition and specialist knowledge of the Orient, J. was a foundation member of modern Marian theology. Author of five volumes on Orthodox Dogmatic Theology, he completed the edition of the works of Scholarios (qv) first undertaken by Mgr. Petit. He edited unpublished homilies from the fourth to the fifteenth centuries, and other texts, especially (for PO 12 and 16), the epoch-making *Sermo in Sanctissimam Deiparam* by Theophanes of Nicaea (qv). J. was a frequent contributor to *Echos d'Orient* and other reviews, and to the *Dictionnaire de Théologie Catholique*. His principal works, *L'Assomption* and *L'Immaculée Conception*, are frequently cited in this work. As a member of the advisory committee on *Munificentissimus Deus* (qv), J. persuaded Pius XII (qv) to leave the question of Mary's death out of the dogma.

[1]Cf. D. Stiernon, A.A., "L'Oeuvre mariologique du P. Martin Jugie," in EphMar, 5(1955), 445-448; *id.*, in *Catholicisme*, VI, 1190-1193. Bibliography of Fr. Jugie, "Mélanges Martin Jugie," 256 items, in REB, 11(1952), 19-32.

JUSTIN MARTYR, ST. (d. c. 165)

Born in Sichem (Nablus) of immigrants of some means, J. was converted to Christianity about 133, after studying philosophies of different kinds. He treated of Our Lady in passing in his work the *Apology*, and in the *Dialogue with Trypho*, a Jew, which contains one long, memorable passage, very probably the first patristic testimony on the Eve (*qv*)-Mary parallel. The recurring theme is the virginal conception.

In the *Apology*, J. noted the parallel between the oracle of Is 7:14 (see EMMANUEL) and Lk 1:31.[1] He rejected pagan myths invoked against the mystery. In the *Dialogue*, he dealt at length with Trypho's opinion that *almah*, in the Isaiah text, should be translated "young woman," and the child to be born was Hezekiah. The *Septuagint*, he reminded his opponent, used *parthenos*, a virgin; if the oracle were to be fulfilled by an ordinary birth, how could this be a sign?[2]

J. thought that Mary was of the Davidic line.[3] Recalling the infancy narrative (*qv*), he expressed the view that Joseph, before being informed by an angel, thought Mary had conceived her Child through human intercourse; he also spoke of the "cave" near Bethlehem, one of the earliest testimonies on the subject[4] and, as in the *Apology*, he answered objections based on pagan mythology.

The Eve-Mary passage seems slightly out of place. It seems to have been joined to a set of remarks on Christ, which end with a list of figurative titles from the Old Testament to continue thus: ". . . and has become man by the Virgin, in order that by the same way in which the disobedience caused by the serpent took its beginning, by this way should it also take its destruction. For Eve, being a virgin and incorrupt, conceived the word spoken of the serpent, and brought forth disobedience and death. But Mary the Virgin, receiving faith and grace when the angel Gabriel brought her the good news that *the Spirit of the Lord would come upon her, and the power of the Most High would overshadow her, so that the holy [one] born of her is the Son of God*, answered, Be it done unto me according to thy word."[5] J. then reverted to Christ the Saviour: "And by her has he been born, about whom we have proved so many Scriptures have been spoken, by means of whom God destroys both the serpent and those angels and men that became like it, but for them that repent of their evil deeds, and believe in him, does he work deliverance from death."[6]

The latter sentence seems to echo Gen 3:15 (see WOMAN IN), and has prompted the opinion by one scholar, T. Gallus, that J. was the first to give a Marian interpretation of the oracles[7]— an opinion challenged, since J. quotes the oracle a little later in a rather vague sense. One must recall, however, that the passage opened with reference to the serpent.

His sureness of touch in the theology of the Incarnation, and the divine maternity is evident in this passage: "But what is really a sign, and what was to become a sure proof to the human race, namely the first-born of all creatures to become incarnate through a virgin's womb, and really to become a child, this he anticipated by the spirit of the prophets in various ways, as I related to you, and he made the proclamation beforehand, in order that, when it took place, it might be known to have taken place by the power and purpose of the maker of the universe."[8]

---

[1]PG 6, 628-629. [2]PG 6, 673. [3]*Dialogue with Trypho, 43, 1, 100, 3.* [4]*Dialogue with Trypho, 78*, in PG 6, 657-660; *Dialogue with Trypho, 84, 1*, in PG 6, 673. [5]*Dialogue . . . , 100, 4-5*, in PG 6, 709-712; tr. by L. Williams, *Justin Martyr, The Dialogue with Trypho*, (London, SPCK, 1930), 210. [6]Cf. G. Jouassard, in BSFEM, 12(1954), 36-37. [7]T. Gallus, *Interpretatio mariologica protoevangelii tempore post-patristico usque ad Concilium Tridentinum*, (Rome, Orbis Catholicus, 1949). Cf. R. Laurentin, in BSFEM, 12(1954), 92-93, 116 for diverse opinions. [8]*Dialogue . . . , 84, 2*, in PG 6, 673.

K

KETWIGH, JOHN BAPTIST, VAN (d. 1746)

Flemish Dominican regent of the Studium Generale in Antwerp, K. published in 1720 a controversial work on Our Lady, aimed at many opponents, with the work of Adam Widenfeld in mind, but opening to wider perspectives. The first words of a very lengthy title are "Panoplia Mariana." It is a work heavily packed with quotations from past writers, some of them of lessened repute, e.g. Pseudo-Albert—whom he understandably took for St. Albert the Great—and Bernardine of Busti (*qv*). K. defended certain phrases applied to Mary, "omnipotent Mother" and "Virgin of unlimited power," for this is an omnipotence which is not a divine attribute,but says that by her prayer and suppliant power, she can obtain all things from God. Cardinal Newman (*qv*) gave such an explanation to E. B. Pusey (*qv*). K. also defended the title Coredemptress: "The most blessed Virgin Mary is in an orthodox manner named Coredemptress or cooperatrix of the salvation of mankind, in so far as she brought forth the Redeemer, offered him hanging on the Cross to the Father for human Redemption, and obtained by her prayers and merits that the Passion of Christ the Redeemer be applied to men."[1] He is likewise explicit on Mary's universal mediation. God grants all good things through Mary's hands to honour her; no creature obtains grace from God, save through Mary's dispensation. The prayers of the saints obtain nothing of good for us unless Mary's suppliant power is added. Devotion to Mary is necessary—at least a certain pious sentiment—and her intercession is necessary to salvation, not absolutely, but from assumption of the divine decree by which God willed and decided that no grace comes from heaven to earth, save through Mary's hands. K. lauded consecration to Mary as her slave. We can, he thought, appeal from God's justice to Mary's mercy. Then he dealt with problems raised by the *Avis*—on the possibility of salvation for hardened sinners who practice some devotion to Mary, and on her power to save those already doomed. He did hedge his conclusion in each case with the necessary safeguards, appealing to the power of Mary to induce a change of heart in the sinner, and the dependence of her power in regard to the damned on God's "suspended divine sentence," (*divina sententia manente suspensa*). He saw the Hidden Life as honour to Mary, and said that the Holy Trinity honours, praises, and glorifies her; he inveighed against those who criticize excesses of Marian piety.

[1](Antwerp, 1720), sect. II, prop. 4, 101ff, and also Cl. Dillenschneider, *La Mariologie de S. Alphonse de Liguori*, I, (Fribourg, 1931), 146. Cf. also *ibid., op. cit.*, 145-150; H. Graef, *Mary*, II, 68-71.

KNOCK

On the evening of 21 August, 1879, several villagers of Knock, County Mayo, Ireland,

saw against the end wall of the church, in heavy rain, a heavenly tableau. On the right, was an altar surmounted by a lamb and cross, with a fluttering of angelic beings around it; on the left were three figures—Our Lady, wearing a crown, holding her hands high in a gesture of prayer, with St. Joseph on her right, and St. John the Evangelist on her left, next to the altar. He held an open book in his hand and seemed to speak. Fifteen of those present gave evidence to a diocesan commission set up soon after the alleged apparition; their statements concurred. In 1936, a second commission examined, on oath, three survivors, two living in Knock, one who testified for them before an ecclesiastical tribunal in New York. The testimony was the same.[1]

An immense movement of piety quickly arose about Knock. After some decades, a decline set in. It has been reversed by a new movement of devotion on a national scale. This was due to organized lay support, guided by the Archbishops Gilmartin, Walsh, and Cunnane, and notably through the Knock Shrine Society founded in 1935 by Mr. Justice W. D. Coyne and his wife. It was owing as well to the enlightened support of parish priests, especially Mgr. James Horan, at present in office, recalling the saintly priest of 1879, Archdeacon Cavanagh, by his devotion and phenomenal ability. He has cleared the approaches to the shrine, built hostels for the sick, and constructed a large church needed for the crowds which are drawn to Knock. Pope John Paul II came for the centenary year, addressed a huge crowd, the sick, and the voluntary helpers. He raised the new Church of Mary, Queen of Ireland, to the rank of a Basilica, and conferred the Golden Rose on the shrine. Theological analysis of the apparition has now a welcome stimulus.

[1]W. D. Coyne, *Cnoc Mhuire in Picture and Story*, 6th ed., (Dublin, 1957); *ibid., Venerable Archdeacon Cavanagh*, (Knock, 1953); T. Neary, *I Comforted Them in Sorrow*, (Knock, 1979); C. Rynne, *Knock, 1879-1979*, (Dublin, 1979); M. Walsh, *The Apparition at Knock*, (Tuam, 1955); *id., Knock, The Shrine of the Pilgrim People of God*, 2nd ed., (Tuam, 1973); *Knock Shrine Annual*, (1938).

KNOWLEDGE, OUR LADY'S

Pseudo-Albert (*qv*) gave consideration to Mary's knowledge over the whole range of things knowable in his age. What is here considered is the knowledge she possessed in relation to her role in salvation history, principally when and how she knew of her Son's divinity.[1] When Erasmus questioned her knowledge of this mystery at the moment of the Annunciation, Suarez replied that such a view went against the whole tradition of the Church. Traditional Catholic doctrine has distinguished three kinds of knowledge in the mind of Mary: *acquired*, that is, the body of ideas and facts which she took from her cultural environment, in the process of education and personal activity; *infused*, truths communicated directly by God to Mary in the order of her destiny, which brought her into a unique relationship with the divine; even, some have maintained, *beatific*, at least in certain moments of her earthly existence.

The recent approach to these problems and theories has been biblical, as a reaction against what some modern writers would think essentialist and conceptualist theorizing: essentialist, because removed from the life situation and problems Mary faced; conceptualist, because it would be an imposed idea to which the facts and texts are made to conform. Nonetheless, present-day exegetes, fully attentive to the demands of the text, and with proper methodology in expounding its meaning, conclude that the dialogue of the Annunciation (*qv*), which is crucially relevant, would have given Mary the idea that her Son was divine. "We do not claim, certainly, that each of the expressions we have studied, if taken in isolation, cannot bear another interpretation; but it seems to us that, having regard to the context which is particular and, if we consider it completely, absolutely unique, the whole passage could scarcely, in the eyes of the Virgin, take on a different meaning . . . . At any rate, supposing that God wished to reveal the mystery to her from this moment— and nothing else seems more suitable—it was without doubt not possible to choose less ambiguous terms."[2] R. Laurentin (*qv*) is not as emphatic, concluding that Mary's knowledge of the divinity of her Son is, "from the point of view of exegesis, the best probability."[3] If he does not find it a certainty, he does think that there can be fruitful encounter between exegesis and theology, the former showing how Mary could, in a concrete way, have grasped such a revelation. The implication, which is quite proper, is that the final solution does not rest with the exegete or biblical theolgian.

Those who reject the possibility of Mary's knowledge, at the time of the Annunciation, have suggested either the Resurrection or Pentecost as the suitable moments for such a revelation. But this is conjecture, for there is no text to inform us. By whom was she told? How did her informant acquire the knowledge?

There are ambiguous texts here and there in the great writings of the ages, but too many explicit assertions not to give substantial support to Suarez's rebuttal of Erasmus. St. Augustine's saying, about Mary conceiving Christ first in her mind and then in her body, is developed thus by St. Leo the Great (*qv*): "A royal virgin of the race of David is chosen who would become pregnant with a sacred offspring and would conceive her *divine and human* offspring in her mind before doing so in her body."[4] St. Bernard returned frequently to the idea that Mary was asked to become the Mother of God's Son. St. Thomas's dictum, that Mary, as representative of all men, contracted a spiritual marriage between mankind and the Son of God, presupposes that she knew who he was. The later doctors proceed from the truth itself as from a starting-point. The great nineteenth and twentieth century theologians do likewise.

The modern Popes did not have any need to speak on the precise problem, for it had not been raised. St. Pius X (*qv*), in *Ad diem illum* (*qv*), showed clearly what answer would have been forthcoming. "Who more than his Mother could have a far-reaching knowledge of the admirable mysteries of the birth and childhood of Christ, and, above all, of the mystery of the Incarnation, which is the beginning and foundation of faith?"[5] The notes to the first Marian *schema*, prepared for Vatican II, mentioned, among other errors needing correction, the opinion that Mary, "at the time of the Annuciation, was wholly ignorant of the fact that the Son, whom she would conceive, was God." The correction was made gently in the text by stating that God did not effect his redemptive plan until the free acceptance of the appointed Mother was forthcoming, "so that the Son of God, by the Incarnation, should also become her Son, the new Adam and the Saviour of the world." Annotation to this sentence states that, in Lk 1, "the divine motherhood is proposed to Mary (30-33), Mary sets forth her difficulties which the angel solves (34-37), and then finally Mary agrees (38)." Quotations given include that previously cited from St. Leo the Great.[6] The finally approved version of the second *schema* contains the words: "The Father of mercies willed that the consent of the predestined Mother should precede the Incarnation, so that as a woman contributed to death, so also a woman should contribute to life." (LG 56). The Council also said: "At the message of the angel, the Virgin Mary received the word of God in her heart and in her body, and gave life to the world" (LG 53); and, "For believing and obeying, Mary brought forth on earth the Father's Son." (LG 63). These texts do not say, in so many words, that Mary knew that her Son was God; they would be difficult to reconcile with the view that she did not know this.

The real source of confusion for modern writers, who speak of the impossibility of Mary living an ordinary human life with one she knew was God, is in their vagueness on the kind of knowledge she possessed. It was the knowledge of faith, of perfect faith, but not vision, **not continuous ecstasy. It was a kind of knowl**edge which became her Jewish character, her upbringing, and culture, her singular personality, her sex, her unique experience, intuitive, experiential, filling her whole existence, integral to her entire conduct.

[1]For recent views, cf. J. de Aldama, S.J., "Gozo de la vision beatífica la Santísima Virgen alguna vez en su vida mortal?" in *Archivo Teologico Granadiano*, 6(1943), 121-140; E. Sutcliffe, S.J., "Our Lady and the Divinity of Christ," in *The Month*, 180(1944), 347-350; *id.*, "Our Lady's Knowledge of the Divinity of Christ," in IER, 66(1945), 427-432; *id.*, "Again Our Lady's Knowledge of Christ's Divinity," in IER, 68(1946), 123-128; *id.*, "Scripture, Tradition and Mariology," in IER, 69(1947), 807-814; H. Pope, O.P., "Our Lady and the Divinity of Christ," in IER, 66(1945), 100-105; Fr. Peter, O.F.M.Cap., "When Did Our Lady Know She Was Mother of God?" in IER, 67(1946), 145-163; *id.*, "Mariology and Exegesis," in IER, 69(1947), 113-124; G. M. Roschini, O.S.M., *Mariologia*, 2nd ed., vol. 2, pt. 2, 184-194; A Martinelli, *De primo instanti conceptionis B. V. Mariae. Disquisitio de usu rationis*, (Rome, 1950); D. Unger, O.F.M.Cap., "When Did Mary First Know of Her Divine Maternity?" in AER, 114(1946), 360-366; *id.*, "Mary's Knowledge of Her Son's Divinity at the Annunciation," in *Univ. Dayton Rev.*, 5(1968), 33-48; *id.*, "Utrum secundum Doctores Ecclesiae Virgo Maria filium suum Dei Filium esse nuntio angelico cognoverit," in MSS, IV, 347-420; S. Lyonnet, S.J., "Le récit de l'Annonciation et la Maternité divine de la Sainte Vierge," in *L'Ami du Clergé*, 66(1956), 33-48; R. Laurentin, *Structure et Théologie de Luc I-II*, (Paris, 1957), 165-175; *id.*, *Jésus au Temple; Mystère de Pâques et foi de Marie en Luc 2:48-50*, (Paris, 1966); C. Kearns, O.P., in *Mother of the Redeemer*, ed. by K. MacNamara, (Dublin, 1959), 38ff. [2]S. Lyonnet, "Le récit de l'Annonciation . . . ," in *L'Ami du Clergé*, 66(1956), 46. [3]R. Laurentin, *Structure et Théologie de Luc I-II*, (Paris, 1957), 175. [4]*Serm. 21*, in PL 54, 191. [5]OL, 170. [6]First Marian *schema*, (Vatican Press, 1962).

KOEHLER, THEODORE, S.M. (1911-)

A diligent research-worker in the history of Marian theology, K. has contributed scores of scholarly articles to specialist reviews. He directed the activities associated with Dayton University Marian Library, and completed a five-volume *Storia della Mariologia*, from the New Testament to modern times.

KOESTER, HEINRICH MARIA, S.A.C. (1911-) — See Supplement, p. 384.

KOLBE, MAXIMILIAN, O.F.M., CONV. BLESSED
(1894-1941)

Founder of the Militia of the Immaculate One, K. was a missionary in Japan. He employed modern methods and means as an apostle of Our Lady. He died in Auschwitz, freely offering his life for another prisoner. His Marian doctrine is in letters, diaries, notes, and lectures, most of which are unpublished.[1] His association was founded and approved, like the Legion of Mary, in the years when Mercier (*qv*) was launching his movement for doctrinal and liturgical recognition of Mary's mediation (*qv*) for all graces (see DUFF, FRANK). "The activity of the Militia is based directly on this truth, that the Immaculate One is the Mediatress of all graces, because, if it were not thus, all our labour and all our strength would be in vain . . . The Most Blessed Virgin is the Mediatress of all graces, without exception . . . . The life of grace depends on the degree of nearness of the soul to the Immaculate One. The nearer the soul is to her, the purer it becomes, the livelier its faith becomes, the fairer its love; all the virtues, being the work of grace, are strengthened and vivified. We cannot look for grace elsewhere, because she is the Mediatress."[2]

K. wished to relate his Marian theses to the doctrine of the Holy Trinity, which preoccupied him greatly. "We say that the heavenly Father is the origin of everything, that everything originates from the Most Holy Trinity. We cannot see God. Jesus descended on earth to make him known to us. The Most Blessed Virgin is the one in whom we venerate the Holy Spirit, because she is his spouse . . . . The third person of the Trinity did not become incarnate. Nevertheless, the expression, 'Spouse of the Holy Spirit,' is much more profound than merely human usage. In a certain kind of way, we can say that the Immaculate one is the incarnation of the Holy

Spirit." K. frequently repeated the latter idea while stating clearly that Mary and the Spirit remain two natures and two persons. He even went so far as to say: "This perfect union of the Immaculate one with the Holy Spirit makes her, in a certain manner, the Holy Spirit himself."[3] There are points of resemblance here with the doctrine of Scheeben (*qv*) and Bulgakov (*qv*). K. also kept his ideas right with Christology. He spoke of the soul not going to Christ from Mary, but with Mary to Christ. Those who find his language excessive, especially on the Holy Spirit, should read St. Paul on the Christian's identity with Christ. His devotional advice matched his lofty ideal; he put special emphasis on consecration.

---

[1]Cf. S. Ragazzini, O.F.M.Conv., *Maria vita dell'anima—itinerario mariano alla SS. Trinità*, (Rome, 1960), 570-594; *ibid.*, "L'Immacolata e lo Spirito Santo, La spiritualità e l'apostolato mariano del Servo di Dio P. Massimiliano M. Kolbe dei frati Minori Conventuali," in EphMar, 10(1960), 223-255; L. di Fonzo, O.F.M.Cap., "Il 'Cavaliere dell'Immacolata' P. M. M. Kolbe," in *Miscell. Frances*, 60(1960), 3-46; A. di Monda, O.F.M.Cap., "Sviluppo e conclusione della tesi mariana scotistica nella dottrina e nella prassi del P. Massimiliano M. Kolbe . . .," in *Giovanni Duns Scoto nel VII centenario della nascita*, (Naples, 1967), 183-214; A. Blasucci, *L'Immacolata e la sua Milizia*, (Naples, 1965), 113-160; *ibid.*, "La consacrazione a Maria negli insegnamenti del P. Kolbe," in *Teologia e Pastorale etc.*, Collegamento Mariano Nazionale, Padua, 1969), 127-147. Cf. esp. E. Piacentini, O.F.M.Conv., *Dottrina mariologica del P. Massimiliano Kolbe*, (Rome, Herder, 1971), xxxiv; *ibid.*, "L'Immacolata nel pensiero di P. Kolbe," in MM, 33(1971), 129-191; *ibid.*, "Maternità divina e spirituale nel pensiero mariologico del P. Kolbe," in *Marian Library Studies*, 2(1970), 33-74; *ibid.*, "Valutazione teologica e ripercussioni ecumeniche nella mariologia del P. M. M. Kolbe," in EphMar, 21(1971), 217-256; H. Manteau-Bonamy, O.P., *La doctrine mariale du Père Kolbe*, (Paris, 1975); F. Villepelée, *Le Bienheureux Père Kolbe, L'Immaculée révèle le Saint Ésprit*, (Paris, 1974). [2]E. Piacentini, in EphMar, 21(1971), 218. [3]EphMar, 21(1971), 231-232.

L

LAURENTIN, RENÉ (1917-   )

Professor at the Catholic University of Angers, theological journalist, author of many works on Church life, on Vatican Council II, on the Episcopal Synod, crisis areas of evangelization, and the charismatic renewal, L. has done his most distinctive and enduring work in Marian theology. A pioneer of the method approved by Vatican II—immensely erudite, strictly scientific —he must be ranked among the very great Marian theologians of this century. He earned a double doctorate for his *Marie, l'Eglise et le Sacerdoce* (from the Sorbonne, for the historical part of the work in Volume I; from the Catholic Institute of Paris, for the theological part in Volume II). His *Court Traité*, which has attained five editions, remains a seminal work. His monograph, *Structure et Théologie de Luc I-II* (1957) made a deep impact; it was followed by *Jésus et le Temple. Mystère de Pâques et foi de Marie* (1966). *La question mariale* (Mary in the Church) was an attempt to assess critically but constructively the Marian movement, to which

L. had made so large a contribution at congresses, in published symposia, in reviews, and which he continues to make. His record and assessment of current Marian publications in various media are comprehensive and valuable; the substantial, two-yearly *Bulletin* in RSPT since 1962 is indispensable. Scholars await with interest his massive monograph on the history of the title "Mediatress."

LAWRENCE OF BRINDISI, O.F.M.CAP., ST., DOCTOR OF THE CHURCH
(1559-1619)

The Marian teaching of this remarkable post-Reformation figure, is homiletic in form, and substantial in content. He wrote eighty-four sermons. They are grouped as follows: 1) on the praise and invocation of the Virgin Mother of God (seven on the vision of St. John, sixteen on *Missus est*, ten on the angelic salutation, ten on the *Magnificat*, five on *Beatus venter*, six on *Fundamenta ejus*, and six on the *Salve Regina*); 2) on feasts of the Blessed Virgin Mary (eleven on the Immaculate Conception, six on the Purification, two on the Visitation, two on Our Lady of the Snows, and three on the Assumption). They are contained in the *Mariale*, volume I in his collected works, edited in the present century.[1]

Despite the religious circumstances of the time, L.'s sermons are largely free of polemics. He had a knowledge of the Fathers (*qv*), particularly St. Augustine, and he liked to quote St. Bernard (*qv*), and St. Thomas Aquinas (*qv*). He seems to have been influenced by St. Bernardine of Siena (*qv*) and perhaps Bernardine of Busti (*qv*), but was more restrained than either. Though committed to two basic theses of Duns Scotus, he never mentioned him.

His essential source, incessantly quoted, is Sacred Scripture. L. was accepted by Jews as a master in Hebrew, and he knew the Latin Vulgate by heart. Much of his interpretation, especially of the Old Testament, was in the accommodated sense. He abounds in types and figures, as he multiplied titles (*qv*) of Mary by the score.

L. saw the need for a "principle or axiom" in science of Mary (see *Fundamental Principle of Mariology*), and formulated it thus: " . . . the first principle of the nobility and dignity of Mary, that she is truly *Theotokos*, the natural, true and own Mother of the living and true God, the only-begotten Son of the Most-High."[2] L. stated boldly the Scotist doctrine of the absolute, universal primacy of Christ: "Christ is then the foundation of every creature, of every grace and every glory, since he is the end of all things, that for which all things have been created." The idea was extended with due proportion to his Marian doctrine, for "Mary was like Christ in predestination, birth, life, death, resurrection, assumption, glorification."[3] "Like" did not mean "equal" for the author, as he explicitly affirmed elsewhere. But he was convinced of Mary's mysterious greatness: "What tongue, even of an angel, could tell how great were the divine benefits, favours, honours, dignities, privileges, prerogatives, the divine excellences of Mary since she has become the daughter of God the Father, the true Mother of God the Son, the spouse and unique comfort of the Holy Spirit, the Queen of heaven, the mistress of angels, the empress of the universe?"[4]

L. defended the Scotist doctrine of the Immaculate Conception also, arguing from suitability and from Old Testament types—Eve to begin with—and especially from Mary's fullness of grace (Lk 1:28), and from Church practice, shown in the Liturgy. The traditional contrast between Eve (*qv*) and Mary did not escape him. "Because Eve believed in the devil, the world perished; because Mary put her faith in the angel, the world was saved."[5] Yet, more than any other idea about Mary, that of "spouse" dominated his thinking of her as a person. The sixteen sermons on *Missus est* deal with this theme from every conceivable angle. The language is at times very human, with biblical reminiscence of Eve, Rachel, Bathsheeba, and Esther. The last-named is mentioned by L. again and again in his sermons. Mary is spoken of as spouse of God, occasionally of the Holy Spirit; she is the associate of God, particularly of Christ in his Passion and glory.

Mary entered into the heart of the redemptive mystery. "Was not Mary, for our sake, in danger of death when she stood by the Cross of Christ, totally possessed by the true spirit of Abraham, truly sacrificing him to God, offering him with true charity for the salvation of the world . . . . The spirit of Mary was a spiritual priest, as the Cross was the altar, Christ the sacrifice; though the spirit of Christ was the principal priest, the spirit of Mary was one with the spirit of Christ, as it were one soul in two bodies. Wherefore the spirit of Mary with the spirit of Christ exercised a priestly office by the altar of the Cross, offered the sacrifice of Christ to the eternal God for the salvation of the world."[6] The passage occurs in support of L.'s statement that Mary "cherishes us with maternal charity, intimate, true, heartfelt love." L. thought that Mary's spiritual motherhood had been due to Christ's word from the Cross, *Behold your mother*.

L. developed the doctrine of the Assumption, calling on the traditional typology of the Ark (*qv*), which he cherished, going on to proclaim Mary "above the choirs and seats of the angels, crowned Empress of the world, Mistress of angels and Queen of all saints."[7] In this context, he dealt with the mediation of Mary: "She is the neck [of the Mystical Body], which, situated above all the other members, is immediately joined with the Head; thus Mary is, to Christ, above all saints. By the neck, the head bows, through Mary, we attain mercy; through the neck, the influence of the head descends to the body, and from the body, vapours mount to the head; thus through Mary, the prayers of the Church mount to God and graces from God descend on the Church."[8]

But always L. remained Christocentric. Mary is "our most sweet Mother and, on our behalf, Mediatress and Advocate with Christ her Son, never powerless in her intercession."[9] Likewise, in regard to the Immaculate Conception, he interpreted Church teaching to show that Mary "has been so redeemed by a most perfect manner of redemption, and has been so because, without the preservation which the grace and merit of Christ obtained for her, she would, without any doubt, have incurred the original stain."[10]

[1]*Mariale*, (Padua, 1928); 2nd ed., (1964), is used here. For bibliography, cf. Felix a Mareto, O.F.M.Cap., *Bibliographia Laurentiana*, (Rome, 1962), 185-194, nn. 1058-1142. Cf. Jerome de Paris, O.F.M.Cap., *La Doctrine mariale de S. Laurent de Brindes*, (Rome, Paris, 1933); B. a S. Joanne Rotundo, O.F.M.Cap., S. Laurentinus a Brundusio et Immaculata Conceptio, (Isola del Liri, 1940); G. M. Roschini, O.S.M., *La mariologia di S. Lorenzo da Brindisi*, (Padua, 1951); Dominic of Herdon Unger, O.F.M.Cap., "The Absolute Primacy of Jesus and His Virgin Mother According to St. Lawrence of Brindisi," in *Collect. Francisc.*, 22(1952), 113-149; *ibid.*, "The Heavenly Queenship of God's Virgin Mother According to St. Lawrence," in *Collect. Francisc.*, 24(1954), 303-328; *ibid.*, "St. Lawrence and the Primary Principle of Mariology," in *Collect. Francisc.*, 31(1961), 5-25; Adrien de Krizovljan, O.F.M.Cap., "Marie et l'Église dans S. Laurent etc.," in *Et. Franc.*, 10(1960), 1-35; Didier de Cre, O.F.M.Cap., *L'Épouse du Saint-Esprit, un peu de théologie avec S. Laurent de Brindes etc.* [2]*Mariale*, 2nd ed., (Padua, 1964), 479. [3]*op. cit.*, 454. [4]*op. cit.*, 297. [5]*op. cit.*, 84, esp. 119, 131, 416 passim. [6]*op. cit.*, 183. [7]*op. cit.*, 576. [8]*op. cit.*, 578. [9]*op. cit.*, 254. [10]*op. cit.*, 498.

LEBON, JOSEPH-MARTIN (1879-1957) —

See Supplement, p. 384.

LEO THE GREAT, ST., DOCTOR OF THE CHURCH
(POPE, 440-461)

Known to history for his achievements in papal government, Pope Leo I intervened in one of the major Christological debates of the early centuries, the heresy of Eutyches (d.454), which was condemned by the Council of Chalcedon in 451. The Pope's dogmatic letter to Flavian, Patriarch of Constantinople (June 13, 449), known as the *Tome of Leo*, was read at the Council, and the truth he stated became official church teaching. Eutyches, in his reaction against Nestorius, had gone so far as to deny the existence of a human nature in Christ, an error which struck at the very meaning of the Incarnation and the validity of the Redemption.

L.'s thought on Our Lady is also found in other letters and in some of his sermons,[1] preached for the feast of Christmas.

L. did not develop certain intuitions of the Latin Fathers who had preceded him. His thinking was principally in the Christological context, but there are valuable suggestions on other aspects of Marian theology in his work. Mary's real motherhood was affirmed. "In the whole and perfect nature of true man, true God was born, complete in his own, complete in ours."[2] Eutyches had argued that if Christ had a true human nature, he would have inherited original sin. L. held the view, which stemmed from St. Augustine, that human intercourse was sinful, transmitting sin. Mary's virginity, he thought, preserved Jesus from contact with sin. "Sin could have no origin where the transmission of paternal seed had not reached."[3] "He was conceived by the Holy Spirit within the womb of the Virgin Mother who brought him forth with her virginity intact, as she had conceived him preserving it."[4] "He was generated in a new nativity, because inviolate virginity, [that] did not know concupiscence, furnished the material of his body. From the Mother of the Lord, nature, not guilt, was assumed; and in the Lord Jesus Christ, born from the womb of the Virgin, because his birth was miraculous, nature was not for that reason different from ours."[5]

L. applied Old Testament prophecies to Mary. He gave a Christological-Marian sense to Gen 3:15 (see WOMAN IN),[6] invoked, as did practically all the Fathers, Is 7:14 (see EMMANUEL) and, with many, he invoked Is 11:1 on the "rod of Jesse." L. adapted Ps 134:12 to the birth of Christ, Is 45:8 to Mary, and Prov 9:1 to the Incarnation.

Like St. Augustine (qv), L. taught that Mary "conceived her divine and human offspring first in her mind and then in her body."[7] He appears to have given a saving role to the Incarnation which would enhance, in his view, the importance of Mary's participation therein.[8] He says for instance: "Truth only saves us in our flesh . . . and thus the Virgin Mary conceived the Word that she should provide, of her substance, flesh to be united with him . . . ."[9] Elsewhere he says that "there is no hope of salvation for the human race unless the Virgin's Son was he who was his Mother's creator."[10]

In one of the sermons, there is an arresting thought on Mary and the Holy Spirit: "Each one in regeneration follows his [Christ's] spiritual origin and, to every man who is reborn, the baptismal font is like the Virgin's womb, with the same Holy Spirit filling the font as filled the Virgin, so that here the mystical washing should take away the sin which the sacred conception then rendered void."[11] Again L. suggested that Mary is the link between us and Christ in his mystical body: "The generation of Christ is the origin of the Christian people, and the birthday of the Head is also the birthday of the body."[12] L. summarized his doctrine with Latin sobriety in his *Communicantes* to the Canon of the Mass. "Communicating with and honouring in the first place the glorious ever Virgin Mary, Mother of God and of Our Lord Jesus Christ...."

---

[1]Sermons and Letters, in PL 54; C. Silva-Tarouca, S.J., *S. Leonis Tomus ad Flavianum ep. constantinopolitanum, Textus et Documenta*, series theologica, (Rome, 1932). Cf. A. Spindeler, "S. Leo Magnus de parte B. Virginis Mariae in Redemptione," in ME, IV, 141-152; K. Balic, O.F.M., "La dottrina mariana di S. Leone inserita nel Canone della Messa," in *L'Osserv. Rom.*, (12 April, 1962); F. Spedalieri, "La madre del Salvatore nella Soteriologia di S. Leone M.," in MM, 25(1963), 23-38; B. Studer, "Consubstantialis Patri. Consubstantialis Matri. Une antithese cristologique chez Léon le Grand," in REA, 18(1972), 87-115; G. M. Polo, O.S.M., *Maria nel mistero della salvezza secondo il papa Leone Magno*, (Vicenza, 1977). [2]*Tome of Leo*, DS, 293. [3]*Serm. 22, 3*, in PL 54, 196C. [4]*Tome of Leo, 2*, in PL 54, 760A. [5]*Tome of Leo, 4*, in PL 54, 768A. [6]*Serm. 22, 1*, in PL 54, 194A. [7]*Serm. 21, 1*, in PL 54, 191. [8]Cf. A. Spindeler, "S. Leo Magnus de parte B. Virginis Mariae in Redemptione," in ME, IV, 149ff. [9]*Ep. 124, 9*, in PL 54, 1068. [10]*Serm. 28, 5*, in PL 54, 224C. Cf. *Serm. 24, 1-3*, in PL 54, 204-206. [11]*Serm. 24, 3*, in PL 54, 206A. [12]*Serm. 26, 6*, in PL 54, 213B.

LEO VI, "THE WISE" (d. 912)

An emperor theologian, not uncommon in Byzantine history, L. gave attention to Marian themes in three homilies on the Nativity of Christ,[1] and in certain other works, expressly in four homilies on Marian feasts (the Nativity, the Presentation, the Annunciation, and the Dormition).[2] The author ranges over many questions in this corpus, mostly those familiar to the Byzantine tradition.

Mary, he thought, was born of sterile parents. His language excludes not only sin but its possibility in her case. The earth, which hitherto had brought forth thorns because of the curse, now "offers with thanksgiving to him who had rendered it fertile, as first-fruits of great price, a fruit which has not the customary bitterness, but the sweetness of blessing. This fruit is Mary; she has been chosen as the resplendent bride of the Only-begotten." Mary is the "root planted by God."

Our Lady's role was of universal moment. Because of her blessed state, she could leave us an inheritance of blessing, changing our sad lot. "God, reconciled to us through her, dispels, in the incomparable bond of fatherly love, the hostility which, as his enemies, we had wrought." A daughter of Eve (*qv*) repairs the ruin she caused, and sadness turns to joy.

Because of this very role as "the cause of our restoration," L. thought that Mary must have died, lest she appear altogether exceptional, her origin enigmatic. He then set forth the theory of the double Assumption (*qv*): "Christ's hands, which contain all things, receive your stainless soul; whereas, your pure and immaculate body is transported to the purest place. Because you have given birth to God clothed in flesh, you are now borne in the hands of God, deprived of your flesh."[3] L. still thought that Mary was received in heaven with exceptional honour.

Such a view does not mean a lessening of the mediatorial and intercessory power attributed to Mary. The ancient Jews had the Ark, her type as their help. But it could be captured, whereas she is safe.[4] Transferred to (the abode of) her Son, and united to him in an ineffable partnership, she does not cease to give help to those on earth. All things are bestowed by God through her. "There is no good fortune which does not happen when she wants it, no harm that is not averted when she resists it."[5] L.'s own prayer, offering his own written work to Mary, whose help encouraged him to undertake it, whom he asks to continue this help in advancing years, illustrated his belief and trust in this mediation.[6]

---

[1]PG 107, 27-60. [2]PG 107, 1-12, 12-21, 21-28, 157-172. Cf. *In deposit, corporis Christi*, in PG 107, 81D-84C, on the sorrows of Mary; *Preces Liturgicae*, in PG 107, 299A-314D, passim. *Canticum Compunctionis*, in PG 107, 309-314; *Espistola ad Omarum*, in PG 107, 315-324. Cf. M. Jugie, A.A., *L'Immaculée Conception*, 180-181; id., *L'Assomption*, 265-268. [3]PG 107, 164D. Cf. M. Jugie, A.A., *L'Assomption*, 268. [4]PG 107, 168C. [5]PG 107, 169C. [6]PG 107, 41A.

LEO XIII (POPE, 1878-1903)

In 1898, L. summed up the intention of his Marian teaching: "We have long desired to promote the welfare of the human race through an increase of devotion to the Blessed Virgin . . . and we have never ceased to encourage the constant use of the Rosary (qv) among Christians, by publishing every year, since 1 September, 1883, an Encyclical Letter on this subject, besides frequently issuing decrees, as is well known."[1] L. developed more fully than his predecessors the doctrine of Mary's mediation (qv), with corresponding emphasis on her intercession (qv). In his greatest Encyclical, *Adjutricem populi*, he related Marian intercession to the cause of Christian unity, especially with the eastern Christians, whose early contribution to Marian theology and devotion is acknowledged.

---

[1] *Diuturni temporis*, in OL, 155-156.

LIBERMANN, FRANCIS MARY PAUL, VENERABLE

(1802-1852)

A Jew, destined to follow his father as Rabbi, L. was baptized a Catholic in his twenty-fifth year. He was attracted to Mary from the moment of baptism: "When the water of Baptism flowed on my Jewish head, in that moment I loved Mary whom previously I had detested."[1] Despite a health handicap and many difficulties, he founded the Society of the Holy Heart of Mary for missionary work, among the Black Race especially. He later united it with the older Congregation of the Holy Ghost. His rule was written, on his avowal, after direct intervention of the Heart of Mary. This became his devotion: "What distinguishes us from all other workers in the Lord's vineyard is a quite special consecration which we make of all our society, of each of its members, of all their works and enterprises to the most holy Heart of Mary, a heart eminently apostolic and all inflamed with desires for the glory of God and the salvation of souls." In his Spiritual Writings, in the Rule, in his Commentary on St. John, and in his voluminous spiritual correspondence, L. set forth a very rich Marian spirituality, which had its origin in his distinctive mystical experience, and had been influenced by the traditions of M. J. J. Olier (qv) at St. Sulpice and St. John Eudes (qv) at Rennes. He was conscious of Mary's constant influence in his life, which was immensely fruitful in the Church.

L.'s work had brought him into close contact with Abbé Desgenettes and Notre Dame des Victoires. When he was at the head of the Holy Ghost Congregation, he enlarged the consecration of the members to the "Holy Spirit, author and perfector of all holiness and inspirer of the apostolic spirit."

The Immaculate Heart was filled "by the divine Spirit with the plenitude of holiness and the apostolate . . . the perfect model of fidelity to all the holy inspirations of the divine Spirit and of the interior practice of the virtues of the religious and apostolic life." Mary was by Jesus so filled with grace "that she had wherewith to give not only to the whole world but to more than a thousand worlds." L. thought that St. Bernard's dictum about all good things given through Mary was more evident in his time than in the saint's. He analyzed perceptively the marriage scene of Cana, showing how it exemplifies Mary's role: "That wedding feast represents the Church in which souls are espoused to the Holy Spirit. It is Mary whose prayer wins strength, joy and consolation for those admitted to that holy banquet. In addition, she provides joy for the divine bridegroom by inspiring our wills with love for him." Mary was proposed as a model for souls in many different callings, particularly for priests. Her power was, in L.'s view, limitless, her maternal care constant, sensitive, and encouraging.

---

[1] *Commentaire de l'Evangile selon S. Jean*, (Paris, Possielgue, 1874); *Lettres spirituelles*, 4 vols., (Paris, 30 Rue Lhomond, 1874); *Écrits Spirituels*, (Paris, Rue Lhomond, 1891); *Notes et Documents relatifs à la Vie et à l'Oeuvre du Vénérable F. M. P. Libermann*, 13 vols., ed. by A. Cabon, C.S.Sp., (Paris, Rue Lhomond, 1929-1941), vol. 13, 1-15. bibliography. Cf. H. Barré, C.S.Sp., "Spiritualité Mariale du Ven. Père Libermann," in *Maria*, III, 381-401; B. Kelly, C.S.Sp., ch. 11, "Devotion to Our Lady," in *The Spiritual Teaching of Ven. Francis Libermann*, (Dublin, 1953), 164-180; P. Blanchard, ch. 10, "L'Expérience mariale," in *Le Vénérable Libermann*, Études Carmélitaines, I, (Paris, 1958), 527-562.

LITTLE OFFICE OF THE BLESSED VIRGIN MARY

This is an abbreviated form of the common office of the Blessed Virgin, which may have arisen parallel with the Votive Masses of Our Lady for Saturday, composed by Alcuin. It was certainly found in the tenth century, recited daily by Bernerius, Provost of Verdun, and Bishop Ulrich of Augsburg (d. 973). St. Peter Damian (qv) reorganized it, and urged its adoption. The contents developed slowly during the eleventh and twelfth centuries to a complete office of all the Hours.[1] The *Ave Maria* (see HAIL MARY), as it then existed, figured prominently, as Antiphon for the *Magnificat*, responsory after the Readings and Invitatorium for Matins. The Little Office became part of the Book of Hours. St. Pius V limited the recitation to certain monastic groups; the Carthusians still add it to their ordinary office. In 1952, it was revised with psalms, canticles, hymns, responsories, little "chapters," antiphons, and collects for the six periods of the year. There were twenty-eight feasts of Our Lady, with proper antiphons for the *Benedictus* and *Magnificat*, or both. According to Vatican II, *Constitution on the Liturgy*, Article 98, the Little Office is now part of the public prayer of the Church; it is mostly recited by non-clerical religious institutes.

---

[1]For Bishop Ulrich, cf. PL 135, 1016D, and cf. his Life by Gerard, Provost of Augsburg Cathedral. Cf. St. Peter Damian, *Opusculum de Horis Canonicis*, in PL 145, 230B. Cf. J. Leclercq, O.S.B., "Formes anciennes de l'office marial," in EphLit, 72(1958), 294-301; EphLit, 74(1960), 89-102; B. Capelle, O.S.B., in *Maria*, I, 234-235; J. M. Canal, C.M.F., "El officio parvo de la Vergen de 1000-1250," in EphMar, 15(1965), 463-475.

LITURGY

Origin and early growth: From the outset, Mary's important place in the Church's living tradition is seen in the primary Christian documents. Reflection on the Christian mystery was closely linked with worship, as homiletics through the centuries clearly shows. In the early age, before liturgical forms were developed and organized, it is not so much separate feasts of Mary which we meet, but an emphasis on her person, appropriate to the moment, a kind of celebration of her essential role vis-a-vis the Saviour. The mystery, which evidently manifested this role, was the birth of Jesus, and it has been well said that, for the Church, Christmas was the first feast of Our Lady.[1]

Papers read at the International Mariological Congress in Lisbon in 1967 tended to show that this liturgical advertence to Our Lady may have been much earlier than had been thought previously. Archaeological research in Nazareth (see ARCHAEOLOGY) has uncovered the remains of a third century Jewish-Christian church, synagogue style, with inscriptions which suggest that it was sacred to Our Lady. One inscription points to a person whose name began with M; another, left by a pilgrim, has the full name *Maria*, with an abbreviation of Luke's *Chaire* (1:28), *Xe*, before it. The grottos beneath this church may have been used for worship directed to Christ Jesus and then probably to his Mother also.[2]

Research into the early Egyptian Liturgy has been summarized thus: "According to available documents, the divine motherhood is being thought of in the second century; in the third, it is invoked liturgically with the *Sub tuum praesidium*; and certainly by the fourth century it is honoured, in the Lord's Nativity, as the subject of a feast."[3] There is still scope for investigation on the precise chronology of this development.

Of special moment was the mention of Mary in the *Communicantes* of the Mass, a perpetual reminder of her closeness to the mystery. As to when it appeared in the Roman Canon, opinions vary—possibly before St. Leo the Great (*qv*), not as late as Gelasius I (492-496) as L. V. Kennedy, C.S.B. maintained.[4] At the Lisbon Congress, Dom G. Frénaud, a true bridge-builder between Marian and liturgical theology, showed that, in the East, it is found in the *Syrian Anaphora of the Apostles* at the beginning of the fourth century, and in the *Anaphora of St. Basil*, some fifty years later.[5]

As to the emergence of feasts of Our Lady in the organized worship of the Church when freed from persecution, the results of research to date may be briefly presented thus. Celebrations took place within the Christmas cycle in the East: a) on a day before that feast, probably Sunday, with the gospel of the Annunciation (Lk 1:26-38), in Cappadocia in the fourth century and in Constantinople before 431; b) on a day in January, between 411 and 548, in Antioch, and in Egypt where the date was the sixteenth, brought forward from the earlier feast. In the West, celebrations took place: a) in Rome, first on the Christmas octave, 1 January, between 550 and 595—then on Wednesday and Friday of what would be Advent Quarter Tense in the seventh century, the earlier feast fading and its readings adopted in the new; b) in northern Italy, on the last Sunday in Advent from mid-fifth century; c) in Gaul, on 18 January in the sixth century; d) in Spain, on 18 December, the octave before Christmas (in 656). Next comes the decisive step by which four feasts, in different ways, involving the person of Mary, were adopted in Rome: the *Hypapante*, or meeting of the Infant Jesus and Simeon, the Presentation of the Lord, later the Purification of the Blessed Virgin Mary which was celebrated in Jerusalem from the end of the fourth century (14 or 2 February, calculated from Christmas on 6 January or 25 December), and in Rome, between 640 and 649; the *Dormition*, known in Jerusalem from about 430 and accepted in Rome about 650, in its origins of a complex if not mysterious import;[6] the *Annunciation*, difficult to date in the East since the gospel had been used for the pre-Christmas commemoration, which was taken up in Rome in the mid-seventh century; the *Nativity of Mary*, one of the feasts taken from the *Apocrypha* (the *Protevangelium*), on 8 September, certainly existing in the East from mid-sixth century, and in Rome, from shortly before the end of the seventh century.

An entry in the *Liber Pontificalis*, I (376), stating that Pope Sergius, a Syrian (687-701), had prescribed a procession for these feasts, was taken to mean that he personally introduced them. The text merely means that he extended the privilege of a procession, already enjoyed by the *Hypapante*, to the other three feasts. Two other feasts were inspired by the *Protevangelium*: the *Conception*, on 9 December, which arose in the seventh century; and the *Presentation of Mary*, known certainly to exist about 700, but originating probably as early as 543. By the middle of the sixth century, Constantinople had another feast of great popular interest, but of local reference, the *Deposition of the Mantle of the Mother of God at Blachernae*.[7] The close links between Church and State in Byzantium affected Marian doctrine and devotion, as entries in the Code of Justinian and homilies by later emperors manifest. In 561, Justinian intervened by a letter to the church in Jerusalem on the celebration of the Annunciation and Christmas. The emperor Maurice, in 600, published an edict on the feast of the Assumption, which had evolved through the analogy with the *dies natalis* of the martyrs, the influence of the Apocrypha (*qv*), and other factors still more ancient, possibly even a tradition deriving from the Virgin's tomb at Gethsemane, with the typology of the Ark as a medium for transmission. The imperial order extended the celebration on 15 August to all the emperor's dominions.[8]

With time, regional or ritual ideas and preferences dictated the emphasis, or lack of it, on the feasts as transmitted by the first centuries; or again added others, for particular reasons, to the universal list. Witness the feast of *Mary Pokrov*, or Protectress, in Slavic lands, or the Ethiopian celebration of *Kidana Mehrat*, the Pact of Mercy.[9] The meaning of a feast would depend on the degree of theological development —hence, the different ways in which the feast of the Conception was seen in the East and West, and the varying vicissitudes of the feast in the West.

Councils in the Germanic lands prescribed, in 800, the celebration of four feasts of Our Lady: the *Purification*, as it was now called; the *Annunciation* (sometimes called the Conception of Jesus); the *Assumption*, the name which had supplanted all others; and the *Nativity*. Sermons on these four feasts become more numerous with time.

What of the *Conception of Mary* and the *Presentation*? The history of the first has been the object of much critical research. There are two Winchester entries about 1060: "The Conception of Mary, the holy Mother of God" (8 December); and "The offering of holy Mary in the Temple of the Lord when she was three years old" (21 November). The second feast disappeared at the time of the Norman conquest, but returned in the fourteenth century. The feast of the Conception had a somewhat similar fate. Suppressed by the Normans, it reappeared in England between 1120-1130, and spread to general use on the continent quickly thereafter.[10] The claim, based on entries in the Martyrology of the Irish eighth-century abbey of Tallaght, has been unfavourably considered; not so the entry in a ninth-century Neapolitan calendar. Still more firm is the evidence, from eighth and ninth-century Benedictine records, which was presented to the Zagreb Congress by Dom Bernard Billet.[11]

From medieval times to Vatican II, the number of Latin feasts of Our Lady increased. The origin varied in each case according to particular need or spiritual insight; papal approval was the decisive factor. The *Visitation*, unknown to the Easterns, and a problem with Martin Luther (*qv*), was heard of at a Franciscan General Chapter in 1263, and was successfully proposed to the Synod of Prague in 1386 by the

Pole, John Jenstejn, as an intercession for Church unity. Urban VI approved it, and Boniface IX, in 1389, extended it to the universal Church. The prevailing schism was an obstacle to his decree, which, renewed by the Council of Basle in 1441, was given effect by St. Pius V.[12]

Two feasts of the Sorrows, or *Dolours of Our Lady*, eventually figured in the Latin calendar: on the Friday after Palm Sunday; and on 15 September. The first took its origin in the medieval sentiment towards the compassionate Mother of the Saviour (see COMPASSION). Established by a provincial synod of Cologne in 1423, it became widely popular, with different titles, and was approved for Rome by Sixtus IV in 1482. It was granted to the Servites in 1714 and, through their influence, was extended to the Latin Church in 1727 by Benedict XIII. The Servites played an important part also in gaining support for the second feast. They received permission, in 1668, to celebrate it in their communities. Pius VII, in 1814, extended it to the universal church. St. Pius X (*qv*) raised its status in the calendar in 1908, and, in 1913, fixed it on 15 September. It had hitherto been celebrated on the third Sunday in the month.[13]

The feast of *Our Lady of Mount Carmel* (16 July) was at first a celebration within the Carmelite Order, whose members obtained permission for it in 1587 from Sixtus V. It was extended to the universal Church in 1726. *Our Lady of the Snows* (5 August) sprang from the belief that the site of St. Mary Major's church in Rome was miraculously indicated by a snowfall in the midst of summer. The feast was granted to other Roman sanctuaries in the fourteenth century, and to the universal Church by St. Pius V. The feast of the *Holy Name of Mary* was suppressed by the same Pope. It had been granted to a Spanish diocese by Julius II in 1513. It was restored by Sixtus V; was due for suppression by Benedict XIV; and was given to the whole Church by Innocent XI, when Vienna was delivered from the Turks on the feastday (12 September, 1683) by John Sobieski. Another crusader, Don John of Austria, by his victory at Lepanto on the feast of the *Rosary* (7 October, 1571), enhanced the importance of this celebration, which St. Pius V had made a day of intercession. Hitherto a confraternity festival, it became universal by decree of Clement XI in 1716. The feast of *Our Lady of Mercy* (24 September) recalls a different kind of rescue, the redemption of those enslaved by the Moors. The order founded to this end, the Mercedarians, for a long while held the feast on 8 September. Altered in the calendar in the seventeenth century, it was granted to the universal Church in 1896.

Five feasts of Our Lady were instituted, or given importance, in the present century: a) *Our Lady of Lourdes* (11 February), approved for the diocese of Tarbes in 1890, was made universal by St. Pius X (1907); b) *Mary Mediatress of All Graces*, granted in reply to Cardinal Mercier's request in 1921, was approved for dioceses or religious institutes who sought the permission from Rome; c) the *Divine Motherhood of Mary*, was conceded to the king of Portugal by Benedict XIV (*qv*) in 1751 (the Mass and Office are the Pope's own composition). It was, on the fifteenth centenary of the Council of Ephesus in 1931, extended to the whole Church by Pius XI (*qv*), but very slight alterations were made in the texts of Benedict XIV; d) *The Immaculate Heart of Mary* (22 August), was instituted by Pius XII (*qv*) in 1944, two years after he had consecrated the world to Our Lady under this title. It was certainly not the first feast of the kind, for three centuries previously, the first Mass had been said in honour of the Heart of Mary at Autun, as the same Pope was to emphasize in a commemorative message, and there were similar feasts in many calendars; e) *Mary Queen* was established by the same Pope after he had proclaimed the queenship of Our Lady in 1954—about the same time he introduced the feast of *St. Joseph the Workman*.

Pre-Vatican II Roman Missals, besides the Saturday Masses of Our Lady, included Masses for certain places, and for feasts approved for certain countries, dioceses or institutes. Twenty of these were feasts of Our Lady, some of them very popular, such as *Our Lady, Help of Christians, Our Lady of Good Counsel, Our Lady of Perpetual Succour*, and *Our Lady of the Miraculous Medal*. There were other Masses, locally approved, which did not figure in the Roman Missal. Finally, the Liturgy included commemorations of saints noted for their Marian doctrine or piety, aspects of their holiness which would be mentioned in the prayers.

Vatican II: The pontificate of Pius XII, which immediately preceded the Council, saw two movements, Marian and liturgical, which did not have many points of contact. Two Benedictine scholars, B. Capelle and G. Frénaud, were bridge-builders between the two movements; it would have served to have had more. But the Council was itself to remove any ideas of opposition between Liturgy and cult of Mary. Theologians and preachers are thus assigned their task in regard to Our Lady: "Pursuing the study of Sacred Scripture, of the holy Fathers and Doctors and of the liturgies of the Church, under the guidance of the Teaching Authority, let them set forth the gifts and privileges of the Blessed Virgin, which always refer to Christ, the origin of all truth, holiness, and devotion." (LG 67).

The importance here, attached to the Liturgy, is reflected in practical terms in the Council's teaching. The first article of the Marian chapter of *Lumen Gentium* quotes from the *Communicantes* of the Roman Missal. The meaning of the mention of Mary in the Canon is thus elsewhere explained: "Celebrating the Eucharistic sacrifice, therefore, we are most closely united to the worshipping Church in heaven as we join with and venerate the memory, first of all of the glorious and ever-Virgin Mary, of Blessed Joseph and the blessed apostles and martyrs, and all the saints." (LG 50). This idea has to be taken with Council doctrine that, "in the earthly liturgy, by way of foretaste, we share in that heavenly liturgy which is celebrated in the holy city of Jerusalem toward which we journey as pilgrims" (*Constitution on the Liturgy*, 8).

The essential link between doctrine and liturgy was admirably stated in the same Constitution: "In celebrating the annual cycle of Christ's mysteries, holy Church honours with special love the Blessed Mary, Mother of God, who is joined by an inseparable bond to the saving work of her Son. In her, the Church holds up and admires the most excellent fruit of the Redemption, and joyfully contemplates, as in a faultless model, that which she herself wholly desires and hopes to be." (Article 103). The directive given in *Lumen Gentium* complements this: "At the same time, it [this holy Synod] admonishes all the sons of the Church, that the cult, especially the liturgical cult, of the Blessed Virgin be generously fostered." (LG 67).

The Council decreed that liturgical reform should be undertaken, within limits clearly fixed. The *Consilium*, set up by Pope Paul, to accomplish this task, had, with the publication of the Roman Missal in 1970, achieved that part of its work which is here relevant. The reform of the Calendar was intended to bring into relief the entire cycle of the mysteries of salvation, without interference with the sequence of seasons by feasts of the saints, primacy being given to feasts which recall the essential mysteries of salvation. Sunday was to be kept free of other celebrations, "unless they be truly of the greatest importance," for it is "the foundation and kernel of the whole liturgical year." (*Constitution on the Liturgy*, 106).

The *Consilium* reduced the total number of feasts which had already been reduced in the 1960 pre-conciliar calendar. In the new list, fourteen feasts are of Our Lord, but five of these (the *Annunciation*, the *Nativity*, the *Epiphany*, the *Holy Family*, and the *Presentation*) involve Mary. Of her feasts, thirteen still remain. The *Holy Name* and one of the *Dolours* have been suppressed. Three are solemnities: *The Mother of God* (now January 1, that of 11 October lapsing); the *Immaculate Conception*; and the *Assumption*. Two, the *Nativity* and *Visitation*, have festive rank. Three are ordinary *memoriae*: the *Presentation*; *Our Lady Queen*; and *Our Lady of the Rosary*. The first was retained, quite properly, out of respect for the Easterns who keep it (along with the *Annunciation of the Blessed Virgin Mary* and the *Dormition*) among the twelve great feasts, with a wealth of ancient homiletics. The remaining four are optional: *Our Lady of Mount Carmel*; *Our Lady of Lourdes*; the *Immaculate Heart of Mary* (now movable, on the Saturday following the feast of the Sacred Heart); and *Our Lady of the Snows* (Dedication of the Basilica of holy Mary). The Saturday Mass of Our Lady still remains and, as Paul VI pointed out in *Marialis Cultus*, is now more frequently available. The Pope also reminded us that local calendars may add to the list of the Roman Missal; this no longer has Masses for local celebration. The Mass for *Mary, Mediatress of all Graces* has been thus eliminated.

Pope Paul, in the *Apostolic Exhortation*, in what is a subtle *apologia* for the Marian content of the new Liturgy, drew attention to the predominantly Marian aspect of the readings in the octave before Christmas. He insisted on the fact that "the Christmas season is a prolonged commemoration of the divine, virginal and salvific motherhood of her, whose 'inviolate virginity brought the Saviour into the world'." Nor must we forget that the feast of St. Joseph is also an occasion for reflection on the Blessed Virgin Mary, his spouse.

Liturgy and Doctrine: Pius XII, in what still remains the major papal statement on the theology of the Liturgy, the Encyclical *Mediator Dei*, warned against a false interpretation of the dictum *Lex orandi, lex credendi.* The Church should approve those truths which, "by means of the Liturgy, have yielded fruits of piety or holiness." The Pope went on to explain how it can be said that "the whole Liturgy contains the Catholic faith, in as much as it is a public profession of the faith of the Church." "In the Liturgy, we make explicit profession of the Catholic faith," he said, and he quoted Pius IX (*qv*), using the Liturgy as a theological source for his arguments when he defined the dogma of the Immaculate Conception. He himself did likewise in *Munificentissimus Deus* and *Ad Caeli Reginam* (*qqv*).

This area of encounter is one that has to be taken and examined with delicacy. The Pope stated that the faith is professed "not only by celebrating the various mysteries, not only by offering the Sacrifice and administering the Sacraments, but also by reciting or singing the Creed (the Christian watchword), by reading other documents and also the divinely inspired Scriptures." Each element, mentioned here, would demand careful historical research and evaluation. Every doctrinal or devotional truth, related to Our Lady, affords scope for such study.

[1]On Mary and the Liturgy, cf. *Marialis Cultus*, by Pope Paul VI; *Maria*, I, 215-416 (on the different rites); PCM, II and V; D. M. Montagna, O.S.M., "La liturgia Mariana primitiva (sec. IV-VI), Introduzione ad uno studio sull' omelitica mariana greca," in MM, 24(1962), 84-128, also separate issue; *id.*, "La lode alla Theotokos nei Testi greci dei secoli IV-VII," in MM, 24(1962), 453-543; *Mariologische Studien* 3, German Marian Society, (Essen, 1964), separate issue; G. Frénaud, O.S.B., "Le Culte de Notre Dame dans l'ancienne liturgie latine," in *Maria*, VI, 159-211; H. Barré, C.S.Sp., "L'Apport marial de l'Orient à l'Occident de S. Ambroise à S. Anselme, 3, Liturgie et Piété mariale," in BSFEM, 19(1962), 44-59; R. Laurentin, *Traité*, V, 52-59, 172-173; *id.*, in RSPT, 52(1968), 512-518; *id.*, "Marie dans le Culte, Ce que l'Occident doit à l'Orient du VIe au XIe siècle," in Zagreb Congress, II, 17-36; J. H. Crehan, S.J., "The Assumption and the Jerusalem Liturgy," in TheolSt, 30(1969), 312-325; R. Caro, *La Homilética*; G. M. Roschini, *Maria Santissima*, IV. [2]E. Testa, O.F.M., "Cultus marianus in textibus nazarethanis primorum saeculorum,' in PCM, V, 21-34. [3]G. Giamberardini, O.F.M., "De primaevo Deiparae festo ex documentis aegyptiacis," in PCM, V, 95. [4]L. V. Kennedy, C.S.B., *The Saints of the Roman Canon*, (Vatican Press, 1938). [5]PCM, II, 459-462 (summary of lecture, in default of text lost when the author was killed in a car accident between Lisbon and Fatima); A. A. Maguire, O.F.M., in PCM, II, 429-438; S. M. Meo, O.S.M., in PCM, II, 439-458. [6]For evidence from the Armenian and Georgian lectionairies and the homiletic background and relevance of Etheria, cf. J. H. Crehan, S.J., "The Assumption and the Jerusalem Liturgy," in TheolSt, 30(1969); see article on *Hesychius* in the present work. [7]Cf. A. Wenger, A.A., *L'Assomption*, 111-139, for relevance to the Assumption. [8]PG 147, 292. For Justinian, cf. M. van Esbroeck, "La lettre de l'empereur Justinien sur l'annonciation et la Nöel en 561," in AB, 86(1968), 351-371. [9]On the feast of the Pokrov, cf. L. Ryden, in AB, 94(1976), 63-82. On *Kidana Mehrat*, cf. E. Cerulli, "La fiesta etiopica del Patto di Misericordia e le sue fonti nel greco 'Liber de Transitu' e nel racconto latino dei Cinque Dolori di Maria," in *Silloge Bizantina*, for S. G. Mercati, (Rome, 1957), 54-57. [10]Cf. A. M. Cecchin, "La Concezione della Vergine nella liturgia della Chiesa Occidentale, anteriore al secolo XIII," in MM, 5(1943), 58-114. [11]Dom Bernard Billet, "Culte et Dévotion à la Vierge Marie dans l'ordre monastique aux VIIIe-IXe siècles," in Zagreb Congress, IV, 203-216. On Ireland, cf. P. Grosjean, S.J., "La prétendue fête de la Conception des Eglises celtiques," in AB, 61(1943), 91-95. [12]Cf. R. W. Pfaff, *New Liturgical Feasts in Later Medieval England*, (Oxford, 1970), 40-61; I. V. Polc, *De origine festi Visitationis B.M.V.*, (Rome, Lateran University, 1967). [13]E. Bertaud, in DSp, III, 1693-1695.

LOURDES

The shrine with the widest international appeal, though probably less frequented than Guadalupe, Lourdes interests the theologian as an example of Marian pastoral theology, place of miracles (*qv*), a focus of the sentiment of the faithful (*qv*), and a center of devotion intimately bound to the life of the Church, where respect for the Liturgy (*qv*) combines admirably with popular piety.[1] The Apparitions are well documented; the commitment to caring, works of relief, reconciliation and compassion, which they have caused, show the social dimension of genuine Marian cult.

The message received by St. Bernadette came four years after the papal dogma of the Immaculate Conception (*qv*). There has been a continuing link since then with the Papacy, particularly close in the pontificates of Pius XII and John XXIII (*qqv*), because of the centenary celebrations in 1958. The principal papal texts are: *Auspicatus profecto* and *Maximopere laetamur* by Pius XI (*qv*) for the seventy-fifth anniversary of the Apparitions; Pius XII's centenary Encyclical, *Le Pèlerinage*, and Apostolic Constitution, *Primo exacto*, announcing the Jubilee; and John XXIII's addresses in 1959 for the closing of the centenary year.

Mary and the Eucharist (*qv*) is a theme evoked particularly at Lourdes.

[1]Cf. R. Laurentin, *Lourdes, Documents authentiques*, 7 vols., Vols. III-VI with B. Billet, O.S.B., Vol. VII by B. Billet with appendices by R. Laurentin; *id., Sens de Lourdes*, (Paris, 1955); B. Billet, O.S.B., "Les dimensions ecclésiales du message de Notre Dame de Lourdes," in PCM, VI, 451-462.

LUKE, ST.

L. was well suited to write of Our Lady, because of his sensitivity to women, his insistence on prayer, and his emphasis on the universality of the gospel message.[1] He treated of Our Lady in the infancy narrative, in short passages dealing with the public life of Christ, and in one sentence of his second work, the *Acts of the Apostles*.

The Infancy Narrative: The many topics arising from his first and second chapters are dealt with separately (see ANGELUS, ANGELS, ANNUNCIATION, ARK OF THE COVENANT, BIRTH OF CHRIST, CHRONOLOGY, CONSENT, DAUGHTER OF ZION, FAITH, FATHERHOOD OF JOSEPH, FINDING IN THE TEMPLE, FULL OF GRACE, HAIL MARY, HANDMAID OF THE LORD, HOLY SPIRIT, JOSEPH, ST., KNOWLEDGE, MAGNIFICAT, MOTHER OF GOD, POOR OF YAHWEH, PRESENTATION OF THE LORD, PURIFICATION OF MARY, QUEENSHIP, SWORD OF SIMEON, VIRGINITY, VOW OF VIRGINITY, VISITATION, WOMAN).

No matter how sophisticated the approach, the materials used by L. cannot be identified with total scientific precision—hence the conflicting views of those who think that he used a pre-existing Hebrew or Aramaic document, and those who think that he composed his own text from traditions which reached him, which he clothed in the language of the *Septuagint*. Was there a birth story of John the Baptist in circulation, and was this the starting-point? Was the Annunciation story the "initial cell" around which the rest grew?

Certain features are noteworthy. The chapters, especially the passages which mention Mary, abound in Old Testament influence. Apart from overt reference to legal prescriptions (2:23-24, 41), the parallel between the Annunciation (1:31) and Is 7:14 (see EMMANUEL) and the

Magnificat, which, like the *Benedictus*, is almost a mosaic of Old Testament phrases, there are numerous textual echoes, as may be seen from a glance at any Bible which gives cross-references. There are differences of opinion on interpretation of some of these parallels. On whether, for example, "overshadow" in 1:35 does have the implication of Ex 40:35, of the *shekinah*, that is; or whether 1:43 really evokes 2 Sam 6:2-11 to support the typology of the Ark.

Within this sense of fulfillment, there is an element of the unexpected, of innovation—the priestly visionary struck dumb, the virgin mother, the two women relatives miraculously pregnant, the journey of the younger one. A series of striking contrasts unfolds, with the difference between John the Baptist and Jesus increasingly evident. John announced in the Temple to one who was bound officially to the old institutions, Jesus to a private individual in the privacy of a village home. John's birth was hymned in his home, Jesus' in the heavens by angels, a sign of Yahweh's presence. John withdrew to the wilderness (1:80), Jesus on the threshold of manhood entered the Temple, his Father's house (2:46). The chronicle of John's infancy closes with the allusion to the desert, while that of Jesus includes the Presentation to the Lord and the Finding in the Temple (*qv*).

The framework used for the vivid narrative of events is a double diptych, that of the Annunciations and of the births. Herein the superiority of Mary, not only to Elizabeth but to all others after her Son, is in many ways affirmed or implied. Her Son is given wonderful titles—Great, Holy, the Lord's Anointed, King, Son of God, Glory, Saviour, Light—which leads R. Laurentin to conclude that the approximation of Jesus to Yahweh is "the final word in Luke's Christology."[2] All this redounds to his unique parent in the flesh. But she too is highly praised—"favoured one," "the Lord is with you," "blessed among women" (1:28;42). She "has found favour with God" (1:30); she is the "Lord's servant" (1:38); "she is blessed to have believed" (1:45). "All generations" will call her blessed, he "who is mighty, has done great things" for her (1:48-49); it is her soul that "will be piercd by a sword so that, out of many hearts, thoughts may be revealed" (2:35). Mary responds fully to God's call in the Annunciation; she takes the initiative in the dialogue (2:48). She is the special recipient of the Spirit, whose presence is so marked in the whole narrative (1:35).

The Public Life: "Is not this the son of Joseph?" (4:22) is L.'s rendering of the question at Nazareth, where Mark has, "Is not this the carpenter, the son of Mary?" (6:3). L. had already made Joseph's position clear, in the infancy narrative and 3:23. He does not mention the "Brothers" in Chapter 4.

Twice, L. states in the infancy narrative that Mary kept things in her heart and pondered them (2:19,51). The phrasing recurs in replies made by Jesus to those who referred in public to his Mother. "My Mother and my brothers are those who hear the word of God and do it" (8:21) was his answer to those who told him that his Mother and brothers were seeking him. To the woman who exclaimed, "Blessed is the womb that has borne you and the breasts you sucked," he replied, "Rather blessed are they who hear the word of God and keep it." (11:27-28). Vatican II picked up this thread of thought: "During his preaching, she welcomed the words by which her Son, exalting a kingdom above the relationships and ties of flesh and blood, declared blessed those who hear the word of God and keep it, as she was doing." (LG 58).

The Acts of the Apostles: "All these, with one heart, were persevering in prayer, as were the women and Mary, the Mother of Jesus and his brothers." (1:14). In the 20,000 items listed in G. M. Besutti's bibliographies, there is no study of the Marian content of this verse; the sole entry concerns its relevance to the Eucharist. It is studied in the article on the Holy Spirit in the present work. John XXIII (*qv*) quoted the text frequently in his prayer for the Council, in his inaugural address. Paul VI did the same in his address to the second session, the Council Fathers in their message to the world, and in LG 59.

[1]Cf. bibliography of article on *Infancy Narratives* in the present work; E. Burrows, *The Gospel of the Infancy*, (London, 1940); H. Sahlin, *Der Messias und das Gottesvolk. Studien zur protolukanischen Theologie* (Uppsala, 1945); R. Laurentin, *Structure et Théologie de Luc I-II*, (Paris, Etudes Bibliques, 1957); S. Munoz Iglesias, "El Evangelio de la Infancia en San Lucas y las infancias de los heroes biblicos," in EstBib, 16(1957), 329-382; M. D. Goulder and M. L. Sanderson, "St. Luke's Genesis," in *Journal Theol. St.*, 8(1957), 12-30; P. Winter, "The Cultural Background of the Narrative in Luke 1 and 2," in *Jewish Quarterly Review*, 45(1954-1955), 159-167, 230-242; *id.*, "On Luke and Lucan Sources," in ZNW, 47(1956), 217-242; *id.*, "The Proto-Source of Luke I," in NovT, 1(1956), 184-199; *id.*, *op. cit.*, in NovT, 12(1970), 348; *id.*, "The Main Literary Problem of the Lucan Infancy Story," in *Anglican Theol. Rev.*, 40(1958), 257-264; J. P. Audet, "Autour de la théologie de Luc I-II," in ScEccl, 11(1959), 409-418; R. M. Wilson, "Some Recent Studies in the Lucan Infancy Narrative," in *St. Evang.*, I(TU 73, Berlin, 1959), 235-253; F. Neirynck, *L'Evangile de Nöel selon S. Luc*, (Paris, Pensee Catholique, 1960); R. J. Dillon, "St. Luke's Infancy Account," in *The Dunwoodie Rev.*, 1(1961), 5-37; R. H. Oliver, "The Lucan Birth Stories and the Purpose of Luke-Acts," in NTS, 10(1964, 1965), 202-226; W. B. Tatum, "The Epoch of Israel: Luke I-II and the Theological Plan of Luke-Acts," in NTS 13(1966, 1967), 184-195; A. Legault, C.S.C., *L'Evangile de l'enfance selon Luc I-II*, (Montreal, Pro manuscripto, University Press, 1968); A. George, "L'Evangile de l'enfance en Luc I-II," in CM, 13(1969), 99-126; D. L. Himmler, *History and Christology in the Lucan Infancy Narratives*, (Dissertation, Catholic University of America, 1971); A. Feuillet, *Jésus et sa Mère d'après les récits lucaniens de l'enfance et d'après S. Jean*, (Paris, 1974), Parts I and II, 15-196; J. McHugh, *The Mother of Jesus in the New Testament*, (London, 1975), esp. 3-36, 125-149; R. E. Brown, *The Birth of the Messiah*, (London, 1977), 235-255; Mary in NT, 105-172.

LULL, RAYMOND (*c.* 1232-1316)

Philosopher, mystic, missionary, Catalan poet and prose writer, perhaps martyr, L. developed a system of achieving the unity of all knowledge, his "Art." He was devoted to the conversion of Moslems.[1] L. was a Franciscan tertiary known because of his many writings as the Enlightened Doctor, *Doctor Illuminatus*. The influence of his ideas was greater than has been known until recently. L. wrote much of Our Lady. He may have been the first to teach the Immaculate Conception (*qv*) openly in Paris. His relevant work is *Disputatio Eremitae et Raymundi super aliquibus dubiis quaestionibus Sententiarum Petri Lombardi* (Paris, 1298; ed. Mainz, vol. IV). L. gave three reasons why Mary should be immaculate. The Son of God could not take flesh from her if she had been in any way stained by sin. There would be greater resemblance and agreement between her and him if her conception resembled his in being entirely sinless. The new creation, beginning with Jesus and Mary, counterpart of Adam and Eve (*qv*), should be marked by innocence, as the first had been, free from every touch of sin. L. also wrote *Liber de Sancta Maria, Plant de Nostra Doña Santa Maria*, and *Horas de Nostra Doña Santa Maria*, a poem in seven parts like the seven canonical hours. Two works sometimes attributed to L. are spurious: *Benedicta tu in mulieribus*, an important defense of the Immaculate Conception; and *De conceptu virginali*, published in 1491.

[1]Works: *Obres*, 21 vols., (Palma,1905-1952); (Mainz, 1721-1742); *Obres essencials*, 2 vols., (Palma, 1951); *Opera latina*, (Palma, 1959). Cf. E. Longpré, O.F.M., in DTC, IX, 1098; M. Caldentey, T.O.R., "'Nuestra Senora Santa Maria' fue Madre por causa del pecado? o el primado universal de Jesucristo y Maria, segun el Doctor Iluminado," in EstM, 8(1949), 363-381; M. Guix, "La Inmaculada y la Corona de Aragon en le baja Edad Media (siglos XIII-XV)," in *Miscelanea Comillas*, 22(1954), 193-326; Andres de Palma de Mallorca, "La Inmaculada en la Escuela Lulist," in *Estudios Franciscanos*, 55(1954), 171-194; M. Alvar de Barcelona, O.F.M.Cap., "Llull i el doctorat de la Inmaculada," in *Est. Lulianos*, 5(1961), 61-97; *Est. Lulianos*, 6(1962), 5-49, 222-255; *Est. Lulianos*, 8(1964), 5-16, separate issue, (Palma de Mallorca, 1964).

LUTHER, MARTIN (1483-1546)

L.'s opinions on Our Lady are not wholly consistent, not altogether free from tension. They are abundant, and it would be possible to select a series of extracts which would make him look like a Catholic. They are contained in his sermons, in biblical commentaries, and in his work on the *Magnificat*,[1] the latter including many things not strictly relevant to Marian theology or piety. He underwent a certain development in his ideas, and we must not forget that, up to his middle thirties, he had accepted—though with some questioning—traditional Catholic ideas and practice in this area. After the year of his challenge to the Church, 1517, he showed no sign of material change until the critical year 1522. In a sermon on the feast of Mary's Nativity that year, he questioned Mary's role in our day-to-day Christian life. To what extent did he change? The question is acute in two areas, the Immaculate Conception (*qv*) and Intercession (*qv*).

L. was emphatic on the divine motherhood: "In this work whereby she was made the Mother of God, so many and such great good things were given her that no one can grasp them." "Not only is Mary the Mother of him who is born [in Bethlehem], but of him who, before the world, was eternally born of the Father, from a Mother in time and at the same time man and God."[2] He returned to the subject frequently, and it stirred him to awe. We must reflect in our hearts what it means to be God's Mother.

Likewise, L. was true to Catholic tradition on the virginity. "It is an article of faith that Mary is Mother of the Lord and still a virgin." "Christ, we believe, came forth from a womb left perfectly intact."[3] That Mary lost her virginity after the Child's birth, he thought a thing to be neither said nor thought. L. inter-preted Is 7:14 in the sense of a prophecy of the virgin birth, and he inveighed against Helvidius. In the commentary on the *Magnificat* (*qv*), he extolled Mary's virginity.

L. saw Mary as the figure of the Church: "Mary represents Christianity after the synagogue. Elizabeth represents the people under the law of the synagogue; although they were a pious people, they were surrounded by external precepts. But Mary, who goes over the mountains, and nevertheless with modesty, represents the Christian people walking freely here below under heaven . . . ." "This undoubtedly means that on earth the Christian Church remains the spiritual Virgin Mary, and that it will not be destroyed, although even its preachers, its faith, and its Gospel, the spiritual Christ, will be persecuted . . . ."[4]

Of Mary's virtues, L. also spoke warmly: "The Blessed Virgin was the most pure worshipper of God, for she glorified God alone above all things." Faith especially was singled out by L. among God's gifts to Mary. Rarely, he thought, is such great faith as hers found in the Scripture, and he related this to his fundamental idea of *Deus solus*. Thus, too, in the commentary on the *Magnificat*, his concept of Mary's humility is such a tribute to God that all merit on her part is excluded, especially in his explanation: "The almighty has done great things for me; holy is his name."

L. did surround his doctrine on the Immaculate Conception with important distinctions—active and passive conception, the latter inchoative and consummated, i.e. by the infusion of the soul. To the latter, the famous passage in the 1527 sermon for the conception of Mary is related. "But the other conception, namely the infusion of the soul, it is piously and suitably believed, was without any sin, so that while the soul was bring infused, she would be at the same time cleansed from original sin and adorned with the gifts of God to receive the holy soul thus infused. And thus, in the very moment in which she began to live, she was without all sin . . . ."[5] The texts which seem irreconcilable with this statement are: "[His] Mother was born from parents in sin like us," in 1532; and "Every man, save Christ, was subject to the vices of original sin,"[6] in 1540. But these texts are explainable on L.'s view of the active conception; the second passage, aimed at those who were denying that Christ was truly man because he did not have original sin and concupiscence,

LUX — LYDGATE

ends with the words, "all seed except Mary was vitiated."

L.'s theory on Mary's intercession was influenced by his idea of *Christus solus*, and by the abuses which, in his Catholic days, had shocked him. But he did not change drastically at once. After 1522, change is perceptible, and commentators differ as to whether in the end he allowed for any intercession on Mary's part, or would have any invocation of her.[7] Though he knew that regard for her was "deep in the heart of man," he distinguished between her power as *Fürbitterin*, which he conceded, and *Fürsprecherin*, which he rejected. L. became more caustic on the word "Mediatress" as the years moved on, taking St. Bernard to task. He talked of the danger of making Mary into an idol, even a "goddess." The "papists" have done so. In the commentary on the *Magnificat*, he had said that she should be invoked, that God, through her may give and do what we ask, ending the work thus: "May she enlighten our intelligences, inflame our hearts, and inspire our whole life. May Christ grant us this grace, through the intercession of his holy Mother." Eleven years later, recalling the "frightful idolatry" which had reached "terrible proportions in the papacy," he warned: "It can be permitted that they can rest content simply with praising her. But to pray to her, to await her intercession and help . . . ." These things should be reserved for Christ alone, he says, quoting Jn 14:13.[8]

L. reduced the feasts of Mary to three: the Annunciation; the Purification, "feasts of the Incarnation of Christ"; and the Visitation, "completely papist" but he would let it stay. Of the feast of the Assumption, he had said: "The feast of the Assumption is totally papist, full of idolatry, and without foundation in the Scriptures." He even said that he would keep the Visitation to "remind us that the [Papists] taught us apostasy." The *Salve Regina*, Europe's most powerful Marian hymn, he dismissed. It said too much. True, he had no part in the iconoclasm of the times, though he reduced the role of images from cultic to pedagogic. And in this last sermon, on 17 January, 1546, as death was approaching, he could thus recall the piety of his early years: "Is Christ only to be adored? Or is the holy Mother of God rather not to be honoured? This is the woman who crushed the serpent's head. Hear us. For your Son denies you nothing. Bernard said too much on the gospel

'An angel was sent' . . . . For of Christ alone, it was said 'Hear him.' Likewise, 'Behold the Lamb of God' etc. Not of Mary, or angels, or Gabriel."[9]

[1]Works, in WA: English translation, ed. by J. Pelikan, (Concordia, St. Louis), esp. Vol. 21 *The Magnificat*, 297-358. For Marian texts, cf. W. Tappolet, *Das Marienlob der Reformatoren*, (Tübingen, 1962), 17-160. Cf. R. Schimmelpfennig, *Die Geschichte der Marienverehrung im deutschen Protestantismus*, (Paderborn, 1952); W. Delius, "Luther und die Marienverehrung," in *Theol. Literaturzeitung*, 79(1954), 409-415; H. D. Preuss, *Maria bei Luther*, (Gutersloh, 1954); E. Stakemeier, in MO, 424-450; T. A. O'Meara, O.P., *Mary in Protestant and Catholic Thought*, (New York, 1966), 112-125; H. Dufel, *Luthers Stellung zur Marienverehrung*, (Göttingen, 1968); B. Gherardini, *La Madonna in Lutero*, (Rome, 1967). Cf. esp. W. J. Cole, S.M., "Was Luther a Marian Devotee?," in MSt, 21(1970), 94-202; D. Bertetto, S.D.B., "La Madonna in Lutero in un'opera recente," in *Divinitas*, 12(1968), 612-617. [2]WA 7, 572; WA 36, 60-62. Cf. article on *Karl Barth* in the present work. [3]WA 11, 319-320; WA 6, 510. [4]WA 10, 405. [5]WA 4, 694. [6]WA 1, 60; WA 39, 11, 107. [7]Cf. W. J. Cole, "Was Luther a Marian Devotee?," in MSt, 21(1970), 152ff. [8]WA 52, 316, 692. [9]WA 51, 128-129.

LUX VERITATIS (31 December, 1931)

This is the Encyclical issued by Pius XI (*qv*) for the fifteenth centenary of the Council of Ephesus (see CYRIL OF ALEXANDRIA, ST.).[1] The Pope, beginning with Christology, went on to teach certain important truths about Mary, particularly her spiritual motherhood, which he related to the motherhood of the Redeemer and the words of the dying Christ (see WOMAN IN JN 19:25-27), adducing Leo XIII's authority herein. Pius exhorted the faithful to invoke Mary confidently. There are references to the separated eastern Christians, and to the social programme of Pius, as set forth in *Casti Connubii* and *Divini illius Magistri*.

[1]AAS, 23(1931), 493-517.

LYDGATE, JOHN, O.S.B. (d. 1450)

An English poet, L. was author of a life of Mary in verse, a work commissioned by King Henry V. The work is in six books: 1) Birth, early years and marriage; 2) Annunciation, Visitation, proof of Mary's virginity; 3) Birth of Christ; 4) The Circumcision; 5) The Magi; and 6) The Purification.[1]

[1]J. A. Lauritis, C.S.Sp., *A Critical Edition of John Lydgate's Life of Our Lady*, (Duquesne University, Pittsburgh, ed. Nauwelaerts, Louvain, 1961); *A Selection from the Minor Poems of Dan John Lydgate*, vol. II of *Early English Poetry, Ballads, and Popular Literature*, ed. by J. O. Halliwell, for the Percy Society, (1840).

M

MAGNIFICAT, THE

This is the hymn of Mary in Lk 1:46-55.[1] It may be considered under these headings: authorship; content; liturgical use; and impact on Christian culture.

It was assumed down to the nineteenth century that the hymn was attributed to Mary by Luke (see INFANCY NARRATIVES). A. Loisy, under the pseudonym Francois Jacobe, proposed the attribution to Elizabeth in 1897. A. Harnack defended the view which has been supported by a number of scholars since then. Three Latin manuscripts from the fourth to the eighth centuries have the reading, "And Elizabeth said." So have one manuscript of St. Irenaeus *Adversus Haereses* (IV, vii, 1), St. Jerome's Latin translation of Origen, and Nicetas of Remesiana, *De psalmodiae bono*. Otherwise, the entire manuscript tradition favoured the reading, "And Mary said." Arguments are adduced for and against from internal evidence. Attribution to Elizabeth offends the whole plan of the two chapters, the diptych of Annunciations and births, wherein Zachary and Mary are parallel. It brings Elizabeth to a prominence which the rest of the narrative denies her; it unjustifiably deprives Mary of a prominent role, which she has in every other incident—Annunciation, Nativity, Presentation, and Finding. A ruling of the Pontifical Biblical Commission (26 June, 1912) favoured the attribution to Mary.

The composition is a cento of Old Testament phrases on the pattern generally of the song of Hannah (1 Sam 2:1-10). But commentators have seen in the hymn a unity of its own, a synthesis of many elements from the era of expectation, which derive their coherence from the fulfillment. Theories of the origin range from P. Winter's suggestion that, like the *Benedictus*, the *Magnificat* was a Maccabean hymn, to P. Benoit's that it was a "pre-Christian hymn originating among the 'Poor of the Lord'

adopted by the first Christian community before Luke took it up." Could Mary as one of the *Anawim* not have known the composition?

The borrowings from the Old Testament remain striking. Understood in the light of Mary's personality and destiny, they reveal or help us to understand the unfolding of the whole plan of salvation. It is on this level that Mary speaks, and this explains the absence of reference to Elizabeth's child. On this level, the hymn is an oracle uniting the mystic intuitions of the *Anawim* with an eschatology proof against every crisis. Thence comes the repeated resonance of these sublime phrases through Christian history.

The destiny of an individual becomes the symbol and the fulfillment of her people's vocation. Identity between Mary and Israel, in its fullness, is implicit in the *Magnificat*, strongly so as it moves to its final notes—not only the ancient Israel, but the new Israel, which is the Church of God.

The *Magnificat*, from about the time of St. Benedict, has been daily recited or sung at Vespers in the Latin Rite, with simultaneous incensing of the altar at Solemn Vespers. It has also a place in the Byzantine, Syro-Maronite, and Armenian liturgies.

The stimulus given by the *Magnificat* to theological, especially spiritual, reflection has been constant and fruitful. Commentaries from the time of Origen and St. Ambrose are supplemented by diverse studies and substantial works such as Martin Luther's, John Gerson's, and St. Lawrence of Brindisi's. It has been found suitable as a song of thanks to the Lord in moments of public rejoicing. In certain communities, recitation of it in such moments evokes a whole spirit, ethos, and corporate memory.

---

[1]Bibliography in R. Laurentin, *Structure et Théologie de Luc I-II*, (Paris, 1957); G. M. Roschini, O.S.M., in MM, 31(1969), 260-323. Cf. F. Jacobe (A. Loisy), "L'Origine du

Magnificat," in *Rev. hist. liter. rel.*, 2(1897), 424-432; A. Durand, S.J., "L'Origine du Magnificat," in RB, 7(1898), 74-77; A. Harnack, "Das Magnificat der Elisabeth (Lk 1:46-55) nebst einigen Bemerkungen zu Luc I und II," in *Sitzung. der Kgl. Preussichen Akad. der Wissenschaft zu Berlin*, 27(1900), 538-556; P. Ladeuze, "De l'origine du Magnificat et son attribution dans le troisième Évangile à Marie ou à Elisabeth," in RHE, 4(1903), 623-644; L. Mechineau, "L'Attribuzione del Magnificat à Maria," in *Civiltà Catt.*, (1913), II, 33-47; L. Pirot, "Commission Biblique et Magnificat," in DBS 2(1934), 1270-1272; L. Suarez, "Soteriologia del Magnificat," in EphMar, 3(1953), 447-466; P. Winter, "Magnificat and Benedictus Maccabaean Psalms," in *Bulletin of John Rylands Library*, 37(1954), 328-347; R. Laurentin, *Structure et Théologie de Luc I-II*, (Paris, 1957), 82-86; G. I. Koontz, "Mary's Magnificat," in *Biblia sacra*, 116(1959), 336-349; J. Forestell, C.S.B., "Old Testament Background of the Magnificat," in MSt, 12(1961), 205-244; R. Schnackenburg, "Das Magnificat, seine Spiritualität und Theologie," in *Geist und Leben*, 38(1965), 342-357; S. Benko, "The Magnificat: A History of the Controversy," in *Journal Bibl. Lit.*, 86(1967), 263-275; R. H. MacGrath, "Who Spoke the Magnificat? An Exercise in Textual Criticism," in *Bible Today*, 33(1967), 2315-2319; L. Ramaroson, S.J., "Ad structuram cantici 'Magnificat'," in *Verbum Domini*, 46(1968), 30-46; J. McHugh, *The Mother of Jesus in the New Testament*, (London, 1975), 73-79, 445; R. E. Brown, P.S.S., *The Birth of the Messiah*, (London, 1977), 334-338, 355-366; S. de Fiores, S.M.M., L. Monloubon, E. Hamel, J. Allemand, P. Blanc, J. Godefroid, in CM, 113(15 June, 1978); A. M. Serra, O.S.M., "Il 'Magnificat' messagio di liberazione e promozione humana," in *La Madonna*, (December 1976); Mary in NT, 137-143; F. Gryglewicz, "Die Herkunft der Hymnen des Kindheitsevangeliums des Lukas," in NTS, 21(1975), 265-273; P. Schmidt, "Maria und das Magnificat," in *Catholica*, 29(1975), 230-246; R. S. Miguel, *Fecit mihi magna qui potens est*, (Rome, 1970); R. C. Tannehill, "The Magnificat as Poem," in *Journal Bibl. Lit.*, 93(1974), 263-275; W. Vogels, "Le Magnificat, Marie et Israel," in *Église et théologie*, Ottawa, 6(1975), 279-296; S. Callahan, *The Magnificat*, (New York, 1975).

MANUEL II PALAEOLOGUS, EMPEROR
(1391-1425)

M. continued an ancient tradition by composing a work on the Assumption (*qv*), an offering in thanks for his cure from serious illness.[1] He had travelled in European countries seeking help against the Turks between 1399 and 1403, and, during two years in Paris, got to know the clergy, and wrote a polemical treatise (157 chapters) on the *Filioque* controversy. Did he know of western theories and debates on the Immaculate Conception (*qv*)? Four points mark his Marian theology: the indescribable majesty of the *Theotokos* (*qv*), and her free consent to the mystery; her constant union with Jesus, before the Incarnation and after the Ascension; and her

joyful death (on which he is lengthy) and exhortation to us to be united with her in joy.

Mary alone of all women, M. thought, had escaped from the condemnation that followed sin. She was always immune from sin,[2] her soul and body free from all stain.[3] What of the initial holiness? M. Jugie, A.A., bases the affirmative answer on this passage: "At the same time as the blessed one was born, I might also say, as she was conceived, he who had predestined her as his Mother, filled her with his own grace . . . he was never not united to her, from the very moment she had her first beginning in the womb of her barren mother."[4] M. argued then that, if John the Baptist had been full of the Holy Spirit in the womb, "how can it not be right to say the same of the all-pure?" Jugie thinks that M. was excessive in regard to John the Baptist,[5] Miss H. Graef, on the contrary, argues that mention of the saint implies only sanctification of Our Lady in the womb.[6] She also contends that a clause omitted by Jugie, "and which the angel Gabriel came from God to bring her," after the descriptive phrase applied to Mary, "a vessel full of the blessing from which the first mother [i.e., Eve] had fallen away," weakens his argument. For, she argues, this is the Greek idea of purification only at the time of the Annunciation. Miss Graef herself omits the first part of the sentence which reads, "The most pure Virgin, all pure in soul and body, who from all ages was superior to the ancient curse coeval with the human race," and the conclusion, "was fittingly all that we have said."[7]

M. insisted on the respect which each of the three divine persons showed to Mary's free consent, "that there should be a place for freedom of will, and violence be entirely absent,"[8] to defeat the wiles of Satan.

M. dealt exclusively with Mary's death, and said nothing of the body after death, of its possible resurrection. He was totally elusive on the subject. Mary's death, he thought, was necessary to establish the reality of human nature. Mary desired to be separated from her body, to contemplate God in death "with the immortal eyes of her soul."[9]

[1]PO 16, 543-566. Cf. introduction, in PO 16, 539-542. Cf. M. Jugie, A.A., *L'Immaculée Conception*, 284-287; id., *L'Assomption*, 335-336. [2]PO 16, 556. [3]PO 16, 555. [4]PO 16, 552-553. [5]M. Jugie, A.A., *L'Immaculée Conception*, 186. [6]H. Graef, *Mary*, I, 347ff. [7]PO 16, 555. [8]PO 16, 555. [9]PO 16, 566.

MARIALIS CULTUS (2 February, 1974)

This is the principal statement by Paul VI (*qv*) on Our Lady since Vatican II.[1] It is an Apostolic Exhortation for the right ordering and development of the cult of the Blessed Virgin Mary. The text is supported by impressive erudition, draws on the conciliar texts, the liturgical books and sacred writers, particularly from the patristic period, with the Eastern Fathers well represented. After an introduction, the first part explains, in Section 1, the place given to Our Lady in the reformed Liturgy. In Section 2, it presents her as the model of the Church in its worship as the Virgin who listened (to the word of God), who prayed and who offered. Inset in the text are very important doctrinal considerations, especially in the conclusion to the second section of this part. Part Two deals with the renewal of Marian piety. Section 1 points to the Trinitarian, Christological and ecclesial basis of Marian cult; there is a valuable passage on Mary and the Holy Spirit. Section 2 gives four directive norms, opening these perspectives—biblical, liturgical, ecumenical, and anthropological. Part 3 deals with the Rosary and the Angelus, treating the second at much greater length. The conclusion expounds the theological and pastoral value of the cult of Our Lady. Throughout, the document manifests realism as well as scholarship—realism e.g. on the subject of Woman and Mary.

[1]Text, in AAS, 66(1974), 113-168. Cf. presentation by J. Galot, S.J., in DCath, (1974), 319-321; A. Kniazeff, Orthodox commentaries, in *La Maison Dieu*, 121(1975), 108-113; Y. M. Congar, O.P., in *La Maison Dieu*, 121(1975), 114-121; M. Thurian, Protestant commentaries, in *La Maison Dieu*, 121(1975), 98-107; "Saggi sulla Esortazione apostolica 'Marialis Cultus'," in MM, (1977), I-II, 7-131, on scriptural, liturgical, ecumenical, and pastoral aspects, and comparison with Vatican II (7 contributors).

MARIE DE L'INCARNATION, BLESSED (1599-1668)

The Teresa of the new world, one of the great mystics, M. was, in her Marian devotion, true to the spirit of her country and time, seventeenth century France, which witnessed a flowering of Marian doctrine and piety. M.'s vocation called for an empirical, experiential approach, rather than exposition of theory. She has bound herself, according to a custom of the time, by an engagement of "slavery" to her heavenly Mother, and bore a little cross as a symbol of this vow. When she spoke of Mary as Mediatress, she was speaking as a highly competent witness. Towards the end of her life, she summed up her attitude: "I still feel myself powerfully strengthened by the protection of the Most Blessed Virgin, who is our divine Superior, by the special choice and solemn vow which our community made in this context many years ago. This divine Mother gives us continual help in all our needs, and guards us as the pupil of her eye. It is she who conducts all our business; she who has helped us to rise again after the fire and a host of other accidents, beneath the weight of which we should, in the normal way, have been crushed .... What fear can I have beneath the wings of so powerful and lovable a Protectress."[1]

[1]Cf. H. de Lubac, S.J., "Marie de l'Incarnation et la Sainte Vierge," in *Maria*, III, 183-204, quotation from letter (12 October, 1668), 184.

MARIOLOGY

The word *Mariologia* was first used as the title of a book by Nigido Placido (*c.* 1570-*c.* 1650), A Sicilian priest who was for twenty-seven years a member of the Society of Jesus. While a Jesuit, he published *Summa Mariologiae* (Palermo, 1602, a second edition following in 1613).[1] Important works dealing entirely and solely with Our Lady had appeared since St. Ildefonsus of Toledo (*qv*) and Pseudo-Albert (*qv*) and Richard of St. Laurent, with Engelbert of Admont, exemplified the same trend in medieval times. St. Thomas and the scholastic theologians treated theological themes on Our Lady within the framework of the Incarnation. Suarez, the first author of a systematic Marian theology, adhered to the context of the mysteries of Christ. Separate treatises have appeared in modern times, homiletic and devotional in the fifteenth century and after, strictly doctrinal in the nineteenth and twentieth centuries. Witness the four-volume works of J. B. Terrien and G. M. Roschini, the latter's Latin volumes entitled *Mariologia*. Scheeben's work, now available separately, was part of his dogmatic theology.

These three theologians gave much attention to the Fathers, as did Cardinal Newman in his controversy with Pusey; they did not neglect Sacred Scripture. With the "return to the sources" as a methodic principle of theology in the forties of the present century, theologians of Our Lady aimed at the presentation of Marian themes to meet this demand. R. Laurentin's

MARK — MARMION

Court traité de théologie mariale was a first successful example of this literature.

The word "Mariology" stirred suspicion in certain quarters—suspicion echoed by Cardinal Koenig in his conciliar speech in October, 1963—that a new discipline, detached from theology, with its own methodology and conclusions of dubious validity, was being created. The search for a fundamental principle of Mariology may have misled people.

Such fears would be allayed by obedience to the directives given to Marian theologians by Pius XII (*qv*) in his address to the International Mariological Congress in October, 1954 and by Vatican II (LG 67). The Council repeated the Pope's warning on the extremes to be avoided, "the falsity of exaggeration on the one hand and the excess of narrowmindedness on the other" (LG 67). Each authority listed the sources to be studied, each urged a Christocentric outlook and respect for the teaching authority. Pius said: "Consequently when we admire the Mother's eminent gifts and rightly praise them, we are admiring and praising the divinity, the goodness, the love, and the power of her Son." *Lumen Gentium* concludes: "Let them rightly explain the offices and privileges of the Blessed Virgin which are always related to Christ, the source of all truth, sanctity, and piety."

---

[1]Cf. A. Segovia, S.J., "Nota sobre el Autor y el contenido de la primera 'Mariologia', Miscellanea Antonio Perez Goyena," in EstEcl, 35(Madrid, 1960); C. Vollert, S.J., *A Theology of Mary*, (New York, 1965), esp. Ch. I "The Structure of Marian Theology."

MARK, ST.

M., in his gospel, says very little about Our Lady.[1] He has no infancy narrative; he does not mention Mary among the "women watching from a distance" on Calvary (15:40). In M.'s narrative of the public ministry, she appears in one incident, and is named in another. The first prompts Jesus' reply: "Here are my mother and my brethren. Whoever does God's will is my brother and sister and mother." (3:35). The phrasing varies from the parallel passage in Matthew: "For whoever does the will of my Father in heaven is my brother and sister and mother." (12:50); and in Luke: "My mother and my brethren are those who hear the word of God and do it" (8:21). Jesus does not reject his mother in this saying but draws attention to the law of the eschatological kingdom, the will of

God. By implication, his presence before the crowd as a prophet showed that she had bred, reared and equipped him for his mission. This was surely the will of God for her. It was the Matthaean version that St. John Chrysostom (*qv*), St. Ambrose, St. Jerome, and St. Augustine chose for comment. Vatican II's explanation of Mary's attitude to the words of Jesus during the public life is in the context of Lk 11:27-28, Jesus' reply to the woman from the crowd who praised his mother. (LG 58).

M. never mentions St. Joseph (*qv*), which has prompted different interpretations of the words, "Is not this the carpenter, the son of Mary?" (6:3). Matthew has, "Is not this the carpenter's son? Is not his mother called Mary?" (13:55). The only Father named of Jesus in M. is his heavenly Father in whose glory he will come with the angels (8:38), to whom he prays, "Abba, Father . . ." (14:36). These texts are compatible with the virgin birth, which is not to say that they teach it explicitly. The difficulty about seeing a reference to the virgin birth in the phrase, "son of Mary," is that M. would scarcely put this on the lips of the villagers. Their choice of words may mean that at the time St. Joseph was dead.

References to the "Brothers of the Lord" in M. (6:3; 15:40; 15:47; 16:1) are considered in the relevant article in this present work.

---

[1]Besides commentaries on St. Mark, cf. E. Stauffer, "Jeschu ben Mirjam: Kontroversgeschichtliche Anmerkungen zu Mk 6:3," in *Neotestamentica et semitica: Studies in Honour of Matthew Black*, ed. by E. E. Ellis and M. Wilcox, (Edinburgh, 1969), 119-128; G. W. Lathrop, *Who Shall Describe His Origin? Tradition and Redaction in Mk 6:1-6a*, Dissertation, (Nijmegen Catholic University, 1969); E. Grasser, "Jesus in Nazareth," in NTS, 16(1969-1970), 1-23; H. K. McArthur, "Son of Mary," in NovT, 15(1973), 38-58; M. Miguens, O.F.M., "Mary a Virgin; Alleged Silence in the New Testament," in MSt, 26(1975), 29-51; Mary in NT, 51-72.

MARMION, COLUMBA, O.S.B. (1858-1923)

Acknowledged as a master in the spiritual life after the appearance of his trilogy (*Christ, the Life of the Soul, Christ in His Mysteries*, and *Christ, the Ideal of the Monk*), M. was a principal influence in the growth of Christocentric spirituality in recent times.[1] This outlook informs his ideas about Our Lady and adds interest to them. They are found in two chapters of the books mentioned, in sermons, retreats which were recorded, and in his correspondence.

232

There is a sobriety in M.'s Marian teaching which resembles that of Vatican II, as some quotations from the first title cited above will show. "God proposes the mystery of the Incarnation which will only be fulfilled in the Virgin when she shall have given her free consent" (p. 372); "The Father of mercies willed that the consent of the predestined Mother should precede the Incarnation" (LG 56). "In the divine plan, Mary is inseparable from Jesus" (p. 382); Mary is "united to him by a close and indissoluble bond" (LG 53). "God is pleased, not so as to derogate from the power of his Son's mediation, but on the contrary to extend and exalt it, to recognize the credit of those who are united to Jesus, Head of the Mystical Body" (p. 382); "The maternal duty of Mary towards men in no way obscures or diminishes the unique mediation of Christ, but rather shows its power" (LG 60). "Christ has associated his Mother . . . with all his mysteries, from the offering in the Temple to the immolation on Calvary . . . . She accepted not only to be the Mother of Jesus, but to be associated with all the mission of the Redeemer" (p. 384); "By decree of divine Providence, she served on earth as the loving Mother of the Redeemer, an associate of unique nobility" (LG 61). "She has received from Jesus Christ himself a special grace of maternity towards his Mystical Body" (p. 384); "Taught by the Holy Spirit, the Catholic Church honours her with filial affection and piety as a most loving Mother" (LG 53). "Is he [Jesus] not our elder brother? Are we not predestined to be like him, so that he may be the 'firstborn among many brethren'?" (Rom 8:29), (p. 378); "The Son whom she brought forth is he whom God placed as the firstborn among many brethren, namely the faithful" (LG 63). "The Virgin Mother has no greater wish than to see her divine Son obeyed, loved, glorified, and exalted" (p. 387); "While honouring Christ's Mother, these devotions cause her Son to be rightly known, loved, and glorified, and all his commands obeyed" (LG 66). There are other points of similarity.

M. served as an adviser to Cardinal Mercier's commission on Mary's mediation; the memorandum he submitted on the subject was profoundly argued. "God," he said, in a sermon as early as 1899, "willed to give us his Son through her. In like manner, it is his will that every grace and every blessing should come to us through Mary."[2] He saw Mary associated with the new Adam, as Eve (qv) had been with the first. M. drew on St. Thomas' dictum: "She, so to speak, gave grace to the world, because she gave him who is the source of it."[3] He also drew on Bossuet's idea of Mary's mediation, and on Leo XIII's Encyclical Octobri mense (22 September, 1891), all in a Christocentric sense; he used the title Co-redemptress.

M.'s own devotion to Our Lady was sensitive and profound. He urged devotion to her in his correspondence with his spiritual disciples. He valued the Liturgy very highly, but would not allow it to be invoked against the Rosary, which he prized. He acted with respect for personal freedom, and the inclination given by the Holy Spirit in such devotions as the consecration taught by St. Louis Marie de Montfort (qv).[4]

[1]Marian doctrine: Ch. XII "The Mother of the Incarnate Word," in Christ, the Life of the Soul, (1922 and following editions), 368-387; Ch. IX "The Blessed Virgin, the Mysteries of the Childhood and the Hidden Life of Christ," in Christ in His Mysteries, (1922 and following editions), 152-173. Cf. Union with God According to Letters of Direction of Dom Marmion, ed. by R. Thibaut, O.S.B., (London, 1934); R. Thibaut, O.S.B., Abbot Columba Marmion, a Master of the Spiritual Life, (London, 1932); M. M. Philipon, O.P., Part V "The Mother of Christ," in The Spiritual Doctrine of Dom Marmion, (London, 1956), 201-216. [2]M. M. Philipon, O.P., op. cit., 209. [3]Summa Theologica, III, 27, 5. [4]Cf. Union with God . . . , ed. by R. Thibaut, O.S.B., (London, 1934), 201-202, n.3.

MARRACCI, HIPPOLYTUS (1604-1675)
Probably the most prolific writer of all time on Our Lady, M. was a member of the Clerks Regular of the Mother of God, engaged in pastoral work in Rome. He composed 115 books on Our Lady, thirty of which were published.[1] The two-volume Bibliotheca Mariana appeared in 1648, in Rome. It contained a vast bibliography (over 3,000 authors), a list of works on Mary from the beginnings to his own century. After M.'s death, the sequel, Appendix ad Bibliothecam Marianam, was published by P. Ketteler in Cologne (1683). The Bibliotheca Purpurea Mariana, listing books or writings on Mary by Cardinals, remained unpublished. M. collected Marian texts of different authors, publishing each as a Mariale. Those of St. Germanus of Constantinople, Leo the Wise (qqv), Isidore of Thessalonica, Adam of Perseigne (qv), and Joseph the Hymnographer (qv) were printed; those of St. John Chrysostom, St. John of Damascus (qqv), St. Andrew of Crete (qv), and St. George of Nicomedia (qv)

were not. Under generic titles, M. traced the history of devotion to Mary, ferreting out the details of over 2,200 clients of Our Lady.

Three compositions are in Bourassé's *Summa Aurea: Polyanthea Mariana; Familia Mariana;* and *Apostoli Marian.* The contents of the first, the best known, are alphabetically arranged titles or words of praise chosen for Mary by writers of all the ages.[2]

M. was limited by the critical deficiencies of his time. Specialists, nonetheless, regret the loss of his work on Mary and the priesthood, *Sacerdotium mysticum Marianum.* He was an ardent believer in the Immaculate Conception (*qv*), but was gravely hampered by opponents in the Curia, notably the Dominican Master of the Sacred Palace, Hyacintho Libello. M. was punished for works published on the subject anonymously, possibly without his consent, being obliged to remain in his community residence for weeks. He wrote then as copiously as ever. After the Bull, *Sollicitudo,* of Alexander VII (8 December, 1661), he enjoyed more liberty. The Pope may have been influenced by his writings. Among his friends was Luke Wadding, O.F.M., theologian to the Spanish royal delegation, seeking a papal definition of the Immaculate Conception.

---

[1]Cf. A. Guerra, *Il P. Ippolito Marracci, CC.RR. della Madre di Dio,* (Rome, 1889); G. M. Roschini, O.S.M., "Un grande precursore dell'Era mariana, il P. Ippolito Marracci, O.M.D.," in ASC, XI, 219-232; R. Laurentin, *Marie l'Église et le Sacerdoce,* I, (Paris, 1952), 332-335; F. Ferraironi, C.R.M.D., "Un grande innamorato di Maria SS., il P. Ippolito Marracci (sec. XVII), instancabile scrittore," in "*Vita Christiana*," 23(1954), 597-600; L. Zver, S.D.B., "Doctrina de Hippolito Marracci sobre o sacerdocio de Maria Santissima," in ME, VII, 81-91. [2]*Summa Aurea,* Vol. IX, letters A to M, cc. 858-1511; *op. cit.,* Vol. X, letters N-Z, cc. 10-594.

MARRIAGE, OUR LADY'S

Leo XIII expressed the Church's teaching on the marriage of Mary in these words: "The motives for which St. Joseph has been proclaimed Patron, especially of the Church, and for which the Church looks for singular benefit from his patronage and protection, are that Joseph was the spouse of Mary and that he was the putative father of Jesus Christ. From these relationships have sprung his dignity, his holiness, his glory. In truth, the dignity of the Mother of God is so lofty that no creature can rank above it. But as Joseph has been united to the Blessed Virgin by the ties of marriage, it may not be doubted that he approached nearer than anyone else to the eminent dignity by which the Mother of God surpasses all created natures. For marriage is the most intimate of all unions, which essentially imparts a community of gifts between those joined together by it."[1]

If some of the Fathers appear hesitant on the reality of Mary's marriage, it is because they wished to emphasize Mary's virginity at the moment of the Annunciation. There was no marriage, they thought, at that time. The idea of a true marriage persisted, nonetheless, and was given a theological basis by St. Augustine. "Every good of marriage was fulfilled in the parents of Christ: offspring, loyalty, and the sacrament. We recognize the offspring in Our Lord Jesus Christ himself; the loyalty, in that no adultery occurred; and the indissolubility, because of no divorce. Only conjugal intercourse did not take place."[2]

Despite opposition later by the twelfth century canonist, Gratian, who was opposed by Peter Lombard, this opinion prevailed. It was defended by St. Thomas Aquinas, who pointed to the twofold perfection due in marriage, present in this sublime instance: consent to the nuptial bond, "but not expressly to the bond of the flesh, save on condition that it was pleasing to God"; and the upbringing of the Child, even though procreation was not by carnal intercourse.

From the outset, the Fathers of the Church sought to discern reasons why Jesus was conceived and born of an "espoused" or married woman. Origen, developing a suggestion made by St. Ignatius of Antioch, thought that it was to conceal the virginal conception from Satan.[3] This view was accepted by, among others, St. Jerome (*qv*), who added three others—so that Mary's ancestry would be indicated by the genealogy of Jesus; lest she be stoned by the Jews as an adulteress; and that she should have the consolation of a husband when fleeing into Egypt.[4] St. Ambrose (*qv*) used a famous phrase: "The Lord permitted that some people should doubt his own origin rather than his Mother's honour."[5]

St. Bernard (*qv*) was at great pains to show the importance of Joseph as a witness to Mary's virginity. St. Thomas Aquinas gathered the reasons adduced for the marriage before him, added some of his own to make twelve in all, and ordered them under these heads: a) in view of the Incarnation; b) with regard to Christ and Mary; and c) with regard to ourselves. St. Joseph was, by his position, to veil the mystery of the Incarnation until the moment God thought fit to reveal it. The marriage saved Christ from charges by impious men that he was illegitimate; established his genealogy through his legal father, according to custom; concealed the virginal birth from Satan; and provided for his upbringing. Mary was saved from dishonour, was not exposed to stoning as an adulteress, and was given the help and protection of Joseph. For us, the virgin birth is confirmed, Mary's words given credence, the espousal of Christ and the Church is symbolized, and both virginity and matrimony are honoured with an example to both virgins and wives alike. St. Thomas added, in the final section, another motive: virgins, victims of ill-repute through carelessness, cannot appeal wrongly to the example of Mary.

[1]*Quamquam Pluries*, in OL, 107. On the marriage, cf. J. C. Didier, "Le mariage de la S. Vierge de la théologie," in *Mélanges de Science Religieuse*, 9(1952), 135-138; O. Graber, "Wollte Maria eine normale Ehe eingehen?," in MM, 20(1958), 1-9; F. Filas, S.J., "The Genuinity of Joseph's Marriage," in *The Man Nearest to Jesus*, (Boston, St. Paul editions, 1962), 103-133; B. Llamera, O.P., "Marriage of St. Joseph and the Blessed Virgin," in *St. Joseph*, (London, St. Louis, Herder, 1962), 17-49; M. O'Carroll, C.S.Sp., *Joseph, Son of David*, (Dublin, Gill, 1963), 61-68; F. G. Llamera, O.P., "El matrimonio de Maria y José," in EstJos, (1965); vol. 19, 37, 53-87; L. M. Herran, "El Matrimonio de San Jose y la Virgen anticipo de la Iglesia bodas del Cordero," in EstJos (1965), vol. 19, 37, 99-197; P. L. Suarez, C.M.F., "Matrimonio de Maria y José a la luz del antiguo Testamento," in EstJos, (1965), vol. 20, 38, 187-202; P. Guion, "El Matrimonio Judio," in EstJos, (1965), vol. 20, 40, 159-161; S. Bartina, S.J., "El Matrimonio y su esencia en el Rabinismo antiguo," in EstJos, (1965), vol. 20,40, 163-175; A. L. Iglesias, C.SS.R., "El Matrimonio y sus Ritos en el Judaismo a través de los tiempos," in EstJos, (1965), vol. 20, 40, 177-216; G. P. Diaz, "Legislaciones y Costumbres Orientales sobre el Matrimonio y su Proyección en el derecho matrimonial judío," in EstJos, (1965), 20, 40, 216-229; H. Frévin, "Le mariage de S. Joseph et de la sainte Vierge," in CahJos, 15(1967), 205-388. [2]*De nupt. et concup. XI, 13*, in PL 44, 421. [3]*Hom. in Luc. 6*, in PG 13, 1814. [4]*Comment. in Mt. 1, 2*, in PL 26, 23. [5]*De Inst. Virg. VI, 42*, in PL 16, 316.

MARTIN OF LEÓN (d. 1203) — See Supplement, p. 384.

MARY OF AGREDA (1602-1665)

A Poor Clare sister, M. was Abbess of her monastery from the age of twenty-five, with an interval of three years, until her death. She wrote *Mystical City of God, The Divine History and Life of the Virgin Mother of God*, which was published in 1670.[1] The work is in three parts: Part I, from the predestination of Mary to the Incarnation (books 1 and 2); Part II, from the Incarnation to the Ascension (books 3 to 6); and

Part III, from the Ascension to the coronation of Mary (books 7 and 8). The aim of the work was to give "new light to the world, joy to the Church, confidence to mortals." Throughout the work, by way of teaching and exhortation, M. reproduced the doctrine which she said the Queen of Heaven taught her. This doctrine comprises the Immaculate Conception, the Assumption (*qqv*), Mary's part in the Redemption, her universal mediation of graces, her queenship, and her role as mother and mistress of the Church. The author accepted the Franciscan doctrine of the Incarnation. Christ would have come if there had been no sin. He came as one capable of suffering because of sin. But in the divine plan, Mary was exempted from the results of the fall of our first parents. The life of Mary, as given in great detail by M., is in the manner of the Apocrypha (*qv*) with a great mass of added material, some of it extravagant. Extraordinary graces, visions, and manifold angelic presence accompany the phases of Mary's conception, infancy, espousal, and Annunciation.

Though not figuring in the works of theologians, as did the revelations of St. Bridget of Sweden (*qv*), M.'s composition was widely read through the eighteenth century. There have been 168 Spanish editions and many translations. The book met with many vicissitudes. In 1681, Innocent XI condemned it, but, at the request of the king of Spain, withdrew the condemnation three months later. It was later placed on the Index, in 1704, but again there was a cancellation of the censure at least for Spain. The Sorbonne objected to it because of the extravagant details added to the account of the Immaculate Conception. Bossuet and Eusebius Amort criticized it. But the Universities of Salamanca, Alcalá de Henares, Toulouse, and Louvain approved it, and, in 1929, the Congregation of Rites permitted reading of it.

[1]Spanish ed. by Santiago Ozcoidi y Udave, (Madrid, 1911, 1912); critical ed. by C. Solagauren, O.F.M., with A. M. Monux, O.F.M. and L. Villasante, O.F.M., (Madrid, 1970). Cf. J. Campos, "La Venerable Madre (Maria) Agreda y dos Obispos de Albarracin," in *Salmanticensis*, 14(1967), 581-606; A. Martinez Monux, O.F.M., "Maria, signo de la creación, receptora de los meritos de Cristo. La cooperación "Suarez, mariologo," in Est. Eccl., 22(1948), 311-337; id., *Posición de Suarez en la controversia conceptionista* in V.I., XI, 268-284; J. Riudor, "Influencia de San Bernardo en la Mariologia de Salmeron y Suarez" in EstMar, XIV, 329-352; J. A. De Aldama, S.J., *El sentido moderno de la Mariologia de Suarez* in *Actas del IV Cent. del naciemento de F.S.*, II (1950), 55-73; id., "Piété et système dans la Mariologie du "Docteur eximius", in *Maria*, II, 975-990; T. M.

mariana a la redención según la 'Mistica Ciudad de Dios'," in *Verdad y Vida*, (Madrid, 1958); *Verdad y Vida*, 26(1968), 135-178; H. Graef, *Mary*, II, 53-55.

MARY OF EGYPT, ST. (Seventh Century)

This is a story of miraculous repentance, of doubtful authenticity, first found in the *Life of Cyriacus* by Cyril of Scythopolis, printed by Migne in the works of Sophronius (BHG 1042).[1] M., an Egyptian who had lived a wicked life in Alexandria from her twelfth to seventeenth year, reached Jerusalem where, on the feast of the Exaltation of the Holy Cross, she sought to enter the Church of the Holy Sepulchre but was mysteriously impeded. She prayed to an image of Our Lady, was then able to enter, was converted by contact with the Cross, and lived a life of penance for forty-seven years thereafter. The prayer was Christological, though offered through Mary. Paul the Deacon, at the request of Charles the Bald, translated the story into Latin, at the time he did likewise for the Theophilus Legend. It was used in homiletics in the West to support exhortation to the faithful to pray to Our Lady.

[1]TU 49, 2; 23, 4-234, 19; PG 87c, 3697C-3726C; PL 73, 671-690. Cf. R. Laurentin, *Traité*, I, 168; *Acta Sanctorum*, (1 April, 1675), 67-90; H. Barré, *Prières Anciennes*, 60; H. Leclercq, O.S.B., in DACL, X, 2, 2128-2136; A. Bujila, *La vie de Ste. Marie l'Égyptienne*, (Ann Arbor, Michigan, 1949).

MASCALL, ERIC L. (1905-   ) — See Supplement, pp. 384-385.

MASS, THE, AND OUR LADY

The Mass as the perfect sacrifice derives its meaning and its efficacy from the sacrifice of the Cross, which it continues. We have had fresh illumination of this wonder in recent times by the theology of the Paschal Mystery of Christ, and by the renewal of the theology of the Resurrection as integral to that mystery. The liturgical movement, fully blessed and wisely directed by Vatican II, will bring us still further enlightenment as the experience of the Church deepens its understanding.

Mary's association with the Mass can be studied in the biblical context, especially of the Paschal event, through which she lived, which, as a faithful Jewess, she understood so fully. Here she is the privileged, the entirely authentic witness.

But the debates of former and more recent times, have not lost their relevance. Mary was, in some not easily defined way, a participant in the sacrifice of the Cross (see REDEMPTION, MARY'S PART IN, COMPASSION, SORROWS, SPIRITUAL MOTHERHOOD, MOTHER OF DIVINE GRACE, PRIESTHOOD). The priest who offered was her Son; the life he offered came, under the Spirit, from her. Her spiritual perfection attuned her to his act, as none else was ever so united with it; her motivation was universally redemptive as was his.

Since sacrifice implies priesthood, Mary's participation in Christ's priesthood is a matter to be clarified, if we are to understand her relationship with the Mass, of which he still remains the High Priest. Meanwhile, as with the Eucharist, we have a firm basis for this relationship in the principle so fully enunciated by the Popes and adopted by Vatican II. There is between Mother and Son an indissoluble bond (LG 53), no less so in the moment of the Mass.[1]

[1]Cf. R. Laurentin, *Our Lady and the Mass*, (Dublin, 1959).

MATTHEW, ST.

M. speaks of Mary in the infancy narrative[1] and in a brief passage later.

THE INFANCY NARRATIVE: (see also BIRTH OF JESUS, BROTHERS OF THE LORD, CHRONOLOGY, DOUBT OF JOSEPH, FATHERHOOD OF ST. JOSEPH, HOLY SPIRIT, JOSEPH, ST., MARRIAGE, VIRGINITY). St. Joseph dominates the Matthean infancy narrative, as Mary does that of Luke. Marian theology in its development has nonetheless drawn on M.'s infancy narrative for the themes above mentioned. A theology of St. Joseph leans still more heavily on these chapters. The debates of scholars on the sources used by M., on the historicity of the events narrated by him, are highly relevant to the virginity. When a factual core has been discerned within the cultural setting and the literary devices used by M., the virginal conception must be part of it, factual and historical also. Attempts to separate the historical elements from the cultural "clothing," such as that made by L. Peretto, justify this view. R. E. Brown's illustration of how, with modern methodology, a pre-Matthean text may be established, does not embody the account of the virginal conception. The omission is not justified, apart from the fact that such reconstructed texts, though stimulating for research, cannot constitute documentary evidence for the historian.

As well as through the Old Testament quotations, the Christology is conveyed in Old Testament ideas of Davidic and divine sonship; and underlying motifs, drawn from the patriarch Joseph and Moses, are discernible. On the obedience of Joseph, "son of David," to the angelic message, depended the transmission of the Davidic inheritance to Jesus. The name-giving (1:21,25), here attributed to Joseph, whereas in Lk 1:31 it is allowed to Mary, marks recognition of legal sonship. The words, "he did not know her until she had given birth to a son," do not mean that he knew her, in the marital sense, afterwards. St. Jerome dealt with this point in his reply to Helvidius. The verb used for "he 'took' her," *paralambanein* (1:24), is also used for Joseph's guidance of the Child and his mother (2:14,21). "Know," in 1:25, may have a spiritual sense.

The Public Life: (12:46-50). Jesus, being told that his mother and brethren were seeking him, replied: "Who is my mother and who are my brethren?" And stretching out his hand toward his disciples, he said: "Here are my mother and my brethren! For whoever does the will of my Father who is in heaven is my brother and sister and mother." St. John Chrysostom misinterpreted this text; he spoke of Mary's ambition and arrogance, as if she wished to show the people that she could order her Son.[2] His contemporaries in the West, St. Ambrose and St. Augustine, on the contrary, based their doctrine of spiritual fecundity on the words of Jesus. "Through the gospel," said St. Ambrose, "there are many fathers and many mothers who bring forth Christ. Who then will show me the parents of Christ? He himself did so when he said: 'Who is my mother, who are my brothers? He who does the will of my Father in heaven is my brother and sister and mother (Mt 12:48-50)'. Do the will of the Father that you may be a mother of Christ. Many have conceived Christ, but did not give birth to him."[3] This idea is, with Ambrose, linked with the Mary-Church typology.

St. Augustine made the typology explicit in the course of his commentary on the Matthean text. Showing how virgins especially reach a kind of maternal fulfillment in obeying the word of Christ, in doing the will of his Father, he urged all categories of the faithful to conceive Christ by faith and to express him in works, "so that what Mary's womb did in the flesh of Christ, your heart may do in the law of Christ. But how should you not belong to the offspring of the Virgin when you are the members of Christ.

Mary brought forth your Head; the Church, you yourselves. For she is also a mother and virgin, a mother in the sentiments of charity, a virgin in the integrity of faith and piety."[4] Elsewhere, quoting M.'s text, Augustine emphasized Mary's own fidelity: "Did not the Virgin Mary do the will of the Father, she who believed with faith, conceived with faith, was chosen as the one from whom salvation among men should be born, was created by Christ before Christ was created in her? Holy Mary did, she certainly did, the will of the Father; and therefore it is greater for Mary to have been the disciple of Christ than the Mother of Christ."[5]

In the passage on the Brothers of the Lord (13:53-55), M. records the question, not as Mark does, but, "Is not this the carpenter's son? Is not his mother called Mary? Are not his brethren James, and Joseph, and Simon, and Judas? And are not all his sisters with us?" In the Calvary narrative, M. speaks of "many women" looking on from afar. He singles out Mary Magdalene, Mary the mother of James and Joseph, and the mother of the sons of Zebedee, but anymore than Luke or Mark, he does not mention Mary, the mother of Jesus.

---

[1]Besides commentaries on St. Matthew and the bibliography to the article on *Infancy Narratives* in the present work, cf. P. Winter, "Jewish Folklore in the Matthaean Birth Story," in *Hibbert Journal,* 53(1954), 34-43; J. Racette, "L'Évangile de l'enfance selon S. Matthieu," in ScEccl, 9(1957), 77-82; S. Munoz Iglesias, "El genero literario del Evangelio de la Infancia en San Mateo," in EstBib, 17(1958), 243-273; M. M. Bourke, "The Literary Genius of Matthew I-II," in CBQ, 12(1960), 160-175; K. Stendhal, *Quis et Unde, An Analysis of Mt 1-2, Judentum, Urchristentum, Kirche* (Festschrift J. Jeremias), ed. by Eltester, (Berlin, Topelman, 1960), 94-105; H. Milton, "The Structure of the Prologue to St. Matthew's Gospel," in *Journal Bibl. Lit.,* 81(1962), 175-181; C. H. Cave, "St. Matthew's Infancy Narrative," in NTS, 9(1962-1963), 382-391; M. Kramer, "Die Menschwerdung Jesu Christi nach Matthaus (Mt 1)," in BB, 45(1964), 1-50; E. Krentz, "The Extent of Matthew's Prologue," in *Journal Bibl. Lit.,* 83(1964), 409-414; J. Ponthot, "L'Évangile de l'enfance selon S. Matthieu. Perspectives doctrinales de MT 1-2," in *Révue Diocésaine de Tournai,* 19(1964), 615-637; W. B. Tatum, *The Matthean Infancy Stories. Their Form, Structure and Relation to the Theology of the First Evangelist,* (Duke University, doctoral dissertation unpublished, 1966); L. Soubigou, "A Narracao da Epifania segundo Sao Mateus," in *Revista de Cultura Biblica,* 4(Sao Paolo, 1967), 104-110, 5(1968), 8-14; R. Balmori, "Anuncio a José y Misterio Pascal," in EstJos, 21(1967), 187-201; D. M. Crossan, "Structure and Theology of Mt 1:18-2:23," in CahJos, 16(1968), 119-135; G. Danieli, C.S.J., "Matteo 1-2 e l'intenzione di narrare i fatti accaduti,"

in *Riv. Bibl.*, 16(1968), 187-199; *id.*, "Le tradizioni di Mt 1-2 e loro origine," Part of dissertation before the Biblical Commission, ed. in *Divus Thomas*, (Piacenza, 1969); *id.*, "Storicità di Matteo I-II: Stato presente della discussione," in CahJos, 19(1971), 53-61; A. Paul, P.S.S., *L'Évangile de l'enfance selon Saint Matthieu*, (Paris, Cerf, 1968); E. Rasco, *Matthew I-II: Structure, Meaning, Reality, St. Evang. IV*, (TU 102; Berlin: Akademie, 1968), 214-230; B. Cardoso, "A forma literaria de Mateus I e II," in *Lumen*, 33(1969), 405-411; G. G. Gamba, S.D.B., "Adnotazioni in margine alla struttura letteraria ed al significato dottrinale di Matteo I-II," in *Bibbia e Oriente*, 11(1969), 5-24; 65-76, 109-124, also in 26th Spanish Biblical Week, *Consejo Superior de Investigaciones científicas*, (Madrid, 1969), II, 59-99; A. Ibanez Arana, "El Evangelio de la Infancia en Mt 1-2," in *Lumen (Vitoria)*, 18(1969), 3-25; E. Nellessen, *Das Kind und seine Mutter. Struktur und Verkündigung des 2 Kapitels im Matthäusevangelium*, (Stuttgart, Verlag Katholisches Bibelwerk, Stuttgarter Bibelstudien 39, 1969); *id., Die Verkündigung der Menschwerdung in Mt 2, in Jungfrauengeburt gestern und heute*, (Essen Verlag Hans Driewer, 1969), 185-204; E. L. M. Peretto, O.S.M. *Lettura esegetica del racconoto di Mt 1-2 (Appunti)*, (Rome, ed. Marianum, 1969); *ibid.*, "Ricerche su Mt 1-2," in MM, 31(1969), 140-247, separate issue, (Rome, ed. Marianum, 1970); A. A. Tavares, *Da mariologia a cristologia, Mt 1:25*, (Lisbon, Portuguese Catholic University, 1972); A. Vogtle, "Die matthäische Kindheitsgeschichte," in *L'Evangile selon Matthieu*, (Gembloux, J. Duclot), 153-183; L. Zani, "Influsso del genere letterario midrashico su Mt 2, 1-12," in *Studia Patavina*, 19(1972), 257-320; J. M. Germano, S.C.J., "Et non cognoscebat eam donec," in MM, 35(1973), 184-240; A. Salas, O.S.A., *La infancia de Jesus (Mt 1-2). Historia o teologia*, (Madrid, Biblia y fe, 1976); B. M. Nolan, *The Christology of Matthew I-II in its Gospel Setting*, (Fribourg, University, 1977); R. E. Brown, *The Birth of the Messiah*, (London, 1977), 45-232; Mary in NT, 73-103. ²*In Mt 44, 1-2*, in PG 57, 463-466. ³*In Lc 10, 25*, in CSEL 32, 4, 412; PL 15, 1810C. ⁴*Serm. 192, 2*, in PL 38, 1012-1013. ⁵"Serm. Denis, XXV, 7," ed. by G. Morin, in *Miscellanea Agnostiniana*, (Rome, 1930), I, 162.

MATTHEW CANTACUZENUS, EMPEROR
(d. 1356)

A Byzantine emperor who retired to a monastery before his death, M. is the author of a commentary on Song of Songs, in which the interpretation is predominantly Marian, though the spousal imagery is applied to the Church.[1] M. praised Mary's eminent purity. She is the only one among the miserable daughters of Adam who has received a message of faith by the voice of an angel.[2] She is the "tower of David, always protected against the attacks of the evil one, who has never been able to approach her."[3] "She comes from Lebanon, from God; since her origin is from him and she has been completely deified, she has escaped the demons."[4]

M. also points very briefly to Mary's role: ". . . the undefiled Theotokos had become the cause of universal salvation";[5] "she is the blessed workshop of the divine economy."[6] But her greatness is related to Christ, all her blessings come from her divine motherhood. Sin withdrew from her because the Sun of Justice made her his tabernacle; she is the vine that brought forth Christ, the Grape. She is enthroned above the seraphim, with the Creator in her arms.[7]

¹PG 152, 997-1084. Cf. M. Jugie, *L'Immaculée Conception*, 224. ²PG 152, 1016A. ³PG 152, 1036D. ⁴PG 152, 1040. ⁵PG 152, 1037D. ⁶PG 152, 1011. ⁷PG 152, 1077C.

MEDIATION, MARY MEDIATRESS
Sacred Scripture: The theology of mediation has been built on New Testament passages. In the light of this theology, mediators are retrospectively identified in the Old Testament, in moments of special divine power or illumination, as with the prophets. Angels also intervene between God and man. A mediator is, in religion, one who unites God and man. Christ is the perfect Mediator as the Son of God and true man. "For there is one God and there is one mediator [*mesites*] between God and men, the man Christ Jesus, who gave himself as a ransom for all, the testimony to which was borne at the proper time." (1 Tim 2:5). What then of Mary as Mediatress?[1] As will be abundantly clear from the historical evidence to be set forth later, the question arises from the life and practice of the Church.

The practice of addressing Mary as Mediatress was not and need not be impeded by the Pauline text. The use of "one" (*eis* not *monos*) emphasizes Christ's transcendence as a mediator, through the unique value of his redemptive death. The context is the salvation of the infidel, as the following verse makes clear: "God, our Saviour, desires all men to be saved and to come to the knowledge of the truth." This is a statement of the universality of salvation, not of Christ's relationship towards those who have already come to him. On this relationship, Paul gave the fullest doctrine found in the New Testament.[2] Existence "in Christ" is a transformation: "If anyone is in Christ, he is a new creation." (2 Cor 5:17). "For me to live is Christ, and to die is gain." (Phil 1:21); "it is no longer I who live, but Christ who lives in me" (Gal 2:20). "Christ is all and in all." (Col 3:11). The absolute character of Paul's affirmation of the unique Mediator is paralleled by Peter's words: "And there is salvation in no one else, for there is no other name under heaven given among men by which we must be saved." (Acts 4:12).

But these ideas must be seen in the full plan of salvation. Therein the initiative lies wholly with God, and this initiative is seen in the mission of the Son. Mediation is linked with mission, and depends on it.[3] Thus St. Paul tells us how the Mediator appeared: "But when the fullness of time had come, God sent forth his Son, born of a woman, born under the law, to redeem those who were under the law, so that we might receive the adoption of sons" (Gal 4:4). The two texts are closely linked by the idea of ransom, the verb *exagerazo* in Galatians and the noun *antilutron* in 1 Timothy. This time our role or status is described, "adoption as sons." A still closer union with Christ is offered us: "And because you are sons, the Spirit of God has sent his Son into our hearts crying, 'Abba! Father!'" (Gal 4:6).

To describe his own lifework, Paul frequently uses the word *apostolos*, radically the same as the word in Gal 4:4 (*exapostello*); he has been given a mission. Though the synoptics often speak of Christ as one sent (Mt 15:24; Mk 12:6-11; Lk 4:18; 9:48; 10:16), it is in John that the mission is explicitly related to the programme of our salvation. "For God sent his Son into the world, not to condemn the world, but that the world might be saved through him." (3:17). "My food is to do the will of him who sent me and to accomplish his work." (4:34; cp. 5:30, 6:38, 10:36; and 1 Jn 4:9-10). This mission Christ formally and explicitly shared with the apostles: "As the Father has sent me, even so I send you" (20:21, the words used are *apostello* and *pempo*). Of the Baptist, John says: "There was a man sent from God whose name was John." (1:6).

It is not only Christ's mission which is shared with men, but his very divine sonship (Jn 1:12), by which gift we are entitled to the name "sons of God" (1 Jn 3:1). The idea is in harmony with Gal 4:4. It is the basis of all our kinship with the incarnate Son of God, with participation in his life and functions, with due attention to his infinite majesty. Participation in his eternal relationship with the Father surpasses immeasurably any share in his temporal function as Mediator. That this should be shared intimately by the one through whom his mission as Saviour was effected, is a truth which was grasped early in Church history.

History: History will show that the truth is complex. The seeds were in the Eve-Mary analogy, though not all proponents of the view saw its implications. St. Irenaeus (*qv*) wrote: "Mary, espoused but yet a virgin, became by her obedience a cause of salvation for herself and the whole human race."[4] The same Irenaeus saw Christ's mediation as a work of obedience: "He was made Mediator of God and men, atoning on our behalf to the Father, against whom we had sinned, and by his obedience effacing our disobedience."[5] Here was an interesting convergence of ideas. By the fourth century, the Eve-Mary doctrine was being expressed thus: "Death *through* Eve, life *through* Mary."[6] The use of this preposition in all languages hereafter will always have some reference to a mediating role. Pseudo-Theodotus of Ancyra (d. *c.* 446) was elaborate: "Through you, the sorrows of Eve have ceased; through you, evils have perished. Error has departed through you; through you, affliction has been abolished, condemnation destroyed."[7]

This formulation needed a wider context than the Eve-Mary idea. The Council of Ephesus provided this context, and the doctor of Ephesus, Cyril, in "the greatest Marian sermon of antiquity," related Mary's mediation to her office as Mother of God, to her relationship with the most Holy Trinity. Cyril's authorship of the sermon has been fully vindicated by R. Caro, S.J.[8] "Hail Mary Theotokos, venerable treasure of the whole world, light unextinguished, crown of virginity, sceptre of orthodoxy, indestructible temple, which contains the uncontainable . . . it is through you that the Holy Trinity is glorified and adored, through you, the precious cross is venerated and adored throughout the whole world, through you that heaven is in gladness, that angels and archangels rejoice that demons are put to flight, through you that the tempter, the devil is cast down from heaven, through you that the fallen creature is raised up to heaven, through you that all creation, once imprisoned in idolatry, has reached knowledge of the truth, that the faithful obtain baptism and the oil of joy, churches have been founded in the whole world, that peoples are led to conversion." The reason is that, through Mary, the only Son of God shone as a light on those who are in darkness and the shadow of death, ". . . the prophets have foretold, the Apostles announce salvation to the nations, the dead are raised . . . ."[9]

Proclus of Constantinople spoke of Mary as "the only bridge between God and men." With Basil of Seleucia (qv), the word "Mediatress" itself appears, and significantly in the context of the Annunciation: "Hail full of grace [highly favoured]: set up as Mediatress [mesiteuousa] of God and men, so that the walls of enmity should be torn down, heavenly and earthly things come together as one."[10] It is in the Annunciation context too that Antipater of Bostra (qv) addressed Mary by the same title: "Hail you who acceptably intercedes as a Mediatress for mankind."[11] These words occur in a section of Antipater's homily considered authentic by R. Caro. The exact word used by St. Paul, in the feminine, was applied to Mary in the sixth century by Romanos the Singer. Mary is pictured speaking to Adam and Eve: "Restrain your tears. Take me as your Mediatress [mesitin] with the one who is born of me."[12] In the same century, a homily attributed to St. Anastasius of Antioch described Mary as "the ladder stretched towards heaven, the gate of paradise, the entry into incorruption, the union and harmony of men with God"[13]—a rhetorical expression of mediation.

The much disputed homily of Modestus of Jerusalem, which certainly is seventh century, contains a passage wherein the author attributes —in the manner of St. Cyril—universal benefits to the Dormition: "O most blessed Dormition of the most glorious Theotokos, [this formula is repeated in each sentence] through whom we have been mystically recreated and made the temple of the Holy Spirit . . . through which we have received forgiveness of all our sins and have been ransomed from the tyranny of the devil . . . through which the whole universe is renewed, earthly things have come together with heavenly, and in unison with them cry out in praise, 'Glory to God in the highest and peace to men of good will' . . . through which the same one is God on earth and made man, is in heaven unchangeably and without division by reason of mercy and the economy [of salvation] . . . through whom we have 'put on Christ' and been made worthy to be 'the sons of God'. (Gal 3:27; Jn 1:12)."[14] Note the Pauline doctrine of life in Christ, to which allusion has been made.

Not later than mid-seventh century, Theoteknos of Livias (qv) styled Mary, "ambassadress [presbis] of mankind with the immaculate king."

The Akathistos Hymn (qv) adopted, for liturgical use, the idea now current of Mary as one "through whom" certain spiritual effects were achieved. "Hail, through whom creation is renewed . . . . Hail, through whom and in whom the Creator is adored . . . . Hail, heavenly ladder, through whom God has descended . . . . Hail, bridge leading those on earth to heaven."

The eighth century eastern Fathers taught the doctrine of Mary's mediation in an explicit plenary manner. St. Andrew of Crete (qv) called her "Mediatress [mesitis] of the law and grace," saying also: "She is mediation [mesiteuei] between the sublimity of God and the abjection of the flesh, and becomes the Mother of her maker."[15] St. John of Damascus (qv) addressed Our Lady thus: "You also by fulfilling the office of Mediatress [mesiteusasa], and being made the ladder of God descending to us, that he should assume our weak nature, and join and unite it to him[16] . . . . You brought together what had been separated."

St. Germanus of Constantinople (qv) is the doctor of Mary's universal mediation. If the Oratio V in Annuntiationem SS. Deiparae, in which he called her "truly a good Mediatress [mesiteia] of all sinners," is of somewhat doubtful authenticity, there is no doubt about the second homily on the Dormition. "Man was made spiritual when you, O Theotokos, became the dwelling of the Holy Spirit. No one is filled with the knowledge of God save through you, O most holy one. No one is saved except through you, O Theotokos; no one is ransomed save through you, Mother of God [Theometros]; no one secured a gift of mercy save through you, who hold God; . . . you cannot fail to be heard, since God, as to everything, through everything, and in everything, behaves towards you as his true and unsullied Mother . . . in you all peoples of the earth have obtained a blessing, for there is no place where your name is not held in honour."[17]

Even with these words, we have not reached the summit of Byzantine Marian theology. In the tenth century, John the Geometer (qv) proclaimed Mary, "second mediatress after the first Mediator." But it was in the fourteenth century that the climax came. Nicephorus Callistus described Mary as an abyss of mercies, and mistress and mediatress of the world. For the Palamites, Mary's mediation is part of their total vision of the cosmic Christ, center and purpose of creation. Thus Gregory Palamas (*qv*) saw her "standing alone between God and the whole human race," making God the son of man, and men the sons of God; no divine gift can reach men or angels save through her. Nicholas Cabasilas (*qv*) also saw Mary as the intermediary (*meses*) between God and man, a moving cause and end of the Incarnation, cause of graces, and mediatress by her intercession.

With Theophanes of Nicaea, we reach the peak; he is unequalled in all literature as an exponent of Mary's universal mediation. "It cannot happen that anyone, of angels or of men, can come otherwise, in any way whatsoever, to participation in the divine gifts flowing from what has been divinely assumed, from the Son of God, save through his Mother." Theophanes used the metaphor of the neck, found in western medieval writing, to express Mary's place in the Mystical Body, "the only way leading to the Head of all." Mary, for him, is the "dispenser and distributor of all the wondrous uncreated gifts of the divine Spirit."[18]

The Latin Tradition: The first mention of the word "Mediatress" in the West occurred in the sixth-century Pseudo-Origen: *Vitae Mediatrix*.[19] It is next found in Paul the Deacon's (*qv*) translation of the Theophilus Legend. There is a solitary text in the tenth century from Geoffrey of Soissons (*c.* 950): "You, who are first before God, be a Mediatress for your own, bearing hope of forgiveness, lest they sink in the guilt of vices."[20] In the next century, Gottschalk of Limburg (*qv*) wrote in his sequence *Fecunda Verbo*: "Mediatress, Mother of the Mediator, in whom man is joined to God, God to man."[21] In a liturgical hymn for the Assumption of the same time, we read: "Our Mediatress, who art, after God, our only hope, present us to your Son, that, in the heavenly court, we may joyfully sing the Alleluia."[22]

A framework of thought was created which would contain the idea of Mary's mediation. Thus St. Peter Damian (*qv*) stated the principle: "As the Son of God has deigned to descend to us through you, so we also must come to him through you."[23] St. Anselm used the word "reconciler of the world," but he was clear that it was "through" Mary that "the elements are renewed, the lower world healed, the demons trodden under foot, men saved and angels restored." This is a comprehensive statement of Mary's mediation. Anselm's disciple, Hermann of Tournai (*qv*), first used the metaphor of the neck to describe Mary's role between the Head and the Mystical Body.

R. Laurentin has counted fifty texts in the twelfth century in which Mary is called Mediatress. Abelard (*qv*) is among the authors. So is St. Bernard, who struck an immortal summary of the doctrine: "God wills us to have everything through Mary."

St. Bonaventure (*qv*) used the title Mediatress —"between us and Christ, as Christ is between us and God," "Mediatress of all with God." St. Thomas Aquinas (*qv*) called Mary "Mediatress" in commenting on the Cana episode. His whole conception of her place in the scheme of things implies a mediatorial function. She took the place of all mankind in the moment of the Incarnation.

The word "*socia*" (see ASSOCIATE) appeared in the literature from about this time. It did not displace "Mediatress," which came almost spontaneously to Pseudo-Albert (*qv*), Richard of St. Laurent, James of Voragine (*qv*), and Engelbert of Admont (*qv*), and appealed too to the author of *The Ancrene Riwle*.[24] Thinking on the subject, most ardent with St. Bernardine of Siena, was not neglected by his namesake, Bernardine of Busti, John Gerson, and Denis the Carthusian (*qv*). From the thirteenth century, the word occurs occasionally in hymns.[25]

From the fifth through the fifteenth century, Fathers, Doctors, preachers, and hymn writers explained or assumed Mary's mediation without contradiction. It was the Easterns, using Paul's own language, who borrowed his word, *mesitis*, without stirring the slightest fear that the dignity of the one *Mesites* would be compromised. The word was not used in a strictly homogeneous sense. The contexts varied from age to age and culture to culture, though certain essential aspects are distinguishable: Mary's essential role in the work of salvation; and her ceaseless, heavenly activity on our behalf. There is, in each, much scope for reflection.

Instead of reflection, the sixteenth century brought rejection in wide areas. But the Counter-Reformation Doctors—Peter Canisius (*qv*), Robert Bellarmine (*qv*), Lawrence of Brindisi (*qv*), and Francis de Sales (*qv*)—continued the tradition, and clung to the title, with the exception of St. Francis, who preferred "treasurer of graces," "advocate," and "collaborator [*coopératrice*] in our salvation." Suarez penned a sober passage: "Thus, therefore, the Church and the Fathers speak to the Virgin whom also as we have already seen, they at times call reparatrix and mediatress, because she brought forth our Redeemer and with him has the greatest influence . . . . Which view is the sense of the Church and known to all."[26]

In the vast output on the subject from the seventeenth century to 1921, some items claim attention. The two most popular books on Our Lady through those centuries—St. Louis Marie de Montfort's work on *True Devotion*, and *The Glories of Mary* by St. Alphonsus Liguori—were composed on the theme of Mary's universal mediation. That would indicate the sentiment of the faithful, an important factor in the development of doctrine. Perhaps M. J. Scheeben may provide the complementary theological judgment: "Not only Mary's whole position as Mediatress, but also her preceding mediatorial functions are entirely designed for a universal mediation of grace, and condition the communication of all grace without exception."[27]

Teaching Authority: Our Lady's mediation has been a fundamental theme in the teaching of the modern Papacy from Pius IX's *Ineffabilis Deus* (*qv*) on. St Bernard's dictum, that God wills us to have everything through Mary, is found in the writings of Pius IX, Leo XIII (*qv*), St. Pius X, Pius XII, and John XXIII (*qqv*).[28] The word "Mediatress" is applied to Mary by each of the six Popes from Pius IX to Pius XII—more than once by each of the last five of these, eight times by Pius XII.[29] Paul VI solemnly promulgated it, as it is included in *Lumen Gentium*. In *Signum Magnum*, he changed the Council wording to make it stronger. "She makes herself their Advocate, Auxiliatrix, Aid-giver, and Mediatress." The Popes deal with different aspects of Mary's mediation, and some of the pronouncements do not present an analysis in depth.

A new phase was opened in 1921 by the initiative of Cardinal Mercier (*qv*). He sought and obtained Roman approval for a Mass and Office of Mary, Mediatress of all Graces, and urged his fellow bishops throughout the world to request them for their dioceses; 450 sent favourable replies. Thereon, Pius XI set up three commissions—Belgian, Spanish, and Roman—to study the possibility of a dogma on Mary's universal mediation. Members of the Belgian commission were: J. Bittremieux, author of a treatise on the subject; J. Lebon, a patrologist and writer on Marian theology; and C. Van Crombrugghe. The Spaniards were: J. M. Bover, S.J.; Canon D. I. (later Cardinal) Goma y Tomás: and A. Ruibal — all writers on the subject. The membership of the Roman commission was not published. A committee, appointed by Pius XI to advise on a possible recall of Vatican I, included Mary's mediation, as well as her Assumption, on a suitable programme.[30] In 1950, the first International Mariological Congress, held in Rome, approved this *votum*, which was submitted to Pius XII: "Since the principal, personal attributes of the Blessed Virgin Mary have been already defined, it is the wish of the faithful that it should also be dogmatically defined that the Blessed Virgin Mary was intimately associated with Christ the Saviour in effecting human salvation, and, accordingly, she is a true collaborator in the work of redemption, spiritual Mother of all men, intercessor and dispenser of graces, in a word universal Mediatress of God and men."[31]

Vatican II: Between 1950 and the announcement of Vatican II by Pope John in 1959, theological interest was centered first on Mary's part in the Redemption, and then on her relationship with the Church. The two themes met in competition at the Lourdes Congress. Yet in the pre-Council consultation of the world's episcopate, 382 bishops asked that Mary's mediation be defined. The first Marian *schema* referred in one section to Mary as "the minister and dispenser of heavenly graces," because she was the noble associate of the suffering Christ in acquiring them. In another section, added after the meeting of the Theological Commission in March, 1962, the wording was firmer and fuller. "Since, therefore, the humble 'Handmaid of the Lord,' for whom 'He that is mighty has done great things' (cf. Lk 1:49), is called Mediatress of all Graces, because she was associated with Christ in acquiring them, and since she is invoked by the Church as our Advocate and as the Mother of mercy, for she always remains the associate of Christ glorious in heaven, she intercedes for all through Christ, in such wise that the maternal charity of the Blessed Virgin is present in the bestowal [*conferendis*] of all graces to men . . . ."

The previous passage had explained Mary's mediation very fully, showing that Christ's unique mediation was not in any way compromised, for, despite the uniquely close bond between Mary and him, and the uniqueness of her share in the Redemption, "in her predestination, holiness, and every gift, she depends on Christ and is wholly beneath him." To the passage quoted above, there is also an addition to state that Christ's mediation is neither obscured nor lessened, but extolled and honoured by Mary's role, which is assigned by divine good pleasure and bounty. It does not spring from any necessity.[32] The notes to the *schema* reveal the problems which Mary's universal mediation raise: Old Testament graces; direct and indirect intervention by her; and Sacramental grace. The phrase, "the maternal charity," was chosen to allow freedom of discussion.

After the *schema* had lapsed in 1963, sharper, more exacting attention was inevitably given to the title and idea of mediatress, for the indirect influence of the non-Catholic Observers was now at its peak. The analysis of opinions, forwarded on the first *schema* to Rome by some 235 Fathers, showed that, already at that stage, the subject was one to stir lively comment. Those drafting the new *schema* would take note of this material and of the different draft-texts submitted. The Spanish hierarchy used the words "Mediatress of all graces" for which they claimed the support of the Popes, the Liturgy, and the sentiment of the faithful (*qv*). Fr. E. Dhanis, S.J., spoke of Mary as a "universal [*generalem*] Mediatress in dispensing the graces of the Saviour." The Chilean bishops, Mgr. Philips, Dom (now Bishop) Butler, O.S.B., and R. Laurentin did not use the title, though the first three applied the abstract word "mediation" to Mary's lifework. The Chileans spoke of "maternal mediation," and Mgr. Philips of "noble [*generosa*] mediation in the order of grace." At a meeting of experts held in Rome on 25 November, 1963, the problem of mediation, as understood by the Easterns, was raised with diverging views. The two experts, responsible for a new text, Fr. K. Balic, O.F.M. (*qv*) and Mgr. Philips, aided by friends, worked through five successive drafts, submitting the fifth to the higher commission on 14 March, 1964, and in revised form on 4 June.

This agreed text referred to Mary's "cooperation and mediation in the order of grace," which, it said, "continues ceaselessly." The phrasing was not considered adequate by the commission,

and an important passage was added. The statement, on Mary's part in the Redemption, was amplified in scope. These words were added: "Wherefore the Blessed Virgin Mary has been customarily adorned [*condecorari consuevit*] in the Church with the title of Mediatress as well as with others." A sentence then followed which gave more significance to this apparently factual, almost superficial, assertion: "The Church does not hesitate to profess such an office of Mary, she constantly experiences it, and commends it to the hearts of the faithful that, relying on this maternal help, they may adhere more closely to the Mediator and Saviour." Though the Pauline text from 1 Timothy was already quoted, and its idea repeated, though Mary's maternal office was related to it, still another restrictive clause was deemed necessary to safeguard the dignity and efficacy of Christ the one Mediator. This repetitiveness of an idea, universally accepted, was to remain, to disfigure textual draftsmanship to the end. Even the notes, supplied with the draft text, restated the idea, while listing some quotations with the word "Mediatress," or its equivalent, from the eastern Fathers of the Church.

Archbishop (now Cardinal) Roy presented the document to the Council on 16 September. Mary's cooperation in universal salvation, he said, was treated in the section on the Blessed Virgin and the Church. "In that context along with other titles, the designation Mediatress is quoted, something not acceptable to several [*pluribus*] members of the commission; it is explained in such wise that the excellence of the unique Mediator is in no way impaired thereby."[33]

Of the thirty-three Fathers who spoke in the *aula*, a number dealt with mediation;[34] a proportionately high number of the fifty-seven written submissions did so.[35] In the *aula*, three Fathers—Cardinals Bea, Leger, and Alfrink—urged the elimination of the title "Mediatress" from the *schema*. The Dutch Cardinal spoke on the last day on behalf of 129 Fathers. Cardinal Leger based his argument on the Pauline text; Cardinal Alfrink wished to emphasize the seriousness of committing the Church to a doctrine, especially a title of Mary, which he thought potentially difficult and divisive. Cardinal Bea, known as president of the Secretariat for Christian Unity, a biblical scholar and adviser of Popes, had, at the 1950 Rome Congress (see CONGRESSES), outlined the theological argument for Mary's mediation of all graces.[36] Now he spoke lengthily to explain why, in asking for the elimination of the title, he was not denying the doctrine which, as taught by the Popes since Leo XIII, he fully accepted. He thought that it was not sufficiently clarified for a conciliar pronouncement, and feared difficulties between Catholics and the separated brethren.

Cardinal Ruffini, Bishop Rendeiro, O.P., Archbishop van Lierde, and Bishop Gasbarri defended the retention of the title, appealing to theological and pastoral reasons. Bishop Rendeiro was supported by more than ninety-eight other Fathers. Bishop Cambiaghi called for fuller, clearer affirmation of Mary's universal mediation. The thesis, as it stood or with additions, would be accepted by others. Thus Archbishop Djajasepoetra, supported by twenty-four others, found the title unhappy, but would be satisfied if it were not exalted—which could be done by setting beside it other titles (Advocate, Helper, and Mother of mercy). Cardinal Silva Henriquez, spokesman for forty-three Fathers, found the phrasing about Mary's mediation sober—more would be inopportune.

One speaker, Cardinal Wyszynski, representing the seventy Polish bishops, referred to Mary as Mediatress of all graces as to an accepted doctrine. Those who did not express any view are assumed to have had no objection.

In the written submissions, some fifteen urged retention of the word "Mediatress," some asking for stronger phrasing, one for other accompanying titles. One of the six statements, which asked that it be dropped, was signed by fifty-six Fathers, another by Bishop (now Cardinal) Willebrands, and another by the Dutch bishops. The eastern Fathers had not made a mark in the public debate, so one submission from Bishop Malanczuk of Syria would have been welcome.[37] He aimed at presenting the oriental doctrine on the subject of Mary's mediation. Though he thought that "the eastern tradition, both ancient and more recent, was, on the whole, silent on Mary's cooperation in the acquisition of graces," he emphasized teaching on her mediation, distributing grace, "not as Christ, but under him, in him, and through him," totally dependent on his mediation. Mary's mediation transcended that of all

others, and, while the inner reality awaited investigation, it was, he thought, a dogma that she participated in the Redemption through her motherhood, and seemed certain that, as Mother of those to be saved, she cooperated in the distribution of grace. Fr. A. Wenger, A.A., the Byzantine scholar, sent a memorandum to the commission, drawing attention to the importance, for the Easterns, of Mary's mediation, but was told by a commission member to practice moderation![38]

The amended text,[39] distributed on 27 October, had the words: "Wherefore the Blessed Virgin is *invoked* [for is *adorned*] in the Church by the titles of Advocate, Helper, Aid-giver, Mediatress." A passage was added to explain this cooperation of Mary in the order of salvation, on the priesthood and divine goodness, used here analogically. The notes indicated the state of opinion within the Council: (i) 191 Fathers asked that the statement on Mary as Mediatress be retained or strengthened. Two others wanted mediation to be of all graces. One sought a definition, another the title dispenser of graces; (ii) 196 wished the title "Mediatress" to be removed; (iii) some forty asked that the title be maintained, but with Advocate, Helper, and Aid-giver added.

Almost unanimously the commission, which was not entering "problems debated by theologians," chose the third solution, as most likely to win a majority. They said that Pius XII never used the word "Mediatress" (he did so eight times); and they thought that, as the "title was declared at the same time as other non-controversial ones," they were attuned to Eastern usage. "They do not construct a theological system," a poor tribute to Theophanes of Nicaea.

With the favourable vote of 29 October, a number of textual amendments (the *Modi* permitted) were submitted. The central sentence was still the prime object of interest: (i) 132 Fathers wanted "by" the Church rather than "in" it, and 121 of these sought to elevate Mediatress above the other titles, adding also after this "deservedly" or "rightly and devoutly." These Fathers would add further Marian privileges; (ii) fifteen, though in agreement, wanted a rephrasing which would appease ecumenical disquiet; (iii) sixty-one still asked for deletion—eight would accept *sequestra*. The commission thought the best hope now was to make no change. Vatican II had not defined, nor unequivocally declared, that the Blessed Virgin Mary is the Mediatress of all graces. Theologians retain the freedom granted them by LG 54. Was the Church thwarted in a great hope by the Council? History will tell.

¹For bibliography, cf. G. M. Roschini, O.S.M., *Maria Santissima*, II, 235-252. Cf. M. J. Scheeben, *Mariology*, II, (English tr., St. Louis, 1956), 238-273; J. B. Terrien, *La Mère des Hommes*, (Paris, 1902), I, 533-606; C. Godts, C.SS.R., *De definibilitate Mediationis universalis Deiparae*, (Brussels, 1904); J. Bittremieux, *De mediatione universali B. M. Virginis, quoad gratias*, (Bruges 1926); C. Friethoff, O.P., *De alma Socia Christi Mediatoris*, (Rome, 1936); J. Lebon, "Comment je conçois, j'établis et je défends la doctrine de la médiation mariale," in ETL, 16(1939), 655-744; *id.*, "Sur la doctrine de la médiation mariale," in *Angelicum*, (1958), 3-35; *id.*, "À propos des textes liturgiques de la fêtes de Marie Médiatrice," in MM, 14(1952), 122-128; Serapio de Iragui, O.F.M.Cap., *La Mediación de la Virgen en la himnografia latina de la Edad Media* (Buenos Aires, 1939); *id.*, "La mediación de la Virgen en la Liturgia," in ASC, II, 193-233; E. Druwe, S.J., "La médiation universelle de Marie," in *Maria*, I, (1949), 417-572; J. M. Bover, S.J., *Mediazione di Maria*, (Florence, 1956); G. Giamberardini, O.F.M., *La mediazione di Maria nella Chiesa Egiziana*, (Cairo, 1952); W. Sebastian, O.F.M., *De B. V. Maria universali gratiarum mediatrice, Doctrina Franciscanorum ab an. 1600 ad an. 1730*, (Rome, 1952); Th. Koehler, S.M., "La foi du XIe siècle en la Médiation de Marie," in *Nouvelle Rev. Mar.*, 6(1955), 144-163; J. Bur, *Médiation Mariale*, (Paris, 1955); *id.*, in *Maria*, VI, 471-512; *id.*, in *Divinitas*, 12(1968), 725-752; A. Louis, "Maria omnium gratiarum mediatrix," in EphMar, 12(1962), 423-494; H. M. Koester, S.A.C., "Maria-Mittlerin aller Gnaden," in *Marianisches Jahrbuch*, 1(1963), 49-80; *ibid.*, *Die Mittlerschaft Mariens*, (Leutesdorf am Rhein, 1967); T. Gallus, "Zur Frage der Mitwirkung Marias am Erlösungswerk," in *Österreich. Klerusblatt.*, (1968), 232-233; *id.*, *Jungfraumutter "Miterlöserin,"* (Regensburg, 1969); M. O'Carroll, C.S.Sp., "Vatican II and Our Lady's Mediation," in ITQ, 37(1970), 24-55; G. M. Roschini, O.S.M., *La mediazione mariana oggi*, (Rome, 1971). Cf. esp. EphMar, (1974), fascicules (i)-(iv), and (1976), fascicules (ii)-(iii) for inter-faith series of articles on Mediation of Mary based on *La Médiation de Marie et la doctrine de la participation* by Pastor H. Chavannes, in EphMar, 24(1974), 29-38. ²Cf. L. Cerfaux, *The Christian in the Theology of St. Paul*, (London, 1967), 312ff. ³Cf. I. Ortiz de Urbina, S.J., in MO, 145ff; J. MacPolin, S.J., in ITQ, 36(1969), 113-122. ⁴*Adv. Haer. III, 22, 4*, in PG 7, 959; SC 34 (M. Sagnard, O.P.), 380. ⁵*Adv. Haer. V, 16*, in PG 7, 1168. ⁶St. Jerome, *Epist. 22, 21*, in PL 22, 408, and others quoted n. LG 56. ⁷PO 19, 331, ed. by M. Jugie, A.A. On authenticity, cf. CMP, IV, 1, 107; R. Caro, S.J., *La Homiletica*, I, 189-194. ⁸*Hom. IV Ephesi in Nestorium habita...*, in PG 77, 992BC; ACO, 1, 1, 8, 104. Cf. R. Caro S.J., *La Homiletica*, II, 269-283. ⁹*Hom. in Deiparam*, in PG 65, 681. ¹⁰*In SS. Deiparae Ann.*, in PG 85, 444AB. On authenticity, cf. R. Laurentin, *Traité*, I, 167; R. Caro, S.J., *La Homiletica*, II, 288-308. ¹¹*In S. Joannem Bapt...*, in PG 85, 1772C. ¹² *Hymn for the Nativity*, in SC 110, 103. ¹³*Serm. II in Annunt. S. Mariae*, in PG 89, 1389. For authenticity, cf. R. Laurentin, *Traité*, I, 169. ¹⁴*In Dorm. SS. Deiparae...*, in PG 86bis, 3293. For authenticity, cf. R. Laurentin, *Traité*, I, 168; A. Wenger, A.A., *L'Assomption*, 103-104. ¹⁵*In Nativ. Mariae, Serm. I* and *Serm. IV*, in PG 97, 808, 865. ¹⁶*Hom. I in Dorm.*, in PG 96, 713A. ¹⁷PG 98, 321, 352-353. ¹⁸*Serm. in SS. Deiparam, 4, 55; 15, 205.* ¹⁹*Hom. in Mt 12:38*, in *Florilegium Cassinense*, II, 154B. ²⁰On *Mediatrix* in Latin authors, cf. H. Barré, C.S.Sp., in BSFEM, 96ff; R. Laurentin, *Traité*, V, 68, n.53, while awaiting the latter's monumental monograph on the subject. ²¹G. M. Dreves. *Hymnolog. Beitr.*, 2, (Leipzig, 1897), 170. ²²E. Druwé, S.J., "La médiation universelle de Marie," in *Maria*, I, (1949), 430. ²³*Serm. 46*, in PL 144, 761B. ²⁴*The Ancrene Riwle*, tr. by M. B. Salu, (London, 1955), 17. ²⁵Cf. Serapio de Iragui, O.F.M.Cap., *La Mediación de la Virgen en la himnografia latina de la Edad Media*, (Buenos Aires, 1939), esp. 182-216; F. J. Mone, *Lateinische Hymnen des Mittelalters*, 2, (Freiburg im Breisgau, 1854), 21, 48, 57, 67, 306; AH 42, 79, 107, 112. ²⁶Fr. Suarez, "De Mysteriis Vitae Christi," *Disp. 22, 3, 2*, ed. by Vivès, vol. 19, 328. Cf. *Disp. 23, 3, 5*, 336. ²⁷M. J. Scheeben, *Mariology*, II, (St. Louis, 1956), 265. ²⁸OL, 57, 132, 185, 241; *Acta Mariana Joannis PP. XXIII*, 29. ²⁹OL, 81, 132, 148, 172, 184, 191, 196, 209, 223, 254, 265, 276, 285, 295, 360-361, 422, 427. ³⁰Cf. G. Caprile, S.J., "Pio XI e la ripresa del Concilio Vaticano," in *Civiltà Catt.*, (1966), 27-39. ³¹ASC, I, 234. ³²Quotations from section 3, *Schema Constitutionis dogmaticae de B. M. V. Matre Ecclesiae*, (Vatican Press, 1963). ³³For text of report, cf. G. M. Besutti, O.S.M., in MM, 28(1966), 32. ³⁴Speeches in *Acta synodalia sacrosancti Concilii Oecumenici Vaticani II*, Vol. III, *Periodus* IIIa, Pars I, 435-544. Cf. G. M. Besutti, O.S.M., in MM, 28(1966), 35-117. ³⁵*Acta synodalia...*, Vol. III, *Periodus* IIIa, Pars 2, 99-188. ³⁶ASC, VI, 1, 31. ³⁷*Acta synodalia...*, Vol. III, *Periodus* IIIa, Pars 2, 139-141. ³⁸BSFEM, 23(1966), 51-52. ³⁹For text of 27 October with notes and report, cf. G. M. Besutti, O.S.M., in MM, 28(1966), 124-138; *Modi*, (Vatican Press, 1964), 16-17.

MERCIER, DÉSIRÉ JOSEPH, CARDINAL (1851-1926)

M., at the peak of his fame as a great educator, pioneer in the synthesis between Thomistic philosophy and modern disciplines and research, a patriotic hero, was inspired by Blessed (now St.) Louis Marie de Montfort's book on *True Devotion* to launch a whole movement for liturgical and dogmatic recognition of Mary's universal mediation.¹ In the Brussels Marian congress of 1921 sponsored by M., the doctrinal section dealt with mediation. At his request, on 12 January that year, the Sacred Congregation of Rites approved for the dioceses of Belgium and others which would request it, a Mass and Office in honour of Mary, Mediatress of all graces. M. received 450 favourable replies, only three unfavourable, to his letter to bishops throughout the world asking cooperation in the use of the Mass and Office. Mgr. J. Lebon has described how the formulas, prepared by him and submitted by the Cardinal to Rome, were altered and diluted. M. published a Pastoral in 1925 expounding the doctrine of mediation and the spirituality of St. Louis Marie. When Pius XI established a Belgian commission, composed of Fr. (later Mgr.) Lebon, Fr. Merkelbach, O.P., and Mgr. Crombrugghe, to investigate and report on the definability of Mary's universal mediation, M. became involved in its work, and secured the help of others—Fr. F. X. Godts, C.SS.R., Fr. Bittremieux (author of the first important modern work on mediation), and Dom Columba Marmion (qv). Belgium was first influenced as were other countries later, by the Cardinal's initiatives. They have particular moment in the light of his pioneering work for Christian unity in the Malines Conversations.

¹D. J. Cardinal Mercier, *La Vierge Marie, pages choisies*, ed. by A. Demoulin, (Liège, 1947). Cf. R. Laurentin, "Intuitions du Cardinal Mercier," in VieSp, 84(1951), 518-522; J. Lebon, 'A propos des textes liturgiques de la fête de Marie Médiatrice," in MM, 14(1952), 122-128; L. de Bivort de la Saudée, *Anglicans et Catholiques*, 2 vols., (Brussels, 1949).

MERIT, OUR LADY'S

Merit is a title to reward, dependent, in the Christian life, on three things—freedom, divine grace, and charity. Christ promised rewards frequently, all of them summed up in eternal life, entry in bliss to the eschatological future. St. Paul insisted on personal reward. Since Our Lady enjoyed personal freedom, was in grace with God, and animated by charity, she truly merited. As to what way, in regard to what divine gifts, in what degree, for whose benefit, are all questions discussed by theologians.¹ Many times the Fathers and medieval writers used the word "to merit" (*mereor*) loosely, with the meaning 'to have the good fortune." But from medieval times, certainly in the writings of St. Albert the Great and St. Thomas Aquinas, it was held that, in some way, Mary merited her divine maternity.

In the seventeenth century, Suarez (qv), by using the distinction of *de condigno*, or in strict justice, and *de congruo*, due to a certain suitability, prepared the way for the theological axiom: "The Blessed Virgin merited for us *de congruo* what Christ merited *de condigno* " This

makes the merit of Mary, in the plan of Redemption, coextensive with that of Christ, though clearly subordinate to it.

The Christian economy is based on transfer of merit. The life of grace originates and grows through our solidarity with Christ, the author of grace. We are saved through the application to us in Christ's merits. Can we, with due proportion, say the same of Mary's merits? St. Pius X's answer to this question has been debated, despite its clarity. "But since she surpassed all in holiness and union with Christ, and has been associated (*ascita*) with Christ in the work of Redemption, she, as the expression is, merits *de congruo* what Christ merits *de condigno*, and is the principal minister in the distribution of grace."²

The degree of Mary's merit depended on the grace she received from God. Theologians have at certain times discussed this spiritual eminence of Mary, comparing the grace she received in the first moment of her sanctification with that of the saints, even with that of all the angels and saints in their final perfection (see SUAREZ; FULL OF GRACE). If it be assumed, as it can be, that she belonged to the hypostatic order physically, directly and immediately, then since God's grace is proportionate to vocation and dignity, she at any moment surpassed all other creatures in this regard, for she existed by right in the world superior to all others. It does not necessarily follow that her merit was *de condigno*, a thesis defended at the *Alma Socia Christi* 1950 Congress by a Spanish Mariologist, M. Llamera, O.P. with what he considered the necessary safeguards for the uniqueness of Christ's meritorious action and with tireless verve and dialectical skill.

Mary ceased to merit after her entry into glory. Henceforth, her acquired merit would give substance to her mediation (qv), her intercession (qv), her diverse, countless interventions in human life, personal and collective.

¹Cf. Cl. Dillenschneider, C.SS.R., *Marie dans l'économie de la création rénovée*, (Paris, Alsatia, 1957), 152-159; R. Laurentin, *Traité*, V, 120-121. ²"Ad diem illum," in OL, 173.

MIECHOW, JUSTIN, O.P. (1590-1649)
The most famous Polish Marian theologian, M.'s principal work is *Discursus praedicabiles super litanias lauretanas Beatissimae Virginis Mariae*, Lyons 1660, and reprinted in Naples,

1856, with the addition of *Regina sine labe originali concepta*.[1] His intention was to pay a debt to Mary for saving his life many times. Each of the *discursus*, on separate titles in the Litany, is really a short treatise on some truth about Our Lady. As a Dominican, he opposed the Immaculate Conception (*qv*), but admitted that the Christian people, the academies, and all religious orders, save his own, supported it. He contended that Mary's initial grace was probably greater than that of all others in the final moment. In the work of Redemption, Christ acted as first cause, Mary as second. Christ's sufficiency must be safeguarded. He it is who wills that none should reach him, save through the consent of Mary and with her help. Her place in the supernatural scheme is expressed by M. by the ancient metaphor of the neck. All prayers should ascend to Christ through Mary.

---

[1]Cl. Dillenschneider, C.SS.R., *La Mariologie de St. Alphonse de Liguori*, I, (Fribourg, 1931), 218-220; J. Wolniak, *De morte et assumptione corporali B. M. V. juxta doctrinam Justini Miechoviensis, O.P.*, (Vatican City, 1955); P. Szelfler, *Mariologia P. Justini Miechoviensis, O.P.*, (Rome, Gregorian University, 1961); J. Szewczyk, *L'Immaculée Conception selon l'enseignement de Justin Zapartowicz de Miechow*, Doctoral Dissertation, (Lyons, Calauire et Cuire, Abbaye de la Rochette, 1968).

MIGNE, J. P. (1800-1875)

The article on the Fathers of the Church in the present work shows the importance of first-hand materials in this section. M.'s *Patrologia Latina* and *Patrologia Graeca* were for a long time the only available editions. With the increase in critical editions, Migne has been supplanted, but, for many authors, remains indispensable. Besides SPL, it is necessary to consult the working aids which indicate authenticity, especially for the Marian patristic and medieval texts.[1]

---

[1]*Clavis Patrum Latinorum* and *Clavis Patrum Graecorum*. Cf. P. Glorieux, *Pour revaloriser Migne, Tables rectificatives*, (Lille, 1952). Cf. esp. R. Laurentin, "Table rectificative des pièces mariales inauthentiques ou discutées contenues dans les deux Patrologies de Migne," in *Traité*, I, 119-173.

MILO OF ST. AMAND (d. *c.* 871)

A Latin poet in the region of modern Belgium or nothern France, M. set down Marian themes in some fifty verses inset in his long poem *De Sobrietate*.[1] He addressed Mary as "praise of the world, glory of heaven," through whom "grace has been spread into the whole world." She has opened the gates of paradise which Eve (*qv*) had closed. M. used the metaphor of the fruit, and applied it to Christ hanging on the tree of the Cross, concluding, "you lead your adopted sons to the heights of heaven."[2] A remarkable verse puts Mary's intercessory, even mediatorial role (using for the first time the title adopted by Vatican II, *Auxiliatrix*): "I ask, beseech you, O ornament of high virginity, to be my protectress, mistress, helper. Your life, whose donor was born of you, is virtuous. May your holy prayer keep this our companion."[3]

---

[1]Poet. Lat., 3," in MGH, 645-647. Cf. Scheffczyk, *Das Mariengeheimnis*, 383-386. [2]MGH, 645-646. [3]MGH, 646-647.

MIRACLES

The theology of miracles has been reviewed in recent times. The elements of the traditional definition have not been substantially altered in the literature dealing with so many aspects of the problem—replying to denials by atheists or agnostics of the possibility of any such thing as a miracle; attempting to solve the epistemological problems which arise, or to establish the relation between nature and the supernatural; or allowing for modern advances in Medicine, Psycho-pathology, Psychiatry, and Para-psychology.[1] The event considered must be perceptible to the senses "within the horizon of human experience," as Fr. K. Rahner puts it. It must be inexplicable, save as the result of direct divine intervention, showing what Archbishop Trench called "extraordinary divine causality"; it must be a sign of the supernatural. Men look for miracles from God and, in this domain, example is potent; one reported miracle sets off a chain of urgent prayer. History abundantly shows that the prayer is offered with special confidence at holy places. This local factor presents its own problem and its challenge to modern science, calling for a scientific attitude that is not determined by prior assumptions of any kind.

Church authorities may intervene when the effects of an alleged miracle are felt in the community of the faithful. The criteria for miracles of healing, proposed by Benedict XIV (d.1758), were summarized in the digest of his work on the procedure for Beatification and Canonization made by Fr. Azevedo (book IV, pt. 1, ch. 8). The disease must be grave, incurable, or very difficult to cure; it must not be at a stage where a cure is naturally to be expected. Medical treatment capable of healing must not have been used; the cure must be at least morally instantaneous. It must be complete; it must not be preceded by a notable change attributable to a known cause. The disease must not return. A warning is given about the possible effects of the imagination, of a kind that could be easily adapted to modern psychological research.

In 1958, on the occasion of the Lourdes (*qv*) centenary, Dr. P. Miest described the fifty-four cures which had taken place through invocation of Our Lady of Lourdes, and had been subsequently recognized as miraculous. The procedure is exemplary. First, the Lourdes Medical Bureau examines the case, demanding full documentation; it repeats the examination after an interval. If they are satisfied, they refer the matter to an international jury of medical specialists and theologians in Paris. If this body certifies a miracle, a report is sent by the bishop of Lourdes to the bishop of the diocese where the person cured resides. It is for him, after the necessary consultation, to publish the fact. Any doctor, irrespective of religion, race or nationality, may serve on the Lourdes Medical Bureau. In 1954, 1,541 doctors from twenty-two nations took part in its sessions. The fifty-four miracles were those found utterly certain. Canon M. G. Bertin reckoned that there may have been more than 3,900 probable miracles.

[1]Cf. *Benedicti Papae XIV doctrina de Servorum Dei Beatificatione et Beatorum Canonizatione in synopsim redacta ab Emm. de Azevedo, S.J., Sacrorum Rituum Consultore*, (Rome, 1751, later ed., 1841); *Les 54 Miracles de Lourdes au jugement du Droit Canon*, (Paris, Encyclopédie Universitaire, Presses Universitaires, 1958); F. Reginal-Omez, O.P., "Psychical Phenomena," in *Faith and Fact Book*, (London, 1959); A. Olivieri and B. Billet, O.S.B., *Y a-t-il encore des miracles à Lourdes? 30 Dossiers de guérisons (1949-1971)*, (Paris, Lethielleux; Lourdes, Oeuvre de la Grotte, 1972); symposium, *"De miraculis atque sanationibus lourdensibus,"* in *ME, XIII, xii-336.*

MISSIONS, THE

Catholic missionary endeavour has been much influenced by Marian idealism.[1] At times, the influence has been by way of direct charismatic action associated with Our Lady personally. Thus the conversion of Russia took place in some areas after an icon (*qv*) had been made known and venerated. In the sixteenth century, Mexico became largely Christian in the years that followed the apparition (*qv*) reported at Guadalupe. The European missionaries to South America brought with them their Marian traditions; so did those who laboured in the Far East. The missionary revival in the nineteenth century, which was turned so much towards Africa, coincided with the emancipation of the slaves overseas and the renewal in Europe of Marian devotion. Most of the new institutes, founded for evangelizing work, were placed under the patronage of Our Lady, or included devotion to her in their spiritual programme. The trend grew in the next important phase of missionary expansion, the decades which followed the First World War. Lay societies, like the Militia of Mary Immaculate, founded by Blessed Maximilian Kolbe (*qv*), and the Legion of Mary, have accomplished wonders in missionary lands.

Pius XI, in the Encyclical *Rerum Ecclesiae* (28 February, 1926), and Pius XII, in *Fidei Donum* (21 April), commended the missionary cause to Mary under the title "Queen of Apostles," as did John XXIII in *Princeps Pastorum* (28 November, 1959), under the popular title "Queen of the Missions."

The decree on the Church's missionary activity, issued by Vatican II, has two references to Mary. The first *schema*, drawn up in 1964, was in that year much abbreviated—to a set of propositions—and as such was rejected by the assembly. Experts in ecclesiology were then called in to provide a new draft, and the result was an important addition to the Council's teaching on the Church. The passage on the Holy Spirit was the answer to criticism voiced by an Orthodox theologian of the previous documents, which he found deficient on this subject.[2]

But the first text they composed contained no reference to Our Lady. Bishop V. J. McCauley of Fort Portal, Uganda, on behalf of the East African bishops, voiced dissatisfaction in the assembly as follows. "In the *schema*, nothing is said of the Virgin Mary. The Blessed Virgin is given as model and mother to all who, in the Church, have a determined place or function, with the exception of missionaries: [to] the laity (*schema* on the Apostolate of the Laity, n° 4 at the end); [to] religious (Dogmatic Constitution, LG n° 46, and *schema* on the renewal and adaptation of the religious life, n° 25 at the end); [to] clerics (*schema* on priestly formation, n° 8);

and priests (*schema* on the ministry and life of priests, n° 15).

Yet if the Church is missionary by her very nature (this *schema*, n° 2), and since Mary has been declared Mother of the Church, that is of the whole Christian people, both faithful and pastors, who call her a most loving Mother (Paul VI, 21 November, 1964; cf. Dogmatic Constitution, LG n° 53), it is of the greatest importance to give Mary as a model and mother to missionaries. Missionaries are sent, as the Apostles were sent from the day of Pentecost, to evangelize the world. She, who by her prayers implored the gift of the Spirit (cf. LG 59), is now imploring the same gift for the missionaries, her most beloved sons. The Queen of Apostles is truly the Mother of the Church, that is especially of missionaries, who evangelize the Christian world.

I propose that there be inserted in number 23 on spiritual and moral formation: 'Let him honour, as the model of this apostolic life, the Blessed Virgin Mary, Queen of Apostles or Mother of the Church, who, with the Apostles, before the day of Pentecost, implored by her prayers the gift of the Spirit (cf. LG 59), and whom the missionary and Catholic Church, taught by the Holy Spirit, honours with filial devotion and affection'."[3]

Two additions referring to Our Lady were made to the text. Showing that the Church takes its origin from the mission of the Son and the Holy Spirit, the Decree goes on: "For it was from Pentecost that the 'Acts of the Apostles' began, just as Christ was conceived by the Holy Spirit coming down upon the Virgin Mary, and as Christ was impelled to the work of his ministry by the same Holy Spirit descending upon him as he prayed." (Article 4). The passage is significant for the theology of Mary and the Holy Spirit.

The following words, relevant to Mary's intercession (*qv*), occur at the very end of the Decree: "But aware that it is God who brings it about that his kingdom should come upon earth, they [the Council Fathers and the Roman Pontiff] pour forth their prayers together with all the Christian faithful that, through the intercession of the Virgin Mary, Queen of Apostles, the nations may soon be led to knowledge of the truth (1 Tim 2:4), and that the glory of God, which is resplendent on the fact of Christ may, through the Holy Spirit, shine upon all men (2 Cor 4:6; Article 42).

The Decree was the last one in which mention was made of Our Lady; it was to be promulgated on the final day of the fourth session. The draft was accepted at the penultimate stage by a substantial majority. Some of the *Modi*, or amendments suggested, bore on Article 4. Fifty Fathers suggested that there should be, after the word Pentecost, reference to Mary's presence to read thus: "In Pentecost, as the Spirit breathed [*Spiritu afflante*] on the Apostles and on the Disciples praying with Mary, the 'Acts of the Apostles' began." The commission thought this would overload the text; they rejected also a suggestion by the same group that the paragraph should begin with the words about Christ's conception, and that the word "agreeing" (*consentientem*) should be inserted after "Virgin Mary." Logical order, they said, demanded that the passage begin with Pentecost, and they did not think that there should be a reference at this place to Mary's consent. One is free to disagree with their verdict. Six Fathers put forward this phrasing: ". . . the same Spirit, leading the Apostles, from whom Christ had been conceived of the Virgin Mary and who, descending on Christ as he prayed, impelled him to the work of his ministry." The aim was to avoid the implication that the Holy Spirit was "the origin of Christ rather than the cause of Mary's sanctification, so that she should become the Mother of God." A grammatical change was made to satisfy this request; a rewording to favour clarity was not accepted, as the commission thought this attained.[4] "Queen of the Missions" is not then a decorative title, but, replete with a theology of the Spirit.

[1]Cf. M. Vodeb, *Iconografia missionaria, Maria Sma., Regina di tutti i Santi*, VIII, *Bibliotheca Sanctorum*, (Rome, 1967); E. Ogge, I.M.C., *La Madonna missionaria*, 2nd ed., (Turin, E. Missioni Consolata, 1968). On Our Lady and the missionary territories, cf. 12 articles on Asia, in *Maria*, IV, 831-1033; 8 articles on Africa, in *Maria*, V, 23-194; 13 articles on South America, in *Maria*, V, 285-480; Oceania, in *Maria*, V, 485-505. Cf. A. V. Seumois, "Maria nei paesi di Missione," in *Enciclopedia Mariana, Theotokos*, 2nd ed., (Genoa, Bevilacqua e Solari; Milan, Ed. Massimo, 1958), 212-220; A. Galli, "Madre della Chiesa," II, in *La Madonna e l'Asia*, (Ascoli Piceno, 1967). [2]Cf. article *Spirit, Holy, and Mary* in the present work. [3]Text communicated by Bishop McCauley. [4]*Modi* to Decree on Church's missionary activity, (Vatican City, 1965), 11.

MODESTUS OF JERUSALEM, ST. (d. 634) Photius stated that he read three discourses under the name of Modestus of Jerusalem: on the women who bore ointment (for the body of the Lord); on the Hypapante, or Presentation to the Lord; and the *Encomium in Dormitionem SS. Deiparae*, the only one of the three to reach us intact.[1] A quotation from this discourse appears in *Munificentissimus Deus*: "As the most glorious Mother of Christ, our Saviour and God, and the giver of life and immortality, has been endowed with life by him, she has received an eternal incorruptibility of the body, together with him who has raised her up from the tomb, and has taken her up to himself in a way known only to him."[2]

The *Encomium*, which is lengthy, contains much that is of interest, on Mary's eminence above creatures as Mother of God, and on her important role in the work of salvation. M. applied to Mary an impressive series of titles, personal praise or eulogy, biblical in origin. The text has, however, been the subject of acute debate as to authenticity. The main objections drawn from internal evidence, were made by Fr. M. Jugie, A.A. It may have been due to his influence—he was a member of the drafting committee—that the text was not attributed to M. in *Munificentissimus Deus*. Vatican II, on the other hand, citing the text in a footnote, attributed it to M. The sermon may be authentic; it certainly belongs to the seventh or eighth century.

---

[1]Text, in PG 86bis, 3277-3312, EMBP, 1255-1279; Italian tr. *La Madonna*, (Rome Opera del Divino Amore, 19(1971), n.2, pp. 2-13 n.6, pp. 2-5. Cf. M. Jugie, A.A., *L'Assomption*, 215-218; R. Laurentin, *Traité*, I, 168; D. Bertetto, S.D.B., "Il culto mariano in S. Modesto di Gerusalemme," in Zagreb Congress, III, 127-159; *id*., "S. Modesto di Gerusalemme (d. 634), dottore dell'Assunzione," in *Mater Ecclesiae*, 8(1972), 154-162. [2]PG 86bis, (14), 3311.

MONTFORT, LOUIS MARIE GRIGNION DE, ST. (1673-1716)

For a long time popularly known as Grignion de Montfort, a Breton, educated by the Jesuits at Rennes, then at St. Sulpice, where he was librarian. He was named a "missionary apostolic" by Clement XI. M. devoted himself to this work and left two new religious societies, the Company of Mary (De Montfort Fathers) and the Daughters of Wisdom. His principal work, *Treatise on the True Devotion to the Blessed Virgin* was not found until 1842, a century and a quarter after his death. It has been widely distributed, over 300 editions in twenty languages. It was translated into English by Fr. Faber, and a later edition introduced by Cardinal Vaughan. Cardinal Mercier wrote a Pastoral Letter on it. Its influence on the *Handbook of the Legion of Mary*, one of the most widely read manuals of the Lay Apostolate, and the choice of its author as patron of this body, considerably enlarged its impact. So did the beatification of M. by Leo XIII and his canonization by Pius XII in 1947.

The saint's other works were issued at irregular intervals: *The Secret of Mary*, in an almost complete text (1868, integral edition, 1898); *The Love of the Eternal Wisdom*, in a satisfactory edition only in 1929. The *Secret* has gone through 350 editions in twenty-five languages. In 1966, for the 250th anniversary of the saint's death, the Montfort Fathers in France brought out a single volume (xxxii, 1904 pages including tables), a critical edition of the saint's entire writings.[1] The annotation enables the reader to trace the quotations and references in M.'s works, some of the former at secondhand. It reveals fully the very wide reading on which his writing was based. Recent studies have examined in depth the spiritual development of the saint and the effect upon him of the controversies of the time (see AVIS SALUTAIRES, LES).[2]

Besides what is contained in the writings already named, the collected writings hold much that is of Marian interest: *The Admirable Secret of the Most Holy Rosary*, some twenty of the 164 hymns, advice on saying the Rosary, and prayers or instructions in the context of his missions or religious families. But the essence of his teaching is found in the treatise on true devotion.[3]

The book is closely-knit and may easily suffer from quotations out of context. M. held the doctrine of universal mediation, and the intrinsic spiritual motherhood. The general plan is Trinitarian, and there is no compromise on divine transcendence. On the other hand, the description of types of false devotion is realistic, and the characteristics of true devotion psychologically sound. Having laid down in article 120 that "our whole perfection consists in being conformed, united and consecrated to Jesus Christ," then he states that the true devotion he is urging "consists in giving oneself entirely to the Blessed Virgin, in order to belong entirely to Jesus Christ through her" (article 121). Thus the soul becomes Mary's slave of love. The engagement must be lived by "performing all one's actions through Mary, with Mary, in Mary, and for Mary, so as to perform them more perfectly through Jesus Christ, with Jesus Christ, in Jesus, and for Jesus." (article 258). The act of consecration composed by the saint is addressed to the eternal and incarnate wisdom.

There is a great deal about the Holy Spirit in the work. The saint broke with thinking in the French school, which saw Mary as spouse of the Father, to speak of her as spouse of the Spirit. "God the Holy Spirit," he says in a striking passage, "being barren in God, that is, producing no other divine Person, became fruitful by Mary, whom he espoused." He worked his masterpiece with her and, "with her and in her, daily to the end of time, he produces the predestined, and the members of the Body of this adorable Head." (article 20). The author made it clear that the Blessed Virgin does not give fruitfulness to the Spirit, that he does not need her. Likewise, when the author says that "she distributes all his gifts and graces to whom she wills, in the measure she wills, how she wills, and when she wills," he first states that it was the Holy Spirit who communicated his gifts to her, "his faithful spouse." (article 25)

The saint glorifies and exalts Our Lady in language of the superlative kind that the Byzantines used. He saw those lovingly enslaved to her as the apostles of the latter times. He was the prophet of the Age of Mary.

---

[1]Oeuvres complètes de saint Louis-Marie Grignion de Montfort, (Paris, Editions du Seuil, 1966). Cf. J. M. Hupperts, S.M.M., "S. Louis Marie de Montfort," in Maria, III, 253-274; symposium on St. Louis Marie's Marian spirituality, in ASC, vol. VIII; L. Perouas, in DSp. IX, 1073-1081; id., Ce que Grignion de M. croyait et comment il a vécu sa foi, (Paris, 1973); M. T. Poupon, Le poème de la parfaite consécration à Marie suivant S. Louis Marie . . ., (Lyons, 1947); P. Gaffney, S.M.M., Mary's Spiritual Maternity According to St. Louis de Montfort, (Bay Shore, New York, 1974). [2]Cf. S. de Fiores, S.M.M., Itinerario spirituale di S. Luigi M. di Montfort nel periodo fino al sacerdozio, (Rome, 1974). [3]Oeuvres Complètes . . . (Paris, Editions du Seuil, 1966), 487-671; English tr. by Fr. Faber, (1862), 5th ed., (1904); 4th Monfortian ed., (1957). Article numbers as in critical edition.

MOTHER OF THE CHURCH

Teaching Authority: On 21 November, 1964, Paul VI, in his concluding address to the third session of Vatican II, proclaimed Mary "Mother of the Church" in the following words: "As we consider the close relations by which Mary and the Church are linked, as they have been set forth so very clearly in this Council Constitution, they lead us to judge the present moment most solemn and especially appropriate to fulfill a wish, which at the end of the last session we expressed, and which very many Fathers made their own, requesting urgently that during this Council the maternal function, which the Blessed Virgin Mary exercises towards the Christian people, should be declared in explicit terms. For this reason, it seems right to us that, in this public assembly, we should formally pronounce a title by which the Blessed Virgin Mary may be honoured, which has been petitioned from many parts of the Catholic world, and to us is, in a special manner, acceptable and pleasing; for with remarkable conciseness, it conveys the conspicuous place which this Council has acknowledged as proper to the Mother of God in the Church.

Therefore, for the glory of the Blessed Virgin and our consolation, we declare most holy Mary Mother of the Church, that is of the whole Christian people, both faithful and pastors, who call her a most loving Mother; and we decree that henceforth the whole Christian people should, by this most sweet name, give still greater honour to the Mother of God and address prayers to her."[1]

The Pope emphasized the logical link between Mary's divine motherhood and her relationship to the Church. "Mary is the Mother of Christ who, immediately that he assumed human nature in her virginal womb, took to himself as Head his Mystical Body which is the Church. Mary, therefore, as Mother of Christ is to be considered as Mother also of all the faithful and pastors, that is of the Church."[2]

Paul VI's intervention was a solution to a problem of Vatican II. The preliminary Marian *schema* for a while bore the title *Mary, Mother of the Church*. After the debate and vote in October, 1963, a new *schema* was ordered, and it appeared for the next session with an altered name. In the conciliar debate in September, 1964, and in written submissions, many Council Fathers objected to the omission of the title and pleaded that it be restored in the *schema*, while others asked that it be not restored in the title, and objected to its use in the *schema*. The official report on the first point gave the number as 195 for a return to *Mater Ecclesiae* and 123 against.[3] The theological commission did not put the title at the head or in the body of the chapter. Their report said that the title was rare, though occurring in church writers and could scarcely be called traditional. It could not be commended from an ecumenical viewpoint; though theologically acceptable, it was thought sufficient to express it equivalently, which was done with words borrowed from Benedict XIV (LG 53).

Several Fathers—hundreds it has been stated—appealed directly to the Holy Father to intervene. On 18 November, he announced at a public audience his intention to proclaim Mary "Mother of the Church." His words at the final assembly of the third session were received with acclamation by the majority of the Fathers. The size of the dissident minority is difficult to establish.

The idea thus imposed by Paul VI had been accepted by Popes before him. Benedict XIV's words are: "The Catholic Church, taught by the authority of the Holy Spirit . . . has always surrounded with expressions of filial homage and devotion the most loving Mother who was bequeathed to her by her dying Spouse."[4] In the Encyclical *Adjutricem Populi*, Leo XIII (*qv*) says: "She was, in very truth, the Mother of the Church, the teacher and Queen of the Apostles, to whom, besides she confided no small part of the divine mysteries 'which she kept in her heart'."[5] St. Pius X, in *Ad diem illum* (*qv*), recalled the union of the faithful with Christ, their Head, in the womb of the Virgin Mary. Pius XII ended his Encyclical *Mystici Corporis* with a passage on Mary in which he said that "she bestowed on it that same motherly care and fervent love with which she fostered the suckling infant Jesus in the cradle." John XXIII (*qv*) used the title five times. Paul VI did so several times before and after the proclamation. This remains the principal pronouncement, made within a Council assembly, addressed by the Pope as its Head.

Sacred Scripture: Before Paul VI's statement, exegetes had discerned the truth in familiar Johannine texts. Thus, A. Feuillet thought that "on Calvary [Mary] is proclaimed at the same time Mother of the Head of the Mystical Body and of all the members of his body."[6] F. M. Braun, O.P. wrote: "At the present moment [the messianic marriage feast symbolized at Cana], his Mother is with him. In the evangelist's eyes, is not this a sign of the maternal role which the Mother of Jesus would one day have to play in the community of believers?"[7] "The basic idea, to which one must always return, is that Mary is the Mother of the Church."[8] A. Feuillet comments more recently on Lk I-II: "The narratives of Lk I-II insinuate that Mary, in becoming the Mother of Christ, became already Mother of the new people of God, and that, in a much more profound way than the Church, she is mother of Christians, though there is a profound likeness between Mary's motherhood and that of the Church. Moreover if it is true that the Church is, in the new economy, the place where normally we receive the grace of Christ the Redeemer, it is still more true to say that we receive this grace of Christ through the intervention and mediation of Mary."[9] There is yet much to explore on the role of the Spirit in the dual motherhood of Mary, in particular on the relation between the descent of the Spirit at the Annunciation and at Pentecost.

History: Little in patristic writings bears directly on the truth here considered. The Augustinian text which is quoted by Vatican II saying that Mary is "truly Mother of the members [of Christ] which is what we are, because she cooperated by charity that faithful should be born in the Church who would be members of that Head, she herself being truly in the body Mother of the Head himself," is the nearest any Father comes to a doctrine of Mary as Mother of the Church.

In medieval times, some attention is given to the collective motherhood. Mary is called "Mother of the nations," and "Mother of the Christian people." St. Peter Damian spoke of the Church coming from Mary. Rupert of Deutz called Mary "Mother of churches"; St. Bonaventure (*qv*) said that the Church took its origin from Mary.

Berengaud, in the twelfth century, seems to have been the first to use the title. On Rev 12, he wrote: "In this passage, we can also see the woman as Blessed Mary, since she is the Mother of the Church [*Mater Ecclesiae*] because she brought forth him who is the Head of the Church."[10] In the next century, an English Cistercian was explicit: "She herself seems to be Mother of the Church, for since she is certainly Mother of the Head, not unfittingly she is understood to be Mother also of the Body. The Church is, therefore, Mother of Mary and Mary is Mother of the Church."[11] St. Albert's work *De Sacrificio Missae*, with authenticity challenged but upheld by the Cologne editors, contains the title also.

The title can also be found in an Irish litany to the Virgin, dating of which is controverted—it cannot be later than the fourteenth century. From then on, either literally or by implication, testimony accumulates on the specific maternal role of Mary towards the Church, important names being Denis the Carthusian, St. Peter Canisius, J. J. Olier, M. J. Scheeben, and J. B. Terrien (qqv). The first substantial work to bear the title as its name was published by H. J. Coleridge, S.J. in the nineteenth century; the contents are the Church in the early age. Fears were expressed that the prominence given the doctrine might embarrass ecumenists. One non-Catholic, John McQuarrie, has proposed it as a suitable rallying center for Catholics, Orthodox, and Protestants.

[1]Cf. "Maria Mater Ecclesiae ejusque influxus in Corpus Christi Mysticum quod est Ecclesia," 18 articles, in ME VI; N. Garcia, "Maria verissima Ecclesiae Mater," in EphMar, 12(1962), 495-524; Th. Koehler, S.M., "Marie, Mère de l'Église," in BSFEM, 11(1953), 133-157; F. M. Braun, O.P., "Marie Mère de l'Église," in BSFEM, 10(1952), 7-12; F. Sebastian Aguilar, C.M.F., "Maria, Madre de la Iglesia," in EphMar, 10(1960), 53-100. For after the proclamation, cf. J. de Aldama, S.J., "Sancta Maria, Mater Ecclesiae," in EphMar, 14(1964), 441-465; id., "Madre de la Iglesia," in Temas de Teologia Mariana, (Madrid, 1966), 68-86; J. Galot, S.J., "Mère de l'Église," in NRT, 96(1964), 1163-1185; G. Geenen, O.P., "'Mater Ecclesiae,' in doctrina Pauli VI," in MM, 26(1964), 331-343; G. M. Roschini, O.S.M., "Maria SS. solennemente proclamata de Paolo VI 'Madre della Chiesa'," in MM, 26(1964), 297-333; D. Bertetto, S.D.B., Maria Madre della Chiesa, (Catania, Ed. Paoline, 1965); G. O'Shea, "Pope Paul VI and the 'Mother of the Church'," in MSt, 16(1965), 21-28; F. de P. Sola, "Maria Madre y Hija de la Iglesia segun Paulo VI," in EphMar, 16(1966), 79-93; R. Spiazzi, La Vergine Madre della Chiesa, (Rome, 1966); J. Esquerda Bifet, Maria Madre de la Iglesia, (Bilbao, 1968); H. M. Manteau-Bonamy, O.P., La Vierge Marie et le Saint Esprit, (Paris, 1971). [2]AAS, 56(1964), 1018. [3]G. M. Besutti, O.S.M., in MM, 27(1965), 125-126. [4]Gloriosae Dominae, 27 September, 1748, Bullarium Romanum, ser. 2, vol. 2, no. 61, 428. [5]OL, 135. [6]A. Feuillet, "Les Adieux du Christ à sa mère (Jn 19:25-27) et la maternité spirituelle de Marie," in NRT, 86(1964), 476-477. [7]id., La Mère des Fideles, (Paris, Tournai), 2nd ed. [8]BSFEM, 10(1952), 7. [9]Jésus et sa Mère, Paris, 1974, 126. [10]PL 17, 876CD. [11]"Distinctiones monasticae," ed. Pitra, in Spicilegium Solesmense, III, 130-131.

MOTHER OF DIVINE GRACE (THE SPIRITUAL MOTHERHOOD)

Sacred Scripture: That the Mother of God is our Mother has been for centuries a truth totally accepted by teaching and believing Catholics. This truth has very often been supported by the Johannine text, 19:25-27 (see WOMAN IN). The Fathers of the Church and early Christian writers did not so interpret the words of the dying Christ. Development of the idea of Mary's spiritual motherhood was slow and did not enter the consciousness of the Church until medieval times. During those early centuries, the sacred text did not immediately convey the notion. Lenghty reflection was needed to reach it, and Catholic biblical scholars do not fear to defend the interpretation in the face of modern non-Catholic exegetes.[1] The New Testament basis has been widened and made more firm by recent research. Patient analysis of all the Johannine texts, the disputed reading of 1:12-13, the Cana episode, as well as 19:25-27 and Rev 12, discerns converging lines of thought towards Mary's universal motherhood. Thus an Angelican exegete, while rejecting the singular number in 1:13, can still write "that the birth of Christians, being bloodless and rooted in God's will alone, followed the pattern of the birth of Christ himself,"[2] which readily accords with Mary's motherhood. Likewise, a strictly scientific analysis of Cana can lead its author to this conclusion: "Here, without any doubt, then, is the clearest teaching of John on the Mother of Jesus, her role as collaborator and associate in the changing of the old economy into the new economy, her function as mother in regard to all believers."[3] Jn 19:25-27 read in the light of Jn 16:21 suggests the same truth, as does a profound understanding of "the rest of her offspring, on those who keep the commandments of God and bear testimony to Jesus" in Rev 12:17. Vatican II, which was deliberately non-committal on unresolved biblical controversies, hints that Rom 2:19, "that he might be the first-born among many brethren," is in harmony with the general idea that Mary, in becoming the physical Mother of the Saviour, became the Mother in grace of the saved.

History: St. Irenaeus (qv), who most powerfully expressed the Eve-Mary intuition, hints elsewhere that our spiritual regeneration relates us to her. It was St. Epiphanius (qv) who applied to her the title "Mother of the living," an extension of the Eve typology.[4] Not long after, St. Nilus speaks of "Mary the Mother of all those who live by the Gospel." In the same century, we meet titles significant for our subject: "Mother of salvation," from Severian of Gabala (qv);

"Mother of the Economy," from Theodotius of Ancyra (d. before 466); "She who has given birth to the mystery," from Proclus of Constantinople.[5] Long before these writers, the *Sub Tuum* (*qv*) was in existence, but it was a prayer addressed not to Mary, our Mother, but to the Mother of God.

There is another precious vein, not yet accurately dated, but certainly prior to the fifth century, the *Transitus* stories. (see ASSUMPTION APOCRYPHA). In the oldest known version, the Ethiopian, John speaks thus to Mary before her death: "Mary, our sister, who has been made mother of the twelve." And later the assembled Apostles, "spoke with one voice: Mary, our sister and Mother of those who have been saved, joy be with you."[6]

In the West, too, the relevant testimony is slight. St. Ambrose (*qv*) thought of Mary as having a parental role, *munus parentis*, towards virgins, and St. Jerome (*qv*) was more explicit in the same line: "She is a perpetual virgin and Mother of countless virgins."[7] St. Peter Chrysologus (*qv*), who died some decades after Jerome, spoke of "her who by nature had been mother of the dying, becoming by grace Mother of men." It is clear that the change is due to Mary. But the idea remains underdeveloped.[8]

More influential than any views of all his contemporaries or near contemporaries in the West was St. Augustine's intuition: "According to the body, Mary is Mother only of Christ. But in so far as she does the will of God, she is spiritually sister and mother. And thus this unique woman is mother and virgin, not only in spirit but bodily—mother in spirit, not of the Saviour, our Head, of whom rather she is born spiritually, for all who believe in him—and she is one of them—are rightly called sons of the Spouse, but she is really Mother of the members who we are, because she cooperated by charity so that there might be born in the Church believers, of whom he is the Head."[9] This text seemed to point the way to a universal motherhood—it is found in LG 53—but in the next century, it is the theme of Mary, Mother of virgins which we find in Leander of Seville.

Through these early centuries, silence continues on any interpretation of Jn 19:25-27 in the sense of the spiritual motherhood. It is broken momentarily by Origen (*qv*) who has this comment. "No one can understand the meaning of this gospel [according to John] if he has not rested on the bosom of Jesus, if he has not received Mary as a mother from Jesus.... In fact, every man who has become perfect no longer lives, but Christ lives in him and, because Christ lives in him, it is said of him to Mary: Behold your son Christ."[10] The focus of interest here, however, is identity with Christ, not the maternal office of Mary. This office and the corresponding duty of children are well explained by George of Nicomedia (*qv*), but the context is limited to the Apostles during Mary's lifetime. "Be for them all that natural mothers are for their children, or rather all that I would be by my presence; all that children are, they will be for you."[11] Despite the limitation, the seminal idea is there.

The pioneer of such an interpretation in the West was Anselm of Lucca (*qv*), who taught that the words were spoken "so that the glorious Mother would intercede for all true believers, with her immense affection ... so that she should keep with special protection, those she has adopted as children, the ransomed captives."[12] Rupert of Deutz (*qv*) read the Calvary text in conjunction with Jn 16:21 to show that since Mary on Calvary, "with the true pains of childbirth, has brought forth, in the Passion of her only Son, salvation for all of us, she is in truth a Mother to all of us."[13]

This was sound exegesis which retains its validity. Medieval thinking on Mary's spiritual motherhood began, however, independently of the last words of the Saviour. A seventh-century anonymous writer used the title "Mother of nations," but it is in the following century that we get a theology of Mary's universal maternal office. In a sermon on the Purification, Ambrose Autpert (*qv*) showed how Mary's intercession is prompted by her motherly interest in us, and he pointed to the doctrinal root of this motherly function and devotion. "She does not cease to the present time to offer him whom she has brought forth: by her holy prayers, she causes the same Redeemer to unite himself with the elect; and, let it be said, it is with maternal affection that she, the most devoted of all [*piisima*], does this. For she considers as her sons all those whom divine grace associates with Christ. How should she not be the Mother of the elect, she who gives birth to their brother? If Christ is the brother of believers, I say, why should she who brought forth Christ not be the Mother of believers?"[14] Ambrose Autpert implores Mary to pray to her only Son for the faults of her many sons.

No one spoke like him for hundreds of years. In the East, Theoteknos of Livias (*qv*) had made a veiled allusion to Mary as Mother of the disciples, i.e. the Apostles, in the manner of the Apocrypha (*qv*). It is John the Geometer (*qv*) who here, as in other areas, made a giant step forward. Mary is not only Mother of God, but "our common Mother and more than our Mother, for as she has a nature above nature, she has likewise for men an affection and interest above nature . . . . After his [Christ's] departure, Mary had, as it were, taken his place and maintained his office; she was Mother to all of them, mistress of doctrine, pastor, head, taking some into her arms, teaching others, defending others again, repelling enemies." In this passage, John the Geometer is thinking of Our Lady's role during her lifetime. Later, he prefaces his passage on her role in the Redemption (*qv*) by the words: "We give you thanks, our common Father, for having arranged that your Mother should become a Mother to all of us."[15]

The idea persisted in the East and found a notable exponent in Theophanes of Nicaea (*qv*): "In the same way as she became the Mother of God incarnate according to the flesh, she is Mother of all those who are divinized according to grace."[16] In the West, the twelfth century brought widespread conviction. Blessed Guerric d'Igny (*qv*) applied and developed at length the principle which he enunciated thus: "She who is the only Virgin-Mother, she who glories in having borne that same only-begotten of the Father, embraces that same only-begotten of hers in all his members, so she can truly be called Mother of all in whom she sees that Christ her Son has been formed or is being formed." Mary was the Mother of the Life, he would go on, and added: "She in some way brought to rebirth all those who were to live by that life . . ."; "she shows herself a mother by her care and loving attention." He contrasts Mary's far more holy and godlike manner of bringing forth children, "by giving birth to the Word himself," with Paul's begetting children by his preaching.[17]

The age of Guerric and of Rupert of Deutz (*qv*) saw a whole litany of Marian titles which expressed Mary's motherhood of divine grace, completing, with those like Mother of Mercy (*qv*), the description which already existed of a manifold reality. With some vicissitudes, the doctrine is henceforth accepted and increasingly clarified. Some authors—e.g. Gerson and especially St. Antoninus of Florence—emphasize it more than others. Spiritual writers, medieval like Raymond Lull and Ubertino of Casale—the French school in the seventeenth century—understandably found it congenial to their purpose. All were encouraged by the commitment of the Teaching Authority to the truth.

Teaching Authority: The modern Popes, from Leo XIII on, have repeatedly taught, even emphasized, the spiritual motherhood of Mary. All of them, who had occasion to refer to Jn 19:26-27, saw the words of Jesus as a scriptural basis for the doctrine. "Now in John," said Leo, "as the Church has constantly taught, Christ designated the whole human race, and in the front rank are they who are joined with him by faith."[18] This is not the sole nor the most profound, theological reason given by the Popes for Mary's spiritual motherhood. St. Pius X (*qv*) notably related it to the divine motherhood: "Now the Blessed Virgin did not conceive the eternal Son of God merely in order that he might be made man . . . but also in order that by means of the nature assumed from her, he might be the Redeemer of men . . . . Therefore, in the same holy womb of his most chaste Mother, Christ took to himself flesh, and united to himself the spiritual body formed by those who were to believe in him. Hence Mary, carrying the Saviour within her, may be said to have also carried all those whose life was contained in the life of the Saviour . . . . Hence, in a spiritual and mystical sense, we are said to be children of Mary and she is Mother of us all."[19]

Mary's association (see ASSOCIATE) with Christ the Redeemer is, for the Popes, a further title to her universal motherhood. Thus says Pius XII in papal documents of more than passing interest, the Encyclicals *Mystici Corporis* and *Mediator Dei*: "Thus [having offered her Son on Calvary] she, who was the Mother of our Head according to the flesh, became, by a new title of sorrow and glory, the spiritual mother of all his members."[20] "She became our Mother when the divine Redeemer was consummating the sacrifice of himself; hence, by this title also, we are her children."[21] The Pope speaks in each case of an additional reason, the primary one being clearly the divine motherhood.

The spiritual motherhood of Mary was the central recurring theme in the teaching of John

XXIII (*qv*). Paul VI (*qv*) related it to Mary's motherhood of the Church, which he proclaimed after the third session of Vatican II; he recalled the truth in *Marialis Cultus* (*qv*), and in his letter to the 1975 Marian Congress.

Vatican II: The spiritual motherhood of Mary is a central theme of LG 8, almost dominant. The truth was affirmed in the preliminary *schema*, and in the first draft of the conciliar *schema*; it was strengthened in the latter without challenge. A biblical point was an exception to this harmony. Each of the three drafts, before the one finally voted, included the words, "a figure [or type] of the faithful," after the sentence, "Finally the same Christ Jesus, dying on the Cross, gave her [Mary] as a mother to his disciple." The first *schema* had read, "she was finally given by the same Christ Jesus dying on the Cross as a Mother to men." At the *Modi*, twelve Fathers asked that "figure of the faithful" be dropped, "as it is not certain from the sacred text nor from the documents of Tradition." One Father suggested "is declared" or "was proclaimed" instead of "was given." The descriptive phrase was dropped—a rejection of the medieval and papal interpretation—and "was given" remained as being "more expressive and intimate," a strange exegetical comment about the most public and significant event in history![22]

In LG 8, Mary is twice called "Mother of God and of men," "especially of the faithful" added the first time (LG 54, 69). Mary's "maternal duty" is mentioned in the section on mediation, wherein one passage ends, "For this reason she is a Mother to us in the order of grace," words taken almost entirely from a *schema* prepared for Vatican I. Before the enumeration of the mediatorial titles, we have a more explicit explanation: "This maternity of Mary in the order of grace began with the consent which she gave at the Annunciation, and which she sustained without wavering beneath the Cross. This maternity will last without interruption until the eternal fulfillment of all the elect . . . . By her maternal charity, Mary cares for the brethren of her Son who still journey on earth surrounded by dangers and difficulties until they are led to the happy fatherland" (LG 62). Contrasting Mary with Eve early in the chapter, the Council recalls her ancient title, "Mother of the living." Dealing with the Mary-Church typology, it returns to the idea: "She was the new Eve who

put her absolute trust, not in the ancient serpent, but in God's messenger. The Son whom she brought forth is he whom God placed as the first-born among many brethren (cf. Rom 8:29), namely, the faithful. In their birth and development, she cooperates with maternal love." (LG 63).

[1]For extensive bibliographies, cf. E. Lamirande, "Bibliographie sur la maternité spirituelle de Marie" (from 1840-1957) in *La Maternité Spirituelle*, (Soc. Mar. Canadienne), I, (1958), 157-172; D. M. Montagna, O.S.M., "Rassegna bibliografica sulla 'maternità spirituale' di Maria (1947-1964)," in MM, 26(1964), 191-207. For collections on the theme, cf. MSt, (1952); EstM, (1948 and 1958); BSFEM, (1959-1961); French National Marian Congress, (1961); *La maternidad espiritual. Estudios teológicos*, (Mexico, Guadalupe, 1961), ed. by Mexican national commission for definition of the doctrine. Cf. W. Sebastian, in *Mariology*, III, 325-376; Th. Koehler, S.M., in *Maria*, VI, 553-638; J. B. Terrien, S.J., *La Mère des Hommes*, I, (Paris, 1902, new ed., 1950); M. Llamera, O.P., "La maternidad espiritual de Maria," in EstM, 3(1944), 68-162; A. Baumann, *Maria, mater nostra spiritualis*, (Brixen, Weger, 1948), papal texts from Council of Trent; L. Marvulli, *Maria, madre del Cristo mistico. La maternita Maria nel suo concetto integrale*, (Rome, 1948); T. M. Bartolomei, O.S.M., "La maternita spirituale di Maria," in *Divus Thomas*, 55(Piacenza, 1952), 289-357; G. Jouassard, "Amorces chez S. Irénée pour la doctrine de la Maternité spirituelle de Marie," in *Nouvelle Rev. Mar.*, (1954), 140-197; F. J. Kenney, S.M., *Mary's Spiritual Maternity According to Modern Writers*, (Washington, 1957); W. J. Cole, S.M., *The Spiritual Maternity of Mary According to the Writings of Fr. Chaminade*, (Dayton, 1958); G. M. Roschini, O.S.M., "La Maternità spirituale di Maria, presso gli scrittori latini dei secoli VIII-XIII," in MM, 23(1961), 225-295. On Vatican II, cf. J. Esquerda, in EstM, 27, vol. II, 147-210; B. le Erois, S.V.D., in CBQ, 13(1951), 422-431 and CBQ, 14(1952), 116-123; F. M. Braun, O.P., *La Mère des Fidèles*, 2nd ed., (Tournai-Paris, 1954); C. P. Ceroke, O.C., in MSt, 11(1960), 123-151; J. M. Salgado, O.M.I., in EphMar, 20(1970), 281-349; *id.*, in *Divinitas*, 16(1972), 17-102, 445-452; MSS, *passim*. [2]C. K. Barrett, *The Gospel According to St. John*, (London, 1955), 138. [3]J. M. Michaud, S.M.M., in MSS, V, 95. [4]*Panarion haer, 78*, in GCS 37, 468-470. [5]*Apud* R .Laurentin, (French National Congress, Paris, 1962), 4-5. [6]*De Transitu Mariae Apocrypha Aethiopice*, ed. by V. Arras, in CSCO 343, 17, 20. For earliest Greek version, cf. A. Wenger, A.A., *L'Assomption*, 220-228. [7]PL 23, 254AB. [8]*Serm. 140*, in PL 52, 576AB. [9]*De Virgin., VI*, in CSEL 41, 239-240; PL 40, 399. [10]*In Jn 1, 4, 23*, in GCS, *Origenes Werke*, IV, 8-9. [11]*Hom. 8 in Jn 19:25-27*, in PG 100, 1475 D. [12]*Oratio I.* [13]*Comm. in Jn 13*, PL 169, 790AB. [14]PL 89, 1297BD. [15]A. Wenger, A.A., *L'Assomption*, 369, 406. [16]*Serm. in SS. Deiparam*, ed. by M. Jugie, A.A., (Rome, 1935), in PG 108, 64. [17]*In Assumpt. I, 3*, in PL 185, 188-189A. Cf. Saturday Office of Our Lady, second lesson in the Roman Breviary. [18]"Adjutricem Populi," in OL, 135. [19]"Ad diem illum," in OL, 171. [20]"Mystici Corporis," in OL, 253. [21]"Mediator Dei," in OL, 282. [22]"Modi," in OL, 13.

MOTHER OF GOD

Teaching Authority: The most important truth about Our Lady is that she is the Mother of God.[1] The doctrine is supported by Sacred Scripture, Sacred Tradition, and the Teaching Authority of the Church. The first decisive intervention of the Teaching Authority on the subject was at the Council of Ephesus. The passage from St. Cyril's letter to Nestorius, approved by the Council, relevant to the divine motherhood was: "For in the first place, no common man was born of the holy Virgin; then the Word thus descended upon him; but being united from the womb itself, he is said to have endured a generation in the flesh in order to appropriate the producing of his own body. Thus [the holy Fathers] did not hesitate to speak of the Holy Virgin as the Mother of God."[2] Twenty years later, the Council of Chalcedon, speaking of "one and the same Son, Our Lord Jesus Christ, the same perfect in Godhead and the same perfect in human nature, true God and true man, the same with a rational soul and body, consubstantial with the Father according to divine nature, consubstantial with us according to the human nature, *like unto us in all things except sin* (cf. Heb 4:15)," added these words, "indeed born of the Father before the ages according to divinity, but, in the latest days, the same born of the Virgin Mary, Mother of God according to the humanity."[3]

Just over a century later, the second Council of Constantinople (553), condemning an erroneous interpretation of Chalcedon, ended thus: "Or, if anyone calls her the mother of the man or the mother of the Christ, as if the Christ were not God, but does not confess that she is exactly and truly the Mother of God, because God the Word, born of the Father before the ages, was made flesh of her in the last days, and that thus the holy Synod of Chalcedon confessed her [to be], let such a one be anathema."[4] The third Council of Constantinople (680, 681), condemning the Monothelites, repeated some of the earlier formulas and affirmed that Jesus Christ was born "of the Holy Spirit and the Virgin Mary, rightly and truly the Mother of God according to his humanity . . . ."[5] This doctrine is constant in Church documents through the centuries. Paul IV taught it in the sixteenth century;[6] Pius XI summed it up admirably in *Lux Veritatis* (*qv*), written on the fifteenth centenary of the Council of Ephesus.[7]

Pius XII referred frequently to the divine motherhood of Mary, seeing it as the source of all her privileges and graces.[8] Vatican II in *Lumen Gentium*, chapter 8, spoke of Mary as Mother of God twelve times, using *Mater Dei, Dei Genitrix*, or *Deipara*, and recalled the divine motherhood in three other documents—on the Liturgy (103), Ecumenism (15), and the eastern churches (30).

Sacred Scripture: It is not stated explicitly in Sacred Scripture that Mary is the Mother of God; the truth is found in equivalent terms. St. Paul, Gal 4:4, says, "God sent forth his son, born of a woman, born under the law"; in Rom 9:5, he says, "of their race, according to the flesh, is the Christ, God who is over all to be blessed forever." An analysis of Lk 1:32, 35, where Mary's future Son is called "Son of the most high," and "the Son of God," will show that in the full context, in which the eternal "reign," proper to God, is promised him, and the symbolism of the Ark of the Covenant is related to the Mother, the inference is as immediate as in the Pauline texts. Mary's son is God, and she is the Mother of God. Again, when Elizabeth calls Mary "the Mother of my Lord" (Lk 1:43), she uses a term which, among Hellenistic Jews, meant God—as is implied in the verses which come shortly after, "what was spoken to her from the Lord" (45), "My soul magnifies the Lord" (46). St. John finally tells us that he wrote his gospel, "that you may believe that Jesus is the Christ, the Son of God, and that believing you may have life in his name" (20:31). The same evangelist calls Mary the Mother of Jesus, never using her own name (2:1; 19:25).

Sacred Tradition: The *Apostolic Tradition* of St. Hippolytus of Rome gives a question put in the Roman rite of Baptism: "Do you believe in Christ Jesus, the Son of God who was born by the Holy Spirit of the Virgin Mary . . . ."[9] Here too we have to make an inference to reach the truth we are considering. In the centuries that followed, specific affirmation of this truth would be made with the use of the title *Theotokos* (*qv*). Present knowledge indicates that it was first used by Alexander of Alexandria in 325, though if the *Sub tuum* papyrus, in the John Rylands library, is put back to 270, then this is the first witness to the title. With St. Athanasius (*qv*), it is fully established. For St. Gregory Nazianzen (*qv*), acceptance of it was a test of orthodoxy: "If anyone does not accept the holy Mary as Theotokos, he is without the Godhead."[10] St. Ambrose first used the title *Mater Dei* in the West. In the next century, St. Cyril of Alexandria brought the question to a church council, which decided to answer in his very terms. The fullest exposition of the theology of the divine motherhood in the patristic period was made by St. John of Damascus (*qv*).

The great medieval scholastic theologians analyzed the philosophical aspects of Mary's motherhood of God, its transcendence and its formal constitutive element, which is the relation between Mother and Son. Another problem, dimly perceived already by St. Ambrose, was brought into debate: how did Mary merit the dignity of Mother of God? The answer was found in the distinction between merit *de condigno*, in the strict sense, which she could not have had, and *de congruo*, by reason of a certain suitability, which, with differing nuances, theologians attributed to her. St. Thomas, with admirable precision said: "The Blessed Virgin did not merit the Incarnation, but, assuming that it would take place, she merited that it would be through her, not with condign merit, but with the merit of suitability, in so far as it was fitting that the Mother of God should be a most pure and perfect Virgin."[11]

The transcendence of Mary's maternal function was a favourite theme of St. Bernardine of Siena (*qv*). It was one of many theses elaborated by Suarez (*qv*), whose work preludes an immense seventeenth-century discussion of certain aspects of the divine maternity. The abstract phrase was used for the first time in this age by Nazario, O.P. Suarez also analyzed in depth the reality of the divine motherhood, the relationship between the office and sanctifying grace, Mary's place in the hypostatic order, and her predestination relative to her motherhood of God. He was the first to deal with the problem of the hypostatic order, which is not to be confused with the hypostatic union.[12]

Speculative investigation pursued subjects which cohere closely with the philosophy of the age, and cannot be dismissed as subtleties— whether the generative power of Mary was raised to a higher degree than is natural;[13] whether Mary can be called an instrumental cause of the hypostatic union, that is, of the Incarnation; whether the divine motherhood is the fundamental principle of Mariology; whether the divine motherhood is in itself an order apart; and especially whether the maternal office was of itself sanctifying, independently of sanctifying grace. The latter *possibility* at least was defended by Juan Martinez de Ripalda, S.J., energetically opposed by the theologians of Salamanca.[14]

Since then, the outstanding contribution to the theory of the divine motherhood has come from M. J. Scheeben (*qv*), the concept of the bridal motherhood, with which the great theologian linked Mary's predestination, her personal supernatural character and her dignity, and her role in our salvation.

Recent Writing: Before Vatican II, attention was being directed to an integral idea of the divine maternity by Fr. M. J. Nicolas, O.P.,[15] and the Trinitarian aspect by J. Alonso, C.M.F.;[16] while G. Rozo, C.M.F. revived the thesis of De Ripalda, extending it from a possibility to fact,[17] and C. Van Biesen, C.SS.R., also defended an extreme view, which would see, in the divine motherhood, a participation in the very fatherhood of God the Father to the Son.[18] On the other side, there has been in at least one case a tendency to blur the distinction between the maternal office of Mary and sanctifying grace.

Since Vatican II and the change from scholasticism to salvation history, there was at first a new emphasis on the concrete term Mother of God and an existential approach. The metaphysical basis still remains open to research and adequate formulation.[19] Conscious of the abiding mystery in the divine motherhood, theologians search for an explanation of that perfection or prerogative in Mary which establishes her relationship with her divine Son. As to the fact that her motherhood essentially consists in a relationship, there can be no discussion. The Son was unique for, as God, he existed before his Mother and could seek her consent to become his Mother. The motherhood was unique for her Son. In the instant of conception, he himself assumed the human nature that she provided, making it his own.

That he made it his own in oneness of person, truly God and truly man, is the faith of the early Councils, which must be explained to modern man. It must be shown that intrinsic to these definitions is the truth that motherhood implies relationship to the person of the child, therefore, in this case, to a divine person, which makes Mary Mother of God.

¹For bibliography, cf. G. M. Roschini, *Maria Santissima*, II, 102-110. Cf. G. van Ackeren, S.J., in *Mariology*, II, 177-227; M. J. Nicolas, O.P., "Le concept intégral de maternité divine," in *Rev. Thom.*, 42(1937), 58-93, 230-272; *id.*, *Theotokos*, (Paris, 1965), 51-107; H. M. Manteau-Bonamy, O.P., *Maternité divine et Incarnation*, (Paris, 1949); J. M. Alonso, C.M.F., "Trinidad-Encarnación-Maternidad Divina," in *EphMar*, 3(1953), 84-102; M. D. Philippe, O.P., "Le mystère de la maternité divine de Marie," in *Maria*, VI, 369-416; *EstM*, 8(1949); *MSt*, 6(1955); C. Wessels, *The Mother of God, Her Physical Maternity: a Reappraisal*, (River Forest, 1964). ²DS, 251. ³DS, 301. ⁴DS, 427. ⁵DS, 555. ⁶DS, 1880. ⁷AAS, 23(1931), 506-507, 511, 513. ⁸"Fulgens Corona," in OL, 350. ⁹*Apostolic Tradition*, ed. by B. Botte, O.S.B., in SC 14, 50-51. ¹⁰*Ep. 101*, in PG 37, 177C. ¹¹*III Sent.*, d. 4, a. 1, ad 5. ¹²Cf. M. J. Nicolas, O.P., "L'appartenance de la Mère de Dieu à l'ordre hypostatique," in *BSFEM*, 3(1937), 147-194. ¹³Cf. Silvestro Saavedra, *Sacra Deipara*, (Lyons, 1655), I, 136-251. ¹⁴Cf. E. Andres, *Es la maternidad divina formalmente santificante?*, typed dissertation, (Washington, Catholic University, 1964). ¹⁵*Art. cit.*, n. 1. ¹⁶J. M. Alonso, C.M.F., "Hacia una Mariologia trinitaria: dos escuelas," in *EstM*, 10(1950), 141-191. ¹⁷G. Rozo, C.M.F., *Sancta Maria Mater Dei*, (Milan, 1943), esp. 120ff. ¹⁸Cf. G. M. Roschini, *Maria Santissima*, II, 90. ¹⁹Cf. R. Laurentin, *Traité*, V, 118ff.

MOTHER OF MERCY

Mercy was from early times associated with Mary. The reconstructed text of the *Sub Tuum* (*qv*) has: "We take refuge beneath your mercy."¹ The Akathist (*qv*) Hymn has: "Let every hymn yield which seeks to match your infinite mercy." The title "Mother of Mercy" is found in Jacob of Sarug's (*qv*) sermon *De Transitu*: "How many terrors did not the Mother of Mercy experience when you were buried and the guards of the sepulchre turned her away, so that she could not approach you."² In the East, too, pseudo-St. Sophronius (*qv*) called Mary "an abyss of mercy,"³ and St. Germanus (*qv*) said that "no one without you will be granted the gift of mercy."⁴

In the West, first intimations were the use of *misericordissima*, most merciful, in prayers to Mary,⁵ and the prayer which gained such popularity because it was part of a sermon attributed to St. Augustine. The author was Ambrose Autpert (*qv*): "Come to the relief of those in misery.... Have pity on the afflicted."⁶

The title "Mother of Mercy" occurs first in Latin writing in the life of St. Odo (d. 942), second abbot of Cluny, the starting-point of tenth-century reform. John of Salerno, the biographer, relates that Odo himself had been converted as a young man when, on a Christmas eve, he addressed Mary as follows: "O Lady,

Mother of Mercy, on this night you gave a Saviour to the world; be to me a worthy intercessor."⁷ A converted robber, who was received by Odo into the monastery, had before his death, a vision of a "woman of most glorious presence [*personae*] and surpassing power."⁸ She revealed herself to him as the Mother of Mercy. The biographer adds: "And from thence, our father [i.e. Odo] kept the custom of calling blessed Mary the Mother of Mercy."⁹ In the tenth and eleventh centuries, the title was increasingly used.¹⁰

It did not always mean that Mary was the merciful mother, but that she was the mother of him who was Mercy. Thus St. Peter Damian (*qv*) writes: "We beg of you, most clement one, Mother of pity and mercy himself [*ipsius*], that we may have the help of your intercession in heaven."¹¹ But the same saint could speak of Mary as herself the merciful one, and "guardian of the treasure of God's mercies." The latter sense was gradually to prevail, as deeper awareness came of Mary's spiritual motherhood, as it was seen than, having given to the world Mercy himself, she shared uniquely in this attribute. With such conviction, the change in the *Salve Regina* from *Salve Regina Misericordiae* to *Salve Regina, Mater misericordiae*, was easily conceived and achieved.¹²

¹Cf. article *Sub Tuum* in the present work, text reconstructed by G. Giamberardini, O.F.M. ²*De Transitu*, ed. by A. Baumstark, in *Oriens Christ.*, 5(1905), 96. ³*Triodion* by Joseph the Hymnographer, in PG 87-3, 3846C; R. Laurentin, *Traité*, I, 169. ⁴*In S. M. Zonam*, in PG 98, 379. ⁵H. Barré, *Prières Anciennes*, 52, 75. ⁶*In Assumpt., II*, in PL 39, 2134. ⁷*Vita Odonis, I, 9*, in PL 133, 47B. ⁸PL 133, 72. ⁹*ibid.* ¹⁰For quotations from writers, many well-known, from 10th to 13th centuries, cf. H. Barré, "Répertoire de Textes," in BSFEM, 16(1959), 105-117. ¹¹*Serm. 46 in Nativ. B. M.*, in PL 144, 761. ¹²Cf. G. M. Roschini, "Il titolo e il culto della 'Mater Misericordiae'," in Zagreb Congress, IV, 473-486; H. Barré, *Prières Anciennes*, 111-113.

MOTHER OF THE MESSIAH — See Supplement, p. 385.

MUNIFICENTISSIMUS DEUS
(1 November, 1950)

This is the Apostolic Constitution in which Pius XII gave his reasons for dogmatically defining the Assumption of the Blessed Virgin Mary and pronounced the definition in binding form.¹ On 30 October, 1950, two days before the definition, the Pope told the Cardinals in Consistory that he had "entrusted the matter to experts." They had been instructed to gather and examine the requests sent to the Holy See. "Furthermore," said the Pope, "at our bidding, they studied, with the greatest diligence, all the attestations, indications, and references in the common faith of the Church, as well as lastly in the writings of the Fathers and the theologians, and with the admirable harmony of this with other revealed truths."[2]

Names of theologians who served on the committee are known: Mgr. (later Cardinal) A. Ottaviani; Frs. P. Parente, A. (later Cardinal) Bea, S.J., H. Lennerz, R. Garrigou-Lagrange, O.P., S. Tromp, S.J., K. Balic, O.F.M. (qv), M. Jugie, A.A. (qv), Compagnone, and Hurt. Frs. Balic and Jugie had written monographs on the history of the doctrine. Fr. Bea was rector of the Biblical Institute. Fr. Garrigou-Lagrange had published a work on Our Lady, and articles on the definability of the doctrine. Fr. Tromp was author of a large work on the Mystical Body, and was said to have helped in drafting Pius XII's Encyclical *Mystici Corporis Christi*. He was editing the works of St. Robert Bellarmine (qv) who is quoted in the Apostolic Constitution. Fr. Lennerz had written a treatise on Our Lady in which, as in articles in the review of his university, *Gregorianum*, he had severely criticized theories of Mary's co-redemption (see REDEMPTION). He later accepted the dogma of the Assumption on faith, for he thought it necessary to establish an unbroken historical tradition to Our Lady's death and Assumption.

Economy of phrase in the dogmatic formula matches the whole tenor of the document, which is in contrast with *Ineffabilis Deus*, from the viewpoint of style (forty-six superlatives to ninety-five in *Ineffabilis Deus*), precision in the historical section, and reserve in the handling of biblical texts. This Apostolic Constitution still bears the imprint of Pius XII's strong devotion and exalted feeling towards Our Lady.

---

[1] See article on the Assumption in the present work. For bibliography, cf. J. Carol, O.F.M., "A Bibliography of the Assumption," in *The Thomist*, 14(1951); J. de Aldama, S.J., "Boletín asuncionista. Los primeros comentarios de la Bula M. D.," in EstEcl, 25(1951), 376-406; B. Capelle, O.S.B., "Théologie de l'Assomption d'après la Bulle M. D.," in NRT, 72(1950), 1009-1027; K. Balic, O.F.M., *De Constitutione Apostolica M. D. Disquisitio-dogmatica-apologetica*, (Rome, 1951); id., "De proclamato Assumptionis dogmate prae Theologorum doctrinis et Ecclesiae vita," in Anton, 3(1951), 3-39; id., in *De Sacra Scriptura et Traditione*, (Rome, 1963), 706ff; J. Bonnefoy, O.F.M., "La Bulle dogmatique M. D.," in EphMar, 1(1951), 89-130; C. Colombo,

"La Constituzione dogmatica M. D. e la teologia," in *Scuola Catt.*, 79(1951), 52-93; M. Jugie, A.A., "La définition du dogme de l'Assomption," in *Année théol.*, (1951), 97-116; K. Rahner, S.J., *Das "neue" Dogma. Zur Definition der Himmelfahrt der hl. Jungfrau und Gottesmutter*, (Vienna, 1951).

MURATORI, L. A. (1672-1750)

The "Father of Italian History," M., a conscientious priest, adopted a critical approach to questions of Marian theology.[1] He and his opponents used pseudonyms. In 1714, he published, over the name Lamindus Pritanius, *De ingeniorum moderatione in religionis negotio*. Having heard a preacher in Modena advocate the "Vow of Blood" (qv), he devoted four pages of chapter VI of this work to criticism of the idea. No one, he thought, could sacrifice his life for a human opinion; one could do it for divinely revealed truth, and for the observance of God's holy laws. M. thought that the Immaculate Conception was not mentioned in Sacred Scripture or by the Fathers of the early centuries, who, he went on, seem rather to deny it. He was not directly attacking the doctrine, but undermining it. His first work was opposed by a clandestine manuscript pamphlet circulated in Rome in 1717, "*Osservazioni*" by Mgr. Giusto Fontanini. A Sicilian Jesuit, Francesco Burgi, with the pseudonym Parthenotimus Candidus, next entered the fray with *Votum pro tuenda immaculata Deiparae Conceptione ab impugnationibus recentioribus Lamindi Pritanii*, published in 1729. M. composed a reply, *De superstitione vitanda sive censura voti sanguinarii*, but, fearing the entourage of Clement XII who were favourable to the Immaculate Conception, he bided his time. He issued the book in 1740 when his friend and protector, Benedict XIV, was Pope. Despite the efforts of the Scotists, he contended, the Immaculate Conception remained a human opinion. The work did but rouse public demonstrations of fervour in Italian cities, with renewal of the vow. M. published in 1743 a collection of Letters against certain of his critics, entitled *Ferdinandi Valdesii Epistolae sive Appendix ad Librum Antonii Lampridii, De superstitione vitanda. Ubi votum sanguinarium recte oppugnatum, male propugnatum ostenditur*. Therein, he was still concerned with the Immaculate Conception. He went further in his next book, *Della regolata divozione de Cristiani*; therein, he devoted a chapter (22) to what he considered excess in doctrine or practice. He did not accept Mary's universal mediation, but tried to allow her some mediatorial role, and rejected such views as that she commands in heaven, and the superstition that devotion to Mary without leading a virtuous life will save. He regretted the multiplication of Marian feasts beyond the number of those for Christ.

[1]Works, (Arezzo, 1768; Venice, 1790-1800). Cf. esp. J. Stricher, C.SS.R., *La voeu du sang en faveur de l'Immaculée Conception*, 2 vols., (Rome, Pontifical Marian Academy, 1959); H. Graef, *Mary*, II, 72-74; G. M. Roschini, O.S.M., *Maria Santissima*, III, 212-214; X. le Bachelet, "Immaculée Conception," in DTC, 1180-1185; E. Amann, "Muratori," in DTC, 2553.

N

NARSES (d.*c.* 502) — See Supplement, p. 385.

NEOPHYTUS THE RECLUSE (1134-1220)

A monk, styled the "Chrysostom of Cyprus," N. was known as the Recluse because for years he lived in the solitude of a cave and then accepted disciples, withdrawing after some time to another cave. He was self-taught. He treats of Our Lady in many passages of his writings, directly in nine: two sermons published by M. Jugie, A.A. (*qv*), on the Nativity of Mary and her Presentation (*qv*) in the Temple;[1] three discourses published by E. Toniolo, O.S.M., on the Presentation, the Annunciation, and the Assumption (*qqv*);[2] and four catecheses from the same editor, on the Annunciation, dormition, Nativity, and Presentation.[3]

Mary is the subject of praise by N. in characteristic Byzantine fashion. Mary is for him most pure, most spotless, immaculate: "You certainly, O illustrious Lady, have no need for praise from mortal lips, you who dwell in the heavenly kingdom, spouse of the Father, Mother of the Son, receptacle of the Holy Spirit, because immaculate."[4] Five sections of the discourse on the Annunciation are given to litanies of praise in the *Chaire* sequence: "Hail, you who undid the condemnation of your ancestor and of your first mother Eve . . . . Hail, gate to paradise who lets in believers and excludes unbelievers, ship guided by God, laden with heavenly goods . . . ," with scores of other titles, laudatory epithets, and practically every Old Testament symbol or type, such as holy Ark, rod of Aaron, promised land, city of God, and others with connotation of a saving role.[5]

N. taught Mary's eternal predestination, "whom God chose before all generations."[6] He appears to have held the Immaculate Conception: "Anne, delivered by the Creator of nature from the bonds of sterility conceives, by her spouse, Mary a daughter of God, to whom today she gave birth as the first-fruits of our salvation and the Immaculate Mother of God the Word, and, as the first-fruits of the renewal of our nature, aged and tarnished by transgression of the divine precept."[7] N. uses a striking metaphor to express Mary's purity. The most pure Baker mixed himself with the most pure leaven and thus remade the whole dough from it.[8] "Had not [Mary] to be purer than the sunrays, she who was to communicate to the Sun of justice flesh pure and all immaculate."[9]

In the account of the Presentation, N. relies on the apocryphal story as he does in part for the Assumption. He believed in the bodily Assumption: "That pure and holy body, placed by the apostles in the sacred place of Gethsemani, was borne to the God of the apostles and delighted in those things 'which eye has not seen, nor ear heard, which have not entered the heart of man'."[10]

Through the titles he uses frequently, we can perceive the role N. attributes to Mary. She is Mistress (*Despoina*), "Mistress of the world."[11] But especially she is Spouse. Probably more than any other writer, N. applies this title to Mary. She is "the Spouse of God," "the virgin Spouse of God," "the Spouse and Mother of God," "Spouse and daughter of the immortal Father," "irreproachable Spouse of the King," "immaculate Spouse," "immaculate Spouse of

Christ," "Spouse of the Father," "pure Spouse of the immortal Father," "blessed, untouched, immaculate Spouse, divinely acceptable to the immortal Father," "holy Spouse," "Virgin-Mother Spouse."[12]

Through the sponsal metaphor, N. sees the parallel between Mary and the Church: "We apply, therefore, the words of the psalm [45] to the Church, spouse and daughter of the king of glory; but they agree fully also with the most pure Virgin, Spouse and daughter of the immortal Father."[13]

In biblical matters, N. has little of note. He takes the "hour" of Jn 2:4 as the hour of his miracles. Mary he looks to as "Mother of life." He intercedes to Christ through her supplication, and he expresses his belief in her "invincible strength" to those in the stress of passion.

[1]PO 16, 528-532, 533-538. [2]MM, 36(1974), 210-236, 238-262, 264-282, Italian tr. facing. [3]MM, 36(1974), 284-290, 292-294, 296-298, 300-302; "Encomium for Hypapante," by same editor, in MM, 36(1974), 304-314, Italian tr. throughout. Cf. Beck, 633; M. Jugie, A.A., *L'Immaculée Conception*, 209-212. Cf. esp. E. Toniolo, *intr. op. cit.*, 184-209. [4]MM, 36(1974), 264. [5]MM, 36(1974), 240-248. [6]PO 5, 531. [7]PO 3, 530. [8]PO 3, 530. [9]PO 1, 534. [10]MM, 36(1974), 282. [11]PO 5, 531. [12]PO 5, 532; MM, 36(1974), 220, 222, 218, 234, 262, 236, 266, 276, 264, 270, 294, 300, 298. [13]MM, 36(1974), 218.

NEWMAN, JOHN HENRY, CARDINAL
(1801-1890)

N.'s writing on Our Lady is comparatively slight: about half a dozen sermons wholly or in part on Mary; basic passages in the *Essay on Development; Letter to E. B. Pusey*; the section on the Immaculate Conception (*qv*) in *On Consulting the Faithful*; a number of letters on the dogma of the Immaculate Conception, defined during his life or which give the background to the controversy with E. B. Pusey; pages of piety in the *Mediations and Devotions*, part of which deals with the Litany of Loreto; and suggestive jottings in the *Sermon Notes*.[1] Interest has been given to this corpus due to N.'s reputation as a prophet for our times, and to his agreement with Vatican II.[2] As a university student, he had difficulties about devotion to Mary.[3] He was helped by Hurrel Froude—"He fixed deep in me the idea of devotion to the Blessed Virgin"—and by Dr. Russell of Maynooth, who explained to him that, in an English

translation of sermons by St. Alphonsus, some passages had been deleted.[4] He saw that what suited Italy was not universally acceptable. These devotional manifestations had been his "great *crux* as regards Catholicism...."" "... they may be fully explained and defended, but sentiment and taste do not run with logic; they are suitable for Italy, but they are not suitable for England."[5]

Between 1832 and 1845, the Anglican, who was emerging as a great religious leader, developed a theology of Mary, not only unexampled in his own communion, but superior to most contemporary thinking on the subject in the Catholic or Orthodox churches. In the first year, he preached a sermon on the Annunciation extolling Mary's dignity and holiness. "In her, was now to be fulfilled that promise which the world had been looking out for during thousands of years."[6] Already we have the patristic parallel and contrast with Eve, which will dominate the thinking of the years ahead. "I observe that in her the curse pronounced on Eve was changed to a blessing."[7] He not only asked, "Who can estimate the holiness and perfection of her who was chosen to be the Mother of Christ?," and spoke of the "transcendent purity of her whom the creator Spirit condescended to overshadow by his miraculous presence," but used a phrase which created difficulties with his fellow Anglicans. Years later, he described the event. To indicate "the sanctity and grace of that human nature of which God had formed his sinless Son," he had recalled that, "what is born of the flesh is flesh," and "none can bring a clean thing out of an unclean." "I was accused of holding the doctrine of the Immaculate Conception, for it was clear that I connected 'grace' with the Blessed Virgin's *humanity*, as if grace and nature in her case had never been separated. All I could say in answer was, that there was nothing against the doctrine in the Thirty-Nine Articles."[8]

The sermon was notable for two other striking insights. Why, asked the preacher, do the Scriptures say so little about Our Lady? The reserve, he thought, is a divine concession to our weakness: "We cannot combine in our thought of her all we should ascribe with all we should withhold."[9] He thought that "by *nature* a sinner, she was raised above the condition of sinful beings . . . brought near to God, yet but a creature," which recalls Paul VI's saying to Vatican

II, later written into *Lumen Gentium*, "she who occupies a place in the Church which is the highest after Christ, yet very near to us."[10] Secondly, the preacher counselled his hearers to follow Sacred Scripture, and to think of Our Lady always as "with and for her Son, never separating her from him"—an essentially conciliar idea—"united with him by a close and indissoluble bond" (LG 53).[11]

In two sermons preached in February, 1843, N., making his own "return to the sources," moved still nearer to a doctrinal synthesis which would surpass any thinking by his contemporaries anywhere. On the feast of the Purification, explaining Lk 2:19, 51, on the text, therefore, which Vatican II used to illustrate the developing process within Sacred Tradition, he spoke of Our Lady's faith, but in a way foreshadowing the great theological work he was to complete before his entry to the Catholic Church. The sermon bore the title *Theory of Developments in Religious Doctrine*.[12]

Some weeks later, N. took up another aspect of biblical theology about Our Lady—the marriage feast of Cana, which he was comparing with the Last Supper. Here he gave the exegesis of the words spoken by Jesus to Mary, "What have I to do with thee," which will recur in the *Letter to E. B. Pusey*, which is commended by a modern specialist.[13] "He seemed to put his Mother from his thoughts as being called to the work of a divine ministry."[14] Thus too, as the text continues, N. understood the "awkward" texts in the synoptic gospels—"Who is my mother and who are my brethren?," and "Yea, rather, blessed are they who hear the word of God and keep it." But things would not remain thus: "While his work was in progress, he turned from his Mother; but in alluding to an hour that was to come, he gave her to understand that her separation from him would end in that hour."[15]

N. was scrutinizing Sacred Scripture closely on the subject of Our Lady, and the *Essay on Development of Christian Doctrine*, which appeared in 1845, gave further proof of his study. It showed especially impartial, comprehensive research on the patristic witness, and on the facts of history within the Catholic communion. The edition here used is that of 1845, which expresses N.'s mind at the time. There was some rearrangement of the matter in the 1878 edition.

Relevant to our subject is section four of chapter seven, "The Office of St. Mary," and pages in sections one and two of chapter eight, entitled respectively, "The Deification of St. Mary" and "The Worship of St. Mary."

The foundation of Mary's "special prerogatives," he discerned already in the patristic doctrine of the new Eve: "St. Justin, St. Irenaeus, and others had distinctly laid it down, that she not only had an office, but bore a part, and was a voluntary agent, in the actual process of redemption, as Eve had been instrumental and responsible in Adam's fall . . . . And certainly the parallel between the "Mother of all living" and the Mother of the Redeemer may be gathered from a comparison of the first chapters of Scripture with the last."[16] The supporting quotations included Irenaeus' classic sentence, "being obedient [Mary] became a cause of salvation both to herself and to all the world."[17]

N. goes on to apply Rev 12 to Mary, sustaining his argument with an original analogy taken from the history of Arianism, concluding: "The votaries of Mary do not exceed the true faith unless the blasphemers of her Son came up to it. The Church of Rome is not idolatrous, unless Arianism is orthodoxy."[18] The work of the Councils is fully appreciated; the Church, in reaction against heresies, was led "to lay down first the conceivable greatness of a creature, and then the incommunicable dignity of St. Mary."[19] "In order to do honour to Christ, in order to secure a right faith in the manhood of the Eternal Son, the Council of Ephesus determined the Blessed Virgin to be Mother of God."[20] Allowance is made for the *sensus fidelium* (see SENTIMENT OF THE FAITHFUL), in the preparation of these teachings, and for the theological speculation on Mary's eternal destiny, "she was predestined in the Eternal Mind coevally with the Incarnation of her Divine Son."[21]

Catholic theory was subjected to a kind of empirical test by the great Tractarian. He found that, contrary to facile prejudice, the European "religious communions, which are characterized by the observance of St. Mary, are not the churches which have ceased to adore her Eternal Son, but such as have renounced that observance."[22] N. noted clear difference between the language of devotion used by Catholics about Our Lady and about the Holy Trinity and Christ.

He made a favourable survey of popular Catholic literature on Our Lady, being particularly happy with Fr. Segneri's *Il Devoto di Maria*, a treatise which throws "light upon the *rationale* by which the distinction is preserved between the worship of God and the honour of an exalted creature."[23]

No Anglican had written thus of Our Lady; few Catholics were, at the time, writing thus about her. The year of the *Essay* was the year of the author's conversion to Catholicism, to which he remained faithful through the next forty-five years, despite heart-breaking experience, and despite the misunderstanding which his towering genius and integrity could not always dispel. He acquired a new sense of Our Lady's guidance in his past life, marked his gratitude to her by taking her name in Confirmation, naming the Oratory at Birmingham "Maryvale," and dedicating the church to the Immaculate Conception. When he preached or wrote on her, it was with the same sure learning, with an occasional flash of deeper insight. Soon after the return to Birmingham, he preached in St. Chad's on the text, "Yea, but blessed are they who hear the word of God and keep it" (Lk 11:27), arguing that Mary's holiness was inseparably linked with her divine motherhood, adding a nuance to his previous exegesis of these synoptic texts, "he taught her and all who heard him that the soul was greater than the body, and that to be united with him in spirit was greater than to be united with him in the body;" he defended the opinion that Mary had a vow of virginity (qv).[24]

In the following year, the *Discourses Addressed to Mixed Congregations* appeared. They included two important papers: *On the Glories of Mary for the Sake of her Son;* and *On the Fitness of the Glories of Mary*—powerfully constructed essays. Mary's grace and glory are not for her own sake, but her Maker's. She has the custody of the Incarnation, as her appointed office which leads to this fine passage: "A mother without a home in the Church, without dignity, without gifts would have been, as far as the defense of the Incarnation goes, no mother at all . . . . If she is to witness and remind the world that God became man, she must be on a high and eminent station for the purpose."[25]

Another striking passage merits study in the light of the recent change in the theology of

Revelation, away from the propositional, essentialist view prevailing in manualistic theology, to a biblical Christocentric doctrine. The passage may be compared with N.'s sermon preached in 1830, on 1 Jn 1:1-3, quoted in the preamble to *Verbum Dei*, wherein he spoke thus: "Here, then, Revelation meets us with simple and distinct *facts* and *actions*, not with painful inductions from existing phenomena, not with generalized laws or metaphysical conjectures, but with *Jesus and the Resurrection* . . . ."[26] Of Our Lady, he now writes: "He became man of her; and received her lineaments and her features as the appearance and character under which he should manifest himself to the world. He was known, doubtless, by his likeness to be her Son. Thus his Mother is the first of the Prophets, for, of her, came the Word bodily; she is the sole oracle of Truth, for the Way, the Truth, and the Life vouchsafed to be her Son; she is the one mold of Divine Wisdom, and in that mold it was indelibly set."[27]

On Mary's intercessory role, he was explicit. "Is it strange that the Mother should have power with the Son, distinct in kind from that of the purest Angel and the most triumphant Saint? If we have faith to admit the Incarnation itself, we must admit it in its fullness; why then should we start at the gracious appointments which arise out of it, or are necessary to it, or are included in it?"[28]

In the order of time, the next contribution to Marian theology was made in the *Rambler* article, *On Consulting the Faithful in Matters of Doctrine*. It appeared in July, 1859. Already in 1849, N., writing from Rome to W. G. Ward, commented on the Encyclical *Ubi Primum*, noting the fact that the people were given a place in the consultation which the Pope, Pius IX, instituted by this letter before defining the dogma of the Immaculate Conception.[29] In the *Essay*, he had judged that "the spontaneous or traditional feeling of Christians . . . had in great measure anticipated the formal ecclesiastical decision."[30] In the *Rambler* article, he drew on the work of G. Perrone, *De Immaculato B. V. Mariae Conceptu*, the Encyclical, and the Bull *Ineffabilis Deus* (qv).

In all, N. found recognition of the *sensus fidelium* which he explained thus, "the body of the faithful is one of the witnesses of the tradition of revealed doctrine, and because their *consensus* through Christendom is the voice of the infallible Church."[31] He held that "the gift of discerning, discriminating, defining, promulgating, and enforcing any portion of that tradition resides solely in the *Ecclesia docens*."[32] This is now the doctrine of Vatican II (LG 12, 34); the phrase of Perrone which N. liked, *pastorum ac fidelium velut in unum conspiratio*, is, with the word *antistitum* substituted for *pastorum*, found in *Ineffabilis Deus, Munificentissimus Deus* (*qv*), and *Verbum Dei* (10), "a common effort on the part of bishops and faithful."

The immediate sequel to the *Rambler* article was deplorable: N. was denounced to Rome for heresy, and we can follow the pitiful details through a whole volume of the *Letters and Diaries*.[33] We can follow, with equally complete documentation, the fortunes of his best-known work on Our Lady, *The Letter to E. B. Pusey*.[34] Cardinal Manning had written an open letter to Pusey on the workings of the Holy Spirit in the Church of England, and the *Eirenicon*, addressed to Keble, was Pusey's reply. It is described in the article on Pusey (*qv*). N. decided to publish a detailed comment on the section of the work which dealt with Our Lady; he felt confident of an audience, and felt that he owed his witness to those who wished to know "what they would, and what they would not be bound to hold concerning her."[35] He wanted to put forward a theology of Mary and of her place in worship which would be orthodox, but clearly different from excesses singled out by Pusey. (see ECUMENISM) He kept up kindly contact, chiefly by correspondence, with the author of the *Eirenicon* before and after his reply; he also wrote to Keble in the same tone.

The basic doctrinal theses of the *Letter* had been set forth in previous works. With some preliminaries and forty pages of notes, the body of it was in three parts: on the belief of Catholics concerning the Blessed Virgin, as distinct from their devotion to her; on belief of Catholics concerning the Blessed Virgin, as coloured by their devotion to her; and on Anglican misconceptions and Catholic excesses in devotion to the Blessed Virgin. In the first part, the warrant is patristic doctrine: "I do not wish to say more than they suggest to me, and will not say less."[36] The doctrine of the Second Eve, as the "great rudimental teaching of Antiquity," is set forth with many testimonies cited from East and West. "We are able, by the position and office of Eve in our fall, to determine the position and office of Mary in our restoration."[37]

N. deduces Mary's holiness from this premise, even her Immaculate Conception, "as an immediate inference," and likewise her dignity.[38] He is led into biblical theology and defends a strictly Marian sense in Gen 3:15 (see WOMAN IN) and Rev 12 (see WOMAN IN), though he is aware of the difficulties in the latter exegesis. He links the ecclesial and Marian interpretations. Jn 19:25-27 (see WOMAN IN) is also, for him, related to the spiritual motherhood. N. calls on patristic support for the title *Theotokos* (*qv*); he thought Origen first used it. Intercession was also recognized by the Fathers.

In the second part of the Letter, N. subtly explains the relation between belief and devotion. The third part has been much quoted. These pages should be read in their entirety, for it is easy to miss the qualifications and the explanation of factors like the unpredictable singularity of saints and the effects of national temperament. The exuberant manifestations of the Easterns are recalled. Pusey had made use of excerpts taken out of context from the well-known works of St. Alphonsus Liguori (*qv*), *The Glories of Mary*, and St. Louis Marie de Montfort (*qv*), *On True Devotion to the Blessed Virgin*. It is surprising that the Oratorian of Birmingham had not come across Faber's translation of the latter work, and that he had not read the other. He had not met either the extravagant effusions of Bernardine of Busti (*qv*). He did know, and made it clear that, for St. Bernardine of Siena (*qv*), St. Alphonsus, and St. Paul of the Cross, devotion to Our Lady did not impede due honour and love of Our Lord. He went into some detail to show the truth of his earlier view that Catholic peoples devoted to Mary had remained strong in faith in the divinity of her Son.

It was with the necessary provisos, therefore, that N. repudiated the phrases which Pusey had extracted from Catholic works, which he found objectionable, because they attributed divine powers, attributes, or privileges to Our Lady. They seemed to him like a "bad dream," and he doubted if the vast majority of English Catholics knew of them.

The author of the Letter remarked in correspondence to his Catholic friends that it might prove a disappointment, since he dealt with things well known and omitted much else that figures in the *Eirenicon*. It was an immediate success, selling two thousand copies in a fortnight, given a full-page review in *The Times*, translated into French within a year. It drew some Ultramontane fire of course, but was defended adequately. It remains the outstanding single exercise in true Ecumenism on the subject of Our Lady. The Catholic reader will know from what genuine Marian piety it sprang: by reading the *Meditations and Devotions*, or going through the *Sermon Notes*,[39] a number of which deal with the *Mater Dolorosa*; or by looking at the title chosen for honour in N.'s exquisite Byzantine church in Dublin, *Sedes Sapientiae*; or by recalling Maisie Ward's biographical item, that a favourite practice of this great Doctor of our times, this imperial intellect, was the Rosary.

[1]Cf. F. J. Friedel, *The Mariology of Newman*, (New York, 1928); H. F. Davis, "La Mariologie de Newman," in *Maria*, III, 535-552; H. du Manoir, S.J., "Marie, nouvelle Eve, dans l'oeuvre de Newman," in BSFEM, 14(1956), 67-90; F. M. William, "Cardinalis Newman Theses de doctrina et devotione Mariana et motus oecumenicus," in MO, 257-274; J. Stern, M.S., "Le culte de la Vierge et des Saints et la conversion de Newman au catholicisme," in VieSp, 117(1967), 156-168; *id.*, "Le Saint Esprit et Marie chez Newman et Faber," in BSFEM, 26(1969), 37-56; *id.*, "L'Action du Saint Esprit dans le mystère du Christ et de sa Mère selon J. H. Newman," in CM, 14(1970), 183-190; G. Velocci, C.SS.R., "La Mariologia di Cardinale Newman," in *Divinitas*, 11(1967), 1021-1046; *id.*, "La Madonna in Newman," in *Ecclesia Mater*, 6(1968), 139-161; M. M. Olive, O.P., "Un petit traité de Mariologie selon les Pères des premiers siècles: La 'Lettre à Pusey' de Newman (1865)," in PCM, III, 303-332; L. Govaert, *Kardinal Newman's Mariologie und sein personnliche Werdegang*, with an unpublished sermon on the Annunciation, (Salzburg, 1975). [2]Cf. M. O'Carroll, C.S.Sp., "Our Lady in Newman and Vatican II," in *Downside Rev.*, 89(1971), 38-63. [3]Cf. S. O'Faolain, *Newman's Way*, (London, 1952), 83. [4]*History of My Religious Opinions*, (ed. 1865), 25. [5]*op. cit.*, 195. [6]*Parochial and Plain Sermons*, (London, 1840), II, 128. [7]*op. cit.* [8]*Letters and Diaries*, XIX, 346-347. [9]*Parochial and Plain Sermons*, (London, 1840), II, 135. [10]AAS, 56(1964), 37. Cf. LG 63, 67. [11]LG 53. [12]*Oxford University Sermons*, (ed. London, 1890), 313-314. [13]*In Certain Difficulties Felt by Anglicans in Catholic Teaching*, (ed. 1876), 72. Cf. F. M. Braun, O.P., *La Mère des Fidèles*, 2nd ed., (Tournai, Paris, 1954), p. 58 and n. 30. [14]*Sermons on Subjects of the Day*, (ed. London, 1873), 33. [15]*op. cit.*, 35. [16]Essay, p. 384. [17]*Essay on the Development of Christian Doctrine*, (London, 1845), 385. [18]*op. cit.*, 406. [19]*op. cit.*, 407. [20]*op. cit.* [21]*op. cit.*, 444. [22]*op. cit.*, 436. [23]*op. cit.*, 443. [24]*Catholic Sermons of Cardinal Newman*, (London, 1957), 94-95, 100. [25]*Discourses to Mixed Congregations*, 3rd ed., (London, 1862), 407. [26]II, "The Influence of Natural and Revealed Religion Respectively," in *Fifteen Sermons Preached Before the University of Oxford*, (ed. London, 1890), 27. [27]*Discourses* . . ., 3rd ed., (London, 1862), 429-430. [28]*op. cit.*, 414. [29]*Letters and Diaries*, vol. XIII, 81. For the Encyclical, cf. M. O'Carroll, C.S.Sp., "Our Lady in Newman and Vatican II," in *Downside Rev.*, 89(1971), 55ff. [30]*Essay* . . ., (London, 1845), 407. [31]*On Consulting the Faithful*, 2. ed. by J. Coulson, (London, 1961), 63; text also in M. Carroll's tr. of *The Church and the Laity*, (New York, 1965). [32]*op. cit.* [33]Cf. *Introduction to Vol. XIX*, subtitled *Consulting the Laity*, January 1859-June 1861, in *Letters and Diaries*, 204ff, 240ff, 276ff, 289ff. [34]Vol. XXII, *Beween Pusey and the Extremists*, July 1865-December 1866, in *Letters and Diaries*, 117-211. [35]In *Certain Difficulties Felt by Anglicans* . . ., (ed. 1876), 25. For Cardinal Manning's letter, cf. his work *England and Christendom*, (London, 1867), 83-133. [36]*op. cit.*, 24. [37]*op. cit.*, 32. [38]On the Immaculate Conception, cf. *Mediations and Devotions*, XIX, *Letters and Diaries*, 346-347, 437-438, 361-370. [39]*Newman's Sermon Notes 1849-1878*, ed. by the Oratory Fathers, (London, 1913), *passim*, esp. 104.

NEUBERT, ÉMILE, S. M. (1878-1967)

A Marianist, pioneer in Marian studies, author of the first doctoral thesis accepted in the university world, N. supported the growing movement of Marian theology in France immediately before and after the Second World War.[1] His published work included doctrinal essays—*Marie dans l'Église Anténicéenne*, and *Marie dans le dogme*—and contributions to pastoral and apostolic Marian literature: *Marie et notre sacerdoce*, *La Mission apostolique de Marie*, and *L'âme de Jésus contemplée avec Marie*. Of special significance in spiritual literature were *Mon idéal, Jésus, fils de Marie*, and *La Vie d'union avec Marie*.

[1]Cf. Th. Koehler, S.M., "Le P. E. Neubert, marianiste," in EphMar, 17(1967), 530-532; B. Wyder, S.M., "L'Oeuvre mariale du P. E. Neubert," in EphMar, 17(1967), 532-538; L. Gambero, S.M., "Un maestro di vita spirituale: E. Neubert, S.M.," in MM, 30(1968), 26-52.

NICEPHORUS CALLISTUS (d. *c.* 1335)

It is probable that N. was born in Constantinople and that he became a monk before he died; he used the library of Santa Sophia. Better known as a historian, his Marian ideas are found in a commentary on the *Troparion* of Cosmas Melodes (the younger adopted brother of St. John of Damascus (*qv*), a work still in manuscript,[1] in passages of his *Church History*, and in poems published in 1929 by M. Jugie, A.A. (*qv*).[2]

M. Jugie thinks that N. was the first eastern theologian to have denied the Immaculate Conception (*qv*). He had contacts with the West and seems to have known of the controversy current on the subject. "She did not then engender through corruption, but by the word of the archangel Gabriel, after the Holy Spirit had come upon her and had purified her of the original stain, if perchance this stain was still found in her in some way."[3] Here N. seems to interpret the Purification (qv) in relation to sin, but this was not the universal opinion. Elsewhere, the author says that the Blessed Virgin Mary was found worthy to become the dwelling of God the Word. "She had been consecrated to God even before her birth, and had come to being as a fruit given by God, born of a womb grown old and knowing no passion."[4] In the same manuscript, from which Fr. Jugie quotes, towards the end, there is a touching prayer for forgiveness to Our Lady, "if I have gone astray in deciding to speak of stain in regard to the all-pure one."[5]

N. extols Mary's total virginity in the manuscript cited. In the poems, he expresses the sense of his own unworthiness in striking terms which contrast with the unimpeded flow of praise of the *Theotokos*, the "undefiled Virgin." There is not the merest suggestion of imperfection and some phrases incompatible with any: "Impure one, as I am, I make bold to address with an unholy tongue thee, who art immune from every stain."[6] "God, most pure and most beautiful, found thee the only pure one."[7]

Titles used in Byzantine literature occur in the poems: Mistress (*despouina*); Queen; Helper; Mediatress of the faithful; Mediatress of the world; Consoler; and, the favourite title, Protectress. Acrostic patterns and, in one poem, *chairetismoi*, provide a chain of eulogy; with the *chairetismoi*, N. used the end title from the *Akathistos* Hymn, unespoused spouse. "Hail, gift of Christians; hail, thou who abolished the devil's strength, who, by your word, brought forth the Word; hail, Mistress, hail, unespoused spouse."[8]

On the bodily Assumption (qv), N. is ambiguous. He has read the Euthymiac History which he reproduces,[9] John the Geometer and Simeon Metphrastes. He seems torn between the theory of the double Assumption[10] and that of total resurrection.[11]

217-221. Cf. *ibid.*, in *L'Assomption*, 327-328. [2]*In Byzantion*, 5(1929), 362-390; intr. 357-362. [3]M. Jugie, A.A., *L'Immaculée Conception*, 218. [4]*Hist. Eccl.*, in PG 145, 1, 7, 651. [5]M. Jugie, A.A., *L'Immaculée Conception*, 219. [6]I, 23, p. 365. [7]V, 12, p. 374. [8]VII, *Chairetismoi*, 4, p. 380. [9]*Hist. Eccl.*, bk. 15, ch. 14, in PG 147, 44-46. [10]*Hist. Eccl.*, bk. 2, ch. 21-23, in PG 145, 809-816. [11]PG 147, 41ff.

NICHOLAS OF CLAIRVAUX (d. after 1176) Nineteen sermons by N. had been lost among those of St. Peter Damian (qv), and are printed with his in the *Patrologia Latina*. Seven of them have matter relevant to Marian theology—three on feasts of Our Lady: the Annunciation; the Assumption; and the Nativity.[1]

N. thought that Mary was sanctified in the womb like St. John the Baptist. He thought that she had an exalted position in the divine dispensation of things. "And immediately, from the treasure of the divinity, the name of Mary is brought forth, and through her, in her, from her, and with her, it is decreed that all this will be done, so that, as without him [God], nothing was made, without her, nothing has been remade."[2] N. says elsewhere that Mary "gave back life to the world." Having been an object of choice and predilection, "the Holy Spirit was to take her totally to himself and mark her with heavenly ornaments."[3] In her, action did not lessen contemplation, and contemplation did not abandon action. N. believed in the bodily Assumption (qv): "The whole multitude of angels assembles to see the queen seated at the right of the Lord of power in golden attire, in her ever immaculate body."[4] In the same sermon on the Assumption, N. pictures Mary leaning on her Son, or reclining between his arms as his spouse (qv): "O what dignity, what special power she has to lean upon him, whom the angelic powers look upon with awe." She is the mistress of the world, the queen of the heavens, even the empress of the heavens, enjoying partnership, *consortium*, with her divine Son.

The emphasis on the queenly dignity and power does not lessen belief in mercy, "the more powerful, the more merciful," says N. "For he, my God, is my mercy, and this sweet lady is the gate of mercy. May the Mother lead us to the Son, the daughter to the Father, the spouse to the Spouse, who is blessed forever."[5]

---

[1]Extracts from the manuscript in the Bodleian Library, quoted by M. Jugie, A.A., in *L'Immaculée Conception*,

[1]Cf. J. Ryan, "Saint Peter Damiani and the Sermons of Nicholas of Clairvaux," in *Medieval Studies*, 9(1947),

151-161; R. Laurentin, *Traité*, I, 144-145; Marian sermons, in PL 144, 557A-563A, 717A-722C, 736B-740D. [2]PL 144, 558C. [3]PL 144, 558C. [4]PL 144, 717B. [5]PL 144, 563A.

NICHOLAS OF ST. ALBANS
(Twelfth Century)

Little is known of N., save that he was Prior and possibly Abbot of the Benedictine Abbey of St. Albans.[1] He is known for his written work, *Liber Magistri Nicolai de celebranda conceptione beatae Mariae contra Bernardum*, and his letter to Peter of Celle to answer Peter's criticism of this work. Genuineness of the *Liber* has been questioned by L. Modric, O.F.M., who placed it at the end of the twelfth century, and by J. de Aldama, S.J., who thought that it was written after N. had replied to Peter, by another Master Nicholas. The arguments used to support these views have not prevailed, so we may accept the text as genuine. C. H. Talbot, the editor, supplies information to distinguish N. from Nicholas of Clairvaux (*qv*).

N.'s purpose was to defend the feast of the Immaculate Conception (*qv*) against the famous letter of St. Bernard to the Canons of Lyons. The feast had recently been raised to most solemn rank in the abbey. He argued that it would enrich the Liturgy, that it would not upset tradition, that, even if based on a private revelation, as Bernard feared, God reveals as he decides and no true revelation can harm the Catholic faith. He disagreed with Bernard also on the opinion that the feast of Mary's Nativity was sufficient to honour her saintly origins; he thought it left the main point ambiguous.

In dealing with Bernard's fifth objection to the feast, N. came to grips with the Augustinian theory on the mode of transmitting Original Sin. He did not have the intuition of Scotus on the difference between preservative and liberating redemption. He proposed two solutions. In the first, Mary's conception did not come from corrupt concupiscence, which was the consequence of Adam's sin, but from natural concupiscence, innate, not experienced before sin. On the second view, if "the Virgin's flesh in seed before the infusion of the soul was as ours, it is lawful to believe that the soul, at the moment of this infusion, was immediately filled by the Holy Spirit, and the flesh was cleansed of the leprosy of corruption."

For a biblical argument, N. used texts taken from the Psalms, Proverbs, and Song of Songs.

He thought that Mary, as her divine Son, was an exception to "in peccatis concepit me mater mea" (Ps 51:5), and he also rejected as irrelevant Mt 11:11, that none born of a woman was greater than John the Baptist. Commentators judge his doctrine as reconcilable with the universal redemption by Christ. "So by a privilege of office, it was granted to the Precursor that his birth, to the Virgin Mother, that both her conception and birth, should be honoured in public worship, for therein the mystery of our redemption is, in a certain way, begun."

Peter replied by a letter (PL 202, 171, 613-622) in which zeal to defend his master, Bernard, outran theological method. He makes a great point of the differences between the French and English, due to climatic factors, seeing therein what he thinks N.'s mistake. The latter's answer was moderate (PL 202, 172, 622-628). He unfortunately mentioned a "stupid little legend" (Fr. H. Barré's word). A Cistercian lay brother, in a dream, saw St. Bernard clad in white, but there was one black stain—the symbol of his error about the Immaculate Conception. N. also left himself open to further criticism by Peter: "As the Father and the Son are equal in heaven, so also the Mother is like the Son on earth, not that I say she was conceived by the Spirit, but that she was filled and sanctified by the Spirit from her mother's womb, just like the Son." To Peter's second letter (PL 202, 173, 628-632), N. did not reply.

He has his place among the theologians of the Immaculate Conception of medieval England. He was influenced, if not inspired, in the development of his doctrine by the feast again restored in England—the Liturgy fulfilling its role as an expression of the sentiment of the faithful, voice of tradition.

[1]J. Bale, *Scriptorum illustrium majoris Britannicae*, (Basle, 1657), 299; Tanner, *Bibliotheca Britannico-Hibernica*, (London, 1748), 546-547. Cf. F. Mildner, O.S.M., "The Immaculate Conception in the Writings of Nicholas of St. Alban's," in MM, 2(1940), 179-193; H. F. Davis, "Our Lady's Conception, A Medieval Manuscript," in CRev, 30(1948), 85-95; *id.*, "Theologia Immaculatae Conceptionis apud primos defensores, scil. in Anglia saec. XII," in V.I., V, 1-12; L. Modric, O.F.M., "Doctrina de conceptione Mariae in controversias.. XII," in V.I., V, p. 21, n. 31; A. J. Luddy, O.Cist., "Nicholas of St. Alban's Among the Prophets," in CRev, 29(1948), 313-319; C. H. Talbot, "Nicholas of St. Alban's and St. Bernard," in RevBen, 64(1954), 83-91; *id.*, "Liber Magistri Nicolai de celebranda conceptione beatae Mariae contra Bernardum," in RevBen, 64(1954), 92-117; P. Bonnar, "Nicholas of St. Alban's:

A Twelfth Century Theologian of the Immaculate Conception," in *Dublin Review*, 72(1958), 54-64; J. Fr. Bonnefoy, O.F.M., *Le Ven. Jean Duns Scot, Docteur de l'Immaculée Conception*, (Rome, 1960), 413-421; J. de Aldama, S.J., "El Tratado de Nicolas de San Albano sobre la fiesta de la Concepción," in MM, 22(1960), 506-511; H. Graef, *Mary*, I, 250-253; G. M. Roschini, O.S.M., *Maria Santissima*, III, 96-118.

NICOLAS, JEAN JACQUES AUGUSTE
(1807-1888)

A French lay apologist for Christianity, N. was author of four volumes on Our Lady: *La Vierge Marie dans le plan divin* (Paris, 1855); *La Vierge Marie dans l'Évangile* (Paris, 1857); and *La Vierge Marie vivant dans l'Église*, two volumes (Paris, 1860)—a work which had considerable influence. Two grandsons of J. J. A. Nicolas—M. J. Nicolas, O.P., author of a substantial work on Our Lady, *Theotokos*, specialist in the theology of the divine motherhood, and dogmatic theologian of the French Society for Marian Studies, and H. Nicolas, O.P., author of an important work on Mary's virginity—continue an exceptional family tradition.[1]

---

[1]P. Lepeyre, *Auguste Nicolas, sa vie et ses oeuvres*, (Paris, 1892).

NILUS THE ABBOT, ST. (d.c. 430) — See Supplement, p. 385.

NOTKER "BALBULUS", THE STAMMERER, ST.
(d. 912)

A monk of the monastery of St. Gall, with an interest in versified biography—of St. Gall and Charlemagne—author of a martyrology, and especially of liturgical hymns, N. may have been influenced by Greek monks with whom he became acquainted. His *Liber Ymnorum* (884) contains three sequences for feasts of Our Lady—the Purification, the Assumption, and the Nativity—while what is said in those for the feasts of Christmas and its octave, and of St. John, has some relevance.[1]

The accent in N.'s compositions is on Mary's powerful intercession. His manner is restrained.

He speaks of angels around Mary singing together the glory of God at Christmas;[2] of Mary, enlightened by her Son on "the painful glory of his power;"[3] of Mary, honoured by the first sign of Christ's divinity,[4] the miracle of Cana.

N. sees Mary in the center of salvation history, hymned by the books of the prophets, the jubilant choir of priests, and preached by the apostles and martyrs of Christ. "The faith of the supreme patriarch, your father [Abraham] possessed you completely"; Aaron's rod prefigured Mary, as did the closed door of Ez 44:2.[5] She herself surpasses all her ancestors, and the poet exclaims: "But why should we recall those [Old Testament] heroes, when your Son excels them and all throughout the world."[6]

In his Martyrology, N. professes belief in the bodily Assumption: "Since it was fitting [*decuit*] that the body, from which God willed to take a body, should be raised more quickly to heaven."[7] This may inspire his confidence. "Therefore we beg you to become our mediatress [*interventrix*] because of our guilt." "The whole Church, honouring you with heart and hymns, shows its devotion to you, imploring you, O Mary, in suppliant prayer, that you deign to be, before Christ the Lord, its help for all time." "On this day, on which you came to the light of the world, keep us, Virgin, close to you who were to bring forth the Light of heaven."[8] With these solemn petitions to one whom he elsewhere sees "resplendent in the presence of God," N. can keep the human touch, speaking of Mary as the one on whom the Child smiles.[9]

---

[1]*Liber Sequentiarum*, in PL 131; critical ed. by W. von den Steinen, *Notker der Dichter und seine geistige Welt*, II, (Berne, 1948); biography and background, in *op. cit.*, I, (Berne, 1948). Cf. L. Scheffczyk, "Das Marien bild in den lateinischen Hymnen des frühen Mittelalters, besonders beim Notker Balbulus von St. Gallen," in Zagreb Congress, III, 479-497; O. Perler, "Die Marienverehrung im Gebiet der heutigen Schweiz," in Zagreb Congress, V, 151-158. [2]*In Natale D. N. J. C.*, in critical ed. by W. von den Steinen, 12. [3]*De S. Joanne*, apud W. von den Steinen, 16. [4]*In Octava Dni. (Die Mutterhymne)*, apud W. von den Steinen, 20. [5]*In Nativ.*, apud W. von den Steinen, 68; *In Purif.*, apud W. von den Steinen, 24. [6]*In Nativ.*, 68. [7]PL 131, 1142. [8]*In Nativ.*, 20, 66, 68. [9]*In Purif.*, 24.

O

OBJECTIONS TO MARIAN DOCTRINE AND DEVOTION

Criticism has been made of Marian doctrine and devotion from without and from within the Catholic body. At the time of the Reformation, such criticism was motivated by the essential theses of Protestantism. Confessional rivalries and antagonisms may have added to the doctrinal criticism.

In the decades before Vatican II (*qv*), the Marian movement had so grown that a certain reaction was to be expected. In the Council entourage, the words "maximalist" and "minimalist" expressed two trends—one which tended to increase the power, privileges, and function of Our Lady to the extreme possible; the other seeking to accord to her only what could be literally and rigorously justified. The clash of opinions was described and analyzed in a preconciliar book which stirred some controversy, R. Laurentin's *La Question mariale*.[1] Echoes of the debate were heard in the Council speeches. The ecumenical movement prompted a more critical attitude towards questions about Our Lady.

The main criticisms of Marian doctrine would be: Mariology is being enlarged at the expense of the unity of Theology, with a methodology of its own, claiming almost independent status; dogmas are being multiplied beyond objective validity—after the Immaculate Conception and Assumption, requests were heard for still more, the doctrinal development has been in excess of the data of Revelation; Marian theologians have been at times influenced unduly by the sentiment of the faithful (*qv*) or by private revelations; and Christ is at times displaced from the center of the Christian mystery and economy.

Complaints about the growth of Marian theology are sometimes prompted by the sheer amount that has been published. Books and substantial studies on Our Lady were, at the time of the dogma of the Assumption, appearing at the rate of a thousand a year. The sight of so much print gives some people the idea that the subject has somehow got out of hand, which does not follow. There are no such complaints when vast numbers of books appear on secular figures or movements. This is a matter of free expression and a free market.

The history of Marian homiletics and theology shows that much has been composed in the immediate context of Christ: homiletics on his feasts; and Marian treatises within the dimensions of the treatise on the Incarnation. Witness the great medieval scholastics, and Suarez, Petau, and Scheeben. The doctrine of Christ's absolute, universal primacy has been notably expounded and defended by giants of Marian theology, East and West, the Palamites and the Scotists.

Theologians have been given firm guidance by Pius XII and Vatican II on how they should advance in study of Mary's destiny and person. The Council proclaimed their freedom as well as encouraging their research. Their desire, in one case or another, for new dogmas remains subject to the Teaching Authority, which, as the same Council tells us, advances in harmony with Sacred Scripture and Sacred Tradition.

Objections to Marian devotion have run parallel to those against doctrine. Critics objected to the number of feasts of Our Lady, or they alleged that devotions to her were competing with or displacing properly liturgical services. Again, it is sometimes said that the cult is excessively papal. The Church, it is thought, is unduly influenced in its forms of piety by the Latin or Celtic or Slav mentality. Adding "new jewels to Mary's heavenly crown" is a characteristic manifestation of this mentality. Disciples of Our Lady, it is felt, are unduly credulous, seeking apparitions, prophecies, and the like. Elsewhere, they are accused of aggressive behaviour. It is a fact that crusades against the Turk, in the sixteenth and seventeenth centuries, were associated with Mary by Popes of the time. Apostles of Our Lady irritate some by their apparent propaganda ardour, their pressure to take up some particular practice or prayer, their willingness to add duties to the Christian life by forming new associations. All the time there is the fear that they take from Christ what they give to Mary.

Cardinal Newman's Letter to E. B. Pusey (*qv*) is a good guide in such matters. He was led to the Catholic Church by the discovery that it was the Catholic peoples who retained the cult of the Mother who remained true to the divine Son. Vatican II has established the primacy of liturgical prayer, while allowing freedom to popular devotions. It will be seen that, in Marian piety, the Popes were true interpreters of the intuition of the People of God. They and the Council have granted a warrant to the variations in devotion which, within the universal norms, local or ethnic conditions demand. Militant attitudes should be related directly to the combat in which all are engaged for the glory of God. All voluntary organizations must proceed from respect for individual freedom and choice.

---

[1]R. Laurentin, *La Question mariale*, (Paris, 1963), many translations. For criticism of the book, cf. J. de Aldama, S.J., *De quaestione mariali in hodierna vita Ecclesiae,* (Rome, Marian Academy, 1964).

ODILO OF CLUNY, ST. (962-1049)

O., fifth abbot of Cluny, spoke on Our Lady in many of his short sermons, especially four on her feasts, the Purification, the Assumption, and the Nativity (2). The last three are composed from pre-existing material, that on the Assumption from a sermon that may go back to the eighth century, the first on the Nativity from a work spuriously attributed to St. Augustine (*qv*), the second literally extracted from St. Ambrose's *De Virginibus*.[1] O. may be assumed to have accepted the ideas in these texts. His life, written by Jotsaldus, in PL 142, contains matter of interest.

O. singled out virtues and attributes in Mary relevant to monastic life. Her life was active but, as in the Visitation (*qv*), to be helpful; for the most part, she was a contemplative, for example in the moment of the Annunciation (*qv*). He thought she had chosen perpetual virginity and delayed on her poverty, evident in the Presentation of the Lord: "She was poor in earthly possessions, but filled with heavenly blessing."[2] Eve and Mary are evoked in traditional sense.

Though the apocrypha are rejected, O., after Sedulius, spoke of Mary in the company of the women who went to the tomb on Easter morning; but with faith she knew he was already risen. After the Ascension, she was accustomed to visit the holy places sanctified by Jesus' sufferings. He could not resist Pseudo-Jerome (*qv*) on the question of the bodily Assumption (*qv*). Mary was closely united with the apostolic "college" (his word twice), and spoke to them of the facts of Christ's life which she especially knew, "thus the apostles learned from her how to believe the secret of so great a mystery so as to teach it more clearly to others."[3]

Mary was a "most holy and most pure mother"; "you are," exclaims O., "after God, the principal cause of human salvation."[4] Hence the power of Mary's intercession: "Whoever is exposed to dangers in the spiritual or bodily life must turn the point of his spirit towards contemplation of this star, whose merit and grace can free him from all danger, let him not doubt it."[5] It was, however, by the special act of consecration to Mary as her slave that O. enriched the Cluniac Marian tradition, though this practice was not new. "O most clement [*piissima*] Virgin Mary, Mother of the Saviour of all the ages, from today and henceforth, hold me in your services, and in all my affairs be with me as a most merciful advocate. From now on, after God, I choose nothing before you, and spontaneously I commit myself forever to your bondage as your slave."[6] Jotsaldus, in his poetic lament for his abbot, describes his devotion to Mary, the fulfillment of the special vow: "O Virgin Mary, how greatly he served your honour. He kept you, the kindly mistress of the world and of the heavens, in all his prayers, you he preferred and loved."[7] Two customs, begun by O., were taken up by many Benedictine monasteries—the inclination or genuflection at the words of the *Te Deum, Non horruisti Virginis uterum*, and the celebration of the Assumption with the same solemnity as Christmas and Easter.

---

[1]Cf. R. Laurentin, *Traité*, I, 144; G. Bavaud, "La dévotion de saint Odilon à la Vierge Marie," in Zagreb Congress, III, 571-582; J. Hourlier, "Saint Odilon Abbé de Cluny," in RHE, 40(1964), 143-145; P. Cousin, O.S.B., "La dévotion mariale chez les grands Abbés de Cluny," in *À Cluny, Congrès scientifique. Fêtes et cérémonies liturgiques en l'honneur des saints Abbés Odon et Odilon 9-11 Juillet 1949,* (Dijon, 1950), 210-218. [2]*Serm. 3, De Purific.*, in PL 142,

1000D. [3]*Serm. 12*, in PL 142, 1026C. [4]PL 142, 1028C. [5]*Serm. 12*, in PL 142, 1003CD. Cf. Pseudo-Jerome, in PL. [6]Jotsaldus, *De vita et virtutibus O. Abbatis, 2, 1, 30*, in PL 142, 124-126; PL 142, 915D-916A. [7]PL 142, 1044D.

ODO OF CLUNY, ST. (d. 942)

The second abbot of Cluny, O. played a notable part in the spiritual renewal initiated by the abbey. His interest in Marian piety is in the title, Mother of Mercy (*qv*). It emerges in two episodes in his life as told by John of Salerno about 945. The more picturesque story is of a robber who had become a monk in Cluny and shortly before death told the abbot of a vision he had. "Last night, father, I was raised up to heaven in a vision. But a woman of glorious appearance and wonderful power met and, as she approached me, she said, 'Do you know me?' I said, 'Not at all lady'. 'I,' she said, 'am the Mother of Mercy.' 'What,' I replied, 'do you wish me to do, lady?' 'You will be coming here at a certain hour after three days,' she said. This is what happened. On the third day, at the hour he had said, he died. What he saw was then clearly real, for he departed this life at the hour he had foretold. Thence our father took the custom of calling blessed Mary the Mother of Mercy."[1]

The other incident is personal to O., and seems to show that he thought of the title himself—a view open to question. His father, to further his conversion, suggested a night's vigil in prayer. The young man chose Christmas night and composed this prayer: "O lady, Mother of Mercy, on this night you gave a Saviour to the world. Deign to intercede for me. To your glorious and singular Child, I fly, O most clement one, and do you bend the ears of your pity to my prayers. I have an intense dread that my life may be displeasing to your Son, and because, O lady, through you, he manifested himself to the world, may he very soon, I pray, have mercy on me, because of you."[2] This prayer was widely diffused and elsewhere given in the plural number. The title "Mother of Mercy" is meaningful in doctrine and devotion.

[1]PL 133, 72AB. Cf. J. Leclercq, O.S.B., in *Maria*, II, 554; P. Cousin, O.S.B., "La dévotion mariale chez les grands Abbés de Cluny," in *À Cluny, Congrès scientifique. Fêtes et cérémonies liturgiques en l'honneur des saints Abbés Odon et Odilon 9-11 Juillet 1949*, (Dijon, 1950), 210-218; H. Barré, *Prières Anciennes*, 111-113; G. M. Roschini, "Maria Santissima," in Zagreb Congress, IV, 475-480. [2]PL 133, 47BC.

OLIER, JEAN JACQUES (1608-1657)

O. was founder of the Seminary of St. Sulpice and of the Society of the same name, which was to have very great influence on the training of the clergy in France and overseas. The Sulpician ideal of sanctity and the practices which derived from it were thus given diffusion and a certain permanence. One such practice was the prayer *O Jesu vivens in Maria*, adapted by O. from a formula composed by Fr. de Condren, many of its elements traceable to Bérulle (*qv*).

O.'s Marian doctrine is contained in a remarkable book, *Vie Intérieure de la Très-Sainte Vierge, ouvrage recueilli des écrits de M. Olier*.[1] This work, in two substantial volumes, was composed from the writings of O. by his biographer, M. Faillon, and published in Rome. It was not reissued, but was replaced by a work of somewhat similar title in 1875.[2] It is a rare publication, but is the indispensable source. M. Faillon added to the body of the work, clearly marked off by chapter headings from O.'s text, passages of his own sometimes by way of explanation, more frequently as practical suggestions. And he set out on page after page, beneath O.'s text, numerous, often lengthy, excerpts from the Fathers, still more from the best known medieval Latin writers, by way of corroborative material. Quotations from the Greek and Syrian Fathers were given in Latin. The book was thus an ordered compilation of the Marian writings of O., and an anthology of patristic and medieval Marian passages; the editions used had the shortcomings of the time and questions of authenticity, since resolved, were not even raised.

O.'s thinking, though related to the successive mysteries in the life of Mary, drew on the master idea of the French school—the interior states of Jesus and Mary. The subtleties and validity of his views depend on a mystical insight, which may be missed or dismissed by hasty isolation of unusual texts. Thus the bridal motif (see SPOUSE, MARY AS) is constant. More than any writer perhaps, O. treats of Mary as spouse of the Father. Thus she was predestined: "For God the Father, who alone can send and give the person of his Son and communicate him to mankind, wills that, in the mystery of the Incarnation, Mary should be his true and unique spouse, since he has destined her to be, with himself, the principle in the temporal generation of the Word, to do with him, in the Incarnation, what he does alone in eternity."³ All that follows is, in O.'s thinking, drawn from this initial insight: "He [the Father] conceives for her all the affection of a spouse."⁴ She is entirely one with him, "from which it follows that she shares in his designs, in his orders, in his works."⁵ "He wills to give the most holy Virgin union with and perfect enjoyment of his person, of all his goods, of his treasures and of his glory, to order with her all his plans."⁶ In this sense, the Old Testament texts, Sir 24:5f and Prov 8:22f, are explained.

O. held that Mary was conceived immaculate and that, "besides being preserved from the crime of origin, she was all filled from the first instant of her conception, with the Holy Spirit and his graces."⁷ He analyzes at length Mary's state of soul after she had been presented in the Temple. "The Word of God, through the love he bore the most holy Virgin, advanced the time of his holy marriage with the Church."⁸ For Mary cried out and longed for the Messiah with power exceeding that of all the prophets.⁹

One after another, the mysteries in Mary's life are thus spiritually interpreted. St. Joseph (qv) is the image of God the Father: "It is in fact God the Father who espouses the most holy Virgin, by the ministry and under the exterior of St. Joseph."¹⁰ The Spirit, at the Annunciation, gives her "the excess of magnificent graces needed to accompany the spouse of the eternal Father, and of Mother of his Son."¹¹ O. analyzes the effects of the divine maternity, relating them to the persons of the most holy Trinity. Of the Holy Spirit, he says: "All the gifts, all the virtues, all the graces of this divine Spirit are administered by the hands of Mary and as she wills"¹²— a thought from St. Bernardine of Siena (qv).

The birth of Christ prompts O. to express his opinion on the spiritual motherhood (qv) of Mary. She forms Jesus in us. In a chapter entitled "The Society of Jesus and Mary," he considers gospel episodes or sayings such as the Finding in the Temple (qv), and Jesus' replies to words spoken about his Mother, and ends with a doctrine of Mary and the Church, which post-conciliar theologians can value, which gives him the opportunity of preparing for a new application of the bridal concept—the espousals of Mary and Jesus. This is brought out in the chapter on Mary on Calvary, when "the Church, in the person of Mary, espouses Jesus Christ on the Cross."¹³ Here O. adopts the idea of Mary as the new Eve (qv): "In her role as new Eve, she

[Mary] must contribute to our reconciliation with God the Father."¹⁴ When he completes the theory in his reflection on the Resurrection, he incorporates the same idea in his synthesis: "He takes her, in his turn, as spouse, so as to beget the Church with her, as the Father had taken her to beget himself . . . he takes the most holy Virgin, as a new Eve, as his helper; and in that moment, he gives her communion with all that he had received from the Father, to make her *Mother of the living*."¹⁵ An interesting subordinate theme developed in these chapters is Jesus' "design" to transform St. John into his own person"—by interior assimilation, according to the French school—so that through him, he should still bestow love on his Mother after the Ascension.¹⁶

Mary received the Spirit in fullness on Pentecost Sunday, whereas the Apostles received him in a certain measure; she cooperated with them in the growth of the Church. This is worked out at great length. Very fully too, O. shows how Mary, assumed into heaven, continues as our Mediatress, as the special advocate of sinners. His book ends with a warm exhortation to devotion to the interior of Jesus in Mary, and reproduces the office of the Interior of the most holy Virgin Mary.

¹J. J. Olier, *Vie Intérieure de la Très-Sainte Vierge, ouvrage recueilli des écrits de M. Olier*, (Rome, 1966); Olier's *Oeuvres complètes*, ed. by Migne, (Paris, 1856). Cf. P. Pourrat, *La Spiritualité chrétienne*, III, (Paris, 1927), 525-574, and *Jean-Jacques Olier*, (Paris, 1932); H. Brémond, *Histoire littéraire du sentiment religieux en France*, III, (Paris, 1921), 420-507, esp. 447ff; Cl. Dillenschneider, C.SS.R., *La Mariologie de S. Alphonse de Liguori*, I, (Fribourg, 1931), 234-238. ²H. J. Icard, *Vie intérieure de la Très-Sainte Vierge d'après les écrits de M. Olier*, 1 vol., (Paris, 1875). Note *"d'après les écrits"* instead of *"ouvrage recueilli des écrits."* ³*op. cit.*, I, ch. 1, p. 57. ⁴*ibid.*, p. 60. ⁵*ibid.* ⁶*ibid.* ⁷*op. cit.*, I, ch. 2, p. 90. ⁸*op. cit.*, I, ch. 3, p. 152. ⁹*ibid.*, p. 143. ¹⁰*op. cit.*, I, ch. 4, p. 174. ¹¹*ibid.*, 185. ¹²*op. cit.*, I, ch. 6, p. 247. ¹³*op. cit.*, II, ch. 13, p. 85. ¹⁴*ibid.*, pp. 86, 74. ¹⁵*op. cit.*, ch. 14, p. 126. ¹⁶*op. cit.*, ch. 12, p. 42; *op; cit.*, ch. 13, p. 72; *op. cit.*, ch. 14, pp. 131ff.

OLIVI, PETER JOHN (1248-1298)

One of the Franciscan Spirituals whose rigorism brought him for a while into difficulties with his order, O. studied under St. Bonaventure (qv) in Paris. His Marian theology is contained in *Four Questions on Our Lady (Quaestiones quatuor de Domina.*¹ The first deals with the virginal consent (qv) of Mary in the Annunciaton (qv); the second with twelve victories of the Blessed Virgin in twelve temptations; the third with the excellence of Mary in glory; the fourth with the sorrow of Mary during the Passion. St. Bernardine of Siena (*qv*) took over much of the first and third questions and a little of the second. With material from the first he fleshed out Sermons 5 and 6 of his treatise on the Blessed Virgin; from the third he took matter for his sermon on the "superadmirable grace and glory of the Mother of God" and for his first sermon on the glorious name of Mary, O. was probably the first Western writer to treat systematically the biblical theology questions concerning St. Joseph; this he did in his *Postilla in Mt 1*.[2]

O. thought that Mary was conceived in original sin, but he held the strongest views on her perfection. He analyses her consent in very philosophical terms, praising in the highest manner the merit it won her. Inset in the second part of the work is a perceptive analysis of OT and NT texts on Mary,[3] especially Rev 12 (see WOMAN IN) which O. applies to Mary and the Church in the manner of Ambrose Autpert (*qv*): "And certainly the woman clothed with the sun, having Christ in her womb and giving birth to him signifies the Church because it refers more properly and specifically to Mary."[4] In the third part, Mary's excellence over all the blessed and angels is stressed.[5] O. rejected, in the fourth question, a view of Mary's compassion which would see in it more joy than sorrow: "For the suffering of Christ entered and pierced the Virgin's heart, in such wise that it cannot be believed that she had any joy, at least so great or of such a kind as would be felt in her heart."[6]

The doctrine of the book is substantial and very reasonable. On questions about St. Joseph, O. had substantial influence after his death, first on Ubertino of Casale (*qv*) and through him on St. Bernardine of Siena (*qv*), and on others less well known—John of San Gemignano, O.F.M., and another Franciscan, Bartholomew of Pisa (d. 1410).[7] Manuscript material awaits further study.

[1]Quaracchi, ed. D. Pacetti, 1954. [2]Cf. for text and commentary A. Emmen, O.F.M., "Pierre de Jean Olivi, sa doctrine et son influence," *CahJos*, 14-2, (1966), 209-270. [3]32ff. [4]Pp. 35-36. [5]Pp. 44, 52. [6]P. 66. [7]Cf. E. Longpré, O.F.M., *Le Patronage de saint Joseph d'après l'école franciscaine du XIIIe siècle*, in *Le Patronage de saint Joseph, Actes du Congrès d'Etudes* (Montreal, 1956), 216-254.

ORIGEN (*c*. 185-254)

The prolific genius of Alexandria, the "father of Greek theology," O. made important contributions to Marian theology, though here, as in other areas of his thought, the loss of so much of his written work deprives us of a complete picture. In medieval times, he was known as a Marian doctor.[1]

O. reconciles the Incarnation with his ideas about the preexistence of souls. Christ is truly man, conceived by the Holy Ghost, and the virginal conception (see VIRGINITY OF MARY) is rooted in the Alexandrian's Christology. In the long passage on the subject, in the *Contra Celsum*, he justifies biblically the *Septuagint* translation of *almah* by *parthenos*, rather than *neanis* in Is 7:14 (see EMMANUEL). "What sort of sign would it be if a young woman, not a virgin, bore a son?"[2] Here too the author deals with the invention that Christ was born of an adulterous union between Mary and a Roman soldier, Panthera; the name ben-Panthera is found in the Talmud.[3] O. saw a relationship between the virginal conception and the divinity of Jesus, for he was pointing the way to a view which, in the West, would be associated with St. Augustine (*qv*). Conjugal relations imply a certain blemish. He upheld the perpetual virginity: "Mary had no other children but Jesus, according to those who think sanely."[4] He first gave at length, as a reason for the marriage (*qv*), the need to conceal the divine origin of the Child—deducing it from a sentence in St. Ignatius of Antioch's Epistle to the Ephesians. "The virginity of Mary was hidden from the prince of this world." To which O. added: "It was hidden by reason of Joseph."[5] Mary would also be preserved from stoning "for having lost her virginity." The fragment on Luke, containing this phrase, is thought doubtfully genuine by Dom Vagaggini.[6] O. took the common eastern view that the "Brothers of the Lord" were children of Joseph by an earlier marriage.

Mary was the firstfruit of women's pure chastity, as Jesus was of men's pure chastity. "It would not be pious to attribute the firstfruits of virginity to any but her."[7] O. highly esteemed virginity, and he wrote: "Every virginal, incorrupt soul, having conceived of the Holy Spirit to engender the will of the Father, is the mother of Christ."[8] The Word is the will of the Father.

On the virginity *in partu*, the relevant texts have been examined carefully by H. Crouzel, who concludes firmly against such an opinion held by O.[9] Mary's personal perfection is exalted, caused by the coming of the Holy Spirit and the divine child-bearing. In the gallery of "spirituals" formed by the great ones of the Old and New Testaments, she is the only woman fully accepted. She meditates assiduously on the Law and the prophets, and is specially enlightened and endowed, enjoying the gift of prophecy in the moment of the *Magnificat*. She is humble, poor, filled with faith, advancing in spiritual knowledge, and sustained in moments of obscurity by the sense of mystery—all of which is expressed in the distinctive O. categories.

Yet there are the texts in which O. seems to attribute imperfection to Mary. In the first homily on Genesis, he insinuates that Mary's question in Lk 1:34 shows a certain incredulity.[10] In *Hom.* 20 on Luke, he speaks of Mary and Joseph going down to Nazareth, because they could not remain on the heights of faith with Jesus[11]—a characteristic allegory with him. The passage which most deeply marked subsequent exegesis, however, is that on the sword of Simeon (*qv*). O. interpreted it as doubt which would pierce Mary's soul in the Passion. "What! Are we to suppose that, when the apostles were scandalized, the Lord's Mother was exempt from scandal? If she did not suffer scandal in the Lord's Passion, Jesus did not die for her sins . . . even thee shall the sword of unbelief pierce, and thou shalt be struck with the spear of doubt, and thy thoughts shall tear thee asunder, when thou shalt see him whom thou hadst heard to be the Son of God, crucified and dying, and subject to human torments, and at last with tears complaining and saying, 'Father, if it be possible, let this chalice pass from me'."[12]

The exegesis here is faulty, and was eventually rejected by tradition. O. did teach that the weakness would be momentary.[13] The sword was not doubt; the warning to the Apostles did not include Mary. The universality of the redemption was not affected. O.'s perspectives are not thereby limited. He has some references to the Eve-Mary typology, deals at length with the Visitation (*qv*), and interpreted the words of the dying Jesus to his Mother in a way exceptional in patristic writings. The passage is sometimes related to medieval and modern, especially papal, doctrine on the universal

spiritual motherhood of Mary, but this is not its main thrust. Singling out the gospels in the whole Bible, and St. John's among the four, he goes on: "Of this, no one can receive the sense if he has not reclined upon the breast of Jesus, and if he has not received, from Jesus, Mary to be his Mother also. He who wishes to become another John must become such, and so great that he will be shown to be Jesus by Jesus himself, as was John. For if, in the judgment of those who think sanely about Mary, there be no Son of Mary, but Jesus, and Jesus said to his Mother, 'Behold thy son' and not 'Behold, he too is thy son,' it is as if he said, 'Behold, this is Jesus whom you brought forth.' For it can be said of everyone who is perfect that he no longer lives, but Christ lives in him, and since Christ lives in him, it is said of him to Mary. 'Behold thy Son, Christ'."[14] This is a view of Mary's spiritual motherhood in highly personalist, mystical, Christocentric terms, more, some contend, a view of the unity of the perfect in Christ.

O. used the word *Theantropos* of Christ. His use of *Theotokos* is controverted, and is dealt with the relevant article.

[1]CMP, I, 73-126; EMBP, 79-108; C. Vagaggini, O.S.B., *Maria nelle opere di Origene, (Orient. Christ. Anal. 131)*, (Rome, 1942); H. Crouzel, S.J., "La Mariologie d'Origène," in SC, 87, 11-63; *id.*, "Marie, modèle du spirituel et de l'apôtre selon Origène," in BSFEM, 19(1962), 9-25. [2]*C. Celsum*, I, 35, tr. by H. Chadwick, (Cambridge, 1953), 34. [3]Cf. H. Chadwick, *op. cit.*, p. 31, n. 3. [4]*In Jo. com.*, in GCS, 10, 8-9. [5]*Hom. VI in Luc 4*, in SC, 87, 144. [6]*op. cit.*, 21-23. [7]*In Matth. com. X, 17*, in GCS, 40, 22. [8]*Fragm. in Matth.*, 281, in GCS, 126. [9]SC, 87. [10]*In Gen. hom. I, 14*, in SC, 7, 84. [11]*In Luc. hom. XX, 4*, in SC, 87, 283-285. [12]*In Luc. hom. XVII*, in SC, 87, 257-259. [13]*Fragm. in Luc. 71*, in GCS, 49, 257. [14]*In Jo. com. I, 4*, in GCS, 10, 8-9; PG 14, 32A-B.

ORTHODOX THEOLOGIANS
Theologians of the eastern churches separated from Rome.[1] There has been continuity with the early ages on the great themes of Marian theology. The Palamite theologians were a high-water mark; at the very end of the Byzantine empire, George Scholarios (*qv*) was true to the tradition of doctrine and eloquence. The principal Orthodox contribution to Marian theology in modern times has come from expatriate Russians. In the same period, from about the seventeenth century on, whether through direct or indirect reaction against Rome, opposition to the Immaculate Conception (*qv*) hardened in certain Orthodox circles. The denial was official,

though Kiev held out for a long time. *Ineffabilis Deus* (*qv*) was the occasion of vigorously hostile essays. As a result of the most extreme of them, written by Alexander Lebedev (1833-1898), the Holy Synod of the Russian Church, in 1884, placed the dogma on the list of differences between Rome and the Orthodox Church. It was to be so presented in seminaries and academies. The Conference of Orthodox Churches held in Moscow in 1948 endorsed the decision. All differences on the subject presuppose a different concept of original sin. (See PURIFICATION MARY'S)

In view of the eastern patristic and Orthodox tradition in favour of the Assumption, reaction in Orthodox circles to the dogma of 1950 was surprising—particularly negative in the Greek church. In 1903, A. I. Bulgakov, of the Kiev academy, had criticized M. J. Scheeben's arguments for the definability of the doctrine, and these were revived. What some Orthodox theologians have found objectionable in *Munificentissimus Deus* was the non-committal attitude to Mary's death (*qv*). For some, the fact of a papal intervention was the difficulty.

Most fruitful in the domain of Marian theology has been the work of the Russians. The determining concept was the sophiological idea elaborated into a system by Vladimir Soloviev (1853-1890), who sought to incorporate his belief about Our Lady into the system. The theological outlook was continued by Paul Florenskij, Eugene Trubeckoj, and Leo Karsavin, and reached a pinnacle in the work of Sergius Bulgakov (*qv*). With varying nuances, these writers treat of Mary as, after Christ, the embodiment of divine wisdom, with an altogether special place in the scheme of things— the heart of the Church, the personification of the Church, endowed with holiness, which, for some, implies the Immaculate Conception. This Bulgakov and Florenskij deny, though Bulgakov's phrasing of his opinion brings him very near the truth.

Before the creation of the world Council of Churches, Bulgakov, a committed ecumenist and member of Faith and Order, raised the Marian question. In the most recent phase of the ecumenical movement, Orthodox theologians participate in inter-faith discussions on Our Lady, in the English Ecumenical Society of Our Lady from the outset, in the French Society for Marian Studies, and at other such meetings.

[1]Cf. G. Florovsky, "The Ever-Virgin Mother of God," in *The Mother of God*, ed. by E. L. Mascall, (London, 1949); V. Lossky, *ibid.*, Panagia, p. 24-36= *Ways of Worship. The Report of a Theological Commission of Faith and Order*, (London, 1951), 67-74; M. Gordillo, *Mariologia Orientalis, (Orient. Christ. Anal. 141)*, (Rome, 1954); A. Wenger, A.A., "Foi et piété mariales à Byzance," in *Maria*, V, 923-981; *id.*, "Les interventions de Marie dans l'Église Orthodoxe et l'histoire de Byzance," in PCM, VI, 423-431; B. Schultze, S.J., "Maria und die Kirche in der russichen Sophiatheologie," in ME, X, 51-141; *id.*, "La Mariologie sophianique russe," in *Maria*, VI, 215-239; *id.*, "Die biblische Grundlage der Marienverehrung in der Exegese der Orthodoxen," in PCM, II, 71-101; P. Sherwood, O.S.B., "Byzantine Mariology," in *Eastern Churches Quarterly*, 14(1962), 384-409; M. J. Le Guillou, O.P., "Les caractères de la mariologie orthodoxe," in BSFEM, 19(1962), 91-121; *id.*, "Corrientes mariológicos en la moderna teologia rusa ortodoxa," in EstM, 20(1961), 9-22; G. Mastrantonis, *The Virgin Mary Theotokos*, 3rd ed., (New York, 1962). Cf. esp. D. Stiernon, A.A., "Marie dans la théologie orthodoxe Gréco-Russe," in *Maria*, VII, 241-315, bibliography, 315-338; Kallistos Ware, *The Mother of God in Orthodox Theology and Devotion*, (London, The Ecumenical Society of the Blessed Virgin Mary); H. M. Koester, S.A.C., "Die Eigenart der orthodoxen Mariologie," in MSS, VI, 37-56; A. Kniazeff, "La place de Marie dans la piété orthodoxe," in BSFEM, 19(1962), 123-143; *id.*, "La Mere de Dieu," in *La Vierge Marie*, (Tours, Mame, 1968), 107-164; *id.*, "The Great Sign of the Heavenly Kingdom and Its Advent in Strength," in *St. Vladimir's Seminary Quarterly*, 13(1969), 53-75; Meletios, "Postura actual de la Iglesia ortodoxa acerca de la doctrina y del culto a la Madre de Dios," in EstM, 32(1960), 275-288; I. Gheorghescu, "La doctrine sur la S. V. dans l'Orthodoxie et le Catholicisme," in *Ortodoxia*, 16(1970), 382-399; P. Evdokimov, "Panagion et Panagia," in BSFEM, 27(1970), 59-71.

OSBERT OF CLARE (Twelfth Century)

A monk who was Prior of Westminster (*c.* 1136), O. was a hagiographer, especially devoted to the cause of Edward the Confessor's canonization, and a theologian of Our Lady.[1] He was a notable defender of the feast of the Conception of Mary, which the Normans suppressed for a while in England. In his *Sermo de Conceptione*, and in his Letter to Anselm of Bury, nephew of St. Anselm, he expressed his reasons for believing in the Immaculate Conception (*qv*). It was the beginning of the Redemption and consequently the uplifting of fallen nature. The destiny of the Mother of God incarnate implied it. The ultimate reason was the Incarnation.

O. also saw a possible argument from the Eve-Mary analogy. He was the author of hymns, prayers, and a sermon on St. Anne, in which he asks her to be on his behalf "sedula mediatrix et propicia interventrix."

[1]Letter 7 in *Letters of Osbert of Clare*, ed. by E. W. Williamson, (London, 1929); *Sermo*, in H. Thurston and T. Slater's *Eadmeri monachi Cantuariensis Tractatus de conceptione Sanctae Mariae*, (Freiburg, 1904), 65-83; texts on St. Anne, "Les compositions de Osbert de Clare en l'honneur de Ste. Anne," ed. by A. Wilmart, O.S.B., in *Annales de Bretagne*, (1926),=1-33 *Auteurs spirituels et textes dévots du Moyen Âge latin*, (Paris, 1932), 261-286. Cf. D. Knowles, *The Monastic Order in England*, (Cambridge, 1949), 511-513; A. W. Burridge, "L'Immaculée Conception dans la théologie de l'Angleterre mediévale," in RHE, 32(1936), 572-579; J. A. de Aldama, S.J., "La fiesta de la Concepción de Maria," in EstEcl, 36(1961), 430.

P

PAGANISM

Was the gospel narrative of the birth of Christ akin to or influenced by "divine" births related in pagan literature?[1] Like that of Perseus born of Danae "still a virgin by him that they entitle Zeus flowing down upon her in the form of gold"? Thus the question was put in the *Dialogue with Trypho* by St. Justin Martyr. Does the story recall legends of divine intervention in the conception of extraordinary men like Plato or Alexander? Or the passage in Virgil's Fourth Eclogue about a virgin and a divinely descended child?

The Jewish idea of divine transcendence, of monotheism, was the basis of the gospel story. It is entirely different from the theogamies of the pagan world, anthromorphic pictures of sensual divinities, themselves contained within a man-designed cosmos. The Annunciation story tells of a moment of divine election, one eminent and unique by reason of the absence of any sensual tendency, any sexual motivation, a descent of the *Ruah* or *pneuma*, oriented towards a plan of universal salvation—issuing in offspring, himself divine and transcendent.

Was there an influence from the cult of goddesses and mother—goddesses on that of the Virgin Mary? Cybele, Artemis, Demeter, Astarte, and Isis come to mind from the contemorary world of early Christianity. It is principally in the cult of the mother-goddess that historians have looked for possible influence. But two essential differences mark the devotion rendered to Mary. She was never given divine honours, they were; she was seen in a world of the supernatural whose term is the hereafter, they were principles of biological fertility here and now.

There is no difficulty in allowing for psychological factors, for the integration of certain social patterns, common in pagan religious practice into the Christian system of worship and piety—after they have been purified. Missionary practice on lines laid down by Pius XII and Vatican II help us to understand what took place in times past. Customs, notions slightly or even seriously mistaken, may, when purified and elevated to the Christian ideal, achieve their true fulfillment. Words may be adapted as the origin of *Theotokos* shows.

[1]Cf. F. J. Dolger, "Die eigenartige Marienverehrung der Philomarianiten oder Kollyridianer in Arabien," in *Antike und Christentum*, I, 2(1929), 107-140; K. Prumm, *Die christliche Glaube und die altheidnische Welt*, I, (1935), 253-333; *id.*, ch. VIII, "Maria im Heilsplan," in *Christentum als Neuheitserlebnis*, (Freiburg im Brisgau, 1939), 145-158; J. Cardinal Daniélou, S.J., "Le culte marial et le paganisme," in *Maria*, I, 161-181; G. Cardaropoli, O.F.M., "Il culto della B. Vergine in relazione al culto delle dee pagane," in PCM, IV, 85-108; G. Söll, S.D.B., "Haben das Heidentum und die Apokryphen die Marienverehrung illegitim beeinflusst?," in PCM, IV, 109-121; D. Fernandez, C.M.F., "Num cultus matrum deorum influxum in terminologiam circa divinam maternitatem habuerit?," in PCM, IV, 123-143.

PASCHASIUS RADBERT, ST. (*c.* 780-*c.* 865).

Benedictine Abbot of Corbie, P. was a principal theologian and scholar of the Carolingian Age. His Marian doctrine is contained in the *De partu sanctae Mariae*,[1] written about 845, in three sermons on the Assumption found among the works of St. Ildefonsus,[2] in the *Libellus de Nativitate sanctae Mariae*, found among the works of St. Jerome (*qv*),[3] in the commentary on Matthew, on the infancy narrative. A famous medieval work, "*Cogitis me*," which had enormous influence because it was attributed to St. Jerome, was indeed composed by P. as a letter by him (see PSEUDO-JEROME). It bore the title "To Paula and Eustochium on the Assumption." Altogether this collection of pieces represents a respectable theology of Our Lady for the time.

Because of an ambiguity, what the critical editor calls a Sibylline quality, some texts of P. have been adduced to support the Immaculate Conception. "But because she is the object of such solemn cult, it is clear from the authority of the Church that, when she was born, she was subject to no sins, nor did she contract original sin, being sanctified in the womb."[4] Later, in the same passage, he says that "it is clear that she was free from original sin," but the whole context is that of the birth and the phrase, "sanctified in the womb," is also used.[5]

P.'s work, subsequently entitled *De partu sanctae Mariae*, on the birth from holy Mary, is a treatise on the *virginitas in partu*, on the preservation, that is, of Mary's physical integrity in the moment of childbirth. It was a reply to the treatise of his junior in the same monastery, Ratramnus (*qv*), which, subsequently also, bore the same title, but contained a different doctrine. P. drew mostly on Latin Fathers, though he used passages from St. Irenaeus (*qv*) and St. Cyril. His concern was with "those" (taken by the best authority to be Ratramnus) who, in their desire to save the idea of genuine motherhood for Mary, contended that the birth of Jesus must be "by the common law of nature and, as is the custom, with all women."[6] The argument against such a view was based ultimately on the mystery of the Incarnation and on the virginal conception, on the "blessing she brought to the world" in reply to the initial curse, on the sanctifying power of the Holy Spirit. Old Testament texts, Ps 21:10, Song 4:12, and Ez 44:2, are adapted by P., who shows at length that the Purification (*qv*), as described in Lk 2:22-23, in no way weakens the traditional view.[7] P. R. adds a second part to his treatise, in which he seeks to enforce his arguments; he may have been urged to do so. The theory, that the treatise of Ratramnus appeared between the first and

second parts of P.'s work, does not appear sustainable.

There are insights of value in *Cogitis me*, on Mary and the Holy Spirit for example, and on the grace which, through her, flowed from him on every creature.[8] The three sermons on the Assumption (taken by P. as of the soul only) contain some passages of high praise for Mary, "a virgin most beautiful and fruitful, in body fair and intact, in spirit resplendent, clear in faith, notable in her life, devoted in her love of virginity, ready to answer every call of virtue, most careful in the office assigned to her."[9] Her ineffable gifts and divine privileges bring her such glory in heaven that "no one on earth can worthily honour her with praise."[10] We cannot grasp her exaltation and magnificence, but at least we can reflect on her humility so that, through her merits, we may reach the glory of her gifts.[11] By the law of species and genus, "grace and happiness are given to her to be spread through the whole genus of the Church."[12]

In the commentary on Matthew, wherein P. also discusses texts from Luke, and shows the influence of St. Jerome, dealing with the marriage (*qv*) between Mary and Joseph (*qv*), he shows how Mary prepared for the coming of the Church, which she foreshadowed. He uses the same law of genus and species: "The blessed evangelist, wishing to foreshadow this grace of election in Mary, first presents her as a spouse [of St. Joseph], and then proclaims that she remained, in every way, a virgin afterwards, and he first fashions *in specie* what would later be so *in genere*."[13]

P., in the *Libellus de Nativitate sanctae Mariae*, tells of Mary's origins—he is in dependence on the Apocrypha (*qv*). The problem arises then whether P. had a hand, at any stage, in the composition of the best-known Latin version of the apocryphal narrative of the birth of Mary, the Pseudo-Matthew.[14]

---

[1]Critical ed. of *De partu sanctae Mariae*, by J. M. Canal, C.M.F., in MM, 60(1968), 113-160; *id.*, 'La virginidad de Maria según Ratramno y Radberto, monjes De Corbie. Nueva edición de los textos," in MM, 60(1968), 53-160; PL 120, 1367-1386. [2]PL 96, 239A-257D. Cf. R. Laurentin, *Traité*, I, 141. [3]PL 30, 297D-305B. Cf. R. Laurentin, *Traité*, I, 125. Cf. C. Lambot, O.S.B., "L'homélie du Pseudo-Jerome sur l'Assomption et l'Évangile de la Nativité d'après une lettre d'Hincmar," in RevBen, 46(1934), 265-282. [4]Critical ed. by J. M. Canal, C.M.F., 16, p. 121. [5]*ibid.*, 17, p. 122. Cf. J. M. Canal, C.M.F., "La virginidad de Maria

según Ratramno y Radberto . . . ," in MM, 60(1968), p. 71, n. 33. ⁶MM, 60(1968), 114. ⁷MM, 60(1968), 118ff. ⁸PL 30, 129. ⁹*Serm., I*, in PL 96, 242D-243A. ¹⁰*Serm. II*, in PL 96, 252BC. ¹¹*Serm. III*, in PL 96, 255. ¹²*ibid.*, in PL 96, 256C. ¹³*In Mt., II*, in PL 120, 104D. ¹⁴Cf. J. M. Canal, C.M.F., "El libro apocrifo 'Nacimiento de Maria' del Pseudo-Yago," in PCM, IV, 313; *id.*, "Antiguas versiones latinas del Protoevangelio de Santiago," in EphMar, 18(1968), 431-473.

PASSAGLIA, CARLO (1812-1887)

A theologian contemporary with the preliminaries of the Bull *Ineffabilis Deus* (qv), P. taught at the Gregorian University, having M. J. Scheeben (qv) among his pupils. P. had a certain influence in the drafting of the Bull. He was author of an immense, three-volume work, over 2,000 pages large format, *De immaculato Deiparae semper Virginis conceptu*, not always marked by a critical sense, amassing much material.[1]

---

¹NCE s.v.

PAUL VI (Pope 1963-1978) — See Supplement, p. 385.

PAUL, ST

A number of Pauline texts are studied for possible reference to Our Lady, and attempts have been made to fit a theology of Mary into the whole Pauline synthesis.[1] The principal text considered—and used in the Liturgy—is Gal 4:4-5: "But when the time had fully come, God sent forth his Son, born of woman, born under the law, to redeem those who were under the law so that we might receive adoption as sons."

Did Paul show by the words, "born of a woman," that he knew of the virginal conception? The answer at one time tended to follow, though not quite, confessional lines; Catholics thought so, Protestants differed. Things have changed. Paul, let us note, uses the word *genomenon* from *ginesthai*, to make, not *gennomenon* born from *gennan*. Did this mean an intention to rule out birth in the ordinary way? There can, apparently, be no certain affirmative. Nor does the phrase, "born of woman," automatically rule out physical paternity. It may come from "man is born of woman" (Job 14:1; cf. 15:14; 25:4). It must be stated that the context in Gal 4:4 is such as to elevate immeasurably the meaning of any personal descriptive phrase used. The highly singular factors are the fullness of time— linked in Eph 1:10 with the summing up of all

things in Christ—the mission by God, the choice of his Son, the incomparable purpose, redemption and adoption as sons of God, and the sending of the Spirit into the hearts of the adopted sons. A reference to the mode of entry by the Son to the human situation must, in this exalted context, be interpreted with great attention to what it contains to render it entirely unique. "Born of woman" can then have a special meaning, so emphasizing the woman that she must be unique before God, a virgin.

The reference to "James, the Brother of the Lord" (Gal 1:19) is dealt with in the relevant article (see BROTHERS OF THE LORD). The phrase used by Paul about Isaac, born "according to the Spirit," has no direct bearing on Mary and has been fully explained by exegetes. They have likewise shown that the words, "born of the seed of David according to the flesh" (Rom 1:3), are absorbed in their own context not directly affecting the story of Mary.

It has been suggested that, from 1 Cor 7:37, Paul would have understood a virginal marriage between Mary and Joseph: "But whoever is firmly established in his heart, being under no necessity, but having his desire under control, and has determined in his heart to keep her as his betrothed, he will do well."

A different approach fits a theology of Mary into the Pauline synthesis with fairly comprehensive results. This has been largely in the area of Christology, with emphasis of different kinds on the "One Mediator," and the new Adam. Attention must be given to Paul's doctrine of the identification of Christ with the Christian. If he could say, "I live, no longer I but Christ lives in me" (Gal 2:20), then how much more justifiably could Mary say that. The Pauline doctrine of faith can also with advantage be applied to Mary as a supreme exemplar, she who "cooperated in the work of salvation through free faith and obedience" (LG 56), who "advanced in the pilgrimage of faith" (LG 58).

---

¹For Pauline texts, cf. R. J. Cooke, *Did Paul Know of the Virgin Birth?*, (New York, 1926); J. M. Bover, S.J., *Teologia di San Pablo, Derivaciones Mariologioas*, (Madrid, 1944), 433-524; G. A. Danell, "Did St. Paul know the Tradition About the Virgin Birth?," in ST, 4(1951), 94-101; E. de Roover, "La maternité virginale de Marie dans l'interprétation de Gal 4:4," in *Studiorum paulinorum congressus internationalis catholicus 1961*, (An. Bib. 17-18: Rome, Biblical Institute, 1963), 17-37; A. Légault, "Saint Paul a-t-il parlé de la maternité virginale?," in ScEccl, 16(1964), 481-493; J. McHugh, *The Mother of Jesus in the New*

Testament, (London, 1975), 275-276; Mary in NT, 33-49. For Pauline theology, cf. C. Stuhlmueller, C. P., "Our Lady and St. Paul's Doctrine on Justification," in MSt, 16(1965), 94-120; M. B. Schepers, O.P., "Mary and the Pauline Doctrine of Justification by Faith and the Law of Sin," in MSS, IV, 50-118; F. Mussner, "Der Glaube Mariens im Lichte des Römerbriefs," in Praesentia Salutis, (Dusseldorf, 1967), 264-288; J. Bligh, S.J., Galatians, (London, 1969), 347-348.

PAUL THE DEACON (Eighth Century)

P. was author of the *Homiliarium* bearing his name, *Paul Warnefried*, composed of items not by himself but by others.[1] PL 95, 1159A-1566C is not the original, which scholars have reconstructed. P. is the author of two sermons on the Assumption (PL 95, 1565D-1569C and 1569D-1574A). A passage eliminated in PL 95, 1573B is of importance in the growth of belief in the Assumption. The absence of Mary's body is noted and the question of its fate raised. Others, rising from the dead, ascended with the Lord; similar or more wonderful things are surmised about her, for she is holier not only than these but than all others on earth. Mary's unique sanctity, her excellence over men and angels, her intercessory power and compassion towards sinners are stressed.

[1]Cf. R. Laurentin, Traité, I, 139-140; H. Barré, C.S.Sp., in DSp, VII, 60; id., in BSFEM, 7(1949), 66-67, for missing passage; id., Prières Anciennes, 46-47; S. Marocco, in MM, 12(1950), 401-403.

PERRONE, GIOVANNI (1794-1876)

A principal theological adviser to Pius IX (*qv*) on the dogma of the Immaculate Conception (*qv*), P. also helped in the drafting of the Encyclical Letter *Ubi Primum*, by which the Pope consulted the Church's hierarchy on the forthcoming dogma.[1] One of the most respected dogmatic theologians of his time, his work, *De Immaculato conceptu. An dogmatico decreto definiri possit?*, was influential. It went into several editions, the tenth in Milan (1852). His *Praelectiones theologiae dogmaticae* went into thirty-four between 1835 and 1842, when the nine volumes appeared in Rome in 1888. Cardinal Newman (*qv*) met P. in Rome, and submitted to him theses explaining his doctrine of development. Newman had been impressed by the recognition of the role of the faithful in the official documentation of *Ineffabilis Deus*. P.'s work was more precise than Passaglia's less ambitious in use of authorities.

[1]DTC, and also NCE, s.v.

PERSONALITY OF MARY, THE — See Supplement, pp. 385-386.

PÉTAU (PETAVIUS), DENYS (1583-1652)

The first notable French theologian of Our Lady, P., a pioneer in positive theology and the history of dogma, expressed his ideas on the theology of Mary in eight sermons, *De festis et laudibus Beatissimae Virginis Mariae* (1642), a paraphrase of the *Magnificat* in Greek with Latin interpretation, and especially in the fourteenth book of his famous *Dogmata Theologica* (1643-1650).[1] Presenting his Marian theses like Suarez, in the context of the Incarnation, P. refers frequently to the Fathers and medieval writers, following the ideas of his time on authorship; there are passing shafts at the Reformers.

P. accepted the Immaculate Conception (*qv*), but not as a matter of faith, or in such wise as to condemn or censure those holding different opinions, "in the way," as he thought, "prescribed by the Roman pontiffs and the Council of Trent, that is, the Roman Catholic Church." He was drawn "especially to this side by the general sentiment of the faithful (*qv*) [*sensus fidelium*]." He deals at length with the virginity; he thought the *virginitas in partu* supported by the Fathers and professed by the Church. He defended St. Joseph's virginity. In dealing with the cult of Mary, P. expounds the divine maternity, "root and origin of her excellence" and dignity. He borrows some of the principles of John Gerson (*qv*). The final chapter deals with Mary's mediation. P. sets forth testimonies that Mary was Mediatress, secondary to and lower than Christ—Easterns: Irenaeus, Epiphanius, and Germanus especially; the Latins with much space for St. Bernard.

[1]*Dogmata Theologica*, Vives ed., (Paris, 1867), ch. I-IX, 35-96, double column. Cf. Sommervogel, *Bibliothèque de la Compagnie de Jésus*, VI, 588-616; Hurter, *Nomenclator*, III, 965-978; P. Galtier, S.J., in DTC, XII, 1313-1337.

PETER OF ARGOS (d. after 920)

Bishop of Argos, P. is known to Marian theology for a sermon on the feast of the Immaculate Conception (BHG 132), one on the Presentation (BHG 1111b), and one unpublished on the Annunciation (BHG 1159g). He is cited as a witness to the Byzantine belief in the Immaculate Conception (*qv*).[1] He thought that the one chosen as the instrument of the Incarnation should surpass all men in purity. Part of his sermon is a lengthy eulogy of Mary's parents.[2] Like many of the Byzantines, he was insistent on Anne's sterility, therefore on the miraculous nature of the conception.[3] The one conceived fills our first parents with joy, for she is "the rose all perfumed, planted in a sterile ground, who is to fill the world with her good odour and chase the stench of their transgression . . . a paradise divine."[4] Nature echoes the cry saying, "A woman until now was the cause of my misfortune, now a woman makes me happy."[5] "The first shoot of the original nobility of our nature" points to freedom from original sin.

The benefits are extended to all. Mary's conception is the first sign of "our reconciliation with God." On this day, all who behold "the foundations of the most pure temple of Christ, king of all, gratefully exult, clap their hands, and worship God, author of all good things, with thanksgiving and praise."[6] Mary is, for us, "the author of all joy, and the one who wins us joy unspeakable."[7] The homily on the Presentation gathers together the traditional biblical imagery, speaks of us as "slaves" of Mary, insists on mediation, her intercession, and especially hails her as the "all-pure one."

[1]*Oratio in Conceptionem Sanctae Annae quando concepit sanctam Dei Genitricem*, in PG 104, 1351-1366; homily on the Presentation, *Alcune Omelie mariane dei sec. X-XIV*, ed. by E. M. Toniolo, O.S.M., (Rome, Marianum, 1971), 18-46, with Italian tr. Cf. M. Jugie, A.A., *L'Immaculée Conception*, 183-185; L'omelia di Pietro d'Argo sull'Annunciazione," in MM, 35(1973), 1-35; *id.*, in MM, 33(1971), 329-409. [2]PG 104, 1361-1364. [3]PG 104, 1361B, D, 1364A. [4]PG 104, 1352A. [5]PG 104, 1360D. [6]PG 104, 1352B. [7]PG 104, 1353A.

PETER AUREOLI (c. 1280-1322)

A disciple of Duns Scotus (qv) and, like him, a Franciscan, P. played an important part in establishing the tradition of the Immaculate Conception (qv). His treatise on the subject, composed in 1314-1315, is the first entirely devoted to the subject.[1] He also treats the subject in the *Repercussorium editum contra adversarium innocentiae Matris Dei*, and especially in the commentary on the *Sentences*, given in Paris, in 1318—the final draft of which was recently published.[2]

P. depends on Scotus for some of his argumentation, but he has insights of his own. He was influenced by the Pseudo-Augustine (qv), and skillful in adapting some of his arguments to his own thesis. A person might contract original sin *de jure*, as being bound by the necessity of nature, but not *de facto* through the effect of a special grace.[3] P. supported this contention by reference to divine omnipotence, to the Scotist argument from the most perfect Redeemer, and especially to the divine motherhood, which implies the privilege. Underlying all his thought is the principle of suitability, or fittingness, in which he was strengthened by Pseudo-Augustine. "Augustine proves that her body was not reduced to dust, because it was not fitting; and it was less fitting that she should be stained by original sin."[4] In regard to venial sin, he applies the same rule of suitability. "Again, according to all the saints, she never sinned venially, for it was not fitting that she should be stained with venial sin; but original sin is certainly a greater stain,"[5] the implication being that it was more fitting that she be preserved from this. "Therefore, he redeemed her more perfectly when he preserved her from sin than if he allowed her to fall into sin and cleansed her afterwards."[6] "Divine power is more effective in bestowing grace than flesh infected is in causing this infection to the soul."[7] Thus the causing this infection to the soul."[7] Thus the essential framework was clarified and strengthened.

[1]Text, "Quaestiones disputatae de immaculata conceptione beatae Mariae virginis," in *Bibl. franc. scholastica medii aevi*, 3, (Quaracchi, 1904), 23-94. Cf. A. di Lella, O.F.M., "The Immaculate Conception in the Writings of Peter Aureoli," in FS, 15(1955), 146-158; L. Rosato, O.F.M., *Doctrina de Immaculata B. M. V. Conceptione secundum Petrum Aureoli*, (Rome, 1959). [2]Cf. E. Buytaert, O.F.M., "Aureoli's Unpublished Reportatio III, Dist. 3, q. 1-2," in FS, 15(1955), 159-174. [3]"Tractatus . . .," in *Bibl. franc. scholastica medii aevi*, 3, (Quaracchi, 1904), 47. [4]*In Sent. Dist. 3, q. 1*, ed. by E. Buytaert, O.F.M., in FS, 15(1955), 166. [5]*ibid.*, in FS, 15(1955), 166. [6]*ibid.*, in FS, 15(1955), 167. [7]"Tractatus . . .," in *Bibl. franc. scholastica medii aevi*, 3, (Quaracchi, 1904), 50.

PETER OF BLOIS (d. after 1204)

From influential posts at the royal courts of Sicily and England, P. came to the priesthood late in life. His Marian doctrine is contained in a number of sermons, some of them on three of the feasts of Our Lady then honoured: the Purification (2); the Assumption (4); and the Nativity (1).[1]

The note of high praise, with superlative terms, is characteristic of P. Translation cannot give the force of the words *elegit et praeelegit, exaltavit et superexaltavit*, and *superbenedicta, superelecta, superspeciosa*. One must add to these words the list of glorious titles such as: "She has become the mistress of the world, the restorer [*reparatrix*] of the temporal sphere, the destroyer of hell, the glory of martyrs, the honour of virgins, the strength of the just, the trust of the lapsed, the hope of the militant, the exultation of angels."[2] He thought frequently in the Eve-Mary framework, using this to introduce a string of eulogies of Mary, or making the contrast in the traditional way. "Let Adam and Eve, our parents, or rather our destroyers, rejoice today for, as Mary enters heaven, entry is opened to her posterity. Eve led us to misery, she raises us to glory."[3] Eve is the mother of crimes, Mary, the Mother of mercy. Mary is the strong woman, who crushed the head of the ancient serpent (see WOMAN IN GEN 3:15), and this is related by P. to her role in "presenting the Church without wrinkle or stain to her Son."[4]

Mary had received the fullness of grace in her mother's womb, which means that P. did not believe in the Immaculate Conception (*qv*). But he immediately states that, when the Holy Spirit (*qv*) "descended on her in the conception of the Word, he poured into her a fullness of heavenly grace."[5] She was freed from sin; the flesh of Mary was sanctified, that of Christ saintly and sanctifying.

No one should wonder that Mary was queen and mistress of angels but, adds P., she was far more closely bound to her Son, since they are two of one flesh—consubstantial with him as he was with the Father. This led him to propose a novel view of the bodily Assumption (*qv*). After the Ascension, "it appeared to Christ that he had not fully ascended into heaven, until he had drawn to him her from whose flesh and blood he had drawn his body. With desire, he had desired to have with him that vessel of election, I mean, the Virgin's body ., . . . Let no angel wonder that the Mother of God, his handmaid, his sister and spouse, his mother and daughter, should be assumed in splendour and glory."[6]

Mary's power on our behalf follows naturally. She is "put before us for our help as an attentive patron and merciful Mediatress to her Son."[7] P. knows that what she asks from God will not go unheeded. "Take Mary out of heaven and what will be among men but blindness in the dark, wandering at the mercy of the cold wind, enveloping blackness."[8] These opinions show that P. deserves more attention than he has thus far received.

[1]PL 207, 592-599, 660-669, 672-677. Cf. N. Jung, in DTC, XII, 1884. [2]*Serm. in Nativit. B. M.*, in PL 207, 674A. [3]*Serm. 34 in Assumpt.*, in PL 207, 665A. [4]*Serm. 33 in Assumpt.*, in PL 207, 662AB. Cf. PL 207, 665A. [5]PL 207, 675C. [6]PL 207, 662B, 663A. [7]PL 207, 665D. [8]PL 207, 662A.

PETER CANISIUS, ST. DOCTOR OF THE CHURCH
(1521-1597)

An active apostle and controversial writer of the Counter-Reformation, P. composed the first major defence of Catholic doctrine and devotion about Our Lady against the Reformers. In the *Summa Doctrinae Christianae*, 1555, his famous catechism, destined to be issued in hundreds of editions, he outlined traditional teaching on the Mother of God. His principal work was *De Maria Virgine Incomparabili*, the fruit of much labour; it appeared in Ingolstadt in 1577.[1] (His earlier edition of works of the Fathers, St. Cyril of Alexandria and St. Leo I, was the first book published by a Jesuit.)

The work is massive—more than 1240 columns in the Bourasse (*qv*) edition. The erudition is considerable: the materials drawn on include the writings of more than 90 Fathers and Doctors of the first eight centuries and over a hundred writers of later ages. In groups or singly, he dealt with over a hundred opponents; 4,000 different biblical texts are quoted; there are more than 10,000 marginal references to patristic or scholastic theologians. Those mentioned or quoted most frequently are St. Augustine (670), St. Jerome (280), St. Ambrose (235), St. Bernard (200), St. John Chrysostom (170) and Tertullian (100). Of references to the Reformers; 140 are Luther, 100 to Calvin, 110 to Brenz and 70 to Melanchton—to mention only the highest names in the list.

The intention of the work was frankly apologetic. The saint, whose personal devotion was free of extravagance, and who felt that abuses which had existed had been corrected by Trent, developed traditional truths. He was in some particulars of history and devotion and limited, and quoted, like other theologians, St. Bridget of Sweden. The book fell into five parts: 1. On the birth, childhood and character of Mary and of her life, perfect in every kind of virtue; 2. On Mary's admirable and perpetual virginity; 3. On Mary the Virgin greeted by the angel Gabriel, on the most holy Mother of God and man; 4. On various passages of the Gospel distorted to the dishonour of Mary, vindicated for Catholics; 5. On the passing of the Blessed Virgin Mary to heaven, and of the cult and honour which to this very day the Church offers to the Mother of God. This last is the longest section, filling almost 400 columns of Bourassé.

P. defends the Immaculate Conception and after setting forth the reasons—of suitability—concludes that she was "preserved or cleansed immediately in the very conception."[2] No one after Christ was so completely or abundantly sanctified. Though rejecting the apocryphal gospel of James, P. accepts the Presentation in the Temple, of which it was the source.

To show the true marriage between virgins (for he holds the traditional view of Mary's vow) he has a succinct phrase, "it is consent not intercourse which makes a marriage." In dealing with gospel texts, he sees a direct Marian sense in Gen 3:15, justifying the mistranslation by centuries-old acceptance. In the OT the Eve typology and other types show Mary's dignity. P. rightly interprets the difficult NT texts as in no way minimizing Mary; but he makes much of translations no longer an issue, such as *gratiosa* instead of *gratia plena* for *Kecharitomene* (Lk 1:28), or "lowliness" instead of "humility" for *tapeinosis* (Lk 1:48). He quite properly objects to any doubt implicit in Mary's words "How shall this be?", in Lk 1:34. The sword of Simeon did not refer to a defect in faith.

P. defends the bodily Assumption, then universally held: "so that exalted above the choirs of angels and all those in heaven, the Mother should see none above her but her Son alone, the queen admire none higher than herself than the King, the Mediatress should revere none beyond herself but the Mediator, as Guerric learnedly says."[3] On the disputed title of Mediatress, P. has very much to say, analysing the Pauline text, quoting many past authorities. He will have no diminution in the dignity of Christ: "All of which must be taken in such wise that Christ always retains primacy since, without any controversy, he destroyed our death and restored our life, holds the primacy in all things. In this manner all the ancient testimonies, several of which we have quoted, must be interpreted when Mary is being preached not only as advocate but also as Mediatress and reconciler of men."[4]

P. expounds the *Salve Regina* at length. He explains the difference between *latria, hyperdulia* and *dulia* in Christian worship. Mary's uniqueness, after Christ, was ever present to him. Quoting a doubtful Athanasian text, he goes on: "This commendaton of Mary is excellent nor is there anyone other than the Mother of the Lord to whom pertains the honour of being called new Eve, Mother of God, Restorer, Queen and Mistress of all, who abides in the very life of body and soul, is in every way most blessed and adorned, dwelling at the right hand of her Son full of grace, whom in the Church the elect and saints implore."[5]

[1]Ed. J. J. Bourassé, *Summa Aurea de laudibus B. M. V.* (Paris, 1862), vols. VIII, IX; cf. J. Brodrick, S.J., *St. Peter Canisius* (Baltimore, 1950) 745ff; K. Schellhass, *Kardinal Marone, Petrus Canisius und dessen Opus Marianum* (1521-1633), in *Miscellanea Francesco Ehrle*, Vatican 1962, V, 473-488, *Studi e Testi* 41; J. Escudero, S.J., "Canisio por la Inmaculada," *Miscel. Comillas* 22(1954), 27-28, 327-48; F. M. Bauducco, S.J., "Influssi di Dionigo il Certosino sulla mediazione Mariologica in S. P. Canisio" La Palestra del Clero 50(1971), 1366-79; A. Troll, *Studien zur Mariologie des hl. Petrus Canisius*, Kicklingen, Selbstverlag des Verfassers, 1971, 885 pp.; id., Die Zeugen der Marienverehrung vom 6-11 Jahrhundert in der gegenreformatorischen Sicht des Hl P. Canisius, Zagreb Congress, II, 183-195. [2]1, X, 750. [3]5, IV, 57. [4]5, XXX, 403. [5]5, XXX, 387, 88.

PETER OF CELLE (d. 1183)

A Cluniac monk who became Abbot of St. Remy and then bishop of Chartres, P. preached 17 sermons on Our Lady; one on the Purification, 7 on the Annunciation, 8 on the Assumption, one also on Mary without reference to a feast—but without saying very much new or important.[1] He replied in a doctrinal letter to Nicholas of St. Albans (qv) who had attempted to rebut the objections of St. Bernard, P's idol, to the feast of the Immaculate Conception: N's answer to this missive occasioned a second letter.[2]

In the sermons, P. has an occasional flash of thought to interest. Mary for him (as for those of his time) is the Star of the sea, the illuminatress, the Lady. She is the one who "intervenes" (*interveniat*), he prays; from her "appeared to the world the true light, eternal healing, copious redemption."[3] Though he speaks of Jesus hastening, after his Ascension, to break the bonds that hold back Mary from him, he remains fundamentally agnostic on the bodily Assumption. "Whether she was taken up in the body is

PETER CHRYSOLOGUS

truly unknown, though it is a matter of pious belief."[4]

In the sermons, P. had shown awareness of the OT figures. In the letters, which turn a good deal on the authority of Bernard and on methodology, he applies most of the OT and NT texts to Mary but angles them to his own thesis, that she did "feel" sin and had to struggle, for without struggle he saw no victory possible. He is most generous in praise of "the saint of saints": "You say that she is the Mother of God, you set her up as our Mediatress (qv) to God, so do I."[5] But he thought that what he believed was based on the gospel, not on dreams; he was ready, however, to accept a future revelation from God. His tribute to Our Lady's greatness is impressive: "I believe and confess that more things are unknown by us about the most holy Virgin than are known, because she is strengthened in grace and glory and we cannot approach her."[6]

---

[1]PL 202, Sermons 13, 22-28, 67-74, 75. [2]PL. 202, Letter 171, 613D-622B; 173, 628B-632B. [3]715CD; 849B. [4]849B. [5]632A. [6]ibid.

PETER CHRYSOLOGUS, ST., DOCTOR OF THE CHURCH.
(c. 400-c. 450)
Archbishop of Ravenna in the generation following the Council of Ephesus, P. treats Marian themes in some passages in sermons not directly relevant to Our Lady, but especially in five sermons on the Annunciation (qv), four on the Incarnation, and in Christmas sermons which have been restored to him by critical scholarship.[1] In regard to the main corpus of nine sermons, there is general agreement among scholars as to authenticity.[2]

P. translates the teaching of Ephesus into the idiom of his hearers:" She was truly blessed, who received the glory of divine seed and was the queen of all chastity. She was truly blessed, who was greater than heaven, stronger than earth, wider than the world, who alone held God whom the world does not hold. She bore him who bears the world, she brought forth the one who brought her forth, she fed him who gives food to all living things."[3] "Let them come, let them hear, those who have sought to cloud Latin clarity by Greek disturbance, saying blasphemously that [Mary] is the mother of man, the mother of Christ, so as to take from her the *Theotokos* [in Greek, as are *anthropotokon* and *christotokon*]."[4] Equally insistent on the

virginity, P. echoes St. Augustine on the threefold aspect: "The Virgin conceives, the Virgin brings forth, the Virgin remains thus."[5] The *virginitas in partu* is compared to the miraculous entry through closed doors by Christ's risen body.[6]

On Joseph's "doubt," P. thinks that the saint knew that something wonderful had happened; he was overcome by the novelty of the matter— "she stood clothed with the office of a mother, but not deprived of the honour of virginity."[7] He could take no step against her. P. puts it more subtly elsewhere: "His [Joseph's] just mind and holy spirit are torn by perplexing thought; he feels but cannot grasp so great a mystery, since he cannot be an accuser and has not the means to undertake a defence before men."[8]

First apparently among the Latins, P. speaks of Mary as spouse (qv) of God. About the angel's mission at the Annunciation (qv), he uses the technical words of espousal and continues; "the swift messenger flies to the spouse, that he may remove and end the affection of human espousal from the spouse of God, nor does he take her from Joseph, but returns her to Christ, to whom she was pledged when she was made in the womb. Christ therefore takes his own spouse, not seizing one belonging to another."[9]

The Eve-Mary idea recurs in P.'s sermons: "The angel deals with Mary about salvation, because with Eve an angel [fallen] had dealt about ruin."[10] Since in them (i.e. women) "Eve accursed brought punishment to the womb, then in them blessed Mary rejoices, is honoured, uplifted."[11] For P., the very Incarnation looks forward to the universal salvation: "A girl takes, receives, attracts God in the shelter of her womb so that . . . peace on earth, glory in the heavens, salvation to the lost, life to the dead, relationship between the earthly and those in heaven, union of God himself with flesh."[12]

---

[1]Nine sermons, PL 52, 575B-598D; Christmas sermons, PL 39, 1992 (*inter op.* St. Augustine); PLS III, 159-60, 161, 180-81; EMBP, 869-890. [2]Cf. R. Laurentin, *Traité*, I, 131-132; J. P. Barrios, "La naturaleza del vinculo matrimonial entre Maria y José segun san Pedro Crisologo," Eph. Mar., 16(1966), 321-335; B. Capelle, O.S.B., BSFEM, 12(1954), 72-76; R. H. McGlynn, *The Incarnation in the Sermons of St. Peter Chrysologus* (Mundelein Seminary Chicago, 1956). [3]*Serm. 143*, PL 52, 584AB. [4]*Serm. 145*, 590B. [5]*Serm. 117*, 521A. [6]*Serm. 84*, 436D-437A. [7]*Serm. 145*, PL 52, 588. [8]*Serm. 175*, PL 52, 658A. [9]*Serm. 140*, PL 52, 576. [10]*Serm. 142*, PL 52, 579. [11]*Serm. 140*, PL 52, 576. [12]*ibid.*, 577.

284

PETER COMESTOR (d. *c.* 1179)
Chancellor of the Cathedral school in Paris, finally a Canon of St. Victor, P. speaks of Our Lady in sermons on the Assumption and in one on the Purification. Two of the former are printed by PL among works of Hildebert of Lavardin[1] (*qv*), one in PL 198 where that on the Purification is also found;[2] a fourth on the Assumption is partially published,[3] and two others are in manuscript.[4] Sermon LIX on the Assumption has most interest, P. thought that the tongues of angels and of men would not be sufficient to praise Mary. P. believed in the bodily Assumption (*qv*): "Today the Blessed Virgin obtained happiness of soul and glorification of body which, lest it be doubted, we shall support by authorities."[5] He concludes: "For as the Blessed Virgin was immune from the curse on woman to whom it was said 'in sorrow you shall bring forth', so she was immune from the common curse on men and women to whom it was said 'To dust you shall return'."[6] Mary, P. continues, was not associated with the angels, but in her beauty exalted above the angels. Her intercession is recognised by the Church, which implores her more affectionately than others.[7] Her crown was a crown of mercy.

---

[1]PL 171, *Serm.* 59, 627B-631A; *Serm.* 60, 631B-636B. Cf. R. Laurentin, *Traité I*, 150; M. M. Lebreton, "Recherches sur les MSS contenant les sermons de Pierre le Mangeur" in *Bulletin d'information de l'Institut de recherche et d'histoire des textes*, 1953, n.2, pp. 25-44. [2]1783-1788; 1744-48. [3]A. M. Landgraff, *Dogmengeschichte der Frühscholastik*, II, 2, Regensburg, 1954, p. 361. [4]Cf. H. Barré, C.S.Sp., ME, V, p. 117. [5]630A. [6]*ibid.* [7]631A.

PETER DAMIAN, ST.
DOCTOR OF THE CHURCH
(1007-1072)
Born in Ravenna into a poor family, a hermit who was appointed bishop and Cardinal, St. Peter was an important personality in the eleventh-century church reform movement. He was conspicuous as a preacher on Our Lady and a promoter of devotion to her in an age which, beginning with St. Fulbert of Chartres (*qv*) and ending with Pseudo-Augustine (*qv*) and St. Anselm of Canterbury (*qqv*) saw a remarkable flowering of Marian doctrine and piety.[1]

P.'s Marian doctrine is found in the two sermons on the Nativity,[2] in passages throughout other sermons, in certain of the *Opuscula*, in the hymns, and in prayers; the last are in the Office for daily use in honour of Our Lady and there are references to Mary in prayers addressed to the persons of the Most Holy Trinity. Recent critical scholarship has shown that the author of some sermons attributed to P. was Nicholas of Clairvaux, St. Bernard's secretary; some fragments, of Marian interest, have been restored to P.[3]

"Mary is *Theotokos* for she truly gave birth to God."[4] With this dogma P. allied a comprehensive view of Mary's perfection. Her destiny was exalted: "it was impossible for the redemption of the human race to take place, unless the Son of God was born of the Virgin."[5] Her dignity surpasses our praise: "For how could the passing word of mortal man praise her who gave forth from herself the Word which remains forever."[6] It is not to be wondered at that praise of her is beyond the power of human language "since by the dignity of her excellent merits she transcends the very nature of mankind."[7] Whence too comes her perfection. None of those who figured in salvation history can be compared with her. "What could have been wanting in holiness, justice, religion, perfection to this unique Virgin who was full of the charism of all divine grace?"[8] No vice could exist in her mind or body since she was like heaven deserving to be "the sanctuary of the most Holy Trinity." The saint's opinion on the Immaculate Conception (*qv*) is not explicit though these phrases are strong.[9] On Mary's personal sinlessness, on the fullness of her virtue, he had no doubt. He seems, however, to assume that Mary was "conceived of sin" and that Christ took his nature, "but not guilt" from her—Original Sin?

No doubt either on the virginity (*qv*), in conception, in childbirth and ever afterwards. She is the "garden locked, the fountain sealed," the rod of Aaron which blossomed though dry, the burning bush which was on fire but not consumed.[10]

Mary's role was capital in salvation. Because she was elected in the eternal divine plan, P. can write of her that she was "the fount of the living fount, the origin of the beginning because he who is the head and principle of all things through the essence of the deity came forth from her through the matter of the flesh."[11] The Eve-Mary (*qv*) parallel fits this concept: "*Blessed art thou among women.* Through a woman a curse fell upon the earth, through a woman the blessing was restored to the earth.

By the hand from which the cup of bitter death is offered the cup of sweet life is held out. The most plentiful flow of the new blessing has wiped away the contagion of the ancient curse."[12] P. speaks of Mary as the "door of paradise," the "ladder of heaven," "the ladder which joins heaven to earth, the depths to the heights."[13] Life lost by men is restored through her and the happiness of angels increased as their depleted numbers are made up by men entering their high company. "She opened heaven to us."

P. considers the links between Mary and the Church, the parallel—"It brings forth, in a certain manner, like his [Christ's] blessed Mother"—and dependence of a filial kind: "The blessed Virgin Mary is therefore a great and happy Mother, from whose womb the flesh of Christ was taken, from whom also came forth the Church through water and blood. In this way the Church seems to have taken its origin from Mary. Each is chaste, each is pure, each is protected by the girdle of perpetual virginity."[14]

Understandably the defender of orthodoxy in regard to the Eucharist (see MARY AND) gave some thought to the relations between the two mysteries: Mary and the Eucharistic Christ. "For the same body of Christ which the most blessed Virgin brought forth, which she nourished in her womb, wrapped in swaddling clothes and brought up with motherly care: this same body I say, and none other, we now perceive without any doubt on the sacred altar.[15] "Through the food which Eve ate we were punished by an eternal fast; but Mary brought forth food for a heavenly banquet."

With such profound insights and strong conviction, P. urged devotion to Our Lady—recitation of the Little Office (he himself composed an office of Our Lady for daily use),[16] daily recitation of the angel's greeting to Mary and of the "Five Joys" of Our Lady, and the Saturday Office and Mass. He liked to relate episodes showing Mary's intervention, including one which centred on a consecration to Mary in the form of a slavery of love. In a beautiful prayer to the most clement one, Mother of compassion and of mercy himself, P. asks that, as we rejoice to manifest signs of praise on earth, we may deserve to have the help of her intercession in heaven "in as much as the Son of God deigned through you to come among us, so also we may be able through you to attain his company."[17]

[1]H. Barré, *Prières Anciennes*, Pt III, *L'Essor marial du XIe siècle*, 125-127. [2]PL 144, *Serm.* 45, 740-748, *Serm.* 46, 748-761; cf. S. Baldassarri, "La Mariologia di San Pier Damiano" in *Scuola Cattolica* 61(1933), 304-312; H. Barré, *op. cit. St. Pierre Damien et les Camaldules*, 216-224; J. Leclercq, O.S.B., *S. Pierre Damien, ermite et homme d'Eglise* (Rome, 1960), 227-229; G. M. Roschini, *Mariologia*, I, 213-7; id., *La Mariologia di S. Pier Damiano*, in *San Pier Damiano nel IX Centenario della morte*, (Cesena, 1972) I, 195-237; R. Laurentin, *Traité*, I, 144-5. [3]Cf. J. Ryan, "St. Peter Damian and the sermons of Nicholas of Clairvaux," in Mediaeval Studies, 9(1947), 151-161; J. Leclercq, *Eph. Lit.* 72(1958), 302-5. [4]PL 144, 860D. [5]PL 144, 741A; G. Lucchesi, *Clavis S. Petri Damiani* (Faenza, 1970). [6]PL 144, 742C. [7]PL 144, 752A. [8]*ibid*. [9]But cf. *Opusc. VI, Liber qui dicitur gratissimus*, 19, PL 145, 129B and G. M. Roschini, *art. cit.*, 216-9. [10]*Serm.* 46, PL 144, 764; *Rythmus de S. Maria Virgine*, PL 145, 938AB. [11]753B. [12]PL 144, 758B. [13]*Rhythmus de S. Maria Virgine*, PL 145, 937D. [14]*Serm. de S. Joanne Ap. et Ev.*, PL 144, 861. [15]PL 144, 743B. [16]PL 145, 935A-937C. [17]PL 144, 761B.

PETER LOMBARD (d. 1160)

One of the most influential figures in medieval theology, P. had spent some time in the Abbey of St. Victor, was a teacher and preacher in Paris, became bishop of the city. He wrote the *Libri Sententiarum* about 1150, but its impact was delayed. Attacked by various people it was by the Lateran Council in 1215 declared orthodox; it became thereafter the chief theological textbook. All the schoolmen wrote commentaries on it. P. determined thinking on the Immaculate Conception (*qv*) through one important passage in book III. He asks whether the flesh of the Word was subject to sin before it was assumed and whether it was so assumed. He answers: "It can truly be said and must be believed, according to the agreed witness of the saints, that it was, like the rest of the Virgin's flesh, beforehand subject to sin, but that by the work of the Holy Spirit it was so cleansed that free from all contagion of sin it could be united with the Word, [capacity for] pain remaining, though this not of necessity but by the choice of the one who assumed. The Holy Spirit coming upon Mary completely cleansed her from sin and freed her from the root (*fomes*) of sin, either by taking it out completely as some think, or by so weakening or reducing it that afterwards no possibility of sin existed; he also prepared in the Virgin the power to have a child without male seed."[1] P. relies on St. John of Damascus, whose view of the purification (*qv*) of Mary needs subtle exegesis. In the next article P. teaches

Mary's sinlessness, quoting St. Augustine's (*qv*) well-known words from *De natura et gratia*.[2]

Two sermons by P. on Our Lady are printed among the works of Hildebert of Lavardin (*qv*) —on the Annunciation and the Purification.[3] The first has worthwhile passages. He insists on the virginity, before, in and after childbirth. He recalls Ez 44:2 on the contrast between Eve (*qv*) and Mary: "Three evils Eve left to her kind: the man's lordship over the woman, conception in sin, and childbirth in pain. In the Virgin's conception there was no carnal desire mingled with it, no sadness in the one who conceived, no difficulty for her who brought forth."[4] On the Mary-Church relationship: "The Virgin Mary became the Church or any faithful soul who is chaste through incorrupt desire, a virgin by the sincerity of faith."[5]

---

[1]*Libri IV sententiarum*, Quaracchi ed., 1917, Lib. III, Dist. III, c. 1, pp. 557-558. [2]*ibid.*, c.2, p. 559. [3]PL 171, 605B-610D; 615C-627B; cf. R. Laurentin, *Traité I*, 149-150. [4]607C. [5]609A.

PETER PASCASIUS, ST.
(*c.* 1225-*c.* 1300)

Born in Valencia, P. studied in Paris where he knew St. Thomas Aquinas. He entered the Mercedarians in 1250; he taught humanities in Paris, philosophy in Barcelona, theology in Saragossa.[1] In three works, *Life of St. Lazarus, Contemplation on Spy Wednesday, A Little Bible* (composed from his materials) he taught the Immaculate Conception (*qv*), one of the first to do so. "You are the woman created by God, so that in you there is not venial, mortal, original, actual sin or any other kind of sin . . . if you had been bound to original sin, our mother Eve could say that she had been been made purer than you, without any stain of sin . . ." Thus the Lord speaks to his Mother. P. returns to the idea of Mary's immunity and attributes her perfection, it would appear, to the redemptive work of Christ.

---

[1]Works (4 vols) ed. Rome 1905-08 by Valenzuela Pietro Armenguado, *Obras de S. Pedro Pascual, Martyr, Obispo de Jaén . . .*; cf. V. Mancini, O.d.M., *Il primo difensore dell'Immacolata Concezione di Maria e stato un Mercedario: S. Pietro Pascasio* (Naples, 1939); M. Ortuzar, O.d.M., *S. Pedro Pascual y el dogma de la Inmaculada Concepción, La Inmaculada y la Merced* (Rome, 1955), I, 383-8; A. Sancho Blanco, O.d.M., *S. Petrus Paschasius, Ep. et Martyr, Immaculatae Conceptionis defensor, ibid.*, II, 1-35 = V.I., VIII, p. 1-35; G. M. Roschini, O.S.M., *Maria Santissima*, III, 148-50.

PETER THE VENERABLE (d. 1156)

Ninth Abbot of Cluny, after St. Bernard (*qv*) the most prominent churchman of his age, friend of Bernard despite moments of tension, and a monastic leader,[1] P. fostered devotion to Mary in his order. In the *Statutes* which he drew up to regulate obervance, he ordered that a Mass be said daily at her alter, that the Little Office of Mary be daily recited in the chapel of the sick which was dedicated to her, that on the feast of the Assumption the *Salve Regina* (*qv*) be chanted during the procession. Doctrine is found in a lengthy letter which P. composed for a certain monk Gregory.[2]

Prompted by reading Pseudo-Jerome (*qv*), Gregory had raised questions about the gifts of grace and knowledge received by Our Lady. Did she receive special added graces as did the apostles, on the day of Pentecost? P. combines a sense of proportion with respect for Sacred Scripture and the necessary distinctions. "There could be no addition to the fullness of justice and holiness" in the coming of the Holy Spirit "to her whom before the concepton and in the conception of the Son of God the same Spirit had filled with sanctification and perfection of all the virtues."[3] She had been chosen not to preach the word of God but to engender the Word of God.[4] Scripture says nothing in her case about the special secondary graces which the apostles needed for their ministry, as they also needed to rise above imperfection.

Gregory had also drawn unwarranted conclusions about Mary's knowledge—surpassing that of the angels—from the Pauline text, "in whom are hidden all the treasures of wisdom and of understanding" (Col 2:3). No, replies P., Mary did not, during her life, have knowledge of all things. "This belongs to God alone and has not been granted to any mortal being in this life."[5] P. cites the obvious Matthaean and Lucan texts. He analyses at length the condition of beatitude. He has no doubt that Mary "had wisdom immense and superior to that of all the saints while they were still living."[6] A third question put to him by Gregory touched on the Incarnation and on this he set forth admirably the orthodox doctrine.

---

[1]Cf. G. Constable and J. Kritzeck, *Petrus Venerabilis in Studia Anselmina*, 40 (Rome, 1956), for 8th centenary of his death. [2]*Statuta*, 54, 60, 76, in PL 189, 1040B, 1041D,

1048A; for letter PL 189, 283-304; critical ed. (used here) n.94 in *The Letters of Peter the Venerable*, G. Constable, ed., Harvard University Press, 1967, I, text, II intr., notes. Cf. P. Séjourné, *Pierre le Vénérable*, DTC, 12, 2, esp. 1070, 71; B. Billet, O.S.B., "L'Oeuvre mariale de Pierre le Vénérable," *Espirit et Vie* 87(1977), p. 466-77. [3]I, 240. [4]I, 241. [5]I, 244. [6]I, 250.

PHILIP OF HARVENGT (d. 1183)

One of the first Premonstratensians, P. expresses his ideas on Our Lady in his commentary on the Song of Songs, and in an unpublished sermon on Assumption.[1] Though he attributes faults to Mary, he thought that she was inferior only to Christ. He describes, in terms of the courtly love of his time, the relations between the divine Spouse and his beloved. Excesses are ruled out: Mary did not see the divine essence while on earth; she surpassed the angels, but in grace. P. thought that Mary was the most beautiful of women. She had purified herself before the Incarnation and Christ assimilated her to himself. Her conception of Christ was free of concupiscence.

P. defended the bodily Assumption (*qv*). "The Mother is, therefore, with the Son not only in spirit, about which there is not even the slightest doubt, but also in the body, which appears nowise incredible, for though the canonical Scripture does not proclaim it with tangible proof, pious belief is led to it by plausible arguments."[2] He insinuates a link between the Assumption and the *virginitas in partu* (*qv*), as with the divine motherhood: "His Mother is there who ministered to him her own flesh, who from her womb, with her virginity intact, gave birth to the Godman."[3] As a corollary P. taught the queenship (*qv*) very fully.

Likewise the mediation: "Therefore the Bride is rightly called Mediatress (*qv*) of us all, and the Mother is not incongruously called the Empress, because asking her Spouse and commanding her Son she turns his fury into grace and his wrath into sweetest love."[4] P. uses the metaphor of the neck which seems to have been first used by Hermann of Tournai: "She seems to hold the middle place between the Head and body . . . The Mother of the Spouse and our handmaid the empress of all joins those separated, keeps them joined as a powerful and efficient Mediatress . . . . A good neck, a good intermediary, a good Mediatress finally who joins what the harmful divider Eve (*qv*) had separated, who invites her Son to largesse and

us to obedience and acts to ensure that we do not forget to offer submission and he not to bestow benefit."[5]

P. picks up easily the concept of Mary's mercy so widespread in his age: "The Virgin has a feeling of more generous kindness towards those whom she sees in need of stronger protection, whom she considers willing to be redeemed by her Son, striving, but impeded from the result by the pressure of their own burden."[6]

[1]*In Cant. Canticorum*, PL 203, 181-490. Cf. R. Laurentin, *Traité* I, 155; for sermon cf. H. Barré, ME, V, 118. [2]VI, 50, 488C. [3]*ibid.* [4]IV, 5, 360D. [5]II, 7, 260BCD. [6]IV, 14, 376C.

PHOTIUS (d. *c.* 897)

Patriarch of Constantinople in a moment of crisis between east and west, when, however, the break was avoided. A scholar of encyclopaedic knowledge P. speaks of Mary in important homilies, two on the Annunciation, one on the birth of the Virgin, one on the church in the imperial palace, one on the icon of the *Theotokos* in Santa Sophia.[1]

P. is in the Byzantine tradition, as this eulogy of Mary will show: "Hail, because thou has made the tree of life bear fruit for us, which withers the offshoots of the tree of decay and yields the sweetness of knowledge. Hail much-graced one, because thou hast stored away the pearl of great price, conveying the wealth of salvation to the ends of the universe. Blessed art thou among women, because thou hast requited the discomfiture of woman's transgression, having turned the reproach of deceit into a laudation of the sex; because in thee, a virgin, he who first moulded Adam out of virgin earth, today remoulds man from thy virginal blood; because, having woven the fleshy garment of the Word, thou hast covered up the nakedness of the first-formed."[2]

P. held the traditional Byzantine view that Mary was born of a sterile mother; he interpreted Gen 3:15 (see WOMAN IN) in a Marian sense and accepted other OT types like the burning bush, and the stone cut by no human hands (Dan 2:45). M. Jugie thought that he held and taught the Immaculate Conception. (*qv*). It is for experts to interpret such passages as these on the one hand: ". . . she is seen not only to be fair in beauty surpassing the sons of men, but elevated to an inexpressible fairness of dignity beyond any comparison beside. All fair is my companion. She has escaped the blows, has been freed of her wounds, has wiped off all blemish, has cast down her detractors into hell, has raised up those who sang her praises,"[3] and the sentence already quoted "thou hast revoked the failing of woman's transgression"; and, on the other hand, "Today the Virgin is being set apart from among men, offered to the Creator as the first fruits of our human clay, and the great and eternal mystery of our re-creation is being accomplished in a wondrous manner. Today Adam's daughter, having retrieved the transgression of the first mother Eve, and cleansed herself of the stain that emanated thence, fair and beautiful in the eyes of the Creator, pledges salvation to the human race."[4] Can "cleansed herself of the stain" be seen as a form of Purification (qv), Katharsis, compatible with initial sinlessness?

P. saw the Annunciation as "the beginning of all the other festivals," and in his Homily VII for it, he lengthily developed his favourite idea of Mary spouse (qv) of God. "For verily, the betrothal of the ever-virgin is the foundation and ground-work of our salvation . . . it does raise, renew and support our entire human race, which had taken a great fall . . . . With good reason does human-kind leap with joy and cry aloud; for it receives the glad tidings that its daughter has been desig-nated as a chosen bride for her Creator. With good reason does humankind bear itself proudly and rejoice; for upon receiving the news of the marriage contract with the Lord, it casts off the shameful yoke of slavery . . . . (The prophets, apostles, martyrs, angels contribute to the marriage festival) . . . For today the Virgin on behalf of our whole race is being betrothed to the common Lord . . . For this reason David also, the ancestor of God, as he holds his spiritual lyre, appears to dance in his soul at his daughter's betrothal . . ."[5]

Mary's unique holiness is emphasised, "steeped in the virtues," "entirely possessed by divine love," "by surpassing human standards she showed herself worthy of the heavenly bride-chambers." She is our model. Her central role in salvation is already evident in the sponsal theme. She is the Mediatress (Mesitis) "the Lord is with thee, delivering through thee the whole race from its ancient sorrow and curse;" ". . . for she, the descendant, was able to repair the ancestral defeat, who brought forth the Saviour of our

race by a husbandless birth, and moulded his body."[6]

In an invasion crisis P. can then pray with characteristic Byzantine trust in the Mediatress: "Let us set her up as our intermediary (Mesitis) before her Son our God, and make her the witness and surety of our compact, her who conveys our requests and rains down the mercy of her Offspring, and scatters the cloud of enemies, and lights up for us the dawn of salvation."[7]

[1]Homilies ed. S. Aristarchos, *Photiou logoi kai homiliai* (Constantinople, 1900). 16 genuine homilies, others of the 83 drawn from other works. Critical ed. B. Laourdas, *Photiou homiliai* (Athens, 1959) 34-70, 88-96; I use transla-tion of Cyril Mango, *The Homilies of Photius, Patriarch of Constantinople (Cambridge, Mass), Dumbarton Oaks Studies, 1958), V, VII,* on the Annunciation, p. 112-122; 139-149; the Nativity, p. 164-76; church, pp. 184-190; the image in S. Sophia, pp. 286-96. Cf. M. Jugie, *L'Immaculée Conception,* 164-69; H. Graef, *Mary,* I, 191-94; B. Schultze, S.J., *Der Marienkult des Patriarchen Photius,* Zagreb Congress, III, 461-78. [2]Mango, p. 121. [3]p. 292. [4]p. 142. [5]p. 140-43. [6]p. 142, 143; p. 143, 175. [7]*Hom III,* p. 95.

PIUS IX (Pope 1846-1878)

The Pope of the Immaculate Conception (qv), which he defined in the Bull *Ineffabilis Deus* (qv). In 1849, the Pope in the Encyclical *Ubi primum,* consulted the hierarchy of the Church who were to report to him "concerning the devotion which animates clergy and people regarding the Immaculate Conception of the Blessed Virgin and how ardently glows the desire that this doctrine be defined by the Apostolic See" as well as conveying their own opinion. He told of the appeals which had reached Rome already and of the conviction of "eminent theologians"; he spoke of his own trust in Mary, quoting St. Bernard's maxim that it is God's will "that we obtain everything through Mary" —a saying frequently repeated by his successors —and gave an account of the preliminary steps he had taken by setting up a committee of experts and Cardinals. The Pope informed the Cardinals in Consistory on 1 December 1858, that "prac-tically all the bishops" wished the definition.

Pius IX spoke of Mary on a few other occa-sions. He had occasion to write about her in the decree *Quemadmodum Deus,* 8 December 1870, by which he proclaimed St. Joseph (qv) Patron of the Universal Church and in the companion decree, *Inclytum Patriarcham,* 7 July 1871, which regulated liturgical honours due to the saint. In a letter to an author of a book on the Virgin Priest Pius IX stated that the title was used by the Fathers: an error.

See D. Bertetto, S.D.B., *Il Papa dell'Immacolata Pio IX*, Preface Luigi Villa, (Brescia, Ed. Civitá Cattolica, 1972).

PIUS X, ST. (Pope, 1903-1914)

Pius X's holiness was marked by very great devotion to Our Lady. His teaching on Mary is found principally in *Ad diem illum* (*qv*), a doctrinal statement much discussed in the literature on Our Lady's part in our Redemption.[1] The Pope also deals with the spiritual (*qv*) motherhood and with Mary's distribution of grace. He applies to the merit (*qv*) of Jesus and Mary the distinction *de condigno* and *de congruo*. The occasion of the Letter was the fiftieth anniversary of the dogma of the Immaculate Conception (*qv*), which the Pope commemorated in other devotional ways too. He spoke or wrote on Our Lady at other times and encouraged consecration (*qv*) to her.

[1]Texts, OL 165-88. Cf. A Basso, O.S.M., *Il B. Pio X, grande anima Mariana* (Vicenza, 1951).

PIUS XI (Pope 1922-1939)

Pius XI was spiritually attracted by St. Thérèse of Lisieux, a saint of Carmel, whom he beatified, canonised, proclaimed Patroness of the Missions and of Russia. His pontificate coincided with the movement in favour of Our Lady's universal mediation (*qv*), launched by Cardinal Mercier (*qv*). The Pope set up three commissions, in Rome, Belgium and Spain, to examine the definability of the truth.[1] Principal Marian documents were: *Ephesinam Synodum*, 25 December, 1930, urging commemoration of the fifteenth centenary of the Council of Ephesus; the Encyclical *Lux Veritatis* (*qv*), 25 December, 1931 on the occasion; the Apostolic Letter *Inclytam ac perillustrem* on the Rosary to Very Rev. M. Gillet, O.P.; the Encyclical *Ingravescentibus malis* on the same topic, 29 September, 1937. In other official documents and addresses there are passages relevant to Marian theology or piety.

[1]G. M. Roschini, O.S.M., *La Mariologia de Pio XI*, MM 1(1939), 121-72; D. Bertetto, S.D.B., "Maria nell'insegnamento di Pio XI", *Salesianum* 20(1958), 596-647; *id.*, "La devozione mariana di Pio XI," in *ibid.* 26(1964), 334-49.

PIUS XII (Pope 1939-1958)

Pius XII made the most significant papal contribution to Marian theology and public piety.[1] The principal acts of piety were the consecration of mankind to the Immaculate Heart (*qv*) on 31 October, 1942; that of Russia likewise in the Encyclical *Sacro vergente anno*, 7 July, 1952; declaration of a Marian Year 1953-54 for the centenary of the dogma of the Immaculate Conception (*qv*); institution of a less formal Marian Year for the Lourdes Centenary, 1957-58 and the *Encyclical Pour Le pèlerinage*, ceremonial crowning of the image *Salus Populi Romani*, 1 November, 1954; institution of the feast of Mary Queen, and extension of it and that of the Immaculate Heart to the whole Church. Pius continued papal teaching and exhortation on the Rosary, especially in the Encyclical *Ingruentium malorum*, 15 September, 1951.

Pius XII's doctrinal acts were chiefly: the definition of the dogma of the Assumption (*qv*); the proclamation of the Queenship (*qv*); the Encyclical *Fulgens Corona* for the centenary of the Immaculate Conception to which many other passages of doctrinal import from many documents and discourses might be added. He encouraged national, regional and international congresses, often speaking to them directly by radio-link. Mariological congresses were added to the international Marian assemblies from 1950, and the Pope gave a notable address to the theologians assembled in Rome in 1954 for the second. Notable too are the passages on Our Lady in four important Encyclicals: *Mystici Corporis, Mediator Dei, Sacra Virginitas* and *Haurietis Aquas* on the Mystical Body, the Liturgy, Holy Virginity and the Sacred Heart of Jesus. In *Menti nostrae* on the priesthood and elsewhere, Pius urged a special attitude towards Mary as helpful to priests. He canonised three saints strongly linked with Marian piety: St. Catherine Labouré the apostle of the Miraculous Medal, St. Louis Marie de Montfort (*qv*) and St. Anthony Mary Claret (*qv*); he commemorated by Encyclicals the Marian doctors, St. Cyril of Alexandria (*qv*) and St. Bernard of Clairvaux (*qqv*); he extolled Fra Angelico as a painter of Our Lady. On Marian themes he spoke a special language to countries where Our Lady is part of the community consciousness—Mexico, and especially Poland.

The first *schema* on Our Lady prepared for Vatican II referred in its annotation 32 times to

Pius XII. The final text, ch. VIII of LG has 7 references to him, the largest number to any non-biblical or patristic author. The guiding lines given to theologians and preachers are borrowed textually from Pius XII's address to the Marian theologians and *Ad Caeli Reginam*.[2] The Council could have drawn abundantly on the Pope's discourses on the subject of woman.[3]

---

[1]D. Bertetto, S.D.B., *Il Magistero Mariano di Pio XII*, ed. Paoline, 2nd ed. 1959, 1015 p; *id., "La Mediazione celeste di Maria nel magistero di Pio XII,"* Euntes docete 9(1956), p. 134-59; G. M. Roschini, O.S.M., "Pio XII il Papa della Madonna," MM 20(1958), 313-35; I. Fabrega, C.M.F., "Doctrina mariologica de Pio XII," *Eph Mar* 9(1959), p. 9-50; B. C. da Silva, C.M., "Pio XII o Papa mariano," *Rev. Eccl. Brasil.* 1958, p. 889-97; C. Balic, O.F.M., "De mariologia Pii Papae XII," *Divin.*, 3(1959), 670-700. [2]OL, pp. 396 and 408. [3]Papal Teachings, *The Woman in the modern world*, Boston, 1958, Pius XII, pp. 43-325 passim and appendices.

POOR OF YAHWEH, (ANAWIM), THE

Vatican II tells us that Mary held a primacy of merit among the Poor of the Lord:[1] "She stands out among the poor and humble of the Lord, who confidently await and receive salvation from him" (LG 55). With the passage of time in OT the word poor had acquired a very distinctive spiritual meaning, the mark of an identifiable suffering section of the Jewish people. "I will leave in the midst of you a people humble and lowly. The shall seek refuge in the name of the Lord" (Zeph 3:12). They are especially dear to the Lord: "But this is the man to whom I will look, he that is humble and contrite in spirit, and trembles at my word" (Is 66:2; cp. Is 49:13). Ps 149:4 almost identifies the *anawim* with the People of God: "For the Lord takes pleasure in his people; he adorns the humble with victory." Thus was built up an image of the "Church of the Poor," humble, faithful, the object of God's love, an Israel, a Remnant of spiritual fibre. The Messiah would be *par excellence* the "Poor One," the suffering servant of Is 53, he who would be sent "to preach good news to the poor," a title which Jesus willingly claimed (Lk 4:18). Of that select company, in that proximity to the Messiah stood Mary as she awaited the fullness of Israel.

---

[1]Cf. A. Gelin, *The Poor of Yahweh*, Collegeville, 1953; articles on *Poor* in biblical dictionaries and encyclopaedias.

PREDESTINATION, MARY'S

Mary's predestination was, like that of all human beings, an act of eternal divine choice which included total respect for her personality, for her freedom therefore, which is the root of personal dignity. It extended to her entire existence as this would unfold and grasped this entity bounded by time and space through the calling which gave it eternal meaning. This calling was divine motherhood. All theories about Mary's predestination must therefore centre on this office or function. This is part of the scheme of the Incarnation as God intended it. Wherein lies mystery: a mystery linked with the primacy (*qv*) of Christ in creation. The theory of Christ's (and with due proportion Mary's) absolute, universal primacy implies a relation of the predestination of all others to them.

Pius IX (*qv*) taught that: "God, by one and the same decree, had established the origin of Mary and the incarnation of Divine Wisdom" (*Ineffabilis Deus* (*qv*).[1] Pius XII took up the same phrase in *Munificentissimus Deus* (*qv*), "... the revered Mother of God, from all eternity joined in a hidden way with Jesus Christ, in one and the same decree of predestination."[2] Vatican II expressed the idea thus: "The Blessed Virgin was eternally predestined, in conjunction with the divine Word, to be the Mother of God" (LG 61).

---

[1]OL, 63. [2]OL, 318.

PRESENCE OF MARY

The problems raised by an affirmation of Christ's presence in the world have not all been rightly stated; consequently not fully answered. Vatican II made a comprehensive affirmation of his presence in the Church: "To accomplish so great a work, Christ is always present in his Church, especially in her liturgical celebrations. He is present in the sacrifice of the Mass, not only in the person of his minister the same one now offering, through the ministry of his priests, who formerly offered himself on the cross, but especially under the Eucharistic species. By his power he is present in the sacraments, so that when a man baptizes, it is really Christ himself who baptizes. He is present in his word, since it is he himself who speaks when the Holy Scriptures are read in the Church. He is present, finally, when the Church prays and sings, for he promised: 'Where two or three are gathered together for my sake, there I am in the midst of them'(Mt 18:20)." (Constitution on the Liturgy, 7).

This presence, in its liturgical aspect, is given fuller warrant by Council doctrine of the Church's liturgy as a sharing, by way of foretaste "in the heavenly liturgy which is celebrated in the heavenly Jerusalem toward which we journey as pilgrims" (*ibid.*, 8). *LG* is equally explicit: "Celebrating the Eucharistic sacrifice, therefore, we are most closely united to the worshipping Church in heaven as we join with and venerate the memory first of all of the glorious ever-Virgin Mary, of Blessed Joseph and the blessed apostles and martyrs, and of all the saints" (LG, 50).

Any theory about Mary's presence must, obviously, be based on the "indissoluble link" which unites her with Christ (LG, 53) and on the resemblance there is between them, resemblance accompanied by the dissimilarity flowing from his Godhead, his mission and his offices. No theory is proposed here for the question has not been singled out for detailed attention by theologians and the evidence—if the word is applicable—found in devotional or mystical writing has to be critically assessed; as has general practice within the Catholic body, which would support valid appeal to the sentiment of the faithful (*qv*). There is not only the question of Mary's presence, but of degrees in that presence. How it varies with objectively fixed moments in the life of the Church and with the different phases in personal spiritual growth would demand much difficult study.

The life of grace constitutes a presence of God and therefore of those whom God decides are linked with grace, in each particular case. The Mass, as the Council teaches, brings the faithful into the presence of Christ and of those glorified with him. His presence has a unique dimension because of his full glorification in body and soul; so has Mary's, again with the necessary qualifications.

PRESENTATION IN THE TEMPLE, THE
(Lk 2:22-38)

The episode narrated in Lk's infancy narrative has given us a proverbial phrase, *Nunc dimittis*, an important feast (see LITURGY), a canticle which like the *Benedictus* and the *Magnificat*, forms part of the Church's official prayer.[1] It introduces an important new idea, the universal mission of the Messiah, "a light for the revelation of the Gentiles," characteristic of Lk, and illustrates the Spirit's action on Simeon as on Zechariah, in a way markedly different from his action on Mary. Lk's regard for the Mother brings her into prominence in a prophetic moment and his feminist outlook is shown in the presence of Anna. The Jewish respect for old age is finely manifest, emphasised by the contrast with the infant Messiah and the youthful parents: a grouping to satisfy all tastes.

The Messiah is central to the development of thought, the Messiah awaited by his people, for the privilege of Israel is not lost in the universalism. This is Jesus' first encounter with the Temple which would have such meaning and symbolism in his life and that of his Mother, his first coming to Jerusalem where the drama of their lives would reach a climax. But Simeon's presence shows that Lk wished also to stress the fulfilment of OT hope.

St. Paul's description "born under the law" (Gal 4:4) is exemplified, but already the fullness which will transcend the law is foreshadowed. Mary accepted the obligation of Lev 12:6-8 and the two parents that of Ex 13:11-16—"their purification" (Lk 2:22) appears to refer to Mary and Jesus. There was no strict obligation to bring the Child to the Temple and Lk adds to the Ex text the word "holy." Why was the decision taken? Did the parents/Lk have Mal 3:1 in mind: "Behold I send my messenger to prepare the way before me, and the Lord whom you seek will suddenly come to his temple"? There are, as elsewhere in Lk's infancy narrative, other OT echoes more relevant to Jesus than to Mary. The proclamation of God's glory, which was a favourite theme of Temple theologians, incarnate, as it were in Jesus, glory of God's people Israel, is noteworthy. So is the evocation of the *Anawim* (*qv*) in the person of Simeon, and especially of Anna.

History: The notion of active offering by Mary which would fit a synthesis on her part in the Redemption appears to originate with St. Bernard, who did not develop it at very great length: "Offer, O consecrated Virgin, your Son and present to the Lord the blessed fruit of your womb. Offer, for the reconciliation of all of us, this holy victim, this victim pleasing to God. God the Father will most willingly receive this new and most precious victim, of whom he himself said: 'This is my beloved Son, in whom I am well pleased (Mt 3:17)'. This offering, brethren, does not appear painful; no sooner is the victim presented to the Lord than it is ransomed with some birds and borne away at once. But the day will come when he will be offered not in the Temple, nor in Simeon's arms, but outside the city between the arms of the Cross. The day will come when he will not be ransomed by the blood of another, but when he himself will ransom others by his own blood. For it is he whom God the Father has sent to be the ransom (*redemptionem*) of his people. That will be the evening sacrifice; today's is the morning sacrifice. This is more joyous, that fuller; this is offered at the time of birth, that in the fullness of age. To one and the other can be applied what the prophet announced: 'He offered himself because he willed it'."[2]

The same idea less developed is found with St. Bonaventure: "For she offered Christ in whom is the fulfilment of all legal offering, according to the word spoken [by St. Paul] to the Romans, 'the righteousness of God through faith in Christ Jesus for all who believe."[3]

Little has come from the Teaching Authority on the passage. Leo XIII writes thus: "Then, that he may offer himself as a victim to his heavenly Father, he desires to be taken to the Temple, and by the hands of Mary he is there 'presented to the Lord'."[4] Vatican II merely paraphrased the gospel: "When she presented him to the Lord in the Temple, making the offering of the poor, she heard Simeon foretelling at the same time that her Son would be a sign of contradiction and that a sword (*qv*) would pierce the mother's soul, that out of many hearts thoughts might be revealed (cf. Lk 2:34-35)" (LG 54).

---

[1] Cf. R. Laurentin, *Structure et théologie de Luc I-II (Paris, 1957)*; E. Galbiati, "La presentazione al Tempio" (Luca 2:22-40), BibOr 6(1964), 28-37; K. Baltzer, "The Meaning of the Temple in the Lukan writings," *Harvard Theol. Rev.* 58(1965), 263-77; A. Cutler, "Does the Simeon of Luke 2 refer to Simeon the Son of Hillel?", *Journal of Bible and Religion*, 34(1966), 29-35; A. George, "Israel dans l'oeuvre de Luc," RB 75(1968), 481-525; M. Schmaus, "De oblatione Jesu in templo (Lc 2:22-24)," MSS IV, 287-95; J. McHugh, *The Mother*, 99-103; R. E. Brown, *The Birth*, p. 435-70; see article Sword of Simeon; *Mary in NT*, 152-57. [2] *Serm. 3 in Purif.*, 2. [3] *Serm. in Purif.*, Ed. Quaracchi, vol 9, 648b. [4] *Jucunda semper*, 8 September, 1894, OL, 126.

PRIESTHOOD OF MARY, PRIESTS AND MARY

There are two separate questions: How did Mary share the priesthood of Christ? What special relationship exists between priests and Mary?[1] The answer to the second depends on that given to the first. The history of the ideas, nonetheless, can be taken separately.

The Priesthood: Thought on this subject has evolved through four stages. Down to 1050 A.D., treatment of it was oratorical and poetic, but not without attention to what divine revelation contained. During the next period, to 1600, progress was generally along the line of the plenitude of grace enjoyed by Mary, with some interesting insights on her act of offering. The third period comprises the seventeenth and eighteenth centuries, during which Mary's role in salvation was closely examined and thought given to her priesthood; the French school first used the title "Virgin Priest." Finally during the nineteenth and twentieth centuries the approach was systematic. But investigation which tended to concentrate on the victim of sacrifice, especially between 1870-1920, was first encouraged, and then frozen for a while by two Roman incidents.

Mgr. Van den Berghe published in 1873 a book entitled *Marie et le Sacerdoce*, of which he presented a copy to Pius IX. The Pope replied with a letter of commendation which contained these words: "She was so closely united to the sacrifice of her divine Son, from the virginal conception of Jesus Christ to his sorrowful Passion, that she was called by some Fathers of the Church the Virgin Priest."[2] No patristic text justifying this assertion has been found. In 1906 St. Pius X approved and indulgenced a prayer which ended with the words: "Mary, Virgin Priest, pray for us."

Roman attitudes were to change before long. In 1911 Fr. Hugon, O.P., a reputable theologian, brought out a book entitled *La Vierge Prêtre*; in the same year a paper was read on the subject at the Marian congress of Guingamp. By a decree published in 1916, the Holy Office forbade pictures of Our Lady clothed in priestly vestments. In 1927 an article appeared in *Palestra del Clero* on true devotion to the Virgin Priest. It dealt mostly with true devotion according to St. Louis Marie de Montfort, and only in passing referred to the Virgin Priest. The Bishop of the diocese was notified by Cardinal Merry del Val, Secretary of the Holy Office that, in accordance with the previous decree of 1916, "the devotion in question is not approved and cannot be spread." Later the Holy Office let it be known that the question must be allowed to lapse "as souls not enlightened would not understand it properly." Fr. Hugon withdrew his book, then in its fourth editon.[3]

Silence was kept on the subject thereafter until the forties, when Spanish theologians revived it. In the early fifties, R. Laurentin chose it as part of the subject presented for two doctorates, the historical aspect at the Sorbonne, the dogmatic at the Catholic Institute in Paris. He suggested using the abstract word priesthood rather than priest in conjunction with Mary. He noted through the ages, save for Salazar and H. Marracci (*qqv*) whose full substantial works he could not discover, a certain reluctance on the part of theologians to go to the limit from positions which seemed promising. Constants in tradition are: Mary did not receive the Sacrament of Orders because she was a woman; she is superior to the ministerial priests.

Not much has been written on the subject since Vatican II. Little, too, on the priesthood of Christ. Yet the Council amplified, without altering, Pius XII's teaching on the priesthood of the faithful or laity "whatever" as the Pope said "is the meaning of this honourable title and claim." The demands of women for some share in the ministry may prompt reconsideration of the problem.

Priests: Since the seventeenth century, literature on the relationship between the priestly life and Mary has increased. Many congregations of priests have made devotion to Mary a central tradition. The Popes, especially Pius XII, have urged priests to this form of piety. Ideas in this context are often more freely expressed than in the theological essays: on the parallel between Mary's life, vocation, consent, activity and those of the priest.

Not surprisingly the subject figured on the agenda of Vatican II. The first *schema* dealing with priests entitled *De Clericis*, distributed in 1963, gave a list of six aids towards priestly sanctification. The third read thus: "Filial love for the Blessed Virgin Mary, who is to be honoured by daily recitation of the Rosary and by other prayers." Comments had been sent to the commission which, in its summary of them, stated: "Others finally wished that no juridical obligation to recite the Rosary should be drawn up for the universal Church, for in the oriental Churches other very ancient and most beautiful prayers to the Blessed Virgin Mary are recited in place of the Rosary." The next version of the

schema entitled *De Sacerdotibus* recommended "filial love and devotion to the Blessed Virgin Mary"

The next phase was those black months of early 1964 when this *schema*, as well as a number of others, was reduced to a set of arid propositions. It now contained no reference to Our Lady. It was rejected *in toto* by the assembly; 78 Fathers asked that in the rewritten text devotion to Our Lady be included among the means of sanctification.

In November a new *schema* was distributed. It has two references to Our Lady. "Devotion to the Most Holy Sacrament and to the Blessed Virgin Mary" was a means to the preservation of priestly celibacy, "that is chastity as understood in the Latin rite." The section on priestly holiness began with an exhortation to continuous prayer under the inspiration of the Holy Spirit and ended thus: "Let them value highly devotion to the Blessed Virgin; for she is the Mother of the High and Eternal Priest and accordingly Queen of Apostles and outstanding image of the Church in the order of faith, charity and perfect union with Christ." A footnote referred to the relevant section of LG.

The passages were criticised in the assembly. Cardinal Suenens said there was too little on the role of Mary in the life of the priest. On behalf of the Polish Hierarchy Bishop Barela asked for clarification of the relationship between Mary, Mother of Christ and Mother of the Church, and the priesthood. Bishop Pechuan of Cruz del Eje suggested a possible explanation. Mary is Mother of Christ and she should be proclaimed Mother of Priests. She is Mother of the Priesthood because it was in her chaste womb that Christ received his priestly anointing and she shared in a unique manner in the redemptive sacrifice of the Cross. Psychologically, Mary fills a void left in the priest's life by the absence of a family. Cardinal Heenan spoke of the arrangement existing between priest and members in the Legion of Mary as a model. Mgr. Falls, a priest auditor, said among other things: "All priests should especially foster a particular devotion to the Holy Spirit, to Jesus the eternal High Priest and to his Mother and ours, the Queen of Apostles and Queen of the clergy."

The next version of the *schema* showed slight effect of these comments, though there was an important addition: Mary was proposed as a model of docility to the Holy Spirit and the aspect noted was that: "she devoted herself wholly to the mystery of the Redemption"—a new idea, for it was not stated in LG that her cooperation was under the impulse of the Spirit. The principal Marian passage was abbreviated: the words "Mother of the High and eternal Priest" were dropped. Dissatisfaction was shown by a massive demand for restoration of the previous wording: 439 votes *juxta modum*. The dissatisfied, singly or in small groups, proposed alternative phrasing. One group of 390 requested these words: "Let priests love and venerate with filial devotion and homage this most loving Mother of the High and eternal Priest and Queen of Apostles." One Father suggested "protectress (*praesidium*) of their ministry."

The commission's answer was this passage: "Nourished by spiritual reading, in the light of faith, they can more sedulously seek the signs of God's will and the impulses of his grace in the different events of life, and thus from day to day become more docile to the mission they have undertaken in the Holy Spirit. They will always find a wonderful example of such docility in the Blessed Virgin Mary who was led by the Holy Spirit to devote herself to the mystery of the Redemption of mankind. Let priests venerate and love with filial devotion and homage this Mother of the eternal High Priest, Queen of Apostles and protectress of their ministry" (art. 19, ref. to LG 57). There was no mention of Our Lady in the passage on celibacy.

Priestly Training: This has been in different ways and in varying degrees influenced by attitudes towards Our Lady, those current in the particular age, milieu, region or institute. The influence is more easily traced in the post-Tridentine period. The Company of St. Sulpice, founded to train future priests, was conspicuous in this regard: the impulse given by Bérulle (*qv*) passed through the work and writings of Olier (*qv*). In the nineteenth century many clerical or religious societies, especially those working in missionary lands, were placed under the direct patronage of Our Lady. The example of a founder imbued with Marian piety such as St. Alphonsus Liguori, or of a heroic figure in the history of an institute like St. Bernard, would be potent on young aspirants. Memoirs or biographies of saintly priests often recount marked devotion to Mary in seminary days.

Such characteristics were found in seminary life during the decades before the Council. The first *schema* on priestly training recognised the fact, as this sentence showed: "Let them perform faithfully, therefore, the pious exercises approved by the seminary rule or tested by usage and let them assiduously cherish the various forms of piety, especially in honour of the Mother of God." Early in 1964 the *schema* like others at the time was reduced to a set of propositions. At that time too Our Lady's name was not mentioned in several documents where it would ultimately appear and, what is worse, deleted from some where it had already figured. It was deleted from the *schema* on priestly training. Nor did it appear in the next version. The needed addition was finally made to article 8: "With filial trust they should love and render homage to the most Blessed Virgin Mary, who was given as a mother to the disciple by Christ Jesus dying on the Cross." (see WOMAN IN JN 19:25-27).

[1]P. Belon, S.M., *La maternité sacerdotale de Marie* (Lyons-Paris, 1939). Cf. N. Garcia-Garces, C.M.F., "La cooperación de Maria a nuestra redención a modo de sacrificio," EstM 2(1943), 195-247; id., "La Santisima Virgen y el sacerdocio," EstM 10(1950), 61-104; id., "Maria, la Iglesia y el sacerdocio, EphMar 5(1955), 441-43; M. Philippe, O.P., *La Très Sainte Vierge et le Sacerdoce* (Paris, 1947); E. Neubert, S.M., *Marie et notre Sacerdoce* (Paris, 1952); J. M. Bover, S.J., *Maria, Mediadora universal o Soteriologia mariana* (Madrid, 1946), 331-54; E. Sauras, O.P., "Fué sacerdotal la gracia de Maria?", EstM 7(1948), 387-424; Basilio de San Pablo, C.P., "Los problemas del sacerdocio y del sacrificio de Maria. Conquistas de los veinte ultimos anos," EstM 11(1951), 141-220; J. M. Alonso, C.M.F., "De B.M.V. mediatione in Eucharistia," EphMar 2(1952), 179-90; *Gracia de unión, sacerdocio, maternidad divina, Studia Mediaevalia et mariologica P. Carolo Balic . . . dicata* (Rome, 1971) 563-73; Esp. R. Laurentin, *Marie l'Église et le sacerdoce*, (Paris, 1952, 1953); ME II, C. Koser, O.F.M., *De sacerdotio B.M.V.* 169-206; E Doronzo, O.M.I., *De sacerdotali ministerio B.V.M.*, 149-167; ME VII, articles by O. Mueller, S.J., A. P. Joannes a Jesu, O.F.M., J. Dos Santos, C.M.F., L. Zver, S.D.B., J. I. Lorscheiter, C. Koser, O.F.M., D. Bertetto, S.D.B., J. M. Goicoechea, O.F.M., H. Rito, O.F.M., S. Matellan, C.M.F., G. de Becker, SS.CC.A. Vallejo, O.F.M., R. Mascarenhas Roxo, J. Martins Terra, S.J., G. van Rooijen, M.S.C.; D. Bertetto, *De B. Maria Virgine et sacerdotio Ecclesiae, Acta Congressus Internat. de Theol. Vaticani II* (Rome, 1968), 225-37; id., "Priesthood of Mary and the Church," Marian Era 9(1969), 37-38, 69-72; W. G. Most, "On the Priesthood of Mary," UnivDaytonRev 5(1968), 15-25; M. P. Pourrat, *Marie et le Sacerdoce* in *Maria I*, 803-24; J. Lécuyer, C.S.Sp., *La Vierge Marie et la formation sacerdotale dans la tradition de l'Ecole française* in *Maria III*, 75-93; Mgr. Duperray *Regina Cleri* in *Maria III*, 661-95; on priestly training special issue Seminarium, 1975, 3, *De Beata Virgine in sacerdotali formatione*, p. 474-723, 13 contributions by well-known

authors with bibliography by G. M. Besutti, O.S.M.; J. Massingberd Ford, *Our Lady and the Ministry of Women in the Church*, MSt 23(1972), p. 79-112. [2]OL, 85.

PRIMACY OF MARY

Mary's primacy in creation depends on that of Christ. Franciscan theologians arguing from the intuition of Scotus (*qv*) that the Incarnation was decreed independently of Adam's fault, that the soul of Christ was, in creation, the first object of divine predestination, went on to attribute to the Godman not only primacy of excellence, but absolute universal primacy.[1] The scriptural basis is in Col and Eph. A succinct statement is from St. Lawrence of Brindisi: "Christ is the foundation of all creation, all grace, all glory since he is the end of all things because of whom all things were created."[2]

Vatican II made the mystery of Christ one of its key concepts: he is not only the "mediator and the fullness of all revelation" (*Verbum Dei*, 2), but "the image of the invisible God and in him all things came into being. He is before all things and all things hold together in him. He is the head of the body which is the Church. He is the beginning, the first-born from the dead, so that in all things he should hold the primacy (cf. Col 1:15-18). By the might of his power he dominates what is in heaven and on earth and by his surpassing perfection and activity he fills the whole body with the riches of his glory (cf. Eph 1:18-23), (LG 7). "For Adam, the first man, was a figure of him who was to come, namely Christ the Lord. Christ, the final Adam, by the revelation of the mystery of the Father and his love, fully reveals man to man himself and makes his supreme calling clear. It is not surprising, then, that in him all the aforementioned truths find their root and attain their crown." (*Gaudium et Spes*, 22).

Mary is brought into this scheme by papal and conciliar insistence on her predestination (*qv*) with Christ. Pius IX and Pius XII used the phrase "by one and the same decree" to signify this eternal bond. Vatican II expresses it thus: "The Blessed Virgin was eternally predestined, in union with the incarnation of the divine Word, as Mother of God and by design of divine Providence was on earth the loving Mother of the divine Redeemer, an associate of unique nobility and the humble handmaid of the Lord." (LG 61). The Council explicitly taught Mary's primacy of excellence: "Because of this gift of sublime grace she far surpasses all other creatures, both in heaven and on earth." (LG 53).

When the theology of the Palamite theologians is fully assimilated by the Latins, the idea of Mary's primacy, absolute and universal as that of Christ, but subordinate to and totally dependent on him, will be more readily acceptable. (See GREGORY PALAMAS, NICHOLAS CABASILAS, THEOPHANES OF NICAEA) It is one of the most fruitful themes awaiting exploration in the field of Marian theology.

---

[1]For the primacy of Christ, cf. D. Unger, O.F.M.Cap., "Franciscan Christology" in *Franciscan St.* 23(1942), 428-75; cf. J. F. Bonnefoy, O.F.M., "La place du Christ dans le plan divin de la création," *Mélanges de Sc.Rel.* 4(1947), 237-84; *id.*,[2]"Marie dans l'Église, ou la Primauté de la Sainte Vierge," BSFEM, 11(1953), 51-73; M. J. Nicolas, O.P., "Appartenance de la Mère de Dieu à l'Ordre hypostatique," BSFEM 1938; *id.*, "De transcendentia Matris Dei," ME II, 73-87.

PROCLUS OF CONSTANTINOPLE, ST.
(d. 446)

One of the great Byzantine sacred orators, P. was secretary to Atticus, Patriarch of Constantinople (*qv*) and was in 426 appointed bishop of Cyzicus. Impeded from the exercise of his office, he remained in Constantinople and enriched sacred oratory. His sermon on the *Theotokos*, preached before Nestorius, was a high moment in the pre-Ephesus controversy; he does not figure in the subsequent council history. In 434 he was named Patriarch of Constantinople.

Scholars have given much attention to the authenticity of the works attributed to P. in PG, and to the possible authorship of other items in PG or elsewhere.[1] This research has been summarised and each separate critical problem considered anew by R. Caro. Of the eight homilies or sermons on Christology—the Incarnation or Nativity—and Our Lady in PG, seven are authentic; one, a composite product, may be in part inspired by P.[2] One item from the mass of Ps-Chrysostom spuria is probably by P.; some others may have been influenced by him.[3]

P. abounds in the figurative language of the Byzantines and in the application to Mary of the OT symbols, not only the Ark (*qv*), which many of the Fathers saw as a Marian symbol, but the golden candlestick, the bedewed fleece, the burning bush and the light cloud, both of which are also found with other authors; and again the incorrupt paradise, the earth in which no seed was sown, or still more vivid, the loom of the "economy" on which the garment of union, i.e. of Christ's two natures, was woven.

The great theme basic to all P.'s thinking is the divine motherhood, the word *Theotokos* a favourite title.[4] Closely linked with this truth is the virginity, treated at great length with a sense of profound wonder, the virginity in conception, the virginity *in partu*.[5] P. applies the Ezek. 44:1-2 text on the closed door to Mary; her childbirth was miraculous. Besides the Is 7:14 (see WOMAN IN) text, P. continues the Eve-Mary parallel and contrast, rooted in patristic tradition. "Adam took a woman who waylaid him, Christ a woman who provided his bridal chamber."[6] "You alone remedied the sorrow of Eve; you alone wiped away the tears of the one who groaned . . . you will bear the price of the world's redemption."[7] Mary's obedience repairs the disobedience of Eve, her obedience to God's plan.[8]

Mary is the "only bridge between God and men," but by her role in the incarnation she enters the "economy," the whole mystery of redemption. Her motherhood is the prototype of all motherhood; as a mother and virgin she honours her sex. Through her, all women are blessed: the ignominy of Eve, Delilah, Jezebel, Herodias is covered; Mary surpasses the mission of Sarah, Rebekah, Elizabeth, Deborah. Women have a title to glory of incomparable excellence.

[1]EMBP, 839-863; CMP, IV, 36-106; PG, 65, 68-757, 841-846; Roschini, *Mariologia* I, 118-122, *Maria Sant.* I, 314-316; R. Laurentin, *Traité*, I, 164-65; F. Leroy, *L'Homilétique de Proclus de Constantinople*, ST, 247, 1967; R. Caro, *La Homiletica*, I, 76-128; Clavis G III, 133-150. [2]R. Caro, *La Homiletica* II, 308-344; R. Laurentin, in RSPT, 52(1968), 545. [3]Ps.-Chrysostom IV. *In Christi diem natalem*, PG, 61, 737-738; R. Caro, *La Homiletica*, II, 398-410; on other items cf. *ibid.*, 347ff, 421ff, 433ff, 452ff; R. Laurentin, *art.cit.*, 541-544. [4]PG, 65, 692, 681, 712. [5]692. [6]696. [7]720. [8]712.

PROTESTANTISM

The outstanding figures in Protestantism from Luther to Karl Barth are dealt with separately, and recent attitudes are dealt with in the article on Ecumenism.[1] With the passage of time, much less importance was attached to Mary in the different Protestant communions than had been allowed by the founding fathers—with the exception of the Caroline divines (see ANGLICANISM). One factor in the decline was the dessicating effect of the official confessions and creeds. Restrictions carefully phrased at the outset became more general, due at times to social and political causes. As Catholic countries increased their devotion to Our Lady, with kings and other notabilities taking the lead, Protestant states tended to react more vigorously. Cultural contrasts had some influence, Anglo-Saxon and Latin, Prussian and Slav. In the nineteenth century the Madonna's clients, the Italians, Spaniards, Irish and Poles, did not bathe in the power and success which was shed on Protestantism by the British and Prussian empires; the French were recovering from the Revolution and the defeat of Napoleon. To an extent that needs careful research, devotion to Our Lady was a victim of Europe's addiction to civil war.

This does not obscure the fact of basic doctrinal differences between Catholicism and Protestantism, which are reflected in the area of Marian doctrine and devotion: *Deus solus, Scriptura sola, gratia sola* summarise the Protestant outlook, which varies from one communion to another. While there has been a characteristic voice like Karl Barth change has also been manifest, and there is a literature on Mary from the Protestant side which is notably different from that of previous ages. Suffice it to mention the names of authors such as F. Heiler, H. Asmussen, F. W. Kunneth and M. Thurian.

[1]Y.-M. Congar, O.P., "Marie et l'Église chez les Protestants," BSFEM 10(1952), 97-106; *id., Mary, Christ and the Church*, London, 1952; W. Tappolet, *Das Marienlob der Reformatoren*, Tübingen, 1962; BSFEM 20(1963) whole issue; R. Laurentin, *La question mariale* (Paris, 1963), 138-50; J. Hamer, O.P., "Marie et le protestantisme à partir du dialogue oecuménique," *Maria* V, 983-1107; E. Stakemeier," "De B. V. ejusque cultu juxta reformatores," MO, 424-50; A. Brandenbourg, "De Mariologia ac de cultu venerationeque Mariae apud christianos disjunctos protestanticos hoc tempore vigentibus," MO, 479-516; W. Cole, "Scripture and the current understanding of Mary among American Protestants" MSS, VI, 95-161; *id.*, "Mary and American Protestants," *Univ. Dayton Review*, p. 49-58. Esp. T. A. O'Meara, O.P., *Mary in Protestant and Catholic Theology* (New York, 1966); S. Benko, *Protestants, Catholics and Mary*, (Valley Forge, 1968); H. Roux, "Le protestantisme et la question mariale," in *La Vierge Marie* (a symposium), Tours, Mame, 1968.

PRUDENTIUS, AURELIUS CLEMENS (348-*c*. 405) — See Supplement, p. 386.

PSELLOS, MICHAEL (1018-1079)

In the midst of a vast output on a variety of subjects, P. composed a homily on the Annunciation, especially noteworthy for its purity of style.[1] After general considerations on the Incarnation and the plan of redemption, the author turns to Mary's person and place in creation. He uses the metaphor of Jacob's ladder to express her sublime character and the way in which our nature is elevated through her motherhood. "Through her God descended to us and we ascend to him. O ladder touching heaven by its height and surpassing nature's manner . . . remaining unapproached even by angels."[2] Her soul most like to God shone in her stainless body. This body was fashioned from the purest elements to be a sanctuary for her soul.

P., boldly, as he says, places Mary "not far removed from the Trinity" and thinks that she saw God even before conceiving him, more clearly than the Seraphim; "in an ineffable manner she conceived, bore and brought him forth in the activity of her mind, as it would later be given to her to do in substantive reality."[3]

Within the scheme of salvation it is the traditional Eve (qv) Mary contrast that P. uses. The title "Blessed among women" replies to the curse, since Mary has been substituted for Eve as Christ for Adam: "Therefore as there the curse followed transgression, so here a blessing has been attached to obedience to the commandments."[4] Mary marked the turning-point in the fortunes of mankind. She would be the dike, the rampart saving us from the torrent and flood of evils. She who did not eat of the tree of knowledge being herself divinised has divinised our race.

The Father and the Holy Spirit entered personally into the Incarnation, "the latter coming close to [Mary] and sanctifying her nature that it might be more brilliant and appear more resplendent to receive the Word, the former overshadowing her to avert every snare, guarding entirely this inviolable sanctuary, protecting this paradise of delights from the heat."[5] Along with this unique intimacy with God, P. does then attribute total sinlessness to Mary.

[1]*Oratio in salutationem angelicam*, PO, 16, 517-525; cf. intr. by editor, M. Jugie, 515-17, id. *L'Immaculée Conception*, 190-194; id. in DTC, 17, 1149-1158. [2]4, 521. [3]ibid. [4]5, 522. [5]7, 524, BHG 1082m; cf. E. M. Toniolo, O.S.M., unpublished homily on the Presentation of the B.V.M., in Alcune Omelie mariane, Rome, 1971, pp. 60-68.

PSEUDO-ALBERT

Down to the fifties of the present century, the *Mariale super missus est* was taken as the work of St. Albert the Great (qv). A. Fries, C.SS.R and B. Korosak, O.F.M. independently established in 1954 that the work was spurious.[1] The main reason was the marked difference between the doctrine in the *Mariale* and that in other works of St. Albert. This assessment has been confirmed since by the publication of genuine Mss of the saint, hitherto not printed.

While there is agreement thus far, there is divergence between the proposed authorship, and dating. Fr. Fries opted for the end of the thirteenth century, Fr. Korosak for a date before St. Bonaventure (d. 1274). Fr. Pelster supports the opinion of Korosak and thinks that the *Mariale* originated in the circle of St. Albert, the author being a German Dominican. A. Kolping, after an examination of the manuscript tradition, concluded that the work appeared in the second half of the century, in the south-east of the Empire, and that it was written possibly by a Benedictine or Cistercian, perhaps even Engelbert of Admont (qv). Detailed comparison with the latter's work will scarcely support that theory.[2]

With the growth of Marian literature in the present century, many had drawn on the Pseudo-Albert; this body of writing was overnight deprived of its importance when the work was proved spurious. There is scope for criticism.[3] Ps-Albert proceeds in general from one idea, the fullness of grace, the explanation of all Mary's privileges and endowment. Some of these privileges may appear arbitrarily affirmed: Mary has any gift possessed by anyone famous for any reason; she received all the Sacraments save Orders—though of this she had the grace and dignity and power; her knowledge covered everything that could be known, revealed truth or secular science; and so on. The author's curiosity in dealing with the Annunciation extends to the angel's sex, age and clothes, to Mary's physical appearance, to the precise hour of the meeting.

Yet there are many valuable and valid insights in the work. The most important is that of Mary as *socia*, associate (qv) of Christ; the theory of association is elaborated as never before.[4] Mary's part in the Redemption was the subject of interest to Ps.-Albert, whose insights and phrases continue in succeeding ages—"helper and associate, partner in the kingdom who was partner in the sufferings for the human race, when as all the servants and disciples fled, she remained beneath the cross, and took into her heart the wounds which Christ had in his body."[5] Mary's faith was firm in the Passion.

The author abounds on the mediation (*qv*) and the spiritual motherhood (*qv*). He defends the bodily Assumption of Our Lady.

The influence of Ps.-Albert on later writers was considerable, notably on St. Antoninus of Florence (*qv*).

[1]A. Fries, "Die unter dem Namen des Albertus Schriften," in *Beiträge zur Geschichte der Philosophie und Theologie des Mittelalters*, 37, Munster, 1954; B. Korosak, *Mariologia sancti Alberti Magni ejusque coaequalium*, Rome, *Bibliotheca mariana medii aevi*, 8, 1954. [2]Cf. F. Pelster, "Zwei Untersuchungen über die literarischen Grundlagen für die Darstellung einer Mariologie des hl. Albert des Grossen," in *Scholastik*, 30(1956), 388-402; A. Kolping, "Zur Frage der Textgeschichte, Herkunft und Entstehungszeit, der anonymen Laus Virginis (bisher Mariale Albert des Grossen), RTAM, 25(1958), 285-328. [3]Text *inter op.* St. Alberti, Borgnet ed., vol 37. [4]Cf. M. O'Carroll, C.S.Sp., "Socia: the word and idea in regard to Mary," *Eph. Mar.* 25, 339-40. [5]*op. cit.*, q. 42, p. 81.

PSEUDO-AUGUSTINE

The treatise on the Assumption is the item most significant for Marian theology among the mass of Pseudo-Augustiniana.[1] It appeared about the beginning of the twelfth century and was to prove a counterweight to Pseudo-Jerome (*qv*). Taking no account of the Apocrypha, it was, in the West, the first hard thinking on the problem. After the event of Pentecost, the author notes, Scripture is silent on Our Lady. But reason has a function and things can be believed on reason with "the suitability of the matter" as a guide; on which foundation the arguments are raised. Christ was exempt from the law of Gen 3:19, "into dust thou shalt return," and in the "nature taken from the Virgin." Mary was exempt from the curse pronounced on Eve (Gen 3:16). Since Jesus can do all things, would it be irreverent to suggest that she died, but was not bound by the ties of death—"through whom God willed to be born and to share in the substance of her flesh." "He could have kept her immune from corruption and the dust, who being born from her could leave her a virgin," he adds later, having first stated that children are bound to honour their parents. "The flesh of Jesus is the flesh of Mary," he says and develops the idea of unity, a special bond between them. To the union which binds all Christ's followers to him is added that special characteristic of nature uniting mother and son, son and mother.

There is abhorrence in thinking of Mary's body, so honoured by contact with Christ, delivered to worms. Again Jn 12:26 is quoted and applied to Mary, the *ministratrix* and *secutrix* par excellence. If Mary received grace beyond all others in life, will she have less in death? No one doubts that the Saviour could have kept his Mother forever without (bodily) corruption, why then doubt that he did it? Summarising his arguments, the Pseudo-Augustine recalls the argument from the *virginitas in partu* (*qv*) and ends with a phrase which is echoed by *Munificentissimus Deus* (*qv*): "let her be with him whom she bore in the womb, let Mary, the Mother of God, the nurse of God, the minister of God and follower of God be with him whom she brought forth nurtured and fed."

The author is still unknown. St. Fulbert of Chartres (*qv*), Ratramnus (*qv*) and Alcuin (*qv*) have been suggested. The present verdict: someone about the beginning of the 12th century, a disciple of St. Anselm (*qv*).[2]

[1]Text PL 40, 1140-48. [2]Cf. H. Barré, C.S.Sp., "La croyance à l'Assomption corporelle en Occident de 750 à 1150 environ," BSFEM, 7(1949), 80-100; G. Quadrio, S.D.B., "'Il trattato De Assumptione B.M.V.' dello Pseudo-Agostino e il suo influsso nella teologia assunzionistica latina," Rome, *Analecta Gregoriana*, 7, 1951; R. Laurentin, *Traité*, 1, 130.

PSEUDO-BONAVENTURE

There is a large amount of apocryphal material linked to the name of St. Bonaventure(*qv*), some of it Marian in content.[1] One sermon, however, included in the Quaracchi edition, the sixth on the Assumption, has been given special attention.[2] If the judgment of J. Beumer, who thinks it spurious, is accepted, then some ideas in the sermon which are not characteristic of B.'s works may be permanently dissociated from him. This does not mean that all ideas in the sermon are negligible. The teaching on universal mediation has continuing support from patristic times. It is particularly the idea of two kingdoms, of justice ruled by Jesus and of mercy by Mary that needs review. The phrasing too of Mary's privilege as Lady, counterpart of Christ as Lord, is excessive. The work is part of a current of thought which also carries along Richard of St. Laurent (*qv*), Pseudo-Albert (*qv*) and Englebert of Admont (*qv*).[3]

[1]Cf. C. Fischer, O.F.M., *Bonaventure (Apocryphes attribues à saint)*, DSp. 1, 1843-56. [2]Cf. J. Beumer, "Eine dem hl. Bonaventura zu Unrecht zugeschriebene Marienpredigt? in *FranziskSt*, 42(1960), 1-26.

PSEUDO-JEROME

A forgery bearing the name of St. Jerome (qv), the letter *Cogitis me*, was addressed to the saint's friends Paul and Eustochium, as if to answer their question about the Assumption (qv).[1] Rejecting the apocryphal tales, the author maintained that nothing certain was known about the passing of the Virgin save that she left the body. The fact of the empty tomb is accepted, but what happened to the body is unknown. With this total scepticism on the Assumption, the letter contained admirable things on the dignity of Mary (above that of angels and archangels), her queenship and intercessory power. Her role in preserving truth was expressed in a famous phrase to which the spurious prestige of St. Jerome gave permanence: "you alone have crushed heresies in the whole world."[2] Devotion was encouraged by the assurance that whatever honour is given to Mary redounds to her Son. The author also attempted a psychological interpretation of Mary's martyrdom of the spirit after the Ascension.

Extracts from this letter figured in medieval and later Breviary lessons. Thus it became widely known and through the name of Jerome, the greatest biblical scholar among the Latin Fathers, with personal knowledge of the Holy Places, it had immense effect. It blocked development of doctrine on the Assumption until the appearance of Pseudo-Augustine, two-and-a-half centuries later.

The author of the letter was Paschasius Radbert (qv). Attempts have been made to question the attribution, but the most reliable scholarship has confirmed it, as has the critical edition of the text.[3]

---

[1]Text among the writings of St. Jerome, PL 30, 122-42. [2]Cf. A. Emmen, O.F.M., "Cunctas haereses sola interemisti. Usus et sensus hujus encomii B.M.Virginis in liturgia, theologia et documentis pontificiis," in ME, 9(1961), 93-159; H. Barré, C.S.Sp., MM 29(1967), 196. [3]For authors expressing the contrary opinion or doubt cf. R. Laurentin, *Traité*, 5, p. 67, n. 50; Cf. H. Barré, C.S.Sp., "La Lettre du Pseudo-Jerome est-elle antérieure à Paschase Radbert?" in *Rev.Ben.* 68(1958), 203-226; critical ed., A. Ripberger, *Der Pseudo-Hieronymus-Brief IX "Cogitis me". Ein erster marianischer Traktate des Mittelalters von Paschasius Radbert* (Frieburg, Universität, 1962).

PURIFICATION (KATHARSIS) OF MARY

A difficulty in the interpretation of passages which are found in writings of the Eastern Fathers and Orthodox theologians on the Annunciation: they speak of Mary as "purified" or "prepurified" in that moment.[1] The texts of St. Ephraem are controverted. St. Cyril of Jerusalem speaks of a sanctifying (*Hagiasmos*). The starting-point is in a text from St. Gregory Nazianzen: "The Word of God became a complete man, with the exception of sin, born of the Virgin who was pre-purified (*protokathartheises*) by the Spirit in her soul and in her body."[2] With the passage of time, the Fathers saw two meanings in the word "sanctification";[3] divine action raising Mary to the level of divine conception.[4] Nicholas Cabasilas could write: "If certain holy doctors have said that the Virgin had been purified beforehand by the Spirit, we must believe that they understood this purification in the sense of an increase of grace. These doctors in fact speak of the angels in the same way; they speak of them as purified, though there is no evil in them."[5] Gregory Palamas (qv) likewise writes: "You are already holy and full of grace, O Virgin, says the angel to Mary. But the Holy Spirit will come upon you again, preparing you, by an increase of grace for the divine mystery."[6] From Nicephorus Callixtus (d. *c.* 1335) dates the interpretation of purification as removal of sin and this does not gain support until the sixteenth century; thereafter in the Orthodox world it was used against the doctrine of the Immaculate Conception. Among the Latins (St. Thomas for example), it was so used too.[7]

The interpretation given here is not universal, unreservedly supported. The Eastern mentality complicates things, the Platonic notion for example of the flesh as "soiled"—even Origen referred thus to Christ's flesh: "You must know that Jesus has been soiled, that of his own will he took a human body for our salvation."[8] Fr. M. Jugie refers to the subject frequently in his basic work, *L'Immaculée Conception*; his attempt to equate the theme with the "Debt of Sin" is not convincing; the latter is a western concept. St. John of Damascus is controverted in the subject. Dom C. (later Bishop) Butler, O.S.B. in his draft Marian *schema* for Vatican II used the concept of *Katharsis* to express an increase of grace: "already before the Annunciation prepurified as none else, but then purified by the Holy Spirit that she should conceive the Word, but as gold needing no refinement and not by the divine fire consumed, in every way free from corruption in her conception . . ."[9]

In the light of this view, St. John of Damascus is proclaimed by Dom Butler "the Doctor of the Immaculate Conception."[10]

---

[1]Cf. D. Stiernon, A.A., *Maria* VII, p. 283-98; for St. John of Damascus, pp.291-2. Cf. also M. Candal, S.J., "La Viergen santisima 'prepurificada' en su Annunciación," OCP, 31(1965), 241-76; R. Laurentin, *Traité* V, 128,29. [2]PG 35, 325B, 633C. [3]Sophronius, PG 87, 3160D. [4]St. John of Damascus, PG 96, 704A; PG 94, 985B. [5]PO 19, 477. [6]*Homily on the Presentation*, ed. Sophoclis, Athens, 1861, p. 123, M. Jugie, *L'Immaculée Conception*, 228, PG 151, 178. [7]III, q. 27, a.3. [8]*In Lc* 14,3; PG 13, 1834B; SC 87, 218-19; cf. 2 Cor 5, 21. [9]Text, *EphMar* 18(1968), 194. [10]*ibid.*, p. 13.

PUSEY, E. B. (1800-1882)

A member of the Oxford Movement P., a friend of Newman, by publishing the *Eirenicon* in the form of a letter to F. C. Keble but directed to Manning prompted Newman's famous *Letter to E. B. Pusey*.[1] P. had occupied 80 pages of his book with criticisms of Catholic ideas and practice about Mary and added 50 pages of notes taken from minority opinions among the bishops consulted by Pius IX on the Immaculate Conception. For him, Mary was "the special crux as to the Roman system." He laid out quotations which he found theologically objectionable from the writings of Bernardine of Busti, Bernardine of Siena, St. Louis Marie de Montfort, St. Alphonsus Liguori (qqv). He rejected the title Mediatress of all graces and the idea that Mary's intercession was necessary to us. After Newman's *Letter* had appeared, P. took up the subject again in the *First Letter to Very Rev. J. H. Newman*; it appeared in 1869 as did P's edition of the treatise of John of Torquemada on the Immaculate Conception, dedicated by the editor to the Fathers of the First Vatican Council soon to meet in Rome.

---

[1]Cf. H. E. Cardinal Manning, *England and Christendom* (London, 1867); J. H. Cardinal Newman, *Letters and Diaries*, ed. S. Dessain; *The Letter to Pusey*, H. Graef, *Mary* II, 110ff.

Q

QUEEN OF PEACE

This title has taken primacy in the present century in a context wherein formerly that of "Help of Christians" dominated: Our Lady's role in the public life of nations. During early attacks on Constantinople, in the ages of the Crusades and of the wars against the Turks, Mary was invoked as a protectress, an ally on the side of Christians. As war became a form of social and international disease, with Christians, Catholics too, engaged on opposing sides, the ideal of peace took on a higher, universally imperative value. Thus it has been proposed by the Popes, who have not confused it with mere absence of conflict, nor with abdication of freedom, justice and human rights: Pius XII (*qv*) is the papal Doctor of peace. Before him, Leo XIII (*qv*) had used the particular title "Queen of Peace"[1] and Benedict XV had added it to the Litany of Loreto, justifying this decision by public statements.[2] Pius XII returned to the topic time and time again.[3] Paul VI has done likewise.

---

[1]OL, 94. [2]OL, 191-192. [3]OL, cf. Analytical Index, *Mary and Peace*, pp. 562-563.

QUEENSHIP, MARY'S

The kingship of Christ is the official teaching of the Church and is honoured in the Liturgy. The queenship of Mary is parallel to and subordinate to Christ's office.[1] It too has been officially taught, in Pius XII's Encyclical *Ad Caeli Reginam*, which gave doctrinal substance to an idea that recurred frequently in church teaching, notably in the same Pope's address to pilgrims at Fatima, 13 May, 1946. The queenship has a feast which is retained in the reformed Liturgy.

The Pope reproduces texts from the Fathers, Doctors and Popes on the queenship, and also draws on the Liturgy and popular prayers for similar supporting quotations. The testimonies are cited from east and west; the witness of iconography since the Council of Ephesus is mentioned.

The basis of the royal dignity and office is "a principle already evident in the documents handed down by tradition and in the sacred Liturgy, without doubt her divine maternity." Linking Lk 1:32-33 and 1:43 with a sentence from St. John of Damascus, the Pope concludes: "And it can likewise be said that the first one who with heavenly voice announced Mary's royal office was Gabriel the Archangel himself."

The Encyclical also adduces Mary's role in the Redemption as a ground of her queenship. The Pope argues from similarity with the kingly dignity of Jesus Christ, which was founded in his redemptive work as well as in his divinity, as Pius XI taught in *Quas primas*. St. Anselm is invoked as is Suarez (*qqv*), but principally the argument is from Mary's association with Christ: "And so it is that Jesus Christ alone, God and man, is King in the full, proper and absolute sense of the term. Yet Mary also, although in a restricted way (*temperato modo*) and only by analogy, shares in the royal dignity as the mother of Christ who is God, as his associate in the work of Redemption, in his conflict with the enemy, and in his complete victory. From this association with Christ the King she obtains a height of splendour unequalled in all creation."

Mary's primacy of excellence places her royal prerogative in stronger relief. It derives, says the Pope, recalling the words of Pius IX, from the abundance of grace with which she was filled from the first moment of her existence. Pius XII then ventures on much debated ground: "The Blessed Virgin has not only been given the highest degree of excellence and perfection after Christ, but also she shares in the power which her Son and our Redeemer exercises over the minds and wills of men. For if the Word of God, through the human nature assumed by him, works miracles and gives grace, if he uses the Sacraments and uses his saints as instruments for the salvation of souls, why should he not use his Blessed Mother's office and activity to bring us the fruits of the Redemption?"

Some theologians will see support, in the Pope's use of the word instrument, for a theory of a physical instrumental causality in Mary's distribution of grace. Pius is not conclusive in his assertion. Nor is Vatican II which here remained true to its intention of not "deciding those questions not yet fully clarified by the work of theologians." (LG 54). It did not go beyond a general affirmation of the queenship: "She was exalted by the Lord as Queen of all (*tanquam universorum Reginam*) in order that she might be more thoroughly conformed to her Son, the Lord of Lords and the conqueror of sin and death" (LG 59). Elsewhere, the Council calls Mary "Queen of Apostles."

Mary's queenship cannot be limited to intercession. How she exercises what Leo XIII called her "almost immeasurable power" in the distribution of graces is an area still to be fully researched.

[1]Bibliographies: *Maria* V, 1072-80; E. Lamirande, in *La Royauté de l'Immaculée* (Ottawa, 1955) 233-42; L. Galati, *Maria, la Regina* (Rome, ed. Paoline, 1962, 341-49); G. M. Roschini, O.S.M., *Maria Santissima*, II, 502-15; *ibid., Maria SS. Regina della Chiesa*, 345-502. Collective works, *Souveraineté de Marie, Congrès marial national* (Boulogne sur Mer, Paris, 1938); ASC III, *De praedestinatione et regalitate B.V.Mariae*, 1952; MSt 4(1953); MM 16(1954), 5; EstM 17(1956). S. G. Mathews, S.M., *Queen of the Universe*, Grail Publications, St. Meinrad, Indiana, 1957; ME V, *Mariae potestas regalis in Ecclesia*, 1959; cf. R. Bernard, O.P., "Le couronnement de gloire de la très Sainte Vierge," *Vie Spirit.* 32(1932), 113-35; L. de Gruyter, *De Beata Maria Regina, isquisitio positivo-speculativa* (Tenlings, 1934); H. Barré, C.S.Sp., "Marie Reine du Monde," BSFEM 3(1937), 19-76; *id.*, "La Royauté de Marie pendant les neuf premiers siècles," RSR 29(1939), 129-162; 303-334; *id.*, "La Royauté de Marie au XIIe siècle en Occident," ME V(1959), 93-120; M. J. Nicolas, O.P., "La Vierge-Reine," *Rev. Thomiste*, 45(1939), 1-29; 207-231; A. Luis, C.SS.R., *La Realeza de Maria* (Madrid, Ed. El Perpetuo Socorro, 1942); *id.*, "La realeza de Maria en los ultimos veinte anos," EstM 11(1951), 221-52; G. M. Roschini, O.S.M., "Royauté de Marie," *Maria* I, 603-18; *id., Maria SS. Regina della creazione e della storia* (Tolentino, 1949); *id., La Regina dell'Universo* (Rovigo, IPAG, 1950); *id., La regalità di Maria nell'innologia liturgica del medioevo, Studia mediaevalia et mariologica P.C.Balic..dicata*, Rome, 1972; D. Bertetto, S.D.B., *Maria Regina* (Turin, L.J.C.E., 1954); J. Galot, S.J., "Reine de l'univers," NRT, 1955, 491-505; Basilio de S. Pablo, C.P., "La teologia de la Realeza de Maria," EphMar 1956, 163-91; T. Bartolomei, O.S.M., *Maria Signora e Regina* (Rome, 1965); C. Sericoli, O.F.M., "De Regalitate B.M.Virginis juxta auctorum Franciscalium doctrinam, Ant. 30(1955), 105-118, 221-224; F. Schmidt, O.F.M., "Mary's universal Queenship in Franciscan Theologians," V.I. XII, 85-111; *id. Mariology*, II, *Universal Queenship of Mary*, p. 493-549.

R

RABANUS MAURUS (c. 784-856)

A Benedictine, taught by Haimon of Halberstadt at Fulda and by Alcuin (qv) at Tours, R. became head of the school at Fulda, Abbot in 842, and in 847 Archbishop of Mainz. Because of his influence he won the title *Praeceptor Germaniae*. Important elements of Marian doctrine are found throughout his works, particularly in the commentary on Mt, in the homilies, and in the hymns and poems.[1]

R. was firm on the essential dogma of the divine motherhood: "The true Son of God was one and the same in each nature"; "Mary brought forth her only-begotten, that is a Son of her own substance."[2] The virginal conception "without the admixture of male flesh," he deemed necessary to the Incarnation.[3] In the controversy between the monks of Corbie (see PASCHASIUS RADBERT: RATRAMNUS) on the *virginitas in partu* (qv), he took no part but his position was clear: Mary had a painless childbirth, was a virgin in the birth.

Mary's role in salvation was linked with her motherhood: "The Virgin brought forth the salvation of the whole world"; "Mary brought salvation to the world."[4] He continues the Eve-Mary theme: "For Eve mourned, Mary exulted, Eve [shed] tears, Mary bore joy in her womb, one brought forth a sinner, the other an innocent one, as a virgin she gave birth and she remained a virgin."[5] R. has the contrasting ideas of the curse and blessing in mind.

"Mary typifies (*significat*) the Church, which is incorrupt in faith."[6] She is brought into the bridal theme in relation to the Church: "The way in which the Father effected a marriage for the King, his Son, was that he associated (*sociavit*) the holy Church with him through the mystery of the Incarnation. The womb of the Virgin Mother was the bridal chamber of this Spouse."[7]

Mary's queenship (qv) is very clear to R.: "Lo you are exalted above the choirs of angels, O happy Mother, as a queen you will reign forever, queen of heaven, mistress of the angels."[8] The note of intercession is found in the homilies—Mary is the mediatress (*interventrix*)—and in the hymns and poems; around Mary, angelic and human society centres.

[1]In PL 107, 110, 111, 112 and MGH *Poetae Lat.*, 2. Cf. J. Huhn, "Das Marienbild in den Schriften des Rabanus Maurus," *Scholastik*, 31(1956), 515-532; H. Barré, *Prières Anciennes*, 89-90. [2]*Comm. in Mt.*, 7:25, and 1:1, PL 107, 1096A, 754A. [3]*In Ez 16:40*, PL 110, 943. [4]*In Mt 1:1*, PL 107, 752A; *Hom 28*, PL 110, 54. [5]*Ibid.*, 54. [6]*De Universo*, 7:1, PL 111, 184. [7]*In Mt 6:22*, PL 107, 1053; cp. *De Universo, 4, 20*, PL 111, 49; hymn *In Solemn. S.M.*, PL 112, 1658. [8]*Hom. 29*, PL 110, 55.

RADULFUS ARDENS (12th century)

A priest of the diocese of Poitiers, theologian and orator, R. has left, among his sermons, two on the Purification of Mary, two on the Annunciation, two on the Assumption and one on the Nativity.[1] Mary, he thought, was most strong and yet spoke of herself preferably as the handmaid and subject. She had received grace abounding: "there is no virtue, no merit, no honour which does not abound in her and the graces which are distributed singly to each of the saints are bestowed collectively on her."[2] These graces may benefit us, for Mary "leads us by her example, enlightens us by her virtues, helps us by her intercessory prayers."[3] She can reconcile us to her Son. "Who" asks R., "figuratively is Jerusalem, a peacemaker as is Mary, the Mediatress between God and men."[4] We should look to her, fly to her, cry out to her when beset by the enemies of our souls. "Let us, my brothers, ask the Mother of graces, that she may obtain that some little stream from the fountain of graces she brings forth be shared with us."[5] R. teaches the queenship (qv) of Mary, occasionally linking it with care for her subjects: "She rejoices and reigns with her Son forever, always interceding with him for us."[6]

[1]PL 155, 1339-45; 1353-64; 1421-1430; 1439-1443. [2]1360B. [3]1359C. [4]1423B. [5]1360B. [6]1430B.

RAHNER, KARL, S.J. (1905-   ) — See Supplement, p. 386.

RATRAMNUS (d. *c.* 870)

A monk of the Benedictine monastery of Corbie, which he entered about 825 and where he spent his life teaching and writing, R. came into conflict with his abbot, Paschasius Radbert (*qv*), not only on Eucharistic doctrine, but on the subject of Mary's virginity. About 844-45 he composed the work, later entitled *De Partu Sanctae Mariae*.[1] The point at issue between monk and abbot, who replied with a similar work, was the *virginitas in partu* (*qv*). R. is a subtle thinker and his view has been differently interpreted. His intention in writing was, from what he tells us, to combat "the poisons of new perfidy" spread by the old serpent through regions of Germany, which sought to undermine by diverse subtlety, "Catholic faith on the birth of the Saviour."[2] R. then wished to demonstrate that Christ was truly born of Mary in a truly natural way, but he was insistent on his adherence to the Catholic faith that Mary "was a virgin before birth, in birth, after birth."[3] Why then the sharp division of opinion? Because he so realistically described the childbirth.[4]

J. M. Canal, the most recent authority, and editor of the critical text here followed, follows Radbert, Dom Mabillon, Dom Cellier (1754), Dom Grenier (1789), and in the present century Dom Cappuyns and Dom E. Schmitz in the opinion that R. defends a childbirth entirely natural, with the customary consequences, though without loss of virginity. Others have held that R. did not depart from the traditional doctrine, that he believed in the "closed womb" and spoke only metaphorically when he used the phrase Christ "opened the womb." The relationship with Radbert's treatise is also in dispute, some contending that they were opponents, others that they agreed and addressed a common enemy; and it has been suggested that R. wrote his booklet after Radbert had published Part One of his, whereon, Part Two was issued to cope with R.'s ideas. These he sought to buttress with arguments from OT and the Fathers, Latin with the exception of St. Cyril of Alexandria. Radbert's work has had the better subsequent support, one sign being that only 5 manuscripts of R's work survive, all in England, Scotland, and Ireland.

[1]Critical edn., ed. J. M. Canal, in MM, 30(1968), 84-112; cf. *intr.*, pp. 53-66. Cf. H. Peltier, *Ratramne*, DTC, XIII/2, 1780-87; R. Laurentin in RSPT, 54(1970), 323-324. [2]MM, 30(1968), 84. [3]*Ibid.*, 87. [4]Cf. J. M. Canal, ed., in MM 30(1968), 56ff.

RAYNAUD, THÉOPHILE, S.J. (1583-1663)

This very erudite writer composed a number of Marian works, grouped as *Marialia*, which are found in volume VII of the 20-volume edition of his writings.[1] They are: *Scapulare marianum illustratum et defensum* (Paris, 1654), *Scapulare Partheno-Carmeliticum, illustratum ac defensum* (Cologne 1658), *De retinendo titulo immaculatae Conceptionis Deiparae Virginis* (Lyons, 1665), and especially *Nomenclator marianus*[2] and *Diptycha mariana*.[3] The books on the Scapular were written at the request of a Carmelite superior. Therein R. defends the story that the Scapular originated in an apparition of Our Lady to St. Simon Stock (d. 1265), a view not now held by scholars. In the *Nomenclator* he gives with comments some 960 titles applied to Mary by the Fathers, church writers, and the Liturgy. In the *Diptycha* he has important things to say about method in Marian theology, reviewing and qualifying Gerson's principles: on how much can be deduced from the divine maternity, how argument should proceed from the graces accorded to other saints. He is restrained in dealing with the initial grace of Mary, though he held that she enjoyed the use of reason from the first moment of her existence. Mary's first grace surpassed that of angels and saints, he thought, but not of all the grace they will collectively possess in final glory. He is moderate too in regard to Mary's mediation and cooperation in the work of Redemption, emphasises the importance of the sentiment of the faithful in the Assumption, and warns against presumption by Our Lady's clients. He was a favourite author of Adam Widenfeld (see AVIS SALUTAIRES).

[1]Cf. R. Brouillard, DTC XIII, 1823; Cl.Dillenschneider, C.S.S.R., *Stalphonse*, 170-76; H. Graef, *Mary*, II, p. 44. [2]*Nomenclator marianus e titulis selectioribus, quibus B. Virgo a sanctis Patribus honestatur, contextus a Theophilo Raynaud, ejusdem ad Nomenclatorem observationes et Glossarium* (Lyons, 1639, Rome 1649), *Marialia*, pp. 337-446. [3]*Diptycha mariana, quibus inanes B. Virginis praerogativae, plerisque novis scriptionibus vulgate, et a probatis*

et veris apud Patres, theologiosque receptis, solide et accurate secernuntur (Lyons, 1654, and 1665), Marialia, pp. 1-240.

REDEMPTION, MARY'S PART IN THE

Sacred Scripture: "God so loved the world that he gave his only Son," (Jn 3:16). Thus St. John explains the divine initiative which he succinctly recorded: "The Word became flesh and he dwelt among us," (1:14). The same evangelist relates the love to the act of laying down one's life. St. Paul also teaches that love was the prime motive of Christ the Redeemer, pointing to his death as the proof: "But God showed his love for us in that while we were yet sinners Christ died for us" (Rom 5:8). Death thus accepted was a fulfilment of Christ's role as unique Mediator and the death was a ransom to benefit all men (1 Tim 2:5-6). The death cannot be isolated from the Last Supper which preceded it and the Resurrection which followed it. All has for believing Christians immeasurable meaning and mystery because they see in Jesus Christ the Eternal Son of God.

Can anyone, even the Blessed Virgin Mary, share in such things?[1] The answer must be found in Scripture, Tradition and the Teaching Authority. Redemption is one aspect of Mediation and what is said, therefore, about the scriptural evidence for Mary's mediation would be relevant to her redemptive role. The particular mode of Christ's Redemption and Mary's part in it demand study of Gen 3:15 (see WOMAN IN), the Annunciation (*qv*) especially Mary's consent (*qv*), the Presentation of the Lord (*qv*) and the Calvary episode related by Jn (see WOMAN IN JN 19:25-27). It is a question of seeing Mary's place in God's plan, but this plan itself has been—within the permissible limits—differently explained by the various schools of thought. None the less, reflection on the words and deeds narrated by the Bible shows a deepening insight, progress towards a satisfactory synthesis.

History: The Fathers did not see the need to consider Redemption apart from the Incarnation, which for them included it. There is little consequently on Our Lady's possible participation in the work of Christ as later theologians would understand it. In the context of the new Eve, St. Irenaeus (*qv*) expressed a suggestive idea that Mary was a cause of salvation to herself and all mankind. St. Ambrose (*qv*) presents theologians with a problem. He sees the link between Incarnation and Redemption: "Alone Mary has worked the salvation of the world and conceived the redemption of all." Through her, "salvation was given to all"; "Mary, who gave birth to the victor, has defeated the devil."[2] But commenting on Mary's presence on Calvary, A. seems suddenly restrictive: "Jesus did not need a helper for the redemption of all, he who said, 'I am become as a man without help, free among the dead'. So he welcomed the love of a mother, but sought no help of man."[3] The idea occurs twice elsewhere in A.'s writings. The quotation given was included in the notes to the drafts of LG, ch VIII, prepared for the Council Fathers of Vatican II before the third session of the Council. These notes and some commentaries did not show the full context of the excerpt. In each case, A. praises Mary highly: she was "intrepid"; "not less than the Mother of Christ should be"; she remained when the men fled. More revealing still is the fact that A. imagines the possibility that Mary wanted to die with her Son, "hoping that by her death something would be added to the public office," and it is with this hypothesis firmly in mind that he offers his judgment.

John the Geometer (*qv*) is the first to express a decisive view on Mary's part in the Redemption: "You (Christ) have not only given yourself as a ransom for us, but, after yourself, have given your mother also as a ransom at every moment, so that indeed you have died for us once, but she died a thousand times in her will, her heart torn for you and also for those for whom she, like the Father, had given her own Son and knew him to be delivered unto death."[4]

Western thinking on the subject was not impeded by the words of St. Ambrose as Pseudo-Jerome halted development of the doctrine of the Assumption and St. Augustine blocked advance in the doctrine of the Immaculate Conception. As Mary's role in the early Church was more fully valued and her continuing intervention in heaven more clearly recognised, attention was logically led to her saving role and this would be studied in the context of Calvary. Milo of St. Amand (*qv*), St. Peter Damian (*qv*) and St. Anselm (*qv*) reflected on Mary's sufferings at the death of her Son.

It was a disciple of St. Bernard, Arnold of Bonneval (*qv*), who sought to show their redemptive effect. Nothing of Christ's unique dignity was sacrificed. The Saviour included his Mother "in the general benefit of his redemption." "No angel, no man could have with him common authority." Yet A. will say: "The Mother's affection cooperated, nevertheless, greatly in her manner, (*cooperabatur tamen plurimum secundum modum suum*) to render God propitious, since the charity of Christ brought to the Father both his own desires and those of his Mother, since what the Mother asked the Son approved, the Father granted." A. goes on to inquire how Mary came to "obtain a common effect with Christ in the salvation of the world." The origin is the Incarnation: "From the moment when she was told the Lord is with you" (Lk 1:28), the promise and gift continued inseparably. The climax came on Calvary: "There was then but one will between Christ and Mary and both together offered one only holocuast, she in the blood of her heart, he in the blood of his flesh." "In this sanctuary could be seen two altars: one in the breast of Mary, the other in the body of Christ. Christ immolated his flesh, Mary her spirit."[5]

The idea of a partnership between Jesus and Mary comes up in writings of thirteenth century theologians. The thinking of the twelfth century had produced two insights which favoured this theory. Ekbert of Schönau saw Mary as the associate of Christ (*qv*): "Uniting you with himself as his associate, completing with you and in you the work of the saving Incarnation."[6] Hermann of Tournai had given a new dimension to the new Eve concept by the use of Gen 2:18, "a helper like himself." Richard of St. Laurent and Pseudo-Bonaventure (*qv*) would adapt the second idea to the theory of the Redemption; Pseudo-Albert would make use of both. "It must be heeded and constantly recalled" says R., "that there was a helper for the redemption of the world so devoted that as there was no suffering like that which the Son endured for the redemption of the world, so there could be none like that which she bore in her heart for the same cause."[7] He uses the phrase "reconciling the guilty and sinners by her compassion."

"But the Blessed Virgin" says Pseudo-Albert "was not taken by the Lord into the ministry but into partnership (*consortium*) and help according to the saying 'Let us make him a helper like unto himself' . . . . But the Blessed Virgin was not Christ's vicar, but his helper and associate sharing in his reign as she shared in his sufferings for the human race, when, as all the ministers and disciples fled, she took her stand alone beneath the Cross and suffered in her heart the wounds he suffered in his body; thus the sword pierced her soul."[8] R. and P-A. use the word *coadjutrix* for helper.

St. Bonaventure (*qv*), insistent on the unicity of Christ's Redemption, still spoke of Mary paying the price of our ransom because of her veneration for God, her compassion with Christ and her pity for the world, especially for the Christian people.[9]

Echoes of the thirteenth century doctrine occur in the next centuries, in Tauler for example and St. Antoninus of Florence (*qv*). In the latter's age, the title Coredemptress appears in the literature. Mary's redemptive role was seen in the closest proximity to that of Jesus, but the greatest defenders of such a view, Salmeron (*qv*) for example, the theologian of the Council of Trent, knew how to safeguard the dignity of Christ the Redeemer. By the seventeenth century, the distinction of merit *de condigno* and *de congruo* was being used to this end: Suarez (*qv*) clarified it and gave it status.

Salazar (*qv*) also adopted the distinction. But he worked out an elaborate theory of Mary's part in the Redemption which in scope and profundity is practically unequalled. Mary was not given to Christ as his Mother only, but as "helper and companion to redeem the human race." "Hence it comes that every grace bestowed on the Virgin, even the very benefit of her first creation, is a grace of redemption and expiation, that is ordered to wiping out sins, not her own but those of others, that is all the transgressions of the human race." S. used two basic principles to justify such a role for Mary: Jesus belonged to her and she could offer him as none other could; her will was a positive force in the accomplishment of the redemptive sacrifice. He justifies titles like *Reparatrix, Mediatrix Redemptrix*, author and cause of our salvation because "she had this in common with Christ that she truly and of herself is said to have given and offered the price of our redemption"; "joining her will in association with the will of Christ she offered him, who was hers, to us and for us."[10] S. theorized also on Mary's priesthood (*qv*).

The next noteworthy name is that of M. J. Scheeben (*qv*). Distrusting the word Coredemptress, which in its proper sense he saw as valid, he argued at great length for Mary's participation in the redemptive work: "All these reasons [four given by him] obviously demand Mary's cooperation, not in order to achieve or complete the intrinsic power of the redeeming work, but only to perfect its beauty and loveliness in all respects, especially its organic connection with mankind to be redeemed, whereby the perfect completion of its application and applicability was conditioned."[11]

The Modern Phase: A vast literature appeared on the subject of coredemption between the end of the second World War and Vatican Council II. It was the theme of the French Marian Congress in 1947 and of the International Mariological Congress in Rome in 1950 (Pius XII did not approve the title *Coredemptrix*, so *Alma Socia Christi* was chosen). The Lourdes Congress in 1958 showed clearly the opposing doctrines which had evolved through the preceding decade. Three points were especially debated: Mary's part in the objective as well as in the subjective redemption; her immediate or remote cooperation in the former; the ultimate basis of her coredemption and, consequently, the pattern it follows, Christ-type (*qv*) or Church-type (*qv*). Since Christ's redemptive act was essentially priestly, the question of Mary's participation in his priesthood logically arises. Allowance must also be made for continuing research into the meaning of Christ's Redemption.

Objective Redemption was the single act completed by the Saviour, valid for all men; the application of its fruits to individual souls constitutes the subjective redemption. All Marian theologians agree that Mary cooperates in the second, as does the Church. As to her cooperation in the first, two moments are distinguished: remote, through her consent (*qv*) to the Incarnation and the redemptive plan outlined in the Annunciation; proximate or immediate through her co-offering with merit of the sacrifice of Calvary.

This final point is the heart of the problem. Could Mary join in this essential work of Christ? Difficulties have been raised. Since redemption is an aspect of mediation (*qv*) the Pauline text 1 Tim 2:5 is urged. That question is dealt with elsewhere; Paul himself applies the very word mediator (*mesites*) to Moses. It is urged that to assign a share in the Redemption to Mary compromises either the universality or the sufficiency of Christ's act. Mary was redeemed by Christ and since "the principle of merit does not fall under merit," she could not have helped to accomplish that from which she benefited. Defenders of the thesis reply that "Christ redeems Mary, and her alone, with a preservative Redemption, then together with her, *in signo posteriori rationis*, he redeems the rest of mankind with a liberative Redemption."[12]

As to sufficiency: either, say the critics, Mary's contribution adds nothing to Christ's, in which case it is not to be considered, or it does add something and then Christ alone did not redeem us. God, reply the proponents, saves us, but his saving act includes our cooperation. Christ redeems us with his infinite merit, but he can bring Mary into the very scheme whereby this merit is implanted in mankind. She represents mankind in the new alliance and her representative role is part of the alliance, which is essentially constituted by divine initiative and munificence.

But on this very point theories of Mary's coredemption diverged in the years before the Council. For stress on the alliance concept leads to a Church-type theory of her lifework. On behalf of the redeemed, Mary (according to this view) accomplished in an eminent manner, what the Church does for each of the faithful. She was, in this as in other things, the prototype of the Church. Advocates of the Christ-type theory see Mary as partner, joint cause, with Christ, so closely united with him as to make one principle. The necessary distinctions are made to safeguard his primacy and transcendence.

Teaching Authority: Those who were criticised for using the word Coredemptress of Mary generally replied that St. Paul calls Christians co-workers of Christ, in the very passage in which he says: "So neither he who plants nor he who waters is anything, but only God who gives the growth" (1 Cor 3:7-9). The Popes have not in recent times, with the exception of Pius XI, used this title of Our Lady. They have none the less quite firmly taught that Mary had an active part in the Redemption. Leo XIII (*qv*) spoke of "the mysteries of our Redemption in which she not only shared, but also took part."[13] St. Pius X (*qv*) was more explicit: "But since she surpassed all in holiness and union with Christ in the work of Redemption, she, as the expression is, merits *de congruo* what Christ merits *de condigno*, and is the principal minister in the distribution of grace."[14] Benedict XV (qv) expressed an idea which was seized upon by Marian theologians: "She renounced her mother's rights for the salvation of mankind and, as far as it depended on her, offered her Son to placate divine justice; so we may well say that with Christ she redeemed mankind."[15] Pius XI (qv), who twice called Mary Coredemptress, adopted the words just quoted of Benedict XV, having stated himself the "fact that the Sorrowful Virgin took part with Jesus Christ in the work of Redemption."[16]

Pius XII (qv), to designate Mary's part in the Redemption, chose phrases such as Associate of the Redeemer, Noble (or loving) Associate of the Redeemer, Associate in the work of the Redeemer. He linked the idea of association (qv) twice with the Eve (qv)-Mary typology. His fullest statement is in *Haurietis Aquas*: "By the will of God, the most Blessed Virgin Mary was inseparably joined with Christ in accomplishing the work of man's Redemption, so that our salvation flows from the love of Jesus Christ and his sufferings intimately united with the love and sorrows of his Mother."[17] Pius XII took over the idea of Mary on Calvary offering her maternal rights.

Vatican II: The first Marian *schema* was Christ-type in orientation. It spoke of Mary's "partnership (*consortium*) in achieving the work of Redemption: "By this consent [the Fiat] Mary, a daughter of Adam, became not only the Mother of Jesus, the only divine Mediator and Redeemer, but also with him and under him she associated her work in achieving the redemption of the human race. The saving consent of the Mother of God, and from it her partnership in accomplishing the work of redemption persisted from the moment of the virginal conception of Jesus Christ to his death, it was especially conspicuous when she stood by the Cross, as God's plan had it (cf. Jn 19:25); she suffered intensely with her only-begotten, with him and through him with great spirit she offered him as the price of our redemption and finally by the same Christ Jesus dying on the Cross she was given as a mother to men (cf. Jn 19:26-27)."[18]

The passage met the request of 54 bishops who wished to have a conciliar pronouncement on Mary as Coredemptress, 36 seeking a definition, 11 a dogma of faith. Deliberately, in formulating the doctrine, the authors of the *schema* avoided the word Coredemptress. Cardinal Santos in the confrontation of October 1963 had asserted that Mary "by the grace of the Redeemer was associated with him in the very objective redemption," whereas Cardinal Koenig had stressed the conception of Mary as "fruit of the redemption" like the Church. She could be shown as "Christ's most sublime cooperator, through his grace, in perfecting and extending the work of salvation," but in the manner of the Church.[19]

In the agreed draft of the new *schema* presented to the Doctrinal Commission, there was a general description of Mary (which was to remain), the handmaid of the Lord, with a full heart and unimpeded by sin, embracing the saving will of God, devoting herself entirely to the person and work of her Son, "in subordination to him and with him, serving, by the grace of Almighty God, the mystery of the redemption" (LG 56). In the additional matter ordered by the Commission (see article MEDIATION), we read: "here on earth she was for Christ the Redeemer a humble handmaid and an associate of unique nobility . . . by conceiving, bringing forth, nourishing her Son and suffering with him as he died on the Cross she cooperated in an altogether unique manner by obedience, faith and burning charity, in restoring supernatural life to souls." This passage should be completed by that earlier, which described Mary suffering intensely with her only-begotten and went on, "she associated herself with maternal spirit with his sacrifice, lovingly consenting to the immolation of the victim she herself had brought forth." Here "freely offering the victim" in the agreed text had been altered.

[1]On the Redemption, cf. L. Richard, *The Mystery of the Redemption* (Dublin, Baltimore, 1965); on Mary and the Redemption cf. J. Lebon, *Comment je conçois, j'établis et je défends la doctrine de la médiation mariale*, in *Eph. Theol. Lov,* 16(1939), 655-744; W. Goosens, *De cooperatione immediata Matris Redemptoris ad redemptionem objectivam* (Paris, 1939); N. Garcia Garces, *Mater corredemptrix* (Rome, 1940); H. Lennerz, S.J., "De redemptione et cooperatione in opere redemptionis," *Greg.* 22(1941), 301-324; id., *De Beata Virgine* (Rome, 1957); Cl. Dillenschneider, C.S.S.R., *Marie au service de la Rédemption*, (Hagenau, 1947); id. *Pour une corédemption bien comprise* (Rome, 1949); id. *Le mystère de la corédemption mariale* (Paris, 1951); *Marie dans l'économie de la création renovée*, 1957; J. B. Carol, O.F.M., *De Corredemptione* (Rome, 1950); id., in *Mariology*, II, 377-425; H. M. Koster, *Unus Mediator* (Limburg, 1950); id. *Die Madg der Herrn* (2nd ed., Limburg,

1954); *id.*, in ME, II, 21-49; ME, IV, 17 articles on *Co-operatio B.V.Mariae et Ecclesiae ad Christi Redemptionem*; G. D. Smith, *Mary's part in our Redemption* (2nd ed. London, 1954); R. Laurentin, *Le Titre de Corédemptrice* (Rome, 1951); J. Bur, *Médiation Mariale* (Paris, 1955); *id.*, "La Vierge Marie dans l'économie du salut" *Divinitas*, 12(1968), 725-752; F. M. Alvarez Herrera, S.Sp.S., *La Madre del sumo y eterno sacerdote* (Barcelona, 1968); M. Cuervo, O.P., *Maternidad divina y corredención mariana* (Villava-Pamplona, 1967); Enrique del Sdo Corazon Llamas, "La cooperación de Maria a la obra de la Redención en la teologia postconciliar" in Est. Mar. 32(1969), 149-230; G. M. Roschini, O.S.M., *Maria Santissima*, II, 116-198; *id., Problematica sulla corredenzione* (Rome, 1969); G. Philips, "Marie dans le plan du salut," in CM 16(1972), 81-100; E. Druwé, S.J., in *Maria* I, 427-538. [2]Cf. Article on Ambrose, St. in the present work. [3]*ibid.* [4]*apud* A. Wenger, A.A., *L'Assomption*, p. 406. [5]Quotations from *De laudibus B.M.V.*, PL 189, 1727-31, and *De septem verbis* PL 189, 1694-95. [6]*Super missus est* in *Die Visionen der hl. Elizabeth und die Schriften der Aebte Ekbert und Emencho*, ed. F. W. E. Roth (Brun, 1884), p. 252. [7]*De laudibus Sanctae Mariae, inter op.* St. Albert the Great, 36, p. 158. [8]*Mariale, inter op.* St. Albert, 37, q. 42, 81. [9]*De Donis Sp. Sncti.*, ed. cit., 5, 484. [10]*Apud* José dos Santos, C.M.F. in ME VII, p. 64, n. 121; pp. 55-56. [11]*Mariology* II, 207; cf. pp. 193-238. [12]*Mariology*, III, J. B. Carol, O.F.M., 418. [13]*Parta humano generi*, OL, 159. [14]*Ad diem illum*, OL, 173. [15]*Inter Sodalicia*, OL, 194. [16]*Explorata Res*, OL, 205. [17]OL, 426. [18]Number 2, pp. 8(94). [19]*Relationes etc.* Vatican Press, 1963.

RELIGIOUS LIFE

In church history, attempts to establish a state of perfection have frequently been related to the person of Mary.[1] Her privilege as a virgin mother was brought into the fourth century debate on the excellence of virginity over marriage. With the institution of religious orders, she was often given prominence in approved prayers and devotional practices, taken as patroness. Religious orders were enriched by the teaching or example of striking personalities devoted to her: Venerable Bede, Ambrose Autpert, St. Anselm, St. Bernard, St. Thomas Aquinas, St. Albert the Great, St. Bonaventure, Duns Scotus, St. Bernardine of Siena, St. Lawrence of Brindisi, St. Antoninus, Suarez, St. Peter Canisius, St. Robert Bellarmine (*qqv*)—to look at the Western church alone prior to the seventeenth century, after which time such figures become more numerous and are well known.

E. Gambari lists over 50 religious institutes of men and over 190 of women which have the name of Mary or some aspect of her life in their official titles. B. F. Morineau listed over 200 religious institutes of men since the seventeenth century which "by reason of their name or their spirit offer a special interest for the history of Marian cult." E. Bergh, dealing with the statistics for congregations of women religious, mentions a figure of 700 with membership of the pontifical bodies alone over 23,000 in 1941. Discrepancies occur through lack of accurate statistics and the difference between pontifical and diocesan institutes.

The Encyclopaedic work *Maria* contains articles on Marian doctrine and devotion in every important order and congregation of men in the Church (Volumes II, III, IV *passim*). Religious have served the Teaching Authority in the preparation of theological texts on Our Lady, notably in the case of *Ineffabilis Deus* and *Munificentissimus Deus* and the Marian passages issued by Vatican II. They have helped to promote congresses, found Marian societies, international academies. *Church Teaching:* Pius XII, especially in *Sedes Sapientiae* and *Sacra Virginitas*, spoke of the help Mary obtains for those consecrated to God—in the second, the Pope quoting St. Athanasius and St. Augustine traces the origin of the virginal commitment to Mary.[2] The passage meets an objection which urges that those committed to virginity invented Mary's virginal motherhood.

Vatican II says of Religious: "As the example of so many saintly founders shows, the counsels are especially able to pattern Christian man after that manner of virginal and humble life which Christ the Lord elected for himself and which his virgin Mother also chose" (LG 46). The history of the Decree on the Adaptation and Renewal of the Religious Life was similar to that on the Priesthood. The first *schema* approved by Pope John in April 1963 was entitled "The States of Perfection." The section on the vow of chastity mentioned "piety towards the Blessed Virgin Mary" next after the Sacraments as a means of obtaining divine help in the cultivation of that virtue. When the *schema* was reduced to a set of propositions, the section on chastity was omitted; there was then no mention of Our Lady in the entire text. An amended version of this short *schema* was given to the Fathers in October, 1964; it was still silent on Our Lady. Between then and the final vote in the fourth session the defect was remedied. The text ended with these words: "Thus, too, with the intercession of the most loving Virgin Mary, Mother of God, religious communities will experience a daily growth in numbers and will yield a richer harvest of fruits that bring salvation" (25).

[1]E. Gambari, Ordini e congregazioni religiose di nome e di orientamento mariani, Theotocos, pp. 607-630; E. Bergh S.J., Les Congrégations féminines des XIXe et XXe siècles in Maria III, 467-488; B. M. Morineau, S.M., Les Congrégations religieuses d'hommes du XVIIe siècle à nos jours, ibid., 339-378; R. Laurentin, La question mariale (Paris, 1963), 16; D. Fernandez, C.M.F., La mision de Maria y la espiritualidad de las almas consagradas, EstM 24(1969), 193-242. [2]Sedes Sapientiae, OL, 427; Sacra Virginitas, OL, 365-67.

RESURRECTION OF CHRIST, THE

From the fourth century on, the idea is found regularly among the Fathers that the Risen Jesus appeared to his Mother.[1] St. John Chrysostom praises the women who followed Jesus in his public ministry and who showed their quality especially by fidelity in his Passion. "Then they contemplated all that happened, how he uttered a cry, how he gave his last sigh, how the rocks opened and all that followed. These same first see Jesus risen. The female sex most condemned taste the first-fruits of the happy reality. This above all shows their courage; the disciples take to flight, they remain in their place. Who were they? His own Mother—for it is the Virgin who is called Mother of James, and the others."[2] The critical position is not clear about George of Nicomedia and Simeon Metaphrastes, but in the same age as Chrysostom, St. Gregory of Nyssa held the view, and a lifetime later St. Ephraem and Hesychius of Jerusalem speaks of the woman "who introduced virginity, contained God in her womb, gave birth in the flesh, to the Creator, first welcomed Jesus coming back from the dead, began to proclaim the Resurrection, revealed joy to the disciples."[3] Two seventh century writers, Severus of Antioch and Romanos the Singer (qqv) continue the tradition. Severus writes: "It was becoming to her to announce the joyous news since she was the cause of joy and she had heard herself addressed in these glorious words: Hail, full of grace." Romanos puts these words on the lips of the dying Jesus: "Be reassured Mother; you will be the first to see me come forth from the tomb."

The origin of the tradition is difficult to trace. The Gospels and Acts are silent on an apparition of Jesus to His Mother. Acts includes her with those who had seen the risen Lord, the Apostles and the "women," and with those who would choose a successor to Judas, one who would be a "witness of the Resurrection" (Acts 1:14;, 22). There is here no explicit affirmation. Yet, though the belief of Chrysostom and others is expressed through a faulty or questionable exegesis—identifying the Mother of James as Mary, the Mother of Jesus—the belief itself was very probably independent of such a setting. It is a belief taken up in age after age by writers or preachers on Our Lady: Rupert of Deutz, St. Albert the Great, Gregory Palamas, John Mauropous, Suarez, Sergius Bulgakov, and, among the Popes, Pius XII and John Paul II (qqv).

[1]Cf. C. Gianelli, "Témoignages patristiques en faveur d'une apparition du Christ ressuscité à la Vierge Marie," REB 11(1953); Mélanges Martin Jugie, 106-119; further bibliography ibid, (D. Stiernon), 234-35; J. D. Breckenbridge, "Et prima vidit: The iconography of the Appearance of Christ to his Mother" in Art Bulletin, 39(1957), 9-32; W. Medding, Erscheinung des Auferstandenen vor Maria, Lexicon der christlichen Ikonographie, 1, 667-73; C. Vona, "L'Apparizione di Cristo risorto alla Madre negli antichi scrittori cristiani," Divinitas, 1(1957), 479-527; D. Squillaci, "L'Apparizione di Gesu Risorto alle madre sua," PalClero, 12(1958), 226-47. For the Syrian tradition, R. Murray, Symbols of Church and Kingdom, (Cambridge, 1975), 329-35. [2]Hom. 88 in Matth, PG 58, 777. [3]Cf. M. Aubineau, S.J., Les Homélies festales d'Hesychius de Jérusalem (Brussels, 1979), 13-15.

REVELATION

Vatican II changed the emphasis in a theology of Revelation from the propositional to a personalist approach. Christ is the "Mediator and the fullness of all revelation"; "Jesus perfected revelation by fulfilling it through his whole work of making himself present and manifesting himself." (Constitution on Divine Revelation, 2, 4). It is at once clear that in this context Mary is brought into the process of revelation as God's self-disclosure to man, with a view to man's salvation. God, Pius XI once said, à propos of St. Thérèse of Lisieux, reveals himself through his saints. Much more through the greatest of them after Jesus Christ, still more so in view of the "close indissoluble bond" between Jesus and Mary. The subject is one which awaits detailed research and development.[1]

A patristic intuition, found already with Origen, is that Mary has a prophetic role, in the plenary sense of the word.[2] Origen thought in the context of the Magnificat. Later writers apply to Mary Is 8:3. Thus Severus of

Antioch: "But who is the prophetess mentioned in the divine books, who brought forth a son . . . if it is not the Mother of God, the Virgin who gave birth to Emmanuel.[3]

Another idea which recurs is that Mary enlightened the Apostles. She is called in medieval times *magistra apostolorum*: the idea appealed to St. Amadeus of Lausanne. Medieval writers and preachers too elaborated on Mary as *Illuminatrix*, among them St. Albert the Great and St. Bonaventure. The notion of a revealing function is implied in Mary's title "Seat of Wisdom," as in the saying "you alone have destroyed all heresies." Eadmer was explicit: "Incomparably, in a more eminent and a clearer way she understood the depth of truth through the same Spirit and thus many things were revealed to the Apostles by her who had in herself learned of the mysteries of the same Jesus Christ, our Lord, not only by simple knowledge but by the very effect and very experience of them."[4] This opinion recalls the word of Vatican II: "Jesus perfected revelation by fulfilling it through his whole work of making himself present" (Const. on Divine Rev., 4).

At the level of anthropology, Christ owed three things to Mary: integration in the community of Israel, which bore his revelation; historical existence at the time and place of her life creating thus the human situations which evoked his thought; his physical nature, the instrument through which his divine message passed to men.

The inter-personal relationship between Mother and Son which conditioned God's self-disclosure was put thus by Newman: "He became man of her; and received her lineaments and features as the appearance and character under which he should manifest himself to the world; He was known, doubtless, by his likeness to her to be her Son. Thus his Mother is the first of the Prophets, for of her the Word came bodily; she is the sole oracle of Truth, for the Way, the Truth and the Life vouchsafed to be her Son; she is the one mould of Divine Wisdom and in that mould it was indelibly set."[5]

[1]Cf. A. Grillmeier, S.J., "Der Titel 'Maria Prophetin' und seine Begründung in der Theologie der Vater," *Geist und Leiben*, 30(1957), 102-115; J. Leclercq, O.S.B., "Maria Christianorum philosophia." *Mélanges de Sc.Rel.*, 1956, 103-106; C.Spicq, O.P., *Ce que Jésus doit à sa Mère selon la theologie biblique et d'après les théologiens médievaux* (Paris, Montreal, 1959); M. Zundel, "La Sainte Vierge témoin et révélation du Christ, *Vie Spirit.*, 1963, 539-550.

[2]*In Luc. Hom 8*, GCS 49, 47-51; PG 12, 1819C. [3]PO, 38, 4, 403. [4]*De Excell. V. M.*, 7, PL 150, 57C. [5]*Discourses to Mixed Congregations* (London 1862) 429-30; see SPIRIT, HOLY AND MARY.

RHODES, GEORGES DE, S.J. (d. 1661)

A dogmatic theologian, R. in his work *Disputationes theologiae scholasticae* deals with Marian questions.[1] On the question of Mary's fullness of grace, he held that initially she surpassed all the grace of angels and saints united. He argues strongly for the Immaculate Conception, emphasising the total extinction of the *fomes peccati* in the first moment of Mary's existence. He thought that she possessed the use of reason also from the beginning of her life. Since Mary is, with her divine Son, the principle of all grace she must possess all fully, even *gratiae gratis datae*. R. deduces Mary's co-operation with her Son in the work of Redemption from her compassion, from the merit of her prayer and of this compassion; her merit is *de congruo*, Christ's *de condigno*. God's grace and gifts are dispensed through her, with the necessary safeguards he applies to Mary the title *Redemptrix*.

[1]Vol. II, Tract. XIII, *De Maria Deipara, Disputatio unica*, q. 1 ad 6um, pp. 184-275; cf. Cl.Dillenschneider, C.SS.R., *S. Alphonse*, pp. 178-82.

RICHARD OF ST. VICTOR (d. 1173)

One of the Victorines, of interest, therefore, to the theology of mysticism. Many Marian passages are found in his works; their value is unequal. Scholars have restored to him 100 sermons heretofore attributed to Hugh of St. Victor (*qv*); ten of these are on various feasts of Our Lady.[1] R. writes of Mary also in several chapters of his *Explanation of Song*, particularly in Ch. 39, and in two other short works, *On the Emmanuel* and *On the difference between the sacrifice of Abraham and of the Blessed Virgin Mary*.[2]

The Marian sermons do not aim at originality, save perhaps in the application of OT and other images to Mary. R. urges imitation of her and speaks of reward proportionate to merit.[3] On *Song* he describes Mary's purity: "Blessed Mary was all fair, because she was sanctified in the womb. Having come forth from the womb she never committed mortal or venial sin. Before conceiving the Son of God she was preserved by grace from sins; after this she was so confirmed and strengthened by the overshadowing power of the Most-High that she could in no way commit sin."[4] Here there is a statement of original sin in Mary and a theory of progressive purification as taught by the Easterns. Writing on the Emmanuel, R. says that "unless she had been thoroughly purified of the contagion of all vices she could not have given birth to the Son of God."[5]

Through her sinlessness, but especially through her likeness to Christ, Mary exercises a saving role: "Being the most like to Christ, not only has she the image of Christ in herself, but she restores it to others .... Not only did she not commit sin, but she wiped out the sins of others. Mary is, therefore, intermediate and mediatress between divine and human things, that she may surpass what is human while accomplishing sublime things through her Son."[6] She sheds light on the Church, which R. compares to the moon beneath her feet.

R. insists on Mary's perfection as a contemplative. Her love was immense; so too was her sorrow. She was bodily assumed and the commentary on Song ends with a hymn to the Assumption; here R. follows Pseudo-Augustine (qv). Mary was raised above the angels; she is Mother of Mercy for it was in view of mercy that she became God's Mother. R. thought of the close bond between her and the Eucharistic Lord: "The same body that was conceived in the Virgin is offered (presentatus) on the altar."[7]

---

[1]PL 177; cf. R. Laurentin, Traité, I, 152. [2]PL 196; cf. A. Sage, Les Victorins, Maria, II, 686-693. [3]Serm. 47, PL 177, 1029A; Serm. 55, 1063B. [4]In Cant. 26, PL 196, 482CD. [5]660A. [6]516D. [7]In Ps 23, 1078D.

ROMANOS THE SINGER, ST.
(c. 490-c. 556)

A Syrian who came to Constantinople early in the sixth century R. is the greatest of Byzantine poets, excelling in the Kontakion. Critical editions are very recent.[1] Relevant hymns are on the Annunciation, on the Nativity, four, of which the first, most famous, was sung for centuries at the Christmas imperial banquet, the Presentation, the Wedding at Cana, and Mary at the Cross. The Akathistos (qv) can no longer be attributed to him.

Striking figures, some biblical such as the "closed door" of Ez 44:2 and the cloud and the ark (qv), recur and R. adopts the traditional sense of Is 7:14. For him Mary is Theotokos (qv)

and ever-virgin. He marks progress in the concepts of intercession and mediation.

Like the Syrians St. Ephraem (qv) and Jacob of Sarug (qqv), R. keeps St. Joseph (qv) prominent. Mary affirms her virginity to him in the tender scene of the Annunciation hymn: "The conception of the Child is beyond my understanding. I am pregnant and you see that my virginity is intact, for you have not known me. Who will be witness to these things if not you, my guardian?"[2] Joseph agrees, "the light of your virginity shines always." On the doubt (qv), the view is that Joseph was restrained by fear: "O luminous one, I see a flame, a fire which surrounds you and I am terrified of it. Mary, protect me and do not consume me. Your guiltless womb is suddenly become a furnace filled with fire; let it not melt me, spare me, I beg of you. You wish that I as Moses of old should also take off my shoes, that I should approach you and listen to you and that, enlightened by you, I should say to you—Hail unespoused spouse."[3] The image of the burning bush is implicit here. When the Magi ask Mary why, though a virgin mother, she has the saint with her, she replies: "This is why Joseph is with me, proving that this little Child is God from before the ages."[4]

Mary's saving role is clear to R.: "The Word made flesh in you. In this flesh I suffer, in it I save." "The past is over and all is new thanks to the Son of Mary." "My Mother, it is for you and through you that I save them. If I had not desired to save them I should not have dwelt in you, I should not have caused my light to arise from you, you would not have been called my Mother . . . ."[5]

R. sets the doctrine of Mary's mediation in a distinctive relation to Adam and Eve. These implore her thus: Adam says—"See me at your feet, virgin mother without stain and in my person the whole race is attached to your steps." Eve—"Hope of my soul, listen to me, Eve also, drive shame far from her who gave birth in pain, for you see that miserable as I am, Adam's laments still crush my heart . . ."[6] Mary's reply brings out two important words: "End your lamentations, I shall be your advocate (presbis) before my Son." "Restrain your tears, receive me as your mediatress (mesitis) with him who is born of me."[7] In the history of the doctrine of Mary's mediation, this text following on those of Basil of Seleucia (qv) and Antipater of Bostra (qv), is capital. Henceforth the word—in the feminine of course—used by St. Paul of Christ (1 Tim 2:5), will be increasingly applied to Mary, first in Paul's own language, and then in Latin translations *mediatrix* (see MEDIATION).

How Mary was invited to join in the redemptive act is described by R. in the hymn "Mary at the Cross." Simeon's prophecy is, in the hymn on the Presentation, interpreted in the tradition of Origen (*qv*)—the sword (*qv*) means uncertainly and doubt. "Yes when you shall see your own Son nailed to the Cross, Immaculate one, with the memory of the words which the angel had spoken to you and the divine conception and the indescribable miracles, you will suddenly doubt. The hesitation in which sorrow will plunge you will be like a sword within you; but then he will send quick healing to your heart and to his disciples unshakable peace, he who is the only friend of men."[8]

In the hymn "Mary at the Cross," it is more a sense of mystery in grief than doubt that Mary shows. The dying Christ urges her to think of Adam and Eve—again taken in representative sense—and to join with him in his redemptive work. In answer to her fear or anxiety that she might not see him after death, he replies: "Be reassured, O Mother, you will be the first to see me leave the tomb."[9]

R. sees Mary's request at Cana as for a miracle. He anticipates the title "Mother of Mercy," saying that to the Merciful One a tender Mother is fitting. And he extends the scope of her intercession universally: "Reconcile the whole world, since you were born through me, my little Child, God from before all the ages."[10] "You have made of me the voice and honour of all my race; the earth which you have made has in me a sure protection, a rampart and a support. Towards me turn their gaze all whom you drove from the paradise of delights, for I bring them back to it that the world may recognise that you have been born of me, my little Child, God from before the ages."[11] Thus, through R., a theory of Mary's mediation inspired by Sacred Scripture was deeply embedded in the Liturgy.

[1]SC 99, 110, 114, 128, ed. J. Grosdidier de Matons; P. Maas-C. A. Trypanis, *Sancti Romani Melodi Cantica* (Oxford, 1963); N. Tomadakis, *Romanou tou Melodou Hymnoi*, I-IV (Athens, 1952-61); ClavisG III, 415; cf. C. Chevalier, "La Mariologie de Romanos," in RSR, 28 (1938), 48-71; Beck, 425-27. [2]*Annunciation* 17, SC 110, 38. [3]*Ibid.*, 15, 36. [4]*I Nativity*, 11, SC 110, 62. [5]*Mary at the Cross*, 6,

SC 128, 168; II Nativity, 6, SC 110, 94; *ibid.*, 13, 104. [6]*Ibid.*, 8, 98; *ibid.*, 9, 98. [7]*Ibid.*, 10, p. 100; 11, p. 102. [8]*Presentation*, 13, SC 110, 190. [9]12, SC 128, 176. [10]*I Nativ.*, 22, SC 110, 74. [11]*I Nativ.* 23, SC 110, 74.

ROSARY, THE

This prayer has been beloved of widely different categories and social groups within the Church, intellectuals and the untutored, contemplatives and apostles, rich and poor, priests and people.[1] Great saints have worked to spread it, St. Peter Canisius, St. Louis Marie de Montfort, St. Alphonsus Liguori, priests or laymen apostles of the Rosary in the present age. It is the form of extra-liturgical prayer most frequently recommended by the Popes from Leo XIII to John Paul II. As at present formed it is biblical in theme and formulas, and a prime example of repetitive prayer.

The history of the Rosary has been complicated by the legend which linked its origins with St. Dominic, a legend supported principally by the writings of Alan de la Roche. Critical scholarship from Dominicans as from others has not sustained the legend. The Dominicans have had a major role in the apostolate of the Rosary.

In the development of the Rosary there was a fusion of different elements. One was the desire to give the laity a form of common prayer which would be modelled on monastic prayer. As this was based on the 150 psalms, the faithful were encouraged to recite 150 Paternosters; they were given beads to help them. In a parallel growth Mary's clients used antiphons in her honour, principally Gabriel's *Ave*, in chaplets of 50, groups of 100 or psalters of 150. As the Hail Mary (*qv*) evolved, it was used in this arrangement. The mysteries were not imposed from the beginning, but evolved with time. First, psalters of Jesus or Mary were formed by adding to each psalm a phrase that referred it to one or the other. With time, the psalms were omitted and the phrases made up a life of Jesus and of Mary from the Annunciation to heavenly glory. The joys dominated at first—the Annunciation, and then other sets of 5, 10, 15 or 20 joys. These joys would be recalled by liturgical antiphons, by brief phrases which might be rhymed. The Hail Mary was adapted to the remembrance of joys, the Annunciation joy for the first chaplet, others for the second or third. In the fourteenth century the Sorrows were considered during a second chaplet, and heavenly joy during a third.

From the psalters of Jesus and Mary chains of 50, 100 or 150 phrases referring to joys were attached to the recitation of *Aves* of the same number. The decision of the Carthusian Dominic of Prussia, soon after 1409, to attach fifty phrases referring to Jesus and Mary to fifty *Aves* was a step in the direction of standardized practice. About the same time another Carthusian, Herny Kalkar, visitator on the Lower Rhine, furthered the development by changing an arrangement whereby 150 *Paters* and 150 *Aves* were recited alternately to one in which the Hail Marys were taken in decades and fifteen Our Fathers were inserted between them. In the same way, chaplets of 50 *Aves* were separated by inserting five *Paters*. The word *Rosarium* had been used in regard to the chaplets of fifty points.

The next step was to simplify the mysteries: fifty points, one for each *Ave*, could not be recalled without a book. In 1480, Rosaries of 50 mysteries were reduced to five, one for each decade. In 1483, a Rosary book written by a Dominican, *Our Dear Lady's Psalter*, reduced the fifty points to fifteen, all of which, except the last two, correspond to the present mysteries: the Coronation was combined with the Assumption and the Last Judgement was the fifteenth mystery. The Dominican, Alberto da Castello, in 1521, in his book *The Rosary of the Glorious Virgin Mary*, tried to unite the old and the new forms of the mysteries. (He first used this term.) A mystery was attached to each *Pater* and the old series of 150 remained, as submysteries, linked with the *Aves*. In that century, none the less, the Rosary of the 15 mysteries became the accepted form. In that century too, St. Pius V, in 1569, officially approved the Rosary which had been completed by the addition of the second half of the Hail Mary and the Glory to the Father; in 1573 the same Pope instituted the Feast of the Rosary in thanksgiving to Our Lady for the Christian victory of Lepanto. Subsequent Popes have richly indulgenced the prayer.

[1]Cf. H. Thurston, S.J., articles in *The Month*, 96(1900), 403-18, 513-27, 620-37; 97(1901), 67-79, 172-88, 286-304; D. Mezard, *Étude sur les origines du Rosaire* (Calmire, 1912); M. M. Gorce, O.P., *Le Rosaire et ses antécédents historiques* (Paris, 1931); A. Duval, O.P., "Les Frères Prêcheurs et le Rosaire," *Maria* II, 768-82; M. Ward, *The Spendour of the Rosary* (New York, 1945); M. Mahé, "Aux sources de notre Rosaire," *Vie Spirituelle, Suppl.* 4(1951), 100-20; F. M. Willam, *The Rosary: Its History and Meaning* (New York, E. Kaiser, 1953); M. Llamera, O.P., "Validez del Rosario en la Iglesia Postconciliar," *Teologia Spiritual* 11(1967), 11-76; *id.*, "El problema de la reforma del Rosario," EstM 35(1970), 209-58; H. J. Carpenter, O.P., "The Rosary: Its doctrinal basis," *Cross and Crown*, 20(1968), 298-307, 429-441; J. Eyquem, O.P., J. Laurenceau, O.P., *Aujourdhui le Rosaire* (2nd ed. Toulouse, Centre National du Rosaire, 1969); R. Masson, O.P., "Le Rosaire après le Concile," MM 30(1968), 218-52; M. Cuervo, O.P., *La mision integral de Maria en el Rosario* (Guadalajara, Editorial Ope, 1970); D. Caloyeras, O.P., *La scuola di Maria nel rosario* (Bologna, Centro Nazionale del Rosario, 1972); symposium, Dominican authors, *Rilanciamo il rosario* (Naples, Ed. Dominicane italiane, 1973); J. N. Ward, *Five for Sorrow, Ten for Joy* (London, 1973).

ROSCHINI, GABRIEL MARY, O.S.M. (1900-1977)

One of the most prolific of all writers on Our Lady, R. was also a promoter of research in Marian theology.[1] He founded *Marianum*, an international scientific review in 1939 and saw it supported by contributions from almost every important expert in the subject in the last forty years. He was first rector of the *Marianum* Institute, which has very great prestige as a centre of higher learning. An adviser to church authorities in doctrinal matters, council member or high official of Marian academies, R. was assiduous as a contributor to congresses at every level. He was author of hundreds of articles in reviews and encyclopaedias, and of very many books among which the four volume *Mariologia* (2nd ed, 1948) is notable. An Italian counterpart, also in four volumes, appeared in 1953, *La Madonna secondo la fede e la teologia*. This was followed in 1969, after the Council and its immediate aftermath, by four large volumes, *Maria SS. nella storia della salvezza*. Substantial works on Marian doctors also came from his pen, e.g. on St. Thomas, St. Bernard, St. Alphonsus, St. Lawrence of Brindisi, as did a *Dizionarario di Mariologia* and a *Vita di Maria*. Occasionally controversial, as with C. Balic, O.F.M., on Duns Scotus, yet intensely loyal to the Teaching Authority, timing his articles or books with papal pronouncements, issuing a booklet on the Marian schema of Vatican II, he was also deeply devoted to his own Order, to furthering Marian piety and learning, and recording past achievement.

[1]Bibliography in MM, 11(1949), 498-505; *Elenco bibliografico dei scritti di G. M. Roschini* (Marianum, Rome,

1965). Cf. G. M. Besutti, O.S.M., *Ricordo del P. G. M. Roschini*, MM 39(1978), 309-20; *id.*, "El P.G.M.Roschini," EphMar 18(1978), 105-109; esp. the commemorative volume of MM fasc. i-iv 1979, with exhaustive bibliography by G. M. Besutti, O.S.M., pp. 5-63.

RUPERT OF DEUTZ (*c.* 1075-1130)

A Benedictine abbot, R. lived in the transition period between monastic and scholastic theology; he was involved in theological controversies. He had important insights in Marian theology, and was, in one area, a pioneer; he was the first to apply the *Song of Songs* (*qv*) entirely to Mary.[1]

R. held that Mary was the spouse of the Father: "Therefore, as we had already begun to say, the blessed Virgin Mary was the spouse of God the Father. In her the cause was fulfilled for which he had, in the Scriptures, called the church of the (old) people his spouse, his Word namely, to which, in the manner already mentioned, he had given expression through the hearts and mouths of the prophets, but had before all ages decided would become flesh through the womb of this blessed Virgin . . . Thus the blessed Virgin, the best part of the former church, deserved to be the spouse of God the Father that she should be the exemplar (*qv*) of the younger Church, the spouse of God the Son, her Son."[2]

In the same work on the Holy Spirit, part of his extensive account of salvation entitled "On the most holy Trinity," he draws out the parallel between Mary and the Church: "For the Holy Spirit who wrought the incarnation of the only Son of God in her womb or from her womb, he from the womb or through the womb of the Church would effect the regeneration of the sons of God through the washing of his grace which gives life."[3]

R. is a landmark in the explanation of Jn 19:25-27, as in biblical theology;[4] he sees the episode in the light of Mary's spiritual motherhood (*qv*). Asking why the beloved disciple should be called Mary's son and she his mother, he recalls the painless birth of Jesus and contrasts with this her birth pangs as our spiritual mother, using the words spoken by Jesus to the apostles on the woman in childbirth, Jn 16:21, 22: "how much more rightly did such a Son say that such a mother, this woman standing by his cross was truly like a woman in childbirth. How, I should say, like her since she is truly a woman and mother and has real offspring in that hour

of her pain? . . . Thus truly, suffering here the pains of childbirth the blessed Virgin brought forth the salvation of us all; she is really the mother of us all."[5]

The same doctrine is expressed in the commentary on the Song of Songs.[6] This work was written between 1117 and 1126, and in it R. divides the 8 chapters of the Song to suit 7 books of commentary. In this commentary he expresses many of the ideas of his time on Mary, giving his attention very particularly throughout to the NT especially to the infancy narratives (*qv*). Mary's dignity and holiness are expounded; so is the Eve-Mary typology in line with R's whole sense of the unity of the OT and NT. Mary is a model of the contemplative and active life; Rupert stresses her ardent longing for her divine Son after he had left this earth.

Despite his remarkable insights he did not grasp the idea of the Immaculate Conception (*qv*). Mary, he thought, did have original sin but was freed at the time of the Incarnation; she had belonged to "the mass which had been corrupted in Adam."[7] Nor did R. teach the bodily Assumption (*qv*), already known in certain areas in the West. He attached considerable importance to Mary's role as a prophetess, as he does in the treatise on the Holy Spirit.[8] Through Mary, Christ is our brother: "Everything that our brother means to us is from the mother . . . that mother is our mother, because that flesh is our flesh and that faith, your faith O Mary, is our faith."[9] The commentary ends with a moving prayer to Mary—". . . to thee especially we turn, to thee before all others we raise our eyes, thy help before all else we long for"[10]—which ends by asking, through her petition, for the light of the holy Trinity.

R. has many other significant passages on Our Lady in his works. In the *De divinis officiis* on the ecclesiastical year, he recalls that "the Virgin Mary gave birth to Christ, God and man, preserving the integrity of her womb";[11] contends that the risen Christ appeared to his Mother;[12] that as the "Mother of our faith" she is helpful in the bringing the nations to Christ through Baptism.[13] In the *Vita S. Hereberti* he relates an apparition of the "blessed queen of angels and all saints" to the saint, during which she indicated the site of a monastery "to God, to me and to all the saints"; he also styles her "Mother of mercy" and "Mother of eternal salvation."[14] In the *De laesione virginitatis* R.

describes Mary's humility, arguing that this was the cause of her vow of virginity (*qv*). More than once he interprets Is 7:14 (see EMMANUEL) in the traditional sense. Of the woman in Rev 12 (*qv*) he writes, "she was a sign of the whole Church, of which the blessed Virgin Mary is, through the blessing of her own womb, the greatest and most excellent part (*portio*)."[15] Like a good biblical theologian he relates Rev 12 to Gen 3:15 (see WOMAN IN).

[1]Cf. M. Peinador, C.M.F., "La Mariologia de Ruperto de Deutz," Eph.Mar. 17 (1967), 121-148; *id.*, "Maria y la Iglesia en la Salvación según R. de D.," EphMar. 18(1968), 337-381; *id.*, "La actitud negativa de R. de D. ante la Inmaculada Concepcion de la Virgen," MM 30(1968), 192-217; *id.*, "El Comentario de Ruperto de Deutz al Cantar de los Cantares," MM 31(1969), 1-58; *id.*, "La maternidad mesianica de Maria en el Antiguo Testamento segun R. de D." MM 32(1970), 521-550. [2]*De Sanct. Trin.* 34, *De operibus Spiritus Sancti*, 1, 8, CCCM 24, 1829; SC 131, 80; PL 167, 1577D. [3]*Ibid.* CCCM 24, 1830. [4]Cf. Th. Koehler, S.M., "Les principales interprétations traditionelles de Jn 19:25-27 pendant les douze premiers siècles," BSFEM 16(1959), 148,9. [5]*In John XIII*, CCCM 9, 743-744; PL 169, 789-790. [6]CCCM 26; PL 168, 837-962. [7]CCCM, 26, 12; cf. *In Mt 1*, PL 168, 1325C. [8]CCCM 26, CCCM 24, 1831. [9]*In Cant.* 7, CCCM 26, 158. [10]*Ibid.*, 171. [11]CCCM 7, 3, 25, 102. [12]7, 25, 256. [13]p. 258. [14]PL 170, 404D-405A. [15]*In Apoc.* 7 c. 12, PL 169, 1043A.

S

SAINTS

All the saints held the common truths of the faith about Our Lady and practised devotion towards her.[1] In each case greater or less emphasis arises from temperament, character, vocation, circumstance. In certain great civilizations—Byzantium, the European Middle Ages, seventeenth-century France—there was a universal consciousness of Mary's personality and power; in some regions and countries the same awareness persists over centuries. Sanctity in such situations has inevitably a Marian character.

The lifework of many saints was directly related to Our Lady, in writing or preaching, furthering particular devotions, founding institutes under her patronage, giving testimony to an extraordinary intervention by her in the life of the Church. Saints devoted to the apostolate differ in devotion to Mary from contemplatives. Men saints have been attracted to Mary as women saints have been to the Saviour, but not in an exclusive way; generalizations on this basis are not valid. Men since St. Paul have had an intensely personal love for Jesus Christ, as women—most of the genuine visionaries of modern times—have had for the Blessed Virgin Mary. Married men and women as well as celibates have loved Our Lady heroically. All true devotion may imply an element of sublimation, as sanctity often gives an increase in psychic energy, a toughening of mental and moral fibre, suppleness of spirit. The saints of Our Lady are no exceptions.

[1]Cf. G. M. Roschini, O.S.M., *Maria Santissima*, IV, *Il culto mariano, passim.*

SALAZAR, QUIRINO DE (1576-1646)

The greatest Spanish Marian theologian of the seventeenth century, S. was brought to deserved notice by R. Laurentin.[1] He taught in Murcia, Alcalá, finally settled in Madrid, a celebrity through his influence at Philip IV's court and his theological writings. He treats of Our Lady in *Pro Immaculata Conceptione Deiparae Virginis Defensio* (Alcalá, 1618), *Expositio in Proverbia Salomonis* (Paris, 1619), *Canticum Canticorum Salomonis allegorico sono et prophetica, mystica, hypermystica expositione productum* (Lyons, 1642). S. made a distinctive contribution to the doctrine of Mary's part in the Redemption and to her participation in the priesthood. Mary cooperated in the objective Redemption: S. thought that the salvation and redemption of the human race must be in a way attributed to her, that with Christ she gave and offered the price of our redemption truly and directly, and that titles given to Christ—redemptress, restorer, mediatress, author and cause of our salvation—are rightly used of her: "Therefore, though the Virgin by prayer and pouring out petitions contributed something to our salvation, that assuredly, in my opinion, is not enough to justify calling her cause of our salvation, its author or mediatress, as is clear of others who also prayed and poured out petitions. What clearly brought the Virgin to this glory and made her a collaborator (*cooperatricem*) and helper with Christ was that joining her will in association with the will of Christ she offered him who was hers to us and for us for which reason, as is clear from Bonaventure, the Virgin especially bound God and men to herself, for she so greatly pleased God by this free offering of her son that in a manner singular and proper to herself she obtained life and salvation for the human race."[2]

S. preserves the essential distinction between Christ and Mary with the concepts of merit *de condigno* and *de congruo*. "If *per impossible*" he says, "the will of Christ the Lord had not been expressed, the will of the Mother would be sufficient to interpret the will of the Son, for the Son could be thought to will what the Mother willed."[3] More boldly still, S. gives, as a purely personal opinion, that if the Saviour had no indication of the Father's will "and the Mother alone had wished and decreed that her Son should die for men," to this he would have bowed and faced death.[4] Yet the transcendence of Christ is preserved: "Therefore Mary was an aid-giver and helper (*adjutrix et auxiliatrix*); not that Christ needed help or assistance since the value of his blood immeasurably surpasses settlement of our debts, but because the authority and dignity of the Mother demanded that her merits, prayers and wishes should be joined with the wishes and merits of Christ so that the salvation of men should be given to each of them."[5]

S. included in Mary's dignity the queenly office. But he was especially preoccupied with her priesthood and it is to be regretted that we have not his complete teaching on the subject. He thought that Mary's priesthood was very different from and far superior to the common priesthood of the faithful. She alone offered herself entirely as a holocaust to God. Her priestly office was active on Calvary: "In this also the Blessed Virgin fulfilled the office of priest in that showing her will in all things conform to the will of her Son she offered and sacrificed him on the altar of the Cross as did Christ himself."[6] "Not only did Christ pour the fullness of his priestly anointing on Mary, but he emptied it on her."[7] With such ideas frequently repeated, it will be expected that S. too held Mary's universal mediation of grace: so excellent was the office of mediatress in Mary that all and each good thing comes from God to men through her and God has never granted any grace to man which was not obtained by Mary . . . "[it was the fathers' reasoning] that all grace must be in Mary because through Mary all grace is to flow on others."[8]

[1]Cf. R. Laurentin, *Marie l'Eglise et le Sacerdoce*, 1 (Paris, 1952), 230-304; O. Casado, C.M.F., "Doctrina Ferdinandi Q.Salazar de B.V.M. Corredemptione," EphMar 9(1959), 101-12; J. Dos Santos, C.M.F., "A doutrina do sacerdocio mariano segundo Fernando Q. de Salazar," ME VII, 39-79; J. Esquerda Bifet, "Maria en Sagrada Escritura según Fernando Quirino de Salazar," MSS III, 179-96. [2]Extracts from J. dos Santos, *op.cit.*, 56. [3]*ibid.*, 52. [4]*ibid.* [5]*ibid.*, 67. [6]*ibid.*, 60. [7]*ibid.*, 61. [8]*ibid.*, 63.

SALVE REGINA

The best-known western anthem to Our Lady, the *Salve Regina* summarizes appropriately medieval themes and aspirations in presence of Our Lady: the mother chosen to replace Eve, the source of mercy, the advocate, the hope of eternal salvation through her power with "Jesus the fruit of her womb," the embodiment of female tenderness.[1] The S. R. entered profoundly into the liturgical and popular prayer of the Latin world. A *Benedicamus Domino* trope in the eleventh century (Karlsruhe MS Aug LV) seems to have been influenced by it. In the twelfth century it was inserted into earlier manuscripts, such as St. Gall 390, as the Magnificat antiphon for the feast of the Annunciation. Its authorship is still uncertain. It is sometimes linked with the *Clamor*, a form of prayer known from the ninth century. It has been attributed to St. Bernard of Clairvaux, Peter of Compostela (among several of the same name, the one born in 930), Adhémar de Monteil of Puy, about 1080, and Hermann the Cripple—the last-named is mostly supported at present despite Fr. J. M. Canal's attempt to reinstate St. Bernard.

About 1135 the S. R. was a processional chant at Cluny. The Cistercian Order used it as a daily processional chant after 1218 and after Compline from 1251; the Dominicans and Franciscans adopted it at about the same time; the Carmelites for a while used it instead of the last gospel at Mass. Gregory IX (1227-41) ordered that it be chanted after Compline on Fridays, and from the fourteenth century it was sung after Compline universally in the Latin Rite. St. Pius V (1568) decreed that it be sung or recited after Vespers from Trinity Sunday to the first Sunday in Advent. Since 1971 it is one of the anthems which may be said after the divine office. From 1884 to 1964, it was one of the prayers prescribed by Leo XIII for recitation after all Masses of the Roman Rite; Pius XI directed that these prayers be offered for the conversion of Russia. Historians relate that recitation of the S. R. dramatically preceded Columbus' warning to his men to look out for land; next morning they sighted the New World.

The S. R. has been wedded to noble plain chant which enhances its appeal, and given many other musical settings.

---

[1]Cf. AH 1, 318f; 50, 308-309. Cf. also J. de Valois, *En marge d'une antienne, le Salve Regina* (Paris, 1912); H. Thurston, "The Salve Regina," *The Month, 128(1918)*, 248-80, 300-14; *Familiar Prayers*, ed. P. Grosjean, S.J., (London 1953) 115-45; J. Maier, *Studien zur Geschichte der antiphon "Salve Regina"* (Regensburg, 1939); R. Baurreiss, *Der "Clamor". Eine verschollene mittelalterliche Gebetsform und das Salve Regina*, in *Mitteilungen zur Geschichte des Benektiner-Ordens und seiner Zweige*, 62, Munich 1950, 24-33; J. Leclercq, O.S.B., *Maria* II, 577-78, *Note sur le Salve Regina*; R. Laurentin, *Traité* 1, 148; I. Cechetti, *Salve Regina* in *Enciclopaedia Cattolica*, X, 1719-21; J. M. Canal, C.M.F., *Salve Regina Misericordiae, Historia y Leyendas en torno a esta antifona* (Rome Edizioni di Storia e Letteratura, 1963); id., "En torno a la antifona 'Salve Regina'", RTAM 3(1966), 342-55 (review of reviews of his book); id., La "Salve Regina" de origen compostelano? in *Anuario de estudios medievales* 4 (1967), 377-84; H. Barré, C.S.Sp., *Saint Bernard et le "Salve Regina,"* 26(1964), 208-16; reply to book by J. Canal; A. M. Mundo, *El origen de la "Salve" visto desde Espana, Anuario de estudios medievales* 4(1967), 369-76.

SATAN

Because of the intimate bonds which unite Mary with Jesus, she participates most perfectly in his struggle with Satan and joins in his victory. A Marian interpretation of the Woman in Gen 3:15 and Rev XII will give this truth a biblical foundation. R. Laurentin found unanimity among Fathers of the Church and ecclesiastical writers during the first twelve centuries on the identity of Satan with the serpent in Gen 3:15.[1] *Ineffabilis Deus* speaks of the "enmity of both (Christ and Mary) against the evil one as significantly expressed," and goes on, "so the most holy Virgin, united with him (Christ) by a most intimate and indissoluble bond, was with him and through him, eternally at enmity with the evil serpent, and most closely triumphed over him, and thus crushed his head with her immaculate foot."[2] *Munificentissimus Deus* says: "We must remember especially that, since the second century, the Virgin Mary has been designated by the Holy Fathers as the new Eve who, although subject to the new Adam, is most intimately associated with him in that struggle with the infernal foes which, as foretold in the protoevangelium, would finally result in that most complete victory over the sin and death which are always mentioned together in the writings of the Apostle of the Gentiles."[3]

Mary crushing the serpent beneath her foot is a common theme in Christian iconography.

---

[1]BSFEM 12(1954), 111. [2]OL, 72. [3]OL, 317.

SCHEEBEN, M. J. (1835-1888)

Matthias Joseph S. studied in Rome under famous professors, in the age of the dogma of the Immaculate Conception; he taught dogmatic theology in Cologne seminary until his death. He edited and contributed to theological periodicals, published important works on divine grace and the mysteries of Christianity; his main work was *Handbuch der Katholischen Dogmatik*, remarkable for profundity and learning. Therein principally his Marian theology is found; it has been made available in a single volume by his modern editor, K. Feckes, himself a key figure in the promotion of Marian studies in Germany.[1] S.'s first contribution to the subject was a patristic and poetic anthology on Our Lady. In 1869 in his review *Das Oekumenische Konzil*, he published a lengthy study of papal infallibility, which he defended at the time, showing the link with the dogma of the Immaculate Conception (qv).

Studying the Bible, with such resources as were then available to him, especially attentive to the testimony of the Fathers, S. dealt with many problems which were to become acute in the present century.

The distinctive theory of S. was the bridal motherhood, which he sought to make the fundamental principle (qv) of Marian theology. "Mary is as much anointed and made the Mother of God as the flesh taken from her is made the flesh of God, for the Logos is so taken up in her that she herself is taken up in him in an analogous way as the flesh taken from her. Consequently the relation of the Mother to the divine Son appears as a marriage with this divine Person. Here now the Bridegroom gives himself to the Bride as her Son and dwells in her in virtue of this gift."[2] S. develops this idea elaborately. He integrates it with the Eve (qv)-Mary parallel, delaying especially on the medieval extension, Gen 2:18, "a helper like himself." He appeals to the Wisdom texts applied to Mary in the Liturgy (qv), to Mary's predestination (qv) as taught in *Ineffabilis Deus* (qv)—"by one and the same decree as the incarnation of divine Wisdom." He looks for evidence in titles (qv) given to Our Lady in the past. He analyses her relationship with each of the divine persons.

With his habitual depth and learning S. deals with Mary's Immaculate Conception (qv) and Assumption (qv). Aware of Epiphanius (qv), he argues subtly about her death (qv), supporting the view that it was not inevitable but accepted in conformity with Christ.[3] Though the bodily resurrection was not yet a dogma he expounded it fully.

It is in the chapters dealing with Mary's role in life and since then that S. is most relevant to the present century. "The distinguishing mark of her person as bride of Christ is conceived fully in her capacity of bearer and temple of the Holy Ghost," he says, and goes on to show how she was "the dynamic and authoritative organ of the Holy Spirit."

On the difference between Mary's mediation and that of the saints, he writes: "Thus she is not only the mediatress who applies the fruits of redemption to individuals, but also the Mediatress who produces and gains these fruits."[4] On the relation of her saving work to that of Christ, he writes: "It is obvious, as the expression 'influence of the Mother of the Redeemer' clearly states, that Mary cannot be a principle co-ordinate to and independent of Christ, called and empowered to complete his redeeming power and might. On the contrary, she is subordinate to and dependent on Christ the Redeemer in such a way that she herself is redeemed by him, and can cooperate in the Redemption only as one redeemed and with a power which she receives from him ... this cooperation is only

one of ministering in Christ's act of Redemption, which is the real act of Redemption and stands by itself."

It is here that S. expresses dissatisfaction with the word Coredemptress, preference for *Adjutrix*, helper, which shows Mary's cooperation as "bridal," brings out its "complete subordination and dependence, as well as her closest union with the Redeemer."[5] He reverts to the Eve-Mary typology. Later he wrestles with the problem of a priestly aspect to Mary's participation in the sacrifice of her Son, suggesting the term "deaconess at Christ's sacerdotal sacrifice."[6]

S. thought that Mary's spiritual motherhood flowed from her part in the Redemption; therein especially she was the type of the Church: "Mary's motherhood remains the root and soul of that of the Church in such unity that the Church can have and exercises its motherhood only in so far as it contains and acts through Mary's motherhood."[7] Likewise dealing with Mary's universal mediation, which he defended, he sets forth the reasons and concludes that "Mary is first, the ideal model of the Church; secondly, the universal mediation of all graces by the Church cannot exist entirely of itself, if Mary is not regarded as the unfailing Mediatress of grace."[8] "Mary's intercession," he thought, "forms an ordinary and indispensable means of salvation for all men." And the highly intellectual and erudite work concludes with a justification of devotion to the heart (qv) of Mary: "In the case of Mary, the heart is the life centre of her person and, as such, it represents the latter even in the maternal distinguishing mark of her person, since her heart is the instrument of her physical and spiritual motherhood."[9]

[1] *Handbuch*, (Freiburg im Breisgau, 1873-1882); reissue ed. K. Feckes, Freiburg, 1954. Marian doctrine, M. J. Scheeben, *La Mère virginale du Sauveur*, French tr. A. Kerkvoorde (Paris, 1954) and English tr. (2 vols, T.L.M.J. Geukers) *Mariology (St. Louis and London, 1946-1953)* and Italian tr., Brescia, 1955. Cf. K. Feckes, "M. J. Scheeben, Théologien de la mariologie moderne" in *Maria*, III, 553-571; *id.*, *Quid Scheeben de B.V.Mariae debito contrahendi maculam senserit*, in V.I., 11, 333-342; H. Muehlen, "Der Personalcharakter Mariens nach J.M.S.," *Wissen. Weish.*, 17(1954), 95-108; *id.*, Maria als "Frucht und Glied" Adams, 18(1955), 95-108; *id.*, "Maria 'Glied Christi' und Zugleich 'Glied Adams'", *Wissen, Weish*, 19(1956), 17-42 (second title to each article, *Zur Frage nach dem Grundprinzip der Mariologie bei M.J.S.*); J. Galot, S.J., "La nouvelle Eve d'après Scheeben, in BSFEM 14(1956), 49-66; D. Flanagan, "Scheeben and the basic principle of Mariology" in *Irish*

Theol. Quart., 25(1958), 367-381; J. I. Lorscheiter, "Doctrina M.J.S. de sacerdotio B.V.M.," in ME, VII, 93-111; K. Wittkemper, *Mariol. Stud.*, I, 267-280 and II, 149-165. [2]*Mariology*, I, 162-163. [3]*Mariology*, II, 151-158. [4]*Mariology*, II, 185, 186, 194. [5]*Mariology*, II, pp. 195-197. [6]Cf. pp. 227-238. [7]*Mariology*, II, 250. [8]*Mariology*, II, 266. [9]*Mariology*, II, 273.

SCHOLARIOS, GEORGE (d. after 1472)

The principal Eastern theologian of the fifteenth century, the greatest in medieval times. S.'s life was caught in the movement towards unity which caused the Council of Ferrara and Florence, 1438-49, which he attended and in the collapse of the Eastern empire with the seizure of Constantinople by the Turks. He had studied Western theologians, St. Augustine (*qv*), St. Thomas Aquinas (*qv*) and later writers like Francis of Mayronis (*qv*). At the Council, he accepted the *Filioque* but later changed his mind and opposed the Latins. A layman until 1450, he was as a monk enslaved by the invader, but in 1454 Mohammed II named him Patriarch; whereon he took the name Gennadius II. S.'s Marian theology is contained especially in homilies on the Annunciation (BHG 1107g), published in Volume I of the collected works,[1] and on the Presentation (BHG 1147g),[2] and Dormition (BHG 1099s),[3] the latter two published by M. Jugie, A.A. (*qv*).

S. understood the Latin theory of grace and of original sin. His praise of Mary is in the Byzantine manner: "O honour of the human race, admiration of angels, ornament of the entire creation, crown of virginity . . ."[4] "O woman most pure one in soul and body, flower not only of all women, but also of all nature, flower most sweet among flowers, because it was made the root and principle of the predestined to salvation, as the first woman was and remains that of the reprobate."[5]

S. emphasised Mary's initial holiness, attributing more therein to divine grace than did other Byzantines: "What conception without seed achieved in her Son, in her divine grace operated, so that in both there should be wondrous purity."[6] "But God's grace freed her completely as if she had been conceived virginally, so that she should provide flesh perfectly pure to the incarnation of the divine Word."[7] The author goes on to describe the full purity of Mary who while in the flesh was the sanctuary of God. His view does seem to reject original sin, but it is clear that he was not at grips with the problems deriving from St. Augustine and others which, somewhat earlier, had obstructed western thought on the subject, and continued to do so (see IMMACULATE CONCEPTION).

As a passage quoted has shown, Mary's role towards others is closely linked with her own purity: "How should you not be blessed, you who not only completely escaped the iniquities of the first curse but will deliver others from these iniquities . . . . And as the shame of the curse taking its origin from a woman brought ruin to human nature, in the same way, now through you the treasure of blessing will be shared with others and you will become the seed of a new life and the beginning of men truly worthy of the name."[8] This previous santification of Mary is recalled by S. when he says explicitly that "she cooperated with God in giving us eternal life, filling the role of an appropriate instrument."[9] S. saw Constantinople, so often saved by its patroness the *Theotokos*, now succumb to the foe. But his confidence is unabated.

On the subject of Mary's bodily Assumption (*qv*), he felt his way cautiously. In the first version of the Dormition homily he was content to state the two possibilities hitherto defended: Mary's soul was assumed and her body taken to the earthly paradise, to await the final resurrection; body and soul were united on the third day. In a final writing of the text just before he died, he added the words: "It is rather with the opinion of the latter that we side as being the wisest and in every way the most plausible."[10]

[1]*Oeuvres completes de Georges Scholarios*, (Paris, 1928-36), 8 vols., ed. L. Petit, X. Siderides, M. Jugie; cf. Vol I, pp. 1-61. [2]PO 19, 513-525. [3]PO 16, 570-587; cf. Beck, 763; M. Jugie, *L'Assomption*, 337-38 and *L'Immaculée Conception*, 301-307; H. Graef, *Mary*, I, 349-50. [4]*In Dormit.*, PO 16, 585. [5]*In Praesent.*, PO 19, 515. [6]*In Dorm.* ed. Petit et al., I, 202; PO 16, 577. [7]*Second Treatise on the origin of the Soul*, 20, ed. Petit, I, 501. [8]*In Annunt.* 43, ed. Petit, I, 40. [9]*In Dorm. 1*, PO 16, 570. [10]*In Dorm.* ed. Petit, I, 205 for both readings.

SCOTUS, JOHN DUNS (1266-1308)

S. a Scottish born Franciscan, teacher at Oxford and Paris, has generally appeared in the history of the doctrine of the Immaculate Conception (*qv*) as the one who marked a great medieval turning point; he provided the solution to an apparently insuperable difficulty, how to reconcile Our Lady's privilege with the universality of the redemption by Christ.[1] Historical research has thrown light on the contribution of others, notably William of Ware (*qv*). Then a major controversy occurred in the nineteen-fifties on the significance of S., between two great Mariologists, G. M. Roschini, O.S.M. (*qv*) and C. Balic, O.F.M. (*qv*).[2]

S. deals with other questions in Marian theology. On the philosophical basis of the divine motherhood he differed from St. Thomas (*qv*) in his analysis of the relationship of sonship to Mary,[3] with the risk that Christ could be the adoptive son of God, a risk which S. foresaw and countered. He held that Mary had made an *absolute* vow of virginity, not a conditional engagement, i.e. "unless God wills otherwise." In the conception of her Son he attributed an active part to her, following Galen, not merely a passive part, as others like St. Thomas who followed Aristotle. He thought that thus he was showing the plentitude of her motherhood and G. M. Roschini, who has questioned the importance of his doctrine on the Immaculate Conception, on this point concludes: "In this way Duns Scotus, in contrast with all the other great scholastic doctors, placed in its true and full light the fundamental mystery of the divine motherhood of Mary and came close to the conclusions of modern biology."[3]

Scotus was moderate in proclaiming Mary's intercessory power: "The Blessed Virgin has authority to intercede by prayer, not to command."[4]

Without entering into the controversy which opposed Franciscans, principally C. Balic, to G. M. Roschini, the essence of Scotus' position —stated after all objections had been fully set out—was rooted in the perfection of Christ: "For the most perfect mediator has the possibility of a most perfect act of mediation in regard to some person for whom he mediates; therefore Christ had, as a possibility, the most perfect degree of mediation in regard to some person for whom he was a mediator. He had a more excellent degree in regard to no one than to Mary; therefore etc. But this would not have been unless he had merited to preserve her from original sin. Proof is threefold: first, by comparison with God to whom he reconciles, secondly by comparison with the evil from which he liberates, thirdly by comparison with the obligation of the person whom he had reconciled."[5] The Subtle Doctor expounds each point succinctly. The Trinity will not be most perfectly appeased

unless offence is entirely prevented in one case. The original fault itself is the greatest penalty and must in some one instance be removed to show the power of the Mediator. Christ who came especially to restore and reconcile from original sin preserved his Mother, as was commonly held, from actual sin. Hence too from original sin. The beneficiary of mediation, if he or she is to have the highest obligation, must receive the highest good possible from the mediation. Only one preserved from original sin can hold this obligation to Christ. Since he has merited for many grace and glory, "why should no soul be indebted to him for innocence, and why, since all the angels are innocent, will no human soul be innocent in heaven save that of Christ."[6]

"If it is not opposed to the authority of the Church or to the authority of Scripture, it seems probable that what is more excellent should be attributed to Mary."[7] This was the granting of as much grace in the first instant as others receive in circumcision or baptism. In this way she had the greatest need of Christ as redeemer, "for as others needed Christ so that through his merit they should be forgiven sin already contracted, so she needed the mediator preserving from sin (*praeveniente peccatum*) lest she should ever have to contract it or should contract it."[8]

Later in the same work he repeats the doctrine in even more positive manner: Mary was never the enemy of God "originally through original sin; she would have been had she not been preserved."[9] True he was less assertive in Paris using the word "perhaps" and there is a much disputed text, in the *Theoremata* where the relevant words read "as it is said, that the Blessed Virgin contracted [original sin], nevertheless was cleansed afterwards."[10] The major contribution had been made; it had been taught in the university world, then so important, first in Oxford, then in Paris. So the historic stature of S. remains. He did not relate his theory explicitly to his doctrine on the motive of the Incarnation, which was to develop into a theory of the cosmic Christ. But the majesty of the Saviour, his universal primacy, are implicit in the texts quoted.

[1]For texts cf. C. Balic, O.F.M., *Joannis Duns Scoti Doctoris Mariani Theologiae Marianae Elementa* (Sibernik, 1933); *Joannes Duns Scotus, Doctor Immaculatae Conceptionis*, I

Textus Auctoris (Rome 1954). [2]For bibliography cf. G. M. Roschini, *Maria Santissima*, III, 257-258 and I, 450. Cf. from the controversial literature, C. Balic, "Il reale contributo di G. Scoto nella questione dell'Immacolata Concezione," *Antonianum*, 29(1954), 475-496, and Joannes Duns Scotus et historia Immaculatae Conceptionis," *Antonianum*, 30(1955), 349-448; also P. Migliore, O.F.M. Conv., "La dottrina dell'Immacolata in Guglielmo de Ware, O.Min. e nel B. Giovanni Duns Scoto, O. Min.," in *Misc. Franc.*, 54(1954), 433-538; K. Koser, O.F.M., "Die Immakulata-lehre des Joannes Duns Scotus," *Franz.St.* 36(1954), 337-384; G. M. Roschini, "Duns Scoto e l'Immacolata," MM 17(1955), 183-258; "Questioni su Scoto e l'Immacolata," Eph. Mar., 7(1957), 491-536; J. Bonnefoy, O.F.M., *Le Ven. Jean Duns Scot, Docteur de l'Immaculée Conception etc.* (Rome, 1960). [3]*Maria Santissima*, II, 59; cf. C. Balic, *Theologiae Marianae Elementa, Ordinatio*, III, d.4 q. 1, 80-112. [4]*Ibid.*, 171. [5]*Ordinatio*, III, d. 3, q. 1, C. Balic, *Doctor Immaculatae Conceptionis*, p. 7. [6]*Ibid.*, p. 10. [7]*Ibid.*, p. 13. [8]*Ibid.*, p. 16. [9]*Ibid.*, p. 21. [10]*Theoremata* XIV, 27, C. Balic, *Theologiae Marianae Elementa*, p. 409; cf. G. M. Roschini, *Maria Santissima*, III, 165-166.

SENSE (SENTIMENT) OF THE FAITHFUL, SENSE OF FAITH

These phrases refer to the participation of the faithful in the prophetic or teaching role of the Church. There has been a change of emphasis on one aspect or another through the centuries. In medieval times, analysis of the faith in the believer brought out the idea of the sense of the faith; in the sixteenth century, the thought was of the sentiment of the faithful or of the Church (*sensus, consensus fidelium, Ecclesiae*) whereas recently the accent is on the faith of the Christian people, the common faith of the Church (*Christiani populi fides, communis Ecclesiae fides*).[1] The general truth that the faithful join with the teaching authority in maintaining the faith of the Church is of biblical and patristic origin. The faithful are not mere passive recipients, nor, at the other extreme, an autonomous source. The Church teaching and the Church that is taught complement each other; at times the weight of the latter has been salutary and corrective. If theologians of Our Lady draw attention to the *sensus fidelium*, this emphasis may occur at a certain stage in all doctrinal development.

Newman is enlightening on the point. Already in his Anglican period he had, in his study of the early Church pronouncement on Our Lady at Ephesus, discerned that "the spontaneous or traditional feeling of Christians had anticipated the formal ecclesiastical decision." While in Rome in 1849 he read the Encyclical of Pius IX,

Ubi Primum, which had appeared that year and noted its revelance to his idea. Pius IX in the letter asked the bishops of the world to inform him "concerning the devotion which animates your clergy and your people regarding the Immaculate Conception of the Blessed Virgin, and how ardently glows the desire that this doctrine be defined by the Apostolic See."

Ten years later Newman published his *Rambler* paper "On consulting the faithful in matters of doctrine."[2] He drew on the work of Giovanni Perrone, S.J., *De Immaculato B.V.Mariae Conceptu*, on the Encyclical, and on the bull *Ineffabilis Deus* (qv). In all he found confirmation of his theory about the *sensus fidelium*.

Newman begins from the fact that the faithful are, on certain occasions, treated "with attention and consideration." He goes on: "Then follows the question, 'Why?' and the answer is, *viz.* because the body of the faithful is one of the witnesses of the tradition of revealed doctrine, and because their *consensus* through Christendom is the voice of the infallible Church."[3] Analysing the ways in which the "tradition of the Apostles" committed to the whole Church in its various constituents and functions *per modum unius*, manifests itself," he declared that "these include the people." Though none of these channels must be treated with disrespect, one must grant fully "that the gift of discerning, discriminating, defining, promulgating and enforcing any portion of that tradition resides solely in the *Ecclesia docens*."[4]

The teaching of Vatican II resembles this theory very closely: "The body of the faithful as a whole, anointed as they are by the Holy One (cf. Jn I, 2:20,27) cannot err in matters of belief. Thanks to a supernatural sense of faith which characterizes the People as a whole, it manifests this unerring quality when from the bishops down to the last member of the laity, it shows universal agreement in matters of faith and morals. All this it does under the lead of a sacred teaching authority to which it loyally defers" (LG 12 and cp. 34).

Giovanni Perrone used the phrase *pastorum ac fidelium velut in unum conspiratio*, (as it were a concerted impulse of pastors and faithful) to show how the *Ecclesia Docens* and *Ecclesia Discens* complement each other. It passed into the Bull with the word *antistitum* substituted for *pastorum*. It is found again in *Munificentis-simus Deus*. This document has a lengthy passage on the common faith of the Church. Significantly, before it was drawn up, Pius XII in the Encyclical *Deiparae Virginis* made a consultation of the world's bishops in which he also inquired "about the devotion of your clergy and people (taking into account their faith and piety)" toward the Assumption, and whether "in addition to your own wishes (on the dogmatic definition) this is desired by your clergy and people."[5] The Perrone phrase is finally found in Vatican II's (*qv*) Constitution on Divine Revelation.[6]

Theologians have been occasionally drawn to consideration of the subject in recent times: it is the theme of one major essay. At the Lourdes Congress (*qv*), the Papal Legate Cardinal Tisserant defended the validity of the *sensus fidelium*, distinguishing it from views put forward by Modernists.[7]

Concern has been expressed over excesses possible in the whole sector; the imprudent organisation of signature campaigns, theology by plebiscite, confusion of emotionalism with genuine adherence to the faith. Despite such dangers, the importance of the *sensus fidelium* is theologically grounded. It is particularly valuable in questions concerning Our Lady. Tradition (*qv*), which it serves, has played a remarkable part in the development of Marian doctrine. There is an affinity, which must be very delicately considered, between the faithful and Our Lady; for she did not enter into the government or official teaching authority of the Church during her life.

Respect for the sentiment of the faithful must also benefit theologians, save them from the danger of professionalism, of "theologians talking to theologians", and of missing the necessary pastoral dimension of all divine revelation (*qv*), the vital links by which theology must enter organically into the life of the Church.

---

[1]Cf. J. H. Newman, *Essay on the Development of Christian Doctrine* (London, 1845), p. 407; *On Consulting the Faithful in Matters of Doctrine*, ed. J. Coulson, London, Geoffrey Chapman, 1961—also in *The Church and the Laity* by J. Guitton, tr. M. Carroll, New York, 1965. Cf. also F. Taymans d'Epernon, S.J., "Le progrès du dogme," NRT, 71(1949), 687-700; Y.-M. Congar, O.P., "Le peuple fidèle et la fonction prophétique dans l'Eglise," *Irenikon*, 3(1951), 289-312 and 4, 440-466; *id., Jalons pour une théologie du laicat* (Paris, Cerf, 1953) 394-407; C. Balic, O.F.M., "Il senso cristiano e il progresso del dogma," *Gregorianum*

33(1952), 106-35; M. Peinador, C.M.F., "El 'sensus fidei' y el progreso dogmatico en el misterio marial," EphMar 6(1956), 463-73; Cl.Dillenschneider, C.SS.R., *Le sens de la foi et le progrès dogmatique du mystère marial* (Rome, Pontifical Marian Academy, 1954); M. Lefebvre, *La valeur du consentement universel de l'Eglise*, Montreal, *Studia Montis Regii*, 1, February, 1958, pp. 61-91; E.(Cardinal) Tisserant, "De Mariologia in ambitu Sacrae Theologiae," ME II, 465-72; A. Leonard, "La foi, principe fondamental du développement du dogme," RSPT 42(1958), 276-86; T. M. Bartolomei, O.S.M.F., "L'influsso del 'senso della fede' nell'esplicitazione del dogma dell'Immacolata Concezione," MM 25(1963), 405-46; L'influsso del 'senso della fede' nell'esplicitazione del dogma dell'Assunzione di Maria," *EphMar* 14(1964), 5-38. [2]Cf. article NEWMAN. [3]*On Consulting the Faithful*, section 2, ed. in article *jam cit.* [4]*Ibid.* [5]OL, 264. [6]Art. 10. [7]"De Mariologia in ambitu sacrae theologiae," ME, II, esp. pp. 468-470.

SEVERIAN OF GABALA (d. after 408)

S., bishop of Gabala in Syria, was first a friend and supporter of St. John Chrysostom, then his adversary. He was of the Antiochene school, but held opinions independently which would not be in its tradition. Critical research has proved his authorship of a number of items attributed to Chrysostom,[1] with judgment pending on one sermon.[2] An inventory of the Marian passages in 11 works exists; as well as the texts, this monograph presents the critical position for each item, and detailed bibliography, with classified analysis of opinions and interpretations.[3]

In the *Oratio IV in mundi creationem* S. expresses an unusual idea: God spared the Jews despite their ancient sins because he foresaw the piety of those to come, foremost among them "the holy Virgin Theotokos": all three words are significant, especially *Theotokos*. The word used in the long Marian passage[4] in the *Oratio VI in mundi creationem* is *Kuriotokos*, perfectly orthodox with S. The passage has given rise to many interpretations on these subjects: the woman in Gen 3:15 (*qv*); Mary's holiness (*qv*); the divine motherhood (*qv*); the Assumption (*qv*); the Eve-Mary contrast (*qv*) the spiritual motherhood (*qv*) and Marian cult.[5] Two singular titles are applied to Mary, "Mother of salvation" and "the source of that Light that is perceptible both sensibly and intellectually, sensibly by reason of his flesh, intellectually by reason of his divinity."[6] The context here is concrete relating to the Saviour, Light of the world.

Mary is for S. "great" (*megale*). He develops a spirited defence of her virginity against the

Jews,[7] attributes to the Holy Spirit the formation of the body of Christ, "the temple of the Word."[8] Mary is *aeiparthenos*, ever-virgin.

In the *Hom. de Legislatore V. et N.T.* at one time attributed to St. John Chrysostom, there is a passage on Mary's intercession. The circumstance is an attack on the city of Constantinople: "We also have Mary, the holy Virgin and Mother of God, interceding for us on our behalf. For if any ordinary woman has gained the victory, how much more the Mother of Christ confounds the enemies of truth."[9] S. recalls that in OT times God overthrew enemies of his people by means of Deborah, Jahel and other heroic women. "In this age there is not lacking to God a Deborah, a Jahel. We also have the holy Virgin and Mother of God interceding for us." The words used, *presbeuo*, to intercede and *kataischuno*, to confound or humiliate (the enemy), imply more than mere intercession, something practically identical with mediation, personal intervention.

Writing at a time when Mary's holiness was not yet fully understood, especially in the Antiochene school, S. does not speak of either original sin or defects in Mary, though to bring the divinity of Jesus into high relief, he does show Mary's request at Cana as unnecessary and inopportune.[10] He proclaimed a very high idea of her holiness, all the more remarkable as he was a contemporary of St. John Chrysostom, preaching in his city. In like manner remarkable was his use of the title *Theotokos*, and his witness to a cult of Mary.[11]

[1]R. Laurentin, *Traité*, I, 162-163. CMP II, 439-454; EMBP, 503; ClavisG, 468-488. [2]*In natale D.N.J.C.*, PG 61, 763-768; cf. R. Caro, *La Homiletica* II, 410-419; R. Laurentin, RSPT, 52(1968), 544. [3]A. M. Gila, O.S.M., *Studi su testi mariani di Severiano di Gabala* (Rome, 1965). [4]PG 56, 496-98; English tr. T. Livius, C.SS.R., *The Blessed Virgin in the Fathers of the first six centuries* (London, 1893), 56. [5]Gila, *op.cit.* 28-29. [6]PG 56, 498. [7]*Hom in S.Crucem*, apud Gila, 51-52. [8]*Hom in illud, Dominus regnavit, exultet terra*, PG 55 (attributed to St. John Chrysostom), 607. [9]PG 56, 409. [10]*Hom. in S. Martyr. Acacium*, apud Gila, 78. [11]Cf. also A. M. Gila, "Esame dei principali testi mariani di Saveriano di Gabala," MM, 26(1964), 113-172; id., PCM, III, 229-242.

SEVERUS OF ANTIOCH (c. 465-538)

S. was a monk who was appointed patriarch of Antioch in 512. Because of his Monophysite leanings, he went through many vicissitudes; he was deposed, took refuge in Alexandria, was finally excommunicated by a synod in Constantinople. Recent scholarship has shown that his differences from Chalcedon were largely in vocabulary, particularly in the use of *phusis*.[1] He gave 125 Cathedratical Homilies and wrote 400 letters. With the exception of fragments in patristic exegetical anthologies, nothing survives in the original Greek; we depend on Syrian translations, which have been appearing with modern versions in PO since 1908. Two homilies treat of Our Lady, 14 and 67.[2] Marian doctrine is also found in the controversial writings, especially against Julian of Halicarnassus, appearing in CSCO since 1929, and in the hymns in PO.[3]

S. was a devoted follower of St. Cyril of Alexandria (qv) and insisted on Mary's claim to the title *Theotokos* (qv): "The word *Theotokos* is a perfect word and it has no need of a heretical addition, by which one would also want to call her *anthropotokos* . . . ."[4] "The Son of God and his Word, who is before the ages, has, at the end of time, become incarnate and was made man of the Holy Spirit and of the Mother of God, Mary ever-virgin."[5] S. cherishes the idea of the union of the Holy Spirit and Mary in the incarnation. There could be no thought of a human father. S. accepts the idea of St. Ignatius of Antioch (qv) that Joseph was present to ensure that the mystery was hidden not only from the Jews, but from demons. Joseph's genealogy was also valid for Mary since they were of the same tribe and family.[6] Mary remained a virgin after the birth of Jesus. "Mary," he tells us, "had brought, from her side, for the divine conception of the Child all that mothers can bring to the birth of children born of them."[7]

Mary stirs S.'s admiration: "What can one contemplate more divine than the Mother of God, or superior to her? To approach her is to approach a holy land and to attain to heaven. In fact she belonged by nature to mankind, and was of the same essence as us, though she was pure of all stain and immaculate and she produced from her womb as from heaven the God who became flesh, because she conceived and gave birth in a manner altogether divine."[8]

S. likes images such as "root of the true vine of which we are become the branches,"[9] or vine from which the grape has grown without seed, to signify Mary. He insisted on the *virginitas in partu* (qv) and to relate it to the Bible he used the image of the closed door from Ezek 44:2, linking it with Is 7:14 "the birth of God, of Emmanuel born of the Virgin, who did not undo even after his birth the closure of the virginal door."[10] Again speaking of the "seal of virginity which this birth did not even violate," S. suggests that this is mysterious, secret and one cannot talk of it: "so astonished by this prodigy, someone will cry out: 'How awesome is this place, it is the gate of heaven'."[11] Again it is the typology of the detached stone, Dan 2:34, which he singles out.[12] But three OT types appeal especially to him: the burning bush, which represents "the union of God the Word with the flesh, or the indwelling in the holy Virgin, so that it should appear, if but feebly, how the human flesh had borne the proximity and indwelling which no one approaches without being absorbed, consumed or perishing";[13] the spiritual mountain, which is in contrast with the OT Sinai, revealing the glory of the Eternal One, but in the new covenant "the Virgin, shining and resplendent through the purity and descent of the Holy Spirit," the mountain which does not have God merely on its summit, but within it;[14] the Holy of Holies, within which everything symbolises Christ, especially the Ark of the Covenant, image of the flesh taken from Mary by Christ like ours but "alone free and withdrawn from the corruption of sin."[15]

S. insinuates a universal role for Mary, but does not elaborate it. In one of the hymns Mary is "the gate of heaven," as "the root of the Resurrection," a different context from the previous use of this image, one in which the author can invite us to pray to her or pray to God through her.[16] Elsewhere he says that the "memory of the Virgin awakens our souls, leading them to consider from what irreconcilable enmity, from what *katastrasis* or condition of war so to speak, to what peace, to what divine familiarity and to what association we have been called through her intervention."[17]

S. shows Mary amidst the elect rejoicing while her Son is on the altar, high priest, sacrifice and victim.[18] He extolled virginity above the married state, but wished to safeguard the latter's dignity: "Since you have been deemed worthy, women of such an honour [he is speaking of the superiority of the second Adam taken from woman over the first from whom the woman was taken] which is first and principal, by the mediation of the Virgin Mother of God, give then to your husbands very wise advice which will lead them to eternal life."[19]

Mary was the glory of her sex. Like Origen, S. attributes a prophetic role to Mary, Commenting on Is 8:3,4 he says: "But who is the prophetess mentioned in the divine books, who brought forth a son called 'The spoil speeds, the prey hastes', a son who as soon as he is born, before he can say papa or mamma, pillages and strips his enemies, if it is not the Mother of God, the Virgin who gave birth to Emmanuel, who from his birth according to the flesh overthrew the calumniator, taking the power of Damascus and carrying off the plunder of Samaria? These words symbolically and, as it were, antonomastically stand for idiolatry . . ."[20]

In the same Hom 14, S. speaks of Mary as apostle and martyr: "On the other hand she is an apostle as she will be called rightly and it will be said that she surpasses all the apostles." With a reference to Acts 1:14 he concludes: "What nation has not been taught by her?"[21] He shows in a truly magnificent passage, patriarchs, prophets, apostles, martyrs in heaven, each seeing a special title to honour her—patriarchs the fulfilment of their hope in giving Christ, prophets the illumination of their prophecies ("she who revealed things secret, hidden, unknown"), apostles recognising the principle of their preaching, martyrs the example (to follow) in their struggles and their crowns. He concludes: "Doctors of the Church, on the other hand, and pastors of Christ's sheep honour her as the one who seals the mouth of heresy and who, from a drinkable and pure spring, causes floods of orthodoxy to gush forth, and in the first place above all dispels the darkness of Manicheism."[22]

By us on earth, the holy Mother of God is honoured by most remarkable means—"she who more than all the saints can send up prayers on our behalf, who sheds glory on us who have obtained her as the ornament of our race." The thought is filled out with a wealth of biblical imagery, all centred on Christ: "What honour then shall we render to the Mother of God, or rather to God who became incarnate of her for our salvation? That is where she finds honour, sacrifice, holocaust."[23]

Finally from this remarkable little known Marian theologian, an idea which anticipates LG 65: "For I was born in the flesh of the Holy Spirit and of a virgin mother and you also will be born not of blood, nor of the flesh, nor of the will of man, but of the Holy Spirit and of water, and you, none the less to have a share in my grace, but for me, on the contrary, it was to have a share in your nature."[24] Elsewhere he couples the Pauline idea of the first-born from the dead and the hope of resurrection, with birth from the Holy Spirit and the Virgin.[25]

[1]Cf. J. Lebon, *Le monophysisme sévérien* (Louvain, 1909); id., *La christologie du monophysisme sévérien*, in Grillmeier-Bacht, *Das Konzil von Chalkedon*, (Wurzburg, 1959), 433-455, 452-465; ClavisG, 327-345. [2]*Hom 67*, PO 8, 349-367, Syrian text with Fr. tr. M. Brière. [3]Cf. M. Brière, PO 29, 7-72; *Hom 14*, PO 38, 400-415, M. Brière, F. Graffin, C. Lash, J. M. Sauget; J. Lécuyer, C.S.Sp., *L'Homélie Cathedrale 67 de Sévère d'Antioche*, Zagreb Congress, III, 1-15. [4]*Liber contra impium Grammaticum*, II, ch. 15, ed. J. Lebon, CSCO, ser. 4, p. 105; cf. *Hom. 58*, PO 219. [5]*Critique du tome de Julien d'Halicarnasse* (tr. R. Hespel), CSCO, 245, *Script. Syri*, 105, p. 18. [6]*Ref.* St. Ignatius, *Hom.* 94, PO 25, 69-71; on Mary's ancestry, *ibid.*, 65-66; *Hom. 63*, PO 8, 297. [7]*Contra Additiones Juliani*, (tr. Hespel), CSCO, *Script.Syri*, 125, p. 132. [8]*Hom. 67*, PO 8, 350. [9]PO 8, 364. [10]*Contra Additiones Juliani*, 136. [11]PO 8, 35. [12]*ibid.*, 354. [13]*Critique du tome de Julien d'Halicarnasse*, 111. [14]PO 8, 353-54. [15]*ibid.*, 357-358. [16]Hymn 117, James of Edessa, *The Hymns of Severus of Antioch and others*, ed. tr. E. Brooks, PO 6, 156-157. [17]PO 8, 365. [18]Hymn 230, PO 7, 685. [19]*Hom. 63*, in PO 8, 303. [20]PO 38, 4, 403. [21]*Ibid.*, 8, 405. [22]*Ibid.*, 10, 407. [23]*Ibid.*, 19, 413. [24]*Hom. 66*, PO 8, 332. [25]*L'Apologie de Philalèthe*, CSCO 136, 108.

SHRINES OF OUR LADY

Shrines of Our Lady have originated in different ways: as sites of images or icons with a particular history; from belief that an apparition of Our Lady occurred at the spot; from a legend or a story of her prayer on behalf of a saintly person or the local community. A shrine or holy peace accords with religious psychology; it preserves the veneration of images approved by the Church; theologically it may manifest the sentiment of the faithful. Shrines have been the starting-point for faith, personal and corporate, and the circumstance of heroic witness. Guadalupe is the origin of Christian Mexico. Czestochowa is the hearth-stone of Polish Catholicism; it was in August, 1956, a year of economic distress and political oppression, the scene of an unexampled public act of faith: over one million people assembled from all over the country.

Recent Popes have encouraged devotion at Marian shrines, issuing letters of commendation, and sending Legates to important religious ceremonies: 400 Marian shrines were represented at Rome for the proclamation of the queenship of Mary on November 1, 1954. On November 21, 1964, Paul VI, before the promulgation of LG, was joined in a concelebrated Mass by 24 bishops in whose dioceses are important Marian shrines. On May 1, 1971 he sent a special Apostolic Letter to Rectors of Marian shrines throughout the world.

[1]Cf. G. M. Besutti, O.S.M., "Santuari, apparizioni, culto locale, ex voto. Rassegna bibliografica 1962-1971," MM 34(1973), 42-141.

SIGNUM MAGNUM (13 May, 1967)

Paul VI's Encyclical issued on the fiftieth anniversary of the events at Fatima in 1917.[1] It is an extension of the teaching of Vatican II and of the ideas in the Pope's proclamation of Mary as Mother of the Church. He deals with Mary's spiritual motherhood, does not hesitate to relate Jn 19:25-27 to this (see WOMAN IN), urges imitation of Mary as a most effective form of devotion to her. He sketches Mary's place in history, points to the influence she can exert in the matter of Christian unity, recalls the consecration of mankind to the Immaculate Heart of Mary and urges each one to renew and live more faithfully "by a life ever more in conformity with the divine will" his personal consecration.

[1]AAS 59(1967), 465-475; cf. H.-M. Manteau-Bonamy, O.P., *La Vierge Marie et le Saint Esprit* (Paris, 1971); J. M. Salgado, O.M.I., "La maternité spirituelle de la T.S.V. Marie," EphMar 20(1970), 343-44.

SIMEON METAPHRASTES (fl. a. 1000) — See Supplement, p. 386.

SIXTUS IV (1414-84, Pope 1471)

A Franciscan Pope, S., despite the controversy and intellectual tension surrounding the doctrine of the Immaculate Conception, took important steps to further its theological development.[1] An active Dominican theologian, Vincenzo Bandinelli, Master General of his order, prompted the papal intervention, B. published anonymously in 1475 a book *Libellus recollectorius auctoritatum de veritate Conceptionis B.V.M.* which, with 200 texts drawn mostly from the Fathers and allegedly opposed to the doctrine, stigmatised it in language extreme and even abusive—"false, impious, rash, more dangerous than the heresies of Pelagius, Celestius and Julian, a pestilent, infamous, diabolical opinion, a lie from the lips of the insane, undermining Catholic dogma." The Pope, in 1476, held a public debate between B. and the Master General of the Conventual Franciscans, Francesco of Brescia. He congratulated the latter on his victory, naming him Samson—B. was nicknamed Goliath! On 27

February of that year S., by the Constitution *Cum Praecelsa*, approved and indulgenced an Office and Mass in honour of the Immaculate Conception, which had been composed by a Veronese prelate, Leonardo de Nogarolis. On 4 October, 1480, by the Constitution *Libenter* he approved and indulgenced the Office for the Immaculate Conception composed by Bernardine de Bustis. Bandinelli was persistent in his opposition to the doctrine. By the Constitution *Grave nimis* (1482), S. condemned those who taxed defenders of the doctrine with heresy and excommunicated them if they continued to do so; but he threatened the same penalties on those who accused opponents of the doctrine of heresy—"for neither the Roman Church nor the Apostolic See have yet decided the question." He stated in the Constitution that "the Holy Roman Church publicly and solemnly celebrates the feast of the Conception of the Immaculate and ever Virgin Mary." As the document was directed mostly to Lombard theologians and preachers, S. issued on 4 September, 1483, another Constitution *Grave nimis*, repeating the same teaching. In twelve other Constitutions or Apostolic Briefs he granted spiritual favours of one kind or another in regard to the feast.

[1]Cf. DS 1400, 1425-26; esp. Ch. Sericoli, O.F.M., *Immaculata B.M.Virginis Conceptio juxta Xysti IV Constitutiones* (Sibenik, Rome, 1945); G. M. Roschini, O.S.M., *Maria Santissima*, I, 253-254; and III, 187-192; R. Laurentin, *L'action du Saint Siège par rapport au problème de l'Immaculée Conception*, V.I. II, 1-98.

SOCIETIES

Groups of theologians specialising in Marian studies have been active since the nineteen-thirties. The Flemish Society, *Mariale Dagen*, was founded in 1931 by Mgr. Bittremieux. A Marianist, B. Morineau, had the chief role in launching the *Société française d'Études mariales* in 1934; it was soon joined by a remarkable group of scholars. In the fifties, the proceedings of its annual sessions ranked very high in Marian theological publications; some bulletins were mentioned in the official documentation of Vatican II. At the Spanish national Marian congress in Saragossa in 1940, it was decided to establish a Spanish Mariological Society. Fr. N. Garcia Garces, C.M.F., was chiefly active in the initial organisation. He was joined by other theologians of repute, some of

whom would also collaborate in the review which he later founded, *Ephemerides Mariologicae*, 1950. The Society's proceedings appear in *Estudios Marianos*. The American Mariological Society has also a regular annual publication, *Marian Studies*, since it was launched at Washington in 1949 by Fr. Juniper Carol, O.F.M. He was fortunate to have the help of biblical scholars in an age of biblical renewal in the United States. Fr. Karl Feckes, a specialist in the writings of M. J. Scheeben, was instrumental in beginning a German Mariological Society which has brought out occasional volumes. Portuguese, Canadian, Colombian and French-speaking Belgian societies have also been noted. Due to the influence of the leading Polish Marian theologian of recent times, B. Przybylski, O.P. (d. 1979) a group of theologians in Poland maintain continuous Marian studies, with occasional assemblies.

SONG OF SONGS, THE

The interpretation of this sublime love song is a task for biblical scholars. Summaries of their work and bibliographies are readily available.[1] Here we are concerned with the Marian interpretation of the composition.[2]

From early times, individual vv were applied to Mary. St. Ambrose was probably the first to do so, in the sense of the Spirit's action, of Mary's fruitful virginity or giving phrases a collective meaning to fit A.'s Mary-Church theory; he uses vv 1:1,2,4; 3:11; 7:1,2. St. Jerome (*qv*) interpreted 4:21 of Mary's virginity and 4:13 of the harmony of other virtues with her virginity. St. Epiphanius (*qv*) also adapts 4:12 to the theme of virginity. Apponius, an early fifth century Jewish Christian writer in Rome, in the course of a commentary on S. applies many passages to Mary. St. Isidore (*qv*) continues with the adaptation of 4:12 to the virginity. St. Germanus (*qv*) finds 3:6 and 4:8 suitable to the opening of his homily on the Presentation in the Temple. His Eastern contemporary, St. John of Damascus (*qv*) in one homily on the Nativity of Mary and in the homilies on the Dormition quotes S. frequently. The quotations seem to run smoothly with the saint's thought on Mary's uniqueness, her attributes and privileges; he uses vv 1:2, 12, 13; 2:1,2,3,5,11,12; 3:6,11; 4:7,8,9,10,12,13,14; 5:1,3; 6:8,9.

In the West, Ambrose Autpert (*qv*) quotes 2:11-14 in reference to Mary's assumption; he sees the "dove" as a symbol of charity. Paul the Deacon (qv) and Paschasius Radbert (qv) invoke the Mary-Church theme in their interpretation of S.

The twelfth century was a great age of Marian commentaries on S. The fact that lessons for the feast of the Assumption and for the Nativity of Mary were chosen from the work may have influenced this trend.[3] There was something deeper, a unique sense of a compelling presence and a powerful movement of the soul of Europe. It was a world which like Byzantium and 17th century Europe seemed to draw its power under God from Our Lady. S. expressed its love in fitting language. The Benedictine, Rupert of Deutz (qv), was probably the first to interpret the work wholly in terms of Mary.[4] About the same time Honorius of Autun (qv) composed his work, *Sigillum Beatae Mariae ubi exponuntur Cantica Canticorum*;[5] he expounds the lessons for the Assumption and gives a short Marian commentary of S. Thereafter application of vv of S. to Mary is fairly frequent. Surprisingly St. Bernard (qv) shows restraint and though he mentions Mary occasionally in the course of his 86 sermons on S. he generally uses another biblical work and almost invariably avoids applying the text of S. to her.[6] Hugh of St. Victor (qv) in a sermon for the feast of the Assumption, gives a Marian commentary on the passages from S. used in the Office.[7] Richard of St. Victor (qv) in his explanation of S. devotes ch. 39 to Mary.[8]

The Victorines were Canons Regular of St. Augustine. The longest Marian commentary of S. was written by Philip of Harvengt (qv) one of the first Premonstratensians.[9] Godfrey of St. Victor (d. 1194) in a sermon for the Nativity of Mary offers a threefold interpretation of S., individual, ecclesiological, and Marian.[10] Thomas of Perseigne (d.1200) in his commentary on the work does likewise.[11] Alan of Lille (qv), a Cistercian, in his commentary relates S. to the Church and especially to Mary.[12]

Somewhat distinctive is the contribution of William of Newburgh (qv).[13] Whatever influence Rupert of Deutz had on other commentators, William was unaware of his or any other work and he was prompted to the Marian interpretation by Abbot Roger of Byland. William of Weyarn used Rupert's commentary; his own has not yet been published.

Thereafter individual verses will be from time to time applied to Mary by writers on the Immaculate Conception—Francis Mayronis for example—or in the liturgy of the feast. One Eastern writer, Matthew Cantacuzenus (qv), in his interpretation gave prominence to Mary while still applying images to the Church.[14] In subsequent literature two writers deserve mention, Denis the Carthusian (qv)[15] and F. Quirino de Salazar (qv).[16] Each has much to say on a Marian sense of S.

If to the Christian S. expresses Christ's love for his Church, then since Mary is a type of the Church, the figurative Marian interpretation is valid and may powerfully help those with true mystical endowment.

[1]Cf. *Jerome Commentary*, 1, 506-510, (R. E. Murphy, O.Carm.); *New Catholic Commentary*, 522-530 (P. P. Saydon and G. Castellino, S.D.B.). [2]Cf. A. Rivera, C.M.F., "Sentido mariologico del Cantar del los Cantares? *EphMar*, 1(1951), 437-468, and 2(1952), 25-42; J. Beumer, *Zeitschrift fur kath. Theol.* 76(1954), 411-39, *Die marianische Deutung des Hohen Liedes in der Frühscholastik*; John G. Gorman, S.M., *William of Newburgh's Explanatio sacri epithalamii in matrem sponsi, A Commentary on the Canticle of Canticles*, Fribourg, *Spicilegium Friburgense*, 6, ch. 3, 36-57; Fidelis Buck, S.J., *The Marian interpretation of the Song of Songs in the Middle Ages*, typescript of paper communicated to International Mariological Congress, Rome, 1976. [3]Cf. J. Beumer, *op.cit.* [4]CCCM 26; PL 168, 837-962. [5]PL 172, 495-518. [6]Cf. 21 extracts from sermons *apud* P. Bernard, O. Cist., *St. Bernard et Notre Dame* (Paris, Sept Fons, 1952) 388-406. [7]PL 177, 1209-1222. [8]PL 196, esp. 516-518. [9]PL 203, 181-490. [10]Paris, Mazarine, MS 1002, 107 and 157. [11]PL 206, 21-862; cf. R. Laurentin, *Traité* 1, 155; J. Leclercq, O.S.B., *Mediaeval Studies* 10(1948), 204-209. [12]PL 210, 51-110. [13]*Commentary on the Canticle*, ed. J. C. Gorman, Fribourg, 1960. [14]PG 152, 997-1084. [15]*Enarratio in Canticum Canticorum de B. Maria, Opera* 7, 291-447. [16]*Expositio in Canticum Canticorum*, Cologne, 1612.

SOPHRONIUS, ST. (d. 638)

Patriarch of Jerusalem, in the history of Christology S. was a resolute opponent of Sergius, the Monothelite Patriarch of Constantinople.[1] The *Life of Mary of Egypt*, (BHG 1042), which contains a prayer to Mary, attributed to him in Migne's Patrology, is of doubtful authenticity. *Triodion* also in Migne is by Joseph the Hymnographer. Relevant to Marian theology are the homilies *In Christi Natalitia*, (BHG 807), *In Annunt Mariae*, (BHG 1098), the *Oratio III in Hypapante*, (BHG 808), and the *Epistola synodica ad Sergium*.

Byzantine exaltation of the *Theotokos* finds full expression in these works, especially in the homily on the Annunciation: S. puts his ideas on the lips of Gabriel and Mary, each as it were expanding the dialogue given by Lk. The well-known themes recur: "Truly you are *blessed among women* for you changed the curse on Eve into a blessing, since you achieved that Adam who first lay stricken by the malediction should through you receive a blessing. Truly you are *blessed among women* since through you the blessing of the Father shone on men and freed them from the ancient curse. Truly you are *blessed among women* for through you your ancestors found salvation. For you were to bring forth a Saviour who made divine salvation available to them."[2] S. extols Mary's primacy over all the choirs of angels concluding "in a word you far outdistanced every creature, for you shone beyond every creature in purity and received within yourself the creator of all creatures, you bore him in your womb and brought him forth and alone of all creatures became the Mother of God."[3] Expounding then the wonders of the divine motherhood S. concludes: "For from you joy was not only given to men, but is also bestowed on the heavenly powers."

It is not surprising that S. has been claimed as a defender of the Immaculate Conception; he states it almost in Western terms. "Others before you have flourished with outstanding holiness. But to none as to you has the fullness of grace been given. None has been endowed with happiness as you, none adorned with holiness like yours, none brought to such great magnificence as yours; no one was ever possessed *beforehand* by purifying grace as were you . . . And this deservedly, for no one came as close to God as you did; no one was enriched with God's gifts as you were; no one shared God's grace as you did."[4] S., in a word, is one of the greatest exponents in history of Mary's primacy of excellence.

---

[1]Works, PG 87c, 3201ff; EMBP, 1283-1339; Cf. ClavisG III, 422-431. R. Laurentin, *Traité* I, 168; H. Usener, *Weinacht-spredigtes Sophronios, Rheinisches Museum*, N.F., 41(1886), 501-551; *id. Sophronii de praesentatione Domini sermo*, ed. University of Bonn, August, 1889, pp. 1-18; M. Jugie, A.A., "Saint Sophrone et l'Immaculée Conception," *Rev. August.* 1(1910), 565-74; *id., L'Immaculée Conception*, 99-105; G. Bardy, DTC 14,2, 2379-83; Beck, 434-36; H. Graef, *Mary* I, 139-40. [2]*In SS Deip Annunt.* 22 PL 87c, 3241. [3]*Ibid.*, 3237. [4]*Ibid.*, 3248.

SPIRIT, THE HOLY

Since Vatican II there has been increasing interest in the theology of the Holy Spirit, with special attention by Marian theologians to the relationship between Mary and the Holy Spirit.[1]

Sacred Scripture: The theology of OT is incomplete on the Trinity and, therefore, on the Spirit of God. Embryonic ideas grow to fullness in NT. The *Ruah* in the OT descends on judges, kings, especially prophets, is promised to the whole people of God, and will be given especially to the Messiah. Change is perceptible in the first NT reference. John the Baptist will be filled with the Holy Spirit, even, adds the angel, "from his mother's womb" (Lk 1:15); this is new; there is no explicit reference to the Spirit in Jer 1:5.

The greatest innovation, which remains unexampled, was in the mystery of the Incarnation. This is the only instance of a descent by the Spirit on a mother before the conception of her child, with the conception attributed beforehand to the Spirit, the sole instance where there is preparatory dialogue followed by a free act of acceptance. Mary, it is assumed, knew about the Spirit, an assumption not made in OT times. When Lk records her words, (1:38,40,46-55, 2:48 or deeds (1:39,56, 2:19,51), he does not think it necessary to refer to the Spirit as with others whose words and deeds he reports. Having received him in such plenitude in the moment of the Incarnation she is deemed to be one with him thereafter.

There is a fundamental reason for this: "In Lk I-II the Spirit which in turn fills the precursor, Elisabeth, Zechariah, Simeon (1:15,17,41,67; 2:25,26,27) is obviously the *OT Spirit of prophecy:* he makes John the Baptist a new Elijah; he informs Simeon about the imminent coming of the Messiah; he impels Elizabeth, Zechariah and Simeon *to speak.* The Spirit who intervenes in 1:35 for the virginal conception of Jesus is the *creative Spirit, the source of a new economy,* the same One who will intervene in the public ministry of Jesus and will show himself powerfully at Pentecost, the One of whom Is 32:15 already spoke (cf. the intervention of the Spirit and of power from on high in Lk 1:35; 4:1; 4:14; 24:49; Acts 1:8; 10:38). Attached by the infancy narratives to the ancient economy, the Virgin Mary bears within her, thanks to the action of the creative Spirit, the very source of the new economy."[2]

With the others Mary awaited the coming of the Spirit at Pentecost her special position emphasised by the title recalling the OT privileged role of the queen mother, *Mother of Jesus*, even the little word *kai* separating her from others in the group (Acts 1:14). The coming in her case was a second one, parallel—motherhood of Christ in the first instance, a maternal office in the messianic community, also born of the Spirit, in the second. R. Laurentin insists that according to Acts 1:14 Mary was seen within the messianic community, the Judeo-Christian body, 120 in all; she belonged to two groups mentioned by Lk in Acts I-II, his account of the infancy of the Church as Lk I-II narrates the infancy of Christ. Yet the meaningful title, Mother of Jesus, sets her not only apart but above the other witnesses of the Resurrection. There is still much to explore in the text, neglected until recently. In 20,000 titles listed in the volumes of G. M. Besutti's *Bibliographia Mariana*, only one deals with the text and that in the context of the Eucharist.

There is much also to explore in the Johannine texts, the theophanies recounted at Cana and on Calvary, explained latterly in the light of Sinai: revelations of the new creation in which the Spirit's role is so important—it is implicit in the narratives.

St. Paul's well-known words in Gal 4:4, "But when the time had fully come, God sent forth his Son, born of a woman, born under the law, to redeem those who were under the law, so that we might receive adoption as sons," are followed immediately by "And because you are sons, God has sent the Spirit of his Son into our hearts, crying 'Abba! Father!'" This action of the Spirit in the souls of the adopted sons is suggestive; so is the proximity of the idea to the thought of Mary's motherhood. So is Jesus' reference to the new birth in the Spirit (Jn 3:5,6,8), if it is taken with his own conception by the Spirit's intervention in Lk 1:35.

History: In the early centuries commentary on the essential gospel datum, Lk 1:35, was mainly Christological. Theodotus of Ancyra speaks of Mary's "entire anointing by the holiness of the Holy Spirit."[3] Similar brief snatches of thought, meaningful titles, occur in St. Jerome. Mary is the "temple of God," "seat of the Holy Spirit."[4] And also in St. Ambrose, for whom Mary is the "temple of the Holy Spirit."[5] Prudentius was the first to imply that Mary was the Spouse of the Spirit: "The unwedded Virgin wedded the Spirit."[6] Isidore of Seville first spoke of her as the "sanctuary (*sacrarium*) of the Holy Spirit."[7] Ildefonsus of Toledo composed a prayer in which the roles of Jesus, the Spirit and Mary are shown: "I beg you, I beg you, O holy Virgin, that I may have Jesus from the Spirit from whom you conceived Jesus. May my soul receive Jesus through the Spirit, through whom your flesh conceived the same Jesus. Let it be granted to me to know Jesus from the Spirit, from whom it was given to you to know, to have and to bring forth Jesus. May I in my lowliness speak exalted things of Jesus in that Spirit, in whom you confess yourself to be the handmaid of the Lord, choosing that it be done unto you according to the angel's word. May I love Jesus in that Spirit in which you adore him as Lord, contemplate him as your Son."[8]

St. Bede the Venerable analyses the twofold operation of the Spirit in the moment of the Annunciation, sanctifying Mary and creating the Redeemer's body;[9] her *fiat* is a prayer that he may make her worthy of the divine mysteries. There was, in subsequent ages, occasional advertence to such mysteries, and clarification too, which eliminated a problem already raised in the time of St. Augustine: How did the Spirit intervene in the creation of Christ's humanity without becoming his father? Mary, in medieval times, was associated with the Spirit in the prayers of the Liturgy. Some writers spoke of her as Spouse of the Spirit. Few saw her union with him in the terms used by Theophanes of Nicaea: "From the outset she was united to the Spirit, author of life: and she did not taste the least particle of existence itself without participating in the Spirit, for participation in the Spirit had become for her participation in being."[10]

Mary was given the title "Prophetess" many times by the Fathers—I. Marracci counted 40 instances; this would clearly be action of the Spirit upon her. If she was more frequently invoked by Catholics than the Spirit, there is no evidence that they identified her with him, made her a goddess.

Without receding altogether the Spirit was in the background of Catholic Marian piety, so that St. Louis Marie de Montfort appears singular through his emphasis on the union between the two.[11] The theological basis of the relationship was expounded by M. J. Scheeben.[12]

The emphasis on the Church as institution, the hardening of the theology of appropriation in manualistic theology, a certain dessication of spirituality proved unfavourable to a personalist approach to the Holy Spirit.

Teaching Authority: Three phases are discernible: prior to Vatican II, within Vatican II, and since its completion. Before the Council there are some references to the Holy Spirit in papal documents. Mary is called the spouse of the Holy Spirit by Leo XIII and Pius XII. There are other occasional mentions, no substantial doctrine.

The first Marian *schema* at the Council was sparing on the subject: Mary in prayer before the coming of the Spirit was referred to in terms similar to the final text. In 1963 nothing was said on the subject in the assembly.

In the *schema* submitted to the Council Fathers for debate in September 1964, there were some brief new passages on the Holy Spirit and some strange omissions: the credal statement, "incarnate by the Holy Spirit from the Virgin Mary"(52); "the Catholic Church taught by the Holy Spirit honours her"(53); "fashioned by the Holy Spirit into a kind of new substance and new creature"(56); the central role is attributed to the Spirit in the exposition of the Mary Church-typology (63,64).

The surprising omissions were Lk 1:35 and Mt 1:18 and the other verses in Lk's infancy narrative which reveal the Spirit's constant presence and influence, Lk 1:41,67; 2:25. The omissions were publicly regretted by one of the draftsmen, Mgr. G. Philips, at a meeting of the French Society for Marian Studies.[13]

In the September debate, Archbishop van Lierde pointed out that the text "was almost silent on the cooperation between Mary and the Holy Spirit, a cooperation that does not cease with the birth of Christ, she remains the model of our ascent to God and of our apostolic zeal"; in the Spirit she helps and assists us in our zeal.[14]

Archbishop (later Cardinal) Jaeger of Paderborn devoted most of his remarkable speech to an appeal to incorporate in the text a passage— drafted by him—on the relation between Mary and the Spirit; it was centred on Mary as type of the Church, and drew on patristic sources, on papal Encyclicals and on M. J. Scheeben.[15] The only relevant addition made, however, was attributed in the official report to Cardinal Suenens. It is found in LG 65. The Church, in her apostolic work, can look to the Mother of Christ, "conceived by the Holy Spirit and born of the Virgin, so that through the Church Christ may be born and grow in the hearts of the faithful also."

Between the third and fourth sessions of the Council an important article appeared in the *Journal of Ecumenical Studies* written from W.C.C. by N. Nissiotis.[16] It voiced the dissatisfaction felt by the Orthodox at the poverty of teaching on the Holy Spirit by Vatican II thus far in subjects like the Church where the Easterns see his primary role. Fortunately two Council documents, on the Missions and the priesthood, were being rewritten in the interval between the third and fourth sessions. Note was taken of the criticism. In the decree on the missionary activity of the Church we read: "For it was from Pentecost that the Acts of the Apostles took their origin. In a similar way Christ was conceived when the Holy Spirit came upon the Virgin Mary. Thus too Christ was impelled to the work of his ministry when the same Holy Spirit descended upon him in prayer." (art. 4). The parallel between the Annunciation and Pentecost implied in LG 59 is here made explicit. The decree on the ministry and life of priests also marks an advance on LG in one point. Whereas therein Mary is said to have "served the mystery of the Redemption" "with the grace of Almighty God" (56), now we read: "They [priests] can always find a model of such docility [to the Holy Spirit] in the Blessed Virgin Mary. Led by the Holy Spirit, she devoted herself entirely to the mystery of man's redemption." (art. 18). The constitution on divine revelation was also issued in the last session of the Council. It says that "tradition develops in the Church with the help of the Holy Spirit," and describes one way by which this happens as "the contemplation and study made by believers, who treasure these things in their hearts." The references to Lk 2:19,51 added to the text strengthen the implication that Mary is the model of this process.

Since the Council, the Teaching Authority has had strong stimulus to pronounce on the living Spirit. Paul VI (*qv*) did so, notably twice. In the Encyclical *Marialis Cultus* (*qv*) he summarised the teaching of the Fathers on the subject (n.26), and, recalling a certain criticism of modern spiritual writings because they lacked a complete doctrine of the Holy Spirit (a matter he left to the judgment of the competent) he urged pastors especially and theologians to take up the subject. "From this research the basis of the hidden relationship between the Spirit of God and the Virgin of Nazareth will stand out conspicuously as will their common action in the Church. From these truths of the faith more profoundly pondered will come a piety more intensely lived." (art. 27).

In the letter *E'con sentimenti* (*qv*) to Cardinal Suenens, Legate to the Marian Congress in Rome 1975, Pope Paul gave the lengthiest and possibly most significant teaching on the theme of Mary and the Spirit so far to issue from the Teaching Authority. The subject of the Congress was the Holy Spirit and Mary. What was significant about the Pope's letter was the detailed explanation of all the events and words in the life of Mary in the light of the Spirit's union with and action on her.

Recent literature: The contemporary interest in the Holy Spirit was evident in the world charismatic congress which was being held in Rome at the same time, for the feast of Pentecost, as the Marian assembly. The Pope's letter matched the scholarly and devotional interest in this theme. Most of the works cited in the bibliography to this article are the product of this movement. The French Society studied the subject at its annual meetings for three years, exploring every aspect of it—biblical, patristic, historical, conciliar, spiritual and ecumenical. A contributor, H. M. Manteau-Bonamy, O.P., has, in his book, contended that Vatican II, for the first time in the Latin Church, taught a visible mission of the third person of the Trinity on the Blessed Virgin at the Annunciation.[17]

Participants at the third meeting of the French Society were Henry Chavannes, Swiss Calvinist, and Paul Evdokimov, disciple of Sergius Bulgakov (*qv*). The latter's contribution to our subject was remarkable. Twenty years before Vatican II, he taught a plenary mission of the Spirit at the Annunciation: "The Annunciation was a complete and therefore hypostatic descent of the Holy Spirit and his entry to the Virgin Mary . . . by his coming into the Virgin Mary identifies himself in a way with her through her God-motherhood . . . he does not at all leave her after the birth of Christ, but remains forever with her in the full force of the Annunciation."[18] This was not, Bulgakov reminds us in his *The Wisdom of God*, an incarnation of the Holy Ghost. "He abides, however, in the ever-virgin Mary as in a holy temple, while her human personality seems to become transparent to him and to provide him with a human countenance."[19] He distinguished stages in the Spirit's action on Mary, one a peculiar and exclusive sanctification, the other the descent by which he consecrated her whole bodily being and made of her the Mother of God.[20] "If there were not an eternal motherless generation from the Father, there would not be a manless generation from the mother. In this the one who joins both 'generations' is the Holy Spirit, in his relation to the Son, whom he eternally bears as the Only-begotten of the Father and, in the strength of this communicates the power of generation to his Mother. Therefore the seedless conception is accomplished by the presence of the Holy Spirit."[21]

[1]For bibliography cf. esp. D. Fernandez, C.M.F. and A. Rivera, C.M.F., EphMar 28(1978), 266-73; collective works, BSFEM, *Le Saint Esprit et Marie*, 1968, '69, '70; *La Madonna*, 5-6, September-December, 1975; *La Madonna e lo Spirito Santo nell'opera salvifica; Lo Spirito Santo e Maria Santissima*, ed. Mgr. P. C. van Lierde, Vatican Press, 1976. *Maria Santissima e lo Spirito Santo*, (Ed. Centro Volontari della Sofferenza, Rome, 1976); EstM 41(1977), *Maria y el Espiritu Santo*; S. Bulgakov, *Le Paraclet*, tr. C. Andronikof (Paris, 1944), 238-239; J. M. Alonso, C.M.F., "Hacia una Mariologia Trinitaria: Dos escuelas," EstM 10(1950) 141-91, and 12(1952), 237-67; *id.*, "Mariologia y pneumatologia," EphMar 21(1971), 115-21 and 22(1972), 395-405; S. Ragazzini, "L'Immacolata e lo Spirito Santo," EphMar 10(1960), 223-55; E. J. Ricuarte, "El Espiritu Santo y la Virgen Maria," *Regina Mundi*, 23(1962), 191-205; T. M. Bartolomei, "Le relazioni di Maria Madre di Dio con lo Spirito Santo," EphMar 13(1963), 5-40; H. Muhlen, *Mystica Persona. Die Kirche als das Mysterium der heilsgeschichtlichen Identität des Heiligen Geistes in Christus und den Christen* (Paderborn, 1968, 2nd ed.), 461-94; R. Laurentin, *Esprit Saint et théologie mariale*, NRT 89(1967), 26-42; *id.*, *Pentecotisme chez les catholiques* (Paris, 1974), 241-50; M. Garrido Bonano, O.S.B., "Actuación del Espiritu Santo en las almas a traves de Maria," MM 32(1971), 227-54; E. Piacentini, "L'Immacolata Concezione nel pensiero del P. Massimiliano Kolbe. Rapporto tra Mariologia e Pneumatologia," MM 33(1971), 123-82; J. M. Salgado, O.M.I., "Pneumatologie et mariologie: bilan actuel et orientations possibles," *Divin.* 15(1971), 421-53; H. M. Manteau-Bonamy, O.P., *La Vierge et le Saint Esprit, commentaire doctrinal du ch. VIII LG* (2nd ed. Paris, 1971); C. Graves, *The Holy Spirit in the Theology of Sergius Bulgakov*, Dissert. Basle University, World Council of Churches, Geneva, 1972; A. Schmemann, "Our Lady and the Holy Spirit," MSt 23(1972), 69-78; L. Pfaller and J. Alberts, *Mary is Pentecostal*, (Pecos, New Mexico, 1973); H. M. Guidon, *Marie et le Saint Esprit* (Ottawa, 1974); L. J. (Cardinal) Suenens, *Une nouvelle Pentecôte* (Paris, 1974), 229-46; M. V. Blat, *La renovación carismatica a la luz de la*

Virgen Maria, (Managua, 1975); D. Fernandez, C.M.F., "El Espiritu Santo, Maria y la Vida Religiosa," *Claretianum*, 15(1975), 39-64; A. de Monléon, O.P., "L'Espirit et Marie à la lumière du Renouveau charismatique," CahMar 90(1973) 217-29; L. Scheffczyk, "Der trinitarischer Bezug des Mariengeheimnisses," *Catholica* 29(1975), 120-31; H. Holstein, S.J., "Le mystère de Marie et de l'Esprit," CahMar 102(1976), 67-92. G. M. Roschini, O.S.M., *Il Tuttosanto e la Tutta santa*. Relazioni tra Maria e lo Spirito Santo, I, *Quadro storico*, Rome, 1976; II, *Sintesi dottrinale*, Rome, 1977, K. Wittkemper, *Dreifaltigheit* and *Braut*, LexMar, 1148, 906-909; *Eph Mar* fasc. II-III, 1978; Mgr. van Lierde, ed., *Lo Spirito Santo e Maria Santissima* Symposium at Genazzano, 1969, Rome, Vatican Press, 1973; D. Bertetto, S.D.B., "L'azione propria dello Spirito Santo in Maria," MM 41(1979), p. 400-444. [2]A. Feuillet, P.S.S., "L'Esprit Saint et la Mère du Christ," BSFEM 25(1968), 56-57. [3]PG 77, 1400. [4]*Adv. Helv.* 6, PL 23, 191. [5]*In Luc, II*, 6, PL 15, 1635. [6]*Apotheosis*, v. 571, 2; CCL 126, 97. [7]*De Ortu et Obitu Patrum* 67, PL 83, 148C. [8]*De Virgin.* 10, PL 96, 95C. [9]*Hom. 1, 1*, CCL 122, p.18; cf. *In Luc*. 1, 1, CCL 120, p. 33,34. [10]*Serm. in SS. Deiparam*, ed. M. Jugie, Rome, 1935, 178-80. [11]*Treatise, Oeuvres Complètes*, Paris, 1966, p. 505-507. [12]Cf. art. S.V. [13]BSFEM, 25(1968), 16. [14]*Acta Synodalia Sacrosancti Concilii Oecumenici Vatican II*, Vol. III, *Periodus tertia*, Pars 1, 513ff; apud G. M. Besutti, MM, 28(1966), 86-87. [15]*Ibid.*, 517-519; Besutti, 90-92. [16]*2* (1965), *The main ecclesiological problems in the Second Vatican Council and the position of the Non-Roman Churches facing it*, 31-62, esp. p. 48. [17]*Op. cit.*, 16ff, and in BSFEM, 27(1970), 8-9. [18]*Le Paraclet*, tr. C. Andronikof, Paris, 1944, 238,9. [19]London, 1937, pp. 176,7. [20]*Ibid*. [21]*Kupina Neopalimaja*, p. 158, apud C. Graves, *The Holy Spirit in the Theology of Sergius Bulgakov*, Dissert. Basle University World Council of Churches, Geneva, 1972.

SPOUSE OF GOD (BRIDE OF GOD), MARY AS

Israel as the Bride of God is a constant theme in OT. Marriage was so often taken as the symbol of God's choice, God's predilection, God's fidelity, that once a woman appeared prominently in salvation history she was bound to be invested with the bridal role. The semitic habit of interchanging personal and corporate roles and attributes made the transference inevitable.[1] Nowhere in NT is Mary called Bride of God or of one of the divine persons. But at the stage of biblical theology, a comparative study of the Annunciation scene and certain OT passages discovers sponsal connotations in the dialogue between the archangel and Mary. Yet in the first centuries the theology of the new Eve developed from the Annunciation scene did not include the sponsal idea. Some authors have tried to trace the beginnings of a doctrine with the idea implied to Fathers as early as Origen, Athanasius of Alexandria and Cyril of Alexandria (qqv). St. Ephraem leaves no room for doubt. With him, Mary is the spouse of Christ, a form of the theory which arouses controversy.

A vague terminology which does not specify the divine person to whom Mary is espoused occurs in many of the Greek Fathers; she is spoken of as "God-wed" (*Theonymphos*). Among those who use this title is St. Germanus of Constantinople.[2] St. John of Damascus in a passage in *Munificentissimus Deus* calls Mary spouse of the Father: "It was fitting that the spouse whom the Father had taken to himself should live in the divine mansions."[3] The earliest specific reference to Mary as spouse of Christ in Greek literature may be in a sermon which is dated before 800.[4]

The Latin tradition already articulate in St. Peter Chrysologus is slow in the elaboration of a theory. P. speaks of Christ who "takes his own spouse and does not snatch one who belongs to another."[5] In the eighth century, Ambrose Autpert; in the ninth, Paschasius Radbert briefly express similar ideas. Already with Prudentius the idea of espousal to the Holy Spirit appears, *Innuba Virgo nubis Spiritui* (the Virgin who is marriageable is espoused to the Spirit), Rupert of Deutz applied the bridal image to the Father and the Son—"the best part of the first church, who merited to be the spouse of God the Father so as to be also the exemplar of the younger Church, the spouse of the Son of God and her own Son."[6] The idea of Mary as the spouse of the Father recurs in that age, as does the notion of Mary as spouse of the Holy Spirit—there was a tendency to reserve the title spouse of Christ to the Church. Spouse of the Father appealed to Ubertino of Casale (qv) and to the French school of spirituality, notably Bérulle. St. Louis Marie de Montfort and St. Lawrence of Brindisi (qqv) think of the Holy Spirit in the sponsal relationship, as do Leo XIII and Pius XII.[7] Though the title was evoked in the conciliar debate, Vatican II did not use the word spouse in any context, preferring "most beloved daughter of the Father," "sanctuary of the Holy Spirit" (LG 53).

Theology: Scheeben's attempt to make the bridal motherhood the basis of all Marian theology, the fundamental principle, has not won wide acceptance. St. Thomas Aquinas saw the solution as a marriage between the Son of God and all mankind, in which Mary was the representative on the human side. Many theologians would have difficulty with the term "spouse of Christ" unless it is taken in a purely spiritual sense, an eminent mode of the sponsal relationship between every soul in grace with the Saviour. In the context of the Incarnation, from which clearly everything flows, Mary is rightly termed spouse of the Holy Spirit; but the context must be retained. The justification of the title spouse of the Father has been seen in the fact that the eternal Father and the predestined Mother have each a parental relationship to God the Son made man. Again this is an aspect of reality, but there is risk in emphasizing it.

---

[1]Cf. M. J. Scheeben, *Mariology* I, Ch IX, *The Bridal Motherhood*, 154-83; J. B. Terrien, *La Mère de Dieu et la Mère des hommes* (Paris, 1900-02), Bk I, 179-88; J. M. Bover, S.J., *EstEccl*, 4(1925), 59-73 (*Tanquam sponsus de thalamo suo*); E. Springer, *Maria als Braut der zweiten gottlichen Person*, *Pastor Bonus* (Trier, 1921), 492ff; J. Bittremieux, "Relationes B. M. V. ad personas SS. Trinitatis," *Divus Thomas* (Placencia), 37(1934), 549-68, and 38(1935), 6-41; J. M. Alonso, C.M.F., "Relationes Immaculati Cordis B.M.V. ad personas SS. Trinitatis," ASC VI, 2, pp. 54-81; A. Piolanti, "*Sicut sponsa ornata monilibus suis*". *Maria come "Sponsa Christi" in alcuni teologi del secl. XII*, V.I., V, pp. 181-93; H. Barré, C.S.Sp., "Marie et l'Église du Ven. Bède à S. Albert le Grand," BSFEM, 9(1951), *Sponsa*, p. 66-72; id., esp. s.v. *sonsa*, Vocabulaire marial, *Prières Anciennes*, p. 340; J. H. Crehan, S.J., "Maria Paredros," *TheolSt* 16(1955), 414-23; D. Daube, *Ruth and Boaz*, *The New Testament and Rabbinic Judaism* (London, 1956) 27-51; A. Rivera, C.M.F., "Maria 'Sponsa Verbi' en la tradición biblico-patristica," EphMar 9(1959), 461-78; D. Flanagan, "The Image of the Bride in the earlier Marian Tradition," ITQ 27(1960), 111-124; id. *Mary, Bride of Christ, ibid.* 28(1961), 233-37; J. Esquerda, "Sintesis de doctrina mariologica en el B. Avila," *EphMar*, 11(1961), 169-91; J. A. de Aldama, S.J., *Maria en la patristica de los siglos I y II* (Madrid, BAC, 1970) 7-32 and 140-66; J. Arnaiz, S.J., "Maria sponsa Spiritus Sancti (Lc 1:35)," MSS IV, 123-28; J. Massingberd Ford, "Mary's Virginitas post partum and Jewish law," BB 54(1973) 270-71; I. Bengoechea, O.C.D., "Maria esposa o Sagrario del Espiritu Santo?" *EphMar*, 28(1978), 339-51; esp. K. Willkemper, *LexMar*, "Braut," 898-910; with caution, I. Marracci, *Polyanthea mariana* s.v. *sponsa*; Didier de Cré, O.F.M.Cap., *L'Épouse du Saint Esprit*, S. Laurent de Brindes (Blois, 1960); H. M. Manteau-Bonamy, *La Vierge Marie et le Saint Esprit* (Paris, 1971) 34. [2]*Oratio IV In praesent. SS. Deip.*, PG 98, 320. [3]PG 96, 741, *Hom II in Dormit.*, 14. [4]PG 43, 485-501, *passim*. Cf. R. Laurentin, *Traité*, I, p. 161. [5]PL 52, 576. [6]*De Operibus Spiritus Sancti*, I, 8, PL 167, 1577D. [7]OL, 150, 268, 432.

STEPHEN OF SALLEY (d. 1252)

Dom A. Wilmart published in 1929 an interesting text from the hands of an English Cistercian, Stephen, Abbot of Salley: *Meditationes de gaudiis Beatae Virginis*, 15 short reflections each followed by a joy and a petition.[1] The grouping falls into three fives, recalling the Rosary (*qv*), and every important event in Mary's life is included: the Nativity, her life, the Annunciation, the Holy Trinity in the Incarnation, the Visitation, the virginity before, during and after childbirth, the visit of the Magi, the Presentation of the Lord, the Finding in the Temple, Cana and other miracles, the death of Christ, the Resurrection, the Ascension, the descent of the Spirit and the Assumption. The petitions at times recall the *Ave Maria* (see HAIL MARY).

The underlying theology is not very profound. Certain Marian titles (*qv*) of the time occur: "Mother of the only Son of God, Queen of heaven, mistress of the world."[2] Mary at the Presentation is said to "offer to God the Father the first-fruits of the human race."[3] With her own eyes she saw and recognised the risen Christ. Mary is "a faithful Mediatress (*qv*) for the salvation of those who belong to her"; "the only hope of human consolation and joy."[4]

The Ascension she beheld as a mystery "in her own true flesh." The Assumption was total "when glorifying you in body and soul he placed you at the right hand of his majesty on high."[5] The meditations excel in sobriety and simplicity. Phrases recall the *Salve Regina* (*qv*).

---

[1]RAM, 10(1929), 368-415, Paris, Bibl.Nat. Latin 10358, s. XIII, ff. 193r-201v; repr. *Auteurs spirituels et textes dévots du moyen-âge latin*, (Paris, 1932), pp. 339-58; intr. 317-338, Cf. also J. M. Canal, C.M.F., *Salve Regina Misericordiae* (Rome, 1963) 273-294. [2]*Auteurs* etc., 344. [3]*Auteurs* etc., 347. [4]*Auteurs* etc., 356-357. [5]*Auteurs* etc., 357.

SUAREZ, FRANCIS (1548-1617)

S. was the founder of systematic or scholastic Mariology. His Marian theology is found in 23 *Disputationes* set within the commentary on questons 27 to 37 of part three of the *Summa Theologica* of St. Thomas (*qv*);[1] to which add the section in vol IV of his works dealing with the Debt of sin.[2] S. was followed by other writers in his treatment of Marian questions. He based his theory on the essential truth that Mary is the Mother of God, her dignity and predestination related to it. This predestination he thought prior to original sin. With the great erudition which characterised all his writing, S. defended the opinion that "the Blessed Virgin was sanctified in the first moment of her conception and preserved from original sin."[3] This was the climate of opinion in Spain in his time; he refused to follow what he thought an extreme view that Mary was free of the "Debt of sin," as he thought it compromised the universality of the Redemption and Mary's dependence on Christ.

S. proceeded from certain principles, which he enunciated as axioms, in defining Mary's privileges: whatever was given to another saint she must have; likewise, whatever was needed for her dignity and office—and especially this guideline, quoted in *Munificentissimus Deus* (*qv*), "the mysteries of grace, which God wrought in the Virgin, are not to be measured by ordinary laws, but by divine omnipotence, with due respect for the propriety of the matter and in the absence of contradiction and inconsistency in the Scriptures."[4] Here there may appear an affinity with St. Bernardine of Siena (*qv*) whom S. often quotes, but his method is strictly scientific, and his erudition, revealed in innumerable references and many texts, is vast if not total.

S. discusses at length the metaphysics of the Mother-Son relationship. He deals with such questions as whether Mary had received the Sacraments of the New Law—denying Orders, Penance and Matrimony (i.e. as a Sacrament of the Church), affirming Baptism with reasons adjoined, Confirmation in some way. About Extreme Unction he was uncertain, but thought she received the Eucharist frequently. He speculates on whether, in the context of "absolute power," she could have been the mother of the Son of God in the ordinary way of human marriage, answering yes categorically. Mary's vow of virginity and her virginity *in partu* and *post partum* in the historical order he defended and expounded at length; he does not consider that the hypothesis of an Incarnation within marriage intercourse would imply an alteration of the entire course of salvation history.[5]

S. deals with other speculative questions which would continue to interest theologians. He was satisfied that the first grace given to Mary was greater than the final grace given to angels or men.[6] Did she at least in the moment of the Incarnation excel in grace all other creatures together? S., though attentive to St. Bernardine, was hesitant: he thought that Mary had "all that perfection radically as it were," but that any one asserting the fullness "would not be too much in error."[7] He held that she had the use of reason from the first moment of her conception; he was influenced by Bernardine in this, but argued

from the case of St. John the Baptist, according to his axiom. From the Incarnation possibly, but certainly from the birth of Christ, she knew "what pertained to the mystery of the Redemption," and at Pentecost what related "to the state of the Church of Christ." She had diverse and many revelations—the Lord appearing to her before the Apostles, likewise after his Ascension —and (this a matter of pious and probable belief) she was occasionally briefly raised to clear vision of the divine essence.[8] She had many *gratiae gratis datae*.[9]

On Mary's role in our regard, S. has his strongest passages when dealing with the perfection of her merits and grace. He quotes the essential texts on the new Eve from St. Irenaeus (*qv*) and other Fathers, and relies especially on St. Bernard (*qv*) whose image of the aqueduct and dictum that on God's will we should have all gifts of grace through Mary he entirely accepts—as he does the title Mediatress from other writers.[10] Later he quotes Bernard on the Mediatress to the Mediator, and on Mary as the neck of the Body.

He remains truly Christocentric. Mary does not receive *latria* which is given to God alone, but *hyperdulia*; her merit on our behalf is not *de condigno* but *de congruo*. If for S. Christ loved Mary more than he loved the Church, the initiative lies with him, for she cannot be the proper or principal cause of our salvation. But "by her advocacy, by meriting *de congruo* and by cooperating in her way in the Incarnation she cooperated in some way in our salvation."[11] Thereon S. assembles some of the strongest passages from the Fathers, especially of the East (e.g. Ephraem, Germanus, Andrew of Crete) and the medieval writers on Mary's mediatorial and intercessory role and concludes his treatise with such dicta as, "In the Virgin we have a universal Advocate, for in all things she is more powerful than the rest are in separate things."[12]

Inset in the section on Our Lady is a scientific theology of St. Joseph (*qv*). It is contained in two Disputations, one on the marriage (*qv*) (which of course S. thoroughly vindicates) and the other on the dignity and sanctity of the "Son of David."[13]

[1] *Opera Omnia* (Vives), Paris 1860, XIX, 1-336, quarto, double column. [2] Pp. 614-622; cf. G. Rodriguez de Yurre, "Suarez y la transcendencia de la maternidad divina" in *Rev. espanola de Teologia*, 1(1941), 873-917; J. M. Bover, S.J.,

Bartolomei, O.S.M., "Relazione dottrinale fra la Bolla 'Munificentissimus Deus' e il pensiero di Suarez sull'Assunzione corporea di Maria Vergine in *Divus Thomas* (Plac.) 54(1951), 334-358; F. de P. Sola, "Doctrina del Doctor Eximio y Piedoso F. Suarez sobre la Concepción Inmaculada de Maria," in *Est. Eccl.*, 28(1954), 501-532; E. Lopera, "De divina maternitate in ordine unionis hypostaticae ad mentem Doctoris Eximii," in *Eph. Mar.*, 4(1954), 66-88; J. M. Moran, "De mysterio Jesu Christi et suae Matris B.V.M. suique corporis mystici secundum theologian P. Suarez" in *Miscel. Comillas*, 27(1957), 257-292. [3]*Disp.* III, 5, 8, p. 35; cf. whole section. [4]*Disput.* 3, V, 31, p. 44. [5]*Disp.* 10, all III. [6]*Disp.* 4, I, 4, p. 57. [7]*Disp.* 18, IV, 9, p. 294. [8]*Disp.* 4, VII, 2, pp. 70, 71; *Disp.* 19, III, 6, 7, pp. 303, 4; 19, IV, 2, p. 304. [9]*Disp.* XX *passim.* [10]*Disp.* 18, IV, 12, 13, pp. 295, 96. [11]*Disp.* 23, I, 4, p. 331. [12]*Disp.* 23, III, 5, p. 336. [13]*Disp.* VII, VIII.

SUB TUUM, THE

The fragment of papyrus reproduced as the frontispiece of this book was acquired by the John Rylands Library, Manchester, in 1917 and published in 1938.[1] In the following year it was identified as an early Greek version of the *Sub Tuum*, hitherto considered a medieval prayer.[2] The commentator, Dom Mercenier, based his judgement on comparison of the words on the torn fragment with the version of the prayer used in the Byzantine liturgy; he also attempted a reconstruction.

This is the first instance of a prayer to Our Lady, expressing belief in her intercessory power, applying to her the word *rysai*, (deliver) of the *Pater Noster*, Mt 6:13. The text contains the word *Theotokos* in the vocative case (*qv*), the title which was to provoke so much controversy at Ephesus.

The dating is debated.[3] M.C.H. Roberts, the editor, quoted E. Lobel, a papyrologist, as favouring the third century. He chose the fourth because he thought it "almost incredible that a prayer addressed so directly to the Virgin in these terms could be written in the third century."[4] G. Giamberardini, specialist in early Egyptian Christianity, maintains that there was no reason, literary or theological, why the papyrus should not be put back to the third century. His reconstruction may be translated thus: "Under your mercy, we take refuge, Mother of God, do not reject our supplications in necessity. But deliver us from danger. [You] alone chaste, alone blessed."[5] The common tr. of the accepted Latin version is: "We fly to thy patronage, O holy Mother of God, despise not our petitions in our necessities, but deliver us from all danger, O ever glorious and blessed Virgin."

LG VIII, 66, has: "Indeed from most ancient times the Blessed Virgin has been venerated under the title of 'God-bearer'. In all perils and difficulties the faithful have fled prayerfully to her protection." The note says "We fly to thy protection" (*Sub tuum praesidium confugimus*).

---

[1]*Catalogue of the Greek and Latin Papyri in the John Rylands Library, Manchester* (Manchester, 1938) III, 46ff. [2]F. Mercenier, O.S.B., "L'Antienne mariale grecque la plus ancienne" in *Le Museon*, 52(1939), 229-233. [3]Cf. O. Stegmüller, "Sub Tuum Praesidium. Bemerkungen zur ältesten Überlieferung" in *Zeitschrift für kath. Theol.* 74(1952), 76-82. [4]*Op. cit.*, 46. [5]Pp. 348ff in "Il 'Sub tuum praesidium' e il titolo 'Theotokos' nella tradizione egiziana" in MM, 31(1969), 324-362.

SUENENS, LEO JOSEPH CARDINAL

(1904-   ) — See Supplement, pp. 386-387.

SWORD OF SIMEON, THE — See Supplement, p. 387.

T

TARASIUS OF CONSTANTINOPLE, ST. (d. 806)

Patriarch of Constantinople, T. called the Second Council of Nicaea (787) to deal with the iconoclastic controversy. His Marian theology is contained in a homily on the Presentation of Mary[1] (BHG 1149). T. is invoked as a supporter of the Immaculate Conception; he speaks of Mary as the "holier than the Cherubim," "entirely stainless," "stainless offering of the human race"; she was so pure that in the Temple as a child she was placed in the Holy of Holies, where even the priests could not enter. To suggest a mystery which he thought both admirable and terrifying, T. uses a series of images—"heaven," "sun," "moon," "throne," "pearl," "Eden," "mount," "table," "sea." Mary he thought elect, predestined from the creation of the world. She was the mirror of prophecies, the happy outcome of them all: he refers to prophetic insights in Ezek, Is, Jer, Dan etc. Mary is the ever virgin Mother of God who "beyond the order of nature brought forth both God and man."[2] Mary was the "abyss of miracles, the fount of good things, the untarnished supply of riches."

T. clearly taught Mary's role in universal salvation: she is "the cause of salvation of all mortals," "the reconciler in the second regeneration with God," "the restoration of the whole world," "the expiation of Adam's curse, price of Eve's debt," "the one who frees us from the curse pronounced against our first parent Eve." Mary is not only the book divinely written of God's great deeds, but in which is written "the mystery of regeneration." Consequently she is queen of the whole universe, "the Mediatress (*mesitis*) of all who are under heaven."[3]

---

[1]PG 98, 1481-99; cf. M. Jugie, A.A., *L'Immaculée Conception*, 128-129; G. M. Roschini, O.S.M., *Mariologia*, I, 191-92; Beck, 489. [2]PG 98, 1495. [3]PG 98, 1499.

TERESA OF AVILA, ST., DOCTOR (1515-1582)

Endowed with a powerful intuitive intellect and a rare mystical gift, T.'s frequent references to Our Lady are related to the order of experience rather than elaborate theory.[1] When as a child she lost her mother, she turned spontaneously to Our Lady. Named Prioress of the Incarnation monastery, she gave her place in choir and the keys of the monastery symbolically to Mary. Carmel was for her the order of the Virgin, as she said repeatedly. She told those who helped Carmel that they were giving service to Mary, told Philip of Spain that he had been chosen by her to protect and raise up her order, warned a Master General of the Carmelites that Mary would be vexed with him if he abandoned those who had toiled to extend her order. T. began *The Foundations* with the words: "I begin in the name of the Lord and of the glorious Virgin whose habit I wear." Some months before her death she wrote: "Now my daughter, like the old man Simeon I can say: I have seen in the order of the Virgin what I desired."

---

[1]Fr. Elisée de la Nativité, O.D.C., *Maria* II, p. 854-855; Archange de la Vierge du Carmel, "La Mariologie de S. Thérèse," *Etudes Carmelitaines*, July-Dec. 1924; Fr.

Emmanuel, O.D.C., *St. Teresa and Our Blessed Lady* in *St. Teresa of Avila*, ed. Fr. Thomas. O.D.C. and Fr. Gabriel, O.D.C. (Dublin, Clonmore and Reynolds, 1963).

TERRIEN, JEAN-BAPTISTE, S.J. (1832-1903)
— See Supplement, p. 387.

TERTULLIAN (d. after 220)

T., a man of wide culture, a convert from paganism, was the first of the Latin Fathers. A rigorist he joined the Montanists, "as if Newman had joined the Salvation Army" (R. A. Knox). His Marian doctrine is found substantially in the *Adversus Marcionem* and *De Carne Christi* and in occasional passages through the other works.[1]

T. is a witness to the Eve-Mary parallel and contrast, though in this his theology does not equal that of St. Justin or St. Irenaeus (*qqv*). "The word [of the devil] which builds up death had crept into Eve, while still a virgin; to a virgin likewise the word of God, building up life, should come, so that what through the female sex had gone to perdition, should through the same sex be brought back to salvation. Eve had believed the serpent. Mary believed Gabriel. What the former did wrong by believing, the latter set right by believing."[2] He then goes into the immediate descendant of Eve, "the diabolical murderer of his brother," whereas the importance of the typology is more comprehensive. T. also thought Eve a type of the Church,[3] invoking for Mary and the Church Gen 2:18.

Other OT passages. Is 11:1-2 are related to Mary: "He shows Christ in the figure of the flower, springing from the shoot that came forth from the root of Jesse; that is from the Virgin of the race of David son of Jesse."[4] Is 7:14 (see EMMANUEL) in its total Marian sense, dominated his thinking.[5] He was particularly insistent—with the aid of this text as of others— on the virginal conception, relating it to the divine sonship: "Besides, there will be two fathers, God and man, if the mother is not a virgin; for she will have a husband not being a virgin, and having a husband, this will make two fathers, God and man to him who would be the son of God and of man . . . If these things are thus distinguished, that is, if he is the son of man from his mother, since he is not from a father, but from a virgin mother, because not from a human father, then he will be the Christ spoken of by Isaiah who announces that a virgin will conceive."[6] "It was not fitting that the Son of God should be born of human seed, lest thus he be wholly the son of man; for he would not then also be the Son of God and would have in him nothing more than Solomon or Jonas . . ."[7] T. employs the image of the virgin earth, from which Adam was formed, a type of the virgin from whom Christ took his origin.[8]

So emphatic on the virginal conception, he rejected the *virginitas in partu*.[9] His preoccupation here was to proclaim the real motherhood of Mary, against the gnostics who asserted that Christ merely passed through the virgin Mary. He approaches one of the so-called difficult texts, Mt 12:48, with a similar outlook—"they wish the Lord himself to have denied that he was born because he had said 'who is my mother and who are my brothers'."[10] He went astray on this and the other similar text in Lk 11:27-28. He thought that Christ rejected his mother and his brethren, preferred those who heard the word of God and kept it. The brethren of the Lord were, in his opinion, the sons of Mary and Joseph, for he did not believe in the perpetual virginity. He thought that Christ in rejecting his mother and brethren was doing what he commanded others to do, to leave them for God's work. He then went further: "the figure of the synagogue was in the mother cut off from him, and of the Jews in the unbelieving brothers."[11]

On a different problem, T. interpreted Jn 19:25-27 as the Lord appointing John as Mary's son in his own place, but ends his theory there.[12]

---

[1]For a list of passages cf. Roschini, *Maria Santissima*, 1, 288; CMF, I, 167-186; EMBP, 55-67. On Tertullian's Marian doctrine cf. E. Madoz in *Est Eccl* 23(1944), 187-200. [2]*De Carne Christi*, 17, 5, PL 2, 782; CCL, 2, 905; CSEL 70, 232. [3]*Adv. Marc.* 2, 4,4-5, PL 2, 289A; CCL 1, 479; CSEL 47, 338. [4]*Adv. Marc.* PL 2, 488B; CCL 1, 686; CSEL 47, 598; cf. *ibid.* 3, 17, 3-4, PL 2, 345. [5]Cf. *Adv. Marc.* 3, 13, 3-5, PL 2, *De carne Christi*, 21, 5, PL 2, 788; 338; *De Resurrect. Mort.*, 20, 3, PL 2, 821B; *De carne Christi*, 17, 1; 21, 1; 23, 1; PL 2, 781, 787, 790. [6]*Adv. Marc.* 4, 10, 7, PL 2, 378. [7]*De carne Christi*, 18:1, CCL 2, 905; CSEL 70, 234; PL 2, 782C. [8]*De carne Christi*, 16, 5, PL 2, 694; 17, 3, PL 2, 782. [9]*Ibid.*, 23, 2, PL 2, 790. [10]*Ibid.*, 7, 1, PL 2, 766. [11]*Ibid.* 7, 13, PL 2, 769. [12]*De Praescr. haeret.* 22, 5, PL 2, 34B.

THEODORE OF STUDION, ST. (c. 759-826)

Ordained priest by Tarasius (*qv*), T. through his monastic life especially as Abbot, through his sermons and writings, and his liturgical texts (hymns found in the *Triodion*) strongly influenced Byzantine spirituality. Mention of Our Lady occurs in his anti-iconoclastic writings, but his ideas are found principally in the homily on the Nativity,[1] published by Migne among the works of St. John of Damascus (*qv*), and in that on the Dormition,[2] BHG 1112, BHG 1157.

Passages by T. are invoked in favour of the Immaculate Conception (*qv*); they certainly exclude all personal sin. "What is purer, more irreproachable than the Virgin? God, sovereign and all immaculate light, found in her so many charms that he united himself to her substantially by the descent of the Holy Spirit."[3] Mary is compared to the earth on which the thorn of sin has never sprouted—on the contrary, it has produced the shoot by which sin has been torn by the root. "It is soil not cursed as the first . . . on which has come the blessing of the Lord, and its fruit is blessed as the divine oracle says." [Mary] "is the new leaven, the all-holy first fruits of the human race."[4]

T. uses the now traditional OT images: the burning bush, the closed door, the stone cut by no human hands, and others such as the incorruptible wood, the light cloud. Mary is the "spouse" whose best man is the Holy Spirit, and spouse Christ, all fair as in Song 4:7. But she has a role in our regard, for "having left the body she is with us in spirit and entering heaven she puts demons to flight, becoming our mediatress with the Lord. Formerly death by the ancestress Eve made entry and held the world in its sway; now having assailed her blessed daughter, it has been routed, being overcome from the very point whence formerly it had taken its power."[5] Thereon T. proclaims that Mary is the glory of her sex, and has removed the curse on Eve; T. employs the metaphor of Jacob's ladder.

Mary enjoys in heaven the royal or lordly power "which through her authority as Mother she obtained from the Lord of all"; she is the propitiation for mortals through which "from the rising of the sun to its going down among the nations and in every place, the name of the Lord is glorified and an offering is made to his name as most holy Malachi says."[6] T. gives an enthusiastic account of the heavenly court, human and angelic, greeting Mary's arrival.[7]

The cult of Mary, especially in the Liturgy, was rich in the monastery of Studion and T. defended the images of Mary as of Christ and the saints. Devotion to the *Theotokos* is constantly evident in the homilies; T. also mentions the special fortnight fast before the Assumption in honour of Mary.[8]

[1]PG 96, 680-697. [2]PG 99, 720-729. Cf. M. Jugie, *L'Immaculée Conception*, 130-32; *L'Assomption*, 255-257; J. Esquerda Bifet, "Culto y devoción mariana en San Teodoro Studita" in *Burgense*, 13(1972), 445-457; *id.*, same title, *Zagreb*, III, p. 383-394; H. M. Guindon, S.M.M., *De la proskynèse chez Saint Théodore le Studite à l'exemplarite mariale de Vatican II*, Zagreb III, 349-382. [3]PG 96, 684C. [4]5, PG 96, 685A-D. [5]2, PG 99, 721BC. [6]4, PG 99, 725C. [7]5, PG 728B. [8]*Doctrina Chronica*, PG 99, 1679A. Cf. BHG 1093c and BHG 1116p).

THEODORE THE SYNCELLUS (early 7th century) — See Supplement, p. 387.

THEODORET OF CYRRHUS (c. 393-c. 466) — See Supplement, pp. 387-388.

THEODOTUS OF ANCYRA (d. before 446)

Bishop of Ancyra in Asia Minor, modern Ankara, T. was a friend of Nestorius but opposed him vigorously at Ephesus (*qv*), he was one of the eight delegates to the imperial court in September, 431. He disappears from history after a letter sent to him by St. Cyril (*qv*) in 438. In his Exposition of the Nicene Symbol, T. deals briefly with the virginal motherhood. His ideas about Our Lady are elaborated in the homilies. Of those preached at Ephesus two are relevant;[1] a third, an attack on Nestorius preached on the feast of St. John the Evangelist, and a fourth, known only in an Ethiopian version, have no interest. Three others are in PG, the first in Greek,[2] the others in Latin only, but of these two M. Aubineau published a Greek text of the first and M. Jugie of the second.[3] Both editors, M. Aubineau perhaps more satisfactorily, defended authenticity against doubts raised by O. Bardenhewer.[4] The order in PG is followed here, with advertence to OCP and PO where necessary.

The context of Ephesus determines the emphasis on the divine motherhood: "Therefore the only-begotten Son of God, who is also called the Word, is born, not taking his beginning as the Word from the birth but that he might become man effecting a beginning from the birth."[5] "God, therefore, today appeared from the Virgin, and the Virgin preserving the integrity of her virginity, became a mother."[6] "He is born of the Father concerning his divine nature, of the Virgin concerning the "dispensation" (*oikonomia*), in the first instance as God, now as man."[7]

With the divine motherhood T. links very closely, as a reality and a sign, the virginity: "The mother of no [mere] man has remained a virgin. Do you see how the very birth presents us with a dual meaning of the one born? For if he were born in our manner, he would be a man, but

if he truly preserved the untouched integrity of his mother, for those who think rightly the one who is born is God."[8] Contrasting the resurrection which opened the tomb with the birth "which did not open the womb," T. goes on to show that the resurrection will be shared by all, but the miraculous virginal birth remains singular.[9] To the virginity, the marriage (*qv*) is related: "Joseph became the guardian of Mary and a witness unexceptionable of her virginity."[10] T. adjusts the ancient reason which was insinuated by St. Ignatius of Antioch (*qv*), that the mystery must be hidden from the evil one: "Joseph marries Mary, and the form of marriage is shown, so that the Virgin, unknown to the devil, should continue as a virgin, keeping virginity by divine decree."[11] T. expounds Is 7:14 at length.

The Eve-Mary contrast begins on the aspect of death and life, "for the virgin Eve who had ministered unto death, the Virgin most pleasing to God and full of God's grace is chosen in service of life"—and goes on to a portrait of Mary's perfection so strongly phrased that it suggests the Immaculate Conception (*qv*). "A virgin innocent, spotless, free of all defect, untouched, unsullied, holy in soul and body, like a lily sprouting among thorns."[12] The passage must be read with that in *Hom IV* which speaks of the two moments of sanctification or purification, initial and at the Annunciation. Interpretation of this is indecisive; T. may also have changed his mind in the interval."[13] The *chairetismoi* section in *Hom IV* insists too on Mary's sanctity as well as her role.

The Eve-Mary contrast is used to express this role. Mary "spouse of God" (*qv*) removes Eve's sadness. Her childbirth will not be sorrowful but "the beginning of a world all of light." "Because of thee Eve's sadnesses have ceased; through thee evils have perished; through thee error has departed; through thee the curse has been abolished; Eve through thee has been redeemed."[14]

[1]*Hom. in die nativ. Salvatoris Jesu Christi* . . . PG 77, 1349-69; ACO 1, 1, 2, 80-90; *Hom* . . . . *in natalem Salvatoris*, PG 77, 1369-85; ACO, 1, 1, 2, 73-80. [2]*In sanctam Deiparam et in Simeonem*, PG 77, 1389-1412. [3]*In Dni. nostri J. C. diem natalem*, Latin, PG 77, 1411-1418; Greek, ed. M. Aubineau, OCP 26(1960) 224-232; *In sanctam Deigenitricem et in sanctam Christi nativ.*, Latin, PG 77, 1418-32; Greek, ed. M. Jugie, PO 19, 318-335. [4]Cf. R. Laurentin, *Traité* I, 166-67; RSPT, 52(1968), 546; M. Aubineau, *op.cit.* 246-249; M. Jugie, *op.cit.*, 292ff; cf. M. Jugie, *L'Immaculée Conception*, p. 81-86; R. Caro, *La homilética*, I, 156-197; EMBP,

812-838; ClavisG III, 192-196; CMP IV, 1, 107-142. [5]Hom I, 2, 1349C; E. M. Toniolo, O.S.M., in *Diaconia Pisteos*, Festschrift J. de Aldama, S.J., (Granada, 1969) 5-30. [6]*Hom II*, 3, PG 77, 1372C. [7]7, PG 77, 1377C. [8]3, PG 77, 1372D-1373A. [9]*Hom V*, 1, OCP, 225. [10]*Ibid.*, 3, 227. [11]*Ibid.*, 4,227. [12]*Hom VI*, 11, PO 19, 329. [13]PG 77, 1396C, 1397-1400; Cf. M. Jugie, *op. cit.*, and R. Caro, *op. cit.*, 185-186. [14]PO 12, 331.

THEOGNOSTUS (d. after 871)

A monk who supported the Patriarch Ignatius in his dispute with Photius (*qv*), which brought him marginally into church affairs, and to the city of Rome, accounting also for one of his works, the letter of Ignatius to Pope Nicholas I; the others are a panegyric on all saints and an *Encomium on the Dormition of the B.V.*[1] Echoing a theme of St. Andrew of Crete (*qv*)— that there is harmony between Mary's privileges T. closely linked her Assumption (*qv*) with her Immaculate Conception (*qv*): "It was truly fitting that she who from the beginning had been conceived by sanctifying action (*hagiastikos*) through saintly prayer in the womb of a holy mother, should also have a holy passing."[2] Her beginning, life and end were holy.

T. describes Jesus "separating the soul of Mary from her body. He undoes the bond which united the two. He undoes it for a short time and then reties them for long duration, for duration is long when one knows its beginning and knows not its end . . . the separation for a few days yields to union forever."[3]

T., a true Byzantine, proclaims Mary's intercessory role, in proportion to her work while on earth to save the world and enlighten the universe: ". . . she now makes entreaty for the salvation of the world, intercedes for those of the true faith" as well as for the people, the king, every principality and power and those celebrating her passing.[4] By praising her conception and glorifying her passing we shall obtain forgiveness for our negligence.

[1]Ed. M. Jugie, PO 16, 457-62 and cf. intr. 455-57; M. Jugie, *L'Immaculée Conception*, 177-79; *id.*, *L'Assomption*, 259-62. [2]1, PO 16, 457. [3]3, PO 16, 460. [4]5, PO 16, 462.

THEOPHANES OF NICAEA (d. 1381)

The one Marian work of this Palamite, archbishop of Nicaea, contains the most daring synthesis ever proposed on the primacy of Mary, her relationship to the three divine persons and her role as Mediatress (*qv*) in all creation. T. sees the whole cosmos turning around Mary.

Behind this synthesis is the conception of creation deriving from Pseudo-Dinoysius and the theology of Gregory Palamas (*qv*). The reader must bear in mind that quotation from a theological treatise—called by the author a "sermon"—is a risk. It must be read in its entirety; it is essentially close-knit. The text was first published in 1935 by Fr. M. Jugie, A.A. (*qv*).[1]

T. distinguishes two moments in creation: being in itself and well-being. The second, to which the first is designed, is achieved through deification and of this the source is the Incarnation. Through the divine motherhood Mary is intrinsically bound with the entire reality. She is compared with the earth from which "our Lord and God, the new Adam become the second Adam, was taken according to the flesh," with heaven[2] "as truly and rightly the throne of the Omnipotent One," as including and containing all the treasures of grace. The first receptacle of the divine fullness is the assumed nature of the Saviour: "But the living tabernacle which brought him forth is acknowledged as the second receptacle, that is receiving immediately from the first receptacle, the assumed nature of the Saviour, all the fullness of divinity . . ."[3] Christ can be approached only through Mary.

Mary's mediation thus rooted in the order of things is universal. "It cannot happen that anyone, of angels or of men, may come otherwise, in any manner whatsoever, to participation in the divine gifts flowing from what has been divinely assumed, from the Son of God, save through his Mother."[4] There is a kind of sacramental character or role assigned to Mary, who is a second bishop (*hierarches*) under Christ, the first bishop. Because of her divine motherhood as T. understands it, he attributes divine titles or names to her—God, Lord, King of kings; as he is led by the theology of Pseudo-Dionysius to see reflected in her divine properties, omnipotence, dominion, wisdom. She is "the universal cosmic and supercosmic good," "the cosmos par excellence," for the abode of the Word is found with her more than in heaven.

T. emphasises the Trinitarian perspective, studying Mary in relation to each of the divine person: with the Father, whose mirror image and all-fair spouse she is, she is linked by their common Son. While repeating that Mary and her divine Son each retain their identity, T.

elaborates powerfully the astonishing union between them, closer than any association (*qv*) described by Western authors. Born of sterile parents she was "from the origin of her existence united to the Spirit, the author of life . . . participation in the Spirit was for her participation in being and her conception was the image and type of the conception of her Son."[5] There are many subtleties interwoven with these ideas.

Surprisingly, a Western image—Mary as the neck of the mystical body of Christ—was also used by T. to illustrate her vital and indispensable role; he concludes his analysis thus: "Since then the Head of every principality and power and of our Church is the only way which leads to the Father, so that sacred neck is the only way leading to the Head of all."[6] As the fountain, the beginning of life, "she receives wholly the hidden grace of the Spirit and amply distributes it and shares it with others, thus manifesting it."[7] All things were created for her and are governed through her. No one attains the fullness and the goal of life in Christ "without her cooperation, or without the Spirit's help." Germanus (*qv*) in the East before him, Bernard (*qv*), Bernardine (*qv*), or Grignion de Montfort (*qv*) in the West were not any more explicit than this on Mary's universal mediation of grace. T links the doctrine with that of the spiritual motherhood, which he first describes powerfully and sensitively: "The Mother of him who through his unspeakable goodness willed to be called our brother is the dispenser and distributor of all the wondrous uncreated gifts of the divine Spirit, which make us Christ's brothers and co-heirs, not only because she is granting the gifts of her natural Son to his brothers in grace, but also because she is bestowing them on these as her own true sons, though not by ties of nature but of grace."[8]

To this so powerful mediatress and mother we owe praise and the tribute of virtue in imitation of her. T.'s doctrine is not weakened by any query on the influence of Pseudo-Dionysius—lower hierarchies participate in divine things through those above them—nor of Gregory Palamas, on whom we may, perhaps, blame T.'s lack of certain theological distinctions.

[1]*Sermo in Sanctissimam Deiparam* in *Lateranum*, nova series, 1, Cf. B. Schultze, S.J., in MO, 389-406; M. Jugie, A.A., *L'Immaculée Conception*, 240-46; M. Candal, S.J., "El 'Sermo in Deiparam' de Teofanes Niceno," in MM 26(1964), 72-103. [2]4, 5, p. 19, 45. [3]5, p. 51. [4]5, p. 55. [5]13, p. 180. [6]10, p. 133. [7]14, p. 195. [8]15, p. 205.

THEOPHILUS LEGEND, THE

An unusual seventh-century Eastern story of repentance and forgiveness, the latter obtained through Our Lady's intercession.[1] T. held a high post in the church of Adana in Cilicia; he was chosen as bishop but refused. The new bisohp dismissed him from his office. Thereon he made a pact with the devil, to whom he was introduced by a Jew, renouncing Jesus and Mary. When it was signed and sealed he got back his post. Later he was seized by remorse and feared for his eternal salvation. In his helplessness he turned to Mary and when she was assured of his repentance she obtained forgiveness for him. "The Lord has heard your prayers and grants your petitions through me." T. asks to have the damning document recovered, which was also done by Our Lady. T. then tells the whole story to his bishop who narrates it to his people, praising God and extolling Mary's intervention. T. dies soon after happily.

The author, who is unknown, claims to have witnessed the events narrated, which he puts in the year 538. His Greek text was translated into Latin by Paul the Deacon of Naples (d.877). The story was versified by the tenth-century Benedictine nun, Hroswitha of Gandershein. Widely diffused in the West, the tale was used as an example of Mary's intercessory power. Eastern preachers did not draw on it. In the West it was cited by Geoffrey of Vendome, Honorius of Autun, Abelard, Richard of St. Laurent, and St. Albert the Great (*qqv*). Some 40 titles of Mary are used, with variants amounting to 60. As well as Mother of God, Mary is called Mediatress (*Mesites* in Greek), *Mediatrix* for the first time in Latin. Mary is called "the strong protection who, with her holy heart, cherishes all Christians" (n.24); "The hope and support of the race of Christians, ransom of those astray, the true way of those turning upwards to her, who intercedes for sinners, mediatress of God and men" (n.29). Mary is the "hope of salvation," "the unique hope of all and the salvation of souls," "the fountain of mercy and mediation," "the universal help and prepared protection of those turning to her, the refuge of Christians" (n.18), "the surest bridge between God and men" (n.36). Finally, these words which anticipate the *Memorare*: "For who hoped in you and was confounded? Or who among men besought the omnipotence of your help and was abandoned?" (n.31).

[1]Editions: *Acta Sanctorum*, February I, die 4, ed. 1863, 489-92; R. Petsch, *Theophilus: ein Mittelniederländisches Drama des Mittelalters in drei Fassungen* (Heidelberg, 1908); critical ed., Greek, G. N. Sola, *Il testo greco inedito della Leggenda di Teofilo di Adana in Rivista storico-critica delle scienze teologice* 3(1907), 835-48; Latin, esp. G. G. Meersseman, O.P., *Kritische Glossen op de griekse Theophilus-Legende (7e eeuw) en haar latijnse vertaling (9e eeux), Mededelingen van de Koninglijke Vlaamse Academie voor Wetenschapen, Letteren en Schone Kunsten van Belgie:* Klasse der Letteren XXV (1963), n.4 (Brussels, 1963). For textual history and commentary, cf. esp. G. Geenen, O.P., *Legenda Theophili—Speculum Historico-doctrinale de mediatione Matris Dei in alto medio aevo* (saec. VII-XII), Zagreb Congress, IV, 313-46.

THEOPHYLACT (d. after 1092)

Archbishop of Achrida in Bulgaria, but from Constantinople, where he had been a disciple of Michael Psellos (*qv*) and tutor to the emperor Michael VII's son. Two points are picked out of his commentary on Lk's infancy narrative (*qv*). He considers that *kecharitomene* (1:28) means pleasing to God, or full of joy (see FULL OF GRACE); and "Blessed art thou" (1:42) means that Mary was blessed as Eve (*qv*) had been cursed.[1] His ideas on Mary are contained in his homily on the Presentation.[2]

T. insisted on Mary's purity and holiness, possibly from the first moment of her existence: "She who is to give birth [to the Word incarnate] is chosen, embellished with all the virtues and raised above every creature . . . she appears like a fruit given by God."[3] Like so many Byzantines T. thinks that the mother was sterile and like them he accepts the legend of Mary's sojourn in the Temple. In describing the decision of the High Priest to allow her to live in the Holy of Holies, where he himself was permitted to enter only once a year, T. thinks that he was convinced that in Mary was fulfilled the typology of the Ark (*qv*). "Her holiness surpassed all nature," "she had been justified from the womb."[4] The Eve contrast is related to the entry to the Temple— she had caused us to be expelled from paradise. Does all this amount to total sanctity? "A fruit given by God" possibly holds the clue.

[1]*In Lc.* 1, PG 123, 701C and D. [2]PG 126, 129-144; cf. M. Jugie, *L'Immaculée Conception*, 197-200. [3]4, PG 126, 133A. [4]7, PG 126, 137A.

THEOTOKOS, GOD-BEARER

The ancient Eastern title for Mary, Mother of God, prominent especially in liturgical prayer in the Orient down to our time.[1] It was formally sanctioned at the Council of Ephesus (see CYRIL OF ALEXANDRIA, ST.). It makes into one word the Lucan title "Mother of the Lord" (1:43) with 2:12, where Lord is taken in a transcendent sense; it is the counterpart of Jn's "the Word was made flesh" (1:14). From the second century, Mary's Son was called God by the Fathers; a Christian interpolation in a Jewish book of the Sibylline oracles reads "a young maiden will bear the Logos of the highest God." The precise origin in time of the word itself is difficult to establish. It is attested by a unique piece of evidence: the papyrus fragment in the John Rylands Library, Manchester, on which, in the vocative case, it is clearly discernible (see SUB TUUM). If this papyrus can be dated in the third century, the title must have existed for some time, possibly a generation, before. A word of such significance would not be invented in a popular prayer.

Since Egypt was the homeland, Christian thinking, or verbal composition, may have been influenced by the existence of the title "Mother of god" for Isis in regard to Orus; the adaptation was possibly first made in Coptic. The differences between Mary and Isis were well clarified: she was "the handmaid of the Lord," the chaste virgin whose Son was true God and true man, whereas Isis was seen as a goddess, one who conceived her son in passion, entirely removed from the mysterious destiny of the Incarnation.

Texts from Hippolytus of Rome and Origen (*qqv*) showing *Theotokos* are controverted, and at present the first certain literary use of the title is attributed to Alexander of Alexandria in 325.[2] Thereafter it is found widely, especially with St. Athanasius and the Alexandrians, in Palestine with Eusebius of Caeserea and Cyril of Jerusalem, with the three Cappadocians, with Eustathius of Antioch and the Council of Antioch in 341, Apollinarius of Laodicea, Diodorus of Tarsus, Severian of Gabala—even Arians like Asterius the Sophist used it.

[1]Cf. V. Schweitzer, "Alter des Titels Theotokos," *Der Katholik*, 28(1903), 97-113; Cl. Dillenschneider, C.SS.R., *Le sens chrétien et la maternité divine de Marie au IVe et Ve siècles* (Bruges, Beyaert, 1929); G. Jouassard, *Maria*, I, 85-86, 122-36; A. Grillmeier, S.J., *Christ in Christian Tradition* (London, 1965), 73-74, 244; G. Giamberardini, O.F.M., *Il culto mariano in Egitto nei primi sei secoli: Origine-Sviluppo-Cause* (Cairo, 1967), ch. 6, art 4; *id.,* "Il 'Sub tuum praesidium' e il titolo 'Theotokos' nella tradizione egiziana," MM 31(1969), (6. *L'Origine del titolo "Theotokos")* 350-58; *id.,* "Nomi e titoli mariani," *EphMar* 23(1973), (5. *Madre di Dio*) 214-17; R. Laurentin, *Traité*, V, 170-71;

R. H. Fuller, "New Testament roots to the Theotokos," MSt 29(1978), 46-68. [2]PG 18, 568C.

THÉRÈSE OF LISIEUX, ST. (1873-1897)

The spirituality of T. based firmly on the gospel and very specially approved by the Church, the ideal of spiritual childhood expressed in love, confidence and self-surrender, logically led to emphasis on Mary's role as exemplar and particularly as Mother of divine grace.[1] The saint's personal experience and the traditions of Carmel favoured development of these ideas. She believed that she had been miraculously cured from illness during an apparition of Our Lady, an apparition of a special kind in which a statue took life; she had the conviction that Our Lady moved towards her and smiled. On the day of her first Holy Communion she made a special act of consecration to Mary; her last poem was *Why I love you Mary*—it has been much analysed and explained. Throughout her life the saint lived in a prayerful union with Our Lady. Her sister, Céline, in evidence at the inquiry for her Beatification, said that in her last months she spoke continually of Mary;[2] her reflections were often inspired by the gospel texts. The spiritual movement inspired by the saint in which priests were prominent, was a factor in the Marian revival of this century so intrinsic to her outlook and spirit was Marian idealism. The eighth French National Marian Congress in 1961 was held in Lisieux on the theme of Mary's spiritual motherhood. It was addressed by John XXIII by radio broadcast.

[1]Cf. autobiography, letters and poetry of the saint, *Novissima Verba* ed. Mother Agnes of Jesus, all available in many editions. Cf. esp. *Manuscrits Autobiographiques* (Lisieux, 1956)-act of consecration II, Notes, p23; Louis de Ste. Thérèse, *La Vie mariale de S. Thérèse de l'Enfant Jesus* (Lisieux, 1946); R. P. Piat, *La Vierge du sourire et S. Thérèse de l'Enfant Jésus* (Lisieux 1951); esp. François de S. Marie, O.D.C., *La dévotion mariale de S. Thérèse de l'Enfant Jésus, Marie plus Mère que Reine*, in *VIIIe Congrès Marial National* Paris, 1962, 129-48; A. Combes, "Marie pour S. Thérèse de Lisieux," *Divinitas*, 14(1970), 75-124. [2]Summarium of the Canonical Process, p. 345.

THOMAS AQUINAS, ST.
DOCTOR OF THE CHURCH
(1225-1274)

The greatest of scholastic, if not of all, theologians expressed his doctrine on Our Lady in: a) the *Summa Theologica*, III, qq. 17-35; b) the *Summa contra Gentes*, IV, 9, 45; c) the *Commentarium in IV Libros Sententiarum*, III, d.3 and 4; d) occasional passages in his commentaries on the Bible; e) the *Compendium Theologiae*; f) the *Expositio Salutationis Angelicae*; g) some other sermons.[1] St. Thomas integrated his Marian theology fully in his Christology and founded it on a rigorously scientific basis.[1]

He writes at length on Mary as Mother of God, bringing metaphysical precision to the traditional doctrine: "Christ is really said to be the Son of the Virgin Mary from the real relation of motherhood towards Christ."[2] "Since the subject of sonship is not nature or a part of nature, but the person or hypostasis only; but in Christ there is no hypostasis or person save the eternal one, there can be in Christ no sonship save that which is in the eternal hypostasis."[3] T. shows that the relation of Mother and Son is real on the part of the mother, notional on the part of the son.

Mary could not merit the incarnation, but assuming that it would take place she could merit, by merit of suitability only, that it would happen through her. The grace she received placed her above angels and men. T. is particularly insistent on the fullness of grace. He went so far, in dealing with Mary's dignity, as to use the phrase "a certain infinite dignity": "The Blessed Virgin from the fact that she is the Mother of God has a kind of infinite dignity from the infinite good which is God."[4]

Much ink has flowed on the subject of T. and the Immaculate Conception. Yet the decisive passage (III, q. 27, a.2 ad 2) appears explicit: "If the soul of the Blessed Virgin had never been stained with the contagion of original sin, this would have taken from the dignity of Christ in his capacity as the Saviour of all." Because he saw this apparently insuperable obstacle, the saint could write that "the Blessed Virgin did indeed contract original sin but was cleansed from it, before her birth."[5] About the feast he wrote: "from the fact that the feast of the Conception is celebrated it is not to be understood that she was holy in her conception, but because it is not known when she was sanctified, the feast of her sanctification rather than of her conception is celebrated on the day of her conception."[6] The debate on T.'s meaning of animation can scarcely nullify these texts, as his acceptance of the biology of his time does not affect his theology of Mary, Mother of God.

Mary's freedom from any personal sin and the triple virginity were defended by T. He gave a lengthy vindication of the marriage (*qv*) from the viewpoint of Christ, of his Mother, and from ours: a logical ordering of the patristic teaching, with some refinements of his own.

On the subject of Mary's part in our salvation, he is sparing. He does apply the word mediatress to Mary in the commentary on the Cana episode, but the context is restricted. It is universal in his use of another concept, Mary as the representative of all mankind. There was to be a kind of spiritual marriage between the Son of God and human nature: "And hence through the Annunciation the consent of the Virgin was sought in the place of the whole human nature."[7] "Was sought" (*expetebatur*) is the critically established reading, not "was awaited" (*expectabatur*). The idea of representation of all here affirmed is a form of mediation. Those who look for a basis for the role in T. will find it perhaps in his admission of lesser forms of mediation not ruled out by the unique office of Christ: dispositive with prophets of the Old Law, ministerial for priests of the New.[8]

The saint is likewise guarded in dealing with Mary's distribution of grace. In the *Summa* he writes: "But the Virgin Mary obtained such a fullness of grace that she was nearest to the author of grace; so that she received into herself him who is full of all grace and by bringing him forth in a certain manner she brought grace to all."[9] In the commentary on the *Ave Maria* preached the year before he died he says: "most wonderful of all is it to have enough [grace] for the salvation of all mankind, and thus it is in Christ and the Blessed Virgin. Thus in every danger you can find a refuge in this same glorious Virgin."[10] The saint's own devotion to Mary was profound and sensitive.

[1]Cf. for bibliography, G. M. Roschini, *Cio che e stato scritto sulla Mariologia di S. Tommaso* in *San Tommaso e l'odierna problematica teologica*, ed. Mgr. A. Piolanti (Rome, 1974) 159-195; *id.*, *La Mariologia di San Tommaso*, (Rome, Studi Mariani 2, 1950); M. Cuervo, *Santo Tomas en Mariologia* (Villava- Pamplona, 1968); *Summa Theologiae*, vol. 51, *Our Lady*, ed. T. R. Heath, London, 1969. [2]III, q. 35, a.5. [3]*Ibid*. [4]S. T. I, q.25, a.6 ad 4. [5]III, q. 27, a. 2, ad 2. [6]*Ibid.*, ad 3. [7]III, q. 30, a.1; for comparison with III Sent. D. 3, q.3, a.1, 1, cf. M.-J. Nicolas, *Theotokos*, 145ff. [8]III, q. 26, a.1, ad 1. [9]III, q. 27, a.5, ad 1. [10]Cf. *The Three greatest prayers* by St. Thomas Aquinas, tr. L. Shapcote (London, 1937) 32-33.

TIMOTHY OF JERUSALEM (4th century) — See Supplement, p. 388.

TITLES OF OUR LADY

Thinking on Our Lady in theology and devotional life has very often turned on the meaning and validity of titles given to her.[1] Some of her titles are biblical: *Kecharitomene*, the angel's word, "Full of grace"; "Mother of my Lord," Elizabeth's; "Mother of Jesus," in Jn and Acts, and especially her own "Handmaid of the Lord." The Fathers pointed the way for the "New Eve," and typological titles from OT "Ark of the Covenant," "Burning Bush," were used explicitly or implicitly of her as she was given the Pauline title Mediatress. Irenaeus already called her "Advocate"—though with a meaning that is debated. The point of controversy settled at Ephesus was contained in the word *Theotokos*. Cardinal Newman culled from patristic writings a list of descriptive names glorifying Mary. The Middle Ages and every subsequent period added to the list. Theological controversy on Mary's part in the Redemption has sometimes turned on the propriety of titles like "Coredèmptress," while within Vatican Council II the debate was whether she should be called Mother of the Church and Mediatress. Church history has added countless names arising from icons, images, shrines or works of art; church authority has sometimes enhanced a title by approving a religious congregation. Usage has sometimes failed striking phrases such as "ladder of heaven" in the East, "neck of the mystical Body" in the West.

There are compilations of Marian nomenclature, the early ones understandably lacking scientific precision. Theophile Raynaud (d. 1663) assembled in his *Nomenclator Marianus* names and epithets given to Mary by the Fathers, medieval theologians and the Liturgy, with a glossary. I. Marracci assembled alphabetically an enormous mass of titles applied to Mary from the earliest times to his day—*Polyanthea Mariana*, published by J. J. Bourasse in vols IX, X, XI of the *Summa Aurea de laudibus B.M.V.* In 1930, for the centenary of the liberation of Greece, the former metropolitan of Leontopolis, Sophronius Eustradiades, published a collection in alphabetical order of the titles given to Mary in Byzantine hymns. Four recent collections are also valuable. R. Laurentin to the second volume of *Marie l'Église et le Sacerdoce*, G. G. Meersseman, O.P., to the second volume of *Der Hymnos Akathistos im Abendland*, H. Barré, C.S.Sp., to *Prières Anciennes*, and D. Casagrande to *Enchiridion*

Marianum, each appended a list of the names or titles applied to Mary in texts reproduced in their books.[1]

The dangers to be avoided in consideration of descriptive words or phrases applied to Mary are nominalism which would fail to establish true meaning and confusion of external honour with valid insight.

---

[1]Besides the works referred to in the text, cf. G. Giamberardini, O.F.M., "Nomi e titoli mariani nella filologia e nell'esegesi degli egiziani," EphMar 23(1973), 205-30.

TITUS OF BOSTRA (d.*c.* 378) — See Supplement, p. 388.

TRADITION, MARY IN, — See Supplement, pp. 388-89.

TRENT, COUNCIL OF

The Council discussed the subject of Original Sin in May, 1546. On the 28th, in regard to its universality, Cardinal Pacheco proposed that there be a definition of the exception in Mary's case.[1] He was opposed by Dominicans, principally Bishop Bertrano of Fano who thought silence advisable in view of the uncertainty of traditions. Others thought that nothing should be said since each opinion was "pious," or that the matter should be put back to a more suitable time, or that the Constitution of Sixtus IV (*qv*) should be approved. In subsequent debates and in drafting by the theologians, Pacheco with his 24 followers could not secure an explicit statement on Mary's privilege. The most that would be agreed on was expressed in these words: "This holy Synod declares, nevertheless, that it is not its intention to include in this decree, where original sin is treated of, the blessed and immaculate Virgin Mary, Mother of God, but that the constitutions of Pope Sixtus IV of happy memory are to be observed, under the penalties contained in these constitutions which it renews."[2]

The time for a full definition was not opportune. The required theological expertise was not available. There was still much controversy—thus the report drawn up by John of Torquemada, O.P., for the Council of Basle was published; in the early editions of the decrees the clause relevant to the Immaculate Conception (*qv*) was deleted. Yet Pius IX could say that, "considering the times and circumstances the Fathers of Trent sufficiently intimated by this declaration that the Blessed Virgin Mary was free from the original stain; and thus they clearly signified that nothing could be reasonably cited from Sacred Scriptures, from Tradition or from any authority of the Fathers which would in any way be opposed to so great a prerogative of the Blessed Virgin."[3]

The Council referred to Our Lady in other contexts. The Canons on Justification say: [If anyone holds] "that throughout his whole life he can avoid all sins, even venial sins, except by a special privilege of God, as the Church holds in regard to the Blessed Virgin: let him be anathema."[4] This statement affirms the personal sinlessness of Mary. By implication she was also included in the teaching on the intercession of the saints and the veneration of sacred images which was passed at the twenty-fifth, final session of the Council unanimously without debate: "The holy Synod commands all bishops and others who hold the office of administration... that they above all diligently instruct the faithful on the intercession and invocation of the saints, the veneration of relics, and the legitimate use of images, teaching them that the saints, who reign together with Christ, offer up their prayers to God for men; and that it is good and useful to invoke them suppliantly and, in order to obtain favours from God through his Son Jesus Christ our Lord, who alone is our Redeemer and Saviour, to have recourse to their prayers, assistance and support."[5] "Moreover, that the images of Christ, of the Virgin Mother of God, and of the other saints, are to be placed and retained especially in the churches, and that due honour and veneration be extended to them, not that any divinity or virtue is believed to be in them, for which they are to be venerated, or that anything is to be petitioned from them, or that trust is to be placed in images, as at one time was done by the gentiles, who placed their hope in idols (cf. Ps 134:15f) but because the honour which is shown them is referred to the prototypes which they represent, so that by means of the images which we kiss and before which we bare the head and prostrate ourselves, we adore Christ, and venerate the saints, whose likeness they bear."[6] The Council refers to Nicaea II, as does Vatican II (LG 67) on the same subject.

---

[1]Cf. M. Tognetti, O.S.M., "L'Immacolata al Concilio di Trento," MM 15(1953), 304-74 and 555-86; J. Sagues, "Trento y la Inmaculada, Natura del dogma mariano," EstEccl 28(1954), 323-68; B. Korosak, O.F.M., *Doctrina de Immaculatae B.V.Mariae Conceptione apud auctores ordinis minorum qui concilio Tridentino interfuerunt* (Rome, Marian Academy, 1958); on Mary's sinlessness, J. de Aldama, S.J., "El valor dogmatico de la doctrina sobre la

immunidad de pecado venial en Nuestra Señora," *Archivo Teologico Granadino* 9(1946), 52-57; also L. von Pastor, *History of the Popes*, XII (London, 1923), 266. [2]DS 1515. [3]OL, *Ineffabilis Deus*, p. 70. [4]DS 1573. [5]DS 1821. [6]DS 1823.

TRINITY, THE MOST HOLY

On the day of the Annunciation, the Holy Trinity entered mankind in a way hitherto unexampled: the Father sent the Son; the Son was made flesh by the power and operation of the Spirit.[1] God, a father in OT, becomes henceforth the father of Jesus Christ; the Messiah awaited by all generations is God himself, the Word; the *Ruah*, representing heretofore God's intervening power, is now the very personal source of that power. NT shows the persons intervening in the economy of salvation. To each person separately, Christian literature has tended to relate Mary. The certain foundation is the divine motherhood of God the Son. This is dealt with, as is her relation with the Holy Spirit, in separate articles in the present work. (See also FATHER)

If it is true that every creature and especially every rational creature raised to the life of grace mirrors the Holy Trinity, this exemplary effect is most perfectly realized in Mary. Vatican Council II teaches: "Redeemed in an especially sublime manner by reason of the merits of her Son, and united to him by a close and indissoluble tie she [Mary] is endowed with the supreme office and dignity of being the Mother of the Son of God. As a result she is also the favourite daughter of the Father and the temple of the Holy Spirit" (LG 53). LG ends with the words: "May she do so [intercede with her Son in the fellowship of the saints] until all the peoples of the human family, whether they are honoured with the name of Christian, or whether they still do not know their Saviour, are happily gathered into the one People of God, for the glory of the Most Holy and undivided Trinity" (LG 69).

---

[1]Cf. Josephus de la Cerda, *Maria effigies revelatioque trinitatis* (Almeria, 1640).

TYPE OF THE CHURCH

Teaching Authority: The Mary-Church typology, fully investigated in recent times, is clearly expressed by Vatican II.[1] LG 63, 64 read: "The Blessed Virgin is also intimately connected with the Church through the gift of the divine maternity and its function, by which she is united with her Son, the Redeemer, and through

her distinctive graces and offices. As St. Ambrose already taught, the Mother of God is a type of the Church, that is in the context of her faith, her charity and her perfect union with Christ. In the mystery of the Church, itself rightly styled a mother and a virgin, the Blessed Virgin Mary has taken precedence; whether as a virgin or a mother she stands out eminently and uniquely as an exemplar. Believing and obeying, not knowing man but overshadowed by the Holy Spirit, she brought forth on earth the very Son of the Father. As the new Eve she affirmed her faith, which was undiluted by doubt of any kind, not in the ancient serpent but in God's messenger. She gave birth to the Son, whom God placed, among many brethren, as the first-born, that is among the faithful, in whose birth and upbringing she cooperates with maternal love. (64). "And now the Church studying her hidden sanctity and imitating her charity, faithfully accomplishes the Father's will and by the word of God, which she has welcomed with faith, she herself becomes a mother; by her preaching and by baptism she engenders to new and immortal life, children conceived of the Holy Spirit and born of God. She is also a virgin who keeps the faith she has pledged to her Spouse in its fullness and purity; as she imitates the Mother of her Lord she guards like a virgin intact faith, firm hope and genuine charity."

This passage is the first and still the most significant to come from the Teaching Authority on the Mary-Church typology. The modern Popes had frequently spoken of Mary's relationship with the Church; but never before Vatican II, of Mary as type or figure of the Church. Reflecting thought which had recently emerged, as will be seen, Fr. Balic and Mgr. Philips had included the theme in the *schema* which they submitted to the Doctrinal Commission. At this stage the following changes were made: "in the context of faith, charity and perfect union with Christ" were added to "type of the Church"; "whom God placed" before the words "firstborn among many brethren"; "by the word of God which she has welcomed with faith" before "she herself becomes a mother"; "for by preaching" before "by baptism."

The explanatory notes provided for the Council Fathers marked clearly the limits of typology: "This appellation [Mary as type of Church] put forward by St. Ambrose is evidently not understood in the context of hierarchical structure or of sacramental signs but, as the Doctrinal Commission has explicitly added, "in the context of faith, charity and perfect communion with Christ." (*Communionis* is used here; *unionis* in the *schema*, where it remained).

The passage drew little comment in the Council assembly: it was well drafted and the Fathers were not familiar with the subject. After the September debate, a quotation from St. Ambrose and St. Augustine—"imitating the Mother of her Lord, since it was not possible bodily, she is nevertheless a mother and virgin in mind," was abridged to take some words from another text of St. Augustine and read thus: "she keeps intact faith, firm hope and genuine charity"—"by the power of the Holy Spirit." At the final *Modi* stage one change was made: the word keeps (*custodit*) was added for faith pledged to her Spouse and guards, (*servat*) for the theological virtues.

Sacred Scripture: The testimony of Tradition, beginning with the fourth century Fathers, is much clearer on the subject than that of Sacred Scripture. The use of the Lucan infancy narrative (*qv*) to support the typology depends on the interchangeable roles and attributes of individuals and corporate personalities, of Mary and Israel, of Mary and the Church. If Mary is portrayed by Lk as the Daughter of Zion then she is also by intrinsic continuity the type of the Church. It was in his commentary on Lk's infancy narrative that St. Ambrose taught that Mary is the type of the Church. Modern commentators on St. John speak convincingly on the interpretation. "Mary like the Church and before her," writes A. Feuillet, "realises the prodigious motherhood of Zion announced by the prophets; this is probably the general meaning of the Johannine texts devoted to Mary."[2] "Two ideas stand out," says F.-M. Braun, O.P., "and bring into relief the others which are prominent: that of Eve-Mary continued in Mary-Church. That is the culmination of all. Mary replaces the old Eve, she is the woman of the Protoevangelium, as Mother of the Saviour, as participant in the victory won over the ancient serpent and as Mother of Christians. From the triple viewpoint she typifies the Church, of which she seems to achieve the whole destiny."[3] On Calvary, says Max Thurian, "the Mother of God becomes the type of the Church. Henceforth it will not be possible to speak of the Church, of her humility, motherliness, her faith or her joy . . . without conceiving of Mary, the Mother of the Lord, as her pure expression, her archetype, and as her first realization."[4]

The strongest biblical support for the typology remains in Rev 12 (see WOMAN IN). Since Ambrose Autpert (*qv*), exegetes have, from time to time, seen the "woman" as representing both Mary and the Church; the idea that one is the type of the other is in harmony with this dual identification.

History: As St. Ephraem (*qv*) was the first known witness to the idea of Mary's sponsal union with Christ, he appears as the first to express the idea that Mary was a type of the Church: "Mary who saw him is a symbol of the Church, which will first see the signs of his coming."[5] St. Epiphanius was less explicit: "Indeed the sentence of Scripture is taken from Mary and we can adapt it to the Church: 'For this reason a man will leave his father and mother and cling to his wife and they will be two in one flesh'; the Apostle says: 'This is a great mystery; I speak in Christ and his Church.'"[6]

Tertullian (*qv*) had an idea of Eve as type of Mary and the Church, but on our subject St. Ambrose is the first clear voice in the Western Church: "Mary is truly espoused but a virgin, because she is a type of the Church which is immaculate but wedded." "What was prophesied of Mary was as a type of the Church."[7]

St. Augustine achieved the full doctrine: "Consider how the Church is the bride of Christ, a thing that is clear. What will be more difficult to understand, yet is true, she is the mother of Christ. The Virgin Mary went before her as her type. Whence I ask you is Mary the Mother of Christ if not because she gave birth to the members of Christ? You, to whom I speak, are the members of Christ; who has given birth to you? I hear the voice of your heart: Mother Church. This Mother is honoured, similar to Mary, she brings forth, yet is a virgin."[8] His words on the virgin Church are written into LG 64: "What is this virginity of mind? Intact faith, firm hope, genuine charity."[9] "It was fitting," he says elsewhere, "that our Head should be born of a virgin in the flesh to signify thereby that his members in the spirit should be born of the Church which is a virgin."[10]

St. Bede the Venerable develops the idea in a remarkable passage: "Which, in the pattern of the blessed ever virgin Mary, is both wedded and immaculate, as a virgin conceives us by the Spirit, as a virgin brings us forth without pain, and as espoused to one but rendered fruitful by another, through its individual parts which make one Catholic body, is visibly joined to the Pontiff placed over her but is filled by the power of the invisible Holy Spirit . . ."[11] The passage was quoted in the annotation to a draft of LG for the Council Fathers.

With the exception of St. Albert the Great, the great Scholastic Doctors did not develop the theme. Nor is it found in subsequent literature until the "return to the sources," and the ecumenical approach of the present age. Luther (qv) had been aware of the idea, as was Sergius Bulgakov in the present century. It throws light on the mystery of Mary and is a valuable insight, provided that it does not decline into literary artifice. It must not lessen Mary's personality. To this end the best safeguard is to relate the typology explicitly to the Holy Spirit, as the Fathers and Vatican II did.

[1]Cf. for bibliography to 1951, R. Laurentin, BSFEM, 9(1951), p. 145-52; M. J. Scheeben, Mariology, II (English tr. London, 1947), 250-53; id., The Mysteries of Christianity (English tr. 1954, St. Louis, London), 546-48; J. B. Terrien, La Mère de Dieu et la Mère des hommes (Paris, 1902), vol III, book VIII, ch. 1-2, pp. 1-84; O. Semmelroth, Urbild der Kirche (Wurzburg, 1950), English tr. Mary, Archetype of the Church (New York, 1963); H. Rahner, S.J., Maria und die Kirche (Innsbruck, 1951), English tr. Mary and the Church (London, 1960); A. Muller, Ecclesia-Maria, Die Einheit Marias und der Kirche (Fribourg, 1951); BSFEM 1951, '52, '53; R. Laurentin, Marie l'Église et le Sacerdoce, (Paris, I, 1952, II, 1953); H. Coathalem, S.J., Le parallélisme entre la Sainte Vierge et l'Église dans la tradition latine jusqu'à la fin du XIIe siècle (Rome, 1954) EstM, 1957; MSt 1958; ME, vol III, De parallelismo Mariam inter et Ecclesiam, Rome, 1959, 668 pp.; M. Thurian, Mary, Mother of the Lord, Figure of the Church (London, 1963); A. Milano, "Maria, figura della Chiesa," Via verita e vita, 15(1966), 37-52; J. Esquerda Bifet, "Significado salvifico de Maria como tipo de la Iglesia," EstM, 145-92; id., "Maria tipo de la Iglesia," EstM 31(1968), pp. 185-239; id., same title (Burgense, 1968), 25-61; P. M. Migliore, O.F.M.Cap., "Maria e la Chiesa: sacramento della salvezza," Miles Immaculatus 4(1968), 159-69; E. Carroll, O.Carm. "Mary and the Church," AER 160(1969), 291-311; B. Rovira, "Maria como tipo de la Iglesia," EstM 32(1969), 125-48; P. de Alcantara Martinez, O.F.M., "Sintesis de los conceptos 'Madre y tipo de la Iglesia' en la teologia y en su proyección espiritual, EstM 34(1970), 75-90; G. M. Roschini, O.S.M., "Analogia tra Maria e la Chiesa," Mater Ecclesiae, 8(1972), 147-53; R. Kugelman, C.P., "The Hebrew concept of corporate personality and Mary, the type of the Church," MSS VI, 179-84. [2]Maria, VI, 66. [3]La Mère des Fidèles, 2nd ed. (Paris-Tournai, 1954), 158. [4]Mary, Mother of the Lord, Figure of the Church, London, 1963, p. 164. [5]Hymns on the Crucifixion, 4, 17, CSCO 249, p. 43. [6]Haer. 78, 19, PG 42, 730. [7]In Luc. II, 7, PL 15, 1555; CSEL 32-IV, p. 45. [8]Serm. Denis, ed. Morin, 8, p. 163. [9]In Jo tr. 13, 12, PL 35, 1499. [10]De S. Virg., PL 40, 399. [11]In Luc. expos. I, cap 2, PL 92, 330.

U

UBERTINO OF CASALE (1259-c. 1330)

A leader of the Franciscan "Spirituals," U. composed in 1305 the Arbor vitae crucifixae Jesu, a work dealing with the principal episodes in the Saviour's life, with doctrinal and spiritual insights and polemical digressions.[1] St. Bernardine of Siena (qv) reproduced in his works, almost literally, some 47 of the 101 chapters in the book: this was especially true of the Marian chapters, so that the very considerable influence of B's Marian teaching on subsequent writers is ultimately traceable to U.[2]

Mary is above all orders of creatures, constituting an order in herself; there is no grace or glory in an inferior creature which she did not have in much more excellent manner. "The Blessed Virgin was the first-born of the redemption of her Son; and he came more to redeem her than any other creature."[3] U. did not teach the Immaculate Conception, however, holding that Mary was sanctified in her mother's womb, and freed of the root of sin (fomes peccati) at the Annunciation. Thereon she received "as great a perfection of grace, abundance of divine charisms and consummation of all virtues" as a creature on earth could receive outside hypostatic union.[4] In the Incarnation she gave her consent for all human nature and was more blessed to conceive in her mind than in her flesh—a Thomistic and Augustinian idea respectively.

Mary is related to each person of the Holy Trinity: "This day [the Annunciation] is the most important solemnity of the Virgin Mother of God, whereby she became the spouse (qv) of God the Father, the mother and associate (socia *genitrix*) of his Son, the wonderful treasure-house of the Holy Spirit: the sanctuary and most fair temple of the whole Trinity, the queen and mistress of angels."[5]

The profound bond between Mother and Son and the immense role *vis a vis* mankind is rarely lost sight of. In a typically Franciscan presentation of the Bethlehem scene, U. can speak of "my most merciful Mother," and refer to Mary's reflective attitude and to her "heart stirred and moved by the Holy Spirit."[6] He wrote with special insight on St. Joseph (*qv*)—St. Bernardine's famous sermon was largely from his work—and also feelingly on Mary's love for Joseph.

The Circumcision evokes thoughts of compassion, as of joy at the promise of future redemption. The offering in the Presentation (*qv*) is made in the context of Mary's coredemption, though the word is not used: "With the fullest and most perfect charity I present my beloved Son Jesus to train, instruct, redeem, remake and glorify those who wish to share in this redemption and benefit. And I promise that I myself shall become with unchangeable charity their advocate, mother, protectress and guardian, apologist and defender from all enemies."[7]

In different contexts U. insists on the association between Mary and Jesus (see ASSOCIATE): Jesus wished to associate his mother in his pain;[8] Mary asks the Father to associate her with the Son in his Passion;[9] the reader is asked in the context of 2 Cor 1, 7, to "measure how much the Virgin was . . . associated with the Resurrection,"[10] or again is reminded of the "stupendous prodigy that a woman is associated with the divine glory."[11] Save the Pseudo-Albert (*qv*) and those directly dependent on him, (St. Antoninus, for example) no other medieval writer emphasised this concept so much: the article referred to shows its importance in recent Marian theology.

U. is abundant on the Compassion (*qv*). He also has the idea of Mary's faith surviving alone in the Passion (see FAITH IN THE PASSION): "Because the Virgin alone worthily sorrowed for Jesus on the Saturday [of the Passion] and was alone the pillar of the Church in the foundation of faith, therefore Saturday is hers both for reverence by the celebration of Masses and for abstinence in veneration of her sorrows."[12] Still more important in this context is the idea of coredemption, already expressed: "One thing is necessary, that I, Jesus your Son, should die in atrocious pain, that you, my Mother should die with me in similar manner and that the world should be generously redeemed."[13]

U. applies the word Mediatress (*qv*) to Mary.[14] He also stated first most explicitly the doctrine of the universal mediation of grace, which is usually attributed to St. Bernardine—who here also borrowed from him. St. Bernard (*qv*) of course had practically prepared the way with his oft-quoted dictum that God wished us to have all things through Mary: "The most grateful Son placed all things in the hand of his Mother, as in the dispenser of all graces"[15] . . . "Mary . . . became the mother of all the elect and thus the plenary treasurer of the charisms of the most blessed Trinity, so that not an iota of any even the least grace is given, unless it pass through Mary's dispensing act."[16]

---

[1]Ed. Venice, 1485; cf. G. M. Colosanti, O.F.M.Cap., "Maria SS. nella vita di Cristo decondo 'L'Arbor Vitae' di Ubertino da Casale, O.Min.," MM, 24(1962), 349-380; *id., "I SS Cuori di Gesu e di Maria nell'Arbor vitae' di Ubertino da Casale, O. Min.,"* in *Miscellanea Francescana,* 59(1959), 1-40. [2]Cf. Emmerich Blondeel d'Isegem, "L'Influence d'Ubertin de Casale sur les écrits de S. Bernardin de Sienne," *Collectanea Franciscana,* 5(1935), 5-44, esp. 27-39. [3]*Arbor vitae,* 4, 38, 199ra. [4]1, 8, 15rb. [5]1, 9, 22rb. [6]1, 11, 36b. [7]2, 5, 51c. [8]4, 11. [9]4, 12, 158d. [10]4, 29, 174d. [11]4, 39. [12]4, 27, 171b; 13, 4, 38. [13]Cf. C. Balic, O.F.M., "Die Corredemptrix-frage innerhalb der franziskanen Theologie," in *Franzis., St.,* 39(1957), esp. pp. 235-237. [14]1, 11, 36rb. [15]3, 6, 84ra. [16]1, 9, 22rb.

UNION WITH MARY

The Christian is united with Mary by the essential bond of the Mystical Body of Christ: a union of grace which transcends time and space, time and eternity. This union is of a special kind by reason of the relationship between Mary and the Church (see MOTHER OF THE CHURCH) and her spiritual motherhood (*qv*). Such things are objective, grounded in the divine economy of salvation. To what extent personality affects them in each case is more difficult to determine. Divine choice and Mary's personal choice under God are the ultimate factors: not subject to any human law, wrapped in the natural and supernatural mystery of Mary and the natural mystery of the human person.

Spiritual writers propose union with Mary as an ideal to the soul seeking perfection and indicate the ways of prayer and self-direction conducive to this end.[1] The lives of the saints and records of devout souls afford evidence which must be sifted and assessed in the light of sound doctrine to show the validity and scope of union with Mary as an extraordinary grace in the mystical order.

[1]Cf. E. Neubert (author of patristic and doctrinal works) *Marie dans le Dogme; Marie dans l'Eglise Anténicéenne; La Vie d'Union à Marie,* 5th ed. (Paris, 1957, with references to his other works, *Mon Idéal, Jésus, Fils de Marie; Marie et notre Sacerdoce* etc.)

V

VATICAN I

Vatican Council I did not publish doctrine on Our Lady. Interest in Marian questions was incidental but not insignificant.[1] Pius IX, who called the Council, had defined the Immaculate Conception. In the preliminaries to the Council he stressed the intercessory role of Our Lady, as John XXIII would later do before Vatican II. He spoke of her patronage "than which there is none more powerful with God." To bishops who echoed this conviction in a letter to him, he wrote of his intention to place the assembly under the special protection of her "beneath whose foot, from the origin of things, the head of the serpent had been subjected and who had, accordingly, alone destroyed all heresies." By *Aeterni Patris,* 29 June, 1868, the Pope announced the opening of the Council on 8 December, 1869, feast of the Immaculate Conception. By *Multiplices inter,* on the 27th, he asked that the Mother of God be especially invoked in Roman churches during the Council.

There was talk about the analogy between the dogma of the Immaculate Conception and that on papal infallibility, and of the suitability of a definition of the former by the Council which was deemed unnecessary. Attention especially was given to the Assumption. Pius XII in *Munificentissimus Deus* stated that "a considerable number of the Fathers of the [first] Vatican Council urgently petitioned the Apostolic See" to define the dogma. One such petition or *Postulatum* was in the name of "about 200" Fathers. The *Postulata* were presented to the Council steering commission by two bishops active in organising them, Joseph Dusmet, O.S.B., of Catania and Louis Maria Ideo, O.P., of Liparia in Portugal. This commission met on 14 March, 1870 and unanimously

rejected the combined request for three reasons: since all believed the truth there was no need for a definition; such a definition would be inopportune in the circumstances; the traditional faith of believers would be endangered by the controversies and historical debates which would be stirred up between Catholics and non-Catholics.[2] A special "Congregation" to deal with petitions, meeting on 8 May following, decided not to submit any such petition to the Council discussions; the Fathers were of opinion that the petition should be preserved in the archives to Our Lady's greater glory.[3] Next day Pius IX approved these decisions and expressed his praise of the bishops who had signed: in number they would be more than a quarter of the total membership.

A clash of opinion inside the Council was thus avoided as a number of bishops—possibly over 130—had come to Rome to oppose the Assumption as some opposed papal infallibility.

The contents of the documents submitted contain a number of theological points which would be debated between 1870 and 1950. The lengthiest submission was by Archbishop Martinez of San Cristobal, occupying 24 columns of Mansi, an extended treatise on Marian theology. There were no Marian theologians in the Council entourage of the quality remarked just before Vatican II. Three are mentioned: A. Vaccarri, O.S.B., author in 1869 of a book on the definability of the Assumption; Fr. Buselli, O.F.M., and S. Hunter, S.J., whose lecture on the subject in Rome at the time was used in one petition.

A draft text, circulated among the Fathers of Vatican I but not then considered, influenced the Marian chapter of LG, the revised *schema, De mysterio Verbi incarnati,* 22 July, 1870, ch. IV. The passage on the divine maternity, which referred to Ephesus, ended thus: "She, therefore, bringing forth Christ our God and Lord became *to us a mother of grace* and triumphing through him over the ancient serpent, was made *mother* of all *the living*, nor does she cease by her powerful *intercession to win us gifts of eternal salvation.*" Italicised words are found in LG. Vatican II preferred "in the order of grace"; it changed "does not cease" (*nec desinit*) to "continues to" (*pergit*) and altered "powerful" (*potenti*) to "manifold" (*multiplici*) in regard to Our Lady's intercession. J. Kleutgen's report says that the affirmation of the divine motherhood was made at the request of Eastern Fathers and continues: "Some other matters were added as suitable to stir the faithful so that, in the iniquity of the present times, they should more confidently implore the help of the Virgin Mary."[4]

Points to note further: 108 Fathers asked that the words *Virgo Immaculata* be added to the Hail Mary, a request not granted; the phrase "Mediatress most close to us" (*praesentissimam mediatricem*) was used in the letter by Bishops Dusmet and Ideo; "Coredemptress" occurs in a document sent by Bishop Laurent of Quersoneso; 27 Fathers led by the Archbishop of Naples submitted a lengthy study on Christ and Mary as the final and exemplary causes of the universe (see PRIMACY).

[1]Sources: Pius IX and the preliminaries, Mansi 49, 248ff; *Postulata*, Synod of Smyrna, 13 June, 1869, Mansi 53, 517-19; Jacinto Maria Martinez, Archbishop of San Cristobal in Havana, 15 August, 1869, *ibid.*, 490-514; Antonio Monescillo, Bishop of Jaen, 8 January, 1870, *ibid.*, 489-90; "About 200 Fathers," 23 February, 1870, *ibid.*, 481-90; Bishop Francesco Majorsini, 2 November, 1870, *ibid.*, 514-18; 108 Bishops asking that the words *Virgo Immaculata* be added to the Hail Mary, 19 February 1870, Mansi 53, 592-96. Cf. M. Garrido, O.S.B., "Doctrina Mariana en las Actas del Concilio Vaticano I," EphMar, 13(1963), 315-69; G. Hentrich-R.G. de Moos, *Petititiones de Assumptione corporea B.V. Mariae in caelum definienda ad Sanctam Sedem delatae* (Rome, 1942, Vatican Press) II, VI, ch. 2, *De Motu Assumptionistico in ipso Conc. Vatc. manifestato*, p. 901-917; G. M. Roschini, O.S.M., *Maria Santissima*, III, 583-584. [2]Mansi 53, 687. [3]Mansi 53, 695. [4]Mansi 53, 289, 290, 303.

VATICAN II.
THE SECOND VATICAN COUNCIL
The Council teaching is contained in chapter VIII of LG and in brief passages or phrases in ten other documents: to which may be added a reference to Mary in the Council address to the world, and the lengthy passage in Pope Paul's address promulgating LG.[1] Teaching in texts other than LG is dealt with in the relevant articles in the present work. Here LG is the subject treated. Ample primary documentation exists, as by now all relevant Council documents have been published. It is not customary to release minutes of Council commission meetings, if they were kept. There is an immense amount of secondary literature on the subject of Mary and Vatican II, individual works and symposia—many of the latter the result of sessions organised by Marian societies. Many books and articles on Marian theology or piety published since the Council refer to its teaching, even if this is not their direct subject. Theological experts responsible for the Council texts or asked to advise on it have made statements. Material of varying kinds distributed by individuals or groups during the Council, or comments by Observers or Lay Auditors then or later have interest.

The Council was announced on 25 January, 1959, by John XXIII who lived to open with a remarkable address the first session, on 11 October, 1962; this session he also officially terminated. His personal part in the Council preliminaries was deeply coloured by Marian piety, in exhortation and in the programme of prayer which he fostered. He visited Loreto before the inauguration which he timed for the feast of Our Lady's divine motherhood; his inaugural speech ended with a prayer which opened, "O Mary Help of Christians, Help of Bishops, of whose love we have recently had particular proof in your temple of Loreto, where we venerated the mystery of the Incarnation, dispose all things for a happy and propitious outcome . . ."

Very many of the future Council Fathers had been, in one way or another, involved in the movement of Marian teaching and piety associated with the pontificate of Pius XII. One third of the Fathers were religious, most of whose orders or congregations have strong Marian traditions. Marian associations of different kinds had claimed the attention or authority of many of the bishops. Theological and devotional congresses, written or homiletic publication, had attained in the nineteen-fifties vast dimensions—written works were of the order of a thousand a year for a time.

The story of Our Lady and Vatican II opens in continuity with this general movement. When the replies sent to an inquiry circularised among bishops and Catholic university faculties by the ante-preparatory commission, whose president was Cardinal Tardini, were analysed, they gave the following result: 570 future Council Fathers wished to include Marian subjects on a conciliar agenda; three of the university faculties in Rome—the Antonianum, S. Bonaventura and Marianum—made a similar request; 382 Fathers asked for a statement on Mary's mediation, the largest number agreeing on any one item of the entire conciliar programme. The next highest figure was 320 who sought a condemnation of communism; 266 desired a dogmatic definition on mediation.

The requests came before the preparatory theological commission which had been set up by Pope John on Pentecost Sunday, 1960. The commission planned four *schemata* and despite an earlier preference for inclusion of the Marian theme in the one on the *depositum fidei*, it was decided in October of that year at a full meeting to take it in the *schema* on the Church. Textual composition fell largely to Fr. C. Balic, O.F.M. and, by July, 1961, he and his associates in the Pontifical Marian Academy, had a third draft ready. It was discussed at a meeting held in the house, *Il Divino Maestro*, in Arriccia by the sub-commission (Mgrs. Colombo, Schauf, Lattanzi, Philips, and Frs. Balic, Gagnebet, O.P., Lécuyer, C.S.Sp., Witte, S.J.). The title of the *schema* was *Mary, Mother of Jesus and Mother of the Church*. Members of the theological commission received the draft text and some sent comments on it. A fourth somewhat altered text emerged with a new title: *Mary, Mother of the Mystical Body*. A fifth with a still lengthier one, *Mary, Mother of the Head and Mother of the members of the Mystical Body*, was examined during two sessions held in the Antonianum University on 21 and 22 September. The idea was now in the air that the *schema* might not remain part of that on the Church, but stand on its own. Among those present at the Antonianum sessions were Archbishop Dubois (author of a substantial work on Marian theology), Bishop Griffiths, Mgrs. Philips, Colombo, Fenton, Lattanzi, and Frs. Laurentin, Gagnebet, O.P., Tromp, S.J., Congar, O.P., Garcia Garces, C.M.F., Bertetto, S.D.B., Philip of the Holy Trinity, O.D.C., and Salaverri, S.J.

Most of these had published important works on Marian theology. Another meeting was held in *Domus Mariae* in Rome on 23 November. Composition was becoming difficult owing to contradictory opinions and uncertainty on the status of the *schema*, whether it would be independent or part of that on the Church. Yet by 20 January 1962, a completed text was sent to the theological commission.

When the commission met, it decided that the Marian *schema* would be independent. Clarification was sought on Our Lady's mediation. The *schema* must then be enlarged. To this end there was much consultation between the responsible sub-commission and other members of the theological commission. The outcome of the joint labours was the addition of a lengthy passage on the titles given to Mary to express her association with Christ in the economy of salvation. In the final hasty drafting, detailed revision was not possible so there were some repetitions. The *schema* with the title *Mary Mother of God and Mother of men* was accepted at the June meeting of the ninety-strong Central Commission, with sixteen members expressing reservation on the title Mediatress. There was no objection to an independent *schema*, nor to the title "Mother of the Church" written into the text. John XXIII approved the *schema* on 10 November; it was given to the Fathers on the 23rd.

This first conciliar *schema* ran to over 1,700 words. In structure and sequence of thought it is in contrast with the Marian chapter finally approved. It deals with Mary's close relationship with Christ, her part in the economy of salvation, the titles whereby her association with Christ therein is expressed, her singular privileges, the cult due to her and her role in promoting Christian unity. There are 29 biblical references in the text and 22 in the annotation; Mary in the gospel from the Annunciation is briefly portrayed, but there is no overt summary of OT and NT texts in order, as in LG 55-59. There are, in the notes, 22 references to the Fathers, Eastern and Western. In the controversy over the "sources" of revelation the solution adopted was reliance on papal teaching.

Despite a strong plea by Cardinal Ottaviani, the *schema* was not considered by the Council during the first session. Beyond brief references to Mary by Cardinals Suenens and Montini (each gave her the title Mother of the Church) and some moving phrases by Pope John in his concluding discourse, there was silence about her. From the date of distribution of the first *schema* and its reissue in the following May under a new title, *The Blessed Virgin Mary, Mother of the Church*, over 130 Fathers individually and about 150 as signatories of group statements sent comments to Rome on the contents. Fr. Balic made a digest of these replies and circulated it to Council Fathers.

The labour of draftsmen, experts and Fathers would not be lost: some 300 words of the *schema* would pass directly into the final document, more than 70 indirectly.

The second session: During September, 1963, and the first days of October, seven Fathers requested that the *schema* on Our Lady be made part of that on the Church: Cardinal Frings, Bishops Ferrero di Cavallerleone, Gargitter, Elchinger and Mendez Arceo, Cardinal Silva Henriquez in the name of the Chilean bishops, and Bishop (later Cardinal) Garrone in the name of the French bishops. Cardinal Arriba y Castro opposed the idea. After some discussion between the Council commission and the Moderators, it was announced on 23 October that next day the Fathers would be asked to hear arguments *pro* and *con* and on the 29th to decide the question by vote.

Cardinal Santos of Manila put the case for an independent *schema* and Cardinal Koenig of Vienna for inclusion in the Constitution on the Church. Each affirmed belief in the doctrine of the Church on Our Lady which was not in question. Cardinal Santos argued from Mary's preeminence over all under God, from her role previous to the existence of the Church, from the call for full doctrine on her for the good of the faithful and out of charity for the separated brethren. Marian theology has links with Christology and Soteriology as well as Ecclesiology. Moreover it would not be possible to relate the Marian text to the topics in the other chapters of the Constitution on the Church as planned. There were other points in his discourse not to be lightly dismissed. Inclusion of the Marian text would appear to commit the Council to Church type Marian theology.

Cardinal Koenig thought that a separate *schema* would give the impression that a new dogma was being proposed which was not the Council's intention. He thought that inclusion need not lead to Church type Marian theology,

treating Mary as a "member among members." The essential theological position, he argued, would be saved by treating Mary as a member, eminent, in the People of God, by emphasising her role as type of the Church, her saving role so like that of the Church.

The Cardinal ordered his arguments under four heads, theological as just stated, historical, pastoral, ecumenical. He picked out points of interest under each head, not with the greatest accuracy or cogency, but easy to follow by those to whom the whole subject was new. The Cardinal thought that the cult of Mary was at times unduly separated from the mystery of Christ and the Church and an integrated *schema* would help restore the balance. The Easterns would recognise the *Theotokos* in the presentation he was urging, and Protestants through the Bible were becoming sympathetic to the theme Mary-People of Israel-Church.

The long week-end between the speeches and the vote was filled with tension and feverish activity. Much hurried briefing was sought and given: there was a spate of lecturing. *Ad hoc* scripts were distributed among the Fathers; in some the language used was vigorous. Some of the Observers desired an integrated *schema* eagerly; most from the separated Western communions would have welcomed it. On the day of the vote the Moderator, Cardinal Agagianian, assured the Fathers that doctrine about Our Lady or devotion to her were not at issue; rewriting of a new text, should this be necessary, would be controlled by the doctrinal commission.

The result of the vote was: votes cast, 2,193; majority required, 1,097 (i.e. 50 per cent plus one); for inclusion, 1,114; for a separate *schema*, 1,074; spoiled votes, 5. The difference was less than 2 per cent, the necessary majority reached with but 17 votes to spare. This was the narrowest majority and the lowest favourable vote in the entire history of the Council: with the exception of two *schemata* favourable votes were generally well over 90 per cent.

The news media had been given an instance of confrontation which they always relish; it was exploited in a way that the bishops did not foresee. It is an event immediately thought of, when people, years after the Council, observe a decline in Catholic devotion to Our Lady, a change that opinion polls have shown undesirable to Catholics in different countries. For the Council could be made to appear divided on the subject of Our Lady. Nor could the faithful understand the failure to issue any substantial teaching on Our Lady during the second session. They would not note the brief, instructive article in the *Constitution on the Liturgy, 103*.

There was a further illogicality. When the new *schema* was presented in the next session, the official report stated that in relation to the mystery of the Word incarnate, "a Mariological exposition goes beyond (*excedit*) a treatise on the Church . . . it had to go beyond the strict limits of the *schema*."

To provide the new text, a committee of four members was appointed: Cardinals Santos and Koenig, Bishops Doumith (a Maronite) and Theas of Lourdes. They were to have Fr. Balic and Mgr. Philips as experts; the two represented the different trends manifest and were collaborators in Marian publications before and since the Council (each has contributed to the other's *Festschrift*).

On the experts fell the burden of work. They were to produce a *schema* that would "satisfy all or nearly all." They had to take account of drafts already in existence: one submitted by the Chilean hierarchy; another by the Spanish Mariological Society, supported by the hierarchy; Dom Butler's, sponsored by the English bishops; the memorandum sent in by the German and Scandinavian bishops, presented by Cardinal Doepfner; the first *schema* and drafts submitted by R. Laurentin, E. Dhanis, S.J. (Rector of the Gregorian University); J. A. Alonso, C.M.F., Mgr, Philips, M. Llamera, O.P. and N. Garcia Garces, C.M.F. (jointly).

One method of work was to attempt a composite product from some of these documents. Another was consultation. On 25 November, theologians of different tendencies met in Rome with the special experts present, in search of common ground. Those who attended were Frs. Ciappi, O.P., Master of the Sacred Palace, Belanger, Fonzo, O.F.M.Conv., Garcia Garces, Grillmeier, S.J., Laurentin, Llamera, Moeller, Ochagabia Larrain, and Schmaus. The biblical, pastoral, ecumenical thrust of Council thinking was evident; there was agreement on nothing textual, but there was agreement on the possibility of a future text. Concluding the whole Council session, Pope Paul used a memorable phrase found later in LG 54: "a place [Mary's] highest after Christ and nearest to us."

The Third Session: The two experts aided by friends were to exchange draft texts and consider mutual objections until Fr. Balic accepted the fifth as an agreed statement for submission to the Doctrinal Commission. It was given general approval on 14 March and examined in detail on 6 June. This meeting was a landmark.

For reasons that are obscure there was a policy of silence about Our Lady in the composition of conciliar texts during the first months of 1964. There was no mention of her in the *schemata* then elaborated on the Missions and the Lay Apostolate; where such a mention had existed in *schemata* prior to this time, on the priesthood, priestly training and religious life, it was now deleted. The omission would be rectified in each case subsequently. In the same spirit, Our Lady's role in salvation was expressed in very moderate terms in the Marian *schema* now submitted. The abstract words cooperation and mediation were used, but Mediatress was omitted. A new title, *The Blessed Virgin Mary Mother of God, in the mystery of Christ and of the Church*, meant deletion of the appellation "Mother of the Church." In the text, the idea in the latter title was insinuated. There is reasonable evidence that at the June Meeting the Commission was informed that if the *schema* did not contain either the title Mediatress or Mother of the Church, it would be denied a majority vote in the assembly; this would affect the entire Constitution on the Church.

On orders from the Commission changes were made. Phrases were altered here and there, some of them significant: "is foreseen" was replaced by "is foreshadowed" for Gen 3:15 (see WOMAN IN); "freely offering, with him and through him, the victim born of her" in regard to Calvary gave way to "lovingly consenting to the immolation of the victim born of her." A short passage on Mary and Christian unity was dropped.

The largest addition was in the section dealing with Mary's saving function. The theological phrasing was strengthened by such words and sentences as: "Associate, noble beyond all others"; "she cooperated, in an altogether singular manner, in the work of the Saviour for the restoration of the supernatural life of souls"; "Accordingly the Blessed Virgin Mary has been customarily honoured [or adorned, *condecorari*] in the Church by the title of Mediatress, as by others." To the latter crucial passage there was a further addition to say that the Church professes this doctrine, experiences it continuously, and commends it to the faithful.

On 16 September of that year, the Council Fathers after an introductory report by Archbishop (now Cardinal) Roy began the debate on the new *schema*. Their response was diverse: 33 speeches in the assembly and altogether 57 written submissions. Until the Acts of the Council were published, preponderant attention was, understandably, given to the speeches; they occupy 120 pages of the Acts, the written submissions taking 89. The swaying opinion from one day to the next in the debate had an element of subdued drama.

In the speeches and the written statements two points recur constantly—mediation and Mary's motherhood of the Church. A number urged silence on the two subjects, while others insisted that they be retained in the text. An Eastern Council Father showed what he considered the difference between the Eastern Conception of Mary's mediation and Western ideas: he did not refer to Theophanes of Nicaea or any of the Palamite theologians.

Some other matters were raised: the chapter should be recast to give greater accuracy; biblical scholars should be brought in to assist in textual composition; the chapter should stand next to that on the mystery of the Church, i.e. as II; Mary should not be relegated to history, her influence on souls should be manifest; there should be a fuller account of her relationship with the Holy Spirit; there should be a reference to St. Joseph; Rev XII (see WOMAN IN) should be treated in the scriptural section; her role in the life of priests was worthy of treatment; the Council should make a formal act of consecration to Mary, Mother of the Church.

A number of speakers had supporting signatures. Three speakers were allowed, with the required number of signatures, to carry on the debate beyond the days fixed—there had been some confusion since the subject was taken up very early in the session. One of these may be named, as his intervention was at the request of Fr. Balic, who feared that with opposing views so bluntly exposed unanimity would be missed. So Cardinal Frings appealed to those on both sides to consent to sacrifice some of their quite properly held ideas so that, with the minor defects eliminated from the *schema*, they should assent to the best possible text—one which had

cost so much labour and perspiration to the responsible commissions and experts. Let all unite "that this decree may be achieved to the glory of God and of him whom he sent and in honour of the Virgin Mary, Mother of God whom we all—Fathers, Observers, Auditors—love most tenderly."

When revision was completed the altered text was again brought to the assembly. Archbishop Roy drew attention to five principal changes: addition of the words "as a most loving mother" as an equivalent statement of Mary's motherhood of the Church (art. 53); Mary's motherhood in the order of grace was more clearly expressed; "is invoked" was substituted for "honoured" in regard to Mediatress, and Advocate, Helper and Aid-giver were added to it; a theological explanation of mediation by analogies with divine goodness and Christ's priesthood was provided (art. 62, paragraph 2, over 50 words); over 50 words were also added to art. 65 on the apostolic activity of the Church modelled on Mary; a passage of over 100 words in the form of a prayer towards the end was deleted—there would be a reference to the "glory of the most holy and undivided Trinity."

Verbal precision was the aim of a number of brief changes, especially in the biblical section; sometimes the exact biblical words were used in place of others which implied a doctrine. "Daughter of Zion" was adopted; Mary was said to advance "in the pilgrimage of faith"; patristic borrowings were rendered more accurate.

The amended text was put to a vote on 29 October, 1964, exact anniversary of the divided assembly in 1963. The result was: voters, 2,091; *Placet* (Yes), 1559; *Placet juxta modum* (Yes with amendment), 521; *Non Placet* (No), 10; Spoiled vote, 1. Unanimity had been achieved.

Textual refining was completed on the basis of the amendments: of 95 presented, 26 were accepted. On grounds of intrinsic merit (in the judgement of the commission, not of supporting numbers) a request by 144 Fathers that "is indicated" from *Ineffabilis Deus* replace "is foreshadowed" for Gen 3:15 was refused. Two biblical corrections, each made by one Father, were accepted: "word" for "words" in Lk 1:38, and the reference to Cana. Several other corrections suggested by in each case one Father were accepted. Requests for change from both sides on the Mediatress text were refused; so was a plea to use the title "Mother of the Church" which some also did not wish to be even implied by the text.

Amendments of interest: "In view of the merits of her Son," for "by her Son," 53; "Mother of *men, especially* of the faithful," 54; readjustment of a text from St. Ambrose which had been dropped in the previous revision, 56; elimination of "figure of the faithful" after disciple, Jn 19:25-27, 58; addition of "Liturgies of the Church," 67; "anyone else" added to "separated brethren," 67; "exalted in heaven above all the saints and angels," 69.

On 18 November, the revised text was accepted by 2,096 votes to 23, with one spoiled vote. Next day LG as a whole received 2,134 votes with 10 against; the formal vote before promulgation was 2,151 for and 5 against; on the same day 39 votes were cast against the decree on the Eastern Churches, and 11 against that on Ecumenism.

Pope Paul, for the concelebrated Mass that ended the third session, chose 24 bishops in whose dioceses important Marian shrines exist. More than one-third of his concluding address was devoted to Our Lady and he solemnly proclaimed Mary "Mother of the Church."

Fourth Session: A number of Council documents which were published in the fourth session have brief passages on Mary; notably the decrees on the missionary activity of the Church (art. 4) and that on the ministry and life of priests (art. 18). She is cited as an example to women in the Council message to women; as she had been recalled by the Fathers in their opening message to the world. "We successors of the apostles have gathered here in singlehearted prayer with Mary the Mother of Jesus"—words not in the first draft text, added as the only amendment.

---

[1] Official text LG VIII, AAS, 57(1965), 58-67. Paul VI's words on Our Lady, AAS 56(1964), 1014-18. On Council preliminaries, official documents in *Acta et documenta Concilio Oecumenico Vaticano apparando* (Vatican City, 1960-1961), *Series I (Antepraeparatoria)*, Vols II. See Appendix Voluminis II, esp. analysis of opinions expressed by bishops consulted, p. 131-42; Vol III, opinions of university faculties; on phases of the Council, *Acta Synodalia*, Vol I, pt. IV, the first *schema*, p. 92-121; comments thereon, Vol II, pt. III, p. 677-857; Vol III, pt. 1, conciliar debate September, 1964, p. 435-544; written submissions, pt. II, p. 99-188. In the extensive literature, cf. collective works, EstM 27, 28 (1966), Spanish theologians, *Doctrina Mariana del Vaticano II*, esp. C. Balic, 1, p. 133-83, G. Philips, *ibid*, p. 187-209; EstM 30, 31 (1968), *Mariologia Conciliar* (LG VIII); BSFEM 22(1965), French theologians, *La Vierge dans la Constitution sur l'Église*; *La Madonna nella Costituzione 'Lumen Gentium'. Commento al capitolo VIII . . . . French theologians* (Milan, Massimo, 1966); CM (1965), p. 74-171; *Maria nel Concilio Vaticano II, Atti della VI settimana mariana nazionale*, Rome, *Opera Madonna Divino Amore* 1966; R. Laurentin, *La Vierge au Concile*, Paris, 1965; C. Balic, O.F.M., "La doctrine sur la bienheureuse Vierge Marie Mère de l'Église, et la Constitution 'Lumen Gentium' du Concile Vatican II," Div 9(1965), p. 464-82; *Animadversiones quoad Caput VIII LG, Mélanges C. de Kininck (Quebec, Laval, 1968) 47-60; Maria* in *Dizionario del Concilio Vaticano II (Rome, 1969)*, 1360-71; E. Carroll, O.Carm., "The Second Vatican Council," *Carmel in the World*, 5(1965), 279-91; G. Barauna, O.F.M., *La SS Vergine al servizio dell'economia della salvezza*, in *La Chiesa del Vaticano II* (Florence, Vallechi, 1965) 1137-1155; G. M. Besutti, O.S.M., *Lo schema mariano al Vaticano II* (Rome, 1966. The most fully documented before the publication of the Council Proceedings, 288 pp.); N. Garcia Garces, M. Llamera, J. de Aldama, in *Commentarios a la Constitucion sobre la Iglesia*, (Madrid, 1966), 924-1084; J. Esquerda, *La Virgen del Vaticano II* (Bilbao, 1966); O. Semmelroth, S.J., in *Das Zweite Vatikan, Konzil, Lex, Theol. Kirche*, 1966, p. 326-47; R. Caro, S.J., "El capitulo VIII de la Constitucion LG, Su contexto historico-teologico," EphMar 17(1967), 241-59; Th. Koehler, S.M., "Commentaire du chap, VIII de LG," CM, 11(1967), 39-44, 109-15, 169-76, 235-42; D. Flanagan, ch. VIII in *The Constitution on the Church*, ed. K. McNamara, Dublin, 1968; S. de Flores, S.M.M., *Maria nel mistero di Cristo e della Chiesa. Commento teologico-pastorale . . .* (Salone-Roma, 1968); A. Nino Picado, C.M.F., "La intervención espanola en la elaboración del capitulo VIII de la constitución LG, 18(1968) 1-2, pp. 5-310; very many documents beyond title; Ortensio da Spinetoli, O.F.M.Cap., *La Madonna della LG* (Rome, ed. Paoline, 1968); D. Bertetto, S.D.B., *Maria con Cristo e con la Chiesa* (Naples, Rome, Libreria ed. redenzione, 1969); E. Carruth, O.S.B., *Mary and the Council* (Glasgow, John Burns, 1969); G. M. Roschini, O.S.M., *Mariologia del Concilio Vaticano II* (Rome, Marianum, 1969), 426 pp.; *Maria Santissima*, I, 3-102; G. Philips, *L'Église et son mystère au II Concile du Vatican. Histoire, texte et commentaire de la Constitution LG*, vol II (Tournai, 1968), 207-89; T. Cranny, S.A., *Is Mary Relevant? A commentary on ch. VIII of LG* (New York, Exposition Press, 1970); M. Garrido Bonano, O.S.B., "Exegesis y valoración de textos patristicos en el capitulo VIII LG," EstM 33(1969), 33-80; Pedro de Alcantara Martinez, O.F.M., "La espiritualidad mariana segun el Concilio Vaticano II," EstM 33(1969), 105-28; M. O'Carroll, C.S.Sp., "Vatican II and Our Lady's Mediation," ITQ 27(1970), 24-55; H.-M. Guindon, S.M.M., *Marie du Vatican II* (Paris, Beauchesne, 1971); H. M. Manteau-Bonamy, O.P., *La Vierge Marie et le Saint-Esprit, Commentaire doctrinal et spirituel du chap. VIII LG*, 2nd ed. (Paris, Lethielleux, 1971); S. Meo, O.S.M., *Note di teologia dommatica sulla 2a parte del simbolo Niceno-Constant. e sulla 2a parte dell' VIII cap. LG* (Rome, Marianum, 1972); W. G. Most, *Vatican II Marian Council* (St. Paul Publications, Athlone, 1972).

VEGA, CHRISTOPHER DE (1595-1672)

Spanish author of *Theologia Mariana, sive certamina litteraria de B.V. Dei Genitrice Maria, quae tam apud theologos scholasticos quam apud sacrorum voluminum interpretes exagitari solent* which appeared at Lyons in 1653.[1] It was reprinted at Naples in 1866, at which Scheeben protested. The work contains some extravagant opinions and immoderate phrasing. V. threatens with the fate of Zechariah theologians who question the praise of Mary. He thought the private revelation made to St. Bridget sufficient ground for a papal definition of the Immaculate Conception, doubted that Mary should be called truly a child of Adam because of the Immaculate Conception. He thought that Mary's universal mediation would not be contrary to Christ's dignity, since her merited *de condigno*, Mary *de congruo* and by her prayers. He sought to reconcile her role, her compassion with the sufficiency of Christ's redemptive work—"the Redeemer infinitely sufficed for our ransom." V. was also the author of a work entitled *Devocion a Maria: passaporto o salvacondotto per una buona morte*, 1650.

---

[1]Cf. Cl. Dillenschneider, C.SS.R., *La Mariologie*, 176-78; J. P. Gransem, DTC, 152, 2611-12; Sommervogel, *Bibli. de la Comp. de Jésus*, VIII, 521-25.

VENANTIUS FORTUNATUS (*c.* 530-*c.* 610) — See Supplement, p. 389.

VIRGINITY OF MARY, THE

Mary of Nazareth conceived her Son Jesus while remaining a virgin; her virginity was not altered by childbirth; she remained a virgin in her marriage with St. Joseph.[1] The virginal conception is affirmed by Sacred Scripture—*virginitas ante partum*; the second was discerned by the Church's intuition—*virginitas in partu*; the third, *virginitas post partum*, the perpetual virginity, is strongly implied in the sacred text and, with the exception of Tertullian, has been held by important theologians from the beginning of Christianity.

Sacred Scripture: With the immense concentration of interest on the infancy narratives, the virginal conception of Jesus has been subjected to exhaustive study, principally its historicity. Mt and Lk drawing on different traditions concur in reporting the moment of conception: it was before Mary was married to Joseph her fiancé; it was directly due to the action of the Holy Spirit. The exclusion of the father is completely opposed to the entire series of biblical birth stories down to that of John the Baptist. This exclusion is evident in Mt's genealogy where a series of forebears called invariably "the father of" gives way to "Joseph the husband of Mary of whom Jesus was born, who is called the Christ" (1:16). Other readings have been proposed but this satisfies critical standards. Mt is explicit: "When his mother Mary had been betrothed to Joseph, before they came together she was found to be with child of the Holy Spirit," (1:18); "he [Joseph] knew her not until she had borne a son" (1:25). The evangelist delays on Joseph's "doubt" as if to emphasise that he was not the father of Mary's Child.

Lk too emphasises Mary's virginity in the moment of the conception. She is twice called a virgin (1:27), says that "she knows not man" (1:34), makes no mention of her future husband, hears the angel say not that she will give him a son, but that she will conceive in her "womb and bear a son" (1:31). The parallel annunciations and birth stories in Lk I and II, much analysed by recent scholars, confirm the event of the virginal conception in many ways. Zechariah is told that "Elizabeth, your wife will bear you a son" (1:13). He went to his home and "after these days his wife Elizabeth conceived" (1:23, 24), whereas after the angel departed from Mary Lk says "In those days Mary arose and went with haste (or "very thoughtfully") into the hill country" (1:39).

The encounter preliminary to conception which in Zechariah's case is on the human level, is in Mary's between her and the Spirit of God. This is the only instance in the Bible where the *Ruah* (*pneuma*, Spirit) descends on a mother to be, descends only after an exchange of views between God and the destined recipient of the *Ruah*, with her consent awaited and given. This intervention of the Spirit to accomplish a new reality within Mary is singular to her; there is no parallel in the words spoken to Zechariah—the sole reference to the Holy Spirit concerns John.

The verb *epiaskiazein*—"to overshadow"—used to express the Spirit's action, can, as D. Daube has shown, refer to conception, without losing its OT connotation of the divine presence. Through its semitic equivalents Hebrew *salal* and Aramaic *tallel*, from which came *tallith*, it can denote marital relations -*tallith* was the cloak of a scholarly or pious man and the Rabbis used the phrase "to spread the wings" (*tallith*) in this sense. The usage is found in Ruth: "I am Ruth, your maid-servant (*doule* in the Septuagint as in Lk 1:38) spread your wing (*pterugion*, "Skirt" in RSV is inaccurate) over your handmaid for you are next of kin." (Ruth 3:9; cp. Ezek 16:8) In Rabbinic literature Ruth's life is often interpreted as prefiguring Messianic events. Another word used by the Rabbis for marital union "to lay one's power" (*reshuth*) over a woman echoes in Lk 1:35, "the power of the Most High will overshadow you." Thus the Annunciation has a bridal character, with insistence on the human spouse as virginal, that is, exclusively given to God.

The descent of the Spirit on Mary is comparable with that promised to the Apostles in Acts 1:8; the same word *dynamis*, power, is used to signify the effect. But it will make the Apostles witnesses, whereas in Mary it is directed to the Child to be born—"therefore the Child to be born will be called holy, the Son of God."

Zechariah and Mary are each promised a miracle. The thrust of the annunciation to Mary is towards someone greater than John the Baptist, so a greater miracle than conception by a barren woman would logically follow, and Mary is given such an indication—"For with God nothing will be impossible" (1:37). Zechariah's son will be "great before the Lord" (1:15), Mary's son "will be great and will be called the Son of the Most High"; Zechariah's son will "turn many of the sons of Israel to the Lord their God (1:16), whereas Mary's son "will reign over the house of Jacob forever and of his kingdom there will be no end" (1:33). Zechariah points out to the angel that he and his wife are elderly; Mary keeps her replies, especially the act of consent, strictly in the singular, "let it be *to me* according to your word" (1:38). Mary's *fiat* closes the mystery within her person. Within a short time another person inspired by the Holy Spirit, her cousin Elizabeth, bears witness to the work of the Spirit exclusively hers: "Blessed is she who believed that there would be a fulfilment of what was spoken to her from the Lord" (1:45).

Lk II, whether from a different tradition or not, is strictly coherent with I on the virginity. Mary is called Joseph's "betrothed," though pregnant (2:5). Joseph is not called father of Jesus until after the birth, after the heavenly hymn which signified God's presence, after the presentation of the Child in the Temple and the recognition by Simeon, representative of Israel. All of Joseph's duties as described in this chapter are strictly legal, obedience to the imperial edict, 2:1,4, to Jewish ordinances, 2:32,41; there is no reference to physical parenthood where for example it would be expected, in the circumcision and naming ceremony: rather we read "he was called Jesus, the name given him before he was conceived in the womb" (2:21), a deliberate reminder surely of 1:31. The personal relationship between Jesus and Mary, founded on the fiat and unique in the Bible, is preserved through the chapter: to Mary not Joseph, Simeon speaks of the future mysteries (see SWORD OF SIMEON); she questions Jesus in the Temple; she guards the revelation, 2:19,51.

Why should the two evangelists narrate the virginal event with such sedulous attention to detail if it were not a fact? Those who do not accept the historical character of the infancy narratives should explain why it was that this particular event was so carefully invented. They must also explain why the pre-natal phase of the Messiah's existence was chosen for such invention, fiction. They must, moreover, tell the source of the idea. Mt quotes Is 7:14 but he did not get the idea in that text, as it was not thus interpreted by the Rabbis. The attempt to show links between pagan divine births and the evangelists fails totally; there is too in such stories a *hieros gamos*, totally absent in Mt and Lk.

Sacred Tradition: The doctrine of the virginal conception is found widely in the second century: a) in the official creeds, that of Hippolytus (*c.* 217) though later being well-known, but the antecedents, *Romanum Vetus* and *Textus Receptus* more ancient as witnesses from near the end of the second century; b) in the popular stories called Apocrypha; c) in the most important inscription of the times, that of Abercius; d) in Christian writing by St. Ignatius of Antioch, Aristides, St. Justin Martyr, St. Irenaeus—these last two the first exponents of Marian theology, interpreters of Is 7:14 in a Marian sense, pioneers of the Eve-Mary doctrine; to these add St. Clement of Alexandria who died before 215.

The idea of the New Eve which was the beginning of Marian theology, sprang from belief in the virginal conception. Justin and Irenaeus, who opened the way, were clear on the point: the former contrasts "Eve, while a virgin incorrupt conceived the word which proceeded from the serpent," with the Virgin Mary "who was filled with faith and joy"; the latter has the phrase "being still a virgin" about both Eve and Mary. The virgin motherhood was a fixed point of reference too in speculation on Mary's fiat, which from the Fathers to Vatican II has furthered thinking on Our Lady.

The debate at Ephesus which was Christological was to involve Mary directly. Without agreement on the virginal motherhood the problem of *Theotokos* could not have arisen. The clash between Nestorius and St. Cyril of Alexandria was within a dialectical area marked out, made possible by belief in the virginal conception, by universal acceptance that only this one human being was fully involved in the physical happening of the Incarnation. In a word what we know as Marian theology has from the outset depended for its existence on belief in a unique parental relationship. Its authentic growth has been continually on this line: witness the Mary-Church typology worked out lucidly by two Fathers, St. Ambrose and St. Augustine, who developed it from the virginal motherhood; in so doing they in no way attenuated the bodily meaning they attached to the word virgin.

In the development of Marian theology, the absence of direct reference to St. Joseph at times when new insights were appearing and being tested is in keeping with the Gospel message. To attribute physical parentage to him at the present stage of our knowledge would imply the rejection of valid doctrines painfully acquired through the ages.

The close link between virginity as an ascetical ideal and Mary as its model, already noticeable in the writings of St. Athanasius of Alexandria, became very prominent in fourth-century Rome. But the ascetics did not invent the doctrine. Its origin was not in that context but in the mystery of the Incarnation—already St. Irenaeus saw it as a sign. Athanasius stated this lucidly: "For who seeing that the body came forth from a virgin alone without a man, would not think that he who was revealed in it was the Creator and Lord of other bodies."[2]

The truth as part of the commonly held faith found a place in every theology, Jewish-Christian, Antiochene, Alexandrian, Augustinian, Thomist, Scotist, Palamite, Orthodox, Lutheran, Calvinist, modern Russian. If the "sentiment of the faithful" supported any doctrine this was one. The ideals of the religious life were constantly nourished by it; the practice of priestly celibacy at times drew sustaining power from it.

Teaching Authority: Because of such unanimity through the ages, there was no need for direct action by the Teaching Authority in regard to the virginal conception; there was such an intervention on the *virginitas in partu*. References to Mary's virgin motherhood occur in dogmatic formulas on other truths; these, because of their cumulative effect and the circumstances do commit the Teaching Authority to the doctrine. Thus the Council of Constantinople, 384 A.D. said in its creed: "He (the onlybegotten Son of God) came down from heaven for us and for our salvation. He was incarnate by the Holy Spirit of the Virgin Mary and became man."[3] The capital phrase in St. Cyril's letter accepted by the Council of Ephesus was "the Holy Fathers did not hesitate to call the holy Virgin Mary the Mother of God."[4] The Council of Chalcedon speaks of the "Virgin Mary, Mother of God according to his humanity."[5] In later times, similar phrases are found in the dogmatic formula of *Ineffabilis Deus*, "the most Blessed Virgin Mary"[6] and *Munificentissimus Deus*, the "Immaculate Mother of God, the ever Virgin Mary."[7]

No direct action by the Teaching Authority was thought necessary either in regard to the perpetual virginity of Mary, which early appealed to the Christian sense. Among the Fathers, Tertullian disagreed but in the same age Origen set the pattern which would persist. The Eastern Fathers tended to solve one objection in the gospel story, the "Brothers of the Lord" considering them sons of St. Joseph by an earlier marriage. The fourth-century Latin doctors repeatedly taught the perpetual virginity in such terms that it was never thereafter questioned.

The Teaching Authority and Tradition combined in all the Christian liturgies, East and West, in massive constant emphasis on Mary's virginity.

Vatican II: Vatican II taught Mary's virginity as an uncontroverted truth in theology. No appeal can be made to LG 54, "those opinions may be lawfully retained which are freely propounded by schools of Catholic thought" for, at the time of the Council, no such opinions as a denial of the virginal conception were current among Catholics. The decree on Ecumenism laid down a normative principle on a "hierarchy of truths" within the Catholic faith. For chronological reasons it could not apply this to Marian teaching for it became official teaching the same day as the Marian chapter of LG. The Council

VIRGINITY OF MARY

texts refer over thirty times to Mary as Virgin, Virgin Mother, ever-Virgin. Three passages are strongly worded: "This association (between the Mother and the Son) was shown also at the birth of our Lord, who did not diminish his Mother's virginal purity but sanctified it" (LG 57); "For believing and obeying, Mary brought forth on earth the Father's Son. This she did, knowing not man, but overshadowed by the Holy Spirit" (LG 63); "In a similar way [to Pentecost] Christ was conceived when the Holy Spirit came upon the Virgin Mary" (*Ad Gentes*, 4).

Recent Theories: Though the founding fathers of Protestantism Luther, Calvin and Zwingli and a principal Protestant theologian of the present century, Karl Barth (*qqv*), defended the virginal conception, a number of recent writers in that communion deny it. Since the *Dutch Catechism* and the controversies following its appearance, some Catholics have treated the question as an open one. The wording in the Catechism was ambiguous and the Commission of Cardinals appointed to examine the work recommended that the words should show that Our Lady was always "adorned with the honour of virginity" which was "supremely in accord with the mystery of the Incarnation."[8] *The Supplement to a new Catechism* puts it thus: "The mystery of this greatest gift of God to man in the person of Jesus can also be seen to be indicated by another event which is also mysterious, the virginal conception of Jesus, of which Matthew and Luke tell us in the Gospel. Jesus was not procreated by the intervention of man. He was conceived of the Holy Spirit, born from a young woman who was full of grace and chosen by God to be the Holy Mother of his Son."[9]

The late sixties and the seventies have seen a theological ferment within the Church, a desire to investigate with the maximum freedom truths long accepted; ecumenical concern was sometimes invoked to justify this procedure. In the flow of writing appear a large number of studies on the virginity of Mary. A distinction is sometimes made between biological and moral or spiritual virginity. The only virginity in the case of a mother with her child, each taken in the concrete circumstances of life, is biological, physical, bodily. That metaphors based on this reality may be valid in other areas is a different matter: witness the Mary-Church typology.

[1]See bibliographies to the articles on *Vow of virginity, Mary's: Virginitas in partu: Marriage, Our Lady's.* Cf. V. Taylor, *The Historical Evidence for the Virgin Birth* (Oxford, 1920); H. Leisegang, *Pneuma Hagion: der Ursprung des Geistbegriffs der synoptischen Evangelien aus der griechischen Mystik* (Leipzig, 1922) 14-72; E. Norden, *Die Geburt des Kindes: Geschichte einer religiosen Idee*(Leipzig and Berlin, 1924); J. G. Machen, *The Virgin Birth of Christ* (New York, 1932, reprint Grand Rapids, Baker Book House, xiii-415 pp., 1967); F. Kattenbusch, "Die Geburtsgeschichte Jesu als Haggada," *Theolog. Studien und Kritiken,* 102 (1930), 454-74; M. Dibelius, *Jungfrauensohn und Krippenkind*, reprinted from proceedings of Heidelberg Scientific Academy, 1931-32 in *Botschaft und Geschichte* I, Tubingen, 1953, p. 1-78; D. Edwards, *The Virgin Birth in History and Faith* (London, 1943); A. M. Sancho, S.J., *La virginidad de la Madre de Dios* (Granada, 1955); K. Barth, *The Miracle of Christmas, Church Dogmatics,* I, 2, (Edinburgh, 1956), 172-202; T. Boslooper, *The Virgin Birth* (Philadelphia, 1962); F. de P. Sola, S.J., 'Semper Virgo Maria," EphMar 12(1962), 353-82; J. H. Nicolas, O.P., *La Virginité de Marie. Étude théologique* (Fribourg, University Press, 1962); J. A. de Aldama, S.J., *Virgo Mater, Estudios de teologia patrística* (Granada, 1963); *La Maternité virginale de Notre Dame, Maria,* VII 119-52; H. v. Campenhausen, *The Virgin Birth in the Theology of the Ancient Church,* Studies in Historical Theology, 2 (London, 1964); J. F. Craghan, C.SS.R., *Mary, the Virginal Wife and the married Virgin* (Rome, Gregorian University Press, 1967); "Mary's 'ante partum' Virginity. The biblical view", AER 162(1970), 361-72; "The Gospel witness fo Mary's 'ante partum' virginity," MSt 21(1970), 28-68; J. Galot, S.J., "La conception virginale du Christ," *Gregorianum* 49(1968), 637-66; *Che cosa pensare della verginità della Madonna?* (Rome, Apes Ed. 1969); F. Salvoni, *Verginità di Maria? Legenda e verità: dal Vangelo al Catechismo olandese* (Genoa, Ed. Lanterna, 1969); *Zum Thema Jungfrauengeburt,* symposium: R. Kilian, O. Knoch, G. Latke, K. Susa Frank, K. Rahner (Stuttgart, Kath. Bibel Werk, 1970); G. M. Roschini, O.S.M., *La Verginità di Maria oggi,* (Rome, Ed. Cor Unum Figlie della Chiesa, 1970); K. Balic, O.F.M., *De conceptione Christi Domini et scientiis naturalibus,* in *Ecclesia a Spiritu Sancto edocta,* Festschrift G. Philips (Gembloux, 1970) 475-502, J. M. Alonso, C.M.F., P. Schoonenberg, "La concepción virginal de Jesus: Historia o leyenda? Un dialogo teológico," EphMar, 21(1971), 161-216; *La concepción virginal de Jesus,* I En autores protestantes; II En autores catôlicos, ibid., pp. 63-109; 257-302; R. Schnackenburg, *Die Geburt Christi ohne Mythos und Legende* (Mainz, 1969); J. N. D. Kelly, *Early Christian Creeds,* 4th ed. (London, Longmans, 1970); B. Bagatti, O.F.M., *La Verginità di Maria negli apocrifi del II-III secolo,* MM 33(1971), 281-92; H. Gese, 'Natus ex virgine' *Probleme biblischer Theologie* (Gerhard von Rad zum 70 Geburtstag) Munich, 1971, 73-89; M. Zerwick, *Verginità di Maria* in Encicdella Bibbia, VI, 1133-39; R. Laurentin, *Sens et historicité de la conception virginale* in *Studia mediaevalia et mariologica P. Carolo Balic O.F.M. . . . dicata,* 515-42; P. Grelot, "La naissance d'Isaac et celle de Jésus" NRT, 94(1972), 462-87, 561-85; R. E. Brown, "The Problem of the Virginal Conception of Jesus," *TheolStud* 33(1972), 3-34, reproduced with introductory notes, *The Virginal Conception and Bodily Resurrection of Jesus,* London, Dublin, New York, 1973; Luke's Description of

the Virginal Conception," *TheolStud* 35(1974), 360-62; *The Birth*, 157-33; J. A. Fitzmyer, S.J., "The Virginal Conception of Jesus in the New Testament," *TheolStud* 34(1973), 541-75; J. M. Ford, "Mary's Virginitas Post-partum and Jewish Law," BB 54(1973), 269-72; F. J. Stein-metz, *Jungfrauengeburt- Wunderglaube und Glaube Orientierung*, 37(1973), 31-34; E. Vallauri, "L'Esegesi Moderna di fronte alla Verginità di Maria," *Laurentianum* 14(1973), 445-80; H. Schurmann, *Die Geistgewirkte Leben-sentstehung Jesu* in *Einheit in Vielfalt* (Festgabe Hugo Aufderbeck), Leipzig, St. Benno, 1974, 156-69; M. Miguens, *The Virgin Birth: An Evaluation of Scriptural Evidence* (Westminster, Maryland, 1975); M. O'Carroll, C.S.Sp., "The Virginal Conception. Some recent Problems," MM 37(1975), 429-64; R. Gauthier, C.S.C., "La virginité de Marie 'ante partum' selon la tradition primitive," MSS IV 475-92; P. J. Donnelly, S.J., *The Perpetual Virginity of the Mother of God* in *Mariology*, p. 228-96; EstMar 20(1960); MarSt, 7(1956), 11(1956), 21(1970); *MariolSt*, IV, *Jungfrau-engeburt gestern und heute*, German Mariological Society, Essen, Hans Driewer, 1969; V, *Mythos und Glaube*, 1972; M. Schmaus, *Die kirchliche Lehre von der jung-fräulichen Empfängnis Jesu*, ibid., p. 477-95. ²*De In-carnat.*, 18, tr. R. W. Thomson, Oxford Texts, p. 178; C. Kannengiesser, S.J., SC 199, p. 322,23. ³DS 150. ⁴DS 251. ⁵Mansi VII, 115b; DS 302. ⁶*Pii IX P. M. Acta, I*, Rome, 1854, 616; DS 2803;OL p. 80. ⁷AAS 42(1950), 770; DS 3904; OL, 320. ⁸AAS 60(1968), 688. ⁹E. Dhanis, S.J. and J. Visser, C.SS.R, (London, 1970), 24-25.

VIRGINITY IN PARTU

The phrase means that in the moment of childbirth Mary, through a special divine action, did not lose the physical signs of virginity.[1] The fact is described, on the evidence of midwives, in the Protevangelium of James, XIX, XX;[2] it is insinuated as a painless birth in the *Odes of Solomon*, XIX (see APOCRYPHA) and by St. Irenaeus in the *Demonstration of the Apostolic Preaching*.[3] Tertullian rejected the idea while about the same time Clement of Alexandria accepted it from the Apocrypha. Zeno of Verona (d.*c.* 372) is the earliest explicit voice on the subject in the West: "O great mystery! Mary, an incorrupt virgin conceived, after conception she brought forth as a virgin, after childbirth she remained a virgin."[4]

St. Jerome avoided the subject because it had been treated by the *Apocrypha*, of which he had a horror. After the synod in Milan which condemned Jovinian, a fugitive from papal sanctions in Rome, Ambrose, in his letter to Pope Siricius, set forth the doctrine fully. Augustine asserted it repeatedly; so did a number of fourth century Eastern Fathers, the Cap-padocians and St. Epiphanius notably. Ambrose said that "Mary had kept the seals of her vir-ginity;"[5] Augustine in one instance expressed

the truth thus: "She had conceived without male seed, brought forth without corruption, retained her integrity after childbirth."[6]

If there was division of opinion on the subject it never took the form of widespread heresy on one side and the Teaching Authority on the other; no ecumenical council was needed. Pope St. Leo I, in the Letter of Flavian, the Tome, wrote: "Mary brought him forth, with her virginity untouched, as with her virginity un-touched she had conceived him."[7] Pope Hormis-das (d.523) used the words "not opening his Mother's womb in birth, by the power of the deity not undoing his Mother's virginity." The idea is found in the third canon of the first Lateran Council, and theologians argue that because Pope Martin I, in a letter addressed to the "holy pleroma," gave his support to the Council, the decree is a dogma of faith though the Council is not ecumenical. The essential words are "[Mary] in the fullness of time and without male seed, conceived by the Holy Spirit God the Word himself, who before all time was born of God the Father and incorruptibly brought him forth, and after his birth preserved her virginity inviolate."[8] Paul IV, in the Bull *Cum quorum-dam*, 1555, condemned those who denied the virginal conception and who taught that Joseph was the father of Jesus. The Pope ended with the assertion that Mary's virginity was threefold, "before birth, in birth and perpetually after birth."[9]

Ten years before Vatican II met, A. Mitterer had in a book, which caused some stir in Catholic circles, questioned the *virginitas in partu—Dogme und Biologie der heiligen Familie*. The first Marian *schema*, which never came to the Council assembly, contained the words "who [the Son] willed the bodily integrity of his Mother to remain, in the moment of birth (*in ipsomet partu*), incorrupt and untouched . . ."; the notes to the text said that this phrasing was meant to counter Mitterer's theory.[10] The final *schema* carried a sentence similar to that pro-posed by Mgr. G. Philips: "the Mother of God showed her firstborn Son, who did not lessen her virginal integrity but sanctified it (*sacravit*) to the shepherds and the Magi" (LG 57).

[1]Cf. G. Jouassard, *Maria* I, 1949, 101-14; J. C. Plumpe, "Some Little-known early Witnesses to Mary's Virginitas in Partu," TheolSt 9(1948), 567-77; A. Mitterer, *Dogma und Biologie der Heiligen Familie* (Vienna, 1952); E. P. Nugent, C.M.F., "The Closed Womb of the Blessed Mother of God,"

EphMar 8(1958), 249-70; O. Graber, "Maria Virgo in partu," *Theol. prakt. Quart.*, 107(1959), 306-16; J. Galot, S.J., "La virginité de Marie et la naissance de Jésus," NRT 82(1960), 449-69; J. Crehan, S.J., "Mary's Virginity and the Painless Birth of Christ," Clergy Rev. 45(1960), 718-25; D. Fernandez, C.M.F., "Maternidad perfecta y virginidad integral. Reflexiones criticas en torno a Mitterer," EstMar 21(1960), 243-96; R. Laurentin, "Le mystère de la naissance virginale," EphMar 10(1960), 345-74; D. Bertetto, S.D.B., "La natura della verginità di Maria SS. nel parto," Salesianum 23(1961), 7-42; J. de Aldama, S.J., "Natus ex Maria Virgine," Gregorianum, 42(1961), 37-62; "La virginidad 'in partu' en la exegesis patristica," Salamanticensis, 9(1962), 113-53; "Virgo in partu, virgo post partum," EstEclest 38(1963), 57-82; "La maternité virginale de Notre Dame," *Maria* VII, 1964, 119-52; *El problema teologico de la virginidad en el parto*, Studia mediaevalia et mariologica P. C. Balic, . . . dicata (Rome, 1971), 497-514; M. Hurley, S.J., "Born Incorruptibly," Heythrop Journal 2(1961), 217-23; A. Michel, "Marie et la naissance virginale de Jésus," Ami du Clergé 71(1961), 171-76; K. Rahner, S.J., *Virginitas in partu*, Theological Investigations, IV (Baltimore, Helicon, (1966), 134-62; J. H. Nicholas O.P., "Vierge jusque dans l'enfantement," EphMar 21(1971), 377-82; A. C. Clark, "Born of the Virgin Mary," The Way, Supplement 25(1975), 34-45. [2]*Papyrus=Bodmer V*, ed. M. Testuz, 1958, 38-41. [3]SC 62, 115. [4]*Tractatus, lib.* 2, tr. 8, 2, PL 11, 415. [5]*Epist.* 63, 33, PL 16, 1198C. [6]*Serm.* 215, 3, PL 38, 1073. [7]Leo 1, ACO 2, 2, 1, 25; PL 54, 759; Hormisdas, *Epist.* 137(79), PL 63, 514. [8]Mansi 10, 1152. [9]DS 1880; *Bullarium Marianum*, Bourassé, VII, 60. [10]*Schema Constitutionis de B.M.V., Matre Dei et Matre hominum*, Vatican Press, 1962, n. 4.

VISITATION, THE

The Visitation in Lk's infancy narrative (1:39-56) links the annunciation narratives with the birth stories; it includes the *Magnificat*. The event brings together the two women each favoured by a miraculous conception and is marked by the action of one Child on the other.[1] This action is dependent on the Mother's decision to make the journey, and the text gives further emphasis to the point: "And when Elizabeth heard the greeting of Mary, the babe leaped in her womb . . . . For behold, when the voice of your greeting came to my ears, the babe in my womb leaped for joy" (1:41,44). This unusual incident recalls the words of the angel to Zechariah, "and he will be filled with the Holy Spirit even from his mother's womb" (1:15), that he would be a prophet. Mary's decision was entirely personal, directly related to the angel's communication to her that Elizabeth was with child and that this was miraculous, "For with God nothing will be impossible." Since the Holy Spirit had come upon her (1:35), she was in this directed by him; *meta spodes* translated "with haste" is sometimes rendered "thoughtfully,"

John the Baptist signified to his mother the presence of the Messiah by the messianic leap, whereon she was "filled with the Holy Spirit" (1:41b). Elizabeth gives Mary a meaningful title, added to those Lk already relates, "Highly favoured," "Handmaid of the Lord." This time it is "Mother of my Lord," *Kyrios* which taken with Mary's self-description and its theological setting, can but mean God. This is the clearly affirmed basis of Mary's superiority to Elizabeth, as in the Annunciation narratives she is shown to be superior to Zechariah. When Mary speaks it is again unnecessary to say that she was filled with the Holy Spirit.

The OT episodes and texts so directly recalled make the moment one of culmination, as the Annunciation was in its unique context, as the Presentation would also be. That, in the Visitation, the fulfilment should be in an encounter between two women is characteristically Lucan and is unique in salvation history (it has scarcely been expounded by Christian Feminists). Thus, rightly or wrongly, 1:43 is related to 2 Sam 6:9, "How can the ark of the Lord come to me," to support the typology of the Ark; 1:42 recalls the words of Deborah to Jael, "Blessed be Jael among women," (Jg 5:24) and of Uzziah to Judith, "Blessed are you daughter . . . among all women on earth" (Jud 13:18); 1:42 "and blessed is the fruit of your womb" has been compared with Dt 7:12,13 "[the Lord God] will love you, bless you and multiply you and will also bless the fruit of your body," especially with Dt 28:4, "Blessed shall be the fruit of your body" which depends on 28:1, "And if you obey the voice of the Lord your God," which Mary had done (1:38).

In this fidelity too Mary's excellence, singled out by Elizabeth, accords with Lk 11:28, "Blessed rather are those who hear the word of God and keep it." The praise of Mary's faith (1:45) is given a certain force when contrasted with the angel's rebuke to Zechariah, Elizabeth's own husband (1:20). Its wider significance is to proclaim her the heiress to Abraham, father of believers, whose memory she will in the Magnificat presently evoke (1:55). The three months of Mary's stay with her cousin is further adduced to demonstrate the parallel with the ark which remained in the house of Obed-edom the Gittite for three months (2 Sam 6:11).

Tradition identifies the spot where the two mothers met as Ain Karim, about five miles west of Jerusalem; it has two churches to commemorate the encounter and the birth of the Baptist. Tradition may see an apostolic or missionary character in Mary's journey, as Is 52:7 speaks of him whose feet "are so beautiful on the mountains, he who brings good tidings... who publishes salvation, who says to Zion, 'Your God reigns'": cp. Ps 66:1, 2; Is 40:9. The episode of John the Baptist's "leap" when seen as sanctification is traditionally associated with Jer 1:5, may also be compared with Gen 25:23, the children struggling in Rebekah's womb. During Vatican II one Council Father spoke of Mary in the Visitation as the model of those engaged in the apostolate.

[1]Cf. P. Gaechter, *Maria im Erdenleben* (Innsbruck, 1953), 98-105; B. Hospodar, "Meta spoudes in Luke 1:39," CBQ 18(1956), 14-18; R. Laurentin, *Structure et Theologie de Luc I-II* (Paris, 1957), 79-82; M. Thurian, *Mary, Mother of the Lord, Figure of the Church* (London, The Faith Press, 1963), 66-83; A .Feuillet, *La Vierge Marie dans le Nouveau Testament*, in *Maria* VI, 36-39; *Jésus et sa Mère* (Paris, Gabalda, 1974), 25-30; J. Galot, S.J., *Mary in the Gospel* (Wesminster, Maryland, Newman Press, 1964), 69-74; S. Bartina, S.J., "Maria en la Biblia y el signo de la Visitación," EstEcl, 45(1970), 99-102; R. W. Pfaff, *New Liturgical Feasts in Later Medieval England* (Oxford, Clarendon Press, 1970) The Visitation, pp. 40-61; P. Termes, "Visita ad Elisabetta," *EncBibbia*, VI, 1971, 1188-90; P.-E. Jacquemin, "La Visitation," *Assemblées du Seigneur*, 8(1972), 64-75; J. McHugh, *The Mother*, 68-72; R. E. Brown, *The Birth*, 330-66; E. Galbiati, "La Visitazione (Luca 1:41-50)," BibOr 4(1962), 139-44; J. K. Elliot, "Does Luke 2:41-52 anticipate the Resurrection?," *Expository Times*, 83(1971), 2, p. 87-89; *Mary in NT*, p. 134-143.

VOLPE, ANGELO, O.F.M.CONV.
(*c.* 1590-1647)
Italian author of a *Summa Sacrae Theologiae* by way of commentary on the work of Duns Scotus, in which one lengthy section (248 pages) dealt with Our Lady, *Disputationes magis scholasticae de Maria vera Christi Parente*.[1] Beginning with Mary's predestination, V. follows a chronological order from the Immaculate Conception to the Assumption and Coronation. Because of his anti-thomistic position and certain extreme views his work was placed on the Index.

[1]Cf. L. di Fonzo, O.F.M.Conv., "La mediazione universale di Maria in un Trattato Mariologico del P. Angelo Volpe O.F.M.Conv. grande teologo scotista del Seicento," *Misc. Franc.* 41(1971), 175-226; A. di Monda, O.F.M.Conv., *L'Immacolata nell'opera mariologica dello scotista Angelo Volpe, O.F.M.,Cap.*, V.I. VII, 242-73.

VOW OF BLOOD, THE
On 3 March, 1497, the Sorbonne University decided that those being admitted to degrees would be obliged to take an oath that they would defend the doctrine of the Immaculate Conception. Other European universities took up the idea. In time the phrase "*usque ad sanguinis effusionem*" (to the shedding of blood) was added. This was the Vow of Blood current in certain Catholic circles in the seventeenth and eighteenth centuries.[1] The subject is historically complicated—the author of the essential monograph on it took twenty years to unravel the story: the literature of the seventeenth century on the Immaculate Conception may never be exhaustively described.

The great Italian historian, L. A. Muratori (*qv*) was the chief critic of the practice, the very idea of the Vow of Blood. The basis of his criticism was that one should shed one's blood for divine revelation and laws and not for opinions; he thought that the Immaculate Conception was but an opinion. On this last point the defenders of the practice took issue with him, contending that the truth was by now church teaching. The practice of the Vow died out gradually, though as late as the nineteenth century we find Pope Gregory XVI stating in a private letter that he was ready to shed his blood for the truth of the doctrine. With the promulgation of *Ineffabilis Deus* the matter ended.

[1]Cf. esp. J. Stricher, *Le voeu du sang en faveur de l'Immaculée Conception* (Rome, Pontifical Marian Academy, 1960) 2 vols.; H. Graef, *Mary*, II, p. 72-74.

VOW OF VIRGINITY, MARY'S
From the time of St. Gregory of Nyssa in the East and of St. Augustine in the West, the opinion has been held that Mary's reply to the angel "How shall this be since I know not a man" (Lk 1:34) meant that she had the intention, though married to Joseph, of remaining a virgin.[1] "The angel," says G., "announces offspring; but she cleaves to her virginity preferring her [bodily] integrity to what the angel manifests. She neither lacks faith in the angel nor departs from her promise . . . Because she was bound to preserve her flesh, which was consecrated to God as a sacred gift, untouched, therefore she says 'though you are an angel, though you come from heaven, though what is shown is beyond human

VOW OF VIRGINITY

nature, it is nevertheless impossible for me to know man.'"[2] St. Augustine wrote: "Before he was conceived, he chose to be born of a woman already consecrated to God. This is the meaning of the words with which Mary replied to the angel's message that she was to bear a child (How shall this be . . .). Surely she would not say that unless she had previously vowed her virginity to God (*nisi Deo virginem se ante vovisset*). But because this the customs of the Jews still refused, she was betrothed to a just man, who would not take her by violence but rather guard against the violent what she had vowed."[3]

Down to recent times this opinion has been accepted, assumed, by Catholic writers. It has been reexamined by Catholic biblical scholars in the age of critical biblical scholarship. Some like R. E. Brown reject the opinion as an interpretation of the words of Mary to the angel, "I know not man"; others, like G. Graystone, see it as quite in keeping with the sense of the text provided this be read in the full context, which deals with a unique individual given by Almighty God a unique vocation.

If Mary did not wish to express more than the fact that she was as yet a virgin why should she use the words at all? For the fact that though betrothed she had not yet conceived a child is implied in the use of the future tense by the angel "you will conceive in your womb and bear a child." It has been suggested that the reply of Mary is a literary device used by Lk to lead to the further revelation by the angel. This apart from being an unproved thesis leaves us with the problem why, in the literary device, did the evangelist express this idea. If, as opponents of the idea of a vow or purpose of virginity maintain, Mary intended to lead an ordinary married life with St. Joseph, why should she do anything but welcome the idea that she would have a child and leave the burden of any further revelation to the angel? On close analysis the view of the opponents deprives Mary's words of any meaning or relevance. Feuillet rightly remarks that if she wished to say that as yet her marriage had not been consummated, she would not have used the present tense. Brown mistranslates, admitting in his notes that in the Greek it is the present that is used. Feuillet rightly says that the use of the present does have a special meaning.

Those who contend that virginity, voluntary childlessness, would not enter the mind of any Jewess at the time are in reality making a factual deduction to a particular instance not only from a general rule that is not certain but without recognition of the uniqueness of the individual about whom they speak or write. Though the Infancy narrative of Lk does speak of Elizabeth's childlessness as a "reproach among men," there are OT and NT examples of women without children honoured—Judith, Anna the daughter of Phanuel, as there are examples of celibacy practised by men—St. John the Baptist, St. John the Evangelist, probably St. Paul (1 Cor 7:8). Paul mentions the practice of virginity in 1 Cor 7:32-38. He in no way gives the impression that it was a revolution in manners, one so vast as would follow from certain views expressed on the possibility of a vow or purpose of Mary.

Assuming that the general pattern of the social milieu at the time was marriage with a view to children, we are perfectly entitled to suggest that great personalities transcend the thinking of their milieu. Mary appears in Lk I-II as such a personality. It is likewise perfectly justifiable to allow that the Holy Spirit would inspire her in the path along which she would eventually travel. We are not to assume that she was, up to the moment of the Annunciation when she was given the highest calling possible to a woman, bereft of any but the most commonplace experience of the divine. The level of the dialogue between her and the angel was immeasurably higher than any similar occurrence in the Bible. The logic of things agrees with a pioneering decision on her part.

---

[1]Cf. D. Haugg, *Das erste Marienwort; Eine exegetische Studie zu Lukas 1:34* (Stuttgart, 1938); J. J. Collins, "Our Lady's Vow of Virginity (Lk 1:34)," CBQ 5(1943), 371-80; P. Gaechter, S. J., *Maria im Erdenleben* (Innsbruck, 1953), 92-98; B. Leurent, "La consécration de Marie à Dieu," RAM 31(1955), 226-49; B. Brodmann, O.F.M., "Mariens Jungfraulichkeit nach Lk 1:34 in der Auseinandersetzung von heute" *Antonianum*, 30(1955), 27-44; S. Lyonnet, S.J., "Le récit de l'Annonciation et la Maternité divine de la Sainte Vierge," *Ami du Clergé* 66(1956), 33-48; O. Graber, *Die Frage Marias an den Verkundigungsenge Eine exegetische-dogmatische Studie* (Graz, 1956); J. Galot, S.J., "Vierge entre les Vierges," NRT, 79(1957), 463-77; R. Laurentin, *Luc I-II* (Paris, 1957), 175-78; M. Villaneuva, C.M.F., "Neuva controversia en torno al voto de Virginidad de N. Senora," EstBibl 16(1957), 307-28; N. Flanagan, O.S.M., "Our Lady's Vow of Virginity," MSt 7(1956), 103-33; C. P. Ceroke, "Luke 1:34 and Mary's Virginity," CBQ, 19(1957), 329-42; M. Zerwick, "Quoniam virum non cognosco," *Verbum Domini* 37(1959), 212-24, 276-88; O. Graber, "Maria, die immerwahrende Jungfrau (Lk 1:31-34)," *Theolprakt. Quartalschrift* 107(1959), 185-99; J. M. Alonso,

C.M.F., "Virgo Corde," EphMar 9(1959), 175-228; P. Franquesa, C.M.F., "Exegesis del'quoniam virum non cognosco' y voto de virginidad," EstM 21(1960), 59-116; J. Gewiess, "Die Marienfrage, Lk 1:34," *Biblische Zeits.* 5(1961), 221-54; H. Quecke, "Lk 1:34 in den alten Uebersetzungen und im Protevangelium des Jakobus," BB 44(1963), 499-520; BB 45(1964), 85-88; BB 47(1966), 113-14; J. B. Bauer, "Philologische Bemerkungen zu Lk 1:34," BB 45(1964), 535-40; J. F. Craghan, C.SS.R, *Mary, the Virginal Wife and the married Virgin. The problematic of Mary's vow of virginity* (Rome, Gregorian University, 1967) 298 pp., *esp.* G. Graystone, S.M., *Virgin of all Virgins* (Rome, 1968) and same title in EphMar 21(1971), 5-20; J. McHugh, *The Mother*, p. 173-99; R. E. Brown, *The Birth*, p. 303-9; A. Feuillet. [2]*De natali Christi*, PG 46, 1140D-1141C. [3]*De Sancta Virginitate*, IV, 4, CSEL 41, 238; PG 40, 398.

W

WADDING, LUKE, O.F.M. (1588-1657) —
See Supplement, p. 389.

WALAFRID STRABO (d. 849)

Disciple of Rabanus Maurus (*qv*), monk in the Benedictine abbey of Fulda and later abbot of Reichenau, W. like other Carolingians wrote of Mary in his poems and also left a homily on the beginning of St. Matthew's gospel, wherein he treats of her role. The *Explanation of the four gospels* (which contains a passage on Mary and the Church) attributed to W. in PL is not authentic.[1]

W. values especially Mary's prayers: his verses on the Assumption (*qv*) express the hope that her Son "with the help of her prayers" will bring us to the rest she enjoys (he does not specify bodily resurrection).[2] He has a sense of her direct intervention, ending a plea to the Holy Trinity with the cry: "Holy Mother of God, have mercy on us, we pray."[3] A still more impressive little poem reminiscent of the *Salve Regina*—"keep safe on all sides with your help those who cry to you with tears and plead vocally"—may not be his, though it comes from a late 9th century St. Gall MS.[4]

Explaining the threefold meaning of Mary's name—Illuminatress, Star of the sea and (in Syrian, he says) Mistress, he interprets the Eve-Mary (*qv*) contrast in terms of darkness and light. The light of the Star he sees as Christ born of the Virgin, linking the idea with "I am the Light of the world." Mary he sees as queen (*qv*) and mistress (*Domina*) for she is the one "through whom receiving the light of faith and of divine grace we are led to the indescribable vision of almighty God . . ."[5] In the poem *De Cultura Hortorum*, praising the virginal motherhood, W. addresses Mary as "spouse, dove, queen of the house, faithful friend" and goes on to speak of the "flower which comes to you from the sceptre-bearing stock of Jesse, the sole restorer and author of the ancient race."[6] Sensitive poetry and sound biblical theology.

---

[1]Cf. R. Laurentin, *Traité*, I, 143. [2]MGH, *Poet. Lat.*, 2, 366. [3]*Ibid.*, 401. [4]*Ibid.*, 399; PL 114, 1090; cf. H. Barré, *Prières Anciennes*, 90. [5]PL 114, 859C. [6]MGH, *op. cit.*, p. 349.

WALTER OF CHATEAU THIERRY (d. 1249)

Chancellor of the diocese of Paris and of the University, W. was author of commentaries on Mt, Mk, Lk, Jn and on Song. He composed a sermon on the Assumption.[1] He left three *Quaestiones de transitu, B.M.V.; 1, de privilegiis ejus sc. quae sunt sive quot sunt; 2. si doluit in transitu sive in morte vel non; 3. si post transitum assumpta fuit in anima et corpore, vel in anima tantum sicut alii sancti.*[2]

---

[1]Ed. among the works of William of Auvergne, Paris, 1674, vol II, 446b. [2]*Gualterri Cancellarii et Bartholomaei de Bononia O.F.M., Quaestiones ineditae de Assumptione B.V.M. quae ad fidem manuscriptorum edidit Augustinus Deneffe, S.J.*, Edition secunda aucta et emendata quam curavit Henricus Weisweiler, S.J., Monasterii, 1951, pp. 23-40. (*Opuscula et Textus historiam Ecclesiae ejusque vitam atque doctrinam illustrantia-Series scholastica* ed. J. Koch and F. Pelster, S.J., Fasc. IX; cf. F. Pelster, LTK X, 742).

WALTER OF ST. VICTOR (d. after 1180)

Five of the sermons by W. recently published by J. Chatillon are nominally on Our Lady, but much of what they contain is of general spiritual or moral interest.[1] What he does say is in the Victorine tradition, with one very strong passage on the Mediation (*qv*). On Mary's sinlessness he is of the school of St. Augustine (*qv*), but he opts for sanctification in the womb, not the Immaculate Conception (*qv*). "For if Jeremiah and John were sanctified in the womb, reborn before being born, how much more so the Virgin, Mother of God. It is not, nevertheless, read when she was sanctified, nor do we affirm it."[2] W. applies verses of the Song of Songs (*qv*) to Mary and is led to flights of highest praise: "Were I to speak with the tongues of men or of angels I cannot express the perfection and beauty of holy Mary. Beautiful in the flesh through permanence of incorruption; beautiful in spirit through humility which marked her especially; most beautiful and fair in the perfection of all the virtues. For all the active and contemplative virtues were united in her and made her admirable before all others."[3] ". . . the form of all perfection shone in her as in a mirror, in her was depicted the pattern of all religion."[4]

Enumerating the titles of power attributed to Mary, "empress, queen of heaven, mistress of angels," he recalls the Pauline text on Christ, the unique Mediator and continues "thus the blessed Virgin Mary is our Mediatress, through whom alone we have access to Christ. She is the gate, Christ the door, the Father the mystery; through the gate we come to the door, through the door to the mystery; through Mary to Christ, through Christ to the Father."[5] Mary is not only our patron and advocate, but our mother. W. adapts Gal 3:29 "If you are Christ's then you are Abraham's offspring" to "you are Mary's offspring" adding "not in the carnal but spiritual sense."[6]

[1]CCCM 30, 1975; V, *De Purific.* pp. 40-46; VI, *De Purific.*, pp. 47-56; X, *De Assumpt.* pp. 85-92; XIII, *Serm. In festo B. M.*, pp. 115-121; XIV, *De Nativ.*, B. M., pp. 122-28; cf. A. Sage, in *Maria*, II, 686-693. [2]p. 125. [3]p. 87. [4]p. 86. [5]p. 88. [6]*ibid.*

WILLIAM OF MALMESBURY
(*c.* 1093-*c.* 1143)
A Benedictine, well-known as a historian. In his book *Liber de antiquitate Glastoniensis Ecclesiae* he speaks of a "certain image of Blessed Mary" (PL 179, 1698C). He also wrote *De miraculis Mariae*, a collection of miracle stories.[1] H. Barré (*qv*) has shown that a work once attributed to Eadmer (*qv*) "*De quatuor virtutibus*" was by William; it contains an allusion to Mary's bodily Assumption (*qv*). An edition of William's work is awaited from P. N. Carter.

[1]Cf. A. Mussafia, *Studien zu den mittelalterlichen Marien legenden. Sitzungsberichte der Kaiserl. Akademie der Wissenschaften in Wien. Philos-histor. Klasse*, 123, n. 18, Vienna 1891, pp. 18-30. H. Barré, C.S.Sp., "Le De quatuor virtutibus' et son auteur," EphMar 3(1953), 231-244; J. M. Canal, C.M.F., "Guillermo de Malmesbury y el Pseudo-Augustin," EphMar, 9(1959), 479-499; H. Farmer, DSp, 6, 1220-1221.

WILLIAM OF NEWBURGH (1136-*c.*1200)
An Augustinian Canon of the abbey of Newburgh, known for his *Historia Rerum Anglicarum*, a chronicle of English history from 1066-1198, he wrote, at the request of Roger, abbot of the Cistercian abbey of Byland nearby, a commentary on the Marian sense of the Song of Songs (*qv*). About 95,000 words, it is the longest of the 12th century Marian commentaries on the OT work, save for that of Philip of Harvengt (*qv*). It has been fully published only in the present century.[1] In the 8 parts of his work, the author expounds many truths of importance about Mary and her role in salvation.

W. spoke of Mary as freed entirely from the first from concupiscence, but as conceived in the "heat of concupiscence" and drawing death from Adam and needing salvation in the blood of her Son; he did not know of preservative redemption.[2] He attached very great importance to her consent on the day of the Incarnation: on her mouth all prophecy and the "salvation of all depends."[3] Her consent gave her a role as cooperator (*cooperatrix*) in the Incarnation and her own sanctity was ordered to the mystery.

Mary had a further part in the redemption (*qv*). Christ was crowned because through obedience in the Passion he completed the work of redemption: of Mary, W. writes "you also shall be crowned, because you were a sharer in the work."[4] He attributes to her the words "that as formerly believing with all my strength I piously cooperated in the mystery of the Incarnation, thus also now suffering with you (*compatiendo tibi*) as fully as I can, I may cooperate devoutly in human redemption."[5]

W.'s teaching on the spiritual motherhood, which is very full, links this office with the Mystical Body: "She is the Mother of Christ, Mother of the head and members, for the head and body are one Christ . . . bringing forth our head corporeally, she brought forth all his members spiritually. Hence also she is called Mother by all and is honoured as a mother by fitting cult."[6] After Christ's Ascension Mary had a special ministry in regard to grace; as she had shared in Christ's death through love, she shared in his resurrection and glory.

An entirely singular point in W's doctrine is the prayer offered specially by Mary for the Jewish people. She reminds her Son that from them he took the flesh in which and by which he worked salvation on earth. They should have been first saved and if they chose Barabbas, let the loss of their birthright suffice and let them come last.[7] Mary helps sinners but they must repent; her clients must enter on a way of real reform.[8]

---

[1]William of Newburgh's Explanatio sacri epithalamii in matrem Sponsi, A Commentary on the Canticle of Canticles, ed. John G. Gorman, Fribourg, 1960. [2]7, p. 305. [3]4, p. 200; cf. ibid, p. 224. [4]4, p. 192. [5]1, pp. 104-105. [6]4, p. 205. [7]3, p. 152. [8]1, p. 96.

WILLIAM OF NOTTINGHAM (d. 1336)

A Franciscan teacher at Oxford, who defended the Immaculate Conception, as William of Ware and Duns Scotus had done, but with a certain moderation.[1] "There are many," he said, "who hold the opinion, not bluntly asserting it, but holding their opinion respectfully."[2] The possibility he accepted, but was not sure of the fact: "I know that that was possible to God, but do not know what took place in fact."[3] God alone who arranged that she should be Mother of God knows this. Yet he quotes Eadmer (qv) whom he takes for St. Anselm (qv), as was, in regard to this treatise, customary: "Until God shows me what can be said which is more worthy of the excellence of my Lady,I say what I said, I am not changing what I have written."[4]

---

[1]Text from III Sent., d. 3, q. 1, a. 4 ed A. Emmen, O.F.M., Immaculata Deiparae Conceptio secundum Gulielmum de Nottingham, in MM 5(1943), pp. 220-60. [2]p. 253. [3]Ibid. [4]p. 255.

WILLIAM OF WARE (d. c. 1305)

A Franciscan, teacher at Oxford, the first, it appears from present knowledge, who in a commentary on the Sentences of Peter Lombard, taught in a university the doctrine of the Immaculate Conception.[1] W. was probably the teacher of Scotus (qv); it is possible that in later years he came under the influence of his famous disciple.[2] W. took note of the existence of the "pious opinion," as it was still called: "There is another opinion, that she did not contract original [sin], which I wish to hold, because, if I am to be mistaken, since I am not certain of either side, I prefer to be mistaken by excess, giving Mary some prerogative, than by defect, lessening or taking from her some prerogative which she had."[3] He proceeds to show first the possibility, secondly the suitability, and thirdly the fact of Mary's privilege, her unique purity (munditia is his word): the argument potuit, decuit, ergo fecit. His argumentation is encumbered by his theory of original sin as contamination of the substance of each one rather than the Anselmian idea of absence of original justice. But he has the idea of preservation, and when faced with the objection arising from Mary's need to be redeemed by Christ he replied: "The whole purity of the Mother was in her through her Son; hence she needed the Passion of Christ not because of sin which was in her, but which would have been in her, unless the Son himself had preserved her by faith."[4]

---

[1]Text in Bibl. Franc. Schol. Med. Aevi, 3, Quaracchi, 1904; cf. P. Migliore, O.F.M.Conv., "La dottrina dell'Immacolata in Guglielmo de Ware, O.Min. e nel B. Giovanni Duns Scoto, O.Min.," in Misc. franc., 54(1954), 433-538; J. Bonnefoy, O.F.M., Le Ven. Jean Duns Scot, Docteur de l'Immaculée Conception, etc. (Rome, 1960); A. Emmen, O.F.M., "Wilhelm von Ware, Duns Scotus' Vorlaeufer in der Immakulatalehre. Neue Indikation in den Werken seiner Zeitgenossen," in Anton., 40(1965), 363-392. [2]Cf. J. Bonnefoy, op.cit., pp. 202-203. [3]Text, p. 4. [4]Text, p. 10.

WILMART, ANDRE, O.S.B. (1876-1941)

Trained by P. Battifol, W. became a Benedictine attached to Farnborough Abbey, though obliged to travel to other countries, with one lengthy sojourn in Rome, because of his work on manuscript material in library collections. A pioneer in the critical study of major liturgical texts and in Latin patristic and medieval literature, his services in this domain to Marian theology were of the highest order. His most notable achievement in regard to authenticity was with the writings of St. Anselm of Canterbury (qv);[1] the frequency of appeals to him by R. Laurentin in Traité, I, shows something of this contribution in regard to other writers. He edited hitherto unpublished texts: of the Latin Transitus, Transitus W, named for him; of St. Anselm of Lucca (*qv*), and of Stephen of Salley (*qv*). Many of the 377 books and articles which figure in his bibliography deal with Marian themes: H. Barré's important work *Prières Anciennes* has over 100 references to W. W's principal work, *Auteurs spirituels et Textes dévots du Moyen Age Latin* (Paris, 1932, reprint, 1970) is a precious source book; his edition of *Precum Libelli quattuor Aevi Karolini* (Rome, 1940) is likewise valuable.

[1] *Traité*, I, 146-48.

WISDOM, SEAT OF

The invocation which occurs in the Litany of Loreto, dates from the eleventh century. The theme of Mary and Wisdom is supported also by evidence from the public, liturgical, prayer of the Church. The historical development is enlightening.[1] The well-known text from Ecclesiasticus "among all things I sought a resting-place" was first adopted for Masses in honour of virgin martyrs, but without the verse "From eternity, in the beginning, he created me." The passage unchanged was at first applied to Mary, Virgin of virgins. In the tenth century when Votive Masses appear, in the Mass for Saturday *per annum* the passage chosen began with the words "From eternity in the beginning . . ." (the opening words in the Vulgate are *Ab initio*); eventually the reading would be used for the feast of the Assumption. Concurrently the parallel text from Proverbs VIII, "The Lord created me at the beginning of his work" was chosen for Mary's Nativity, where it was significantly offset by the genealogy of Jesus as the gospel reading— the parallel between the two OT passages was emphasised by the opening words of the Proverbs reading as in the Vulgate, *In initio*.

"Seat of Wisdom" a descriptive phrase first found with St. Augustine was taken up by others. St. Bernard used it three times; the nearest the latter comes to an application to Mary is *Domus divinae Sapientiae*, House of divine Wisdom. The notion of a special relationship between Wisdom and Mary grows through medieval times. It was fully expressed in a remarkable text discovered some twenty years ago, the work of Odo (d. *c.* 1200) Benedictine Abbot of Battle Abbey: "Philosophy is called the pursuit or love of wisdom. Mary is, therefore, the philosophy of Christians for whoever desire to find true wisdom must direct all their love and endeavour

towards Mary. But Christ who is called the power and the wisdom of God, is the true Wisdom. He is strictly the true Wisdom of Christians for to another beyond him the Christian cannot go. Whoever desires to have this wisdom must direct his study towards the Mother for in Mary must he study who is to find Christ. For through Mary we come to Christ as through a mother to a son, through the Mother of mercy to Mercy himself."[2]

The theme of Mary and Wisdom is known to Richard of St. Laurent, is developed and repeatedly taken up by Denis the Carthusian, J.J. Olier treated the subject. St. Louis Marie de Montfort, in his short work on *The Love of the Eternal Wisdom*, showed that a means to obtain it was a "tender and true devotion to the Blessed Virgin." Newman liked the title Seat of Wisdom and chose it for the statue of Our Lady in the Byzantine church which he built in Dublin. Mary, he wrote, was the "one mould of divine Wisdom and in that mould it was indelibly set."[3] Modern Russian Orthodox writers, foremost among them Sergius Bulgakov have sought to include the person of Mary in the sophiological system within which their theology is cast.

The modern Popes have made occasional references to the subject. The longest is by Pius IX in *Ineffabilis Deus*: "And hence the very words with which the Sacred Scriptures speak of uncreated Wisdom and set forth his eternal origin, the Church both in its ecclesiastical offices and in its Liturgy, has been wont to apply likewise to the origin of the Blessed Virgin, inasmuch as God, by one and the same decree, had established the origin of Mary and the incarnation of divine Wisdom."[4]

Speaking on the queenship of Mary, Pius XII used these words: "So now may she deign to shelter all men and all people in her watchful tenderness; may she deign as Seat of Wisdom to manifest the truth of the inspired word which the Church applies to her: 'By me kings reign and lawgivers decree just things. By me princes rule and the mighty decree justice.'"[5] The same Pope introduced his Apostolic Constitution on the training of religious with these words: "The Seat of Wisdom, Mother of the God of all knowledge and Queen of Apostles, the most holy Virgin Mary, to whose veneration we have dedicated an entire Holy Year, is rightly held to be, in a special way, the Mother and Teacher of all who embrace the state of acquiring perfection while striving to carry on the apostolic warfare of Christ the High Priest."[6]

A synthesis on the theme of Mary and Wisdom must show the effect on her destiny and lifework of her maternal association with Christ, the Wisdom of God pre-existent and incarnate, reflected in all creation for whom all creation exists, from whom it derives a meaning.

[1]Cf. R. M. de la Broise, S.J., "La Sainte Vierge dans les Livres Sapientiaux," *Etudes*, 89(1899), 289-311; Jean-Chrysostome de S. Etienne de Fursac, O.F.M., *Les trois grands privilèges de Marie: puissance, sagesse, miséricocrde* (Toulouse-Blois, 1915); M. Zundel, *Notre Dame de la Sagesse* (Paris, 1935, 2nd ed, 1957); B. Capelle, O.S.B., *Les Epîtres sapientiales des fêtes de la Sainte Vierge*, in *Questions liturgiques et paroissiaies*, 1946, pp. 42-49; *id.*, *Maria* I, 236-37; L. Poirier, O.F.M., *La Révélation et Marie 'a travers la Sagesse de l'Ancien Testament*, Québec, 1954; C. de Koninck, *Ego Sapientia . . . La Sagesse qui est Marie* (Quebec, 1943); L. Bouyer, "Marie et la Sagesse de Dieu," *Nouvelles de l'Institut Catholique de Paris*, April-May, 1954; *Le trône de la Sagesse?* (Paris, 1957); J. Leclercq, O.S.B., "Maria Christianorum Philosophia," *Mélanges de Sc.Rel.*, 1956, 104ff; E. Catta, "Reine de la Sagesse," *Rev. Facultés catholiques de l'Ouest*, April, 1956; *id.*, esp., *Sedes Sapientiae, Maria*, VI, 691-866; Didier de Crc̓, O.F.M.,Cap., *Notre Dame de la Trinité*, 3 vols. (Blois, 1959). [2]*Apud* J. Leclercq, O.S.B., *op.cit.*, p. 104. [3]*Discourses to Mixed Congregations*, 3rd ed. (London, 1862) p. 430. [4]OL, 63. [5]OL, 411. [6]OL, 427.

WOMAN AND OUR LADY

Judaeo-Christian literature gave the world thought on womankind which was highly singular in all antiquity and was to influence subsequent ages profoundly.[1] The OT as well as oracles and didactic passages offers a series of remarkable Jewish heroines. These culminate in the Jewess who has been accepted as the supreme heroine, the ideal woman, of Christendom. The name of the first woman in the OT has become a symbol of her sex; she and the others who followed her foreshadow and typify the greatest woman of the NT.

The effect of Christian ideals associated with the person of Mary has been seen very clearly in the female saints and great Christian women of history. Was this effect limited to women's private lives? Here we enter an area where there has been hasty generalization on every side. When the Catholic Church, the Christian communion most fully committed to Marian idealism, refused for over a lifetime to espouse the feminist cause, to support women's claims in cultural, social, political and economic life, and by its attention to woman's domestic role and its apparent wish to consider religious life as the only alternative female vocation, appeared to discourage public activity by women, then the uninstructed would draw a facile conclusion—that Mary's example to women is valid in a restricted way. It is the plain duty of theologians of Our Lady to remove entirely this grave misunderstanding.

There have been errors in Catholic views and attitudes towards the whole feminist movement, in regard to woman's dignity and status in society and in the Church. It is for social historians to explain such things, to tell us why the post-Tridentine Church, at least in its ultimate stage, would scarcely prompt the tribute which medieval Catholicism received from the rationalist historian, Lecky: "Whatever may be thought of its theological propriety there can be little doubt that the Catholic reverence for the Virgin has done much to elevate and purify the ideal of woman, and to soften the manners of men. It has had an influence which the worship of the pagan goddesses could never possess, for these had been almost destitute of the kind of moral beauty which is peculiarly feminine. It supplied, in great measure, the redeeming and ennobling element in that strange amalgam of religious, licentious and military feeling which was formed around women in the age of chivalry, and which no succeeding change of habit or belief has wholly destroyed."[2]

On the subject of woman and Our Lady the teaching authority was reserved until quite recently. Papal teaching on *The Woman in the Modern World* down to 1957 runs to 338 pages of text; matter before the pontificate of Pius XII takes up about 12 pages—of little relevance to Feminism. First drafts of texts for Vatican II on the Lay Apostolate and Religious Life were composed without any consultation of women—though the text on Religious would legislate for more than a million nuns! The Council did not deal in any exhaustive sense with the subject. John XXIII had included two brief passages on the subject of woman in his popular Encyclical *Pacem in Terris*. Pius XII, the greatest of Marian Popes, first authoritatively accepted Feminism and expounded its values; his principal statement on the subject was an address to Italian women on 21 October, 1945. The Pope spoke frequently at great length on the dignity, duties, and role of women. He very often related his thought to Our Lady.

Paul VI carried papal thinking further ahead. The movement for women's liberation had advanced during his pontificate. On 3 May, 1973, he set up a special commission for the study of woman in society and in the Church, answering thus the desire expressed by the Episcopal Synod of 1971. For International Woman's Year a special committee served as liaison between the papal commission and the United Nations body. In the course of addresses to meetings of these commissions or to the United Nations representative, Pope Paul developed his thought on the theology of woman and generally referred to Mary.[3]

The Pope's thinking was, however, most fully expressed in *Marialis Cultus*. In the section where he gave anthropological guidelines, he stated a difficulty in the way of devotion to Our Lady: "The picture of the Blessed Virgin presented in a certain type of devotional literature cannot easily be reconciled with today's lifestyle, especially the way women live today." The Pope then outlines the changes achieved by the feminist revolution. "In consequence of these phenomena," he says, "some people are becoming disenchanted with devotion to the Blessed Virgin and finding it difficult to take Mary of Nazareth as an example because the horizons of her life, so they say, seem rather restricted in comparison with the vast spheres of activity open to mankind today."

Theologians, pastors and the laity are to examine these difficulties, while the Pope himself offers his own contribution. Imitation of the Virgin, he points out, has never been proposed "in the type of life she led and much less for the socio-cultural background in which she lived and which today scarcely exists anywhere." Mary is to be imitated because "she heard the word of God and acted on it and because charity and a spirit of service were the driving force of her actions . . . because she was the first and most perfect of Christ's disciples." Paul VI also emphasised the fact that it was "certain aspects of the image of Mary found in popular writings" that caused difficulties, not the image of her found in the Gospel. He then pointed to the obligation on our time as on any other to test its knowledge of reality by the word of God. In developing these different ideas Paul VI gave a Marian anthropology.

During his pontificate there appeared the Declaration *Inter Insigniores* by which the Congregation for the Doctrine of the Faith with the Pope's approval rejected the plea for priestly ordination of women. The biblical section has this passage on Mary: "His Mother herself, so clearly associated with his mystery and whose peerless role is emphasised by the gospels of Luke and John, was not invested with the apostolic ministry, which will lead the Fathers to present her as an example of the Saviour's will in this matter. 'Although the Blessed Virgin Mary surpassed all the Apostles in dignity and excellence,' Pope Innocent III will repeat again at the beginning of the thirteenth century, 'it was not to her but to them that the Lord entrusted the keys of the kingdom of heaven.'"[4]

Paul VI spoke at times of "the precious function of women in the whole plan for the kingdom of God and the temporal kingdom." He asked for their "incomparable and indispensable cooperation," urged them to acquit themselves fully of their "mission of piety, wisdom, virtue, love through which they are in a wonderful way 'queens with Mary'"; "if the testimony of the Apostles establishes the Church, the testimony of women contributes greatly to nourishing the faith of the Christian community." Great saints and servants of God have, under God, got their faith from their mothers.

[1]Bibliography to 1966 on anthropology of woman *Spiritus* review, *Femmes et Mission*, 29(2), 1966, 432-440, 244 titles; cf. L. Krinetzki, O.S.B., *Der Aufstieg der Frau in der Heiligen Schrift*, in *15 August. Aufnahme de Mariens in den Himmel*, Stuttgart, Kath. Bibelwerk, 1965, 43-56; R. Laurentin, "Marie et l'anthropologie chrétienne de la femme," NRT 89(1967), 485-515; C. Sean, O.S.F., "Mary, model of modern woman," MSt 20(1969), 29-40; A. Martinelli, O.F.M., *Il mistero della donna consacrata* (Bologna, 1969); *id., Origine, natura, missione della donna*, 1970; J. Galot, S.J., "Culto mariano e emancipazione della donna," *CivCatt*, 1970, II, 123-132; *id., Marie et la femme d'aujourdhui*, Festschrift C. Balic, Rome, Antonianum, 1971, 669-83; F.-J. Steinmetz, S.J., "Maria als Jungfrau und Mutter," *Geist und Leben*, 44(1971), 336-41; J. Massingberd Ford, "Our Lady and the ministry of Women," MSt 23(1972), 79-112; L. Pinkus, O.S.M., "Il femminile e la Chiesa," MM, 34(1972), 386-95; H. Rollet, *La condition de la femme dans l'Eglise* (Paris, Fayard, 1975); For recent abundant literature, cf. R. Laurentin RSPT, 60(1976), 459-71; *id.*, RSPT, 62(1978), 278-84. [2]*History of European Morals* (London, 1911), vol. 2, p. 367. [3]Cf. address to committee, 18 April, 1975, *DCath*, 404; to Mme Helvi Sipila, general secretary UNO, International Woman's Year, 6 November, 1974, *DCath*, 1007. [4]*L'Osservatore Romano*, 28 January, 1977; *DCath*, 1977, 180; cf. article *Marialis Cultus*.

WOMAN IN GENESIS 3:15
"I will put enmity between you and the woman, and between your seed and her seed;

he shall bruise your head and you shall bruise his heel."[1] CB

The translation of this text has its own history. The Hebrew text was written down, as part of the story of Paradise and the Fall, in the ninth century B.C. *Zera* (seed) is a masculine noun and *hu* (he) matches it as a pronoun. The Septuagint translated *zera* by *sperma*, a neuter, but used the masculine pronoun, *autos*, rather than *auto*, neuter—a *constructio ad sensum*, a decision as to meaning which implies that the "seed" who will crush the serpent will be male (cp. 2 Sam 7:12; 1 Chron 17:11). The verb *shuph* (to bruise or crush) is also used for the action of the serpent; but it is possible that the second apparent use of the word may come from a verb which derives from *sha af, shafaf*—"to snap," "to snatch at," "to lie in wait." St. Jerome though conscious of the problem, used, in the Vulgate, *conteret* "will crush" for the seed of the woman, *insidiaberis*" will lie in wait" for the seed of the serpent: in the *Liber hebraicarum quaestionum* he says that *conteres* better renders the Hebrew in the second case also.[2] Whether Jerome himself used *ipsa*, feminine, before conteret, "she will crush," it is found in most Vulgate manuscripts and prevailed; it does not seem to have been linked with a Mariological interpretation at the outset; eventually it fitted this view. *Zera* generally has a collective meaning; but in Gen 4:25 Eve calls the son given her in place of Abel a "new seed." NEB and the Anchor Bible (E. A. Speiser) take a risk with the plural "they."

History: exhaustive analyses have been made of the opinions expressed by the Fathers and later writers. From such studies, notably R. Laurentin's which is exemplary, it emerges that the dominant interpretation in the early centuries is of a collective struggle between the human race and the demon. Within the collective sense one individual, Jesus Christ, will be singled out by some writers. This is giving the oracle a messianic sense. It is more explicitly stated when the issue of the struggle is seen as victory. Though St. Irenaeus saw that in this victory of Christ Mary too is involved, the Marian interpretation was not unanimously held by the Fathers; nor was the messianic sense. They are at one in identifying the serpent as the devil. The Reformers rejected the *ipsa* rendering and any Marian sense. The Marian interpretation was defended by Catholics irrespective of translation differences; for the verb *conteret* had a continuing effect. The Bull *Ineffabilis Deus* was a landmark, for the oracle was quoted; writing and sermons thereafter were influenced by the fact.

Teaching Authority: the context in the Bull was "the Fathers and writers of the Church," of whom Pius IX said: "These ecclesiastical writers in quoting the words by which at the beginning the world God announced his merciful remedies prepared for the regeneration of mankind—words by which he crushed the audacity of the deceitful serpent and wondrously raised up the hope of our race, saying, 'I will put enmities between thee and the woman, between thy seed and her seed'—taught that by this divine prophecy the merciful Redeemer of mankind, Jesus Christ, the only begotten Son of God, was clearly foretold; that his Blessed Mother, the Virgin Mary, was prophetically pointed out (*designatam*)." The Pope went on to say that Mary most closely united to Christ was "with him and through him, eternally at enmity with the evil serpent, and most completely triumphed over him and thus crushed his head with her immaculate foot."[3] The idea did not occur in the dogmatic formula. But before that passage the Pope repeated the idea in the name of the Fathers: "They also declared that the most glorious Virgin was Reparatrix of the first parents, the giver of life to posterity; that she was chosen before the ages, prepared for himself by the most high, foretold by God when he said to the serpent, 'I will put enmities between thee and the woman', unmistakable evidence that she has crushed the poisonous head of the serpent."[4]

Pius XII used the oracle in *Munificentissimus Deus*: Mary, the new Eve subject to the new Adam "is most intimately associated with him in that struggle against the infernal foe which, as foretold in the *protoevangelium*, would finally result in that most complete victory over sin and death which are always mentioned together in the writings of the Apostle of the Gentiles."[5] The same Pope wrote in *Fulgens Corona*: the biblical foundation of the doctrine of the Immaculate Conception was "in these words, which not a few Fathers, Doctors of the Church and many approved interpreters applied to the Virgin Mother of God: 'I will put enmities between thee and the woman, and thy seed and her seed'." He goes on to say that if at any time the Blessed Virgin were destitute of divine grace even for the briefest moment through Original Sin "there would not have come between her and the serpent that perpetual enmity spoken of from earliest times" down to the dogma, "but rather a certain subjection."[6]

Vatican II marked a slight recession from these views. Cardinal Bea in the 1964 debate on LG VIII, changing his own previous opinion, noted lack of agreement among Catholic scholars on the text. LG 55 says that Mary "is already prophetically *foreshadowed* (adumbratam) in that victory over the serpent which was promised to our first parents after their fall into sin (cf. Gen 3:15)." The statement, moreover, is qualified by the previous words "these earliest documents, as they are read in the Church and are understood in the light of a further and full revelation." At the *Modi* stage, 144 Council Fathers asked that Pius IX's word *designatam* be put in the place of *adumbratam*. The responsible commission replied: 'Is prophetically foreshadowed' is deliberately used, as it accurately fits the oracle."[7]

Recent interpretations: Between 1854 and 1948 over 160 authors had published work on the subject, among them Newman, Scheeben and Terrien (*qqv*). After *Divino Afflante Spiritu* (see PIUS XII) the Catholic approach was increasingly scientific. On the principle that the Bible is a unity the identity of the serpent as the devil is, in one way or another, shown in Wis 2:23, 24; Lk 10:18, 19; Jn 8:44; Rom 16:20; Rev 12:9; 20:2. In different ways also the association of a woman with a man in the inauguration of the messianic age, which will be a new creation, is subtly conveyed through the OT.

Non-Catholic exegetes still dismiss any messianic or Marian sense in Gen 3:15, speaking mostly of myths. Among Catholics, J. Coppens argued that "woman" is used generically; the oracle refers to the future of the whole female sex, within which certain individuals stand out, Mary principally because she is linked with the victor. Coppens sees her included in the oracle only indirectly, by connotation.

B. Rigaux reaches the conclusion that Mary is designated in the strict literal sense. Eve cannot be overlooked, but since this is a prophecy she must be brought forward to the moment of victory. Analysis of the text as part of the Yahwist document shows how this will be done. The Yahwist, conscious of the promise of universal salvation which was strong at the time, habitually summed up the achievements of a

group or line of descendants in one person; he associated a woman (Sara, Rebecca, Rachel) with the saving work of such chosen male figures. Eve victorious is therefore Mary Mother of the Messiah, for we are reading an "eschatological and messianic oracle of unique spiritual value."

[1]Cf. G. Arendt, *De Protoevangelii habitudine ad Immaculatam Deiparae conceptionem* (Rome, Typ. artificum a S. Joseph, 1904); L. Drewniak, *Die Mariologische Deutung von Gen 3:15 in den Vaterzeit*, (Wroclaw [Breslau], R. Nickowsky, 1934); F. X. Pierce, "Mary alone is the 'Woman' of Gen 3:15," CBQ 2(1940), 245-52; *id.*, "The Protoevangelium," CBQ, 13(1951), 239-52; T. de Orbiso, O.F.M.Cap., "La Mujer del Protovangelio," Est.Bib. 1(1941), 187-207 and 273-89; P. Hitz, "Le sens marial du Protévangile," BSFEM 5(1947), 33-83; G. M. Roschini, O.S.M., "L'Interpretazione Mariologica del Protovangelo (Gen 3:15) dal tempo postpatrisitico al Concilio di Trento," MM 12(1950), 308-13; P. Bonnetain, "Immaculée Conception," SDB 19 t. IV, 1943, 240-54; H. Lennerz, S.J., "Consensus Patrum in interpretatione mariologica Gen 3:15? Greg 27(1946), 300-18; T. Gallus, S.J., "Assumptio B.M.V. ex Proto-evangelio definibilis," *Divus Thomas* (Plac.), 42(1949), 121-41, *Interpretatio mariologica Protoevangelii (Gen 3:15) tempore postpatristico usque ad Concilium Tridentinum*, xvi-21 pp., (Rome, Orbis Catholicus, 1949); *id., Interpretatio mariologica Protoevangelii postridentina usque ad definitionem dogmaticam Immaculatae Conceptionis*, 2 vols, I, to 1660, xvi-288 pp.; II, 1661 to 1854, xlii-384 pp. (Rome, Ed. di storia e letteratura), 1953, 54; *id.*, "Beata Maria Virgo Protoevangelio praesignata," ASC, II, 58-67; *id.*, "Observationes ad novam Protoevangelii mariologicam interpretationem," *EphMar* 2(1952), 425-37; *id.*, "Quaestiones de Protoevangelio in Bulla Munificentissimus Deus," MM 17(1955), 305-331; J. M. Bonnefoy, O.F.M., *Le Mystére de Marie selon le Protévangile et l'Apocalypse* (Paris, 1949); J. Coppens, "Le Protévangile. Un nouvel essai d'exegése," ETL 26 (1950), 5-36, V. G. Bertelli, "L'interpretazione Mariologica del Protovangelo (Gen 3:15) negli esegeti e teologi dopo la Bolla 'Ineffabilis Deus' di Pio IX (1854-1948)," MM 13 (1951), 257-91 and 369-95; G. Calandra, "Nova Protevangelii mariologica interpretatio," *Anton* 26(1951); A. Gugliemo, "Mary in the Protoevangelium," CBQ 14(1952), 104-115; *esp.* J. Michl, "Die Weibsame (Gen 3:15) in spätjudischer und frühchristlicher Auffassung," BB 33(1952), 371-401 and 476-505; S. Stys, S. J., "De antithesi Eva Maria ejusque relatione ad Protoevangelium apud Patres," Collect. Theol. 23(1952), 318-365; F. Spedalieri, S.J., "Il Protovangelo. Nuovo saggio di interpretazione mariologica," MM 15 (1953), 528-54; *id.*, "Giustizia e peccato originale nel commento patristico di Genesi 3:15," *Renovatio* 5(1970), 337-74; A. Bea, S.J., *Bulla "Ineffabilis Deus" et Hermeneutica Biblica*, V, I, III, pp. 1-17; *id.*, "Maria santissima nel Protoevangelio," MM 15(1953), 1-21; D. J. Unger, O.F.M.Cap., *The first Gospel, Genesis 3:15* (New York, Franciscan Institute, 1954); *esp.* R.Laurentin, "L'Interprétation de Genèse 3:15 dans la tradition jusqu'au début du XIIIe siècle," BSFEM 12(1954), 78-156; B. Rigaux, O.F.M., "La femme et son lignage dans Genèse 3:14,15," RB 61(1954) 321-48; H. Cazelles, "Genèse 3:15, Exégèse contemporaine," BSFEM, 14(1956), 90-99; P. G. Dunckner O.P., in *Mother of the Redeemer*, ed. K. MacNamara, (Dublin, 1959), pp. 5ff; T. Gallus, S.J., *Der Nachkomme der Frau (Gen*

3:15) in der altlutheranischen Schriftauslegung 2 vols. (Klagenfurt, 1964 and 1972). ²PL 23, 981. ³OL, 71, 72. Cf. Leo XIII, Augustissimae Virginis, ASS, 30(1898), 129; Pius X, Ad diem illum, ASS 36(1904), 462; Pius XI, Divini Redemptoris, AAS 29(1937), 96; Biblical Commission, 1909, Enchiridion Biblicum, 3, 38. ⁴OL, p. 75. ⁵OL, 317. ⁶OL, 348. ⁷Modi etc., ch. VIII LG, Vatican Press, 1964, pp. 8 and 9.

WOMAN IN JOHN 19:25-27

A wide variety of opinions have been expressed on this passage.¹ The fact that John alone reports the episode has prompted some recent commentators to question its historicity. Why should John put a fact about the most important member of the messianic community —given the prestigious title Mother of Jesus, evocative of the ancient mother of the king—in a factual record about the death of Jesus if it was not of a piece with this record? What motivated invention, fiction? Mary, as we know from the independent evidence of Acts, was in Jerusalem at the time of the Ascension (1:14), the time of climax in Jesus' life. She is spoken of then as one of a community present at Jerusalem for some time, not as one newly arrived.

Catholic and Protestant commentators have seen in the incident and words support for the Eve-Mary, Mary-Church themes. The appellation "woman" and the connotation of the word "son" are central to all interpretation of the passage. Since medieval times and especially in papal documents the doctrine of Mary's universal motherhood has been seen in the words spoken by Christ. Here Vatican II showed some reserve; it showed less on Mary's union of spirit with her Son on Calvary.

Interpretation of the passage reflects the general critical attitude taken towards the fourth gospel as well as characteristic confessional views. Catholic Marian theology, ideals of priestly holiness, and ascetical practice give ample evidence of this. So does iconography.

History: Generally the Fathers interpreted the text to show Jesus' thoughtfulness for his Mother, his intention to provide for her. They also saw the words of Jesus as praise of John, of his virginity, as an indication of Mary's perpetual virginity. Origen had an intuition of something more: "The gospels have primacy among the Scriptures; among the gospels, in turn, it is the gospel according to John which has primacy. None can grasp its meaning if he has not reclined on Jesus' breast, if he has not received from Jesus Mary for mother. He who will become another John must then be so like

John that he be pointed out by Jesus as being Jesus. For if Mary, according to those who judge her sanely, had no other son but Jesus, and if Jesus, nonetheless, said to his Mother, 'here is your son' and not 'this is also your son' it is as if he had said 'this is Jesus to whom you have given birth.' In fact every man who has become perfect lives no longer, but Christ lives in him. Because Christ lives in him is the reason why it is said of him to Mary: 'this is Christ your son.'."²

The emphasis here is on the unity of the perfect with Christ. After the patristic period George of Nicomedia (*qv*) marks an advance; he thought that as well as John the other disciples were entrusted to Mary: "For through him I also bequeath the rest of my disciples. And as long as you live with them, by my will, you will assure your presence bodily in place of mine. Be for them all that mothers are by nature for their children, or rather all that I should be by my presence; all that sons and subjects are, they will be for you." The words of the dying Christ to John are similarly interpreted by George: "O honour beyond honour for the disciple! O inheritance richer than all things together! O grace of which the beloved [disciple] has become the herald! to be called the brother of the Creator of the universe, to receive as mother the one who is sovereign of all! . . . Henceforth I establish her as guide of the disciples, as mother not only for you but for all the others and it is my will that she be honoured fully as of right with the dignity of mother."³

Anselm of Lucca's view was not known until his prayers were published by Dom Wilmart (*qqv*). He interpreted the Saviour's words in the sense of spiritual motherhood: "'Mary' he said 'here is your son; apostle, here is your mother'—so that the glorious Mother would intercede for all true believers in her great loving clemency, that she should watch over with special protection those whom she has adopted as children, redeemed captives."⁴ Anselm says that Christ substituted us "in the person of his favourite disciple" for himself so that Mary would have the greatest maternal love for us.

A turning-point was reached in the next century with Rupert of Deutz (*qv*). He used the Johannine text (16:21) on the woman in travail to explain Mary's sufferings as oriented to a new motherhood, different from the painless one when she gave birth to "the cause of salvation for all, when she brought forth of her flesh God made man." "Thus suffering here truly the pains of childbirth (Ps 47), in the Passion of her only Son, the Blessed Virgin brought forth our universal salvation; that is why she is mother to us all. He was, therefore, rightly attentive to his Mother in what he said about the disciple: 'Woman, behold your son.' And the word to the disciple, 'Here is your mother', could have been said, properly, of any other disciple who would be present."[5]

In the same age Gerhoh of Reichersberg and Odo of Morimond (*qqv*) make this interpretation their own, enuntiating it more explicitly. In subsequent times it has been widely adopted.

Teaching Authority: The first reference to the text in a papal document interprets Christ's words of the Church. Benedict XIV, in words echoed by LG 53, expressed the idea: "The Church has encompassed this most loving of Mothers, entrusted to her by the last words of her dying Spouse, with expressions of filial homage and devotion."[6] Pius IX and Leo XIII, saw John as the representative of the faithful and the human race. "Now in John," says Leo, "as the Church has constantly felt, Christ designated the human race, especially those joined to him by faith."[7] The Popes of the present century, Pius XII especially, take the interpretation for granted. Thus Pius XII: "He thus entrusted all Christians, in the person of the beloved disciple, to the most Blessed Virgin." And John XXIII: "the last testament of the Lord, who, in the supreme moment of death, leaves his Mother to the world as universal Mother."[8]

Vatican II was, by comparison, non-committal. From the comments sent to Rome on the first *schema* which was not brought to the assembly, to the final *Modi* prior to the vote on the completed text of LG VIII, objections were made to a conciliar decision on a biblical text still in dispute among scholars. The penultimate draft contained the words, "as a figure of the faithful" after "disciple" in article 58. Twelve Council Fathers asked that they be deleted. This was done, so now we read "by the same Christ Jesus dying on the Cross she was given as a mother to the disciple by the words, 'Woman behold your son' (Jn 19:26, 27)." Something more is implied in the brief passage in the *Decree on Priestly Training*, article 8: "With filial trust they should love and honour the most blessed Virgin Mary, who was given as a mother to his

disciple by Christ Jesus as he hung dying on the Cross."

Recent interpretations: The words of Christ constitute a "revelation formula," disclosure of profound truth, deeper than the obvious sense of the words. The words echo Gen 3:15 (see WOMAN IN) in the use of the word "woman," Jn 16:21, the woman in travail. How much can be drawn from such findings is debated.

Those who believe in the historicity of the incident and words may still look for symbolism; those who reject the historicity have little else but symbolism to discuss. Bultmann, following Loisy, sees in Mary Jewish Christianity and in the beloved disciple Gentile Christianity, a view not adequately sustained. C. H. Dodd rejects symbolism outright: "Attempts to give a symbolic meaning are, in general, singularly unconvincing."[9]

[1]Commentaries on St. John's gospel are important: E. Hoskyns, ed. F. N. Davey, *The Fourth Gospel* (London, 1940) and cf. *id.* JTS, 21(1920), p. 210; C. K. Barrett, *The Gospel according to St. John* (London, 1955), p. 458; C. H. Dodd, *The Interpretation of the Fourth Gospel* (Cambridge, 1953), p. 428; *id., Historical Tradition in the Fourth Gospel* (Cambridge, 1963), pp. 126ff; R. Bultmann, *The Gospel of John* (London, 1971), pp. 671-73; *esp.,* R. E. Brown, *The Gospel according to John*, II(XIII-XX) (Anchor Bible, London, 1971), pp. 922-27; cf. P. Gaechter, *Maria im Erdenleben* (Innsbruck, 1953), pp. 201-26; F.-M. Braun, O.P., *La Mère des Fidèles*, (Paris, Tournai, 1954), pp. 75-129; K. H. Schelkle, *Die Mutter des Erlösers* (Dusseldorf, 1958), pp. 36-37; esp. Th. Koehler, S.M., "Les principales interprétations traditionelles de Jn 19,25-27 pendant les douze premiers siècles," BSFEM 16(1959), pp. 119-55; M. Thurian, *Mary, Mother of the Lord, Figure of the Church* (London, 1963), pp. 144-66; A. Feuillet, Les Adieux du Christ à sa Mère (Jn 19,25-27) et la maternité spirituelle de Marie," NRT, 86 (1964), pp. 469-89; *id.,* "L'heure de la femme (Jn 16:21) et l'heure de la Mère de Jésus," BB, 47(1966), pp. 169-84 and 361-70 and 557-73; *id.,* "De muliere parturiente et de maternitate spirituali Virginis Mariae secundum evangelium S. Joannis," MSS V, pp. 111-23; *id., L'heure de la Mère de Jésus,* (Prouilhe, 1970); *id., Jésus et sa Mère* (Paris, Gabalda, 1974), pp. 134-40; A. Dauer, "Das Wort des Gekreuzigten an seine Mutter und den 'Junger den er liebte'. Eine Traditionsgeschichtliche und theologische Untersuchung zu Joh. 19:25-27," BiblZeitschr 11(1967), pp. 222-39 and 12(1968), pp. 80-93; *id., Die Passionsgeschichte im Johannesevangelium* (Munich, 1972), pp. 318-33; H. Schurmann, *Jesu letzte Weisung,* Jo 19:26-27a, *Sapienter ordinare:* Fest. E. Kleineidam, Leipzig, 1969, pp. 105-23; M. Zerwick, "La hora de la Madre (Jo 19:25-27)," *Revista-Biblica* 30(1968), pp. 197-205; J. McHugh, *The Mother,* pp. 370-404; esp. I. de la Patterie, S.J., "La parole de Jésus 'Voici ta Mère' et l'accueil du Disciple, Jn 19:27b," MM 36(1974), pp. 1-39. Articles in MSS V, A. Mercado, O.F.M., pp. 123-37; P. Gutierrez Osorio, S.J., pp. 151-60; H. Barré,

C.S.Sp., pp. 161-71; J. Nguyen Cong Ly, O.P., pp. 173-80; D. Bertetto, S.D.B., pp. 181-99; P.-R. Masson, O.P., pp. 201-23; R. Struve Haker, pp. 225-33; B. Duda, O.F.M., pp. 235-89: articles deal with many aspects. Cf. also *ibid.*, B. Schultze, S.J., on Greek and Russian Orthodox, p. 401; *Mary in NT* pp. 206-218. [2]*In Jo I, 4, 23, GCS Origenes Werke*, 10, 8-9; PG 14, 32A-B. [3]*Hom in "Stabant autem,"* PG 100, 1476D-1477AB. [4]*RAM 1938*, p. 53, 62. [5]*In Joh XIII*, PL 169, 789C-790C. [6]*Apos. Const. Gloriosae Dominae*, OL, p. 26. [7]*Adjutricem Populi*, OL, p.135; *Acta Leonis XIII*, 15, p. 300. [8]Pius XII, All. July 17, 1954, AAS 46, 491; cf. *Fulgens Corona*, AAS 45(1953), 577; John XXIII, All. to congress at Lisieux *Acta Mariana Joannis PP XXIII*, p. 254. [9]*op.cit.*, in Note 1., p. 428.

WOMAN IN REVELATION 12, THE

One of the most difficult passages in a difficult book.[1] It may be considered from these aspects:

Origin: A legend in the ancient Near Eastern world told of a marvellous birth, prelude to universal salvation. A goddess was pursued by a horrible monster, but being protected gave birth to a son who slew the evil one and brought happiness to the world. Did the author of Rev XII know of the legend or a Jewish version of it, this latter possibly influenced by Gen 3:15? Another extra-bibilical parallel which will be mentioned bears more on interpretation.

History: Recent literature on the subject deals in large part with the history of previous interpretations—the identification of the mysterious "woman" principally concerns Marian theologians. The word was given a collective meaning by most ancient writers, under the influence probably of the biblical custom of describing the people of God as a female figure. Already in the fourth century St. Epiphanius discussing the end of Our Lady's life wrote: "Elsewhere though, we read in the Apocalypse of John that the dragon rushed against the woman who had brought forth the male child and wings of an eagle were given to her and she was borne into the desert lest the dragon seize her."[2] There is in the same age a vague reference in Andrew of Caeserea to people who identified the woman with Mary. In the next century Quodvultdeus, friend and disciple of St. Augustine, was explicit: "None of you is ignorant of the fact that the dragon was the devil. The woman signified the Virgin Mary, who remaining intact brought forth our intact Head, she who also showed forth in herself the image of the holy Church, so that as she remained a virgin while bringing forth a son so [the Church] for all time should bring forth members without losing its virginity."[3] In the

sixth century the philosopher Oecumenius, Greek author of the earliest extant commentary on the whole book of the Apocalypse, interprets the passage in a Marian sense without mentioning the Church. He thinks that the vision rightly shows Mary as heavenly, pure in soul and body, sublime, though she shares our human nature and being. The sun which clothes her is Christ, the twelve stars the Apostles; her travail he explains not as of childbirth, but as due to Joseph's suspicions (see DOUBT OF JOSEPH): the vision, he repeats, is "about our Lady, the holy, ever-virgin and *Theotokos* Mary."[4]

The collective sense may in early writers mean the people of God on earth, the Church of the OT and NT, or only the second. Ambrose Autpert (*qv*) has the fullest interpretation of Rev XII in a Marian and ecclesial sense, that is related to the Church of the New Law. The passage in Alcuin expressing a similar idea is spurious.[5] St. Bernard in his great sermon *In signum magnum* takes the opinion as his starting-point: "the whole sequence of the prophetic vision shows that it is to be understood of the Church, but I see no inconvenience in applying it to Mary." St. Bonaventure thought that the literal sense was Marian and the mystical sense ecclesiological. From the seventeenth century a "Jesuit" interpretation has seen the woman as the Church in final glory. A survey of 88 post-Tridentine writers has shown that 62 favoured the Church as the meaning intended by woman, 26 Mary—the compiler thought that the latter conclusion was not always scientific.[6] Newman held that "the Holy Spirit would not have spoken of the Church under this particular image, *unless* there had existed a blessed Virgin Mary, who was exalted on high and the object of veneration to all the faithful."

Teaching Authority: St. Pius X in *Ad diem illum* taught: "Everyone knows that this woman signified the Virgin Mary, the stainless one who brought forth the Saviour."[7] He interpreted the pains of childbirth in relation to Mary's spiritual motherhood. Pius XII made a reference to the history of interpretation in *Munificentissimus Deus*: "Moreover, the scholastic doctors have recognised the Assumption of the Virgin Mother of God as something signified, not only in the various figures of the OT but also in the woman clothed with the sun, whom John the Apostle contemplated on the island of Patmos."[8] There is a hint in the last clause that the Pope himself identified the woman as Mary. He did not include this opinion in the strict argumentation preceding the dogmatic formula, nor in the latter, though some members of the advisory committee favoured it, notably Fr. M. Jugie, A.A. (qv).

Vatican II did not mention Rev 12 in LG. Cardinal Koenig had made a fleeting allusion to the passage as a basis of the Mary-Church theme acceptable to non-Catholics in the October 1963 debate on the status of the Marian schema. In the debate in September 1964, a plea was vainly made by Bishop Kempf of Limburg for inclusion of the text in the Marian chapter because of its "Christological, ecclesiological, eschatological, Mariological elements" especially suited to the Council teaching.[9]

Paul VI opened *Signum Magnum* thus: "The great sign which the apostle St. John contemplated in the heavens, the woman clothed with the sun (cf. Apoc. 12:1) is rightly, in the holy Liturgy of the Catholic Church, interpreted of the Blessed Virgin Mary, by the grace of Christ the Redeemer Mother of all men."[10]

In the footnote to this sentence, reference is to the epistle for the feast of the Apparition of the Immaculate B.V.M., 11 February. In the Roman Missal approved some years later by the Pope, the following excerpts are taken from Rev 12: the entrance antiphon for the Mass of the Assumption, v 1; the first reading for the same Mass vv 1-6 and 10 with v 19 of the previous chapter; the same reading is among those for the Common of Our Lady. The following are in the reformed Breviary: reading for the midday hour on the feast of the Assumption, v 1; the same as a reading for Morning Prayer on Our Lady's Saturday.

Catholic iconography has drawn heavily on Rev 12.

Recent interpretations: With an occasional exception like Max Thurian, non-Catholic opinion fails to support the identity of Mary and the woman; the collective sense is preferred, whether this be realised in the Church of the Old or the New Law or both. Two Catholics, J. Dillersberger and J. Bonnefoy, see the woman as Mary exclusively. A large number of others either do not rule out reference to the Church or firmly defend the dual meaning. There is not unanimity on how Mary and the Church are each represented.

Some exegetical points to note: this is a series of tableaux with action interspersed. The woman and the dragon, each described as a "sign" (semeion) figure in most of the tableaux. The scene changes from heaven to earth. OT echoes are easily traced. The sun recalls the image of light to signify divine presence, Ps 104; 2, "who coverest thyself with light as with a garment"; Wis 7:26, "For she [wisdom] is a reflection of eternal light." The sun and moon echo Is 60:19-20, "Your sun shall no more go down, nor your moon withdraw itself; for the Lord will be your everlasting light . . ." and Song, 6:10, "Who is this that looks forth like the dawn, fair as the moon, bright as the sun, terrible as an army with banners?" The serpent of Gen 3 is recalled by the dragon. Israel's place of retreat from Pharaoh in Ex is evoked by the desert to which the woman flees.

The parallel between Gen 3:15 and Rev 12 is much discussed: the woman and her seed *vis a vis* the serpent in the former; the woman and the male child *vis a vis* the dragon in the latter. There is one very great difference, rarely if ever mentioned. In Gen 3:15 it is the seed of the woman who is in conflict with the serpent, whereas the vision of Rev 12 is of Michael and his angels fighting with the dragon and his angels.

There are other differences. Gen 3:15 is a cryptic oracle referring to the future, a punishment on the serpent for his part in the initial disobedience, punishment through the woman whom he tempted and misled; no such previous relationship existed between the woman and the dragon in Rev 12. Since, however, it is written in the past tense the later action of the dragon against the woman is told. Thrown down from heaven, he still threatened her: she fled to the desert where he pursued her and when she flew on "the wings of the great eagle" he poured water like a flood after her, whereon this time she was saved by the earth which "swallowed the river which the dragon had poured from his mouth." But how was the woman, first seen as a sign in heaven, exposed on earth to pursuit by the dragon? What mean the words "her child was caught up to God and his throne?" And these "Then the dragon was angry with the woman, and went off to make war on the rest of her offspring, on those who keep the commandments of God and bear testimony to Jesus?"

There is an apparent difficulty about identifying the woman with Mary, with the people of God or Church of OT, with the Church of NT. The words "she cried out in her pangs of birth" (v.2) are opposed to the entire Christian tradition of the painless birth in Bethlehem; the words "she brought forth a male child" (v.5) cannot be reconciled with constant OT teaching that Israel as a community does not give birth to an individual child—the Messiah as an individual is to be born of an individual mother; nor can the Christian Church be the mother of this child in v.5 for it did not exist when he was born—the child "one who is to rule all nations with a rod of iron" is the Messiah, (cp. Ps 2:9), Jesus of Nazareth.

Answers are proposed to these objections. Jn 19:25-27 is invoked with Jn 16:21 and its antecedent texts in Is 26:16-17; 66:7-9 on the metaphorical childbirth of Zion to show the full spiritual dimensions of the word woman in Rev 12; in Jn the woman has the beloved disciple as a son, in Rev posterity "who keep the commandments of God and bear testimony to Jesus" —are the birth pangs thus explained? Is the woman endowed with dual motherhood, one physical, the other spiritual? Is the latter the painful one experienced on Calvary?

A Qumran hymn speaks of Israel as a community being the mother of the Messiah; it does not then seem untenable that the woman represents the people of God of OT: "For amid the throes of Death/ she shall bring forth a man-child, and amid the pains of Hell/ there shall spring from her child-bearing crucible/ a Marvellous Mighty Counsellor;/ and the man shall be delivered from out of the throes."[11] The passage is controverted.

In Rev generally, symbols are interchangeable. The author of Rev 12 could have seen that the mystery of Israel in the essential moment of transition to a new and final destiny could still be conveyed by the figure of a woman, still more cogently because in the same moment a woman was at the heart of the mystery.

[1]As well as commentaries cf. B. le Frois, S.V.D., *The Woman Clothed with the Sun (Apoc 12): Individual or Collective?* (Rome, 1954); id., "The Woman Clothed with the Sun," AER 126(1952), 161-80; F. M. Braun, O.P., *La Mère des Fidèles*, 2nd ed. (Paris, Tournai, 1954), 133-76; id., "La Femme vêtue de soleil (Apoc. 12). Etat du problème," *Rev. Thomiste*, 55(1955), 639-69; L. Cerfaux, "La vision de la femme et du dragon de l'Apocalypse en rélation avec le protévangile," ETL 31(1955), 21-33; A. Dubarle, *La Femme couronnée d'Étoiles, Apoc. 12, Mélanges Andre Robert*, Paris, 1957, 512-18; A. Dupont-Sommer, "La Mère du Messie et la Mère de l'Aspic dans un hymne de Qumran," *Rev. de l'histoire des Religions* 147(1955), 174-88; J. Dillersberger, "Das Weib und der Drache," *Wort und Warheit* 2(1947), 257-68; J. F. Bonnefoy, *Le mystère de Marie selon le Protévangile et l'Apocalypse* (Paris, 1949); A. Trabucco, "La Donna ravvolta di sole," MM 19(1957), 1-58; A. Th. Kassing, *Die Kirche und Maria: Ihr Verhältnis im 12 Kapitel der Apokalypse* (Dusseldorf, 1958); A. Feuillet, "Le Messie et sa Mère d'après le chapitre 12 de l'Apocalypse," RB 66(1959), 55-86, and *Johannine Studies* (Staten Island, Alba, 1964) 257-92; id., *Jésus et sa Mère*, (Paris, 1974) 30-46, 94-95; id., "Le Cantique des Cantiques et l'Apocalypse," RSR 49(1961), 321-53; S. Lyonnet, S.J., "Maria santissima nell'Apocalisse," *Tabor*, 25(1959),. 213-22; P. Prigent, *Apocalypse 12: Histoire de l'éxègese* (Tübingen, 1959); M. Thurian, *Mary, Mother of the Lord, Figure of the Church* (London, 1963) 176-88; F. Montagnini, "Le 'signe' de l'Apocalypse 12 à la lumière de la christologie du Nouveau Testament," NRT, 99(1967), 401-16; J. Ernst, "Die 'himmlische Frau' im 12 Kapitel der Apokalypse," *Theologie und Glaube* 58(1968), 39-58; H. Gollinger, *Das "Grosse Zeichen" von Apokalpyse 12* (Stuttgarter Biblische Monographien 11), Würzburg and Stuttgart, 1971; A. Vogtle, "Mythos und Botschaft in Apokalypse 12," *Tradition und Glaube, Festschrift K. G. Kuhn*, Göttingen, 1972, 395-415; J. M. Salgado, O.M.I., "Le chapitre XII de l'Apocalypse à la lumière des procédés de composition littéraires de S. Jean," MSS V, 293-360; id., *EphMar* 20(1970), 327-34; F. W. Koester, *Apokalyptisches Weib*, LexMar; J. McHugh, *The Mother of Jesus*, 404-432; *Mary in NT*, 219-239. [2]*Haer.* 78, 11, PG 42, 716C. [3]*De Symbolo* 3, PL 40, 661. [4]*The Complete Commentary of Oecumenius on the Apocalypse*, ed. H. C. Hoskier (Ann Arbor, 1928), 135-37. [5]PL 100, 1152D-53; cf. R. Laurentin, *Traite'*I, p. 142. [6]A. Trabucco, *op.cit.*, in Note 1. [7]OL, 180. [8]AAS 42(1950), 763. [9]Cf. R. le Déaut C.S.Sp., BSFEM 22(1965), p. 72, nn. 57, 58. [10]AAS 59(1967). [11]G. Vermes, *The Dead Sea Scrolls in English* (London, 1965) (= 1 QH iii); T. H. Gaster, *the Scriptures of the Dead Sea Sect* (London, 1957), 140.

Z

ZAMORO, GIOVANNI MARIA, O.F.M.CAP. (1579-1649)

Italian professor of Philosophy and Theology, author of a work on the unity and trinity of God, Z., a convinced scotist, issued in 1629 in Venice, a three-volume treatise on Marian theology: *De eminentissima Deiparae Virginis perfectione.*[1] It aroused bitter controversy, as Z. contended that Mary was free of the proximate "debt of sin"; in 1636 the work was put on the Index where it remained until Leo XIII ordered a revision of the list in 1900. The work was planned for seven books, three of which appeared, dealing with: (1) "the supreme perfection of Mary"; (2) "the predestination, prophecies, ancestry, parents, conception, perfections of soul and body and many other privileges granted to the Virgin from the first moment of her conception"; (3) "the life of Mary from her birth to her espousal." In the four unpublished books the author dealt with the Annunciation, the conception of the divine Word, the Visitation, the Purification after childbirth, the flight into Egypt, the most blessed passing, the resurrection, Assumption and Coronation of the Blessed Virgin Mary. Z. also left five treatises on the Immaculate Conception of the B.V.M.

---

[1]Arcangelus a Roc O.F.M.Cap., "Joannes Maria Zamoro ab Udine, praeclarus mariologus," *Collect. Franc.*, 16(1945), 117-63; 17(1946), 125-85; 19(1949), 143-223. Adalberto da Postioma, O.F.M.Cap., "De summa Deiparae Virginis perfectione apud Joannem M. Zamoro Utinensem, O.F.M. Cap.," EphMar 9(1959), 497-502.

ZENO OF VERONA (d.*c.* 372) — See Supplement, p. 390.

ZWINGLI, ULRICH (1484-1531)
The Swiss Reformer expressed views somewhat similar to Luther's; but there were certain differences due to his singular outlook. His ideas on Mary are found mostly in a *Marienpredigt*[1] and in his commentary on Lk and the controversial writings. The sermon is praise of the divine motherhood and perpetual virginity: "it was given to her," he says, "what belongs to no creature, that in the flesh she should bring forth the Son of God."[2] On the virginity, he might be St. Augustine (*qv*): "I firmly believe that Mary, according to the words of the gospel as a pure Virgin brought forth for us the Son of God and in childbirth and after childbirth forever remained a pure, intact Virgin."[3] He believed that *Scriptura sola* was "the guide and mistress"; but in the virginity—as well as in his erroneous doctrine on the Eucharist—he relied on a special illumination of the Spirit. Thus he saw the Marian meaning of Is 7:14 and thus he solved the difficulty of the Matthean 1:25 "until she brought forth." He was opposed to the Papists who thought "that the perpetual virginity of the divine *Theotokos*, that is the *Deipara*, could not be proved from holy writ, but was established by the Church's assertion (by Church, he adds, they mean that of Rome, wealthy heretofore)."[4] Throughout his life he continued to teach the perpetual virginity of Mary.

On Z.'s attitude to the Immaculate Conception and Assumption (*qqv*) of Mary there is no lengthy evidence. In a debate in Zurich in 1523 he said: "It was publicly decreed in the Council of Basle that the Mother of God was conceived without original sin, nevertheless no monk is so inept and stupid that he would not dare to contradict it publicly."[5] This may have been refusal to accept a Council, for at other times he used such words as: "When the Saviour of all men was born of a holy immaculate Virgin Mary, the angel spoke to the shepherds" . . . ; "I esteem immensely the Mother of God, the ever chaste, immaculate Virgin Mary". . . ; "Christ . . . was born of a most undefiled Virgin."[6] Elsewhere he speaks of God sanctifying and purifying the Mother of the Saviour "for it was fitting that such a holy Son should have a holy Mother." And one of his associates, Pastor Amman, held the doctrine: "Mary was preserved from all stain and sin, from original sin, from mortal sin and from actual sin."[6] As to the Assumption, the authorities in Zurich forbade unseemly entertainment on the eve of the feast presumably with Z.'s approval; he had retained the feast.

In the *Marienpredigt* he said: "The more the honour and love for Christ grows among men, the more esteem and honour for Mary grows, for she brought forth for us so great, but so compassionate a Lord and Redeemer."[7] Z. kept the Angelus in Zurich (it was forbidden in Berne) and also the Hail Mary, but the latter as greeting and praise. For he was against all invocation of Mary. He denied, on the Reformation principle of *sola gratia*, all merit on Mary's part and any power of mediation or intercession on our behalf. He waged war on all images.

---

[1]The sermon in *Zwinglii Opera, Corpus Reformatorum*, (CR), Berlin, 1905 . . . vol I, pp. 391-428; *Opera completa*, Zurich, 1828-42. Marian texts in W. Tappolet, *Das Marienlob der Reformatoren* (Tübingen, 1962), pp. 221-260; cf. K. Federer, "Zwinglii und die Marienverehrung," in *Zeitschrift fur Schweizer Kirchengeschichte*, 45(1951); G. W. Locher, "inhalt und Absicht von Zwinglis Marienlehre" in *Kirchenblatt für die reformierte Schweiz*, 107(1951), pp. 34-37; R. Schimmelpfennig, *Die Geschichte der Marienvererehrung im deutschen Protestantismus* (Paderborn, 1952); K. Algermissen, "Mariologie und Marienverehrung der Reformatoren" in *Theol. und Glaube*, 49(1959), pp. 1-24; *esp.* E. Stakemeier in MO, pp. 450-59; T. A. O'Meara, O.P., in *Mary in Protestant and Catholic Theology* (New York, 1966), pp. 143-144. [2]*In Evang. Luc., Op. compl.*, 6, 1, 639. [3]CR 1, 424. [4]*Apologia complanationis Isaiae*, in *Op. compl.*, 5, 616; W. J. Hollenweger, *Zwingli's devotion to Mary, One in Christ*, 1980, 1-2, pp. 59-68. [5]E. Stakemeier, *op.cit.*, p. 455. [6]*Ibid.*, p. 456. [7]CR, I, pp. 427-428.

Supplement

ANGELUS, THE

A prayer traditionally said three times a day, about six in the morning, at midday and at six in the evening, the Angelus is ideally structured for popular prayer, is in its versicles and in the first part of the Hail Mary (*qv*) taken verbally from Holy Writ. The origins are western and medieval and here our most reliable authority is Fr. H. Thurston, S.J. The recitation of three Hail Marys in the evening marked the tolling of a curfew bell in some areas: this custom probably dates from the eleventh century. Pope Gregory IX (d. 1241) ordered the ringing of the bell to remind people to pray for the Crusades. We find St. Bonaventure (*qv*) in 1269 asking that the faithful be urged to follow the Franciscan custom of saying three Hail Marys as the bell rang in the evening. Pope John XXII indulgenced this practice in 1318 and 1327. The morning custom seems to have been prompted by the monastic habit of saying three Hail Marys as the bell rang during Prime. The noontide habit was apparently linked with the memory of the Passion, at first on Fridays, with the intention of peace predominant: thus it was proposed by the Synod of Prague in 1386; it was extended to the whole week by Callistus III in 1456 with the special intention of praying for victory over the Turks. By the sixteenth century the prayer is standardised. It has been recommended by Benedict XIV, Leo XIII, Pius XI and, to the Lourdes Congress of 1958, by Pius XII. No Pope wrote of the Angelus as extensively as Paul VI (*qv*) in *Marialis Cultus* (*qv*): it needed no reform, he said, was entirely biblical, was oriented to the Paschal Mystery, a most potent and relevant form of invocation, prompting contemplation.[1]

---

[1]Cf. esp. H. Thurston, S.J., DSp I, 1164, 65; W. Henry, DACL, I, 2069-78.

AVE MARIS STELLA

The most popular hymn in honour of Our Lady.[1] Widely translated, widely sung, especially at great shrines like Lourdes, it phrases with simplicity and sobriety a whole theology of the Mother of God and of men: "establish us in peace, changing Eve's name"; "set prisoners free, give sight to the blind"; "show yourself a Mother, may he who was born for us, took you for his own, hear our prayers through you"; "free us from our faults, make us meek and chaste"; "keep us pure through life, protect us on the way, to eternal joy with Jesus.".

The hymn is found in the ninth century Codex Sangallensis, which may put its origin in the previous century. Paul the Deacon is sometimes suggested as author. The Roman Breviary once gave it as hymn for Second Vespers of the Common of Feasts of Our Lady, it still includes it among those optional.

---

[1]Text AH 51, pp. 140-42; cf. A. dal Zotto, '*Ricerche sull'autore dell'Ave Maris Stella* in *Aevum*, 25(1951), pp. 494-503; S. de Ibero, O.F.M.Cap., J. Garcia Garcia, E. R. Panyagua, C.M., *Estudio del "Ave Maris Stella"*, in *Helmantica*, 8(1957), pp. 421-75.

CASSIAN, JOHN (*c.* 360-*c.* 435)

Cassian, an important figure in the early history of monasticism, was brought into the controversy previous to Ephesus (*qv*) when the future Leo the Great (*qv*) urged him to write on the Incarnation; C. was also given the documentation of the controversy between St. Cyril and Nestorius.[1] In this work there is a defence of the title *Theotokos* with comments also on Pauline texts applied to the problem, on Is 7:14 and, at some length, on the Annunciation (*qv*) scene.

[1]Works PL 50; also ed. M. Petschenig, CSEL 17, for *De Incarnatione* pp. 233-291; *Collatio* V, 6, 3, CSEL 23, p. 125; EMBP, 675-684; E. Schwartz, *Konzilstudien,* Strasbourg, 1914, 20, I, pp. 1-17, Cassian und Nestorius.

CHARISMATIC RENEWAL, THE

Cardinal Suenens (*qv*) had an important role in effecting harmony and mutual exchange between the Marian movement and the Charismatic Renewal movement as this began, in recent decades, to take on worldwide dimensions: he was so prominent as presiding prelate at international congresses, so steadfast in help, that he came to be considered the patron. He urged participants to a positive attitude towards Mary, devoted a chapter of his work *A New Pentecost* to her role vis a vis the Spirit, in particular seized the opportunity given him to further this outlook by the simultaneous occurrence in Rome, 1975, of the International Marian Congress, held on the theme Mary and the Spirit, to which he was Papal Legate and the International Charismatic Congress, in which he had a leading part. Exchange of lecturers between the two congresses augured well for the future; this trend was enhanced at the Dublin congress, 1978, when R. Laurentin (*qv*), lecturing on Mary as a charismatic, had to repeat his lecture before a second crowded audience. Here is an excellent instance of the existential approach to the mystery of Mary.[1]

[1]Cf. bibliography to Spirit, the Holy; E. D. O'Connor, NCE, XVII, 104-106; *id. Pope Paul and the Spirit,* Notre Dame, Indiana, 1978, esp. pp. 220-223, letter, 13 May, 1975 to Cardinal Suenens, pp. 228-230, address to charismatic congress; R. Laurentin, *Les charismes de Marie, Ecriture, Tradition et Sitz im Leben,* EphMar, 28 (1978), pp. 309-321; M. G. G. Guerra, C.M.F., *Maria, la primera carismática en la Iglesia, ibid.,* pp. 323-337.

CHRISTOLOGY, RECENT.

It would be a herculean task to analyse and assess in detail the explosion of literature on Christology in recent times.[1] One trend mentioned in the article *Primacy of Mary* continues; here Teilhard de Chardin joins Duns Scotus.[2] Many divergent views have been expressed, and met the predictable criticism. In the ferment reductionist theories mingle with novel syntheses projecting on to the sacred figure of the God-man all the mental categories fashioned from the agony of our times. In such a volume of invention and debate the statement issued by the International Theological Commission will prove salutary and enlightening.[3] Theologians of Our Lady have been at work on the problems which arise for them. They should not forget the findings of the early Fathers and the conclusions of the Councils on the need to retain Mary in any truly enlightening doctrine on Christ.[4]

[1]Solely for the general situation and bibliography cf. J. Sobrino, S.J., *Christianity at the Cross-roads,* London, 1978; J. D. G. Dunn, *Christology in the Making,* esp. bibliography, pp. 354-403, London, 1980; L. Bouyer, *The Eternal Son,* Huntingdon, Indiana, 1978; K. Rahner with W. Thusing, *A New Christology,* London, 1982. [2]Add to bibliography on *Primacy of Mary,* J. F. Bonnefoy, O.F.M., *Christ and the Cosmos,* Paterson, N.J., 1965; M. Meilach, *Mary Immaculate in the Divine Plan,* 1981; esp. J. Carol, O.F.M., *The Absolute Primacy and Predestination of Jesus and his Virgin Mother,* Chicago, 1981; cf. also A. Feuillet, P.S.S., *Le Christ, Sagesse de Dieu d'après les épitres/pauliniennes,* and important preface by Y.-M. Congar, O.P. [3]Text DCath, 1981, 222-231. [4]Cf. issue EphMar, 30(1980), Fasc 1, *Maria en las Cristologias actuales,* J. M. Alonso, C.M.F., J. Galot, S.J., and D. Fernandez, C.M.F., *Maria en las recentes cristologias holandeses,* EphMar, 32(1982), pp. 9-32.

COMMUNION OF SAINTS

Implied in the NT, becoming quickly in the first ages and since then a living truth, its effects on the Liturgy soon explicit in the *Communicantes* prayer in the Mass in which Mary was prominent (LG 50, 52), this reality, whether it is taken to refer to a fellowship of persons or a sharing of spiritual goods, is highly relevant to Mary. Because the basis of the communion is the Mystical Body of Christ, her Son, and its author is the Spirit (*qv*) with whom she has a totally singular relationship, her place in the Communion is superior to that of all others and her role in the maintenance of its continuous beneficent vitality is marked by her office of spiritual Mother and her royal function.[1]

[1]Cf. J. Cahill, S.J., *Mary's present role in the Communion of Saints* 18(1967), pp. 31-45; E. Carroll, O.Carm., *The Mother of Jesus in the Communion of Saints: Challenge to the Churches;* Proceedings of the 21st Annual Convention of the Catholic Theological Society of America, 21(1967), pp. 29-65; R. Laurentin, *Mary in the Communion of Saints,* London, *Ecumenical Society of the Blessed Virgin Mary,* 1973.

DILLENSCHNEIDER, CLEMENT, C.SS.R. (1890-1969)

Prominent member of the French Society of Marian Studies, author first of a remarkable monograph on the Marian theology of St. Alphonsus Liguori, seen against a very wide, carefully composed canvas, D. went on to specialize in the theology of Mary's coredemption: *Marie au service de notre Rédemption,* 1947; *Pour une corédemption mariale bien comprise,* 1949; *Le mystére de la Corédemption mariale,* 1951. With time he changed his approach, turning from Christ-type theory to Church-type (*qv*). This change marks his work *Marie dans l'économie de la création renovée,* 1957. He also published a monograph on the development of Marian doctrine, *Le sens de la foi et le progrès dogmatique du mystère marial,* 1954; and considered the question of a first principle in Marian theology in *Le principe premier d'une théologie mariale organique,* 1956. Interested also in the theology and sanctification of priests.[1] Erudite, balanced in his conclusions, with a capacity for fresh synthesis, lucid in exposition.

---

[1] M. Benzerath, C.SS.R., EphMar 20(1970), pp. 245-251 with bibliography.

EASTERN LITURGIES

This outline of liturgical origins and development will not enter into detail on the liturgies of the different rites in the eastern churches. This is a subject of wide ramifications, illuminating and rewarding. What is given here is a series of bibliographical indications. It is hoped that therein the reader will acquire an idea of the riches of the compositions which feature Mary Theotokos so abundantly and so beautifully, in every aspect of the liturgical observance.

The Byzantine liturgy, which has been called the most Marian of all liturgies: S. Salaville, A.A., *Marie dans la liturgie byzantine ou gréco-slave, Maria,* I, pp. 249-326; C. Cumbinger, O.F.M.Cap., *Mary in the Byzantine Liturgy, Mariology* I, pp. 188-209; A. A. King, *The Rites of Eastern Christendom,* Rome, 1948, Vol. 2, *Byzantine Rite with Variants,* pp. 1-250; J. Nasrallah, *Marie dans la sainte et divine liturgie byzantine,* Paris, 1955; J. Ledit, S.J., *Marie dans la liturgie de Byzance,* Paris, 1976; Kallistos Archmandrite Ware and Sister Mary, *The Festal Menaion,* tr. from the Greek, London, 1969; G. Gharib, *La Madonna Assunta nella chiesa Byzantina, Mater Ecclesiae,* 10(1974), pp. 75-83; *id., Theotokos, Madre di Dio nella chiesa Bizantina, ibid.,* pp. 54-64.

The Alexandrian Liturgy, rooted in the city which was once the most important see and greatest intellectual centre in the eastern Mediterranean, has a splendour which matches this history; it is abundantly and nobly Marian: C. Gumbinger, *The Alexandrian Liturgy, Mariology,* I, pp. 210-215; esp. G. Giamberardini, O.F.M., *Marie dans la liturgie copte, Maria,* V, pp. 75-116; *id., San Giuseppe nella tradizione copta,* Cairo, 1966; *id., Il culto mariano in Egitto,* vol. II, Sec. VII-X, Jerusalem, 1974 and vol. I, Sec. I-VI, 2nd ed., Jerusalem, 1975.

Ancient popular devotion to Mary, exemplified in the *Sub Tuum* (*qv*) has amply supported the Liturgy; it has recently received a striking impetus in the very singular series of Apparitions (*qv*) of Our Lady, witnessed by hundreds of thousands at Zeitoun near Cairo, 1968-1971, declared authentic by leaders of all religious denominations; the first witnesses were Moslems, one of whom was instantaneously cured of an injured finger.

The Ethiopic Liturgy: The immense place given to Mary in the devotional life of the Ethiopian people is fully reflected in their liturgy. Those impeded by language difficulties with oriental liturgies have translations of the Ethiopian synaxaria: PO, I, fasc. 5; VII, 3; IX, 4; XV, 5; XXXVI, 1, tr. I. Guidi, A. Singlas, S. Gregaut. Works by E. A. Wallis Budge in the article on him; King, *op. cit.* pp. 497-658; J. M. Harden, *The Anaphoras of the Ethiopic Liturgy;* G. Nicollet, *Marie dans la liturgie éthiopienne,* Maria, I, pp. 374-413; C. Gumbinger, *op. cit.,* pp. 215-223; Mario da Abiy-Addi, O.F.M.Cap., *La seconda Anafora Mariana del Messale Etiopico,* MM 30(1968), pp. 181-191.

The Antiochene Liturgy: Source of the Armenian, Byzantine and Maronite liturgies, possibly of the Chaldean. C. Gumbinger, *op. cit.,* pp. 224-232; P. Hindo, *Disciplina Antiochena antica,* appendix, Rome, 1943; *Anaphorae Syriacae,* Rome Pontifical Oriental Institute, 1939-1951.

The Armenian Liturgy: Synaxaria with translations PO V, fasc. 3; VI, 2; VI, 2; XV, 3; XVI, 1; XVII, 1; XIX; 1; XXI, 1, 2, 3, 4, 5, 6, tr. G. Bayan, and Prince Max of Saxony; P. Vartan Tekeyan, *La Mère de Dieu dans la liturgie arménienne,* Maria I, pp. 355-361; C. Gumbinger, *op. cit.* pp. 233-239; King, *op. cit.* II, pp. 521-646.

Syro-Maronite Liturgy: M. Doumith, *Marie dans la liturgie Syro-Maronite, Maria,* I, pp.

329-340 with bibliography p. 340.

The Chaldean Liturgy: C. Gumbinger, *op. cit.* pp. 240-244; King, *op. cit.* II, pp. 251-520.

Useful information in general in G. Frénaud, O.S.B., ME, V, pp. 57ff and general works, E. Renaudot, *Liturgiarum Orientalium Collectio,* 2 vols., Paris, 1716; F. E. Brightman, *Liturgies, Eastern and Western,* Oxford, 1896; I. H. Dalmais, *Eastern Liturgies,* tr. D. Attwater, New York, 1960.

GALOT, JEAN, S.J. (1919-   )

Belgian Professor in the Gregorian University G. has written much on Christology, important studies in Marian theology: two remarkable essays on the Immaculate Conception and the Assumption in Maria, VII; *Mary in the Gospel* (tr. *Marie dans l'evangile,* Paris, Louvain, 1958); *Le Coeur de Marie,* Louvain, 1955; *Etre né de Dieu, Jean 1:13,* Rome, 1969; *La fede di Maria e la nostra,* Assisi, 1973; a stream of review articles in Italian and French on contemporary Marian problems, papal and conciliar Marian teaching, Mary and the Holy Spirit, aspects of the virginity, Mary and womankind. G. presented *Marialis Cultus* (qv) to the press, possibly helped in drafting same.

GARCIA GARCES, NARCISO, C.M.F. (1904-   )

A leading figure in the Spanish Marian movement, G. founded the Spanish Mariological Society and from 1941 to 1954 edited its annual proceedings, *EstM,* resuming this task in 1957.[1] Founded with religious colleagues in 1951 *EphMar.* Author of substantial, thoroughly argued works on Marian theology, *Maria Corredemptrix,* 1940; *Titulos y grandezas de Maria,* 3rd ed. 1959; *La Virgen de nuestra Fe,* 1967; shorter works on Marian themes; over 70 review articles; papers for national and international congresses. G. was adviser to Spanish hierarchy during Vatican II (qv).

[1] EphMar, 25(1975), pp. 13-18.

GERMANUS II (d. 1240)

Experienced the hardship following the capture of Constantinople by the Latin Crusaders in 1204. Patriarch of Constantinople from 1222 to his death. His contribution to Marian theology is in the long *Sermon on the Annunciation,*[1] wherein characteristic Byzantine ideas find expression. So does the Traditional Eve-Mary parallel. All in Mary is related to her role as *Theotokos.*

[1] PG 140, 677-736; cf. M. Jugie, *L'Immaculée Conception,* 212-216; H. Graef, *Mary,* I, 327-329.

GIAMBERARDINI, GABRIELE, O.F.M. (1917-1978)

Italian by origin, G. spent from 1950 to 1969 in Egypt, where he specialized in Coptic Christian literature.[1] Highly qualified, he taught in higher institutes in Egypt, the Holy Land and Rome. Member of many cultural societies, national and international; editor of the annual of Christian Studies Centre, Cairo. His most valued work was in Marian theology and liturgy related to the Coptic church, on Our Lady and St. Joseph (qqv: see articles SUB TUUM, EASTERN LITURGIES). Author of over 100 articles and papers based on research into primary sources and wide erudition. Adviser to Coptic bishops during Vatican II (qv).

[1] G. Marinangeli, O.F.M., MM, 40(1978), pp. 217-220.

GILLETT, MARTIN (1902-1980)

An Anglican deacon who became a Catholic, G. manifested interest in and devotion to Mary. At the suggestion of Pius XII he undertook the two volume *Famous Shrines of Our Lady,* 1949, later added *Shrines of Our Lady in England and Wales,* 1957. Devotional and organising activity centred on the revived Walsingham shrine. At the Golden Jubilee of the Malines Conversations in Brussels, in 1966 (see Mercier, Cardinal) G. was persuaded by Cardinal Suenens and others to found the Ecumenical Society of the Blessed Virgin Mary: from 1967 to his death he was Honorary General Secretary, travelled widely to found new branches, organised the highly successful international conferences, the last of which at Canterbury was held after his death. Proceedings of last three, 1975, 1979, 1981 have appeared as special issues of *The Way* (1975, 1981) or *One in Christ* (1979); papers earlier presented appeared as single pamphlets or review articles. Contributions are varied, of very high quality, with increasing U.S. participation. G. was indefatigable in administration; also lectured.[1]

[1] E. Carroll, O.Carm., *Our Lady and Ecumenism in the English-speaking World*, MM 41(1979); A. Stacpoole, O.S.B., Introduction to *One in Christ*, issue of 1979, also as separate booklet, ESBVM; *id*. Introduction to *Mary's Place in Christian Dialogue*, twenty five selected papers given to the Society, London, 1982.

HERMANN OF TOURNAI (d.c. 1147)

Author of a *Tractatus de incarnatione Jesus Christi* H. had notable insights in Marian theology.[1] He dealt with her eternal predestination but particularly, in his treatment of the mediation (*qv*) theme, he was the first to use a metaphor that passed into wide currency: "Our Lady is rightly understood to be the neck of the Church, because she is the mediatress between God and men."[2] In the east Theophanes of Nicaea (*qv*) hit upon the same idea. H. also considerably widened the Eve Mary parallel by applying to Mary the words of Gen 2:18 "a helper like unto himself." From that acquisition a whole doctrine of Mary as *"adjutrix Redemptionis"* would follow.[3] Mary was "spouse and mother of God." H. wished to show in the same passage how we had been brought into filial relationship to God by Mary. He is also author of *De miraculis S. Mariae Laudunensis*.[4]

[1] PL 180, 9-38. [2] PL 30. [3] PL 36. [4] PL 156, 961-1018; cf. H. Graef, *Mary I*, p. 234.

ISIDORE OF SEVILLE, ST., DOCTOR OF THE CHURCH (c. 560-636)

His encyclopaedic writings had immense influence in medieval times.[1] Influenced by his elder brother, St. Leander, archbishop of Seville, who supervised his education: I. himself the author of a treatise on virginity wherein he speaks of Mary as the "Mother of incorruption," who spiritually brought forth their sister, St. Florentina, as a nun and who will pray for her. I. in the *Etymologiae* fixes the threefold meaning of Mary's name, *Illuminatrix,* Star of the Sea, Mistress (alleged from the Syrian)[2]: this trilogy would form the basis of countless sermons for centuries. To these, in the *De ortu et obitu Patrum*, he adds a number of titles, "enclosed garden, sealed fountain, Mother of the Lord, temple of God, sanctuary of the Holy Spirit."[3] This is the first usage known of the title "Sanctuary of the Holy Spirit," lasting to the present,

preferred designation of Vatican II. I. has a curious exegesis of Simeon's prophecy (see SWORD),[4] mentions Mary elsewhere in his works especially in the *Homilia 22 in Nativitatem Christi*.[5] His commentary on Song of Songs is spurious.[6]

[1] Works PL 81-84; cf. R. Laurentin, *Court Traité* I, pp. 136, 139; J. Fontaine in DSp, VII, 2104-2116. [2] PL 82, 289. [3] PL 83, 148. [4] *Ibid*. [5] R. Laurentin, *l.cit.*. [6] PL 83, 1119A-1132C.

JOHN OF EUBOEA (d.c. 750)

Author of what may have been the first sermon for the feast of Mary's conception. Therein he uses language which can scarcely be interpreted other than affirmation of the Immaculate Conception. The homily (BHG 1117) has been definitely established as his.[1]

[1] R. Laurentin, *Traité* I, p. 171; M. Jugie *L'Immaculee Conception*, pp. 126-128; text PG, 96, 1460-1500.

JOHN OF GARLAND (d.c. 1272)

Poet and grammarian J., born in England, living in France, was the author of two works on Our Lady, *Epithalamium Beate Marie Virginis,* a 6,000 line poem unpublished and the *Stella Maris*, composed between 1248/1249.[1] It is a collection of 61 Mary legends in Latin verse, apparently the first such collection made by a layman. There may have been, at the time, some 2,000 Mary legends in circulation, most of them in the North of France. One large compilation was the *Mariale Magnum*, deemed lost, the other was based in the Paris monastery of Ste. Geneviève: J. drew on the second, reducing it apparently. His collection of miracles and edifying episodes is an excellent illustration of the genre, which can be compared with that of Vincent of Beauvais.

[1] ed. E. F. Wilson, with admirable, detailed introduction, which also covers the whole question of Mary Legends in medieval times, Cambridge, 1946.

JOHN PAUL II (Pope 1978-)

In formal papal documents, the Encyclicals *Redemptor Hominis, Dives in Misericordia,*

Laborem exercens, or Apostolic Exhortations on Catechetics, the Family, and in lengthy addresses at the great shrines, which are always prominent in his apostolic journeys, John Paul insists on Mary's place in Christian life:[1] his sermons at Czestochowa, Guadalupe, Knock, Ephesus, Aparecida, Altotting, Loreto, Fatima, Lujan and other less well-known Marian centres are pastoral in character, but enriched with Marian theology; influenced too by Marian saints, especially his Polish hero, St. Maximilian Kolbe (*qv*). His ideal is living contact with Mary as a loving supremely caring Mother. His fundamental idea is the divine motherhood, but he is particularly attentive to Council teaching, especially of Vatican II and to that of Paul VI; he returns to the idea of Mary, Mother and model of the Church. In the commemorative ceremonies for Ephesus and Constantinople he went into the theology of Mary and the Spirit.[2]

---

[1]*This is your Mother*, Marian texts of John Paul II, ed. S. Byrne, Athlone, 1981; Bishop K. McNamara, *John Paul II: Mary, the Mother of God*, London CTS, 1982. [2]AAS 73(1981), 485-497.

JOUASSARD, GEORGES (1895-1982)
A founding member and, for ten years, president of the French Society for Marian Studies, noted patrologist, J. specialized in the theology of the patron of his university city, St. Irenaeus of Lyons. A regular contributor to the Society's annual sessions, author of a truly seminal work, *Marie à travers la patristique,* in *Maria* I. Immensely erudite, balanced in interpretation with sure intuition in vexed areas of scholarship.[1]

---

[1]R. Etaix, *Catholicisme,* VI, 1041-1042.

KOESTER, HEINRICH MARIA, S.A.C. (1911-   )
Contributor to many reviews and to theological encyclopaedias, esp. LexM as to national and international congresses, K. entered the debate on Mary's part in our Redemption in the forties with two substantial works, *Die Magd des Herrn,* 1947; *Unus Mediator,* 1950; later published *Die Frau die Christi Mutter war,* 2 vols., 1963-1964; *Die Mittlerschaft Mariens,* 1967 and several lengthy articles or papers (e.g. for the German Mariological Society's meetings) rele-

vant to present-day problems, especially the ecumenical question, the relationship between Scripture and Tradition, the place of the Bible in Marian theology.

---

[1]EphMar 20(1970), pp. 251-252.

LEBON, JOSEPH-MARTIN (1879-1957)
A member of Cardinal Mercier's immediate circle in the promotion of the doctrine of Mary's mediation (*qv*), one of the committee members established by Pius XI to study the definability of the doctrine, L. brought to these and other Marian projects his singular prestige as a patrologist and Oientalist.[1] Specialist in Athanasius and especially in Severus of Antioch he was a key figure in the publication of CSCO. Of his articles on Mary's mediation the most stimulating — though not universally accepted in one of its theses — was *Comment je conçois, j'établis et je défends la doctrine de la médiation mariale,* in ETL 16(1939), pp. 655-744; the controverted idea was that Mary enjoyed a grace from God directly as well as the grace of Christ.

---

[1]G. Rotureau, O.P., *Catholicisme,* VII, 134; F. X. Murphy, NCE, VIII, 596.

MARTIN OF LEÓN (d. 1203)
Canon Regular of St. Isidore of Leon, M. has left a number of sermons on liturgical feasts, especially on the Nativity of the Lord, two on Our Lady — the Assumption and the Nativity — in the course of which he deals with Marian themes, the divine motherhood, Mary's holiness.[1] In explaining Revelation XII (see WOMAN IN) he adopts the Woman-Church identification.

---

[1]Works PL 208, 209; cf. G. M. Roschini, O.S.M., *Maria Santissima,* I, pp. 416, 17.

MASCALL, ERIC L. (1905-   )
A principal Anglican theologican of Our Lady, collaborator in two pioneer works, *The Mother of God* and *The Blessed Virgin Mary* appearing in England from that communion in the present age. M. was a founder member of the Ecumenical Society of the Blessed Virgin Mary, 1967, has contributed to its proceedings as to other congresses. To all this intellectual activity he

brought his theological talent, shown over a wide field, his ability to resist modern error and his clarity in expression.

MOTHER OF THE MESSIAH
A title which demands research and synthesis over the whole of the OT, related to a unique thread of interest which runs through these books and finds its culminating point in the NT. It is tentatively suggested in this work that only by an understanding of this title and its roots in the OT prominence given to the king's mother —as shown in a remarkable study by H. Cazelles, P.S.S.[1] — can one explain the substitution of *Mother of Jesus* for Mary's own name in Acts and John: partially in the former, entirely in the latter. The messianic kingdom was in being and she was the King's Mother, the *gebirah*.

---

[1]*La Mère de Roi-Messie dans l'Ancien Testament*, ME V, pp. 39-56; id., *La fonction maternelle de Sion et de Marie*, MDD, VI, pp. 165-178.

NARSES (d.c. 502)
Founder of the Nestorian school at Nisibis N. following his credal allegiance did not give Mary the title *Theotokos*.[1] He did praise her highly, calling her a "second heaven," admiring her especially for her poverty. He taught that it was through her that the Lord of the universe resolved to descend to release and deliver Adam.

---

[1]F. Feldmann, *Syrische Wechsellieder von Narses*, Leipzig, 1896; cf. H. Graef, *Mary I*, p. 124.

NILUS THE ABBOT, ST. (d.c. 430)
The works of this saintly man, who exercised considerable influence through his correspondence, are not satisfactorily edited.[1] Enough survives in accepted condition to give an idea of his Marian theology. Writing probably well before Ephesus (qv) he repeatedly calls Mary Theotokos (qv). He believed not only in the virginal conception, commonly held, but in the *virginitas in partu* (qv), "the seals of virginity were in no way broken."[2] Likewise in the perpetual virginity. Not long after St. Epiphanius (qv) he spoke of Mary in these terms: Eve was called life that she should signify the second (Eve) "Mary, that is, who brought forth Christ the Lord of glory as

the life of men. She indeed is shown as the true mother of all who live in harmony with the precepts of the gospel, not allowing their souls to fail in unbelief."[3] N. also thought that there was a parallel between Adam's creation, the making of Eve, on the one hand, and, on the other, Christ's birth from Mary, but the Church's from the open side on the Cross.[4] He enlarges on Mary as a prophet (see REVELATION, MARY AS[5]).

---

[1]PL 79, CMP, II, pp. 468-472; EMBP, pp. 662-667; cf. J. Quasten, *Patrology*, III, pp. 496-504. [2]PG 79, 182B. [3]PG 179D. [4]PG 182A. [5]PG 294 A-B.

PAUL VI (Pope 1963-1978)
Because of the tensions within the post-conciliar Church Paul's contribution here as in the pursuit of Church unity has not been fully appreciated (see MARIALIS CULTUS, MOTHER OF THE CHURCH, SIGNUM MAGNUM, VATICAN II, WOMAN AND OUR LADY).[1]P. had the habit of preaching on Our Lady as bishop; he kept up this habit as Pope, preaching many homilies on her, in tune with the Council themes emerging or proclaimed. Besides the documents already mentioned he issued an Encyclical — *Christi Matri*, 1966 — and an Apostolic Exhortation — *Recurrens mensis October*, 1968 — on the Rosary, was attentive to congresses held during his pontificate, usually sending a letter to his Legate and giving an address to the participants by radio-link when necessary. He encouraged devotion at Marian shrines (qv). His address to the Rome Congress in 1975 on the *Via pulchritundinis* was noteworthy.[2] He visited many shrines, notably Fatima in 1967.

---

[1]Texts published periodically in MM and EphMar; cf. D. Bertetto, S.D.B., *La Madonna nella parola di Paolo VI*. Rome, 1972; Th. Koeller, S.M., annually in *Cahiers Marials*. [2]AAS 67(1975), 334-337.

PERSONALITY OF MARY, THE
The problem of analyzing a personality about whom there is little factual knowledge has been solved in many ways; by reconstruction on the basis of the historical background, by projecting on to the figure of Mary the ideals of one culture or another, the personal mental categories of one writer or another, by identifying with the historical figure the attributes of the woman in heavenly glory, by attaching to her person a schema

of theological and moral virtues, each justified by such facts as the gospels yield, by transcription of mystical experience related to the Queen of heaven, by an intuitive search for her secret, a search which is inevitably conditioned and limited by the writer's own personality. Is the problem beyond solution? Can no woman achieve a portrait of the perfect woman? Are all impeded by sinfulness in understanding a sinless personality? Are the contrasts too challenging between the outer frame of her life and the mysterious destiny? Does she embody as her divine Son striking contrasts, total purity and compassion for sinners, sensitivity and strength, gentleness and power, absorption in the present and a gaze fixed unalterably on eternity, simplicity in the spirit and endless versatility? The mystery of Mary is the mystery of all human personality magnified by the unimpeded intrusion into her being, an intrusion loving and wholly accepted, of the divine beyond our evaluation.[1]

---

[1]By way of illustration of the problems cf. Jean Guitton, *The Blessed Virgin*, London, 1962; Caryll Houselander, *The Reed of God*, London, 1944; Adrienne von Speyr, *The Handmaid of the Lord*, EphMar 31(1981) Fasc i-2, *Maria en la experiencia mística de Santa Teresa*.

PRUDENTIUS, AURELIUS CLEMENS (348-c. 405)

P., born in Spain, greatest of early Christian poets, only layman accepted as a Church Father, conveyed in his poems the great truths about Mary.[1] Among his personal intuitions was the idea of Mary as Spouse (qv) of the Holy Spirit (qv), "the unwedded Virgin wedded the Spirit, nor felt any defect of love."[2] P. lauds Mary's virginity. As an interpreter of Gen 3:15 (see WOMAN IN) in a Marian sense he writes of her as the conqueror of the "serpent."[3] P. is one of the first to address praise directly to Our Lady: "O what real joys (your) chaste womb contains, from which the new age proceeds and the golden light."[4]

---

[1]Works PL 59, 60; CSEL 61; CCSL 126; EMBP, pp. 446-447; CMP pp. 193-200; cf. I. Rodriguez, *Mariologia en Prudencio*, EstM, 5 (1946), pp. 347-358. [2]CSEL, 104. [3]CSEL 18. [4]CSEL 65.

RAHNER, KARL, S.J. (1905-)

R.'s prestige in theological circles lends interest to his writing on Mary. It concludes *Mariologie,*

Innsbruck, 1959; *Mary, Mother of the Lord,* 1962; profound essays on the Immaculate Conception, in Theological Investigations I, and III; on the Assumption in T.I. I and on the Virginity *in partu*, T.I. IV, as well as reflections on Mary and the Apostolate (qv). Sobriety in affirmation does not lessen the profundity of the insights.

SIMEON METAPHRASTES (fl. a. 1000)

Known and named for his adaptations of early works in his lives of the saints M. was also author of Marian texts, one particularly significant.[1] He gave an account of the life and "falling asleep" of Mary and added to it the story of the miraculous mantle venerated in Blakhernae (BHG 1047, 1048, 1048a, 1048b); excerpts from this composition are printed in PG.[2] His principal work is *"In lugubrem lamentationem Deiparae"* (BHG 1148).[3] The theme is Mary's compassion; it is here expressed at a length and with a depth of feeling not found in the east save among the Syrians. Mary is shown holding the dead Christ in her arms, expressing her pain at the thought of his every pain, contrasting her present lot with her mighty privileges and with the joy of Jesus' childhood. "Your side has been pierced but my heart, too, has been pierced at the same time."[4] S. is reputedly author of a *"Commentarius de imagine Deiparae Romanae."* (BHG 1067).

---

[1]Works PG 114, 115; cf. H. Graef, *Mary*, I, pp. 200-201; Beck, pp. 570-75; J. Gouillard, A. A., in DTC XIV, 2, 2959-71. [2]PG 115, 531-44, 547-550. [3]PG, 209-217. [4]PG 216C.

SUENENS, LEO JOSEPH CARDINAL (1904-)

As a young auxiliary bishop of Malines the future Cardinal was attracted to the Legion of Mary, formed a deep friendship with its founder, Frank Duff (qv), wrote the life of one of its heroines, Edel Quinn, composed a theological commentary on the legionary promise, *The theology of the Apostolate*, to which book *The Gospel to every creature* was a sequel, as was *The Nun in the World*. S. took part in the debate on chapter VIII LG, is responsible for the passage on Mary and the apostolate, LG 65. He has written much on Our Lady from *Mary, the Mother of God* to a passage in his most recent work, *Renouveau et Puissances des Ténèbres*, 1982. He proposed Frank Duff to Paul VI (qv) as a Lay Auditor at the Council. Because of his interventions on such subjects as Charisms in the Christian life and the need to have woman Lay Auditors, his sponsorship of the Pastoral Constitution on the Church in the Modern World and the wide diffusion of his books, he enjoyed during and after the Council, at which he was a Moderator, quite exceptional prestige inside and outside the Church: he presented *Pacem in Terris* on behalf of John XXIII to U Thant, Secretary General of UNO; he received the Templeton Award. He has been a powerful link between the Charismatic Movement (*qv*) and the Marian movement.

---

[1]Cf. Elizabeth Hamilton, *Cardinal Suenens, A Portrait*, London, 1975 and international reference books s.v.

SWORD OF SIMEON, THE

A puzzling saying which some of the Fathers misunderstood — they thought that it forecast a breakdown in Mary's faith (*qv*) during the Passion. The student has the benefit of an exhaustive survey of patristic opinion, thoroughly scientific.[1] One striking modern opinion expressed by a great biblical scholar, Pierre Benoit, O.P., that Mary represented the people of Israel has not rallied unanimity.[2] Another equally eminent scholar maintains the view that the oracle is related to the sufferings of Mary in the Passion, not a breakdown of faith: A. Feuillet, P.S.S.,[3] can quote five Protestant or independent scholars who thus interpret the words. J. M. Alonso found five views among the patristic writings: doubt or scandal during the Passion; the final divine judgement; the word of God searching hearts; the sword of the Cherubim at the gate of the Paradise, due to the first Eve, removed by the new Eve (*qv*); Mary's maternal sorrow in the Passion.

Epiphanius (*qv*) thought that the sword possibly referred to a violent death for Mary, for which there is no evidence. Other views see Mary as Mother of the Messiah sharing the rejection met by her Son; or again it is suggested that the fall of many in Israel was foretold, and this Mary lived to see; or that this prophecy refers back to the conflict or enmity foretold in Gen 3:15 (see WOMAN IN). A. Feuillet's opinion has certainly widespread support in Christian literature on the *Mater Dolorosa*.

---

[1]J. M. Alonso, C.M.F., *La espada de Siméon (Lc 2:35a) en la exégesis de los Padres*, MSS, IV, pp. 183-285. [2]"*Et toimême, un glaive te transpercera l'âme*" (Lc 2:35) CBQ

25(1963), pp. 251-61. [3]*Jésus et Marie d'après les récits lucaniens de l'enfance et d'après saint Jean*, Paris, 1973, pp. 60-69, 100-102; R. E. Brown, *The Birth of the Messiah*, pp. 441, 460-466; *Mary in NT*, pp. 154, 55.

TERRIEN, JEAN-BAPTISTE, S.J.
(1832-1903)

Theological professor whose work *La grâce et la gloire*, 2 vols., 1897, established his reputation. His four volume *La Mère de Dieu et la Mère des hommes*, 1902, several editions, the last with preface by H. Rondet, S.J., was for decades the quarry of students: extensive treatment of every important theme based on wide, solid erudition; a synthesis of positive and scholastic theology.[1]

---

[1]DTC XV, i, 129-130.

THEODORE THE SYNCELLUS
(early 7th century)

A priest of the great church of Constantinople during the patriarchate of Sergios (610-638) T. is author of a homily on the finding of the mantle of the Theotokos preserved in the church at Blakhernae in Constantinople (BHG 1058)[1] and of a discourse on the miraculous preservation of the city in 619: authenticity in each case is guaranteed by the authority in Byzantine studies, A. Wenger, A.A.;[2] the homily on the mantel was for a time attributed to George of Nicomedia. Both homilies constitute evidence for a most important dimension of devotion to the Theotokos. Byzantium was a "wholly Marian civilization" (A. Wenger). T. speaks of innumerable temples mostly to the Theotokos — he says that there was "no public place, no princely house, no monastery, no residence of civic notability" without a sanctuary or an oratory to the Theotokos. A. Wenger thinks there may be 200 unpublished Byzantine Marian homilies, and Byzantine Marian liturgy is the most beautiful of all.[3]

---

[1]*Homilia in depositionem vestis sanctae Deiparae in Blachernis*, Combefis, *Bibliotheca Patrum novum auctarium*, II, Paris, 1648, pp. 751-788. [2]For second homily Mai, *Nova Patrum Bibliotheca*, VI, 2, 423-437; cf. A. Wenger, *L'Assomption*, pp. 111-139; id. esp. in *Maria* V, pp. 963-967; Beck, 545. [3]For a list of the 124 Marian churches in Constantinople itself cf. R. Janin, A.A., *Les Eglises et les Monastères de Constantinople*, III, Paris, 1953, pp. 164-253.

THEODORET OF CYRRHUS (*c.* 393-*c.* 466)
Antiochene and controversial Father of the Church, T. writes movingly of Our Lady in his

commentaries on Scripture, wherein he treats of her predestination and her many privileges and holiness.[1] He is the author of the *De Incarnatione Domini* for long attributed to St. Cyril of Alexandria (*qv*) and there he takes his stand for the title of Theotokos.

---

[1]Works PG 80-84, SC 57, 98, 111, A. Möhle, *Theodoret von Kyros Kommentar zu Jesaia,* Berlin 1932; EMBP, 933-943; CMP IV, 1, pp. 440-486.

TIMOTHY OF JERUSALEM (4th century)

Timothy, a priest of Jerusalem, is author of a homily on the prophet Simeon and the Blessed Virgin (BHG 1958),[1] which has special relevance to the debate on Mary's death (*qv*). He asserts explicitly that she is "immortal to the present time through him who had his abode in her and who assumed and raised her above the higher regions."[2] The dating of the homily which contains this important text is controverted, Fr. M. Jugie, A.A. (*qv*) opting for the fourth century against Dom Bernard Capelle, O.S.B., an eminent liturgical historian, who defends the sixth or seventh centuries as the probable time.[3]

---

[1]PG 86, 237-252, EMBP pp. 1140-1144. [2]PG 245-248. [3]Cf. M. Jugie, *L'Immaculée Conception,* p. 74; B. Capelle, *Les homélies liturgiques du prétendu Timothée de Jerusalem* in *EphLit,* 63(1949), pp. 5-26; Beck, 400.

TITUS OF BOSTRA (d.*c.* 378)

T. Bishop of Bostra, capital of the Roman province of Arabia, defended the real motherhood of Mary against the Manicheans, in the fourth book of his treatise against this sect, and in his *Homilies on Luke*, fragments of which survive.[1] He had the idea of special sanctification of Mary by the Holy Spirit. Like a number of other Fathers he considered Mary a prophet: "Let us therefore hear what the virgin in all respects now says, and what is her marvellous prophecy; for as she is above nature mother and virgin, so she also shows herself a prophetess and speaker of God."[2] He probably taught the *virginitas in partu* (*qv*) and certainly the virginity *post partum*.

---

[1]*Contra Manichaeos,* ed. P. A. Lagarde, Berlin, 1859; *id.* Syriac translation, Berlin, 1859; PG 18, 1065-1204; Lucan fragments TU, 21. [2]*Op. cit.* p. 145; cf. E. Amann, DTC XV, 1143; H. Graef, *Mary* I, p. 54.

TRADITION, MARY IN

In the question of Mary, who is of the highest import in the theology of Tradition, the classic Tridentine text, with its sequel in Catholic Protestant polemics, must be studied; therein the important words "this same truth and code of morals is contained in written books and in unwritten traditions" had a textual history within the Council and has had a divisive effect, even among Catholic theologians, since.[1] Some clung to the idea that a two source theory of revelation was an integral part of Catholic doctrine; others held "that the saving gospel is contained entirely in the Scripture, as it is contained entirely in Tradition."[2]

In the changing climate of the Second Vatican Council certain fixed positions were abandoned and after considerable tension, the rejection of a "two source" text prepared by the preparatory theological commission, and the nomination of a new drafting commission to bring in ecumenists by Pope John, a text was eventually drawn up, amended and passed with wide opening to free theological debate on the relationship between Scripture and Tradition.

It is for theologians to advance from this teaching, without, be it said, forgetting the important role assigned to Tradition in the eastern Church.

Among many fine things in the Council document one may be of interest to Marian theologians: "The tradition which comes from the Apostles develops in the Church with the help of the Holy Spirit. For there is a growth in the understanding of the realities and the words which have been handed down. This happens through the contemplation and study made by believers, who treasure these things in their hearts (cf. Luke 2:19, 51), through the intimate understanding of spiritual things they experience, and through the preaching of those who have received through episcopal succession the sure gift of truth."[3]

The same Council issued directives to "theologians and preachers of the divine word" on how they should prepare themselves to treat of the "unique dignity of the Mother of God." They were to "pursue the study of sacred Scripture, the holy Fathers, the doctors, and liturgies of the Church, under the guidance of the Church's teaching authority."[4]

The importance given to the Fathers of the Church (*qv*) here, as that given to "the study made by believers" (cf. Sentiment of the Faithful) is encouraging for those who have resolutely striven to achieve a renewal of Marian theology in accord with, not only sacred Scripture, but with the documents of history, especially the Fathers scientifically studied: for what they meant and taught in the intellectual world of their time, not for what we may be able to extract from their writings and adjust to our preference. Vatican II rightly invokes the Teaching Authority as a complement to both Scripture and Tradition: "It is clear, therefore, that, in the supremely wise arrangement of God, sacred Tradition, sacred Scripture and the Teaching Authority of the Church are so connected and associated that one of them cannot stand without the others."[5]

In the light of such teaching Marian theologians must study especially the truths about Mary which *seem* to derive more from Tradition than from Scripture: the perpetual virginity, the Immaculate Conception, the bodily Assumption and the spiritual motherhood (*qqv*). But it is important to take full account of the constant reliance of Tradition on Scripture.[6] It is a vast field and when fully developed will help a new understanding of the meaning of Tradition.

[1]Of the many works on the subject of Tradition cf. J. R. Geiselmann, *Die Heilige Schrift und die Tradition*, Freiburg, 1962 (first three chapters tr. *The Meaning of Tradition*, London, 1966); H. Holstein, *La Tradition dans l'Eglise*, Paris, 1962; J. Mackey, *The Modern Theology of Tradition*, London, 1962; Y.-M. Congar, O.P., *Tradition in the Life of the Church*, London, 1964; *id. Tradition and Traditions*, London, 1966; on Mary in Tradition, the following articles in *De Scriptura et Traditione*, ed. K. Balic, O.F.M., Rome, 1963: A. de Aldama, on the dogma of Mary's virginity, pp. 613-633; Th. Koehler, S.M., on the Immaculate Conception, pp. 635-648; H. Rondet, S.J., on the bodily Assumption, pp. 649-661. [2]Y.-M. Congar, *Tradition in the life of the Church*, p. 43. [3]*Constitution on Divine Revelation*, art. 8. [4]*Constitution on the Church*, art. 67. [5]*Constitution on Divine Revelation*, art. 10. [6]Cf. for further bibliographical aid, J. McHugh, *The Mother*, Introduction; C. Pozo, S.J., *Maria en la obra de la salvación*, Madrid, 1974, *Introducción*, esp. pp. 10, 11.

VENANTIUS FORTUNATUS (*c.* 530-*c.* 610)

The author of the two most popular Passion hymns, *Vexilla Regis* and *Pange lingua*, also composed beautiful tributes in verse to Our Lady.[1] His hymn *"Quem terra, pontus, aethera..."* was for long part of the Roman Breviary, is still optional in a rendering by Mgr. R. Knox, in the English Breviary. Mary figures in his hymn for the Nativity, with clear echoes of patristic exegesis, the Isaian Emmanuel oracle, and the "root of Jesse." His two lengthy hymns on virginity, the second in praise of Mary, inspired subsequent authors abundantly:[2] so did another great Christian poet, Sedulius (d. 450), whose Marian passage in the *Carmen Paschale* resounds through the liturgy unendingly: "Salve, sancta parens, enixa puerpera regem...."[3]

[1]Works, PL 88; *Quem terra.*. 265. [2]PL 266-276; 276-286. [3]PL 19, 599A-600A; for the other Breviary hymn from Sedulius, *"A solis ortus cardine"* PL 19, 763A-770A; cf. B. de Gaiffier, S.J., *S. Venance Fortunat.*. AB 70(1952), pp. 262-284; J. Szoverffy, *Die Annalen der lateinischen Hymnendichthung*, 1(1964), pp. 128-40; Works of Sedulius, CMF, III, pp. 200-205; on Venantius cf. H. Barré, *Prières Anciennes*, pp. 26, 27.

WADDING, LUKE, O.F.M. (1588-1657)

Irish scholar and patriot, W. came from the College of Salamanca to Rome in 1618 as theologian to the Spanish embassy sent by Philip III to urge the Pope to define the Immaculate Conception as a dogma. His scholarship was internationally recognised on the publication of the monumental *Annales Minorum*, 8 vols., 1625-1654, of the first critical edition of the works of Scotus and of *Scriptores Ordinis Minorum*, 1650. His part in the campaign which achieved the Bull *Sollicitudo* of Alexander VII (*qv*) four years after his death was significant.

W.'s writings: *Presbeia, sive Legatio Philippi III et IV...ad SS. SS. DD. NN. Paulum V. et Gregorium XV PP. de definienda controversia Immaculatae Conceptioni B. Virginis Mariae*, Louvain, 1624; *De morte B. Mariae Virginis: Immaculatae Conceptioni B.M.V. non adversari ejus mortem corporalem*, Rome 1655; *De redemptione Deiparae semper Virginis*, Rome, 1656; *De Baptismo B.M.V.*, Rome 1656. W.'s friend I. Marracci (*qv*) mentions a work by him entitled *Tractatus de scandalis exortis in controversia Conceptionis* and F. Casolini another *De mente Scoti in controversia Conceptionis*. W.'s influence on his order, on his country and on the general Catholic world of his time was certainly enhanced by his great personal sanctity.[1]

[1]F. Casolini, *Luca Wadding, l'annalista dei Francescani*, Milan, 1936; D. Stiernon, A.A., *L'annaliste Luc Wadding*, EphMar 8(1958), pp. 291-312; C. Gutierrez, *Espana por el dogma de la Immaculada. La ambajada a Roma de 1659 y la Bula "Sollicitudo" de Alejandro VII. Miscellanea Comilas*, 24(1955), 480pp; for W. pp. 48ff; *Fr. Luke Wadding, Com-*

memorative volume, Franciscan House, Killiney, 1957, esp. B. Millet, O.F.M., *The writings*, pp. 235-242; C. Balic, O.F.M., *Wadding the Scotist*, pp. 463-507.

ZENO OF VERONA (d.c. 372)

Z. born in Africa became bishop of Verona. In his 93 *Tractatus* there are occasional passages of Marian interest. He develops the Mary–Eve parallel and contrast turning it also to the Church; he was particularly insistent on Mary's virginity.[1] He seems to have been the first Latin Father to affirm explicitly the *"virginitas in partu."* "O great mystery! Mary an incorrupt virgin conceived, after conception she brought forth as a virgin, after bringing forth she remained a virgin."[2] "She would not believe such a Son was born of her, unless having been an incorrupt virgin after conception, she remained likewise after childbirth."[3]

[1]Works, PL 11. [2]PL 415. [3]PL 417.

About the Author

Theotokos is the magnum opus of Michael O'Carroll C.S.Sp., Irish theologian and educator. He has written widely and well, over the last three decades, on theological and ecumenical topics, and is internationally known as a specialist in Marian Studies.